DICTIONARY OF AMERICAN BIOGRAPHY

AMERICAN COUNCIL OF LEARNED SOCIETIES

DICTIONARY
OF
AMERICAN BIOGRAPHY

PUBLISHED UNDER THE AUSPICES OF
THE AMERICAN COUNCIL OF LEARNED SOCIETIES

The American Council of Learned Societies, organized in 1919 for the purpose of advancing the study of the humanities and of the humanistic aspects of the social sciences, is a nonprofit federation comprising forty-five national scholarly groups. The Council represents the humanities in the United States in the International Union of Academies, provides fellowships and grants-in-aid, supports research-and-planning conferences and symposia, and sponsors special projects and scholarly publications.

MEMBER ORGANIZATIONS

AMERICAN PHILOSOPHICAL SOCIETY, 1743
AMERICAN ACADEMY OF ARTS AND SCIENCES, 1780
AMERICAN ANTIQUARIAN SOCIETY, 1812
AMERICAN ORIENTAL SOCIETY, 1842
AMERICAN NUMISMATIC SOCIETY, 1858
AMERICAN PHILOLOGICAL ASSOCIATION, 1869
ARCHAEOLOGICAL INSTITUTE OF AMERICA, 1879
SOCIETY OF BIBLICAL LITERATURE, 1880
MODERN LANGUAGE ASSOCIATION OF AMERICA, 1883
AMERICAN HISTORICAL ASSOCIATION, 1884
AMERICAN ECONOMIC ASSOCIATION, 1885
AMERICAN FOLKLORE SOCIETY, 1888
AMERICAN DIALECT SOCIETY, 1889
AMERICAN PSYCHOLOGICAL ASSOCIATION, 1892
ASSOCIATION OF AMERICAN LAW SCHOOLS, 1900
AMERICAN PHILOSOPHICAL ASSOCIATION, 1901
AMERICAN ANTHROPOLOGICAL ASSOCIATION, 1902
AMERICAN POLITICAL SCIENCE ASSOCIATION, 1903
BIBLIOGRAPHICAL SOCIETY OF AMERICA, 1904
ASSOCIATION OF AMERICAN GEOGRAPHERS, 1904
HISPANIC SOCIETY OF AMERICA, 1904
AMERICAN SOCIOLOGICAL ASSOCIATION, 1905
AMERICAN SOCIETY OF INTERNATIONAL LAW, 1906
ORGANIZATION OF AMERICAN HISTORIANS, 1907
COLLEGE ART ASSOCIATION OF AMERICA, 1912
HISTORY OF SCIENCE SOCIETY, 1924
LINGUISTIC SOCIETY OF AMERICA, 1924
MEDIAEVAL ACADEMY OF AMERICA, 1925
AMERICAN MUSICOLOGICAL SOCIETY, 1934
SOCIETY OF ARCHITECTURAL HISTORIANS, 1940
ECONOMIC HISTORY ASSOCIATION, 1940
ASSOCIATION FOR ASIAN STUDIES, 1941
AMERICAN SOCIETY FOR AESTHETICS, 1942
AMERICAN ASSOCIATION FOR THE ADVANCEMENT OF SLAVIC STUDIES, 1948
METAPHYSICAL SOCIETY OF AMERICA, 1950
AMERICAN STUDIES ASSOCIATION, 1950
RENAISSANCE SOCIETY OF AMERICA, 1954
SOCIETY FOR ETHNOMUSICOLOGY, 1955
AMERICAN SOCIETY FOR LEGAL HISTORY, 1956
AMERICAN SOCIETY FOR THEATRE RESEARCH, 1956
SOCIETY FOR THE HISTORY OF TECHNOLOGY, 1958
AMERICAN COMPARATIVE LITERATURE ASSOCIATION, 1960
AMERICAN ACADEMY OF RELIGION, 1963
AMERICAN SOCIETY FOR EIGHTEENTH-CENTURY STUDIES, 1969
ASSOCIATION FOR JEWISH STUDIES, 1969

DICTIONARY OF American Biography

Supplement Eight

1966–1970

John A. Garraty
Mark C. Carnes
Editors

WITH AN INDEX GUIDE TO THE SUPPLEMENTS

Charles Scribner's Sons
NEW YORK
Collier Macmillan Publishers
LONDON

The preparation of the original twenty volumes of the Dictionary was made possible by the public-spirited action of the New York Times Company and its president, the late Adolph S. Ochs, in furnishing a large subvention. The preparation and publication of Supplement 8 have been supported by the sale of those volumes and the preceding Supplements. Entire responsibility for the contents of the Dictionary and its Supplements rests with the American Council of Learned Societies.

Library of Congress Cataloging-in-Publication Data
(Revised for Suppl. 8)

Dictionary of American biography.

Includes index.
Supplements 1–2 comprise v. 11 of the main work.
Contents: —3. 1941–1945—[etc.]—
7. 1961–1965—v. 8. 1966–1970.
1. United States—Biography. I. Garraty, John
Arthur, 1920–
E176.D563 920′.073 77–2942
ISBN 0–684–18618–7 (Suppl. 8)

Published simultaneously in Canada
by Collier Macmillan Canada, Inc.

1 3 5 7 9 11 13 15 17 19 B/C 20 18 16 14 12 10 8 6 4 2

Printed in the United States of America

The paper in this book meets the guidelines for
permanence and durability of the Committee on
Production Guidelines for Book Longevity of the
Council on Library Resources.

Editorial Staff

PREFACE

With this supplement, which contains biographies of 454 persons, written by almost 300 authors, the *Dictionary of American Biography* extends its coverage through December 31, 1970, and reaches a total of 18,110 sketches. As with earlier volumes, this one could not have been completed without the generous and unremunerated cooperation of dozens of experts in various fields. These scholars have assisted both in deciding which persons to include in *Supplement Eight* and in locating authors for the biographies. We wish to thank them most sincerely for their help.

As was the case with *Supplements Five, Six,* and *Seven,* the authors of the sketches have been asked to fill out data sheets for their subjects covering the following information: Section I: full date of birth and death; place of birth; full name of father; full name of mother; father's occupation; economic and social position of the family at the time of the subject's birth; education; institutions attended, dates, degrees earned; full name of spouse or, if never married, mention of this fact; date of marriage; number of children, names of any of apparent historical importance; place of death. Section II: number of siblings, number of each sex; order of birth of subject, order among those of same sex; economic and social position of mother's family; names of close relatives who achieved distinction; nationality and time of migration to the United States of ancestors; religious affiliation of subject; religious affiliations of father and mother; religious affiliation of spouse; economic and social position of spouse at time of marriage; highest education of spouse; names and dates of birth of children; cause of subject's death; place of burial; date of spouse's death.

Authors were asked to include in their essays all the facts in Section I, but only such details from Section II as seemed relevant. The purpose was to gather the material in a form convenient for researchers, but to keep most of it out of the biographies themselves. The data sheets will be placed on file, along with other *DAB* papers, in the Library of Congress so that sociologists, psychologists, and other researchers interested in collective biography can have access to them.

When the first volume of the *Dictionary of American Biography* was published in December 1928, it contained an article on the Maryland jurist Richard Henry Alvey (1826–1906), written by a young historian named Broadus Mitchell. As the succeeding volumes of the original set appeared over the years, Mitchell continued to contribute essays. All together he wrote biographies of fifty-five distinguished Americans. Since then, he has written many articles for the supplements. Thus, Professor Mitchell, who died on Apr. 28, 1988, is the only scholar who has been part of this vast enterprise from the beginning; this volume contains his estimations of Waddill Catchings and Bray Hammond. For this reason we wish to dedicate *Supplement Eight* to him.

We also wish to thank the board of the American Council of Learned Societies and Council President Stanley N. Katz for their many kindnesses and wise guidance.

JOHN A. GARRATY
MARK C. CARNES

DICTIONARY
OF
AMERICAN BIOGRAPHY

DICTIONARY OF

AMERICAN BIOGRAPHY

Aandahl—Zorach

AANDAHL, FRED GEORGE (Apr. 9, 1897–Apr. 7, 1966), congressman and governor of North Dakota, was born in Litchville, Barnes County, N.Dak., the son of Soren (Americanized to Sam) Jörgen Aandahl, a Norwegian immigrant farmer, and Mamie C. Lawry, a teacher. His mother, a daughter of English immigrants, taught school and insisted on high standards of education for her family. In 1906 the Aandahls moved to Kingsbury, Calif., where they owned and operated a five-acre fruit farm. Returning to Barnes County in 1909, Sam Aandahl constructed a farmhouse on 960 acres and engaged successfully in diversified agriculture. From 1916 to 1920 he served two terms as railroad commissioner, elected on the Republican ticket with the support of the Nonpartisan League. Disillusioned with the league as an unselfish political movement concerned with the plight of the North Dakota farmers, Sam Aandahl retired from public life. Fred Aandahl learned much from his father's political experience.

Aandahl attended a one-room country school in Litchville and completed three years at Litchville High School. In 1916 he enrolled at the model high school of the University of North Dakota and entered the university in 1917. He won a position on the debating team and gained widespread campus recognition. In June 1921 he received his B.A.

After college Aandahl returned to Barnes County and entered into a farming partnership with his father (who died in 1922). This was the outset of what has been called North Dakota's "Years of Despair," the period between the two world wars when agricultural crises and economic depression destabilized farm life. From 1922 to 1927, Aandahl taught school in the county, served as principal of the Svea Township Consolidated School, and spent three years as superintendent of schools in Litchville. On June 28, 1926, Aandahl married a fellow teacher, Luella Brekke; they had three children. Aandahl and his wife continued as teachers until June 1927, when they moved permanently to the Aandahl livestock and grain farm. Aandahl supplemented his income in the 1930's by serving on Agricultural Adjustment Administration (AAA) boards.

In 1930, Aandahl won a seat in the state senate, defeating a twelve-year incumbent who had Nonpartisan League backing. Two years later, in a recall election, the league won and Aandahl lost his seat. In 1934, Aandahl failed to regain his seat, losing to a league candidate by eleven votes. The 1938 contest for the seat was also close, but this time Aandahl won by twenty-one votes. To break the authority exercised by the Nonpartisan League in the Republican party, Aandahl and other Republicans formed the Republican Organizing Committee (ROC) in 1943. Conservative in outlook, Aandahl consistently voted against legislation favoring one group or segment of the population over another. He thus opposed most league-sponsored measures to ease the plight of farm families. He argued that he had entered the legislature "with no thought of revolutionizing the state government or immediately curing all the ills that confronted the people."

Between his legislative terms, Aandahl concerned himself with agricultural matters, implementing federal farm legislation, improving relations between farmers and businessmen, and seeking new ways to finance public education. Allying himself with Milton R. Young, the individual most responsible for the political success of the ROC, Aandahl led the fight for a bill for more-equitable distribution of education funds among school districts, many of which had assessed valuations so low that it was impossible to maintain schools at minimum standards. He also secured an initial appropriation of more than $4 million to support the state equalization fund.

Aandahl became the first ROC governor in 1944 and was reelected by impressive majorities in 1946 and 1948. His victories marked the decline of the Nonpartisan League and Republican senator William Langer, a former league official. While Aandahl was governor, North Dakota benefited from wartime prosperity and adequate rainfall. Following his conservative bent, Aandahl insisted upon legislative restraint, vetoing some appropriations endorsed by ROC legislators. His approach, he explained, was "to bring efficiency into government in caring for the common welfare, to use government so that free enterprise can thrive, and to make the advantages of free enterprise available to all of the people." He called for diversification as the key to the future of North Dakota but was unwilling to sponsor or support programs, aside from road construction and buildings at state institutions, to ensure that goal.

In 1950, running on his six-year record as governor, Aandahl won a seat in the United States House of Representatives. His victory enabled him to challenge incumbent William Langer in the June 1952 Republican primary for the United States senatorial nomination. While the ROC had taken power away from the Nonpartisan League, Langer himself seemed invincible. Appointed to the influential House Appropriations Committee, Aandahl was at first reluctant to run for the Senate. When drafted by the ROC executive board, however, he agreed to challenge Langer. Aandahl proved a surprisingly weak candidate and lost decisively (107,905 to 78,359).

Dwight D. Eisenhower's victory in 1952 and the support of Milton R. Young (whom Aandahl, when governor, had appointed to the United States Senate) led to Aandahl's appointment as assistant secretary of the interior for water and power development in 1953. He held that post until the end of the Eisenhower administration, despite the fact that he had been an enthusiastic supporter of Senator Robert A. Taft in Taft's bid for the 1952 Republican presidential nomination.

Aandahl, who as a congressman had voted to cut appropriations to the Tennessee Valley Authority and favored state control of offshore oil drilling, now supervised the Bureau of Reclamation as well as the Bonneville, Southwestern, and Southeastern power administrations, which were the marketing agencies for the sale of surplus power generated at federal dams. Aandahl advocated granting private companies a larger role in distributing power from government-built projects. He was also one of the first officials to see the possibilities of desalting and using seawater, utilizing the Office of Saline Water for this purpose. By 1957 this office enjoyed a $10 million appropriation, and Aandahl claimed it had reduced the cost of converting salt water to sixty cents a thousand gallons. Aandahl was also a strong opponent of the "preference clause" in government power contracts; the clause favored municipalities, public corporations or agencies, and rural electric cooperatives in purchasing power from federal installations. In the Department of the Interior he had an opportunity to press his views, but in 1955 an opinion by Attorney General Herbert Brownell, Jr., suggested that the government was obliged to uphold the preference clause.

At the end of the Eisenhower administration, Aandahl returned to his farm near Litchville. He died in Fargo, N. Dak.

[Aandahl's political papers up to 1951 are at the North Dakota capitol in Bismarck. The remainder are in the Orin G. Libby Manuscript Collection of the Chester Fritz Library at the University of North Dakota. Aandahl's official reports, beginning in 1954, are in the annual reports of the secretary of the interior. See Dan Rylance, "Fred G. Aandahl and the ROC Movement," in Thomas W. Howard, ed., *The North Dakota Political Tradition* (1981). An obituary is in the *New York Times*, Apr. 8, 1966.]

RICHARD LOWITT

AKELEY, MARY LEONORE (Jan. 29, 1878–July 19, 1966), explorer, author, and educator, was born Mary Leonore Jobe, in Tappan, Ohio, the daughter of Richard Watson Jobe, a farmer, and Sarah Jane Pittis. She received her Ph.B. in 1897 from Scio (Ohio) College. From 1901 to 1903 she pursued graduate studies at Bryn Mawr and taught at Temple College in Philadelphia. Her interest in exploration was sparked during her Bryn Mawr years, when she served as an assistant on a botanical expedition to the Selkirks, British Columbia. After teaching history from 1903 to 1906 at Cortland Normal School, New York City, she returned to graduate studies in history and English at Columbia University and received her M.A. in 1909. While teaching at Hunter College, New York City, from 1907 to 1916, she conducted major explorations of the Canadian Northwest.

In 1909 Jobe joined an exploring party in British Columbia and in 1913 studied Indian tribes there. In 1914 and 1915 she explored the headwaters of the Fraser River and the glaciated region of Mount Sir Alexander, making the first two attempts to ascend this hitherto unnamed and unmapped peak, one of the highest in the Canadian Rockies. She continued her climbing, photography, and botanical collecting in the winters of 1917 and 1918. The Canadian government sponsored her work, published her maps, and in 1925 gave the name Mount Jobe to a high peak at 54°10′ north latitude. Accounts of her explorations appeared in travel and popular magazines.

Jobe advocated a strenuous outdoor life for girls and was active in the Camp Fire Girls. She believed that human beings found their highest development in the outdoor life. From 1916 to 1930 she operated Camp Mystic in Mystic, Conn., where she taught outdoor skills, athletics, and the arts to affluent urban girls and exposed them to her world of exploration through such speakers as Vilhjalmur Stefannson.

Jobe married another famous explorer, Carl Ethan Akeley, on Oct. 18, 1924. A noted inventor, taxidermist, and sculptor for the American Museum of Natural History in New York City, he was internationally known for his four expeditions to Africa. In 1926–1927 she accompanied him on the Akeley-Eastman-Pomeroy expedition to East Africa and central Africa, serving as safari manager and secretary. After ten months in the field, Carl Akeley died of fever on Nov. 17, 1926, at Mount Mikeno in the Congo. Mary Akeley directed the safari for the remaining five months, collecting museum specimens and completing gorilla observations and a park survey. She also led the party to Lake Hannington in Uganda to study and photograph its wildlife.

After her return to the United States, Akeley devoted herself to her husband's work. From 1927 to 1938 she was special adviser and assistant for the African Hall in the American Museum of Natural History and dedicated the Akeley African Hall when it opened in 1936. In 1938 she was appointed to the trustees' committee on the African Hall and African Collections. She also completed, with Belgian zoologist J. M. Derscheid, her husband's report on Parc National Albert, the Congo. For this and in memory of her husband, in 1929 she was awarded the Cross of the Knight, Order of the Crown, by King Albert of Belgium. From 1929 to 1936 she was the American secretary of the International Committee for Conservation in Parc National Albert.

Akeley wrote and lectured extensively about her African experiences. In *Carl Akeley's Africa* (1929) and *The Wilderness Lives Again* (1940), she described the expedition and exhibit plans. *Rumble of a Distant Drum* (1946) described, through the eyes of a native boy, her struggle to continue the expedition alone. She also edited her husband's field notes and stories in *Adventures in the African Jungle* (1930) and *Lions, Gorillas and Their Neighbors* (1932). She stressed the need to study and preserve vanishing human cultures, flora, and fauna. She opposed unregulated slaughter of wildlife and called herself a hunter with a camera.

In 1935–1936 Akeley journeyed through Swaziland, Zululand, the Transvaal, and Portuguese East Africa, a trip she described in *Restless Jungle* (1936). She made ethnographic observations and photographed the Swazi and Zulu people but was disturbed by their modernization. She also surveyed the wildlife of the Natal Reserves and Kruger National Park, and traveled with an elephant herd through the Maputo swamps of Portuguese East Africa.

Akeley returned to the Canadian Northwest in 1937, traveling up the Canoe River on what she called "a journey of rediscovery." In 1941 she conducted a survey of the women's war effort in Canada and made a study of Alaskan defenses, including Kodiak Island. Akeley was invited by the Belgian government to return to the Congo in 1946 to visit her husband's grave, to see the recently expanded Parc National Albert, and to prepare a report on all the wildlife sanctuaries in the Congo. She described this trip in *Congo Eden* (1950). In 1952 she made her fifth and last expedition to Africa, traveling through the Congo and East Africa, southern Africa, and central Africa.

Akeley was known as the woman who

"brought the jungle to Central Park West." She used her international fame to advocate preservation of wildlife and respect for primitive cultures. Her seven books, all on Africa, reflected a romantic view of traditional African cultures and stressed the dangers posed by unchecked hunting of wildlife and by economic development. She encouraged the establishment of a system of nature reserves throughout Africa and documented vanishing cultures, habitats, and wildlife through still and motion pictures. She retired to her home at Great Hill in Mystic, Conn., remaining independent and aloof from her neighbors. She died in Stonington, Conn.

[Akeley's correspondence, diaries, manuscripts, news clippings, photographs, and movies are in the American Museum of Natural History, New York City. A biobibliography by Janet M. Harbour is in the Schlesinger Library, Radcliffe College, Cambridge, Mass. For information on her girls' camp see Carol W. Kimball, "Camp Mystic in the Good Old Summertime," *Historical Footnotes: Bulletin of the Stonington (Ct.) Historical Society*, Feb. 1978. Obituaries are in the *New York Times*, July 22, 1966; and *Geographical Journal*, Dec. 1966.]

PAMELA M. HENSON

ALLEN, FLORENCE ELLINWOOD (Mar. 23, 1884–Sept. 12, 1966), jurist and feminist, was born in Salt Lake City, Utah, the daughter of Clarence Emir Allen, a teacher of classics, and Corinne Marie Tuckerman, whose father was an early advocate of higher education for women. Shortly before her birth her father, who had tuberculosis, moved the family to Salt Lake City, where it lived in genteel poverty until he became a manager of a mine, a lawyer, and the first member of the House of Representatives from Utah.

Allen attended the New Lyme Institute in Ohio from 1895 to 1897 and Salt Lake College from 1897 to 1899. In 1900 she entered the College for Women of Western Reserve University, where she studied the piano and was elected to Phi Beta Kappa. She received her B.A. in 1904. Allen continued her musical studies at the University of Berlin from 1904 to 1906 and served as correspondent for the *Musical Courier* of New York. Because she was not good enough, she abandoned plans for a career as a concert pianist.

After Allen returned to Ohio in 1906, she served as music critic for the *Cleveland Plain Dealer* for three years and lectured on music at the Laurel School, a prep school for girls. She earned an M.A. in political science from Western Reserve in 1908. She next decided to study law, a profession that then admitted few women. Because Western Reserve barred women from its professional schools, in 1909 she entered the University of Chicago Law School, where she was one of a handful of women.

In 1910, Allen became an investigator for the New York League for the Protection of Immigrants and continued her studies at New York University. She also lectured on music for the New York Board of Education. She received her LL.B. cum laude in 1913 and was admitted to the Ohio bar the next year.

Even before she began practicing in Cleveland, Allen worked for women's rights, especially for woman's suffrage. Between 1911 and 1919 she worked in New York City and later in Ohio and other states for female equality. As counsel after 1914 to the Ohio Woman Suffrage party, she contributed extensive legal services to that cause. In 1916 she appeared twice before the Ohio Supreme Court, which accepted her arguments that women in East Cleveland, Lakewood, and Columbus were entitled to vote. Not until the Nineteenth Amendment was passed, however, did all Ohio women get the vote.

In 1919, Allen was appointed an assistant prosecutor by Cuyahoga County, Ohio, the first woman in the state to hold that post. In 1920 she was elected judge of the Court of Common Pleas of Cuyahoga County, and in 1922 she was elected to the Ohio Supreme Court and reelected in 1928. Allen was the first woman in the nation to hold these two positions. In 1926 she lost the Democratic primary for the United States Senate. In 1932 she won the Democratic primary for the House of Representatives but lost the general election.

In 1934 the Roosevelt administration, which sought to appoint women to office, named Allen to the Court of Appeals for the Sixth Circuit, encompassing Ohio, Michigan, Kentucky, and Tennessee. She served for twenty-five years, writing numerous important decisions and gaining the grudging respect of male colleagues. She was particularly proud of her opinion in 1937 upholding the law establishing the Tennessee Valley Authority, a decision affirmed by the Supreme Court. In 1958 she became the first woman to serve as a chief judge of a federal appellate court. A year later she retired from active status but continued as a senior judge of the Court of Appeals.

Every time a vacancy on the Supreme Court occurred during a Democratic administration, women's groups called for Allen's elevation. On occasion, Eleanor Roosevelt gave her some support, but both the Roosevelt and Truman administrations always picked men. Allen clearly wanted the position but recognized that the nation was not yet ready for a woman on the Supreme Court.

Allen often wrote and spoke for human rights and for outlawing war. After World War II, she was a member of the International Bar Association and the International Federation of Woman Lawyers. In both associations she worked extensively for human rights, world peace, and international laws regulating the uses of outer space.

Allen was a fellow of the American Bar Association, and she received numerous awards and honorary degrees. Ironically, one of her honorary degrees came from Western Reserve University, which had denied her admission to its law school. In 1960 she received the Albert Gallatin Medal, given by New York University for service to humanity, the first time it was awarded to a woman.

Allen, who never married, had little interest in women's traditional pursuits. She commented frequently on the problems career women faced in seeking acceptance by men. She stressed the necessity of working steadily and conscientiously. She also recommended a sense of humor, tact, and above all a lack of emotion. She enjoyed the out-of-doors, mountain climbing, and daily walks with her dogs. She died in Waite Hill, a suburb of Cleveland.

[Most of Allen's personal papers are at the Western Reserve Historical Society, Cleveland, Ohio. Others are in the Manuscript Division of the Library of Congress; the Sophia Smith Collection at Smith College Library; and the Schlesinger Archives of Women's History in the Radcliffe College Library. Her books and articles include *This Constitution of Ours* (1940); *The Ohio Woman Suffrage Movement* (1952), written with Mary Welles; *The Treaty as an Instrument of Legislation* (1952); and *To Do Justly* (1965), a memoir. The texts of her opinions can be found in the *Ohio Reports*, 1923–1928, and the *Federal Reporter*, 1935–1965. Biographical information may be found in Virginia C. Abbott, *The History of Woman Suffrage and the League of Women Voters in Cuyahoga County, 1911–1945* (1949); Beverly B. Cook, "The First Woman Candidate for the Supreme Court," *Supreme Court Historical Society Yearbook 1981* (1981), and "Women as Supreme Court Candidates: From Florence Allen to Sandra Day O'Connor," *Judicature*, 65 (1982); Jeanette E. Tuve, *First Lady of the Law* (1984). An obituary is in the *New York Times*, Sept. 14, 1966.]

WALTER A. SUTTON

ALLEN, GEORGE VENABLE (Nov. 3, 1903–July 11, 1970), diplomat and federal administrator, was born in Durham, N.C., the son of Thomas Ellis Allen, a merchant, and Harriet Moore. He attended local schools, received a B.A. from Duke University in 1924, and worked for the next four years as a high school teacher and principal in Buncombe County, N.C. In addition, he was a reporter for the *Asheville Times* and the *Durham Herald-Sun*. In the fall of 1928 he entered graduate school at Harvard, where the following year he received an M.A. and won the Charles Sumner Prize for International Relations.

In 1930 Allen entered the United States Foreign Service as vice-consul in Kingston, Jamaica. He attended the Foreign Service school in 1930–1931, moving from there to vice-consulships in Shanghai from 1931 to 1934 and Athens and Patras, Greece, from 1934 to 1936. He was married on Oct. 2, 1934, to Katherine Martin. They had three children. Allen was named consul and third secretary of the legation at Cairo, Egypt, in 1936, and after two years at that post he returned to Washington, D.C., as a staff member of the Division of Near Eastern Affairs in the State Department. In 1943 he became assistant chief of that division; the following year he was promoted to chief, remaining in that position until 1946. While in the Near Eastern Division, he attended the Moscow and Cairo conferences in 1943 and the Potsdam Conference in 1945. He was also a member of the United States delegation to the United Nations Conference on International Organization in San Francisco in 1945.

In May 1946 Allen became United States ambassador to Iran, replacing Wallace S. Murray. Allen had dealt with Iran since the end of World War II as a special adviser to Secretaries of State Edward Stettinius and James F. Byrnes, and Byrnes in particular had come to like his "fellow Carolinian." As ambassador, Allen agreed with other State Department policy makers, such as Loy Henderson, that the Soviet Union was trying to exploit Iranian instability to its own territorial advantage, and that Moscow's reluctance to withdraw Soviet troops from Iran contributed to the difficult situation. Allen's youth (he was the youngest American ambassador at this time) and lack of prestige made it harder for him to work with the Iranian prime minister, Ahmad Qavam. Allen was nevertheless successful in blunting Qavam's desire for a more activist American policy, which Allen felt was too interventionist, while still making it clear that the United States considered Qavam's apparent appeasement of the Soviet Union unsatisfactory.

In the fall of 1946, Allen contributed to a reorganization of Qavam's cabinet, in which leftist Tudeh and pro-Tudeh members were replaced by members of anti-Soviet factions. He also recommended a show of support for Iran through an increase in economic aid. In 1947, to quiet Iranian opposition, Allen firmly stated America's desire for Iranian self-determination. Allen's tenure in Iran was important in promoting better United States–Iranian relations and influencing Iranian leaders to distance their country from the Soviet Union.

In 1948 Allen returned to Washington as assistant secretary of state for public affairs. In this position he directed the State Department's information and exchange programs in the face of budget cuts. The next year President Harry S Truman named him ambassador to Yugoslavia, and he spent the remainder of the Truman years there articulating American support for the sovereignty of Yugoslavia and for its independence from the Soviet bloc. With the coming of the Eisenhower administration in early 1953 Allen was transferred to the embassy at New Delhi, a relatively uneventful tour marked by his advocacy of increased economic aid for India.

Returning to Washington in 1955, Allen assumed the post of assistant secretary of state for Near Eastern, South Asian, and African affairs. The highlight of his relatively brief tenure was his trip to Egypt in September 1955. Dispatched by Secretary of State John Foster Dulles, Allen was to try to dissuade Egyptian president Gamal Abdel Nasser from completing an arms agreement with Czechoslovakia. He was to deliver what was rumored to be an ultimatum from Dulles threatening a cutoff of all American aid and trade. Allen doubted the mission could be successful and when, after some delay, he was able to interview Nasser, he did not read Dulles' note but talked off the cuff to Nasser for two hours. In the end, his mission still failed.

Following a short period as ambassador to Greece from 1956 to the fall of 1957, Allen assumed his most significant role, as director of the United States Information Agency (USIA), a position he held from November 1957 until his retirement after John F. Kennedy's election in November 1960. At this time, the USIA was obliged to counteract the spectacular success of the Soviet Union's orbiting satellite, *Sputnik*, which had dealt a blow to the American image abroad. Moreover, Allen's predecessor, Arthur Larson, had made a highly partisan political speech that angered the Democratic majority in Congress. Allen accepted the post reluctantly; he did not believe in strident propaganda but instead adopted what he called a "positive, objective, and long-range approach, emphasizing the full and fair picture of American life and culture and seeking to find areas of mutual interest." He felt that a subtler approach would yield greater support for American foreign policy. Under his leadership, more English was taught overseas, more English broadcasting was carried over the Voice of America, and more attention was paid to American participation in trade fairs. Although Allen sat on the National Security Council and was effective in relating the work of the USIA to the making of foreign policy, in practice he tried to detach the agency from an overly close identification with specific foreign policy positions.

In 1958 President Eisenhower sent Allen to Brussels to investigate charges that the United States pavilion at the World's Fair was not as impressive as the Soviet pavilion. The following year Allen coordinated the United States National Exhibition in Moscow, where the highly publicized "kitchen debate" between Vice-President Richard Nixon and Soviet Premier Nikita Khrushchev took place. During the 1960 presidential campaign Allen found himself embroiled in partisan politics when results of USIA polls showing a decline in American prestige were leaked to the press after he had refused a Democratic request for them. After the information became public, he refused a Republican request to issue a statement asserting that American prestige had never been higher. On the whole, however, for the USIA Allen's tenure marked an improvement in congressional relations, an increase in cultural operations, and a move in the direction of greater professionalism. In both his diplomatic and his administrative work, Allen was cautious but effective. Without flair or extravagance, he moved quietly and loyally within both Democratic and Republican administrations and reflected the bipartisan Cold War views of his era.

In 1960 Allen became president of the Tobacco Institute and spent the next six years defending the industry against research reports linking smoking with cancer. President Lyndon Johnson called Allen out of diplomatic retirement in 1966, naming him Career Ambassador (one of sixteen then to hold that honorific title) and appointing him to head the Foreign Service Institute. He retired from that position in February 1969 and died the following year at his farm near Bahama, N.C. Allen was a founding member of the Middle East Institute. He is frequently confused with George E. Allen, the author of *Presidents Who Have Known Me.*

[Allen's papers at Duke University contain an unpublished paper on his years in Iran. See also Robert E. Elder, *The Information Machine* (1968); Thomas C. Sorensen, *The Word War* (1968); Michael K. Sheehan, *Iran* (1968); and Bruce R. Kuniholm, *The Origins of the Cold War in the Near East* (1980).]

JOHN E. FINDLING

ALLPORT, GORDON WILLARD (Nov. 11, 1897–Oct. 9, 1967), social psychologist, was born in Montezuma, Ind., the son of John Edwards Allport, a businessman and later a country doctor, and Nellie Edith Wise, a schoolteacher. Allport graduated second in a class of one hundred from Glenville High School, Ind., in 1915. His home life was marked by Protestant piety and hard work.

Allport received a B.A. from Harvard in 1919. In 1919–1920 he was an instructor in English at Robert College, Istanbul, Turkey. He received an M.A. in 1921 and a Ph.D in 1922, both from Harvard. From 1922 to 1924 he visited Europe on a Harvard fellowship. In his first year he attended the universities of Berlin and Hamburg, where he met the influential psychologists Wolfgang Köhler, Louis William Stern, Carl Stumpf, Heinz Werner, and Max Wertheimer, whose ideas had an enduring impact. His second year was spent at Cambridge, England.

On his way back from Turkey to graduate school, Allport met Sigmund Freud, an encounter he later described as a "traumatic development episode." Freud greeted him silently and Allport told him about a boy he had just seen on a trolley car who had shown an extreme fear of getting dirty. Freud asked, "And was that little boy you?" (Allport's oft-reprinted account of this meeting appeared in his "Trends in Motivational Theory" [1953].) Although Allport never regarded himself as anti-Freudian, he did feel strongly that manifest and conscious motives should be fully explored before probing for latent and unconscious ones.

After his return to America, Allport served as an instructor of social ethics at Harvard from 1924 to 1926. There, probably for the first time in an American college, he taught a course entitled "Personality." On June 30, 1925, he married a fellow graduate student, Ada Lufkin Gould, who later worked in clinical psychology. They had one child.

From 1926 to 1930 Allport was assistant professor of psychology at Dartmouth and also taught summer classes at Harvard. He returned to Harvard as assistant professor of psychology (1930–1937), associate professor (1938–1942), and, thereafter, professor. He became the first Cabot Professor of Social Ethics in 1966. He died in Cambridge, Mass.

Allport's most influential book, a gracefully written volume entitled *Personality: A Psychological Interpretation* (1937), stressed the normal rather than the pathological. It was standard reading for twenty-five years and was revised as *Patterns and Growth in Personality* in 1961. In the book, Allport stated that the goal of the new science of personality was to derive a better understanding of a person than could be gleaned by using "unaided common sense" alone. In the chapter "The Ability to Judge People," he wrote that the best way to measure progress toward this goal was by the accuracy of predictions made about the feelings, thoughts, and actions of the subject. Allport's ideas were quick to gain popularity and stimulated considerable research. The results invariably showed that psychologists were no better than laymen in their predictive accuracy and that psychological training did not improve accuracy.

The book also introduced the controversial concept of the functional autonomy of motives, which held that adult motives are infinitely varied because, although they grow out of earlier motives, they become independent of them. His book described fifty-two ways of studying personality, including the use of gestures and graphology, but emphasized the central importance of the single-case method. In 1933 Allport wrote, with P. E. Vernon, *Studies in Expressive Movement*.

In 1939 Allport was elected president of the American Psychological Association. His presidential address, "The Psychologist's Frame of Reference," presented trends in psychological research that were based on a content analysis of 1,600 articles in the fourteen most important journals published between 1888 and 1938. The analysis showed declines in studies of social betterment, of single cases, and of comprehensive theories. It showed an increase in studies concerned with "diminutive theories implemented with great precision," and a striking rise in the employment of statistical aids, the use of animal subjects, and the spread of physiological research. Allport concluded that "operationism is the current watchword of an austere empiricism."

Allport's own approach was counter to all these trends. He was a global but imprecise theorizer. His quantitative contributions were limited to widely used inventories for measuring differences in ascendancy that he developed with his brother, Floyd, and to a scale for measuring differences in religious, theoretical, social, economic, political, and religious values that he developed with P. E. Vernon. He did no work with animals or in physiological psychology. He was neither an applied nor a clinical psychologist.

Allport viewed theories and methods as means for solving significant human problems. He was especially interested in the problems of immaturity and maturity, rumor and prejudice, science and religion, and war and peace. In 1956 he examined the South African racial issue as a visiting consultant for the Institute for Social Research. He predicted that white supremacy would not be maintained.

Allport's national and international visibility and influence continued to rise. In 1944 he became president of the Society for the Psychological Study of Social Issues. He gave Lowell Lectures in Boston, Terry Lectures at Yale, and the Hoernle Lecture in South Africa. He became a member of the National Committee for UNESCO, a member of the Social Science Research and National Research Councils, and director of the National Opinion Research Center. In 1963 he received the Gold Medal of the American Psychological Foundation. The same year fifty-five of his former students presented him with two bound volumes of their writings. Many of Allport's publications concerned with social issues were collaborations with students. Among these was *The Psychology of Radio* (1935), with Hadley Cantril; *Personality Under Social Catastrophe* (1941), with Jerome S. Bruner and E. M. Jandorf; and *The Psychology of Rumor* (1947), with Leo J. Postman.

Allport stressed the importance of using many methods to study one person. His most original contribution in this area was *The Use of Personal Documents in Psychological Science* (1942), in which he analyzed the advantages and disadvantages of using autobiographies, diaries, letters, and artistic creations as ways of understanding an individual.

Allport viewed theory as a means to improve the understanding of a particular person. *Letters from Jenny* (1965) was an effort to apply this view. It began with 300 letters written by a mother over a twelve-year period, largely about her relationship with her son. Allport provided a variety of theoretical analyses, none of which he considered entirely satisfactory, of the mother's personality and problems. Allport considered differential, Gestalt, organismic, and personalistic theories as especially relevant for understanding individual lives. He maintained a lifelong personal and professional interest in religion. The best known of his writings in this area is *The Individual and His Religion* (1950).

While psychologists have become increasingly involved in problems that individuals and society regard as important, the researchers in psychology have not followed Allport's lead. Rather, the trends he identified in 1939 have accelerated. Diminutive theories implemented with precision have given way to even more diminutive theories implemented with still greater precision. The use of sophisticated statistical analysis has continued to expand, and animal and physiological research dominates many more research journals. Consequently, Allport, who was a major influence on psychology in his time, is little known to graduate students today. Following the trend, their research has become increasingly theory-centered and method-centered. Studies of the ability to understand a person as measured by predictive accuracy that Allport advocated have largely faded from the contemporary research scene. Psychology has made little progress toward the goal that Allport set for it—predicting the single person more accurately than can be done by common sense alone.

[Allport's autobiography is in E. G. Boring and G. Lindsey, eds., *A History of Psychology in Autobiography*, V (1967). R. I. Evans, *Dialogues with Gordon Allport* (1981), an edited transcript of filmed interviews, includes a tribute by T. J. Pettigrew. An obituary is in the *New York Times*, Oct. 10, 1967.]

HENRY CLAY SMITH

ANDRUS, ETHEL PERCY (Sept. 21, 1884–July 13, 1967), educator and founder of both the National Retired Teachers Association and the American Association of Retired Persons, was born in San Francisco, the daughter of George Wallace Andrus, a lawyer, and Lucretia Frances Duke. When Andrus was an infant, the family moved to Chicago so that her father could continue his legal studies at the University of Chicago. Andrus grew up in that city, graduating from Austin High School in 1900 and the University of Chicago (Ph.B.) in 1903.

Andrus taught English and German at Lewis Institute (later the Illinois Institute of Technology) from 1903 to 1910. While teaching, she also took courses at the institute and was awarded her B.S. in 1918. In her spare time, she served as a volunteer at Hull House and at the Chicago Commons, two settlement houses. In an autobiographical sketch, she attributed this "urge to serve" as "an extension of what I daily was seeing in my father's life—a conviction that we must give of ourselves, to our fellows—must do some good, somewhere, for which we would receive no pay other than the satisfaction of the doing."

Because of her father's failing health, Andrus moved with the family back to California in 1910. She taught for a year at Santa Paula High School and then, from 1911 to 1916, at Manual Arts High School in Los Angeles, also serving for one year as acting principal. She went to Abraham Lincoln High School in Los Angeles as vice-principal in February 1916 and, the following June, became principal, a position she held for twenty-eight years. Andrus thus became the first woman high school principal in California.

Lincoln was a large urban school with students from varied ethnic, racial, and cultural backgrounds; it had a high delinquency rate and tension often existed between parents and teachers. Andrus therefore dedicated herself to the twin goals of helping "our many nationalities" to respect "their own roots and the traditions alike of America and the land and faith of their forefathers" and of bringing together the school and community. She established at Lincoln the Opportunity School for Adults in the evening to serve the immigrant parents of her pupils. This soon developed into a full-fledged adult evening school that offered courses leading to a high school diploma. In 1940 the Juvenile Court of East Los Angeles awarded a special citation to Andrus and the school for their roles in reducing the rate of juvenile delinquency in the neighborhood. So successful was her attempt to meld school and community that the section of eastern Los Angeles in which the school was located came to be called Lincoln Heights. In 1940 the National Education Association chose Lincoln as one of the schools to be used as a case study for the textbook *Learning Ways of Democracy*.

Andrus herself returned to school, earning her M.A. in 1928 and her Ph.D. in 1930 from the University of Southern California. During summer sessions from 1930 to 1940, she taught guidance, educational philosophy, and school administration at the University of Southern California, Stanford University, and the University of California at Los Angeles. Her career as an educator seemingly ended when she resigned her position as principal of Lincoln in 1944 in order to nurse her invalid mother.

In retirement Andrus received a pension of $60 a month. Although she had additional income, she began to wonder how other retired teachers lived. Her position as welfare director of the southern section of the California Retired Teachers Association made her more sharply aware of the problem. As she began to investigate how different states financed teachers' pensions, it became obvious to her that a national organization was needed. Thus, in 1947 she founded the National Retired Teachers Association (NRTA) and became its president. Besides lobbying across the country for better-funded pension systems, the NRTA published a quarterly journal (beginning in 1950); established a teachers' retirement home (Grey Gables) in Ojai, Calif. (1954); initiated a travel program geared to the needs of the elderly; and opened a mail-order pharmaceutical program to provide prescription medicines at low cost.

The most significant of the NRTA's actions was the introduction of a low-cost health and accident insurance program for those over sixty-five. The pilot program, sponsored by the Continental Casualty Company of New York, was offered nationally in 1956 to NRTA members. The first of its kind, the insurance program quickly became so popular that retired persons from other professions wanted access to it. This led Andrus in 1958 to found the American Association of Retired Persons (AARP), which was open to all retired people over the age of fifty-five. With Andrus as its president, the AARP extended to its members all the benefits won for teachers through the NRTA. Both organizations became powerful lobbying forces in Congress. In 1961, Andrus formed the Retirement Research and Welfare Association, a nonprofit foundation to channel funds provided by gifts or legacies into research and philanthropy. That same year she was appointed to the advisory council of the White House Conference on Aging. In 1963 she established the Institute of Life-Time Learning in Washington, D.C., to offer classes and seminars for senior citizens; other branches were soon opened in California and Florida. She also established and edited the monthly magazine of the AARP, *Modern Maturity*.

In 1964, at the age of eighty, Andrus still traveled up to 16,000 miles a month on behalf of the NRTA and the AARP. She continued to oppose mandatory retirement laws and to crusade for wider job opportunities for older people, urging others to follow her own example by embarking on a second career. She died in Long Beach, Calif.

[Andrus' numerous published articles include "An Experiment in Social Living," Jan. 1935; "Core Curriculum at the Lincoln High School," Jan. 1937; and "Social Living Classes for the Underprivileged," Nov. 1939, all in *California Journal of Secondary Education*. She also wrote many articles for the magazines she edited: *Journal of the Association of Retired Persons International*, *Dynamic Maturity*, and *Modern Maturity*, the Jan. 1968 issue of which was dedicated to her and provides the most comprehensive information concerning her work. Her feelings are best revealed in an unpublished autobiographical sketch, available from the AARP headquarters in Washington, D.C., and all quotations above are taken from it. See also Dorothy Crippen, ed., *The Wisdom of Ethel Percy Andrus* (1968). A valuable popular article is Jean L. Brock, "Dynamic Retirement Is Their Goal," *Reader's Digest*, Jan. 1964. An obituary appeared in the *New York Times*, July 15, 1967.]

MELBA PORTER HAY

ANTHONY, JOHN J. (Sept. 1, 1898–July 16, 1970), radio personality and human-relations adviser, was born Lester Kroll in New York City. His family background and early years are shadowy, in part because he was always secretive about his family background. He dropped out of school at an early age and held a variety of jobs in New York during the 1920's. According to one rumor, he was, among other things, a taxicab driver, though he claimed to have been an editor of a "taxicab publication."

Anthony married young and in 1929 was divorced from his first wife, Stella; they had two children. He was unable or unwilling to make his alimony payments and served a jail sentence for his refusal. After his release, he founded the Marital Relations Institute and made himself its director. He provided counseling and information to persons seeking marital advice, charging a $5 fee. It was at this time that he began to use the name John J. Anthony, feeling that it had a more dignified sound than his legal name. He also began to fabricate impressive educational credentials for himself, claiming to hold three university degrees and to have studied with Sigmund Freud in Europe, all of which he later denied.

By the mid-1930's the Marital Relations Institute was beginning to show some signs of success. In 1935 it issued the first of a series of reports on alimony and divorce that purported to prove that 69 percent of the women who sent their husbands to jail for nonpayment of alimony were pathological. The next year, the Marital Relations Institute submitted to the New York State legislature several reports calling for changes in New York marriage and divorce laws, including premarital blood tests, the extension of the waiting period between the issuance of a marriage license and the wedding ceremony, and the establishment of a separate court to deal with marital and domestic problems.

As early as 1930, Anthony was heard on New

York radio station WMCA, offering advice on marriage and domestic life, but the Marital Relations Institute occupied most of his time until 1937. In September 1936 a WMCA program called "The Goodwill Court" had gone onto a national network and had enjoyed tremendous audience success. By December, however, the show had drawn such sharp criticism from the legal profession that the New York Supreme Court ruled that judges and lawyers who went on the show (which specialized in dispensing legal advice in response to listeners' queries) would be disbarred, and therefore, the show was canceled that month, leaving a large hole in WMCA's program schedule. Anthony went to WMCA with a proposal to do a show similar to "Goodwill Court," but instead of having lawyers and judges respond to listeners' inquiries about legal matters, he would answer the audience's questions about domestic and marital problems. WMCA's management was eager to find a replacement for their highly successful—and lucrative—show, and in August 1937, Anthony's program "The Goodwill Hour" premiered on the Mutual Network.

The show drew considerable criticism from various psychiatric and psychological organizations, but it was popular with Sunday-night listeners, and in 1938, Ironized Yeast became its national sponsor. The format of the show was simple. An announcer (Roland Winters) would open the show with a line such as "You have a friend and adviser in John J. Anthony." Anthony would then say, "What is your problem, madam [or sir]?" A client, selected by Anthony from the cards and letters sent to him, would then deliver a three- or four-minute monologue, typically describing a problem with sex, alcohol, money, infidelity, or another source of domestic stress. Anthony would then make a suitably pious or general suggestion, advising the person to try harder, pray, or be more forgiving. He would then go on to the next guest.

The program was extremely successful. By 1939, Anthony was being paid $3,000 a week and his radio show was being carried on 700 stations. His minimum fee for a counseling session at the Marital Relations Institute had gone to $25, and his book, *Marriage and Family Problems and How to Solve Them* (1939), was selling well. In 1940 his show jumped from the Mutual Network to the National Broadcasting Company's Blue Network, and in 1943 it moved back to Mutual, picking up Clark Chewing Gum as its sponsor.

Anthony's show lost its network distribution in 1953, and he moved to Los Angeles. In 1954, Los Angeles station KTTV gave Anthony a half-hour weekly television show with essentially the same format as the one he had developed for radio, but the program did not receive network distribution and was canceled after a brief run.

Anthony was a moderately competent nonobjective painter, and he had a show at the Arthur Brown Gallery in Manhattan in 1949. After moving to Los Angeles, he tried to develop his artistic talent commercially by investing in a product called Talking Pictures, which used phonograph records as a system for teaching people how to paint. The project was unsuccessful.

After the demise of his television program and the failure of his art project, Anthony continued to lecture and to work on West Coast radio, but he was basically in retirement. His second wife, the former Etille Sorella, produced most of his radio shows. They had one child. In 1964, Anthony was appointed a commissioner of the Human Relations Board for Los Angeles County. In 1967 he played a divorce-court judge in the movie *Divorce, American Style,* and he continued to appear on radio and television shows and to lecture. He died in San Francisco.

Anthony was among the first and most successful of America's many media psychologists, and the success of "The Goodwill Hour" helped to establish a small but enduring niche in radio and television for "human interest" shows such as "Queen for a Day" and "This Is Your Life." But Anthony's persistent claims to have been a moving force in the reform of marriage and divorce laws and in the establishment of premarriage courses in college curricula are hard to credit.

Certainly, Anthony was among the first to recognize the commercial potential of popular psychology. An inveterate showman given to exaggeration, braggadocio, and—when useful—outright lies (he gave his birthdate variously as 1896, 1898, 1900, and 1902, depending on which age seemed more expedient), he saw that advice, packaged correctly, could make good money. He was one of the most successful practitioners of the psychological self-help tradition that has since become so thoroughly entrenched in American popular taste.

[Although Anthony claimed authorship for a number of titles, most of them seem to have been pamphlets issued by his Marital Relations Institute. His only published book, *Marriage and Family Problems and How to Solve Them* (1939), was reissued as *Mr. Anthony Solves Your Personal Problems* (1945).

Sources of information on Anthony are sparse and often contradictory. The Billy Rose Theater Collection of the New York Public Library at Lincoln Center has some publicity photographs and three scrapbooks of clippings on Anthony. The Broadcast Pioneers Library in Washington, D.C., has a letter from Anthony dated 1961 that purports to summarize his career. In fact, it is devoid of useful facts or information. See Richard Lamparski, *Whatever Became of . . .* (1967); and John Dunning, *Tune in Yesterday* (1976). An obituary is in the *New York Times*, July 18, 1970.]

NICHOLAS A. SHARP

ARDEN, ELIZABETH (Dec. 31, 1878–Oct. 18, 1966), beautician and cosmetics manufacturer, was born Florence Nightingale Graham in Woodbridge, near Toronto, Canada, the daughter of William Graham, a market gardener on a leased farm, and Susan Tadd, who died when Arden was six.

Her education in local schools ended before she completed high school. Propelled by her name, Arden entered nursing, but she quickly abandoned the profession, declaring years later that she preferred helping well people maintain their health to caring for those who had lost it. The restlessness that ultimately helped make Arden the most successful woman entrepreneur in American history drove her from one low-paying job to another.

She joined her brother William in New York City in 1907, continuing her erratic employment pattern until 1908, when she secured a clerical job from Eleanor Adair, who specialized in facial massages. Sensing the possibilities in the beauty treatment field, Arden asked Adair to teach her how to give facials. Having learned the technique, she was further encouraged when those on whom she practiced declared she had healing hands.

Intent on capitalizing on her new skill, Arden joined Elizabeth Hubbard in 1909 and opened an upper-floor salon under Hubbard's name at 509 Fifth Avenue, New York City. When the two strong-minded women parted in 1910, Arden kept the salon with a $6,000 loan from her brother and found a pleasing name for her enterprise by borrowing "Elizabeth" from her former partner and a surname from Tennyson's poem "Enoch Arden." She furnished her salon with antiques and an Oriental rug, and after a four-year quest, ending in Paris, perfected a facial with which she was satisfied.

Using a scientific approach, which was new to cosmetics, Arden conducted a parallel quest for a light, fluffy cleansing cream. She succeeded in 1914 when a chemist, A. Fabian Swanson, compounded the preparation she named Amoretta. That same year Arden launched her first branch salon in Washington, D.C. In the years that followed, Arden opened more branches (including one in Paris in 1922) and developed new cosmetics and additional beauty treatments as she moved her premier salon up Fifth Avenue—to 673 in 1915 and 691 in 1930. In 1938 a reporter for *Fortune* magazine wrote that Arden "built her business on swank, ultraexclusiveness and a line beautifully packaged and styled."

On Nov. 29, 1915, Arden became an American citizen when she married Thomas Jenkins Lewis. They had no children. For fifteen of the nineteen years of their marriage (which ended in divorce in 1934) he managed the wholesale department of what was fast becoming the Arden cosmetics empire, which in time would boast 300 products sold in forty-four countries. The most popular of Arden's products was Velva Moisture Film, applied before makeup. Another best-seller was an astringent lotion called Ardena Skin Tonic. Arden, who had an excellent sense of color, mixed every new shade and tried each new preparation on herself, friends, and employees. Declaring that "every woman has the right to be beautiful," she insisted (despite the costly inventory) on providing a complete beauty service for a wide range of complexions and skin types. She introduced eye shadow and mascara to the United States in 1917, and in 1932 she began a line of lipsticks and other makeup to match the user's clothes. Arden was the creator of the cosmetics industry and changed the appearance of American women.

Although cosmetics sales brought Arden the bulk of her fortune, she also pioneered a system of exercises to maintain the body, some choreographed to popular music and others inspired by yoga. She made the first record on how to do exercises and had the first exercise room associated with a beauty salon. Procedures purporting to restore the skin included a course of thirty-two electrical shortwave treatments with her pink Ardena Youth Masque and a sweat-inducing coating of paraffin, applied from head to toe. Elizabeth Arden salons, located in the world's principal cities, were often unprofitable, but they gave her business the panache to put and keep it at the forefront of the cosmetics trade. The company, which prided itself on being exclusive, was a giant in reputation rather than in production.

Aware early of the importance of advertising, Arden told the American Advertising Federation that "repetition makes reputation and reputation makes customers." She exhibited an excellent sense of timing and based her business decisions on a shrewd knowledge of the psychology of women and on a practical grasp of what they would find appealing. Most of her customers were women over forty years old who reached for youth and beauty through her treatments. Appearing far younger than her years, Arden, slim and five feet, two inches tall, with a legendary vitality, beautiful skin, and hair that slowly changed from reddish brown to blondish beige, was her firm's best advertisement. Although all her salons had red doors, she considered pink the most flattering color in the spectrum. She usually wore pink and used it to decorate her homes and salons and in the packaging of all her products. Once she refused to use $100,000 worth of cosmetics jars because they deviated slightly from the soft, pale, fabled shade of Arden pink.

While vacationing in Maine in the early 1930's, Arden purchased a farm next to the home of her friend Elisabeth Marbury, a prominent literary agent who had introduced her to society. Ever the entrepreneur, Arden named it Maine Chance Farm and by 1934 used it as a restorative beauty treatment center, where in luxurious surroundings clients were given individually prescribed low-calorie diets and exercises. The nutritionist Gaylord Houser worked out appetizing menus more reliant on vegetables and fruit than on meat and sweets. By insisting that youthfulness was an important ingredient of beauty, Arden contributed to the youth craze. But by advocating moderate exercise and a healthy diet she also helped older women remain active. In 1947 she opened a winter center, Arizona Maine Chance Farm, in Phoenix, where customers included Ava Gardner and Mamie Eisenhower.

Arden also established a Maine Chance Farm in Lexington, Ky., for racehorses, making it possible for a biographer to say that she "made her fame and fortune from rich women and fast horses." She bought her first racehorse in 1931 and remained an important figure in racing circles through the early 1960's, using the name Elizabeth N. Graham and often owning as many as 150 horses. In 1945 her stables topped all others in prize money. The next year her horses got her featured on the cover of *Time* magazine, and in 1947 her horse Jet Pilot won the Kentucky Derby. Arden, who united cherry pink with white and blue for her racing colors, usually visited her horses twice a week and bought them cashmere blankets. She named her largest-selling perfume and her yearly charity ball Blue Grass in her horses' honor, and prescribed her own cosmetic preparations for their minor injuries and rubdowns. She was said to treat "her women like horses and her horses like women" (Whitman, 1971).

When a favorite horse to whom she was feeding an orange bit the tip off her right index finger in 1959, her arch rival Helena Rubinstein queried, "What happened to the horse?" In their fifty-year feud Rubinstein hired Thomas Lewis, Arden's former husband and sales manager, after Arden had coaxed away a dozen Rubinstein employees including Harry Johnson, whom Arden paid $50,000 a year to be her general manager. After Rubinstein married a prince, Arden married Prince Michael Evlanoff, a Russian émigré, on Dec. 30, 1942; they were divorced in 1944.

Arden employed a number of noble expatriates, including a Persian prince and a Russian general and later, during World War II, hired many Europeans whose lives had been disrupted by the war. In her cosmetics factories she also employed numerous blind workers and a much larger percentage of women than worked in similar jobs. In keeping her company the most efficient in the cosmetics industry, Arden was always exacting and often petulant and tyrannical. Although she readily fired workers and according to *Fortune* magazine she had a deserved reputation for training more people for "the competition than any other manufacturer in the business," Arden consistently paid top wages and had many long-term employees on whom she lavished presents.

Always innovative and a firm believer in what she called "the concept of total beauty," Arden started a fashion business in 1943. Oscar de la Renta was among those who created exclusive collections for her salons. In the 1950's Arden opened the first men's boutique attached to a beauty salon; earlier she had been the first major manufacturer of women's cosmetics to put out a line for men.

Although Arden was fluttery in her movements and sometimes asked males for advice with a docile air, she was the absolute dictator and sole owner of her company. She argued and in her career proved that women were not incapable because of their sex or temperament of assuming managerial and executive duties. Arden, who insisted she was much younger, was nearly eighty-eight when she died in New York City.

As the dowager empress of the beauty business Arden remained in command of her company until her death. "There's only one Elizabeth like me, and that's the queen," she told a reporter for the *Saturday Evening Post*. She was badgered by the Federal Trade Commission, limited by the Food and Drug and Robinson-Patman acts, and harassed by competitors, yet her company's sales ultimately reached over $60 million yearly. Arden left $4 million to numerous long-term employees, but the bulk of her $30 million to $40 million estate went to her family, particularly to her sister Gladys, Vicomtesse de Maublanc, who ran the Arden business in France, and to her niece and residual heir, Patricia Young, who for years had been her companion. To satisfy inheritance taxes, the business was sold to Eli Lilly and Company for $37.5 million.

[See *New Yorker*, Apr. 6, 1935; *Fortune*, Oct. 1938; *New York Times*, June 22, 1939; *Time*, May 6, 1946; *Saturday Evening Post*, Apr. 24, 1948; *Cosmopolitan*, June 1956; *Business Week*, Oct. 17, 1970; and *Fortune*, Jan. 1977. See also Alden Whitman, *The Obituary Book* (1971); Alfred Allen Lewis and Constance Woodworth, *Miss Elizabeth Arden* (1972); and Alden Whitman, *Come to Judgment* (1980). Obituary notices are in the *New York Times*, Oct. 19, 1966; *Time* and *Life*, both Oct. 28, 1966; and *Newsweek*, Oct. 31, 1966.]

OLIVE HOOGENBOOM

ARMOUR, THOMAS DICKSON ("TOMMY") (Sept. 24, 1895–Sept. 11, 1968), professional golfer, was born in Edinburgh, Scotland, the son of a confectioner with an avid interest in golf (his parents' names are unknown). Armour's childhood was spent primarily in the company of his older brother Alexander, a golfer who later won the Scottish Amateur Championship. The two boys also became friends with Bobby Cruickshank, from whom Tommy Armour learned the effective use of long irons and woods, which later characterized his game.

When he was about eighteen years old Armour matriculated at Edinburgh University, but his formal education was cut short by World War I. He enlisted in 1914 and served with the Black Watch Highland Regiment as a machine gunner. He was severely gassed at the Battle of Ypres and lost the use of his left eye. Later in the war a shell hit his tank and shattered his arm. His golfing style, which included many waggles, was influenced by these injuries.

Rather than resuming his studies, after the war Armour competed in British amateur golf tournaments. His excellent long game enabled him to rise immediately to the forefront in the amateur ranks. In 1919 he finished second in the Irish Amateur Open and won the Dispatch Trophy. By playing privately between tournaments against many of the top British professionals, he further sharpened his skills and was able to win four titles the next year, including the Scottish and French amateur championships. In 1919 he married Consuelo Carrera, whose wealth enabled him to concentrate exclusively on golf. They had two children.

His early successes enabled Armour to represent Britain on a team in a pre-Walker Cup international competition against the United States, where he won his match. The growing popularity of golf in America and the large number of tournaments there prompted Armour to emigrate in 1921. He won three minor tournaments that year (the New London, the Engineers, and the Nassau Amateurs). Two years after becoming an American citizen in 1924, Armour represented America in a match against Britain, thus becoming the only golfer to compete on national teams from both countries.

The height of Armour's competitive career came after he turned professional in 1924. In the next eleven years he won fourteen major titles, including the United States Open in 1927, the Canadian Open three times between 1927 and 1934, the U.S. Professional Golfers

Association (PGA) Championship in 1930, and the Miami Open in 1932 and 1935. His most important and gratifying victory came in the British Open of 1931, which was played for the first time at Carnoustie, Scotland, on a course that the London *Times* called "fierce enough and long enough" to defeat all but the most intrepid and long-driving competitors.

Armour, who was prematurely gray, became known in the 1920's as the "Silver Scot," a sobriquet that could just as readily have referred to his growing reputation as a raconteur. His love of sport and talent for telling stories became an increasingly important source of revenue in the interwar years, when he was a regular speaker on the banquet circuit. It also brought him into contact with wealthy Americans, one of whom, Estelle D. Andrews, the widow of an iron manufacturer, became his second wife soon after he divorced his first wife in 1929. Armour adopted Andrews' son.

After his competitive years, Armour established a reputation as a keen student of golf and one of its most successful teachers. Despite the fact that he was a stickler about the rules, correcting other players who tended to bend them, he was well liked and highly regarded by fellow professionals. His students included the great golfers of his day, including Bobby Jones, as well as the rich and famous, notably Richard Nixon. Perhaps Armour's success came about because he was the most expensive instructor of his time, charging $50 an hour even though he provided only a few minutes of personal instruction in each lesson. He also wrote three well-received books on golf: *How to Play Your Best Golf All the Time* (1953), *A Round of Golf with Tommy Armour* (1959), and *Tommy Armour's ABC's of Golf* (1967).

Armour was elected a charter member of the PGA Hall of Fame in 1940. His impact on the sport for forty years was rivaled by few and surpassed by none. He died in Larchmont, N.Y.

[In addition to articles from 1922 to 1935, obituaries appeared in the *New York Times*, Sept. 14, 1968; the *Times* (London), Sept. 14, 1968; *Time*, Sept. 20, 1968; and *Newsweek*, Sept. 23, 1968. Armour's career is summarized in Len Elliott and Barbara Kelly, *Who's Who in Golf* (1976).

CHARLES R. MIDDLETON

ARNO, PETER (Jan. 8, 1904–Feb. 22, 1968, cartoonist, was born Curtis Arnoux Peters, Jr., in New York City, the son of Curtis Arnoux Peters, a New York State Supreme Court justice, and Edith Theresa Haynes. He attended the Hotchkiss School in Lakeville, Conn., and Yale College (1922–1923). Although his father expected him to prepare for a career in law or banking, Arno preferred art and music, contributing drawings to the *Yale Record* and organizing the Yale Collegians, a nine-man band with Rudy Vallee as lead singer. Arno played piano, banjo, and accordion and performed with the group at Gilda Gray's Rendezvous, one of the first postwar New York nightclubs. He also wrote music, achieving minor Tin Pan Alley success with a song entitled "My Heart Is on My Sleeve." Later he coauthored a Broadway musical satire, *Here Comes the Bride* (1931).

Arno wrote that he was "a painter at heart" in the early 1920's, although he never formally studied painting or drawing. Several restaurants and cafés offered him employment decorating screens and panels, including the Bulldog Grille in New Haven, where he painted a mural satirizing Yale football heroes. He began submitting cartoons to *Life* and *Judge*, but none was accepted. In 1923, Arno left Yale for the artists' milieu of Greenwich Village, changed his name to Peter Arno, and continued his panel painting.

After more of Arno's cartoons were rejected, he was about to accept an offer from a band in Chicago when the *New Yorker* bought one of his drawings in 1925. Arno's work appeared regularly in the *New Yorker* for the next forty-three years, helping to establish the magazine's distinctive voice and style. Robert Benchley credited Arno with revitalizing the joking cartoon: "With the advent of the *New Yorker*, and with the *New Yorker*, Peter Arno, the entire technique of picturized jokes underwent a sudden and complete change. The old, feeble, two-line joke practically disappeared and in its place came a fresh and infinitely more civilized form—the illustrated single remark."

Although he refused credit for inventing the one-line caption, Arno admitted to being "one of the first to use it consistently, so that it became a trademark." The "Whoops Sisters," his first successful cartoon characters, were, however, still captioned in dialogue. Attired in muffs and silly hats, the sisters were gin-soaked harridans who, according to Arno, "cavorted about town yelling 'Whoops,' followed by appropriate remarks, at the pop of the nearest button."

The urbane cartoons for which Arno became best known retained the irreverence and earthiness of the Whoops Sisters but were rendered with more visual and verbal economy. His favorite subjects were old roués, generously proportioned dowagers, curvaceous showgirls, haughty maître d's, and brainless ingenues, all of whom he depicted with powerful black lines and crisp silhouettes. With this cast of images, which also includes his "Cadwallader," a balding little man who never quite catches the drift of an innuendo, Arno relentlessly skewered the pretensions, prejudices, and hypocrisies of New York café society.

Well known as a Manhattan bon vivant, Arno was on intimate terms with his subject matter. Tall, strikingly handsome, and impeccably dressed, he was voted the best-dressed man in America by the Custom Tailors Guild in 1941. His social life was chronicled in the gossip columns, especially after an altercation in 1931 with Cornelius Vanderbilt, Jr., over his attentions to Mrs. Vanderbilt. At the time, Arno had only recently been divorced from Lois Long, whom he had married on Aug. 12, 1927, and who wrote for the *New Yorker* under the pen name Lipstick; they had one child. In August 1935, Arno married Mary ("Timmie") Livingston Lansing, a celebrated debutante, from whom he was divorced in 1939.

In the 1920's Arno's relationship with the milieu he satirized was equivocal, but by the late 1930's it was clearly negative. "At no time in the history of the world have there been so many damned morons gathered in one place as here in New York right now," he said in 1937. "I had a really hot impulse to go and exaggerate their ridiculous aspects. That anger, if you like, gave my stuff punch and made it live."

Technically Arno's drawings delivered their punch through a carefully weighted interdependency of picture and caption—which was, in his mind, the most important characteristic of the *New Yorker* cartoon. "The reader had to examine the picture," he explained, "before the joker in the caption made its point, or vice-versa. The quick revelation of incongruity (actually the sudden realization by the reader that he'd been hoodwinked) brought the laugh."

An Arno cartoon for the *New Yorker* began with rough sketches, which were reviewed at weekly meetings of the magazine's art staff. Some would be picked out for finishing, often with suggestions from the staff for improving the picture or rewording the caption. Back at the drawing board, Arno would pencil in the layout, swearing that he used more erasers than all other artists at the magazine combined. The skeleton of the drawing was then laid down in heavy india ink, followed by a laying-on of wash (an ecclesiastical-sounding process, in Arno's mind). The final product, according to one of his *New Yorker* colleagues, was an image so distinctive that that "bold signature of his was the only unnecessary thing in any Arno drawing."

Arno spent the last years of his life living with his mother in Harrison, N.Y. Although ill with emphysema, he continued to contribute regularly to the *New Yorker*, which published one of his cartoons the week of his death. In this drawing, a middle-aged Pan plays his pipes and cavorts before a scantily clad nymph. Clearly unimpressed, she looks at him and says, "Oh, grow up."

[Arno published several collections of his cartoons, among them *Whoops Dearie!* (1927); *Peter Arno's Parade* (1929); *Hullabaloo* (1930), with an introduction by Robert Benchley; *Peter Arno's Circus* (1931); *Peter Arno's Favorites* (1932); *Bride for a Night* (1934); *For Members Only* (1935); *Cartoon Revue* (1941); *Peter Arno's Man in the Shower* (1944); *Peter Arno's Pocket Book* (1946); and *Peter Arno's Ladies and Gentlemen* (1951). Arno's relationship with the *New Yorker* is described in James Thurber, *The Years with Ross* (1959), and Brendan Gill, *Here at the New Yorker* (1975). An obituary is in the *New York Times*, Feb. 23, 1968.]

PATRICIA FAILING

ARNOLD, THURMAN WESLEY (June 2, 1891–Nov. 7, 1969), lawyer, educator, social analyst, and government official, was born in Laramie, Wyo., the son of Constantine Peter Arnold, a prosperous lawyer and rancher, and Annie Brockway. He attended the University of Wyoming preparatory school, spent a year at Wabash College in Indiana, and in 1911 received a B.A. at Princeton University. After earning an LL.D. from Harvard Law School in 1914, he began legal practice in Chicago. As a member of the Illinois National Guard, he was among those mobilized for Mexican border duty in 1916.

During World War I Arnold served as an artillery officer. On Sept. 7, 1917, he married Frances Longan; following his return to civilian life in 1919, they moved to Laramie, had two children, and settled into a genial, small-town life. Arnold became a prosperous lawyer and rancher involved in civic affairs and in the Lions Club, the Elks Club, and the chamber of commerce. He lectured at the University of Wyoming, became a vestryman in the Episcopal church and a leader in the Democratic party, was elected to a term in the state legislature and a term as mayor, and ran for the office of county prosecutor.

In 1927 Arnold's relationship with a former Harvard classmate led to the offer of a deanship at the University of West Virginia Law School; he thus began an academic career that would soon earn him a national reputation. His innovations included curricular reform, faculty upgrading, and the promotion of quantitative research on court procedures. The last brought him into association with Charles Clark, the dean of Yale Law School, and in 1930 he moved to Yale, then the center of legal realism and innovative legal education. At Yale the focus of legal scholarship was on discovering the "real" as opposed to the formal or "paper" rules of judicial behavior, on effecting reforms that would make the legal system more responsive to social needs, and on replacing exercises in formal deductive logic with an empirically grounded and pragmatically applied sociological science. In that milieu, Arnold became a professor noted for his unconventional classroom techniques, his attacks on traditional legal theory, and his efforts to bring social scientific and psychological insights into legal study and training.

While at Yale, Arnold wrote two major works of social analysis, *The Symbols of Government* (1935) and *The Folklore of Capitalism* (1937). In them, he exposed the myths surrounding established institutions, especially those about the evils of government intervention and those allowing large business corporations and other "private governments" to disguise themselves as individuals, posited in traditional market and democratic theory. Yet, unlike most legal realists, he held that such myths performed important social functions and that effective government must come not through popular enlightenment but through an elite engaged in constructive kinds of myth management. Some critics detected totalitarian overtones or at least a refusal to confront ethical questions. But many read with glee his witty, Veblenesque puncturing of conservative shibboleths, and *Folklore* unexpectedly became a best-seller and was widely quoted in the popular media.

Between 1933 and 1937 Arnold's academic contacts also led to special governmental assignments in which he worked with a number of New Deal lawyers and administrators. In March 1938, on the recommendation of Robert Jackson, he was chosen to spearhead the administration's new drive against anticompetitive business practices. Although in *Folklore* Arnold had poked wicked fun at the antitrust myth, he now became the New Deal's "trustbuster in chief," bent on using the myth to serve reform purposes. During the next five years, as assistant attorney general in charge of antitrust enforcement, Arnold led what some historians call the "great antitrust revival."

Arnold succeeded in turning his gift for satire, wit, and disarming eccentricity into an appealing personal mystique accompanied by high public drama. In one contemporary characterization, he was said to combine the attributes of a small-town storekeeper with those of "a native Rabelais"; in another, he was a "cross between Voltaire and the cowboy." And to the consternation of opponents on both the right and the left, he was successful in quadrupling antitrust appropriations, making antitrust seem compatible with modern economic needs, and securing nearly as many indictments as during the whole previous history of the Sherman Antitrust Act. He also proved highly innovative as a prosecutor, pioneering the use of massed indictments, industrywide campaigns, economic analyses, and consent decrees as substitutes for regulatory law.

Arnold's actions are generally credited with helping to strengthen and preserve the nation's antitrust apparatus. But assessments of the wisdom of this and its effects on anticompetitive organization and behavior have varied greatly; and in two major areas—his efforts to deal with labor-union abuses and to make antitrust a working part of wartime economic management—Arnold had little success. He became increasingly disillusioned and frustrated, and in March 1943 he accepted President Franklin Roosevelt's offer to appoint him to the United States Court of Appeals for the District of Columbia. As an appellate judge, he wrote several important opinions, notably on the issues of censorship, insanity, and patent rights. But the work, he found, was ill suited to his temperament, and in 1945 he returned to private practice, first in a short-lived partnership with Arne Wiprud and then as senior member of the Washington firm of Arnold, Fortas, and Porter.

After 1946 Arnold's firm became one of the nation's preeminent practitioners of corporate law and representation. But in speeches and writings he continued to defend the antitrust laws, and during the McCarthy era he became a staunch defender of civil liberties, handling for little or no fee a series of celebrated loyalty, security, and censorship cases. His tolerance in this regard, however, did not extend to the civil disobedience that characterized the 1960's, and he remained a strong supporter of President Lyndon Johnson's Vietnam policies. Arnold died in Alexandria, Va.

[Arnold's papers are in the University of Wyoming Library at Laramie. His writings include *Report on West Virginia Procedure and Legal Reform* (1927); *Cases on Trials, Judgments, and Appeals* (1936); *Bottlenecks of Business* (1940); *Democracy and Free Enterprise* (1942); *Cartels or Free Enterprise?* (1945); *The Future of Democratic Capitalism* (1950); and the autobiographical *Fair Fights and Foul* (1965). He also wrote numerous articles.

The best biographical accounts are in Edward N. Kearny, *Thurman Arnold, Social Critic* (1970); and Gene M. Gressley, *Voltaire and the Cowboy: The Letters of Thurman Arnold* (1977). See also Joseph Alsop and Robert Kintner, "Trust Buster," *Saturday Evening Post*, Aug. 12, 1939; Richard L. Strout, "The Folklore of Thurman Arnold," *Christian Science Monitor* magazine, May 11, 1940; William B. Huie, "Thurman Arnold," *American Mercury*, June 1942; Corwin Edwards, "Thurman Arnold and the Antitrust Laws," *Political Science Quarterly*, Sept. 1943; and Louis Cassels, "Arnold, Fortas, Porter and Prosperity," *Harper's*, Nov. 1951.

On Arnold's career, see Gene M. Gressley, "Thurman Arnold, Antitrust, and the New Deal," *Business History Review*, Summer 1964; Ellis W. Hawley, *The New Deal and the Problem of Monopoly* (1966); Wilfrid E. Rumble, Jr., *American Legal Realism* (1968); and Wilson D. Miscamble, "Thurman Arnold Goes to Washington," *Business History Review*, Spring 1982. An obituary is in the *New York Times*, Nov. 8, 1969.]

Ellis W. Hawley

BABSON, ROGER WARD (July 6, 1875–Mar. 5, 1967), business forecaster, statistician, and author, was born in Gloucester, Mass., the son of Nathaniel Babson, a dry-goods merchant and wholesaler, and Ellen Stearns. Nathaniel Babson was stern, demanding, and exacting, whereas his wife had a warm and gentle disposition. Young Roger spent summers on his grandfather's farm. "I owe more to that farm than any educational institution, including MIT [Massachusetts Institute of Technology]," Babson later wrote. He attended Collins Elementary School for six years. An indifferent student who was quite rowdy and belonged to a number of gangs, Babson entered Gloucester High School in 1890. At his father's insistence, he studied bookkeeping at the expense of required courses, resulting in his diploma being marked "special course" when he graduated from high school in 1894.

That year Babson again acceded to his father's wishes and entered MIT to study engineering. During summer vacations he worked mostly on road-building projects.

Upon receiving his B.S. in 1898, Babson began looking for a career in what his father called a "repeat" business, like insurance or investment banking. He worked for an investment house in Boston but was soon fired for being too independent. Thereafter he set up a profitable bond-selling business in New York City and eventually became associated with a bond firm that specialized in utilities. In 1900 Babson married Grace Margaret Knight, the daughter of a clergyman. They had one child. His first wife died in 1956, and on June 1, 1957, Babson married Nona Margaret Dougherty.

Babson always claimed that he was a rugged individualist who wanted to make a living by furnishing "protection to the investor in relation to his capital and income." From his bond-selling experience Babson knew that little care was given to investigation when securities were purchased and that many uninformed people were hurt financially. With this in mind, in 1904, he set up the Business Statistical Organization, Inc. (later Babson Statistical Organization, Inc.), with capital of $1,200; Babson became the president and his wife the treasurer. They were the sole stockholders. The Babsons started to collect, analyze, and index business information on five-inch-by-eight-inch cards. They then issued to subscribers the *Composite Circular*, which provided information on bond offerings.

After the 1907 financial panic, Babson launched his *Babsonchart*. Similar to the earlier *Composite Circular*, the *Babsonchart* advised clients on when to buy and sell stocks, bonds, and commodities. It traced the ups and downs of the stock market in vertical red bars. A solid black line indicated the movements of the bond market. The course of commodity prices was traced by a dotted black line. In addition to the *Babsonchart*, the *Supervised List* suggested what to buy and sell. The *Babsonchart* reflected what Babson referred to as his "area theory" of the business cycle, which was based on Newton's law of action and reaction. The normal line was on the x-axis, and the y-axis recorded the scale of stock prices, the scale of business and commodity prices, and an inverted bond yield scale. The black areas above the normal line represented prosperity, characterized by abnormal expansion of production. The red areas below the normal line represented depression, marked by abnormal curtailment of output. In Babson's view, every period of business prosperity would be followed by an equal and opposite period of depression. To break this cycle, Babson suggested that abnormal booms be minimized by timely contraction of credit.

In 1914 Babson launched the first annual clients' conference, wherein he discussed his business forecasts, analyzed business conditions, and took questions from the floor. As a result of these meetings, Babson's fame and influence spread across the nation. In 1919 Babson established the Babson Institute (later Babson College) in Wellesley Hills, Mass. At that time it was the only undergraduate business school in the United States. He also set up Webber College in Babson Park, Fla., in 1927 to train women for business. A prolific writer, Babson had published thirty-nine books by 1935, when his autobiography came out.

Babson prospered by selling business information. He provided real estate, commodity, bond, stock market, and wage forecasts, as well as political trends. However, his belief that emotions, rather than statistics and information, ruled the world prompted Babson to refer to himself as a "mere statistician." He liked to work with estimates and approximations, and he insisted that in business forecasting one cannot demand too much exactness. In an era when computers and huge data banks were not available, Babson helped generate the knowledge and information that guided many businessmen during the first three decades of the twentieth century. He died in Lake Wales, Fla.

[Babson's papers are in the Horn Library, Babson College, Wellesley, Mass. See Roger W. Babson, *Actions and Reactions* (1935); and *Business Barometers and Investments* (1945). See also the obituary, *New York Times*, Mar. 6, 1967.]

NICHOLAS W. BALABKINS

BACCALONI, SALVATORE (Apr. 14, 1900–Dec. 31, 1969), opera singer, was born in Rome, Italy, the son of Joaquin Baccaloni, a building contractor, and Ferminia Desideri. His musical training began at the San Salvatore in Lauro School in Rome when he was five. In 1906 he began a five-year period of service as chorister at the Sistine Chapel, where he received further vocal training. Soon after his twelfth birthday his voice changed, and he temporarily abandoned music to study architecture at the Academy of Fine Arts in Rome, graduating in 1920. These studies were interrupted during World War I, when Baccaloni served in the signal corps of the Italian army.

Giuseppe Kaschmann, a baritone with the Metropolitan Opera in New York, convinced Baccaloni that his destiny lay in singing. Baccaloni studied voice with Kaschmann for two years (1920–1922) before making his opera debut in April 1922 as Bartolo in *The Barber of Seville* at the Teatro Adriano in Rome. He served his operatic apprenticeship with various Italian companies during the next four years. In 1926, Arturo Toscanini engaged him for Milan's La Scala, where Baccaloni remained for fourteen years. At Toscanini's suggestion, Baccaloni began assuming basso buffo roles. He achieved international renown for his sharply defined characterizations and comedic talent as well as for his vocalism, notably in the title roles in *Don Pasquale* and *Falstaff* and as Dulcamara in *L'elisir d'amore*, Bartolo in *The Barber of Seville* and *The Marriage of Figaro*, and Leporello in *Don Giovanni*.

On Nov. 17, 1928, Baccaloni married Elena Svilarova; they had no children. Following his first tour of South America in 1930, he made his debut in the United States with the Chicago Civic Opera in 1930–1931, when his talent passed unnoticed. More eventful were his appearances at the festivals at Glyndebourne, England, and Salzburg, Austria, from 1936 to 1939 and his return to America in October 1938, when he made his debut with the San Francisco Opera as Leporello. His first appearances with the Metropolitan Opera took place in Philadelphia on Dec. 3, 1940, and in New York City four days later, as Bartolo in *The*

Marriage of Figaro. He scored a personal triumph in New York City on December 21 in the title role of *Don Pasquale,* an opera that had been revived for him.

For more than two decades Baccaloni was the principal basso buffo at the Metropolitan Opera and was heard 297 times in New York City and 146 times on tour, in fifteen roles, though his repertory consisted of more than 150 roles in five languages, in serious as well as comedic parts. During his years at the Metropolitan Opera, Baccaloni made many successful appearances with other opera companies in concerts in America and Europe. At the San Francisco Opera he was heard in the seasons from 1941 to 1954 and from 1958 to 1960. He last performed at the Metropolitan Opera as Fra Melitone in *La forza del destino* on Feb. 14, 1962.

Baccaloni made his film debut in a nonsinging role in *Full of Life* (1957). He subsequently appeared in nonsinging character roles in films such as *Merry Andrew* (1958), *Rock-a-Bye Baby* (1958), *Fanny* (1961), and *The Pigeon That Took Rome* (1962). In 1962 he retired to New York City, where he died.

[See *Time,* Jan. 6, 1941; *Saturday Evening Post,* Nov. 29, 1947; and David Ewen, *Musicians Since 1900* (1978). An obituary is in the *New York Times,* Jan. 1, 1970.]

DAVID EWEN

BAKER, DOROTHY DODDS (Apr. 21, 1907–June 17, 1968), novelist, was born in Missoula, Mont., the daughter of Raymond Branson Dodds, chief division dispatcher for the Northern Pacific Railroad, and Alice Grady. The family moved to California when Dorothy was young so her father could go into the oil business. She studied the violin until she went to college, and she was interested in jazz most of her life. She received her B.A. in 1929 from the University of California, Los Angeles, and her bachelor of education in 1930 from Occidental College in Los Angeles. In college she was especially interested in languages, particularly French. She traveled to Paris and began to write a novel about an unusual romantic triangle set in a college town. While in Paris, on Sept. 2, 1930, she married the poet and novelist Howard Baker, who had been living there among the expatriates. They had two children.

The Bakers moved to Berkeley, Calif., where he was an instructor at the University of California and she a Latin, Spanish, French, and English teacher in a private preparatory school in Oakland. She earned her M.A. at the University of California at Berkeley in 1934. The Bakers next moved to Cambridge, Mass., where Howard Baker was an instructor in English at Harvard from 1937 until 1943. They then returned to California, settling in Terra Bella, where they raised oranges, olives, and cattle.

"When I first began to write," Baker recalled, "I was seriously hampered by an abject admiration for Ernest Hemingway, and I found that the only way I could grow up and get over it was simply to quit writing any direct discourse." She said she studied the nonfiction method of film critic Otis Ferguson. "In fiction I admire above all else simplicity and clarity in both phrase and story," she commented. She also was grateful for the constant helpful criticism of her husband and of Yvor Winters, the poet and critic.

Baker's major work was *Young Man with a Horn* (1938), a sensitive, expert novel about jazz music and musicians. Clifton Fadiman believed it "darned near perfect." The novel, inspired by the jazz music of Leon (Bix) Beiderbecke, was true to the lives and to the music of real jazz musicians. "Jazz music," Baker said, "was one of the very few things I knew much about, and the only thing, except writing, that I had a consistent long-term interest in." The book, a best-seller, was turned into a popular Warner Brothers motion picture in 1950 with Kirk Douglas, Lauren Bacall, Doris Day, and Hoagy Carmichael.

Baker's writing experiments in Paris in 1930 resulted in her 1943 novel *Trio* and her (and her husband's) 1944 play of the same title. The novel and the play dealt honestly with a mature woman's mental and sexual control over a female student. Eventually the girl breaks away from the relationship through the intervention of a young man with whom she is in love. Over all the years devoted to *Trio,* Baker seems to have struggled for a perfect form. She did not fully succeed. Reviewer John Chamberlain thought the novel "first-rate" technically, but "hardly worth a decade of agonizing over its form and content."

Whereas the novel *Trio* was called theatrical, the play was at least once called novelistic. In his review, Stark Young noted that "the play itself went slow at times, as if it were a novel." The play premiered on Dec. 29, 1944, and ran for sixty-seven performances at the Belasco Theater in New York City. It was forced to close after the city's license commissioner, who considered the play immoral, declared the Belasco's license forfeit unless *Trio* was withdrawn.

Baker also wrote the novels *Our Gifted Son* (1948) and *Cassandra at the Wedding* (1962). In addition, she wrote, with her husband, a television play called "The Ninth Day." And she contributed numerous short stories to *Harper's*, *New Republic*, *McCall's*, and other periodicals. Baker occasionally lectured about writing at, among other schools, Stanford University and Pomona College. She died in Springville, Calif.

Baker's honors and awards include the Houghton Mifflin Literary Fellowship in 1937 (for the manuscript of *Young Man with a Horn*), a Guggenheim Fellowship in 1942, the General Literature Gold Medal of the Commonwealth Club of California in 1943 (for the novel *Trio*), and a National Institute of Arts and Letters Fellowship in 1964.

[The Oral History Collection of Columbia University contains the transcript of a tape-recorded autobiographical interview with Baker (this transcript is partially restricted). See John Chamberlain, "Books of the Times," *New York Times*, July 10, 1943; Stark Young, "New Year Start," *New Republic*, Jan. 15, 1945; Jane Rule, *Lesbian Images* (1975); and Lina Mainiero, ed., *American Women Writers*, vol. 1 (1979). See also the obituary, *New York Times*, June 19, 1968.]

DOUGLAS J. MCMILLAN

BANKHEAD, TALLULAH (Jan. 31, 1902–Dec. 12, 1968), actress, was born in Huntsville, Ala., the daughter of William Bankhead, a lawyer and Speaker of the United States House of Representatives, and Adelaide Eugenia Sledge. Bankhead was named for her grandmother, who had been named after a waterfall—Tallulah Falls, Ga. Because her mother died from complications of childbirth when Tallulah was three weeks old, Tallulah's early upbringing was left to aunts in Montgomery and Jasper, Ala. She attended various private schools, including the Convent of the Sacred Heart in New York City, the Mary Baldwin Academy in Staunton, Va., and Fairmont Seminary in Washington, D.C., where she was best known for her tantrums and other attention-getting behavior. Bankhead won a contest in *Picture-Play* magazine, which awarded her a screen contract in New York, and at fifteen she left school for good.

Tallulah Bankhead was a natural actress, as a lifetime of self-dramatization demonstrated. Even as a child she was fascinated by entertainers and took to imitating them for her family. Will Bankhead, who had once hoped to become an actor, encouraged his daughter's theatrics. In *Exiles from Paradise*, Sara Mayfield compared the young Bankhead and Zelda Fitzgerald, another celebrated southern belle: "Even in those days, both of them had dash, a style and daring that left me wide-eyed and open-mouthed with admiration, for Zelda and Dutch, as we called Tallulah, were personalities and performers long before they became famous."

Bankhead's first acting job, compliments of the *Picture-Play* contest, was in the film *The Wishful Girl* (1918), where she went unnoticed. But the movie director Ivan Abramson spotted her in a nonspeaking role on Broadway in *The Squab Farm* (1918) and cast her in *When Men Betray* (1918). The first notice of her work highlighted the qualities that propelled her to stardom. "Miss Tallulah Bankhead," wrote the reviewer, is "exquisite of feature, dainty of form, deliciously feminine. . . . Her appearance brings with it the feeling that the very atmosphere is surcharged with energy." Bankhead continued briefly in films with a featured role in Samuel Goldwyn's *Thirty a Week* (1918) and a walk-on in *The Virtuous Vamp* (1919), but she had her greatest success on the stage.

Bankhead had her first speaking part on Broadway in *39 East* (1919). She made only six appearances before the play was closed by an actors' strike. After a brief run in *Footloose* (1919), a comedy, Tallulah did not work again until 1921, when she went into *Nice People* for 120 performances. She did five more Broadway shows, including *Everyday* (1921), written for her by Rachel Crothers, and then set out for London in quest of theatrical opportunities and Lord Napier Alington, whom she had met in New York.

Bankhead's affair with Alington ended badly, but the move to England advanced her career. Uninvited, Tallulah presented herself backstage to Sir Gerald du Maurier, one of England's great leading men, who cast her in *The Dancers* (1923). She soon established herself as a great favorite of London playgoers. Indeed, she became the object of a Tallulah craze. Her appearance onstage often inspired tumultuous reactions from an adoring public. "What is heard," wrote Arnold Bennett, who witnessed such an occasion, "is terrific, wild, passionate, hysterical roar and shriek." The demonstration would be repeated at curtain call and again at the stage door when Bankhead left the theater. Bennett found it difficult to explain her appeal: "What is Tallulah's secret? If she is beautiful, and she is, her beauty is not classical. How many wayfarers would look twice at her in the street? Her voice is not beautiful. It has, however, the slight seductive huskiness which lent so much enchantment to the acting of Pauline Lord." He neglected to mention that she was bright, witty, and outrageous. To many she personified the exuberance of the 1920's. And to catch a part of that spirit for themselves, women copied her fashions, affected her manner, and even imitated her husky voice, while men sought her company or admired her from the gallery.

Bankhead did sixteen plays during her eight years in England, most notably Noel Coward's *Fallen Angels* (1925), Michael Arlen's *The Green Hat* (1925), and Sidney Howard's *They Knew What They Wanted* (1926). She returned to the United States in 1931 for a film contract with Paramount. In *Tarnished Lady* (1931), *My Sin* (1931), *Thunder Below* (1932), and *Devil and the Deep* (1932), Bankhead portrayed a succession of jaded women. But the vitality she brought to the stage was not evident on the screen. Although "talkies" were the rage, even her famous voice did not save her. Her pictures failed, and Paramount did not renew her contract. Believing herself to be a victim of miscasting, she decided to return to the stage.

Bankhead established herself as one of Broadway's leading ladies during the 1930's, though she had some notable flops. Her *Antony and Cleopatra* (1937) is best remembered for the famous opening line of John Mason Brown's review: "Tallulah Bankhead barged down the Nile last night as Cleopatra—and sank." Yet, her performance as Regina Giddens in *The Little Foxes* (1939) was widely hailed and earned her *Variety*'s best-performance award. Bankhead often appeared with the actor John Emery, whom she married on Aug. 31, 1937, and divorced in June 1941, after a predictably stormy marriage; they had no children.

During the 1940's and 1950's, Bankhead remained busy in the theater. She was praised for her performance in *The Skin of Our Teeth* (1942), for which she won the New York Drama Critics' Circle Award, and enjoyed a long run in *Private Lives* (1948). She worked infrequently in films, most of them mediocre, but was outstanding in Alfred Hitchcock's *Lifeboat* (1944), for which she was named best actress by the New York film critics. Bankhead frequented radio and television talk shows, usually discussing baseball or politics: she was a passionate fan of the New York Giants and was a staunch Democrat. During this period she was best known as the hostess of "The Big Show" (1950–1952), network radio's much-touted effort to compete with variety programs on television. Radio lost the competition, but the program was an effective vehicle for Bankhead's wit and unique voice.

In the 1960's, however, Bankhead was seldom in demand for plays and films. Age, abetted by cocaine, alcohol, and tobacco, had diminished her beauty, and she had gained a reputation for being difficult to work with. There is merit in Brendan Gill's assessment that Bankhead "invented by trial and error an exceptional self, which with a child's impudent pretense of not caring she flung straight into the face of the world." But her colorful personality enabled her to remain a celebrity long after her acting career had faded. She died in New York City.

[Bankhead's best-selling autobiography, *Tallulah* (1952), was in fact written by publicist Richard Maney from materials provided by the actress. *Tallulah, Darling* (1980) is a biography by Denis Brian. Most valuable is Brendan Gill, *Tallulah* (1972). An obituary is in the *New York Times*, Dec. 13, 1968.]

WILLIAM HUGHES

BARBEY, DANIEL EDWARD (Dec. 23, 1889–Apr. 11, 1969), naval officer, was born in Portland, Oreg., the son of John Barbey and Julia Anna Chlopeck. He attended local schools and graduated in the bottom third of his class at the United States Naval Academy in 1912. He served in politically troubled Central America and Mexico aboard the armored cruiser *California* in that year, the destroyer

Lawrence in 1914, and the gunboat *Annapolis* during 1916–1917. As executive officer of the new destroyer *Stevens* during World War I, he escorted a convoy to Ireland in June and July 1918 and coastal convoys in British waters until the Armistice and then served ashore at Cardiff, Wales, and London. In November 1919 he became naval port officer at Constantinople, transferring there the following October to be operations officer and flag lieutenant to Rear Admiral Mark L. Bristol, the United States high commissioner to Turkey during that country's struggle for political survival. Barbey was concurrently an American delegate to the Allied commission for control of trade with Turkey and an observer with the White Russian armies in the Crimea during the Russian civil war. His affable personality and ability to cut through bureaucratic tangles were essential in these delicate situations.

Returning to sea duty in 1922, Barbey spent one year in the Pacific as assistant engineer on the battleship *Oklahoma*, followed by two years on recruiting duty in Portland, Oreg. He married Katherine Graham on June 16, 1927; they had no children.

Barbey was chief engineer of the cruiser *Cincinnati* in the Atlantic (1925–1927), executive officer of the oiler *Ramapo* in the Pacific (1927–1928), and aide and flag secretary to the superintendent of the Naval Academy, Rear Admiral Samuel S. Robinson (1928–1931). Barbey then served on the west coast in command of the destroyer *Lea* (1931–1933), as chief ordnance inspector at the Mare Island ammunition depot in San Francisco (1933–1935), as first lieutenant and damage-control officer of the battleship *New York* (1935–1936) and later (second half of 1940) its captain, and in command of a division of destroyers (1936–1937). In June 1937 he was placed in charge of the war plans section of the Bureau of Navigation. There he developed an interest in amphibious warfare from pictures of a ramped boat used by Japan in its war against China and initiated a similar design for the United States Navy. During this tour of duty he was promoted to captain.

In January 1941, Barbey became chief of staff to the commander of the Atlantic Fleet's service force, Rear Admiral Randall Jacobs, who that summer charged him with organizing an amphibious force. Already a pioneer in this theretofore neglected aspect of naval operations, he used his primitive landing craft for the first major prewar amphibious maneuvers along the North Carolina coast. As a result of his success, in May 1942 he was appointed head of the new amphibious-warfare section at the Navy Department. Barbey oversaw the development and tactical employment of specialized assault craft, notably the DUKW (pronounced "duck"), his own invention, which he dramatically introduced by running a prototype into a pond in downtown Washington, D.C.—only to see its occupants arrested for violating a bird sanctuary. He tackled the problems of offloading transports and supply ships of men and matériel at beachheads, ultimately shortening the time from five days to five hours. After he introduced his revolutionary concepts in battle, he earned from a newspaperman the sobriquet "Uncle Dan, the Amphibious Man."

Promoted to rear admiral in December 1942, Barbey reported the next month to Australia to command the amphibious forces in the Southwest Pacific theater; he was responsible for landing the ground forces of General Douglas MacArthur on enemy-held beaches. Men and equipment arrived slowly, but he forged them into an efficient combat team officially designated VII Amphibious Force. His calm demeanor enabled him to serve closely and without difficulty with the controversial and headstrong MacArthur.

Barbey successfully initiated the Southwest Pacific offensive in the summer of 1943 by landing army forces along the coast and offshore islands of northeastern New Guinea, moving on to New Britain and the Admiralty Islands between December 1943 and February 1944. Though his flagship was a destroyer for most of these operations, during the spring of 1944 he shifted to the specialized amphibious command ship *Blue Ridge* for MacArthur's invasion of the Hollandia region of New Guinea's north coast. In May 1944 he was transferred to Washington, D.C., where his expertise was utilized by the planners of the D-day landings at Normandy the next month.

As MacArthur closed in on the Philippines, Barbey, again aboard the *Blue Ridge*, commanded the assaults on Morotai in the Moluccas in September 1944; the northern assault force at San Pedro Bay, Leyte, in October; and, with the rank of vice-admiral, the San Fabian attack force at Lingayen Gulf, Luzon, in January 1945. As overall amphibious commander of the Seventh Fleet, he coordinated the landing operations that liberated the southern Philippines in the spring of 1945. Barbey then commanded the assault on Balikpapan, Borneo, during June and July 1945. By the time of Japan's surrender the next month, VII Amphibious Force had put ashore more than 1 million men in fifty-six landings over a two-year period; and in September, Barbey placed occupation forces ashore at Inchon, Korea. The following month he landed marines at Tsingtao, China, and moved Nationalist Chinese troops from Indochina and southern China to occupy northern China, where, however, they ran afoul of Communist Chinese forces claiming control of the region. He also repatriated Japanese troops to Japan. Barbey assumed command of the Seventh Fleet in November 1945 and began to train the Nationalists in amphibious techniques, but was glad to be relieved of trying to help resolve the China problem the following January.

Appointed to command the Atlantic Fleet's amphibious forces in March 1946 and then the Fourth Fleet in September, Barbey returned to China in February 1947 as chairman of the Joint Military Board to study America's strategic requirements in the Far East. He then served in the dual role of commandant of the Tenth Naval District and Caribbean Sea Frontier (1947–1950) and of the Thirteenth Naval District (1950–1951). He retired with the rank of vice-admiral in June 1951 and published his wartime memoirs, *MacArthur's Amphibious Navy* in 1969. He died in Bremerton, Wash.

[In addition to his memoirs, which cover only the period 1943–1946, Barbey's career is traced in a mimeographed outline biography at the Naval Historical Center, Washington, D.C. See Samuel Eliot Morison, *History of United States Naval Operations in World War II*, VI (1950), VIII (1953), XII (1958), and XIII (1959); and Clark G. Reynolds, *Famous American Admirals* (1978). An obituary is in the *New York Times*, Apr. 13, 1969.]

CLARK G. REYNOLDS

BARDEN, GRAHAM ARTHUR (Sept. 25, 1896–Jan. 29, 1967), attorney and United States congressman, was born in Sampson County, N.C., the son of James Jefferson Barden, a farmer, and Mary Robinson James. Barden attended local public schools and graduated from the University of North Carolina with a law degree in 1920 after serving as a seaman in the United States Navy in 1918–1919. Following graduation, he began to practice law in New Bern; at the same time, he taught social studies and mathematics at the New Bern high school for one year and was its athletic coach for two years. His teams won several state titles in 1922. While working as an attorney, teacher, and coach, he was appointed recorder's court judge of Craven County, a position he held from 1921 to 1924. During his term as judge, Barden actively fought the Ku Klux Klan and helped destroy it in Craven County. On Dec. 22, 1922, he married Agnes Foy; they had two children.

In 1932, Barden was elected to the North Carolina House of Representatives, where he achieved an outstanding record. As chairman of the Appropriations Committee, Barden led the fight to reduce taxes. Although he believed in racial segregation, he sought to increase the pay of black teachers and to provide better school facilities for black children. He secured passage of his bill to make teachers' salaries standard, regardless of race.

Barden first won a seat in the United States Congress in 1934 and served continuously until 1961, when he retired. In the House he served as a member of the Rivers and Harbors, Education and Labor, and Library committees. Barden generally supported New Deal legislation, including the 1938 Wage and Hour Act. He did not support the antilynching bills, and as a result, the *Raleigh News and Observer* referred to him as early as 1938 as a Dixiecrat.

As World War II began, Barden used his growing influence to secure military installations for his district. By the time the United States entered the war, construction of a number of bases such as Camp Lejeune had begun. Early in the war, Barden became interested in veterans' benefits and the rehabilitation of veterans and disabled civilians. In 1946 he and Senator Robert M. La Follette, Jr., of Wisconsin persuaded Congress to pass the Vocational Rehabilitation Act, to provide training for disabled veterans. In that year, he and Senator Walter George of Georgia cosponsored the Vocational Education Act, to provide federal aid for vocational education and home economics programs. Almost single-handedly Barden secured the passage of the Library Service Act, which established a federal program to provide books and songs for the blind.

Barden broke with the Roosevelt administration in 1944, and by 1948, he had become a Dixiecrat. After 1944, he generally voted with the right wing of the Republican party, opposing most administration bills. These included such social reform measures as fair employment practices and federal aid to education. He also voted against the Marshall Plan and military aid to Europe. He took pride in authorship of Section 14 of the Taft-Hartley Act (1947), a clause enabling states to pass right-to-work laws. While Barden supported the cold war, he opposed the draft. In March 1956, Barden joined ninety-five other congressmen in signing the "Southern Manifesto," which denounced the Supreme Court's school-desegregation decision in *Brown* v. *Board of Education* (1954) as a "clear abuse of judicial power."

As chairman of the House Education and Labor Committee from 1952 to 1960, he considered his toughest fight the passage of the Landrum-Griffin Labor Management Act (1959), which sought to control labor-union corruption.

While serving on the Education and Labor Committee, Barden tangled with Cardinal Francis Spellman when seeking passage of the 1949 Barden bill whereby the federal government would contribute $300 million annually to the states in support of elementary and secondary public, but not private or parochial, schools. The cardinal denounced the bill as anti-Catholic legislation. Eleanor Roosevelt strongly backed Barden in this fight.

In 1960, Barden announced that he would not stand for reelection. A hundred of his House colleagues asked that he reconsider. He declined, and in January 1961 he returned to New Bern to fish, hunt, and visit with friends. An extrovert, Barden rarely offended people, and his nickname, "Hap," indicates something of the feeling friends and supporters felt for him. He died in New Bern.

Barden proved an able representative of his district and state. He knew parliamentary procedures well, and he used this knowledge to achieve his purposes. Yet, as is the case with some other southern congressmen, Barden's record is difficult to appraise. Had he continued as a political moderate, he would have faced certain defeat in his traditionally conservative district. He therefore chose a course of drift on issues of race and attended to local affairs very well.

[Barden's papers are at Duke University. The only biography is Elmer L. Puryear, *Graham A. Barden* (1979). See also Paul J. Puryear, "Graham A. Barden and the Struggle over Federal Aid to Elementary and Secondary Schools, 1949–1960" (M.A. thesis, University of North Carolina, 1973). An obituary is in the *New York Times*, Jan. 30, 1967.]

BENNETT H. WALL

BARTLETT, EDWARD LEWIS ("BOB") (Apr. 20, 1904–Dec. 11, 1968), United States senator, was born in Seattle, Wash., the son of Edward C. Bartlett, the manager of a freight business, and Ida Florence Doverspike. He grew up in Fairbanks, Alaska, and graduated from Fairbanks High School in 1922. An average student, Bartlett briefly attended the University of Washington, the University of Alaska, and the University of California at Los Angeles. From 1924 to 1933 Bartlett worked as a reporter and editor for the *Fairbanks Daily News-Miner*. He also served as the Alaskan stringer for the *New York Times* during the early 1930's. On Aug. 14, 1930, Bartlett married Vide Marie Gaustad; they had two children. In 1933 Bartlett, a Democrat, was appointed secretary to Alaska's nonvoting delegate to the United States Congress. Feeling homesick for Alaska, he accepted an administrative position with the Federal Housing Administration in Juneau in 1934. He resigned from that position in 1936 to take over his parents' mining operation at Independence Creek.

After three difficult seasons, during which the mine produced low-grade ore, Bartlett gave up mining and the part-time jobs needed to support his family to accept the position as secretary of Alaska, an administrative position under the territorial governor. He held this office from 1939 until 1944, when he was elected Alaska's delegate to the United States Congress. He assumed his duties in Washington in early 1945 and served until 1959, lobbying effectively to obtain federal monies for the territory. Between 1945 and 1952 Bartlett authored sixty-one bills that were passed by Congress, more measures signed into law than could be claimed by any congressman then in office. While in Washington he had no hobbies, took no vacations, and became a workaholic. In addition to promoting various federal expenditures for Alaska, Bartlett worked in Congress to improve the health and housing of Alaska's Inuit population.

During the 1950's Bartlett labored tirelessly

to gain statehood for Alaska. After numerous disappointments and delays, Congress passed the Alaska Statehood Act in 1958. On Jan. 3, 1959, President Dwight D. Eisenhower signed the proclamation officially admitting Alaska as the forty-ninth state of the Union. It was a triumph for Bartlett, who had advocated statehood for many years. Bartlett and former territorial governor Ernest L. Gruening were elected United States senators from Alaska and began to serve in 1959. By virtue of a coin toss, Bartlett was designated the senior senator to serve a two-year term. He was reelected in 1960 and 1966.

As senior senator, Bartlett was a loyal Democrat who largely supported the programs of Presidents John F. Kennedy and Lyndon B. Johnson. Bartlett described himself as "a liberal Democrat who is not remotely removed from a center position." During his years in the Senate Bartlett was a strong supporter of the fishing and maritime industries, two enterprises that were important to Alaska. As a member of the Senate Commerce Committee, he advocated federal appropriations for both industries.

In May 1964 President Johnson signed into law a Bartlett-sponsored bill that restricted foreign fishing in United States territorial waters and subjected violators to criminal penalties. Later Bartlett cosponsored a bill that in 1966 extended United States fishing rights to an area twelve miles from its coastline. He also supported a bill that promoted research and development of fish protein concentrate as a possible food source.

Bartlett gained national prominence for his efforts to establish stricter regulations to reduce the levels of permissible radiation from medical and dental equipment and color televisions. His hearings on the danger of radiation led to passage of the Radiation Control for Health and Safety Act in 1968. Senator Warren G. Magnuson of Washington summed up Bartlett's contribution to the act when he stated that the "Senate is in essence paying tribute to the senior senator from Alaska, Mr. Bartlett, who more than any member of Congress has led the fight for radiation safety."

Bartlett and Senator Mike Mansfield of Montana were the first senators to call for a negotiated settlement in Vietnam. In March 1964 Bartlett maintained that a peaceful settlement in Vietnam was "neither passive nor surrender. It is more an attempt to combine active hope with cool realism." He opposed extending the war into North Vietnam, arguing that an expansion of the conflict might lead to a major war. Although Bartlett voted for the Tonkin Gulf Resolution of 1964, he continued to criticize America's policy in Southeast Asia. He was among fifteen Democratic senators who sent a letter to President Johnson on Jan. 27, 1966, asking for a continued pause in the bombing of North Vietnam.

A heavy smoker and often a heavy drinker, Bartlett suffered a heart attack in 1966 and died in Cleveland in 1968, nine days after undergoing heart surgery. His biggest regret in life was being born outside the territory of Alaska.

[Bartlett's papers are in the University of Alaska Archive, Fairbanks, Alaska. A biography is Claus-M. Naske, *Bob Bartlett of Alaska: A Life of Politics* (1979). For Bartlett's career in the Senate, see Nelson Lichtenstein, ed., *Political Profiles: The Kennedy Years* (1976) and *Political Profiles: The Johnson Years* (1976); and Claus-M. Naske, *Alaska: A History of the Forty-ninth State* (1979). An obituary is in the *New York Times*, Dec. 12, 1968.]

JOHN M. CARROLL

BARTON, BRUCE FAIRCHILD (Aug. 5, 1886–July 5, 1967), advertising executive, author, and United States congressman, was born in Robbins, Tenn., the son of William Eleazar Barton, a Protestant minister, and Esther Treat Bushnell, a schoolteacher. Barton grew up in rural Tennessee, where his father was a circuit-riding preacher, and Oak Park, Ill., where his father later was given his own congregation. Barton retrospectively exaggerated the poverty of this period in order to make his life seem a rags-to-riches story. "We were not poor," he wrote. "We just didn't have any money."

In fact, his youth was spent comfortably; his father even served as moderator of the National Council of Congregational Churches and wrote a well-known biography of Abraham Lincoln. True to the Horatio Alger myth, however, Barton sold newspapers at nine, and by sixteen he was earning $600 a year selling his uncle's maple syrup.

In 1903, Barton entered Berea College in Berea, Ky., but the next year transferred to Amherst College, financing his education by selling pots and pans. He graduated in 1907, having been elected to Phi Beta Kappa and named "most likely to succeed." In the recession year in which he graduated, the only job he could find was as timekeeper in a Montana railroad camp. He went from there to Chicago, where he worked as an editor at the *Home Herald*, a small religious paper, and *Housekeeper* magazine, both of which failed.

In 1912, Barton went to New York City, where he became assistant sales manager at *Collier's* magazine. He had his first taste of advertising success, selling 400,000 sets of the Harvard Classics by promising that one could "earn more and enjoy life more than many college men" by reading from them for just fifteen minutes a day. On Oct. 2, 1913, Barton married Esther Maude Randall; they had three children.

During World War I, Barton edited a magazine called *Every Week*. His own magazine writing, with which he would continue throughout his life, consisted mostly of sunny, uplifting essays, collected in *More Power to You* (1917), *It's a Good Old World* (1920), *Better Days* (1927), and *On the Up and Up* (1929).

While doing volunteer work for the Salvation Army during the war, Barton coined his first famous slogan: "A man may be down but he is never out." In 1918 he was asked by the federal government to supervise publicity for the United War Work fund drive. As chairman, Barton raised $220 million and met two advertising men, Roy Durstine and Alex Osborn. In 1919, Barton joined them to form an advertising agency. After a merger in 1928 with the George Batten Company, this agency became Batten, Barton, Durstine and Osborn (BBDO), later one of the largest agencies in the United States.

Described as "suave and hearty," Barton proved to be a successful advertising man from the start. Within four years of its founding, his agency had a client list that included General Electric, General Motors, Dunlop Tires, and Lever Brothers. During the 1920's, the years in which the advertising industry rose to its present prominence, no advertising executive rose higher than Barton. He created the character Betty Crocker, the archetypal housewife, and improved public opinion of United States Steel with advertisements that celebrated the virtues of Andrew Carnegie: "He came to a land of wooden towns and left a nation of steel."

Barton's personal fame increased with the publication of *The Man Nobody Knows* (1925), in which he portrayed Jesus Christ as the first great businessman. "A failure!" Barton wrote. "He picked up twelve men from the bottom ranks of business and forged them into an organization that conquered the world." The book was a huge success, topping the nonfiction best-seller list for two years. Barton became the most forceful spokesman for the view that religious faith could lead one to business success, which was a dominant theme of the decade. Barton followed this book with a less successful sequel about the Bible called *The Book Nobody Knows* (1926).

Despite his public displays of spunk and boosterism, Barton was no Babbitt. He expressed doubts in private letters about the course of American business and the worth of advertising. In a 1926 letter he wrote, "It seems to me that a very large percent of the current advertising is merely representative of the most wasteful phases of the competitive system." In the 1930's he turned his attention increasingly away from advertising and toward politics.

Barton, a conservative Republican, was one of a group of New York businessmen whose support Franklin Roosevelt sought in the early days of the New Deal, but support was not forthcoming. Barton's opposition to the New Deal and to Roosevelt was unshakable. In 1932 he had dismissed Roosevelt in a letter to Herbert Hoover as "a name and a crutch." Barton ran successfully for Congress in 1936, and for two terms he represented Manhattan's affluent "silk-stocking district." In his first campaign, he told the *New York Times*, "I would like to be known as the Great Repealer. . . . I would move to repeal a law a week." Roosevelt parried in 1940 with some phrasemaking of his own, rebuking Republicans for their isolationism and claiming his staunchest foes in Congress to be "Martin, Barton, and Fish," referring to Joseph W. Martin of Massachusetts and Hamilton Fish of New York.

A losing campaign for a Senate seat ended Barton's political career in 1940, and he returned to advertising, serving as chairman of BBDO until his retirement in 1961. He died in New York City.

[Barton's papers are at the State Historical Society of Wisconsin in Madison. Barton wrote two books other than those mentioned: *What Can a Man Believe?* (1927) and *He Upset the World* (1955), a study of St. Paul. There are brief biographical sketches of Barton in Stephen Fox, *The Mirror*

Makers (1984); and Warren I. Sussman, *Culture as History* (1984). References to his political career can be found in Arthur M. Schlesinger, *The Age of Roosevelt*, III (1960); and Robert S. McElvaine, *The Great Depression* (1984). An obituary is in the *New York Times*, July 6, 1967.]

ANDREW BOHJALIAN

BEAN, LEON LENWOOD (Nov. 13, 1872–Feb. 5, 1967), businessman, was born in Greenwood, Maine, the son of Benjamin Warren Bean, farmer and horse trader, and Sarah Swett. He became world famous as L. L. Bean. His parents died when he was twelve and he, his sister, and his four brothers were cared for by relatives in South Paris, Maine. Later Bean lived with an uncle in West Minot. Early in life he developed an avid interest in hunting and fishing. When he was nine years old his father offered him a choice between going to the county fair or receiving money for five steel traps. He chose the traps and earned his first dollars. His formal education was limited and included a commercial course from 1891 to 1893 at Kent's Hill Academy and one semester at Hebron Academy. In 1898 he married Bertha Porter. They had three children. His first wife died in 1939 and in 1940 Bean married Claire L. Boudreau.

Bean maintained that his life prior to age forty was uneventful, since he never stayed in one place long enough to establish himself. He worked as a farmhand, an itinerant soap peddler, and later a partner in his brother's store in Freeport, Maine. Bean's first break came in 1911, when he sought a practical way to keep his feet warm and dry on hunting trips. Leather boots gave good support but became heavy when wet; rubber boots were too clumsy. So he designed what he called the "Maine Hunting Shoe," which had leather uppers and rubber overshoe bottoms. After testing the shoes himself, Bean began selling them in 1912. He obtained the names of Maine hunting-license holders and sent them a three-page brochure stating, "You cannot expect success hunting deer or moose if your feet are not properly dressed."

Bean fully guaranteed his shoes and refunded the purchase price on ninety of the first 100 pairs when the shoes developed cracks. To improve his product he visited the United States Rubber Company in Boston and got them to make a light, rubber, low-heeled shoe strong enough that he could attach leather tops. By 1917 business was so good that Bean moved into the quarters on Freeport's main street that his firm would occupy until 1962. He hired people to cut and stitch the shoes and in 1918 obtained United States and Canadian patents. Mail orders provided most of his business. Slowly he added other products to an expanding catalog, and before long Bean was providing 70 to 90 percent of the business of the Freeport post office. The company had twenty-five employees in 1924 and recorded $135,000 in annual sales. Its basic products were outdoor and casual clothing and footwear; hunting, fishing, camping, and winter-sports equipment; canoeing gear; and camp furnishings.

In 1932 Bean expanded his factory and on July 1, 1934, he incorporated the business. All but three stockholders were members of his family. The business grew and in 1937 sales reached $1 million. During World War II Bean served as a consultant to help design boots for the army and navy; his company received war contracts for military versions of the Maine Hunting Shoe and for other products. He also constructed a new building and warehouse. He poured profits back into advertising and expanded his mailing lists. The L. L. Bean Catalog, the showcase for his business, was also enlarged. By 1950 Bean employed more than 100 people, and sales reached $1,848,000.

National magazines began to publish articles on this Yankee mail-order enterprise with its homey philosophy. Customers responded to the old-fashioned character of L. L. Bean, Incorporated, where the owner seemed "more interested in hunting and fishing than in shopkeeping." Bean's prescription for success was "Sell good merchandise at a reasonable profit, treat your customers like human beings, and they'll always come back for more." Bean's book *Hunting, Fishing, and Camping* (1942) ran through twenty editions by 1963.

During the 1950's and 1960's Bean's retail store in Freeport was open twenty-four hours a day to accommodate the varied schedules of hunters and fishermen. The Yankee trapper who had started on a shoestring now had a concern doing $2 million in business each year. He resisted further expansion, holding instead to the personal language in his catalog and to the personal manner in which orders were handled. The business, however, was not adapting to new techniques and opportunities.

By 1961 the average age of Bean's employees was over sixty, and Bean was spending most of his time in his winter home in Miami Shores, Fla. He died there in 1967. *My Story: The Autobiography of a Down-East Merchant* was first published in 1960. Like Bean's catalog, it was highly personal, a rambling, disconnected account of his life and convictions.

L. L. Bean, Inc., continued as a family enterprise after Bean's death. Sales in 1980 reached $121 million and 1,472 people worked for the company in a new factory and distribution center on the outskirts of Freeport. *The L. L. Bean Guide to the Outdoors* was published in 1981 and *The L. L. Bean Game and Fish Cookbook* in 1983.

[See "Maine's Bean Outfits Sportsmen Everywhere," *Life*, Oct. 13, 1941; Webb Waldron, "Bean, the Happy Hunter," *Reader's Digest*, Dec. 1941; Arthur Bartlett, "The Discovery of L. L. Bean," *Saturday Evening Post*, Dec. 14, 1946; *Business Week*, Sept. 6, 1952; Earle Doucette, "The Super-Salesman of Freeport, Maine," *Coronet*, June 1953; *Sports Illustrated*, Aug. 27, 1956, and Feb. 20, 1967; "Retail Trade," *Time*, Dec. 7, 1962; and "Salesman," *ibid.*, Feb. 17, 1967. See Leon A. Gorman, *L. L. Bean, Inc.* (1981). See also the obituary in the *New York Times*, Feb. 7, 1967.]

HOMER E. SOCOLOFSKY

BEARY, DONALD BRADFORD (Dec. 4, 1888–Mar. 7, 1966), naval officer, was born in Helena, Mont., the son of Lorenzo Dow Bradford, a civil engineer, and Melinda Ervin. After graduating from Helena High School in 1906, he entered the United States Naval Academy at Annapolis, and completed his studies in 1910. In common with all Naval Academy graduates of the time, he was then appointed a passed midshipman and, having served satisfactorily for two years, was commissioned an ensign on Mar. 7, 1912. He served on the armored cruisers *Tennessee*, *Washington*, and *Maryland* until September 1915. During the next two years, he studied electrical engineering, first at the Naval Postgraduate School at Annapolis and then at Columbia University in New York, where he was awarded an M.S. degree in 1917.

Beary returned to sea on the destroyer *Warrington* in the spring of 1917. He assumed his first command, that of the destroyer *Remlik*, in February 1918. He was promoted to the temporary grade of lieutenant commander in July 1918. For most of that year, he was engaged in patrolling North Atlantic waters infested with enemy submarines and mines, escorting convoys carrying troops and supplies while participating in offensive and defensive actions. He was awarded the Navy Cross for his wartime activities.

Beary briefly reported for fitting-out duty on the destroyer *Edwards* at the Bethlehem Shipbuilding Yards in Squantum, Mass., in December 1918 but was detached before that vessel was commissioned. On Jan. 15, 1919, he married Alice Lovett Keene, the daughter of a retired army officer; they had one child. From January 1919 until March 1921, he was assigned to the Officers Records Section of the Bureau of Navigation, in the Navy Department in Washington, D.C. He returned to sea in April 1921 and was made a permanent lieutenant commander that June. In the next twenty-nine months, Beary successively commanded the destroyers *Talbot*, *Parrott*, and *Sumner* in the Pacific. Returning to Washington, he was assigned to duty in the Division of Fleet Training in the Office of the Chief of Naval Operations. He remained in that post until December 1925, when he was named navigating officer on the battleship *New Mexico*.

From August 1928 until February 1930, Beary was an instructor in the Department of Electrical Engineering and Physics at Annapolis. Promoted to the rank of commander in April 1930, he served as aide to the superintendent of the academy until reassigned in July 1931. For the next three years, he served as assistant chief of staff to the commander in chief of the Asiatic Fleet, on the heavy cruisers *Houston* and *Augusta*, successively flagships for the fleet. In July 1934 he was reassigned to the Navy Department in Washington for duty in the Fleet Maintenance Division of the Office of the Chief of Naval Operations. He remained there until June 1936, when he was assigned to undertake the senior course at the Naval War College in Newport, R.I.

From June 1937 until April 1938, Beary was executive officer of the battleship *Colorado;* he was then placed in command of the light cruiser *Richmond*. In June 1938 he was promoted to captain. One year later he returned to the Naval Academy as officer in charge of buildings and grounds and aide to the superintendent. In May 1941 he took command of a former United States Army transport, the *Washington*. The vessel was renamed the *Mount Vernon*, and

Beary assumed command of it on June 16, 1941.

In September of that year, while retaining this command, Beary was designated commander of Transport Division 19. Two months later the *Mount Vernon*, under Beary's command, was assigned to Convoy WS-12X, under Rear Admiral Arthur B. Cook, with orders to help transport nearly 20,000 British troops from Halifax, Nova Scotia, to support the British garrison at Singapore. The troops were landed at the latter port in mid-January 1942, in the midst of the Japanese attack. Beary evacuated women and children from the city despite continuing Japanese air raids and the difficulties of negotiating some of the heavily mined waters south of the city. Beary was then detached from the convoy and steamed for Suez via Aden, where he picked up some 4,500 Australian troops for transport to Fremantle, Australia. There the *Mount Vernon* took on some survivors from the Corregidor and Java Sea operations, together with refugees from the Netherlands East Indies, and took them to San Francisco, arriving at the end of March 1942. Two months later Beary was promoted to the temporary grade of rear admiral. He was the first native of Montana to have reached flag rank.

Following the disbandment of Transport Division 19 in June 1942, Beary served as commandant of the Naval Operations Base in Iceland. Then, in February 1943, he was made commander of the Fleet Operational Training Command, Atlantic Fleet, headquartered at Camp Allen, near Norfolk, Va. This assignment entailed supervision of all training facilities, except for those having to do with submarines and landing craft. In this capacity, Beary served, in effect, as "Chancellor . . . of the United States Antisubmarine University" (Morison, 1956). He had charge of some eighteen sound schools and antisubmarine training and refresher centers from Newfoundland, Canada, to Recife, Brazil. For his performance in this post, he received the Distinguished Service Medal.

In November 1944, Beary reported for duty with the Pacific Fleet, where he assisted with the organization of a logistic support group known as Service Squadron 6. Operating under strict secrecy for the remainder of the war in the Pacific, Beary's command served in direct logistic support of the Iwo Jima and Okinawa invasions mounted by the Fifth Fleet under Admiral Raymond S. Spruance, the amphibious force under Vice-Admiral Richmond K. Turner, and the fast carrier forces under Vice-Admiral Marc Mitscher. Under Beary's leadership, Service Squadron 6 became a revolutionary new mobile underway replenishment logistical support force. This naval element made the traditional and time-consuming return of the fleet to port for resupply unnecessary. Instead, the highly mobile vessels of Service Squadron 6 brought all needed logistical support to the combat units. Beary and his staff overcame the problems posed by the enormous distances involved in the Pacific war. With his replenishment forces at sea, the fleets he was supporting could retire a few hundred miles for refueling, rearming, and reprovisioning and then strike again at the enemy with minimal delay. In the words of a navy press release, his command was the fleet's "ace in the hole." Within a short period of time, Service Squadron 6, originally organized on an experimental basis, became an established naval logistical unit. Beary was awarded the Legion of Merit with a Gold Star for his actions during the period from January to September 1945.

Squadron 6 ultimately supported Admiral William F. Halsey's Third Fleet as it ranged up and down the coast of Japan in the closing months of the war. During this period Beary's flagship was the light cruiser *Detroit*. He later reported that his operations were "limited only by battle damage and human and mechanical endurance." Beary was present for the Japanese surrender aboard the battleship *Missouri* in Tokyo Bay on Sept. 2, 1945. Beary was then made administrator of the United States Naval Shipping Control Authority for the Japanese merchant marine. He had responsibility for the repatriation of some 5 million Japanese troops from their final duty stations in Asia and the Pacific.

On Apr. 1, 1946, Beary became commandant of the Twelfth Naval District at San Francisco, which over the next two years included command of the San Francisco Naval Base, the Western Sea Frontier, and the Pacific Reserve Fleet. Promoted to vice-admiral in October 1948, Beary was assigned on November 1 of that year as president of the Naval War College at Newport, R.I. He retired on Oct. 1, 1950, concluding forty years of active duty.

Beary settled in Coronado, Calif. His wife

died in March 1953, and in October 1955 he married Mary Louise Robnett, a widow. Beary died in San Diego, Calif.

[Beary's papers include only a brief journal covering the early months of World War II and some correspondence and photographs in the family's possession. A few speeches made by him during his tenure as president of the Naval War College are in the archives there. Beary's work in World War II is mentioned in W. R. Carter, *Beans, Bullets, and Black Oil* (1953), and Samuel Eliot Morison, *History of United States Naval Operations in World War II*, I (1947), X (1956), and XIV (1960). See also three naval administrative histories of World War II: Commander in Chief, United States Atlantic Fleet, *Naval Operating Base, Iceland*, IV (1946), and *Commander Fleet Operational Training Command*, VIII (1946); and Commander in Chief, United States Pacific Fleet, *History of Service Force* (1946). An obituary is in the *New York Times*, Mar. 10, 1966.]

KEIR B. STERLING

BEGLEY, EDWARD JAMES ("ED") (Mar. 25, 1901–Apr. 28, 1970), actor, was born in Hartford, Conn., the son of Michael Joseph Begley, a laborer, and Hannah Clifford. His father was a natural entertainer with a wide repertoire of dialect stories and songs. Young Begley shared his father's flair for entertaining and at age eleven ran away to Stamford, Conn., and New York City, hoping to get into show business. Returned to Hartford by the juvenile authorities, he attended St. Patrick's Parochial School through the fifth grade.

When he was thirteen, Begley, by then a practiced runaway, left home for good to join a traveling carnival. "I was looking for something," he later recalled. "I didn't find it then, but it started me on the road that finally led to acting." Begley spent many years working at odd jobs, usually leaving them for brief turns in vaudeville, circus, and carnival. But his burning desire to act was frustrated by his impulsiveness and lack of direction.

It was not until 1931 that he found a show-business niche on radio station WTIC in Hartford, where he was announcer, actor, writer, producer, and disc jockey. In 1943 he moved on to network radio and became one of radio's busiest actors. He starred in "Charlie Chan," "Official Detective," "Family Doctor," and other popular series. On "State of the Union" he often portrayed President Franklin D. Roosevelt.

Thirty years after running away from home to become a stage actor, Ed Begley finally realized his ambition. He first appeared on Broadway as a German general in *Land of Fame* (1943), a play about Greece under Nazi rule. He also had roles in *Get Away, Old Man* (1943) and *Pretty Little Parlor* (1944). In 1947 he starred in Arthur Miller's *All My Sons*, a breakthrough play for both actor and playwright. Begley won critical acclaim for his portrayal of Joe Keller, a corrupt defense contractor whose shoddy products had caused the death of some aviators during the war. "Ed Begley," wrote Brooks Atkinson of the *New York Times*, "dramatizes the whole course of the father's poignant ordeal without losing the basic coarseness of the character."

Earlier that year, Begley was in Hollywood for a supporting role in *Boomerang*, a semi-documentary film directed by Elia Kazan, who staged *All My Sons*. In his screen debut Begley etched "a remarkable portrait of joviality, venality and fear." He worked primarily in films between 1948 and 1952 and then was prominent in the so-called golden age of live television drama. During the 1950's he appeared on most of the new medium's major drama anthologies, including "Armstrong Circle Theatre," "Goodyear Playhouse," "Robert Montgomery Presents," "Kraft Theatre," "Philco Playhouse," "Alcoa Hour," and "U.S. Steel Hour."

Begley re-created two of his memorable television roles in films made from teleplays. In *Patterns* (1956), Rod Serling's drama about conflicts among corporate executives, Begley portrayed Bill Briggs, a man of ability and principle who is ruined by his efforts to observe standards of decency and kindness in a business guided by a ruthless and manipulative chief executive. In *Twelve Angry Men* (1957), a tense jury-room drama, Begley was a racially prejudiced juror. The film critic of the *New York Times* found his performance "properly warped and rabid."

Between film and television roles Begley returned to Broadway for what proved to be his greatest success—the role of Matthew Harrison Brady in *Inherit the Wind* (1955), a play inspired by the famous Scopes trial. William Jennings Bryan was the model for Begley's character, and Brady's antagonist, Henry Drummond, a defense attorney modeled after Clarence Darrow, was portrayed by Paul Muni. Playing opposite Muni's much-heralded performance, Begley more than held his own. Brooks

Atkinson of the *New York Times* declared Begley's acting "superb" and added, "His benevolent warmth, his nice synthesis of sincerity and vanity, his counterfeited divine strength radiate throughout the theatre." The critic Walter Kerr wrote that Begley's performance "has been widely praised, but is likely never to be praised enough." For his effort Begley received the Donaldson, Variety, and Tony awards. Two years later, in a major tour de force, Begley assumed the Drummond role. His other Broadway plays included *Look Homeward, Angel* (1958) and *Advise and Consent* (1960).

Begley added to his movie laurels as Boss Finley in the film version of Tennessee Williams' *Sweet Bird of Youth* (1962). Finley, wrote Bosley Crowther of the *New York Times*, is "a horrible, howling Southern roughneck, a strong reminder of Huey Long, splendidly played by Ed Begley, who makes you cringe every time he grins." For his performance Begley won an Academy Award as best supporting actor. *The Unsinkable Molly Brown* (1964), a Hollywood musical, afforded the actor a rare opportunity to clown, sing, and dance.

Throughout the 1960's Begley remained active in television and films. The drama anthologies had nearly vanished from the small screen by then, but Begley made guest appearances on many popular series, including "Ben Casey," "The Defenders," "Naked City," "Route 66," "Wagon Train," "Gunsmoke," and "The Fugitive." He also did *Inherit the Wind* on television for "The Hallmark Hall of Fame" in November 1965. His films of this period include *Billion-Dollar Brain* (1967) and *Wild in the Streets* (1968).

Begley's career encompassed 12,000 radio roles, more than 200 television appearances, a dozen Broadway plays, thirty-five films, and recordings of "Great American Speeches" and *Leaves of Grass*. He was an instinctive actor who drew upon personal experience for his characterizations. A bulky man, with heavy brows, sharp eyes, and a toothy grin, the actor made the most of his appearance in shaping his characterizations. Begley always tried to find more than a single dimension in a role. "In playing a role," he told Jesse Zunser of *Cue*, "a villain role, for example, I try to make him a little sympathetic somewheres. . . . The thing is to make each character individual and at the same time an image of all humanity. So, good or bad, we recognize ourselves in him."

Although known for his villainous roles, the actor was, according to an acquaintance, "a gay, merry soul" and a warmhearted family man. He married actress Amanda Huff in Philadelphia on Apr. 1, 1922. They had three children, one of whom, Ed, Jr., became an actor. Widowed in 1957, Begley married Dorothy Bates on June 7, 1961; they were divorced in January 1963. On Dec. 12, 1963, Begley married Helen Jordan, his agent's secretary; they had one child. Begley maintained homes in Merrick, Long Island, and Manhattan for many years, but resided in Van Nuys, Calif., at the time of his death.

[There is no published biography of Begley. The Margaret Herrick Library of the Academy of Motion Picture Arts and Sciences has an extensive clippings file on the actor. The *New York Times Film Reviews, 1913–1968*, 6 vols. (1970), contains reviews of most of his films. Many of his television appearances are listed in James Robert Parish, *Actors' Television Credits* (1973). An obituary is in the *New York Times*, Apr. 30, 1970.]

WILLIAM HUGHES

BERG, GERTRUDE EDELSTEIN (Oct. 3, 1899–Sept. 14, 1966), actress, author, and producer, was born in Harlem, New York City, the daughter of Jacob Edelstein, a restaurant and hotel owner, and Diana Goldstein. She attended public schools in New York City and wrote skits for the guests of her father's resort hotel in the Catskill Mountains. After graduating from Wadleigh High School, she enrolled in extension courses in drama at Columbia University. She married an engineering student, Lewis Berg, on Dec. 1, 1918. They had two children.

Lewis Berg became chief technologist for sugar refineries near Reserve, La., where the couple lived for three years. The family returned to New York City in 1928. Berg's first effort to write for radio, a series called "Effie and Laura," was canceled by the Columbia Broadcasting System (CBS) after the opening show.

In 1929 Berg devised another radio show, based upon her observations and memories of her parents and immigrant grandparents. The series was intended to chronicle the rise of a family called the Goldbergs. The central figure in the family was Molly, the mother. Berg recalled that when she first submitted her script to the National Broadcasting Company (NBC) she made it illegible so that she would have to read it aloud, thus auditioning for the main role of Molly at the same time. "The Rise of the Goldbergs" was inaugurated, at first only in New York City, on Nov. 20, 1929.

Only a month later, laryngitis forced Berg to allow a substitute to play Molly. More than 11,000 letters of protest deluged NBC. By 1931 the program was broadcast nationally five evenings a week, from 7:30 till 7:45. Among radio series only "Amos 'n' Andy" exceeded it in popularity and longevity. Beginning at a salary of $75 per week, out of which she was expected to pay her cast, Berg earned at her peak 100 times that amount, a trajectory quite different from that of the Goldberg family itself, whose rise was thwarted by the Great Depression.

From its familiar opening, when Molly greeted her tenement neighbor with "Yoo-hoo, Mrs. Bloom!" the program was bathed in good cheer and informal humor. Unlike its rival, "Amos 'n' Andy," "The Goldbergs," as it was soon retitled, exuded lower-class authenticity. Berg had grown up in a home in which Yiddish was rarely spoken; and ethnic expressiveness percolated through the scripts not so much in vocabulary as in syntax and intonations. More than 200 characters, drawn from Berg's relatives and friends, gave the shows immediacy and buoyancy. Sometimes nothing in particular seemed to happen, except demonstrations of Molly Goldberg's domestic skills. Though Berg used various professional actors, including such future stars as John Garfield, Joseph Cotten, Anne Bancroft, and Van Heflin, amateurs who were really delivery boys, grocery clerks, and elevator operators were hired to play themselves.

The heart of "The Goldbergs" remained its creator and protagonist; and as Molly, Berg became the operational definition of the Jewish mother, warm, nurturing, omnicompetent, but with a special flair for nagging her husband and children. In dispensing wisdom as well as blintzes, in soothing tensions that her own manipulations often provoked, Berg—as Molly—contributed to the formation of an American stereotype.

Berg later wished to transcend such material, but her close identification with "The Goldbergs" did not permit much distance. In 1935, with the series temporarily off the air, Berg wrote and produced a radio series set in the Catskills. But "The House of Glass," though moderately successful, was dropped that same season. "The Goldbergs" returned in 1936, this time on CBS. The series enjoyed an uninterrupted run until 1945, and then reappeared from 1949 until 1951. By then Berg had written more than 5,000 scripts in longhand. They rarely needed to be rewritten, although alterations were made during rehearsals.

In 1948 Berg wrote and starred in a stage version of "The Goldbergs," *Me and Molly*, which ran for 156 performances on Broadway. Brooks Atkinson, the drama critic of the *New York Times*, observed that "Mrs. Berg is a real human being who believes in the people she writes about and is not ashamed of their simplicity. . . . The result is a leisurely, intimate, cheerful portrait."

With N. Richard Nash, Berg wrote the screenplay for *Molly* (1951), a Paramount motion picture in which she again played Molly Goldberg. An estimated 13 million television viewers watched "The Goldbergs" on CBS from 1949 to 1951. But Philip Loeb, the actor who played Molly's husband, was associated with left-wing causes, and this led to pressure to fire him. Berg resisted, but in June 1951 General Foods dropped its sponsorship "for economic reasons." When NBC picked up "The Goldbergs" in 1952, Loeb was not rehired; three years later he committed suicide. By then the series itself was off the air, despite Berg's efforts to eschew controversy: "I don't bring up anything that will bother people. . . . I keep things average. I don't want to lose friends."

An affable, kindly, roundish person who seems to have aroused little jealousy or animosity in show business, Berg could not escape the sentimental persona of the Jewish mother. Back on Broadway in 1959, she won an Antoinette Perry (Tony) Award for her portrayal of Mrs. Jacoby, a Brooklyn widow who became involved with a Japanese widower, in Leonard Spigelgass' *A Majority of One*. Though she appeared in many other roles on television and in summer stock, Berg was so closely identified with Molly Goldberg that fans usually called her Molly, and autograph seekers wanted her to sign as Molly Goldberg. She obliged, but signed her own name as well. Berg died in New York City.

[The library at Syracuse University holds the papers of Gertrude Berg, including correspondence and clippings. Excerpts from the television version of "The Goldbergs" can be seen in the National Jewish Archive of Broadcasting, New York Jewish Museum. Her books include *The Molly Goldberg Cookbook* (1955); an autobiography, *Molly and Me* (1961); and *The Rise of the Goldbergs* (1971). See also Morris Freedman, "The Real Molly Goldberg," *Commentary*, April 1956; Erik Barnouw, *A Tower in Babel* (1966); and Jim Harmon, *The Great Radio Comedians* (1970). An obituary notice is in the *New York Times*, Sept. 15, 1966.]

STEPHEN J. WHITFIELD

BIDDLE, FRANCIS BEVERLEY (May 9, 1886–Oct. 4, 1968), lawyer, judge, and United States attorney general, was the third of four sons of Algernon Sydney Biddle, a law professor, and Frances Robinson. He was born in Paris, France, while the family was on a tour of Europe. Biddle's mother had wanted this child to be a girl, which may partially explain his being christened Francis Beverley. If his given names proved an embarrassment and provided a motivation for his becoming the champion pugilist of his school, his family name provided him with all the advantages that an American aristocracy could offer. His mother brought added distinction to the Biddle family of Philadelphia in being of the Randolph family of Virginia.

Upon completing his preparatory training at Groton, Biddle entered Harvard, from which he received his B.A. cum laude in 1909 and his LL.B., also cum laude, two years later. Because of his outstanding academic record he was chosen to be the personal secretary of Associate Justice Oliver Wendell Holmes during the Supreme Court term of 1911–1912. Holmes proved to be one of the great, enduring influences of Biddle's life. The young man was thoroughly indoctrinated in the Holmesian brand of liberalism, which carried with it a compelling sense of noblesse oblige. When Biddle returned to Philadelphia in 1912 to enter the law firm of Biddle, Paul, and Jayne, he abandoned the traditional Republicanism of his family and campaigned for Theodore Roosevelt and the Bull Moose Progressives. He was a delegate to the 1916 Progressive convention, but lost interest in politics when the Progressives obediently endorsed the regular Republican ticket. On Apr. 27, 1918, Biddle married the poet Katherine Garrison Chapin. They had two children.

Biddle initially evinced little enthusiasm for participating in World War I. It was not until President Woodrow Wilson announced his Fourteen Points that Biddle saw purpose in the war. In the summer of 1918, a year after joining the law firm of Barnes, Biddle, and Myers, Biddle began artillery officers' training in Kentucky, but the Armistice was signed and he was discharged before seeing any action. He returned to his law firm, where over the ensuing two decades he had a great variety of clients, ranging from the Pennsylvania Railroad to the Dionne quintuplets. Encouraged by his wife, he also found time to write his only novel, *Llanfear Pattern* (1927), an unflattering portrait of Philadelphia society, which the *New York Times* praised as being reminiscent of *The Forsyte Saga*.

Although still nominally a Republican, Biddle became increasingly disaffected with the party as his concern grew for the plight of the Pennsylvania coal miners during the early years of the Great Depression. In 1932 he actively campaigned against President Herbert Hoover in Pennsylvania. Two years later Franklin D. Roosevelt rewarded Biddle for his political support and for his reputation of being a friend of labor by naming him chairman of the newly created National Labor Relations Board. During his brief tenure in that post, Biddle energetically carried out the mandate to give a new deal to organized labor.

In 1935 Biddle returned to private law practice in Philadelphia, but in 1938 he was asked to serve as legal counsel for a special congressional committee investigating charges against the Tennessee Valley Authority (TVA) of corrupt practices and of engaging in unfair competition with private utility companies. So effectively did the committee under Biddle's direction refute all charges that the TVA did not again come under serious attack during the Roosevelt administration. Biddle always considered the service he rendered to the TVA as his most important contribution to the New Deal program.

A grateful President Roosevelt appointed Biddle to the United States Court of Appeals for the Third Circuit in 1939. Although this was a life-tenure position, Biddle quickly became bored with the job. He much preferred being on the other side of the bench, arguing rather than judging a case. Biddle's dissatisfaction became known to Roosevelt, and so, after less than one year as a federal judge, Biddle was appointed United States solicitor general. Biddle returned to Washington, D.C., which would be his home for the remainder of his life.

As solicitor general, Biddle argued before the Supreme Court fifteen major government cases testing the constitutionality of New Deal legislation, most notably the Wage and Hour Act (*United States* v. *Darby*, 1941). He won all fifteen cases. In 1940 Biddle was also given the added responsibility of heading the Immigration and Naturalization Service, which had been transferred to the Justice Department as an independent administrative section.

When Attorney General Robert Jackson was appointed to the Supreme Court in 1941, Biddle was the obvious choice as his successor. In this office he held the position that his great-great-grandfather, Edmund Randolph, had first occupied in the Washington cabinet. One of the most dramatic incidents to occur during Biddle's tenure was the forcible removal in 1944 of the chairman of Montgomery Ward, Sewell Avery, when he refused to leave his office in compliance with a decree from the War Labor Board. As Avery, still seated in his desk chair, was carried out of the building by two soldiers, he turned to Biddle, who was supervising the operation, and hurled at the attorney general the most blistering epithet in his vocabulary, "You New Dealer!" Biddle accepted this intended curse as the finest encomium he could receive.

Shortly after the death of Roosevelt in 1945, President Harry S Truman reorganized the cabinet and asked for Biddle's resignation. Truman later asserted in his memoirs that Biddle had voluntarily left office and had urged the appointment of Assistant Attorney General Tom Clark to be his successor. Biddle vigorously denied this account, insisting that he had specifically counseled against Clark's appointment when Truman asked for his resignation.

At the conclusion of the war Truman appointed Biddle as the chief American representative on the international tribunal to try Nazi leaders for crimes against humanity. When the Nuremberg trials were concluded, Biddle in his report to the president recommended that hereafter the instigation and conduct of all aggressive wars be made a crime under international law, a recommendation that Truman enthusiastically endorsed. Following this assignment, Biddle was nominated by Truman to be the American representative to the newly created United Nations agency UNESCO, but when the Senate delayed action because Senator Arthur Vandenburg regarded the nominee as being "too advanced a New Dealer," Biddle asked that his name be withdrawn.

Except for serving as chairman of the national committee to plan a memorial in Washington, D.C., for Franklin Roosevelt, Biddle's years of public service ended with the Nuremberg trials. He remained active in politics, however, and served as chairman of Americans for Democratic Action from 1950 to 1953. He was also national chairman of the American Civil Liberties Union. In both his private law practice and his public service Biddle was a defender of civil liberties. Upon his appointment as attorney general, he stated that "the most important job an attorney general can do in time of emergency is to protect civil liberties." He found it necessary, however, during his years in the Justice Department to carry out directives that he would later regret, especially his enforcement of the Smith Act of 1940 (later used to prosecute members of the American Communist Party) and the military order in 1942 to remove Japanese-Americans from their homes on the West Coast to internment centers.

During his years of semiretirement Biddle wrote *The Fear of Freedom* (1951), a vigorous attack on McCarthyism; *Justice Holmes, Natural Law, and the Supreme Court* (1961), a supplement to his earlier biography of his great mentor; and a candid two-volume autobiography. He died at his summer home on Cape Cod, Mass.

[Biddle's correspondence is in the Franklin D. Roosevelt Library and the Harvard Law School Library. The papers of George Biddle, Francis Biddle's brother, are in the Library of Congress; the Biddle family papers are in the Historical Society, Pennsylvania. See his autobiography, A *Casual Past* (1961) and *In Brief Authority* (1962). An obituary notice is in the *New York Times*, Oct. 5, 1968.]

JOSEPH FRAZIER WALL

BIFFLE, LESLIE L (Oct. 9, 1889–Apr. 6, 1966), secretary of the United States Senate, was born in Boydsville, Ark., the son of Billie B. Biffle, a storekeeper and local public official, and Ella Turner. The letter "L" is his full middle name. He attended high school in nearby Piggott and the Keys Business Institute in Little Rock. He grew up talking local politics with his father, a Democrat, who was elected clerk and later sheriff of Clay County. The efficiency with which young Biffle distributed campaign literature for Senator James P. Clarke brought him to the attention of Congressman Bruce Macon, who in 1908 hired Biffle as his secretary in Washington, D.C.

When Macon retired in 1912, Biffle became secretary to Senator Clarke. Upon Clarke's death in 1916, Biffle was appointed superintendent of the Senate folding room, where papers are prepared for mailing. After serving as an army auditor in France during World War I, he returned to the folding room. He married Mary Glade Strickling in October 1921. They had no children.

In 1925 Biffle was appointed minority assistant secretary of the Senate and, with the Democratic takeover in 1933, became majority secretary under majority leader Joseph T. Robinson of Arkansas. In this position Biffle earned a lasting reputation as a shrewd nose counter, skilled parliamentarian, and discreet confidant. He won respect from both parties and often interceded to smooth relations between competing personalities. Once, when Robinson and the fiery Huey Long were about to come to blows on the Senate floor, Biffle rushed between them, shoved Long into his seat, and kept him there until tempers cooled. In another instance Biffle intervened to prevent an armed, drunken senator from shooting a reporter. He devoted most of his energy, however, to such mundane but crucial chores as pairing the votes of absent senators, monitoring the parliamentary maneuvers of the opposition, and anticipating Senate voting patterns. He also took freshmen Democratic senators under his wing, providing guidance in protocol and help in getting desired committee assignments.

One such freshman Biffle befriended in 1935 was Harry Truman. Biffle and Truman had much in common and over the years developed a close personal relationship. It is said that Biffle helped arrange Truman's appointment as chairman of the Special Committee to Investigate the National Defense Program, a forum that brought Truman his first national exposure and led to his selection as vice-president in 1944.

In February 1945 Biffle was unanimously elected secretary of the Senate. It was a tribute to his bipartisan appeal that for the first time in history the minority party did not run an opposing candidate for this important housekeeping post. As Senate secretary Biffle assigned members their floor seats and took charge of more than 1,000 employees, including pages, clerks, and the Capitol police, as well as the parliamentarian and sergeant-at-arms. He also served on the American Battle Monuments Commission. During one inspection tour his life was saved by a black cat that crossed his path and tripped a land mine just seconds before his advance.

When Truman succeeded Franklin Roosevelt as president in April 1945 the first person he called was Biffle. In an unprecedented gesture the president conducted his first meeting with congressional leaders not in the White House, but over fried chicken in Biffle's office. Because of his close association with Truman, Biffle emerged as the Senate's chief liaison with the White House. He conferred with the president daily over a hot line and helped smooth passage of administration programs. His office, dubbed "Biff's diner," quickly became a favorite watering hole for lobbyists, office seekers, and others after the president's ear. His behind-the-scenes direction earned him such nicknames as "the sage of Capitol Hill," "the 97th senator," and, less flattering, "prince of wire-pullers." With the Republican takeover of the Senate in 1947 Biffle became executive director of the Democratic Policy Committee. He resumed his duties as secretary of the Senate when a Democratic majority returned in 1949.

Relations between Biffle and Truman were strained briefly during the 1948 Democratic National Convention. As sergeant-at-arms of the convention, Biffle angered the president by promoting Senator Alben Barkley for vice-president at a time when Truman was trying, unsuccessfully, to convince Supreme Court Justice William O. Douglas to join the ticket. During the campaign Biffle conducted an informal poll that contradicted the prevailing notion that Truman had little chance of defeating Thomas Dewey that year. Dressed in overalls and a straw hat, Biffle drove a pickup truck through several states in the East and Midwest, striking up conversations with people along the way and carefully recording their views each night. At the end of six weeks he returned to Washington, D.C., to announce that, contrary to national public-opinion polls, Truman would win the election. He also advised the president that a majority approved of temporary assistance to war-torn Europe but opposed a long-term commitment. In 1953 Biffle retired, a victim of the Republican sweep the previous year, but he remained in the capital as a consultant.

Unassuming in appearance, Biffle stood five feet, seven inches tall, weighed about 135 pounds, and had brown hair and blue eyes. He was modest, soft-spoken, and courteous to all. He moved swiftly though discreetly about the Senate, quietly signaling orders to pages and slipping reminders to senators. His ability on a crowded Senate floor to whisper out of earshot of everyone but his interlocutor was legend on Capitol Hill. An avid fisherman, he adorned his office wall with a prize catch, a sixty-nine-pound sailfish he landed off Miami. He processed tomatoes grown in his own rooftop garden into "Biffle's Tomato Juice," which became a popular hangover remedy on the Hill. Biffle died in Washington, D.C.

[Articles on Biffle are in the *New York Times*, Aug. 26, 1945, VI:18; *Life*, June 10, 1946; and *Colliers*, Jan. 29, 1949. See also the obituary, *New York Times*, Apr. 7, 1966.]

WILLIAM A. DEGREGORIO

BIGELOW, HENRY BRYANT (Oct. 3, 1879–Dec. 11, 1967), oceanographer, was born in Boston, Mass., the son of Joseph Smith Bigelow, a banker, and Mary Cleveland. His parents, who encouraged him in intellectual pursuits and outdoor activities, spent summers at Cohasset, on Massachusetts Bay, where Bigelow developed an interest in sailing. In 1895 Bigelow graduated from Milton Academy, near Boston, and then spent a year at the Boston Natural History Museum, studying under Alpheus Hyatt, learning German, and taking a course in biology at the Massachusetts Institute of Technology.

In 1897 Bigelow enrolled at Harvard College, where he was a good student, especially in natural history, but he did not consider himself a social success. In the summer of 1900 he was one of four students who accompanied Reginald A. Daly of Harvard and Edmund B. Delabarre of Brown University on a sailing exploration along the coasts of Newfoundland and Labrador.

Bigelow graduated with a B.A. in 1901. In the fall of that year he accompanied Alexander Agassiz of the Harvard Museum of Comparative Zoology on an oceanographic cruise from Ceylon to the Maldive Islands in the Indian Ocean. He was in charge of large collections of jellyfish, about which he published an article in 1904.

In 1902 Bigelow enrolled at Harvard for graduate work and carried out physiological studies of fish under George H. Parker and E. L. Mark. He joined Agassiz for six months in 1904 and 1905 to sail on the *Albatross* from Panama to the Galápagos Islands, Easter Island, and the west coast of Mexico. Bigelow received his Ph.D. in 1906 and that same August married Elizabeth Perkins Shattuck; they had four children. In 1907 Bigelow and his wife accompanied Agassiz on a cruise to the West Indies to investigate coral reefs. The previous year he had been an assistant to Agassiz at the Museum of Comparative Zoology, and he was named curator of coelenterates in 1913, lecturer at the college in 1921, associate professor and curator of oceanography in 1927, and professor in 1931.

After Agassiz's death in 1910, Bigelow was at loose ends until Sir John Murray, on a visit to the Harvard museum, suggested that Bigelow study the oceanography of the Gulf of Maine. Bigelow arranged to use the schooner *Grampus*, belonging to the United States Fish Commission, and from 1912 to 1928 he conducted many cruises, nearly single-handedly, in the Gulf of Maine. He determined water temperatures and salinities at several hundred stations, captured living organisms in 10,000 net tows, and set 1,000 drift bottles to determine surface currents. He summarized this research in three monographs from 1925 to 1927 and in shorter papers thereafter. During these years he continued to publish on coelenterates.

When the International Ice Patrol was established in 1913 following the sinking of the *Titanic* from a collision with an iceberg, Bigelow became a special consultant to the United States Coast Guard. During World War I he was a navigation officer on an army transport ship and an instructor in navigation.

In 1921 Bigelow became a member of the North American Council of Fisheries Investigations and attended many meetings of the International Council for the Exploration of the Sea, although the United States was not a member. He thus became widely acquainted with European leaders in oceanography.

Bigelow's experience in oceanic studies placed him in the forefront when the federal government was becoming interested in oceanography. At the instigation of Frank R. Lillie, of the Marine Biological Laboratory, the National Academy of Sciences established a Committee on Oceanography in 1927. Bigelow was appointed secretary, and in 1928 he prepared a report on the role of the United States in worldwide oceanography. This effective summary led to the establishment of the Woods Hole Oceanographic Institution in Massachusetts, through a large grant from the Rockefeller Foundation. Bigelow became its first director in 1930 and served for ten years. He assembled a staff of scientists interested in ocean studies, he had a laboratory building constructed (later named for him), and he had a research vessel, the *Atlantis*, built in Denmark. That vessel was used for systematic cruises in the North Atlantic Ocean to acquire basic information on physical oceanography and marine organisms.

After his retirement from Woods Hole, Bigelow continued to serve as a trustee. He was widely honored during his lifetime by scientific societies. After 1939 Bigelow served as editor in chief of the series Fishes of the Western North Atlantic, sponsored by the Sears Foundation for Marine Research of Yale University. Working closely with William C. Schroeder, he published extensively on fish, especially sharks and related species, and he wrote many articles for early volumes in the series. He was pursuing this research when he died, in Concord, Mass.

[Bigelow's records are at the Woods Hole Oceanographic Institution, Woods Hole, Mass. His summaries on oceanography are in *Bulletin of the United States Bureau of Fisheries*, 1925, 1926, and 1927. A revision of the monograph (1925) by Bigelow and W. C. Schroeder is *Fisheries Bulletin*, 53 (1953). Bigelow published a summary of his report to the National Academy of Sciences Committee on Oceanography as *Oceanography* (1931). See Bigelow and W. T. Edmondson, *Wind Waves at Sea, Breakers, and Surf* (1947); and *Fishes of the Western North Atlantic* (1948–1968). His autobiography is *Memories of a Long and Active Life* (1964). The biography by Alfred C. Redfield, *Biographical Memoirs of the National Academy of Sciences*, 48 (1976), includes a bibliography. *Oceanus*, 14 (1968), includes reminiscences by Bigelow's colleagues.]

ELIZABETH NOBLE SHOR

BILLINGSLEY, JOHN SHERMAN (Mar. 10, 1900–Oct. 4, 1966), nightclub owner, was born in North Enid, Okla., the son of Robert Billingsley and Emily Collingsworth. The father was an indifferent provider, and the family was so poor that Sherman Billingsley's schooling ended after the fourth grade. His first earnings came from the sale of discarded whiskey bottles at a penny each to bootleggers, who flourished in the "dry" state of Oklahoma. In 1912, Billingsley moved to Anadarko, Okla., to work with his older brothers in their chain of drugstores, where whiskey was sold under the counter.

Leaving Oklahoma in 1917 to see America, Billingsley settled in Detroit, just across the river from an abundant supply of Canadian whiskey. In 1923, with $5,000 in cash accumulated from the operation of grocery stores in Detroit, Billingsley moved east and acquired a drugstore in the Bronx, New York City, where during the Prohibition years he dispensed whiskey by medical prescription; eventually he owned a chain of twenty such stores in the Bronx and nearby Westchester County. He also invested in real estate and built a number of apartment houses and private homes.

Shortly before the stock-market crash in 1929, Billingsley opened a speakeasy in New York City on West 58th Street, the first of three establishments to bear the name Stork Club. This Stork Club was closed by Prohibition agents, but in 1932 a second version was opened at Park Avenue and 51st Street. With the repeal of Prohibition in 1933 the club moved to its last location, 3 East 53rd Street. There Billingsley's gift for showmanship made his supper club famous.

One social phenomenon of the 1930's and 1940's was the mingling in cafés of society figures and entertainers. Billingsley capitalized shrewdly upon the new chic of "café society." By creating an atmosphere of exclusivity in his club, he attracted a clientele that wished to see, or be, celebrities. Pretty young women with a Social Register background, people in the news, syndicated gossip columnists, stage and motion-picture stars, and decorous, well-dressed out-of-town visitors were swept past the red velvet rope in the foyer and seated in one of the club's five rooms. Those deemed sufficiently important or attractive dined in the plush Cub Room, where dinner checks were sometimes not presented. On holidays and anniversaries, or when "Sherm" was in a genial mood, favored patrons received gifts, ranging from Napoleon brandy to a pedigreed puppy or even an automobile.

Billingsley made it easy for even his less notable customers to remember that they had been at the Stork Club. Upon them he bestowed lipsticks embossed with the Stork insignia, powder compacts, gold cigarette holders, tie clasps, golden keys to the club's front door, neckties, garters, and champagne—all appearing unannounced at the patrons' tables accompanied by the owner's card. "This is a place unique unto itself," Billingsley said. "No other place in the world can duplicate it." His customers confirmed this judgment by stealing each year about 2,000 of the black ashtrays inscribed *Stork Club* in white letters—and they were welcome to their plunder.

At the next table one might see Ginger Rogers, the Darryl Zanucks, Tommy Manville about to announce his latest marital intentions, or Ann Sheridan with Steve Hannagan, the flamboyant press agent who advised his friend Billingsley to "make the customers [his] floor show." It was at the Stork Club that General Douglas MacArthur was feted after his return from Korea. There Grace Kelly and Prince Rainier announced their engagement, and Lana Turner and Artie Shaw their divorce. J. Edgar Hoover was a frequent visitor, as were the duke and duchess of Windsor and Ethel Merman, for whom a waiter was especially detailed to light cigarettes. One regret that Billingsley openly expressed was, "If I could only get the Roosevelt boys to bring their mother!"

The Billingsley formula for attracting well-heeled patrons included advertising in Ivy League college publications and offering $1 debutante luncheons. When a newsworthy person arrived in New York, Billingsley sent a special invitation along with orchids, a bottle of premium whiskey, perfume, or champagne. One device for keeping the Stork Club in the news was to refuse admittance to a public figure for some alleged misbehavior. Among those banished were Elliot Roosevelt, Humphrey Bogart, and the editor of the *New Yorker*, Harold Ross, who had published an unflattering profile of the Broadway columnist Walter Winchell. Winchell had his own permanent table in the Cub Room and certified that the Stork Club was "the New Yorkiest place in town." Two dance bands played in shifts in the mirrored blue and gold main dining room, and two crews of press agents worked around the clock to keep the Stork Club in the news. In addition to all this, Steve Hannagan advised that "one good fight a year is swell for a nightclub." Among the patrons who obliged were Ernest Hemingway and Johnny Weissmuller, each of whom became annoyed with a convivial stranger and threw a punch.

During the Stork Club's best years it grossed more than $3 million annually, but in the 1950's a long decline set in. Josephine Baker, the black entertainer, charged in 1951 that she was discriminated against at the club. A city investigation did not support the charge, but there was picketing by civil rights demonstrators and more picketing by the restaurant workers' union in a labor controversy that dragged on from 1957 to 1962. The 1960's marked the appearance of a new kind of nightclub, the discotheque, which appealed to a new generation of fashionable people who did not feel the need for Billingsley's imprimatur. When the pacesetters deserted the Stork Club, so did the followers. The club closed on Oct. 5, 1965.

Billingsley married twice. His first marriage, to Ina Dee, ended in divorce in 1924. On Aug. 25, 1924, he married Hazel Donnelly, a former Ziegfeld Follies chorus girl; they had three children. He died in New York City.

[See Jerome Beatty, "Sherman Packs 'Em In," *American Magazine*, June 1941; Annette Kutner, "Your Name Is Jacqueline Billingsley," *Good Housekeeping*, July 1944; *Time*, Aug. 7, 1944, and Oct. 15, 1965; Russell Whelan, "Inside the Stork Club," *American Mercury*, Sept. 1944; *New York Journal-American*, Sept. 4, 1962; and *Newsweek*, Oct. 18, 1965, and Oct. 17, 1966. Obituary notices are in the *Enid* (Okla.) *Daily Eagle*, Oct. 4, 1966; *New York Times*, Oct. 5, 1966; and *National Review*, Oct. 18, 1966.]

GERALD CARSON

BINFORD, JESSIE FLORENCE (Jan. 20, 1876–July 9, 1966), social worker, was born in Marshalltown, Iowa, the daughter of Thaddeus Binford, a lawyer, and Angelica Beasley. From 1895 to 1897 she attended Smith College, then transferred to Rockford College, where she received her B.A. in 1900. Returning to her family home, she led a boys' club that met in her backyard. In 1902 Binford heard Jane Addams speak and requested permission to visit her famous settlement, Hull House, in Chicago. Addams told her to come the following summer. From 1905 until 1963, Binford was a Hull House resident. She also worked for the United Charities and Legal Aid Society in Chicago from 1906 to 1909 and for the Juvenile Protective Association (JPA).

Binford's most significant contributions to social work were in connection with the JPA. A voluntary child-welfare organization, it was formed in 1906 as the Juvenile Protective League to support the juvenile court, promote reform, and provide casework services to families of neglected or delinquent children. Binford joined the year it was formed and worked as an investigation or probation officer. Based at Hull House, the league changed its name to the Juvenile Protective Association in 1909. While working with delinquent boys, Binford discovered that people connected with neighborhood drugstores were supplying youngsters with cocaine. She joined forces with another Hull House resident, Dr. Alice Hamilton, a pioneer in industrial medicine. Hamilton analyzed the drugs, and the women then confronted the legal system with their findings. The inability of the courts to deal effectively with the drug problem left them angry and frustrated. However, Binford continued to speak out, occasionally accusing influential people of harming Chicago's youth; and she advocated various reforms, especially in the juvenile justice system. Binford was promoted to assistant superintendent and, in 1916, to superintendent of the JPA, a post she held until 1952. During World War I, she also served on the United States Interdepartment Social Hygiene Board and the War Department's Commission on Training Camp Activities, for which she was Midwest regional director for protective work with girls at naval stations and military camps.

As head of the JPA, Binford worked to stop the sale of liquor to minors in dance halls. She joined with Louise de Koven Bowen, a wealthy Hull House and JPA board member, in organizing the Dance Hall and Ball Room Managers' Association. This organization hired chaperones approved by Binford and Bowen and paid for a dance hall officer to ensure that all of its member dance halls were decently run. In 1929, even though the JPA was in financial straits, it adopted a policy of not accepting donations from dance halls of which it disapproved.

In addition to the drug and liquor traffic aimed at juveniles, Binford took up other issues. In 1917 she served as one of three civil service examiners hiring twenty county officials. She also questioned the Red Cross's campaign to salvage junk because she was concerned that youngsters would go into the business of selling junk to dealers. In 1920 Binford chaired the Women's City Club's Police Committee, which did a thorough study of Chicago's police stations and then recommended that voters reject a bond issue for new jails because it did not reflect careful planning. Binford also fought the black market in babies, advocated local censorship of movies, attacked gamblers, and pressured the police and the courts into doing a better job of law enforcement. She was variously called "Miss Jessie" and "the conscience of Chicago." Law enforcement officials listened to what she had to say, and some credited her efforts with diverting as many as 75,000 youngsters from lives of crime and poverty.

The professionalization of social work in the 1920's undermined the effectiveness of those like Binford who lacked graduate professional training. Funding problems also contributed to the haphazard nature of JPA activities. In the late 1930's the agency decided to focus on neglected and abused children. However, the JPA did not acquire a professionally trained staff until after Binford's resignation took effect in 1952.

Binford became a fixture at Hull House. When Addams was away, Binford was one of a small group of residents who, with Bowen, made decisions and handled emergencies. Binford continued to make Hull House her home after retiring as head of the JPA. In 1961 Hull House sold its site to the city for use as the future home of the Chicago campus of the University of Illinois, an action that was opposed by the neighborhood. Binford and Florence Scala, a Hull House neighbor, cochaired the Harrison-Halsted Community, a group that fought the settlement's deal with the city. When Binford's and Scala's speeches and marches failed to change the decision, they launched an unsuccessful two-year campaign in the courts. In 1963 Binford was the last to move out of Hull House. However, the publicity that she and Scala generated led the University of Illinois to restore the original Hull House building. Binford, who never married, returned to Marshalltown but maintained an active interest in the use of the Hull House restoration until her death. She died in Marshalltown, and left her family home, Binford House, to Marshalltown's Federation of Women's Clubs.

Binford possessed a lifelong commitment to her adopted slum neighborhood and tremendous tenacity in speaking out for, and on behalf of, her neighbors. In the end, she truly became one of them.

[Material on Binford is in the manuscript collections of the Juvenile Protective Association and Hull House Association, both in the University of Illinois, Chicago Library. Binford published several pamphlets, including *The Return of the Saloon* (1935) and *Fifty Years of Pioneering* (1951). Articles about Binford include "New Honorary Members for 1949," *Journal of Social Hygiene*, Mar. 1949; and Karl Detzer, "Miss Jessie Fights for the Kids," *Reader's Digest*, Dec. 1950, condensed from an article in *Christian Herald*, Dec. 1950. See Paul G. Anderson, "Juvenile Protective Association" in Peter Romanofsky, ed., *Social Service Organizations* (1978). Obituary notices are in *Chicago Tribune* and *Chicago Daily News*, both July 11, 1966, and *New York Times*, July 12, 1966.]

JUDITH ANN TROLANDER

BLOCH, CLAUDE CHARLES (July 12, 1878–Oct. 6, 1967), naval officer, was born in Woodbury, Ky., the son of Adolph Bloch, a broker; there is no record of his mother's name. He attended Ogden College in his home state before entering the United States Naval Academy in 1895. During the summer of 1898, as a naval cadet aboard the battleship *Iowa*, he received the Specially Meritorious Medal for rescuing Spanish sailors from their burning ships in the battle off Santiago, Cuba. He graduated in the top third of his class at Annapolis in January 1899, and for the next two years, he served aboard the gunboat *Wheeling* in operations related to the Philippine Insurrection and the Boxer Rebellion. On Mar. 3, 1903, while serving as customs officer and captain of the navy station yard in American Samoa, he married Augusta Kent; they had one child.

Assigned to important billets in gunnery, then considered essential for advancement in the navy, Bloch had many duties at the prestigious Bureau of Ordnance. He was the inspector of powder for the entire East Coast during 1905; an aide from 1907 to 1909 to the commanders in chief of the Pacific Fleet; and a tester of guns at the Naval Proving Grounds at Indian Head, Md., from 1909 to 1911. He also served along the Atlantic seaboard and in Cuban waters on the battleships *Virginia* (1906–1907), *Delaware* (1911–1913), *Maine* (1913), and *Arizona* (1916–1918). During the summer of 1918 he commanded the *Plattsburg*, which convoyed American troops to Europe. After commanding the battleship *Massachusetts*, he completed his World War I service at the Office of the Chief of Naval Operations. From December 1918 until May 1921, Bloch was assistant to the chief of the Bureau of Ordnance, after which he commanded mine forces and the minelayer *Baltimore* in the Pacific.

Bloch held key staff positions on battleships in the Pacific before inspecting ordnance in Virginia and Maryland during 1923. He held the permanent rank of captain but was temporarily advanced to rear admiral in October 1923, when he was appointed chief of the Bureau of Ordnance, the highest administrative post in the battleship branch of the navy. He occupied this post for four years.

Reverting to the rank of captain, Bloch commanded the battleship *California* in the Pacific between 1927 and 1929, attended the Naval War College in 1929, and spent the next year as commandant at the Washington Navy Yard.

Although the tall, ruddy-faced, and mild-mannered Bloch was known as a trim, quietly efficient officer who avoided publicity, he became a major figure in the navy during the 1930's. He argued so forcibly for preparedness in order to "beat the enemy to the punch" that the press dubbed him the "Jack Dempsey of the Navy." Promoted in 1931 to rear admiral, then the highest permanent rank in the navy, he commanded the training squadron of the scouting force until May 1933. He then became budget officer for the Navy Department, and from 1934 to 1936 he was judge advocate general of the navy.

In the words of his colleague Admiral J. O. Richardson, Bloch "had no peer in the handling of committees of Congress," and "it was generally believed in the Navy that, no matter where Bloch was assigned, he and his command would do a superior job." Especially adept at tactics, Bloch was given command of a battleship division in June 1936 and the following January took over the battle force in the temporary rank of full admiral. On Jan. 29,

1938, he became commander in chief of the United States Fleet, based on the West Coast. In the spring of 1939, with his flag on the battleship *Pennsylvania*, he took the fleet to the Caribbean for annual war games. However, the deepening crisis with Japan caused the fleet's premature return to the West Coast. In accord with normal command rotation, Bloch was relieved as fleet commander by Admiral Richardson on Jan. 6, 1940, and was returned to his permanent rank of rear admiral.

To finish out his career, Bloch was given a typical last assignment as commandant of the Fourteenth Naval District and was based at Pearl Harbor. His responsibility for the defense of the Hawaiian Islands was complicated when the United States Fleet was transferred from California to Pearl Harbor in the spring of 1940 to act as a deterrent to Japan. Admiral Husband E. Kimmel assumed command of the fleet early in 1941 and constantly interfered when Bloch tried to strengthen Hawaii's defenses. Bloch was present when the Japanese attacked Pearl Harbor on Dec. 7, 1941, but he was one of the few senior officers not criticized during subsequent investigations of the disaster. However, he then ran into trouble with his superiors for trying to tell the new Pacific commander, Admiral Chester W. Nimitz, how to direct operations against the Japanese. In April 1942, Bloch was recalled to Washington, where he served on the navy's General Board until he retired on August 1 with the rank of full admiral. He spent the remainder of World War II as chairman of the navy's board for giving production awards to wartime industries. He died in Washington.

[Bloch's papers are in the Library of Congress. A listing of his assignments may be found in an outline at the Naval Historical Center, Washington, D.C. The history of his ships is traced in the Naval Historical Center, *Dictionary of American Naval Fighting Ships* (1959–1981). See also Samuel Eliot Morison, *History of United States Naval Operations in World War II*, III, *The Rising Sun in the Pacific* (1947); James O. Richardson, *On the Treadmill to Pearl Harbor* (1973); and E. B. Potter, *Nimitz* (1976). See also the obituary notice in the *New York Times*, Oct. 7, 1967.]

CLARK G. REYNOLDS

BOGAN, LOUISE MARIE (Aug. 11, 1897–Feb. 4, 1970), poet, short-story writer, and critic, was born in Livermore Falls, Maine, the daughter of Daniel Joseph Bogan, who held various white-collar jobs in paper companies, and Mary Helen Shields. Bogan spent her childhood in New England mill towns. Her family was not a happy one, and Bogan found refuge from constant domestic turmoil in *Grimm's Fairy Tales* and adventure stories. In 1907, Bogan spent a year at Mount St. Mary's Academy in Manchester, N.H. In 1909 the family moved from Ballardvale, Mass., to Boston, where, from 1910 to 1915, Bogan received a rigorous classical education at Girls' Latin School. At fourteen she began to write, and by seventeen she had become an accomplished metrist in the style of Algernon Charles Swinburne, William Morris, and Christina Rossetti.

After graduating from high school, Bogan spent one year at Boston University (1915–1916). On Sept. 4, 1916, she married a young army officer, Curt Alexander, and accompanied him to the Panama Canal Zone, where their only child was born. After one separation, she left Alexander permanently, and at his death in 1920 she had been living alone in New York City for at least a year.

Bogan began to publish her poems in 1917 and by 1921 was contributing frequently to the *New Republic*, the *Measure*, the *Liberator*, and other small magazines. After a six-month sojourn in Vienna in 1922, she published her first book, *Body of This Death* (1923), which established her as one of the foremost lyric poets of her generation. She began friendships with the critic Edmund Wilson and the poet Rolfe Humphries, and in July 1925 she married the poet Raymond Peckham Holden. After spending most of 1926 in Santa Fe, N.Mex., to improve Holden's health, the couple bought a fruit farm in Hillsdale, N.Y., where they moved in 1928. Bogan's second book, *Dark Summer* (1929), contained her two longest poems, "The Flume" and "Summer Wish," in addition to shorter lyrics (among them "Simple Autumnal" and "Come, Break with Time") that, according to the critic Yvor Winters, demanded comparison "with the best songs of the sixteenth and seventeenth centuries."

After a fire destroyed the Hillsdale house in December 1929, Bogan and Holden moved back to New York City. In the spring of 1931, shortly after publishing her first poetry review for the *New Yorker*, Bogan sought hospital treatment for depression. After traveling in Europe on a Guggenheim Fellowship in 1933, she returned home to find her marriage broken, and she again suffered from a severe depression. She recovered with a new outlook of acceptance and reconciliation, sentiments captured in the poems of *The Sleeping Fury* (1937). She and Holden were divorced in 1937.

In the late 1930's, Bogan became a vigorous and outspoken opponent of political cant, especially on the Left, and in reviews and essays she persistently upheld the autonomy of art and the freedom of the artist. The light verse of *Poems and New Poems* (1941) took a satiric view of the current scene. From 1942 to 1948, Bogan did not write a single poem. She occupied the chair in poetry at the Library of Congress in 1945–1946, and in 1948 she began a new career as a teacher with visiting lectureships at the University of Washington in Seattle and the University of Chicago. In 1948 she also collaborated on a translation of Goethe with Elizabeth Mayer; in later years, she translated Valéry with May Sarton, and Jules Renard with Elizabeth Roget.

Bogan also published a brief critical history, *Achievement in American Poetry, 1900–1950* (1951); *Collected Poems, 1923–1953* (1954); and *Selected Criticism: Poetry and Prose* (1955). As a critic, Bogan emphasized maturity in the artist, the work, and the age. Her essays on Yeats, Rilke, James, and Auden are major contributions to the criticism of these writers. Her judgments are clear, detached, and marked by insight, humor, and generosity, qualities equally evident in her letters to Rolfe Humphries, Edmund Wilson, Morton Dauwen Zabel, Theodore Roethke, William Maxwell, and May Sarton.

Throughout the 1950's and 1960's, Bogan continued to write reviews for the *New Yorker*, to teach, and to work sporadically on her memoirs. Writing few poems, she nevertheless produced important lyrics in her later years, including "Song for the Last Act," "After the Persian," "March Twilight," and "Psychiatrist's Song." A visit to Boston in 1965 revived painful childhood memories that precipitated a severe depression from which she never fully recovered. Her final collected edition, *The Blue Estuaries: Poems 1923–1968*, was published in 1968. Living in increasing seclusion, Bogan resigned from the *New Yorker* in 1969, after an association of thirty-eight years. She had only recently approved the text of her collected criticism, *A Poet's Alphabet* (1970), when she died in New York City.

Often placed in the tradition of seventeenth-century metaphysical verse, Bogan's austere, formal lyrics have traditional themes. Yet, her treatment of them is thoroughly modern, nourished by symbolist aesthetics, twentieth-century views of the unconscious, and the concerns of Yeats, Rilke, Eliot, and Auden. William Maxwell wrote after her death, "She was a handsome, direct, impressive, vulnerable woman. In whatever she wrote, the line of truth was exactly superimposed on the line of feeling." Her best poems, predicted Theodore Roethke, "will stay in the language as long as the language survives." She was a professional woman of letters in the fullest sense, conscientious in her critical tasks and faithful to her art. Her voice remains not only one of the strongest in mid-twentieth-century American literature but among the few that actually define the age.

[Bogan's papers are in the Amherst College Library. Some correspondence is in Ruth Limmer, ed., *What the Woman Lived* (1973). See William Jay Smith, *Louise Bogan* (1971); Jane Couchman, "Louise Bogan," *Bulletin of Bibliography* (1976); "Louise Bogan," *New Yorker*, Jan. 30, 1978; Ruth Limmer, *Journey Around My Room: The Autobiography of Louise Bogan* (1980); Martha Collins, ed., *Critical Essays on Louise Bogan* (1984); and Elizabeth Frank, *Louise Bogan* (1985). Obituaries are in the *New York Times*, Feb. 5, 1970; and the *New Yorker*, Feb. 14, 1970.]

ELIZABETH FRANK

BORING, EDWIN GARRIGUES (Oct. 23, 1886–July 1, 1968), psychologist and teacher, was born in Philadelphia, Pa., the son of Edwin McCurdy Boring, a pharmacist, and Elizabeth Garrigues. Boring was raised in a Moravian-Quaker household and attended the Friends Select School, an orthodox Quaker institution. His childhood was a lonely one, dominated by a matriarchal family, a delicate nervous disposition, and a constant feeling of inferiority. Boring intended to become an engineer and in 1908 graduated from Cornell with an M.E. degree.

Boring worked for a year at Bethlehem Steel as an apprentice electrician. When offered a promotion, he quit because he had grown to dislike engineering. He then turned to teaching science at the Moravian Parochial School in Bethlehem, Pa. (1909–1910). He considered himself lacking as a teacher and returned to Cornell to pursue a doctorate in psychology, a subject he had enjoyed earlier. Boring became part of a group of young scholars influenced by E. B. Titchener, a structuralist concerned with exploring human consciousness and opposed to behavioral studies. Although Boring often disagreed with Titchener, he never broke with him personally; indeed, Titchener arranged for Boring to receive a series of fellowships so that he could complete his education. Boring received his M.A. in 1912 and his Ph.D. in 1914. While at Cornell, he met Lucy May Day, who took her doctorate in psychology in 1912. They were married on June 18, 1914, and had four children.

When the United States entered World War I, Robert M. Yerkes recruited Boring to help test the intelligence of draftees. Boring was appointed a captain in the medical department of the army and soon became a chief psychological examiner. At the end of the war, he helped write a report of the surgeon general indicating that the average inductee had a mental age of thirteen and that low levels of intelligence were especially noticeable among blacks and other minorities. These tests were later seen as grossly biased; in the 1950's, Boring admitted that they had been "culture-bound" but even later professed admiration for the testers and saw the program as honest and useful work.

At the conclusion of the war, Boring accepted a position at Clark University as professor of experimental psychology. In opposition to Wallace W. Atwood, the university's president, he supported the right of a radical to speak to the student body. His contract was not renewed, and in 1922 he was invited to Harvard, where he began a long and productive career. From 1924 until 1949 he was director of the psychological laboratory and was named full professor in 1928. In 1925 he became coeditor of the *American Journal of Psychology*, a position he held until 1946. At Harvard, Boring undertook to free psychology from its status as part of the Department of Philosophy. A separate Department of Psychology was established in 1934, and he was named its chairman.

In 1925, Boring became involved in the investigation of a famous Boston medium named Margery (Mrs. L. R. G. Crandon), who claimed to possess extraordinary psychic powers. Boring and a number of Harvard associates witnessed her séances and declared that her claims were false. A year later Boring wrote an article for the *Atlantic Monthly* discussing the case and the difficulties of dealing with supernormal phenomena in scientific terms.

Boring published his first and most important book, *A History of Experimental Psychology*, in 1929 (revised and enlarged in 1950). He followed it with *The Physical Dimensions of Consciousness* (1933), *Sensation and Perception in the History of Experimental Psychology* (1942), *History, Psychology, and Science* (1963), and *Source Book in the History of Psychology* (with R. J. Herrnstein, 1965). He also collaborated in writing a number of textbooks in basic psychology and wrote a large number of articles for both professional and popular journals.

During World War II, Boring was chairman of a National Research Council committee assigned to write a textbook on the psychology of soldiers. It was decided that a nonscholarly book directed to the soldiers themselves was needed; *Psychology for the Fighting Man* (1943) was the result. Nearly 400,000 copies were sold, and it was rewritten for a more professional military audience as *Psychology for the Armed Forces* (1945).

Boring claimed that the 1950's were the best years of his life. His administrative duties had finally ended, and an intellectual maturity had finally dissipated his chronic feeling of inferiority. From 1956 to 1961 he edited a new journal, *Contemporary Psychology*. He was appointed Edgar Pierce Professor Emeritus upon retirement from Harvard and continued to teach classes until he was nearly seventy-one. He was chairman of the American Psychological Association Committee on Freedom of Enquiry from 1954 to 1956, at the end of the McCarthy era, and was appointed the Lowell television lecturer on psychology for a Boston educational station (1956–1957).

Boring was an associate editor for Basic Books from 1961 to 1968. In 1961 he published a brief autobiography, *Psychologist at Large*, in which he traced his personal and academic development. The title of the book was an apt summation of Boring's contribution to psychology. He was not a serious researcher, a problem that caused him a good deal of anxiety during much of his career, even leading him to undergo psychoanalysis in the 1930's. Boring believed that he never had the time for research and that he simply was "not an experimentalist at heart." According to a colleague, he was "perhaps the last universalist of the profession," devoting himself with enormous energy and erudition to writing about the history of psychology, editing professional journals, and guiding the psychology department at Harvard. He died in Cambridge, Mass.

[Boring's autobiography includes a sampling of his correspondence and professional papers. A collection of his work is *History, Psychology, and Science: Selected Papers* (1963), edited by R. J. Watson and D. T. Campbell. His writings on military intelligence testing are in his *History of Experimental Psychology* (1950). A discussion of the Margery case is in R. Laurence Moore, *In Search of White Crows* (1977). Obituaries are in the *New York Times*, July 2, 1968; the *American Journal of Psychology*, Aug. 1968; and *Contemporary Psychology*, Mar. 1969.]

ERIC JARVIS

BRACKETT, CHARLES WILLIAM (Nov. 26, 1892–Mar. 9, 1969), writer and motion-picture producer, was born in Saratoga Springs, N.Y., the son of Edgar Truman Brackett, a lawyer and New York State senator, and Mary Emma Corliss. After receiving a B.A. from Williams College in 1915, Brackett entered Harvard Law School. His studies were interrupted by World War I, in which he served as an assistant liaison officer on the staff of the French general Michel Henri Martin Coutanceau. Brackett was decorated with the *Médaille d'honneur en argent*.

Returning to the United States, Brackett married Elizabeth Barrows Fletcher on June 2, 1919. They had two children. Upon receiving his LL.B. from Harvard in 1920, Brackett joined his father's law firm. His first novel, *The Counsel of the Ungodly*, appeared serially in the *Saturday Evening Post* in 1920. In the 1920's and early 1930's Brackett published over thirty-five short stories and five more serialized novels, primarily in the *Saturday Evening Post*.

When his novel *Week-end* (1925) attracted the attention of Harold Ross, the editor of the *New Yorker*, Brackett was offered a post as the magazine's drama critic. He held this position from 1926 to 1929, but he also continued writing novels: *That Last Infirmity* (1926), a comedy of manners about a nouveau riche widow breaking into society; *American Colony* (1929), about the decadent life of wealthy American expatriates on the French Riviera; and *Entirely Surrounded* (1934), a roman à clef treating satirically a weekend at the summer home of a famous radio broadcaster and newspaper columnist patterned after Brackett's friend Alexander Woollcott.

Brackett resigned from the *New Yorker* in 1929 to write full-time. In 1932 he accepted an offer to become a screenwriter for Paramount Pictures. After a six-week stint in Hollywood he briefly returned East, then went back to the film industry. His career blossomed when he was assigned by Paramount story editor Manny Wolf to collaborate with a young Viennese writer, Billy Wilder, in July 1936. Their first screenplay, *Bluebeard's Eighth Wife* (1938), began a fourteen-year, thirteen-film collaboration between Wilder and Brackett that made them one of the most famous screenwriting teams in Hollywood history, renowned as "the happiest couple in Hollywood."

After co-writing *Midnight* (1930) and, with Walter Reisch, *Ninotchka* (1939), for which they received an Academy Award nomination, Brackett and Wilder began to achieve creative independence, a status enjoyed by few screenwriters during the studio era. Beginning with *Five Graves to Cairo* (1943), they became a writing-directing-producing team; both wrote, Wilder directed, and Brackett produced. Under this arrangement they made their two most famous films. *The Lost Weekend* (1945), a powerful film about an alcoholic writer (Ray Milland), won Oscars for best film, director, actor, and screenplay, while *Sunset Boulevard* (1950), a portrayal of the relationship between an aging movie queen (Gloria Swanson) and a youthful, down-and-out screenwriter (William Holden), won the respect of critics and earned three Oscars, including the award for best screenplay. *Sunset Boulevard* also marked the end of the Brackett-Wilder collaboration.

The personalities and writing skills of Brackett and Wilder complemented one another. Bracket was calm, suave, and urbane; Wilder was buoyant and mercurial. Whereas Wilder paced and talked incessantly while writing, Brackett preferred to relax on a couch, discarding some of Wilder's suggestions and writing down others as he thought about the development of the story and the tone of the dialogue. Wilder was the more cynical of the two, Brackett the more cautious. Wilder's biographer, Maurice Zolotow, has suggested that though Brackett seemed the more dependent member of the team, he was probably stronger and more stable than Wilder.

Brackett was active in the Screen Writers' Guild, serving as its president from 1938 to 1939. In 1949 he became president of the Academy of Motion Picture Arts and Sciences, continuing in that position until 1955 (the longest presidential term in academy history). Brackett's first wife died in 1948, and in 1953 he married her sister, Lillian Fletcher. He continued as a writer and producer for Twentieth Century–Fox in the 1950's. His best-known films during this decade were *Titanic* (1953), for which Brackett, Walter Reisch, and Richard Breen received an Oscar for best screenplay, *The King and I* (as producer, 1956), and *Journey to the Center of the Earth* (as producer-screenwriter, 1959). In 1957 he was given a special Oscar for outstanding service to the academy. Brackett retired from Twentieth Century–Fox in 1962.

Brackett retained his ties to Saratoga Springs throughout his life as a partner in the law firm of Brackett, Eddy and Dorsey, and as vice-president of the Adirondack Trust Company in the same community. Like a character in his novel *Entirely Surrounded*, he claimed to abhor physical exercise and was passionately devoted to cribbage. Accomplished in many fields, he was most clearly successful as a movie screenwriter and will be remembered by film historians as a member of the famous screenwriting team of Brackett and Wilder. He died in Bel Air, Calif.

[See Richard Corliss, *Talking Pictures* (1975); and Maurice Zolotow, *Billy Wilder in Hollywood* (1977). An obituary is in the *New York Times*, Mar. 10, 1969.]

CHARLES J. MALAND

BRENNAN, FRANCIS JAMES (May 7, 1894–July 2, 1968), Roman Catholic canon lawyer, jurist, and cardinal, was born in the coal-mining town of Shenandoah, Pa., the son of James Brennan, a dentist, and Margaret Connor. Brennan attended public school in Shenandoah until 1910, when he entered St. Charles Borromeo Seminary near Philadelphia. Eight years later Brennan was chosen for advanced study at the Pontifical Roman Seminary. In 1920 he received his D.D. and was ordained a priest. After four years of additional study at the Juridical Seminary of St. Apollinare in Rome, he received his doctorate in civil and canon law.

Brennan returned to Philadelphia in 1924, served as assistant pastor at St. Charles Borromeo Church and then at St. Carthage Church, and taught Latin at West Philadelphia High School for Boys. In 1928 he went to St. Charles Borromeo Seminary as professor of canon law and moral philosophy. In 1937, Brennan became a member of the Philadelphia Archdiocesan Court and director of the conference of clergymen that advised the archbishop on moral cases under canon law. His judicial work came to the attention of the apostolic delegate (papal representative) in the United States, Archbishop Amleto Cicognani, who had been one of Brennan's teachers in Rome and who later became a cardinal and the Vatican's secretary of state. Cicognani recommended him for a post in the Sacra Rota, the Vatican court of appeals from diocesan tribunals.

In 1940, Brennan became the first American appointed an auditor (judge) in the Rota, which had been established in 1171. While it had once played a key role in the Vatican's relations with secular rulers and states, in modern times it dealt primarily with appeals for church annulment of marriages. After nineteen years of service in the Rota, Brennan became its dean (chief judge), with the title of monsignor. In that capacity, he carried the pope's miter, a symbol of law, in papal processions and served as president of the Vatican Court of Appeal, a civil court. Between 1959 and 1967 he served in administrative, financial, and legal posts in several congregations (governing committees) of the Roman Catholic church, including the Congregation of the Discipline of the Sacraments, which governs legislation on ritual; the Congregation of the Council, which administers many aspects of discipline in the church; the Congregation for the Propagation of the Faith, which directs work in missionary areas; and the Congregation of Sacred Rites, which oversees the performance of the liturgy. In 1962, Brennan served as a consultant to the central commission of the Second Vatican Council.

In May 1967, Brennan was nominated by Pope Paul VI to the College of Cardinals, an unusual honor for a nonprelate. A month later he was consecrated as titular bishop (bishop of a see that no longer exists) of Tubune, Mauritania, and given the red biretta, red cape, and sapphire ring of the cardinal's office. As titular bishop, Brennan remained in Rome working in the Curia, the collective title given to the administrative, judicial, and legislative bodies that govern the Roman Catholic church. In September 1967 he was appointed an assistant to the president of the new Cardinals Commission for the Prefecture of Economic Affairs, which was to supervise the economic assets of the Vatican. In January 1968, when he was named head of the Congregation of the Discipline of the Sacraments, Brennan became the first American to chair a congregation. He became ill five months later. In June he returned to the United States for tests and treatment at Philadelphia's Misericordia Hospital, where he died.

Although Brennan was little known outside the Roman Curia, he rose higher in its ranks than any American before him. Called in Rome "the quiet American," Brennan was self-effacing and shunned publicity. Yet, he cultivated a reputation within the Curia as a careful administrator and jurist who handled a heavy work load without strain. A priest who knew Cardinal Brennan described him as "so extremely proper, extremely quiet, so extremely strait-laced and cautious that his demeanor might be summed up as almost saturnine." Nevertheless, after a talk he gave in a papal audience, Pope John XXIII complimented Brennan for his simplicity of speech. It was fitting, said the pope, "for one who, possessing the art of weighing the value of words, gives to each great importance."

[See the *New York Times* and the *Washington Post*, both May 30, 1967. An obituary is in the *New York Times*, July 3, 1968.]

RALPH E. LUKER

BRERETON, LEWIS HYDE (June 21, 1890–July 19, 1967), military aviator, was born in Pittsburgh, Pa., the son of William Denny Brereton and Helen Hyde. He attended St. John's College, Annapolis, for two years before entering the United States Naval Academy in 1907, after having failed to gain admission to West Point. Upon graduation in 1911, he resigned his ensign's commission and transferred to the army. He served one year as second lieutenant in the Coast Artillery Corps and then transferred to the aviation section of the Signal Corps and learned to fly at its school in San Diego.

Brereton qualified for an Aero Club license as American pilot number 211 on Jan. 23, 1913, and, as military aviator, on March 27. The next month he escaped unharmed from a seaplane crash in which his passenger was killed. It was the first of eight plane crashes during his career as a pilot. In 1913 he married Helen Willis; they had two children.

Brereton was sent to the Philippines for duty in the Field Artillery but managed to change back to flying duty there in 1915. He returned to the army's aviation section in Washington on the eve of American entry into World War I. After additional flight training, he was sent to France in October 1917 in the rank of captain. The following March he assumed command of the 12th Aero Squadron, which he led into battle along the Western Front, rising in rank to temporary lieutenant colonel as a wing commander and First Army Corps air chief. He was shot down over St. Mihiel. By the time of the Armistice, he was operations officer to Major General Mason M. Patrick, who commanded the United States Air Service in Europe. After duty at Air Service headquarters in Washington, he returned to France as an air attaché at the American embassy in Paris during 1919–1922, serving the first two years on the Inter-Allied Control Commission for Aviation.

"Pug-nosed, unhandsome, 5 ft. 10 in. tall," as *Time* described him, Brereton was known for his tireless energy, remarkable memory, firm views, and outspoken defiance of military orthodoxy. A master of profanity, the good-humored flyer was nicknamed by his peers "Looy, dot Dope." He became a leading advocate of strategic bombing while training pilots at Kelly Field, Tex., and Langley Field, Va., where in 1925 he took command of the Second Bombardment Group. The next year he acted as a defense counsel in the court-martial of Brigadier General "Billy" Mitchell. The resulting controversy helps to account for Brereton's not being promoted beyond the permanent rank of major from 1920 to 1935. After a year as student at the Command and General Staff School, Fort Leavenworth, Kans., he commanded the 88th Observation Squadron and also instructed in field artillery at Post Field and Fort Sill, Okla., between 1928 and 1931.

Brereton and his wife were divorced in 1929. On Feb. 20, 1931, he married Icy V. Larkin, from whom he was later divorced, and that year he was transferred to Panama for four years in command of Army Air Corps operations there.

Brereton

Brereton returned to Fort Leavenworth as instructor in the rank of lieutenant colonel in 1935 and was advanced to the temporary rank of colonel a year later. During 1939–1940 he commanded Barksdale Field, La., and in October 1940 became brigadier general at the head of the 17th Bombardment Wing at Savannah. With the approach of war, he was promoted to major general in July 1941 and assumed command of the Third Air Force at Tampa.

That November Brereton took charge of the Far Eastern Air Force under General Douglas MacArthur at Manila. On December 7 his B-17 bombers were caught on the ground at Clark Field and destroyed by Japanese planes, and the Philippines' defenses were badly compromised. A bitter controversy ensued between MacArthur and Brereton over responsibility for this debacle. Though no censure of any senior officer followed, historians have concluded that both men must share the blame. Ordered to evacuate his remaining bombers, Brereton departed with them on Christmas Eve and operated out of Darwin, Australia, and Lembang, Java, as Allied air commander and commander of the Fifth Air Force. His bombers attacked Japanese forces in Indonesia during the fruitless Allied defense of the region.

Brereton was withdrawn to New Delhi, India, in February 1942 to be commanding general of the Tenth Air Force, which he organized the next month. He worked in concert with the Royal Air Force to initiate air strikes on Japanese positions in Burma and the Andaman Islands and to begin the aerial supply of United States forces in China. He inspired the forces under his command by flying with them in battle. In June of that year he was transferred to Cairo, Egypt, to command the United States Middle East Air Force, soon redesignated the Ninth Air Force. In this capacity he continued to fly while directing air attacks on Axis forces in Tunisia and Libya, and in February 1943 he was given the additional command of all United States Army forces in the Middle East supporting the British Eighth Army during the final defeat of Field Marshal Erwin Rommel's forces in North Africa.

Brereton's greatest achievement was the great bombing raid on the Axis oil refineries at Ploesti, Romania. He trained his air crews during the spring and summer of 1943, and on August 1 he sent 177 B-24 Liberators across the Mediterranean to destroy nearly half of Ploesti's refining capacity, although navigational difficulties led to the destruction of fifty-four planes by heavy German antiaircraft fire. Relieved of his army command in October, Brereton continued to head the Ninth Air Force in the European Theater of Operations and was promoted to lieutenant general in April 1944. That August he was assigned command of the First Allied Airborne Army. On September 17 United States and British airborne forces were airdropped by glider and parachute around Arnhem, the Netherlands, in an effort to reach the Rhine River, but stiff German resistance and a sluggish cooperative Allied advance along the ground led to the offensive's being repulsed with heavy losses. Brereton remained in Europe until final victory in May 1945.

Brereton again commanded the Third Air Force at Tampa during the latter half of 1945. On Jan. 24, 1946, he married Zena A. Groves. Also in 1946 he published his wartime memoirs, *The Brereton Diaries*, and served in the Office of the Secretary of War. In 1947–1948 he was senior Air Force member of the military liaison committee with the Atomic Energy Commission. After retiring in 1948, he became president of the Overseas Service Corporation.

An energetic and generally successful army air leader during both world wars, Brereton was almost unique in commanding air power in all three theaters of World War II. Aside from the Clark Field disaster in 1941, his record was one of aggressive leadership, culminating in the great Ploesti raid, his only major contribution to the strategic bombing campaign. The Arnhem defeat was due to circumstances beyond his control, namely, his subordination to senior Allied commanders who made the key decisions and the factor of bad weather.

[The Lewis H. Brereton papers are at the Dwight D. Eisenhower Library, Abilene, Kan., and are supplemented by archives at the Office of Air Force History. Useful biographical sketches may be found in *Time*, May 4, 1942; *Who Was Who in American History: The Military* (1975). References to his earliest feats in aviation are in *Aero and Hydro*, Apr. 19, 1913. See also Wesley Frank Craven and James Lea Cate, eds., *The Army Air Forces in World War II*, I (1948); Charles B. MacDonald, *The Siegfried Line Campaign* (1963); and D. Clayton James, *The Years of MacArthur*, II (1975). An obituary notice is in the *New York Times*, July 20, 1967.]

CLARK G. REYNOLDS

BRIDGES, THOMAS JEFFERSON DAVIS ("TOMMY") (Dec. 28, 1906–Apr. 19, 1968), major-league baseball pitcher, was born in Gordonsville, Tenn., the son of Joseph G. Bridges, a country doctor, and Flossie Davis. He attended elementary school at New Middleton, Tenn., and graduated from the Gordonsville high school. At the age of ten he was playing baseball and could throw a sinking curveball, the pitch that became the key to his professional success. He entered the University of Tennessee in 1925, and although he remained four academic years, he left in 1929 without a degree. A right-handed thrower and batter, Bridges was a star pitcher for the varsity baseball team and its captain during the 1928 and 1929 seasons.

Bridges' family wanted him to be a physician. However, Billy Doyle, a scout for the Detroit Tigers, saw Bridges pitch at Tennessee and signed him to a contract with Wheeling, W.Va., in the Middle Atlantic League. Bridges reported to Wheeling in June 1929 and during the season won ten games and lost three, striking out 106 batters in 129 innings. In 1930 he moved to Evansville, Ind., a Tiger farm team in the Three-I League. He won seven games and lost eight at Evansville before joining the Tigers toward the end of the season on the recommendation of the Tiger scout Wish Egan. He won three games and lost two during the partial season at Detroit. On Mar. 21, 1930, Bridges married Carolyn Jellicose. The marriage ended in a divorce; they had one child.

Bridges spent his entire sixteen-year major-league career with the Tigers. He played under four managers—Bucky Harris, Mickey Cochrane, Del Baker, and Steve O'Neill. He won 194 games, including 33 shutouts, and lost 138. His career earned-run average was 3.57. His tendency to wildness hindered him somewhat early in his career. In a game against the St. Louis Browns on Aug. 25, 1930, he walked twelve players. Bucky Harris worked with him patiently, and Bridges gained control and confidence. He continued to be a bit wild, but this often worked to his advantage by making batters uneasy at the plate. The sharp-breaking curve became his forte, but despite his size (155 pounds; five feet, ten inches) he had a very good fastball. Cochrane, Detroit's catcher at the peak of Bridges' career, claimed he won most of his games with his fastball. And Bridges agreed that "a curve isn't worth a hoot unless the batter respects your fast ball."

During his second full season with the Tigers, Bridges, in a game with the Washington Senators on Aug. 5, 1932, pitched until two were out in the ninth inning without allowing a man to reach first base. With the score 13–0, the Washington manager Walter Johnson, a former pitching great, sent the outfielder Dave Harris up as a pinch hitter. Harris, one of the league's best curveball hitters, rapped a single to left field and broke up Bridges' perfect game. Johnson was criticized in some quarters for putting in a skilled curveball hitter under the circumstances. But Bridges would have none of it. "I don't want credit for a perfect game unless I honestly earn it. I wouldn't get any satisfaction if someone deliberately laid down on his job to hand it to me." On May 24, 1933, again against the Senators, the first baseman Joe Kuhel hit a home run off Bridges in the ninth inning and broke up a no-hitter. It was not until 1947, after Bridges had returned to the minor leagues, that he pitched his only no-hitter, for the Portland Beavers in the Pacific Coast League.

Opposing players, after a swinging third strike, sometimes accused Bridges of throwing a spitball, banned since 1920, but he was never officially charged with it. "Have you ever watched a ball roll across a table, then fall to the floor?" one player asked. "If so, then you have seen Bridges' curve." Some credibility is lent to the batters' complaints by an unauthenticated story that has it that Cochrane one day rolled the ball back to Bridges on the ground after a pitch. Spike Briggs, Jr., the Tigers' owner, the story goes, asked Cochrane after the game why he did it. "Well," the catcher said, "I had to do something to get the chewing gum off the ball."

In the 1934, 1935, and 1936 seasons Bridges won a total of sixty-six games. He led the American League in strikeouts in 1935 (163), and in 1936 in both strikeouts (175) and victories (23). He pitched in four World Series—in 1934, when the Tigers lost to the St. Louis Cardinals; in 1935, when the Tigers defeated the Chicago Cubs; in 1940, when the Tigers lost to the Cincinnati Reds; and in 1945, when the Tigers again bested the Cubs. In World Series competition Bridges won four games and lost one. He lost to Paul Dean in the third game of the 1934 series, 4–1, but beat Dizzy Dean, 3–1, in game five. In 1935 he won the second game, 8–3, against Charlie Root, and the sixth and deciding game, 4–3, against Larry French. In the 1940 series he won the third game against Jim Turner, 7–4. Bridges pitched less than two innings in the 1945 series. His World Series earned-run average was 3.52.

Bridges was selected for the all-star game for a number of years and was credited with winning the 1939 game. Of the 332 games Bridges pitched to a decision in his sixteen years with the Tigers, he completed 207. He profited during the 1934 and 1935 seasons from the great hitting of teammates Charlie Gehringer, Goose Goslin, Hank Greenberg, and Cochrane, all of whom were elected to the Baseball Hall of Fame.

Bridges was well liked by Detroit fans and by his teammates. He was a dependable, hardworking player, unwilling to speak unkindly of anyone. He had a drinking problem, but it usually did not affect his ability to function. In the off-season he hunted pheasant and quail. After his release from the Tigers in 1946, Bridges pitched three seasons for Portland, compiling a 33–25 record. In 1950 he pitched in a total of eleven games for Seattle and San Francisco in the Pacific Coast League. On May 17, 1950, he married Iona Veda Kidwell; they had no children. In 1951 he worked as a coach for the Toledo Mud Hens. He retired to Lakeland, Fla., to work as a salesman for a Detroit tire firm and as a scout for the Tigers (1958–1960) and the New York Mets (1963–1968). Later, he instructed young pitchers at the Tiger spring training camp at Lakeland. He died in Nashville, Tenn.

[The statistics of Bridges' career are in Joseph L. Reichler, ed., *The Baseball Encyclopedia* (1985). See also Clifford Bloodgood, "Tom Bridges of the Tigers," *Baseball*, Apr. 1933; Frederick Lieb, *The Detroit Tigers* (1946); and Fred T. Smith, *The "995" Tigers* (1981). An obituary is in the *New York Times*, Apr. 20, 1968.]

WILLIAM MCCANN

BRINTON, CLARENCE CRANE (Feb. 2, 1898–Sept. 7, 1968), historian and teacher, was born in Winsted, Conn., the son of Clarence Hawthorne Brinton, a dry-goods clerk, and Eva Josephine Crane. Brinton disliked his first name and never used it. Educated in the public schools of Pittsfield and Springfield, Mass., he entered Harvard University in 1915. There he came under what he called the "fantastically contradictory influences" of the conservative Irving Babbitt and the radical Harold J. Laski, as well as two specialists in French history, Charles Homer Haskins and Robert M. Johnston. He graduated summa cum laude in 1919, receiving a prize for an essay on Lord Acton's philosophy of history and winning a Rhodes Scholarship. Brinton spent a year traveling in Europe before he began his studies at New College, Oxford University, where he received a Ph.D. His thesis, *The Political Ideas of the English Romanticists*, was published in 1926.

Brinton returned to Harvard in 1923 to begin a teaching career. Rising from instructor to full professor by 1942, he was named McLean Professor of Ancient and Modern History in 1946, a position he held until 1968. He was strongly influenced in his thinking by the physiologist Lawrence J. Henderson, who directed his attention to the work of the Italian sociologist Vilfredo Pareto. Brinton was also drawn to the "new history" of James Harvey Robinson, which substituted the analysis of social and cultural development for the narrative of politics and war.

During the 1930's Brinton published a succession of books that established him as an authority on modern European history. *The Jacobins: A Study in the New History* (1930), based on extensive research in French archives, applied statistical methods to the membership of the radical clubs of the French Revolution. Inspired by Laski, Brinton's *English Political Thought in the Nineteenth Century* (1933) presented critical portraits of major theorists of government. *A Decade of Revolution, 1789–1799* (1934), a general study written for the Rise of Modern Europe series, emphasized social and cultural change but did not neglect political, military, and religious affairs. In *French Revolutionary Legislation on Illegitimacy, 1789–1804* (1936) Brinton examined the laws passed to deal with bastardy, and in *The Lives of Talleyrand* (1936), he attempted to rescue the French ecclesiastic and diplomat from accusations of betrayal and immorality. Applying sociological theory to history on a grand scale, *The Anatomy of Revolution* (1938) compared upheavals in seventeenth-century Britain, eighteenth-century America and France, and twentieth-century Russia. Brinton used the analogy of an intense fever to demonstrate that all four revolutions passed through a similar sequence: from the breakdown of a weak and ineffective old regime through a moderate first stage and then a more radical second phase, or crisis, to the inevitable Thermidor, or return to normal but permanently altered conditions.

The rise of Adolf Hitler and the outbreak of World War II led Brinton to write *Nietzsche* (1941), a biography of the German philosopher whose ideas he believed contributed to Nazi ideology. Brinton despised Nazism and, after the Germans invaded Russia, predicted that Hitler would follow Napoleon into defeat. After America's declaration of war, he left academic life to work for the Research and Analysis branch of the Office of Strategic Services (OSS). He spent the years 1942–1944 in London carefully sifting through the information available on occupied France. Two months after D day he undertook a 1,600-mile journey through liberated France to investigate local conditions and sample public opinion.

Brinton left the OSS in 1945 to resume his teaching at Harvard, where he helped to develop its new general education program. On Dec. 18, 1946, he married Cecilia Washburn Roberts, widow of his longtime friend Penfield Roberts, and later adopted her three children. Brinton subsequently became a recognized expert on intellectual history, which he defined as the "relations between the ideas of the philosophers, the intellectuals, the thinkers, and the actual way of living of the millions who carry the tasks of civilization." His wide-ranging survey *Ideas and Men: The Story of Western Thought* (1950) traced the development of major cosmological and ethical questions from ancient Greece through the twentieth century. In *The Portable Age of Reason Reader* (1956) he focused on the Enlightenment and the growth of rationalism. He studied changes in social behavior in *A History of Western Morals* (1959) and concluded that if the ethics of the twentieth century were little better than those of ancient times, they were at least no worse. Examining the fundamental beliefs of Western civilization and seeking to offer guidance for the future, he collected important philosophical texts in *The Fate of Man* (1961). It called for a "multanimity" of ideas, or cultural pluralism, that allowed for diversity of opinion.

Brinton's experiences overseas stimulated his interest in contemporary affairs. He drew upon his wartime stay in London for *The United States and Britain* (1945), which described how conditions in England and relations with America had been transformed by the conflict. Two series of lectures on world conditions were published as books: *From Many One* (1948) discussed the possibilities of international political unity, and *The Temper of Western Europe* (1953) analyzed Europe's recovery from World War II and praised its renewed vitality. His last work, *The Americans and the French* (1968), a general survey of the Fifth Republic, reflected on the reasons for Charles de Gaulle's hostility toward the United States.

Brinton did much to develop "intellectual history," a term he was among the first to employ, as a recognized discipline. His numerous publications in the field gained him wide readership because of their lucid style and cosmopolitan outlook. Rational and tolerant, Brinton felt a strong affinity for the refined world of the Enlightenment. "I have kept to the basic belief of my youth in the rightness . . . of human reason," he declared. "You may write me down as born in the eighteenth century and yet not too uncomfortable . . . in the mid-twentieth." A Wilsonian liberal in his youth, he remained a moderate in his politics, favoring peaceful social change and condemning all forms of extremism, whether Jacobinism, Nazism, or Communism, as sources of conflict and terror. Brinton was a confirmed optimist about the fate of humanity and derided the "prophets of doom" who doubted its survival. He held that intellectuals had the obligation "if not to change the world, at least to diagnose it clearly and realistically." In a farewell lecture at Harvard he reaffirmed his faith in human reason and praised the diversity of modern democratic society.

Brinton retained a youthful physique and appearance that belied his white hair. He was a restless traveler who enjoyed motoring and hiking. While most comfortable in the company of intellectuals, he preferred the quiet of his summer home in Peacham, Vt., where he could garden and write.

Brinton served as president of the American Historical Association and the Society for French Historical Studies. Other honors included designation as a chevalier of the Legion of Honor and membership in the American Philosophical Society, National Institute of Arts and Letters, and Royal Historical Society. He died in Cambridge, Mass.

[Brinton's papers are in the Harvard University archives. He described his studies at Oxford in *The*

American Oxonian, Apr. 1926. With John B. Christopher and Robert L. Wolff, he wrote *A History of Civilization* (1955), a popular textbook. His friendship with Lawrence J. Henderson is recalled in *The Saturday Club: A Century Completed, 1920–1956* (1958). Brinton also published *The Society of Fellows* (1959). For Brinton's travels in France in 1944 see his "Letters from Liberated France," *French Historical Studies*, Spring and Fall 1961. Brinton summarized his attitude toward revolutionary movements in "The Nature of Revolution," *Hearings Before the Committee on Foreign Relations, United States Senate, Ninetieth Congress, Second Session. February 19, 21, 26, and March 8, 1968*. Appreciations of Brinton by his colleagues are John K. Fairbank, *The American Oxonian*, Apr. 1969; William L. Langer, *American Philosophical Society Year Book, 1968* (1969); and Arthur Schlesinger, Jr., *Proceedings of the American Academy of Arts and Letters and the National Institute of Arts and Letters*, 1969. The tribute by David D. Bien, *French Historical Studies*, Spring 1969, assesses Brinton as a teacher and historian. See also the *New York Times* interview with Brinton on Apr. 1, 1968, and obituary, Sept. 8, 1968.]

James Friguglietti

BROPHY, THOMAS D'ARCY (Oct. 18, 1893–July 29, 1967), advertising executive, was born in Butte, Mont., the son of Patrick Jerome Brophy and Margaret D'Arcy. His father, a merchant, was fuel administrator for Montana during World War I. Young Brophy graduated with a B.A. from Gonzaga College in Spokane, Wash., in 1912 and with a B.S. from the Massachusetts Institute of Technology in 1916. Trained as an architect, he retained close ties with MIT, serving on its board of visitors even after entering the advertising industry.

During World War I Brophy was an artillery instructor at Fort Monroe, Va., rising to the rank of major before his discharge in 1919. Brophy then joined the South Atlantic Maritime Corporation and in 1921 became a marketing manager for Anaconda Copper Company. On Oct. 9, 1923, he married Jessie Stewart Mulligan; they had three children. Brophy joined the advertising firm of Kenyon and Eckhardt in New York City in 1931. Within two years he was a vice-president.

On Aug. 23, 1933, Brophy was driving home from a sales meeting when his car was hit in the gas tank by a truck and burst into flames. Engulfed in fire, he walked slowly to the side of the road and rolled in a ditch until the flames were extinguished. He then flagged down a surprised motorist who took him to the hospital. He underwent extensive plastic surgery in Jersey City, Baltimore, and New York City. For nearly eighteen months, as doctors tried to reconstruct his eyelids, he was blind.

While recuperating, Brophy listened to radio broadcasts and studied the commercials. "Radio wasn't familiar in those days," he explained later, "and we were all feeling our way—like the early days of television." Early radio had been geared primarily to the hard sell, with announcers reading from station-prepared scripts. A particularly unfelicitous commercial proclaimed, "There's no spit in a Primo cigar." Brophy theorized that well-known personalities would deliver the most effective ads. He returned to Kenyon and Eckhardt in 1935, took up the Chase and Sanborn coffee account, and persuaded ventriloquist Edgar Bergen to deliver the on-the-air commercial for his sponsor's product. The novelty caught on and it became one of the most successful sales tools of radio and television.

Although he enjoyed great success as an advertising account executive and by 1937 had become president of Kenyon and Eckhardt, Brophy claimed that the 1933 accident had given him a particular set of values. He had developed a sense of public service and a belief that advertising could become a factor in the improvement of the public welfare. In 1940, Brophy helped establish the Advertising Council, a public-relations group for advertising agencies. The following year, with the United States mobilizing for war, Walter Hoving, president of Lord and Taylor's department store, approached Brophy about the newly formed United Service Organizations. The USO, designed to assist servicemen, needed $13 million, and Brophy assumed the position of advertising chairman. USO chairman Thomas E. Dewey enthusiastically endorsed Brophy's suggestion that the USO be marketed by the same sales techniques used to sell household products. Brophy then enlisted the services of the Advertising Council. Using the most modern methods of the time, the council surveyed the public attitude toward the USO and considered how people could be persuaded to support the organization. A staff of copywriters implemented the campaign, which exceeded its goal by $2 million during a period when Americans were struggling with war shortages. In July 1945 Brophy lost his only son in the sinking of the USS *Indianapolis* in the Philippine Sea.

In 1947 Brophy was elected chairman of the American Association of Advertising Agencies. The "4As" had been concerned that advertising would decline after the war, when consumer goods once again became abundant. Brophy allayed the fears of the advertisers, stressing that there was no sign that ad placements were falling off. His view, as he expressed it the following year, was that "advertising has the public's eye and ear. . . . As a consequence, advertising people must ask themselves when looking at an advertisement not only 'Will it sell?' but also 'Does it serve?'"

Also in 1947 Brophy formed the American Heritage Foundation. Its first significant accomplishment was the outfitting of a special train with American historical documents. Called the Freedom Train, it was then sent around the country to enable persons in many cities to view the artifacts. Brophy might be accused of a certain conflict of interest on this occasion, however, as the Chesapeake and Ohio Railroad was a leading Kenyon and Eckhardt account during this period and part of its track was used on the train's route.

In 1949 Brophy became chairman of Kenyon and Eckhardt and retreated somewhat from the public eye. In 1955 and 1956 he headed an outdoor advertising group just as the movement to ban signs along public highways took shape. He retired from Kenyon and Eckhardt in May 1957 to devote his time to a trip around the world and activities with MIT and the American Heritage Foundation. Two years later he received the first Distinguished Service Award of the Advertising Federation of America. On July 29, 1967, Brophy took his two young grandsons to the supermarket. He parked his car in the lot, leaving the children alone in the vehicle. It started to roll; Brophy tried to reach the driver's side of the car but he was pinned between the car and a parked truck. He died in Poughkeepsie, N.Y., not far from his retirement home in Pawling, N.Y.

[See *Advertising Age*, May 27, 1957; and the obituary notice, *New York Times*, July 30, 1967.]

JOHN DAVID HEALY

BROWN, JOHN MASON, JR. (July 3, 1900–Mar. 16, 1969), theater critic, writer, and lecturer, was born in Louisville, Ky., the son of John Mason Brown, a lawyer, and Carolyn Carroll (Carrie) Ferguson. His parents were divorced in 1902, and after a year in Switzerland, Brown and his older sister returned to the house on Louisville's Park Avenue, facing fashionable Central Park. There they were raised largely by a nursemaid under the guidance of their maternal grandmother. In 1913, a year after the death of their father, their mother, who has been described as "a perpetual southern belle," married James C. Stone, an agriculturalist.

Brown had a happy childhood, marked by careful schooling in manners, including dancing classes. He became stagestruck at eight after seeing Robert B. Mantell play King Lear at Macauley's Theatre in Louisville. This led to a puppet theater and live performances in the attic, and regular attendance at every play that came to Louisville.

In 1917, after two years at Louisville Male High School, Brown enrolled at the Morristown School in Morristown, N.J. In 1919 he entered Harvard to study drama in Professor George Pierce Baker's already famous 47 Workshop. He joined the Dramatic Club in his freshman year, acted in several of its productions, and became its president in his senior year. He appeared in several workshop productions. In the summer of 1920 he joined the staff of the *Louisville Courier-Journal* and began reviewing plays and books about the theater for the *Courier-Journal*, the *Harvard Advocate*, and the *Lampoon*. He also tried his hand, not too successfully, at writing plays for the workshop. Baker apparently dissuaded him from pursuing a career on the stage, either as actor or as playwright, but did encourage him to prepare for a career in criticism.

After graduating cum laude from Harvard in 1923, Brown secured, with Baker's help, an assignment to teach courses in Shakespeare and dramatic presentation at the University of Montana in Missoula that summer. He then took off on a year-long tour of European theaters with his Harvard classmate and closest friend, Donald M. Oenslager, who became a successful scene designer. Brown revisited the European theaters a number of times thereafter to keep abreast of the modern spirit on the stage.

In New York City the following fall, Brown joined the staff of the magazine *Theatre Arts*, newly become a monthly, as an assistant and within a year was its drama critic and associate editor. He resigned in 1928, and in 1929 he became drama critic for the *New York Evening Post*, a position he held until 1941. He then worked for one year as drama critic for the *New York World-Telegram*.

In 1925, Brown joined the staff of the American Laboratory Theater, an acting school, at which he taught courses on the history of the drama. His career as a lecturer began at the Cosmopolitan Club in New York; the talk was such a success that he scheduled a lecture in Louisville as a way of paying for a visit home in 1925. That marked the first of his many appearances before women's clubs. In 1928 he signed up with the James B. Pond lecture bureau, one of the world's largest. Brown's popularity grew, especially with women's clubs, prompting the *New Yorker* magazine to feature a Helen Hokinson cartoon that depicted a woman standing on a platform and announcing, "Next week, our intellectual cocktail—John Mason Brown." Brown stayed with the American Laboratory Theater until its demise in 1931. On Feb. 11, 1933, he married Catherine (Cassie) Meredith, an acting student who met Brown while attending his lectures; they had two children.

A 1928 European trip, this time including Russia, prompted Brown's first book, *The Modern Theatre in Revolt* (1929), which in turn secured his job with the *New York Evening Post*. Though ballasted with a long historical survey, chiefly of the French theater, it is still interesting for his estimate of theater in Russia: "Crude, infantile, noisy, obstreperous, cheap, confused, and formless . . . [but] magnificently successful in what it set out to be—a propagandistic theatre." That experience probably prepared him for his subsequent sympathetic responses to the American plays of revolt and "social significance" of the 1930's, whose "overstated opinions" he disagreed with, even abhorred, but which had widened both his and the theater's horizons.

From 1942 to 1944, Brown served as a lieutenant in the United States Naval Reserve. During the invasions of Sicily and Normandy he was on the staff of Vice-Admiral Alan G. Kirk. Brown made broadcasts to his fellow crewmen on the flagship *Ancon;* thirty of these broadcasts were gathered into a book, *To All Hands* (1943), which includes impromptu remarks the night of the invasion of Sicily. *Many a Watchful Night* (1944) is an attempt to capture the emotions of war as Brown had experienced them from his vantage point on Kirk's staff during the preparations for the Normandy invasion and the invasion itself, this time while on the flagship *Augusta*.

Most of Brown's writing concerns the theater; many of his books, in fact, are collections of his reviews of Broadway seasons, such as *Upstage* (1930), *Two on the Aisle* (1938), and *Broadway in Review* (1940). From 1944 to 1964 he wrote a column for the *Saturday Review*, "Seeing Things," which increasingly surveyed larger vistas in the creative arts or issues of the moment, like the Nuremberg trials. These essays were also collected into books: *Seeing Things* (1946), *Seeing More Things* (1948), *Still Seeing Things* (1950), and *As They Appear* (1952). He served as editor-at-large of the *Saturday Review* from 1955 to 1969.

Brown's other books include the slim *Letters from Greenroom Ghosts* (1934), five imaginary letters from theatrical personages of the past to their present-day counterparts (such as Christopher Marlowe to Eugene O'Neill); *The Art of Playgoing* (1936), designed to instruct an audience; and two lightweight efforts, *Insides Out* (1942), an account of his hernia operation (to ready him for naval service), and *Accustomed as I Am* (1942), a humorous assault on some of the absurdities of the lecture platform. *Through These Men* (1956), revisions of pieces that had first appeared in the *Saturday Review*, focuses on the political scene in the early 1950's and includes portraits of Dwight D. Eisenhower, Adlai Stevenson (half the book), Henry Cabot Lodge, Felix Frankfurter, Walter Lippmann, and J. Robert Oppenheimer. This book prepared Brown for his most ambitious undertaking, a full-scale biography of the playwright Robert E. Sherwood, *The Worlds of Robert E. Sherwood: Mirror to His Times, 1896–1939* (1965) and the posthumous *The Ordeal of a Playwright: Robert E. Sherwood and the Challenge of War* (1970), which was prepared from Brown's unfinished manuscript by his friend Norman Cousins and includes the full text of Sherwood's play *There Shall Be No Night*. *Dramatis Personae*, an omnibus collection of Brown's writing on the theater (including the whole of *The Modern Theatre in Russia*), appeared in 1963.

Brown had become a popular figure, extending his public personality from the lecture platform to the airwaves. He conducted the radio discussion program "Of Men and Books" from 1944 to 1947. He was an interviewer and narrator on the Columbia Broadcasting System television program "Tonight on Broadway" from 1948 to 1949 and also appeared on the American Broadcasting Company television program "Critic-at-Large" the same year. He also worked as an editor for the Book-of-the-Month Club from 1956 until his death, and he served on the advisory committee for the Pulitzer Prize until he resigned in 1963 to protest the denial of the award to Edward Albee's *Who's Afraid of Virginia Woolf?* In these and many other roles, Brown became a respected molder of public taste in the creative arts and of decency and decorum in public life.

Brown was tall, handsome, auburn-haired, and impeccable in dress and manner. A "Kentucky thoroughbred," he impressed people with his spontaneity, wit, effervescence, and charm. These traits, reflected in his style of writing, may have been the source of the mixed reviews of him as a critic. Touted by Brooks Atkinson as the only drama critic to have deliberately prepared himself for that career, Brown nevertheless seemed too appreciative and undiscriminating in his judgments. His reputation remains secure, however, as a genial apologist and exemplar of good taste. He died in New York City.

[Brown's correspondence is at the Houghton Library, Harvard. The correspondence between Brown and Baker is at Yale's Sterling Library. Other materials are in the Harvard Theater Collection and the theater collections at Princeton and the New York Public Library at Lincoln Center.

George Stevens, John Mason Brown's Harvard classmate and longtime friend, published a personalized and anecdotal biography, *Speak for Yourself, John* (1974); it contains a list of all his published books. See also Herbert Warren Wind, "Circuit Rider," *New Yorker*, Oct. 18 and 25, 1952; Serrell Hillman, *One-Man Chautauqua* (1960); Brooks Atkinson's imaginary interview in the *New York Times*, June 25, 1963; and *New York Times Book Review*, July 14, 1963, and Sept. 19, 1965. Obituaries are in the *New York Times*, Mar. 17, 1969; and the *Saturday Review*, Mar. 29, 1969.]

JAMES R. VITELLI

BRUCE, LENNY (Oct. 13, 1925–Aug. 3, 1966), comedian, was born Leonard Alfred Schneider in Mineola, N.Y., on Long Island, the son of Myron Schneider, a podiatrist, and Sadie Kitchenburg, a nightclub and vaudeville entertainer. He was raised in Mineola and nearby Bellmore. His parents were divorced when he was five, and he was shuttled back and forth from one parent to the other. Bruce's stormy childhood remained part of nearly everything he undertook throughout his life. He quit high school in 1942 to enlist in the navy, where he remained until after World War II, serving most of his time on the USS *Brooklyn* during the Italian campaign.

In the late 1940's, Bruce began to frequent the lunch counter at Hanson's drugstore in New York City, famous in show-business circles as a gathering place for aspiring comedians and older, struggling ones. Here Bruce began to solidify his comedy act, learning much about delivery and timing from various people in the business. Perhaps even more important was his friendship with Joe Ancis, reputedly a richly comic talent who developed stage fright whenever he tried to perform in public. From Ancis, Bruce learned the techniques of improvisational comedy. Bruce's reputation grew to the point that he was able to win the top prize on the radio program "Arthur Godfrey's Talent Scouts" in 1948, after which he began working small nightclubs in the New York area. Realizing that he had not yet developed enough material to work consistently in major cabarets, Bruce worked what was called the "borscht circuit" of Catskill Mountains resorts. On June 15, 1951, Bruce married the striptease performer Honey Harlowe; they had one child.

Bruce and his wife moved to the West Coast in 1953. The next five years were pivotal for Bruce. He spent most of this time as the master of ceremonies and comedian for the various burlesque theaters where his wife performed. He was constantly sharpening his act, and since he worked largely before audiences that were not present primarily to watch comedy acts, he was permitted the freedom to develop his material in a way that would have been exceedingly difficult in more traditional circumstances.

During this period, Bruce also acquired his lifelong dependency on narcotics, including heroin. Bruce suffered from a nervous disorder, and most of the drug charges later brought against him were dropped when the authorities discovered that he had legal prescriptions for the drugs. In 1956, Bruce's wife was arrested and convicted in Hawaii for possession of heroin and was sentenced to two years in prison on Oahu. Bruce and his wife were divorced in

1957, and he was awarded custody of their child.

The years 1958–1961 mark the high point of Bruce's popularity and creativity. San Francisco, the heart of the beat literary movement, had gained the reputation as the artistic center of the avant-garde by this time. There, literate—and sometimes even literary—comedy entered something of a golden age, with the rise of satirists such as Mort Sahl, Richard ("Lord") Buckley, Mike Nichols and Elaine May, Jean Shepherd, Jonathan Winters, and Bob Newhart. In the vanguard was Lenny Bruce, who gained notoriety from his appearances at the hungry i and other bistros in San Francisco.

Bruce's routines usually took the form of dramatic skits in which he spoke all the parts, catching the essence of each character in broad relief. Much of the humor derived from the incongruity of the language and situation chosen for the characters developed in a sketch. For instance, in one routine two German theatrical booking agents have been given forty-eight hours to find a dictator. After listening to, and rejecting, the candidates sent by central casting, one agent turns to the other and says, "Don't look right away, but dig the guy on the right that's painting the wall. Don't look right away; he'll think you're putting him on." After changing the name of the young painter from Schicklgruber to Adolf Hitler ("five and six for the marquee"), the agents make arrangements for him to go on the road, and everyone departs happily.

This sketch was one of Bruce's milder ones; most of his skits wove jazz idioms, Yiddish slang, and profane language into a surrealistic comic vision, much of which was improvised. Also, he often rode roughshod over the feelings of anyone he thought hypocritical. As one critic put it, "He offends so many people that at some time, someone will probably cause him trouble." In retrospect, this seems an understatement.

Beginning in late 1961, Bruce was repeatedly arrested for giving obscene performances. By later standards his arrests seem hard to understand, since far more offensive material was presented in less reputable establishments throughout the country. Also, his arrests had an unquestionable aura of persecution, whether intentional or not. He would be cleared of charges in San Francisco only to be arrested in Chicago or New York. At one point, he was in trouble with some courts merely because he was required to be in two courts at once, two thousand miles apart. He was found innocent of all obscenity charges.

As noted, Bruce was arrested several times for possessing narcotics, charges on which he was convicted and given probation in 1965. During the course of his many trials, Bruce became obsessed with the law, the legal system, and the necessity of justifying himself judicially.

During the last year of his life, the always high-strung Bruce displayed definite signs of being mentally unbalanced, no doubt because of the cumulative effects of continued drug abuse, coupled with his having been effectively deprived of his livelihood. Unable to secure work, he had declared bankruptcy, and on the day of his death a notice of foreclosure on his house arrived in the mail. Bruce's body was discovered by friends in his home. An autopsy revealed traces of narcotics in his system, and the official record states that he died of an apparently accidental overdose of narcotics, though some believe he committed suicide in a fit of despondency.

Throughout his career Bruce was labeled a "sick" comedian. In reality, his humor was by no means deranged, as the term implies, but rather, it focused on hypocrisy wherever Bruce saw it. His extreme profanity was actually a form of catharsis for his audience, allowing them to bypass the superficial aspects of language to arrive at comic truths lying beneath surface appearances.

Bruce's legacy includes a number of recordings of his performances, a film of a late cabaret appearance, the largely fanciful and humorous autobiography *How to Talk Dirty and Influence People* (1965), and a collection of Bruce's finest routines, edited by John Cohen as *The Essential Lenny Bruce* (1967), though much is missing without Bruce's masterful timing. In 1974 the biographical film *Lenny* appeared, directed by Bob Fosse, starring Dustin Hoffman in the title role.

[The most complete biography of Lenny Bruce is Albert Goldman, *Ladies and Gentlemen: Lenny Bruce* (1974). Bruce's performance recordings are available on the Fantasy and United Artists labels.]

ARTHUR P. LIVINGSTON

BRUCKER, WILBER MARION (June 23, 1894–Oct. 28, 1968), secretary of the army, was born in Saginaw, Mich., the son of Ferdinand Brucker, a lawyer and Democratic congressman, and Roberta Hawn. Just nine years old when his father died, Brucker helped support the family by selling newspapers, waiting tables, and working nearby sugar-beet fields. After losing a high school debate to a girl, he vowed to improve his speaking skills and ultimately won a place on the varsity debating squad at the University of Michigan. He graduated from high school in Saginaw in 1912 and the University of Michigan Law School in 1916. That year he enlisted in the Thirty-third Infantry of the Michigan National Guard and served under General John J. Pershing in his Mexican expedition against Pancho Villa. As a lieutenant in the army's Forty-second ("Rainbow") Division during World War I, he saw action at Château-Thierry and took part in the Saint-Mihiel and Meuse-Argonne offensives. He was awarded the Silver Star.

Admitted to the Michigan bar in 1919, Brucker set up law practice in Saginaw and, spurning the party of his father, became active in Republican affairs. Over the next decade he served as assistant prosecuting attorney for Saginaw County (1919–1922), county prosecutor (1923–1926), and assistant state attorney general (1927–1928). As attorney general of Michigan during 1928–1930, he obtained federal licensing for the first radio communications equipment for the state police. He married Clara Helen Hantel on Aug. 18, 1923; they had one child.

In 1930, Brucker was elected governor of Michigan over Democrat William A. Comstock. Brucker insulated the state police from political pressures, increased its manpower, and promoted construction of its new headquarters at Lansing. During the Great Depression, Brucker provided some public-works jobs for those already on the welfare rolls but was unwilling to undertake major relief projects for the growing numbers of unemployed. In the face of shrinking state revenues, he imposed an austerity budget that included a 10 percent pay cut for himself. In a rematch with Comstock in 1932, Brucker was defeated. He settled in Detroit, where for the next two decades he practiced law and remained active in Republican party affairs. He was a delegate to the party's national conventions in 1932, 1936, and 1948. In 1936 he successfully challenged Senator James Couzens for the Republican nomination to the United States Senate but lost in the general election to Democrat Prentiss M. Brown.

In 1954, President Dwight D. Eisenhower appointed Brucker general counsel for the United States Defense Department. Although he cooperated with the Senate investigation of alleged subversion in the military, he gained national attention when, during testimony before the committee, he laughed aloud at Senator Joseph McCarthy for his accusation that President Eisenhower and others were conspiring to cover up military disloyalty. Brucker helped tighten security procedures in the Defense Department and urged defense contractors to screen employees more carefully. But he also deplored the tendency to suspend defense workers on the slightest suspicion of security risk and took steps to expedite the review process in such cases.

In 1955, Brucker was appointed to succeed Robert T. Stevens as secretary of the army. Brucker approved the strategy of maintaining the capability for massive nuclear retaliation as a deterrent to a first strike but warned that conventional forces must also be strong enough to combat tactical probes by Communist forces around the world. He argued persuasively that Quemoy and Matsu should be maintained as a buffer between Taiwan and the Communist government on the mainland of China and that United States forces should remain in West Berlin to protect that democratic enclave from Communist aggression. Following the Soviet Union's successful launch of *Sputnik*, the first artificial space satellite, Brucker carried forward research that placed the first United States satellites in orbit in 1958. He also offered improved military housing and other incentives to make a career in the army more attractive.

With the outbreak of violence in Little Rock, Ark., over court-ordered school desegregation in 1957, Brucker supervised federal troops dispatched by President Eisenhower to maintain order in that city throughout the tense school year. Brucker succeeded in working effectively with the unit's outspoken commander, Major General Edwin Walker, an ultraconservative who had little taste for his assignment. When Walker resigned his commission abruptly in 1959, saying in his letter of resignation that he could no longer serve amid the "fifth-column conspiracy and influence in the United States," Brucker personally convinced him to reconsider, assuring him that he shared his opposition to Communism and that the army desperately needed men of his caliber. Years later, Walker charged that Brucker's appeal was a deliberate effort to keep him from speaking out against Communism.

Brucker was among those under consideration for secretary of defense by presidential candidate Richard Nixon in 1960, but after Nixon's defeat Brucker returned to Detroit to practice law in partnership with his son, Wilber M. Brucker, Jr. He died in Detroit and was buried at Arlington National Cemetery.

Brucker earned a reputation for intelligence and caution and took pains to avoid publicity. An avid outdoorsman, he enjoyed the camaraderie of hunting trips with friends but could not bring himself to shoot anything.

[Brucker's papers are in the Michigan Historical Collections at the University of Michigan. See also the "Man in the News," *New York Times*, June 10, 1958; and the Facts on File compilation *Political Profiles: The Eisenhower Years* (1977). An obituary is in the *New York Times*, Oct. 29, 1968.]

WILLIAM A. DEGREGORIO

BUCHANAN, SCOTT MILROSS (Mar. 17, 1895–Mar. 25, 1968), philosopher, author, and educator, was born in Sprague, Wash., the only child of William Duncan Buchanan, a country doctor, and Lillian Elizabeth Bagg. Raised in Jeffersonville, Vt., he was much involved in the town's Congregational church, which his father helped to found. Buchanan attended high schools in Worcester and Pittsfield, Mass. After his graduation in 1912, he entered Amherst College, where he majored in mathematics and Greek and excelled at long-distance running. Buchanan took his B.A. at Amherst in 1916 and stayed on at the college for two additional years, serving as secretary of the Christian Association from 1916 to 1917 and as an instructor in Greek from 1917 to 1918.

During his college years, Buchanan distanced himself from the church but remained "pretty deeply Christian" throughout his life. Although his religious persuasion made him a pacifist and a conscientious objector, he nevertheless entered the United States Navy in June 1918; he was discharged as an ensign six months later. Having won a Rhodes Scholarship in 1917, Buchanan went to England from 1919 to 1921 to study philosophy at Balliol College, Oxford University. Owing to his mother's illness, Buchanan returned to the United States sooner than expected and was unable to complete an Oxford degree. On Feb. 5, 1921, Buchanan married Miriam Damon Thomas, a teacher and social-welfare worker; they had one child.

For a year and a half, Buchanan taught high school at Amherst, but, determined to obtain a doctorate in philosophy, he entered Harvard University as a graduate student in 1922. While working on his Ph.D., which he received in 1925, Buchanan taught as an assistant in Harvard's philosophy department from 1922 to 1924 and then for a year as an instructor in philosophy at the College of the City of New York.

Buchanan's doctoral dissertation, a study of the philosophical question of possibility, became his first book. *Possibility* (1927) explores "three kinds of possibility—imaginative, scientific, and absolute." This well-received study was described by John Dewey as "a first-class piece of much-needed intellectual work." Meanwhile, Buchanan had become assistant director of the People's Institute in New York City, and in this position, which he occupied from 1925 until 1929, Buchanan worked with the director, Everett Dean Martin, to implement educational programs for adults. These programs—many of them held in branches of the New York Public Library—included an emphasis on the "Great Books" as they were studied in the newly established general honors course at Columbia University. During this period, Buchanan intensified his lifelong commitment to approaches that break down conventional boundaries between the intellectual disciplines. One result was *Poetry and Mathematics* (1929), in which he suggested that "mathematics . . . is often poetry," while poetry can become mathematical by "joining words and images into a world of hard persuasive fact."

In 1929, Buchanan became associate professor of philosophy at the University of Virginia and, the following year, professor. He then studied in England for a year and, stimulated by the work of George and Mary Boole, explored the advances made by a group of Cambridge mathematicians who called themselves the Analytic Society. One result of his stay was *Symbolic Distance in Relation to Analogy and Fiction*

(1932), which analyzes how the intellectual arts are essentially concerned with symbols.

Buchanan remained at the University of Virginia until 1936. Then Robert Maynard Hutchins, the president of the University of Chicago, invited him and Stringfellow Barr, Buchanan's longtime friend, fellow Rhodes Scholar, and colleague at the University of Virginia, to join the Chicago faculty. As chairman of the Committee on the Liberal Arts, Buchanan played a major part in organizing the university's Great Books program.

When Barr became president of St. John's College in Annapolis, Md., in 1937, Buchanan joined him as dean. Buchanan's leadership was instrumental in transforming the nearly moribund college into a vigorous intellectual center whose curriculum was based on a Great Books program in which students and faculty together studied about 120 classics in virtually all of the academic disciplines. Concurrently, Buchanan's writings continued to reflect his interdisciplinary concerns. After considerable study at the Johns Hopkins Medical School, he published *The Doctrine of Signatures: A Defense of Theory in Medicine* (1938). This study in the philosophy of medicine appraised the relations between medicine and modern scientific theory and also the place of philosophy in the thought of Hippocrates and Galen.

Buchanan left the St. John's deanship in 1947 and served until 1949 as director of Liberal Arts, Inc., in Pittsfield, Mass. His consistent passion for the philosophy of Plato and for the Socratic method of inquiry in particular was made evident to a wide audience when he wrote the introduction to, and edited, *The Portable Plato* (1948), a very successful volume in the Viking Portable series.

From 1948 to 1958, Buchanan's political orientation led him to be a consultant, trustee, and secretary of the Foundation for World Government. During this period, he published *Essay in Politics* (1953), which stressed the need to evaluate how large institutions, such as corporations, negatively affect the perception that the republican form of government depends on the consent of the governed.

After spending the 1956–1957 academic year as professor of philosophy and chairman of the Department of Religion and Philosophy at Fisk University in Nashville, Tenn., Buchanan was reunited with Robert Maynard Hutchins, then president of the Fund for the Republic. Hutchins invited him to help direct the fund's project to clarify how a free society could best be preserved in the United States. In that capacity, which took him to Santa Barbara, Calif., Buchanan became one of the founders of the Center for the Study of Democratic Institutions, where he was a senior fellow until his death.

Buchanan left unpublished a manuscript entitled *Truth in the Sciences*, which he had written in 1950. As he introduced the book (it appeared posthumously in 1972), Buchanan aptly summed up his philosophical investigations by professing that "I am not aware of deliberate membership in any school of philosophy, but . . . I am by will, and now by confirmed habit, a teacher of the Socratic persuasion." By insisting that sound learning and teaching depend on critical inquiry that takes time to reflect on the classics of art, literature, philosophy, science, and mathematics in the Western tradition, he left a lasting mark on American thought and education.

[The best source for supplementary detail about Buchanan is *Embers of the World* (1970), edited by Harris Wofford, Jr. Buchanan's 1962 introduction to *Poetry and Mathematics* is particularly helpful for understanding his life and thought from 1925 to 1937. For a representative sample of Buchanan's writings from 1952 to 1967, see *So Reason Can Rule: Reflections on Law and Politics* (1982). An obituary is in the *New York Times*, Mar. 29, 1968.]

JOHN K. ROTH

BULEY, ROSCOE CARLYLE (July 8, 1893–Apr. 25, 1968), historian, was born in Georgetown, Ind., the son of David Marion Buley and Nora Keithley. He received a B.A. (1914) and an M.A. (1916) from Indiana University, and then served for a year during World War I in the United States Army Signal Corps. On June 21, 1919, he married Esther Giles, who died in 1921; on Aug. 3, 1926, he married Evelyn Barnett. He had no children.

After teaching for eight years in the public schools of Indiana and Illinois, Buley did graduate work at the University of Wisconsin, from which he was awarded a Ph.D. in 1925. At Wisconsin he came under the influence of Frederic Logan Paxson, who won the Pulitzer Prize in 1924 for *History of the American Frontier*. Paxson opened to Buley the possibilities for research and writing on the history of the Old Northwest and emphasized the usefulness of local newspapers.

Buley taught history at Indiana University from 1925, after 1944 as full professor, until his retirement in 1964. His lectures were dotted with humorous, down-to-earth anecdotes, and he became one of the most popular members of the Indiana faculty. A leading authority on the states of the Old Northwest, especially Indiana, he wrote his first major book, *The Midwest Pioneer: His Ills, Cures and Doctors* (1945), with Madge E. Pickard. Buley's writing was characterized by sensible, artistic organization and interesting narrative. In the book, as in his articles in the *Mississippi Valley Historical Review*, he included long extracts from the primitive literature of the times.

After two decades of extensive research, Buley found that his manuscript on the Old Northwest frontier from 1815 to 1840 would require at least two volumes for its 1,314 pages. The cost of publishing a book of this length by a scholar not yet widely known would be excessive for commercial publishers and questionable for university presses. Compression was unthinkable; the work's strong point was its very abundance and depth of detail. Even the footnotes, in which Buley expressed his views on conflicting evidence, were informative and useful. The J. K. Lilly Foundation and the Indiana Historical Society concluded that the work should be published regardless of its cost. Their enthusiasm resulted in a lavish edition with many maps and illustrations of early prints, pen and watercolor drawings, and contemporary sketches. Published in 1951, the book was distributed free to all members of the Indiana Historical Society.

The Old Northwest: Pioneer Period, 1815–1840 was praised by scholars for its emphasis on the details of social and family life of the pioneer settlers, their customs, beliefs, habits, food, health and illnesses, and medical practices. Others held that it lacked interpretation, theoretical discussions, and evaluation but was nevertheless a valuable contribution to historical scholarship. Like many university publications, it was not reviewed in the *New York Times*, which, in its May 6, 1951, feature story announcing the Pulitzer Prize winners for 1951, had sparse information about the author and no photograph of him.

Insurance groups wishing the aid of historians to work through their archives and to produce histories useful to business schools came to Buley, who had shown a marked ability to assimilate massive collections and to produce readable accounts of them. He published *The American Life Convention, 1906–1952: A Study in the History of Life Insurance* (1953) and *The Equitable Life Assurance Society of the United States, 1859–1964*, in 1967. Because the latter project was delayed, Buley wrote a preliminary volume, published in 1959 as *The Equitable Life Assurance Society of the United States: One Hundredth Anniversary History, 1859–1959*. Based on extant original documents and on the company's journals, these books naturally reflect a company and conservative point of view toward business legislation. Critics found them unduly discursive, descriptive, and weak on analysis. Yet, with their excellent indexes, as with *The Old Northwest*, readers could find details they needed. Buley died in Indianapolis, Ind.

[See Fulmer Mood, "The Theory of the History of an American Section and the Practice of R. Carlyle Buley," *Indiana Magazine of History*, Mar. 1952; "Tribute to R. Carlyle Buley," *ibid.*, Dec. 1964; Thomas D. Clark, *Indiana University, Midwestern Pioneer* (1970); and Lana Ruegamer, *History of the Indiana Historical Society* (1980).]

PAUL W. GATES

BULLITT, WILLIAM CHRISTIAN (Jan. 25, 1891–Feb. 15, 1967), diplomat, was born in Philadelphia, Pa., the son of William Christian Bullitt, a lawyer who had become wealthy from investments in Virginia and West Virginia coal, and Louisa Gross Horwitz, the granddaughter of the medical pioneer Dr. Samuel Gross. Bullitt attended DeLancey preparatory school prior to enrolling at Yale, where he was a member of the class of 1912. (Owing to illness, he did not actually graduate until 1913.) A year at Harvard Law School was cut short by his father's death; Bullitt returned to Philadelphia and joined the staff of the *Philadelphia Public Ledger*, soon rising to the position of associate editor.

Bullitt went to Europe as a correspondent on Henry Ford's peace ship in 1915. The following year he traveled extensively, especially in Germany and Austria. On March 18, 1916, he married Ernesta Drinker; they had no children. Bullitt's knowledge of the Central Powers led to his appointment as chief of the Bureau of

Central European Information in the State Department in 1917, where he interpreted events, including the Russian Revolution, and prepared reports for President Woodrow Wilson and his top aide, Colonel Edward M. House.

In December 1918 Bullitt went to Paris with Wilson's peace delegation as chief of the division of current intelligence. Early the next year he headed a secret mission to Moscow, apparently to explore with Lenin and other Soviet leaders the conditions under which they would agree to a peaceful settlement of the civil war in the Soviet Union, in which Allied troops were aiding the opponents of the Bolsheviks. Lenin agreed to terms that included an in-place armistice, the evacuation of Allied troops, and Soviet recognition of the imperial Russian debt. These terms, however, were not well received in Paris. Both Wilson and British prime minister David Lloyd George were encountering a good deal of domestic political opposition over other issues at the conference. Wilson was also distracted by a quarrel with Georges Clemenceau, the premier of France, over the disposition of the Saar region, and Colonel House was unwilling to antagonize the president further by pushing Bullitt's proposals. Meanwhile, proponents of accommodation favored the more cautious plan sponsored by the explorer Fridtjof Nansen to give food to the Soviet Union in exchange for a less comprehensive peace agreement.

Distressed over the failure of his mission and the content of the Treaty of Versailles, Bullitt resigned from the delegation and returned home. In the fall of 1919, his testimony before the Senate Foreign Relations Committee was an important factor in the failure of the treaty to win ratification.

During the Republican ascendancy of the 1920's and early 1930's, Bullitt traveled much and entered the film industry as a story editor for Famous Players–Lasky Corporation. He and his wife divorced in 1923, and he married the journalist Louise Bryant, the widow of John Reed, the same year. In 1926 he published the novel *It's Not Done*, which satirized high society in Philadelphia. The book was notable for its frank treatment of sexual themes. In 1924 Bullitt had met Sigmund Freud, who psychoanalyzed him in 1926. Thus began a close association that resulted in a collaboration on a psychobiography of Wilson. (Not published until 1967, *Thomas Woodrow Wilson, Twenty-eighth President of the United States:* A *Psychological Study* received devastating reviews from historians and Freud scholars alike.) In 1930 Bullitt and his second wife were divorced, and he gained custody of their only child.

Bullitt was an early supporter of Franklin Delano Roosevelt, whom he had met during World War I. Following Roosevelt's election as president in 1932, Bullitt was appointed a special assistant to Secretary of State Cordell Hull and served as the executive officer of the American delegation at the London Monetary and Economic Conference of 1933. In the fall of that year Bullitt was deeply involved in the negotiation of the Roosevelt-Litvinov Agreements, which established diplomatic ties between the United States and the Soviet Union. His appointment as the first ambassador to Moscow was announced immediately after the signing of the agreements.

Bullitt received an enthusiastic welcome upon his arrival in the Soviet Union in December 1933. However, his ardor for the Soviet experiment cooled as he found himself isolated in Moscow and became ever more convinced that Stalin was not abiding by the terms of the Roosevelt-Litvinov Agreements. Bullitt began taking a harder line toward the Soviets. While this stance was agreeable to his embassy staff, Roosevelt began to avoid Bullitt's advice on Soviet policy. The embassy, one of the first to deal seriously with security matters in a hostile locale, was, by all accounts, well run, but Bullitt's disillusionment with his service in Moscow gradually developed into a strident anti-Communism that he cultivated the rest of his life.

By 1936 Bullitt was happy to move to the post of ambassador to France. Roosevelt's disdain for Bullitt's advice from Moscow during his last months there had not affected the close personal relationship between the two men, and in Paris Bullitt became Roosevelt's most valuable adviser on European affairs, accurately predicting German moves into Austria, the Sudetenland, and Czechoslovakia. Fluent in French, he developed excellent relations with national leaders, especially Édouard Daladier and Paul Reynaud. Roosevelt's secretary of the interior, Harold Ickes, quipped, "Bullitt practically sleeps with the French cabinet." Bullitt's fondness for the French led to some controversial allegations that he had promised American intervention on the side of France if war broke out in Europe, but published diplomatic correspondence suggests that the allegations were untrue.

After the fall of Paris in the summer of 1940, Bullitt returned to the United States and joined the preparedness debate, advocating all-out aid short of war to Britain and France. A major speech in August was published as *Report to the American People* (1940). From November 1940 until November 1941 Bullitt sought a responsible appointment from the president, but despite promises and hints, nothing came until he was sent to North Africa and the Middle East as an ambassador-at-large on a fact-finding mission. While he made detailed and cogent reports that helped the development of the North African campaign in 1942, Bullitt found his welcome at the White House wearing thin because of a controversy surrounding Undersecretary of State Sumner Welles. As early as April 1941, Bullitt had urged the president to dismiss Welles, whom he thought weak and subject to blackmail because of alleged homosexual activities. Roosevelt did not fully share these feelings, and after 1942 Bullitt never received another appointment.

In May 1944 Bullitt joined the Free French forces as an infantry commandant attached to the staff of General Jean de Lattre de Tassigny and served in France until the end of the war. He returned to the United States in July 1945 and spent the rest of his life in private business, occasionally writing articles or giving speeches that contained a strong dose of anti-Communism. He advocated a blockade of mainland China during the Korean War, and later supported Chiang Kai-shek's desire to return to the mainland. Bullitt switched his party affiliation to Republican, supported the presidential aspirations of Senator Robert A. Taft in 1952 and Vice-President Richard Nixon in 1960, and wrote an unpublished autobiography.

Bullitt was a bright, charming, and sophisticated individual who had an unusual talent for bringing people into his confidence. At the same time, however, he was impulsive, idealistic, and aggressively ambitious, and these qualities led to a premature retirement from public life that was not without bitterness. He died in Neuilly, France.

[The main body of Bullitt's papers, including his unpublished autobiography, are in private hands. See William C. Bullitt, *The Great Globe Itself* (1946); and Orville H. Bullitt, ed., *"For the President: Personal and Secret": Correspondence Between Franklin D. Roosevelt and William C. Bullitt* (1972). See also Janet Flanner, "Mr. Ambassador," in M. Balch, ed., *Modern Short Biographies* (1940), pp. 338–358; Beatrice Farnsworth, *William C. Bullitt and the Soviet Union* (1967); Lloyd C. Gardner, *Architects of Illusion* (1970); Virginia Gardner, *Friend and Lover* (1982); and Robert Dallek, *Franklin D. Roosevelt and American Foreign Policy, 1932–1945* (1979). An obituary is in the *New York Times*, Feb. 16, 1967.]

JOHN E. FINDLING

BURCHFIELD, CHARLES EPHRAIM (Apr. 9, 1893–Jan. 10, 1967), painter, was born in Ashtabula, Ohio, the son of William Charles Burchfield, a merchant tailor, and Alice Murphy. Burchfield's father died in 1898, leaving the family destitute. His mother returned with her six children (Charles was the fifth) to her birthplace in Salem, Ohio, where relatives bought them a house. Beginning in the seventh grade and throughout high school Burchfield worked part-time at a drugstore and also at the W. H. Mullins Company, a metal fabricating plant. He graduated from Salem Public High School as class valedictorian in 1911, winning a $120 scholarship. With this and his own earnings he enrolled at the Cleveland School of Art in 1912.

Burchfield planned to become an illustrator, but he decided midway through his art program "to be an artist and just paint pictures." He graduated in June 1916 and in October enrolled at the National Academy of Design in New York City, where he had received a scholarship. He did not stay long, however, for he decided after attending one life drawing class that he was finished with schools. He returned to Mullins as an accountant, painting during his off hours. The next eighteen-month period was one of his most productive as an artist. He felt at home in Salem physically as well as spiritually, and he believed that his paintings inspired by the Salem countryside showed a spontaneity lacking in his later work. Late in World War I, Burchfield was inducted into the army and sent to Camp Jackson, S.C., in July 1918; he was discharged as a sergeant in January 1919.

In 1921 Burchfield lost his job at Mullins because of a drop in business, and he left Salem to design wallpaper at M. H. Birge and Sons in Buffalo, N.Y. Prior to this move he met Bertha Kenreich; they were married on May 20, 1922. By 1925 they had moved into the home in

Gardenville (a Buffalo suburb) where they remained thereafter. They had five children. With the encouragement of Frank Rehn, owner of the New York City–based Rehn Galleries (which became his sole dealer), Burchfield quit his job at Birge in 1929 and began to paint full-time.

Burchfield produced relatively few paintings between 1922 and 1929 due to his work and family commitments, yet he gained a reputation as one of the new realist painters. His work was associated with that of Edward Hopper and Andrew Wyeth, who depicted provincial American life, sometimes nostalgically. Burchfield's work was also likened to that of Grant Wood, Thomas Hart Benton, John Steuart Curry, and other American scene painters, or regionalists, popular during the 1930's. Burchfield did not consider himself a regionalist, however, so much as a romantic realist, a label that reflected the diverse and conflicting strains of his art. Burchfield's paintings fluctuated between surrealism and realism. Overall, he was most concerned with mood, especially with his nature paintings.

Burchfield dated his career from 1915, when he began to paint outdoors. He saw nature's complex patterns and seasonal changes as poetic, and he translated the sounds, movements, and what he saw as the emotions of nature into pictorial form. Black check marks represented cricket sounds in *Crickets in November* (1917), and vibrating lines conveyed hot air rising in *Noonday Heat* (1917). He executed a series of pen drawings in 1917 called "Conventions for Abstract Thoughts," and thereafter he implemented some of these symbols for emotions in his pictures. For example, the wavelike spirals surrounding the church steeple in *Church Bells Ringing—Rainy Winter Night* (1917) represented fear as well as sound vibrations. Burchfield experimented with double images wherein natural objects resembled themselves and also something more menacing. Windows and doors appeared as eyes or mouths. Flowers become strange creatures in an eerie evening garden. Even though Burchfield had no exposure to modernist painting in the early years of his career, his fanciful symbolic mode and his use of distortion to capture mood and emotion were similar to the techniques of Edvard Munch, Vincent van Gogh, and other European expressionists.

By 1920 Burchfield had become dissatisfied with his work. The surrealistic paintings that he rendered upon his return from Camp Jackson in early 1919 had "not a single redeeming feature," Burchfield said, and he destroyed them so as to move toward the realism of his middle period. Burchfield's more realistic pictures, however, retained brooding and anthropomorphic qualities. His *House of Mystery* (1924) conveyed the sense that, as Burchfield described it, "anything might have happened, or be happening," in this house. As Burchfield began to paint the subjects more typical of the regionalist school his style became less calligraphic. He used strong brushstrokes and tones of gray and black to depict deserted streets and shabby buildings. In Buffalo, N.Y., he made use of such industrial motifs as grain elevators and train depots. *Freight Cars Under a Bridge* (1933) and *Black Iron* (1935) revealed the patterns and textures of city life: the way the bridge girders crisscross, or the way light hits wet pavements or steel beams. Burchfield seldom portrayed people in his paintings, and this sometimes intensified a work's dismal air.

In 1943 Burchfield reassessed his realistic paintings in light of his earlier works. He wrote Frank Rehn that his 1920–1940 period was a necessary "digression" no longer in the "main stream" he felt "destined to travel." He had been searching for the "form and solidity" that his earlier, more ephemeral paintings lacked, he said, but now he was "in danger of painting too realistically." He determined "to recapture the first imaginative and romantic outlook, and even go beyond the scope of that period." As he returned to nature paintings, which were interpretive and emotional, his work became increasingly abstract and fantastic. He sometimes reworked an earlier painting by enlarging it and exaggerating its abstract and repetitive patterns. He reintroduced bright colors into his paintings, and he continued to use the play of light and motion to evoke mood. Burchfield's critics and collectors felt uncomfortable with his shift in style, and for a period in the late 1940's and early 1950's sales of his paintings slumped. Some critics saw his nature fantasies as overblown and too contrived; others believed he had successfully fused his early fantastic manner with the realism of his middle period, bringing technical mastery to his mature works.

From the 1950's until his death Burchfield continued to gain critical attention, with major exhibitions of his work staged throughout the

United States. He had had several one-man shows in the 1920's and 1930's at galleries in New York City, Cleveland, London, and Philadelphia. His watercolors of 1916 to 1918 were exhibited at the Museum of Modern Art (1930) and at the Phillips Memorial Gallery in Washington, D.C. (1934). He had retrospective exhibits at the Albright Art Gallery in Buffalo (1944), the Cleveland Museum of Art (1953), the Whitney Museum of American Art (1956), and the University Gallery, Tucson, Ariz. (1965–1966). Following Burchfield's death, the American Academy of Arts and Letters in New York City had a memorial exhibition in 1968; the Kennedy Galleries in New York City staged one-man shows almost yearly beginning in 1974. Most of Burchfield's paintings were in watercolor, which he tended to use like oil, with heavy overlapping strokes and (in his later paintings) on oversize paper. In this way Burchfield went beyond typical color washes, and he extended the traditional dimensions and scope of watercolor painting.

Burchfield was an introvert, uncomfortable around people other than his family. He also experienced radical mood shifts that affected his art. Essentially, his profoundly romantic personality found its outlet in nature, which he wanted to paint as he experienced it. He preferred the drama of storms and abrupt seasonal changes, and he sometimes experienced transcendent visions during his outdoor rambles. Although he joined the Lutheran church with his wife in 1944, he found an almost pantheistic religion in the beauty and mystery of nature. His acute sense of sound, which he tried to incorporate into his paintings, was related to his love of music, particularly that of Sibelius, Beethoven, and Mozart. An avid reader, he credited Sherwood Anderson's *Winesburg, Ohio*, which Burchfield read in early 1919, for his shift to realism. Anderson's bleak picture of midwestern American life prompted Burchfield to paint contemporary life as he knew it. In the journal that he kept since he was fifteen, Burchfield said that if he had not become a painter, he would have been a writer. He died in Buffalo, N.Y.

[Burchfield's personal papers and journals are at the Charles Burchfield Center, State University College, Buffalo, N.Y. Burchfield's correspondence with Edward Root is in the American Archives, the Philadelphia Museum of Art. See John I. H. Baur, *Charles Burchfield* (1956); and Edith H. Jones, ed., *The Drawings of Charles Burchfield* (with text by Burchfield). For a catalog of his paintings, see Joseph S. Trovato, *Charles Burchfield* (1970). An obituary is in the *New York Times*, Jan. 11, 1967.]

LINDA PATTERSON MILLER

BURKE, BILLIE (Aug. 7, 1886–May 14, 1970), stage and screen actress, was born Mary William Ethelbert Appleton Burke in Washington, D.C., the daughter of William E. ("Billy") Burke, a circus entertainer, and Blanche Hedkinson. Soon after Billie's birth her father left the Barnum and Bailey Circus to form his own small traveling circus. After that venture failed, William Burke did vaudeville in New York. When Billie was eight, her father moved the family to London, where he launched a new troupe—Billy Burke's Barnum and Great London Circus Songsters.

In London, Billie Burke attended Mrs. Bailie's school. Despite her father's profession, Billie was not a stagestruck child. But Blanche Burke, who had no theatrical background herself, decided that her daughter should become an actress. To further her plan, she arranged for Billie to have singing, elocution, and ballet lessons. Billie's father objected to his wife's campaign, but she persisted. Billie herself was too young and retiring to have theatrical ambitions. As she later put it, "I was a shy, wistful sort of moppet who never in this world would have got ahead if it had not been for my mother."

When she was fourteen, Billie Burke debuted as a vaudeville singer at Berkhampstead. At Sheffield she appeared briefly in a pantomime, *The Sleeping Beauty and the Yellow Dwarf*, and then sang at the London Pavilion for £10 a week. In 1902 the composer Leslie Stuart offered her a small part in his new show, *The School Girl*. Billie's musical number was the hit of the show, which ran for eleven months in London and established the young actress as one of the great beauties of the day. Later she had supporting roles in several productions, such as *Duchess of Danzic* (1903) and *Blue Moon* (1905), before the London showman Sir Charles Hawtrey gave her the female lead in *Mr. George* (1907), a hit comedy.

In 1907 the impresario Charles Frohman brought Burke to New York to be John Drew's leading lady in *My Wife*. Next, Frohman, who was to guide Burke's stage career for many years, starred her in *Love Watches* (1908). She subsequently appeared in *Mrs. Dot* (1910), *Suzanne* (1910), *A Marriage of Convenience* (1918), *Caesar's Wife* (1919), *Intimate Strangers* (1921), *Rose Briar* (1922), *Annie Dear* (1924), *The Marquise* (1927), *The Happy Husband* (1928), *Truth Game* (1930), and *The Vinegar Tree* (1931), in which she portrayed the first of those scatterbrained ladies for which she became noted in her later films. She noted in her memoirs that at the pinnacle of her stage career, "I was earning more than $50,000 a season, a fine fortune in those days, had an estate at Hastings-on-the-Hudson, a Rolls-Royce, a nice Packard for my mummy, and went to Europe every season for my clothes."

At a costume party on New Year's Eve 1913, Burke met Florenz Ziegfeld, Jr., the great Broadway showman. They were married on Apr. 11, 1914; they had one child. The Ziegfelds lived lavishly at their Westchester County, N.Y., estate, complete with a collection of exotic animals that might have stocked a small zoo. But their domestic life was often troubled, for Ziegfeld, well known for his womanizing, did not change his habits after marrying Burke. His affairs with showgirls made headlines and generated much public speculation about the Ziegfeld-Burke marriage.

Burke cast herself in the role of the long-suffering but steadfast wife. She granted interviews about her husband's peccadilloes and even wrote articles advising wives on how to hold on to straying husbands. "Don't react in hurt anger and dismay," she cautioned. "Act as if you don't know what's going on. . . . Your gambit is to be so good to come home to."

Shortly after marrying Ziegfeld, Burke signed a movie contract with Triangle for $10,000 per week, reputedly the highest salary yet paid to a film star. Her first picture, *Peggy* (1915), was made in Hollywood. She declined a five-year deal with the producer Thomas Ince because she wanted to be with her husband in New York. Eventually she signed with Famous Players–Lasky, which had a New York studio. She was busy in silent films from 1917 until 1921, when she turned her attention exclusively to the stage.

The Ziegfelds lost heavily in the 1929 stock market crash, and with the onset of the Great Depression the producer's outdated shows no longer enjoyed their former success. Despite these setbacks, Ziegfeld did not curb his extravagance. When he died in July 1932, Burke was left with a debt-ridden estate.

Shortly before her husband's death, Burke returned to Hollywood, hoping that a renewed film career would enable her to pay Ziegfeld's debts. She credited Will Rogers and Sam Goldwyn, old family friends, with getting her reestablished in movies, which by then had become "talkies." Her first important sound film was *A Bill of Divorcement* (1932), with John Barrymore and Katharine Hepburn. Burke made more than sixty feature films between 1933 and 1960, including *Dinner at Eight* (1933), *Topper* (1937) and its sequels (1938, 1941), *The Wizard of Oz* (1939), *The Man Who Came to Dinner* (1942), *Father of the Bride* (1950), *Father's Little Dividend* (1951), and *Sergeant Rutledge* (1960). In addition to her film work, the actress did occasional stage and television dramas. She starred on "The Billie Burke Show" on radio in 1944–1946 and hosted "At Home with Billie Burke" on television in Los Angeles during the early 1950's.

Burke thought her best role was Glinda, the Good Witch of the North, in *The Wizard of Oz*. She was also known for the daffy, fluttery, but always well-intentioned characters she played in so many films. She was typecast in these roles, but the results were inspired. The film scholar David Shipman has observed that "Billie Burke's bird-witted lady was one of the perfect things in an imperfect world."

Burke spent her later years in the Brentwood section of Los Angeles, where she lived next door to her daughter and grandchildren. Her home was filled with theatrical mementos, and she retained connections with the Ziegfeld Club, a group of former Follies performers. Always an animal lover, she kept many pets and was an active antivivisectionist. She died in Los Angeles.

[Burke's autobiographical *With a Feather on My Nose* (1949) and *With Powder on My Nose* (1959), written with Cameron Shipp, provide the fullest accounts of her career and marriage. See also Patricia Ziegfeld Stephenson, *The Ziegfelds' Girl* (1964); and David Shipman, *The Great Movie Stars: The Golden Years* (1970). An obituary is in the *New York Times*, May 16, 1970.]

WILLIAM HUGHES

BUSHMAN, FRANCIS XAVIER (Jan. 10, 1883–Aug. 23, 1966), actor, was born in Baltimore, Md., the son of John and Mary Bushman. His father was a traveling salesman. Bushman received a parochial school education and then attended Ammendale College in Maryland. Although his mother had forbidden him from going to the theater, Bushman sneaked out of school to do so. In 1899 he joined the Fawcett Stock Company in Baltimore, and appeared in many plays as an extra.

In 1902 Bushman met and married Josephine Fladune. By 1909 they had five children, one of whom became an actor known professionally as Francis X. Bushman, Jr. Although Bushman took various odd jobs to support his family (he was a sculptor's model, for statues of Lord Baltimore and Nathan Hale), he continued to work in stock companies. In 1907 he made his Broadway debut playing a featured role in *Queen of the Moulin Rouge*. His good looks led to film offers, and in 1911 he signed a contract with Essanay Studios in Chicago. His first film, *His Friend's Wife*, a one-reeler with Dorothy Phillips, was released on June 6, 1911. Almost immediately he became a favorite of movie audiences. He made sixteen additional films in 1911 and more than thirty in 1912, emerging as a major film star.

In 1912 Bushman was cast opposite Beverly Bayne in *A Good Catch* and they proved immensely popular. In 1915 he and Bayne starred in *Graustark*, his most popular film. Hailed as "the handsomest man in the world" and "the king of the movies," he employed eighteen secretaries to answer his fan mail. Bushman purchased a large estate in Maryland, which he called "Bushmanor." There he raised Great Danes and horses and maintained an aviary. He quickly developed a lavish life-style, characterized by $100 tips, a lavender boudoir, a lavender Rolls-Royce, and lavender cigarettes. His glamorous life-style was heavily publicized, but his contract forbade any public mention of his wife and children.

After Bushman left Essanay in 1915, he signed with the Metro Film Company, later part of Metro-Goldwyn-Mayer (MGM). Three years later he established his own studio, Quality Pictures, and seemed poised for even greater success. However, when his wife filed for divorce his career suffered a setback from which it never fully recovered. The revelation that he had a wife and five children seriously eroded his appeal as a romantic idol. His marriage on July 29, 1918, to costar Bayne soon after the divorce did not rekindle that interest. They had one child. Bushman made only two films in 1919 and by 1926 only two more, one of which, *Modern Marriage* (1923), was filmed by his second company, FXB Pictures.

In 1926 Bushman had an opportunity for a comeback when he was cast as the villain, Messala, in Louis B. Mayer's *Ben-Hur*. This role brought him to Hollywood, the new center of the motion picture industry. The film was a success and Bushman's performance was well received by critics. However, Mayer felt that Bushman had deliberately stolen scenes from Mayer's protégé Ramon Novarro. When Bushman's butler subsequently snubbed Mayer, Bushman's career went into eclipse. While he appeared sporadically in serials and in minor roles in B pictures, he never recaptured his star status. The final blow to Bushman's motion-picture career was the introduction of sound. His flamboyant acting style, developed for and suitable to silent films, did not transfer well to the new medium. Bushman's inability to find work and the stock market collapse led him to declare bankruptcy in 1929. During these proceedings it was revealed that Bushman, who had earned some $10 million as a movie actor, was $100,000 in debt.

Bushman's marriage to Beverly Bayne had ended in divorce and in 1932 he married Norma Atkins, who owned a chain of beauty salons. During the 1930's and 1940's Bushman played many roles in radio dramas, especially soap operas, which allowed him to live comfortably if not lavishly. Later he appeared frequently on television but never in a starring or continuing role, except as the host of a late-night movie series on a local station in Los Angeles. In 1951 his fame was briefly rekindled when he played King Saul in the film *David and Bathsheba* and went on a national tour to promote the picture for Twentieth Century–Fox.

Bushman's third wife died in 1956 and on August 15 of that year he married Iva Richardson. Together they won $30,000 on the television quiz show "The Big Surprise." He continued to appear as a character actor in films, most notably in *Sabrina* (1954), and he was in a television production of *Peer Gynt*. His last film, *The Ghost in the Invisible Bikini*, was released in 1966. He died in Pacific Palisades, Calif., soon after finishing a guest role on the television series "Voyage to the Bottom of the Sea."

Bushman was the first great romantic lead in the history of motion pictures and part of the first great romantic film team. He helped establish film as the major American entertainment medium, not only because of his popularity, but because his off-screen exploits captured the enthusiasm of the public.

[See David Carroll, *The Matinee Idols* (1972); and K. C. Lahue, *Gentlemen to the Rescue* (1972). An obituary is in the *New York Times*, Aug. 24, 1966.]

WILLIAM H. MULLIGAN, JR.

BYRD, HARRY FLOOD (June 10, 1887–Oct. 20, 1966), governor of Virginia and United States senator, was born in Martinsburg, W.Va., the son of Richard Evelyn Byrd, a newspaper publisher and lawyer, and Eleanor Bolling. He was a direct descendant of William Byrd, who immigrated to Virginia from England in 1670 and became one of the colony's most influential figures. Byrd was always immersed in politics and government. His father was Speaker of the Virginia House of Delegates and two uncles were United States congressmen from Virginia. One of his two brothers was Admiral Richard Evelyn Byrd, the explorer. Byrd grew up in Winchester, Va., where his father published the *Evening Star*. In 1903, Byrd dropped out of the Shenandoah Valley Academy to take over management of the paper, which was then financially troubled. Byrd never resumed his formal education. He paid off the newspaper's debts and established a policy of pay-as-you-go advertising that assured a constant cash flow. His thrift and abhorrence of debt later became the dominant themes of his political career. In Winchester, Byrd bought out and closed the competing newspaper, and in 1907 he established a newspaper in Martinsburg, W.Va. In 1923 he purchased the *Harrisonburg* (Va.) *Daily News-Record*.

Beginning in 1906, Byrd was also an apple grower. He got his start by leasing a group of small orchards, but eventually he acquired his own Shenandoah Valley orchards in partnership with his brother Thomas. The Byrds owned one of the largest apple warehouses in the nation, sold their crops throughout the Middle Atlantic region, and exported apples to England.

Active in local Democratic politics, Byrd launched his political career in 1908, when he was elected to the Winchester City Council. From 1908 until 1918 he served as president of the Valley Turnpike Company, which managed Virginia's first paved highway. He married Anne Douglas Beverley on Oct. 7, 1913; they had four children.

From 1915 to 1925, Byrd served in the Virginia state senate, where he rose to prominence as a fiscal conservative and a moderate on social issues. He supported legislation for workmen's compensation, protection for child laborers, and increased aid for education. During World War I he served as Virginia's fuel commissioner. As chairman of the state senate's Roads Committee, Byrd took a leading role in the development of the state's highway system. He sponsored legislation establishing the Virginia Highway Commission and introduced a law that turned the Valley Turnpike into a freeway. Troubled by Virginia's staggering Civil War debt and concerned that a bond issue would put an undue burden on taxpayers, Byrd successfully led the opposition in 1923 to a statewide $50 million bond issue for the construction of highways.

Overcoming the opposition of Virginia's regular Democratic organization, Byrd was elected governor in 1925 and became Virginia's youngest chief executive since Thomas Jefferson. Although Byrd is remembered as a conservative stalwart, he was a progressive governor by the standards of his era. Under his Program of Progress, he streamlined governmental institutions by merging 100 loosely knit and autonomous bureaus, departments, and boards into fourteen departments directly under gubernatorial control. By implementing his pay-as-you-go policy in state expenditures, Byrd transformed a $1.25 million deficit into a $2.6 million surplus by the end of his term. He established tax incentives to attract new industry and eliminated the state tax on land to help farmers. He confronted oil companies and telephone companies to press for lower consumer rates, and he promoted rural electrification and conservation. In 1928, Byrd gained the passage of the South's first antilynching law, making all members of a lynch mob subject to murder charges.

Although he was limited to only one four-year term as governor under the Virginia Constitution, Byrd nevertheless established his dominance in statewide politics when his gubernatorial candidate, John Garland Pollard, defeated the old guard's standard-bearer, Patrick

Byrd

Drury. For the next four decades, Byrd was the major force in Virginia's political affairs.

In 1932, Byrd was a favorite-son presidential candidate at the Democratic National Convention that nominated Franklin D. Roosevelt. Byrd supported Roosevelt, an old friend, and following the election, Roosevelt offered to appoint Byrd secretary of agriculture. Byrd declined and another Virginia Democrat, Senator Claude Swanson, was named to the Roosevelt cabinet as secretary of the navy. Governor Pollard then appointed Byrd to suceed Swanson in the United States Senate.

During his years as a United States senator, Byrd rose to power as a leader of southern conservatives. Elected to six terms in the Senate, Byrd consolidated his influence and became one of the Senate's ranking oligarchs, partly because of his seniority and partly because of his affable, even-tempered personality. Arthur Krock of the *New York Times* observed in 1953 that Byrd's "rare combination of integrity, ability, courage" and "specialized knowledge of complex subjects" made him a force to be reckoned with in the Senate. From 1955 until his resignation a decade later, he was chairman of the Senate Finance Committee, and he used his position to urge presidents from Dwight Eisenhower to Lyndon Johnson to hold the line on federal expenditures. For much of his Senate career, he was chairman of a largely ceremonial panel called the Joint Committee on Reduction of Nonessential Federal Expenditures.

Although friendly with Roosevelt, Byrd became one of the earliest Democratic critics of the New Deal. He supported the Emergency Banking Act of 1933 and early efforts to cut federal expenditures, but he disagreed with Roosevelt's decisions to devalue currency and to abandon the gold standard. Byrd also opposed the National Recovery Act and the original Social Security Act, although he later supported the revision that provided for contributions by employees and employers. Byrd supported the administration's soil-conservation and rural-electrification programs, but he helped forge the bipartisan coalition that blocked Roosevelt's attempt to increase the number of justices on the Supreme Court in 1937. Between 1933 and 1945, Byrd voted with Republicans 45 percent of the time. After endorsing Roosevelt's reelection in 1936, Byrd never supported another Democratic national ticket.

Despite his sharp differences with Roosevelt over domestic policy, Byrd generally backed the administration's foreign policy. He favored Roosevelt's effort to revise the Neutrality Act in 1939 in order to permit military aid to victims of Nazi aggression. Byrd also voted for the nation's first peacetime draft in 1940 and for lend-lease aid to the Allies in 1941. During the Truman administration, Byrd voted with isolationists, opposing the Marshall Plan for aid to postwar Europe and the Point IV foreign-aid package. He supported American participation in the North Atlantic Treaty Organization and helped draft legislation establishing the Atomic Energy Commission.

An opponent of civil rights reforms, Byrd was jolted by the Supreme Court's 1954 ruling that segregation in public schools was unconstitutional. "If we can organize the southern states for massive resistance to this order," Byrd declared, "I think that in time the rest of the country will realize that racial integration is not going to be accepted in the South." Influenced by Byrd, the Virginia legislature voted to have the governor close schools that were ordered to integrate by federal courts or cut off state funding for schools that integrated. But in 1959 the Virginia Supreme Court of Appeals struck down the segregationist closing laws, and a federal court in Norfolk ruled that such resistance was unconstitutional. Governor J. Lindsay Almond, Jr., a Byrd ally, then persuaded the Virginia General Assembly to repeal the school-closing laws, and in February 1959 the color line was broken in Norfolk and Arlington schools without incident. Byrd's political organization was dealt another blow in 1964 when the Twenty-fourth Amendment to the Constitution outlawed the poll tax, which had restricted black participation in southern elections.

In the 1960 presidential election, Byrd, while not a candidate, received six electoral votes from Alabama, eight from Mississippi, and one from Oklahoma. Byrd had supported Lyndon Johnson for the Democratic presidential nomination but was neutral in the election between John F. Kennedy and Richard Nixon. During Byrd's final years in the Senate, he opposed Kennedy's 1962 tax cut and clashed with Presidents Kennedy and Johnson over Medicare. Byrd was reelected to the Senate in 1964, but because of his wife's death and his own failing health, he resigned on Nov. 6, 1965; his son Harry F. Byrd, Jr., succeeded him. Byrd died at his country estate in Berryville, Va.

[Byrd's papers are in the Library of Congress and at the University of Virginia. See V. O. Key, Jr., *Southern Politics in State and Nation* (1949); *Time*, Aug. 17, 1962; J. Harvie Wilkinson III, *Harry Byrd and the Changing Face of Virginia Politics, 1945–1966* (1968); Alden Hatch, *The Byrds of Virginia* (1969); and Jack Bass and Walter DeVries, *The Transformation of Southern Politics* (1976). Obituaries are in the *New York Times* and the *Washington Post*, both Oct. 21, 1966.]

STEVE NEAL

CANTRIL, ALBERT HADLEY (June 16, 1906–May 28, 1969), social psychologist and public-opinion analyst, was born in Hyrum, Utah, the son of Albert Hadley Cantril, a physician, and Edna Mary Meyer. Cantril was raised in Douglas, Wyo., and graduated from Dartmouth College in 1928. He attended the universities of Munich and Berlin in 1929 and 1930 before enrolling at Harvard, where he graduated in 1931 with a Ph.D. in psychology. He returned to Dartmouth for a year as an instructor in sociology. There he met Mavis K. Lyman, whom he married on June 18, 1932. They had a daughter and a son, Albert Hadley, who became a public-opinion analyst. Cantril taught psychology at Harvard from 1932 to 1935, the next year moving to Columbia University Teachers College as an assistant professor.

In the fall of 1936 Cantril joined the psychology faculty at Princeton. By 1944 he was a full professor, and in 1953 became Stuart Professor and chairman of the psychology department. In 1955 he left the university to head the Institute for International Social Research with his associate Lloyd Free. The institute, sponsored by the Rockefeller Brothers Fund, gave Cantril the freedom to research the relation between public opinion and governmental policy. His first book, *The Psychology of Radio* (1935), coauthored with Gordon W. Allport, examined the formation of opinion.

While preparing a series of newspaper articles for the *New York Times* in 1936, Cantril visited George Gallup, who had realized that the *Literary Digest* poll predicting a landslide victory for presidential candidate Alf Landon would be wrong. Gallup influenced Cantril to move to Princeton, where they continued to collaborate, Cantril adding psychological insight to Gallup's technique. The two perfected the method of selecting a stratified sample.

In 1940 Cantril established the Office of Public Opinion Research with Rockefeller Foundation funds. He continued to experiment in methodology but also searched for the reasons that motivated changes in public opinion. In *The Invasion from Mars* (1940) he examined why some people were frightened by the famous Orson Welles radio broadcast "The War of the Worlds," while others accepted it as science fiction. He further explored opinion formation in *The Psychology of Social Movements* (1941).

Cantril also studied attitudinal changes on United States involvement in World War II. President Franklin D. Roosevelt found Cantril's work interesting and depended upon him for an analysis of American opinion throughout the war. While involved in this effort Cantril pursued methodological improvement, publishing his early results in *Gauging Public Opinion* (1944). In the work, which explored the factors determining opinion formation, Cantril considered the way issues were posed in the form of questions, the influence of interviewers, and sampling problems.

Cantril contributed to the genesis of transactional psychology in *Understanding Man's Social Behavior: Preliminary Notes* (1947), which was published the same year that he collaborated with Muzafer Sherif to write *The Psychology of Ego-Involvements: Social Attitudes and Identifications*. Cantril wrote that each individual creates a reality shaped by past experiences of success at judging other people's responses. In Cantril's view, while any one respondent has a unique reality world, that person shares many assumptions with those who have had common experiences.

Cantril's transactional perspective, which was influenced by George Herbert Mead, was further developed in collaboration with Adelbert Ames, Jr. Ames had studied how people perceive an event, and Cantril asked how this perception affected an individual's transaction with the environment. Their approach was a break with conditioning theory and with the idea that people simply react to a situation. Cantril developed this view into a general theory that is described in *The "Why" of Man's Experience* (1950); he later expanded the theory with additions from physiological psychology.

Even in this period of theory building, Cantril never lost interest in the practical study of public opinion. In 1951 he met W. Averell Harriman, then director of the Mutual Security Agency, who secured government support for experimental research in polling abroad. Cantril sought to determine the state of the national mind of Italy and Holland to discover what kinds of appeals would be most credible. He then measured the effects of these appeals, focusing on the American effort to build support for the North Atlantic Treaty Organization (NATO).

This work served as a forerunner for Cantril's first project within the Institute for International Social Research, a study of voter attributes in France and Italy. Cantril was puzzled by the strong showing of Communists, and he wanted details on the attitudes of voters who supported them. His research revealed that citizens of one nation were hostile to other nations not because of unfavorable stereotypes but because they perceived these other nations as interfering with their goals. Details of this research were published in *How Nations See Each Other* (with William Buchanan, 1953) and in *The Politics of Despair* (1958). Cantril's concern was not limited to American interests, as was illustrated by a book he edited, *Tensions That Cause Wars* (1950). In this work he offered his services to the United Nations Educational, Scientific, and Cultural Organization (UNESCO) in the hope of achieving world peace.

The last fifteen years of Cantril's life reflected a growing synthesis of social psychology and public-opinion polling. In his *Soviet Leaders and Mastery Over Man* (1960) Cantril reported on his visit to Russia, where he talked with psychologists and others to determine their attitudes about socialism and their views of the United States. He concluded that the United States should refrain from attacking Communist ideology while commending Russians whenever they emulated the United States. Cantril synthesized even further in *Reflections on the Human Venture* (1960), coedited with Charles H. Bumstead. In their analysis of various literary selections, Cantril and Bumstead introduced basic principles of transactional analysis and demonstrated how these theories could be applied to specific situations.

Cantril, who sensed the turbulence of the coming decade, believed that technology and science created unique tensions in the contemporary world. He hoped to improve the quality of life by prescriptions spelled out in *Human Nature and Political Systems* (1961), which urged an end to policy that was formulated only as a defense against Soviet expansion, and a beginning of long-range policy based on the worldwide revolution of rising expectations. *The Pattern of Human Concerns* (1965) elaborates on theories presented in *Human Nature and Political Systems.*

In 1967 Cantril and Lloyd Free compiled the data from their 1964 campaign polling of Americans into a widely used source, *The Political Beliefs of Americans: A Study of Public Opinion.* The same year saw publication of *The Human Dimension: Experiences in Policy Research*, in which Cantril devised projects that exemplified his goals and methods. His approach, which correlated polling results with policy formulation, may be taken for granted today, but Cantril faced major obstacles when he pioneered the field. He was still advancing its cause when he died at Princeton, N.J.

[Cantril's correspondence with President Roosevelt is at Dartmouth College, Hanover, N.H.; the remainder of his correspondence is in the custody of Albert H. Cantril of Washington, D.C. The most extensive obituary is F. P. Kilpatrick, "Hadley Cantril," *Journal of Individual Psychology*, Nov. 1969.]

ERNEST L. SCHUSKY

CARLSON, CHESTER FLOYD (Feb. 8, 1906–Sept. 19, 1968), inventor and patent lawyer, was born in Seattle, Wash., the son of Olof Adolph Carlson, an itinerant barber, and Ellen Josephine Carlson. The family lived in various locations in Arizona, Mexico, and California before settling in San Bernardino, Calif., in 1912. Carlson's father became disabled by arthritis, and Carlson worked at odd jobs to support the family while in high school.

Carlson developed an early interest in the graphic arts and observed linotype machines while working as a janitor in a printing shop. He was given an old printing press and used it to print a newsletter for amateur chemists at his high school. After taking a high school course in chemistry, he also worked part-time in a testing laboratory in a local cement plant. He graduated from high school in 1925 and enrolled at Riverside Junior College, where he studied chemistry and physics. Carlson participated in a cooperative program in which he alternated every six weeks between attending classes and working in the testing laboratory of the Riverside Cement Company. After three years of study at Riverside, he enrolled as a junior at the California Institute of Technology, graduating with a B.S. degree in physics in 1930.

In July 1930, Carlson accepted a job with the Bell Telephone Laboratories in New York, where he worked on the development and testing of carbon used in telephone microphones. After a few months, he transferred to the patent department at Bell as an assistant to a patent attorney. A reduction in the work force during the Great Depression cost him his job in 1933, but he soon found another job in a New York patent law office. In 1934 he joined the patent department of P. R. Mallory and Company, a manufacturer of electrolytic condensers, rectifiers, and batteries. Carlson remained at Mallory until 1945 and eventually became head of the patent department. He took night courses at the New York Law School and was admitted to the New York State bar in 1940. In 1934 he married his landlady's daughter, Linda (her maiden name is unknown); the marriage ended in divorce in 1945.

Carlson's perception of the need for an office copying machine grew out of his patent-related work at Mallory, where numerous copies of patent specifications were needed. Multiple carbon copies were often unsatisfactory and valuable time was lost if documents were sent out to a photocopying firm. Carlson investigated existing methods used in printing and duplicating documents and decided to concentrate on the photoconductive effects of light on matter. He gained an important insight from reading an article by Paul Selenyi, a Hungarian inventor who had developed a method of sending pictures to remote locations by wire or radio. Selenyi had managed to create an electrostatic image on a rotating drum coated with an insulating material.

After corresponding with Selenyi and obtaining copies of other Selenyi publications, Carlson theorized that he could produce an electrostatic image on a photoconductive plate that had been exposed to light and then possibly transfer the image as a copy of the original. He arrived at the basic concept of this method of electrophotography (later called xerography after the Greek for "dry writing") by 1937 and filed a patent application on his revolutionary invention in the fall of that year.

It took Carlson several months to convert the concept of electrophotography into practice. Initially, while testing sulfur as a material that became more conductive when exposed to light, he managed to coat a zinc plate with a thin layer of sulfur. In October 1938, Carlson hired Otto Kornei, an unemployed Austrian immigrant with a background in physics, to assist in the electrophotographic experiments. Using a rented room in Astoria, Long Island, as a laboratory, they performed the crucial experiment of producing a copy of an image on Oct. 22, 1938. The image of a slide inscribed "10-22-38 Astoria" was produced on a surface of sulfur after it had been charged by rubbing and illuminated by a flood lamp.

Kornei soon discovered that anthracene worked better than sulfur as the photoconductive material, and he and Carlson worked out a technique to transfer an image from the photoconductive plate to a sheet of paper by using lycopodium powder. Kornei fabricated a demonstration kit that Carlson used to attempt to interest various potential sponsors who might help to develop the invention to the commercial stage. Carlson found no one who was willing to invest, and Kornei ultimately took another job. Carlson filed additional patent applications, the most important of which was his basic xerography patent, issued in October 1942.

Carlson's prospects began to improve in 1944 when he disclosed the essence of his invention to Russell W. Dayton, an employee of the Battelle Memorial Institute in Columbus, Ohio. Carlson was invited to demonstrate his copying process at Battelle, a nonprofit research organization. In August 1944, Carlson and Battelle negotiated an agreement under which the institute would undertake to improve the copying process and share in any future profits. Roland M. Schaffert and other Battelle researchers made several significant improvements, such as the adoption of selenium for the photoconductive plate and a more effective way to transfer powder from the plate to paper.

In 1946 the Haloid Company of Rochester, N.Y., a manufacturer of photographic paper and related products, learned of Carlson's invention and decided that it had commercial potential. Haloid entered an agreement with Battelle under which Haloid assumed most of the cost of development, manufacture, and marketing of copying machines. Carlson became a consultant to Haloid and assigned several additional patents to the company. In October 1948, Haloid and Battelle publicly announced the commercial availability of xerography. The first copier was introduced to the market in 1950 and enjoyed modest success in specialized applications. However, it was not until the Xerox 914 came on the market in 1959 as a convenient and simple office copier that the revolutionary impact of Carlson's invention became fully evident. The Haloid Company changed its name to Haloid Xerox in 1958 and to Xerox in 1961. The company's net income increased from about $2 million in 1959 to about $22.6 million in 1963. Carlson shared in the success of the Xerox copying machines and became a multimillionaire from royalties and stock. He received a total of forty-two United States patents, most of which covered improvements in xerography.

During the 1960's, Carlson became a philanthropist and made generous donations to the Center for the Study of Democratic Institutions, the California Institute of Technology, and other institutions. With his second wife, Dorris Hudgins, he became interested in Zen, and they met weekly at their home in Pittsford, N.Y., a suburb of Rochester, with a small group that shared this interest. He died in New York City.

[An edited typescript of Joseph J. Ermenc's tape-recorded interview with Carlson, conducted Dec. 16, 1965, is in the collection of the Center for the History of Electrical Engineering at the headquarters of the Institute of Electrical and Electronics Engineers, New York City. See also John Jewkes, David Sawers, and Richard Stillerman, *The Sources of Invention* (1969); and John H. Dessauer, *My Years with Xerox* (1971). An obituary is in the *New York Times*, Sept. 20, 1968.]

JAMES E. BRITTAIN

CARMICHAEL, OLIVER CROMWELL (Oct. 3, 1891–Sept. 25, 1966), educator, was born near Good Water, Clay County, Ala., the son of Daniel Monroe Carmichael and Amanda Delight Lessley. He grew up on the family's small farm and began his education at a country school. He attended Alabama Presbyterian College from 1907 to 1909, but he received his B.A. in 1911 and his M.A. in 1914 from the University of Alabama. He taught French and German at the University of Alabama in 1911–1912, and in 1912–1913 he was acting professor of modern languages at the Florence Normal School in Birmingham. He attended Oxford University as a Rhodes Scholar from 1913 to 1917, earning a B.S. and a diploma in anthropology. These studies were interrupted by service in the Commission for Relief in Belgium, the British Young Men's Christian Association, the British army, and the United States Army. On July 13, 1918, Carmichael married Mae Crabtree; they had two children.

Following World War I, Carmichael returned to Alabama and became head of the foreign-language department at Birmingham Central High School. He was principal of Henley Grammar School (1920–1921) and Woodlawn High School (1921–1922), and in 1922 he was appointed dean and assistant to the president of Alabama State College for Women (now the University of Montevallo). As its president from 1926 to 1935, Carmichael directed a fund-raising drive to improve the college and provide for its continued growth.

Carmichael began his association with Vanderbilt University in 1935, when he became dean of the graduate school and senior college. He assumed the additional post of vice-chancellor in 1936 and served as chancellor from 1937 to 1946. Carmichael's tenure in Nashville was characterized by expansion of the school's curriculum and the addition of research and academic facilities. Vanderbilt University joined with Scarritt College and George Peabody College to endow and construct a central university library. A $9 million campaign for building and endowment funds for Vanderbilt's liberal arts college was launched, and Carmichael helped raise money for a school of law.

During 1946–1953, Carmichael was president of the Carnegie Foundation for the Advancement of Teaching. Carmichael expressed his concerns with international studies in his annual reports to the foundation's board of trustees. During these years he was also vice-chairman of the Temporary Commission on the Need for a State University of New York, and he was chairman of the board of trustees of the New York State university system from 1948 to 1953.

As president of the University of Alabama in Tuscaloosa, a post he assumed in 1953, Carmichael faced perhaps his greatest challenge. His leadership was tested in the turmoil brought about by the civil rights movement. Labeled a "southern moderate" by the *New York Times*, Carmichael was caught in the middle of the conflict over racial segregation.

In 1956, after attending classes for three days, Autherine Lucy, the university's first black student, was expelled for accusing university officials of conspiring with rioters. Following an investigation, several white students believed to have incited mob outbursts on the Tuscaloosa campus were also expelled. In public, Carmichael spoke of maintaining the order and decorum befitting an educational institution and of obeying the law of the land. While Carmichael denied published reports of his differences with University of Alabama trustees, one member of the board was quoted as saying, "If that —— says 'integration' again, we'll fire him." Carmichael resigned in 1957; for the remainder of his life he was a consultant to the Fund for the Advancement of Education.

Carmichael's first major book was *The Changing Role of Higher Education* (1949), in which he reviewed the expansion of higher education since 1900. He found growth in the numbers attending colleges and universities, as well as in support, subsidies, and endowments. Additionally, he recorded an increase in the number of American junior colleges and professional schools and a broadening of the curriculum. Universities, he stated, were assuming a more strategic role and accepting broader responsibilities than were envisioned in 1900. He saw increased growth in every aspect of higher education in the future. Four problem areas he discussed were balance in the curriculum; the recruitment, selection, training, and improvement of teachers for college; international studies; and appraising educational results. His clarion note was the role of higher education as "society's Number One agency for promoting fundamental social progress."

For his second major book, *Universities, Commonwealth and American: A Comparative Study* (1959), Carmichael visited eight nations of the British Commonwealth and fifty-six universities. After talking with hundreds of faculty members and administrators, he recommended the establishment of a Commonwealth-American Commission on University Education to explore the needs of higher education and serve as a clearinghouse for the exchange of ideas.

Graduate Education: A Critique and a Program (1961), probably Carmichael's most influential book, earned him the American Council Book Award gold medal and the American Council on Education's $1,000 prize for best book on higher education in 1961–1962. He saw graduate school as the most strategic segment of higher education, as well as the most inefficient and ineffective part of the university. Graduate schools, he said, were badly organized, too amorphous, and prone to "the cult of objectivity," which leads to an ethical neutrality and the proliferation of courses and of degrees. He stressed that the most urgent need of American education was reform of graduate education.

In 1960, Carmichael was appointed to the commission established by the Southern Regional Educational Board to chart a course for higher education in the South. The commission's report, *Within Our Reach* (1961), contains many of Carmichael's tocsins: broadening educational opportunity; educating people to be citizens responsive to their time's social, economic, and political needs; achieving excellence in teaching, scholarship, and research; helping the South to advance economically; and providing guidance in the solution of social problems. Carmichael, known to friends and family as "Mike," died in Asheville, N.C.

[Carmichael's papers are at the University of Alabama Library, the Heard Library at Vanderbilt University, the Ford Foundation, and the Carnegie Corporation of New York. His most important writings, other than those cited in the text, include "Education and the New Deal," *Journal of Health and Physical Education*, 5 (1934); "The Relation of the Endowed University to Our Democracy," *Southern Association Quarterly*, 4 (1940); "The Contribution of Liberal Education to Professional Studies," *Association of American Colleges Bulletin*, 27 (1941); "Education for the New Era," *Hispania*, 29 (1946); "What Constitutes an Educated Man," *American Mercury*, 66 (1948); *Education and International Understanding* (1950); "Some Educational Dilemmas," *American Association of University Professors Bulletin*, 37 (1951); "The State University: Its Problems and Prospects," *National Association of State Universities Transactions and Proceedings*, 1954; "Major Strengths and Weaknesses in American Higher Education," *Association of American Colleges Bulletin*, 39 (1953); *Racial Tensions: A Study in Human Relations* (1959); and "College for Americans: A Hundred Years of the Land-Grant Movement," *Saturday Review*, Apr. 21, 1962.

See also John Leslie Carmichael, *The Saga of an American Family* (1950), chap. 13. The Columbia University Oral History Research Project contains an oral history of the Carnegie Corporation of New York that includes numerous mentions of Carmichael. An obituary is in the *New York Times*, Sept. 27, 1966.]

JACOB L. SUSSKIND

CARNAP, RUDOLF (May 18, 1891–Sept. 14, 1970), philosopher and educator, was born in Ronsdorf, near Barmen, in northwest Germany, the son of Johannes S. Carnap, a prosperous merchant, and Anna Dörpfeld, a teacher. Both parents were deeply religious. When her husband died in 1898, Carnap's mother moved with her two children to Barmen. There Carnap attended the gymnasium; mathematics and Latin were his favorite subjects. From 1910 to 1914 he studied physics, mathematics, and philosophy—its neo-Kantian strands in particular—at the universities of Jena and Freiburg im Breisgau. One of Carnap's teachers at Jena was Gottlob Frege, a logician and philosopher of mathematics who, along with Bertrand Russell, most strongly affected Carnap's thinking. During this period, Carnap increasingly viewed religion as irreconcilable with modern science. According to his autobiography, he began to form "a clear naturalistic conception." Theology and metaphysics, Carnap eventually concluded, were "devoid of any cognitive content."

Carnap's plan to write a doctoral dissertation in physics ended abruptly with the outbreak of World War I. Although military service was contrary to his political thinking, he served more than four years in the German army. In quiet moments at the front, Carnap read poetry and studied Albert Einstein's theory of relativity. After the war, he resumed his studies and received his doctorate in philosophy at Jena in 1921. His thesis, *Der Raum: Ein Beitrag zur Wissenschaftslehre (Space: A Contribution to the Theory of Science)*, appeared the following year as a monograph in *Kantstudien*. It stressed a recurring theme in Carnap's work—namely, that philosophical disputes commonly occur when proper logical and empirical analysis is lacking.

In the early 1920's, Carnap intensively probed Bertrand Russell's philosophy. He also became friends with Hans Reichenbach, a philosopher of science, who introduced him to Moritz Schlick, one of the leaders of the Vienna Circle. This group of logical positivists included mathematicians, scientists, and philosophers such as Kurt Gödel, Friedrich Waismann, and Herbert Feigl. They held that philosophy's proper task is to analyze and clarify meaningful language, language that can legitimately be placed within the domains of empirical science or mathematics. All other language, they argued, lacks cognitive significance. Carnap accepted Schlick's invitation to become an instructor of philosophy at the University of Vienna, a position he held from 1926 to 1931. He also joined the Vienna Circle and emerged as its leading thinker and the most precise formulator of its views. Through the circle's discussion, he became familiar with Ludwig Wittgenstein, "who, besides Russell and Frege, had the greatest influence on my thinking," Carnap wrote in his autobiography.

Carnap achieved recognition in 1928 when he published his first important book, *Der logische Aufbau der Welt (The Logical Structure of the World)*. It argued for a theory of knowledge that regarded private, subjective sense-data as the foundations upon which a system of logic could be constructed; such a system would embrace all knowable objects and thereby solve philosophical problems. In the same year, he published an influential monograph, *Scheinprobleme in der Philosophie: Das Fremdpsychische und der Realismusstreit (Pseudo Problems in Philosophy: Other Minds and the Realism Controversy)*, in which he contended that metaphysical problems in general, and the issue of realism versus idealism in particular, are fictitious.

In 1931, Carnap accepted a chair in natural philosophy at the German University in Prague, Czechoslovakia. Two years later he married Elizabeth Ina von Stöger; they had four children. Carnap explored logic and mathematics and achieved major breakthroughs with the publication of *Logische Syntax der Sprache (The Logical Syntax of Language)* in 1934 and *Philosophy and Logical Syntax*, which appeared the next year. Building on his claim that "the only proper task of *Philosophy* is *Logical Analysis*," Carnap utilized the distinction between "metalanguage" (language about language) and "object language" (language about objects) to elucidate and formalize the basic structure of object languages.

When the Nazis came to power, Carnap, who found their ideology loathsome, decided to leave Czechoslovakia. Encouraged by the philosphers Charles W. Morris of the University of Chicago and W. V. Quine of Harvard University, Carnap immigrated to the United States in December 1935. He was appointed professor of philosophy at the University of Chicago in 1936. Soon he joined Morris and Otto Neurath to found and edit the *Interna-*

tional Encyclopedia of Unified Science. One of its most important entries was Carnap's monograph *Foundations of Logic and Mathematics* (1939).

Carnap spent the 1940–1941 academic year as a visiting professor at Harvard University. Bertrand Russell was there for part of that time, and along with Quine and Alfred Tarski, Carnap and Russell carried on significant investigations concerning the nature of logic and truth. Carnap became a naturalized citizen in 1941. From 1942 to 1944 he lived near Santa Fe, N.Mex., where a Rockefeller Foundation research grant enabled him to advance his work both on the logic of modalities and, later, on the problems of probability and induction. During this period he published *Introduction to Semantics* (1942) and *Formalization of Logic* (1943). After returning to the University of Chicago in 1944, Carnap wrote *Meaning and Necessity: A Study in Semantics and Modal Logic* (1947); *Logical Foundations of Probability* (1950), the culmination of his exploration of the logic of empirical knowledge; and *The Continuum of Inductive Methods* (1952).

Except for the spring semester in 1950, when he taught at the University of Illinois in Urbana, Carnap remained at the University of Chicago until 1952. He then went to the prestigious Institute for Advanced Study in Princeton, N.J. He left the institute in 1954 to accept the chair in philosophy at the University of California at Los Angeles (UCLA) that had been vacated by the untimely death of his old friend Hans Reichenbach. Carnap retired from teaching in 1961 but stayed on as a research professor at UCLA until his death in Santa Monica, Calif.

In the history of Western philosophy, Carnap holds a distinguished place. Arguably, he is the most prominent representative of the logical empiricist school in the philosophy of science and logic, which dominated much of the philosophical world of the twentieth century. The technical nature of his work makes it largely inaccessible to all but the philosophically trained specialist. Nevertheless, Carnap's logically oriented empiricism and his analytical approach have permanently influenced what philosophy can and should be.

[An invaluable source of information about Carnap is his autobiographical essay in Paul Arthur Schilpp, ed., *The Philosophy of Rudolf Carnap* (1963). This volume also contains essays about Carnap's thought, his replies to them, and a bibliography of his writings compiled by Arthur J. Benson. Other works on Carnap's life and philosophy include Arne Naess, *Four Modern Philosophers: Carnap, Wittgenstein, Heidegger, Sartre* (1968); Roger C. Buck and Robert S. Cohen, eds., *Proceedings of the 1970 Biennial Meeting, Philosophy of Science Association* (1971); and Jaakko Hintikka, ed., *Rudolf Carnap, Logical Empiricist* (1975). An obituary is in the *New York Times*, Sept. 15, 1970.]

John K. Roth

CASSIDY, MARSHALL WHITING (Feb. 21, 1892–Oct. 23, 1968), racing official, was born in Washington, D.C., the son of Mars Cassidy, a well-known race starter, and Inez King. Cassidy's brothers also continued the family Thoroughbred racing tradition: Wendell worked as presiding steward and head of racing at Hollywood Park in California, and George served as starter at tracks operated by the Greater New York Racing Association. As a youth, Cassidy became an exercise boy, jockey, and assistant starter at Thoroughbred racing tracks in Brooklyn, N.Y. He excelled at several sports before graduating from a Brooklyn high school. Hoping to become a mining engineer, he worked at a gold and silver mine in Chihuahua, Mexico. When revolutionary forces under Francisco Madero took over the mine, Cassidy joined their successful effort to overthrow the dictatorial government of Porfirio Díaz in 1911. Cassidy then returned to the United States and, on Nov. 2, 1916, married Carelotta Busch; they had one child. Cassidy became an assistant starter for his father until enlisting in the United States Army in 1918. After World War I, he resumed his position as assistant starter until becoming a starter at the Bowie racetrack in Maryland in 1921. From 1921 to 1934, Cassidy worked mainly as a starter at tracks in Canada, Mexico, California, Ohio, West Virginia, and Maryland. He helped plan two racetracks, including the Agua Caliente track in Tijuana, Mexico, and served variously as a track superintendent, patrol judge, entry clerk, paddock judge, clerk of scales, racing secretary, steward, handicapper, and racetrack manager. During the 1930's, he was steward at the Hialeah track in Florida and then state steward for New York.

The energetic Cassidy was executive secretary of the Jockey Club of New York City from 1941 to 1964, enabling him to become an undisputed leader of Thoroughbred racing in New York State and across the United States. During this period, the interests of the elite horse-racing set were defended over those of nonclub owners, racing professionals, and the public. As executive secretary, Cassidy held the right to deny licenses. His rulings were accepted almost without question until 1950, when Cassidy refused to renew the license of the Marlet Stable because its owner, Jule Fink, was accused of "associating with gambling interests." The lower New York courts upheld Cassidy's action, but the New York Court of Appeals overruled the decision. The court argued that the licensing power of the Jockey Club was an unconstitutional delegation of legislative authority.

Nevertheless, the Jockey Club and Cassidy both retained considerable authority over Thoroughbred racing. The *American Stud Book* was owned by the Jockey Club. Without a listing in the register, no horse foaled in the United States, Cuba, or Mexico could race in the United States. Cassidy helped develop blood-typing, thus reducing the number of double parentages listed in the *American Stud Book*. In 1949, Cassidy established the Jockey Club's school to train Thoroughbred racing officials. For more than twenty years, he moderated the Jockey Club's roundtables at the Saratoga racetrack to discuss ways of improving Thoroughbred racing.

From 1955 to 1960, Cassidy was vice-president and director of racing for the Greater New York Racing Association. This nonprofit organization reorganized Thoroughbred racing at the Aqueduct, Belmont, Jamaica, and Saratoga racetracks. Cassidy helped design several major North American Thoroughbred racetracks, including an elaborate facility at Aqueduct, and modernize the Belmont and Saratoga racetracks. In addition, he was director of Thoroughbred Racing Associations, Inc., and a trustee of the Turf Foundation and the Horsemen's Benevolent and Protective Association Foundation. In 1963, Ogden Phipps, the chairman of the Jockey Club, called Cassidy "the most important figure in the development of horse racing in the last decade."

Cassidy modernized Thoroughbred horse racing as a sport. He pioneered the mechanical stall starting gate, which separates horses by partitions at the starting line, gives them equal space, and releases them by machine. Cassidy perfected the photo-finish camera and provided motion-picture records of entire races, which made it nearly impossible for jockeys to use rough tactics without being spotted. His installation of electronic timing devices ensured the more precise recording of race finishes. Cassidy developed the use of mirrors in photofinishes, (so that horses can be seen from both sides), encouraged the use of machines to figure odds for each race, and pioneered the method of identifying horses by night-eyes (growths on a horse's legs). At Cassidy's insistence, tracks throughout the nation adopted saliva and urine tests to determine if horses were being given drugs. Cassidy recognized that these changes reduced much of the traditional glamour and color of the sport. In 1953, Cassidy said, "Jockeys used to be more spectacular. We won't let them take chances with their lives or the horses' lives anymore. Betting used to be more fun when you could shop for odds among the bookmakers. . . . The start of the race was more exciting and dramatic, a mad scramble with horses kicking each other and the assistant starters."

The Jockeys' Guild, the Turf Benevolent Association, the Horsemen's Benevolent and Protective Association, the Thoroughbred Club of America, and the National Turf Writers Association honored Cassidy at various times for his enormous contributions to Thoroughbred racing. Cassidy held a transport pilot's license and engaged in boxing and acting. Cassidy sustained serious injuries in an automobile accident on Aug. 8, 1968, and died two and a half months later in Glen Cove, N.Y.

[Cassidy outlined his Thoroughbred racing innovations in "Recollections," *Blood Horse*, Sept. 30, 1967. For articles about Cassidy's career, see the Cassidy file at the National Museum of Racing, Saratoga Springs, N.Y. Cassidy's Jockey Club activities are described in Bernard Livingston, *Their Turf* (1973). Obituaries are in the *New York Times*, Oct. 24, 1968; and *Time*, Nov. 1, 1968.]

DAVID L. PORTER

CASTLE, IRENE FOOTE (Apr. 7, 1893–Jan. 25, 1969), exhibition ballroom dancer and actress, was born in New Rochelle, N.Y., the daughter of Hubert Townsend Foote, a physician and dog breeder, and Annie Elroy Thomas. When Foote was seven, she joined her older sister, Elroy, at St. Mary's Episcopal

Convent at Peekskill, N.Y., and later attended the National Park Seminary, near Washington, D.C., but did not graduate. On May 28, 1911, Foote married Vernon Castle, a twenty-four-year-old Briton whom she met when she pulled herself up on a float at the New Rochelle Rowing Club beach just as he pulled himself up on the other side. He had graduated from the University of Birmingham (England) with a degree in engineering before going on the stage, where he exhibited a talent for farce and original dancing. He had already shed his family name, Blyth, for Castle when he helped his future wife secure a minor part in Lew Fields's Brooklyn production of *The Summer Widowers*.

In 1911 the Castles performed in *The Hen-Pecks*, which introduced jazz to the American stage. Vernon Castle later did a scene from that play in a Paris revue in which the Castles danced. When the revue failed, they agreed to dance at the Café de Paris to bolster their finances. While seated at the café the evening before their act was to start, they were urged to dance by a Russian nobleman who had seen them in the revue. So popular was this unplanned performance that the Castles' other appearances were patterned on it. Unable to compete with the bejeweled customers who flocked to see them, Irene Castle wore refreshingly simple clothes designed for easy dancing.

The Castles' fame preceded them to New York, where their \$300-a-week salary for dancing at the Café de l'Opéra was soon doubled. They became the leaders of the dance craze sparked by Irving Berlin's popular new tunes. Exhibiting grace and a style all their own, they enjoyed enormous success. By making imported dance steps less rowdy and vulgar-looking, they refined the dance craze and broadened interest in it, managing to appease excited moralists without offending the public. While dancing in 1913, the innovative couple stepped up rather than down on the beat, and the "Castle walk" became an instant rage. Among other dances that the Castles helped popularize were the Castle waltz, the one-step, the hesitation waltz, the tango, the maxixe, and the fox-trot. By encouraging an informal social exchange between men and women, these lighthearted dances had a liberating influence.

That the Castles "determined the course dancing should take is incontestable," the critic Gilbert Seldes wrote in *The Seven Lively Arts*. Vernon Castle's innovations transformed ballroom dancing, Seldes maintained, while Irene Castle's cool abandon and "absolute identity with music" was "all that one ever dreamed of flight." She was said to give the sense of moving without effort.

The Castles capitalized on their fame. They expanded a dance school they had started into Castle House, across from the Ritz-Carlton Hotel, where they popularized afternoon tea dances. While society matrons poured tea, the Castles danced to a ragtime orchestra in one packed ballroom and then danced in a second ballroom to tunes played by a Latin orchestra. Individual lessons in the latest dance steps were also available. The Castles briefly operated a popular restaurant, Sans Souci, and a nightclub called Castles in the Air. Using a private three-car train, they toured thirty-two cities in twenty-eight days in 1914, accompanied by an orchestra of black musicians led by James Reese Europe and Ford T. Dabney. After each performance, the Castles conducted and judged dancing contests, gave "Castle Cups" to the winning couples, and later brought the winners to Madison Square Garden for a final contest. In the same year, they also wrote a dance instruction book, *Modern Dancing*, issued a popular instructional dance film, and starred in Irving Berlin's first musical, *Watch Your Step*, written especially for them. The next year, they appeared as themselves in the film *Whirl of Life*.

Irene Castle was as innovative in her dress as Vernon Castle was in his dance steps. Slim and elegant, she was one of the most-photographed women of the World War I era. *Vanity Fair* ran at least one picture of her in each issue, and her clothes, which doomed the hobble skirt and simplified the silhouette, were regularly featured in newspapers and magazines. Her Dutch lace caps became the rage. When she cut her long auburn hair, thousands of women rushed to get a "Castle clip." When she fashioned a narrow band to tame her curly bob, the "Castle band" became wildly popular. Preferring to ride a horse astride, Castle adopted men's riding attire, and other women rushed to buy jodhpurs.

Except for a few special performances, the Castles' dancing partnership ended when, in 1916, Vernon Castle joined Britain's Royal Flying Corps, serving in France. In her husband's absence, Irene Castle continued her career; she remained in *Watch Your Step* and starred in the stirring, fifteen-episode wartime film serial *Patria* (1917–1918). Vernon Castle received the Croix de Guerre for his bravery in combat. He was killed on Feb. 15, 1918, in an airplane crash in Fort Worth, Tex., where he was training pilots.

Irene Castle kept secret her marriage to Robert E. Treman, a captain in the Aviation Section of the Army Signal Corps, on May 21, 1918, three months after Vernon Castle's death. Her book about Vernon, *My Husband*, was published in 1919. On May 4, 1919, she married Treman in a public ceremony and continued her acting career during their marriage, which ended in divorce in 1923. She starred in seventeen silent movies and in 1921 toured the United States with William Reardon in a vaudeville dance routine, arranged by Fred and Adele Astaire. On Nov. 26, 1923, Castle joined Chicago society by marrying Frederic McLaughlin, a polo-playing millionaire.

During her dancing days, Castle popularized the lapdog and often carried a monkey. Throughout her life she was a special friend to animals. In 1928 she established with Helen Swift in Deerfield, Ill., a shelter for stray dogs and cats, calling it Orphans of the Storm after the famous film starring the Gish sisters. To help support this shelter, Castle held an annual "Pooch Ball." She also fought vivisection and continually campaigned against it, often in well-publicized court battles. In 1937, Castle left McLaughlin and began divorce proceedings, but two years later she settled for a separation with shared custody of their two children. McLaughlin died in 1944.

In 1939, Fred Astaire and Ginger Rogers played the Castles in the film *The Story of Vernon and Irene Castle*. Irene Castle was credited as dress designer and technical consultant for the film. That same year, Castle was cheered by 6,000 spectators when she danced the Castle walk and Castle waltz during the New York World's Fair's Irene Castle Day. For nearly three more decades she continued her work for animals, wrote a frank autobiography, *Castles in the Air* (1958), and twice appeared in summer stock. On Nov. 26, 1946, she married George Enzinger, an advertising executive, whom she outlived. She died in Eureka Springs, Ark.

[The Castles' scrapbooks are in the Billy Rose Theater Collection of the New York Public Library at Lincoln Center. Irene Castle's autobiography, *Castles in the Air* (1958), was written with Bob and Wanda Duncan. See *New York Times*, Aug. 21–22, 1919; Frederick Lewis Allen, "When America Learned to Dance," *Scribner's*, Sept. 1937; D. Duncan, *Dance Magazine*, Oct. 1956 and Mar. 1958; and Lewis A. Erenberg, "Everybody's Doin' It: The Pre–World War I Dance Craze, the Castles, and the Modern American Girl," *Feminist Studies*, Fall 1975. Some of Castle's costumes are in the collections of the Metropolitan Museum of Art's Fashion Institute and the Museum of the City of New York. Obituaries are in the *New York Times*, Jan. 26, 1969; and *Dance Magazine*, Mar. 1969.]

OLIVE HOOGENBOOM

CATCHINGS, WADDILL (Sept. 6, 1879–Dec. 31, 1967), investment banker, economist, and writer, was born in Sewanee, Tenn., to which his parents, Silas Fly Catchings and Nora Belle Waddill, had gone to escape a yellow fever epidemic. He received a B.A. from Harvard, in 1901 and an LL.B., in 1904. In the financial-panic year of 1907 he was hired by a New York City law firm at $10 a week. His subsequent success in assisting firms in bankruptcy led to his becoming a director of numerous corporations. During World War I he was a member of the advisory council to the United States secretary of labor and was chairman of the war committee of the United States Chamber of Commerce. He married Helen Weaver on Nov. 7, 1914. They had three children. They were divorced in 1930, and on April 29 of the same year he married May Francis.

Catchings' business associations were in a variety of fields, the first being mainly iron and steel, including the Central Foundry Company, the Platt Iron Works, and Sloss Sheffield Steel and Iron. After working in the export department of J. P. Morgan and Company from 1915 to 1917, he joined the banking firm of Goldman, Sachs and Company in 1918. By the time he resigned in 1930 he was the firm's president and largest shareholder. In 1929 he created the Goldman Sachs Trading Corporation, a holding and investment company with assets in excess of $250 million. Eight years later, he testified at a Securities and Exchange Commission hearing that during the Great Depression the corporation lost more than $289.5 million.

By the early 1930's Catchings directed corporations in a number of diverse fields, including leather, motion pictures (Warner Brothers), radio, television, recorded music (Muzak), tin cans, dry goods, rubber, pharmaceuticals, automobiles (Studebaker and Chrysler), typewriters, breakfast cereals, lumber, mail-order merchandising, music publishing, and electric power. He was knowledgeable about these industries as well as concerned with their financing. Catchings was tall and slender, and had in later years a shock of white hair. He never lost a lingering southern accent. Despite his extraordinary successes he remained modest, reporting his business achievements sparingly in biographical dictionaries.

Prominent as Catchings was in commerce, finance, and industry, he is best remembered for his books. *Money* (1923) was the first of six volumes of similar import. All but one, *Money, Men, and Machines* (1953), written with Charles F. Roos, were written in collaboration with William Trufant Foster, his classmate at Harvard. In addition to *Money*, the two published *Profits* (1925), *Business Without a Buyer* (1927), *The Road to Plenty* (1928), and *Progress and Plenty* (1930). To the collaboration Foster contributed the structure of economic principles, while Catchings supplied wisdom from his business experience and probably most of the actual writing. The earliest books, *Money* and *Profit*, created a sensation in academic circles due to the works' lively, clear exposition and apt illustrations from daily life.

Money was inspired by the postwar depression of 1920–1921, believed to have been caused by consumers' refusal to continue purchasing goods at inflated wartime prices. Catchings' manner as business practitioner turned professor recalled the example of economist David Ricardo, with the difference that Catchings always addressed the multitude, whereas Ricardo addressed the fraternity of economic initiates. Also, Ricardo's language was condensed, while Catchings had the gift of an engaging clarity of words. His approach was friendly and inviting, not monitorial or condescending.

Foster and Catchings' economic theories recalled Alexander Hamilton's policy of abundant circulating media. They anticipated by a decade John Maynard Keynes's stress on the demand side of economics, but without Keynes's obfuscating equations and his advocacy of deliberate deficits in public finance. Foster and Catchings also had an influence on the spend-lend program of Franklin D. Roosevelt's New Deal. A nation "one-third ill-fed, ill-clothed, ill-housed" was one of Catchings' expressions. His last books were *Do Economists Understand Business?* (1955), *Bias Against Business* (1956), and *Are We Mis-managing Money?* (1960).

Like the English economist Alfred Marshall, Catchings abhorred revolutionary change. He had a tenuous faith in the ability of gradual adjustment in the economy to bring demand into harmony with supply and keep it there. Contrivance must "modify the structure year after year in various ways so that human beings . . . will be enabled gradually to create and enjoy better products and more of them," he wrote. The great desideratum was a price level as nearly stable as possible. Catchings supported the Federal Reserve System, but he believed that its ability to control the price level by indirect regulation of the rate of interest was limited. In Catchings' view, the only viable currency was United States notes. "The volume of these notes in circulation," he said, "could be increased promptly as the price-level fell and decreased promptly as the price-level rose." Catchings felt that gold reserves would prove adequate to redeem all currency needed under this plan. He had total faith in his theory that the price level rose and fell directly with the money supply. Catchings lamented underconsumption, including unwise saving. Catchings died in Pompano Beach, Fla.

[See the Harvard Class of 1901, Twenty-fifth Anniversary Report; and Alan H. Gleason, "Foster and Catchings," *Journal of Political Economy*, Apr. 1959. The *New York Times*, 1937–1940, has numerous stories about Catchings' business dealings; see especially June 3, 1937, p. 4, for testimony before the Securities and Exchange Commission. See also the obituary notice, *New York Times*, Jan. 1, 1968. The assistance of Elizabeth N. Chitty, George Dyer, and Sidney Mitchell is gratefully acknowledged.]

BROADUS MITCHELL

CAYTON, HORACE ROSCOE (Apr. 12, 1903–Jan. 22, 1970), sociologist and writer, was born in Seattle, Wash., the son of Horace Roscoe Cayton, a newspaper reporter, editor, and publisher who had been born a slave, and Susie Sumner Revels, who had been educated at Alcorn College and Rust College, where she taught. The well-to-do Caytons had five children and lived in a solidly middle-class white neighborhood. Cayton's father's newspaper and political influence were respected throughout the city and state. Poor investments and decreased newspaper sales, however, drastically reduced the family's income, and so they moved to a working-class neighborhood. Growing racism in the region sharpened young Cayton's awareness of the inferior status of blacks in America.

Cayton's youth as he described it in his autobiography, *Long Old Road* (1965), was troubled and conflict-ridden. He was jailed for sitting downstairs in a movie house that permitted blacks in the balcony only, and he was arrested for driving the getaway car in an abortive filling station robbery. His father's influence obtained his release without trial or police record, on condition that Horace spend time in a training and reform institution. In the eighth grade he was elected school forum president by his mainly white classmates, but racial discrimination became far more prevalent and painful during his sporadic years at Franklin High School. In his junior year (1919) he left school to work on a steamer and wander through Alaska. He returned to Seattle later that same year and through accelerated course work rejoined his class, but he plunged into renewed troubles and felt increasingly dispirited, frustrated, and hostile. He left school in 1920 and entered upon a four-year odyssey of hard manual labor, often frightening adventures, and a journey of self-discovery. He worked as a ship's steward, in a railroad camp, and as a scab longshoreman, and traveled throughout most of the Northwest and Southwest, Mexico, and Hawaii.

At twenty Cayton attended a Young Men's Christian Association college preparatory school in Seattle and then entered the University of Washington (1925). Working his way through college as a sheriff's deputy (the only black deputy), he graduated in 1931 with a B.A. in sociology, and moved the same year with his new wife and fellow student, Bonnie Branch, to Chicago. He was awarded a fellowship at the University of Chicago, and intellectually his career began to blossom. Although he never completed his Ph.D., within a few years he distinguished himself as a researcher, administrator, and writer, primarily in what would be called today "black studies."

For over two years Cayton was a research assistant in the graduate sociology program. The staff advocated intense study of Chicago as a laboratory subject. In the summer of 1932, Cayton edited a newsletter at Tuskegee Institute, but he found life there was too greatly affected by racism. In 1934 and 1935 he served as special assistant to Secretary of the Interior Harold Ickes, with the special task of studying how New Deal legislation affected black laborers. His office was in New York, but his field of study ranged across the United States. In 1935 he sailed for the first time to Europe and arrived in Paris when French fascists were storming the Chamber of Deputies. At a left-wing protest meeting he was hailed as a spokesman for blacks.

Returning to America, he taught economics at Fisk University (1935–1936), but at school's end he went back to Chicago with his second wife, Irma Jackson. His first marriage had dissolved, partly as a result of vocational and racial differences (she was a white social worker). In Chicago from 1936 to 1939, Cayton headed a research unit funded by the Works Progress Administration, under the guidance of the sociologist W. Lloyd Warner, studying the black community in Chicago. He returned to Europe as a Rosenwald Fund Fellow in 1939 and was nearly trapped there by the spreading war. Late that year, he accepted the directorship of Chicago's Parkway Community House, a position he held until 1949. For much of the 1940's he wrote a column for the *Pittsburgh Courier* and from 1952 to 1954 was the paper's correspondent at the United Nations.

An alcoholic, Cayton suffered several psychological breakdowns during the 1940's and 1950's. He wrote about this time in detail in his frank—though sometimes factually cloudy—autobiography. He pieced together jobs during the 1950's and 1960's, performing research for the American Jewish Committee (1950–1951) and for the National Council of Churches of Christ (1954–1958). He taught at the City College of New York (1957–1958) and performed various jobs for the Langley Porter Clinic in San Francisco (1959–1960) and at the Institute for the Study of Crime and Delinquency, Berkeley, Calif. (1960–1961).

Cayton divorced, remarried, and again divorced Irma Jackson, and then married and divorced his third wife, Ruby (Jordan) Wright during this time. All of his marriages were childless. Early in the 1960's he lived briefly with his brother Revels, who had been a distinguished labor leader, in San Francisco and then established his own home in Santa Cruz, Calif. Sturdily built, Cayton was relatively light-complexioned, a matter of some importance to him as it affected his personal relationships. A frequent lecturer at universities and cultural symposia, he taught his last course, "Roots of Revolt," at the University of California at Berkeley shortly before his death in Paris, where he had gone to do research for a biography of his friend Richard Wright.

Cayton's first book, *Black Workers and the New Unions* (1939), written with George S. Mitchell, studies the history, role, and status of blacks in American labor unions, often depicting the racism engrained in many American labor organizations. *Black Metropolis* (1945; rev. ed., 1962), written with St. Clair Drake, is a history and spirited social analysis of the black community in Chicago. Expressing hope for an end to racism to match the defeat of worldwide fascism, the book also exposes the pervasive prejudice and discrimination confronting blacks in Chicago and, by implication, all American blacks. Both works have been praised consistently by critics and authorities, particularly *Black Metropolis*, which won the Anisfield-Wolf Award for 1945. Cayton's periodical essays and reviews reveal sharp perception of the special pressures affecting black figures such as Richard Wright and Paul Robeson. Often ironic and caustic, a journeyer in black, white, and racially mixed worlds, he seems always the maverick, unable finally to be anything but an American black, though doubting that blacks as a group would ever be accepted as equals in their homeland; reminding white Americans during World War II that American blacks were not always displeased by Japanese triumphs over their white enemies in the Pacific; and telling black Americans there was little of the African in them anymore. Though Cayton quarreled bitterly with the fate imposed for so long upon American blacks, he never stopped attempting to better their lives through his research and writing. When he was not flattened by despair, he lived and wrote fully and passionately.

[Cayton had difficulty retaining his papers in the last decades of his life, but those that were still in his possession when he died are now in the Vivian G. Harsh Collection at the Carter Woodson Branch of the Chicago Public Library. The Julius Rosenwald Fund Archive at Fisk University contains limited pertinent materials, and the Chicago Historical Society houses the records of the Parkway Community House during Cayton's term as director. Many of Cayton's letters to Richard Wright are in the Beinecke Library at Yale University.

Works by Cayton not mentioned in the text include "Negro Housing in America," *Social Action*, Apr. 15, 1940; "A Psychological Approach to Race Relations," *Reed College Bulletin*, Nov. 1946; *The Changing Scene*, vol. II of the three-part series Churches and Social Welfare, written with Setsuko Matsunaga Nishi (1955); and "Ideological Forces in the Work of Negro Writers," in Herbert Hill, ed., *Anger and Beyond* (1966).

Arna Bontemps and Jack Conroy, *They Seek a City* (1945), and Bontemps, *We Have Tomorrow* (1945), describe Cayton's family background. See also John H. Bracey, Jr., August Meier, and Elliott Rudwick, eds., *The Black Sociologists* (1971); and Michel Fabre, *The Unfinished Quest of Richard Wright* (1973), and "The Last Quest of Horace Cayton," *Black World* (May 1970). An obituary is in the *New York Times*, Jan. 25, 1970.]

JACK B. MOORE

CHAFFEE, ROGER BRUCE (Feb. 15, 1935–Jan 27, 1967), naval officer and astronaut, was born in Grand Rapids, Mich., the son of Donald L. Chaffee. After graduating from Central High School in Grand Rapids, he attended the Illinois Institute of Technology for one year and then transferred to Purdue University; he received a B.S. in aeronautical engineering in 1957. Commissioned an ensign in the navy that same year, he went through flight training and was subsequently assigned to a photographic squadron in Florida. In January 1963, Chaffee entered the Air Force Institute of Technology to work toward a master's degree. When the National Aeronautics and Space Administration (NASA) announced that it would recruit a third group of astronaut trainees, he applied and was selected on Oct. 18, 1963.

By the time he had completed basic astronaut training, the Gemini program was well under way and Apollo flights were being planned. Like his fellow astronauts, Chaffee was assigned one technical area of primary responsibility, his being flight-control communications systems and spacecraft control systems. On Mar. 21, 1966, he was named to the crew of the first Apollo spacecraft to be tested in flight. He and his wife, Martha Louise Horn, had two children.

For the circumstances of his death, see the article on Virgil Ivan Grissom.

W. D. COMPTON

CHAMBERLIN, EDWARD HASTINGS (May 18, 1899–July 16, 1967), economist and educator, was born in La Conner, Wash., the son of Fred Hastings Chamberlin, a Methodist Episcopal minister, and Irene Dugan. In 1903 his father died and his mother moved the family to Iowa City, Iowa. Chamberlin was editor of his high school yearbook. He also was interested in political affairs and had "a concern for religious life." In 1916 he enrolled at the University of Iowa, where, under the aegis of Frank H. Knight, he became interested in economics. While in college, Chamberlin helped to support his family by writing for the *Iowa City Citizen*; he also contributed to the university newspaper. His studies were interrupted by his service as a second lieutenant in the infantry during World War I, but he received the B.S. in 1920.

In 1922, Chamberlin enrolled at the University of Michigan to study accounting but turned to economics, which he studied with Fred Taylor and Leo Sharfman. He received an M.A. degree in 1924. Later that year he entered Harvard to pursue a Ph.D. degree in economics. On Aug. 16, 1924, he married Marcelle Foubert, a Frenchwoman. Chamberlin converted to Catholicism after their marriage. They had one child.

Chamberlin's doctoral thesis, written under the tutelage of Allyn Young, innovatively analyzed the matters of costs and prices of firms in markets characterized by branded goods and promotional activities. He received his degree in 1927, and his thesis was awarded the David A. Wells Prize (1928). A revised version, published as *The Theory of Monopolistic Competition* (1933), was hailed as a major contribution to microeconomic theory. The book went through eight editions in English and was translated into several languages. In 1929, Chamberlin was named an assistant professor in the Department of History, Government, and Economics at Harvard. He was chairman of the department from 1939 to 1943. During World War II he served as a lieutenant colonel in the Office of Strategic Services.

It was alleged that Chamberlin drew too liberally from the work of his mentors, an allegation spawned by a singular lifelong devotion to his initial subject. Paul A. Samuelson has conjectured that if Chamberlin had died at thirty-five, he would have been mourned as a "Mozart of economics and then no note of anticlimax would have dulled his reputation." The revolutionary aspect of the theory of monopolistic competition as Chamberlin's contribution was specifically underscored by his colleagues at Harvard, and his devotion to the refinement of the theory was applauded by the editor of the volume of essays in his honor.

Until Chamberlin wrote of it, the subject of interfirm rivalry had been largely neglected. In the received wisdom of Alfred Marshall's *Principles of Economics* (1890), the competitive firm, as distinguished from the monopolist, was an atomistic unit unable to influence either price or quality in the marketplace. Matters of pricing, product quality, promotion, and other marketing topics; wages; and personnel management were assumed to be beyond the control of the individual firm. The insight of John Atkinson Hobson, a British economist, in *The Problem of the Unemployed* (1896) that business competition often turned on advantages of promotion rather than production was overlooked until Chamberlin's work.

Chamberlin posited a firm with some ability to attract and maintain patronage through promotional activities for branded products. This monopoly element (the branded product) initially generated high profits, but the firm's inability to prevent rivals from entering the market tended to reduce those profits to a "normal" level. The result was a more or less stable equilibrium with a large number of firms producing at less than capacity because the market was shared by firms with plants constructed to serve larger market shares. Prices were higher than in a market served by numerous firms with undifferentiated wares, but these higher prices yielded only normal profits. This model, which occupied Chamberlin for the rest of his career, was complemented by Joan Robinson's work *The Economics of Imperfect Competition* (1933), which emphasized a market comprising only a few sellers.

Although Chamberlin paid little attention to the public-policy implications of his work, he did not hold himself totally aloof from affairs of state. In 1934 he joined with the Harvard economists Seymour Harris, Joseph Schumpeter, and Edward Mason in writing *The Economics of the Recovery Program*, a book critical of President Franklin D. Roosevelt's National Recovery Administration. In 1945 and 1946, Chamberlin wrote letters to the editor of the *New York Times* dealing with the threat of inflation under policies of the Office of Price

Administration, government railroad rate rulings, wage rates and inflation, and the folly of cutting federal research funds. In 1958 his concern about the adverse effects of labor monopoly power led him to write *The Economic Analysis of Labor Union Power.* In 1959 he served as a consultant to the President's Council of Economic Advisers.

In 1950–1951, Chamberlin taught at the University of Paris and, while in France, lectured at many of the provincial universities. The University of Copenhagen honored him as its Rask-Orsted lecturer in 1951. Chamberlin became David A. Wells Professor in Political Economy in 1951, the post he held until his retirement. His students and peers regarded him as a diligent and effective teacher who used the Socratic method to good advantage. He elected to continue teaching even after he suffered a massive stroke in December 1959, but paralysis forced him to stop four years later.

The American Marketing Association awarded Chamberlin the Paul D. Converse Award in 1953; he was named a Simon Guggenheim Memorial Foundation Fellow in 1958–1959. Other honors included his serving as vice-president of the American Economic Association (1944) and as the editor of the *Quarterly Journal of Economics* (1948–1958). In 1965 the profession bestowed its highest honor on him by making him a Distinguished Fellow of the American Economic Association, and in 1967 he was honored further by colleagues with a book of essays, *Monopolistic Competition Theory: Studies in Impact*, edited by Robert E. Kuenne.

Chamberlin was a member of the American Academy of Arts and Sciences, the Institut Internationale d'Étude et de Documentation en Matière Concurrence Commerciale of Brussels, the Catholic Commission on Intellectual and Cultural Affairs, the Institut de Science Économique Appliquée of France (corresponding member), the American Economic Association, the Royal Economic Society of England, the Catholic Economic Association, and the Real Academia de Ciencias Económicas y Financieras of Barcelona. He died in Cambridge, Mass.

[Chamberlin published forty-eight professional articles, papers, and reviews, and six books, reports, and monographs, including those already mentioned and *The Consumer Services of the Government* (editor, 1936), *Monopoly and Competition and Their Regulation: Papers and Proceedings of a Conference Held by the International Economic Association* (editor, 1954), and *Towards a More General Theory of Value* (1957). Robert Kuenne's preface to the essays in honor of Chamberlin is brief but useful. The *Harvard University Gazette*, Mar. 23, 1968, carried a tribute from his colleagues. Chamberlin's theory is discussed in Mark Blaug, *Economic Theory in Retrospect*, 3rd ed. (1978). Obituaries are in the *New York Times*, July 17, 1967; and the *Harvard Summer News*, July 18, 1967.]

HAROLD L. WATTEL

CHOATE, ANNE HYDE CLARKE (Oct. 27, 1886–May 17, 1967), clubwoman and a leader of the Girl Scout movement, was born at Hyde Hall, her ancestral family home in Cooperstown, N.Y., the daughter of George Hyde Clarke, a lawyer and director of the State Agricultural Experiment Station at Geneva, N.Y., and Mary Gale Carter. Her mother's friend Juliette Gordon Low, founder of the Girl Scouts of America, was both godmother and mentor to young Anne.

After her education at private schools in Albany, N.Y., and Catonsville, Md., Anne Clarke entered New York City society in 1905. A grand tour of the East ended the next year at the home of Mrs. Stanford White in Cambridge, Mass., on the eve of the architect's sensational murder. Anne Clarke later recalled her stay in Cambridge as a "very interesting experience." Juliette Low then invited Anne to travel with her to London, a journey on which they were accompanied by Arthur Osgood Choate, an investment banker and nephew of Judge William G. Choate, founder of the Choate School, and Joseph H. Choate, United States ambassador to the Court of St. James's. Anne Clarke and Arthur Choate became engaged in London. They were married at Cooperstown on Oct. 16, 1907, and moved to his estate in Pleasantville, N.Y. They had five children; three lived to maturity.

In 1915 Juliette Low called upon Choate for help with the new Girl Scout troop in Pleasantville. By 1916 Low had persuaded her to accept election as national vice-president of the Girl Scouts, although Choate protested that her responsibilities as a mother and charity worker did not permit her to take on more.

Choate met James E. Russell, dean of Teachers College, Columbia University, in the fall of 1916. A supporter of American preparedness for war, Russell was a champion of Boy Scouting as a way to increase patriotism and instill discipline. Choate introduced him to Girl Scouting, which he adopted enthusiastically as a cause. Although Low diligently avoided commitments on most social issues (she was particularly opposed to affiliating Girl Scouting with woman suffrage), she, too, had seized upon patriotism and preparedness as themes that could rally support for her movement. With Russell's help, Choate raised money that opened the way for what she called a "tremendous mushroom growth" of Girl Scouting in 1916 and 1917. Meanwhile, she became engrossed in scouting, relishing the training and the camping, and gleefully practicing the skills that were taught to the girls. A friend later recalled that Choate and her associates did not work for the Girl Scouts, "they *were* Girl Scouts."

Her duties as hostess to Lord and Lady Baden-Powell on their first visit to the American Girl Scouts in 1919 exposed Choate to international scouting, which became her passion thereafter. Nevertheless, she succeeded Low as president of the national organization in 1920 and served until 1922. She held the national vice-presidency again from 1922 to 1937, and was honorary vice-president for twenty more years. In addition, she served on the Girl Scouts' board of directors and its executive committee, as well as on the Pleasantville and Westchester County scouting councils. But she concentrated on the international committee, of which she was a member from 1920 to 1955, and on the Juliette Low World Friendship Committee, which she chaired from 1927 to 1955. When in 1939 World War II interrupted plans for an encampment at the Girl Scouts' international chalet in Switzerland, Choate sought to convert that facility into a refuge for displaced children. She was also involved in American efforts to aid civilian victims of the Sino-Japanese War in China.

Another of Choate's interests was historic preservation. She was active in county and state historical societies, and she worked to protect the historic value of her own homes in Cooperstown and Pleasantville. She crusaded to make Juliette Low's birthplace in Savannah, Ga., a historic site, and to maintain it once that goal had been achieved.

Although her husband continued his family's tradition of membership in the Republican party, Choate was an active Democrat. In 1924 she convened a luncheon at the Colony Club in New York City for socially prominent women who endorsed the presidential candidacy of David F. Houston, a former secretary of agriculture and secretary of the treasury under Woodrow Wilson. An opponent of the Ku Klux Klan, Houston briefly attracted attention as a possible compromise candidate who might break the disastrous deadlock at the 1924 Democratic National Convention in New York City. While she never again took as prominent a political role as she did in Houston's brief campaign, Choate was personally close to other women with noteworthy political careers. It was Choate to whom Eleanor Roosevelt confided her concern about Secretary of Labor Frances Perkins, Choate's close friend, when Perkins faced threats of impeachment from conservative opponents.

When resting from her work, Choate returned to Pleasantville and her hobbies of horseback riding and English country dancing, the latter a pastime she learned at a Girl Scout training camp and which she valued because it demanded good posture. Tall and athletic, she loved to ride sidesaddle, which she found "much the best way; safer when you take the jumps and more elegant, too." She took up fox hunting at the age of forty-six, continuing well into her sixties. Widowed in 1962, she sold some of her estate to nearby Pace College but retained the right to ride over the jumps on the land. Choate deeply regretted the property's acquisition by the local public-school district a year later. She continued to ride almost daily until a fall from her horse in January 1967 left her with a broken clavicle and ended her jumping days in her eighty-first year. That accident came soon after her return from a Girl Scout conference in Tokyo that she had insisted on attending, as she had attended earlier meetings around the world. She was described then, and surely she thought of herself, as "the oldest Girl Scout in the United States." She died in Pleasantville, N.Y.

[An interview with Choate, conducted by Ethel Dermady in January 1967, is located at the Girl Scouts of the United States of America Historical Project. See Anne H. Choate and Helen Ferris, eds., *Juliette Low and the Girl Scouts* (1928); and *New York Times*, Mar. 12, 1967. See also the obituary, *New York Times*, May 18, 1967.]

RICHARD A. HARRISON

CICOTTE, EDWARD VICTOR (June 19, 1884–May 5, 1969), baseball pitcher, was born in Detroit, Mich., the son of Ambrose Cicotte, a railroad foreman, and Archangel Cicotte. He completed eight years of schooling at St. Anne's Elementary School in Detroit and then worked as a plumber's helper and a furrier and pitched sandlot baseball in the Detroit area. A promising pitcher and right-handed thrower, he was signed by the Detroit Tigers in 1905, but spent most of that season in Augusta, Ga., in the South Atlantic League. There he played with Ty Cobb, whom he recommended as a good prospect to the Tiger management. Late in the 1905 season, Cicotte pitched for Detroit but was released after appearing in three games; his size (five feet, five inches) was a factor in his release. Cicotte spent the next two seasons pitching in the minor leagues. On May 19, 1905, he married Rose Freer; they had three children.

In 1908 Cicotte was acquired by the Boston Red Sox and thus began a thirteen-year major-league career. His four seasons with the team produced a 51–45 win-loss record, but his low earned-run average (ERA) was excellent. The Red Sox were en route to a world championship in 1912 when Cicotte was traded to the mediocre Chicago White Sox. Five years later, however, owner Charles Comiskey assembled a championship White Sox team with Cicotte as its ace pitcher.

A crafty pitcher, Cicotte mastered a variety of deliveries, including a spitball and his mysterious "shine ball." Opposing batters like Ty Cobb feared the shine ball, which Cicotte delivered after first rubbing the ball on his flannel uniform. According to Cobb, the pitch "arrived at the plate looking like nothing. . . . Yet it was almost impossible to get the bat on the pitch." Cicotte also enjoyed excellent control; only once in his major-league career did he issue as many as 80 bases on balls in a season, and during the seasons of 1918 and 1919 he issued only 97 walks in 556 innings.

In 1917 and again in 1919, with Cicotte winning fifty-seven games, the White Sox won two American League pennants and a World Series. Cicotte's lifetime pitching record, compiled over fourteen seasons, included a 210–148 win-loss record, a 2.37 ERA, 36 shutouts, and 1,374 strikeouts. In his two World Series appearances he won two games and lost three.

Were it not for Cicotte's involvement in the notorious 1919 "Black Sox scandal," such feats might have won him a place in the Baseball Hall of Fame. However, Cicotte admitted to being one of eight White Sox players who were involved in a conspiracy with gamblers to throw the 1919 World Series to the opposing Cincinnati Reds and were thereafter stigmatized as "Black Sox." For his motive, Cicotte blamed owner Comiskey's stingy salary policy; he had received less than $6,000 in salary in 1919. After Comiskey rejected a plea from some of the players for more money, White Sox first baseman Charles ("Chick") Gandil used his contacts with gamblers to hatch the plot. Cicotte joined Gandil's conspiracy in July and helped to recruit others. Eventually Gandil, Cicotte, Joe Jackson, Swede Risberg, Lefty Claude Williams, Buck Weaver, Happy Felsch, and Fred McMullen were involved. Cicotte admitted getting $10,000 of the $100,000 put up by the gamblers and said he used his share to pay off a $4,000 mortgage on his farm.

The scandal came to light only after the heavily favored White Sox lost the series. The plot was a poorly kept secret and rumors were rife. Investigations frightened Cicotte into admitting his role and naming others. Late in September 1920, Cicotte told a Cook County, Ill., grand jury how he helped to throw the first game of the series, which the White Sox lost 8–1, by pitching ineffectively and how his two costly errors helped lose the fourth game by a 2–0 score. Cicotte's confession was followed by teammate Jackson's and led to the suspension of the eight accused players. At the time of the suspensions the White Sox were in the thick of the 1920 pennant race and Cicotte's pitching record was 20–10.

The highly publicized scandal rocked baseball, prompting officials to replace the game's governing national commission with a high commissioner. Federal District Court Judge Kenesaw Mountain Landis accepted the post and took office in January 1921, charged with the task of cleaning up the game's tarnished image. During the following summer seven of the eight accused White Sox players were indicted on charges of conspiracy to commit a confidence game and tried in Chicago. During the much-criticized proceedings, Cicotte and others repudiated their confessions after those and other grand jury records were mysteriously lost. As a result, the jury returned not-guilty verdicts for the seven indicted players.

However, none of the eight accused players ever again played in the major leagues. Commissioner Landis immediately barred the eight men from organized baseball, but over the years his ruling has been much criticized. His harsh edict deprived the players of their civil rights and cast them as lifelong pariahs; as such, they became a part of American folklore.

Cicotte lived most of the rest of his life in semiseclusion on his small farm near Detroit. He worked as a game warden and in the Service Department of the Ford Motor Company. Retiring from Ford in 1944, he spent his last years growing strawberries. In one of his rare interviews, he admitted his guilt, adding, "I've tried to make up for it by living as clean a life as I could. . . . Everybody who has ever lived has committed sins." He died in Detroit.

[The Baseball Library at Cooperstown, N.Y., has an extensive clippings file on Cicotte. See Fred Lieb, *The Story of the World Series* (1949); Eliot Asinof, *Eight Men Out* (1963); Victor Luhr, *The Great Baseball Mystery* (1966); Harold Seymour, *Baseball* (1971); David Q. Voigt, *America Through Baseball* (1976); and Richard C. Crepeau, *Baseball* (1980). An obituary is in the *New York Times*, May 9, 1969.]

DAVID Q. VOIGT

CLARK, FELTON GRANDISON (Oct. 13, 1903–July 5, 1970), educator, was born in Baton Rouge, La., the son of Joseph Samuel Clark, the founder and first president of Southern University in Baton Rouge, and Octavia Eleanor Head. Clark received his early education at Baton Rouge College. In 1922 he graduated from Southern University (High School Department), with a two-year diploma. He received a B.A. (1924) from Beloit College in Wisconsin. His M.A. (1925) and Ph.D. (1933) were awarded by Columbia University.

Clark taught at Wiley College in Marshall, Tex. (1925–1927), Southern University (1927–1930), and Howard University (1931–1933) until he returned to Southern in 1934 as dean of the university. In 1938, Clark succeeded his father as president of Southern University, a post he held until 1969.

Clark's doctoral dissertation gave direction to his career as a university president. He wrote, "Despite the fact that the Negro is a member of a segregated, underprivileged, minority group in American life, his state-supported institutions of higher education have been externally controlled in accordance with principles designed for the group at large." Among his several conclusions is the recommendation that "schemes for control of state-supported higher-education of Negroes should provide for direct representation of the Negro group." Clark presided at the Land Grant College Presidents' Conference in 1940 and again in 1941 and championed the visibility of blacks at local, state, and national levels.

Southern University grew and prospered during the thirty-one years of Clark's leadership. In 1938, Southern had 40 buildings, 139 faculty members, and more than 1,500 students. While he was president the university added campuses at New Orleans in 1956 and in Shreveport in 1964. In addition, new programs and new degrees were added to the university's offerings. A law school offering the LL.B. was established in 1948, and ten years later a graduate-degree program was founded. At the time of Clark's retirement in 1969, the university's physical plant was valued at $52 million, it had an annual budget of $12 million, and more than 11,000 students were enrolled.

Clark's major challenge came when he was placed in the difficult position of apparently quelling attempts at integration. On Mar. 28, 1960, seven Southern University students protested segregation by sitting at the S. H. Kress variety-store lunch counter in Baton Rouge and were arrested. The next day brought more sit-ins and more arrests. To protest the arrests, thousands of students marched through the streets, and Clark, bowing to the demands of Governor Earl K. Long, suspended eighteen students. Hundreds of students withdrew from the university. Clark closed the university in 1962 for a short time because of racial conflict. Later, under Clark's guidance, the university was enlarged and Clark attracted a number of industrial firms to Louisiana and encouraged their managers to hire graduates of the university.

While president of the university, Clark served on a number of national bodies. He was a member of several committees in the Education Department, including the National Conference of Problems of Education of Negroes (1934), the advisory committee of the Graduate Fellowship Section of the Division of Higher

Education (1936–1937), an advisory panel on educational statistics (1954–1960), and the advisory committee on Federal Programs on Higher Education (1961–1963). He served as a consultant to the Educational Policies Commission of the Office of Education (1946–1950); he directed the National Survey of Vocational Education and Guidance of Negroes (1936–1938), and he was a member of the Board of Foreign Scholarships (1956–1963). Clark was also active, nationally and internationally, in the Young Men's Christian Association.

Clark said at his retirement, "Back in the early days, the students had a feeling the students should not stand as tall as they were capable. But now they see themselves as human beings endowed with all the qualities of any man. Up until recently, the Negro has had to think about food and shelter before astronomy and physics. You can't do much creating while digging a ditch. Now Negroes are working in the chemical labs instead of sweeping them out."

Clark married Allene J. Knighten on Aug. 22, 1958; they had no children. He died in New Orleans.

[The Felton G. Clark Collection at Southern University contains papers covering 1938–1968, including minutes of meetings, files, campus publications, books, artifacts, and photographs. Clark's published writings include "Administrative Control of Public Negro Colleges," *Journal of Negro Education*, 3 (1934); "The Control of State-Supported Teacher-Training Programs for Negroes" (Ph.D. diss., Columbia University, 1934); "Findings of the Conference of Presidents of Negro Land-Grant Colleges," *School and Society*, 52 (1940); "Negro Higher Education and Some Fundamental Issues Raised by World War II," *Journal of Negro Education*, 11 (1942); "Four Barriers to Higher Education," *National Education Association Journal*, 40 (1951); and "Development and Present Status of Publicly Supported Higher Education for Negroes," *Journal of Negro Education*, 27, no. 3 (1958). An obituary is in the *New York Times*, July 6, 1970.]

JACOB L. SUSSKIND

CLARK, GRENVILLE (Nov. 5, 1882–Jan. 13, 1967), peace advocate, was born in New York City, the son of Louis Crawford Clark, a business banker, and Marian deForest Cannon, whose father, Le Grand Bouton Cannon, was a railroad builder and early Republican party supporter. Clark was raised in wealthy circumstances and attended Harvard University, from which he graduated in 1903. After earning his law degree at Harvard three years later, he entered the New York City law firm of Carter, Ledyard and Milburn, where Franklin D. Roosevelt also served as a clerk. Although a generalist in law and not outstanding for brilliant legal readings and innovations, Clark gained a reputation for energy, hard work, and results. In 1909 he set up a law firm with two college friends, Elihu Root, Jr., son of the United States secretary of state, and Francis W. Bird, who encouraged Clark in Republican affairs. Tall, athletic, and with a jutting jaw, Clark proved formidable in advancing his interests, which soon involved Bull Moose politics and Harvard. (He was later on the seven-man corporation that governed the university.)

In 1915, with Europe already involved in World War I and American military forces understaffed, Clark became a founder, and then secretary, of the Military Training Camps Association. The effort was supported by the army chief of staff, Major General Leonard Wood, and other preparedness advocates but was denounced by radicals as a rich man's patriotic charade. Attention focused on the elite Plattsburgh, N.Y., training camp, which attracted many professionals and businessmen. However, the association, in fourteen locations across the country, trained an urgently required 16,000 or more officers. It was estimated that 80 percent of the American combat officers in World War I came from the camps. The association was a forerunner of the Reserve Officers Training Corps.

Clark served as a lieutenant colonel in the adjutant general's office, where he was responsible for the recruitment and training of 130,000 technicians. While he supported President Woodrow Wilson's emphasis on preparedness, he also believed that peace demanded forceful efforts and evident gains. Clark opposed selective service in peacetime, and during the 1930's he espoused world-government proposals, which evolved into larger plans for peace based on world law. In 1940 Clark became chairman of the National Emergency Committee for Selective Service, for which he wrote the Selective Service Act of that year; and in 1944–1945 he chaired the Citizens Committee for National War Service.

Although Clark received a number of public

awards, including the Distinguished Service Medal, he kept a low public profile, preferring to stay behind the scenes and help advance others. He interested John Foster Dulles in Clarence Streit's "Union Now" program, which would have limited national sovereignty in a union of free states. He contributed a book, *A Federation of Free Peoples* (1939), to the cause. With Felix Frankfurter, a friend from law school, Clark was influential in the appointment of Henry L. Stimson as secretary of war in 1940. Clark also gained the appointment of John J. McCloy as a disarmament adviser to the War Department and kept close watch through associates on United Nations issues. Clark's World Law Fund issued innumerable publications, and he subsidized many others covering aspects of war and peace. He became famous among policymakers for his telephone calls around the world, through which he put pressure on administrators and heads of state to direct peacemaking efforts.

Clark's most durable work was prompted by the explosion of the atom bomb in 1945. He held a conference of prominent persons at his Dublin, N.H., home. Working closely for many years with Louis B. Sohn, a Harvard law professor, he explored means for ensuring peace through law. *A Plan for Peace* (1950) grew into Clark and Sohn's privately printed *Peace Through Disarmament and Charter Review*, which involved detailed proposals for revision of the UN Charter, including compulsory membership. Clark distributed 2,000 of the 3,000 copies to influential people throughout the world. A digest of this work by Robert H. Reno was widely read. Clark and Sohn's proposal encompassed courts, a revenue system, privileges and incentives, and a bill of rights. The book became *World Peace Through World Law: Two Alternative Plans* (1958). One plan was based on a revision of the UN Charter; the other projected "a new world security and development organization" that would supplement the work of the UN. Although the book did not lead to control of military outbreaks and armed conflict, many agreed that no future peace efforts could be made without recourse to the Clark-Sohn texts.

Clark's social interests extended into government and beyond. He fought Franklin D. Roosevelt's Court-packing plan in 1937, through a committee comprising lawyers who had voted for Roosevelt in 1932 and 1936. Civil rights were a major cause throughout Clark's career. In October 1961 he provided $20,000 bail for blacks arrested in freedom-ride cases. Indifferent to accusations of leftist sympathies, he affirmed the right of academic freedom for known partisans and worked with the National Emergency Civil Liberties Committee on related issues. In his will he left $500,000 to the NAACP Legal Defense Fund and $750,000 to the World Law Fund. Certain that a world at peace would require accommodation with the Soviet Union and the People's Republic of China, he discussed peace freely with representatives and friends of both nations. In 1960 he sponsored a Soviet-American conference.

Clark's private life included a variety of interests, ranging from bird-watching to Harvard affairs. His first wife, Fanny Pickman Dwight, died in 1965; they had five children. His second wife was Mary Brush, the widow of the painter William James. In the 1960's Clark suffered from a lymphatic and throat condition. Earlier ailments had caused him to give up his law practices from 1946 to 1953, and later heart ailments forced him to curtail visits to New York. Friends discussed a campaign for Clark to receive a Nobel Prize, an effort that he first opposed but then agreed to, in order to publicize his peace proposals. His deteriorating health, however, slowed efforts in that direction. He died at his home in Dublin, N.H. No Nobel Peace Prize was given in 1967.

[Clark's papers are at Dartmouth College Library; they comprise an inventory of fifteen microfiches (n.d.) and include an introduction by J. Garry Clifford. Clark's daughter, Mary Clark Dimond, collected essays regarding his life and work in *Memoirs of a Man* (1975), edited by Norman Cousins and J. Garry Clifford. Samuel R. Spencer, Jr., composed an incomplete volume of memoirs concerning Clark as a follow-up to "Clark and the Selective Training Service Act of 1940" (Ph.D. diss., Harvard University, 1947). See Irving Dilliard, "Grenville Clark: Public Citizen," *American Scholar*, Winter, 1963–1964. An obituary is in the *New York Times*, Jan. 13, 1967.]

LOUIS FILLER

CLAYTON, WILLIAM LOCKHART (Feb. 7, 1880–Feb. 8, 1966), business executive and government official, was born near Tupelo, Miss., the son of James Monroe Clayton, a cotton farmer, and Martha Fletcher Burdine. In 1886 the family moved to Jackson, Tenn., where James Clayton had contracted to build a railroad bed. Hard times followed and William Clayton left school at the age of thirteen to work as a clerk. His remarkable proficiency in stenography attracted the attention of Jerome Hill, a cotton merchant from St. Louis, and Clayton went there as Hill's private secretary. In 1896 he moved to New York City to work for the American Cotton Company, rising to the position of assistant general manager by 1904. He married Sue Vaughan on Aug. 14, 1902; they had four children.

On Aug. 1, 1904, Clayton joined his brother-in-law, Frank Anderson, and Anderson's brother, Monroe, in founding Anderson, Clayton and Company, a cotton marketing firm located in Oklahoma City. In 1905 Clayton's brother, Benjamin, also became a partner. The company's headquarters were moved to Houston in 1916 in order to take advantage of the port facilities there. In the next fifteen years the company grew to be the largest cotton-trading enterprise in the world, with branches in several major United States cities and with a number of foreign subsidiaries. America's dominant financial position after World War I provided the capital that Anderson, Clayton and Company needed for expansion into markets formerly controlled by European cotton brokers. By World War II the company was handling 15 percent of the United States cotton crop, and Clayton, who had become chairman of the board in 1920, was acknowledged as one of the country's most successful business leaders.

Clayton's first government service came in 1918 as a member of the Cotton Distribution Committee, part of the War Industries Board, headed by Bernard Baruch. A lifelong Democrat, Clayton remained out of public life in the 1920's and 1930's. In 1934 and 1935 he was associated with the anti–New Deal Liberty League because of his opposition to New Deal agricultural policies, but Secretary of State Cordell Hull's liberal international trade policy revived Clayton's loyalty to the Roosevelt administration, and he publicly supported Roosevelt's reelection in 1936.

In October 1940 Clayton reentered government service as an official of the Reconstruction Finance Corporation with the title of deputy federal loan administrator, and also as a vice-president of the Export-Import Bank. Working under his good friend and fellow Texan Jesse Jones, Clayton was responsible for overseas procurement of materials connected with strategic defense needs. He was particularly effective in his work with the United States Commercial Company, which was entrusted with the task of purchasing large quantities of critical materials, thus denying these goods to the Germans. An administrative shuffle in 1942 brought Clayton to the post of assistant secretary of commerce, although his responsibilities remained much the same. In the summer of 1943 he was placed under the authority of Vice-President Henry Wallace, who headed the Board of Economic Warfare. Unable to get along with Wallace, Clayton resigned in January 1944.

In February 1944, upon the urging of Bernard Baruch, Clayton was named Surplus War Property Administrator under the direction of James F. Byrnes and the Office of War Mobilization. Here Clayton had final authority over the sale and disposal of surplus war plants, equipment, and food. This was a controversial post because of the special interests involved, and Clayton resigned on Dec. 1, 1944, after a dispute with congressional leaders over the nature of agency administration.

On December 20 the Senate confirmed Clayton as assistant secretary of state for economic affairs. Over the next three years as assistant and, in 1946, undersecretary of state, Clayton made valuable contributions as the most significant economic foreign-policy maker in the Truman administration. At the Mexico City Conference in February 1945, Clayton promoted equal access to trade and raw materials, lower tariffs, and the elimination of economic nationalism. He struck a theme that formed the basis of his economic negotiations elsewhere: that steps should be taken whenever and wherever possible to produce the greatest degree of free trade among nations. At the Potsdam Conference in July 1945, Clayton was head of the Reparations Committee and worked out a compromise formula with the Soviet delegates concerning the value of dismantled German industrial facilities to which the USSR would be entitled.

His postwar travels in Europe convinced Clayton that the economic recovery of America's wartime allies could be accomplished only with a large amount of American aid. To this end he worked hard to induce Congress to appropriate substantial funds for the United Nations Relief and Rehabilitation Administration (UNRRA) in 1945 and 1946. He was also the principal United States negotiator in an important Anglo-American trade agreement, signed in December 1945, in which the British received a $3.75 billion loan at 2 percent interest. In return the British accepted a set of trade principles designed to weaken imperial preference and other forms of trade discrimination and to make possible freer trade with the United States. Clayton's effective lobbying with Congress was of great importance in securing ratification of the agreement in 1946.

In early 1947, while in Europe participating in the General Agreement for Trade and Tariffs (GATT) negotiations, Clayton was shocked at the severity of the economic crisis on the Continent. Believing that the free-world economy was in jeopardy because of the preponderant strength of the American economy, Clayton concluded that the United States was obliged to both restore international economic balance and help preserve democracy in the free world. He strongly supported the aid to Greece and Turkey that comprised the Truman Doctrine, and in late May, returning from another trip to Europe, he wrote a memorandum urging that the United States transfer to Europe surplus goods and services in the amount of $6 million to $7 million over a three-year period. Priority would be given to essential items such as coal, food, and cotton, and their use would be based on a plan worked out by the Europeans themselves.

This memorandum found its way to Charles E. Bohlen, the State Department official who drafted Secretary of State George C. Marshall's famous speech at Harvard University on June 5, 1947, in which he outlined what became known as the Marshall Plan. For this reason, some historians have credited Clayton with being the "father of the Marshall Plan," although others point out that Marshall's speech incorporated not only Clayton's memorandum, but also one by George Kennan of the State Department's Policy Planning Committee, as well as some ideas of Dean Acheson. At any rate, Clayton was sent to Britain and France to explain the new direction of American foreign policy; he was later involved in the planning talks held in Paris in August. There he made a key concession to the French regarding international control of Ruhr coal, coke, and steel production.

Clayton's last major service for the State Department was his participation in the November 1947 Havana Conference to establish the International Trade Organization (ITO), a multilateral body dedicated to the elimination of international trade barriers. Although the goal was important to Clayton, the agreement worked out in Havana was unacceptable to Congress, which felt that the free-trade character of the ITO had been too greatly diluted by political compromises.

In late 1948 Clayton returned to Houston and Anderson, Clayton and Company, where he remained until 1961, overseeing the company's diversification into food processing, manufacturing, and insurance. He became involved with the Atlantic Union, an organization devoted to the creation of a much more closely knit free world centered around the North Atlantic Treaty Organization (NATO) alliance. In this forum Clayton stressed the importance of economic cooperation in the struggle against Communism, a struggle he felt was primarily economic rather than military. He remained active in these endeavors until shortly before his death in Houston.

Tall, courteous, and soft-spoken, Clayton was a model of southern courtliness. But his fierce adherence to the principles of free trade and economic cooperation among the Western allies, and his effectiveness as both an international negotiator and an administration lobbyist with Congress, earned him an important place in the making of postwar foreign policy.

[Clayton's papers are at Rice University, Houston, Tex. Other collections are at the Truman Library, Independence, Mo.; the National Archives, Washington, D.C.; and the Cossitt Library, Memphis, Tenn. See also Ellen Clayton Garwood, *Will Clayton* (1958); Fredrick J. Dobney, ed., *Selected Papers of Will Clayton* (1971); David G. McComb, *Houston* (1981); Jordan A. Schwartz, *The Speculator* (1981); and Alan S. Milward, *The Reconstruction of Western Europe, 1945–1951* (1984). See also the obituary, *New York Times*, Feb. 9, 1966.]

JOHN E. FINDLING

CLEMENT, FRANK GOAD (June 2, 1920–Nov. 4, 1969), governor of Tennessee, was born in Dickson, Tenn., the son of Robert Samuel Clement, a lawyer, and Maybelle Goad. Reared in hard times in a deeply religious fundamentalist Christian household, Clement became a political populist and a devout "Bible toter" at an early age. He also developed a special talent for old-style oratory with the help of his father's half-sister, Dockie Shipp Weems. While other schoolboys dreamed of success in sports or country music, Clement's ambition was to become governor of Tennessee.

After attending public schools in Kentucky and Tennessee, Clement entered Cumberland University in 1937. A young man in a hurry, he transferred to Vanderbilt Law School in 1939 and passed the state bar in 1941. The following year, he received his LL.B. On Jan. 6, 1940, Clement married Lucille Laverne Christianson, the daughter of a lumber dealer and politician; they had three children.

Clement eschewed private practice and became an agent for the Federal Bureau of Investigation, working on wartime internal security and selective-service cases out of the bureau's Chicago office. He was inducted into the army as a private in November 1943 and was discharged in 1946 a first lieutenant and commander of a military police battalion in Texas. Upon his return home, political friends maneuvered Clement's appointment as general counsel for the Tennessee Railroad and Public Utilities Commission. Serving from 1946 to 1950, he gained a reputation as a "people's lawyer" for his handling of rate cases. At the same time, Clement took on numerous civic and charitable tasks. In addition to becoming a popular speaker on the high school commencement circuit, he was chairman of the Young Democrats of Tennessee and of the state March of Dimes and was chosen state commander of the American Legion, all in a relatively short span.

In 1950, just as Clement was preparing to make a bid for the governorship, the Korean War intervened, and he was called back into the army. Before he left, he announced his intention to run for governor in 1952. As in World War II, Clement was spared from overseas duty and became a civilian again in late 1951. He immediately mounted a campaign against Governor Gordon Browning, who had served six terms in Congress as well as three two-year gubernatorial terms. Clement proved successful in courting the state's teachers as well as Ed Crump of Memphis, one of the last great machine bosses, and other foes of Browning. As a result, the challenger defeated the incumbent impressively (47 percent to 38 percent) in the Democratic primary. He then won the general election by the largest popular vote in Tennessee history to become, at thirty-two, the youngest governor in the United States. In 1954, Clement captured 68 percent of the vote in a primary rematch with Browning and went on to win Tennessee's first constitutionally mandated four-year term.

Clement was a forceful, charismatic campaigner whose rhetorical repertoire included florid biblical phrases, matter-of-fact indictments of opponents' records, and substantial plans of action for Tennessee. He often wore white linen suits to speak at rallies, which had all of the fervor of evangelistic revival meetings. When critics questioned his unabashed religiosity on the stump, Clement generally responded, "If a man's religion and politics don't mix, there is something wrong with his politics."

As governor, Clement was regarded as a liberal social spender by conservative Tennessee standards. In his first term, he engineered a $5 million bond issue for free textbooks for schoolchildren, created a new department of mental health and a division of services for the blind, and worked to increase teachers' salaries, old-age pensions, and aid to the disabled. The trend toward expansion of services continued in Clement's four-year term. As a result, the state debt limit had to be raised more than once and the sales tax had to be boosted.

After the United States Supreme Court's decision on school integration in *Brown* v. *Board of Education* (1954), racial tension in Tennessee heightened. Adopting a moderate stance, Clement vetoed hard-line segregationist bills sent to him and authorized the National Guard to help restore order in the town of Clinton, where white rioting had occurred during the implementation of a federal judge's desegregation order in the late summer of 1956. In 1957, in an eloquent speech before the legislature, Clement told Tennesseans, "We must not overlook that the Negro is equal to the white in the eyes of the law and in the sight of God." At the same time, however, Clement promoted legislation providing for educational choice for whites, clearly violating the spirit of the *Brown* ruling.

In 1956, Clement won the assignment of delivering the keynote address at the Democratic National Convention in Chicago in August. He hoped that a rousing performance might bring him the vice-presidential nomination, as Alben Barkley's keynote address had earned him the nomination in 1948. In his familiar bombastic style ("How long, oh how long, America?"), Clement recited a long litany of sins allegedly committed by the "opposition party of privilege and pillage." Especially notable was his portrayal of the Eisenhower-Nixon ticket as the "vice-hatchetman slinging slander and spreading half-truths while the Top Man peers down the green fairways of indifference." Clement received only mixed reviews for his speech and lost out to a Tennessee rival, Senator Estes Kefauver, in the race to be Adlai Stevenson's running mate.

Forbidden by law to succeed himself, Clement endorsed the gubernatorial candidacy of his longtime campaign manager and commissioner of agriculture, Buford Ellington, who prevailed in the election of 1958. Virtually ignored during the fiscally conservative Ellington years, Clement returned to the political wars in 1962, securing a third term as governor by defeating two opponents in the Democratic primary and besting retired *Nautilus* commander William Anderson, an independent candidate, in the final election. Clement's agenda again called for substantially increased spending for education and social services. Consequently, he had to guide through the legislature an extremely unpopular revenue package that included a sales tax on utilities. He also appointed a racially mixed human-relations commission and made a serious effort to find places for blacks in his administration. Still, he failed to sign a state code of fair practices drawn up by his own commission in 1964 in the midst of the critical struggle for passage of federal civil rights legislation. An interesting highlight of Clement's last term was his impassioned crusade against the death penalty. After fruitlessly proposing its abolition in the legislature, he commuted the sentences of five men facing execution.

In 1964, Clement entered the race to fill out the remaining two years of the term of Senator Kefauver, who had died in 1963. Clement lost narrowly to Congressman Ross Bass in the Democratic primary because white voters were alienated by the utilities tax and black voters were repelled by the rejection of the fair-practices code. Clement tried again in 1966 and upset Senator Bass in the primary. Clement was in turn upset in the general election by Howard Baker, Jr., the scion of a family of Republican lawyer-politicians and son-in-law of United States Senate minority leader Everett Dirksen. Baker benefited from steady Republican advances in Tennessee over the years, and his cool urbanity seemed better suited to the age of television than Clement's unbridled passion. Clement took his defeats hard and never completely resigned himself to private law practice. Before he could make another political comeback, however, he died in an automobile accident in Nashville.

[Clement's papers are at the Tennessee State Library and Archives, Nashville. There is also a collection of Clement manuscripts at his birthplace in Dickson. Clement's 1956 keynote address is in *Vital Speeches of the Day*, Sept. 1, 1956. A full-scale biographical study of Clement is Lee Seifert Greene, *Lead Me On* (1982). See also Stephen D. Boyd, "The Campaign Speaking of Frank Clement in the 1954 Democratic Primary: Field Study and Rhetorical Analysis" (Ph.D. diss., University of Illinois, 1972); and James Bailey Gardner, "Political Leadership in a Period of Transition: Frank G. Clement, Albert Gore, Estes Kefauver and Tennessee Politics, 1948–1956" (Ph.D. diss., Vanderbilt University, 1978). Articles on Clement include Harold H. Martin, "The Things They Say About the Governor," *Saturday Evening Post*, Jan. 29, 1955; Wilma Dykeman, "Too Much Talent in Tennessee?" *Harper's*, Mar. 1955; C. Arthur Larson, "Frank Clement: Governor for God," *American Mercury*, 1956; "The Keynoter: What Makes Him Run," *Newsweek*, Apr. 13, 1956; Flora Schreiber, "Frank Clement: Tennessee's Political Evangelist," *Coronet*, July 1956; Noel E. Parmentel, Jr., "Tennessee Spellbinder: Clement Runs on Time," *Nation*, Aug. 11, 1956; "Ole Frank," *Time*, Aug. 10, 1962; Bill Kovach, "Racism Wasn't the Issue in Tennessee," *Reporter*, Sept. 24, 1964; Stephen D. Boyd, "Delivery in the Campaign Speaking of Frank Clement," *Southern Speech Communication Journal*, Spring 1974; William L. Davis, "Frank Clement: The First Campaign," *Tennessee Historical Quarterly*, Spring 1976; and Robert E. Corlew III, "Frank Goad Clement and the Keynote Address of 1956," *Tennessee Historical Quarterly*, Spring 1977. Accounts of Clement's death and obituaries are in the *Nashville Banner* and the *Nashville Tennessean*, both Nov. 5–7, 1969. An obituary is in the *New York Times*, Nov. 5, 1969.]

RICHARD H. GENTILE

CLEMENT, MARTIN WITHINGTON (Dec. 5, 1881–Aug. 30, 1966), railroad executive, was born in Sunbury, Pa., the son of Charles Maxwell Clement, a lawyer, and Alice Virginia Withington. After graduating from Trinity College with a B.S. in 1901, Clement joined the engineering staff of the Pennsylvania Railroad (PRR) in New York City, where he participated in surveying tunnels the company was building under the Hudson River. On Apr. 14, 1910, he married Irene Harrison Higbee; they had three children. His wife died in 1929, and on Feb. 14, 1931, he married Elizabeth Wallace.

Clement was promoted to track supervisor in the office of the general manager in Philadelphia in 1910. He held the same post on the PRR Manhattan and Pittsburgh divisions in 1913 and, the following year, was named division engineer of the New York, Philadelphia and Norfolk Railroad, a PRR subsidiary. In 1916 he became chief engineer of the heavily traveled New Jersey division. Two years later, when the PRR was controlled by the United States Railroad Administration, Clement was appointed superintendent of freight transportation for lines east of Pittsburgh, his first nonengineering assignment. The next year, he served as lines-east superintendent of passenger traffic, and in 1920, when the railroad was returned to private control, he was named superintendent of the Lake Division, with headquarters in Cleveland.

His rapid advance through the operating ranks continued in 1923, when he moved to Pittsburgh as general manager of the PRR Central Region, which encompassed divisions from Crestline, Ohio, to Altoona, Pa. Two years later he returned to the PRR general offices in Philadelphia as assistant vice-president in charge of operations. In that capacity and as vice-president in charge of operations from 1926 to 1933, Clement had systemwide responsibility for the efficient running of trains. In October 1933 he became vice-president, with jurisdiction over all departments of the railroad.

The poor health of William Wallace Atterbury, the PRR president, led to Clement being named acting president in 1934 and, following Atterbury's resignation in April 1935, president. Clement served in that post until 1949, when he became the first chairman of the board, a position fashioned largely by Clement himself. As chairman he served as a spokesman for the PRR and the entire railroad industry on issues of political, financial, and public interest. The president of the PRR (Walter S. Franklin was Clement's immediate successor) thereafter handled routine operations. This arrangement lasted through the Penn Central era (1968–1976).

Clement retired in 1951 and spent his remaining years at his Rosemont estate, Crefeld, in suburban Philadelphia.

Clement was one of the most skillful of America's railway managers. He resembled Atterbury and virtually all previous PRR presidents in that he had spent most of his career as an engineer and operating man. By the time he became chief executive, he had acquired an intimate knowledge of all aspects of running what by most standards was the nation's largest railroad. Also in keeping with PRR tradition, Clement ruled in a dictatorial manner. He had a large, hulking frame and an equally formidable will. "Imposing in presence, positive in opinion, quick in decision, and unrelenting in drive—the complete generalissimo," was the way *Fortune* characterized him in 1948.

As vice-president of operations, Clement directed one of the largest capital improvement programs in railroad history—the electrification of the PRR mainline between New York and Philadelphia. Atterbury had inaugurated the project in 1928, but his attention had been diverted by proposals for railroad consolidations then under consideration in industry and government circles and by the financial exigencies of the Great Depression. It was left to Clement to implement the electrification scheme, as well as to pare operating expenditures. Subsequent reductions helped placed the PRR among the relatively few lines that remained profitable.

Early in Clement's presidency, the railroad reached its peak of efficiency, posting an operating ratio of 71.2 percent in 1939. Clement also presided over extensions of electrification from Philadelphia west to Harrisburg, improved passenger service (for example, most cars on through trains received air-conditioning), and expanded the PRR trucking business. At the height of World War II, in what was one of its finest hours, the railroad carried twice the freight tonnage and four times the passengers that it had carried in 1939, without the kind of congestion that had brought rail traffic to a standstill in World War I. However, aside from electrification, capital improvements lagged; Clement followed a financially conservative course that favored debt reduction over modernization of the physical plant. The PRR did not begin large-scale replacement of steam locomotives with diesels until 1947, by which time 80 percent of its 4,500-unit steam fleet was more than twenty years old. The higher costs of using obsolete motive power, combined with a failure to renew a physical plant worn out by heavy war traffic, were among the reasons why the railroad suffered the first annual deficit ($8.5 million) in its history in 1946—ironically, its centennial year.

Although not as prominent an industry spokesman as Atterbury, Clement did serve on several Association of American Railroads and government committees examining problems relating to railroad retirement, labor relations, and government regulation. In 1938, President Franklin D. Roosevelt appointed him to the joint labor-management Committee of Six, whose recommendations contributed to the Transportation Act of 1940. Although a strict Republican, Clement greatly reduced the PRR role in Pennsylvania state politics, where it had been the right arm of the Republican party for decades.

Clement had a sense of history. At his direction, the railroad preserved a number of passenger cars and steam locomotives, a priceless collection that ultimately found its way into the state-owned Railroad Museum of Pennsylvania at Strasburg. Clement died in Rosemont, Pa. It was only fitting that, at the hour Clement's funeral was to begin, all trains on the PRR thirteen-state system were brought to a brief halt.

[Some of Clement's papers are in the PRR archives, held by the Pennsylvania Historical and Museum Commission. Biographical profiles are in *Railway Age*, Apr. 27, 1935, and June 11, 1949. See also "Pennsylvania Railroad," *Fortune*, May–June 1936; "Pennsy's Predicament," *ibid.*, Mar. 1948; and G. H. Burgess and M. C. Kennedy, *Centennial History of the Pennsylvania Railroad* (1949). Obituaries are in the *New York Times* and the *Philadelphia Inquirer*, both Aug. 31, 1966.]

MICHAEL BEZILLA

CLEMENT, RUFUS EARLY (June 26, 1900–Nov. 7, 1967), educator and civic leader, was born in Salisbury, N.C., the son of George Clinton Clement, a bishop of the African Methodist Episcopal Zion (AMEZ) church, and Emma Clarrissa Williams. When Clement was less than four months old, his family moved to Kentucky; he was educated in Louisville public schools. Entering Livingstone College in North Carolina, he established an outstanding record as a scholar and athlete; Clement also took part-time jobs to help finance his education. In 1919 he graduated as valedictorian and in 1920 married his fellow student Pearl Ann Johnson, the daughter of a plantation owner reputed to be the wealthiest black in Mississippi; they had one child.

In 1919 Clement entered Garrett Biblical Institute in Evanston, Ill., to prepare for the ministry. He also took graduate courses in history at Northwestern University. In 1922 he received a B.D. from Garrett and an M.A. from Northwestern. That same year, he was ordained a minister in the AMEZ church, joined the faculty of Livingstone College, and began work toward a doctorate in American history from Northwestern, which he received in 1930. From 1922 to 1925 Clement was an instructor in history at Livingstone, and from 1925 to 1931 he was a professor of history and dean of the college. On weekends he conducted services in rural AMEZ congregations.

At Livingstone, Clement proved himself an effective administrator. This quality, coupled with his articulateness, his ability to deal respectfully but unobsequiously with whites, and his academic credentials, made him a respected figure in black higher education. More significantly, his abilities brought him the good will of the agents of the white secular and religious philanthropies that played so crucial a role in funding and shaping southern black education.

In 1931 Clement became dean of the newly opened Louisville Municipal College for Negroes. This institution, a segregated extension of the all-white University of Louisville, was created to quiet charges by Louisville's blacks that their taxes were used to support an educational institution that excluded them. Coming into a tense and volatile situation, Clement shaped the new school into a significant educational institution that was an asset to Louisville's black community. Simultaneously, his success pleased whites by muting black resentment against the University of Louisville without challenging its whites-only policy. Here again Clement demonstrated an ability to deal with whites and blacks without losing the respect of either.

In 1929 Atlanta University had abolished its undergraduate college, reorganized itself as a graduate institution, and affiliated with two strong neighboring undergraduate schools, Spelman and Morehouse colleges. These changes were encouraged by the General Education Board, a Rockefeller philanthropy, in the hope that a new, comprehensive black center of higher education would emerge. In 1937 the board of trustees of Atlanta University, passing over several older, more distinguished black scholars and educators, invited Clement to become the school's sixth president. The qualities of the new president were seen as a key component in making this possible.

Clement agreed to go to Atlanta, believing that the school's location, its strong alumni association, and the interest of the Rockefeller philanthropies provided him an opportunity to build an important institution. During his thirty years as president (for part of this time he was also president of the Atlanta Center of Colleges) Clement turned Atlanta University into a major educational center. Under his leadership new advanced-degree programs were established in the arts and humanities, the social sciences, and the professions, and existing programs were strengthened. His efforts to recruit faculty, secure scholarship funds, expand the school's physical plant, and build the school's endowment forced him to devote much time to fund-raising, something he did with skill and success. In addition to increasing the support from alumni groups, long-standing white supporters, and northern philanthropic agencies, Clement secured sizable new gifts from the southern white community, the Jewish community, and the federal government. These successes caused *Time* magazine to describe him in 1966 as one of the nation's most influential university presidents.

Clement's most difficult moment came in 1944, when he forcibly retired W. E. B. Du Bois from the Atlanta faculty. Du Bois, a brilliant, volatile scholar, had, in an effort to retain special privileges, clashed with him. Clement's action was motivated as much by a need to demonstrate control as by his belief that the university could not allow preferential treatment to select faculty members in regard to pay and duties. Although the public outcry that followed never threatened Clement's position, to Du Bois and his supporters Clement's reputation as an educator was forever compromised.

The respect of the Atlanta community for Clement was demonstrated in 1953, when he became the first black member of the city's board of education. His campaign succeeded because of the support he received from both black and white voters who were attracted by his prestige, credentials, and reputation as a racial moderate. Returned to office in every subsequent election, he was a member of the board at the time of his death. Although his position led to membership on the boards of numerous organizations, he was particularly active in the United Nations Association, the AMEZ church, the Georgia Conference on Interracial Cooperation, and the Young Men's Christian Association (YMCA). A staunch Democrat, he served on the National Science Board and the State Department's Council on African Affairs during the administrations of John F. Kennedy and Lyndon B. Johnson.

Clement was a handsome, athletic-looking man of great dignity and civility. He died in New York City, where he had gone to attend a meeting of his university's board of trustees.

[The Clement papers are in the Woodroofe Library and in the Presidential Archives of Atlanta University. Clement's correspondence is in the General Education Board Papers, Rockefeller Archive Center, North Tarrytown, N.Y. See also *Time*, Feb. 11, 1966. Obituaries are in the *New York Times* and the *Atlanta Constitution*, both Nov. 8, 1967.]

ALFRED MOSS

CLIFT, EDWARD MONTGOMERY (Oct. 17, 1920–July 23, 1966), actor, was born in Omaha, Nebr., the son of William Brooks Clift, a banker and broker, and Ethel Anderson. In 1925 William Clift joined a Chicago investment firm and moved his family to Highland Park, Ill. Clift's parents chose to live apart from each other most of the time, and the children were brought up by their willful, socially ambitious mother. Determined that her children should absorb Old World culture, Ethel Clift took Montgomery, his twin sister, and his older brother for extended stays in Europe in 1928 and 1929. There the children studied under private tutors, and Clift became fluent in German, French, and Italian. Between these European forays Clift briefly attended public school in Highland Park. In later years he criticized his unsettled upbringing for failing to provide him with roots.

Although the stock market crash of 1929 left the Clifts in financial difficulty, Ethel Clift was able to return to Europe with the children between June and November 1930. In 1931 William Clift moved the family to Greenwich Village in New York City, but in the fall of 1932 his wife and children went to live in Sarasota, Fla. At the suggestion of a tutor, twelve-year-old Monty, as he was known, auditioned for a local theater group and, in March 1933, made his first stage appearance in *As Husbands Go*. The next year Ethel Clift and the children took a house in Sharon, Conn. By then, Monty was eager for a theatrical career. Though inexperienced, he landed a part in *Fly Away Home* at the Berkshire Playhouse, a summer theater in nearby Stockbridge, Mass. He portrayed one of four children who were attempting to reunite their divorced parents. He remained with the play, which starred Thomas Mitchell, when it moved to Broadway in January 1935. The producer, Theron Bamberger, wrote of his fledgling actor, "The boy turned out to be both handsome and intelligent; he read for me and I liked him. The first day of rehearsal proved that Monty was an actor."

When the play closed, Clift modeled for advertisements but soon landed a small role in *Jubilee* (1935), a short-lived Cole Porter musical. Then, after a brief stay at the Dalton School in Newport, R. I., he returned to Broadway in *Yr. Obedient Husband* (1938). Clift's youthful success launched him on a busy stage career but deprived him of a formal education. He told an interviewer in 1957, "My formal education was a mess. I even skipped high school. . . . I've done nothing but act since I was fourteen." He grew up on stage, moving from juvenile roles, such as Prince Peter in *Jubilee*, to the young Canadian airman in *You Touched Me!* (1945).

Clift may have been deficient in schooling, but his professional training was exemplary, for the young actor worked with some of the theater's finest talents. He appeared with Fredric March in *Yr. Obedient Husband* and *The Skin of Our Teeth* (1942), and with the Lunts in *There Shall Be No Night* (1940). Clift greatly admired Alfred Lunt, even to the point of taking on his mannerisms and speech patterns. Another mentor was the character actor Dudley Digges, who worked with Clift in *The Searching Wind* (1944). Clift's directors included Worthington Miner for *Dame Nature* (1938), and three future stalwarts of the Actors Studio—Sanford Meisner for *Out of the Frying Pan* (1941), Robert Lewis for *Mexican Mural* (1942), and Elia Kazan for *The Skin of Our Teeth*.

Before going to Hollywood, Clift did thirteen plays on the New York stage, but it was not until *Mexican Mural* that critics noticed his development. Clift made a breakthrough with his portrayal of a wounded soldier in Lillian Hellman's antifascist tract *The Searching Wind*. He was a soldier again in *Foxhole in the Parlor* (1945), a minor melodrama that Clift turned into a personal triumph. He continued his string of young soldiers with *You Touched Me!*, adapted by Tennessee Williams and Donald Windham from a story by D. H. Lawrence. Critics generally agreed that Clift's stage work displayed intelligence, sensitivity, and personal charm. Yet he was an actor who insisted on naturalistic speech, sometimes at the expense of a play's verbal richness. His speech mannerisms sometimes made him inaudible. Robert Lewis, who coached Clift for his role in *You Touched Me!* and later had Clift in his classes at the Actors Studio, recalled his attempts to keep the actor "from cutting every speech of his that was longer than a grunt." According to Lewis, Clift's refusal to develop his verbal range kept him from becoming "the great American Hamlet we all hoped he would be."

Though Clift never fulfilled his promise as a stage actor, he had a powerful effect on film acting. After declining several offers to work in Hollywood, he agreed to appear opposite John Wayne in *Red River* (1948), directed by Howard Hawks. The contrasting temperaments and acting styles of Wayne and Clift heightened the film's drama, making it one of Hollywood's most memorable westerns. Clift received his first best-actor Academy Award nomination for *The Search* (1948), his second film (though the first to be released), in which he portrayed a young American soldier in post–World War II Germany who tries to reunite a little boy with his mother.

After just two pictures Clift had become a major star, but he had not yet clearly defined his screen persona. It was not until *A Place in the Sun* (1951) and *From Here to Eternity* (1953)—both of which earned him Academy Award nominations as best actor—that the public saw the intense, troubled, vulnerable hero that was to become Clift's specialty. After these great successes the actor was much in demand for film roles, but he chose to work sparingly. In 1954 he returned to the New York stage with a production of Chekhov's *The Sea Gull*. His next film, *Raintree County* (1957), a lifeless Civil War epic, was an expensive failure. The thirty-seven-year-old Clift was miscast as a twenty-year-old Indiana youth. Before the picture was completed, the actor had a serious automobile accident that left his face disfigured and partially paralyzed. Thereafter he did interesting work in *Wild River* (1960), *The Misfits* (1960), *Judgment at Nuremberg* (1961, for which he was nominated for a best-supporting-actor Academy Award), and *Freud* (1962), but otherwise lacked the intensity he had displayed in his early films.

Clift, who was homosexual, never married. He died of a heart attack at his New York City apartment.

[See Robert LaGuardia, *Monty* (1977); Patricia Bosworth, *Montgomery Clift* (1978); and Judith M. Kass, *The Films of Montgomery Clift* (1979). See also James Goode, *The Story of "The Misfits"* (1963); Robert Lewis, *Slings and Arrows* (1984); and Foster Hirsch, *A Method to Their Madness: The History of the Actors Studio* (1984). *The Rebels: Montgomery Clift* (n.d.), a film portrait of the actor written and directed by Claudio Masenza, contains rare candid film footage of Clift from boyhood to manhood. An obituary is in the *New York Times*, July 24, 1966.]

WILLIAM HUGHES

CLUETT, SANFORD LOCKWOOD (June 6, 1874–May 18, 1968), inventor and industrialist, was born in Troy, N.Y., the son of Edmund Cluett, who sold musical instruments, and Mary Alice Stone. Cluett, who grew up in economically comfortable circumstances, attended the Troy Academy, from which he graduated in 1894. He continued his studies at the Rensselaer Polytechnic Institute in Troy during the next four years and received a degree in civil engineering in 1898.

In 1897 he joined the New York National Guard as a private. Soon thereafter he participated in the Spanish-American War as a member of the New York Volunteer Infantry. In June 1898 he was transferred to the First United States Volunteer Engineers, where he was ultimately promoted to captain. He also served in the Puerto Rican campaign in July 1898. From 1904 he served in the New York National Guard, advancing to major before his retirement in 1917. On Feb. 2, 1916, he married Camilla E. Rising; they had four children.

Always full of curiosity and with an inventive mind, Cluett was awarded more than 200 patents, the first in 1900, when he designed a self-operating valve for the locks in the Big Sandy River Dam in Kentucky. In 1901 he joined the Walter A. Wood Company of Hoosick Falls, N.Y., which produced mowers, reapers, and other farm machines used in the agricultural region of upper New York State. There Cluett developed one-horse and two-horse mowers with a vertical lift on the cutting bar, operable from the driver's seat.

Another of his inventions was Clupak, a stretchable paper, difficult to tear. It found extensive use in shopping bags and as wrapping paper for magazines, catalogs, tires, meat, and furniture. At first, Cluett found no manufacturers who were interested in such a paper, but after he was turned down by four companies, the West Virginia Pulp and Paper Company began production. Clupak was later manufactured by many American and foreign companies.

In 1919 Cluett became a member of Cluett, Peabody and Company, a textile firm that had been started by three of his uncles and that produced men's clothing and accessories, including Arrow shirts. He was in charge of manufacturing and research for more than two decades, and became a director in 1921 and a vice-president in 1927.

Cluett's most significant invention was the processing of cloth to reduce shrinkage. His business was in a critical period around 1928, when the detachable shirt collar was going out of fashion. Shirts with permanently attached collars suffered in appearance after shrinkage from washing. Cluett studied the manufacture of cloth and recognized that it was stretched lengthwise while moving through the spinning and finishing mills. He believed that the pulling action during manufacturing had to be adjusted by a pushing counteraction. If he laid a piece of cloth on his knee and pressed a stretched rubber band against it while slowly letting the rubber band contract against the cloth, the cloth returned to an unstretched condition without being wrinkled.

The resulting preshrinking of the cloth was developed on a manufacturing scale by designing a high-speed machine in which the cloth was passed over a contracting elastic felt blanket. This process was designated by the use of Cluett's first name with the *d* dropped. At the time of his death, Sanforized cloth was licensed for manufacture by 448 mills operating in fifty-eight countries, and 3 billion yards of treated cloth were being produced annually. Shrinkage was less than 1 percent.

The National Association of Manufacturers awarded Cluett its Modern Pioneer Award in 1940, and he received the Edward Longstretch

Award from the Franklin Institute of Philadelphia in 1945. The American Institute of Mechanical Engineers conferred on him the Holley Medal in 1952. He held directorships in several railroad companies, was a trustee of Rensselaer Polytechnic Institute, and was a member of the Sons of the Revolution and the Society of Colonial Wars.

[Cluett's papers are in the Troy, N.Y., office of Cluett, Peabody and Company. See "ASME Honors Engineers," *Mechanical Engineering* (Jan. 1953); and Floyd Tifft, "Mr. Cluett Makes 90th," *Rensselaer Review* 1, no. 1 (1964). An obituary is in the *New York Times*, May 19, 1968.]

AARON J. IHDE

COLLIER, JOHN (May 4, 1884–May 8, 1968), community organizer and reformer noted for his role in federal Indian policy, was born in Atlanta, Ga., the son of Charles Allen Collier, a lawyer, banker, and mayor of Atlanta, and Susie Rawson. In 1902, after he graduated from Atlanta High School, Collier attended Columbia University, where he took noncredit classes in literature and French drama. He also studied philosophy, sociology, political theory, and natural sciences under Lucy Graham Crozier, a free-lance tutor in New York City.

Collier became the executive secretary of the Associated Charities of Atlanta in March 1905 but resigned when the board of directors rejected his proposal to focus on creating job opportunities for poor people rather than on the traditional forms of public relief.

In 1906 Collier went to Paris to study abnormal psychology under Pierre Janet at the Collège de France. In Paris, Collier met Lucy Wood, whom he married on Oct. 22, 1906; they had three children. They were divorced in 1943, and later that year he married Laura Thompson.

Collier became civic secretary of the People's Institute in New York City in 1908 and worked with immigrants on the Lower East Side. He promoted the idea of cultural pluralism in order to create a neighborhood community where art, drama, and spiritual values were integrated to combat the disruptive social forces that had accompanied the industrial revolution.

In 1909 the People's Institute sponsored the National Board of Censorship, which encouraged voluntary efforts within the film industry to improve the quality of films. He also edited the *Civic Journal*, a publication of the institute that supported progressive reform, and associated with Mabel Dodge and others involved in bohemian and radical activities in Greenwich Village. He resigned from the People's Institute in March 1914. During the next few months, he camped with his family in the North Carolina mountains, where he wrote poetry and journal articles on the use of drama in community work.

The Colliers then returned to New York City and set up the Home School, a teaching experiment patterned on the educational philosophy of John Dewey. Collier resumed his activities at the People's Institute and in 1915 organized a training school for community workers. He also helped establish the National Community Center Conference (April 1916), became its secretary, and edited its journal, the *Community Center*.

In 1919 Collier ended his association with the People's Institute, having become disillusioned by the antiradical and anti-immigrant hysteria in New York City during World War I. He then moved to California, where he became director of Americanization for the California State Housing and Immigration Commission.

In 1920 Collier joined a group of artists and writers in Taos, N.Mex., who were alienated from the business ethos of modern American civilization. After watching tribal dances and Christmas ceremonies at Taos Pueblo, Collier concluded that the Indians had created a utopian "Red Atlantis." He sought to preserve Indian culture because he believed that it provided an example of harmonious communal life for the rest of society. After five months at Taos, he returned to California to lecture in sociology at San Francisco State College for the 1921–1922 academic year.

Collier began his crusade to reform federal Indian policy in May 1922 when he was named research agent for the Indian Welfare Committee of the General Federation of Women's Clubs. He gained national prominence by helping defeat the Bursum bill, which posed a threat to the land and water rights of the Pueblo Indians. In 1923 he founded the American Indian Defense Association (AIDA), serving as its executive secretary for the next ten years.

During the 1920's Collier was a brilliant propagandist for Indian causes. Beginning in 1925, he employed articles in *American Indian Life* and other AIDA publications to discredit land allotment, to criticize the government for failing to protect Indian water rights and provide necessary social services, and to chastize the Indian Bureau for banning certain tribal dances. In 1927 he worked for the passage of the Indian Oil Act, which guaranteed Indian royalties from subsurface minerals on executive-order reservations.

In April 1933 Collier was appointed commissioner of Indian affairs by President Franklin D. Roosevelt. He became the architect of the Indian Reorganization Act of 1934, which provided a tribal alternative to the previous federal policy of assimilation. It ended land allotment, authorized funds for the purchase of new tribal real estate, increased federal assistance for reservation economic development, and encouraged formal tribal self-government.

Collier initiated other reforms that were directly related to the act. He brought Indians under New Deal relief programs, issued policy statements that upheld Indian religious freedom, and implemented a progressive curriculum and bilingual program for Indian schools. Collier also helped set up the Indian Arts and Crafts Board at the Interior Department and an applied anthropology unit at the Indian Bureau. Furthermore, he asked Felix S. Cohen, a legal scholar, to codify federal Indian law. In 1940 he helped establish the Inter-American Institute of the Indian in Mexico City to encourage contact and the exchange of information among Indian tribes throughout the Western Hemisphere.

Collier encountered many setbacks during his tenure as Indian commissioner. An extroverted and self-righteous person, he was intolerant of criticism of his programs by Indians. In addition, he failed to persuade Congress to appropriate enough money to begin widespread economic development on Indian reservations. His greatest achievement was to demonstrate how the land-allotment system had violated tribal sovereignty and the vested rights that Indians had obtained in previous treaties.

In January 1945 Collier resigned as Indian commissioner. He then organized, and became president of, the Institute of Ethnic Affairs in Washington, D.C. He used the institute to defend the right of self-government and cultural autonomy for the people who lived under American colonial rule in Guam, Samoa, and Micronesia. Between 1947 and 1954, while continuing to direct the Institute of Ethnic Affairs, he taught sociology and anthropology at the City College of New York.

Collier divorced his second wife in 1955. He was visiting professor of anthropology at Knox College in Illinois in 1955–1956. He then moved to Taos, where he married Grace Volk on Jan. 27, 1957. Collier spent his remaining years writing columns for *El Crepúsculo*, a local newspaper, and a memoir of his life, *From Every Zenith*. Collier died in Taos.

[Major collections of Collier's papers are the People's Institute Papers, Manuscript and Archives Division, New York Public Library; the John Collier Papers, Yale University Library; and the Office Files of Commissioner John Collier at the National Archives.

Collier's important writings include "The Red Atlantis," *Survey*, Oct. 1, 1922; "The Indian Bureau's Record," *Nation*, Oct. 5, 1932; "United States Indian Administration as a Laboratory of Ethnic Affairs," *Social Research*, Sept. 1945; *Indians of the Americas* (1947); *Patterns and Ceremonials of the Indians of the Southwest* (1949); *On the Gleaming Way* (1962); and *From Every Zenith* (1963).

Books and journal articles containing significant data about Collier are: *The Navajo Indians and Federal Indian Policy* (1968); Stephen J. Kunitz, "The Social Philosophy of John Collier," *Ethnohistory*, Summer 1971; J. P. Kinney, *Facing Indian Facts* (1973); "The Indian Reorganization Act: The Dream and the Reality," *Pacific Historical Review* 44 (1975); Donald L. Parman, *The Navahos and the New Deal* (1976); "John Collier and the New Deal: An Assessment," in Jane F. Smith and Robert M. Kvasnicka, eds., *Indian-White Relations* (1976); Kenneth R. Philp, *John Collier's Crusade for Indian Reform, 1920–1954* (1977); "John Collier and the Indians of the Americas," *Prologue*, Spring 1979; Graham D. Taylor, *The New Deal and American Indian Tribalism* (1980); Laurence M. Hauptman, *The Iroquois and the New Deal* (1981); "John Collier and the Pueblo Lands Board Act," *New Mexico Historical Review*, Jan. 1983; "Termination: A Legacy of the New Deal," *Western Historical Quarterly*, Apr. 1983; Laurence C. Kelly, *The Assault on Assimilation* (1983); and Francis Paul Prucha, *The Great Father* (1984).]

KENNETH R. PHILP

COLTRANE, JOHN WILLIAM (Sept. 23, 1926–July 17, 1967), jazz musician and composer, was born in Hamlet, N.C., the son of John Robert Coltrane, a tailor, and Alice Blair. His father died when Coltrane was twelve years old; to support the family Alice Coltrane worked as a domestic in white households (the

Coltranes were black), and John earned money at odd jobs while learning to play the clarinet in school.

After the family moved to Atlantic City, N.J., in 1940, and before relocating to Philadelphia, Pa., in 1943, Coltrane switched primarily to alto saxophone. Drafted into the navy in 1945, he spent more than a year in the navy band. After his discharge in 1946, he began his professional career in a cocktail lounge trio, but backed many well-known blues performers when they played Philadelphia. In this way he came to the attention of Eddie ("Cleanhead") Vinson, who hired him on the condition that he play tenor saxophone. After Coltrane played briefly with Howard McGhee in 1948, Dizzy Gillespie called for him to fill a vacant altoist's chair in his orchestra; he stayed on until late 1951.

Coltrane spent the next year and a half in the rhythm and blues band of Earl Bostic, then was asked by Johnny Hodges to join his small band in 1953. Through all these moves, Coltrane remained basically a sideman, usually getting only a few solo opportunities each evening and hardly ever on the recordings of these bands.

During this period a mystical streak in his character became apparent, and Coltrane began to read philosophy voraciously. Although he seldom soloed in public, in private he was practicing and developing the harmonic ideas that were to dominate the middle part of his career. During this early period, Coltrane became addicted to heroin, but in 1957, with help from his family, he was able to overcome this problem and devote the rest of his life to music.

The most important break of his career came in 1955, when Coltrane joined the Miles Davis Quintet, historically one of the most influential jazz groups. Davis used withdrawn, melodic lines; Coltrane, on the other hand, captured critical attention with his highly arpeggiated approach to music. At first some critics disparaged his insistence on making the sixteenth note the rhythmic basis of his music, for this was perhaps the one innovation that was original with Coltrane, the one that made him sound peculiar to many ears when he first came to prominence. Only a decade earlier, Charlie Parker had startled the jazz public by employing the eighth note for the basic rhythmic impetus rather than the traditional quarter note, and many had trouble adjusting to Coltrane's further development. After leaving Davis for a year to free-lance in the New York City area, Coltrane rejoined the group that, because of the addition of Julian ("Cannonball") Adderley on alto, had become the Miles Davis Sextet. From 1957 to 1960 this group pioneered the basic jazz grammar of many subsequent jazz styles.

Easily the most important of these additions was Davis' decision to incorporate modal scales rather than chordal structures in many pieces as the basis for improvising. The scalar approach was to become the foundation for most of Coltrane's playing and composing, freeing him from the intricate complexities inherent in the chordal progressions he had set for himself in such pieces as his "Giant Steps" (in which at the quarter bar a chord change occurs). Coltrane was also able to give free rein to his harmonic ideas without the confinement of running the chords. Because of his freedom within a modal framework, his music sounded progressively more reflective and meditative. At about this time he began a correspondence and an exchange of ideas with Indian sitar player and composer Ravi Shankar; many of Coltrane's later ideas approximated Indian musical concepts placed in a jazz context.

After striking out with his own group, Coltrane explored many jazz innovations, including some uses of the atonalism associated with Ornette Coleman and his followers, basically the application to jazz of twelve-tone musical concepts. Coltrane began doubling on the soprano saxophone, a difficult instrument that, except for the masterful work of Sidney Bechet, had seldom been heard in jazz. Coltrane established the soprano saxophone as a standard jazz instrument.

Coltrane signed a contract in 1961 to record exclusively for the Impulse label. Bob Thiele, the musical supervisor at Impulse, permitted Coltrane the freedom for the remainder of his life to record his music however he saw fit. Coltrane played in a fifteen-piece orchestra exploring the African roots of jazz, backed the song-stylist Johnny Hartman, played with Duke Ellington, and performed free-jazz outbursts with tenor saxophonist Pharoah Sanders.

By far the most famous of Coltrane's recordings, however, were made with his working quartet, the best-known version of which included pianist McCoy Tyner, bassist Jimmy Garrison, and drummer Elvin Jones. Among the many recordings with the group, Coltrane did an extended work in four movements that, according to his notes, represents his spiritual testimony and aspirations. After his death these notes became the religious literature of a cult that views Coltrane as the avatar of God, a position denounced by his family.

Coltrane was planning to form a new group with African percussionist Michael Babatunde Olatunji when the saxophonist was stricken with a liver ailment determined after his death to have been acute hepatoma. He died in New York City.

In 1945 Coltrane married Juanita ("Naima") Peabody. One of his best-known compositions was named after her. They were divorced in 1948. His second wife, Alice Jones, whom he married in 1953, was the pianist and occasional harpist in his band for the last two years of his life. Coltrane is a member of the *Downbeat* Hall of Fame. He is universally acknowledged as one of the enduring masters of jazz music.

[The best and most complete source on Coltrane is J. C. Thomas, *Chasin' the Trane* (1975). An obituary is in the *New York Times*, July 18, 1967.]

ARTHUR LIVINGSTON

CONNOLLY, MAUREEN CATHERINE (Sept. 17, 1934–June 21, 1969), tennis player and coach, was born in San Diego, Calif., the daughter of Martin Connolly, a lieutenant commander and athletics officer at the Naval Training Center, and Jassamine Wood. Connolly's father deserted the family when she was about four years old. Her mother subsequently married August Berste, a musician; they in turn divorced. As a child, Connolly was guided by an overly dominating mother who, frustrated in her own desire to become a concert pianist, pushed her daughter into the study of dancing and singing. But a poorly performed tonsillectomy ended Connolly's chance of a singing career.

Horseback riding was Connolly's first love, but the family's poor financial position precluded her owning a horse. She met an aggressive tennis stylist, Gene Garret, while playing on the neighborhood tennis court, and decided that tennis would be a substitute for horseback riding. In 1944 she started playing tennis. She was left-handed, but her first tennis coach, Wilbur Folsom, instructed her to play right-handed. She began practicing her game at least three hours a day, five days a week, all year long. She later commented, "Any championship career has foundation stones. Mine were slavish work and driving determination."

As Connolly's play progressed she switched coaches. She was introduced to Eleanor ("Teach") Tennant, who had instructed such tennis greats as Helen Wills, Bobby Riggs, and Alice Marble. In May 1947, while playing in the Southern California Invitational Tennis Championship, Connolly won the tournament for girls of fifteen years and under.

She achieved only average grades at Cathedral High School, having begun her professional tennis career in 1949. By the age of fifteen she had won more than fifty championships, suffering only four defeats. During this period she became the youngest person ever to win the national junior title. *American Magazine* described her as "an all-round player with a strong forehand stroke and terrific ability to concentrate . . . deliberately and deceptively unspectacular with a racquet."

In 1950 Connolly repeated her junior-division triumphs and was ranked tenth among American women players; she was the youngest person of either sex to appear among the first ten. Upon graduation from high school in 1951, she was selected to play on the United States Wightman Cup team, again the youngest player ever to be so honored. She helped defend the international trophy by defeating Kay Tuckey of England 6–1, 6–3.

Sportswriters dubbed her "Little Mo" after the battleship *Missouri*, its decks loaded with powerful weapons. At sixteen, she defeated Shirley Fry for the 1951 United States Women's Singles Championship, the second youngest champion in history. Connolly remarked to coach Tennant after the match, "Now we can go home and work on the offensive game." Her ground strokes, especially her backhand, were her strength. Between 1951 and 1954 she was nearly unbeatable. She was United States Singles Champion in 1952 and 1953, French Singles Champion in 1953 and 1954, Wimbledon Singles Champion from 1952 through 1954, Australian Singles Champion in 1953, and United States Clay Court Singles Champion in 1953 and 1954. She was ranked number one in the world from 1952 to 1954. Connolly was never beaten in the singles at Wimbledon and, uniquely, became in 1953 the first woman to achieve the grand slam of tennis, the national championships of the

United States, Great Britain, France, and Australia. The feat has never been duplicated. She was named female athlete of the year three times (1952, 1953, and 1954) by the Associated Press.

In July 1954 while riding her horse, Colonel Merryboy, she suffered a broken right leg and deeply gashed muscles and tendons. Unable to continue tournament play, Connolly announced her retirement in February 1955. Later that year she married Norman Brinker, a businessman and former member of the United States Olympic equestrian team. They had two children.

Philosophical about her forced retirement, Connolly devoted herself to coaching youngsters. "Tennis is a wonderful game and I leave it with no regrets," she said. "I've had a full life with lots of travel and I've met lots of wonderful people. Now I'm going to be a little housewife. It's a new career and I'm awfully happy with it." Her love for the game never died. She established the Maureen Connolly Brinker Foundation for the advancement of tennis achievement among junior players in Texas.

Although she was a bubbling young lady, full of gaiety and friendliness, her relationships with her mother and Tennant were often marked by heated disagreements and misunderstandings. After her 1952 Wimbledon victory she severed all ties with Tennant. When asked by a reporter, "What was your most amusing experience in the sport?" she replied, "I never had one." Personal friction strengthened her aggressiveness and determination on the court and helped make her the dominant female player of her day. In 1968 she was elected to the International Tennis Hall of Fame. She died of cancer in Dallas, Tex.

[Scrapbook collections and memorabilia are in the International Tennis Hall of Fame, Newport, R.I. Brief autobiographical portraits are in Maureen Connolly, *Power Tennis* (1954); and *Forehand Drive*, with Thomas Gwynne (1957). An NBC television program, "Little Mo," was broadcast Sept. 5, 1978. See Owen Davidson and C. M. Jones, *Great Women Tennis Players* (1971); Allison Danzig and Peter Schwed, eds., *The Fireside Book of Tennis* (1972); Gianni Clerici, "The Short and Happy Life of Maureen Connolly," in *The Ultimate Tennis Book* (1978); Virginia Wade with Jean Rafferty, *Ladies of the Court* (1984). See also *American*, Sept. 1949; *Newsweek*, May 28, 1951; *Collier's*, Sept. 1, 1951; *Washington Post*, Sept. 6, 1951; *New York Times Magazine*, Sept. 16, 1951; *Life*, Sept. 17, 1951; *Time*, Sept. 17, 1951, and July 14, 1952; *Scholastic*, Sept, 26, 1951, and Jan. 23, 1952; and *New York Times*, June 6, 1952, and June 24, 1954.]

CHARLES F. HOWLETT

COPE, ARTHUR CLAY (June 27, 1909–June 4, 1966), organic chemist, was born in Dunreith, Ind., the son of Everett Claire Cope, who had a grain-storage business, and Jennie Compton, who worked on the local Young Women's Christian Association office staff. His parents moved the family to Indianapolis to enhance their son's educational opportunities. Cope received a bachelor's degree in chemistry at Butler University in Indianapolis in 1929 and enrolled at the University of Wisconsin for graduate work. Cope's thesis adviser was S. M. McElvain, who, among other things, researched the synthesis of organic compounds for pharmaceutical uses. Cope's thesis, completed in 1932, led to a useful local anesthetic and three independent publications. He obtained a National Research Council Fellowship at Harvard University (1932–1934) under the sponsorship of Harvard's leading organic chemist, E. P. Kohler. At Harvard he wrote several papers that reflect Kohler's influence. On Aug. 22, 1930, Cope married Bernice Mead Abbott.

In 1934, Cope became associate in chemistry at Bryn Mawr College; he was promoted to assistant professor in 1935 and to associate professor in 1938. At Bryn Mawr he further studied the synthesis of substances with potential pharmaceutical applications. He developed new reactions and found novel combinations of substituents for barbiturates and amino alcohols as local anesthetics. He received support and a consultantship from the Sharpe and Dohme Laboratories in Philadelphia. One result was a commercial barbiturate, Delvinyl Sodium. More important for organic chemistry was Cope's discovery of a thermal rearrangement of an allyl group from one carbon to another in a three-carbon system. Although analogous processes were well documented, the unique carbon-to-carbon feature and the clarity with which Cope delineated the details prompted chemists to describe this reaction as the "Cope rearrangement."

In 1940–1941, Cope spent part of a Guggenheim Fellowship doing research at Bryn Mawr and the rest visiting organic chemistry research groups at universities in the United

States. In 1941 he moved to Columbia University as an associate professor. When the United States entered World War II, he joined the Office of Scientific Research and Development and became technical aide and section chief of Division 9 of the National Defense Research Committee, with responsibility for diverse projects ranging from chemical warfare agents and insect repellents to antimalarial drugs. For his contributions to the war effort, he received the Certificate of Merit in 1948.

In 1945, Karl Compton, then president of the Massachusetts Institute of Technology (MIT), asked Cope to become chairman of the Department of Chemistry. Cope's research up to that time was recognized in 1944 by the coveted American Chemical Society Award in Pure Chemistry. He was elected to the National Academy of Sciences in 1947. At MIT, Cope, working with C. G. Overberger, was able to repeat the classical 1911 Willstätter synthesis of the extraordinary polyolefin called cyclooctatetraene. It was a massive effort and led Cope and his coworkers into studies of the chemistry of medium-sized ring compounds. As part of this work, he discovered the change from 1,3,5-cyclooctatriene to bicyclo[4.2.0]-2,4-octadiene at temperatures of 80°–100°, which was the first example of "valence tautomerism," where one compound isomerizes reversibly, without intervention of external agents (except heat) by processes in which connections are made and broken, usually simultaneously. One of Cope's later achievements was an ingenious resolution of the optical isomers of *trans*-cyclooctene and *trans*-cyclononene. The possibility of stable existence of such chiral forms had been recognized long before, but it took imagination and enormous skill to carry the project to successful completion.

At MIT, Cope was appointed in 1945 to the editorial board of *Organic Syntheses*, and in 1947 he joined the editorial board of the influential Organic Reactions series. He was a consultant to the Central Research Department of the Du Pont Company from 1946 until his death. He served the American Chemical Society with particular distinction as chairman of the Division of Organic Chemistry (1946–1947), councillor (1950–1951), northeastern section chairman (1955–1956), member of its board of directors (1951–1966), president (1960–1961), and chairman of the board (1959–1960, 1962–1966). Cope also served for nine years on the important Committee on Professional Training. He had been chairman of the chemistry section of the National Academy of Sciences and served on the academy's Committee on Science and Public Policy. In 1965 he was named the first Camille Dreyfus Professor of Chemistry at MIT. During this period, one of his chemical colleagues described him as the "busiest organic chemist in the world." His widespread activities apparently strained his marriage, for he and his wife were divorced. On July 2, 1963, he married Harriet Packard (née Osgood) and in the process acquired a stepson.

When Cope became president of the ACS, he was described as "mild-mannered," but his courteous and affable facade covered a strong temperament. His students called him "the iron fist in the velvet glove." He was single-minded about chemical education. He did not compromise his belief in the importance of thoroughness and of breadth, feelings surely reinforced by service on the ACS Committee on Professional Training. When MIT made a decision to reduce the hours required for chemistry in the undergraduate curriculum, Cope resisted strongly. This, along with what some faculty members perceived as arbitrary decisions, led to the end of his two-decade tenure as chairman of the chemistry department.

Cope received many honors and awards for his achievements in research, including election to the American Academy of Arts and Sciences and the American Philosophical Society, the Chandler Medal of Columbia University, the W. H. Nichols Medal of the New York Section of the ACS, and the Roger Adams Medal and Award of the ACS.

Because of the royalties on his pharmaceutical patents, Cope became a relatively wealthy man. He bequeathed the bulk of his estate to the ACS to stimulate research in organic chemistry through the Cope Award. He died in Washington, D.C.

[Cope's vast output of scientific publications includes forty-four papers on the proximity effect in ring compounds and forty-six on cyclic polyolefins, published in various scientific journals. Obituaries are in the *New York Times*, June 7, 1966; and *Chemical Engineering News*, June 13, 1966.]

JOHN D. ROBERTS

CORDON, GUY (Apr. 24, 1890–June 6, 1969), United States senator, was born in

Cuero, Tex., the son of Jacob Cordon, a merchant, and Caroline Terry. During Cordon's youth, the family moved to Roseburg, Oreg., where Cordon attended elementary and secondary schools. From 1909 through 1916, he served as deputy assessor of Douglas County, of which Roseburg is the county seat. On Sept. 30, 1914, he married Ana Lucille Allen; they had three children.

Cordon, a Republican, launched his political career in 1916, winning election as county assessor. Two years later, during World War I, he took a leave of absence and enlisted as a private in the field artillery. On his return from military service, Cordon became active in the American Legion, a dominant force in Oregon politics for the next three decades, and served a term as the legion's state commander.

Teaching himself law, Cordon was admitted to the Oregon bar in 1920 and opened a law practice in Roseburg. He was elected district attorney of Douglas County in 1923 and served until 1935, when he resumed private practice of law. His clients included the Interstate Association of Public Land Councils, with members from eleven western states, and the Association of Oregon Counties. Beginning in the 1920's, he was a close friend and confidant of Senator Charles L. McNary and worked closely with the Oregon congressional delegation on issues dealing with public lands. Cordon directed a protracted legal effort that prompted Congress in 1937 to enact legislation granting seventeen western Oregon counties the largest share of federal timber receipts ever made to local governments, as much as 50 percent of the receipts from the sustained-yield management of the Oregon and California Railroad timberlands.

Cordon advised Governor Earl Snell of Oregon on tax and revenue measures. McNary died early in 1944, and on March 4, Snell appointed Cordon to succeed him in the Senate. Two months later, with Snell's active support, Cordon fought back a powerful challenge from the former governor, Charles A. Sprague, to win the Republican nomination for the remainder of McNary's term. In the general election, Cordon easily defeated Democrat Willis Mahoney. He won a second term in 1948 by an even wider margin.

Within the Senate, Cordon's long association with McNary gave him an advantage over other freshmen legislators. He hired the late minority leader's staff to work for him and received choice committee assignments, including membership on the powerful Appropriations Committee and on the Committee for Interior and Insular Affairs.

Lacking a flamboyant style and disdainful of the news media, Cordon never achieved public prominence. But in the Senate he quickly stepped out from McNary's shadow and became the Republican party's leading authority on public lands and the development of natural resources. He was respected by colleagues for his mastery of detail and parliamentary skills. The *Newsweek* columnist Raymond Moley, a conservative, wrote that few senators could match Cordon's ability "to discern the hidden enemy in innocent-looking bills." In 1946, Senator Robert A. Taft named Cordon to the Republican Policy Committee, which dictated the legislative agenda for Republican opposition to the Truman administration.

A fiscal and social conservative, Cordon supported reductions in federal income taxes and across-the-board cuts in federal spending. He voted for the Taft-Hartley (Labor-Management Relations) Act but opposed amendments to curb industry-wide bargaining and to outlaw the union shop and the closed shop. He opposed the extension of wartime price controls and rent controls and the increase of federal aid to the elderly and to the poor. He voted against legislation to eliminate segregation among military draftees in 1950. He cast his vote against President Harry Truman's nominations of Henry A. Wallace as secretary of commerce in 1945 and David Lilienthal as chairman of the Atomic Energy Commission in 1947. In foreign policy, Cordon frequently voted with the isolationist bloc and opposed United States membership in the North Atlantic Treaty Organization and foreign military aid. But he supported the United Nations Charter, the Bretton Woods Agreement, and the Marshall Plan.

Cordon was an early proponent of Hawaiian statehood. In 1948, as chairman of the Senate Subcommittee on Territories and Insular Affairs, he conducted hearings in Hawaii and issued a report that recommended statehood and debunked claims by statehood opponents of Communist infiltration and racial unrest in the Pacific islands. Cordon sponsored statehood legislation that was blocked in committee in three successive congresses.

In 1947, Cordon was chairman of a Senate

committee that investigated the mine explosion on March 25 that killed 111 miners in Centralia, Ill. His report concluded that state and federal regulators had been negligent and also placed partial blame on the mine's management and the mine workers' union.

Cordon supported Taft's 1952 presidential candidacy but switched his loyalties to Dwight D. Eisenhower after the Republican National Convention. As the senior member of a group of western Republican politicians that advised Eisenhower on water and mineral resource issues and public lands, Cordon received prominent mention as a likely choice for secretary of the interior. After Eisenhower's election, however, Cordon made it known that he had no interest in joining the cabinet, stating that he would be more valuable to the new administration in the Senate. Cordon recommended Oregon's governor, Douglas McKay, a longtime political ally, for the post. Eisenhower complied.

During the Eighty-third Congress, Cordon was Eisenhower's senior adviser on resource issues, shaping the so-called "partnership" policy that was designed to reduce the federal government's supervision of resources and to increase the participation of private industry. In 1953, Cordon was the floor manager of the administration's tidelands oil bill that recognized state rather than federal control of offshore oil deposits. He usually supported the administration's foreign and domestic policies.

Cordon had planned not to seek reelection in 1954 but was persuaded by Eisenhower to change his mind. His Democratic challenger, Richard L. Neuberger, forced Cordon on the defensive by making the campaign a referendum on the Eisenhower administration's resource policies. Despite a late campaign appearance by Eisenhower, Cordon lost by 2,500 votes, which cost Republicans their control of the Senate. For the next thirteen years, Cordon practiced law in Washington, D.C., where he died.

[There are materials related to Cordon's political career in the Charles L. McNary papers at the Library of Congress and in the Douglas McKay and Richard L. Neuberger papers at the University of Oregon. See also A. Robert Smith, *The Tiger of the Senate* (1962); Elmo Richardson, *Dams, Parks and Politics* (1973); and Gary W. Reichard, *The Reaffirmation of Republicanism* (1975). Obituaries are in the *New York Times* and the *Oregonian*, both June 10, 1969.]

STEVE NEAL

CRAWFORD, SAMUEL EARL (Apr. 18, 1880–June 15, 1968), baseball player, was born in Wahoo, Nebr., the son of Stephen Crawford, manager of a general store, and Mary McNulty. Crawford left school after the seventh grade and took a job as a shoeshine boy in a barbershop where he also apprenticed as a barber. A left-handed pitcher and outfielder, he played baseball for the Killian Family Company team in Wahoo. With a wagon provided by the sponsor, the team traversed eastern Nebraska, challenging other town teams and passing the hat to cover expenses. In 1898 Crawford was hired for two months to play for Superior, Nebr. Later that year he traveled to West Point, where he helped that club win the state championship. He adopted the nickname "Wahoo Sam"; throughout his career, Crawford signed all his letters and autographs "Wahoo Sam Crawford," even requesting that this full citation be placed on his Hall of Fame plaque.

In 1899 Crawford was recruited by John McIlvaine, a pitcher and friend, to play for the Chatham (Ontario) Club of the Canadian League for $65 per month. Crawford hit .370 in forty-three games before the club disbanded in July. His next job was with the Columbus, Ohio, team in the Western League; the club moved to Grand Rapids, Mich., in midseason. Crawford batted .333 for sixty games. Recruited by Cincinnati in the National League, he earned $150 for the final month of the season. His major-league debut in a September doubleheader was auspicious, with five hits in eight times at bat. In thirty-one games he hit .307, with two doubles and eight triples.

Crawford completed three full seasons with Cincinnati. After batting .270 in 1900, Crawford, six feet tall and 190 pounds, developed as a leading power hitter of his day. In 1901 he ranked third in the league, with 104 runs batted in and first in the league with 16 home runs; his batting average was .335. The following seasons he achieved star status, with twenty-three triples, 256 total bases, a slugging percentage of .461, a .333 batting average, 185 hits, and seventy-eight runs batted in. His full career with Cincinnati encompassed 403 games, batting .314, with 498 hits, including twenty-seven home runs, sixty-two triples, and fifty-two doubles. He scored 278 runs and drove in 261. In October 1901 Crawford married Ada Lattin of Wahoo; they had two children.

Still earning $150 per month in Cincinnati, Crawford looked for bigger and better things; the rivalry between the established National League and the new American League gave him his big opportunity. A bidding war developed for the services of Crawford and other National League stars. On the eve of the 1903 season he signed contracts with both Cincinnati and the Detroit Tigers of the American League. Rather than engage in a costly legal struggle, the two leagues made peace, and in the negotiations that followed Crawford was awarded to Detroit, where he would earn $3,500 for the season.

Crawford's outstanding career with the Detroit Tigers lasted from 1903 through 1917. He played in 2,114 games, averaging 141 games per season. With Detroit his batting average was .309, including seventy home runs, 250 triples, and 403 doubles, accounting for 1,115 runs scored and 1,264 runs batted in. Seven times he was either first or second in the league in runs batted in and total bases; six times in hits and triples; and three times in batting average, home runs, doubles, and slugging percentage. He was an adequate defensive outfielder, but his foot speed was deceptive. In accumulating his record 312 triples, his baserunning skills became evident. In his career he stole 366 bases, with a season high of 41 in 1912.

Crawford's achievements were overshadowed by his illustrious teammate Ty Cobb, who joined the Tigers late in the 1905 season. During Detroit's pennant-winning years (1907–1909), whenever Crawford ranked second in batting average, runs batted in, hits, doubles, runs, slugging average, or total bases, it was Cobb who ranked first. The two outfield stars were intense rivals. Davy Jones, the third Detroit outfielder from 1906 to 1912, observed that "playing by the side of two fellows like that was a good deal like being a member of the chorus of a grand opera where there are two prima donnas."

The two heroes were at their best when the Tigers emerged as league champions. In 1907 Hughie Jennings became the Detroit manager, and his skill at handling Crawford and Cobb resulted in three consecutive American League pennants. Regretably, Crawford was unable to sustain his play in the World Series. He batted just .243 for the seventeen games, with five doubles, one home run, and six runs batted in. In the 1907 World Series the Chicago Cubs defeated the Tigers four games to none, with one tie. The next year the same clubs met in the fall classic, but the Tigers won only one of five games. In 1909 the Pittsburgh Pirates bested Detroit four games to three.

After 1909 the Tigers remained competitive but failed to win a league title, finishing third in 1910 and second in 1911 and 1915. But Crawford's batting achievements continued, and he achieved personal bests in 1910, with 120 runs batted in, and in 1911, with 217 hits, 109 runs, a slugging average of .526, and a batting average of .378, third in the league to Cobb and Joe Jackson, who each hit over .400. From 1913 to 1915 Crawford led the league in triples.

When the club fell to third place in 1910, Crawford, speaking for his teammates, blamed the fall on "too much Cobb," claiming that Cobb had received special treatment from the management and played for himself and not the team. Not until many years into retirement did Crawford and Cobb mellow toward each other. Cobb even lobbied actively for Crawford's election to the Hall of Fame.

After the 1910 season Crawford and many of his teammates, including Cobb, toured Cuba. They played an all-star team that included black American players who took advantage of every opportunity to show their skills outside their own segregated leagues and teams. The American leaguers won seven of twelve games. Three years later Crawford joined a postseason round-the-world tour organized by John McGraw. From Oct. 18, 1913, to Mar. 6, 1914, two teams of players traveled and played exhibition games in Japan, China, Australia, Egypt, Italy, France, England, and Ireland.

Fortunately for Crawford, still productive late in his major-league career, the new Federal League began in the 1914 season. This upstart league, trying to sign established stars, approached Crawford with an attractive offer. Crawford's salary with the Tigers had reached $4,000 in 1908 and $5,000 in 1912 and 1913. World Series shares for the Tigers had added about $2,000 to his earnings in 1907, $870 in 1908, and $1,275 in 1909. The Tigers' owner, Frank Navin, welcoming Crawford back from his world tour, signed him in 1914 to a four-year contract at $7,500 per year.

In 1914 and 1915 Crawford led the league in triples and runs batted in. In 1915 he appeared in 156 games, one less than the previous year, and batted .299. Crawford struck out only eighty-eight times in 1,803 times at bat from 1913 through 1915. Nevertheless, Jennings announced at the start of the 1916 season that Crawford was slowing down and hurting the team. That year Crawford appeared in 100 games and batted .286. Many of his appearances were as a pinch hitter, and his eight hits led the league in that category. For his final major-league season in 1917, Crawford played in sixty-one games and batted .173. In late August, a traditional testimonial game for him was held in Detroit. Crawford received $1,200 in gifts and left for Los Angeles.

He then began a four-year stint with the Los Angeles Angels of the Pacific Coast League, accumulating a .326 batting average. In 1919 he peaked at .360, with fourteen home runs, forty-one doubles, and eighteen triples. Two years later, Crawford hit .318, with 199 hits in 175 games. His playing days over, he moved to other baseball pursuits. In 1924 he became the first official baseball coach at the University of Southern California in Los Angeles. During his six-year tenure, the team registered fifty-nine victories, forty-six defeats, and three ties. In 1927 Crawford began a lifelong affiliation with the Association of Professional Baseball Players of America. Organized in Los Angeles in 1924, the association was formed to provide services to retired ballplayers in need. From 1939 to 1942 Crawford served as treasurer. From 1935 to 1938 he returned to organized baseball as an umpire in the Pacific Coast League. During World War II he worked in a defense plant. His first wife having died, he married Mary Blazen in July 1943.

Throughout his Southern California "retirement," Crawford lived in a number of communities, but in his last years he divided his time between Hollywood and a small home in the desert community of Pearblossom. After the war he became something of a recluse. He would spend long periods of time alone in the desert while his wife remained in Hollywood. He did not have a telephone or read the newspapers, and the television was turned on only for an occasional World Series game. During this period Crawford read Balzac and the nineteenth-century philosopher Robert G. Ingersoll.

When the news arrived in 1957 that Crawford had been elected by the special committee on veterans to the Hall of Fame, his neighbors knew nothing of his baseball exploits. At the induction ceremony on July 22, 1957, in Cooperstown, N.Y., Crawford was overcome by emotion and said only a few words. He died in Hollywood.

Crawford was one of the premier power hitters of baseball's deadball era. He played in 2,505 major-league games and batted .309, with 9,579 times at bat and 2,964 hits, including 95 home runs and 455 doubles. He was the only player to lead both major leagues in home runs; he still holds the record for most triples in a career, 312. Crawford's slugging awed contemporaries, who later insisted that he would have rivaled Babe Ruth had they played at the same time.

[Biographical sketches are in Frederick G. Lieb, *The Detroit Tigers* (1946); Lawrence S. Ritter, *The Glory of Their Times* (1966); and Martin Appel and Burt Goldblatt, *Baseball's Best: The Hall of Fame Gallery* (1977). Considerable material on Crawford is in the Baseball Hall of Fame library in Cooperstown, N.Y. Obituaries are in the *New York Times*, June 17, 1968; and the *Sporting News*, June 29, 1968.]

DAVID BERNSTEIN

CROUSE, RUSSEL McKINLEY (Feb. 20, 1893–Apr. 3, 1966), news reporter, columnist, author, playwright, and producer, was born in Findlay, Ohio, the son of Hiram Powers Crouse, a prominent editor and publisher, and Sarah Schumacher. Crouse began school in Findlay. In 1900 his family moved to Toledo, Ohio, where his father owned and edited the *Toledo News-Bee*. Crouse graduated from Monroe (grade) School in 1906 and attended Central High School for one year. In 1907 his family, having lost money, moved to Enid, Okla., where he attended Enid High School. During his senior year he received an alternate's appointment to the United States Naval Academy, Annapolis. In the spring of 1910 he entered Wilmer and Chew's Prep School, Annapolis, to prepare for the entrance examinations for the academy. He failed geometry and had to withdraw.

Returning home, Crouse stopped in Cincinnati to visit an uncle, who helped him find a job as a reporter on the *Cincinnati Commercial-Tribune*. With a natural talent for news-gathering and writing, Crouse nevertheless made plans to attend college. In the summer of 1911 he joined his family in Kansas City, Mo., where he worked briefly as a police reporter on the *Kansas City Star*. When an illness, incorrectly diagnosed as tuberculosis, prevented him from entering college, he returned to the *Star* and remained there until 1916.

With the approach of World War I, Crouse resigned from the *Star*, rejoined his family, now in Cincinnati, and took a temporary position as political reporter on the *Cincinnati Post*. In 1917, the year that Crouse enlisted in the navy, the city council passed a laudatory resolution for his news coverage of city hall. For two years he served as a yeoman second class at the Naval Training Station in Great Lakes, Mich., remaining for the duration of the war. An officer whom he had known in Kansas City made him the night editor of the *Great Lakes Bulletin*, the official newspaper of the station. Discharged on Jan. 20, 1919, he returned to the *Cincinnati Post*.

Two months later Wesley Stout, a friend who had known Crouse in Kansas City, wrote that he was leaving the *New York Globe*. Crouse went to New York City, got Stout's old job, and stayed. By April 6 Crouse had written his first signed story. On March 17, 1923, he married Alison Smith, a drama critic and feminist and a friend of the writers and newspeople who frequently ate lunch at the Algonquin Hotel. Alison Smith died on Jan. 7, 1943, and on June 23, 1945, Crouse married Anna Erskine, the daughter of John Erskine. They had two children, one of whom, Lindsey Crouse, became an actress.

Careless in dress, tactful, and gentle, Crouse, an inveterate talker and punster, knew the members but was never part of the Algonquin Round Table. A teetotaler, he preferred going to speakeasies with Frank Sullivan and Robert Benchley or playing poker with Harpo Marx and Harold Ross. Defiant of good health habits, he hated fresh air and vegetables. He always carried coins for telephone calls—a legacy from his reporter days.

Crouse stayed with the *Globe* until it suspended publication in June 1923, then worked briefly on the *Evening Mail*. In 1924 he joined the *New York Evening Post;* his column "Left at the Post" was a regular feature from 1924 to 1929. Although he remained with the *Post* until*September 1931, he began writing scenar*arios for short films on newspaper life. He also contributed to "The Talk of the Town" in the *New Yorker*.

Long interested in the theater, Crouse accepted an eight-line role as Bellflower, a reporter, in *Gentlemen of the Press*, which opened on Aug. 17, 1928. In his first try at writing the libretto for a musical, he collaborated with Morrie Ryskind and Oscar Hammerstein on *The Gang's All Here*, which opened Feb. 18, 1931. From 1932 to 1937 Crouse served as press agent for the Theatre Guild and befriended many writers and actors, including Eugene O'Neill.

Crouse's interest in America's past led to his writing *Mr. Currier and Mr. Ives: A Note on Their Lives and Times* (1930) and *It Seems Like Yesterday* (1931), which he and Corey Ford turned into the successful musical *Hold Your Horses* (1933). In 1932 he compiled *The American Keepsake* and wrote *Murder Won't Out*.

Crouse's meeting with Howard Lindsay began one of the most successful collaborations in theater history. In September 1934 the producer Vinton Freedley was seeking someone to assist Lindsay in adapting a Guy Bolton and P. G. Wodehouse story to the music of Cole Porter; Neysa McMein, the illustrator, suggested Crouse. With the opening of *Anything Goes* on Nov. 21, 1934, the pair began a working relationship that lasted thirty-two years. "If any two people can be said to think alike," Lindsay declared, "we do." Lindsay is said to have possessed a greater knowledge of the theater; Crouse, a sharper sense of humor. *Red, Hot, and Blue* opened on Oct. 29, 1936, and *Hooray for What!* on Dec. 1, 1937.

Summoned to Hollywood, Lindsay and Crouse, over the next several decades and usually with other writers, collaborated on a number of screenplays, including *Artists and Models Abroad* (1938), *The Big Broadcast of 1938* (1938), and *The Great Victor Herbert* (1939). They wrote the film adaptations of *Anything Goes* (1936), *Life with Father* (1947), *State of the Union* (1948), and *Call Me Madam* (1953), and the remake of *Anything Goes* (1956).

Life with Father, Crouse and Lindsay's first straight play, brought them enduring recognition. They had talked about dramatizing Clarence Day's stories ever since they had read them in the *New Yorker* in 1936. As scenes began to take shape, they shouted lines at each other and tested phrasing. Lindsay paced the floor; Crouse recorded ideas and dialogue on his typewriter. They wrote the script in seventeen days. The play opened on Broadway on Nov. 8, 1939, and ran for 3,224 performances. As producers, their touches of warm humor and zany horror turned Joseph Kesselring's *Arsenic and Old Lace* (1940) into a highly successful murder comedy. In addition, they produced *The Hasty Heart* (1945), *Detective Story* (1949), and *One Bright Day* (1952).

Their plays were both timely and critical. *State of the Union* (1945), a political satire, was rewritten from day to day to keep it current. *The Sound of Music* (1959), for which they wrote the book, ended with the escape of the Trapp family singers from Nazi Germany. Other plays included *Strip for Action* (1942); *Life with Mother* (1948), based on the book by Clarence Day; *Remains to Be Seen* (1951); *The Prescott Proposals* (1953); *The Great Sebastions* (1956); *Happy Hunting* (1956); *Tall Story* (1959), adapted from the novel *The Homecoming* by Howard Nemerov; and *Mr. President* (1962). Lincoln Barnett called Lindsay and Crouse "probably the most successful team of dramaturgists since Gilbert and Sullivan." Crouse died in New York City.

[The Crouse papers are in the Theater Collection, University of Wisconsin. With Anna Erskine Crouse he wrote two books for children: *Peter Stuyvesant of Old New York* (1954) and *Alexander Hamilton and Aaron Burr* (1958). The most thorough biography is Cornelia Otis Skinner, *Life with Lindsay and Crouse* (1976). See also Henry I. Pringle, "Life with Lindsay and Crouse," *Saturday Evening Post*, May 27, 1941; Thomas Brady, "'Father' in Hollywood," *New York Times*, May 19, 1946; Anna Erskine Crouse, "Life with Timothy's Father," *Good Housekeeping*, September 1946; Lincoln Barnett, "Lindsay and Crouse," *Life*, Nov. 11, 1946; Lincoln K. Barnett, *Writing on Life* (1951); Gilbert Millstein, "First Twenty-five Years of Lindsay and Crouse," *New York Times Magazine*, Nov. 22, 1959.]

JOHN E. HART

CUDAHY, EDWARD ALOYSIUS, JR. (Aug. 22, 1885–Jan. 8, 1966), meat packer, was born in Chicago, Ill., the son of Edward Aloysius Cudahy, a meat-packing plant supervisor, and Elizabeth Murphy. In 1887 his father, his uncle Michael, and Philip D. Armour purchased from Sir Thomas J. Lipton a new, small packing plant (with a daily capacity of 1,000 hogs) in South Omaha, Nebr., which Cudahy's father then managed. In 1890 Michael bought out Armour and with Edward established the Cudahy Packing Company. Michael remained in Chicago as president while Edward stayed in Omaha as vice-president and general manager in charge of plant operations.

While Cudahy attended local schools, his uncle and father expanded Cudahy Packing so rapidly that by 1900 it was one of the four largest American meat-packing companies, along with Swift, Armour, and Morris. Edward Cudahy, Sr., reputedly became a millionaire. On Dec. 18, 1900, young Cudahy was kidnapped and held in chains for twenty-four hours by James Callahan and Pat Crowe, a garrulous swindler and train robber whom Cudahy's father had often aided financially. Threats to blind Cudahy with acid moved his distraught father to pay a $25,000 ransom in gold. After releasing Cudahy unharmed, Crowe escaped and spent the money, but Callahan was captured, tried for robbery (there was no law in Nebraska against kidnapping an adolescent), and acquitted. Apparently the $50,000 reward offered for a conviction undermined the credibility of prosecution witnesses, and the jury felt that Cudahy's father could well afford the ransom. Callahan was later tried and acquitted for perjury. After Crowe surrendered he was acquitted of felonious assault in 1905 and of robbery in 1906, went straight, lectured on the evils of lawbreaking while boasting he had kidnapped Cudahy, wrote an autobiography entitled *Spreading Evil*, and died destitute in New York City in 1938.

The episode seems to have caused Cudahy little harm. He attended Chicago Latin School and Creighton University, Omaha, from 1900 to 1904. In 1905 he entered the family's Omaha plant and learned the business from the ground up. He also became prominent in society. When Cudahy's uncle Michael died in 1910, Cudahy's father became president of Cudahy Packing and Cudahy moved to Chicago to join him at company headquarters. There he learned the business from the top down, becoming first vice-president in 1916. His tutelage was interrupted by service in the army during World War I as captain of a machine-gun company.

After the war Cudahy played a wider role in managing the company, gradually relieving his father of many duties. In 1919 the public accused meat packers of war profiteering, and the Federal Trade Commission charged them with price fixing and attempting to monopolize the food industry. Though the announcement of Cudahy's engagement in December 1919, followed by a congratulatory telegram from dead broke but irrepressible Pat Crowe, amused the nation, Cudahy aroused its ire a few days later when he blamed the high cost of meat not on price fixing but on the demand for expensive steaks and roasts and scolded people for not eating corned beef.

The big five meat packers (Wilson and Company was the addition) soon capitulated and consented to a federal court injunction issued in February 1920 restricting them to the wholesale meat business. On Dec. 27, 1920, Cudahy married Margaret Carry; they had two sons, who entered the family business, and a daughter, Sheila Cudahy Pellegrini, who became a publisher of books under imprints carrying both her maiden and married names.

Cudahy became president of Cudahy Packing (his father becoming chairman of the board) in January 1926. The company operated nine plants, had distribution facilities in nearly 100 cities, and owned a fleet of refrigerator and tank cars. It also manufactured Old Dutch Cleanser, soap, and cottonseed oil. Its sales in 1926 were $232 million, and its $4 million net profit was the highest in its history. It prided itself on its laboratories at each plant and boasted of its "conservative management" that insisted that meat packing was not dependent for success on general industrial activity.

Despite this claim the meat-packing industry was hurt by the Great Depression. In 1932 the company netted only $906,000 on sales of $133 million, though its 12,000 employees had taken two 10 percent wage cuts. Seeking unsuccessfully to modify the consent decree of 1920 that restricted meat-packing operations, Cudahy testified in November 1930 that collusion among meat packers to buy livestock or sell meat was both impractical and impossible. He stressed that in the late 1920's competition among the meat packers increased because pork exports to Europe had declined, chain stores (tending to purchase from smaller packers) had grown, and the highway system (enabling small packers to purchase livestock and sell meats over a wider area) had expanded.

At first Cudahy was pleased with President Franklin D. Roosevelt's New Deal. Its currency manipulation improved meat exports in 1933, and in 1934 National Recovery Administration regulations, while increasing operating costs, raised market prices; Cudahy's net profit rose to almost $2 million. Cudahy's enchantment with the New Deal evaporated in 1935 when a shortage of hogs led to declining meat prices. In 1936, after the Supreme Court declared the Agricultural Adjustment Administration unconstitutional, Cudahy Packing attempted unsuccessfully to recover the $11.9 million it had paid in processing taxes on slaughtered hogs. With the 1935 National Labor Relations Act, labor difficulties intensified. The Meat Cutters Union complained that Cudahy Packing had denied its newly guaranteed rights and by 1939 the National Labor Relations Board ordered Cudahy to disestablish its company union. Ominously, the Robert M. La Follette Civil Liberties Committee included Cudahy Packing among those companies with stores of munitions and tear gas, presumably for use against strikers. Cudahy Packing, which had failed to show a profit only once before, blamed a 25 percent rise on labor costs, a severe drought that cut corn and hog production, and the recession of 1937–1938, when it lost $1.8 million in 1937 and almost $3 million the next year. Contradicting his company's earlier testimony, Cudahy found that "factory payrolls bear a very close relationship to the price of meats and by-products."

Despite these losses, Cudahy was personally wealthy; his salary (almost $50,000 in 1941) did not indicate his worth. His father had distributed some of his wealth before he died in 1941. In 1937 the Joint Congressional Tax Evasion Committee used Cudahy to illustrate loopholes in the tax structure. His personal holding company, Lothair Development, held $5 million of his securities and from 1929 to 1935 they earned $3 million, which Cudahy neither touched nor paid taxes on.

Meat packing revived before World War II but so did federal antitrust activity. Along with other packers, Cudahy was indicted in 1941 for fixing hog prices in Iowa and Nebraska and Easter ham prices throughout the nation. Wartime demands and the need for cooperation led the government to ignore these indictments and to drop them in 1949. World War II brought prosperity to Cudahy Packing (in 1942 and 1943 its profits were $3.4 million), but during the war Cudahy's involvement in the daily operations of the company began to slacken. His wife died in 1942, a few months after they were divorced. Beginning in 1943 Cudahy wintered in Phoenix, Ariz. On Jan. 25, 1944, he married Eleanor Peabody Cochran, and later that year he gave up the presidency of Cudahy Packing to become its board chairman.

The postwar inflation increased Cudahy's net profits to a high of $7.1 million on sales of $573 million in 1947. These profits of one and a quarter cents on each sales dollar, or less than a quarter of a cent per pound of meat sold, were, as Cudahy argued, not exorbitant. Cudahy Packing, however, was inefficient. Its profits declined to $1 million in 1948 because of a disastrous, violent, two-month strike, and, while still fourth among packers, the company showed less growth in sales than did the next five largest packers. Rising operating costs lost Cudahy Packing $4.7 million in 1949, the same year many packers operated in the black.

During Cudahy's last years as board chairman, sales declined from $640 million in 1951 to $313 million in 1962. Occasional profitable years, like 1956 ($6 million), were overshadowed by losses ($7 million in 1954 and almost $1 million in 1962). Cudahy had fallen to seventh place in the packing industry. Struggling for efficiency, the company began in 1951 to close outmoded plants, unprofitable distributing branches, and egg and poultry plants. It also staved off deficits briefly by selling its profitable Old Dutch Cleanser and soap divisions. In the late 1950's, Cudahy began to modernize its facilities and in the early 1960's automated its Omaha plant. Anxious to improve its earnings through diversification, Cudahy Packing in 1956 again tried to obtain release from the restrictions of the 1920 consent decree, but in 1960 Judge Julius J. Hoffman rejected the petition.

After Cudahy, whose health was declining, resigned in 1962, analysts blamed his company's problems on its ingrown, narrow-minded, top-heavy management, which had preferred slaughterhouse to educational experience ("not a single graduate engineer in the company," as his son Edward put it). It had no personnel policy, no job descriptions, and much duplication of effort. Its obsolete marketing strategy snubbed chain supermarkets and relied on independent retailers, requiring an expensive distribution system. As president and then board chairman from 1926 to 1962, Cudahy failed to foster research, long-range planning, or diversification. By hanging Cudahy Packing's fortunes almost totally on the volatile livestock market, Cudahy presided over the disintegration of the company his uncle and father had created. He died in Phoenix, Ariz.

[For information on Cudahy's father, uncle, and the early years of Cudahy Packing, see Consul W. Butterfield, "History of South Omaha," in James W. Savage and John T. Bell, *History of the City of Omaha, Nebraska, and South Omaha* (1894); and William Kane, *The Education of Edward Cudahy* (1941). The Cudahy Packing Company *Yearbook* (1926–1931) and *Annual Report* (1943–1957) provide data on the company and information about Cudahy. On his kidnapping, see Patrick T. Crowe, *Spreading Evil: Pat Crowe's Autobiography* (1927). On Cudahy Packing's problems in the 1960's, see *Fortune*, 67, Feb. 1963; and *Business Week*, Feb. 13, 1965. See also the obituary in the *New York Times*, Jan. 9, 1966.]

Ari Hoogenboom

CUMMINGS, WALTER JOSEPH (June 24, 1879–Aug. 20, 1967), banker and industrialist, was born on his family's farm near Springfield, Ill., the son of Walter Joseph Cummings and Mary Doyle. He attended elementary school in Springfield and high school in Chicago after the family moved to that city. Cummings briefly attended, in succession, Northwestern, Loyola, and De Paul universities but received no degree.

His first job was as a teller for Illinois Merchants Bank (later Continental Illinois National Bank and Trust Company), which was headed by his parents' friend John J. Mitchell. He left this position seeking higher wages in order to better support a family. On Nov. 27, 1915, he married Lillian Garvy; they had three children.

During World War I, Cummings bought the McGuire Streetcar and Bus Manufacturing Company in Paris, Ill., and changed the name to McGuire, Cummings Company (later Cummings Car and Coach Company). Initially the company manufactured streetcars and buses but by the 1920's was also successfully manufacturing trackless trolleys and trucks.

In the 1920's Cummings was active in transit-related businesses. He purchased the Des Moines Railway Company and the Des Moines and Iowa Central Railroad Company, a short-line railway. He also formed the Chicago and West Towns Railway Company, which served Chicago's western suburbs with buses and streetcars. He purchased the Hammond, Whiting and East Chicago Railway, a traction company that served northern Indiana towns, and invested in the Terre Haute, Ind., traction system.

With the onset of the Great Depression, Cummings was appointed bankruptcy trustee of the Chicago, Milwaukee and St. Paul Railroad and the Chicago Railways Company, the streetcar and bus company that served Chicago residents. He also began investing in Chicago real estate, which he continued to do most of his life.

In the early 1930's, Cummings acquired several Chicago-area transit companies. In August 1931, he bought the Calumet Railways Company, South Shore Line Motor Coach Company, and Midwest Coach Company from Midland United Company. In June 1932, he acquired Gary Railways Company. On Mar. 4, 1933, Cummings was elected president of Electric Railway Equipment Securities Corporation and was made a director and member of the executive committee of American Car and Foundry Motors Company.

On Apr. 8, 1933, Cummings entered government service at the behest of William H. Woodin, a former chairman of American Car and Foundry who had been appointed secretary of the Treasury by President Franklin D. Roosevelt. After the president had declared a "bank holiday" on Mar. 6, 1933, closing all the nation's banks, Woodin asked Cummings to serve as his executive assistant to supervise a staff of 1,500 examiners who would screen the banks to determine which were sufficiently sound to be quickly reopened. Within one week 12,000 banks were reopened. Later 3,000 weak banks were liquidated, and 2,000 others were merged with solvent institutions. These actions helped restore faith in the nation's banking system.

On Sept. 7, 1933, Cummings was selected as the first chairman of the Federal Deposit Insurance Corporation (FDIC). By early 1934 he was able to report to the president that 95 percent of the unrestricted banks had begun deposit insurance. On Jan. 30, 1934, Cummings left the FDIC, and on Mar. 14, 1934, he was appointed treasurer of the Democratic National Committee. During his tenure in that position, a long-standing party deficit was eliminated and the party's treasury was placed on a sound footing.

In February 1936, a Senate subcommittee investigated Cummings' income from positions with concerns in which the Reconstruction Finance Corporation (RFC) had an interest, but it found no evidence of wrongdoing. On Nov. 18, 1936, Cummings was elected a class-A director of the Chicago Federal Reserve Bank. (He was reelected to a second term in 1939.) Later in 1936, at the suggestion of the RFC, Cummings returned to Chicago as chairman of the Continental Illinois Bank.

In 1939 the Securities and Exchange Commission (SEC) suggested to the New York Stock Exchange that brokerage banks be established. The SEC opposed the practice of brokers accepting customers' cash and securities for deposit, since, in effect, the brokers were engaged in banking but were not subject to banking regulations. On July 13, 1939, the president of the New York Stock Exchange selected Cummings to serve on an examining board that made a detailed study of the effectiveness of brokerage banks in their relation to protection of brokers' customers.

In June 1946, President Harry Truman appointed Cummings to a commission charged with surveying and making recommendations to the president regarding reconstruction finance and world trade in the postwar period. In 1959 Cummings retired as chairman of the Continental Illinois Bank. He died in Chicago.

[There are no Cummings papers and no published biographies. The *New York Times* reported his career activities regularly between 1931 and 1956. On his role in the banking crisis, see C. B. Upham and Edwin Lamke, *Closed and Distressed Banks* (1934); C. D. Bremer, *American Bank Failures* (1935); and James F. T. O'Connor, *Banking Crisis* (1938). An obituary is in the *New York Times*, Aug. 21, 1967.]

STEPHEN D. BODAYLA

CUPPIA, JEROME CHESTER (Sept. 29, 1890–Sept. 20, 1966), securities and commodities trader, was born in Pelham Manor, N.Y., the son of Caesar Augustus Cuppia and Josephine Clementine Klugkist. The family moved to New Jersey, where he attended public schools and graduated from high school in 1907. Ambitions to attend Princeton were thwarted when his father suffered business reverses in the panic of 1907. Instead, Cuppia began working on Wall Street in that year as a runner for the brokerage firm of Craig and Jenks and quickly rose to the post of trader. While interested in stocks and bonds, Cuppia was more concerned with commodities. In 1916 he was a partner in Robertson and Company and became a member of the New York Cotton Exchange. An astute speculator, by 1917 he was believed to be worth more than half a million dollars. He enlisted in the navy that year and served as a stoker aboard the USS *Massachusetts*. On June 12, 1918, he married Helen Raymond; they had two children.

After World War I, Cuppia returned to commodities speculation, becoming a principal in the Taylor Cotton Company of Macon, Ga. In 1920 he moved to New York, where he formed the firm of Cuppia and Robertson. Three years later he organized a new firm, J. C. Cuppia and Company, which in 1926 was merged with E. A. Pierce and Company. In 1940, E. A. Pierce merged with other firms to form Merrill Lynch, E. A. Pierce and Cassatt. In 1925, Cuppia purchased a seat on the New York Curb Exchange (which became the American Stock Exchange in 1953) and started speculating in stocks and commodities.

In 1929, Cuppia became a member of the Curb Exchange board of directors; he was reelected in 1932 and 1935, heading a liberal group called "the Young Turks." Cuppia had few friends among the generally conservative membership but was respected because of his wealth and contacts. Always ambitious, Cuppia became active in Democratic politics in the early 1930's, supporting the presidential bid of Franklin D. Roosevelt in 1932. He later claimed to have turned down an offer of a position on the newly formed Securities and Exchange Commission (SEC). In 1938 he called for a new constitution for the exchange that would give the president new powers and create the office of chairman. Cuppia made it clear that he intended to seek that position, but the membership rallied behind the sitting president, Fred Moffatt. While a new constitution was adopted, Cuppia lost his bid for the chairmanship.

On Mar. 28, 1940, Cuppia was served with a warrant of attachment, applied for by William J. Plate, a fellow member of the Curb Exchange and a broker at Pierce and Company. Plate alleged that Cuppia had fraudulently obtained $101,647 from him between 1932 and 1939. According to Plate, Cuppia had advanced him $22,500 in 1932 for the purchase of a seat on the Curb. In return, Plate had opened a checking account, giving one of Cuppia's friends, Marion Shade, power of attorney to draw on it. From 1932 to 1939, Plate had earned $159,853 in commissions, all of which had been deposited in the account, and from which Shade had withdrawn $101,647. Plate contended he was left with about $65 a week.

Cuppia denied any wrongdoing, hinting broadly that Plate had brought suit at the suggestion of the conservative faction at the Curb, which was intent on ruining him. Friends urged Cuppia to countersue, but he held back, saying he would defend himself before the Curb Business Conduct Committee. However, in a letter to the committee dated Apr. 1, 1940, Cuppia wrote that Plate's charges "are not wholly untrue." The two men agreed that they would accept the committee's verdict and that the hearings should be held in camera to avoid scandal.

The hearings began on April 3. Initial testimony supported Plate's contention. Cuppia had told Plate that the money would be kept for his financial future, perhaps for a partnership at Pierce and Company. Plate testified that he sued once he learned that there was only $692.03 in an account he believed had close to $100,000. Investigation revealed checks drawn to Mrs. Cuppia, one to a hotel in the Bahamas to pay for a vacation, and a total of $5,000 that was used to purchase Cuppia's automobiles.

In his defense, Cuppia produced a document signed by both men in 1932, indicating that Plate owed Mrs. Cuppia $164,500. Plate claimed the document was false. It soon seemed that Cuppia would face new charges, but his allies on the committee found inconsistencies in Plate's testimony, which set the stage for Cuppia's appearance.

Cuppia testified that his wife and the wife of another broker, Frank Hubbard, had invested in the brokerage house of Locke, Andrews and Forbes, among whose assets were seats on the New York Stock Exchange and the Curb Exchange. Since Plate had purchased one of the seats from the brokerage firm, there was no direct connection between Cuppia and Plate. Cuppia also testified that the checking account had been opened on Plate's insistence and that the withdrawals had been made to defray Plate's debt. Within a few days it became evident that the matter was far more complicated than originally thought and that both men had behaved strangely, as though they had something to hide. It was later revealed that Plate and Cuppia had engaged in commission splitting, a practice forbidden by both the SEC and the Curb. Cuppia had purchased a seat for Plate, in return for which he received a portion of his commissions out of the joint checking account.

Cuppia resigned from his firm in 1940 and announced that he would cooperate with the committee, provided he was permitted a graceful exit from the financial community. Cuppia conceded he had violated Curb rules and told associates he planned to leave the country and move to South America. The contest with Plate was settled on July 31 with the payment by Cuppia to Plate of $7,500.

In 1941 the SEC investigated the matter, and it appeared that other officials, including members of both Curb factions, had been engaged in illegal practices. Cuppia testified on the condition that none of his testimony before the Committee on Business Conduct be made public. He admitted that he had arrangements not only with Plate but several other brokers as well. Within a few weeks it seemed the SEC itself was on trial for having failed to uncover the wrongdoing.

The Cuppia scandal was soon forgotten. Cuppia, who returned to the United States to testify before the SEC, was never indicted. He settled in Montclair, N.J., a broken man, and died there. Curiously, none of his obituaries mentions the scandal.

[See Robert Sobel, *Amex: A History of the American Stock Exchange, 1921–1971* (1972). An obituary is in the *New York Times*, Sept. 21, 1966.]

ROBERT SOBEL

CUSHING, RICHARD JAMES (Aug. 24, 1895–Nov. 2., 1970), Roman Catholic clergyman, was born in South Boston, Mass., the son of Patrick Cushing, a blacksmith, and Mary Dahill, immigrants from Ireland. Cushing attended public schools and then transferred to the Jesuit-run Boston College High School, from which he graduated in 1913. He spent two years at Boston College before entering St. John's Seminary, in Brighton, Mass., and was ordained a priest in 1921.

After a few months as a curate in a series of parishes, Cushing, who had long thought of becoming a foreign missionary, persuaded William Cardinal O'Connell to assign him to the Boston office of the Society for the Propagation of the Faith; in 1928 he was named director of the office with the title monsignor. His talents and temperament were admirably suited to this work; a manifest selflessness, combined with energy and enthusiasm, made him an effective solicitor of gifts. He sympathized warmly and instinctively with both the missionaries and their charges. Cushing became a friend to Francis J. Spellman, a priest who was to become auxiliary bishop of Boston. When Spellman became archbishop of New York in 1939, Cushing was named to replace him, and when O'Connell died in 1944, Cushing was named archbishop. The contrast between O'Connell and Cushing was striking. Whereas O'Connell had been urbane, intellectual, and aristocratic, Cushing was proud of his South Boston roots; was disposed to exaggerate his intellectual limitations; spoke vigorously, frequently at great length and occasionally with a breathtaking casualness, about complex theological questions; lived and died indifferent to material possessions; and derived apparently endless gratification from mingling with people.

As an administrator, Cushing valued imagination and enterprise more than he did prudence or extended financial planning. He added more than eighty churches and brought into the archdiocese more than sixty religious orders. He helped build many secondary schools and chartered three colleges. He worked to increase the number of vocations to the priesthood, designing the Pope John XXIII Seminary in Weston, Mass., for men who late in their lives decided to prepare themselves for ordination. He did not think parochially; just as the new seminary was meant to serve all the American dioceses, Cushing also arranged for priests trained in Boston to serve whichever diocese most needed help. In 1958 he founded the Missionary Society of St. James the Apostle, which sent priests to Peru, Bolivia, and Ecuador.

Throughout his life Cushing felt a special empathy for the helpless. He built six new hospitals. He frequently visited jails. He got great satisfaction from visiting homes for the aged, sometimes joining in a song or a jig or exchanging his episcopal hat for one of the women's. In 1947 he established St. Coletta's School for mentally retarded children in Hanover, Mass.; he visited it often and arranged to be buried there. He strongly supported the

Kennedy family in building Memorial Hospital for handicapped children in Brighton, Mass. He twice led a pilgrimage of children to Lourdes.

For much of the nineteenth and early twentieth centuries, Boston Catholics and Protestants had regarded each other warily. O'Connell in his long reign had demanded that Protestants give, and Catholics deserve, respect; cooperation (let alone warm friendship) was to be neither expected nor sought. Cushing, more than any other man, was responsible for an increasingly cordial tone; no one, the historian Walter Muir Whitehill declared, was more successful in "breaking down fences."

In the late 1940's, a Jesuit scholar, Leonard Feeney, attacked Boston College—and, by implication, Cushing—for watering down the traditional teaching that "there is no salvation outside the Church," and thereby exacerbated non-Catholics' fears of Catholic exclusivism and potential intolerance. Cushing effectively demonstrated that Feeney did not speak for Boston's Catholics. Cushing was not dismayed that Catholic young people attended non-Catholic colleges, and he helped create a chapel at Brandeis University, in the face of bitter protests that to do so would signify the church's indifference to religious error. In 1963 he took part in a Roman Catholic–Protestant colloquium at Harvard University. "I'm all for Catholics being identified with Protestants and Jews . . . in every possible friendly way," he said. "Nobody is asking them to deny their faith, and they shouldn't be asking anybody to deny their faith." He spoke in synagogues and Protestant churches and arranged for televising midnight mass at St. John's Seminary with a commentary that would help non-Catholics understand and appreciate the service. Episcopal Bishop Anson Phelps Stokes was to declare that the Protestant community had come to consider Cushing as "in a special way our own."

When John XXIII became pope in 1958, Cushing sensed a deep affinity with him. Like Cushing, John came from a family of modest means, was notably unpretentious, and was given to self-deprecating humor. Moreover, John's commitment to *aggiornamento* helped articulate and define Cushing's deep conviction, expressed in 1961, that "the Church is a dynamic, not a static institution. . . . It cannot be frozen in set forms. There are essentials of its life, but beyond these there must always be innovation, enterprise, new vision." In 1958, in Pope John's first consistory, Cushing was made a cardinal. He was deeply interested in the pope's purposes for the Second Vatican Council, which began its protracted labors in 1962, particularly in the clarification of Catholic teaching on religious liberty and on the relations of the church to Jews and to Protestants. He took only a small part in the proceedings, professing difficulty in understanding the Latin. He was frustrated by the complex procedures and impatient with what must have seemed to him an unenlightened opposition. But he was enormously gratified with the results, which he eloquently endorsed. When leaving for Rome in 1963 for the conclave that would elect Pope John's successor, Cushing expressed the hope that "the new Pope will be living in the twentieth century, and will think the twentieth century, and not the fourteenth or sixteenth century."

On many occasions as priest and archbishop, Cushing had turned to Joseph P. Kennedy for gifts to charities, and very early he developed a special fondness for John F. Kennedy. The latter seemed to symbolize for Cushing the success of Irish Catholics in America; the cardinal greatly admired the younger Kennedy's easy confidence that Catholicism and Americanism were wholly compatible. When Kennedy announced his candidacy for the presidency, Cushing, though fearful that America was not yet ready for a Catholic president, helped out. In the middle of the campaign, the Catholic bishops of Puerto Rico advised their people not to reelect Governor Luis Muñoz Marin because of his support of birth control and because he had secularized the public schools. Non-Catholics in the United States expressed concern that Kennedy, if elected, would be obliged to heed episcopal pressure of this sort. Cushing promptly issued a statement: "Whatever may be the custom elsewhere, the American tradition, of which Catholics form so loyal a part, is satisfied simply to call to public attention moral questions with their implications, and leave to the conscience of the people the specific political decision which comes in the act of voting."

When Kennedy, as president, proposed to give federal aid to public schools, many Catholic clergy and laity vigorously contended that unless Catholic parochial schools were also to be aided, Kennedy's legislation should be blocked; Cushing again spoke out: "I feel that as long as the majority of the American people" oppose giving federal money to parochial schools "Catholics should try to prove their rights to such assistance, but neither force such legislation through at the expense of national unity, nor use their political influence . . . to block legislation . . . because they do not get their own way." Though the bill did not pass, Cushing had done much to vindicate the right of a Catholic politician to work for what he regarded as the general welfare, even if that involved denying the conscientious claims of fellow Catholics. After Kennedy's death, Cushing found it praiseworthy that "under no conditions" would Kennedy have been "influenced in any way by the Catholic Church or the Vatican in the fulfillment of his official duties."

Cushing continued to give full support to the Kennedy family. When the president's widow proposed to marry a divorced man, Cushing defended her actions. He was criticized by some American Catholics, and protests were sent to Rome. But Cushing, though hurt, never doubted his right to approve the action of a person he was convinced was acting conscientiously.

Cushing's last years were often discouraging; his old age was made difficult by cancer, asthma, shingles, and ulcers. Furthermore, he was dismayed by some of the innovations called for by the "renewed" church. When seminarians at St. John's protested vigorously against traditional discipline, Cushing, who took authority and order for granted, summarily expelled those he regarded as "ringleaders." He was also saddened at the growing number of priests who were renouncing their vocation.

Cushing was not very comfortable with the papacy of Pope Paul VI. *Humanae Vitae*, Paul's encyclical banning artificial contraception, legislated on the kind of matter that Cushing had concluded could safely be left to the instructed conscience of the individual. Finally, his archdiocese was faced with mounting debts, a consequence of Cushing's energetic expansionism and the relative failure of his last fund drives. Cushing resigned his post in September 1970; he died in Boston.

Strikingly unconventional in his public life, Cushing was the sort of man about whom a myriad of anecdotes were told. But, despite his convivial demeanor, he was often lonely. Renowned for his matter-of-fact speech, he was a man of simple piety and deep faith. Wonderfully unpretentious, he occasionally went beyond self-deprecation to declare that he did not really understand himself. The baffling complexity of his persona probably contributed to his impact on American life. This "tough-talking saint" succeeded in speaking to, and for, working-class Catholics in South Boston as well as the Kennedys; and he won the affection and trust of unprecedented numbers of non-Catholics.

On social issues Cushing was conservative. Although long a member of the National Association for the Advancement of Colored People, he shared the opinion of his friend J. Edgar Hoover that Martin Luther King, Jr., was a dangerous radical. He liked Robert Welch, the founder of the John Birch Society, though he was distressed when the society called John F. Kennedy a Communist. But he had a deep respect for American constitutional guaranties of religious liberty, and he understood non-Catholic sensibilities about the exercise of ecclesiastical power.

[Cushing ordered the destruction of his personal papers. The archives of the Archdiocese of Boston contain a small collection of speeches and other public documents. Biographies are M. C. Devine, *The World's Cardinal* (1964); and John H. Cutler, *Cardinal Cushing of Boston* (1970). See also Francis J. Lally, *The Catholic Church in a Changing Society* (1962); Kenneth A. Briggs, "A Catholic Original," *Notre Dame*, Feb. 1983; and John Tracy Ellis, *Catholic Bishops: A Memoir* (1983). An obituary notice is in the *Boston Evening Globe*, Nov. 2, 1970.]

ROBERT D. CROSS

DARWELL, JANE (Oct. 15, 1880–Aug. 14, 1967), actress, was born Patti Woodard in Palmyra, Mo., the daughter of W. R. Woodard, a contractor and president of the Louisville and Southern Railroad, and Ellen Booth. She spent her childhood in Chicago, St. Louis, and Louisville, where her father had business interests, and at the family ranch near Iron Mountain, Mo., where he kept a string of racehorses. At the ranch she indulged a fondness for animals and practiced to become a bareback rider. She was educated at private schools in Chicago and Louisville and at Dana Hall, a finishing school in Boston.

While in school, Patti Woodard decided to become an actress. Though her parents objected—her father had already dissuaded her from seeking a career as a circus performer—they compromised and allowed her to study voice and dramatics so that she could sing roles in light opera. Not long out of finishing school, she joined a stock company in Chicago, making her professional stage debut in a production of *The Stubbornness of Geraldine*. After two years of apprenticeship with the company, she went to London and Paris, studying and playing a number of minor stage roles. She chose the stage name Jane Darwell, she later told an interviewer, so that her "wicked career" would not disgrace her family.

Darwell's European stay was cut short by the death of her father. After her return to America she went to Hollywood, where she appeared in a number of films, including *Rose of the Rancho* and *Brewster's Millions* (both 1914). Soon returning to the stage, she remained on the West Coast except for a summer with the Keith-Albee stock company at Providence, R.I., and two seasons on Broadway. Darwell had a role in *Swords*, Sidney Howard's first play, which opened on Broadway in September 1921. After Henry Duffy took over the Alcazar in San Francisco in 1924, she appeared there in a series of plays. She also did repertoire in Duffy's company in Seattle and Portland.

Darwell did not really embark on a film career until 1930, when she appeared in Paramount's *Tom Sawyer*. In motion pictures, as well as on the stage, she played character roles. By the mid-1930's she had graduated from playing bit parts, such as neighborhood gossips, to contract-player status with Fox (later Twentieth Century–Fox).

During the 1930's Darwell became well known for her roles as the housekeeper or grandmother in a number of Shirley Temple films: *Bright Eyes* (1934), *Curly Top* (1935), *Captain January* (1936), and *Poor Little Rich Girl* (1936). She also appeared in such Twentieth Century–Fox films as *One More Spring* (1935), *Navy Wife* (1935), *Life Begins at Forty* (1935), *Paddy O'Day* (1935), *The Country Doctor* (1936), *White Fang* (1936), *Ramona* (1936), *Nancy Steele Is Missing* (1937), *Slave Ship* (1937), *Dangerously Yours* (1937), *Three Blind Mice* (1938), and *Time Out for Murder* (1938). On loan to Metro-Goldwyn-Mayer (MGM), Darwell played the Atlanta matron Dolly Meriwether in *Gone with the Wind* (1939).

By 1939 most of Darwell's roles were depressingly similar. Since Twentieth Century–Fox did not seem to have anything else for her, she contemplated leaving. Then the studio gave Darwell a screen test for the role of Ma Joad in John Ford's *The Grapes of Wrath* (1940), a character that she had wanted to play since encountering her in John Steinbeck's novel. Though scarcely the image of a gaunt Okie, Darwell effected a remarkable characterization, with a wan look and pulled-back hair, and won the part over fifty other actresses who tested for it. She won the Academy Award for best supporting actress for her portrayal of Ma Joad, her most celebrated role. Darwell later claimed that she never had much luck until she gave up dieting and got plump.

An admirer of John Ford, Darwell appeared in a number of the director's subsequent films: *My Darling Clementine* (1946), *Three Godfathers* (1948), *Wagonmaster* (1950), *The Sun Shines Bright* (1953), and *The Last Hurrah* (1958). In a variety of films, she was used to strike a note of Americana: as Mrs. Samuels in *Jesse James* (1939), as Eliza in *Brigham Young, Frontiersman* (1940), as Mrs. Clemm in *The Loves of Edgar Allan Poe* (1942), and as the title character in *Captain Tugboat Annie* (1945). By the mid-1940's, Darwell had left Twentieth Century–Fox and was working as a free-lancer in Hollywood. Still making occasional stage appearances, she played in the comedy *Suds in Your Eye* in New York City in 1944.

Darwell continued to appear regularly in films throughout the 1950's, though not as frequently as during the prior two decades. She played her last screen role as the Bird Woman in *Mary Poppins* (1964). Darwell never married. She died in Woodland Hills, Calif.

Darwell was one of the most familiar character actresses in the history of Hollywood motion pictures. Known in much of her work for the maternal strength of her characterizations, she was easily the most famous of the motherly and grandmotherly types on the screen between 1930 and 1960.

[See the *Palmyra* (Mo.) *Spectator*, May 8, 1940; Alfred E. Twomey and Arthur F. McClure, *The Versatiles* (1969); Alex Barris, *Hollywood's Other Women* (1975); James Robert Parish *et al.*, *Hollywood Character Actors* (1978); *Hannibal* (Mo.) *Courier-Post*, Oct. 17, 1985; and the obituaries in the *St. Louis Post-Dispatch* and the *New York Times*, both Aug. 15, 1967.]

L. MOODY SIMMS, JR.

DAVIS, BENJAMIN OLIVER, SR. (July 1, 1877–Nov. 26, 1970), army officer, was born in Washington, D.C., the son of Louis Davis, a messenger in the Department of the Interior, and Henrietta Stewart. An avid reader, Davis was a bright student in the public schools of the District of Columbia. His strong interest in the military and in American history manifested itself in his high school days. Davis was in his first year at Howard University when the United States declared war against Spain in April 1898. After completing his final examinations for the year, he joined the infantry. Because he had been in the military training program at Howard, Davis was appointed temporary first lieutenant in the Eighth Volunteer Infantry in July 1898. His battalion moved south and was stationed at Key West, Fla., when the war ended.

Mustered out of the service in March 1899, Davis opted for a military career. He enlisted as a private in Troop I of the Ninth Cavalry, one of four black units in the regular army. His regiment became part of the military force used to put down the insurrection in the Philippines. By the end of his first year, Davis had been promoted to sergeant major. When the army's officer corps was expanded in 1901, having been encouraged by several officers, Davis took the officer candidate examination. Placing third, he was awarded the permanent rank of second lieutenant of cavalry in February 1901. Many considered him the protégé of Colonel Charles Young, then the ranking black officer in the American army.

In October 1902, while stationed in Wyoming, Davis married Elnora Dickerson of Washington, D.C.; they had three children. (Their son, Benjamin Oliver Davis, Jr., became an army general.) In 1916, Davis' wife died from complications following the birth of their last child, and in 1919 he married Sadie Overton.

Prior to World War I, Davis' career was typical of that of the few black officers in the American military establishment. He served as a cavalry officer at various forts within the continental United States. He assisted in the training of black National Guardsmen and was an instructor in military science at black colleges, including Wilberforce University in Ohio and Tuskegee Institute in Alabama. From 1909 until 1912, Davis served as the military attaché to Liberia. Though suffering from recurring bouts of blackwater fever, he made a number of recommendations for the reorganization of the Liberian military and national constabulary. When Pancho Villa raided along the United States–Mexican border, Davis was assigned there, reaching the rank of major by the time the United States entered World War I. Davis saw no combat service during the war; his unit, the Ninth Cavalry, remained in the Philippines, decimated of experienced personnel to staff the growing number of black troops in the army.

After World War I, Davis was reassigned to the teaching of military science at black colleges. He also conducted parties of visitors to France's battlefields and American military cemeteries there, a service for which he received more than one commendation. When he was promoted to colonel in 1930, he was the only black line officer in the United States Army.

In 1938, Davis was appointed to the command of the 369th (N.Y.) National Guard. During the 1940 presidential election campaign, the Roosevelt administration was under pressure from black voters because of continued segregation in the military. Davis was promoted to brigadier general in October 1940, becoming the first black to achieve the rank of general. (At that time, the only other regular black officer was his son.) Davis was assigned command of the Fourth Cavalry Brigade. In June 1942, approaching the retirement age of sixty-five, Davis was mustered out of the service. Because of the expansion of the military with the spread of the war in Europe, Davis was immediately reactivated and assigned to the Inspector General's Office, a move that also had the effect of removing him from an active field command.

During World War II, Davis was primarily involved in inspecting the conditions of black troops, investigating incidents involving possible racial conflict in the military, and making recommendations concerning the involvement of blacks in the army. He was a member of the Advisory Committee on Negro Troop Policies (commonly called the McCloy Committee). Davis also made several trips to Europe, including England, Italy, and France, where he served as special adviser to theater commanders and to other important American military personnel.

Though Davis was sometimes castigated by the growing number of militant blacks for remaining in a segregated army, the evidence indicates that he worked tirelessly, if quietly, to improve the position of blacks in the army. He exerted constant and intense pressure to reduce racial animosity in the armed forces. Through his efforts, responsibility for improving the racial climate of the army was squarely placed on commanding officers. Through Davis' exertions, blacks were admitted to all branches of the American military. He insisted that black troops receive active combat assignments. Davis deserves a major share of the credit for the desegregation of the United States armed forces, even though he was no longer on active service when that occurred.

In 1948, with Davis' retirement pending, Senator Clyde H. Hoey of North Carolina introduced a bill to give Davis the permanent rank of brigadier general. On July 20, 1948, his official retirement ceremony was held in the White House, presided over by President Harry Truman. Following his fifty years of active military service, Davis and his wife resided in northwest Washington. He died at the Great Lakes Naval Hospital in Lake County, Ill.

[See *New York Times*, July 21, 1948; and James J. Flynn, *Negroes of Achievement in Modern America* (1970). An obituary is in the *New York Times*, Nov. 27, 1970.]

ARTHUR E. BARBEAU

DAVIS, WATSON (Apr. 29, 1896–June 27, 1967), science writer, editor, and popularizer, was born in Washington, D.C., the son of Charles Allan Davis, founder and principal of Washington's Business High School, and Maud Watson, a teacher. After attending public schools in Washington, Davis went to George Washington University, where he received a bachelor's degree in civil engineering in 1918 and a civil engineering degree in 1920. On Dec. 6, 1919, he married Helen Augusta Miles, who had received a bachelor's degree in chemistry from the same school; they had two children.

While in school, Davis worked at various jobs simultaneously, a habit that persisted throughout his life; his interests ranged so broadly that he could not confine himself to a single task. In 1917 he began working as an assistant engineer-physicist for the National Bureau of Standards, and three years later, he took an evening job as science editor for the *Washington Herald*. A year later, he left the National Bureau of Standards and became news editor of the newly created Science Service, a syndicated news agency founded by the newspaper magnate E. W. Scripps and the zoologist William E. Ritter. In 1922, Davis left the *Herald* to devote full time to Science Service and edit its new *Science News Letter* (later *Science News*). Although Science Service was directed by the chemist-turned-popularizer Edwin E. Slosson, Davis served (from 1923) as managing editor and secretary for the entire organization.

Slosson died in 1929, and Davis was named acting director. He did not become director until 1933, a delay he attributed to the trustees' desire to find someone with stronger scientific credentials than his own. They also may have been put off by Davis' personality, for he was already known as a desk-pounding, foul-mouthed, "feisty little man." At the same time, he was considerate, kept candy in his desk for visitors, and would quickly forget his rages.

By the early 1930's, Davis had established Science Service as the standard for science journalism. More than 100 newspapers published its regular columns of science news. The circulation of *Science News Letter* grew from 6,000 in 1930 to 30,000 in 1940. In 1930, on the Columbia Broadcasting System, Davis established a nationwide "Adventures in Science" radio interview program that continued until 1959. In 1934 he helped create the National Association of Science Writers (NASW); so many of its potential members were Science Service reporters that NASW founders decided to explicitly limit the organization's voting influence.

Davis' commitment to the popularization of science became something of a personal mission. "Science reporting and interpretation does not accomplish its purpose . . . if it does not bring about an appreciation and a utilization of the method of science in everyday life," he later wrote. Realizing that newspaper reports of science could play only a part in this mission, in 1941 he turned to three activities intended to stimulate an interest in science among young people: the Science Talent Search, science fairs, and Science Clubs of America. Although funded and operated independently, the three activities fed each other. Through a series of competitions, the Science Talent Search brought the nation's most promising high school science students to Washington for lectures and seminars; many went on to prominent and award-winning careers in science. The science fairs were regional events, originally sponsored by New York's American Institute, but Science Service enlarged the program and sponsored the International Science Fair at the peak of the competitive pyramid. And the Science Clubs of America, provided with ideas, badges, and other paraphernalia by Science Service, often served as the locus for talent-search and science-fair activities.

While developing these new programs, Davis maintained his day-to-day involvement with *Science News Letter* and the syndication service. In 1940 his wife began working regularly at Science Service to handle business affairs and, later, editorial work on *Chemistry*, a popular magazine that the organization published from 1944 to 1962. In 1941, Science Service established its independence from its sponsoring organizations by moving out of the National Academy of Sciences building into its own headquarters.

Davis continued his outside activities. In 1926, he and Slosson had started experimenting with new bibliographic techniques. In 1935, Davis applied his organizational skills to bring together similar activities from Science Service, the United States Department of Agriculture, and elsewhere to create the American Documentation Institute (ADI), devoted to innovations in bibliography and library work, especially micropublication and microfilm (a word credited to Davis). From 1937 to 1947 he served as president of the ADI. Other outside activities included the National Inventors Council (from 1940) and active trustee positions with George Washington University (1949–1961), Jackson Laboratory in Bar Harbor, Maine (1949–1967), and the National Child Research Center.

By the time World War II ended, Davis had become an autocratic leader, the undisputed embodiment of Science Service. The board of directors was not active, and Davis delegated no significant power to other staff members. Because he paid low wages and granted vacations only grudgingly, he lost many of his experienced staff members and failed to retain new ones. His devotion to science pleased the scientific community, but his growing involvement in youth activities and education took him away from Science Service's journalism base. At the same time, many journalists and scientists unconnected with Science Service began to recognize the value of science journalism. As a result, Science Service lost its preeminence and did not play a major role in the booming response to the postwar demand for popular science.

Finances at Science Service became strained in the 1950's as sales of the syndicated news service fell, the quality of *Science News Letter* dropped, and funding for many of the youth activities proved insufficient. To bring in money, Davis took on administrative contracts for National Science Foundation (NSF) seminars, as well as other government contract work. By the time NSF established its Public Understanding of Science program in the late 1950's, Davis was unable to present proposals sufficiently well argued to be funded. Science Service continued to drift for the next decade.

Davis' wife and partner died in 1957, and on Nov. 21, 1958, he married Marion Shaw Mooney, a widowed teacher. Unwilling to retire gracefully, Davis was forced to leave Science Service in 1966. He died in Washington, D.C.

[Davis' papers are in the Smithsonian Institution Archives, Washington, D.C. In addition to his thousands of newspaper columns and *Science News Letter* articles, he wrote or edited several books, including *The Story of Copper* (1924), *The Advance of Science* (1934), *Science Picture Parade* (1940), *Atomic Bombing* (1950), and *The Century of Science* (1963). For additional information on science writing and Science Service, see Hillier Krieghbaum, "American Newspaper Reporting of Science News," *Kansas State College Bulletin*, Aug. 15, 1941, and *Science and the Mass Media* (1967); Carolyn Hay, "A History of Science Writing in the United States and of the National Association of Science Writers" (M.A. thesis, Medill School of Journalism, Northwestern University, 1970); David J. Rhees, "A New Voice for Science: Science Service Under Edwin E. Slosson, 1921–1929" (M.A. thesis, University of North Carolina at Chapel Hill, 1979); and Bruce V. Lewenstein, "'Public Understanding of Science' in America, 1945–1965" (Ph.D. diss., University of Pennsylvania, 1987). See also *Science*, Sept. 3, 1948. Obituaries are in the *New York Times*, June 28, 1967; *Science News*, July 8, 1967; and *Chemical and Engineering News*, July 10, 1967.]

BRUCE V. LEWENSTEIN

DAWSON, WILLIAM LEVI (Apr. 26, 1886–Nov. 9, 1970), United States congressman and political power on Chicago's South Side, was born in Albany, Ga., the son of Levi

Dawson, a barber whose parents were slaves, and Rebecca Kendrick. Dawson attended the Albany Normal School and in 1905 went to Fisk University, where he was a star athlete. He received his B.A. magna cum laude in 1909. Three years later he left Georgia for Chicago, where he worked as a bellhop while attending Chicago-Kent School of Law. When the United States entered World War I in 1917, Dawson enlisted in the army as a first lieutenant. He was gassed and wounded in France while fighting with the 365th Infantry in the Vosges Mountains and in the Meuse-Argonne offensive. In 1919 he enrolled at Northwestern University to complete his legal studies. The following year he graduated and was admitted to the Illinois bar. Dawson married Nellie M. Brown in December 1922; they had two children.

Dawson entered politics as a precinct worker in the machine of Republican mayor William Thompson and served on the Republican state central committee from 1928 to 1930. He was elected alderman of the Second Ward in 1933. After serving on the city council for six years as a Republican, he switched parties and became a Democratic national committeeman in 1939. When Arthur W. Mitchell, the first black Democrat to be elected to Congress, decided not to seek a fifth term in 1942, Dawson won the Democratic primary and the general election in the state's First Congressional District. In Congress, Dawson represented the overwhelmingly black South Side slum wards of Chicago from Jan. 3, 1943, until his death.

The only black in Congress during his first term, Dawson actively opposed the poll tax, fought for the integration of the armed forces, and introduced legislation for the establishment of a fair employment practices committee. In 1944 he became the first black to be elected vice-chairman of the Democratic National Committee. The soft-spoken Dawson soon gained a reputation as a diligent party loyalist. He worked harmoniously with the southern democratic leadership in the House of Representatives, and in 1949 he was elected chairman of the House Committee on Government Operations, becoming the first black to head a standing committee in Congress. Unlike the flamboyant black fighter for civil rights, Adam Clayton Powell, Jr., who was elected a congressman from New York City in 1944, Dawson eschewed speaking out on the major postwar racial issues and chose to operate on the personal and committee levels in Congress, claiming that his mission was to win friends for his race and to create an understanding of black grievances. While moderate blacks endorsed him as an effective politician who opened job opportunities and who gained recognition for blacks within the Democratic party, more-militant blacks denounced him as an "Uncle Tom" who neither championed civil rights nor improved the lot of his constituents.

Dawson increasingly retreated into silence as the civil rights movement gathered momentum. Nevertheless, he increased his tight hold on his district by careful organization, patronage, vote-buying, and accessibility to his supporters; he maintained his black political machine as a dominant element in Chicago Democratic affairs. Popularly called "The Man," the only politician on the South Side from whom to seek favors and jobs, Dawson in 1955 helped engineer the dumping of an incumbent reform mayor in Chicago in favor of his friend and ally on the Cook County Democratic Central Committee, Richard Daley. In 1960 his aid in delivering Chicago's black votes in the presidential contest led John F. Kennedy to offer him the post of postmaster general. Dawson turned down the chance to be the first black cabinet member because he believed that he could be more effective in Congress. Throughout his final decade, however, Dawson remained aloof from the racial crusades and turmoil of the 1960's, offering neither eloquence nor legislation to the cause of civil rights. To the end, Dawson continued to exemplify his faith in political power, rather than in protest, as the path to progress for his people. Because of ill health he chose not to seek a fifteenth term in 1970; he died in Chicago shortly after the election of his handpicked successor, Ralph Metcalfe.

[See Harold F. Gosnell, *Negro Politicians* (1935); James Q. Wilson, *Negro Politics: The Search for Leadership* (1960); and Chuck Stone, *Black Political Power in America* (1968). For biographical sketches, see "Negro America's Top Politician," *Ebony*, Jan. 1955; and the obituary in the *New York Times*, Nov. 10, 1970.]

HARVARD SITKOFF

DEBYE, PETER JOSEPH WILLIAM (Mar. 24, 1884–Nov. 2, 1966), physicist and physical chemist, was born Petrus Josephus Wilhelmus

Debije in Maastricht, the Netherlands, the son of Joannes Wilhelmus Debije, a foreman in a metalware manufacturing plant, and Maria Reumkens. After attending the Maastricht schools, Debye began his higher education at the Technical University in Aachen, Germany, twenty miles from his home. He was given a solid grounding in mathematics and classical physics, and in 1905 he received a diploma in electrical engineering. His work included a study of eddy currents in a rectangular conductor; he developed a mathematically elegant solution that in 1907 became his first published paper. He was strongly influenced at Aachen by Arnold Sommerfeld, a brilliant theoretical physicist, who said years later that his most important discovery was Peter Debye.

In 1906, when Sommerfeld received a professorship at the University of Munich, he took Debye with him as an assistant, and the young scholar moved easily into the rapidly changing world of modern physics. Wilhelm Röntgen, the discoverer of X rays, was on the Munich faculty; J. J. Thomson's discovery of the electron, Max Planck's enunciation of quantum theory, and Albert Einstein's formulation of relativity had all taken place during the previous decade. Debye completed a doctoral dissertation on radiation pressure on small spherical particles (1908), published ten other articles, and served for a time as privatdocent. In 1911, when Einstein moved from Zurich to Prague, Debye was selected to succeed him as professor of theoretical physics at the University of Zurich, and from then on, he was recognized as a member of the small international elite of physicists pioneering in the study of electricity, radiation, and molecular structure.

From 1911 to 1939, Debye held professorships at six universities: Zurich (1911–1912), Utrecht (1912–1913), Göttingen (1913–1920), the Federal Technical University in Zurich (1920–1927), Leipzig (1927–1934), and Berlin (1934–1939). In Berlin, as professor of theoretical physics and director of the Kaiser Wilhelm Institute for Physics, he supervised the construction of new laboratories for the institute, succeeded in changing its name to the Max Planck Institute (1938), and held one of the most prestigious and remunerative positions in European science. During these three decades, he conducted a tremendous amount of basic theoretical research and trained numerous scholars in areas where the boundaries between physics and chemistry became blurred or nonexistent. On Apr. 10, 1913, he married Mathilde Alberer, whom he had met in Munich; they had two children.

Debye's wide-ranging research, which ultimately led to the publication of nearly a score of books and well over 200 articles, was at times closely related to work done by contemporaries. In 1910 he developed what Planck agreed was a simpler method than his own of deriving his radiation formula. Two years later, using Planck's quantum concept, Debye derived an equation that extended Einstein's theory of specific heat to include a much lower temperature range. The following year, he presented a broader version of Bohr's first paper on atomic structure, which contributed to the idea of elliptical electron orbits. During the 1920's Debye developed theoretical concepts that, conceived independently and developed more fully by two American scientists, led to Nobel Prizes for Arthur Compton (in physics, 1927) and William Giauque (in chemistry, 1949).

Meanwhile, Debye's major research progressed in three areas: molecular electric dipole moments, X-ray diffraction, and electrolytes. All involved interactions between electric fields or radiation and molecular or atomic structures; all, begun within the field of physics, also contributed to the understanding of fundamental conditions and processes in chemistry.

In 1912 and 1913, Debye introduced the concept of the molecular electric dipole moment and laid the foundation for its calculation and application. While in some molecules the electrical charges are symmetrically distributed, in many cases the arrangement is asymmetrical, resulting in a polarization, and a dipole moment, which can be studied under various conditions. Debye developed an equation relating dipole moment, dielectric constant, temperature, and other factors. The calculation and comparison of the dipole moments of different substances can assist in the determination of their geometric structure—especially helpful in the study of isomers—and in the explanation of other physical characteristics. The practical applications were not immediately realized, but in the 1920's and 1930's, especially after Debye's publication of further studies in 1925 and 1929, dipole moments were calculated for hundreds of substances and were widely used in the development of fuller understanding of their molecular structure. The unit commonly used in the measurement of dipole moments was aptly named the debye.

In the course of intensive and widespread study of the nature of X rays, Max von Laue and others discovered around 1913 that when X rays are passed through crystals, the resultant refraction patterns can reveal information concerning the crystalline structure. Recognizing the sensitiveness of the procedure, in 1914 and 1915 Debye calculated the influence of temperature on the diffraction pattern. With Paul Scherrer he discovered in 1916 that crystalline and molecular structures could be deduced from the scattering of X rays from powder as well as from crystals, which greatly extended the scope of X-ray analysis. This led to his investigation, with several coworkers, of the structure of molecules in gases and liquids and the electron distribution within individual atoms. Later Debye developed a similar light-scattering procedure for the study of larger molecules.

The theory of ions, introduced by Svante Arrhenius in the 1880's, for many years explained electrical conductivity in weak electrolytes but not in strong electrolytes. In the early 1920's, Debye and an assistant, Erich Hückel, developed a more complete picture of ion behavior. Instead of accepting the earlier assumption that electrolytes ionize only partially in solution, Debye postulated that strong electrolytes ionize completely but ions of each polarity are to some extent held in place by the attraction of ions of opposite charge around them and thus impede the flow of electricity through the solution. The corresponding mathematical statement for electrical conductivity is known as the Debye-Hückel equation (1923). This equation—modified slightly in 1926 by another Debye associate, Lars Onsager, to take into account the Brownian movement of the ions—has remained fundamental to the physical chemistry of electrolytes.

Whereas nineteenth-century classical physical chemistry dealt with the properties of substances in the mass, modern physical chemistry seeks also to understand the arrangement of atoms within molecules and the forces that hold them together. Perhaps as much as anyone, Debye the physicist had contributed to this inward shift of emphasis. In recognition of this fact, he was awarded the Nobel Prize in chemistry in 1936 "for his contributions to the study of molecular structure," mainly through his work on dipole moments and X-ray diffraction.

For Debye, as for many others, these years of achievement were disrupted by political events. He had retained his Dutch citizenship and had been assured by the German government that he would not be required to change. However, in the fall of 1939 he was told that he could not retain his position unless he became a German citizen. He refused and was barred from his work.

Debye had visited the United States professionally several times and had declined offers of positions from a number of American universities, but now he accepted a long-standing invitation to deliver a series of lectures at Cornell University, and in January 1940 he moved to the United States. Debye became an American citizen in 1946, and he and his wife made Ithaca, N.Y., their home for the rest of their lives. He headed the Cornell chemistry department from 1940 until 1950, and in 1952 he became a professor emeritus, remaining actively engaged in research until the year of his death.

In 1940, American chemists were intensively engaged in a search for synthetic rubber, a quest that required a fuller understanding of polymers. To advance the study of the large polymer molecules, Debye drew on his X-ray-scattering experience to develop a light-scattering process that proved useful in determining the size, the molecular weight, and other characteristics of proteins and other large molecules. Over sixty of his articles were published after 1952, most of them dealing with some aspect of the ongoing development and utilization of the light-scattering process.

Throughout his life, Debye demonstrated a remarkable ability to formulate mathematically the physical essentials of a problem, often in the light of some new hypothesis. And though his own work was primarily concerned with the derivation of theory, he was intensely interested in the experimental testing and application of his theoretical conclusions. It was consistent with his early training as an engineer that he retained an interest in the theoretical reasons for industrial problems and in industrial applications of scientific theory. He was acclaimed as a lecturer, primarily for the clarity of thought that enabled him to penetrate to the heart of a problem and then to explain his conclusions but also for the aptness of his examples and the good humor that enlivened his presentations. A robust, cheerful man, he loved his work, enjoyed the company of his family and colleagues, and was remembered by them with great admiration and affection.

Debye was the recipient of many honors besides the Nobel Prize. Among them, the honor that is said to have pleased him most was the placing of a bust of him in the Maastricht City Hall in 1939. He died in Ithaca.

[Most of Debye's papers are in the Gemeentelijke Archiefdienst in Maastricht; there are also some materials in the Cornell University Archives. His several books include *Polar Molecules* (1929); *The Dipole Moment and Chemical Structure* (1931); *The Structure of Molecules* (1932); and *The Collected Papers of Peter J. W. Debye* (1954), fifty-one selected papers published, with introductory material, in honor of Debye's seventieth birthday. For additional information on Debye and his work, see F. A. Long, "Peter Debye: An Appreciation," *Science*, Feb. 24, 1967; Henri Sack, "In Memory of Professor Peter Debye," *American Chemical Society Journal*, June 5, 1968; Mansel Davies, "Peter Joseph Wilhelm Debye," *Biographical Memoirs of Fellows of the Royal Society*, 16 (1970); and J. W. Williams, "Peter Joseph Wilhelm Debye," *National Academy of Sciences Biographical Memoirs*, 46 (1975). An obituary is in the *New York Times*, Nov. 3, 1966.]

MAURICE M. VANCE

DELL, FLOYD JAMES (June 28, 1887–July 23, 1969), novelist, editor, playwright, and social critic, was born in Barry, Ill., the son of Anthony Dell, a butcher, and Kate Crone, a schoolteacher. It was a restless, poverty-stricken family. Dell attended the local schools in Barry and in Quincy, Ill., where the family lived from 1899 to 1903, when they moved to Davenport, Iowa. Dell loved books, which provided an idealized world finer than the real world of poverty and sameness that surrounded him. He joined the Socialist party when he was barely sixteen. In 1904 he dropped out of high school and began working at odd jobs.

Dell had a quick grasp of ideas and a photographic memory. In January 1905 he became a reporter for the *Davenport Times;* in 1906 he moved to the *Democrat*, edited by Ralph Cram. Dell was better at feature stories than at straight reporting because he liked to express his own feelings and opinions. He began writing stories, poetry, and articles. He edited several issues of the *Tri-City Workers* magazine. His rebellious ways, Socialist leanings, and love of poetry impelled him toward nonconformity. In the spring of 1908 he lost his job on the *Democrat*. During the summer, he worked on a farm, and in November he left for Chicago to look for a job.

The editor of the *Chicago Evening Post* offered Dell only free-lance writing assignments, not a steady job. But Dell's inventive, humorous, and whimsical style attracted the attention of Francis Hackett, editor of the *Friday Literary Review*, a supplement to the *Post* that first appeared on Mar. 5, 1909. Hackett made Dell his assistant. The *Review* aimed to encourage good literature and civilized criticism, and to bring social ideas to bear upon aesthetic products. Dell's job was to review briefly thirty to one hundred books each week and to read one book and criticize it. After Hackett left the *Post* in July 1911, Dell served as editor until September 1913. The *Review* made a significant contribution to the revival of the arts in Chicago.

Dell met Margery Currey, a teacher and journalist, in Davenport. They were married on Aug. 26, 1909, but after a few years the marriage failed. An amicable separation brought them to separate dwellings in buildings left over from the Columbian Exposition of 1893. Their studios became the center for a group of writers and artists that included Margaret Anderson, Eunice Tietjens, Sherwood Anderson, and Maurice Browne. Dell's critical insights and breadth of knowledge, his charm and conversational abilities, and his free and rebellious ways gave him a lasting place in what became known as the Chicago Renaissance. He recounted many of these experiences in *The Briary-Bush* (1921), a novel, and in *Homecoming* (1933), his autobiography. *Women as World-Builders* (1913), his first published book, a study of ten feminist leaders, reveals his lifelong interest in equal rights for women.

In November 1913 Dell moved to New York City and settled in Greenwich Village. He soon achieved a prominent role in Village life. He joined the staff of the radical magazine the *Masses* as managing editor and wrote plays for the Liberal Club and the Provincetown Players. Love affairs, including one with Edna St. Vincent Millay, earned him the title of archetypal bohemian. He wrote at length about Village life in his autobiography and in the essays of *Looking at Life* (1924); the short stories of *Love in Greenwich Village* (1926); and *Intellectual Vagabondage* (1926), a history of the intelligentsia in the eighteenth and nineteenth centuries and in his own time.

Changing events were pushing Dell in new directions. In April 1918, with other members of the *Masses* staff, he was indicted and tried for conspiring to obstruct military recruiting and enlistment under the Espionage Act of 1917. A first and a second trial ended with a hung jury, and the government abandoned prosecution of the case. After the *Masses* had ceased publication in October 1917, Max and Crystal Eastman formed a new magazine, the *Liberator,* in March 1918, and Dell became associate editor. Still radical in his beliefs, he was, he said, "a moralist, a believer in good and evil, in right and wrong."

In June 1918 Dell was inducted into the army, but was discharged because he was still under indictment. Having divorced Margery Currey in 1916, he married Berta Marie Gage on Feb. 8, 1919. They moved to Croton-on-Hudson, N.Y., and had two children.

Aside from his work as editor, book reviewer, and social critic, Dell devoted much of the next fifteen years to writing fiction. *Moon-Calf* (1920), his first and best novel, is the story of an idealist who grows up in a small midwestern town; his character is formed "by his having been uprooted from one environment after another." The protagonist reads books, studies Socialist doctrine, drops out of school, and works on a newspaper. When he heads for Chicago, he has achieved more intellectual than emotional maturity. In writing about his own life, Dell had written, as Orrick Jones said, "about the life of all of us."

The sensitive, lonely, idealistic dreamer who learns to sacrifice rebellious ideals for conventional realities became the typical Dell character. In a succession of novels, he explored the problems of growing up: *Janet March* (1923), *This Mad Ideal* (1925), *Runaway* (1925), *An Old Man's Folly* (1926), *An Unmarried Father* (1927), *Souvenir* (1929), *Love Without Money* (1931), and *Diana Stair* (1932). His nonfiction includes *Were You Ever a Child?* (1919), a work on education; *Upton Sinclair* (1927), a critical analysis; and *The Outline of Marriage* (1926) and *Love in the Machine Age* (1930), studies in social psychology.

In 1935, failing health and lack of money prompted Dell to accept a job with the Works Progress Administration in Washington, D.C. He continued to work in nonsensitive government jobs until his retirement in 1947. Up to the time of his death in Bethesda, Md., he maintained an extensive correspondence with friends and scholars. His deep interest in intellectual and educational issues, his championing of social and human rights, his role in the artistic and Bohemian life of Greenwich Village during World War I and after, have given Dell a permanent place in American literary history.

[The Floyd Dell Collection is in the Newberry Library, Chicago. His published one-act plays include *The Angel Intrudes* (1918); *Sweet-and-Twenty* (1921); and *King Arthur's Socks and Other Village Plays* (1922). Two plays written with Thomas Mitchell, performed but never published, are "Little Accident" (1928) and "Cloudy with Showers" (1931). His government reports include *Final Report on WPA Program, 1935–43* (1947).

See G. Thomas Tanselle, "Faun at the Barricades: The Life and Work of Floyd Dell" (Ph.D. diss., Northwestern University, 1959), which contains a complete bibliography. Useful is Judith Nierman, *Floyd Dell: An Annotated Bibliography of Secondary Sources, 1910–1981* (1984). The most complete analysis of Dell is John E. Hart, *Floyd Dell* (1971). See also Bernard Duffy, *The Chicago Renaissance in American Letters* (1953); Allen Churchill, *The Improper Bohemians* (1959); Daniel Aaron, *Writers on the Left* (1961); and Dale Kramer, *Chicago Renaissance* (1966). Reminiscences are in Harry Hansen, *Midwest Portraits* (1923); Susan Glaspell, *The Road to the Temple* (1927); Art Young, *On My Way* (1928); Joseph Freeman, *An American Testament* (1936); and Max Eastman, *Enjoyment of Living* (1948) and *Love and Revolution* (1964).]

John E. Hart

D'HARNONCOURT, RENÉ (May 17, 1901–Aug. 13, 1968), museum director, was born in Vienna, Austria, the son of Hubert d'Harnoncourt, an amateur historian and watercolorist, and Julianna Mittrowsky. The family, which had served the Hapsburgs, had extensive landholdings. Born with the title of count, d'Harnoncourt dropped it when he became an American citizen in 1939. He was tutored at home, and from 1918 to 1921 he studied chemistry at the University of Graz, where he also enjoyed writing poems and plays, painting and drawing, and collecting old prints. He became especially interested in Austrian folk art and French modern art. After World War I, he continued his studies at the Technische Hochschule in Vienna. He never received a degree, but his thesis, "The Creosote Contents of Certain Soft

Coals of Southern Yugoslavia," was published in the German technical journal *Brennstoff-Chemie.*

The family's landholdings were lost in the Austrian economic collapse of the 1920's, and in 1925, d'Harnoncourt went to Mexico, where he unsuccessfully sought employment as a chemist. Instead, he eked out an existence retouching news photos, designing shop displays, and painting. He found a vocation advising American collectors on antiques, and in time he became knowledgeable in pre-Columbian and Mexican folk art. Frederick Davis, a Mexico City dealer and collector, hired d'Harnoncourt as a salesman and buyer. For Davis' shop, the Sonora News Company, d'Harnoncourt arranged exhibits of Mexican modernists such as Diego Rivera and Miguel Covarrubias. His activities helped stimulate the Mexican folk-art revival of the 1920's. He also became close to the American ambassador Dwight W. Morrow and his wife, Elizabeth Reeve Morrow. He painted a mural for them and advised them on furnishing their private residence in Cuernavaca. D'Harnoncourt illustrated two of Elizabeth Morrow's books, *The Painted Pig* (1930) and *Beast, Bird, and Fish* (1933). He also wrote and illustrated two books based on his Mexican experiences, *Mexicana* (1931), a picture book for adults, and *Hole in the Wall* (1931), for children.

In 1929, at the invitation of the Mexican Ministry of Education, d'Harnoncourt assembled several collections of Mexican folk art to tour American schools. Late that year, the Carnegie Foundation asked him to organize a major exhibition of 1,200 objects of Mexican art and crafts to be shown first at the Metropolitan Museum in New York and then to travel to various American cities. D'Harnoncourt wrote the catalog, *Mexican Arts*, and made important contacts while traveling with the exhibit for two years. In 1932 he returned to Austria long enough to obtain an immigration visa for the United States. While with the Mexican exhibition he met Sarah Carr of Chicago, an advertising copy editor; they were married on May 29, 1933, and had one child.

A "gentle giant," d'Harnoncourt impressed people with his knowledge of art, impeccable dress, courtly European manners, witty conversation, and size—he stood over six feet, six inches and weighed about 230 pounds. Nelson Rockefeller consulted with him on primitive art in the mid-1930's and became his most prominent sponsor and a close friend. D'Harnoncourt straddled several jobs in the mid-1930's: he taught art history at Sarah Lawrence College and the New School for Social Research, and from 1933 to 1934 he directed a radio program, "Art in America," sponsored by the American Federation of Arts. His interest in native folk art prompted John Collier, the commissioner of Indian affairs of the Department of the Interior, to appoint him assistant manager and then general manager of the department's newly created Indian Arts and Crafts Board.

With the assistance of Frederic H. Douglas of the Denver Art Museum, d'Harnoncourt assembled a major exhibition of Indian art that was shown in 1939 at the Golden Gate International Exposition in San Francisco and then expanded and installed at the Museum of Modern Art in 1941. D'Harnoncourt and Henry Klumb designed the New York exhibit, which was called Indian Art of the United States. It ranged over three floors and featured background colors and lighting that suggested the Indians' native environment, objects juxtaposed for thematic and dramatic qualities, Navajo Indian sand painters demonstrating their craft, and a totem pole in front of the museum. The highly praised show led to a new style of American museum exhibit design, of which d'Harnoncourt was the acknowledged leader.

The Museum of Modern Art suffered a crisis in the 1940's; its founding director, Alfred H. Barr, Jr., encountered administrative difficulties and failed to get along with trustees. He was removed in 1943 and the museum was managed through a committee of trustees. That year Nelson Rockefeller, then coordinator of the Office of Inter-American Affairs, borrowed d'Harnoncourt from the Indian Board to run the art section. He personally paid d'Harnoncourt's salary. The Rockefellers had always played a major role in the Museum of Modern Art: Abby Aldrich Rockefeller had been a founder, the museum was built on Rockefeller land, and Nelson had served as president from 1939 to 1941. In 1944, d'Harnoncourt joined the museum as vice-president in charge of foreign activities and director of the Department of Manual Industries. His unstated assignment was to bring peace among staff, curators, and trustees. Nelson Rockefeller again paid his salary. D'Harnoncourt was appointed director in 1949.

Under d'Harnoncourt's leadership, the museum consolidated its position as the leading modern-art museum in the world. He directed numerous exhibitions, many of which were known for their innovative installation techniques, such as Art of the South Seas (1946), in collaboration with Ralph Linton and Paul S. Wingert; Modern Art in Your Life (1949); Ancient Arts of the Andes (1954), in collaboration with Wendell C. Bennet; and shows on the sculpture of Henry Moore (1946), Jacques Lipchitz (1954), Jean Arp (1958), and Pablo Picasso (1967). D'Harnoncourt excelled at fund-raising, and the museum expanded both in collections and space. One of his most important acts was to rehire Barr, the preeminent authority on modern art in America, as curator of collections. Barr made the museum's aesthetics the taste of modern America. D'Harnoncourt soothed the frequently ruffled feelings of prima-donna curators, wealthy collectors, and trustees. In addition to his charm, he had a connoisseur's judgment, much in contrast to Barr's scholarly approach. And d'Harnoncourt was at least the social equal, if not the superior, of the trustees. He retired from the museum on July 1, 1968. Several weeks later, he was killed by a drunken driver while walking at his summer home at New Suffolk, Long Island.

D'Harnoncourt is credited with saving the Museum of Modern Art from incestuous warfare. He also reaffirmed Barr's belief that modern art was essentially European. Although the museum did show American artists, it acknowledged some American trends only belatedly and missed others altogether. Under d'Harnoncourt the museum lost some of its early avant-garde quality, and exhibits tended to be retrospectives of established artists. His personal leadership lacked an institutional foundation, and his two immediate successors lasted only a short time. Beyond the museum, he made substantial contributions to the art program of the United Nations Educational, Scientific, and Cultural Organization, and he helped Nelson Rockefeller to found the Museum of Primitive Art.

[D'Harnoncourt's papers are at the Museum of Modern Art. Aspects of his career are treated in Elizabeth Morrow, *Casa Mañana* (1932) and *The Mexican Years* (1953); Russell Lynes, *Good Old Modern* (1973); and Robert Fay Schrader, *The Indian Arts and Crafts Board* (1983). Articles include Geoffrey T. Hellman, "Profiles," *New Yorker*, May 7, 1960, which contains some inaccuracies; Museum of Modern Art, *René d'Harnoncourt: A Tribute* (1968); and Elizabeth Shaw, "René d'Harnoncourt," *Art News*, Oct. 1979. An obituary is in the *New York Times*, Aug. 14, 1968.]

RICHARD GUY WILSON

DIRKSEN, EVERETT McKINLEY (Jan. 4, 1896–Sept. 7, 1969), United States congressman and senator, was born in Pekin, Ill., one of twin sons of Johann Frederick Dirksen, a design painter, and Antje Conrady, German immigrants and staunch Republicans who named their children after the leading Republican politicians of the day. Despite a childhood marked by poverty and hard work, Dirksen graduated with honors from the local high school in 1913. Involved in many activities, he was a finalist in a national oratorical contest. After working for a year, he entered the University of Minnesota with the objective of becoming a lawyer but left to enlist in the army, primarily to demonstrate the patriotism of his German-speaking family. He was, however, destined for the bar, to which he was admitted in 1936 after attending law school at night in Washington, D.C.

Sent to France in 1918, Dirksen saw action as a balloon artillery observer and then served with occupation forces in Germany. He was discharged in October 1919 and settled in Pekin, where he worked in a grocery store owned by his two brothers, went into an unsuccessful venture to manufacture electric washing machines, and became a partner in the family bakery. He was active in local theatrical productions and also wrote about a hundred plays, short stories, and poems, only one of which was ever published. On Dec. 24, 1927, he married Louella Carver. They had one daughter, Danice Joy, who in 1951 married Howard H. Baker, Jr., of Tennessee, later to become Republican majority leader of the United States Senate and then President Ronald Reagan's chief of staff.

Dirksen entered politics in 1926 by winning election to the Pekin City Commission. He narrowly lost the Republican primary for the United States House of Representatives in 1930, but two years later defeated incumbent William Hull and subsequently won the general election. In Washington, mindful of President Franklin D. Roosevelt's strength in his district, Dirksen supported many New Deal measures, but in foreign policy he hewed to a steady isolationist, anti-administration line, reflecting his German background, the outlook of the voters at home, and Roosevelt's declining popularity in his district. In September 1941, however, he delivered a speech in which he pledged to back the president's anti-Axis policies.

Through hard work and an amiable personality well suited to the folkways of the House, Dirksen won rapid prominence among the small band of Republicans who survived the early New Deal. He was appointed to the powerful Appropriations Committee in 1937 and a year later became chairman of the Republican National Congressional Committee, a position he held until 1946. Widely considered one of the ablest members of the Republican delegation and positioned near the ideological center of his party, he undertook an abortive candidacy for the Republican presidential nomination in 1944. Actually, he aspired to the vice-presidency, but his hopes for a vice-presidential offer in 1952 and 1960 proved to be equally futile.

After World War II, Dirksen played a key role in drafting the Legislative Reorganization Act of 1946. He usually supported President Harry S Truman's foreign policies but opposed most of Truman's Fair Deal measures. He announced his retirement in 1948 as a result of a serious eye disease, but he recovered after several months of therapy and rest. In 1950 he ran for the Senate against Scott Lucas, Senate Democratic leader.

The campaign against Lucas brought about a political metamorphosis that illustrated the changing center of gravity in Dirksen's party and the special imperatives of Illinois Republicanism: Dirksen became a conservative isolationist and McCarthyite, and his reward was the support of the influential *Chicago Tribune*, then the voice of right-wing Republicanism in the Midwest. The Democrats were hampered at the national level by reverses in the Korean War and at the local level by scandals in Chicago. Dirksen won the election by nearly 300,000 votes.

He began his first term in the Senate as a loyal supporter of the conservative wing of the party, exemplified by Senators Robert A. Taft and Joseph McCarthy, and, as such, regularly flailed away in extreme fashion at the Democrats and their programs. He bitterly opposed the Eisenhower movement in 1952 and continued to be a leading McCarthyite through 1954. In the process, he lost the respect of many independent observers who had praised him in earlier years.

The Eisenhower victory, the death of Taft, the censure of McCarthy, and Dirksen's upcoming 1956 reelection campaign all effected another change of heart. Wooed by a White House that appreciated his abilities and needed his Senate vote, he became an Eisenhower loyalist, a course made all the easier by the death of Colonel Robert McCormick, publisher of the *Chicago Tribune*. Dirksen was easily reelected in 1956, and was chosen Republican whip in 1957 and Republican leader in 1959.

For the next ten years Dirksen functioned as a strong, effective leader of his party. In many ways, he emulated his Democratic counterpart, Lyndon Johnson, but never resorted to the occasional strong-arm tactics for which Johnson was known. His methods included rational persuasion, consensus-building, calling in personal favors, and assiduous logrolling. He displayed in his office the motto, "The oil can is mightier than the sword." Typically working a sixteen-hour day despite precarious health, he achieved mastery over both the tactics of political maneuver and the substance of major legislation.

His tenure under Presidents John F. Kennedy and Lyndon B. Johnson was the high point of his career. Although by then the minority leader, he tended to overshadow Johnson's self-effacing successor, Mike Mansfield of Montana, and became the most powerful and respected Republican in Washington. In return for recognition, patronage, occasional substantive compromise, and administration abandonment of other objectives, he delivered key Republican votes on major issues, among them the Test Ban Treaty of 1963, the 1964 tax cut, and the Civil Rights acts of 1964, 1965, and 1968. He won considerable praise for his statesmanship, and both Kennedy and Johnson avoided giving significant help to his Democratic opponents in 1962 and 1968.

During the 1960's Dirksen became a public figure almost as visible as the president. He instituted weekly televised press conferences with House Republican leader Charles Halleck (succeeded by Gerald Ford in 1965). The "Ev and Charlie Show" drew mixed reviews, but Dirksen appears to have benefited from it considerably. Young Republicans lamented his aged, ruffled appearance, his verbosity, and his old-fashioned oratorical style, but television effectively projected his essential warmth and good humor. He acquired the nickname Wizard of Ooze, an apt description of a speaking style that most of his listeners found entertaining—so much so that in 1966 he even made a record album, *Gallant Men*, a collection of patriotic readings that sold 500,000 copies. (He followed it with two less successful efforts, a group of biblical readings and a recitation of traditional Christmas carols.)

Still, he remained controversial. At times he lapsed into clownish parodies of himself that seemed unbecoming a Senate leader, as when he undertook a tongue-in-cheek crusade to make the marigold the national flower. Investigative journalists delved into his finances time and again, especially his connections with a Peoria law firm. (Dirksen had never actually practiced law, and his relationship with the firm was unclear.) Despite allegations, it was never proved that he accepted payments for his legislative influence, and his life-style was in fact relatively modest.

With Richard M. Nixon's accession to the presidency in 1969, Dirksen's influence diminished. He was overshadowed by the new president and became the object of restlessness from a large number of young Republicans who owed him no favors. He died in Washington of complications following surgery for lung cancer.

A consummate politician of the old school, Dirksen was admired by traditional Republicans and considered an engaging old rogue by many of his opponents. As he once remarked, "I am a man of principle, and one of my basic principles is flexibility."

[Dirksen's papers are in the Everett McKinley Dirksen Congressional Leadership Center in Pekin. Louella Dirksen, with Norma Lee Browning, *The Honorable Mr. Marigold* (1972), is a personal memoir by his widow. The best biography is Neil MacNeil, *Dirksen: Portrait of a Public Man* (1970). See also Edward L. Schapsmeier and Frederick H. Schapsmeier, *Dirksen of Illinois* (1985). An obituary is in the *New York Times*, Sept. 8, 1969.]

ALONZO L. HAMBY

DISNEY, WALTER ELIAS ("WALT") (Dec. 5, 1901–Dec. 15, 1966), film producer, animator, and amusement park creator, was born in Chicago, Ill., the son of Elias Disney, a building contractor, and Flora Call, a former schoolteacher. Walt, as he was always called, one of five children, seems to have had a close and continuous relationship only with his brother Roy, who was eight years older. When Disney was five his family moved to Marceline, Mo., to try farming. Walt and Roy spent most of their time on farm chores, but the younger brother remembered these days with affection. It was here that he first began to draw and paint.

After four years the Disneys moved to Kansas City, Mo., where Elias Disney opened a newspaper delivery service. The two boys again did much of the work, rising at 3:30 A.M. to start their paper routes before attending the Benton School. For amusement, on Saturdays, Disney went to the Kansas City Art Institute, where he received a smattering of formal instruction and met Walter Pfeiffer. They started a vaudeville team that performed in local theaters.

In 1917, Elias Disney returned to Chicago to become one of the directors of a small factory. Walt remained for a time in Kansas City, serving as a news butcher (vendor) on the Santa Fe Railroad, thus acquiring a lifelong fascination with this form of transport. On rejoining his mother and father in Chicago, he attended McKinley High School, where he contributed cartoons and pictures to the school paper. By this time, the United States had entered World War I and Walt tried to follow Roy into the navy. Rejected as underage, Walt instead became an ambulance driver for the Red Cross after he altered the birth date on his application. Assigned to duty in France, he spent his idle hours painting medals and ribbons on uniforms, decorating the walls of ambulances, and contributing drawings to the army paper *Stars and Stripes*.

Disney returned to the United States in 1919 determined to be a commercial artist. In Kansas City he joined the studio of an advertising firm where he met a gifted young Dutch draftsman named Ub Iwerks. Disney, still in his teens, and Iwerks hastily decided to strike out on their own. They failed, and Disney took a job with the Kansas City Film Ad Service. It was, he later said, "the most marvelous thing that ever happened" to him.

The ad service, having recently entered the primitive field of animated film, made cartoon advertisements shown for one or two minutes between movies at local theaters. These projects provided Disney with an elementary understanding of the new medium, prompting Disney and Iwerks to go into business for themselves again. They made a series of short films called Laugh-O-Grams for a local theater and then produced a set of familiar fairy stories in a modern idiom. There followed some very difficult years while Disney sought new ways to exploit his novel process. He looked for craftsmen who were competent to realize his ideas, searched for theaters that would accept his product, and tried to find reliable distributors who could help finance the expanding venture.

In 1923, Disney moved his studio to Hollywood, Calif., starting out in a garage owned by an uncle. From there, with the help of Roy as principal administrator, he gradually enlarged his working space and staff. They first developed a new series called Alice in Cartoonland, which brought together real people and animated creatures in various comic situations. This was followed by another series devoted to the adventures of Oswald the Rabbit, a character whose features anticipated some of the animals in the Disney menagerie.

In this period Disney also made some significant changes in his personal and professional life. On July 13, 1925, he married Lillian Bounds, who had joined his staff to work on the Alice series. They had two children. In 1927, Disney ceased to do any of the actual drawing in his animations, devoting himself entirely to production and the development of the business. Indeed, by then his primary need was money. A trip to New York designed to solve this problem produced instead a falling-out with his principal distributor that left Disney's entire venture in jeopardy.

But the trip was not in vain. On the train back to California, Disney conceived of a series of films built upon the escapades of an animal who would resemble Oswald the Rabbit. Disney described his idea to Iwerks; together they developed a concept that Iwerks then expressed in his skillful drawings. After silent prototypes failed, Disney proposed that the high jinks of his new hero be set to musical accompaniment. In November 1928, Mickey Mouse made his first appearance in a sound film, *Steamboat Willie.* (A silent incarnation of Mickey had appeared earlier that year in *Plane Crazy* and *Gallopin' Gaucho.*) The financial foundation of the Disney enterprises was secured for ever after.

Mickey Mouse went on to become a national figure, an international attraction, and finally a cultural totem. In the 1930's he opened the way for a varied cast of characters, including Minnie Mouse, Donald Duck, Pluto, Goofy, the Three Little Pigs, and the Big Bad Wolf. He also made possible the further exploitation and extension of animation in films such as the Silly Symphony series and, in Technicolor, *Trees* (1932). The first feature-length cartoon, *Snow White and the Seven Dwarfs* (1937), followed. Its immense success led to, among others, *Pinocchio* (1940), *Fantasia* (1940), *Dumbo* (1941), and *Bambi* (1942). Through these exciting new departures, Mickey Mouse and his fellows made a widening impact and more money. Under the shrewd and careful management of Roy Disney, they gave their names and shapes, in return for royalties, to countless objects of art and diversion, from Cartier diamond bracelets to marmalade.

In 1941 the Disney studios began to make training and instructional films for the armed services, an exercise that further refined their ability to combine live actors, animation, color, and sound. The value of this experience was demonstrated in the varied stream of productions that began to flow from the studios in the postwar years. Some were skillful realizations of familiar tales, such as *Cinderella* (1950), *Alice in Wonderland* (1951), *Peter Pan* (1953), and *Sleeping Beauty* (1959). Others were studies of nature; if in the editing they became less than faithful documentaries, the photography was stunning. Disney's first completely live-action film, *Treasure Island* (1950), was followed by *20,000 Leagues Under the Sea* (1954), *Old Yeller* (1957), and *Pollyanna* (1960). There were also a few witty short comments on aspects of contemporary human life and an early entry into the new field of television. The culmination of this experimental activity can be seen in the full-length film *Mary Poppins* (1964), which exploited the full resources of the studios by joining live action, animation, and dazzling special effects.

By the 1960's, Disney had become one of the most powerful men in motion pictures; his company was making a great deal of money and Disney himself was a very rich man. In all, he received over 700 honors and awards, including thirty Oscars, the Presidential Medal of Freedom, and honorary degrees from Harvard and

Yale. He was also said to be the only man in Hollywood to be praised by both the American Legion and the Soviet Union. After such achievements and rewards it seemed to some that Disney was slowing down, repeating past procedures, and waiting at the top with nowhere else to go. Such appeared to be the case to Bosley Crowther, the film critic of the *New York Times,* who visited Disney in the early 1950's and found him "wholly, almost weirdly," absorbed in building a miniature railroad. Crowther came away from the visit "feeling sad."

It became apparent in 1955 that what Disney had been working on at the time was one of the essential elements in the remarkable combination of carnival, small midwestern town, and sheer fantasy that was to be Disneyland. He created in Anaheim, Calif., at a cost of more than $50 million, an extraordinary installation where millions of people have been transported from the routine of daily life to a spotless world of fantasy.

The success of this venture soon turned Disney's mind to a more ambitious enterprise, the construction of an environment that would include transport, housing, dining, and recreational facilities. Attached to this complex Disney envisioned a place he called the Experimental Prototype Community of Tomorrow (EPCOT), a product of his dismay at what was happening to American cities. EPCOT was to be a home for industrial workers situated in an industrial park. It was to demonstrate how people could learn to use technology wisely to create a safe, comfortable, satisfying, and clean environment. Since technology was always changing, the city would never be finished. It would serve as a continuing model for the imaginative organization of technical resources. Disney, who died in Los Angeles, did not live to see the fulfillment of his plan on 27,000 acres of land in Orlando, Fla., and while Walt Disney World, as it is called, is in the great Disney tradition, EPCOT is not exactly what he envisioned.

The course of Disney's extraordinary career did not always run smooth. In the early days he pawned his belongings, lived with friends, and gambled that his schemes would eventually pay off. For a considerable period there was formidable resistance in the industry to what he wanted to do; and opinion remained divided on what he had done. Critics contended that the early Mickey Mouse was flawed by a streak of sadism; *Fantasia* was considered by some to be a pretentious hodgepodge. In almost anything Disney laid his hands on, the discerning eye could find breaches of taste, philistine wisecracks, a milking of the nostalgic mood, slipshod cultural references, a growing dependence on received folklore and other people's classics, and an increasingly slick technical achievement of rather tawdry effects. Beyond that, as fame and fortune multiplied, Disney, some said, became self-satisfied, intractable, and arrogant. As the strike of employees at the Disney studios in 1941 suggested, he was probably never quite the generous father of a gifted flock that he seemed on the surface. Yet, he had made himself, as David Low, the British cartoonist, said, "the most significant figure in graphic arts since Leonardo."

The development of Disney's art depended on the painstaking application of many technological advances and special skills. Not as good a draftsman as Iwerks and untutored in engineering, he nevertheless provided for the interaction of diverse machines and for the dovetailing of various human talents with increasing ingenuity and sophistication. To organize the disparate elements in the new medium of animated cartoons and to take full advantage of its potential, Disney began by throwing familiar things—a tone poem, line drawings of animals, abstract forms and striking colors—into new combinations. A heightened effect was obtained by the exercise of Disney's intuitive capacity as a fabulist. He could take a flattened image, say, Mickey Mouse, and by engaging it in a variety of familiar mishaps and minor triumphs invest the character with, as William Lyon Phelps said, "a soul."

The creative process at the Disney studios began with the statement of a hypothesis—for example, a princess incurs the wrath of a witch—and proceeded to alteration of the hypothesis through argument, mock-ups of the constituent parts, construction of storyboards, dry runs in the studio, sneak previews to see how the public responded, and continuous modification of the product. Disney put his own points across in discussion, staff conference, and conversation. In the end, his characters usually were created in the images he had proposed for them (he once said, "There is a lot of the Mouse in me"), and the amusement parks beyond all doubt came to reflect his peculiar view of things. Disney in some singular way could fortify his own intuitive capacities with the power of technology to appease the residual wistfulness and stimulate the capacity for wonder in his huge audience.

[The Walt Disney Archives in Burbank, Calif., contain a large manuscript collection dealing mostly with business transactions. On his life and work, see Robert D. Feild, *The Art of Walt Disney* (1942); Richard Schickel, *The Disney Version* (1968); and Christopher Finch, *The Art of Walt Disney* (1983). An obituary is in the *New York Times*, Dec. 16, 1966.]

ELTING E. MORISON

DODD, BELLA VISONO (Oct. 1904–Apr. 29, 1969), union representative and renouncing Communist, was born Maria Assunta Isabella Visono, in Picerno, near Potenza, Italy, the daughter of Rocco Visono, a stonemason who emigrated to the United States and became a grocer in East Harlem, New York City, and Teresa Marsica. Visono did not join her family in New York until she was five. She attended public schools in New York and Westchester; her entry into Evander Childs High School, in the Bronx, was delayed for a year by a trolley accident that resulted in the amputation of her left foot. She graduated in 1921, won a state scholarship, and attended Hunter College in New York with the intention of becoming a teacher. She received her B.A. with honors in 1925. Visono spent one semester as a substitute teacher in the history department of Seward Park High School in Manhattan. In February 1926 she joined the Department of Political Science at Hunter, where she taught while working toward her M.A. (1927) at Columbia University and her law degree (1930) at New York University. Later in 1930 she was admitted to the bar. On a trip to Europe in that year, she met John Dodd, whom she married in September 1931; they had no children.

In 1932 economic pressures brought Dodd back to teaching at Hunter, where she helped organize the Hunter College Instructors Association to fight for bread-and-butter issues for low-rank personnel. Attempts to extend that organization citywide proved short-lived but led Dodd into the Anti-Fascist Literature Committee; members of the committee, in turn, introduced her to Communist individuals and organizations. Although she wished to join the Communist party, she was advised to avoid formal association. Dodd instead became legislative representative of Teachers' Union Local 5 of the American Federation of Teachers. She also served as a delegate to the American Federation of Labor Central Trades and Labor Council. There, according to her account, she operated as an agent for Communist interests.

In 1938 she resigned from Hunter to work full-time for the union. She pressured the New York State Board of Education to regularize the employment of substitute teachers who actually worked full-time without commensurate benefits. That effort proved unsuccessful, as did her bid in 1938 for election to the New York State Assembly as the American Labor party candidate in the Tenth Assembly District of New York City.

Dodd worked particularly hard after the 1939 state-aid-to-education bill authorized the Rapp-Coudert investigation into the subversive activities of New York City teachers. She helped organize the Friends of the Free Public Schools to raise funds to distribute information, tried to rally community support through Save Our Schools clubs, and advised teachers who were to be questioned about their left-wing political affiliations. In 1940 she separated from her husband; he obtained a divorce about two years later.

Dodd continued as legislative representative of the Teachers' Union after the American Federation of Teachers expelled Communist-associated locals in 1940. She unsuccessfully advocated the establishment of public nursery schools, a proposal primarily intended to employ teachers. As liaison to various unions, she collected campaign funds for such candidates as the leftist congressman Vito Marcantonio—usually, she later testified, to advance Communist goals. And she helped establish the School for Democracy, an adult-education project intended to give jobs to teachers displaced by the Rapp-Coudert investigation. This school evolved into the Jefferson School of Social Science.

In 1943 Gil Green, the New York State chairman of the Communist party, asked Dodd to formally join the Communist party; her membership was announced at the party's national convention in 1944. In June 1944 she left her position with the Teachers' Union but remained a contact with various teachers' groups. She established a law office in midtown Manhattan and was elected to the New York State Board of the Communist party and to the National Committee of the Communist party. She later said that she was troubled when the Communist party expelled its one-time leader Earl Browder and several thousand others between 1945 and 1947. Dodd also faced party charges on a number of occasions. In 1946 the Communist party first proposed, and then unaccountably withdrew, her name as a candidate for attorney general of New York State.

The party rejected her expressed desire to leave, but she withdrew from most party activities except contact with teachers' groups. In June 1949 she was expelled on charges of being antiblack, anti–Puerto Rican, anti-Semitic, antilabor, and the defender of a landlord—accusations that she found incredible in view of her record. Dodd's legal practice declined; her party and teacher friends withdrew; and she experienced great confusion, refusing to write newspaper articles on her break with the party. Subpoenaed by Abe Fortas to appear before the Tydings Committee in defense of Owen Lattimore, who had been accused of being a Soviet agent, Dodd testified that she had not known Lattimore to be a Communist. This experience caused her to reassess her thinking.

At Easter 1952 Dodd rejoined the Roman Catholic church. Over the next five years she testified several times before the Senate Internal Security Subcommittee, receiving considerable publicity in 1953 for her revelations about Communism and teachers. In January 1953 she was named a visiting lecturer in political philosophy at St. John's University Law School in New York City and continued to teach courses in labor law and legislative law as an adjunct faculty member there until 1961. In 1954 she published a confessional autobiography, *School of Darkness*. The following year she formed the law firm of Dodd, Cardiello, and Blair, within which she concentrated on advocacy for the disadvantaged. Dodd stood unsuccessfully for election to the New York State Supreme Court as a Conservative in 1965 and 1966. In 1968 she ran, again as a Conservative, for the United States House of Representatives in the Nineteenth Congressional District, garnering 29.4 percent of the vote; Leonard Farbstein, a Democrat, won with 38.9 percent. Dodd died in New York City.

[Obituaries are in the *New York Times*, Apr. 30, 1969; and *National Review*, May 20, 1969.]

SUSAN ESTABROOK KENNEDY

DONALDSON, JESSE MONROE (Aug. 17, 1885–Mar. 25, 1970), United States postmaster general, was born in Hanson, Ill., the son of Moses Martin Donaldson, a merchant and postmaster, and Amanda Saletha Little. Donaldson attended public schools in Oconee, Ill., and furthered his education at Sparks Business College, Shelbyville, Ill., and at the Shelbyville Normal School. In 1903 he began teaching in one-room schoolhouses in Shelby, Montgomery, and Christian counties. After five years of teaching, Donaldson became one of the first letter carriers in Shelbyville, where he earned $50 a month.

In 1910, Donaldson left the United States Post Office Department to become a clerk in the War Department. On Aug. 14, 1911, Donaldson married Nell Fern Graybill; they had three children. That same year, he was appointed to the position of post-office clerk and supervisor in Muskogee, Okla. He worked there until 1915, when he became an inspector in the Kansas City, Mo., division of the Post Office Department. Donaldson remained in Kansas City from 1915 to 1932, and it was there that he became acquainted with Harry Truman (then a judge) in the 1920's. While in Kansas City, he also investigated postal fraud. He gained some notoriety when he helped convict a polar explorer of mail fraud and won a promotion for finding an elusive train robber. On Aug. 1, 1932, he was appointed inspector in charge of the Chattanooga, Tenn., division.

In 1933, Donaldson was transferred to Washington, D.C., as deputy second assistant postmaster general. From 1936 to 1943 he served as deputy first assistant postmaster general, and from 1943 to 1945, as chief post-office inspector. On July 5, 1946, Donaldson was appointed first assistant postmaster general and became the chief spokesman for the department before Congress.

In November 1947, Postmaster General Robert E. Hannegan, the chairman of the Democratic National Committee and a longtime friend and associate of President Truman, retired because of poor health. The Republican-controlled Congress had attacked Hannegan and the Post Office Department for being too political and providing substandard service.

The department was also subjected to intensive study in 1947–1948 by the Commission on Organization of the Executive Branch of Government (the Hoover Commission), headed by former president Herbert Hoover and appointed by Truman. The Hoover Commission recommended that the postmaster general be a cabinet member but not an official of a political party. As a result of these circumstances, Truman named Donaldson postmaster general in November; the appointment was confirmed by the Senate on Dec. 16, 1947. He was the first bona fide career official appointed to the position of postmaster general since Horatio King, who served briefly in 1861, and the first to assume cabinet rank.

As postmaster general, Donaldson worked to improve the efficiency of the department and reduce its annual deficit. Acting upon a recommendation of the Hoover Commission embodied in a 1949 congressional act, Donaldson created the position of deputy postmaster general and eliminated the numerical order of precedence of the four assistant postmasters general, designating them instead by their functions—operations, transportation, finance, and facilities. The innovation was designed to protect the deputy, who was to be a career man, from the political turnover that generally affected the department. Subsequent administrations ignored the reform and continued to treat the deputy posts as patronage positions. Donaldson also appointed a seven-member advisory board from various areas of business and established a research-and-development section. To improve efficiency, he created a new money-order system and set up new accounting procedures. During his tenure, a highway post-office service was established, railroad transportation was expanded, and air parcel post was extended to eighty-two countries.

Donaldson's most controversial move came on Apr. 18, 1950, when, in response to a Truman order to reduce the traditional post-office deficit, he severely cut back postal services. He cut home deliveries in residential areas from two to one per day, reduced the number of street collections, curtailed window service in post offices, and cut by half the deliveries of parcel post to business firms. Donaldson claimed that the reductions in service would save $80 million a year and help reduce the deficit. Donaldson's economy moves angered postal patrons and employees alike. His critics claimed that Donaldson's acquiescence in postal budget cuts constituted "the Rape of the Mail Service." Moreover, postal layoffs and a temporary moratorium on wage increases prompted the National Association of Letter Carriers to adopt a resolution asking their leaders to "extend every effort in the direction of securing a new Postmaster General with a background of fairness to labor." Despite Donaldson's economy measures, the deficit continued to climb in his final year in office. Truman later described Donaldson as "the best we had." Donaldson died at Kansas City, Mo.

[On Donaldson's early life, see Robert I. Vexler, *The Vice-Presidents and Cabinet Members* (1975); and Robert Sobel, ed., *Biographical Directory of the United States Executive Branch, 1774–1977* (1977). For his tenure as postmaster general, see Gerald Cullinan, *The Post Office Department* (1968); Arthur Summerfield, *U.S. Mail* (1969); and Donald R. McCoy, *The Presidency of Harry S. Truman* (1984). Obituaries are in the *New York Times*, Mar. 27, 1970; and the *Kansas City Times*, Mar. 26, 1970.]

JOHN M. CARROLL

DONOVAN, JAMES BRITT (Feb. 29, 1916–Jan. 19, 1970), lawyer and educator, was born in the Bronx, N.Y., the son of John D. Donovan, a surgeon, and Harriet F. O'Connor, a piano teacher. He was educated at All Hallows Institute in New York City and Fordham (B.A., 1937), and received his law degree from Harvard in 1940.

Donovan's early ambition was to become a newspaperman, and his father agreed to buy him a midwestern newspaper if he attended law school. After completing his law degree, Donovan took his first job with a New York City law firm that had a number of newspapers as clients. He was admitted to the New York bar in 1941 and practiced law for the rest of his life. "The practice of law got into my blood," he explained. He married Mary E. McKenna on May 30, 1941; they had four children.

Donovan left private practice in 1942 to become general counsel for the United States Office of Scientific Research and Development, where he handled legal matters relating to the development of the atomic bomb. In 1943 he entered the navy as an ensign and by 1945 was a full commander. During this period he was general counsel to the Office of Strategic Services under William J. Donovan (no relation). After the war he was an associate prosecutor at the International Military Tribunal in Nuremberg, Germany. Donovan was in charge of all the visual evidence—such as photographs and motion pictures—presented at the war crimes trials of 1945–1946.

After the Nuremberg trials, Donovan became general counsel for the National Bureau of Casualty Underwriters and was well known for his work in insurance law. In 1951 he formed the successful law firm of Watters, Cowen, and Donovan in New York City.

Donovan became a public figure in 1957 when he was appointed by the Brooklyn Bar Association to defend Colonel Rudolf Abel, the highest-ranking Soviet intelligence agent ever tried in the United States, against charges of conspiracy to obtain and transmit American defense secrets. Donovan accepted the assignment "as a public duty" and donated his $10,000 defense fee to several law schools. Abel was found guilty of conspiracy in late 1957 and was sentenced to thirty years in prison and fined $3,000. Before sentence was passed, Donovan argued successfully that Abel's life should be spared so that he might be exchanged for condemned American spies in the Soviet Union at some future time.

During the trial, Donovan was subjected to numerous abusive telephone calls and letters addressed to "the Commie lover." He responded to cranks and critics by saying that "if the free world is not faithful to its own moral code, there remains no society for which others may hunger." He unsuccessfully appealed Abel's conviction before the Supreme Court in 1959.

In 1962, at the request of the United States government, Donovan conducted secret negotiations in an effort to exchange Abel for Francis Gary Powers, the captured American U-2 pilot whose plane was shot down in the Soviet Union in May 1960. Donovan went to East Berlin and negotiated an agreement with the Soviets. On Feb. 10, 1962, Abel was exchanged for Powers and Frederic L. Pryor, an American student accused of espionage, on a West Berlin bridge. President Kennedy praised Donovan's efforts and called the negotiations "unique."

Several months later, the Cuban Families Committee asked Donovan to negotiate with Fidel Castro in order to free prisoners who were arrested or captured during the abortive Bay of Pigs invasion of April 1961. In 1962–1963, Donovan made numerous unofficial trips to Havana, where he talked with Castro "about everything under the sun." In the spring of 1963 he worked out a settlement whereby 9,700 Cuban and American prisoners were eventually released in exchange for drugs, medicine, and baby food. During the Havana negotiations Donovan was nominated by the New York Democratic party to run for the United States Senate. Preoccupied with the Cuban negotiations, he ran an indifferent campaign, losing to Jacob Javits, the incumbent, in November 1962.

In December 1963, Donovan was elected president of the Board of Education of New York City. He faced continuous controversy because of the board's plan for racial integration in the city. Civil rights groups contended that Donovan was not committed to integration, but he countered by stating that he was committed to education. After an unsuccessful effort by civil rights groups to remove Donovan or force his resignation in 1964, he was reelected as president of the board, a move that he interpreted as a vote of confidence. In 1968, Donovan became president of Pratt Institute, where he faced campus disruptions over black students' demands and antiwar protests. He took a hard line against student protests and vandalism but modified his approach after the Pratt faculty went on strike as a protest against his policies. He died in Brooklyn, N.Y.

[Donovan gives an account of Abel's trial and his exchange for Powers in *Strangers on a Bridge* (1964). A collection of Donovan's speeches outlining his public career is *Challenges* (1967). See Louise Bernikow, *Abel* (1970); and Francis Gary Powers, *Operation Overflight* (1970). An obituary is in the *New York Times*, Jan. 20, 1970.]

JOHN M. CARROLL

DOS PASSOS, JOHN RODERIGO (Jan. 14, 1896–Sept. 28, 1970), novelist and historian, was born in Chicago, Ill., the illegitimate son of John Randolph Dos Passos, a corporation lawyer, and Lucy Addison Sprigg Madison. Because of the boy's illegitimacy, in 1897 his mother took him to Europe, where they could be with his father, who took frequent trips to England and the Continent, more openly. Dos Passos and his mother lived in Brussels until 1901, then returned to Washington, D.C., where he attended Sidwell Friends School for a year. The two returned to London in 1902 and remained there until 1906. During his childhood Dos Passos was frequently apart from his mother; these lonely years he termed a "hotel childhood" in his autobiographical novel *Chosen Country* (1951).

After attending school at Peterborough Lodge in the suburbs of London through the first half of 1906, Dos Passos returned to the United States, where Washington, D.C., became his home. In January 1907 he began four and one half years at the Choate School in Wallingford, Conn. He excelled academically, but felt out of place with his foreign accent, his strange manners, and his lack of athletic skill. "I hated boardingschool," he recalled in his memoir *The Best Times* (1966), "being called Frenchy and Four-eyes and the class grind."

In 1910 Dos Passos' parents were married, after the death of his father's first wife. The tall, shy, introverted boy was pleased to have enough credits to qualify for Harvard University by June 1911, but because he was only fifteen his father decided a grand tour was advisable first. From November 1911 through April 1912 Dos Passos traveled with a tutor in Europe and the Near East. If his "hotel childhood" had not instilled in him the desire for traveling, this trip did; thereafter he was a peripatetic traveler, often, it seemed, using a trip as an excuse to avoid some social or political confrontation.

Intensely intellectual, Dos Passos was as much interested in art and ideas as in people. His friend Edmund Wilson characterized the public side of him in the novel *I Thought of Daisy* (1929). Dos Passos—Hugo Bamman in the novel—seemed close to no one. By the late 1920's Dos Passos had become politically radical. Bamman, Wilson wrote, sampled social groups but distrusted them, whether they were his family, early friends, or the bohemians of Greenwich Village, "so tough remained the insulation between himself and the rest of humanity." Uneasy with others, he would often lurch abruptly away from some party, first expressing his "stooped, stuttered, and bubbled good nights."

Dos Passos grew up as John Madison but took his father's name when he entered Harvard in 1912. At Harvard he had a reputation as being detached and remote, but he could also enjoy life and be sociable, and he thrived amid the college's intellectual ambience. With friends such as e. e. cummings, Robert Hillyer, R. Stewart Mitchell, and Dudley Poore he discovered "the new" in the arts. Writing for the *Harvard Monthly*, of which he was secretary during his senior year, he developed his talents in prose and poetry, moving toward the simple, clean style that marked his later work, and toward a satiric tone.

Harvard was an important training ground for Dos Passos, not only literarily, but politically. When he graduated with a B.A. in June 1916 he considered himself a socialist and actively opposed United States entry into World War I. Nevertheless he wished to experience the war, the great event of his generation, and to serve in some volunteer capacity, but to please his father he agreed instead to study architecture in neutral Spain. He remained in Spain only until the death of his father in 1917. After a brief return to New York City, where he got his first real taste of literary radicalism when he moved among figures like Emma Goldman and Max Eastman, he sailed for France with the Norton-Harjes Ambulance Corps on June 20, 1917. Two months later his section participated in a major offensive against the Germans in the Verdun sector.

The sights and sounds of war horrified Dos Passos. "I want to be able to express, later—all of this—all the tragedy and hideous excitement of it. . . . The vast despair of unavoidable death, of lives wrenched out of their channels—of all the ludicrous tomfoolery of governments," he scrawled in a notebook during the offensive. Ideas for fiction swirled in his mind. One became his first novel, *One Man's Initiation: 1917* (1920). His experiences also became the substance of *Three Soldiers* (1921), the antiwar novel that brought him fame.

When the American Red Cross took over the Norton-Harjes unit, Dos Passos traveled as a Red Cross driver to Italy in November 1917. In the spring of 1918 he was charged with disloyalty for writing letters critical of the war. He returned to the United States to settle his imbroglio with the Red Cross, then enlisted in the Army Medical Corps. At home he was bemused by "the grotesques, the farce-like quality of American life"—seeds of *Manhattan Transfer* (1925) and the trilogy *U.S.A.* (1938), as well as for his expressionistic dramas *The Garbage Man* (1926), *Airways, Inc.* (1928), and *Fortune Heights* (1934). His Medical Corps section left for Europe on Nov. 11, 1918, the day the armistice was signed.

In March 1919 Dos Passos was released from duty to study in Paris at the Sorbonne. Paris that spring, he recalled in a foreword to his translation of Blaise Cendrars' poem *Panama, or The Adventures of My Seven Uncles* (1931), was a city "already in the disintegration of victory," a place that had absorbed the "creative tidal wave" of the previous fifty years. Modern painting—the work of the cubists, the fauvists, Modigliani, Gris, and Picasso—was pouring out fresh and startling, as were new music and ballet, and he was deeply influenced by them. His sketches and paintings, the work of a talented amateur, reflect the techniques of the impressionists more than those of the cubists. With *Manhattan Transfer* and *U.S.A.* Dos Passos attempted to render concepts of simultaneity, collage, montage, and multiple perspectives juxtaposed with one another.

Dos Passos was discharged from the army in July 1919. The next years were his most nomadic. He was constantly on the move between Europe and New York City, a place that he decided in 1920 was like "Babylon gone mad." To a French friend he wrote that New York City was "a city of cavedwellers, with a frightful, brutal ugliness about it, full of thunderous voices of metal grinding on metal. . . . People swarm meekly like ants along designated routes, crushed by the disdainful and pitiless things around them."

With *Three Soldiers* (1921); his first collection of travel reportage, *Rosinante to the Road Again* (1922); and a volume of poems, *A Pushcart at the Curb* (1922), ready for publication, Dos Passos returned to Europe in March 1921. After adventures in such places as Constantinople, Tiflis, Teheran, and Baghdad, he rode a camel across the Sahara Desert to Damascus as part of a thirty-nine-day caravan trip. This experience became the subject of *Orient Express* (1927).

During the 1920's Dos Passos was an inconspicuous member of the literary scenes in Greenwich Village and Paris. His friends were the famous and near-famous: e. e. cummings, Edmund Wilson, Scott and Zelda Fitzgerald, John Howard Lawson, Donald Ogden Stewart, Gerald and Sara Murphy, Ernest Hemingway, and artists such as Fernand Léger. He became a member of the editorial board of the *New Masses* in 1926 and that year joined Lawson and others on the board of an experimental, left-wing, expressionist theater group, the New Playwrights. His increasing commitment to the political left peaked with the executions in August 1927 of the Italian anarchists Sacco and Vanzetti. "America our nation has been beaten by strangers who have turned our language inside out," he wrote eight years later. "We are two nations," he continued, ". . . we stand defeated, America."

These lines are from the next to last "Camera Eye" section of *The Big Money* (1936), the third volume of *U.S.A.*, which attempted to present a panoramic chronicle of the United States from 1900 until the stock market crash of 1929. *U.S.A.* charted what Dos Passos termed the nation's course from competitive to monopoly capitalism. In 1928, before beginning the first volume, *The 42nd Parallel* (1930), he journeyed to the Soviet Union to see "the great experiment" for himself. He was intrigued by the vigor of the Communist movement but not convinced that it was viable for the United States. Despite his doubts, he threw himself into left-wing, even Communist party, activities. During the early 1930's he was generally thought to be America's leading proletarian writer. Dos Passos was married on Aug. 19, 1929, to Katharine Foster Smith. Her house in Provincetown, Mass., became their home and provided a basis for more order and stability in his life.

Dos Passos' political recipe in the late 1920's and early 1930's called for something between socialism and Communism, with a strong dash of anarchism thrown in. Although it was not apparent at the time, Thorstein Veblen's economics, more than those of Karl Marx, influenced him. Moreover, once Franklin Roosevelt's New Deal had begun to take hold, the distance between Dos Passos and the Communists widened. But the publication of *1919* (1932) and of *The Big Money* kept most people from recognizing his drift away from the left until 1937. That year, Dos Passos returned from a trip to Spain to observe the Spanish Civil War feeling betrayed by the Communists, whom he blamed for the execution of his friend José Robles Pantoja. Over this and other political issues Dos Passos and Hemingway had a falling-out. With the publication of his anti-Communist novel *Adventures of a Young Man* (1939), Dos Passos' reputation began to decline. Only the year before Jean-Paul Sartre had acclaimed Dos Passos "the greatest writer of our time," but *Adventures* was seen as the bitter attack of a disillusioned man. Also, in contrast to his inventive earlier works, it was entirely conventional. What he intended as satire appeared to be merely vituperation. Rarely thereafter did he avoid heavy doses of the same political invective in his fiction.

Dos Passos believed that the critics attacked him because of his increasing conservatism. That was partly true. More important was that his fiction after *U.S.A.* lacked complexity. By the late 1940's he was preaching a brand of Jeffersonian agrarianism that eventually took him from the New Deal to the conservative Republicanism of Senator Barry Goldwater.

In the late 1930's Dos Passos turned to American history. Beginning with *The Living Thoughts of Tom Paine* (1940), he wrote frequently about the nation's founding fathers. His developing interest in Thomas Jefferson led him back to Westmoreland County, Va., where he owned land inherited from his father. His wife's death on Sept. 12, 1947, in an automobile accident in which he lost his right eye caused him to leave Provincetown for good. He married Elizabeth Hamlin Holdridge on Aug. 6, 1949. During his last two decades Dos Passos continued to publish and travel widely. Even the birth in 1950 of a daughter did not keep him and his wife from their trips, nor, for that matter, did his health, which began a slow decline during the mid-1960's. He died in Baltimore.

Dos Passos' importance is substantial. Never a flamboyant personality like his contemporaries Fitzgerald and Hemingway, he influenced writers through the innovative style of *Manhattan Transfer* and *U.S.A.* and through the nonfiction-novel style of the latter work. Most critics now consider him to be one of the two or three most important American political novelists of the twentieth century. He struggled throughout his career to chronicle his nation—to, as one observer remarked, "swallow America whole."

[The chief collection of Dos Passos' papers is at the Alderman Library, University of Virginia. Other important collections are at the American Academy and Institute of Arts and Letters in New York, and at the Beinecke Library, Yale University. Important published works in addition to those mentioned above are the novels *Streets of Night* (1923); *Number One* (1943); *The Grand Design* (1949); *Most Likely to Succeed* (1954); *The Great Days* (1958); *Midcentury* (1961); and *Century's Ebb* (1975). Historical studies include *The Ground We Stand On* (1941); *The Head and Heart of Thomas Jefferson* (1954); *The Men Who Made the Nation* (1957); *Prospects of a Golden Age* (1959); *Mr. Wilson's War* (1962); *The Shackles of Power* (1966); and *The Portugal Story* (1969). His travel and political reportage are in *In All Countries* (1934); *Journeys Between Wars* (1938); *State of the Nation* (1944); *Tour of Duty* (1946); *The Prospect Before Us* (1950); *The Theme Is Freedom* (1956); *Brazil on the Move* (1963); *Occasions and Protests* (1964); and *Easter Island* (1971). His report on the Sacco-Vanzetti case is *Facing the Chair* (1927). The only collection of letters is Townsend Ludington, ed., *The Fourteenth Chronicle* (1973). Biographies are Townsend Ludington, *John Dos Passos* (1980); and Virginia Spencer Carr, *Dos Passos* (1984). See also Melvin Landsberg, *Dos Passos's Path to "U.S.A."* (1972). The two major bibliographies are Jack Potter, *A Bibliography of John Dos Passos* (1950); and John Rohrkemper, *John Dos Passos* (1980). Critical studies include Georges Albert Astre, *Thèmes et structures dans l'oeuvre de John Dos Passos* (1956); John H. Wrenn, *John Dos Passos* (1961); Allen Belkin, ed., *Dos Passos, the Critics, and the Writer's Intention* (1971); David S. Sanders, ed., *The Merrill Studies in U.S.A.* (1972); Andrew Hook, ed., *Dos Passos* (1974); Linda Wagner, *Dos Passos* (1979); and Robert C. Rosen, *John Dos Passos* (1981).]

TOWNSEND LUDINGTON

DOWLING, NOEL THOMAS (Aug. 14, 1885–Feb. 11, 1969), constitutional scholar and law professor, was born in Ozark, Ala., the son of Angus Dowling, a Methodist circuit-rider, and Laura Lavinia Boswell. He attended the Bowen Preparatory School in Nashville, Tenn., and then worked his way through Vanderbilt University in three years. His classmates voted him the most popular man on campus. After receiving his B.A. in 1909, he studied law at Columbia, earning an M.A. in 1911 and an LL.B. in 1912. He then held several quasi–public service jobs, including positions with the Columbia University Legislative Drafting Research Fund and the United States Commission on Industrial Relations. During World War I he served as a major in the judge advocate general's office of the army and as an associate director of the War Risk Insurance Bureau, a forerunner of the Veterans Administration. On June 19, 1918, he married Elizabeth Brown Molloy, the daughter of a Presbyterian minister; they had two children.

With the conclusion of the war, Dowling began his long career as a teacher of law. He joined the faculty of the University of Minnesota in 1919. Three years later he returned to Columbia, where he remained the rest of his life, becoming professor of law in 1924, Nash Professor of Law in 1930, and the first occupant of the Harlan Fiske Stone chair in constitutional law in 1946. He retired from active teaching in 1958 but continued his work with the university's Legislative Drafting Research Fund until his death.

Dowling's writings encompass a number of fields, but he is best remembered as a constitutional scholar. His *Cases on Constitutional Law* first appeared in 1931 and went through six more editions in his lifetime. Gerald Gunther took over the editorial duties beginning with the seventh edition in 1965, and the book remains one of the most widely used of all law school texts.

According to colleagues and students, Dowling was an exceptional classroom teacher. He excelled in the Socratic approach, but where the Socratic method usually involves a question-and-answer interchange to move the students to the "right" conclusion, Dowling wanted them to realize that in certain areas of the law there is no single right answer. Dowling emphasized the complicated process by which constitutional doctrine is developed, especially the broader matrix of powers shared by the various branches of the federal government, as well as those shared by the state and national governments. According to Louis Lusky, who knew him as both a teacher and a colleague, Dowling "was a gentleman. He treated his students as gentlemen and ladies. And, so doing, he taught them more than the law."

During the constitutional turmoil of the 1930's, Dowling firmly allied himself with the liberal bloc on the Supreme Court, at least in part because of his friendship with, as well as high regard for, Justice Harlan Fiske Stone, who as dean of the Columbia Law School had been instrumental in bringing Dowling to the faculty. Like Stone, Dowling believed in a broad interpretation of the federal commerce power. But he also believed in the doctrine that the Court serves as the ultimate arbiter of the validity of both federal and state laws and that it plays a key role in balancing the federal system.

Throughout his teaching career, Dowling remained active in a variety of public services. He retained a strong interest in the Columbia Legislative Drafting Research Fund, and during the 1930's helped to establish legislative drafting bureaus in both houses of Congress. The Roosevelt administration consulted him in drafting the Agricultural Administration Act and the Tennessee Valley Authority legislation. A number of private insurance companies retained him to advise them regarding the constitutionality of federal and state legislation that affected their business. He also found time in 1937 to aid his native state in testing the constitutionality of the Social Security Act, and in 1941 he was able to resolve a crippling transit strike in New York City at the request of Mayor Fiorello La Guardia.

During World War II, Secretary of the Navy James Forrestal named Dowling to a special board to review the organization and practice of naval courts. For this work, he received in 1948 the Distinguished Public Service Award, the highest honor the navy can bestow upon a civilian.

Outside of the law, Dowling devoted a great deal of his time to church affairs. Although the child of Methodists and married to a Presbyterian, Dowling, along with his wife, joined the nominally Baptist Riverside Church near Columbia University, where the renowned Harry Emerson Fosdick served as senior minister to a congregation that many of its members considered "interdenominational." In 1939, Dowling was elected to the board of trustees, which included John D. Rockefeller, Jr., Winthrop W. Aldrich, and several other members of New York's most prominent families. They quickly came to respect Dowling's good sense and in 1945 elected him president of the board. He found the demands of the church and his teaching to be too great, however, and so in 1946 gave up the church office. He died in New York City.

[Dowling's constitutional ideas are expressed in the several editions of *Cases on Constitutional Law*, as well as in his article "Interstate Commerce and State Power: Revised Version," *Columbia Law Review*, 47 (1947). See also his "The Methods of Mr. Justice Stone in Constitutional Cases," *Columbia Law Review*, 41 (1941). There is no biography of Dowling, but see the articles by Herbert Wechsler, Stanley Reed, William T. Gossett, and others in "A Tribute to Noel Thomas Dowling," *Columbia Law Review*, 58 (1958), on the occasion of his retirement. An obituary is in the *New York Times*, Feb. 13, 1969.]

MELVIN I. UROFSKY

DRAPER, DOROTHY (Nov. 22, 1889–Mar. 10, 1969), real estate stylist and interior decorator, was born Dorothy Tuckerman in Tuxedo Park, N.Y., the daughter of Paul Tuckerman, a descendant of Oliver Wolcott, one of the signers of the Declaration of Independence, and Susan Minturn. She attended the Brearley School in Manhattan. She had no formal training in art or interior decoration, but she traveled extensively in Europe and enriched her knowledge and appreciation of the decorative arts. She married Dr. George Draper in 1912; they had three children before their divorce in 1930.

Draper, a statuesque, beautifully dressed, and meticulously groomed society woman, decorated her own house with such success that her friends asked her to decorate their homes. Her professional career began in earnest when Douglas Elliman, one of New York's best-known realtors, commissioned her to decorate the Hotel Carlyle. Her talents in the field of interior design soon came to the attention of architects and real estate developers.

By the 1930's, Draper had established Dorothy Draper and Company and had added several staff designers. Her firm influenced the design of the interiors of hotels, hospitals, offices, restaurants, and apartment-house lobbies. She introduced bold colors; large, overscaled architectural elements; and carefully selected accessories. Dark green walls with white plaster appliqués and consoles, swagged draperies and upholstery materials with patterns of large cabbage roses, and wallpapers in broad white and pink or shiny black stripes soon became trademarks of Draper's work. "Draperized" was the begrudging approval given by her rivals in the decorating profession.

Draper was able to secure commissions to redecorate apartment buildings by telling owners that "low-cost but intelligently applied cheerfulness" would boost rentals. She would combat dullness by selling "imagination and paint-and-color jobs." She styled the exteriors of a New York row of brownstones on Sutton Place by painting the outsides a shiny black with white trim, giving each entrance door a different vibrant color. Within three months, all units had been rented. Even more successful was the rejuvenation of tenement housing belonging to the Henry Phipps Estates. Her renovations of eleven buildings made the property an income-producing project, not only amortizing the improvement costs but also bettering the neighborhood. For this project and for her originality in the decoration of River Club, Draper won the Hall of Fame award for 1933.

The largest and best-known work of the Draper firm was New York's Hampshire House apartment hotel at 150 Central Park West, which opened in 1937. Every item in this thirty-six-story building was custom-designed, including the stationery. The goal was to create a London town-house atmosphere. The lobby floors were composed of large black and white marble squares. The doors, flanked by metal espaliered trees, were mahogany with egg-and-dart carvings. The second-floor lobby of the banquet and function rooms was designed as an outdoor space and resembled a Georgian garden. One large room called the Cottage became a popular setting for debutante parties. The dining room, which had a wood-burning fireplace, high-backed chairs, and a crystal chandelier, opened through a paneled glass wall to a neobaroque garden fountain setting with urns, flowers, and shrubs. The effect was dramatic and theatrical. Draper moved into the tower apartment of the Hampshire House and continued to supervise the maintenance of the interior decor throughout her professional career.

In 1939, Draper wrote *Decorating Is Fun! How to Be Your Own Decorator*, which showed readers how to economize on floor coverings and to reupholster furniture. In *Entertaining Is Fun! How to Be a Popular Hostess* (1941), Draper emphasized the art of enjoying oneself as hostess. A third book, *365 Shortcuts to Home Decorating* (1965), returned to subjects of her professional interests.

Draper, who eschewed the term "lady decorator," was considered the foremost woman decorator and real estate stylist of her day. "All that anyone needs to become a good decorator is a sense of beauty, a sense of fun, and some common sense," Draper asserted. She was the director of the Studio of Architecture, Building, and Furnishing of *Good Housekeeping* magazine from 1941 to 1946. She also wrote for *Vogue* and *House and Garden*. In 1959, she began a syndicated newspaper column, "Ask Dorothy Draper," which included advice on self-improvement and "self-refurbishing" as well as on home decorating.

Besides the projects in New York City, Draper did the interiors of a number of hotels elsewhere, including the Drake in Chicago; the

Mayflower in Washington, D.C.; the Greenbrier in White Sulphur Springs, W.Va.; the Arrowhead Springs in California; and the Quitainha in Petropolis, outside Rio de Janeiro, Brazil. She was the color coordinator of the 1952 Packard automobile, and in 1960 she designed the interior of the Convair 880 airplane. In addition to decorating the New York homes of many society leaders, she designed the interior of the Westinghouse Dream House in the Better Living Center of the New York World's Fair in 1964.

In 1960, Draper sold her firm to Leon Hegwood and for a time operated a smaller concern called Dorothy Draper Enterprises. Ill health forced her retirement, and she died in Cleveland, Ohio.

Draper began her career at a time when browns and greens were customarily used for public spaces; her use of vivid colors, new materials, and well-chosen accessories broke with tradition. She gave painstaking attention to detail in everything from carpets to matchbook covers and helped pioneer a modern concept of total design coordination of all objects in a room.

[See Katharine Tweed, ed., *The Finest Rooms* (1964); José Wilson, *Decorating American Style* (1975); and C. Ray Smith, *Interior Design in Twentieth-Century America* (1987). An obituary is in the *New York Times*, Mar. 12, 1969.]

KENNETH H. CARDWELL

DRESSEN, CHARLES WALTER (Sept. 20, 1898–Aug. 10, 1966), baseball player, coach, and manager, was born in Decatur, Ill., the son of Philip Dressen, a tavern manager, and Katherine Driscoll. A natural athlete, Dressen was only fourteen when he began pitching semiprofessional baseball at $7.50 a game. While attending Assumption High School in Decatur he played baseball and football, becoming the star quarterback.

In 1919 Dressen began his professional career in both baseball and football. In the summer he played second base with Moline, Ill., in the 3-I League, batting .306 in forty-two games. That fall he was a quarterback for the Decatur Staleys (which later became the Chicago Bears). In 1920 Dressen played baseball with Peoria in the 3-I League, appearing in 138 games and batting .283. The next year he again played in 138 games with Peoria, raising his batting average to .301.

Dressen continued his dual sports life, but baseball began to establish its preeminence. As a third baseman with St. Paul in the American Association, Dressen batted .304 in both 1922 and 1923. The following year he enjoyed his best season in professional baseball. In 164 games he batted .346, with 212 hits, 110 runs scored, 18 home runs, and 151 runs batted-in. In 1925 the twenty-six-year-old Dressen was signed to a major-league contract by the Cincinnati Reds. He remained with the Reds for six years, enjoying his most successful seasons in 1927 and 1928, when he batted .292 and .291 respectively.

In 1931 Dressen returned to the minor leagues, drifting to Minneapolis in the American Association and then to Baltimore in the International League. Dressen's final baseball-playing experience came with the New York Giants in the last sixteen games of the 1933 season. In his mediocre eight-season major-league playing career Dressen appeared in 646 games and batted .272, with 123 doubles, 29 triples, and 11 home runs. He scored 313 runs and batted-in 221.

Meanwhile, in the middle of the 1932 season, he began his managerial career with the Nashville Volunteers of the Southern League. He got the job by promising that he would forfeit his pay for the season if the club did not win half their remaining contests. He won the gamble by a single game. Dressen's brashness also paid off in the 1933 World Series when, in the eleventh inning, the Giants were leading 2 to 1 and the Washington Senators had the bases loaded. As Giant manager Bill Terry stood on the pitcher's mound, Dressen sprinted from the dugout, uninvited, to advise Terry to play the infield back for a double play. When a double play then ended the game, Dressen gained a reputation as a shrewd strategist.

In 1934 Dressen directed the Volunteers to a league championship for the first half of the split-season format. That July Larry MacPhail, the general manager of the Cincinnati Reds, gave Dressen his first major-league managerial position. Under Dressen the Reds won a total of 218 games while losing 284, never achieving a winning season or finishing higher than fifth in the league standings. Dressen left the club before the 1937 season was over. The next year he was back in Nashville, where he led the Volunteers to a second-place finish.

In 1939 MacPhail, then general manager

of the Brooklyn Dodgers, hired Dressen as a coach under field manager Leo Durocher. Dressen's duties involved handling pitchers, conducting pregame warm-ups, and coaching third base. After finishing third in 1939, the Dodgers climbed to second place in 1940 and won the National League pennant in 1941, losing to the New York Yankees four games to one in the World Series. On Jan. 8, 1942, Dressen married Ruth Sinclair; they had no children.

At the end of the 1942 season baseball commissioner Kenesaw Mountain Landis urged Branch Rickey, who had become president of the Dodgers following MacPhail's departure for the army, to rid the ballclub of anyone associated with gambling. In November 1942 Dressen, hardly more than a $2 bettor at the racetrack, was fired despite Durocher's protests. Eight months later, in July 1943, Dressen was quietly rehired, and he remained on the Dodger coaching staff through the 1946 season.

In 1946–1947 Dressen managed a team of major leaguers who played exhibition games in the United States and Cuba. In October Rickey asked Dressen to contact Roy Campanella after a game in Newark, N.J., between the Negro League All Stars and Dressen's barnstorming team. Jackie Robinson had been signed by the Dodgers the year before, and now Dressen set up an appointment for Campanella to meet Rickey in Brooklyn. Campanella and pitcher Don Newcombe became the next black stars to excel for the Dodgers.

In 1947 Dressen began a two-year stint as a pitching coach with the New York Yankees, but not without controversy. Rickey claimed that Dressen had promised to stay with the Dodgers unless he secured a managerial post. Commissioner A. B. "Happy" Chandler settled the dispute by suspending Dressen for thirty days at the beginning of the season. That year the Yankees won the American League pennant and World Series, defeating the Dodgers four games to three. However, the next season the Yankees fell to third place, and when Casey Stengel was hired to manage the team, Dressen replaced him as manager of the Oakland Acorns of the Pacific Coast League. The Acorns won the league championship in 1950 after finishing second in 1949.

Dressen's success with the Acorns led to his return to the Dodgers—this time as manager. He remained from 1951 to 1953, winning a total of 298 games and losing only 166. During his three-year tenure he guided the Dodgers to two league championships and presided over an agonizing near miss for a third title. On Aug. 11, 1951, the Dodgers held a thirteen-and-a-half-game lead over the New York Giants. But during the season's climactic weeks the team's fortunes reversed. The Dodgers struggled while the Giants won thirty-seven of their last forty-four games, forcing a playoff series. In what was perhaps the most memorable game in baseball history, Bobby Thomson hit a home run off Dodger relief pitcher Ralph Branca to capture the National League pennant for the Giants.

The Dodgers won the National League championship in 1952, but lost the World Series to the Yankees, four games to three. In 1953 the Dodgers got off to a phenomenal start, with ten successive wins. They sustained their performance throughout the season, capturing the pennant on September 13, the earliest date up to that point. In the process they broke thirty-five National League records and won 105 games, hitting .285 for the season with 208 home runs. Nevertheless, the Yankees won the 1953 World Series, four games to two, their record-breaking fifth world championship in a row.

Dressen's sojourn with the Dodgers marked the pinnacle of his baseball career. His self-confidence, almost total recall of baseball facts, and willingness to talk baseball at any hour made him popular with the media in New York City. However, following a disagreement over his request for a two-year contract, Dressen left the Dodgers in 1954 to return to the Acorns as manager and general manager. He led the Acorns into the league playoff championship series, but left in 1955 to manage the Washington Senators. After two unsuccessful years, he was fired early in the 1957 season. He spent the remainder of the year in the Senators' front office as assistant to the president in charge of scouting. In 1958 he returned to the Dodgers, now located in Los Angeles, as a coach under manager Walter Alston.

Three weeks after the Dodgers won the 1959 World Series, Dressen signed a two-year contract to manage the Milwaukee Braves. He continued with the Braves until late in the 1961 season. After piloting Toronto in the International League to a 91–62 finish in 1962, Dressen rejoined the Dodgers as a special assistant to the general manager, handling scouting chores.

On June 18, 1963, he was named manager of the ninth-place Detroit Tigers. He remained with this club until his death, winning a total of 245 games and losing 207, and placing fourth in the ten-team league in 1964 and 1965. During his career Dressen managed five major-league teams, won 1,037 games, and lost 993, for a winning percentage of .511. He died in Detroit, Mich.

[Short biographical sketches are in Tommy Holmes, *The Artful Dodgers* (1953) and *The Dodgers* (1975); Harold Rosenthal, *Baseball's Best Managers* (1961); Gene Karst and Martin J. Jones, Jr., *Who's Who in Professional Baseball* (1973); and Peter Golenbock, *Bums* (1984). Obituaries are in the *New York Times*, Aug. 11, 1966; and *Sporting News*, Aug. 27, 1966.]

DAVID BERNSTEIN

DUFF, JAMES HENDERSON (Jan. 21, 1883–Dec. 20, 1969), lawyer, governor of Pennsylvania, and United States senator, was born in Mansfield (now Carnegie), Pa., the son of Joseph Miller Duff, a Presbyterian minister, and Margaret Morgan. He attended public schools in Carnegie and Princeton University, where he received a B.A. in 1904. After two years at the University of Pennsylvania Law School, he completed his law studies at the University of Pittsburgh and received an LL.B. in 1907. He married Jean Kerr Taylor on Oct. 26, 1909; they had no children.

Duff was an avid outdoorsman, and although he opened a law practice in Pittsburgh, he was attracted to the oil and gas fields of western Pennsylvania. Duff borrowed $5,000 to buy an oil driller's rig, struck oil, and went on wildcat ventures in Texas and Mexico. He lost everything in the stock market crash of 1929 and returned to the full-time practice of law. These experiences left him unintimidated by men of great wealth. "Any damn fool can make a million dollars," he later commented.

Duff held no elected office until he was sixty-three, but he was long active in Pennsylvania politics. In 1912 he was a presidential elector for Theodore Roosevelt's Progressive party. Later he returned to the Republican party and served as its chairman for the Twelfth Legislative District in Pittsburgh and as a delegate to the Republican conventions of 1932, 1936, and 1940, when he actively supported Wendell Willkie. In 1943 Governor Edward Martin appointed him attorney general of the commonwealth. Duff used that post to draw attention to the pollution of Pennsylvania's rivers and streams, and he won enactment of protective legislation over the opposition of the coal industry.

In 1946 Governor Martin, constitutionally barred from succeeding himself, ran for the United States Senate. Republican factions headed by Joseph R. Grundy and Joseph N. Pew, frequently at odds with each other, met to choose a gubernatorial candidate acceptable to both sides. Duff agreed to run, and with the support of Grundy and Pew he won the governorship by a wide margin; he then began to establish his political independence.

In addition to an anti-water-pollution program, Duff initiated ambitious and costly plans for highway and bridge building, increased teachers' salaries, and improved state mental health facilities. To pay for these programs, he recommended taxes on cigarettes, soft drinks, and corporate capital stock. When the Pennsylvania Manufacturers Association (founded by Grundy) protested the new corporate taxes, Duff responded with characteristic bluntness, "If you think I'm going to give you a free seat in the grandstand at the same time I'm going to raise the price of bleacher seats, you're crazy." He also drew fire from organized labor by signing legislation that prohibited public-utility workers from striking. Once he dispersed striking truckers, who had used their vehicles to block the Pennsylvania Turnpike, by ordering the highway department to bulldoze the trucks off the road.

Duff's break with Grundy was sealed at the 1948 Republican National Convention. Duff worked for the nomination of Arthur Vandenberg, while the Grundy forces, including Senator Martin, threw their support behind Thomas E. Dewey. Routed at the convention, Duff confronted the Grundy machine directly when he ran against its candidate for the Republican senatorial nomination in 1950. He campaigned against Grundyism, which he defined as "government by a few, for the benefit of a few, at the expense of the public." Duff won the nomination by a landslide and went on to defeat the Senate Democratic whip, Francis Myers. Duff's victory was attributable to his progressive record as governor and to his popular personal style. All any citizen needed to get in touch with Duff was a nickle and a phone booth, Duff asserted. "I believe in keeping myself close to the average guy."

Duff arrived in the United States Senate with a reputation as "rough, tough Duff," a no-holds-barred, bare-knuckle political fighter, but he found the adjustment to a legislative arena difficult. As governor, he had shunned cabinet meetings, met with department heads individually, and made decisions on his own. Now, as a sixty-seven-year-old freshman, he had only a small staff and minor committee assignments. His relations with Senate Republican leaders Robert Taft and Kenneth Wherry were polite but cool, and he got along poorly with his conservative senior colleague, Ed Martin. Senate traditions also required junior members to keep silent during their first years. Consequently, Duff turned his energies to presidential politics and became a founder of the movement to draft Dwight D. Eisenhower.

Duff swallowed his dislike of Dewey and met regularly with Dewey, Herbert Brownell, Henry Cabot Lodge, Hugh Scott, and other eastern internationalist Republicans who were determined to prevent the midwestern isolationist Robert Taft from receiving their party's nomination. Duff built up support for Eisenhower and tore into those who opposed him. Lodge recalled that in 1951 Duff "virtually single-handedly kept the Eisenhower movement alive . . . by going on a speaking tour and frequently saying printable things—and here and there a few unprintable things." President Eisenhower owed Duff a great debt, but Duff rarely tried to collect on it. He made few patronage demands and seemed content with access to the White House.

With the Republican victory in 1952, Duff received more-important assignments on the Armed Services and Commerce committees. He also spoke out against Senator Joseph R. McCarthy and voted in favor of censure of McCarthy. But Duff's Senate term lacked notable achievement, and he was often absent during roll-call votes. Eisenhower's memoirs credit Duff with 100 percent support of administration programs in 1953, the only senator to achieve a perfect score, but in subsequent years the conservative Martin voted more in line with the administration than did Duff. Nevertheless, when Duff ran for reelection in 1956 Eisenhower campaigned for him as an exemplar of modern Republicanism.

Duff's disenchantment with the Senate showed in his uninspired campaign. His opponent, Joseph Clark, the mayor of Philadelphia, toured with an empty chair representing Duff's absenteeism. The charge made Duff furious, but he could not refute it. In spite of Eisenhower's 600,000-vote margin in Pennsylvania, Duff lost by 17,900 votes, less than 1 percent of the total. He retired from politics to his law practice and his gardening, and he remained vigorous right up to the moment when he collapsed and died at Washington, D.C., National Airport.

Like Theodore Roosevelt, Duff enjoyed a good fight and saw politics as a bully pulpit. An independent, middle-of-the-road politician, he charted a course remarkably free of organized interests, either business or labor. He opposed "free government handouts" but believed that government should do for people what they could not do for themselves. He cited Theodore Roosevelt, Woodrow Wilson, and Harry Truman as his political heroes because "they were willing to fight the trend if they believed in something else." That description fit Duff himself.

[Duff's papers are in the Pennsylvania Historical and Museum Commission in Harrisburg. Material on the draft-Eisenhower movement is in the Eisenhower Library in Abilene, Kans. Additional material is in the Joseph Clark and Hugh Scott oral histories in the Library of Congress; and an interview with Hugh Scott, the transcript of which is on file in the Senate Historical Office. See also Walter Davenport, "Pennsylvania's Rough, Tough Duff," *Colliers*, Oct. 14, 1950; Joe Alex Morris, "That Guy Duff!" *Saturday Evening Post*, Aug. 18, 1951; Jay Franklin, *Republicans on the Potomac* (1953); and Henry Cabot Lodge, *The Storm Has Many Eyes* (1973); Obituaries are in the *Philadelphia Evening Bulletin*, Dec. 20, 1969; and the *Philadelphia Inquirer* and the *New York Times*, both Dec. 21, 1969.]

Donald A. Ritchie

DUKE, VERNON (Oct. 10, 1903–Jan. 16, 1969), composer, was born Vladimir Alexandrovich Dukelsky in Parfianovka, near Pskov, in northern Russia, the son of Alexander Dukelsky, a civil engineer, and Anna Kopylov, whose family had become successful in the sugar business. In 1913, after Alexander Dukelsky died, the family moved to Kiev. There Duke studied music with Reinhold Glière at the Kiev Conservatory. In December 1919, because of increased revolutionary activity in Kiev, the Dukelsky family left for Odessa. When the fighting reached Odessa late in 1920, the family made a daring escape from the city and sailed to Constantinople. Here Duke earned an income playing piano in restaurants, cabarets, and movie theaters, and organized concerts and recitals of serious music. In Constantinople he discovered American popular music, including works by George Gershwin, and began composing melodies in the new American idiom. He also met Pavel Tchelitchew, Nicolas Slonimsky, and Boris Kochno, who later became his artistic colleagues.

In the autumn of 1921, Duke sailed with his mother and brother to New York City. There he played piano in restaurants and conducted and composed for vaudeville and burlesque. Despite the inglorious work, Duke noted in his autobiography that "I was under twenty, not unattractive, and wore my secondhand or borrowed clothes with an air, though without a cent. Obliging mentors turned up on all sides." The singers Eva Gautier and Nina Koshetz encouraged him to compose serious music and performed his art songs. During his first years in America, Duke met both George Gershwin and Artur Rubinstein. Gershwin suggested he adopt the name Vernon Duke for his popular-music persona. Rubinstein encouraged Duke to go to Paris, the Mecca for all young composers of serious music, and so, in 1924, Duke sailed for France.

Shortly after his arrival in Paris, Duke renewed his acquaintance with Tchelitchew and Kochno. Upon hearing Duke's Piano Concerto, Kochno arranged a meeting between Duke and Serge Diaghilev, impresario of the Ballets Russes de Monte Carlo. Diaghilev asked Duke to compose a new ballet to showcase the dancer Serge Lifar. The result was *Zéphire et Flore* (1925), first performed in Monte Carlo with choreography by Leonide Massine, sets by Georges Braque, and costumes by Coco Chanel. Performances followed in Paris, London, and Berlin. Although there were tentative plans for a second ballet, Duke never seemed completely comfortable in his role as a Diaghilev protégé. During this European sojourn, Duke traveled with the ballet company. He played one of the four pianos at the London premiere of Stravinsky's *Les noces*, the other three pianists at this notable performance being Francis Poulenc, Georges Auric, and Vittorio Rieti.

In 1925 Slonimsky introduced Duke to the conductor Serge Koussevitzky in Paris. Koussevitzky conducted Duke's Sonata for Piano and Orchestra and Symphony no. 1 in Paris shortly thereafter. The latter work was performed in 1929 by the Boston Symphony under Koussevitzky, and the next year Duke's Symphony no. 2 was performed in Boston. Koussevitzky remained a champion of Duke's serious music for many years.

Duke also enjoyed some success during this period on the London popular stage; he wrote songs for *Katja the Dancer* (1925), *Yvonne* (1925), and *The Yellow Mask* (1928). Duke used his Russian name on his serious works and his American pseudonym on his popular songs.

After returning to New York in 1929, Duke wrote film music for the Paramount studios in Astoria, Queens, and composed songs for the musical theater. His first notable song was "I'm Only Human After All," for the *Garrick Gaieties* (third edition, 1930), with Ira Gershwin and E. Y. Harburg collaborating on the lyrics. Duke contributed songs to *Three's a Crowd* (1930) and *Shoot the Works* (1931), but his first complete score was for *Walk a Little Faster* (1932), a revue that starred Beatrice Lillie and included what would become his most famous song, "April in Paris." He supplied most of the music for the 1934 and 1936 editions of the *Ziegfeld Follies*. Important songs from these shows include "I Like the Likes of You," "What Is There to Say?" "Suddenly," "I Can't Get Started," "Words Without Music," and "That Moment of Moments." "Autumn in New York," for which Duke wrote both words and music, appeared in *Thumbs Up* (1934). His other New York theatrical projects from this period were *The Show Is On* (1936), *A Vagabond Hero* (closed in tryouts, 1939), *Keep Off the Grass* (1940), and *It Happens on Ice* (1940). Upon the death of George Gershwin in 1937, Duke completed the film score for *The Goldwyn Follies*, to which he contributed two ballets, both choreographed by George Balanchine, and the song "Spring Again."

In 1940 Duke's most important musical, *Cabin in the Sky*, opened in New York with Ethel Waters, Todd Duncan, Rex Ingram, Dooley Wilson, and Katherine Dunham in the all-black cast. Lynn Root wrote the book, and John Latouche, the lyrics; Balanchine choreographed and directed. Its notable songs include "Cabin in the Sky" and "Taking a Chance on Love." Duke also wrote scores for *Banjo Eyes*

(1941); *The Lady Comes Across* (1942); *Jackpot* (1944); and *Sadie Thompson* (1944), an unsuccessful musical version of the play *Rain; Two's Company* (1952), with lyrics by Ogden Nash and starring Bette Davis; and *The Littlest Review* (1956), which included an important Duke song, "Born Too Late." In addition, Duke wrote both music and lyrics for the first American production of Jean Anouilh's play *Time Remembered* (1957); the highly acclaimed production starred Helen Hayes, Susan Strasberg, and Richard Burton. Duke musicals that closed during pre-Broadway tryouts were *Dancing in the Streets* (1943), *Sweet Bye and Bye* (1946), *The Pink Jungle* (1959), and *Zenda* (1963). In 1952 Duke supplied ballet music for the film *She's Working Her Way Through College*. Duke songs were also used in the 1952 film *April in Paris*.

In 1936 Duke became an American citizen, and during World War II he served three years in the United States Coast Guard. His musical revue for the Coast Guard, *Tars and Spars* (1944), was one of several collaborations with the lyricist Howard Dietz.

Duke continued composing serious music for the concert stage and ballets. Most successful was *Le bal des blanchisseuses* (1946), a ballet produced by Kochno in Paris and starring Roland Petit. Throughout his life Duke supported the music of young composers and in 1948 founded the Society for Forgotten Music. With the publication of his autobiography in 1955, Duke announced that he would no longer use his Russian name on any composition.

While Duke's serious music now generates little interest and his theatrical career lacked notable successes, his songs for revues and musicals stand as important achievements. His best songs reflect strong musicianship, a distinctive style, and innovative and often complex melodies.

On Oct. 30, 1957, Duke married Kay McCracken, a singer; they had no children. Duke composed two additional ballets in his later years and in 1958 he finally saw the première of his opera, *Demoiselle paysanne*, written thirty years earlier. Duke published a volume of music criticism as well as essays on the music scene. He also translated American song lyrics into Russian. He died in Santa Monica, Calif.

[The bulk of Duke's papers are housed in the Music Division of the Library of Congress. Published works by Duke include his autobiography, *Passport to Paris* (1955); and *Listen Here! A Critical Essay on Music Depreciation* (1963). For lists of published popular songs, see Nat Shapiro and Bruce Pollock, eds., *Popular Music, 1920–1979* (1985); and Steven Suskin, *Show Tunes, 1905–1985* (1986). For biographical details and critical appraisals, see Hugo Leichtentritt, *Serge Koussevitzky: The Boston Symphony Orchestra and the New American Music* (1946); Igor Stravinsky, "A Cure for V.D.," *Listen*, (Sept. 1964); Stanley Green, "The New Russian Hit Parade," *Saturday Review*, Aug. 26, 1967; Alec Wilder, *American Popular Song: The Great Innovators, 1900–1950*, edited by James T. Maher (1972); Stanley Green, *The World of Musical Comedy*, 4th ed. (1980); and David Ewen, *American Composers: A Biographical Dictionary* (1982). An obituary is in the *New York Times*, Jan. 18, 1969.]

CRAIG S. LIKNESS

DULLES, ALLEN WELSH (Apr. 7, 1893–Jan. 29, 1969), lawyer, foreign-service officer, and intelligence official, was born in Watertown, N.Y., the son of Allen Macy Dulles, pastor of the local Presbyterian church, and Edith Foster, the daughter of one secretary of state, John Watson Foster, and sister-in-law of another, Robert Lansing. Extremely precocious, Dulles produced his first publication, *The Boer War: A History*—with his grandfather Foster's assistance—when he was eight years old. Family trips to Europe whetted his appetite for travel, and so, after graduating from Princeton University in 1914, he went to India, China, and Japan. In 1916, Dulles entered the foreign service. His first post was in Vienna, but with America's entry into World War I, he was transferred to Bern in neutral Switzerland. Dulles was put in charge of intelligence. He did not distinguish himself; indeed, in 1917, evidently failing to grasp the potential significance of a phone call from Lenin urgently requesting a meeting, Dulles chose to keep a prior engagement. By the following morning the Russian Revolution was en route to the Finland Station.

At Versailles, as part of the American Commission to Negotiate the Peace, Dulles helped to redraw the boundaries of Eastern Europe. Subsequent diplomatic assignments took him to Berlin, Constantinople, and Geneva, and back to Washington, D.C. On Oct. 16, 1920, he married Clover Todd; they had three children. Having found it difficult to make ends meet, he attended evening classes at George Washington University, passed the bar, and resigned from the State Department in 1926. He then joined his older brother, John Foster Dulles, in the prestigious Wall Street law firm of Sullivan and Cromwell, becoming a partner in 1930.

Because of the German orientation of many of Sullivan and Cromwell's major clients, Dulles watched the rise of Adolf Hitler with great concern. Breaking ranks with other leading Republicans, he criticized America's neutrality legislation in *Can We Be Neutral?* (1936; written with Hamilton Fish Armstrong). When the United States entered World War II, he enlisted in his longtime friend William J. Donovan's fledgling Office of Coordinator of Information, which was soon expanded and renamed the Office of Strategic Services (OSS). In November 1942, after a short time as head of the New York City office, Dulles was stationed again in Bern.

During the war, Bern became the most important nexus of continental intelligence activities. All but advertising his presence, from a fifteenth-century house overlooking the Aar River, Dulles established liaisons with enemy dissidents and received credit for penetrating the Abwehr, the Nazi intelligence service. Nevertheless, since the Allies had broken the German code ("Ultra"), his work produced few tangible rewards, and the abortive attempt on Hitler's life on July 20, 1944, broke up his network of informants.

Dulles' most controversial project was Operation Sunrise, the secret surrender of the German forces in Italy. SS Obergruppenführer Karl Wolff approached Dulles with a last-minute offer of peace. Dulles, excited by the prospect of such a coup and hoping to minimize the postwar influence of the leftist resistance in Italy as well as of the Soviet Union in Germany, jumped at the opportunity. Wolff, however, promised more than he could deliver. Not until May 2, 1945, only five days before the formal Nazi capitulation at Rheims, were the negotiations concluded, but in the process, relations between the Allies and the Soviets were strained. Still, Operation Sunrise confirmed Dulles' reputation as America's spymaster and enhanced his enthusiasm for covert operations.

Disappointed that President Harry Truman had disbanded the OSS after the war, Dulles returned to Sullivan and Cromwell. But his infatuation with espionage was undiminished, and the escalation of the cold war increased his conviction that the security of the non-Communist world required an American intelligence service. He helped to draft the 1947 National Security Act, which created the Central Intelligence Agency (CIA), and then chaired a commission to evaluate the agency's performance. The commission recommended that the Office of Policy Coordination (OPC), the State Department's clandestine arm, be transferred to the CIA. When Dulles became the agency's deputy director for plans in 1951, he acquired responsibility for OPC projects.

In February 1953, President Dwight D. Eisenhower appointed Dulles the first civilian director of the CIA. With his brother, John Foster Dulles, serving as secretary of state, the agency achieved unprecedented power and prestige. Allen Dulles' convivial personality, orientation toward action, and defense of his personnel against Senator Joseph McCarthy's red-baiting generated intense esprit de corps. Dulles believed that America "was not really 'at peace'" with the Communists and that it had to "fight fire with fire." He masterminded covert projects to overthrow governments in Iran (1953) and Guatemala (1954). In 1956 came the CIA's greatest triumph, the U-2 overflights of the Soviet Union.

Even as Dulles basked in his successes, the legend of the CIA's invincibility began to unravel. Its intelligence-gathering capabilities came under severe criticism during the Suez crisis in 1956. Simultaneously the agency's program to liberate Eastern Europe contributed to an uprising in Hungary that the Soviets ruthlessly suppressed. A 1958 operation in Indonesia ended in abject failure. In May 1960 the Soviets shot down a U-2, capturing the pilot, Francis Gary Powers, alive. Eisenhower took the responsibility, but it was Dulles who suffered the humiliation.

The Bay of Pigs fiasco in April 1961 brought Dulles' active career to an end. Planning for this paramilitary invasion of Cuba had begun prior to John F. Kennedy's election, and although it was the new president himself who had scaled down the air strikes, he blamed Dulles for concealing from the White House the unacceptably high risks of the operation. Before the year was out, Dulles had to resign. The CIA never regained the stature it had held under Dulles' leadership. He has been "the last great Romantic of Intelligence." After his forced retirement Dulles spent much of his time writing about his exploits and defending the intelligence establishment. In 1967 he suffered the first of a series of strokes. He died in Washington, D.C.

[Dulles' papers at Princeton University give little information about his CIA career. More fruitful are his brother's, also at Princeton, and the collections at the Dwight D. Eisenhower Library in Abilene, Kans., and the John F. Kennedy Library in Boston, Mass. The John Foster Dulles Oral History Collection is also at Princeton. Dulles' own writings include *The Craft of Intelligence* (1963) and *Secret Surrender* (1966).

Dulles' CIA activities are treated in reports of the Senate Select Committee on Government Operations with Respect to Intelligence Activities: *Alleged Assassination Plots Involving Foreign Leaders* (1975), *Covert Action Report* (1975), *Hearings* (1976), and *Final Report* (1976). A biography of Dulles and his siblings is Leonard Mosley, *Dulles* (1978). See also R. Harris Smith, *OSS* (1972); Bradley Smith and Elena Agarossi, *Operation Sunrise* (1979); Bradley Smith, *The Shadow Warriors* (1983); John Prados, *Presidents' Secret Wars* (1986); and John Ranelagh, *The Agency* (1986). An obituary is in the *New York Times*, Jan. 31, 1969.]

RICHARD H. IMMERMAN

DURYEA, JAMES FRANK (Oct. 8, 1869–Feb. 15, 1967), automobile inventor, was born in Washburn, Ill., the son of George Washington Duryea, a farmer, and Louisa Melvina Turner. He attended high school in Wyoming, Ill., helped on the family farm, and shared his older brother Charles's early interest in mechanics. Duryea claimed to have made designs for a steam vehicle as early as 1883.

After graduating from high school in 1888, Duryea took up machine work in Washington, D.C., where Charles was designing a bicycle. In 1889 the brothers moved briefly to Rockaway, N.J., and then to Chicopee, Mass., where they worked at the Ames Manufacturing Company. There Charles had his bicycles made, and Frank worked on toolmaking and mechanical drawing. They also acquired information on Daimler and Benz cars and began to read books on gas engines.

Late in 1891 Charles showed Frank designs for a one-cylinder, free-piston gasoline engine and friction transmission. Frank did not like either, but Charles persuaded Erwin F. Markham, a Springfield, Mass., businessman, to provide $1,000 to build the vehicle.

At that point Charles moved to Peoria, Ill., leaving Frank in charge of construction. He redesigned the engine to eliminate the free piston. The car was built in Russel's machine shop in Springfield and made its first trial run on Sept. 21, 1893. Although it did not run well and was clearly inferior to contemporary German and French automobiles, it was unquestionably the first operational American gasoline-powered highway vehicle. (There was much friction between the brothers and their children later over credit for this feat. The issue can be considered settled by a statement made by their younger sister, Atina, who said that Charles had the original concept but that Frank provided the technical skill necessary to implement it.)

The poor performance of this car discouraged Markham, who gradually withdrew from the venture except for paying shop and material costs. Duryea replaced the original transmission with a friction clutch and geared transmission, and hc found another sponsor in Springfield, Henry W. Clapp, for a second car that was completed early in 1895. A four-cycle engine replaced the original two-cycle design. With Duryea driving, it won the *Chicago Times-Herald* Thanksgiving Day race on Nov. 28, 1895—fifty-four miles through snow-covered streets. Of the six vehicles that entered, only Duryea's and a Benz finished.

Meanwhile, in 1894, a syndicate of Springfield investors had organized the Duryea Motor Wagon Company. The Duryea brothers each had a one-third share; Charles was a director and Frank was in charge of design and construction. The company built thirteen cars, with continuing improvements in design. One of these won the second major American automobile race, from New York City to Irvington-on-Hudson and back, fifty-two miles, on May 30, 1896. Duryea again was the driver. On Nov. 14, 1896, he came in first in the Liberty Day Run from London to Brighton. This event celebrated the repeal of Britain's red flag law, which for thirty years had limited the speed of self-propelled highway vehicles to four miles an hour.

Continuing conflict between the brothers led to the dissolution of the Duryea Motor Wagon Company in 1895. Frank left to join the Automobile Company of America, a purely speculative enterprise that failed. In 1900 he formed his own company, the Hampden Automobile and Launch Company. A year later he contracted to design and build automobiles under the name Stevens-Duryea for the Stevens Arms and Tool Company of Chicopee, Mass. This operation was separated from the parent company in 1904 and became the Stevens-Duryea Motor Car Company.

One of the luxury cars of its day, the Stevens-Duryea had a four-cylinder engine in 1903 and a six-cylinder motor after 1906; prices ranged from $2,500 to $6,500. It was a profitable line, but in 1915 Duryea, with unusual prescience, saw that the moving assembly line had doomed the small-scale, luxury-car producer. He was also in poor health, so when he received a good offer from Westinghouse for his factories in Chicopee Falls and Springfield, he accepted. Westinghouse subsequently used the plants for military production.

Duryea's retirement lasted for fifty-two years. He resided in Greenwich, Conn., until 1938 and then in Madison, Conn., where he died. In 1945 he received a testimonial from the American Automobile Association, signed by Captain E. V. Rickenbacker, chairman of the board, stating that he had won America's first race in a car of his own design and construction. Duryea was married twice (names of spouses unknown) and had one child.

[The most detailed account is in Duryea's own memoir, "America's First Gasoline Automobile," *Michigan Business Review*, March 1960. See also J. B. Rae, *American Automobile Manufacturers* (1959).]

J. B. RAE

EASTMAN, MAX FORRESTER (Jan. 4, 1883–Mar. 25, 1969), writer and political activist, was born in Canandaigua, N.Y., the son of Samuel Elijah Eastman and Annis Bertha Ford, both Protestant ministers. He was educated at Mercersburg Academy from 1898 to 1900 and at Williams College, receiving his B.A. in 1905. From 1907 to 1910 he studied philosophy at Columbia University under John Dewey, completing all requirements for his Ph.D. except the dissertation, which he wrote but declined to submit. He married Ida Rauh on May 4, 1911. They had one child, and were subsequently divorced in 1922.

While living in Greenwich Village, Eastman became interested in feminism and socialism. In 1912 he received a telegram from a group of artists and writers that included Louis Untermeyer and Mary Heaton Vorse. The message read: "You are elected editor of the *Masses*. No pay." The *Masses* was a foundering Socialist monthly that Eastman immediately transformed into a lively left-wing periodical. At that time many of the best American artists and writers were Socialists or Socialist sympathizers, and Eastman got a number of them, including John Sloan, Art Young, Floyd Dell, John Reed, Sherwood Anderson, Stuart Davis, Boardman Robinson, George Bellows, Carl Sandburg, and Randolph Bourne, to contribute to and edit his magazine.

Eastman and the *Masses* opposed American entry into World War I. In August 1917, the government put the *Masses* out of business by denying it second-class mailing privileges. Eastman was one of seven editors and contributors indicted for conspiring to obstruct military recruiting. Unlike most defendants in such trials, he escaped prison, two juries in succession failing to agree on a verdict. His eloquence on the stand was crucial to his freedom.

After the Bolshevik Revolution in Russia, Eastman supported the war against Germany. He founded the *Liberator* early in 1918 to advance that end. The *Liberator* was stern and less interested in art and personal freedom than in the Revolution.

In 1922 Eastman went to the Soviet Union to see the great "experiment" in action. There he learned Russian, met many leading Bolsheviks, and sided with Leon Trotsky in the struggle for power following Lenin's death. In 1924 Eastman married Eliena Vassilyenva Krylenko and left for Western Europe. He took with him a copy of "Lenin's Testament," in which Lenin warned against Joseph Stalin and named Trotsky as his heir. Eastman published parts of it in *Since Lenin Died* (1925), an attack on the new Soviet leadership, which he believed was betraying the Revolution.

In 1927 Eastman returned to the United States, where he continued to serve as Trotsky's translator and literary agent. He supported himself by lecturing. His connection with Trotsky and the left-oppositionists isolated Eastman from his former constituency, as most Americans on the left supported Stalin. In the "red decade" of the 1930's his estrangement intensified. Stalin personally attacked Eastman, calling him a "gangster of the pen," the only American writer so named. Eastman regarded this as a "title of nobility conferred by the tyrant himself." Eastman never formally joined the

Trotskyists, and fell out with Trotsky in time. He associated mainly with a few independents and leftists, such as Edmund Wilson and Sidney Hook, who rejected Stalinism while remaining socialists.

In 1940 Eastman published two important political books. In *Marxism: Is It Science?* he answered his own question in the negative, renouncing Marxism and his belief in socialism. *Stalin's Russia and the Crisis of Socialism* was an analysis of Soviet misrule, chronicling it in detail and explaining, for the first time, the meaning and function of the great purges of the 1930's. Reviewing these books, Edmund Wilson said that they were "the best-informed discussion of the implication of the Marxist movement and the development of the revolution in Russia that has yet appeared in English," and that by writing them Eastman had justified his "anomalous role of preacher-teacher-critic-poet," and stood "as primarily a writer to be read."

In the 1940's Eastman moved steadily to the right. In 1941 he joined the *Reader's Digest* as a roving editor. He became a contributor to the *National Review* and supported Senator Joseph McCarthy. He built a home on Martha's Vineyard, visited New York City in the spring and fall, and spent winters in the Caribbean. His second wife died in 1956. On Mar. 22, 1958, he married Yvette Szekely. Eastman died in Barbados.

Eastman was a man of striking good looks and great personal charm. These attributes won him many friends throughout his life, and many lovers for much of it. Self-indulgence made him a bad father, and a poor husband to his first wife, and also at times to his second, who seems not to have fully entered into the spirit of what he regarded as an open marriage. He was a better friend, thoughtful, generous, and dependable. Eastman is most admired as a leader of the antiwar movement in 1917 and 1918, for editing the *Masses*, and as the chief anti-Stalinist on the American left from 1924 to 1939. He wrote twenty-six books, including poetry and fiction, made five major translations from the Russian, and edited two anthologies and a film documentary of the Russian Revolution.

[The Lilly Library of Indiana University is the repository of Eastman's papers. Yvette Eastman also has a large collection, which has not been made public. See Eastman's memoirs, *Enjoyment of Living* (1948) and *Love and Revolution* (1964); his biographical essays, *Heroes I Have Known* (1942) and *Great Companions* (1959); and also his *Seven Kinds of Goodness* (1967). His last interview is in the *New York Times*, Jan. 9, 1969. See also Edmund Wilson, *Classics and Commercials* (1950). Daniel Aaron, *Writers on the Left* (1961); and John P. Diggins, *Up from Communism* (1975). William L. O'Neill, *The Last Romantic* (1978), is the only full biography. A brief study in the Twayne United States Authors Series is Milton Cantor, *Max Eastman* (1970). An obituary is in the *New York Times*, Mar. 27, 1967.]

WILLIAM L. O'NEILL

EDDY, NELSON (June 29, 1901–Mar. 6, 1967), singer and actor, was born in Providence, R.I., the son of William Darius Eddy, a machinist, and Isabel Kendrick, a church soloist. At the age of five, he began attending the Dartmouth Street Primary School in New Bedford, Mass., and he continued his early schooling in Providence and Pawtucket, R.I. Between the ages of nine and fourteen, he sang as a soprano in a Providence church choir and also as a soloist in several churches there. In 1915, Eddy's parents separated, and he accompanied his mother to Philadelphia, where out of financial necessity he left school and took a job as a telephone operator in the Mott Iron Works. He subsequently worked for three Philadelphia newspapers and then for N. W. Ayer and Sons as an advertising copywriter. During his leisure hours he attended evening school, took correspondence courses, read, and listened to the recordings of eminent baritones.

Eddy's initial stage appearance was in the musical *The Marriage Tax* in January 1922. That same year, he won a Gilbert and Sullivan competition and appeared as Strephon in a Savoy Opera Company production of *Iolanthe*. In 1924 he won a competition that enabled him to make his debut in grand opera as Amonasro in *Aida* with the Philadelphia Civic Opera Company. With the help of the company's conductor, Alexander Smallens, he learned twenty-eight operatic roles. Édouard Lippé, another member of the company, who became Eddy's longtime singing coach and friend, persuaded him to give up his nonmusical employments and become a student of William Vilonat. Borrowing money from a banker friend, Eddy joined Vilonat in Dresden in 1927 and studied with him there for a number of months. The Dresden Opera Company offered Eddy a position, but he declined in favor of pursuing his singing career in America. Once back in the United States, he appeared again with the Civic Opera and also with its successor, the Philadelphia Grand Opera Company, in such works as Richard Strauss's *Feuersnot* and *Ariadne auf Naxos* and Wagner's *Parsifal*, the last under Stokowski.

But opera was not the only vehicle used by Eddy to display his singing talent. On his return from Europe, he decided to take up concert singing, signed a contract with Columbia Concerts, and made his debut in Norristown, Pa. He increased his repertoire of songs to 500, went on tour, and by 1933 had visited almost every major city in the country. During the 1930's and 1940's he also appeared on numerous radio programs, notably "The Voice of Firestone," "The Electric Hour," and "The Bell Telephone Hour."

In 1933, Eddy signed a seven-year contract with Metro-Goldwyn-Mayer (MGM). During the next two years, he played only minor roles and was ready to give up movies when Louis B. Mayer advised him to be patient and to secure a drama coach. After taking acting lessons, Eddy was teamed with the soprano Jeanette MacDonald in *Naughty Marietta* (1935). The movie was very successful, and the Eddy-MacDonald duo were hailed as "America's singing sweethearts." They made eight films, including *Rose Marie* (1936), *Sweethearts* (1938), and *I Married an Angel* (1942), their last. Eddy also appeared in three other MGM musicals: *Rosalie* (1937), with Eleanor Powell; *Balalaika* (1939), with Ilona Massey; and *The Chocolate Soldier* (1941), with Risë Stevens. In 1942, Eddy left MGM and during the next five years made films such as *The Phantom of the Opera* (1943), for Universal Studios; *Knickerbocker Holiday* (1944), for United Artists; and *Northwest Outpost* (1947), for Republic Studios. Reportedly he earned $5 million from his films.

In March 1935, Eddy made his first commercial recording for RCA Victor. During the next thirty years, he recorded 25 albums and 284 songs for RCA Victor, Columbia Records, and Everest Records.

Eddy was just over six feet tall, weighed 180 pounds, and had blue eyes and white-blond hair. On Jan. 19, 1939, he married Ann Denitz Franklin, the former wife of the producer Sidney Franklin. Eddy and his wife had no children. During World War II, Eddy toured with a United Service Organizations (USO) unit and presented shows in Brazil, Egypt, and Iran.

Eddy made his television debut on "The Alan Young Show" in October 1951. During subsequent years, he appeared on "The Ed Sullivan Show," "What's My Line," "The Big Record," and many other programs. In 1952, he developed a nightclub act, and the following year he opened in Las Vegas with the Canadian singer and comedienne Gale Sherwood. During the next fourteen years, Eddy and Sherwood performed their act forty weeks a year, traveling around the United States and touring Canada, Mexico, and Australia.

Eddy was known as a private person who disliked disorderly fans and sensationalism. However, he possessed a sense of humor and was friendly and courteous. He strove for perfection in his work, but he was not vain or temperamental. Although he loved singing, he knew that he did not possess a voice sufficiently loud or high enough to become a first-rate operatic baritone. He died in Miami Beach, Fla.

[Eddy's scores, his sheet music, and the books of his musical library are at Occidental College in Los Angeles. See Robert Sabin, "Nelson Eddy, Story-Teller in Song," *Musical America*, Jan. 15, 1951; Harry Banta, "Nelson Eddy," *Films in Review*, Feb. 1974; Eleanor Knowles, *The Films of Jeanette MacDonald and Nelson Eddy* (1975); and Philip Castanza, *The Films of Jeanette MacDonald and Nelson Eddy* (1978). An obituary is in the *New York Times*, Mar. 7, 1967.]

ALLAN NELSON

EDISON, CHARLES (Aug. 3, 1890–July 31, 1969), businessman, United States Navy secretary, and governor, was born in Llewellyn Park, N.J., the son of Thomas Alva Edison, the inventor, and Mina Miller. Raised in a mansion, Edison attended several prep schools, graduating from the Hotchkiss School in 1909. He matriculated at the Massachusetts Institute of Technology (MIT) for three years because "Father wanted me to be able to read a blueprint." Having a dominant, famous father was a mixed blessing. Charles once revealed that "my father's fame cast a giant shadow. I hope . . . to cast a small shadow of my own."

On his father's advice Edison left MIT before

graduation for a $15-a-week job to gain administrative training at Boston Edison Company. One year later he joined the Edison Illuminating Company. Edison had earlier worked for his father as a common laborer. The twelve-hour-a-day, six-day-a-week schedule, lack of dispensaries in the plant, and low wages appalled him. Consequently, as a young executive he strove to improve working conditions, exhibiting compassion, managerial talent, and a capacity for hard work.

Handsome, distinguished, and witty, Edison showed his independence by pursuing artistic interests in Greenwich Village, New York City, where he helped establish a literary magazine and a theater. He wrote poetry and befriended such luminaries as Edna St. Vincent Millay.

In 1915 he became chairman of the board of Edison Illuminating. Two years later, after President Woodrow Wilson named Thomas Edison chairman of the wartime Navy Consulting Board, formed to develop new weapons, Charles Edison became his father's governmental assistant. These World War I experiences put Edison in contact with Assistant Secretary of the Navy Franklin Delano Roosevelt. On Mar. 27, 1918, Edison married Carolyn Hawkins. They had no children.

During the depression of 1921, Edison clashed with his father over the latter's desire to cut back Edison Industries' staff. Edison nearly left the company, only to concede later that his father was right. In 1926 Edison officially replaced his father as president and reorganized the company, enabling it to survive the Great Depression.

Following Roosevelt's election as president in 1932, Edison joined the Democratic party, the only Edison to do so. He parried the criticisms of fellow businessmen by responding: "I believe in the new experiments going on. It takes courage to try new things . . . and to stop them if they are not successful." Between 1933 and 1936 he was vice-chairman of the New Jersey State Recovery Board, state director of the National Emergency Council, compliance director for the National Recovery Administration (NRA), and a member of the NRA board. He also served ably as regional director of the Federal Housing Administration for New Jersey.

On Nov. 17, 1936, Roosevelt appointed Edison, an advocate of a strong navy, assistant secretary of the navy. Edison supervised naval expansion and assisted Secretary Claude Swanson, who was in poor health. Edison assumed most of Swanson's work for the next three years. Following Swanson's death, Roosevelt appointed Edison navy secretary on Dec. 30, 1939. Despite delays in construction schedules, he secured a larger fleet, and construction standards improved. He also instituted significant reorganization. Edison prevented the sale of 162 obsolescent destroyers for junk. Fifty of these ships later went to England in the Destroyer–Naval Base Agreement. He was also responsible for the introduction of PT (patrol torpedo) boats into the navy and for the continuation of blimps, which were used as submarine spotters during World War II. By October 1939 he supervised naval neutrality patrols in the Atlantic Ocean. Displeased with Edison's initial efforts, Roosevelt ordered him to employ forty additional destroyers. In June 1940 the president replaced Edison with Frank Knox.

Why Roosevelt removed Edison is unclear. His dilatoriness in implementing the patrol policy might have been a factor. His hearing impairment (his father also suffered from deafness) caused Roosevelt to remark that Edison was "too deaf to be effective." But political considerations were perhaps more important. Roosevelt could broaden support for his interventionist foreign policy by appointing Republicans, such as Knox, to his cabinet. Moreover, by persuading state Democratic boss Frank Hague of Jersey City to favor Edison's nomination for the governorship, Roosevelt could capitalize on the popular Edison's race that fall by carrying New Jersey in the presidential contest.

Edison, who detested the political corruption associated with Hague's machine, cut himself off from Hague during the gubernatorial campaign. After winning the election, Edison nominated to the New Jersey Supreme Court a Republican who had led the opposition to the appointment in 1939 of Hague's son to the Court of Errors and Appeals, the state's highest tribunal. Hague vowed to break Edison as the latter sought to destroy Hague's financial and political power. Roosevelt nevertheless continued to channel patronage through Hague, angering Edison.

Edison never eliminated Hague. Lacking political sagacity, Edison failed to win over New Jersey's political leadership or control the legislature; and he faced an antiquated constitution, which limited his power as governor. It was not until 1947, three years following Edison's term, that the state adopted a new constitution. In 1949 Hague was overthrown as mayor, vindicating Edison.

After his governorship Edison resumed the presidency of Thomas A. Edison, Inc., which merged in 1957 with the McGraw Electric Company. Politically Edison became increasingly antistatist. A rabid anti-Communist and promoter of the China lobby in the 1950's, he opposed the Eisenhower presidency for its liberalism. In 1963 Edison joined the New York Conservative party and became an ardent backer of Barry Goldwater's unsuccessful presidential race in 1964. Afterward, deteriorating health kept him close to his Waldorf Towers apartment in New York City until his death.

[The Edison correspondence is at the Charles Edison Fund, Inc., West Orange, N.J. Edison's oral history is in the Columbia Oral History Project, New York City. For the Edison family see Matthew Josephson, *Edison: A Biography* (1959). The major work on Edison is John D. Venable, *Out of the Shadow* (1978). See Warren E. Stickle, "Edison, 'Hagueism,' and the Split Ticket in 1940," *New Jersey History* (1979); Allison W. Saville, "Charles Edison," in Paopo E. Coletta, ed., *American Secretaries of the Navy*, II (1980); and Edward L. Shapiro, "Charles Edison," in Paul A. Stellhorn and Michael J. Birkner, eds., *The Governors of New Jersey, 1664–1974: Biographical Essays* (1982). See also the obituary, *New York Times*, Aug. 1, 1969.]

JAMES N. GIGLIO

EISENHOWER, DWIGHT DAVID (Oct. 14, 1890–Mar. 28, 1969), army officer and president of the United States, was born in Denison, Tex., the son of David Jacob Eisenhower, a railroad worker, and Ida Elizabeth Stover. A year after the boy's birth the Eisenhowers moved to the former cow town of Abilene, Kans., where the father worked as an engineer in the Belle Springs Creamery, an enterprise of the Mennonite River Brethren. The family lived in a small two-story frame house surrounded by a large garden where in summer the six Eisenhower boys grew produce to sell to townspeople.

Eisenhower's early years are of interest only because of the modest circumstances of his upbringing and the pervasive yet curiously undefinable importance of religion. The elder Eisenhower read the Bible in Greek, but none of the boys was notably religious; Dwight Eisenhower did not join a church until he became president of the United States and for many years rarely attended church services. Yet the memory of their devout parents was by all testimony a formative influence upon the sons. Among other qualities, it enforced a modesty that marked their adult lives when they succeeded in worldly affairs—Arthur as a banker, Edgar as a lawyer, Milton as a university president, and Dwight as a general and president of the United States.

Dwight Eisenhower graduated from Abilene High School in 1909, by which time he had achieved a local reputation as a reader of history. According to a classmate, Edgar Eisenhower was going to become president of the United States and serve two terms and Dwight would be a professor of history at Yale. Dwight made an agreement with Edgar to work and earn enough money to put Edgar through school, whereupon Edgar would work and assist Dwight. For two years Dwight worked at the creamery. Then an alternative plan arose. A friend was applying to the United States Naval Academy and proposed that the two of them apply together. However, Eisenhower was too old to be accepted at Annapolis; hence he applied, and was admitted, to West Point. As he left for the military academy in the summer of 1911, his mother, a pacifist, broke down and wept.

Eisenhower's years at West Point (1911–1915) were formative in the sense that being from "the Point" was always thereafter a part of his outlook. He was an officer of the United States Army, the regular army at that, and even in the White House, certainly in retirement, he was known as "the General." He enjoyed athletics at West Point until a knee injury in his sophomore year took him out of football and threatened to remove him from the academy because of his inability to handle some of the school's physical requirements. His academic standing was fair—he was sixty-first out of 164 in the class of 1915—and he gave little indication of the studiousness he had displayed in high school.

After graduation, Eisenhower was posted to San Antonio and thence to other domestic assignments. During World War I he commanded a tank encampment at Camp Colt near Gettysburg, Pa. He rose rapidly in rank, becoming first lieutenant in July 1916, captain in May 1917, major in June 1918, and lieutenant colonel in October 1918. He received embarkation orders in October 1918, but the war ended before he could board ship. In June 1920 he reverted to captain and in December of that year became a major. He remained a major for sixteen years.

While at San Antonio, Eisenhower met Mamie Doud of Denver, and they were married on July 1, 1916. The first of their two sons died in childhood. A second son, John Sheldon Doud Eisenhower, born in 1922, attended West Point and eventually served as his father's White House assistant.

A crucial point in Eisenhower's career occurred inauspiciously when in 1922 he was posted to the Panama Canal Zone. There he served until 1924 as aide to Brigadier General Fox Conner, who had been chief of operations to General John J. Pershing during World War I. Conner had seen the inner workings of the Allied Expeditionary Forces and was a close student of American and European military history. He turned Eisenhower's mind back toward books, at the outset virtually assigning reading. This experience seems to have sparked Eisenhower's interest in writing. He eventually obtained a reputation in the army of being an "academic," which led to his drafting of papers and speeches for General Douglas MacArthur during the 1930's.

Conner groomed Eisenhower for high command and arranged for him to attend the Command and General Staff School at Fort Leavenworth, Kans., in 1925–1926. Eisenhower came out first in his class. He also attended the Army War College in 1927–1928. After a stint in Paris with the American Battle Monuments Commission, which was headed by General Pershing, Eisenhower served in Washington (1930–1935) in the office of the assistant secretary of war and then of Chief of Staff MacArthur.

When President Franklin D. Roosevelt sent MacArthur to the South Pacific to train an army for the new Commonwealth of the Philippines, which was organized in 1936 as a way station toward independence, MacArthur took Eisenhower along as his chief of staff. Army rumor had it that MacArthur, having crossed the president, was being sent into exile. Eisenhower could hardly have refused the assignment, but he did not like it. He asked for a fixed period of duty, which MacArthur refused. At the outset the assignment seemed to go well, but disagreements arose between the two men. Relations became cool, almost formal. When war broke out in Europe in September 1939, Eisenhower, who considered the Philippines of small strategic importance, asked for permission to return to the United States. MacArthur reluctantly granted the request.

Eisenhower's Philippine years have led some writers to search for critical remarks or irritable encounters, but the truth is plain enough: Eisenhower and MacArthur did not get along. Although critical comments that circulated may well have been apocryphal, MacArthur allegedly described Eisenhower as "the apotheosis of mediocrity," and Eisenhower supposedly claimed that he "studied dramatics under MacArthur."

Upon his return to the United States in early 1940, Eisenhower received a series of assignments, most of them in Washington State. He became a full colonel in March 1941 and then chief of staff for Lieutenant General Walter Krueger, just in time for the Third Army's first large peacetime maneuvers. Eisenhower figured prominently in the maneuvers and was raised to brigadier general.

A few days after the Japanese attack on Pearl Harbor, Eisenhower was called to Washington to assist in mobilization. From that point on, his star was in the ascendant. One important duty after another came to him, each of increasing magnitude. His first Washington duties were in the War Plans Division, soon renamed the Operations Division. Working closely with Chief of Staff General George C. Marshall, Eisenhower helped elaborate the details of the "Europe first" strategy set forth by President Roosevelt and British Prime Minister Winston Churchill.

In early summer 1942 Marshall sent Eisenhower, by then a major general, on a mission to London and soon afterward assigned him as commander of American and Allied forces in England, with the rank of lieutenant general. Roosevelt had promised Soviet premier Joseph Stalin that the Anglo-American forces would create a second front that year to remove some of the pressure from the Russian front. Upon British insistence that the Western Allies were not strong enough to invade France in 1942 and President Roosevelt's insistence upon some sort of action that year, Eisenhower organized the invasion of North Africa in November 1942. Eisenhower hoped to catch the

Axis forces in a pincers movement as General Bernard Montgomery's Eighth (British) Army moved against German forces in western Egypt. The campaign, though difficult, finally brought victory in May 1943, by which time Eisenhower had become a full general. Next came the attack on Sicily, followed by the invasion of Italy. In December 1943, when Roosevelt was returning from the Teheran Conference, he stopped in Tunisia and informed Eisenhower of a new task: "Well, Ike, you are going to command Overlord."

The invasion across the English Channel, Operation Overlord, was Eisenhower's greatest military achievement, one of the most notable in the history of American arms. And yet Eisenhower was roundly criticized for his tactics; General Montgomery, for example, charged after the war that Eisenhower was a mere military manager who had never seen a shot fired in anger until the North African invasion. There was a difference between the science and the art of war, he added. Eisenhower might know the former but not the latter. Observing the European war from his "lofty perch" as supreme commander, he was unqualified for the burden of direct command.

Eisenhower and his supporters argued that the supreme commander's decisions were crucial to Overlord. For example, Eisenhower decided to increase the attack force on D day (June 6, 1944) from three to five divisions. This decision was crucial, for the Americans encountered heavy German resistance on the part of the Normandy coast code-named "Omaha Beach." Eisenhower's second decision, to attack on June 6, had to be made a day before, when weather in the English Channel was terrible. Eisenhower went with the forecast, which turned out to be correct, that the weather would improve. The Allies thereby attained a considerable surprise. Eisenhower's third decision was for a parachute and glider drop on the night of June 5–6, which turned out well. Last, Eisenhower, seeking to prevent German reinforcements from reaching the invasion areas, ordered the bombing of French rail centers, a measure that many advisers feared would kill thousands of French civilians. The tactic was successful.

In the months of fighting that followed the invasion, Eisenhower's forces literally ran out of gas, and the war bogged down into the winter because of the inability of the Allies to open the port of Antwerp. The Germans tenaciously held a fortified island that controlled the approaches to Antwerp via the river Scheldt. Montgomery pleaded for enough supplies to mount an offensive into Germany. Eisenhower refused, probably rightly, and insisted that the Allies move into Germany on a broad front from the North Sea to Switzerland, rather than try to make a single thrust north of the Ruhr toward Berlin, which would invite a flank attack.

During the winter and spring of 1944–1945, Eisenhower came in for additional criticism. During the Battle of the Bulge, which opened on Dec. 16, 1944, a heavy concentration of German troops broke through the Western front. It appeared that Eisenhower had overextended his lines and manned frontline positions with green divisions. At the time and later, many critics described the battle as a near catastrophe, for which Eisenhower was directly responsible. In retrospect, it seems clear that no blame should attach to anyone on the Allied side, for bad weather prevented aerial reconnaissance, and any commander of a huge front cannot cover the entire line. Eisenhower brought the German breakthrough—the "Bulge"—under control in ten days, after heavy, but not catastrophic, casualties.

After the war Eisenhower was criticized for failing to take Berlin during the war's last days. He insisted, at the time and later, that Berlin was not a military target. Furthermore, it had been apportioned to the Russians at the Yalta Conference. Even though the Americans reached the Elbe, fifty miles from Berlin, on April 11, they had only 50,000 men. The Russians were within easy reach of Berlin and possessed a force of 1.25 million. Moreover, German resistance in Berlin was fierce. Eisenhower saw no reason to lose thousands of American lives for a city that lay in the future Soviet zone.

The European war ended May 8, 1945. By that time Eisenhower had received the rank of General of the Army, with five stars, and was a world-renowned figure. He received the plaudits of admirers at a series of triumphal receptions in London, Paris, Moscow, Washington, New York, West Point, Kansas City, and Abilene. He returned to Europe to greet Roosevelt's successor, President Harry S Truman, upon the latter's arrival in Antwerp en route to the Potsdam Conference. According to Eisenhower, the president remarked to him, "General, there is nothing that you may want that I won't try to help you get. That definitely and specifically includes the presidency in 1948."

In November 1945 Eisenhower succeeded General George C. Marshall as chief of staff of the United States Army, an office that he held until February 1948. Eisenhower's task was to preside over the demobilization of the army. The wartime supreme commander in Europe found the duty "frankly distasteful." Demobilization, moreover, was disorderly; troops in the Far East demonstrated in favor of getting home more quickly, and senators telephoned Eisenhower almost daily with complaints from constituents eager to be reunited with their loved ones. During this time the army declined from its V-E Day peak of 8.3 million (eighty-nine divisions) to a little over 1 million (twelve divisions).

Eisenhower retired on May 2, 1948, to take up the presidency of Columbia University, a post he held until 1952. While at Columbia, he helped organize the American Assembly, a series of conferences on public issues, and dealt effectively with Columbia's alumni, but he made little impression upon the academic work of the university.

During the Columbia years the army's problems were constantly with Eisenhower. In 1948, after President Truman's personal chief of staff, Fleet Admiral William D. Leahy, became ill, Eisenhower began to spend one or two days a week, and sometimes more, in Washington as the informal chairman of the Joint Chiefs of Staff. This work plunged him into the rivalries of the three services, which quarreled over distribution of appropriations, quite small in those years.

With the onset of the Korean War in 1950, Truman, who feared that Soviet forces would attack in Europe while the United States was involved in Asia, arranged Eisenhower's appointment as supreme commander of the armed forces of the North Atlantic Treaty Organization (NATO). Eisenhower left for Paris on Jan. 1, 1951, and began to organize NATO headquarters. In February 1952 he presided over the Lisbon meeting of NATO members, which looked forward to a NATO force of 100 divisions, half of them ready for immediate service and half subject to mobilization. (NATO forces never reached more than half of that figure.)

The choice of Eisenhower as the Republican candidate for the presidency in 1952 was almost foreordained; the GOP needed a candidate who could win, and Eisenhower was available. Actually, there had been talk of his candidacy by members of both parties in 1948. His politics were uncertain, for while in the army he had never voted. But not long before the 1952 campaign he allowed a supporter to reveal that he had voted Republican in the 1950 New York elections. After suitable preliminaries—delegations of prominent party members visited NATO headquarters—Eisenhower allowed his name to go forward in 1952. He was nominated on the first ballot, following a brief struggle at the Republican National Convention that summer with the supporters of Senator Robert A. Taft of Ohio. In November he easily defeated the Democratic candidate, Governor Adlai E. Stevenson of Illinois.

The "mandate for victory," as Eisenhower later entitled the first volume of his memoirs, arose out of the nation's increasing conservatism. But Eisenhower was no reactionary. After appointing a cabinet composed, as a wag described it, of "eight millionaires and a plumber" (Secretary of Labor Martin P. Durkin had headed a plumbers' union), the new president spoke carefully of "dynamic conservatism." He distanced himself from Republican conservatives, who gathered around former President Herbert Hoover, and from the Hoover record, which many Americans still associated with the Great Depression. Eisenhower also moved quietly but effectively against conservative leaders in the Senate and House, whom he sought to have replaced with moderates. The worst of the conservatives, from his point of view, was the red-baiting Senator Joseph R. McCarthy of Wisconsin. At the time, critics believed that Eisenhower did little or nothing to stop McCarthy, while supporters argued that it was impossible to attack McCarthy openly and that Eisenhower's subtle tactics of marshaling support against McCarthy eventually succeeded. The president's White House diary and the diary by his press secretary and senatorial hatchetman, James C. Hagerty, reveal that Eisenhower stage-managed the senator's downfall after McCarthy sought to discredit the United States Army in televised hearings.

In fiscal policy Eisenhower was staunchly conservative. He feared that government deficits would cause inflation. In the fiscal years 1956 and 1957 his administration produced surpluses, the first since before the New Deal. The president drastically reduced the military budget after the end of the Korean War in 1953, and when the army's chief of staff, General Matthew B. Ridgway, objected, Eisenhower refused to give Ridgway the customary second two-year term in the office. "Now, everything points to the fact that Russia is not seeking a general war and will not for a long, long time, if ever," Eisenhower told Hagerty. "Everything is shifting to economic warfare, to propaganda, and to a sort of peaceful infiltration. Now, we must be fully aware of these threats, but we must not sap our own strength by trying to build too much at the present time." In the late 1950's, deficits appeared, caused by farm surpluses that the government was forced to purchase because of farm-price supports dating from the Roosevelt administration. In fiscal 1959, federal expenditures for agriculture totaled $7.1 billion, up from $2.9 billion in 1953; the total deficit that year was $12.5 billion. (Franklin D. Roosevelt, sometimes called a spendthrift, never spent more than $9 billion in a peacetime budget.) But whatever the difficulties, the Eisenhower budgets seemed to work: during his presidency the rate of inflation was very low, and perhaps for that reason, the country in those years commenced an economic "takeoff," to use the economist Walt W. Rostow's term.

In accord with his own beliefs and those of his party, Eisenhower sought to stop the government from competing with private business. Here his failure was epitomized by the case of the Dixon-Yates syndicate, a group of private power interests that had contracted to build a coal-burning steam-generating plant to furnish power to the city of Memphis, Tenn. The plant originally was to have been built by the Tennessee Valley Authority, which had run out of sites for hydroelectric plants. The much-heralded private project was derailed when an officer of the bank that was financing Dixon-Yates was found to be in a conflict of interest, and Memphis decided to construct the plant itself.

Eisenhower's stance on the rights of black Americans was in theory correct and in practice unenthusiastic. Since he did not believe that civil rights could be legislated, he disagreed with the landmark decision of the Supreme Court in *Brown* v. *Board of Education of Topeka* (1954), announced by a chief justice whom he had appointed, Earl Warren. But when Orval E. Faubus, the governor of Arkansas, reneged on his promise to the president to allow court-ordered desegregation of Little Rock's Central High School, Eisenhower brought in regular-army troops and nationalized the Arkansas National Guard to put down what he regarded as a challenge to federal authority.

Eisenhower may have felt more at ease in the area of foreign policy, and, in any event, the decade of the 1950's offered several challenges. Foreign policy and national security, he told one congressman, occupied 80 percent of his attention. At the time, his actions, which were subjected to considerable criticism, often centered on the hard-line pronouncements of Secretary of State John Foster Dulles, who appeared to dominate administration foreign policy until shortly before Dulles' resignation and death in May 1959. Eisenhower's personal papers reveal, however, that the president controlled his prominent secretary of state and that in no important arena did Dulles act without consulting Eisenhower.

Public concern that Eisenhower might emulate Truman and take the country into another undeclared war or become entrapped in some foreign intrigue prompted Senate conservatives, led by John W. Bricker of Ohio, to challenge the president's constitutional authority. For several years Bricker had been proposing a constitutional amendment to limit presidential treaty-making. One clause in this so-called Bricker Amendment held that a treaty could "become effective as internal law . . . only through legislation which would be valid in the absence of a treaty." Eisenhower protested that this would make it impossible for the executive to conduct foreign affairs. For example, if he concluded an agreement with the Soviet Union on control of nuclear weapons, individual states within the United States could stop inspections under a plan of control. In 1954 the proposal failed, by a single vote, to obtain the two-thirds majority required for passage.

Critics also maintained that Eisenhower's policy turned all large international disputes into nuclear threats. Part of the contention rested upon the president's demand that the army reduce its size after the Korean War. When General Matthew Ridgway objected, Eisenhower replaced him with General Maxwell Taylor, who likewise resisted. Ridgway, Taylor, and their many supporters in and out of

Eisenhower

the army and in both political parties accused the president of resting the country's defense on nuclear arms. Eisenhower had indeed achieved a cease-fire in Korea by threatening the People's Republic of China in 1953 with nuclear war. When the French fortress of Dien Bien Phu in Vietnam was besieged by Communist forces the next year, the Eisenhower administration again considered the use of nuclear weapons. However, Eisenhower required that any American action be predicated upon consent of the British, who opposed American involvement in the Southeast Asian conflict. The next year, the question of the use of nuclear weapons arose again, this time over the administration's decision to support the Chinese Nationalists in their claim to two islands, Quemoy and Matsu, and their islets, which controlled entrance to two mainland ports. When the Chinese Communists threatened the islands, Eisenhower weighed a nuclear defense, perhaps by bombing mainland China. He considered using nuclear weapons again when mainland forces again bombarded the islands in 1958. Fortunately, no Communist invasion materialized.

Unknown to his critics at the time, Eisenhower took a firm position within his administration against the actual use of nuclear weapons. "You know," he told Hagerty, "if you're in the military and you know about these terrible destructive weapons, it tends to make you more pacifistic than you normally have been." In 1954 the president of South Korea, Syngman Rhee, visited Washington and, in a private White House meeting, proposed a defensive war ("some positive action at the front," he described it) against the Communist regime in North Korea. Eisenhower, aghast, told Rhee that "if war comes, it will be horrible. Atomic war will destroy civilization. It will destroy our cities. There will be millions of people dead. War today is unthinkable with the weapons which we have at our command. If the Kremlin and Washington ever lock up in a war, the results are too horrible to contemplate. I can't even imagine them."

Some months later the chief of naval operations, Admiral Robert B. Carney, gave an off-the-record interview to newspapermen that hinted at nuclear war, and the president treated him the same way he had Ridgway, by refusing to reappoint him to a second term as chief of naval operations. Meanwhile, Eisenhower privately lectured his service chiefs. "We are not looking for war, and I think the stories like the ones they get from Carney, when published, are a great disservice to the United States," he explained to Hagerty. He also detected insubordination: "By God, this has got to stop. These fellows like Carney and Ridgway don't yet realize that their services have been integrated and that they have, in addition to myself, a boss in Admiral Radford, who is chairman of the Joint Chiefs of Staff."

In 1955, Eisenhower met the new post-Stalin leadership in Geneva at the first summit conference since the Potsdam Conference ten years earlier. He quickly sensed that Party Secretary Nikita Khrushchev, although nominally second to Premier Nikolai Bulganin, was the real leader of the Soviet Union. Eisenhower advanced a proposal for "open skies," which would have made airspace free to all. The Soviets rejected the proposal as a ploy to open Soviet airspace, but the president firmly believed that it would have advanced international relations.

The years after Geneva unfortunately did not fulfill the promise of world peace, which had come to be known as "the spirit of Geneva." Soviet-American relations were racked by crisis after crisis: Suez and Lebanon, Berlin, and the U-2 incident. The Middle East was a fertile field for international intervention. When President Gamal Abdel Nasser of Egypt nationalized the Suez Canal after failing to obtain an American loan to build a higher dam on the Nile River at Aswan, Britain and France connived with Israel and, without informing the United States, attacked Egypt. This melee, which came just before the presidential election of November 1956, infuriated Eisenhower. Acting with steely resolution and in cooperation with the Soviet Union, he forced a cease-fire. The Suez affair coincided with uprisings against Soviet domination in Poland and Hungary, and thus obscured the world's perception of the Soviets' brutal suppression of the revolt in Hungary. The next year, the Eisenhower Doctrine promised financial and military support to Middle Eastern countries threatened by Communism. Soviet and Egyptian intrigue produced the Lebanon crisis of 1958, in which the United States landed the equivalent of a division of troops to prevent an Egyptian takeover of Lebanon. Observers speculated that American ships off Beirut might be carrying nuclear bombs, but the president carefully avoided comment.

Eisenhower

That the demands of the presidency had strained Eisenhower's health became apparent when, on Sept. 24, 1955, he suffered a massive heart attack that required many weeks of recuperation. In June 1956 he underwent surgery for ileitis, a digestive disorder, and in late November 1957 he was afflicted by a mild stroke. Meanwhile, Eisenhower had been reelected for a second term. After the heart attack he had been uncertain whether he could run, but recovery persuaded him to be a candidate. The ileitis attack did not change his mind. His opponent again was Adlai Stevenson, and again Eisenhower won easily.

In 1957, with the Soviet lofting of *Sputnik*, the first artificial earth satellite, the Russians directly challenged America's reputation for scientific prowess. After the miniaturization of the H-bomb in 1954, the American military had abandoned large-thrust missile programs, but the Soviets, who had not made a useful H-bomb before 1955, were unable to miniaturize their H-bomb warheads and hence required large-thrust missiles. By failing to ask permission of the United States and other countries to send *Sputnik* across their skies, the Soviets unwittingly provided the United States with a precedent to launch the first spy satellite in 1960, but Eisenhower could do little to distract people from what seemed a marvel of Soviet science.

Perhaps emboldened by *Sputnik*, Khrushchev (who had become premier in 1957) announced a showdown over Berlin in November 1958: six months thereafter, he said, he would turn the Soviet sector over to East Germany, which would force Western recognition of that nation. But the deadline came and went quietly, and when Khrushchev sought in the autumn of 1959 to visit the United States, Eisenhower reluctantly invited him.

In the spring of 1960 Eisenhower made what appeared to be a gross miscalculation when he allowed a U-2 photoreconnaissance plane to overfly the Soviet Union. On May 1 the plane was shot down and its pilot, Francis Gary Powers, was captured. Allen W. Dulles, the head of the Central Intelligence Agency (CIA), had categorically assured the president that no U-2 pilot would ever be taken alive. The Soviets played the affair carefully, trapped the American government into concocting a cover story, and then triumphantly produced Powers. Eisenhower took personal responsibility, but at the Paris Summit Conference shortly afterward he refused to apologize. Khrushchev abruptly returned to Moscow.

Out of his sometimes rueful experiences in foreign policy, President Eisenhower came to fear a powerful lobby of veritable merchants of defense, who aided and abetted the arms race with the Soviet Union. In his farewell address of January 17, 1961, he adopted the speechwriter Malcolm Moos's phrase about the dangers of a "military-industrial complex." Eisenhower believed it was the most important challenge he could make to the American people: "This conjunction of an immense military establishment and a large arms industry is new in the American experience. . . . We must not fail to comprehend its grave implications. . . . In the councils of government we must guard against the acquisition of unwarranted influence, whether sought or unsought, by the military-industrial complex. The potential for the disastrous rise of misplaced power exists and will persist. We must never let the weight of this combination endanger our liberties or democratic processes. We should take nothing for granted."

Eisenhower operated differently from any earlier president. He installed a staff system based on his military experience. When Harry S Truman discovered that Eisenhower would have not merely a staff but a chief of staff as well, Truman was both appalled and amused. But what might have been a rigid allotment of duties and responsibilities became, under Eisenhower, a reasonable arrangement—and it did not lead to a serious dilution of the president's authority. He kept close control over his chief of staff, Sherman Adams, a former governor of New Hampshire. Contrary to appearances, Adams did not control access to the chief executive, and he had nothing to do with foreign affairs. The presence of such military aides as Colonel Andrew Goodpaster and the president's son, John, did not betoken military control. Like most presidents, Eisenhower liked to have about him individuals whom he knew and could work with easily.

Eisenhower unintentionally inaugurated what became known as the imperial presidency. This was a peculiar result considering that, despite his military background, the president was in no way imperial. Though known to the public and army intimates as "Ike," he was not really an easy person to understand. Nonetheless, he had long exercised a charming presence in public, and he quickly discovered that he could exploit his popular appeal nationally and internationally through the medium of television and the convenience of jet airplanes. He had first used television in the 1952 presidential campaign, both in "spot" commercials and in speeches. The convention of 1952 had been televised, with great success because of the Taft-Eisenhower rivalry. Press Secretary Hagerty easily persuaded the president in 1954 to allow the televising of press conferences, a hugely successful enterprise that brought the president's convincing personality into living rooms across the country. For a while Eisenhower permitted Secretary Dulles to do most of the administration's traveling, but when the secretary became ill, and especially after his death in mid-1959, the president frequently took to the road. In the last two years of his presidency, Eisenhower went on six international goodwill trips, logging 320,000 miles and visiting twenty-seven countries. These trips endowed the presidency with an aura of grandeur that later presidents capitalized on.

When his second term ended, Eisenhower retired to a pleasant house near the Gettysburg battlefield in Pennsylvania, surrounded by fields and a cattle barn. The general established an office on the campus of Gettysburg College, where, with a team of writers, he put together his memoirs. Eisenhower sold the rights for a lump sum of $635,000, and obtained a ruling from Internal Revenue authorities that because he was not a professional author the sale could not be treated as a capital gain and subjected to a 25 percent tax. Because of the resulting outcry, Congress in 1950 passed the so-called Eisenhower amendment, which required any writer, whether professional or amateur, to pay capital gains taxes.

An avid golfer, Eisenhower often appeared on the links of the National Golf Course near Augusta, Ga. As the years passed, and the rigors of Gettysburg winters became difficult, he frequented the Eldorado Country Club near Palm Springs, Calif., where early in 1968 he realized the dream of all golfers: he shot a hole in one. He also took part in the raising of funds to establish a museum in Abilene, on what was once the family garden plot. Eventually the family house was refurbished for visitors, and his military and presidential papers filled an adjoining library, also built with private funds. In the mid-1960's Eisenhower's health deteriorated. He died at the Walter Reed Hospital in Washington, D.C., and was buried on the grounds of the Eisenhower Library and Museum in Abilene.

Eisenhower's accomplishments are not easy to assess. Because he was at the time the oldest man to be president and was succeeded by the extraordinarily charismatic John F. Kennedy, the youngest elected president, his reputation passed under a historical cloud soon after he left office. A typical early appraisal was that of the journalist Marquis Childs, who portrayed Eisenhower as a "captive hero." The Republican party needed Eisenhower, Childs wrote, and apotheosized him, but he turned out to be more like General Ulysses S. Grant than General George Washington. Childs portrayed Eisenhower as a political naïf, and a lazy one at that. This appraisal was apparently buttressed by the president's much-photographed fascination with golf, his well-known interest in bridge and western novels, and his occasionally muddled syntax during televised press conferences.

The assessment of Eisenhower began to change as more information became available. Far from being a captive hero, he seemed the man who converted the Republican party from a befuddled collection of "outs" dominated by conservatives of the Hoover era into a party that was close to the center of American opinion. Eisenhower had transformed the GOP, his admirers claimed, by flattering the conservatives, who basked in his company, and by giving actual power to middle-of-the-roaders. Eisenhower was decidedly not a lazy, unintelligent man. He was at his White House desk early each morning and worked hard and efficiently, dictating detailed letters, correcting the prose of his speechwriters, and meeting with politicos and prominent figures from the business world who could assist the administration. In the evenings he frequently gave "stag dinners" in the White House, which were wondrously effective among the predominantly male leaders of his time. He played both golf and bridge well, for he worked hard at anything he did.

Eisenhower genuinely liked most people, but his geniality masked an inner intensity and a mind that could calculate matters coldly and efficiently. On rare occasions the intensity gave way to anger. Eisenhower possessed little artistic feeling, although he took up painting while chief of staff and produced attractive canvases of a representational outdoor type. Music did not interest him, nor did literature. If he ever read any fiction other than western potboilers, the names of the books are not known. "The folks' tastes," his son once remarked, "are strictly cornball." He did not enjoy the company of scholars and preferred to socialize with successful businessmen. Critics said this showed that he worshiped money and success. The former is arguable, but it is quite possible that he was indeed drawn to those whose success had come through the same application of effort that he had made in the military and politics. It might therefore be said of him that he was not "complete" in the eighteenth-century sense, but he was an extraordinary technician in the two areas in which he chose to excel.

[Eisenhower's papers are at the Dwight D. Eisenhower Library in Abilene, Kans., which also contains papers of leading administration figures, oral histories, and audiovisual materials. For published papers, public and personal, see *Public Papers of the Presidents of the United States: Dwight D. Eisenhower, 1953–61*, 8 vols. (1960–1961); Robert L. Branyan and Lawrence H. Larsen, eds., *The Eisenhower Administration, 1953–1961: A Documentary History*, 2 vols. (1971); especially Alfred D. Chandler, Jr., and Louis Galambos, eds., *The Papers of Dwight David Eisenhower*, 11 vols. to date (1970–), covering the years to 1952; Joseph P. Hobbs, ed., *Dear General: Eisenhower's Wartime Letters to Marshall* (1971); John S. D. Eisenhower, ed., *Letters to Mamie* (1978); Robert H. Ferrell, ed., *The Eisenhower Diaries* (1981) and *The Diary of James C. Hagerty* (1983); and Robert Griffith, ed. *Ike's Letters to a Friend: 1941–1958* (1984).

Eisenhower wrote of his World War II experiences in *Crusade in Europe* (1948); of the presidency in *Mandate for Change, 1953–1956* (1963) and *Waging Peace, 1956–1961* (1965); and of early life in Abilene and the army in *At Ease: Stories I Tell to Friends* (1967).

Memoirs touching his career include Harry C. Butcher, *My Three Years with Eisenhower* (1946); Omar N. Bradley, *A Soldier's Story* (1951) and *A General's Life: An Autobiography* (1983); A. Merriman Smith, *Meet Mr. Eisenhower* (1955) and *A President's Odyssey* (1961); Matthew B. Ridgway, *Soldier* (1956); Walter Bedell Smith, *Eisenhower's Six Great Decisions* (1956); James M. Gavin, *War and Peace in the Space Age* (1958); Maxwell D. Taylor, *The Uncertain Trumpet* (1960) and *Swords and Ploughshares* (1972). See also George E. Allen, *Presidents Who Have Known Me* (1960); Sherman Adams, *Firsthand Report* (1961); Ezra Taft Benson, *Cross Fire* (1962); Richard M. Nixon, *Six Crises* (1962); Lewis L. Strauss, *Men and Decisions* (1962); Milton S. Eisenhower, *The Wine Is Bitter* (1963) and *The President Is Calling* (1974); E. Frederic Morrow, *Black Man in the White House* (1963); Robert Cutler, *No Time for Rest* (1965); Emmet John Hughes, *The Ordeal of Power* (1963); Arthur Larson, *The President Nobody Knew* (1968); John S. D. Eisenhower, *Strictly Personal* (1974); George B. Kistiakowsky, *A Scientist at the White House* (1976); J. Lawton Collins, *Lightning Joe: An Autobiography* (1979); Virgil Pinkley, with James F. Scheer, *Eisenhower Declassified* (1979); Ellis D. Slater, *The Ike I Knew* (1980); William B. Ewald, Jr., *Eisenhower the President* (1981) and *Who Killed Joe McCarthy?* (1984).]

ROBERT H. FERRELL

EISLER, GERHART (Feb. 20, 1897–Mar. 21, 1968), Soviet espionage agent and East German Communist party official, was born in Leipzig, Germany, the son of Rudolf Eisler, a professor of philosophy at the University of Leipzig, and Marie Edith Fischer. The family moved to Vienna shortly after Eisler's birth. Eisler attended the University of Vienna but interrupted his studies to enlist in the Austrian army during World War I. After his discharge from the army in 1918, he joined the Austrian Communist party. In 1920 Eisler, at the urging of his sister Elfriede (who had adopted the name Ruth Fischer), transferred his membership to the Communist party in Berlin, where he worked as an organizer and propagandist for the party during the 1920's. Sometime during the early 1920's, Eisler married Hede Tune (later known as Hede Massing); they had no children and separated in 1923. In 1928 Eisler became involved in an attempt to depose the German party leader, Ernst Thaelmann. Joseph Stalin thwarted the move, and Eisler fell into disgrace within the party.

In the late 1920's Eisler was called to Moscow, where he was allowed to attend an espionage training school. He then was dispatched to China in 1930 or 1931 to serve as liaison between the Comintern and the Chinese Communist party. After the arrest of two Comintern agents, Eisler decided to leave China. His sister later claimed that his mission was to purge rebellious Chinese Communists, a task that, she maintained, he performed cruelly and effectively. He returned to Europe and married Ella Tune, the sister of his first wife, on Nov. 2, 1931, in Vienna; they had one child. The marriage did not last.

In 1933 Eisler, traveling under forged passports, entered the United States. He reputedly became the top Comintern agent in America. He used various aliases, including "Edwards" and "Hans Burger" and remained in the United States until 1936. In that year Eisler went to Spain, where he served with the Spanish Loyalists as a "political commissar" to a battalion of antifascist Germans fighting against Francisco Franco. Eisler, who was in France at the outbreak of World War II, was detained in an internment camp by the Vichy government as a suspicious character of German origins. During this period he is reputed to have led Comintern-supported missions to aid antifascist underground movements in Czechoslovakia, Austria, and Switzerland.

In 1941 a relief organization arranged Eisler's return to the United States via Mexico. He was stopped at Ellis Island and told that Communists could not be granted transit visas. Eisler explained later that he lied about his past and, after a ten-week investigation, won permission to stay in the United States on a visitor's visa. He married Bruenhilde Rothstein during the early 1940's. Although the couple lived quietly in Queens, N.Y., Eisler resumed his former position as liaison between the Comintern and the United States Communist party. Eisler's main missions were to infiltrate labor unions and liberal organizations and to form front organizations for the party. On an Oct. 13, 1946, radio broadcast from Detroit, Louis Budenz, the former managing editor of the *Daily Worker*, who had turned anti-Communist, alluded to Eisler as one of the Soviet Union's top agents in America. Budenz maintained that "this man never shows his face. Communist leaders never see him, but they follow his orders or suggestions implicitly." After the broadcast Eisler and his wife attempted to leave the country, but they were stopped by immigration officials and their exit permits were canceled.

Eisler was called before the House Un-American Activities Committee (HUAC) on Feb. 6, 1947. During a stormy session he refused to be sworn before reading a prepared statement. After a fifteen-minute shouting match with the committee chairman, J. Parnell Thomas, Eisler was cited for contempt. He was sentenced to one year in jail and received an additional one to three years for having falsified his record in seeking to leave the United States. During the same HUAC session, his sister testified against him, calling him "a most dangerous terrorist, both to the people of America and to the people of Germany." She also claimed that during the Soviet purges of the 1930's Eisler was responsible for the deaths of Hugo Eberlein, a German Communist, and Nikolai Bukharin, the great Soviet theorist. In September 1947 Eisler's brother, Hanns, a composer, was brought before HUAC as a suspected member of the Communist party.

While appeals to both of his convictions were pending, Eisler jumped a $23,500 bail bond by stowing away on the Polish liner *Batory* when it sailed from New York for England on May 7, 1949. When the *Batory* landed in Southampton, Eisler was arrested, but a London court declined to extradite him to the United States. He proceeded to East Germany, where he became a professor at the University of Leipzig.

Eisler became a leading Communist propagandist and a member of East Germany's Central Committee; he also served as chairman of the state radio and television committee. A small, bespectacled man who looked like an underpaid bookkeeper, Eisler was a classic espionage agent who hid in the shadows and frequently altered his identity while guiding revolutions in four countries. Eisler died in Yerevan, in the Armenian Soviet Socialist Republic, while attending to a contract between the East German and Soviet radio networks.

[Sources on Eisler's career are few, and many of them are vague and contradictory. The best available works are Louis Budenz, *Men Without Faces* (1948); Robert Stripling, *The Red Plot Against America* (1949); Hede Massing, *This Deception* (1951); F. W. Deakin and G. R. Storry, *The Case of Richard Sorge* (1966); Earl Latham, *The Communist Controversy in Washington* (1966); Walter Goodman, *The Committee* (1968); and Eric Bentley, ed., *Thirty Years of Treason* (1971). See also U.S. House, Committee on Un-American Activities, *Hearings on Gerhart Eisler*, 80th Cong., 1st sess., 1947; *Annual Report for the Year 1949*, Mar. 15, 1950; and U.S. Senate, Committee on the Judiciary, Subcommittee on Immigration and Naturalization, *Hearings on Communist Activities Among Aliens and National Groups*, 81st Cong., 1st sess., 1949. An obituary is in the *New York Times*, Mar. 22, 1968.]

JOHN M. CARROLL

ELMAN, HARRY ("ZIGGY") (May 26, 1914–June 26, 1968), trumpeter, composer, and bandleader, was born Harry Aaron Finkelman, in Philadelphia, Pa., the son of Alek Finkelman, owner of a delicatessen and a construction business, and Minnie (maiden name unknown). Gifted with perfect pitch, at about the age of three Finkelman began to emulate his brothers and show an interest in the piano. In 1918 his family moved to Atlantic City, N.J. In his teens Finkelman was proficient on several brass and woodwind instruments and played in the Atlantic City high school band, before leaving school in 1928 to perform in nightclubs. He first publicly played the trumpet in Sol ("Sonny") Kendis' group.

Finkelman's nickname may have been given to him by show girls in Atlantic City. Purportedly he told them that he would someday be a big man in show business. They replied that he might become another Florenz Ziegfeld and began to refer to him as "Ziggy." At the age of sixteen, Elman began to work on the Steel Pier in Atlantic City as a trombonist with the Alex Bartha band. He also performed an act called the One-Man Show.

When Benny Goodman was appearing with his orchestra on the Steel Pier in 1936, he needed a replacement trumpet player, and Elman came to his attention. Goodman borrowed him from Bartha and at the close of the engagement invited Elman to join his band on a long-term basis. Shortly thereafter Finkelman legally changed his last name to Elman. He married Blanche Georgette Hammerer on Oct. 18, 1937; they were divorced in 1940.

During his time with Goodman, Elman was a member of the trumpet section, which also included Harry James and Chris Griffin. Each could play whatever part the arrangement or director called for, and most listeners could not tell which one had the lead. This trio was part of the band that appeared in a famous Carnegie Hall jazz concert on Jan. 16, 1938. According to George Simon's review of the event, Elman's performance in "Swingtime in the Rockies" sparked the group to a memorable climax in "Sing, Sing, Sing," a swing classic. When Harry James left to form his own band, Elman became the principal trumpet soloist.

Elman had grown up in an ethnic household where only Yiddish was spoken. This background led him to incorporate the Jewish *fralich* (wedding dance) style of music into his work. In the late 1930's Elman made a series of recordings under the name "Ziggy Elman and His Orchestra"; one of these arrangements was entitled "Fralich in Swing." When words were added by Johnny Mercer, it was renamed "And the Angels Sing." This number, with a trumpet solo featuring Elman, became a hit for the Goodman band in 1939.

Goodman held Elman in high esteem and relied on him to rehearse the group before recording sessions. Late in 1939, when Goodman began to suffer from back problems, Elman led the band. The following year, when Goodman took time for surgery, Elman remained on salary and returned to New York City, where he played for a month with Joe Venuti's group. Tiring of the relative inactivity, Elman joined Tommy Dorsey in August 1940. With the Dorsey band Elman occasionally doubled on trombone while Dorsey played trumpet. One of his outstanding performances with this band in 1942 was his trumpet part in "Well, Git It."

Elman left Dorsey in 1943 for military service and spent most of the next three years in California. He was in the Army Air Force Band at Long Beach and achieved the rank of staff sargeant. Also in 1943 he married Ruby Morie; they had one child. Following his military discharge early in 1946, Elman played baritone saxophone with the Dorsey band prior to rejoining the band's trumpet section. In January 1947 he formed his own short-lived band and later appeared in the movie *The Fabulous Dorseys.* After settling on the West Coast, in 1948 Elman again formed a band and began to specialize in studio work, although his band appeared at the Hollywood Palladium and on midwestern tours in the early 1950's. He also played with Van Alexander's orchestra and free-lanced for movies and television.

In 1953 Elman rejoined Goodman for a tour and again fronted the band after Goodman became ill. In 1956, Elman appeared in the movie *The Benny Goodman Story* but was sick and could not play. The song "And the Angels Sing" was actually played by Manny Klein. For approximately the last ten years of his life Elman considered himself semiretired but continued some musical activities and ran his own music store, though illness curtailed his playing. In the early 1960's he was temporarily hospitalized for a nervous breakdown, but for several months in 1962–1963 he toured with the Tommy Dorsey orchestra under the direction of Sam Donahue. Elman died in Los Angeles.

His performing style and tone together with his use of the *fralich* element gave Elman a strong musical identity. He earned honors on his instrument with *Down Beat* poll victories in 1940–1941, 1943–1945, and 1947, as well as in the *Metronome* magazine poll for 1941–1942. Elman has been characterized as a florid, brash soloist; a big-toned, blasting trumpeter; a colorful, enthusiastic, cigar-smoking extrovert; and a musical genius who could play any instrument. Among the tunes associated with Elman, "Bublitchki" was an illustration of his use of the *fralich* (adapted to swing performances).

[Bio-discographical information is in D. Russell Connor and Warren W. Hicks, *BG on the Record* (1969). See George T. Simon, *Simon Says* (1971) and *The Big Bands* (1981); David Meeker, *Jazz in the Movies* (1977); Brian Rust, *Jazz Records: 1897–1942* (1978); Leo Walker, *The Big Band Almanac* (1978); and Orrin Keepnews and Bill Grauer, Jr., *A Pictorial History of Jazz* (1981). See also the obituary notices, *New York Times*, June 27, 1968; and *Newsweek*, July 8, 1968.]

BARRETT G. POTTER

ELMAN, MISCHA (Jan. 20, 1891–Apr. 5, 1967), violinist, was born in Talnoye in the Ukraine, the son of Saul Elman, a teacher of Hebrew and an amateur violinist, and Yetta Fingerhood. In 1893 his family moved to Shpola. Upon noting Elman's musical precocity, his father gave the five-year-old boy a miniature violin. After several months of paternal instruction, Countess Urusova provided the money for private violin lessons. In 1897, Elman received a scholarship to the Imperial Academy of Music in Odessa, where he studied for five years under Albert Geiger and, principally, Alexander Fidelmann.

In 1901 the eminent violinist and pedagogue Leopold Auer heard Elman play in Odessa and was so complimentary that the following year Elman's father took his son to Elisavetgrad to audition for Auer. Impressed anew, the enthusiastic Auer immediately arranged for Elman's admittance in January 1903 to the St. Petersburg Conservatory of Music as a scholarship student.

After sixteen months of concentrated study, Elman had made such remarkable progress that Auer pronounced him ready for a concert career. Following a series of recitals for the Russian aristocracy, Elman journeyed to Berlin, where Auer had arranged for a concert on Oct. 14, 1904, in which his young protégé would perform for a specially invited audience of influential musical figures. On the eve of the concert Elman, whose humble origins had acquainted him only with oil lamps, failed to turn off his hotel room gas jet completely and was nearly asphyxiated. Unconscious when discovered by his father the next morning, he revived barely an hour before the noon concert. Although ill, Elman insisted upon playing, and his masterful performances of Tchaikovsky's Violin Concerto and Bach's Chaconne so enraptured the audience that he was promptly engaged for a series of concerts in several German cities during the winter of 1904–1905.

In the spring of 1905, Elman visited England, where on March 21 he performed in the first of three orchestral concerts with the London Symphony Orchestra. Following a command performance for King Edward VII shortly thereafter, Elman's British success was assured. For the next three years, Elman resided in London while concertizing in England, France, central Europe, and Scandinavia.

In the winter of 1908–1909, Elman was taken to the United States by Oscar Hammerstein, for whom he performed a series of programs in the Manhattan Opera House. Elman's American debut took place on Dec. 10, 1908, when he played Tchaikovsky's Violin Concerto with the Russian Symphony Orchestra at Carnegie Hall. Acclaimed by critics and concertgoers, Elman went on to complete ninety-two American concerts by June 1909.

During the next five years, Elman divided his time between New York City and London while performing extensively throughout America and Europe. With the outbreak of World War I he settled in the United States, where, in addition to regular concert work, he gave many benefit recitals for various humanitarian causes.

After the war, Elman embarked upon a twenty-year period of artistic achievement that carried him to the summit of his career. Between 1920 and 1940 he concertized in Europe almost annually, one tour alone encompassing sixteen months. Elman spent the greater part of 1921 performing in China, Japan, and other Far Eastern countries, the first artist of major stature to do so. During the 1930's he also played in Mexico, Central and South America, the Near East, and South Africa. Elman became a naturalized United States citizen on

May 17, 1923. He married Helen Frances Katten on May 6, 1925; they had two children.

Elman repeatedly toured America as a recitalist or as the featured soloist on orchestral programs. He also played first violin in the Elman String Quartet during its brief (1924–1927) existence. He made the bulk of his more than 200 recordings during the interwar period. Eventually, more than 2 million of his records were sold.

World War II curtailed Elman's overseas travel but brought no diminution of his American activities. Besides his normal concert schedule, he toured the United States on behalf of refugees, performed for American servicemen, and played a series of Lewisohn Stadium summer concerts with the New York Philharmonic.

In the spring of 1946, Elman returned to Europe for a series of British recitals, and for the next twenty years he included periodic European tours on his concert agenda. He made the five-thousandth appearance of his sixty-two-year concert career on June 29, 1966.

Elman contributed a number of articles to music periodicals, mostly on violin technique or the virtues of diligent practice and self-discipline. A short man, compactly built and prematurely bald, Elman strode onstage with confidence and determination. He seemed almost pugnacious when he lifted his bow, but when he began playing his "Recamier" Stradivarius, listeners heard the world-renowned Elman tone, the rich and sensuous product of innate musical sensivity, proper vibrato, left-hand dexterity, and a strong bowing arm. He could move an audience to tears with his performances of nineteenth-century masterpieces. Although he had a repertory of 600 compositions, the staples were the Beethoven, Mendelssohn, Tchaikovsky, and Brahms concertos and the Franck, Debussy, and Beethoven sonatas.

Elman's interpretations of Bach, Mozart, and other preromantic composers were more controversial. Audiences were pleased, but the critics often berated him for sentimentalizing or otherwise distorting the rhythmic structure of the works. To these charges, Elman had a stock reply. "How do you know how Bach wanted his music played? Were you there?"

Elman lived for his music and his family. With the exception of chess and reading, he had few other interests. He died in New York City.

[Some of Elman's articles may be found in *Étude*, July 1935, Jan. 1939, Jan. 1945, and July 1953; *Violin and Violinists*, Aug.–Sept. and Oct. 1952; and *Music Journal*, Apr.–May 1958 and Apr.–May 1960. *Music Journal* also published posthumously a three-part Elman series, "Mediocrity Glitters but Is Not Gold," May, June, and Sept. 1967. See Leopold Auer, *My Long Life in Music* (1923); Saul Elman, *Memoirs of Mischa Elman's Father* (1933); *New York Times*, Dec. 5, 1948; McDonnell Carpenter, *Mischa Elman and Joseph Szigeti* (1955); and David Ewen, *Musicians Since 1900* (1978). A complete list of Elman's recorded output may be found in James Creighton, *Discopaedia of the Violin* (1974). An obituary is in the *New York Times*, Apr. 7, 1967.]

LOUIS R. THOMAS

FAIRCHILD, FRED ROGERS (Aug. 5, 1877–Apr. 13, 1966), economist and educator, was born in Crete, Nebr., the son of Arthur Babbitt Fairchild, an educator, and Isabel Amanda Pratt. Fairchild attended local schools and earned a B.A. from Doane College in Crete in 1898 and began teaching at Glenwood Collegiate Institute (Matawan, N.J.) in the following fall. He then served a two-year instructorship at the Gunnery School in Washington, Conn. After earning a Ph.D. from Yale in 1904, he joined the faculty as an instructor in economics and political economy. He was promoted to assistant professor in 1908 and to professor in 1913. While at Yale, he chaired the Department of Social and Political Science (1920–1924), the Department of Economics, Sociology, and Government (1924–1925), and the Department of Economics (1937–1939). In 1933 he was named a fellow of Calhoun College and in 1936 the Seymour H. Knox Professor of Economics, a post he held until his retirement in 1945.

Fairchild's professional career was marked by meritorious service as a teacher and author of a popular text in introductory economics, as an expert in public finance, and as a spokesman for business on tax matters. His two-volume text *Elementary Economics* (1926) was written in collaboration with Edgar S. Furniss and Norman S. Buck. (It ran through five editions; the 1954 edition listed as authors Fairchild, Buck, and Reuben Emanuel Slesinger.) When the work was first published, Harry Elmer Barnes described it as "an almost ideal textbook," but noted that it was in the conventional, rather than the emerging institutionalist, tradition. Fairchild's other academic works include *Essentials of Economics* (1923), *Economic Problems* (with R. T. Compton, 1928), *Economics* (1932), *Understanding Our Free Economy* (with Thomas Shelley, 1952), and *Principles of Economics* (with others, 1954). He also wrote the brief *Description of the New Deal* (with Furniss, Buck, and Chester Howard Whelden, Jr., 1935), which one reviewer claimed was "an excellent and objective study of the New Deal," characterizing its main conclusions as "disturbing or gratifying (depending upon one's point of view)." Of these conclusions, the most prescient was that "the vast machinery set up by the 'New Deal' will in all likelihood become more or less permanent."

Much of Fairchild's work in the field of public finance is reflected in numerous published reports, including *The Factory Legislation of the State of New York* (1905); "Taxation of Timberlands," in the *Report of the National Conservation Committee* (1909); *Report of Study of Connecticut Tax System* (for the Connecticut Chamber of Commerce, 1917); *National Survey of School Finance* (prepared for the United States Commissioner of Education under the direction of Dr. Paul R. Mort, with Fairchild one of many expert contributors, 1933); and *Forest Taxation: A Report of the Forest Taxation Inquiry* (1935). He also contributed to *Tax Policy* (edited by Mabel Walker, 1944).

The school finance report's principal recommendations were that states, rather than local communities, should bear the cost of public education, in order to equalize educational opportunities; that the property tax ought not to be the sole source of educational funds; and that, in assuming the educational cost burden, states should separate the matter of control from subvention. The forest taxation report (authorized in 1924 and issued in 1935) attempted to deal with the claims of timber growers that they were being subjected to unjust and burdensome taxation. Conflict had arisen out of the government's need to derive revenue from continuous property taxation and from the growers' irregular earnings resulting from the sporadic cutting and marketing of timber. One reviewer, noting the recommendations of the investigators, welcomed the report but pessimistically concluded, "There is little ground for hoping that either tax relief or any other measure likely to be accepted will induce private owners to engage in socially advantageous behavior."

Fairchild's domestic contributions were augmented by foreign service. In 1917–1918 he was consulted by the Dominican Republic on problems of taxation and public debt. In 1923, Colombia asked him and four others to help advise on the reorganization of its financial system.

Fairchild's general economic orientation was neoclassical and conservative. Consequently, he was asked by such organizations as the United States Chamber of Commerce, the National Association of Manufacturers, the Manufacturers' Association of Connecticut, and the Connecticut Bankers' Association to represent them. He advocated governmental frugality, balanced governmental budgets, low rates of taxation, and tax simplification. He favored a federal sales tax to supplement the federal income tax. He fought against government regulations that tended to stifle private enterprise, and he testified against resale price maintenance. In 1929, Fairchild served as president of the National Tax Association.

On one tax issue, Fairchild changed his mind: in 1923 he advocated revision of the Constitution to permit federal taxation of interest generated by state and municipal securities. His arguments in favor of President Calvin Coolidge's proposal were that "tax exemption destroys the personal character of the income tax and builds up a tax-exempt class of the wealthier citizens." Fourteen years later, in a column for the *Herald Tribune* (Sept. 4, 1942), Fairchild opposed levying taxes on the income from these securities, fearing that the tax burden at the lower governmental levels would rise and that such taxation would threaten the integrity of state and local governments. The change is explicable insofar as the national government of the 1920's seemed to have limited historical functions, whereas in the 1930's it was viewed by Fairchild as a burgeoning, power-hungry leviathan. Fairchild was not a Keynesian. "I am convinced that the supposed benefits of Government spending are an illusion," he wrote. "Government has no magic power to raise the standard of living by spending money."

On June 23, 1917, Fairchild married Ruth Loraine Evans; they had two children. Fairchild, who made his home in Fairfield, Conn., was not affiliated with any political party. His avocational interests included traveling, carpentry, tennis, and swimming. He died in Bridgeport, Conn.

[There is no published biography of Fairchild. An obituary is in the *New York Times*, Apr. 15, 1966.]

HAROLD WATTEL

FALL, BERNARD B. (Nov. 11, 1926–Feb. 21, 1967), historian and war correspondent, was born in Vienna, Austria, the son of Léon Fall, an engineering materials salesman, and Anne Seligman. He grew up in southern France, losing both parents in World War II: his mother was deported as a hostage and never returned; his father was tortured to death by the Nazis. Fall joined the resistance as a teenager. He transferred to the regular army and fought with the Allies in the liberation of France and the drive into Germany. He worked briefly as an investigator for the Nuremberg War Crimes Tribunal and studied at the University of Paris in 1948–1949; at the University of Munich, 1949–1950; and in the United States at Johns Hopkins University and Syracuse University. He received his M.A. from Syracuse in 1953 and his Ph.D. in political science in 1955. In 1956 he accepted an academic appointment at Howard University in international relations, which he retained until his death. In 1954 he married Dorothy Winer, an American designer. They had three children.

Fall became a Vietnam specialist by accident. One of his teachers suggested that he study Vietnam because his French background ideally prepared him to do so and because no one was currently studying the area. Fall went to Indochina in 1953 at his own expense to research a doctoral dissertation (published in 1954 as *The Viet-Minh Regime*) on the Vietminh insurgents. He accompanied French troops on operations in the field, and his letters to his wife describing these operations provided the basis for his classic study of the First Indochina War, *Street Without Joy* (1961).

Thus began Fall's reputation as one of the foremost authorities on Vietnam. He returned to Southeast Asia numerous times, and in 1961–1962 he was a visiting professor at the Royal Institute of Administration, Cambodia. His *The Two Vietnams: A Political and Military Analysis* (1963) was one of the first efforts to put the conflict in Indochina into historical perspective. When the American phase of the war began in the early 1960's, Fall wrote more than 250 newspaper and magazine articles that examined the war and the experiences of those who fought it. Some of his articles and essays were collected and published in *Viet-Nam Witness* (1966). That same year he published *Hell in a Very Small Place*, a study of the battle of Dien Bien Phu.

Fall brought to his work enormous energy and a powerful intellect. A brash and flamboyant man, he cut a dashing figure as a war correspondent. His ambition was to be the foremost writer of his generation. He spoke French, English, Polish, Hungarian, German, and some Vietnamese, and had total recall. He also had great zest for field research, and he was openly contemptuous of those who wrote about the war from the safety of the United States. After he was diagnosed as having retroperitoneal fibrosis, a rare, incurable disease, he returned to Vietnam. While accompanying United States Marines on a mission north of Hue, he was killed by a Vietminh land mine.

Fall, who prided himself on being an independent scholar, was a major contributor to the debate on Vietnam in the 1960's. Highly critical of what he regarded as America's abandonment of France in the First Indochina War, he was sometimes dismissed as a French apologist. Yet he was a harsh critic of French colonialism. Although he admired Ho Chi Minh and the Vietminh, he was firmly anti-Communist. He was neither hawk nor dove, and he rejected both escalation and an American withdrawal from Vietnam. He was sharply critical of American policy, which he felt was based on abstractions divorced from the realities of Vietnamese history and was victimized by chronic and usually unwarranted optimism.

Fall early exposed the flaws in the official American explanation of the war, and he was among the first to warn of the strength of Vietnamese nationalism and of the Vietminh's ability to absorb great punishment. He developed deep empathy for the victims of the wars in Vietnam, the soldiers on all sides, and the Vietnamese people. He remained a French citizen, but he had great affection for both the United States and Vietnam, and he endlessly agonized over the grief each visited on the other.

Although a critic of American policy in an age when criticism was not encouraged, and frequently, in his own words, "the unwelcome bearer of ill tidings," Fall had considerable influence. His books were popular with the American military in Vietnam. Few American officials agreed with him, but increasingly they listened to him and read his work. Much of his writing has become dated through the explosion of scholarship on Vietnam, but it remains important for the light it sheds on the contemporary debate.

[See Fall's *Last Reflections on a War* (1967). See also the obituaries in the *New York Times*, Feb. 22, 1967; and *Commentary*, Mar. 1968.]

GEORGE C. HERRING

FARRAR, GERALDINE (Feb. 28, 1882—Mar. 11, 1967), opera singer, was born in Melrose, Mass., the only child of Sydney D. Farrar, first baseman for the Philadelphia Phillies, and Henrietta Barnes. After receiving vocal training from Mrs. J. H. Long in Boston, Emma Thursby in New York City, Antonio Trabadelo in Paris, and Francesco Graziani in Berlin, she was coached by Lilli Lehmann. Farrar first appeared on the operatic stage on Oct. 15, 1901, as Marguerite in *Faust* at the Berlin Royal Opera, where she received tumultuous acclaim. Despite strong prejudice against American artists she became an operatic idol during her five years with the company. She was also a favorite of the royal family, after a command performance for Kaiser Wilhelm II, and was rumored to have been romantically involved with Crown Prince Friedrich Wilhelm. Further successes followed in Monte Carlo, Warsaw, Paris, Munich, and Salzburg between 1904 and 1906.

Farrar's reign as prima donna assoluta at the Metropolitan Opera in New York City began with her American debut, on Nov. 26, 1906, in *Romeo and Juliet* and ended on Apr. 22, 1922, with the title role in *Zaza*. During these sixteen seasons she made 517 appearances in New York City and 147 on tour in 34 roles. She was famous as Marguerite in *Faust*, Violetta in *La Traviata*, and Mimi in *La Bohème*, and in the title roles of *Tosca, Mignon, Louise, Carmen, Manon*, and *Madama Butterfly;* she was the first American Cio-Cio-San in a production supervised by the opera's composer, Giacomo Puccini, on Feb. 11, 1907, and conducted by Arturo Toscanini, with Enrico Caruso as Pinkerton. To all her roles she brought a lyric soprano expansive in range, pure in texture, and sensitive in phrasing. Her acting left much to be desired, prone as she was to posturing, but her physically attractive stage presence brought glamour to her performances. In addition to the standard repertory, she was heard in the world premieres of Engelbert Humperdinck's *Königskinder* (1910), as the Goose Girl; Umberto Giordano's *Madame Sans-Gêne* (1915), as Caterina; and in the title role of Puccini's *Suor Angelica*, on Dec. 14, 1918. She also starred in several American premieres, including those of *Le Donne Curiose* and *The Secret of Suzanne*, both by Ermanno Wolf-Ferrari, and in the title role of Jules Massenet's *Thaïs*.

While at the Metropolitan Opera she also performed for three seasons at the Chicago Opera, from 1910 to 1911, and from 1915 to 1917. At the same time she became the first opera singer to star in motion pictures, making her screen debut in *Maria Rosa* (1915), directed by Cecil B. De Mille. Among her many films were *Carmen* (1915), *Temptation* (1916), *Joan the Woman* (1917), *The Woman God Forgot* (1917), *Flame of Desert* (1919), and *The Woman and the Puppet* (1920). In her first film, and in several subsequent ones, she was starred with Lou Tellegen, whom she married in 1916. They were divorced in 1923 and were childless; she never remarried.

Following her retirement from opera in 1922, Farrar toured America in recitals and in a condensed version of *Carmen*. She also made appearances on network radio programs, including "The Packard Hour" and "The General Motors Hour." Her final singing performance took place at a recital in Carnegie Hall, New York City, in November 1931. In the early 1930's, during the Great Depression, she returned to the Metropolitan to make several appeals for financial contributions. She published her autobiography, *Such Sweet Compulsion*, in 1938. In 1940 she served as program annotator for the Saturday-afternoon radio broadcasts of the Metropolitan Opera, for which she wrote her own material. She later retired to her home in Ridgefield, Conn., where she died.

[See Edward Wagenknecht, *Geraldine Farrar* (1929); Francis Robinson's memoir in *Opera News*, Apr. 15, 1967; and David Ewen, *Musicians Since 1900* (1978).]

DAVID EWEN

FAY, SIDNEY BRADSHAW (Apr. 13, 1876–Aug. 29, 1967), historian and educator, was born in Washington, D.C., the son of Edward Allen Fay, a Dante scholar, and Mary Bradshaw. Fay received a B.A. from Harvard in 1896. His first love was the classics, but he soon became attracted to history and he chose it for graduate study at Harvard. He received an M.A. in 1897 and studied at the Sorbonne in 1898. After bicycling from Paris to Berlin, Fay enrolled for three semesters at Berlin. Using Brandenburg and Hanoverian archives, he wrote a dissertation on the League of Princes, Frederick the Great's defensive alliance against Emperor Joseph II. Fay mailed the dissertation to Cambridge and received a Ph.D. from Harvard in 1900.

After two years as a teaching fellow, he went to Dartmouth, where he remained until 1914. He married Sarah Proctor in 1904. They had three children. Fay became an active citizen of Hanover, N.H., serving on the school board and as coeditor of the town's early records. In 1898 he had published in the *American Historical Review* (AHR) a prizewinning essay on Napoleon's abduction and execution of the duc d'Enghien, and at Dartmouth he became a prolific reviewer of works on European history, particularly in the *AHR* and the *Nation*.

In 1914 Fay became a professor at Smith College. He founded with John Spencer Bassett the *Smith College Studies in History*, contributing in 1916 an essay on the early Hohenzollern household and administration; and a year later he published in the *AHR* a study of the creation of the standing army in Prussia. But World War I drew him toward contemporary history. He strongly opposed German policy from 1914 to 1918, favored American entry into the war, and supported the breakup of Austria-Hungary. The first of his many studies of the war's background appeared in the *AHR* in October 1918; using the recently published "Willy-Nicky correspondence," he criticized sharply the Kaiser's naive attempt at a Russian alliance in 1904 and 1905. In reports to the House Commission at the Paris Peace Conference, he recommended independence for Poland and Finland and autonomy for the Baltic peoples and the Ukraine, pending later federation with the Soviet Union.

As documentary publications continued to pour forth, Fay grew increasingly dissatisfied with the accepted versions of the war's genesis. In 1920 and 1921 he published in the *AHR* three articles entitled "New Light on the Origins of the War," dealing with the events of July and August 1914. He soon argued that Article 231 of the Versailles Treaty, which attributed the cause of the war to "the aggression of Germany and her allies," was historically untrue in its implication of Germany's sole guilt. His reviews became a continuing commentary on the massive new evidence on prewar diplomacy. In 1927 he interviewed many participants in the events of 1914, including the Kaiser and Admiral von Tirpitz. A year later he published *The Origins of the World War*.

The book was widely read, and many scholars greeted it with enthusiasm; a French translation, which appeared in 1931, elicited some disagreement. Some otherwise favorable reviews, notably in the *AHR* and the *Times Literary Supplement*, criticized Fay's strictly documentary approach and his neglect of such imponderables as popular emotions. Recent scholarship indicates that Fay underestimated German pressure on Austria to act against Serbia and overestimated Germany's last-minute efforts to avert general war.

As an internationally acclaimed authority on diplomacy, Fay was a natural choice for a new joint Harvard-Radcliffe professorship. He returned to Cambridge in 1929 and became very much a public figure. He lectured, attended conferences, and wrote scores of reviews and articles, especially in *Current History*.

With Hitler's accession in 1933, Fay's concern with contemporary Germany increased greatly. After hoping for the moderation of Nazi policies, he firmly opposed the regime, without identifying Germans with Nazis, and without changing his views about World War I. In the mid-1930's his brand of revisionism—though he dissociated himself from the extreme revisionists of left or right—became widespread. Young American scholars especially favored his views, just as contemporary politicians reflected American disillusionment with foreign involvements. But with the outbreak of World War II, Fay favored aid for the Allies and American intervention, if necessary. He argued that 1939 was not 1914; that the old, though fragile, unity of the Euro-American world was lost; and that Hitler's Reich was in essence different from and outside of our civilization. However, Fay maintained that a decent Germany might be restored and he opposed destructive peace measures that would prevent Germany's revival. After 1945 he favored Adenauer's policies, the Schuman plan, and the emergence of a real European community.

Fay retired from Harvard and Radcliffe in 1945, spent a year as visiting professor at Yale, and was elected president of the American Historical Association for the 1946–1947 term. He continued his scholarly activities and was instrumental in founding the Radcliffe Seminars, a program of adult education in which he taught for several years. He died in Lexington, Mass.

Fay's *Origins of the World War* sparked considerable controversy but was for years the foremost scholarly treatment of the subject. Although he published no other work of similar scope, his many articles, his participation in the editing of the *Guide to Historical Literature* (1931), and *The Rise of Brandenburg-Prussia to 1786* (1937) were important contributions. Fay, a wise and gracious man, was loved and respected by students and colleagues alike.

[The Harvard University Archives contain some of Fay's correspondence, manuscripts, including his dissertation, prize essays written as a student, and the texts of hundreds of reviews and numerous articles; notes for and on lectures and bibliography; official academic records; anniversary reports of the class of 1896; and scrapbooks. Annual reports of Smith College during his professorship list his publications. See *A Syllabus of European History*, edited with Herbert D. Foster (1904) and frequently reprinted; his translation of Eduard Fueter, *World History* (1922); the preface to Ruth Fischer, *Stalin and German Communism* (1948); and his translation of Friedrich Meinecke, *The German Catastrophe* (1950). Klaus Epstein published a revised edition of *The Rise of Brandenburg-Prussia* (1964). See also the obituary notice in *American Historical Review*, Dec. 1967.]

REGINALD H. PHELPS

FERBER, EDNA JESSICA (Aug. 15, 1885–Apr. 16, 1968), novelist and playwright, was born in Kalamazoo, Mich., the daughter of Jacob Charles Ferber, a storekeeper who had emigrated from Hungary, and Julia Neumann, the daughter of a prosperous Chicago family. Jacob Ferber sold his dry-goods business in Kalamazoo in 1888 and moved his family first to Chicago and then to Ottumwa, Iowa, a town that at that time, Ferber said later, possessed all the sordidness and none of the picturesqueness of the frontier. Her earliest memories there were of witnessing a lynching and enduring a constant stream of anti-Semitic epithets. Though Ferber practiced no religion, she was proud of her Jewish heritage, but was to write only one work that had anything to do with Jews or Judaism, *Fanny Herself* (1917).

In 1897 the family moved to Appleton, Wis., a more settled, serene place with a substantial Jewish minority, which Ferber called "the American small town at its best." Here she completed her formal education, graduating from a good high school. At the age of seventeen she began her career as a writer, earning $3 a week as a reporter on the *Appleton Crescent*. She later said that her eighteen months in this job were worth any college education, and though she did not realize it then, she was acquiring the skills of observation and characterization that would be of value in her later career. From there she went on to a job with the *Milwaukee Journal*, writing police-court news until 1905, when overwork and anemia caused a collapse, which forced her to return to Appleton.

There Ferber wrote her first book, *Dawn O'Hara* (1911). Though it sold well, she disliked the novel and began to write short stories. When her father died in 1909 and her mother sold the store, she moved with her mother and sister to Chicago. Her stories, revealing the influence of O. Henry, were selling well, and she created a memorable character in the stories of Emma McChesney, the first female sales representative in fiction.

Ferber's second novel, *Fanny Herself*, the story of a Jewish girl growing up in a Wisconsin town like Appleton, also dissatisfied her, and it was not until she published *The Girls* (1921) that she had any real confidence in her ability to write a novel. By this time she had perfected her methods as a writer: a thorough knowledge of the background, an emphasis on characterization rather than plot, a tendency to present strong women and weak men, and an ability to excite the emotions of her readers without offending them.

In 1912, Ferber first visited New York City; after World War I she lived there or at her home in Connecticut. She reported on the political conventions of 1912 and 1920; during both world wars she wrote propaganda; and in World War I she spoke frequently at bond rallies. But, for the most part, her life was that of a writer, punctuated by extensive traveling. In 1924 her novel *So Big* was awarded a Pulitzer Prize, and she began her collaboration with George S. Kaufman, the first fruit of which,

Minick, was an unsuccessful play based on one of her short stories.

The writing of *Show Boat* (1926), an immensely popular work that inspired a radio series, three film adaptations, and a long-running musical, reveals a pattern that Ferber followed for the rest of her career. Wanting to write a novel about a theater riverboat, she went to North Carolina for background and lived and worked on such a vessel for several months. The result was an episodic novel, more or less plotless, but rich in characterization, local color, and historical authenticity. In *Cimarron* (1930) she dealt with the Oklahoma land rush and the state's early development. *American Beauty* (1931) presents the history of a Connecticut house and its owners from its colonial builders, through the decadence of their descendants, to the Polish tobacco farmers who finally supplant them. In *Come and Get It* (1935) she returned to Wisconsin for her subject—three generations of lumber barons. *Saratoga Trunk* (1941), perhaps her best novel, tells the story of a Texas gambler and a Creole adventuress who pool their talents and win their fortune at nineteenth-century Saratoga Springs. In her last three novels, *Great Son* (1945), *Giant* (1952), and *Ice Palace* (1958), she portrayed, with varying degrees of success, the histories of the Pacific Northwest, Texas, and Alaska. *Giant*, which was adapted as a successful film, is the best of these. *Ice Palace*, written in her last years, when her health was failing, is marred by interminable dialogues on Alaska's problems, but it may have played some part in the achievement of Alaskan statehood. Ferber died in New York City.

Ferber nurtured a lifelong interest in the theater, wrote short stories about it, longed to be an actress, and collaborated on nine plays, six of them with Kaufman. Of these, three—*The Royal Family* (1927), *Dinner at Eight* (1932), and *Stage Door* (1936)—were tremendous hits, with *The Royal Family* and the musical based on *Show Boat* beginning their long runs in the same month.

Throughout her career Ferber remained steadfastly American and even middle western in the attitudes she revealed in her life and in her writing. In Chicago in her early years she rejected the Russian writers who were models for many of her literary friends, asking, "Why not write in American?" To her, the Middle West was less European and therefore "fresher, more vital, an integral part of the American way of life." She once said she liked to write about working men and women "perhaps because I really am one of them." At the same time, she never understood why most of her readers seemed unaware of her satiric purposes and social message. She conceived *Cimarron* as a satire of sentimentality and American womanhood as it was usually understood, but the public saw it as a western romance. In most of her novels there is an implicit condemnation of materialism and an idealization of art, social consciousness, and the life of the mind. But her readers generally admired her work for other reasons. When it is considered in its entirety, her work should be remembered for a remarkable gallery of figures who, in richness of characterization, illuminate crucial stages in American history during the twentieth century.

[The Ferber papers are at the State Historical Society of Wisconsin. Her other works include two autobiographies, *A Peculiar Treasure* (1939) and *A Kind of Magic* (1963), and several volumes of short stories, the best of which she collected in *One Basket* (1947). An incomplete list of her writings is Vito J. Brenni and Betty Lee Spencer, "Edna Ferber: A Selected Bibliography," *Bulletin of Bibliography*, Sept.–Dec. 1958.

See Julie G. Gilbert, *Ferber: A Biography* (1978); and Malcolm Goldstein, *George S. Kaufman: His Life, His Theater* (1979). An obituary is in the *New York Times*, Apr. 17, 1968.]

ROBERT L. BERNER

FISCHER, LOUIS (Feb. 29, 1896–Jan. 15, 1970), journalist and writer, was born in Philadelphia, the son of David Fischer, a factory laborer and fish and fruit peddler, and Shifrah Kantzapolsky, a laundress, who were Orthodox Jews from Shpola in the Ukraine. Fischer claimed that the poverty of his childhood instilled in him a dedication to the eradication of want. In 1914, Fischer graduated from Philadelphia Southern High School, where he was an honor student. After two years at the Philadelphia School of Pedagogy, he graduated with a teaching certificate in 1916. He taught only until the end of 1917, when a newfound but intense involvement with Zionism led him to join the British army's Jewish Legion. If Fischer's sojourn in Palestine dimmed his enthusiasm for Zionism, his growing interest in the Soviet Union ended it. Fischer, in *Men and Politics* (1941), wrote that he came to view

Zionism as merely "Jewish Nationalism nailed to a territorial objective."

After World War I, Fischer traveled about Europe. The chaos and disillusionment of postwar Europe nurtured sympathetic feelings on Fischer's part toward Soviet Russia, which seemed to offer certainties and a way out of the chaos. In 1920 he married Bertha Mark-Markoosha, a Latvian who further encouraged Fischer's sympathy toward the Bolsheviks. When Fischer arrived in Moscow in the spring of 1922 as a free-lance writer for the *New York Evening Post*, he hoped to find in Russia an answer to the malaise that had gripped the West.

In 1923, Fischer secured a staff position as the *Nation*'s foreign correspondent in the Soviet Union. From 1924 to 1935, Fischer reported on events in Stalin's Russia for American readers. Like his colleague from the *New York Times* Walter Duranty, Sidney and Beatrice Webb, and other pilgrims to Stalin's Russia, Fischer portrayed the changes brought by the revolution in the most favorable light. Fischer deliberately covered up the severity of Russian social and economic conditions in certain cases, such as the famine of 1932–1933. In that instance, he hoped to avoid jeopardizing the Roosevelt administration's pending formal diplomatic recognition of the Soviet government. Fischer was in the Soviet Union during the collectivization of Soviet agriculture and merely hinted at the resulting hardships. Explaining not only such deception but his attraction in general toward the Soviet system, he wrote in his contribution to Richard Crossman's symposium *The God That Failed* (1949), "I preferred fresh sweeping winds to stale stagnant air, and well-intentioned pioneers to proved failures." Until 1933, Fischer thought Stalin was not only a pioneer in social engineering but also a humane and well-intentioned leader.

After 1933, Fischer suppressed his growing doubts about the Soviet government. He first began to have misgivings about Stalin when he attended the Moscow purge trials. Stalin's use of the secret police to banish Leon Trotsky had also furthered Fischer's suspicions. But he regarded these as "sores on a healthy body" and preserved his faith in the essential virtue of the regime. While some intellectuals withdrew their support of the Soviets after the Red Army's brutal suppression of rebellious sailors at Kronshtadt in 1921, Fischer did not abandon the regime until the Spanish Civil War.

With the onset of the Spanish conflict in 1936, Fischer left a Russia whose government increasingly disturbed him. He joined the International Brigades (the first American to do so) and fought for the Loyalists against Franco. The Soviet execution of Russians who had served in Spain and the Nazi-Soviet Nonaggression Pact of 1939 ended forever his faith in the regenerative, moral power of the Soviet government. In 1939 he met with Eleanor Roosevelt to seek her help in securing American passports for his wife and two sons, who were still in Moscow. Her influence proved decisive, and the Fischers were thus able to settle in America.

For the next thirty years, Fischer was an independent writer and world traveler. He wrote biographies of Gandhi and Lenin, for which he won the National Book Award. Though he renounced the Soviet Union, he never abandoned his optimism concerning man's capabilities and his future. Although Fischer's Jewish background did not seem to translate into overtly religious leanings, he apparently entertained longings for absolute answers to political and social problems. He found his new embodiment of virtue in Gandhi and political nonviolence. Fischer's transfer of affection from Stalin to Gandhi is not as incongruous as it might seem, since both leaders held rigid beliefs and had few doubts as to their spiritual powers and authority.

Fischer believed that writers and journalists should be involved with political causes and contribute to the improvement of the human condition. He belonged to a generation of distinguished Western intellectuals whose admiration for the Soviet system stemmed, in Fischer's words, "more from discontent with conditions in their own countries than from knowledge of conditions inside Russia." For him and many others the attraction of the Soviet system transcended its material shortcomings: "How could you complain about the scarcity of potatoes when you were building Socialism?"

Unlike many political pilgrims and seekers of utopia of a later generation, Fischer earnestly, if with some delay, confronted the moral implications of his political position and, after some quiet agonizing, made a clean break with the Soviet system and its Western supporters. But the attitudes and susceptibilities that Fischer personified outlived him. Although the Soviet Union no longer appeals to many Western intellectuals, other political systems, such as Castro's Cuba and Mao's China, have come to play the same part in the affections of many Westerners disenchanted with their own society. Thus, his work and especially his writing on the Soviet Union and his own feelings toward it remain highly relevant and instructive for political pilgrims and tourists.

[Fischer's writings include *Oil Imperialism* (1926); *The Soviets in World Affairs* (1930); *Machines and Men in Russia* (1932); *Soviet Journey* (1935); *The Great Challenge* (1946); *Gandhi and Stalin: Two Signs at the World's Crossroads* (1947); *The Life of Mahatma Gandhi* (1950); *The Life and Death of Stalin* (1952); *This Is Our World* (1956); *Russia Revisited* (1957); *The Story of Indonesia* (1959); *Russia, America, and the World* (1961); *The Life of Lenin* (1964); *Fifty Years of Soviet Communism* (1968); *Russia's Road from Peace to War* (1969); and *The Road to Yalta* (1972). An obituary is in the *New York Times*, Jan. 17, 1970.]

PAUL HOLLANDER
MARK MENSH

FITZPATRICK, DANIEL ROBERT (Mar. 5, 1891–May 18, 1969), editorial cartoonist, was born in Superior, Wis., the son of Patrick Fitzpatrick, the owner of a millwork factory, and Delia Ann Clark. Fitzpatrick wanted to be a cartoonist from the age of ten. During his years in Blaine High School in Superior, he drew for the school paper and submitted cartoons to the *Telegram*. At the local library he found early sources of inspiration in volumes of *Puck*, *Judge*, and *Life* that contained the work of such illustrators and cartoonists as Joseph Keppler, James Montgomery Flagg, Dan Gibson, and Eugene Zimmerman ("Zim"). In 1906 he dropped out of high school. He said that his early interest in history had not been encouraged, because teachers emphasized dates and statistics rather than meaning. Later, his work would be distinguished because he chose to emphasize the significance of events in broad strokes rather than cluttering his drawings with distracting details.

Fitzpatrick learned dexterity with tools working in his father's plant, in a Superior shipyard, and on a Great Lakes iron-ore carrier. He studied for three years at the Chicago Art Institute. When his family stopped providing financial help, he supported himself with odd jobs and with drawings that were occasionally accepted by the *Chicago Daily News*. In 1911, L. D. Bradley, the *Daily News* editorial cartoonist and head of the art department, hired Fitzpatrick to do sports layouts, comic panels, and illustrations.

During his three years at the *Daily News*, sophisticated newspapermen encouraged him to see his work in a larger context and encouraged his reading. After serving for nine months as editorial cartoonist while Bradley was ill, Fitzpatrick did not want to return to a lesser position. Therefore, in September 1913, having just married Lee Anna Dressen, Fitzpatrick moved to St. Louis, where he continued his art studies at Washington University and began a forty-five-year, 14,000-cartoon career with the *St. Louis Post-Dispatch*.

Fitzpatrick's mature work was influenced by Goya, Forain, Daumier, Hogarth, Rembrandt, and Doré, as well as by the cartoonists he followed as a youngster. Perhaps the greatest influence was the tradition already established at the *Post-Dispatch* by Robert Minor, Jr., who preceded Fitzpatrick as editorial cartoonist. Minor's drawings, like Boardman Robinson's cartoons for the *New York Sun*, which Fitzpatrick also admired, represented a radical departure from the sentimental style of the "bucolic school" of midwestern cartoonists such as John T. McCutcheon of the *Chicago Tribune* and Jay ("Ding") Darling of the *Des Moines Register*. McCutcheon's and Darling's panels, filled with detailed figures, cross-hatching, and labels and words in balloons, all drawn in fine-line pen and ink, were most frequently local, good-natured, and only mildly critical. With the rise of realism, urbanism, the ashcan school of art, and post–World War I disillusionment, Fitzpatrick followed Robinson and Minor, further developing their dramatic "dripping mud" style. Fitzpatrick's cartoons featured a few bold symbolic figures drawn in grease pencil on heavy, grained paper. Although he could also be amusing, the most effective of Fitzpatrick's drawings are somber in mood and subject.

The new simplified shadowy style that made the editorial point primary was appropriate to Fitzpatrick's indignation at social wrongs and oppression. He won his first Pulitzer Prize in 1926 for *The Laws of Moses and the Laws of Today*, which depicted the mass of statutes, such as prohibition laws, that plagued the contemporary justice system; he won another Pulitzer Prize in 1955 for *How Would Another Mistake Help?*, which portrayed Uncle Sam marching into the swamp of French Indochina. More typical of his dark style were his compassionate portrayals of lost men suffering from poverty after the Great Depression and his ominous World War II drawings of giant swastikas rolling relentlessly across Europe.

Fitzpatrick was a liberal Democrat, but his opposition to injustice crossed partisan lines. While his international reputation was based on his stark cartoons dealing with global issues, he sometimes adopted a fussier nostalgic style to expose local corruption. He was convicted of contempt after supporting the editorial policy of the *Post-Dispatch* with a cartoon from his *Rat Alley* series that chastised the courts for releasing an alleged extortionist. The Missouri Supreme Court reversed the conviction.

In the citation accompanying a 1949 degree from Washington University, he was credited with an "instinctive intolerance of self-interest and bigotry" and for speaking "eloquently for a better community and a better world." His agreement with Joseph Pulitzer that he would not have to draw cartoons to support editorial policies with which he could not agree led him to take special leave only twice in his career—when the *Post-Dispatch* supported Alfred M. Landon against Franklin D. Roosevelt and again when the paper favored Thomas E. Dewey over Harry S Truman. He retired in 1958 and was succeeded by Bill Mauldin.

Fitzpatrick cartoons were syndicated in thirty-five newspapers in the United States and have been reproduced, collected, and exhibited all over the world. In the 1930's his works were hung in the Moscow Museum of Modern Western Art, and his *No Place for a Kiddie Car* (Mar. 29, 1940) became part of the White House collection during the Truman administration.

Fitzpatrick's wife died in 1965, and he married Beulah O. Hawthorne in December 1968. He died in St. Louis. The obituary in the *Post-Dispatch* described Fitzpatrick as "an incisive interpreter of the times and a fearless crusader" who brought to his daily work "a controlled passion, a mordant sense of humor, an informed skepticism, and above all the fierce independence of a man not easily tamed to conventional rhetoric and conventional ideas."

[The Missouri State Historical Society has a large collection of Fitzpatrick cartoons. The best introduction to Fitzpatrick is his *As I Saw It* (1953), which contains a foreword by Joseph Pulitzer and an extensive profile of the cartoonist by Thomas B. Sherman. See also William Murrell, *A History of American Graphic Humor* (1938; repr. 1967); Stephen Hess and Milton Kaplan, *The Ungentlemanly Art* (1975); and Charles Press, *The Political Cartoon* (1981). Brief discussions of Fitzpatrick's art appear in *Newsweek*, Apr. 6, 1935, and Apr. 28, 1941; and in *Time*, May 5, 1941. Obituaries are in the *St. Louis Post-Dispatch* and the *New York Times*, both May 19, 1969.]

NANCY POGEL

FITZSIMMONS, JAMES EDWARD ("SUNNY JIM") (July 23, 1874–Mar. 11, 1966), horse trainer, was born in the Sheepshead Bay section of Brooklyn, N.Y., the son of George Fitzsimmons, a farmer, and Catherine Murphy. At the age of eleven he began working at the Brennan Brothers Stable in Sheepshead Bay, washing dishes and cleaning stalls. During this time he met George ("Fish") Tappan, who remained with him for seventy years as his assistant. Fitzsimmons was an exercise boy for the Dwyer brothers in Sheepshead Bay, and he became a jockey in 1889, the year that he took a job at a small track in Gloucester, N.J. In 1890 he rode his first winner, a horse named Crispin. It is reported that he rode for Frank James, Jesse James's brother. Fitzsimmons married Jennie Harvey on Dec. 29, 1892; they had six children.

Despite a desperate struggle to keep his weight down, Fitzsimmons became too heavy to be a jockey, and in 1894 he began training horses. For years thereafter he endured hardships on the training circuit. He kept a public stable and owned a few horses, but it was not until his middle age that his luck changed; he always emphasized the importance of luck. In 1914 he began to attract attention as the trainer for the Quincy Stable, which was owned by James F. Johnson. Because Johnson missed a yearling auction in 1918, he missed getting Man o' War; Fitzsimmons, representing him, was the last man to drop out of the bidding.

Becoming the trainer for William Woodward's Belair Stud Farm in 1924 was Fitzsimmons' great opportunity. The next year, he also took on the new Wheatley Stable of Mrs. Henry Carnegie Phipps and her brother, Ogden L. Mills, who later became secretary of the treasury in Herbert Hoover's cabinet. Fitzsimmons picked Dice as a yearling, along with Diavolo and Distraction. In 1927, Dice was unbeaten in five starts.

No horse did as much to advance Fitzsimmons' career as Gallant Fox, who was named Horse of the Year in 1930. Earl Sande came out of retirement that year to ride him, and Gallant Fox won $308,165 in purses, making Fitzsimmons the leading trainer in money won. In 1930 his horses earned $397,355, of which Fitzsimmons' share was 10 percent. Called "a phenomenal race horse" in the Jockey Club's *Racing in America*, Gallant Fox won the Triple Crown, finishing first in the Kentucky Derby, the Preakness, and the Belmont Stakes.

Faireno's victory in the Belmont Stakes in 1932 was one of sixty-eight that year for Fitzsimmons; again, his horses won more money than any other trainer's. Dark Secret, winner of fifteen stakes races, was trained by Fitzsimmons as an outstanding distance horse. On Sept. 15, 1934, Dark Secret broke his leg winning the Jockey Club Gold Cup at Belmont Park.

During this period, Fitzsimmons trained other notable horses. Omaha won the Triple Crown in 1935, as well as the Dwyer and the Arlington Classic. Granville was named Best Horse of the Year by the *Daily Racing Form* in 1936; he won the Belmont Stakes, Arlington Classic, Lawrence, Realization, Travers, and Saratoga Cup. Johnstown, one of Fitzsimmons' fastest horses, won the Kentucky Derby, Belmont Stakes, Withers, and Dwyer in 1939.

During winter seasons, Fitzsimmons raced his horses in Florida. He also owned a company that manufactured Bigeloil (a cure-all for horses and people), and he invented several devices, including a special plate for injured hooves and a diathermy machine. Two of his sons, John and James, worked as his assistant trainers.

Fillies developed by Fitzsimmons included Vagrancy, the champion three-year-old filly of 1942. Busanda was one of the few fillies to win the Suburban (in 1951), and she won the Saratoga Cup twice. High Voltage was the champion two-year-old filly of 1954, and Misty Morn, the champion three-year-old and handicap filly of 1955.

Modest and cheerful, Fitzsimmons was a favorite of the press. George Dailey of the *New York World* is credited with giving him the nickname Sunny Jim. He was also called Mr. Fitz. The sportswriter Red Smith wrote, "One of the greatest privileges was to be with him around the barns in the morning." Fitzsimmons was even popular with owners who had been beaten by his horses. Alfred Vanderbilt remarked, "Sometimes he has the better horse, and sometimes the better-conditioned horse."

Fitzsimmons' horses excelled at distances of 1.5 miles and more, where conditioning is the key to success. On Oct. 13, 1956, Nashua, in his last race, won the two-mile Jockey Club Gold Cup in the record time of 3:20 2/5. The jockey was Eddie Arcaro, who rode another Fitzsimmons horse, Bold Ruler, to victory in the Futurity later that day. Nashua, who in 1955 had won the Preakness and Belmont Stakes and who had beaten Swaps in a match race, earned a record total of $1,288,565 in three years of racing. Bold Ruler was named Horse of the Year in 1957.

When he was over eighty, Fitzsimmons was not only still working but still at the top of his field. He revealed his secret for longevity in a *New York Times Magazine* interview: "Keep regular hours, eat simple foods, get plenty of fresh air, and remember that humans are inconsistent." He often watched television (he preferred westerns) and sometimes commented on the horses.

Severe arthritis—which he blamed on the punishing weight-loss regimen of his jockey days—had bent his back so far that he stooped over almost double. Fitzsimmons retired in 1963 after a seventy-eight-year career that included winning the Kentucky Derby three times, the Preakness four times, the Belmont Stakes six times, and the Wood Memorial eight times. His horses won over 2,000 races and over $13,000,000 in purses. But Fitzsimmons did not want his grandsons working at the track. He explained to his biographer, Jimmy Breslin, "What sense does it make to get into a business of pure luck? That's all the race track is. Now I'm a winner at it. But I keep tellin' you, all them horses could've lost." Fitzsimmons died in Miami, Fla.

[Jimmy Breslin, *Sunny Jim* (1962), is the best source of information, especially on Fitzsimmons' early years. See Arturo Gonzalez and Janeann Gonzalez' interview with Fitzsimmons in the *New York Times Magazine*, June 22, 1958; and Red Smith, "Mr. Fitz," in *To Absent Friends from Red Smith* (1982). Material on Fitzsimmons' horses is in John Hervey, *Racing in America* (1937). See also George Ryall, "Sunny Jim," *Blood-Horse*, July 13 and 20, 1963. Obituaries are in the *New York Times*, Mar. 12, 1966; and *Blood-Horse*, Mar. 19, 1966.]

RALPH KIRSHNER

FLANAGAN, HALLIE (Aug. 27, 1890–July 23, 1969), playwright and national director of the Federal Theatre Project (FTP), was born Hallie Mae Ferguson in Redfield, S.Dak., the daughter of Frederic Ferguson, a businessman, and Louisa Fischer. She received a B.S. in 1911 from Grinnell College in Iowa. She married John Murray Flanagan on Dec. 25, 1912; they had two children. Upon her husband's death in 1919, Flanagan returned to Grinnell College as an instructor of English. While there she wrote an award-winning play, *The Curtain*, which became her ticket of admission to George Pierce Baker's 47 Workshop at Harvard. During 1923–1924 Flanagan served as production assistant to Baker and took a master's degree at Radcliffe. The following year she resumed teaching at her alma mater as an associate professor of drama and founder of the college's experimental theater. On the strength of a production there of *Romeo and Juliet*, as well as a year of work as director of Vassar College's experimental theater, she became one of the first women to win a Guggenheim Foundation Fellowship. Flanagan spent a year visiting European theaters and described her travels in *Shifting Scenes of the Modern European Theatre* (1928). The book particularly celebrated Soviet efforts, which confirmed Flanagan's view of theater as a vital social force.

Between 1925 and 1942 Flanagan directed Vassar College's experimental theater, staging 100 plays, an experience later chronicled in *Dynamo* (1943). Like Aristophanes, she assumed that theater possessed the ability "to stir up life and infuse it with power." She therefore employed the plays of Chekhov, Pirandello, and Wilder for experiments in form, with Euripides and Shakespeare interpreted in terms of the present. Animated, too, by the desire to introduce students to the latest techniques of the European avant-garde, she brought the works of T. S. Eliot, Ernst Toller, and Alexander Afinogenov to the college stage.

Flanagan could not remain oblivious to the initial ravages of the Great Depression, especially given her conviction that the effectiveness of democracy, like that of education, depended upon popular action to better society. A 1931 story by Whittaker Chambers in the *New Masses* led her and a former Vassar teaching assistant, Margaret Clifford, to write the theater piece *Can You Hear Their Voices?* By using official statistics, newspaper accounts, film slides, loudspeakers, and blackouts, the two women captured the grim plight of tenant farmers in a drought-stricken South. This agit-prop vehicle, like those applauded by Flanagan on a second trip to the Soviet Union, in 1930, found later resonance in the call, projected in her play *Breed Power*, for government control of machines on behalf of the public.

The New Dealer Harry Hopkins first invited Flanagan to "spend money" on a contemplated program for unemployed actors in early 1934. But Flanagan, recently married to her Vassar colleague Philip Haldane Davis, was leaving to establish an experimental theater at England's Dartington Hall and to study productions on the Continent. The trip bore additional fruit when she met T. S. Eliot, who had seen the premiere at Vassar of his *Sweeney Agonistes*. The poet promised her a play about Thomas à Becket, which later became *Murder in the Cathedral*, the first major success of the FTP. Flanagan also heard from Eliot about Auden's *Dance of Death* and saw a production of Marlowe's *Dr. Faustus*, both of which she would later champion. Hopkins did not forget his fellow Grinnell graduate. Having made the then-revolutionary decision that actors' skills were as worthy of conservation as those of millions of other destitute Americans, the head of Franklin Roosevelt's Works Progress Administration ultimately prevailed, securing Flanagan's leave from Vassar and appointment in May 1935 as national director of the newly established FTP.

With this short, feisty redhead at its helm, the FTP achieved considerable success. At a gross cost of $46 million, some 10,000 people on the project's rolls supported an average of 4 dependents at $20 a week for four years. Actors, dancers, directors, scene designers, electricians, and seamstresses regained faith in themselves, and before long, 2,600 project employees returned to private industry. In all, 63,728 performances were given to over 30 million spectators, a vast new audience that had paid less than $2 million in low-price admissions.

Flanagan encouraged almost any form of creative activity and especially pressed for dramatizing the nation's social conscience. Plays ranged from the Orson Welles–John Houseman production of a *Macbeth* in a Haitian setting to a *Swing Mikado;* from Marc Blitzstein's *The Cradle Will Rock* to the simultaneous appearance in twenty-one cities of Sinclair Lewis' *It Can't Happen Here.* The project's "Living Newspaper," a novel compound of montage, native journalism, radio technique, commedia dell'arte, and factual drama, pilloried intolerance, poverty, and disease in the memorable *One Third of a Nation, Power,* and *Spirochete.* The FTP helped to make Eugene O'Neill and George Bernard Shaw, among others, household names. And, at its best, the project's support for American dramatists of the past and present inspired a federation of many theaters catering to different regions, much as Flanagan had advocated when helping found the National Theatre Conference in 1932.

The dynamic experiment faced numerous difficulties. Created foremost as a relief project, the FTP battled bureaucracy, uneven artistry, and local censorship. Conservative critics attacked its alleged boondoggling and the candid Living Newspapers. In hearings on Capitol Hill, one irate congressman made headlines by asking Flanagan if Christopher Marlowe was a Communist. His like-minded colleagues, identifying the FTP with everything they detested in the New Deal, closed the project down in June 1939.

Flanagan never relinquished her faith that an enduring democracy needed the arts, "one of the great mediums of understanding" and, hence, of increased public participation. Back at Vassar and again widowed, she continued to create a theater of ideas while writing a sprightly project memoir, *Arena* (1940), and *Dynamo.* In 1942 Flanagan became dean of Smith College and, in 1946, professor of drama, a position she held until her retirement in 1955. During her tenure at Smith she used the Living Newspaper technique in the play $E=mc^2$ to warn about atomic energy's potential for both good and evil.

Flanagan's efforts and her consistent crusade in diverse periodicals and other forums for a national theater brought honorary degrees from Williams College (1941) and Grinnell College (1956), as well as one of the first annual Brandeis University Creative Arts Awards (1957). In 1968 she received the first annual citation of the National Theatre Conference for "distinguished service" to the American theater. Tragically, neither of her two children lived to see her receive this special honor. She died in Old Tappan, N.J.

[Flanagan's papers are in the Billy Rose Theatre Collection at the New York Public Library at Lincoln Center. See Jane De Hart Mathews, *The Federal Theatre, 1935–1939* (1967). An obituary is in the *New York Times,* July 24, 1969.]

MONTY N. PENKOWER

FLANDERS, RALPH EDWARD (Sept. 28, 1880–Feb. 19, 1970), mechanical engineer and United States senator, was born in Barnet, Vt., the son of Albert Wellington Flanders, a farmer and woodworker, and Mary Lizzie Gilfillan. His family moved to Rhode Island, where he attended Pawtucket High School and in 1896 received a diploma from Central Falls High School.

The following year he became an indentured apprentice in Browne and Sharpe's machine-tool factory, where over a three-year period he secured a grounding in mechanical engineering. After being transferred to the drafting room, he studied mechanical drawing at night school and mechanical engineering by correspondence. He began contributing articles to machine-shop journals, and this led to his employment in New York City from 1905 to 1910 as associate editor of *Machinery.*

He returned to Vermont in order to resume his career as a mechanical engineer. On Nov. 1, 1911, he married Helen E. Hartness, daughter of the president of the Jones and Lamson Machine Company in Springfield, Vt. They had three children. Soon after his marriage Flanders became manager of Jones and Lamson, and later its president. As an engineer, a business executive, and the author of articles on public affairs, by the 1930's he had gained national recognition.

In 1933 Flanders was appointed to the Business Advisory and Planning Council. He soon became a critic of New Deal policies and in 1940 ran unsuccessfully for the United States Senate as a Republican. During World War II he served on the War Production Board, and from 1944 to 1946 he was president of the Federal Reserve Bank of Boston.

In 1946 Flanders was elected to the Senate. As he later wrote in his autobiography, his actions in the Senate were based on a faith in an economy that looked to "production of more, not redistribution of limited wealth"; in education that looked to self-discipline and competition instead of "enjoyment of life" and "togetherness"; in moral or natural law instead of pragmatism; and in a world order based on mutual self-interest instead of individual national interest.

Flanders served on such important Senate committees as Banking and Currency, Finance, Joint Economy, and Armed Services, as well as the powerful Armed Services Appropriations Subcommittee. He voted to override President Harry S Truman's veto of the Taft-Hartley bill, and to enact the Taft-Ellender-Wagner housing bill and the civil rights bill of 1957.

In foreign affairs he held a qualified international outlook. He supported the bold initiatives of the Truman Doctrine, the Marshall Plan, and peacetime conscription. Favoring extension of the Monroe Doctrine to Western Europe and doubtful as to military commitments, he voted against the NATO Treaty. During the Eisenhower administration he supported the Eisenhower Doctrine and the Atoms for Peace Treaty. He voted in favor of the Bricker amendment that sought to limit presidential power to negotiate treaties and executive agreements.

Flanders was reelected to the Senate in 1952 by an overwhelming majority. He made an enduring contribution to the nation in this second term. Republican Senator Joseph McCarthy of Wisconsin had created a climate of fear in America with his reckless charges of Communist penetration of the government and the army. President Dwight D. Eisenhower and prominent Republican leaders failed to rebuke him. Believing that no threat of internal Communist subversion existed, and deeply disturbed by McCarthy's disreputable conduct, Flanders introduced a resolution to censure McCarthy. It was referred to a special committee headed by Senator Arthur V. Watkins.

Senate debate on the resolution began July 30, 1954. Speaking in a calm voice, unperturbed by the tension in the chamber, Flanders urged the Senate to pass his resolution. He was immediately followed by Republican colleagues; Senator Guy Cordon argued for "orderly procedure," and Senator Everett Dirksen savagely attacked the resolution as a contrivance of Communists and left-wingers. When Flanders indignantly rose to reply, Majority Leader William T. Knowland moved for a recess. Upon adjournment it appeared that Flanders was a lonely complainer doomed to defeat.

That the opposite occurred was a result of several factors: televised hearings of the army-McCarthy inquiry, which exposed McCarthy's true character; the support of the National Committee for an Effective Congress; the careful procedures of the Watkins committee; and the November elections, which gave the Democrats control of the next Congress. On December 2, acting on the unanimous recommendation of the Watkins committee, the Senate voted 67–22 to condemn McCarthy's conduct. During the months since he had introduced his first resolution, Flanders had been virtually ostracized by his colleagues; in the debate on the Watkins committee report he had been bitterly assailed. Now he became a hero, earning praise from politicians and the press. The politics of fear had ended. More than any other person Flanders had effected salutary results, restoring the Senate as an institution of repute and responsibility and dissipating hysteria.

In 1958 he chose not to run for a third term. He devoted his remaining years to writing his autobiography, *Senator from Vermont* (1961), and to raising bacon pigs, saying Vermont had too many pigs raised for their lard. Flanders died in Springfield, Vt.

[The Flanders papers are in the Syracuse University Library, which has published a register. Additional manuscript material is in the Vermont Historical Society. Flanders wrote "The New Age and the New Man," in Charles A. Beard, ed., *Toward Civilization* (1930); "Limitations and Possibilities of Economic Planning," *Annals of the American Academy of Political and Social Science*, July 1932; "Business Looks at the NRA," *Atlantic Monthly*, Nov. 1933; *Platform for America* (1936); *Toward Full Employment* (1938); *The American Century* (1950); and *Letter to a Generation* (1956). Ben Pearse, "The Case of the Unexpected Senator," *Saturday Evening Post*, July 31, 1954, is based on an interview during the McCarthy crisis. See also the obituaries in the *Boston Herald Traveler* and the *New York Times*, both Feb. 20, 1970.]

JAMES A. RAWLEY

FLY, JAMES LAWRENCE (Feb. 22, 1898–Jan. 6, 1966), lawyer and government administrator, was born in Seagoville, Dallas County, Tex., the son of Joseph Lawrence Fly, a farmer, and Jane Ard. After graduation from high school in Dallas in 1916, he entered the United

States Naval Academy and graduated in 1920. He served with the Pacific Fleet until 1923, when he resigned from the navy, and on June 12 of that year he married Mildred Marvin Jones; they had two children. He entered the Harvard Law School in 1923 and graduated with an LL.B. in 1926.

Fly then entered private law practice and was associated with the firm of White and Case of New York City from 1926 to 1929. In the latter year, he was appointed a special assistant to the United States attorney general, and during the next five years in this position he represented the federal government in several court cases involving questions of restraint of trade under federal antitrust laws and regulatory measures affecting interstate commerce. When private utility companies began a systematic attack on the constitutionality of the power program of the Tennessee Valley Authority (TVA) in 1934, Fly was selected by David Lilienthal, a TVA director, to be general solicitor and head of the TVA legal department. After 1937 his title was general counsel.

Fly, like Lilienthal, had studied under Felix Frankfurter at Harvard; as the TVA's chief legal officer, he recruited for his staff a number of Frankfurter students. Under Lilienthal's general direction, he conducted legal work in two major constitutional challenges to TVA's power program, beginning in September 1934. The first of these arose when George Ashwander and thirteen other shareholders filed suit to nullify a contract for the sale of electric energy from a TVA-owned dam to nearby Alabama cities. The suit raised the issue of whether a federal agency constitutionally could sell energy (as property) to public as well as private purchasers. Fly and his staff won the suit in appeals to a United States circuit court and the Supreme Court, which ruled that the energy sale was constitutional.

In the second challenge, begun in May 1936, the Tennessee Electric Power and other companies, including five controlled by Wendell Willkie, charged coercion, fraud, malice, and conspiracy in TVA's power operations. These charges, representing a broader challenge to TVA authority than in the Ashwander case, were fought by Fly and rejected by a panel of three federal judges, a newly required body in constitutional cases under a provision of the Judiciary Act of 1937, which Fly had helped to draft. The charges were rejected also by the Supreme Court. By 1939, Fly's legal work had helped greatly to establish firmly the constitutionality of the TVA's power program.

Fly's demonstrated legal talent in the TVA cases came to the attention of President Franklin D. Roosevelt, who in 1939 appointed him chairman of the Federal Communications Commission (FCC). This agency, created to regulate interstate and foreign communication by wire or radio, had been ineffectual since its establishment in 1934. Under Fly's direction, it conducted a strong regulatory program. The chairman initiated public hearings to obtain information for establishing federal regulation of radio networks to foster broadcast competition; he continued the hearings for several months, in spite of protests from the broadcast industry and members of Congress, who opposed stricter regulations. As a result of the hearings, the FCC discovered a broadcasting monopoly and ordered the National Broadcasting Company (NBC), a subsidiary of the Radio Corporation of America, to divest itself of one of its networks. The order was contested by NBC in an appeal to the Supreme Court, which in 1943 upheld the order and gave the FCC broad power to regulate individual licensed broadcasting companies. Accordingly, NBC sold its Blue Network, which became the American Broadcasting Company.

As chairman of the FCC, Fly also proposed prohibiting the operation of more than one broadcast station in any service area by a single interest or group of interests, and insisted that station programming should reflect the licensee's concern for the public interest. He conducted hearings that led to the adoption of engineering standards governing commercial and experimental television stations, the allocation of the first channels to frequency modulation (FM) broadcasting, and the approval of the merger of the Postal Telegraph and Western Union companies, which resulted in stabilization of the telegraph industry and lower rates for users. Despite frequent criticism of Fly by some broadcast executives and congressmen, he was widely credited with greatly improving FCC regulatory efficiency and commended for his administrative competence and industry.

In 1940, Fly's responsibilities were increased with his appointment, concurrently with his FCC duties, as chairman of the Defense Communications Board, renamed the Board of War Communications in 1942. In this position, he directed efforts to establish and coordinate priorities for use of communication facilities essential to national defense. He resigned from the board and the FCC in 1944 with notable recognition, if not praise, for his important accomplishments in defending and promoting the mission of two controversial New Deal agencies, the TVA and the FCC.

After 1944, Fly lived in Florida, where he established a law firm and became an executive in citrus-processing and television companies. He married Phyllis Beckman on Dec. 19, 1950. As a private lawyer, he was a frequent critic of wiretapping by the Federal Bureau of Investigation and was an active member of a national committee of the American Civil Liberties Union. He died at Daytona Beach, Fla.

[Fly's work as a government attorney and administrator is documented in the records of the Department of Justice and the FCC in the National Archives, Washington, D.C., and in records of the TVA at the Federal Records Center, East Point, Ga. His role in cases challenging the constitutionality of the TVA power program is described in Thomas K. McCraw, *TVA and the Power Fight, 1933–1939* (1971), and as chairman of the FCC in Erik Barnouw, *History of Broadcasting in the United States*, II (1968), and Henry F. Pringle, "Controversial Mr. Fly," *Saturday Evening Post*, July 22, 1944. An obituary is in the *New York Times*, Jan. 7, 1966.]

HAROLD T. PINKETT

FORBES, ESTHER (June 28, 1891–Aug. 12, 1967), novelist and historian, was born in Westborough, Mass., the daughter of William Trowbridge Forbes, a judge, and Harriette Merrifield, a historian who wrote *Gravestones of Early New England and the Men Who Made Them* (1927). Esther Forbes grew up in a household in Worcester, Mass., that encouraged both her fascination with the past and her interest in writing. As a child she enjoyed hearing New England legends, poring over old books, family papers, and issues of *Godey's Lady Book* in the family attic, and making up stories. When she was nine years old she joined her brothers and sisters in producing a small magazine that they called *Chronapax* and printed on a hand press their mother had given them for Christmas. During her teenage years Forbes wrote several historical novels with settings in Renaissance Europe and ancient Troy; these unpublished works reveal a precocious mind caught up in romantic melodrama.

Forbes graduated from Bradford Academy in Haverhill, Mass., in 1912. From 1916 to 1918 she took writing courses at the University of Wisconsin. But Forbes did not devote her energies to formal education; she was the only one of five Forbes children who did not complete college and go on to graduate school. From December 1919 until mid-1926 Forbes worked on the editorial staff of Houghton Mifflin in Boston. She said that her most important accomplishment there was the discovery of Rafael Sabatini, whose historical romances were extremely popular in the 1920's. Nevertheless, it is likely that the editorial experience she gained helped Forbes develop her craft.

Forbes's first important success was "Breakneck Hill," a short story that won an O. Henry Award in 1920. Her first novel, *O Genteel Lady* (1926), garnered critical acclaim and sold well. Set in Boston in the mid-nineteenth century, it centered on a young woman struggling to reconcile her literary aspirations with her sexual passions and the social conventions of the era. Forbes married Albert Learned Hoskins, a lawyer, in January 1926. They resided in New York City and then Boston until 1933, when they were divorced. Forbes returned to Worcester, where she lived in her family home with her mother, a brother, and a sister.

Forbes added to her critical reputation with *A Mirror for Witches* (1928), which many consider to be her finest work of fiction. In this remarkable fusion of the historical novel and psychological realism, Forbes told the story of a tormented girl in seventeenth-century Salem, Mass., from the point of view of an apologist for the Salem witchcraft trials. By adopting the style of the great Puritan diarists, Forbes gained sufficient distance to write skillfully and subtly about emotional deprivation and the perversion of sexual desire in a repressive society. *Miss Marvel* (1935), which traced the life of a spinster who retreats into a world of fantasy and imaginary lovers, further illustrated Forbes's concern with imaginative women who allow their lives to be wasted. Forbes was less successful in the long, panoramic novel *Paradise* (1937), which focused on a colonial Massachusetts community during the time of King Philip's war. *The General's Lady* (1938) was a less substantial work set during the final years of the American Revolution.

Forbes intended to write a novel about a man who remained neutral during the Revolution, but the Nazi invasion of Poland and the Japanese bombing of Pearl Harbor radically changed her views and her plans. World War II led Forbes to explore the nature of freedom and warfare. The result was *Paul Revere and the World He Lived In* (1942), a biography that reflected her extraordinary ability to capture the details of everyday life. Her mother collaborated on the extensively researched book, which won a Pulitzer Prize for history. Forbes also used a Revolutionary War setting for *Johnny Tremain: A Novel for Young and Old* (1943). This story of a silversmith's apprentice, who adjusts to both the personal dilemma of a maimed hand and the political turmoil of revolutionary Boston, won the Newbery Medal in 1944 and has become a classic of American children's literature.

Forbes's later books were well received, but they are not among her most interesting works. *America's Paul Revere* (1948) recast her earlier biography for children. *The Running of the Tide* (1948) focused on a Salem family in the early nineteenth century, and *Rainbow on the Road* (1954) paid tribute to American folk art by describing the experiences of an itinerant limner. In 1960 Forbes became the first woman member of the American Antiquarian Society. At the time of her death in Worcester, she was at work on a history of witchcraft in New England.

Forbes earned the respect of historians and reviewers, who praised her lively re-creation of the past, her meticulous treatment of historical detail, and her skillful delineation of character. Forbes preferred life in Worcester with her family and dogs to the literary circles of large cities, but she was a serious artist whose best work added new dimensions to the historical novel. *A Mirror for Witches* and *Johnny Tremain* seem likely to endure.

[The Forbes papers (unpublished works and correspondence) are in the Goddard Library, Clark University, Worcester, Mass. Her uncompleted study of witchcraft is in the American Antiquarian Society, Worcester, Mass. The Houghton Library, Harvard University, has her correspondence with editors. Forbes wrote "Why the Past?" in Dale Warren, ed., *What Is a Book?* (1935); "The Newbery Medal Acceptance," *Horn Book*, July–Aug. 1944; and "The Historical Novel," in Herschell Brickell, ed., *Writers on Writing* (1947). See Margaret Erskine, *Esther Forbes* (1976). Obituaries are in the *Proceedings of the American Antiquarian Society*, Oct. 18, 1967; and the *New York Times*, Aug. 13, 1967.]

ALFRED BENDIXEN

FORESTER, CECIL SCOTT (Aug. 27, 1899–Apr. 2, 1966), biographer and historical novelist, was born Cecil Lewis Troughton Smith in Cairo, Egypt, the son of George Smith, a British official in the Egyptian Ministry of Education, and Sarah Troughton. He attended Dulwich College from 1915 to 1918 and studied medicine at Guy's Hospital in London from 1918 to 1921. However, he left medical school after failing a crucial examination, declared his intention to become a professional writer, and assumed the name Cecil Scott Forester.

During his literary apprenticeship, Forester wrote several potboilers and hack biographies of such figures as Napoleon, the empress Josephine, Victor Emmanuel of Italy, Louis XIV of France, and Admiral Nelson. Most of these works he later repudiated. After his thriller *Payment Deferred* (1926) was dramatized in stage and screen versions featuring Charles Laughton, he contracted to write screenplays and moved to Southern California. As he said later, "I don't believe I ever went hungry again." His work in motion pictures "provided the money that set me free to do what I wanted." Over the years, he worked on films such as *Born for Glory* (1935), *Eagle Squadron* (1942), and *Captain Horatio Hornblower* (1951), all based on his original stories. Forester resided in California at least nine months a year for the remainder of his life, though he never became an American citizen.

In the 1930's, Forester found his métier as a historical novelist. During this decade, he wrote *The Gun* (1933), a story of the Peninsular War, in which the British fought against Napoleon in Spain, and *The African Queen* (1935), a novel set in central Africa early in World War I; in 1951, the latter work was adapted to film with Humphrey Bogart and Katharine Hepburn in the leading roles. Forester followed these successes with *The General* (1936), a novel about the foibles of the British high command during World War I. This work enjoyed unusual critical celebrity: Adolf Hitler presented copies in German translation and bound in vellum to Nazi leaders for Christmas in 1938. Forester also worked briefly as a foreign correspondent on the eve of World War II, covering the Spanish Civil War in 1936–1937 and the German occupation of Czechoslovakia in 1939 for the *Times* of London.

The approach of world war also supplied Forester with the inspiration for the Hornblower Saga, the series of seafaring novels for which he is best remembered. His initial trilogy about the intrepid Captain (later Commodore, Admiral, and Lord) Horatio Hornblower—*Beat to Quarters* (1937), *A Ship of the Line* (1938), and *Flying Colours* (1938)—celebrate English naval heroism during the Napoleonic Wars. Forester received the James Tait Black Memorial Prize for the second volume in the trilogy. By his own testimony, Forester was fascinated by the possibilities for historical fiction of the "man alone," the strong-willed and humane leader prone to decisive action. He said later that the fictional Hornblower "was one of my closest friends." The next two novels in the series, *The Commodore* (American title *Commodore Hornblower*, 1945) and *Lord Hornblower* (1946), first appeared serially during the waning months of World War II and were thinly disguised Allied propaganda. As his biographer, Sanford Sternlicht, notes, "Forester used Napoleon as a surrogate Hitler. Both men had been archenemies of England, both had conquered almost all of Continental Europe, both had been kept at bay by the British Navy." After suffering a bout of arteriosclerosis in 1943 and a heart attack in 1948 that left him a semi-invalid until his death, Forester credited the character of Hornblower with saving him from "the life of a cabbage in a wheelchair."

In all, Forester wrote twelve Hornblower books, including a fragment that appeared posthumously under the title *Hornblower and the Crisis* (1967). Sales totaled over 8 million copies in Great Britain and the United States. The books were also translated into nearly fifty languages. Though a popular hero, Hornblower was no mere stereotype. He fretted before battle, suffered from seasickness, and once while intoxicated committed adultery with a Russian countess (and as a result contracted typhus from a flea). As Francis X. Connolly of *Commonweal* explained in 1946, Hornblower was "essentially a sensitive, uncertain, and complicated figure," a modern hero set against "a romantic background," whose "observations on the age of Napoleon" were delivered "in the accent of twentieth-century liberalism."

Though his reputation largely rests on the Hornblower Saga, Forester wrote a total of forty-two books and experimented with a variety of literary forms. In *The Captain from Connecticut* (1941) he invented an intrepid American privateer in the Hornblower mold. While employed by the British Ministry of Information during World War II, he wrote his best-selling novel *The Ship* (1943), the fictionalized account of a single day aboard a British cruiser on duty in the Mediterranean. His novel *The Sky and the Forest* (1948), devoted to the African slave trade in the mid-nineteenth century, is an allegory of human greed. *Randall and the River of Time* (1950) is a novel of ideas, a study of the role of chance and contingency in human affairs set in the London of Forester's own adolescence. *The Good Shepherd* (1955) is a type of cold-war social commentary on the virtues of duty and sacrifice, exemplified in this case by the Allied commander of a North Atlantic convoy in 1943. Forester also wrote popular histories of naval engagements: *The Age of Fighting Sail* (1956), set during the War of 1812, and *Hunting the Bismarck* (1959), about the Allied search for the mainstay of the German fleet in May 1941.

Forester sought above all to tell an entertaining story, and he harbored few pretensions about the artistic quality of his work. "I have had a remarkably happy life—I doubt if anyone could have had a happier [one] during the twentieth century," Forester once told an interviewer. He married Katherine Belcher in 1926; they had two children before their divorce in 1944. Forester married Dorothy Ellen Foster in 1947. He died in Fullerton, Calif.

[Hornblower novels not mentioned in the text are *Mr. Midshipman Hornblower* (1950); *Lieutenant Hornblower* (1952); *Hornblower and the Atropos* (1953); *Admiral Hornblower in the West Indies* (1958); and *Hornblower and the Hotspur* (1962). Forester also compiled *The Hornblower Companion* (1964), a collection of charts and a personal memoir about the novels. See Forester's autobiography of his first thirty-one years, *Long Before Forty* (1968); and Sanford Sternlicht, *C. S. Forester* (1981). See also *Saturday Review of Literature*, Feb. 9, 1935; *Commonweal*, Nov. 22, 1946; *New York Times Book Review*, Apr. 6, 1952, Mar. 27, 1955, and Apr. 3, 1955; and *Newsweek*, Sept. 1, 1958. An obituary is in the *New York Times*, Apr. 3, 1966.]

GARY SCHARNHORST

FOSDICK, HARRY EMERSON (May 24, 1878–Oct. 5, 1969), author, preacher, and churchman, was born in Buffalo, N.Y., the son of Frank Sheldon Fosdick, a secondary-school teacher and administrator, and Amie Inez Weaver. His brother Raymond enjoyed a distinguished career as a civilian military aid during World War I and then as president of the Rockefeller Foundation.

Fosdick matured in an undogmatic evangelical Baptist household that relished the life of the spirit and of the mind. While his parents were devout, the family freely discussed the heterodox novels and challenges of the Victorian era. An excellent student and orator, Fosdick attended local schools before entering the then-Baptist Colgate University in Hamilton, N.Y., in 1895. He dropped out in 1896 in order to help his family through his father's brief psychological collapse. He returned to Colgate the next year, and graduated with a B.A. in 1900. By this time, Fosdick had resolved his considerable religious doubt, and he opted for the ministry. To that end, he enrolled at Hamilton Theological Seminary to study with the evangelical liberal William Newton Clarke.

While the liberal theological modifications of Clarke and the evolutionist theologian John Fiske made belief possible for Fosdick, he nonetheless sought still wider opinion and experience. After a year at Hamilton, he transferred to Union Theological Seminary in New York City, which was then in the vanguard of progressive theological thought. At the end of the fall semester, however, Fosdick suffered a severe mental breakdown, resulting either from a congenital psychic fragility (his mother suffered from acute depression) or from the enormous pressure he placed upon himself. After four months in a psychiatric hospital and a tour of Europe, he regained his stability. He returned to Union and graduated with a B.D. in 1904. He married Florence Allen Whitney on Aug. 16, 1904. They had three children.

Fosdick's first pastorate was at the First Baptist Church of Montclair, N.J. He left this post in 1915 to assume a professorship at Union Seminary, where he had taught part-time since 1908. His homiletic gifts quickly won a large audience, especially at universities (he was awarded his first honorary doctorate in 1912). These sermons and lectures earned him a national reputation because he adapted them into articles in major periodicals and in six best-selling books. The works all reflected Fosdick's interest in consequential belief and apologetics. In each he took care always to argue for the pertinence and reasonableness of Christian faith. *The Second Mile* (1908), *The Assurance of Immortality* (1913), and *The Manhood of the Master* (1913) sought to encourage fortitude in faith and conduct amid the innumerable stresses of modern life. *The Meaning of Prayer* (1915), *The Meaning of Faith* (1917), and *The Meaning of Service* (1920) explored the intellectual feasibility and practical benefit of Christian devotion. While all were widely read, the book on faith initiated Fosdick's fame as a religious liberal and controversialist.

Questions about Fosdick's orthodoxy occasioned a national debate during his tenure as preaching minister at the First Presbyterian Church in New York City. In order to occupy this important pulpit, Fosdick in 1918 reduced his teaching load at Union Seminary. His status as a Baptist in the employ of a Presbyterian church did not become an issue until conservatives in the denomination tried to oust him for heresy. Investigative committees were formed, and the issue twice went to the national General Assembly, with the opposition led by William Jennings Bryan. The denomination finally agreed that Fosdick could retain the First Presbyterian pulpit if he became a Presbyterian and ascribed to the orthodox Westminster Confession. Fosdick's lifelong refusal to assent to any creed—which applied as well to the Apostles' Creed—dictated that he resign, which he did in 1925.

With Fosdick refusing Presbyterian membership, his admirers among Baptists in New York City, led by John D. Rockefeller, Jr., quickly moved to procure his services for the Park Avenue Baptist Church. The congregation, again led by Rockefeller, promised to erect a new interdenominational sanctuary to accommodate the thousands who came to hear Fosdick preach each Sunday. The result was the erection of Riverside Church in Morningside Heights. The church was dedicated in 1931, and Fosdick remained there until his retirement in 1946.

The zenith of Fosdick's career coincided with the massive realignment of American Protestantism in the aftermath of the new science of evolution and biblical higher criticism. In the 1920's virtually every mainline American denomination was rent by acrimonious disputes over these new perspectives. While conservatives dug in their heels, with some forming the new fundamentalist movement, liberals pleaded for tolerance and harmony. The fates of ministers and churches hung on the outcome of official intradenominational debates. Clearly liberal in his opinions, Fosdick in 1922 challenged conservatives with the sermon "Shall the Fundamentalists Win?" He argued for tolerance for those who doubted the Virgin birth, biblical inerrancy, bodily resurrection, and a Second Coming. He understood these historic doctrines to be no longer credible. He argued that if the church were to prosper and remain evangelical, it must strip historic Christianity to its essential theological and experiential core—the love of God and the possibility of spiritual and ethical help and renewal. These realities, clearly manifest in the Bible and especially in Jesus, were obscured by the reactionary doctrinalism of fundamentalists. In the modern age, theological reaction deterred countless seekers from serious consideration of Christianity.

While Fosdick never retreated from his theological liberalism, in the mid-1930's he criticized religious modernism. In a sermon in 1935, "Beyond Modernism," he accused himself and others of excessive intellectualism, naive cultural optimism, implicit humanism, and moral accommodation. World War I and the clear approach of Nazi and Soviet tyranny revealed the persistence of sin and guilt and the fragility of the reigning progressive optimism. Necessary and cogent in its day, modernism needed to take on sobriety and moral rigor if it were to sustain its appeal. So repulsed was Fosdick by the evils of militarism that during World War II he became one of America's foremost proponents of pacifism.

Fosdick was endowed with an ardent and articulate preaching style. In 1922 he began a radio ministry that culminated in the nationally broadcast "National Vespers," which ran for decades. He published nearly forty books, including such best-sellers as *Adventurous Religion* (1926), *On Being a Real Person* (1943), and his autobiography, *The Living of These Days* (1956), which takes its title from his hymn "God of Grace and God of Glory" (1931). Fosdick poured enormous energy into his sermons and publications. While not an original thinker, he was a major intellectual, moral, and spiritual leader. His concern always was to show how the Gospel met the real challenges of his national audience. In his last years Fosdick's activities were curtailed by severe arthritis. He died in Bronxville, N.Y.

[Important collections of Fosdick's papers and secondary materials are at Union Theological Seminary, Riverside Church, and the First Presbyterian Church in New York City. Works by Fosdick include *The Modern Use of the Bible* (1925) and *The Man from Nazareth* (1949). A collection of his sermons is in Paul H. Sherry, ed., *The Riverside Preachers* (1978). The only lengthy treatment of Fosdick is Robert M. Miller, *Harry Emerson Fosdick* (1985). For periodical literature on Fosdick see Miller. An obituary is in the *New York Times*, Oct. 6, 1969.]

ROY M. ANKER

FOULOIS, BENJAMIN DELAHAUF (Dec. 9, 1879–Apr. 25, 1967), army officer and aviator, was born in Washington, Conn., the son of Henry Foulois, a plumber, and Sarah Augusta Williams. After eleven years in public schools, he became an apprentice in his father's shop. With the outbreak of the Spanish-American War, he ran away from home and, using his older brother's birth certificate, enlisted in the First United States Volunteer Engineers in July 1898. Foulois enjoyed military life. Discharged as a sergeant in January 1899, he joined the regular army the following June. His combat leadership during campaigns in the Philippines led to a field commission as second lieutenant of infantry in February 1901.

In 1908, while attending the Signal Corps School at Fort Leavenworth, Kans., Foulois became interested in aeronautics and wrote a graduation thesis entitled "The Tactical and Strategical Value of Dirigible Balloons and Aerodynamical Flying Machines." Ordered to Washington, D.C., for aviation duty, he gained practical experience as the pilot of the army's first dirigible balloon. His initial flight, Foulois recalled, "sent a surge of joy through my whole body that defied description." This marked the beginning of a lifetime commitment to aviation.

A member of the Aeronautical Board that evaluated the first airplane accepted by the army, Foulois concluded that the future lay with airplanes rather than with balloons. In January 1910, with less than one hour of instruction, he was given command of *Military Aeroplane No. 1* and ordered to San Antonio, Tex. He was the only army officer on flying status for the next fourteen months, and he learned to operate the Wright biplane by trial and error and through correspondence with the Wright brothers.

Foulois served two years of compulsory ground duty and then returned to aviation and organized the army's first tactical air unit. Between March and August 1916 he commanded the First Aero Squadron in operations in Mexico, where his airmen flew reconnaissance and liaison missions for General John J. Pershing during the fruitless pursuit of Pancho Villa.

Foulois was assigned to Washington, D.C., in March 1917, shortly before the United States entered World War I. Over the next six months, he was responsible for drawing up and implementing plans for the rapid expansion of the air arm. Foulois considered this work—which laid the foundation for the postwar Air Service—his most significant contribution to military aviation.

In November 1917, Foulois went to France as a temporary brigadier general to serve as chief of the air arm of the American Expeditionary Force. He immediately clashed with Colonel William ("Billy") Mitchell, who had been in charge of American aviation in France since April 1917 and who viewed Foulois as an interloper. The dispute between the two aviators finally led Pershing in May 1918 to appoint Mason M. Patrick, a nonflyer, as chief of the air arm. Foulois became Patrick's deputy, while Mitchell took charge of combat operations.

Both Foulois and Mitchell emerged from the war as air-power enthusiasts; however, Foulois tried to work through regular army channels, whereas Mitchell became the master of flamboyant gestures. "I have no quarrel about Mitchell's championing the need for air power before the American public," Foulois pointed out. "It was his methods and lack of judgment about what he said that I deplored."

Foulois served in Europe from 1920 to 1924, chiefly as assistant military attaché in Berlin. His marriage to Ella Van Horn ended in divorce in 1921, and he married Elisabeth Shepperd-Grant on Apr. 28, 1923. There were no children by either marriage.

Foulois commanded Mitchel Field, N.Y., from 1925 to 1927 and was then promoted to assistant chief of the Air Corps. In 1931 he gained public recognition during the annual Air Corps maneuvers when he led a provisional air division of 670 aircraft in a test of mobility. The exercise proved a perfect forum for his talents. As John F. Shiner has noted, "A 'doer' rather than a great thinker, he performed best when dealing with the real and tangible." He won the National Aeronautic Association's Mackay Trophy for his successful handling of the largest air exercise ever attempted in the United States.

Appointed chief of the Air Corps (the first pilot to hold the position) and promoted to major general in December 1931, Foulois assumed command at a time of rapid change in air doctrine, organization, and equipment. Supporting the idea that strategic bombing could achieve decisive results in a war, he consolidated all tactical units into an offensive striking force and, despite severe budgetary limitations, pushed for development of long-range bombers. By 1935 he had won approval for a strategic role for air power and had introduced into service the powerful B-17.

Foulois came under criticism in 1934 when the Air Corps attempted to fly the mail after President Franklin D. Roosevelt canceled the Post Office's contracts with commercial airlines. Foulois had assured Roosevelt that the Air Corps could do the job, but a number of fatal accidents raised serious questions about its ability to operate in bad weather. Although Foulois later claimed that the episode had a positive result in that it led to increased appropriations, he was not so sanguine at the time.

Foulois also faced a congressional committee that accused him of violating the law by favoring negotiated contracts over competitive bidding in aircraft procurement. He argued that he had followed established—and sensible—procedures. An inquiry by the inspector general cleared him of legal improprieties but acknowledged that he had made misleading statements to the committee. Foulois left his position at the end of 1935 with a bitterness that did not abate with time.

The "little general," as he was known because of his slight stature (he was five feet, five inches tall), lived quietly in retirement. In 1961, following his wife's death, he moved to the visiting officers' quarters at Andrews Air Force Base in Maryland. He enjoyed his role as "last of the first" and spoke frequently on the early history of aviation and on air power. He died at Andrews Air Force Base.

[The Library of Congress houses the major collection of Foulois papers, but significant items can also be found at the United States Air Force Historical Research Center, Maxwell Air Force Base, Ala., and in the library of the United States Air Force Academy, Colo. His autobiography, written with the assistance of C. V. Glines, is *From the Wright Brothers to the Astronauts* (1968). The best scholarly account of his career is John F. Shiner, *Foulois and the U.S. Army Air Corps, 1931–1935* (1983).]

WILLIAM M. LEARY

FOXX, JAMES EMORY (Oct. 22, 1907–July 21, 1967), baseball player, was born near Sudlersville, Md., the son of Samuel Dell Foxx, a farmer, and Mattie Smith. Called Jimmy from infancy, Foxx tended to farm chores and engaged in hunting and fishing. At the high school in Sudlersville, Foxx excelled in athletics. When he was fourteen, he finished first in the 220-yard and high-jump competitions at the state track and field championships in Baltimore and was voted the outstanding athlete at the meet. He also played baseball for his high school and for local semiprofessional teams.

Soon word of Foxx's ball-playing reached John Franklin ("Home Run") Baker, formerly an outstanding player in the American League, who now managed Easton in the Eastern Shore League. In 1924, Foxx signed his first professional contract, to play for Baker's team.

Foxx appeared in seventy-six games for Easton, batting close to .300 with ten home runs. After the season Baker sold Foxx's contract to Connie Mack, and in 1925 Foxx went into spring training with the Philadelphia Athletics. Mack kept Foxx for a good portion of the season before optioning him to Providence in the strong International League. There he appeared mainly as a pinch hitter and substitute catcher, but hit well enough to earn another trial with the big-league team. In 1926 and 1927, as Mack carefully rebuilt the once powerful Athletics, Foxx spent most of his time on the bench. In 1928 he became a regular player, alternating at catcher, first base, and third base and hitting for an average of .328, with thirteen home runs. That year he married Helen Heite; they had four children.

Foxx reached stardom in 1929, when the Athletics won the first of three straight American League pennants and two straight World Series. In 1929–1930 the Athletics, featuring, besides Foxx, such future Baseball Hall of Fame players as pitcher Bob ("Lefty") Grove, catcher Gordon ("Mickey") Cochrane, and outfielder Al Simmons, were one of the finest baseball teams. Foxx hit .354, .335, and .291 in those pennant-winning years and in 1930 batted in 156 runs. His best all-around season was 1932, when the Athletics yielded the pennant to Babe Ruth, Lou Gehrig, and the New York Yankees. Foxx hit .364, drove home 169 runs, and came within two of tying Ruth's all-time season home run record of 60. Foxx had become a highly capable fielder as well. Dividing his playing time between first and third base, he made only eleven errors in a full 154-game season. The Baseball Writers Association voted Foxx the American League's Most Valuable Player for 1932 and again for 1933, when he topped the league in batting average, runs scored, home runs, and runs batted in.

The Great Depression brought dwindling crowds and shrinking revenues throughout baseball. The Philadelphia American and National League franchises, handicapped until 1933 by Pennsylvania laws prohibiting baseball on Sundays, were especially hard hit. Mack felt that he had no choice but to unload the high salaries of his star players. Foxx was the last to go. Late in 1935 Mack traded him to the Boston Red Sox for $150,000 and two nondescript players.

Foxx was with Boston for the next seven-and-a-half seasons. Although the Yankees dominated the American League nearly all of that time, the presence of Foxx, as well as Grove and subsequently Ted Williams, made the long downtrodden Red Sox one of the circuit's consistently strong teams. Foxx's hitting continued to be prodigious. From 1936 through 1941 he averaged nearly thirty-eight home runs and 130 runs batted in per season and had a combined batting average of .322. In 1938, after hitting fifty homers and driving in 175 runs (nine short of the league record that Gehrig had established seven years earlier), Foxx received his third Most Valuable Player trophy.

Foxx had started in professional baseball at a trim 175 pounds, with exceptionally big biceps and forearms. Over the years he indulged his appetite for steaks and beer, so that by the time he was thirty he weighed 225 pounds during the season and considerably more in the off-season. Excess weight was one reason for the rapid decline of his abilities in the early 1940's. Struggling at bat and afield, Foxx was waived out of the American League in May 1942 and released to the National League Chicago Cubs. Discouraged, he stayed out of baseball in 1943, only to return the next year as the Cubs, like all the other teams, sought to replace players lost to military service in World War II. Foxx made only one hit in twenty times at bat, became a nonplaying coach, and then left to finish out the season as manager of the Portsmouth, Va., minor league team. In 1945 he tried one more time, with Philadelphia's National League team, before retiring.

Like other players who reached their prime in the 1930's, Foxx was a victim of the financial stringency of the Great Depression. Although Boston owner Thomas A. Yawkey paid him as much as $32,500 toward the end of the 1930's, Foxx never got the money commanded by baseball greats in the 1920's; easygoing and amenable, Foxx never held out for a better contract. In the postwar years Foxx struggled to support his family without great success. He moved to St. Petersburg, Fla., where he had become co-owner of two golf courses. But World War II, imposing restrictions on travel and gasoline, ruined his prospects. Eventually he sold all his properties and options.

Foxx did some radio commentary on minor-league games, drove a gasoline truck, and worked for a Miami fishing-equipment manufacturer. He was always an easy mark for barroom acquaintances. Following the death of his wife in the late 1950's, Foxx went to Phoenix, Ariz., and then to Galesburg, Ill. (for an ill-fated restaurant venture), before returning to Florida. He died in Miami, after choking on a fishbone.

Until 1966 when Willie Mays surpassed his record, Foxx's 534 career home runs were the most ever hit by a right-handed batter and the most by any player except Babe Ruth. Foxx's lifetime batting average was .325, and at the time of his death he ranked fourth among the all-time leaders for runs batted in. Foxx was named to the Baseball Hall of Fame in 1951, six years after he stopped playing.

[See James Foxx, "When I Was a Boy," *St. Nicholas*, Nov. 1935; and *Sporting News*, Feb. 23, 1933. Impressions of Foxx by contemporaries are in Donald Honig, *Baseball* (1975). Foxx's career records are in Paul MacFarlane, ed., *Daguerreotypes of Great Stars of Baseball* (1981). See also the obituary notices, *New York Times*, July 22, 1967; and *Sporting News*, Aug. 5, 1967.]

CHARLES C. ALEXANDER

FRANCIS, KAY (Jan. 13, 1905–Aug. 26, 1968), actress, was born Katherine Edwina Gibbs in Oklahoma City, Okla., the daughter of Joseph Sprague Gibbs, a businessman, and Katherine Clinton Franks, an actress. Upon completion of a private-school and convent education, she worked for brief periods as a stenographer and as a real-estate agent. Her first marriage, in 1922, to Dwight Francis, a member of a prominent Massachusetts family, soon ended in divorce, but she continued to use Francis' name throughout her career. Subsequent marriages to William Gaston, a lawyer, in 1926, and to Kenneth MacKenna, a Broadway actor, in 1931, also ended in divorce. Court records mention another husband, John Meehan, but his name appears in no other records. She had no children.

In 1927 Francis started her acting career on Broadway in *Crime*, followed by *Venus*. The next year she appeared in *Elmer the Great* opposite Walter Huston, who arranged her 1929 movie debut in Paramount's *Gentlemen of the Press*. In 1931, at the urging of talent scout Myron Selznick, she transferred to the Warner Brothers studio, where, although often on loan to other studios, she remained for most of her acting career. She appeared in a total of sixty-eight films, sometimes making as many as seven a year.

In her first movies Francis frequently was teamed with William Powell. Two of their best films were *Jewel Robbery* (1932) and *One-Way Passage*, which won the Academy Award for the best story of 1932–1933. Then, on loan to other studios, she starred in two more successful pictures, *Trouble in Paradise* and *Cynara*, both released in 1932. After these movies Francis' career flourished; throughout the 1930's she was one of Hollywood's most popular and highest-paid actresses, a star in the grand tradition. The press, to whom she was not always polite, zealously reported all of her activities. Her name frequently appeared in "ten best" compilations, including the list of best-dressed women and, along with Katharine Hepburn and Helen Hayes, a list of the brainiest women in motion pictures.

Ignoring her ability as a comedienne, revealed in the early scenes of *Living on Velvet* (1935), Warner Brothers generally cast Francis with George Brent, Powell's successor as her leading man, in movies that emphasized her ultrasophistication and her flair for modeling chic styles. A tall, slender woman with lustrous dark hair, expressive brown eyes, and stately carriage, she epitomized tasteful elegance. Her image was flawed only by a lisp that caused her *r*'s to sound like *w*'s, a problem that apparently did not detract from her appeal.

Francis' movies were mostly society dramas of the soap-opera variety, often designated "women's movies," with shallow plots and contrived happy endings. In several of these films Francis, immaculately groomed and self-assured, portrayed successful professional women: a famous fashion designer in *Street of Women* (1932); an obstetrician in *Mary Stevens, M.D.* (1933); and a physician in *Dr. Monica* (1934). In others, like *The Keyhole* (1934), which carried the provocative advertisement, "Don't come if you're afraid to see what's on the other side of the keyhole," and *The Goose and the Gander* (1935), Francis and the equally urbane Brent became involved in intricate romantic tangles that somehow managed to unravel, with the heroine remaining composed and elegant. In two of her most popular films, *The House on 56th Street* (1933) and *Give Me Your Heart* (1936), billed as "the picture every woman [would] want some man to see," Francis portrayed sensitive women who endured the agonies of lost romance and frustrated mother love.

Although repetitious and sentimental, her films nonetheless won unfailing audience approval. The Francis movies, which accorded with the motion-picture magnates' goal of conveying positive themes and images, provided a welcome escape from the oppressive atmosphere of the Great Depression. Indeed, audiences and critics alike rejected her 1936 venture into realistic drama in *The White Angel*, a somber biography of Florence Nightingale.

Francis presumably did not object to being stereotyped. However, she did object when in 1937 Warner Brothers gave the lead in *Tovarich*, a role she had expected, to Claudette Colbert, and also gave several other choice roles to Bette Davis, the studio's newest star. When Francis threatened to leave at the expiration of her contract, under the terms of which she earned $227,000 a year, Warner Brothers officials retaliated by casting her in six mediocre films.

During the next few years, Francis enjoyed a few more successes. Her friend Carole Lombard secured her a role in the RKO production *In Name Only* (1939). She was featured in *Charley's Aunt* (1941), with Jack Benny, for Twentieth Century–Fox, and she played opposite her longtime friend Walter Huston in *Always in My Heart* (1942), for Warner Brothers. She also costarred again with George Brent in a Lux Radio Theatre production of "The Lady Is Willing." The severing of her association with Warner Brothers, however, began the decline of her career. Until her death she expressed bitterness over the action of the studio officials.

From 1944 to 1946, in an effort to revive her career, Francis coproduced and starred in three movies at Monogram. These melodramas, *Divorce* (1945), *Allotment Wives* (1945), and *Wife Wanted* (1946), provided an ironic conclusion to her once-sparkling career. In 1946 she returned to Broadway as a replacement for Ruth Hussey in *State of the Union*, the Howard Lindsay–Russel Crouse Pulitzer Prize–winning play. Then, after recovering from an overdose of sleeping pills taken while on tour in Ohio, she made a few more public appearances on television and in summer stock productions, including *The Last of Mrs. Cheney* in 1948 and, in 1952, the final one, *Theatre*.

For the remainder of her life Francis lived in semiseclusion in a New York City apartment. The bulk of her estate of more than $1 million went to the training of guide dogs for the blind.

[See Daniel Blum, *A New Pictorial History of the Talkies* (1968); Marjorie Rosen, *Popcorn Venus* (1973); James Robert Parish, *Hollywood's Great Love Teams* (1974); Lawrence J. Quirk, *The Great Romantic Films* (1974); George Eels, *Loretta, Ginger, and Irene Who?* (1976); and Karyn Kay and Gerald Peary, *Women and the Cinema* (1977). See also the obituary, in the *New York Times*, Aug. 27, 1968; and *ibid.*, Dec. 17, 1968.]

DOROTHY KISH

FRANK, LAWRENCE KELSO (Dec. 6, 1890–Sept. 23, 1968), social scientist and author, was born in Cincinnati, Ohio, the son of August A. Frank, a prosperous retail grocer, and Grace Kelso. He received a B.A. in economics from Columbia in 1912 and first worked as a systems analyst for the New York Telephone Company. During World War I he worked for the War Industries Board in Washington, D.C.

In 1923, Frank made a fateful shift to foundation work, a change that had significance not only for his own career but for the emerging field of the behavioral sciences. He was first associated with the Laura Spelman Rockefeller Memorial (1923–1930). Later he became a member of the Laura Spelman Rockefeller Fund (1930–1931); the General Education Board (1931–1936); the Josiah Macy, Jr., Foundation (1936–1942); and the Caroline Zachry Institute of Human Development (1945–1950).

Frank's primary interest during these years was in the field of human development, with special emphasis on infancy and adolescence. He was a prolific writer whose work ranged from chatty and informal columns on child-rearing and family relationships, to erudite and provocative essays for professional journals and abstract theoretical discussions of human development, the interaction of culture and personality, methodology, and testing techniques. His style was as varied as his subject matter. Thus, his works include *Babies Are Puppies, Puppies Are Babies* (1953); *How to Be a Woman* (1954), coauthored with his wife Mary; and such substantial works as *Nature and Human Nature* (1951) and *Feelings and Emotions* (1954).

In 1947, Frank shared the Lasker Award with Catherine MacKenzie of the *New York Times* for his contribution to popular adult education in mental health, especially parent-child relations. In 1950 he received the *Parents Magazine* Award for his article "How to Help Your Child in School," written with his wife Mary.

Frank became a professional generalist, with interests encompassing psychology, sociology, anthropology, culture, and politics. He was interested as well in the assessment of intelligence and personality and in new tools (such as the Rorschach test) that were evolving to achieve this. He was one of the first to discuss projective testing and was a pioneer in the interdisciplinary approach to personality studies and a valued collaborator with many of the liveliest minds of his day in the social sciences. He not only was privy to the new thinking in many fields but was a catalyst in their interaction. His role of intellectual guru was enhanced by his creativity as a powerful foundation director with an ability to channel funds into the various projects he believed in. As Margaret Mead put it, "He used foundations in the way the Lord meant them to be used." Certainly he expanded and enriched the role of the foundation both in research and in the implementation of new ideas in social theory. He subsidized research and writing projects, child-study groups, and experimental nursery schools as well.

The line between Frank's professional and personal life was vague. His country house, Coventry, on Squam Lake in New Hampshire, became the center of the lively and productive Holderness intellectual community, among whose members were the sociologists Helen and Robert Lynd; the psychologists Ruth Munroe, John Levy, Lois and Gardiner Murphy, and Dorothy Fisher; the anthropologists Margaret Mead and Gregory Bateson; the psychoanalyst Peter Blos; and the educator Harold Taylor. He was also involved in the work of Ruth Benedict, Caroline Zachry, Lloyd Warner, and John Dollard. He converted friends into colleagues and colleagues into friends. His house in Greenwich Village in New York City was a center for shoptalk and an informal commune in which Margaret Mead and her daughter, who was often left in the care of the Franks, lived for many years.

On Apr. 14, 1917, Frank married Alice Bryant; they had three children. She died in 1928, and on Jan. 5, 1929, he married Dorothea Dairs; they had two children. His second wife died in 1934, and on Jan. 27, 1939, he married Mary Hughes, his collaborator on many articles and books; they had two children. In 1955, Frank retired from the Caroline Zachry Institute and moved to Melmont, Mass. He lectured at the Massachusetts Institute of Technology and continued to write until his death.

Ironically, Frank is remembered less for his prolific output than for his stimulating, critical and widely acknowledged effect on his peers. He is spoken of fondly as a "generative man" and often quoted. If it is an overstatement to say, as Margaret Mead put it, that "he invented the behavioral sciences," certainly he left his thumbprint on effective foundation work in those areas.

[Frank's papers are at the National Medical Library in Washington, D.C. Among his notable writings not mentioned above is *Society as the Patient* (1948). See also Jane Howard, *Margaret Mead: A Life* (1984); and Catherine Bateson, *Through a Daughter's Eyes* (1985). An obituary is in the *New York Times*, Sept. 24, 1968.]

EDNA ALBERS LERNER

FRANK, PHILIPP G. (Mar. 20, 1884–July 21, 1966), mathematician, physicist, philosopher of science, and educator, was born in Vienna, Austria, the son of Hans Frank, a chemist, and Marta Hoffman. Frank began his studies at the University of Vienna in 1901, expecting to pursue a career in experimental psychology and physiology, but decided that he could not progress in these fields without a solid grounding in physics and mathematics. While studying physics, he came under the influence of Ludwig Boltzmann, the successor of Ernst Mach as professor of physics at the University of Vienna. Frank decided to change his major to theoretical physics. In 1906, in order to learn about new developments in physics and mathematics, he visited the University of Göttingen, where David Hilbert and Felix Klein interested him in the problems of the logical reconstruction of experimental science.

Frank received a Ph.D. under Boltzmann in 1906. From that time on he was a productive theoretical physicist, publishing numerous articles in the new field of special relativity as well as in the more traditional areas of classical mathematical physics, such as variational calculus, the principle of least action, the theory of small vibrations, and geometrical optics. His major interest became the interrelationship between science and philosophy. "I used to associate with a group of students who assembled every Thursday night in one of the old Viennese coffee houses," he later recalled. "We stayed until midnight and even later, discussing problems of science and philosophy. Our interest was spread over many fields, but we returned again and again to our central problem: How can we avoid the traditional ambiguity and obscurity of philosophy? How can we bring about the closest possible rapprochement between philosophy and science?" Other participants in these discussions were Hans Hahn, the mathematician, and Otto Neurath, the economist. The issues they raised and the interdisciplinary approach they used typified Frank's work.

Frank and his colleagues perceived a decline in the belief that classical (mechanistic) science provided a valid means of interpreting the events of the physical and social sciences; they felt that this was partly the result of a misunderstanding of the true nature of science and scientific explanation, and partly an unwillingness on the part of traditional philosophers to take full account of recent developments in science, particularly relativity and quantum theory. Building on the works of Abel Rey, Ernst Mach, Henri Poincaré, Pierre Duhem, David Hilbert, Albert Einstein, and others, they concluded that the main factor keeping science and philosophy apart was that both had become encumbered with metaphysical concepts that had once served well as models for organizing phenomena, but had now become ossified into dogma, preventing the creation of new concepts appropriate to new discoveries.

Frank suggested that the very concept of causality, at the heart of both science and philosophy, was one such outmoded convention; causality, he said, was merely a construct of the human mind, used in habitually associating one event or group of events with another. His thoughts on causality, particularly as it applied to quantum mechanics, were published in a 1907 paper that was later enlarged into an influential book, *Das Kausalgesetz und seine Grenzen* (1932).

Frank and his colleagues felt that the most effective way to reunite science and philosophy, and to prevent their estrangment in the future, was to base the fundamental ideas of science and philosophy on the sensory experience of observation and experiment in as direct a way as possible. They also suggested making extensive use of logical, and especially mathematical, tools in extending the concepts that had been invented to represent the "facts" and events of observation. For this reason they were referred to as logical positivists or logical empiricists. Although their movement was not favorably viewed by most German philosophers, men such as Moritz Schlick, Friedrich Waismann, Edgar Zilsel, Béla von Juhos, Felix Kaufmann, Herbert Feigl, Victor Kraft, Karl Menger, Kurt Gödel, and Rudolf Carnap joined them; by the late 1920's their group became widely known as the Vienna Circle.

Frank's formal academic career began in 1910 when he was appointed privatdocent (lecturer) in theoretical physics at the University of Vienna. In 1912 he was appointed *ausserordentlicher* (associate) professor of physics at the German University of Prague, succeeding Einstein, who had recommended Frank partly on the basis of the correspondence that had arisen between them over Frank's paper on causality, as well as on Frank's impressive record as a theoretical physicist. Frank was promoted to *ordentlicher* (full) professor at Prague in 1917, where he remained until 1938.

As director of the Institute of Theoretical Physics, Frank maintained close ties with both the Institute of Experimental Physics and the Institute of Mathematics. On Nov. 16, 1920, Frank married Anna Avramovna. They had no children.

Frank's publications during this period reflect his wide-ranging interests in relativity, quantum mechanics, statistical mechanics, and celestial mechanics, as well as the associated philosophical issues. Perhaps his most influential contribution to theoretical physics while at Prague was his revision and expansion, with Richard von Mises of the University of Bonn, of Riemann and Weber's monumental study, *Die Differential- und Integralgleichungen der Mechanik und Physik* (1925–1927), a standard text for generations of European physics students.

In the fall of 1938 Frank embarked on a lecture tour of twenty American colleges and universities, during which he set forth his ideas of logical empiricism and the unity of science. By the end of the tour in December 1938 Hitler had annexed the Sudeten region of Czechoslovakia. Frank, who had survived and had helped others to survive the troubles of World War I and its tense aftermath, decided to stay in the United States. In 1939 he obtained a position at Harvard University, where he remained under a variety of appointments until his retirement in 1954.

Frank's interest and activity in the philosophy of science continued during his years in the United States. In 1947 he helped found and then served from 1948 to 1965 as first president of the Institute for the Unity of Science; he served as editor of *Synthèse* from 1946 to 1963, and as associate editor of the *Journal of Unified Science* from 1939 to 1940 and of *Philosophy of Science* from 1941 to 1955. In addition to his numerous books and articles on the philosophy of science, he wrote *Einstein: His Life and Times* (1947), a biography authorized by Einstein. Frank helped establish the Boston Colloquium for the Philosophy of Science, and contributed regularly to Harvard's general education program by offering a course for both science and nonscience students. Frank's book *Philosophy of Science* (1957) is a cogent summary of this course, expressing clearly his overall views on science and philosophy, and his vision of a philosophy of science capable of encompassing the physical and biological as well as the scientific aspects of human behavior.

[Frank's papers are in the Pusey Library, Harvard University. A complete bibliography (through 1963) of his works is in Robert S. Cohen and Mark W. Wartofsky, eds., *Boston Studies in the Philosophy of Science*, II (1965). A tape of an interview of Frank by T. S. Kuhn for the *Sources for History of Quantum Physics* (1967) is at the Library of the American Philosophical Society, Philadelphia. Sixteen of Frank's papers and his historical summary of his philosophical development and the activities of the Vienna Circle are in his *Between Physics and Philosophy* (1941), enlarged as *Modern Science and Its Philosophy* (1949). An extension of his views on science and philosophy to religious and spiritual concerns is his *Relativity* (1950). See the introduction to Frank's "Théorie de la Connaissance et Physique Moderne," *Actualités Scientifiques et Industrielles*, 1934; and "In Memory of Philipp Frank," *Philosophy of Science*, Mar. 1968. Obituaries are in the *New York Times*, July 23, 1966; and *Physics Today*, Sept. 1966.]

RICHARD K. GEHRENBECK

FRANK, WALDO DAVID (Aug. 25, 1889–Jan. 9, 1967), writer, was born in Long Branch, N.J., the son of Julius J. Frank, a lawyer, and Helene Rosenberg. He grew up in the family brownstone on Manhattan's West Side in an atmosphere of upper-middle-class comfort and cultivation. After attending the De Witt Clinton High School in New York from 1902 to 1906, he spent a year at a preparatory school in Lausanne, Switzerland. In 1907 he entered Yale University, where he won a number of literary prizes. He received concurrent B.A. and M.A. degrees in 1911. He worked briefly as a ranch hand in Montana and Wyoming and as a reporter for several New York newspapers. He then spent nearly a year in Paris reading Spinoza, Nietzsche, and Freud, absorbing recent avant-garde movements in the arts, and befriending important European writers and artists. He returned to New York in 1914 and launched his career as an experimental writer and radical cultural critic of the American scene. On Dec. 20, 1916, Frank married Margaret Naumberg, the founder of the Walden School; they had one child.

In 1916, Frank joined James Oppenheim in founding *The Seven Arts* and served as an editor, along with Van Wyck Brooks and Randolph Bourne, of the short-lived but influential new journal. Because of its stand against America's entry into World War I, the journal folded under government pressure in 1917. Frank registered as a pacifist in 1917, the year of his first published novel, *The Unwelcome Man*, a psychological study of an "outsider" patterned on his own life. After a cross-country tour, he wrote *Our America* (1919), in which he examined the seemingly contradictory decay and vitality of American life. In the same year, he worked as an organizer for the Nonpartisan League in Kansas, establishing a lifelong pattern of activism coupled with prolific writing.

Frank reached the peak of his reputation and influence in the 1920's and 1930's. After a trip through the South in 1920 with the black writer Jean Toomer, he wrote *The Dark Mother* (1920), *Rahab* (1922), *City Block* (1922), and *Holiday* (1923), works that explored themes of American race relations, urban alienation, prostitution, and the quest for faith. In these novels he extended his narrative experiments toward a greater concern with the psychology of the self, with Freudian analysis, and with a concept of wholeness and harmony with the cosmos that verges on mysticism. A regular contributor to the *New Yorker*, the *New Republic*, and the *New Masses*, he published several collections of essays and proclamations, including *Salvos* (1924), *Time Exposures* (1926), and *In the American Jungle* (1937).

In 1923, Frank inspired a book-length study by Gorham Munson, who praised him as a visionary prophet and "America's most significant novelist." Six years later, Frank published what many consider his major critique of American culture, *The Re-discovery of America*, which had appeared serially in the *New Republic* in 1927–1928. During these years, his friends included writers, artists, and thinkers such as Alfred Stieglitz, Lewis Mumford, Paul Rosenfeld, Leo Ornstein, Hart Crane, and Reinhold Niebuhr.

In 1926, the year of Frank's divorce from Margaret Naumberg, *Virgin Spain* appeared, the first of a number of books interpreting the history and culture of Spanish-speaking countries. In March of the following year, he married Alma Magoon; they had two children. In 1929, he traveled and lectured throughout South and Latin America. He maintained his remarkable reputation in Hispanic America, where he traveled often and widely, until his death. In the next two decades he published *The Death and Birth of David Markand* (1934), a novel about a disaffected businessman in search of faith; *The Bridegroom Cometh* (1938); *Summer Never Ends* (1941); *Island in the Atlantic* (1946), a historical novel about New York City; *The Invaders* (1948); and books of cultural and political interpretation, such as *America Hispana* (1931), *Dawn in Russia* (1932), *Chart for Rough Waters* (1940), *South American Journey* (1943), and *The Jew in Our Day* (1944).

In 1932, Frank joined Edmund Wilson and fifty other writers and artists in endorsing the Communist party presidential candidate. Calling himself "a philosophical social revolutionary," Frank supported a number of radical political causes during the Great Depression. As chairman of a committee of writers investigating conditions in Harlan County, Ky., in 1932, he was jailed and beaten by vigilantes; he also led a protest against the assault on the bonus marchers in Washington, addressed the American Writers' Congress in 1935, and the next year traveled widely in support of Earl Browder, the Communist party candidate for president. In the late 1930's, he was also associated with the Group Theatre in New York, and in 1937 he visited Mexico as the guest of the government. Frank divorced Alma Magoon in 1943 and that August married Jean Klempner; they had two children.

Frank lectured throughout the United States in 1947, and in 1951 published a study of Simón Bolívar, *Birth of a World*. He was elected to the National Institute of Arts and Letters in 1952 but encountered increasing hostility for his political views. He published *Bridgehead* (1957), a book of impressions of Israel, and *The Rediscovery of Man* (1958), which presented his argument for a "deep revolution" in man's relation to himself, others, and the cosmos. In 1960 he chaired the Fair Play for Cuba Committee and the next year wrote *Cuba: Prophetic Island*.

A prolific, wide-ranging writer whose interests reflect the experiences of twentieth-century American intellectuals, Frank was neglected and isolated in the last decades of his life. Once at the center of a vital American movement, he was virtually forgotten at his death. In his *Memoirs* (1973) he expressed a deep sense of failure, particularly because his fiction never won the recognition he believed it deserved. He died in White Plains, N.Y.

[Frank's papers are in the Rare Book and Manuscript Collection of the University of Pennsylvania. *Memoirs of Waldo Frank* (1973) was edited by Alan Trachtenberg, with an introduction by Lewis

Mumford. See M. J. Benardete, ed., *Waldo Frank in America Hispana* (1930); Claire Sacks, *The Seven Arts Critics* (1955); William Bittner, *The Novels of Waldo Frank* (1958); Frederick Hoffman, *Freudianism and the Literary Mind* (1959); Henry May, *The End of American Innocence* (1959); Daniel Aaron, *Writers on the Left* (1961); Jerome W. Kloucek, *Waldo Frank* (1958); and Paul J. Carter, *Waldo Frank* (1967). An obituary is in the *New York Times*, Jan. 10, 1967.]

ALAN TRACHTENBERG

FRARY, FRANCIS COWLES (July 9, 1884–Feb. 4, 1970), chemical engineer, was born in Minneapolis, Minn., the son of Francis Lee Frary, a merchant, and Jeanette Cowles. Frary worked in his father's store while attending Lyndale Public School and Central High School in Minneapolis, graduating in 1901. He later said that his career as a research scientist began in this period, when he "caught the bug" after using a homemade battery to electroplate a key.

Frary attended the University of Minnesota, where he conducted research, worked as an instructor, and received an A.C. in 1905, an M.S. in 1906, and a Ph.D. in 1912, all in chemistry. In 1906–1907 he studied in Berlin. On June 12, 1908, he married Alice Hall Wingate; they had two children.

While at Minnesota, Frary gained a reputation for the breadth of his interests and an impressive capacity for work. Pursuing a childhood interest in photography, he developed and offered a course in photochemistry. Drawn to glassblowing through his acquaintance with broken chemical beakers, he learned the art well enough to teach it and write a manual. Tall and athletic, he was, in the words of his colleague James G. Vail, a memorable figure, "racing down the stairs with a long gangling lope from the attic storeroom, his arms full of dusty, broken condensers, distilling flasks, and whatnots—all of which he would carefully repair for further use."

Frary's career as an academic researcher reflected his commitment to work of practical significance. He developed and patented five age-hardened lead alloys, one of which was marketed by the National Lead Company under the name Frary Metal. He also devised a safe process for making phosphorous sesquisulfide, the substance used to make matches ignite. In 1915, Frary was offered a position with the Oldbury Electrochemical Company, the sole American producer of phosphorous sesquisulfide, as director of its new research laboratory. "Much as I enjoyed teaching," he later wrote, "the opportunity to give all attention to research, with adequate facilities, was too good to pass by."

In 1917, Frary's experience at Oldbury and his work with alloys helped him to win a job setting up and directing a research organization for the Aluminum Company of America (Alcoa). Frary was hired at an attractive salary and with the assurance that his work would be "of an original nature," independent of short-range operational concerns. Before he could assume his new position, he was drafted into the army. During World War I he organized and managed production of toxic chemicals. The laboratory that he established at Edgewood Arsenal in Maryland was a model research facility. When he was discharged from the service in 1919, Frary brought five members of his Edgewood staff with him to Alcoa to form the core of the new research organization.

At the beginning of his long Alcoa career, Frary was only one—and not the most powerful or prominent—of several figures in the company's technical community. Moreover, for a decade his organization, called the Research Bureau, was housed in cramped conditions in a building on the grounds of Alcoa's New Kensington, Pa., fabricating plant. Branch laboratories operated under his direction at three other production sites, each focusing on research problems related to the processes and products of its plant. As a result, Frary's job required extensive travel.

Nevertheless, Frary was granted independence in shaping his organization and its program, and he jealously guarded that independence throughout his career. To direct the various divisions of the Research Bureau, he selected people trained for, and committed to, basic research and allowed them considerable freedom to work on problems of scientific importance. He encouraged his staff to publish their findings and to be active in scientific and technical societies. Under his leadership, researchers established aluminum metallurgy on a firm scientific foundation, from which Alcoa was able to make radical improvements in its process technology and pioneer in broad application of "the wonder metal." In 1928 the company's research and development functions were restructured into a single, centralized organization under Frary and renamed Aluminum Research Laboratories (ARL). The following year, ARL moved into a new building in New Kensington, equipped with the most up-to-date research technology.

Frary's own research was mainly on primary processes. Some of his most important work, patented in 1925–1926, related to development of an electrolytic process for refining aluminum to a purity of more than 99.9 percent. Eliminating the complicating influence of trace impurities, this advance made it possible to obtain basic information about the characteristics and properties of aluminum and its alloys. In 1930, Frary coauthored *The Aluminum Industry*, the standard text for almost forty years. He was active in numerous professional societies and was president of the Electrochemical Society (1929–1930) and the Institute of Chemical Engineers (1941). He also received many awards, most notably the prestigious Perkin Medal of the joint British and American Society of Chemical Industries (1946). With the $1,000 prize from the Electrochemical Society's Acheson Medal, he established an education fund to provide tuition loans to ARL staff members.

Frary retired as director of research on Dec. 31, 1951, but he remained with Alcoa as a technical adviser until 1954 and as a consulting engineer until 1967. In the latter position, he served primarily as a translator of technical literature. During his career he had learned German, French, Italian, and the Scandinavian languages, and at the age of seventy-five he returned to college to study Russian, in order to keep up with the growing body of Soviet research. He died in Oakmont, Pa.

[Manuscript sources on Frary and his career are at Alcoa Archives, Alcoa Building, Pittsburgh, Pa.; and Alcoa Laboratories Archives, Alcoa Center, Pa. Frary published extensively in chemical and metallurgical journals. Several articles by and about him appear in *Industrial and Engineering Chemistry*, Feb. 1946. An obituary is in the *New York Times*, Feb. 5, 1970.]

BETTYE H. PRUITT

FRIEDLAENDER, WALTER FERDINAND (Mar. 10, 1873–Sept. 6, 1966), art historian and educator, was born in Berlin, Germany. Little is known about his parents or early life. He studied Indology under Wösslin at the University of Berlin, from which he received a Ph.D. in Sanskrit in 1898. His doctoral dissertation was on the *Mahabharata*, an Indian epic poem. During the early 1900's, he became interested in the rapidly developing discipline of art history. From 1907 to 1911 he studied in Rome as a staff member of the Prussian Historical Institute. In 1912 he published a monograph on the Casino of Pope Pius IV. Soon afterward, Friedlaender began what would become his lifelong study of the paintings of the seventeenth-century French artist Nicolas Poussin. From 1912 to 1914, Friedlaender lived in Paris, where he wrote *Nicolas Poussin* (1914), the first of several books on the subject. He then returned to Germany, where he joined the art history faculty of Freiburg University, his academic home from 1914 to 1933.

Friedlaender, inspired by Alois Riegl's sympathetic studies of late Roman art, began to explore Italian mannerism, a sixteenth-century style that art historians, following Bernard Berenson, disparaged as an affected and exaggerated imitation of Michelangelo's generation. In 1914, Friedlaender challenged this assessment in his inaugural address, "The Anticlassical Style," at Freiburg University. He argued that sixteenth-century painting was "not merely a conjunction between Renaissance and Baroque, but an independent age of style, autonomous and most meaningful." Friedlaender subsequently distinguished between an initial phase of mannerism (1520–1550), dominated by the Florentine painters Rosso, Pontormo, and Parmigianino, who rejected the High Renaissance classical norms, and a second period (1550–1600), when Lodovico Carracci, Cigoli, and Caravaggio brought about a return to simplicity, objectivity, and truth to nature. Friedlaender alluded to this phase's return to the foundations of the Renaissance as the "grandfather law," whereby a generation of reformers disregarded the teachings of their parents and adopted instead the norms of their grandparents.

Friedlaender, who also served as acting director of the Freiburg Kunsthistorische Institut, taught and published with prolific regularity. His interests included music, literature, travel, and most especially his students. Though Poussin continued to dominate Friedlaender's studies, he wrote with erudition on Claude Lorrain, Carracci, and Rubens. In 1933, anticipating his upcoming retirement from the university, his students gathered papers for a festschrift for him. Nazi officials banned publication of the essays in honor of a Jewish scholar, dismissed Friedlaender from the Freiburg University faculty—one year short of retirement—and expelled him from Germany. In July 1935, Friedlaender, assisted by a grant from the Committee in Aid to Displaced German Scholars, immigrated to the United States. He was appointed lecturer in art history at the University of Pennsylvania that same month. The following autumn, Friedlaender was appointed to the faculty of New York University. The university's nascent Institute of Fine Arts, then known as the Graduate Center, selected him as a visiting professor along with his fellow émigré Karl Lehmann. The institute's scholars included Henri Focillon, Marcel Aubert, Erwin Panofsky (Friedlaender's former student), Adolph Goldschmidt, and Richard Ettinghausen. Walter Cook, the founder of the institute, commented, "Hitler shakes the trees, and I pick up the apples." Their collective endeavors greatly advanced America's reputation in art history. For his part, Friedlaender established the institute's reputation in baroque art.

Friedlaender defined scholarly fulfillment as "the conquest of provinces." At the age of sixty-three, beset by failing eyesight and hearing, illnesses, financial worries, and displacement from his homeland, he embarked on a second art-history career. He faced these adversities with good-humored stoicism, saying, "I never stick my nose in my own business." Friedlaender's publications continued unabated with major works on Poussin (several in collaboration with Anthony Blunt and Rudolf Wittkower), on Caravaggio, and on David and Delacroix. Students and colleagues recall his professionalism, generosity, and unfailing gregariousness. Though Friedlaender, a naturalized American citizen, was fluent in several languages, his heavy German accent permeated all his spoken words and was gently mocked by students and professors as "Friedlaenderese." Friedlaender's enthusiastic mentorship informed the early studies of the American art historians John Coolidge, Jane Costello, Creighton Gilbert, Robert Goldwater, Frederick Hartt, and Donald Posner.

In 1960, Friedlaender organized a major Poussin exhibit at the Louvre. In 1963 he was honored with an international festschrift. That same year, he was elected honorary senator of the University of Freiburg, and he lectured there while publishing a final volume on Poussin (1966). He completed a monograph on Titian just days before his death in New York City. At the time of his death, Friedlaender was working on a festschrift essay dedicated to a colleague. Friedlaender's contribution to the collection was called "Exemplum Virtutis," a theme that much concerned him.

[Friedlaender's major works include *Claude Lorrain* (1921); *The Drawings of Nicolas Poussin: Catalogue Raisonné*, Parts 1 (1939) and 2 (1949), both in collaboration with Rudolf Wittkower and Anthony Blunt, Part 3 (1953), with Blunt, Ellis K. Waterhouse, and Jane Costello, and Part 4 (1963), with Blunt, John Shearman, and Richard Hughes-Hallett; *David to Delacroix* (1952), translated by Robert Goldwater; *Caravaggio Studies* (1955); and *Mannerism and Anti-Mannerism in Italian Painting* (1957). On his life and work, see Colin Eisler, "Kunstgeschichte American Style: A Study in Migration," in Donald Fleming and Bernard Bailyn, eds., *The Intellectual Migration: Europe and America, 1930–1960* (1969); and Donald Posner, "Walter Friedlaender," *Art Journal*, Spring 1967. An obituary is in the *New York Times*, Sept. 8, 1966.]

SUSAN J. GEORGINI

FRIEDMAN, WILLIAM FREDERICK (Sept. 24, 1891–Nov. 2, 1969), cryptologist, was was born Wolfe Frederic Friedman in Kishinev, Russia, the son of Frederic Friedman, a Romanian Jew in the Russian postal service, and Rosa Trust, daughter of a Moldavian merchant. Two years later the family moved to Pittsburgh, Pa., where his father became a sewing-machine salesman. The Friedmans were naturalized in 1896; and in that year Wolfe was renamed.

After graduating from Pittsburgh's Central High School in 1909, Friedman entered Michigan Agricultural College. After one year he transferred to Cornell University, earning B.S. and M.S. degrees in plant breeding in 1914 and 1915. In Geneva, Ill., from 1915 to 1917 and from 1919 to 1920 he headed the genetics department at the Riverbank Laboratories of the eccentric tycoon George Fabyan; while there he also began research in cryptology.

On May 21, 1917, he married Elizebeth Smith, a cryptanalyst at Riverbank. They had two children. By 1917, because of World War I, various federal offices were calling upon the Friedmans for deciphering; the couple set up a school in cryptology for military personnel at

Riverbank. They also wrote a series of landmark treatises, *Riverbank Publications on Cryptography and Cryptanalysis* (1917–1920). Commissioned as a first lieutenant in the army, Friedman worked on solving German codes and ciphers while at American headquarters in Chaumont, France, from July to November 1918. He was demobilized in April 1919 and returned to Riverbank.

In January 1921 Friedman moved to Washington, D.C., as a civilian cryptologist at Army Signal Corps headquarters. That December he was appointed the War Department's chief cryptanalyst. He was commissioned as a captain in the reserve, gaining promotions to major in 1926, lieutenant colonel in 1936, and colonel in 1940. He rationalized the army's cryptologic program; pioneered research linking cryptology to mathematics and statistics; and made numerous cryptographic inventions in electromechanical enciphering equipment. In addition to many articles, he wrote several books that became standard references, including *Elements of Cryptanalysis* (1926) and *The History of the Use of Codes and Code Language* (1928), which became the army's cryptologic bible when it was published in its expanded four-volume form by World War II. His services were often in demand by other federal agencies, and he became a leader in many international communications activities. Meantime, his wife became a noted cryptanalyst in the Treasury Department, deciphering smugglers' messages.

When the Signal Corps established the Signal Intelligence Service (SIS) in 1930, Friedman was chosen as its chief. A primary function of the unit was "black chamber" work (covert interception and analysis of other governments' messages). In addition to setting up a global network of radio-intercept stations, Friedman's group also developed new codes and ciphers and established the Signal Intelligence School. Friedman proved adept at selecting gifted subordinates, notably Frank Rowlett, Abraham Sinkov, and Solomon Kullback, who would become renowned in cryptology.

SIS began work in 1937 on solving "Purple," the code name given to the new, complex Japanese cipher for top-priority diplomatic messages. In early 1939 Friedman was freed of many administrative chores so that he could lead the team trying to break Purple. By August 1940 Friedman's group had achieved significant progress and had built a mock-up of the Purple machine. Eventually they could read a high proportion of Purple texts. These included messages between Tokyo and Japanese embassies around the world, which provided valuable data for the conduct of the war. Many writers have lauded Friedman's role in breaking Purple, but he himself claimed it was "a collaborative, cooperative effort" at SIS.

Friedman suffered a nervous breakdown in January 1941. He was discharged from the army for health reasons that spring but returned to SIS as director of communications research. (In 1946 he was restored to active duty as a colonel.) During the years from 1941 to 1945 he also worked on breaking other Japanese codes and ciphers and on improving American cipher machines. For his SIS services he received the War Department's Commendation for Exceptional Civilian Service in 1944, and President Harry S Truman bestowed the Medal for Merit on him in 1946. During the same interval, his wife continued her work, setting up and heading the cryptographic section of the Office of Strategic Services.

After World War II Friedman was active in reorganizing cryptologic activities in the American defense establishment, while also serving on Allied intelligence bodies and undertaking special missions to Europe. In the period from 1945 to 1951 he was director of communications research in the Army Security Agency and then consultant to the Armed Forces Security Agency. When the National Security Agency (NSA) was established at Fort Meade, Md., in 1952, he was appointed special assistant to the director.

Upon Friedman's retirement from NSA on Oct. 12, 1955, he was awarded the National Security Medal. Friedman and his wife were also interested in alleged literary ciphers. They coauthored *The Shakespearean Ciphers Examined* (1957), which won several awards. In 1958 they journeyed to Yucatán to study Mayan hieroglyphs. Long subject to severe depression, Friedman was hospitalized in neuropsychiatric units on numerous occasions, especially after 1948. He also suffered two heart attacks in 1955. He died in Washington, D.C. The NSA auditorium at Fort Meade was later named for him.

[Friedman's papers are in the George C. Marshall Library, Lexington, Va. Many remain classified but some of his treatises have appeared in *Signal Corps*

Bulletin and *Philological Quarterly*. The only biography is Ronald Clark, *The Man Who Broke Purple* (1977). See Dulany Terrett, *The Signal Corps* (1956–1966); David Kahn, *The Codebreakers* (1967); Ladislas Farago, *The Broken Seal* (1967); and Ronald Lewin, *The American Magic* (1982). See also the obituary, *New York Times*, Nov. 3, 1969.]

D. CLAYTON JAMES

FUNK, CASIMIR (Feb. 23, 1884–Nov. 20, 1967), biochemist, was born in Warsaw, Poland (then part of Russia), the son of Jacques Funk, a dermatologist, and Gustawa Zysan. As a child, Funk was sent to Germany for treatment of a congenital dislocation of the hip. After some improvement, he returned to Warsaw speaking German and had to relearn Polish.

In 1885, as part of the intense Russification of the "Land of the Vistula" (Poland), all public schools had been placed under control of the state. The education offered was poor, and admittance without the help of someone influential was difficult. In spite of home tutoring, Funk at first failed to gain admittance, but when he did, he did well. But the education proved so unsatisfactory that in 1894 his parents sent him to the gymnasium in Warsaw, from which he graduated in 1900.

Funk then began to study biology under Robert Chodat at the University of Geneva in Switzerland. From 1901 to 1904 he attended the University of Bern, where he studied organic chemistry under Carl Friedheim and Stanislaw Kostanecki, a fellow Pole with whom Funk later published an article on the synthesis of stilbestrols. In July 1904, Funk received his Ph.D. for a thesis on the chemistry of two organic dyes ("Zur Kenntnis des Brasilins und Hämatoxylins") and was accepted for postgraduate work in biochemistry at the Pasteur Institute in Paris. He worked there under Gabriel Bertrand. During his year at the institute, Funk enjoyed Paris life and gained valuable experience working with amino acids and organic bases.

From 1906 to 1907, Funk did unpaid work in Emil Fischer's laboratory at the University of Berlin. Several publications on protein chemistry and protein metabolism resulted from Funk's collaboration with Emil Abderhalden, Fischer's assistant. These endeavors with Abderhalden were continued from 1907 to 1908, when Funk was employed as the biochemist at the Municipal Hospital in Wiesbaden, Germany, earning his first salary. In their experiments, they fed dogs synthetic diets of isolated proteins or amino acids. Contrary to Abderhalden's expectations, the animals on this diet lost weight. When Funk substituted a diet of dried horsemeat and powdered milk, the animals gained weight. Abderhalden believed the weight loss had been caused by Funk's methods rather than diet, and rejected the results of the experiments. Funk returned to Berlin in 1908, again to continue unpaid work with Abderhalden, but relations between the two men remained strained, and Funk transferred to the pediatric clinic at the Charité, the hospital of the University of Berlin.

In 1910, Funk was appointed a scholar in the biochemical department of the Lister Institute of Preventive Medicine in London. His first paper in English, on the synthesis of dihydroxyphenylalanine (DOPA), was published in 1911. The head of the institute, Charles Martin, assigned Funk the problem of the causation of beriberi. In his first article on this subject, "On the Chemical Nature of the Substance which Cures Polyneuritis in Birds Induced by a Diet of Polished Rice" (*Journal of Physiology*, XLIII [1911]), Funk made a solution from an extraction of rice polishings that was free from proteins, phosphorus, and carbohydrates but contained the curative substance. While unable to determine its chemical nature, Funk stated that the curative dose was very small.

In 1912, Funk published a summary of modern investigations on the etiology of diseases caused by a deficiency of essential substances in food. His conclusion was that all such diseases, except pellagra, could be prevented or cured by "the addition of certain preventive substances; the deficient substances, which are of the nature of organic bases, we will call 'vitamines' and we will speak of a beri-beri or scurvy vitamine, which means a substance preventing the special disease." (The term "vitamines" was coined from *vita*, meaning "life," and *amines*, which are chemical compounds containing nitrogen. Later, when it was discovered that amines are not always present, the *e* was dropped.)

The next year, he succeeded in preparing extracts of the substance that prevented beriberi from rice polishings, yeast, milk, and ox brain. The "chemical properties of the curative substance suggested that it was a pyramidine base, forming a constituent of a nucleic acid" (*Journal of Physiology*, XLV [1912–1913]).

As a result of the interest aroused by his publications, Funk received a Beit Fellowship and a D.S. from the University of London. Discontented with the research possibilities of the laboratory at the Lister Institute, in 1913 Funk accepted a position at the London Cancer Hospital Research Institute, where he had an assistant as well as the use of a microanalytic laboratory. His reputation was enhanced with the appearance of *Die Vitamine* (1914), the first monograph on the subject. (It appeared in English in 1922 as *The Vitamins*, translated by H. E. Dubin.) On June 19, 1914, Funk married Alix Denise Schneidesch of Belgium; they had two children.

With the outbreak of World War I, Funk sensed a British distrust of German-speaking foreigners and therefore accepted a position at the Harriman Research Laboratory in New York City. Upon his arrival, he found to his dismay that his laboratory was without equipment or research funds, and the effort to secure funds was such a severe strain that his health suffered. Funk was constrained to accept a full-time industrial position, first with the Calco Company in Bound Brook, N.J. (1916), and then with Metz and Company in New York City (1917–1923). When the war interrupted shipments of Salvarsan and Neosalvarsan from Europe, he was able to supply these needed products. He also worked on the synthesis of adrenaline and held an academic appointment at the College of Physicians and Surgeons at Columbia University from 1918 to 1923.

Funk became a citizen of the United States in 1920, but in 1923 he returned to Warsaw, under the sponsorship of the Rockefeller Foundation, to be the chief of the Department of Biochemistry at the State Institute of Hygiene. One of his accomplishments was the production and distribution of a good-quality insulin. The financial and political crisis in Poland that culminated in the Pilsudski military coup of May 1926 caused Funk to uproot his family again in 1927.

Accepting a part-time position with the pharmaceutical house of Grémy, Funk moved to Paris in 1928. Here, with the help of his family, he established his own private laboratory for the preparation of biochemical products, Casa Biochemica. He also served as a biochemist for the Roussel Company from 1927 to 1936. In 1936 he became a research consultant to the U.S. Vitamin Corporation of New York.

After the German invasion of Poland in September 1939, Funk returned to New York City, where he again worked for the U.S. Vitamin Corporation. In 1947, as a result of the corporation's sponsorship, he became head of the Funk Foundation for Medical Research; he retired in 1963.

His bibliography of more than 140 articles, including works on vitamins, nutrition, gonadotropic hormones, and the biochemistry of cancer, ulcers, and diabetes, is impressive, but none of his later work approached the importance of his accomplishments between 1911 and 1914. His attempts to isolate an antiberiberi substance and his declaration of the "vitamine hypothesis" stimulated worldwide interest in the role of vitamins in health and disease. In *Science* (Apr. 30, 1926), Funk wrote, "As regards my own role in the vitamine field the only claims I can put forward are: (1) the recognition of the existence of several vitamines; (2) the right conception about the importance of vitamines for nutrition; (3) the first chemical study of vitamine B (1911), which unfortunately for the problem has not been improved on yet; (4) general stimulation of researches in this field through expressed ideas, experimental and summarizing work."

[Funk's principal contributions aside from those named in the text are "Synthesis of *dl*-3:4-Dihydroxyphenylalanine," *Journal of the Chemical Society*, XCIX (1911); and "The Etiology of the Deficiency Diseases," *Journal of State Medicine*, July 1912. The biography by Benjamin Harrow, *Casimir Funk: Pioneer in Vitamins and Hormones* (1955), is the best source on Funk's life and publications. See also the biographical sketch by Paul Griminger, *Journal of Nutrition*, CII (1972). An obituary is in the *New York Times*, Nov. 21, 1967.]

RUTH J. MANN

GAMOW, GEORGE (Mar. 4, 1904–Aug. 20, 1968), physicist, was born in Odessa, Russia, the son of Anton Gamow, a teacher of Russian language and literature, and Alexandra Lebedinzev, a teacher of history and geography. Between 1914 and 1920 Gamow attended the Odessa Normal School, where he excelled as a student despite the political disruptions of the period. In 1922 he began to study physics and mathematics at Novorossia University, Odessa, but within a year he transferred to the University of Leningrad. There, experiencing little success in experimental work, he discovered his true métier, theoretical physics. He briefly studied relativistic cosmology under Alexsandr Alexandrovich Friedmann. He and his friends Lev Davidovich Landau and D. Ivanenko also formed a self-study group and mastered the new theory of quantum mechanics that was just then, in 1925–1926, being created by Werner Heisenberg and Erwin Schrödinger. Gamow's first publication in 1926 involved an attempt to extend Schrödinger's theory from four to five dimensions.

In the summer of 1928, the year that he received his Ph.D., Gamow traveled to Göttingen, Germany, to pursue his studies at Max Born's institute. It was there that he made his first major contribution to physics, his theory of radioactive alpha decay. His immediate stimulus was a paper by Ernest Rutherford, who presented an essentially classical theory of this process. Gamow realized, instead, that the alpha particles within a heavy radioactive nucleus such as uranium were being confined by a nuclear potential barrier, and that they were capable of tunneling through this barrier quantum mechanically to the outside. This same theory was proposed independently and virtually simultaneously in Princeton, N.J., by Ronald W. Gurney and Edward U. Condon. It represented the first successful application of the new quantum mechanics to nuclear physics.

Gamow's theory inaugurated his career, and he subsequently made a series of fundamental contributions to theoretical nuclear physics. In the fall of 1928 he received fellowship support from Niels Bohr that enabled him to spend the 1928–1929 academic year at Bohr's institute in Copenhagen. There, within a few months, Gamow conceived the liquid-drop model of the nucleus, which a decade later would serve as the basis for understanding nuclear fission. Gamow also theoretically analyzed what would happen when charged particles strike a light nucleus from the outside; that was precisely the inverse of the alpha-decay problem he had solved earlier. Gamow's results encouraged John D. Cockcroft and E. T. S. Walton at the Cavendish Laboratory, Cambridge, England, to construct an accelerator for protons with which they successfully disintegrated a lithium nucleus in 1932—a milestone in the history of nuclear physics. In 1928–1929 Gamow also contributed to the theory of thermonuclear reaction rates in stellar interiors.

During the academic years 1929–1930 and 1930–1931 Gamow received further fellowship support to carry out research in theoretical nuclear physics, first at the Cavendish Laboratory and later again at Bohr's institute. He then returned to Russia in the spring of 1931 to renew his visa so that he might attend a conference on nuclear physics that Enrico Fermi had arranged for that fall in Rome. The Soviet authorities denied Gamow a visa, and he was forced to remain in Russia. He spent the next two academic years, 1931–1933, as a professor of physics at the University of Leningrad. In the fall of 1933 he and his wife, Lyubov Vokhminzeva, whom he had married in 1931, were permitted to travel to Brussels to attend the seventh Solvay Conference. They took their child and never returned to Russia. After the conference they spent successive two-month periods in Paris, Cambridge, and Copenhagen before going to the United States. There, in the summer of 1934, while attending the University of Michigan's summer school for theoretical physics in Ann Arbor, Gamow received an offer to go to George Washington University in Washington, D.C., as professor of physics. He held this position until 1956, when he moved to the University of Colorado at Boulder. That same year he was divorced; in 1958 he married Barbara Perkins. Gamow became an American citizen in 1940.

Shortly after taking up his position at George Washington University, Gamow persuaded Edward Teller to join him there. Together with Merle A. Tuve of the Department of Terrestrial Magnetism of the Carnegie Institution, Washington, D.C., Gamow and Teller began to organize annual conferences on theoretical physics that would stimulate much important work between 1935 and 1940. At the same time Gamow continued his own theoretical researches, often in collaboration with Teller. In 1936 the two formulated the Gamow-Teller selection rule for beta decay. This was Gamow's last contribution to theoretical nuclear physics as such; in subsequent years, he applied his knowledge of nuclear physics to astrophysical processes. Among the interrelated subjects he studied in the prewar period were stellar evolution, the expanding-universe theory, and stellar energy production.

In 1937 Gamow applied his talents to popular-science writing. His new career was launched when C. P. Snow, then editor of *Discovery*, published an article of Gamow's, "A Toy Universe," that grew into Gamow's first popular book, *Mr. Tompkins in Wonderland* (1939). In all, Gamow wrote about twenty popular books in addition to several advanced monographs and textbooks. In 1956 he received UNESCO's Kalinga Award for his popular-science writing.

Gamow served as a consultant to the United States Navy during World War II, studying conventional explosives. In 1948 he was granted top security clearance, which enabled him to work with Teller and Stanislaw Ulam at Los Alamos, N.Mex., on the hydrogen bomb project. His deepest interests, however, remained in the fundamental problems of astrophysics. In 1948 he proposed a theory of the origin of the universe that, when developed in detail, led to the prediction of a residual black-body radiation spectrum, the remnant of the primordial big bang. This remnant was first detected in 1965 by Arno A. Penzias and Robert W. Wilson of Bell Laboratories.

Gamow had a remarkable ability to enter a new field of research at its forefront and to make a significant contribution to it. This ability was perhaps most clearly demonstrated in 1954 when, shortly after James D. Watson and Francis Crick discovered the double-helical structure of deoxyribonucleic acid (DNA), Gamow saw that the information contained in the four different nucleotides making up the DNA chains could be translated into a sequence of twenty amino acids, forming protein molecules, by counting all the possible triplets that could be formed from the four different quantities. This was a fundamental insight into the nature of genetic coding, and Gamow arrived at it similarly to the way in which, at the beginning of his career, he applied his knowledge of quantum theory to the new field of nuclear physics.

Gamow received many honors for his work, including election to the United States National Academy of Sciences and the Royal Danish Academy of Sciences and Letters. He was widely traveled, spoke six languages, enjoyed poetry, and had a legendary sense of humor. He died in Boulder, Colo.

[Gamow's autobiography is *My World Line* (1970). For Gamow's early work on nuclear physics see Roger H. Stuewer, "Gamow's Theory of Alpha Decay," in Edna Ullman-Margalit, ed., *The Kaleidoscope of Science*, I (1986). Obituary notices are in *Physics Today*, Oct. 1968; and *Nature*, CCXX, 1968.]

ROGER H. STUEWER

GARDEN, MARY (Feb. 20, 1874–Jan. 3, 1967), opera singer, was born in Aberdeen, Scotland, the daughter of Robert Davidson Garden, an engineer, and Mary Joss. Garden's father established himself in the United States and sent for his family when Garden was a child. The family lived in Brooklyn, N.Y., and Chicopee, Mass., before moving around 1888 to Chicago, where Garden, whose regular schooling was sporadic, began taking voice lessons when she was sixteen. She had studied violin and piano earlier and had sung before groups as a child. In 1897 her teacher, Sarah Robinson-Duff, took Garden to Paris to study and arranged for her to be sponsored by a Chicago patron. When her stipend stopped, Garden was instructed without charge by her teachers Antonio Trabadello and Lucien Fugère. The American opera star Sibyl Sanderson invited her to share her home and introduced her to Albert Carré, the director of the Opéra-Comique.

In 1900, Sanderson took Garden to a rehearsal of Gustave Charpentier's *Louise*, and Carré gave her a score of the opera, which she practiced constantly. Carré, who had heard Garden sing and had contracted with her to join the Opéra-Comique in October, asked her to attend the performance of *Louise* on April 13, since its star, Marthe Rioton, appeared ill. When Rioton could sing only the first two acts, Carré insisted, over the protests of the conductor, André Messager, that Garden complete the performance. She was an instant success, captivating operagoers with her clear, sweet soprano voice, blue eyes, red hair, and American accent, which sounded exotic to Parisian ears. A dedicated worker and an instinctive actress, she was endowed with beauty and a remarkable stage personality.

Garden remained with the Opéra-Comique for eight years, singing Louise more than 100 times, and from the beginning she identified totally with each character she portrayed. "Others 'acted' a role; I *was* the role," she wrote. Garden was chosen to create the role of Mélisande in Claude Debussy's *Pelléas et Mélisande*; indeed, Debussy had her in mind when he composed the work, which premiered on Apr. 30, 1902. Her interpretation was so convincing that the composer declared, "I have nothing, absolutely nothing, to tell her. In some mysterious way, she knows or senses everything." Mélisande became the role for which she is most remembered.

In 1907, Garden left Paris to sing at the Manhattan Opera House for the impresario Oscar Hammerstein, who billed her as the greatest singer and actress in the world. She opened there in the American premiere of Massenet's *Thaïs* and again was an immediate success, although she was praised chiefly for her acting. The American premieres of *Louise* and *Pelléas et Mélisande* followed, and praise of Garden's performance, especially in the latter, was almost unqualified. In her second New York season, she sang Massenet's *Le Jongleur de Notre Dame*. She was the first woman to appear in the part of Jean, written for a tenor.

Garden was honored by the French government for popularizing modern French opera in the United States. She nearly always sang in French, even when the other roles in an opera were sung in Italian. She returned to Paris yearly, often singing in European opera houses and learning new roles while in France.

Garden created each new part with care. She planned her own stage action and chose her clothes and wigs. She sent to Brittany for the long blond hair of peasant girls for the wig she toyed with seductively as Mélisande. She also negotiated her own contracts. Insisting on doing her own dancing in the second New York production of Richard Strauss's *Salome*, which was staged in 1909, she asked the chief dancing teacher at the Paris Opéra to work out the "Dance of the Seven Veils" with her. The result was a sensual, suggestive dance. *Salome* was twice withdrawn in Chicago after two performances in response to protests concerning its sexuality and gory realism.

Garden began her twenty-year career with the Chicago Opera Association in the fall of 1910 when Hammerstein sold his opera company to the directors of the Metropolitan Opera, who moved their newly acquired competition to Chicago. With Cleofonte Campanini continuing to conduct its company and with Garden its star, Chicago became the American production center of modern French opera. Traveling with the Chicago company, Garden also performed throughout the United States, including New York from 1911 to 1922.

When, in 1921, the Chicago Opera Association floundered after Campanini's death, Garden was asked to head it, becoming the first woman in the world to direct a leading opera company. Her tenure, during which she continued to sing, lasted a year and made her unpopular with singers and staff. Lucien Muratore, a leading French tenor who often sang with Garden, resigned in midseason, and other singers and executives also left. Garden received so many threats that a detective was assigned to protect her. Despite these problems, her year at the helm won her the Legion of Honor and was artistically exciting; it was also expensive. The deficit from the year before had reached $350,000, and during her year as director it topped $1 million. The following season the association was reorganized as the Chicago Civic Opera Company. In 1925, Garden had her last outstanding personal success, in the American premiere of Franco Alfano's *Risurrezione*. She continued singing with the company until 1931.

Garden made her home in Paris and sang occasionally until 1934. She returned to Aberdeen during World War II, and Scotland became her principal home in later years. For the five seasons between 1949 and 1954, she traveled in the United States to lecture in forty cities and to audition singers for the National Arts Foundation. With the music critic Louis Biancolli, she published an autobiography, *Mary Garden's Story* (1951). Garden, who never married, wrote of the men in her life as well as the music. Despite liaisons and numerous suitors, she wrote that her "private life was empty" compared with the lives she lived through her operatic roles.

Garden was often called a singing actress. She defied convention, insisting on original and realistic theater emancipated from tradition. She sang few established roles, preferring modern French operas. During her thirty-one-year career, she sang thirty-four roles. (Sixteen, she claimed, had been written for her.) Despite her innovative work and the influence she had upon the operatic repertoire during her lifetime, many of the roles she sparked grew dim when she no longer sang them. Buoyed in old age by letters from her fans, Garden died in Aberdeen.

[In addition to Garden's autobiography, see James Gibbons Huneker, *Bedouins* . . . (1920); the profile of Garden in the *New Yorker*, Dec. 11, 1926; Edward C. Moore, *Forty Years of Opera in Chicago* (1930); Oscar Thompson, *The American Singer* (1937); G. Whelan, "The Recorded Art of Mary Garden," *Gramophone*, Apr. 1952, which contains a discography; Edward Wagenknecht, *Seven Daughters of the Theater* (1964); Quaintance Eaton, *The Boston Opera Company* (1965); Ronald L. Davis, *Opera in Chicago* (1966); and Henry Pleasants, *The Great Singers* (1966). Press clippings and pictures of Garden from the beginning of her career to Oct. 1923 are in the Robinson Locke Collection of Dramatic Scrap Books in the Billy Rose Theatre Collection at the New York Public Library. An obituary is in the *New York Times*, Jan. 5, 1967.]

OLIVE HOOGENBOOM

GARDNER, ERLE STANLEY (July 17, 1889–Mar. 11, 1970), writer, was born in Malden, Mass., the son of Charles Walter Gardner, a mining engineer, and Grace Adelma Waugh. In 1899 his father's work took the family to Oregon and, in 1902, to Oroville, Calif., where Gardner began his lifelong identification with California. For a brief period, the family lived in Alaska. Gardner began his writing career in Malden. In the *City of Malden Public School Souvenir*, commemorating the city's sesquicentennial, there appears "Atalanta's Race," a retelling of the myth of the golden apple, signed "Earle S. Gardner, Grade Four." (Gardner's parents spelled his name Erle, but he used various spellings until he was in high school.)

Gardner attended Oroville schools but was expelled from Oroville Union High School for pranks. He planned a career in law, and during one of his suspensions he worked in the law office of the deputy district attorney of Butte County. He graduated from Palo Alto High School in 1909. Gardner resisted going to college, preferring instead to read law in a lawyer's office, but in the fall of 1909 he went to Valparaiso University in Indiana. Before the term was out, he left the school after being falsely accused of participating in a dormitory bottle-smashing episode. He worked briefly and then began to read law in Santa Ana, Calif., where he was admitted to the bar in 1911. He moved to Willows and then to Oxnard, a brawling town in Ventura County, where in 1911 he practiced in the office of I. W. Stewart. On Apr. 9, 1912, Gardner married Natalie Frances Beatrice Talbert, Stewart's secretary; they had one child.

In 1915, Gardner formed a partnership with Frank Orr, a leading attorney in Ventura. Gardner briefly left the practice of law to pursue a career in sales. Broke, he returned in 1921 to his practice with Orr. That year he made his first attempts at writing fiction, but he was unable to produce anything marketable, save two brief, suggestive sketches that he sold to the magazine *Breezy Stories*. In 1923 he sold the novelette "The Shrieking Skeleton" to *Black Mask*, a leading pulp magazine. He was paid $160 for the story, which was published under the name Charles M. Green.

During the 1920's, Gardner practiced law during the day and then wrote furiously until he finished his daily stint of 4,000 words. By 1930, he had begun to dictate his fiction, and in 1932 he completed 224,000 words while practicing law two days a week. He wrote dozens of short stories and novelettes for magazines such as *Black Mask, Western Stories, Argosy*, and *Detective Fiction Weekly*. He also completed "Reasonable Doubt," published as *The Case of the Velvet Claws* (1933), and "Silent Verdict," published as *The Case of the Sulky Girl* (1933), the first two Perry Mason mystery novels. Both were rejected by popular magazines and by several book publishers but were accepted by Thayer Hobson of William Morrow and Company. They marked the beginning of a successful publishing record and popular-culture phenomenon.

Gardner had no illusions about the literary quality of his writing. In unpublished autobiographical fragments he conceded that he had "no natural aptitude as a writer. In fact, I don't consider myself a very good writer. I do consider myself a good plotter. And I consider myself one hell of a good salesman as far as manufacturing merchandise that will sell is concerned."

The Perry Mason series centers on a brilliant, skilled lawyer who inevitably solves a crime in a dramatic courtroom denouement; Della Street, his efficient and devoted secretary; and Paul Drake, his detective friend. After the third novel, *The Case of the Lucky Legs* (1934), Gardner abandoned his law practice. For five years he wrote in house trailers parked at various sites in his beloved desert country. Meanwhile, he built several writing retreats in remote places. In 1938 he began buying 1,000 acres of land at Temecula, in the high desert country southeast of Los Angeles, for a ranch and fiction factory called Rancho del Paisano.

There Gardner dictated for three hours each morning, penciled revisions of the typescripts produced by as many as six secretaries, and dictated again later in the day. He began two other series, the Doug Selby novels, about a young, effective district attorney, and, under the name A. A. Fair, the Bertha Cool novels, about a middle-aged woman private investigator and her brash young assistant, Donald Lam. The Selby novels had nearly identical titles, such as *The D.A. Calls It Murder* and *The D.A. Goes to Trial*, while the Bertha Cool titles stressed alliteration, such as *Widows Wear Weeds* and *All Grass Isn't Green*. At his best, Gardner finished a novel within four weeks, even while working on other projects.

In 1957, "Perry Mason," with Raymond Burr as Mason, began a nine-year run on television. It was produced by Gardner's Paisano Productions. The show initially used Gardner's material and then that of other writers supervised by Gardner. Eventually it was dubbed or subtitled in sixteen languages, all of which contributed to what Gardner called a "gigantic" dollar volume, "enormous" profits, and "astronomical" taxes. On the last episode of the show, Gardner played the judge.

In 1947, Gardner secured evidence that a man named William Marvin Lindley had been sentenced to death for a crime committed by someone else. Gardner secured a reprieve, then commutation, and finally freedom for the man. This led to the establishment of the Court of Last Resort, a panel of experts formed by Gardner and supported by *Argosy* magazine that met regularly to review such cases. Gardner eventually broke with *Argosy*, which had published his reports of cases reviewed and resolved, and he retired from the court.

On Feb. 26, 1968, Gardner's wife died. Although they had been separated for thirty-five years, they had remained friends. On Aug. 7, 1968, he married Jean Bethell, his secretary since 1930, who had been the model for Della Street. In March 1969 he finished his last Perry Mason novel, *The Case of the Fabulous Fake*, and he began a nonfiction work, *Cops on Campus and Crime on the Streets*. He finished his last A. A. Fair novel, *All Grass Isn't Green*, in July, just before his eightieth birthday. Years earlier, Gardner had learned that he had cancer, but he kept the diagnosis a secret. In October 1969 he entered the hospital for cobalt treatments but returned to his ranch to die.

Gardner produced more than 140 books in his lifetime, including 80 in the Perry Mason series. His 15 works of nonfiction include *The Court of Last Resort* (1952; expanded, 1954), and travel books such as *The Hidden Heart of Baja* (1962), *Off the Beaten Track in Baja* (1967), and *Mexico's Magic Square* (1968). He was proud of his status as perhaps the best-selling writer of all time. "I write to make money, and I write to give the reader sheer fun," he commented, a critical assessment with which most reviewers agreed.

[Gardner's papers are at the Humanities Research Center, University of Texas, Austin. Other well-known Perry Mason titles include *The Case of the Curious Bride* (1934), *The Case of the Howling Dog* (1934), and *The Case of the Careless Kitten* (1942). Nonfiction titles include *The Desert Is Yours* (1963) and *Hunting Lost Mines by Helicopter* (1965). Biographies of Gardner include Alva Johnson, *The Case of Erle Stanley Gardner* (1947); and Dorothy B. Hughes, *Erle Stanley Gardner* (1978), which contains a thorough bibliography of Gardner's writings compiled by Ruth Moore.

An obituary is in the *New York Times*, Mar. 12, 1970.]

DAVID D. ANDERSON

GARLAND, JUDY (June 10, 1922–June 22, 1969), singer and actress, was born Frances Ethel Gumm in Grand Rapids, Minn., the daughter of Frank Avent Gumm and Ethel Marion Milne. Her parents were entertainers and operated the New Grand Theater, a motion picture house, but contrary to later reports, she was not born in a vaudeville trunk. Her earliest years were spent in a middle-class, small-town environment. She made her first stage appearance at the age of thirty months when she joined her two older sisters, Mary Jane and Dorothy Virginia, in singing "Jingle Bells" at their parents' theater.

In 1926 the family moved to Los Angeles, where Frank Gumm bought the nearby Valley Theater. Frances made numerous appearances at the theater and in local events billed as "Baby Gumm" and in 1927 she sang with her sisters on "The Kiddies' Hour," broadcast on KFI and later KNX radio. In 1929 the girls performed as the Hollywood Starlets Trio, and in 1931 they were featured at the Ebell Theater on Wilshire Boulevard in a show called *Stars of Tomorrow*.

Metro-Goldwyn-Mayer (MGM) signed Frances to a contract for $100 a week when she was thirteen. Her first film for the studio was a short, *Every Sunday Afternoon* (1936), with Deanna Durbin. Soon after Frances signed her first contract her father died, an event she later said was the worst thing that ever happened to her. Her first feature film, *Pigskin Parade* (1936), was made when she was on loan to Twentieth Century–Fox. From that time on, she was known as Judy Garland.

Louis B. Mayer, after some hesitation, decided to publicize the young singer. She sang "Dear Mr. Gable" in *Broadway Melody of 1938* (released in 1937); the song became a hit that created considerable attention for her. Although her singing range was limited, she presented a bright, energetic personality on the screen. She had clarity and excellent enunciation combined with a natural, free and easy style. In 1937 she graduated from Bancroft Junior High School and enrolled at University High School. Three pictures followed quickly; although they were not distinguished, they gave her an opportunity to develop her skills as a comedienne. A movie with Mickey Rooney, *Love Finds Andy Hardy* (1938), made a greater impression upon the moviegoing public. She played an innocent, awkward young girl whose infatuation with Andy Hardy was not reciprocated.

Garland made her New York City stage debut at Loew's State in 1938. The next year she reached undisputed stardom in the role of Dorothy in *The Wizard of Oz*. The film, directed by Victor Fleming with assistance from King Vidor, also cast veteran actors Bert Lahr, Jack Haley, and Ray Bolger. Garland, her fresh, sweet voice touched with impudence, created a sensation with the song "Over the Rainbow." This song, which she sang wistfully, became almost a symbol for her career. Her performance in *The Wizard of Oz* won her a special Oscar in 1939, when she was seventeen. Ray Bolger said that her charisma was evident at that early age.

While making *The Wizard of Oz*, Garland was paid $350 a week. After it was done MGM gave her a contract for $150,000 a picture. Another successful film with Mickey Rooney, *Babes in Arms*, was released in the fall of 1939, and this association continued with *Andy Hardy Meets Debutante* (1940) and *Strike Up the Band* (1940), in which she sang "Our Love Affair." She also appeared in *Little Nellie Kelly* (1940), with George Murphy, and was regularly on Bob Hope's weekly radio show. It is believed that MGM gave her amphetamines and barbiturates, initially unaware of their side effects, to see her through this hectic schedule. On July 28, 1941, Garland married David Rose, a composer and pianist.

For Me and My Gal (1942), with Gene Kelly, was Garland's fifteenth feature film. But success at the box office as one of the top Hollywood attractions did not give her peace of mind. Her emotional difficulties increased and analysis did not furnish any substantial comfort. Nevertheless, she worked under pressure and continued to exhibit remarkable gifts. Producer Joe Pasternak said she combined emotion with hysterical talent. She learned her lines quickly, sang with perfect timing, and had a good memory.

Under the direction of Vincente Minnelli, Garland starred in another picture, *Meet Me in St. Louis* (1944), playing a role closely identified with her public image as a sweet young woman. The songs that she sang in the film, "The Boy Next Door," "The Trolley Song," and "Have Yourself a Merry Little Christmas," endured throughout her career. Her first marriage ended in divorce, and on June 15, 1945, she married Minnelli. They had one child, the singer and actress Liza Minnelli.

Garland's first nonsinging role was in *The Clock* (1945), with Robert Walker, Keenan Wynn, and James Gleason. As a girl who meets and marries a soldier during his one-day leave, she was able once again to project a sincere personality. During the late 1940's Garland firmly established herself as a leading musical star in motion pictures. She put her distinctive stamp on Cole Porter songs in *The Pirate* (1948), with Gene Kelly, and on Irving Berlin songs in *Easter Parade* (1948), with Fred Astaire. In the latter film her rendition of "A Couple of Swells" was especially memorable. By now her emotional troubles had become more evident and caused long delays in production. In 1950 MGM suspended her contract and she made one of many suicide attempts. When her personal problems became public knowledge, her fans seemed to become increasingly devoted to her.

In March 1951 she divorced Minnelli and left Hollywood for London, where she appeared onstage at the Palladium. Her triumph in London was duplicated in the fall of 1951 when she performed at the Palace Theater in New York City. She was held over for nineteen weeks and set a New York City vaudeville record of 184 performances. Nevertheless, her physical and mental problems had a telling effect and some of the earlier quality in her voice disappeared. It is possible that a siege of hepatitis complicated by tranquilizers, diet pills, and other drugs was an underlying cause.

On June 8, 1952, she married Sidney Luft. They had two children, including the actress Lorna Luft. Despite all adversity, often self-imposed, Garland continued to work. Her part in *A Star Is Born* (1954), with James Mason, was probably her greatest dramatic achievement. The film, however, was not a commercial success and her delays and irregular behavior contributed to the high cost of production. Once again she sang a torch song, "The Man That Got Away," that deeply impressed the public, and she was nominated for an Academy Award.

Illness and personal problems, added to the growing belief that Garland was too risky to employ, often prevented her from working during the next few years. She refused to give up, especially since her money had been badly managed and she needed a source of income. In 1955 she appeared on a television special, "The Ford Star Jubilee." In the next two years she was onstage again at the Palace in New York and at the New Frontier and Flamingo in Las Vegas, but under ever-increasing strain. In 1960 she returned to the London Palladium, where her reception exceeded the warmth of her previous appearance. She also made a heartrending and impressive appearance filled with nervous excitement at Carnegie Hall.

Garland received a second nomination for an Academy Award for her small but important part in *Judgment at Nuremberg* (1961). She played a young German woman who had suffered at the hands of the Nazis. Her last film was *I Could Go On Singing* (1963). During her career she made more than thirty-five motion pictures and produced innumerable records for Decca, Columbia, Capitol, and other labels.

"The Judy Garland Show," a television series shown on the Columbia Broadcasting System (CBS) during 1963–1964, was a treat for her followers, but her confused behavior during production created enormous anxiety for her associates. The series was regarded as a failure. This was followed by a near-disastrous tour of Australia, during which Garland was booed by audiences in Melbourne. After a long separation, she divorced Luft and in November 1965 married Mark Herron, an actor. The marriage lasted two years. Occasional personal appearances in the United States in 1967 were generally well received, but her erratic behavior continued. In late 1968 she appeared at the Talk of the Town, a London nightclub, with a degree of success. On Jan. 9, 1969, she married Mickey Deans, a singer, pianist, and discotheque manager. After legalities were cleared up in California concerning her last divorce, she married Deans a second time on Mar. 15, 1969. Shortly after this marriage, she made a brief tour of Scandinavia with the singer Johnnie Ray. According to Deans, insomnia was one of her major problems. Her death, in London, was attributed to an accidental overdose of barbiturates.

[Materials on Garland's career are in the Performing Arts Research Center, New York Public Library. See also Vincent Canby, "Judy Garland," *New York Times*, June 29, 1969; Mel Torme, *The Other Side of the Rainbow* (1970); Al DiOrio, Jr., *Little Girl Lost* (1973); Basil Wright, *The Long View* (1974); Richard Schickel, *The Men Who Made the Movies* (1974); and Christopher Finch, *Rainbow: The Stormy Life of Judy Garland* (1975). An obituary is in the *New York Times*, June 23, 1969.]

ERNEST A. MCKAY

GARNER, JOHN NANCE (Nov. 22, 1868–Nov. 7, 1967), vice-president of the United States (1933–1941), was born in Red River County, Tex., the son of John Nance Garner III, a farmer, and Sarah Guest. Garner attended local schools and played semiprofessional baseball. He attended Vanderbilt University briefly but returned to northeast Texas to read law in Clarksville. There he was admitted to the bar in 1890 and was an unsuccessful candidate for city attorney in 1892. Suffering from a chest ailment, he moved in January 1893 to the drier climate of south-central Texas, settling in Uvalde, from which he worked the courthouse circuit in nine counties. Since much of his payment for legal services was in kind, Garner was soon plunged into commercial transactions involving land, commodities, and livestock. He expanded his business interests over the years, especially into the areas of personal loans and banking. These enterprises and his frugality eventually made him wealthy. Although he considered himself a good Methodist, he made no secret of his enjoyment of bourbon, cigars, and poker. On Nov. 25, 1895, Garner married Mariette ("Ettie") Rheiner, the daughter of a prosperous rancher. She served as his legislative secretary and political confidante. They had one child.

Garner entered politics again in 1893, when he was appointed Uvalde County judge, largely an administrative position; he was elected as a Democrat to the post in 1894. Defeated for reelection in 1896, he soon sought membership in the Texas House of Representatives, to which he was elected in 1898 and reelected in 1900. Garner made a name for himself in Austin as an opponent of pork-barrel legislation and a champion of increased regulation of corporations. During his second legislative term, he served as the chairman of the redistricting committee that created a huge new congressional district in his part of Texas. He then appealed successfully to the bankers, cattle barons, Spanish-speaking people, and county political bosses of the new Fifteenth District in seeking nomination and election to Congress in 1902. Garner's constituents regarded him as a homespun man of the people (among his many sobriquets was "Cactus Jack") and consistently returned him to Congress. Although his district changed considerably, he served in Congress for thirty years.

Although Garner was an able debater, he seldom spoke publicly. As he told his successor in Congress, "It was a good many years before any remarks of mine got in the *Record*; and I hope you won't make a damn fool of yourself either." Moreover, Garner did not introduce much legislation. Most of what he sponsored were private bills relating to his constituents and measures concerning Texas, such as legislation advancing the construction of the Gulf Intercoastal Waterway.

Garner made his mark in Washington, D.C., by being a diligent and studious legislator and an effective negotiator. He soon became popular in Congress. He was amiable and honest, spoke pithily and often colorfully, and was well-informed. Garner was not petty or mean, and he avoided taking extreme positions. Consequently, he gained a remarkable number of friends among both Democrats and Republicans.

Garner initially served on the House Railways and Canals Committee, but he soon moved up to the Foreign Affairs Committee. He became Democratic whip in the House in 1911 and a member of the powerful Ways and Means Committee in 1913. Although an advocate of economy, Garner was usually considered a moderate liberal, espousing independence for the Philippines, improved agricultural credit, marketing, and road programs, currency expansion, and antimonopolistic measures. He was a leading figure in the successful revolt in 1910 against the authoritarian management of the House by Speaker Joseph G. Cannon. An advocate of equitable taxes, Garner was instrumental in incorporating the graduated income tax into the Underwood Tariff Act of 1913. He also supported enactment of the Federal Reserve System and of a federal inheritance or estate tax.

Although by 1913 Garner had become an authority on fiscal matters in Congress, he was not close to the new Democratic president, Woodrow Wilson. As Wilson's relations with Speaker Champ Clark and Chairman Claude Kitchin of the Ways and Means Committee deteriorated by 1917, the president made Garner his spokesman on financial legislation in the House. Garner consequently played a key role in securing passage of the administration's war finance measures in 1917 and 1918. By the end of World War I Garner was highly influential in Congress, especially on tariff, tax, and trade matters. He was also esteemed as a party loyalist and a mediator among his fellow Democrats in the House.

During the 1920's Garner generally opposed American involvement abroad and demanded the payment of foreign debts to the United States, although he resisted tariff increases. He opposed Prohibition and the Ku Klux Klan, was instrumental in legislating a federal inheritance or estate tax in 1926, and worked with some effect for a more equitable income tax reduction policy. In 1923 Garner became the ranking Democrat on the Ways and Means Committee and chairman of the House Democratic Committee on Committees, which allowed him to determine his party's committee assignments.

Garner succeeded Finis J. Garrett as the Democratic leader in the House in 1929. He worked smoothly with his close Republican friend, Speaker Nicholas Longworth, in running the affairs of the House during the Seventy-first Congress. Operating what pundits dubbed "the Board of Education," Garner and Longworth minimized partisan disagreements among their colleagues, and thus facilitated the passage of legislation in the House. Garner relied considerably on "striking a blow for liberty" (having a drink with his colleagues) in order to discuss legislative business under relaxed conditions.

In December 1931 Garner was elected speaker by a majority of three votes. Given his party's narrow majority in the House and the crisis of economic depression, he decided to cooperate with the Republican administration of President Herbert Hoover whenever possible. This resulted in 1932 in the establishment of the Reconstruction Finance Corporation, the strengthening of the Federal Reserve System and Federal Land Banks, and tax increases designed to balance the budget. Yet Speaker Garner also pressed, unsuccessfully, for a federal sales tax and payment of a bonus to World War I veterans and, successfully, for expanded public works projects, farm relief, and a tax on gasoline.

Garner ran for the Democratic presidential nomination in 1932. Backed by publisher William Randolph Hearst, he won the California presidential primary over New York's Franklin D. Roosevelt and Alfred E. Smith. He also had the support of the Texas delegation. It became clear after the third ballot at the Democratic National Convention that Garner could not win the nomination, so he released his delegates to Governor Roosevelt, who was nominated on the fourth ballot. Garner did win the vice-presidential nomination, and provided geographical balance and additional name recognition to the ticket. He was otherwise little involved in the successful 1932 Democratic campaign.

As vice-president, Garner was relatively influential. He worked effectively to obtain enactment of many administration proposals during President Roosevelt's first term, and he was an active member of Roosevelt's circle of advisers. Garner also played a significant role in the establishment of the Federal Deposit Insurance Corporation, despite the president's opposition to it. Roosevelt and Garner were renominated and overwhelmingly reelected in 1936. After that they increasingly split on policy matters. Their differences began over the president's proposal to alter the composition of the Supreme Court and his unwillingness to discourage sit-down strikes in 1937. The division between the two leaders continued over the issues of the mounting federal deficit, Roosevelt's opposition to Democratic dissenters in the 1938 elections, and the president's decision to run for a third term.

By 1940 Garner had become the symbol of traditionalist opposition among Democrats to the administration, and he became a candidate for his party's presidential nomination. His challenge to Roosevelt infuriated organized labor and liberal Democrats. John L. Lewis of the Congress of Industrial Organizations (CIO) characterized Garner as "a poker-playing, whiskey-drinking, labor-baiting, evil old man." Garner attracted only sixty-one votes at the 1940 Democratic National Convention, and Roosevelt handily won renomination for president. Garner did not run for renomination for vice-president, an office that he concluded "isn't worth a pitcher of warm piss." (That statement has been widely bowdlerized as "a pitcher of warm spit.")

In 1941 Garner retired to Uvalde, never to return to Washington. He tended to his many business interests and engaged in some philanthropy. Garner also often held court for admiring fellow citizens, usually commenting on public affairs good-naturedly and sensibly, if conservatively. He died in Uvalde. Garner was a person of notable integrity and of outstanding ability in handling legislative matters. Where there was room for negotiation between conflicting interests, he was remarkably adept at striking honest bargains.

[Garner burned his papers in 1950. A significant amount of correspondence relating to him is in the Franklin D. Roosevelt Library, Hyde Park, N.Y. Other material may be found in the Garner Museum, Uvalde, Texas. Popular biographies are Marquis James, *Mr. Garner of Texas* (1939); Bascom N. Timmons, *Garner of Texas* (1948); and Ovie Clark Fisher, *Cactus Jack* (1978). See also Jordan A. Schwarz, "John Nance Garner and the Sales Tax Rebellion of 1932," *Journal of Southern History*, May 1964; and Michael J. Romano, "The Emergence of John Nance Garner as a Figure in American National Politics, 1924–1941" (Ph.D. diss., St. John's University, 1974). An obituary is in the *New York Times*, Nov. 8, 1967.]

DONALD R. MCCOY

GENOVESE, VITO (Nov. 31(?), 1897–Feb. 14, 1969), reputed Cosa Nostra boss, was born in Ricigliano, near Naples, Italy, the son of Phillip Anthony and Nancy Genovese. Educated in Italy through the equivalent of fifth grade, Genovese entered the United States on May 23, 1913, at New York City. He resided with his family in Little Italy, the Italian section of Greenwich Village. Young Genovese became involved in the Italian underworld and quickly established himself as a reliable and ruthless mob soldier. In 1931 Genovese allied himself with Charles ("Lucky") Luciano to arrange the demise of their leader, Giuseppe ("The Boss") Masseria, and make Salvatore Maranzano "The Boss of All Bosses." In classic fashion the unsuspecting Masseria was wined, dined, and shot to death, and less than six months later Maranzano was assassinated—leaving Luciano and Genovese in control.

That same year Genovese's first wife (her name is unknown) died, and the rising leader chose as his second bride Anna Petillo, who was already married to Gerard Vernotico. Vernotico's body was subsequently discovered on a rooftop, and two weeks later, on Mar. 30, 1932, Genovese married the widow. They had two children. In 1950 Anna left Genovese, and in a court battle over alimony she described her husband as a wealthy man who brought home $20,000 to $30,000 a week in proceeds from the "Italian lottery." She testified that Genovese kept caches of money all over Europe and that she had seen half a million dollars in his safe-deposit box in Switzerland.

During the 1920's Genovese had been arrested several times, but his only two convictions were for the relatively minor crime of carrying a concealed weapon. He was one of the first underworld figures to establish and operate legitimate businesses in order to protect himself. His enterprises included imports, wastepaper, and steel straps. In 1934, however, Genovese was involved in an extortion plot in which one collaborator, Ferdinand ("The Shadow") Boccia, demanded a large share of the $160,000 proceeds. They quarreled, Boccia was murdered, and the police questioned Genovese, but the prosecution stalled when witnesses could not be found. In 1937, a year after Genovese was naturalized, he became concerned about a possible indictment for Boccia's murder and fled to Italy. He reportedly took $750,000 with him and gave one-third of it to Mussolini, who decorated him.

Genovese remained out of the public eye until 1944, when a United States Army investigation of black markets in Italy implicated him, and he was jailed while employed as an army interpreter. While he was in custody in Italy, word came from New York that he had been indicted for Boccia's murder. The indictment was possible because prosecutors had finally located two corroborative witnesses. Genovese fought extradition until January 1945, when witness Peter LaTempa was poisoned while in protective custody in a Brooklyn, N.Y., jail. Genovese then returned to New York City, and the charges were dismissed.

Genovese found that his long absence from the United States had weakened his influence with the Cosa Nostra. Luciano had made a deal with Governor Thomas E. Dewey and had accepted deportation to Italy, where Luciano continued to operate until he moved to Cuba. Frank Costello, who had involved the crime organization in a number of legitimate businesses, had become the Cosa Nostra leader. Genovese bided his time until 1957, when he allegedly ordered Costello's murder. The rival miraculously survived a bungled shooting, and Genovese fled to his home with forty armed guards.

Fearing that Costello and Albert Anastasia, another powerful mob leader, would join forces against him, Genovese called a general meeting of the Italian underworld to announce that he would take Costello's place and that the new underboss would be Gerardo ("Jerry") Catena. Costello's attacker went free when Costello declined to identify him, and Costello was received back into Genovese's organization as an underling. Genovese then allegedly plotted the murder of Anastasia, whose assassination in a fashionable New York City hotel barbershop on Oct. 25, 1957, provided a memorable photograph of mob bloodshed. Two weeks later more than 100 mobsters convened at Apalachin, N.Y., to endorse Genovese's return to power. A poorly organized police raid captured about sixty underworld leaders, including Genovese; many others escaped into the woods.

The publicity about Anastasia's killing and the Apalachin meeting hurt Genovese, and the authorities began to close in. In 1958 Senator John L. McClellan's select committee gave Americans a detailed look inside the Cosa Nostra. In testimony before the committee Genovese took the Fifth Amendment more than 150 times. The committee concluded that Genovese had amassed a fortune worth $30 million. Shortly afterward Genovese was indicted in a federal narcotics smuggling case in New York City, and on Apr. 3, 1959, he was convicted. He was sentenced to fifteen years. On Feb. 11, 1960, he became the first mob boss since Luciano to be jailed. Even from his federal prison cell in Atlanta, however, Genovese continued to run the Cosa Nostra.

It was in prison that Genovese's cellmate, mob soldier Joseph Valachi, learned the details of Genovese's operations. Valachi came to believe that Genovese had marked him for death, and in 1963 Valachi turned state's evidence against his former boss. Valachi's testimony confirmed many allegations concerning Genovese, solved a number of murders and disappearances, and developed the first complete portrait of the inner workings of the Cosa Nostra. Genovese was transferred to the federal prison in Leavenworth, Kans., but he continued to exert influence on the mob. He died in the prison hospital at Springfield, Mo.

Had Genovese lived to be paroled, he would have been deported to Italy, since his citizenship had been revoked in 1955 for lying about his arrest record. Also, narcotics conviction is a deportable crime. He was succeeded as mob boss by Catena and Thomas ("Tommy Ryan") Eboli. Physically Genovese was short, stocky, and undistinguished. He was well liked in Atlantic Highlands, the New Jersey suburb where he lived, and he donated money to the local Catholic church.

[See Peter Maas, *The Valachi Papers* (1968). See also the *New York Times*, Nov. 25, 1944; Mar. 3, 1953; Apr. 4, 1959; Aug. 5, 1963; Sept. 28, 1963; and Dec. 25, 1968. Obituary notices are in the *New York Times* and the *New York Daily News*, both Feb. 15, 1969.]

W. J. Rorabaugh

GERNSBACK, HUGO (Aug. 16, 1884–Aug. 19, 1967), publisher, editor, inventor, and author, was born in Luxembourg City, Luxembourg, the son of Maurice Gernsback, a wealthy wine merchant, and Berta Durlacher. His early education was provided by tutors. He later attended a boarding school in Brussels and the École Industrielle in Luxembourg, and studied electrical engineering at the Technikum in Bingen, Germany.

An ambitious and imaginative youth, Gernsback came to the United States by himself in 1904 with $100 furnished by his family, vowing not to ask for additional financial help. He brought with him an improved dry battery he had invented, but it proved to be too costly to produce commercially. In 1905 he started the Electro Importing Company, probably the first American radio supply house. He then designed and produced a wireless telegraphic sending-and-receiving set with a range of a mile or two. It was sold at department stores for $7.50 and was said to be the world's first commercially built home radio. For mail-order customers, Gernsback published a catalog with instructive articles on new and unfamiliar radio equipment. This was followed in April 1908 by a magazine, *Modern Electrics*, with the lead article entitled "Wireless Telegraphy," and with the latest wireless news.

Gernsback continued his exporting company in New York City but henceforth his main efforts were in publishing and invention. He sold *Modern Electrics* in 1912 and started a larger periodical, *Electrical Experimenter*. In 1919 he began the first American magazine devoted exclusively to radio, *Radio Amateur News*, which in 1920 became *Radio News*.

Throughout much of his career Gernsback continued to invent. He patented about eighty electronic devices. Some were manufactured profitably, but he made little effort to commercialize many of them, allowing others to do so if they wished. His compression-type condenser was licensed to Powel Crosley, Jr., for the Crosley Radio Corporation. Gernsback was perhaps proudest of his bone-conduction hearing aid, the "Osophone," patented in 1928. A scholarly experimenter in electronics, Gernsback corresponded with outstanding scientists who shared his interests, among them David Sarnoff, Lee De Forest, Nikola Tesla, and Thomas A. Edison.

However, it was as a publisher, prophet, and instigator in the field of "science fiction," a phrase he coined, that Gernsback achieved an enduring reputation. He initiated the publication of more than fifty periodicals, many of them pulp magazines devoted to radio, humor, sex, aviation, economics, crime detection, and science fiction. The first issue of *Amazing Stories*, a monthly pulp, in April 1926 signaled the ultimate direction of his career. It consisted largely of tales reprinted from the works of Edgar Allan Poe, Jules Verne, and H. G. Wells but it gained him the title "father of science fiction." The designation was strongly disputed by some devotees of the genre. But his reputation as the publisher of the first science fiction magazine in the United States seems beyond contradiction.

As early as 1911 Gernsback had published serially, in *Modern Electrics*, a long story he wrote, "*Ralph 124C41* +," describing "thrilling adventures of the year 2660." Although poorly written, the tale is memorable for its astonishingly accurate and detailed predictions: radar, solar power, space travel, microfilm, tape recorders, synthetic fabrics, stainless steel, plastics, and numerous advances in other fields of technology. The serial was published as a book in 1925 and translated into French, German, and Russian. Gernsback also wrote *The Wireless Telephone* (1908); *Radio for All* (1922), a how-to book; and a posthumous novel, *Ultimate World* (1970).

Gernsback contended that true science fiction must be scientifically feasible; otherwise it is mere fantasy. "What I detest," he wrote, "is the parading of pure fantasy as science fiction. . . . I consider it an out-and-out fraud." Those who disagreed argued that Gernsback's insistence on technical plausibility discouraged and retarded imaginative writers. They called his demand for scientific validity "the Gernsback delusion."

Gernsback was reputed to be slow and stingy in paying contributors to his science fiction magazines. H. P. Lovecraft and Fletcher Pratt were among the writers who complained. Pratt said he was tardily paid only $250 for a 40,000-word story. Although Gernsback seemed prosperous, he was in fact sometimes in financial trouble. In 1929 he was forced into bankruptcy and lost his magazines and his radio station, WRNY in New York, which he had founded in 1925 and from which in 1928 he instituted telecasts with crude but effective equipment. He quickly regained solvency and resumed publication of science fiction pulps, among them *Wonder Stories*, *Air Wonder Stories*, and *Science Wonder Stories*, as well as other periodicals on a variety of subjects, including *Sexology* (1953), the most successful of his several biomedical magazines. Beginning in 1953, the prestigious achievement award annually presented at the World Science Fiction Convention was called a "Hugo" in Gernsback's honor.

Gernsback became a naturalized citizen in 1927. He was married three times: on May 27, 1906, to Rose Harvey, with whom he had two children; on Jan. 21, 1921, to Dorothy Kantrowitz, with whom he had three children; and on June 11, 1951, to Mary Hancher. He lived and dressed with elegance, collected art, spoke several languages, and dined at fine restaurants. Although he was usually grave—even forbidding—of demeanor, he had a lively sense of humor and made jokes of his misfortunes. In his later years he was still energetic and creative. He died in New York City.

[Bound volumes of all Gernsback's publications, with some of his letters and papers, are in the George Arents Research Library, Syracuse University. On Gernsback and his career, see Sam Moskowitz, *Explorers of the Infinite* (1963); Paul O'Neil, "Barnum of the Space Age," *Life*, July 26, 1963; Theodore Peterson, *Magazines in the Twentieth Century* (1964); Brian W. Aldiss, *Billion-Year Spree: The True History of Science Fiction* (1973); Brian Ash, *Faces of the Future* (1975); James Gunn, *Alternate Worlds: The Illustrated History of Science Fiction* (1975); Tony Goldstone, ed., *The Pulps: FIfty Years of American Pop Culture* (1976); Neil Barron, *Anatomy of Wonder: Science Fiction* (1976); Paul A. Carter, *The Creation of Tomorrow: Fifty Years of Magazine Science Fiction* (1977); Sam J. Lundwall, *Science Fiction* (1977); and Lester Del Rey, *The World of Science Fiction* (1980). See also the obituary notice, *Radio-Electronics*, Oct. and Nov. 1967. *Radio-Electronics*, Aug. 1984, has an article commemorating the centennial of Gernsback's birth.]

WILLIAM MCCANN

GIFFORD, WALTER SHERMAN (Jan. 10, 1885–May 7, 1966), corporation executive and diplomat, was born in Salem, Mass., the son of Nathan Poole Gifford, who operated a lumber mill, and Hariet Maria Spinney. Gifford attended the public schools of Salem and entered Harvard at the age of fifteen, in September 1901, completing the four-year course in 1904 but taking his degree with the class of 1905. Rejecting the advice of his father, who reflected the anticorporation bias then prevalent among small businessmen, Gifford took a job as an accounting clerk with the Western Electric Company in Chicago. His starting pay was $10 a week.

Gifford quickly showed a tendency to think innovatively and soon introduced improved ways of doing the simple arithmetical calculations that the work of his office required. He had an innate respect for data of all kinds and constantly analyzed figures to derive previously obscure facts about the efficiency of the company. In a rapidly growing enterprise, his initiative and steady devotion to work were quick to be noted. (He routinely upset the timekeeper by coming to work before the time-clock cards were in place and departing long after they had been taken up.) Just before his twenty-first birthday, he was made assistant secretary and treasurer of the company, to the news of which his father replied, "Any damn fool can make a success in a corporation." Suspecting that his father might be right, Gifford left Western Electric for six months in 1911 to run an Arizona copper mine. Theodore N. Vail, who had helped set up the American Telephone and Telegraph Company (AT&T) in 1885, had had his eye on Gifford for some time. When Gifford decided to return to the company, Vail made him chief statistician at a salary of $7,000 a year.

In 1915, Gifford enrolled in the civilian military training school at Plattsburgh, N.Y., but this was as close to a uniform as he would ever get. At the recommendation of Howard E. Coffin of the Hudson Motor Car Company, President Woodrow Wilson named Gifford supervising director of the Committee on Industrial Preparedness of the Naval Consulting Board. Gifford's task was to make a survey of the capacities of American factories for production of war matériel. The report led to the creation of the Council of National Defense and a related advisory commission. Gifford, who had married Florence Pitman on Oct. 28, 1916, ended his honeymoon early in order to move to Washington, D.C., to organize the council. Just before the war ended, he went to France to organize the Inter-Allied Munitions Council to coordinate aircraft production.

When Gifford returned to AT&T after the Armistice, his responsibilities increased quickly. He was named controller of the company and, in 1920, vice-president in charge of finance. It was his job to raise the money to finance the Bell System's phenomenal growth, and during the 1920's the modern telephone system took shape. He scored a notable triumph in placing a $90 million stock issue directly with small investors by selling the shares, which he knew would have more appeal than savings bank accounts, through local offices of the telephone company. He emphasized the unique position of the company in the American business world, which was virtually that of a natural monopoly. In 1922, Gifford became a director of AT&T, then executive vice-president, and, on Jan. 20, 1925, the third president of the company.

The sheer size of the Bell System and its scientific complexities and social ramifications made organization Gifford's chief concern. He saw the need for fundamental organizational changes and policy rethinking. He initiated a policy of divestment of all activities that did not fit an avowed policy of furnishing a network, both local and long-distance, of wired voice communication facilities and the design, manufacture, and installation of the equipment such a network required. He sold International Western Electric, having concluded that AT&T would do well to remain aloof from government-dominated foreign telephone enterprises; the Graybar Electric Company, a wholesale jobber that had been set up to market and maintain a host of unrelated electrical equipment; and radio station WEAF in New York City, which the company had established early in the 1920's, when commercial radio was in its infancy. (AT&T thought, mistakenly, that radio would be a competitive threat to the telephone.) Western Union, the giant telegraph company that had been acquired a few years before, was also dropped because it did not fit Gifford's plans. Meanwhile, such inventions as the teletype and the telephoto were acquired.

The attainment of nearly universal residential subscribership (which America achieved almost two generations before any other country) and conversion to the dial system of automatic switching were the most important developments during Gifford's long presidency. The switch to dialing was accomplished, moreover, without discharging a single operator. During the depression, AT&T profits sometimes failed to equal the dividend rate, but Gifford showed that his longtime policy of adding surplus profits to retained surplus made it possible to avoid cutting dividends. However, executive salaries were cut 12 percent and then another 10 percent.

Gifford's one major failure in his career was his inability to coordinate unemployment relief in the fall of 1931 at the request of President Herbert Hoover, who was determined to keep such relief on a state and local basis. In World War II, Gifford was again active in war production planning. Returning to AT&T in 1945, he set the company on a course of expansion that made all previous records seem petty. At the age of sixty-three he became chairman of the board and two years later he retired. Although he was a lifelong Republican, President Harry

S. Truman appointed him ambassador to Great Britain.

Gifford and his wife, who had two children, were divorced in 1929, for Gifford, a quiet, reserved man who detested large social gatherings, failed to give his wife the kind of life she wanted. A neat, conservative dresser who was unswervingly loyal to dark suits and bow ties, Gifford lived a rather lonely life in a city town house and on weekends at his country estate in North Castle, Westchester County, N.Y., But on Dec. 22, 1944, he married a widow, Augustine Lloyd Perry. He died in New York City.

Gifford represents the ideal of the master strategist combined with the "hands-on" executive, his head filled with a mass of statistics about the company on which he is the unquestioned authority. His administrative talents created the modern telephone company, but his diplomatic talents and prestige helped preserve it in its natural monopoly form. For twenty years he persuaded America's political leaders, who had the power of life and death over all his policies, that AT&T's guiding principle was service to the telephone user, not profits. His successors, facing a more firmly entrenched and less sympathetic government bureaucracy and a judiciary devoted to intervention in the structure of the industry, have not been so successful. Their stiff-lipped resolve to make the best of the consent decree that split AT&T from the Bell operating companies would, however, have earned his admiration.

[The AT&T archives contain voluminous material, including Gifford's personal papers. Gifford wrote three articles that were printed as brochures: "Does Business Want Scholars?" (1928), "Pensions, Charity and Old Age" (1930), and "Can Prosperity Be Managed?" (1930). There is no biography of Gifford, but a profile by Jack Alexander in the *New Yorker*, June 5, 12, and 19, 1937, is rich in detail and obviously had Gifford's cooperation. An obituary is in the *New York Times*, May 8, 1966.]

ALBRO MARTIN

GIMBEL, BERNARD FEUSTMAN (Apr. 10, 1885–Sept. 29, 1966), retail merchant, was born in Vincennes, Ind., the son of Isaac Gimbel and Rachel Feustman. His grandfather, Adam Gimbel, an immigrant from Bavaria, founded his Palace of Trade at Vincennes in 1842. Successful there, he moved to Philadelphia in 1865, leaving his sons in charge of the family store in Indiana.

The Gimbel brothers prospered. After experimenting with branch stores in nearby small communities, they moved their operations to Milwaukee in 1887. Young Bernard began his education in the public schools of that city. In 1894 Isaac Gimbel moved the family to Philadelphia, where be became manager of a newly founded Gimbels store. Bernard attended the William Penn Charter School until 1903. In 1904 he entered the Wharton School of the University of Pennsylvania. Nearly six feet tall and of robust physique, he excelled in sports, especially football and boxing. He enjoyed athletics all his life. As a young man he regularly sparred with prominent boxers, including world heavyweight champion Gene Tunney, who became a lifelong friend.

After graduating from college in 1907 with a B.S. in economics, Gimbel began work at the family store in Philadelphia. He served briefly in a variety of positions before becoming a vice-president in 1909. That same year he played a major role in convincing his father and uncles to open a branch in New York City. There they rented a ten-story building on Broadway between Thirty-second and Thirty-third streets. Macy's, the store that became their chief (albeit friendly) rival, stood a block away. Superbly sited at the confluence of the Pennsylvania and Long Island railroads, four subways, and the Hudson Tubes (an underground railroad connecting Manhattan and several New Jersey communities), the new Gimbels opened in 1910 and proved an immediate success. Not long after, in an astute move, Bernard persuaded his reluctant elders to purchase for $9 million the building on which they were paying an annual rent of $655,000.

On April 4, 1912, Gimbel married Alva Bernheimer. They had five children, including a son, Bruce, who succeeded Bernard as president of Gimbels. In 1923 the family moved to Chieftans, a 200-acre estate, in Greenwich, Conn. In the 1920's Gimbel's love of athletics, travel, and high living earned him a reputation as a member of the so-called "international sporting set." But during these years he also helped expand Gimbels. In 1922 he persuaded the family to convert Gimbel Brothers into a public corporation. He engineered Gimbels' purchase of the Saks Thirty-fourth Street and Saks Fifth Avenue stores in 1923, and of

Kaufmann and Baer of Pittsburgh in 1925. The Saks Thirty-fourth Street store closed in 1965, but the other two proved to be highly profitable acquisitions.

In 1927, following a riding accident, Isaac Gimbel retired from the active management of Gimbels to chairmanship of its board of directors. Bernard became president, although he never considered himself as able a merchant as his father. His success in business was due less to attention to detail than to his grasp of broad issues and his ability to sense the public's mood. He avidly read the newspapers and daily traveled the subways of his beloved New York City to keep abreast of the tastes and interests of his customers.

Under his leadership, Gimbels weathered the Great Depression, but not without losses. Profits tumbled from $1.5 million in 1927 to a loss of $4.4 million in 1932. But red ink gave way to profits of $347,000 in 1934 and $1 million in 1935. A shrewd guess that World War II would create shortages led Gimbel to borrow $21 million to lay in stocks of hard-to-obtain items such as nylon and silk stockings and toy electric trains that were sold at considerable profit in 1942 and 1943. At the war's end Gimbels marketed surplus military items, including small flare parachutes and field telephones, as toys for children.

During and after the war Gimbel stressed thrift, deliberately keeping the main store rather dowdy in appearance. "Nobody, but nobody," he boasted in his ads, "undersells 'plain old Gimbels.'" Sensing a growing affluence in the country, Gimbel refurbished the New York City store in 1949, giving it a smart, more fashionable appearance. Even so, the company continued to cater to every economic level, from its basement stores for bargain hunters to its Saks Fifth Avenue stores for those seeking luxury items.

Under Bernard Gimbel's direction, talented outsiders gradually moved into many top positions in the firm. Those whom he put in charge of branch stores were given freedom to adapt to the particular needs and tastes of the communities they served. Gimbel, on occasion, erred in business decisions. He was very slow to join the movement of department stores to the suburbs, for example, beginning only in 1953, the year he stepped down as president. By 1966, however, the firm was operating twenty-seven Gimbels stores and twenty-seven Saks stores across the nation, many in the new shopping malls that were revolutionizing the retail business.

Gimbel continued as chief executive officer of the company until 1961 and as chairman of the board until his death. Except for two years during the depression, Gimbels grew steadily during his association with the firm. Sales were $122 million in 1927, the year he became president. They exceeded those of Macy's for the first time in 1944, reaching $194.5 million. *Fortune* that year hailed Gimbel as the nation's top merchant. By the end of his presidency, in 1953, sales stood at $286 million; in 1966, the year of his death, they totaled $600 million.

Unlike many of his business associates, Gimbel voted for Franklin D. Roosevelt and contributed to all four of his presidential campaigns. Gimbel's labor policies were characterized by *Fortune* as "enlightened expediency." Instead of fighting unionization when his employees began to organize in 1936, Gimbel simply hired an exceptionally skillful negotiator who over the years kept wages competitive with those of rival firms.

Gimbel served on a large number of civic projects, notably the New York World's Fair committees of 1939 and 1964–1965 and the New York Convention and Visitors Bureau. An energetic man who required but five hours of sleep a night, he compensated for an overly hearty appetite by regular and vigorous exercise. He died in New York City.

[See *Fortune*, July 1945; *Life*, Dec. 12, 1949; and *New York Times Magazine*, Apr. 4, 1965. For information about Gimbel's career, see the obituaries in the *New York Times* and the *Washington Post*, both Sept. 30, 1966.]

GERALD EGGERT

GISH, DOROTHY (Mar. 11, 1898–June 4, 1968), actress and younger sister of Lillian Gish, was born in Dayton, Ohio, the daughter of James Leigh Gish, a confectioner, and Mary Robinson McConnell. After business failures in Dayton and Baltimore, James Gish moved his wife and daughters to New York City, where he abandoned them. Mary Gish worked as a store demonstrator and actress (under the name Mae Barnard) and rented a room in the family's apartment to other actresses. At the suggestion of one of these boarders, she allowed Dorothy and Lillian to appear in children's roles onstage.

Dorothy toured with her mother, starting her career as Little Willie in a road-company production of *East Lynne* (1902).

For several years the two girls alternated on tour with Mrs. Gish or an "aunt." They spent rest periods at the Massillon, Ohio, home of Emily McConnell Cleaver, their mother's sister. Dorothy did manage a period at boarding school in Alderson, W.Va., but, as Lillian recalls, lessons were held "in dressing rooms, stations, rented rooms," and at the various historical sites they visited with their mother. The Gish fortunes were at their lowest when *At Duty's Call* closed, stranding them in a southern town and forcing Mary Gish to appeal to her father for help. Fortunately, Dorothy was signed to tour with producer Fiske O'Hara, playing Gillie Morgan in *Dion O'Dare* (1907). Both girls devoted attention to their blooming careers while outwitting the Gerry Society, which was concerned with protecting employed children.

Roles became scarcer as the girls approached adolescence. To make ends meet Mrs. Gish opened an ice-cream parlor in East St. Louis. Here the girls spotted an old friend, Gladys Smith (under her new name, Mary Pickford), playing in *Lena and the Geese* at the local nickelodeon in 1911. When they returned to New York City they renewed their acquaintance with Pickford at the Biograph film studio and, through her, were introduced to D. W. Griffith. He cast them in *An Unseen Enemy* (1912). Dorothy preceded Lillian to California, where Griffith had moved his production facilities, and both girls finally enjoyed financial security with their featured roles in Griffith's films. Dorothy's success before 1916 can only be evaluated by the number of films made (about sixty), since most of the prints have been lost.

Dorothy's first real success came with her role as the bewitching Little Disturber in *Hearts of the World* (1918), made in World War I London and France. Dorothy's comic persona dominated the beginning of the film and created an image she popularized in later movies. Her captivating performance brought her to the attention of Paramount Pictures, which offered her a $1 million contract. Dorothy refused the offer with the flip comment, "Why, it would have ruined me." She signed with Griffith, but she did star in a series of comedies that were later released by Paramount under the banner The Dorothy Gish Artcraft-Paramount Series. Films such as *Battling Jane* (1918), *The Hope Chest* (1919), and *Boots* (1919) won her unqualified praise for her comic pantomime genius. According to a film critic for the *New York Times*, "She can make a motion of hand or foot, a look, a leap, or a fall through the floor more amusing than almost any other screen actress known." The same critic wrote that *The Country Flapper* (1922) "includes in its cast two of the best comedy pantomimists of the screen, Dorothy Gish and Glenn Hunter." *Remodeling Her Husband* (1920), directed by Lillian, was the second-biggest money-maker of Dorothy's Paramount pictures. Her clever pantomiming was balanced by that of a handsome, talented leading man, James Rennie, whom she married on Dec. 26, 1920. The marriage ended in divorce in 1935.

In addition to her comic portrayals, Dorothy joined Lillian in a dramatic role as the blind Louise in *Orphans of the Storm* (1922). She was a sultry Cuban dancer in *Bright Shawl* (1923), a characterization that disturbed fans and critics who preferred her in less worldly roles. She also appeared as Tessa in *Romola* (1924). These films came to be considered classics, but they do not convey Dorothy's comic talent. Her last silent films, all made in England, were *Nell Gwyn* (1926), in which she was acclaimed by *Variety* as "Gish, Pickford, Negri and Swanson in one"; *London* (1926); and *Madame Pompadour* (1927).

As the "talkies" era emerged, Dorothy Gish lost interest in Hollywood. She had enjoyed the improvisation and creative freedom offered by the silents and found the new methods stultifying. She also thought that films should be more daring and creative and should not settle for the merely popular. Her acting was still geared to the demands of silent films, however; *Wanted Men*, not released until 1936, six years after it was made, was a failure, at least partly because of the cast's heavily stylized acting.

She then returned to the stage. In 1928 Gish starred as Fay Hilary in *Young Love*, with James Rennie, recreating the role in London the next year. During the 1930's she played in several productions, some short-lived, including *The Pillars of Society* (1931), *Brittle Heaven* (as Emily Dickinson, 1934), *Morning's at Seven* (1939), William Congreve's *Love for Love* (1940), a touring company of *Life with Father* (as Vinnie, 1940), and *The Magnificent Yankee* (as Fanny Holmes, 1946). Of her title role in *The Story of Mary Surratt* (1947), Stark Young wrote in the *New Republic*, "She works wonders in holding together scenes that are literary and not theatrical; like a good trouper, she never sells the author down the river." She was Mrs. St. Maugham in a summer theater production of *The Chalk Garden* (with Lillian as the governess, 1956). She also made a brief return to Hollywood, appearing in the films *Our Hearts Were Young and Gay* (1944), *Centennial Summer* (1946), *The Whistle at Eaton Falls* (1951), and *The Cardinal* (1963).

Gish performed frequently in radio dramas, such as WJZ's Apr. 22, 1935, production of *Little Women*, in which she played Meg. Her career included appearances on television drama series in the 1950's, such as "Ford Theater," "Robert Montgomery Presents" ("Harvest," with James Dean, Nov. 23, 1953), and "The U.S. Steel Hour" ("The Rise and Fall of Silas Lapham," Apr. 27, 1954). She also starred in *The Story of Mary Surratt* on "Philco Television Playhouse" (Feb. 13, 1949), and *Morning's at Seven* on "The Alcoa Hour" (Nov. 4, 1956). Gish enjoyed travel and during her last years made her home abroad. She died in Rapallo, Italy.

The blue-eyed, fair-haired actress was lively and outspoken, never the perfectionist that her sister Lillian was. Although she seemed sturdier and sunnier than her more fragile-looking, introspective sister, she suffered from severe apprehensions about clothes, her appearance, scripts, and roles. Performances were ordeals. According to Lillian, "Before the curtain went up on opening night, Dorothy was often ready for the hospital." Offstage she was fun-loving; Lillian said of Dorothy, "The world to her [was] a big picnic." Lillian further characterized her sister as having "little common sense," but "fiercely independent," "intuitive about human nature . . . enjoyed making herself ridiculous, . . . [and] a bright flag flying in the breeze." Above all, she was a comedienne. Although she objected to playing comedy because it was often misunderstood by audiences and not regarded as art, and because she thought audiences preferred women in more feminine roles, Gish was, in the words of Richard Schickel, "by far the most naturally charming of Griffith's comediennes." Had her comic films survived, she might well have challenged Charles Chaplin, Harold Lloyd, and Buster Keaton in film history—"she was laughter."

[For further information see clippings and scrapbooks in the New York Public Library Theater Collection, Lincoln Center, in the National Film Information Service, Academy of Motion Picture Arts and Sciences, and in the Harvard Theater Collection. See also Dorothy Gish, "And So I Am a Comedienne," *Ladies Home Journal*, July 1925; and Lillian Gish's two autobiographical studies, *The Movies, Mr. Griffith and Me* (1969); and *Dorothy and Lillian* (1973). Mel Schuster, *Motion Picture Performers* (1971) lists magazine articles. James Parish, ed., *Actors' Television Credits 1950–1972* (1972); and Evelyn M. Truitt, ed., *Who Was Who on Screen* (1977) list performances. Also helpful are Anthony Slide, *The Griffith Actresses* (1973); and Richard Schickel, *D. W. Griffith* (1984). Obituaries are in the *New York Times*, June 6, 1968; *Variety*, June 12, 1968; and *Newsweek* and *Time*, both June 17, 1968.]

ELIZABETH R. NELSON

GOLD, MICHAEL (Apr. 12, 1893–May 14, 1967), radical journalist and writer, was born Itzok Isaac Granich on New York City's Lower East Side, the son of Chaim Granich, a peddler and suspenders-fixtures manufacturer, and Gittel Schwartz. His impoverished Jewish immigrant parents were from Romania and Hungary, respectively. At Manhattan's P.S. 20, Itzok adopted or was given the forename Irwin. He was valedictorian of his grade-school class, but the family's poverty forced him to drop out of school at age twelve.

From 1905 to 1914, Granich worked long hours as a night porter, clerk, and driver for the Adams Express Company. He first became attracted to the radical movement in 1914, when he heard Elizabeth Gurley Flynn speak in Union Square, New York City. At this time his brother Emannuel (Manny) was becoming active in the Industrial Workers of the World. From 1915 to 1917 Granich contributed poems to *The Masses*, edited by Max Eastman, and to the socialist paper the *New York Call*. During the Palmer Raids and Red Scare of 1919–1920, Granich assumed the pen name Michael Gold, borrowing the name of a friend's father who had been a Civil War corporal.

Until the early 1920's Gold lived the transient life of a Bohemian anarchist intellectual. He became involved with George Cram ("Jig") Cook and Cook's Provincetown Players, who produced his one-act plays *Down the Airshaft* and *Ivan's Homecoming* (both 1917), as well as plays by Eugene O'Neill, Floyd Dell, and John Reed. After attending rehearsals, Gold would join O'Neill, and *Catholic Worker* publisher Dorothy Day and anarchist friends, at the Hell-Hole, a writers' saloon in Greenwich Village, where they talked of art and revolution. O'Neill praised *Down the Airshaft* as "the short, simple flannels of the poor," and Gold's later dramas showed his commitment to proletarian art. *Hoboken Blues* (1928) was a fantasy of Harlem life based on the constructivist theories of Vsevolod Meyerhold. It was produced by the New Playwrights Theater, established by Gold, John Dos Passos, and John Howard Lawson. A second full-length play, *Fiesta* (1929), was based on his experiences from 1917 to 1919 while working on the Tampico oil fields in Mexico, where he became further acquainted with Marxism. Neither of these plays was successful as literature. Nevertheless, Stark Young, who in a review of *Fiesta* acknowledged Gold's weaknesses in craftsmanship and "lack of maturity in meaning," also took note of his "genuine poetic instinct for types . . . contrasts of personality, raw color, youth, and pressing life."

These artistic characteristics, and Gold's lifelong dedication to proletarian causes, were prominently exhibited in his most important work, *Jews Without Money* (1930). This novel, an episodic, fictional account of Gold's impoverished childhood, was an impassioned plea for a socialist transformation of American society. He described the sweatshops as "ghastly and dim as an inferno," the "dark sinks of all the evil in the world."

Gold's preoccupation with the frightening experiences of his ghetto youth often resulted in a lack of aesthetic distance in his work, especially the poems. Yet *Jews Without Money* had an intermittent irony that deflated his tendency toward sentimentality, as in his description of his "humble funny little East Side mother" who "hobbled about all day in bare feet, cursing in Elizabethan Yiddish."

Together with *Jews Without Money*, Gold is most noted for his theoretical pronouncements on "proletarian literature," the most important of which are "Towards Proletarian Art" (*Liberator*, February 1921) and "Proletarian Realism" (*New Masses*, October 1930). Based as much upon Walt Whitman as upon Lenin, Gold's theories advanced nineteenth-century utopian idealism toward radical political change. Unlike many middle-class radicals, Gold thought that a proletarian literature would aid in bringing the worker to class consciousness and thus prepare him for the coming class revolution.

Gold allied his theoretical positions with practical commitment to social reform, working with the Communist party as a journalist and editor long after many literary radicals had left the movement following the revelation of Stalin's repressive acts in the 1930's and 1940's. After his studies in journalism at New York University and an unhappy semester as a special student at Harvard in 1914, Gold reported on a factory strike for the magazine *Blast*, and there he met Bartolomeo Vanzetti. In 1920 Gold became a contributing editor of the *Liberator*, the successor to *The Masses;* in 1926 he became editor of *New Masses*, where, through the first half of the 1930's, he enjoyed his greatest literary and editorial influence. In 1933 he became a regular columnist with the *Daily Worker*, producing thousands of columns until almost the end of his life. Since bursts of essay-length work seemed to appeal to him more than long compositions, and since he devoted much time to daily involvement with radical movements, Gold never produced another major novel like *Jews Without Money*. He left several unfinished novels at his death.

In his critical and polemical essays (frequently venomous and, in Daniel Aaron's words, "passionate, flamboyant, and inchoate"), Gold exerted a strong influence both upon the Communist movement and upon the critical life of his time. He attacked the "uncommitted" liberal writers—Max Eastman, James T. Farrell, and the *Partisan Review* editors—in such essays as "Go Left, Young Man" (*New Masses*, January 1929) and "Notes on Art, Life, Crap-Shooting, Etc." (*New Masses*, September 1929), and he sought to preserve the intellectual aspects of Communism in "John Reed and the Real Thing" (*New Masses*, November 1927) and "America Needs a Critic" (*New Masses*, October 1926). In his famed "Prophet of the Genteel Christ" (*New Republic*, Nov. 22, 1930), Gold ridiculed Thornton Wilder's novels as reactionary, and attacked New Humanism and T. S. Eliot's adherence to the traditional in art. Some of Gold's acerbic political articles were collected in *120 Million* (1929) and *Change the World!*

(1937). *The Hollow Men* (1941) gathered five of his most vitriolic essays against those "renegades" who had been alienated from Communism by the Hitler-Stalin Pact of 1939.

In the last decade of his life Gold retired to San Francisco, where despite decreasing vision he continued to write for the *Worker* (the successor to the *Daily Worker*) and the *People's World*. He died in San Francisco. He was remembered by Edmund Wilson as the most dedicated and most "naturally gifted" of the American Communist writers, for whom the workers' revolution represented, as Gold wrote at the conclusion of *Jews Without Money*, "the true Messiah."

[Gold's works include *Life of John Brown* (1924); the plays *Money* (1929) and *Battle Hymn* (with Michael Blankfort, 1936); and the children's book *Charlie Chaplin's Parade* (1930). Stories, poems, journalistic columns, essays, and critiques are in anthologies: Granville Hicks et al., eds., *Proletarian Literature in the United States* (1935); Samuel Sillen, ed., *The Mike Gold Reader* (1954); Joseph North, ed., *New Masses* (1969); and Michael Folsom, ed., *Mike Gold* (1972). See Edmund Wilson, *The Shores of Light* (1952); Walter Rideout, *The Radical Novel in the United States, 1900–1954* (1956); Irving Howe and Lewis Coser, *The American Communist Party* (1957); Daniel Aaron, *Writers on the Left* (1961); Michael Folsom, "The Education of Michael Gold," in David Madden, ed., *Proletarian Writers of the Thirties* (1968); John Pyros, *Mike Gold* (1979); and Paul Berman, "Mike Gold, the Communist, and the Jews," *Village Voice Literary Supplement*, Mar. 1983. An obituary is in the *New York Times*, May 16, 1967.]

FRANK R. CUNNINGHAM

GOLDBERG, REUBEN LUCIUS ("RUBE") (July 4, 1883–Dec. 7, 1970), cartoonist and sculptor, was born in San Francisco, Calif., the son of Max Goldberg, a German immigrant who was successful in real estate, banking, and local politics, and Hannah Cohen. His interest in drawing was evident by the time he was four. At twelve he was taking art lessons from a sign painter. Following graduation from San Francisco's Lowell High School, he entered the University of California at Berkeley to major in engineering. He drew illustrations for the student paper, and as a reward for a prize cartoon in the class yearbook, he received a trip to Yosemite. After taking his B.S. degree in 1904, Goldberg took a job with the city engineering department. For almost a year he shaped sewer lines and water mains, but the work did not appeal to him and he left his municipal post to try his hand at newspaper art.

The consequence was a career as unique as the odd characters he developed on his drawing board. First came a brief period (1904–1905) as a sports cartoonist with the *San Francisco Chronicle*. For the *San Francisco Bulletin* (1906–1907) he visited prizefight training camps to make "action" sketches. He also wrote about what he saw; what he produced, he said, was "a sort of mild, semi-sarcastic ridicule, not of individuals but of situations and actions."

In 1907, Goldberg was hired as a sports cartoonist and columnist for the *New York Mail*, where he remained for nineteen years. After Franklin P. Adams, the humor columnist of the *Mail*, suggested that Goldberg take notice of "what funny questions people ask," the young cartoonist produced *Foolish Question No. 1*. It showed a man who had fallen from the top of the Flatiron Building in New York City being asked if he was hurt. "No, you idiot. I jump off this building every day to limber up for business," was the reply. Thus began the highly successful Foolish Questions series. Goldberg knew that the wild drawings and texts that characterized the series "had struck that human note which gets anything of this kind over, whether it is a drawing, a song, or a piece of writing." Countless readers submitted suggestions, and the series ultimately ran to the tens of thousands. On Oct. 17, 1916, Goldberg married Irma Seeman; they had two children.

The Foolish Questions series was followed by *Phony Films*, *I'm Cured*, and the incredibly complex *Inventions*, which resulted in Goldberg's name being used as an adjective. According to *Webster's Third New International Dictionary*, a Rube Goldberg contrivance achieves "by extremely complex roundabout means what actually or seemingly could be done simply." In the words of the writer William Murrell, these "lunatic devices to prevent anyone from stealing the milk or pulling your hair are fearfully and wonderfully made of pulleys, ropes, knives, cats, bees, sponges, pieces of cheese, revolvers, and other articles. . . . The mere sight of any one of them, even before following the minute a-b-c-d, etc., of the 'Key,' puts the spectator in a happy condition, ready for the leap into the utterly irrational."

Goldberg's comic-strip creations include *Mike and Ike—They Look Alike*, *Boob McNutt*,

The Weekly Meeting of the Tuesday Ladies' Club, and *Lala Palooza*. Perhaps his best-known character was the inventor known as Professor Lucifer Gorgonzola Butts, whose origins can be traced back to Goldberg's student days in mine engineering and his first contacts with complicated machinery. An amiable session with the literary scholar William Lyon Phelps led to the creation of *Lala Palooza*. *Boob McNutt* was syndicated in scores of Sunday comic sections from 1915 to 1934.

As his comic strips became increasingly popular, Goldberg's income grew commensurately—from $30 a week in 1907 to more than $60,000 a year after 1915. For more than a decade and a half Goldberg earned $150,000 annually, and syndication of his work boosted his income to $1.5 million a year. Then, in an abrupt career shift, the nationally popular comic artist joined the *New York Sun* as a political cartoonist in 1938. In their history of American political cartooning, *The Ungentlemanly Art* (1968), Stephen Hess and Milton Kaplan credit Goldberg with being "the only major figure ever to move completely from the comics to political cartooning."

Complicated as Goldberg's comic drawings had been, it was a simple editorial cartoon that brought him a Pulitzer Prize in 1948: *Peace Today* showed a typical American home resting on an atomic bomb, the bomb tottering dangerously on the edge of a cliff labeled "World Control" with a chasm labeled "World Destruction" below.

Many other honors came to Goldberg during his long life. Sigma Delta Chi, the national professional journalism fraternity, awarded him its distinguished service medal in 1945. In 1942 his work was exhibited by the Citizens Committee for the Army and Navy. He was a member of the National Cartoonists Society, the Artists and Writers Golf Association, the Society of Illustrators, and other organizations, several of which he served as president. His many interests included pugilism and vaudeville.

During a brief sojourn in Hollywood in 1930, Goldberg wrote the scenario for a film called *Soup to Nuts*. At the age of eighty he turned to sculpture, and in 1970 his work was exhibited at the Smithsonian Institution. He died in New York City. In an obituary, *Time* magazine reported that "shortly before he died, Goldberg drew a prophecy of the year 2070. The things he foresaw: 'Politicians kissing babies and making promises, women demanding equal rights, and fathers misunderstood by their sons.' "

[Goldberg's books include *Is There a Doctor in the House?* (1929); *The Rube Goldberg Plan for the Post-War World* (1944); *Rube Goldberg's Guide to Europe* (1954), with Sam Boal; *Famous Artists Cartoon Course* (1956), with others; *How to Remove Cotton from a Bottle of Aspirin* (1959); and *I Made My Bed* (1960). Articles by Goldberg appeared in *American Magazine*, Mar. 1922; *Collier's*, Feb. 7, 1925; *Vanity Fair*, May 1925; *Cosmopolitan*, Apr. 1928; *Saturday Evening Post*, Dec. 15, 1928; and *Redbook*, Mar. 1934.

See also William Murrell, *A History of American Graphic Humor* (1938); Clark Kinnaird, ed., *Rube Goldberg vs. The Machine Age* (1968); and Peter C. Marzio, *Rube Goldberg* (1973). Obituaries are in the *New York Times*, Dec. 8, 1970; and *Time*, Dec. 21, 1970.]

IRVING DILLIARD

GOLDFINE, BERNARD (*ca.* Oct. 1889–Sept. 21, 1967), industrialist and influence peddler, was born in Avanta, Russia, the son of Samuel Goldfine, a junk dealer, and his wife, Ida. Goldfine's father emigrated from Russia to the United States in the early 1890's, and Goldfine, his mother, and his siblings followed about three years later in the steerage section of the SS *Rotterdam*. The family settled in a tenement in East Boston. Goldfine attended Lyman Elementary School and entered Mechanics Arts High School in September 1904. He dropped out of high school after a year to work in his father's junkyard. Goldfine later worked as a messenger for a hatter and as a shoeshine boy. In September 1909 he was indicted with nine others for conspiracy to conceal assets in a bankruptcy case. He cooperated with federal prosecutors, pleaded guilty, and was the only defendant who did not stand trial; four of his coconspirators were convicted, and two served prison terms.

With savings of $1,200, Goldfine formed a partnership in 1910 with a friend, Gordon Wayness, and established the Strathmore Woolen Company in Boston. Goldfine purchased remnants from woolen mills in Maine and sold them to Boston tailors and hatmakers. In 1917 he married Charlotte Goldblatt; they had four children. During World War I, Goldfine made a considerable fortune selling cloth to the Allies for uniforms. He acquired the Georges River Woolen Company in Maine in 1929; the Lebanon and Lebandale mills in New Hampshire in 1931; and, later, the Northfield Mills in Vermont. Goldfine also became active in industrial and commercial real estate and formed two companies, the East Boston Company and the Boston Port Development Company. He bought a mansion in Chestnut Hill, a suburb of Boston, for his wife and children.

Goldfine cultivated the friendship of New England political figures and was a generous contributor to candidates of both parties. Among his political friends were Senator Norris Cotton of New Hampshire, who owned 10 percent of Goldfine's Lebandale Mills and lived in a house owned by Goldfine; Governor Sherman Adams of New Hampshire; Senator Styles Bridges of New Hampshire; Senator Frederick Payne of Maine, who was defeated for reelection in 1958 partly because of his association with Goldfine and who later served as Goldfine's lawyer; Representative John W. McCormack of Boston; Mayor James Michael Curley of Boston; and Massachusetts governors Foster J. Furcolo, Paul A. Dever, Maurice J. Tobin, and Joseph B. Ely. In 1951, Goldfine furnished chartered planes for each New England governor to attend a conference hosted by him at Montpelier, Vt.

Goldfine extended a $400,000 line of credit to the *Boston Post* in 1952 on the condition that it endorse Governor Dever's candidacy for reelection. The newspaper met Goldfine's condition, but Dever was defeated. In 1955, Goldfine gave bolts of vicuña to all forty-eight of the governors attending the National Governors' Conference in Chicago. "You operate in the state and you have problems," Goldfine told *Time* magazine in 1958. "Who do you go to? Why, you go to your Congressman or your Senator or to your Governor, not to some schmo."

Through his political connections, Goldfine gained many favors. Mayor Curley arranged a $60,000 tax credit for Goldfine when he purchased a downtown office building. Without asking for public bids, Curley also granted Goldfine the option to build a parking garage under the Boston Common. Governor Dever and Curley's successor as mayor, John Hynes, persuaded President Truman to support a $12 million Reconstruction Finance Corporation loan to Goldfine by promoting the garage as an air-raid shelter. The loan was dropped, though, when Goldfine declined to put up $3 million in collateral. Dever tried unsuccessfully to gain legislative approval for public bonds to finance Goldfine's garage. Goldfine later forfeited his option to build the garage.

Goldfine's lifelong disregard for federal and state regulations resulted in the revocation of the charters of two of his companies. He was also reprimanded by the government's Renegotiation Board for not complying with regulations on more than $2 million in Korean War defense contracts.

During the 1950's, Goldfine sought the help of his longtime friend Sherman Adams, then White House chief of staff, in easing difficulties with the Federal Trade Commission (FTC) over alleged mislabeling of textiles and with the Securities and Exchange Commission (SEC) over failure to file financial reports for his real estate companies. On Dec. 4, 1953, the FTC accused Goldfine of claiming that his products were 90 percent wool and 10 percent vicuña, when in fact nylon fibers had been detected in them. Goldfine got Adams to phone FTC chairman Edward F. Howrey about the alleged violations. Adams then shared confidential FTC information with Goldfine, who agreed to comply with FTC regulations.

But Goldfine continued to mislabel his products, and the FTC received ten more complaints in the next year and a half. On Apr. 14, 1955, Goldfine had Adams set up a meeting with Howrey. Goldfine then negotiated a consent order with the FTC, and the charges were dropped in 1956. In addition, the SEC had filed suit against Goldfine's East Boston Company on May 24, 1954, charging that it had not filed financial reports in six years. Adams asked the White House counsel, Gerald Morgan, to discuss Goldfine's problems with the SEC.

In the summer of 1958, Goldfine gained notoriety as the central figure in the Eisenhower administration's biggest political scandal. On June 10 the House Special Subcommittee on Legislative Oversight linked Goldfine to Adams, disclosing that the industrialist had paid $1,642.28 in hotel bills for Adams between 1955 and 1958. The investigator for the committee, Francis X. McLaughlin, alleged that Goldfine had received preferential treatment from the FTC and SEC as a result of his friendship with Adams. The committee later disclosed that Adams had received a vicuña coat and an Oriental rug from Goldfine and that Goldfine had claimed tax deductions for his gifts. *Look* magazine reported that "to goldfine" had entered the political vocabulary as a verb that meant "to express friendship to influential public officials through expensive gifts." Adams resigned as the White House chief of staff on Sept. 22, 1958, his credibility seriously tarnished by his dealings with Goldfine.

A combative Goldfine accused his congressional interrogators of "hypocrisy" and refused to answer questions about how he had spent $776,879.16 in certified and treasurer's checks between 1941 and 1958. On July 7, 1959, he pleaded no contest to contempt-of-Congress charges and was fined $1,000 and sentenced to a year in prison; the sentence was suspended.

In July 1960, Goldfine began a two-month prison term stemming from a December 1958 contempt-of-court conviction for failing to produce financial records for the Internal Revenue Service. In May 1961 he pleaded guilty in federal court in Boston to the evasion of $790,000 in income taxes and was later sentenced to prison for a year and a day and fined $110,000. Goldfine was also sentenced to an eighteen-month term for refusing to disclose how he had spent the treasurer's checks drawn on his companies and for nonpayment of $5 million in taxes, penalties, and interest. While serving his second one-year prison term, Goldfine pleaded guilty to violating probation rules in receiving smuggled letters. Three prison officials were suspended for assisting him. In 1962, Goldfine consented to sell all of his assets to settle $10.3 million in federal tax claims. He died in Boston. Until the end of his life, Goldfine was an enigmatic character. The United States Office of Immigration and Naturalization has no record that Goldfine ever became a citizen. And despite his zest for politics, he was never registered to vote.

[Sherman Adams describes his relationship with Goldfine in *Firsthand Report* (1961). See also *Newsweek*, July 14, 1958; *Look*, Jan. 20, 1959; David A. Frier, *Conflict of Interest in the Eisenhower Administration* (1969); and Stephen E. Ambrose, *Eisenhower the President* (1984). An obituary is in the *New York Times*, Sept. 23, 1967.]

STEVE NEAL

GORCEY, LEO (June 3, 1917–June 2, 1969), actor, was born in New York City, the son of Bernard Gorcey, an actor, and Josephine Gorcey. (Bernard Gorcey had played Papa Cohen in *Abie's Irish Rose* onstage during the 1920's and was cast in the same role in the 1928 film.) Gorcey left school to become an apprentice in his uncle's plumbing shop in Manhattan. In 1935, Gorcey's father encouraged him to try out for a part in Sidney Kingsley's play *Dead End*. Gorcey recalled, "They wanted real kids. So I got a very close shave and put on kid's knickers and went over. I got the part. I began with a couple of lines and wound up as Spit." One reviewer described Spit as "the littlest, the one most stunted by cigarette smoking, a venomous expectorator for whom the eye of an enemy was like a flying quail to a huntsman."

Gorcey played the same role in the film version of *Dead End* (1937), which featured Humphrey Bogart in a story about the slums and the youngsters who fight for survival there. This film, directed by William Wyler, introduced the Dead End Kids, a group that included Gorcey and Huntz Hall. In 1938 the Kids appeared in *Angels with Dirty Faces*, in which James Cagney played a gangster who pretends to be a coward as he goes to the electric chair in order that he not be a hero to the boys. Cagney observed about working with Gorcey and his friends, "Just tell them you look forward to working with them but you'll slap hell out of them if they do one thing out of line." In 1939, Ronald Reagan appeared in *Hell's Kitchen* and *Angels Wash Their Faces* with the Kids. He commented, "It was an experience similar to going over Niagara Falls the hard way—upstream." By this time, Gorcey and his companions had turned to comedy, and the second film with Reagan and Ann Sheridan was to be their last with recognized movie stars.

In the mid-1940's, Gorcey and Hall formed a new group, the Bowery Boys, which included Gorcey's brother, David, and his father. In the next ten years they made close to fifty low-budget features that became increasingly comical. The film historian Leslie Halliwell called the Bowery Boys movies "quite awful" but noted that "they have retained a certain nostalgia." These movies usually played in second-class, run-down theaters and included *Bowery Bombshell* (1946), *Spook Busters* (1946), *Lucky Losers* (1950), *The Bowery Boys Meet the Monsters* (1954), and *Bowery to Bagdad* (1955).

Gorcey's first films had focused upon social injustice and efforts to defeat crime and expose crooked politicians. By 1940, only his acting style remained as his films became largely slapstick. In some ways, the later Gorcey seemed to be re-creating a kind of back-street "Our Gang." If his first roles suggested a modern-day Artful Dodger, plagued by social rot, his character quickly degenerated into a slouching, good-hearted roughneck. But he and his partners lacked the comic ability of the Three Stooges.

Gorcey retired from films in the mid-1950's and moved to a ranch near Red Bluff, Calif. He married and divorced Catherine Marvis, Evalene Bankston, and Amalita Ward, with whom he had two children. He then married his children's governess, Brandy; they had one child before their divorce in 1962. Five years later he wrote a book about his marriages, a somewhat crude description entitled *An Original Dead End Kid Presents: Dead End Yells, Wedding Bells, Cockle Shells, and Dizzy Spells.* In 1968 he married Mary Gannon. He died in Oakland, Calif.

[An obituary is in the *New York Times*, June 4, 1969.]

ROBERT S. ALLEY

GRAY, HAROLD LINCOLN (Jan. 20, 1894–May 9, 1968), cartoonist, was born in Kankakee, Ill., the son of Ira Lincoln Gray, a farmer, and Estella M. Rosencrans. As a boy he began to draw and placed cartoons in the *Lafayette Journal* in nearby Indiana. After basic education in his home community, he worked his way through Purdue University to a B.S. degree in 1917. That same year he landed a $15-a-week job on the *Chicago Daily Tribune* news staff but soon moved to the art department.

After the United States entered World War I, Gray joined the army in May 1918 and reported to Camp Zachary Taylor in Kentucky. He was transferred to officers' training at Camp Gordon in Georgia, where he served as a bayonet instructor. Discharged with the rank of second lieutenant in December, he rejoined the *Tribune*.

A venturesome spirit caused Gray to break away from the *Tribune* and open his own art studio in Chicago. Although he devoted himself at first to commercial projects, he became a sideline assistant draftsman for the cartoonist Sidney Smith's daily feature, *Andy Gump*. This work, which he said gave him "the finest training any apprentice cartoonist could dream up," became his commanding interest for five years. The *Gump* success, through wide syndication, induced Gray to try a comic strip of his own. He created strips known as *Private Lives, Maw Green,* and *Little Joe* but settled on *Little Orphan Annie.*

Appearing first on Aug. 5, 1924, under the joint auspices of the *New York Daily News* and the *Chicago Tribune*, *Annie* became a sensation and was soon carried by about 400 newspapers. Between 1926 and the late 1940's, Gray also produced a dozen *Annie* books—collections of the strip and his own commentary. In all, *Annie* brought Gray a $5 million fortune.

Gray often said that "Annie narrowly missed being an Andy." Captain Joseph Medill Patterson, the founder of the *New York Daily News*, was credited with recommending that Gray "put skirts on the kid and call her Little Orphan Annie." Gray found it sound advice, for many other strips were using boys. As an orphan, Annie would have "no extraneous relatives, no tangling alliances, and the freedom to go where she pleased." Her automatic exclamation was "Leapin' lizards!" uttered frequently in the presence of her close companion, the dog Sandy, whose response, equally automatic, was "Arf! Arf!" Yet, Annie's world was by no means benign, and Gray defended the strip's violence. "Sweetness and light—who the hell wants it?" he said.

Stephen Hess and Milton Kaplan described *Little Orphan Annie* as "through the years the most blatantly political of the comic strips." Though they tag Gray as an "ultraconservative," they credit him with keeping politics out of the strip for its first ten years. But by 1934, Gray's "strong distaste for Franklin D. Roosevelt burst onto the comic page." In various episodes, Gray manifested his opposition to gasoline rationing, income taxes, and the welfare state. "Communists" and "Democrats" were often indistinguishable epithets in Annie's vocabulary.

Gray made his views on national politics evident largely through a leading character, Daddy Warbucks, the business-world benefactor of the strip's "adult child." As his name suggested, Warbucks was "a munitions tycoon if not an outright war profiteer." In the mid-1930's, Richard L. Neuberger, who later became a United States senator, wrote, "Daddy Warbucks is on trial for cheating the government out of its taxes. Of course, everyone knows he is not guilty; he is being railroaded by agitating politicians, malcontents and dangerous college professors . . . while [in real life] Samuel Insull awaits trial for the collapse of his utilities empire at the hands of a government whose President is influenced by insidious university pedagogues" (*New Republic*, July 11, 1934). In June 1967, Gray's moppet ran a campaign for the passage of a congressional bill to make the penalty for burning an American flag as much as a year in prison. One drawing showed "babbling ninnies" tearing down the flag and setting it on fire.

Through the decades, Annie and Daddy Warbucks adjusted to a changing world. But not having grown up, Annie looked about the same, and she confronted various imbroglios with a persistent inquisitiveness. Al Capp, who became known for his conservative views in his later years, went so far as to say that Gray was "a sharper observer of American trends than Walter Lippmann," created characters that have "endured longer than Upton Sinclair's," and drew "better pictures in his seventies than Picasso."

Gray married Doris C. Platt on Oct. 22, 1921; she died in 1925. On July 17, 1929, he married Winifred Frost, who helped him with his work. He resided mostly in his rural home near Southport, Conn., with winters in La Jolla, Calif., to which he moved in his last year. This was consistent with his oft-repeated message that people should leave crowded cities and enjoy the freedom of the countryside. He traveled about the nation during part of almost every year to keep informed on popular attitudes, a practice that allowed him little social life.

At Gray's death, Little Orphan Annie, with the frizzy hair and magnetic eyes, had become an American institution. Her endurance was proved when, in the late 1970's, *Annie* was successfully adapted as a Broadway and Hollywood musical. By 1986, Leonard Starr, who succeeded Gray as *Annie*'s artist, depicted Annie moving wide-eyed into the future, coping with digital technology and laser beams.

[Gray's unpublished works and papers are at Boston University. His books include *Little Orphan Annie* (1926); *Little Orphan Annie in the Circus* (1927); *Little Orphan Annie and the Haunted House* (1928); *Little Orphan Annie Bucking the World* (1929); *Little Orphan Annie, Never Say Die* (1930); *Little Orphan Annie Shipwrecked* (1931); *Little Orphan Annie, Willing Helper* (1932); *Little Orphan Annie in Cosmic City* (1933); *Little Orphan Annie and Uncle Dan* (1934); *Little Orphan Annie and the Gila Monster Gang* (1944); *Arf! Arf! The Life and Hard Times of Little Orphan Annie, 1935–1945, and Leapin' Lizards* (with Al Capp, 1945); and *Little Orphan Annie and the Gooneyville Mystery* (1947).

See Richard L. Neuberger, "Hooverism in the Funnies," *New Republic*, July 11, 1934; Frank L. Mott, *American Journalism* (1941); and Stephen Hess and Milton Kaplan, *The Ungentlemanly Art: A History of American Political Cartoons* (1968). Obituaries are in the *New York Times*, May 10, 1968; *Time*, May 17, 1968; and *Newsweek*, May 20, 1968.]

IRVING DILLIARD

GREEN, THEODORE FRANCIS (Oct. 2, 1867–May 19, 1966), governor and senator from Rhode Island, was born the son of Arnold Green, a lawyer, and Cornelia Abby Burges, in Providence, R.I. Heir to a textile fortune, Theodore Green was educated at private schools. He graduated from Providence High School, received his B.A. (1887) and M.A. (1890) from Brown University, and attended Harvard University Law School and the universities of Bonn and Berlin. From 1894 to 1897 he was an instructor in Roman law at Brown. He never married. He devoted his long life to the practice of law and business. He served as president of J. P. Coats from 1912 to 1923 and of the Morris Plan Bankers' Association from 1924 to 1927.

Green entered politics in 1906 as a member of a reform party that fused with the Democratic party, and he became active in efforts to reform his state's government. He served in the Rhode Island House of Representatives in 1907 and was an unsuccessful candidate for governor in 1912 and 1930 and for Congress in 1920. He was elected governor of Rhode Island in the Democratic landslide of 1932, running ahead of the state ticket. From a legislature in which the Republicans held a small majority, he was able to secure a compromise relief bill before Franklin Roosevelt took office; the bill enabled the state to borrow Reconstruction Finance Corporation (RFC) funds to afford work for the unemployed and rebated debts owed by towns and cities. In the next two years he strengthened the governor's office by wielding vetoes, assuming administration of RFC funds, controlling federal patronage, and taking charge of the legislative program.

Reelected in 1934 by a larger plurality than in 1932, Green staged a coup that gave the Democrats control of both houses of the legislature, opening the door to further reform. Like Roosevelt, Green effectively used the radio to win public support for his actions and policies.

In 1936, Green was elected to the United States Senate, beginning a long career characterized by devout faith in democracy and humanitarianism, party loyalty, and internationalism. In his first year he supported the New Deal measures on housing, taxation, and unemployment. Despite opposition from his constituents, he supported Roosevelt's Court-packing plan and voted to confirm Hugo Black's nomination to the Supreme Court.

Green voted for Harry Truman's Fair Deal measures and to sustain presidential vetoes. During the legislative struggle over the civil rights bill of 1957, the Senate majority leader, Lyndon B. Johnson, turned to Green to win eastern support for the compromise by which jury trials were to be used in criminal cases but not in civil ones.

Believing the United States had made a mistake by not joining the League of Nations, Green favored revision of the neutrality laws in the late 1930's in order to aid democratic governments in Western Europe and supported the Lend-Lease Act. During World War II he introduced the companion to a House bill that provided absentee voting for members of the armed forces in the continental United States and suspended poll taxes for these voters. After it was enacted over strenuous southern opposition, he devoted his efforts to extending the ballot to overseas service personnel. However, Green vigorously opposed the watered-down Absentee Voting Act of 1944.

It was as a member of the Senate Foreign Relations Committee that Green made his most important contribution. Assigned to the committee in 1938, he served until 1959, the sole interruption occurring during the Eightieth Congress (1949–1951). He upheld Truman's foreign policies, including the Truman Doctrine, the NATO alliance, the Marshall Plan, and the Korean intervention. Green opposed the Bricker amendment to restrict executive power in foreign relations.

Green's twenty years of service came to a climax in 1951 when he became committee chairman. As chairman, he generally supported President Eisenhower, but he looked askance at Secretary of State John Foster Dulles' wide range of activities outside the United Nations. His maxim was, "In the field of foreign policy, if in doubt, support the President."

A notable exception occurred in 1958 when it appeared to him that the Eisenhower administration was preparing to exceed a joint congressional resolution by extending the commitment to defend the Formosa (Taiwan) area to include intervention in the islands of Quemoy and Matsu, which lie just off the Chinese mainland and 200 miles distant from Formosa. Green wrote to the president and expressed his concern that the nation might become involved in hostilities in defense of Quemoy and Matsu, which he thought were not vital to the defense of Formosa. Eisenhower assured him that the United States would not become "involved in military hostilities merely in defense of Quemoy or Matsu." He further recognized that the joint resolution looked to the defense of the Formosa area. The exchange of letters was publicized and apparently served to moderate the administration's policy.

During the first year and a half of his committee chairmanship, Green discharged his duties with vigor. Late in 1958 his hearing and vision became impaired; on Jan. 30, 1959, he tendered his resignation as chairman.

He had experienced no difficulty in being thrice reelected to the Senate in 1942, 1948, and 1954. On May 27, 1957, at the age of eighty-nine years, seven months, and twenty-six days, he became the oldest man ever to serve in the Congress. In January 1960, his health failing visibly, Green announced he would not again be a candidate. He died in Providence.

A patrician in politics, in Truman's words, "a leader in the fight for social progress," an advocate of a responsible internationalist foreign policy, Green was also a wit, a social favorite, a dandy in dress, and an athlete who played tennis until he was eighty-eight.

[The Green papers are in the Library of Congress. Numbering approximately 350,000 items, they cover mainly the period from 1937 to 1960. The John Hay Library at Brown University has collected his miscellaneous writings. An excellent biography is Erwin L. Levine, *Theodore Francis Green*, 2 vols. (1963). Obituaries are in the *New York Times*, May 20, 1966; and *Time*, May 27, 1966.]

JAMES A. RAWLEY

GREENBAUM, EDWARD SAMUEL (Apr. 13, 1890–June 12, 1970), lawyer, was born in New York City, the son of Samuel Greenbaum, a New York State Supreme Court justice, and Selina Ullman. He attended the Horace Mann School and Williams College, receiving his B.A. in 1910. After graduating from Columbia Law School in 1913, he was admitted to the New York bar and practiced law in New York City for two years. He then joined his older brother Lawrence, Herbert A. Wolff, and Morris L. Ernst to form the firm Greenbaum, Wolff and Ernst. In 1920 he married Dorothea Rebecca Schwarcz, who later became a well-known sculptor; they had two children.

When the United States entered World War I, Greenbaum joined the army as a private after his color blindness kept him out of an officers' training program. At Camp Upton on Long Island, he set up a night school to teach English to immigrant recruits. Because of the success of his program, on Feb. 6, 1918, the army promoted him, the first person commissioned a captain from the ranks.

Returning to civilian life, he built up a prosperous practice. In 1933 a bankruptcy court named him trustee for the American estate of Ivar Kreuger, the Swedish financier known as the world's match king, who had committed suicide in Paris after going broke and who left debts in the hundreds of millions of dollars. Over the next six years, Greenbaum built up the estate's assets from less than $84,000 to more than $3 million. His long friendship with Arthur Hays Sulzberger, the publisher of the *New York Times* from 1935 to 1961, led to Greenbaum's service as counsel for the trust that controlled the *Times*. He helped develop a pension fund for *Times* employees and helped to mediate disputes between the newspaper and its workers.

Greenbaum became involved in two major literary cases. The Russian expert George F. Kennan, a neighbor of Greenbaum's in Princeton, N.J., put him in touch with Svetlana Alliluyeva, Joseph Stalin's daughter, when she moved to the West in 1967. After journeying to Switzerland and advising Alliluyeva on the intricacies of publishing contracts, Greenbaum returned to the United States with the manuscript of her *Twenty Letters to a Friend* and offered it to Harper and Row, which his firm had represented for many years. He later became Alliluyeva's close friend and counsel.

In 1967, Greenbaum also defended Harper and Row in its efforts to publish *The Death of a President*, William Manchester's account of the assassination of President John F. Kennedy. Jacqueline Kennedy, the book's original sponsor, objected to parts of the book and brought suit to block its publication; she eventually dropped the suit.

Greenbaum's involvement in public service and legal reform began in 1928 when he headed a lawyers' committee working with the new Institute for the Study of Law at Johns Hopkins University. The committee focused on problems relating to litigation of civil cases. Greenbaum maintained his interest in these problems and in 1952 chaired a special committee of the Association of the Bar of the City of New York that helped realize a state commission on court reform. This led to the establishment of the New York State Judicial Conference to oversee the administrative work of the courts. Greenbaum worked with the conference; in 1961 its studies resulted in a constitutional amendment that overhauled the state's court system.

In 1933, Governor Franklin D. Roosevelt selected Greenbaum to head the New York Alcohol Control Commission after the repeal of Prohibition. Greenbaum was an assistant to the United States attorney general from 1934 to 1938 and a member of the United States delegation to the United Nations in 1956–1957. He was also active in Jewish communal affairs and in local bar groups in New York and New Jersey, to which he moved in 1954.

Between the two world wars, Greenbaum retained a commission as an officer in the army reserves. In 1940 the army promoted him to lieutenant colonel. He served during World War II as an executive officer to Robert P. Patterson, undersecretary and then secretary of war. He negotiated many major contracts between the government and private defense firms. In 1945 he left the army with the rank of brigadier general. Greenbaum died in Princeton after a long illness. He worked at his firm until his death, although he had gone into semiretirement a few years earlier.

Greenbaum never specialized in a particular branch of law, but he was a noted trial attorney. He liked to describe himself as "an old-fashioned lawyer" and had a reputation as a man who could cut through the complexities of a case and lay bare its essentials.

[Greenbaum's autobiography is *A Lawyer's Job* (1967). See also the obituary in the *New York Times*, June 13, 1970.]

MELVIN I. UROFSKY

GRISSOM, VIRGIL IVAN ("**GUS**") (Apr. 3, 1926–Jan. 27, 1967), United States Air Force officer and astronaut, was born in Mitchell, Ind., the son of Dennis D. Grissom, an employee of the Baltimore and Ohio Railroad, and Cecile King. Grissom was fascinated by aviation and determined to become a pilot. He enlisted in the Army Air Corps in 1944 and spent a year in flight training. When World War II ended, he returned briefly to civilian life and married Betty L. Moore on July 6, 1945; they had two children.

Anticipating a need to better prepare himself for a career in military aviation, Grissom enrolled at Purdue University and earned a B.S. in mechanical engineering in 1950. He again enlisted and was commissioned a second lieutenant in the air force in March 1951. During the Korean War he flew 100 combat missions, winning the Air Medal with oak-leaf cluster and the Distinguished Flying Cross. When the war ended, he was assigned to duty as a flight instructor. Seeking new challenges, Grissom completed the Air Force Test Pilot School course at Edwards Air Force Base in California in 1957. He was serving as a test pilot at Wright-Patterson Air Force Base in Ohio when the National Aeronautics and Space Administration (NASA) was seeking pilots to explore the problems of manned space flight for Project Mercury. Grissom volunteered for this project and was one of seven military test pilots chosen on Apr. 9, 1959, to become the first American astronauts.

After two years of training, Grissom was chosen to fly the second suborbital test flight of a Mercury spacecraft (*Liberty Bell 7*) on July 21, 1961. The flight was without incident until after the spacecraft landed, as planned, in the ocean. While helicopters approached to retrieve the capsule and its pilot, the hatch blew off prematurely (an accident that was never satisfactorily explained), but Grissom managed to leave the spacecraft before it sank.

After his Mercury flight Grissom was assigned to the second manned project, Gemini, with special responsibility for monitoring the development of the spacecraft. He was named command pilot on the first manned flight; his crewmate was pilot John W. Young. Their flight (in the spacecraft that Grissom named *Molly Brown*, after the eponymous "unsinkable" heroine of the Broadway musical) on Mar. 23, 1965, lasted nearly five hours. It accomplished some important objectives of manned space flight, including a change of the spacecraft's orbital plane; the controlling of the craft's landing point was less successful, but the attempt contributed essential information for later flights.

Assigned to Project Apollo following his Gemini flight, Grissom was named on Mar. 21, 1966, to command the first test flight of the three-man Apollo spacecraft. Less than a month before the mission was scheduled to fly, a fire at the launch site during a preflight simulation killed the entire crew, Grissom, Edward White, and Roger Chaffee. Their Apollo mission was to have been the first manned test in earth orbit of the first model of the spacecraft that would eventually take men to the moon. On the day of the accident, the crew was conducting a routine simulation of prelaunch activities in their command module at the Kennedy Space Center. Six hours into the exercise a fire broke out in the spacecraft and spread with incredible speed, for the atmosphere in their vehicle was pure oxygen at slightly more than atmospheric pressure. Within half a minute all three crewmen were unconscious and probably dead, asphyxiated by toxic gases. They thus became the first American astronauts to die in an accident directly related to space activity. An investigating board concluded that the fire was probably started by a spark from an electrical short circuit.

[*We Seven: By the Astronauts Themselves* (1962) is a compilation of commentaries by the first group of seven astronauts. Virgil Grissom discussed his experiences in *Gemini* (1968). An account of the life of an astronaut is Michael Collins, *Carrying the Fire: An Astronaut's Journeys* (1974). Loyd S. Swenson, Jr., James M. Grimwood, and Charles C. Alexander, *This New Ocean: A History of Project Mercury* (1967), details the selection of the original seven astronauts and Grissom's flight. Barton C. Hacker and James M. Grimwood, *On the Shoulders of Titans: A History of Project Gemini* (1977), contains an account of Grissom's Gemini mission.

The Apollo fire and its aftermath are discussed in Courtney G. Brooks, James M. Grimwood, and Loyd S. Swenson, Jr., *Chariots for Apollo* (1979); John Noble Wilford, *We Reach the Moon* (1969); and

Hugo Young, Bryan Silcock, and Peter Dunn, *Journey to Tranquility* (1970). Eric Bergaust, *Murder on Pad 34* (1968), is a somewhat sensationalized account of the fire. The detailed results of NASA's investigation of the fire are in the House Subcommittee on NASA Oversight of the Committee on Science and Technology, *Investigation into Apollo 204 Accident*, 3 vols. (1970). Betty Grissom, *Starfall* (1974), written with Henry Still, is a personal account of her experiences before and after her husband's death. Obituaries are in the *New York Times*, Jan. 28, 1967.]

W. D. COMPTON

GROPIUS, WALTER ADOLF GEORG (May 18, 1883–July 5, 1969), architect, was born in Berlin, the son of Neffen Walther Gropius, an architect who served as head of the Berlin Art School and director of education in Prussia, and Auguste Pauline Manon Scharnweber. Gropius grew up amidst the Prussian bourgeoisie of Berlin. He began his professional training at the Technische Hochschule in Charlottenburg, Munich, in 1903 but interrupted his studies in 1904–1905 to tour Spain, where he worked in a ceramic factory. After spending a year in the army, he went in 1906 to the Technische Hochschule in Berlin.

In 1907, Gropius entered the office of Peter Behrens, famous for his transformation of the industrial plant into a dignified place of work. Ludwig Mies van der Rohe and Le Corbusier also gained early experience in Behrens' atelier, which was the most important in Germany. The distinguished turbine factory for A.E.G. (Berlin General Electric Company) was completed while Gropius was working in Behrens' office. Gropius took part in the discussions held by the Deutscher Werkbund, which had been formed in 1907 to refine workmanship and enhance the quality of production. The artist, the workman, and the industrialist were to collaborate in producing goods of artistic value. The Werkbund is comparable to the attempts of William Morris and his followers to improve the products of the industrial process and stem the tide of Victorian design exuberance.

In 1910, Gropius opened his own office. His first major commission—for the Fagus works (1911), a shoe-last factory at Alfeld on the Leine—set new standards for industrial building and became the initial statement of the principles of modern architecture and the "international style." Three years later Gropius designed a model factory and office building, the Fabrik, for the Deutscher Werkbund exhibition in Cologne. Its walls were developed as planes of glass using curtain wall construction, and it introduced new design concepts in forming interior and exterior architectural spaces. On Aug. 18, 1915, Gropius married Alma Schindler Mahler, who was the widow of the composer Gustav Mahler and the daughter of the Viennese painter Emil Jacob Schindler; they had one child, Manon. (Alban Berg dedicated his violin concerto of 1935 to Manon after she died of polio at the age of eighteen.) The marriage ended in divorce, and in 1923, Gropius married Ise Frank; they had one child.

In spite of the distinguished quality of his architectural designs, Gropius is best known for his role in design education. At the end of 1914 he was appointed by the grand duke of Saxe-Weimar to reorganize the Weimar Art School. The new school, the Staatliches Bauhaus, opened in 1919 and combined an academy of art with a school of arts and crafts. At the Bauhaus under Gropius, an effort was made to unite art and industry, art and daily life, using architecture as the intermediary. For more than a decade, the Bauhaus was the center of creative energy in Europe. It was a laboratory for handicraft and for standardization, a school and a workshop. Architects, master craftsmen, and abstract painters all worked for a new spirit in building.

Among the first instructors Gropius hired were the Swiss painter Johannes Itten, the German sculptor Gerhard Marcks, and the American painter Lyonel Feininger. All students of the Bauhaus were trained as apprentices, were permitted at the end of their course the freedom of the trade, and were then admitted to a building site to gain practical experience and to the studio of experimental design. Bauhaus students were first taught the psychological effects of form, color, texture, contrast, rhythm, and light and shade. They were familiarized with the rules of proportion and human scale and were encouraged to explore the fascinating world of optical illusions, indispensable to the creation of form. The students were led through many stages of creative experiences with various materials and tools to make them aware of the potentialities of each. Gropius proposed to train students to bridge the gap between the rigid mentality of the businessman and technologist, on the one hand, and the imagination of the creative artist, on the other.

He wanted his students to come to terms with the machine without sacrificing their initiative, and thus to bring a sense of order and beauty to mass production, architecture, and community planning.

In 1921 the abstractionist painter Paul Klee joined the Bauhaus staff. He was followed by Oskar Schlemmer, Wassily Kandinsky, and László Moholy-Nagy. In 1925 the school moved into a new complex of buildings designed by Gropius at Dessau, where it came in closer contact with industry. Former students Josef Albers, Herbert Bayer, and Marcel Breuer were added to the staff. Although successful and influential in the world of industrial design and contemporary art, the school came under attack from political ideologues of both the Left and the Right. Leftists did not see the need for this type of art school; rightists thought it nonsensical to teach the seemingly unrelated activities of industrial craft and abstract art theory in the same institution. Gropius resigned his position in 1928, and the Nazi government, after denouncing the faculty as degenerate Bolsheviks, closed the school in 1933.

After his return to private practice, Gropius found few commissions. In 1929 he was involved in housing developments in Berlin, but projects for an engineering school, office buildings in Germany, and public buildings in Kharkov and Moscow went unconstructed. With Marcel Breuer he designed a two-story club lounge interior in an apartment building for the first official foreign exhibition of the Werkbund after World War I, at the Salon des Artistes Décorateurs in Paris in 1930. In 1934 he left Germany to join Maxwell Fry in architectural practice in England and three years later was asked to go to the United States to become the head of the Department of Architecture at Harvard's Graduate School of Design. (He became an American citizen in 1944.) There he developed a curriculum that brought the school to a position of leadership in American architectural education. The curriculum, based on Bauhaus ideas about the integration of the arts and sciences into architectural design, emphasized group study of psychological and biological phenomena to gather facts for a science of design; it broke with the traditional studio practice of studying prototypical buildings.

When Gropius retired from the Harvard faculty in 1952, he formed an architectural firm called the Architects' Collaborative. The name reflects his belief that design for the environment must be a collaborative effort of all professions, crafts, and arts concerned. In 1959, Gropius was awarded the gold medal of the American Institute of Architects. In the last decade of his professional practice, he received commissions that in size and scope exceeded all of those previously undertaken. Though disciplined in thought and methodical in habit, Gropius was a gentle nonconformist who integrated into his designs and his philosophy of education the disparate elements of twentieth-century culture, the repetitive forms of mass-production industries, and the iconoclastic images created by modern artists. He died in Boston.

[Gropius' design philosophy is discussed in his books *The New Architecture and the Bauhaus* (1937) and *Scope of Total Architecture* (1955). For biographical detail and critical evaluation of his buildings, see Sigfried Gideon, *Walter Gropius* (1931) and *Space, Time, and Architecture* (1941); and Nikolaus Pevsner, *Pioneers of Modern Design* (1936). For details of the Bauhaus, see Herbert Bayer, Walter Gropius, and Ise Gropius, eds., *Bauhaus, 1919–1928* (1938). An obituary is in the *New York Times*, July 6, 1969.]

KENNETH H. CARDWELL

GROSVENOR, GILBERT HOVEY (Oct. 28, 1875–Feb. 4, 1966), editor and naturalist, was born an identical twin in Constantinople (now Istanbul), Turkey, the son of the Reverend Edwin Augustus Grosvenor, a professor of history at the American-sponsored Robert College in Constantinople, and Lilian Hovey Waters. The Grosvenor twins, Gilbert and Edwin, spent their childhood in Turkey. The boys absorbed an intense interest in history and archaeology from their father and even assisted him in the preparation of a two-volume history of the area. The work's numerous photographs stimulated Gilbert's interest in photography.

In 1890 the Grosvenor family returned to the United States. The twins attended Worcester Academy and then enrolled at Amherst College, where their father had accepted a position. Enjoying their status as twins, Gilbert and Edwin dressed alike and were not above switching places in an occasional lark. Yet both young men were Phi Beta Kappa scholars and, though of only moderate build, competent athletes, especially on the tennis court. They received the B.A. magna cum laude in 1897, and Gilbert began teaching languages, history, and mathematics at the Englewood (N.J.) Academy for Boys while continuing to study at Amherst for his M.A., which he received in 1901.

Edwin entered law school, but the event that truly separated the twins' destinies was almost happenstance. In 1899, Alexander Graham Bell, the second president of the National Geographic Society, needed an editorial assistant for the *National Geographic Magazine*, a publication then distributed only to its membership. The Grosvenor twins attracted Bell's interest, and he offered the position to whichever of them might be interested. Gilbert accepted, and the man whose name became almost synonymous with the society and its publication began his work.

Another inducement to Gilbert may have been his attraction to Bell's daughter, Elsie May Bell, whom he had met at a graduation social; they were married on Oct. 23, 1900. Elsie Grosvenor became known as the "first lady" of the society, and she accompanied her husband on his wide-ranging travels. (The Grosvenors had seven children, one of whom, Melville Bell Grosvenor, became editor of the *National Geographic* not long after his father's retirement.)

Grosvenor transformed the *National Geographic* from a dull, dry, scholarly journal into a colorful and interesting mainstay of home and school libraries. With intuitive knowledge of the impact of fine graphics, especially photographs and maps, he unerringly picked attractive and informative visuals. *National Geographic* photographs, first in black and white and then in color, became the standard of excellence for generations of photographers. Grosvenor trained himself in photography, and over 400 of his pictures appeared in the magazine, including the first ever taken of the North Pole.

Grosvenor ruled the *National Geographic* with a firm editorial hand. When advertising was finally accepted, long after it had become common in other magazines, he not only carefully segregated advertisements from content pages but refused advertising for liquor, tobacco, patent medicines, real estate, stocks, and bonds because of the educational use of the publication in schools. Though the text increasingly became an accompaniment to the fine illustrations (a ratio of three pages of graphics to one of text), Grosvenor insisted on accurate, clear, and inviting writing. To that end, he developed the seven guiding principles of the *National Geographic*: its contents were to manifest absolute accuracy, maximum timeliness, permanent value, an abundance of instructive and beautiful illustrations, a kindly nature, and freedom from anything trivial, partisan, controversial, unduly critical, or of a purely personal nature. And when Grosvenor was criticized for publishing photographs of nude primitive peoples of the world, he defended the practice as truthful.

Under Grosvenor's editorship, the *National Geographic* grew from a dull technical journal seldom read even by the 900 members of the society to a colorful mass publication enjoyed by more than 4.5 million households and institutions, which obtained the magazine only through membership in the society, not through newsstands or subscriptions. Grosvenor provided readers with their first look at natural color photography in 1910, underwater color photography in 1927, and full-color map supplements that not only provided some of the best general-purpose maps ever printed but were so scientifically accurate that the United States and its allies used *National Geographic* maps in both world wars.

Perhaps even more important than the materials published in the magazine were the policies of the society itself. By 1907, Grosvenor had so increased the revenues of the society that it was possible to send teams of explorers and scientists high into the stratosphere and deep into the oceanic trenches, from pole to pole, up into the Himalayas and deep into the canyons and caverns of the earth. Much of what Americans know of the physical world and its peoples has come from such *Geographic*-sponsored activities.

Grosvenor was elected president of the society in 1920, and no fewer than nine discoveries made in the natural or scientific world now bear his name, including mountains, lakes, rivers, islands, trails, a glacier, and a natural arch. Two birds, one in Nepal and one in New Britain, a shell from Greenland, a fish from Peru, and a drug from China also bear his name. An avid bird-lover, Grosvenor introduced the birds of the world in several series, which he collected into the two-volume *Book of Birds*, one of numerous publications he edited from the society's files.

Grosvenor led an active life in addition to his travels, for he was a tennis and golf player, a blue-water sailor, and a founder of the Cruising Club of America, which established the Bermuda Cup yacht races. He retired as editor in chief and president of the society in 1954, but he continued to serve as chairman of the board of trustees until his death, in Baddeck, Nova Scotia.

[Grosvenor's personal papers are in the Library of Congress, while photographs, writings, and professional correspondence are in the library and archives of the National Geographic Society. No full-length biography has been published, but commemorative issues of the *National Geographic* are informative, especially those of Aug. 1949 (his fiftieth anniversary as editor) and Oct. 1966 (his retrospective and memorial). See also Geoffrey T. Hellman, "How to Disappear for an Hour," *New Yorker*, Sept. 23, 1943. An obituary is in the *New York Times*, Feb. 5, 1966.]

DOROTHY S. SCHMIDT

GROVES, LESLIE RICHARD, JR. (Aug. 17, 1896–July 13, 1970), army officer and director of the Manhattan Project during World War II, was born in Albany, N.Y., the son of Leslie Richard Groves, Sr., an army chaplain, and Gwen Griffith. The family lived on army bases in Cuba, the Philippines, and the western United States. Groves enrolled at the University of Washington in 1913 and transferred to the Massachusetts Institute of Technology the following year. In 1916 he was appointed to the United States Military Academy. In 1918, having graduated fourth in his class, he was commissioned a second lieutenant in the Army Corps of Engineers.

Groves was stationed in Hawaii, Nicaragua, and Washington, D.C., and at other army posts. Whenever possible he attended service schools to complete his civil engineering education. On Feb. 10, 1922, he married Grace Wilson; they had two children. Groves, a brusque man who remained aloof from army politics, was not promoted to the rank of captain until 1934. After Pearl Harbor he was made a provisional colonel and assigned to the War Department to supervise construction of army barracks nationwide. Soon he was given the job of completing the Pentagon in Arlington, Va. By 1942 he was supervising all military construction in the United States.

Groves became known as a hard-driving and efficient engineer, but he longed to lead combat troops. In September 1942 he was offered such a command, but Lieutenant General Brehon Somervell, his superior officer, blocked the assignment, informing Groves that Secretary of War Henry L. Stimson and President Franklin D. Roosevelt had selected him to head the intensive research project, known by the code name Manhattan District, to build an atomic bomb. "If you do the job right," Groves was told, "it will win the war." Groves, who had heard rumors about the unpromising venture, muttered, "Oh, that thing." As consolation he was promoted to brigadier general.

Groves seemed an unlikely choice to direct the Manhattan Project, the most ambitious scientific enterprise in the nation's history. After meeting him for the first time, Vannevar Bush, a senior atomic adviser, expressed concern that Groves would antagonize the scientists. "We are in the soup," Bush wrote James Conant, the president of Harvard University and a scientific adviser to the project. Groves's early performance confirmed Bush's doubts. During his first briefing with scientists at the University of Chicago, Groves noticed that an equation had been improperly copied. Believing that the scientists were trying to trick him, he pointed out the error and proclaimed that his engineering study in the military was the equivalent of two Ph.D.'s. When Groves left the room, Leo Szilard, a key project physicist, raged, "How can you work with people like that?" Groves wrote in his memoirs, "They sure didn't fool me. There were a few Nobel prizewinners among them. But I showed them, just the same, where they were wrong and they couldn't deny it. They never forgave me for that."

Groves's first tour of the project's laboratories was discouraging for another reason: no one knew how to produce sufficient fissionable material for the bomb. Harold Urey's team at Columbia University, which was working on a gas-diffusion process, was badly divided over the procedure, and the plans of Arthur Compton of the University of Chicago to produce plutonium had scarcely advanced beyond the theoretical stage.

Then Groves inspected Ernest Lawrence's electromagnetic separation process at Berkeley. "Everything was going very badly," one of Lawrence's associates recalled, "but Lawrence was saying things were never better. Groves believed every word he said." Although Groves's own scientific panel concluded that Lawrence's process was the least likely to succeed, Groves decided in January 1943 to fully fund Lawrence's electromagnetic plants at Oak Ridge, Tenn. In all, Groves spent $544 million on the electromagnetic program, by far the largest item in the Manhattan Project's $2 billion budget. The electromagnetic process fell far short of projections, and the procedure was abandoned in 1946.

In late 1942 Groves made up for these early mistakes by naming J. Robert Oppenheimer to direct the central laboratory for bomb design and development. Oppenheimer, a brilliant physicist from the University of California at Berkeley, commanded the respect of the scientists. But army intelligence, after learning that Oppenheimer had been closely associated with members of the Communist party during the 1930's, refused to confirm his appointment. Groves for the first time made use of his special Manhattan Project powers to overrule army intelligence, and Oppenheimer remained as director. In turn, Oppenheimer became Groves's adviser and staunch defender, much to the bewilderment of the other scientists.

Groves, now preoccupied with security, recommended that the bomb-development scientists be sequestered from outside contacts; Oppenheimer, eager to defer to Groves on all matters of security, endorsed his proposal to build the new laboratories at Los Alamos, N.Mex. There Groves confined the scientists and their families to the base, censored their mail, planted security officers in the laboratories, and tried to keep the scientists from conferring with their counterparts at Oak Ridge and Hanford, Wash., where plutonium was being manufactured in giant nuclear reactors. Many scientists spent much of their time devising stratagems to circumvent Groves's "compartmentalization" of the project.

With even less success, Groves tried to exclude British scientists from the project. When the War Department insisted on fuller cooperation, Groves instructed his liaison with the British to "hold the fort and give nothing, but be amiable about it." Groves's judgment, ridiculed at the time, was later confirmed: the project's most serious security breach occurred when Klaus Fuchs, a member of the British scientific team, passed atomic secrets to the Soviets. Groves maintained that the British were responsible for failing to conduct an adequate security check.

By the spring of 1945 the gas-diffusion plants at Oak Ridge and the plutonium plants at Hanford were producing enough fissionable material for several bombs; the first full shipment of fissionable materials arrived at Los Alamos in early July. On July 16, 1945, Groves watched as the first atomic bomb was exploded at Alamogordo, near Los Alamos. His terse comment was characteristic: "One or two of those things and Japan will be finished."

Groves never doubted that the bombs would be used against Japan, and his resolution influenced President Harry S Truman. Groves also selected the first atomic targets; he objected, to no avail, when Secretary Stimson deleted from the list Kyoto, an ancient religious capital with well over a million inhabitants. On Aug. 6, 1945, a 400-pound atomic bomb destroyed Hiroshima, a military center, and killed more than 70,000 people. Four days later, when clouds obscured Kokura, the primary target, an atomic bomb was dropped on Nagasaki, killing more than 35,000 people.

Groves assumed that atomic weapons would continue to play a major role after the war. "If there are to be atomic weapons in the world," he wrote, "we must have the best, the biggest, and the most." Accordingly, his peacetime budget for 1946 matched his expenditures during the war. Moreover, Groves helped draft the May-Johnson bill, which would have ensured a strong military presence in the postwar Atomic Energy Commission.

Politicians and statesmen came to rely on the judgment of the "Atom General," as Groves was now described in the press. Groves assumed—wrongly—that the atomic bomb would force the Soviets to capitulate in postwar negotiations. He also opposed the Acheson-Lilienthal plan to share atomic secrets with the Soviets. Most important, in 1945 Groves persuaded President Truman, Secretary of State James F. Byrnes, and congressional leaders that the American monopoly on atomic weapons would last fifteen to twenty years. The Soviets, he insisted, would not have access to sufficient supplies of uranium. Groves's assurances were cited by politicians who proposed an aggressive policy toward the Soviet Union. (In 1949 the Soviet Union, having exploited uranium deposits in East Germany and Czechoslovakia, detonated an atom bomb.)

Groves left the army in 1948 to become vice-president in charge of research for the Remington division of the Sperry Rand Corporation. He retired in 1961. He died in Washington, D.C.

Groves was a heavy but tireless man who pursued his goals relentlessly. "I hated his guts and so did everybody else," recalled Major General Kenneth Nichols, Groves's chief aide on the Manhattan Project. Still, Groves was an effective leader and, in Nichols' words, "one of the most capable individuals I've ever met." Groves's achievements in overcoming production and bureaucratic obstacles during war were impressive and at times ingenious. Once, with War Department permission, he deposited $37.5 million into his own bank account to guarantee a uranium contract. Moreover, his controversial decision to contract the gas-diffusion and plutonium operations to private chemical corporations was justified: the government lacked the organizational resources for huge industrial operations.

But Groves frequently erred when political and scientific problems called for reflection rather than determination. When questioned about civilian casualties at Hiroshima and Nagasaki, for example, Groves said that he had heard that death from radiation poisoning was "pleasant." Once he chilled a congressional committee by stating that a victorious nuclear war might result in "only" 40 million American casualties. His blunder on the duration of the American atomic monopoly and his pronouncements on foreign relations needlessly exacerbated cold-war tensions.

[For reasons of security Groves wrote as little as possible during the war. His wartime diary is deposited with the National Archives, Modern Military Branch, Washington, D.C. See also the manuscript collections at the Archives entitled "Manhattan Engineer District History" and "Manhattan Engineer District Records." Other papers can be found at the Harry S Truman Library Institute, Independence, Mo. Groves's own history of the Manhattan Project is *Now It Can Be Told* (1962).

There is no scholarly biography of Groves. See United States Atomic Energy Commission, *In the Matter of J. Robert Oppenheimer* (1954); Arthur Compton, *Atomic Quest* (1956); Robert Jungk, *Brighter than a Thousand Suns* (1958); Richard G. Hewlett and Oscar E. Anderson, Jr., *The New World, 1939/1946* (1962); Nuel Pharr Davis, *Lawrence and Oppenheimer* (1968); Richard G. Hewlett and Francis Duncan, *Atomic Shield, 1947/1952* (1969); John L. Gaddis, *The United States and the Origins of the Cold War, 1941–1947* (1972); Martin Sherwin, *A World Destroyed* (1973); Robert J. Donovan, *Conflict and Crisis* (1977); Daniel Yergin, *Shattered Peace* (1977); Gregg Herken, *The Winning Weapon* (1980); and Peter Goodchild, *J. Robert Oppenheimer* (1981). An obituary is in the *New York Times*, July 15, 1970.]

MARK C. CARNES

GUNN, ROSS (May 12, 1897–Oct. 15, 1966), physicist, was born in Cleveland, Ohio, the son of Ross Delano Aldrich Gunn, a physician, and Lora A. Conner. While still in high school Gunn built a wireless receiver and one of the first long-range radio stations in Ohio.

Gunn enrolled at Oberlin College in 1915 and later transferred to the University of Michigan, from which he received a B.S. in electrical engineering in 1920. He completed his M.S. in 1921 at Michigan and was awarded a doctorate from Yale in 1926. While at Yale he was an instructor in engineering physics and in charge of the high-frequency laboratory. On Sept. 8, 1923, he married Gladys Jeannette Rowley; they had four children.

From 1927 until 1947, Gunn worked at the Naval Research Laboratory in Washington, D.C. He began as a research physicist and in 1938 was named superintendent of the mechanics and electricity division and in 1943 and 1946, respectively, superintendent of the aircraft electrical division and superintendent of the physics division.

In 1944 Gunn became technical director of the Army-Navy Precipitation Project, which studied ice-crystal formation on airplanes. In 1944 Gunn joined the United States Weather Bureau as director of physical research and served as assistant chief of the bureau for technical services during 1955–1956. From 1958 until his death, he was on the physics faculty at American University.

Gunn held forty-five patents, among them a frequency-selective transformer that aided the development of pilotless aircraft, an improved altimeter, and a vacuum-tube modulation system later used in television. While at the Weather Bureau he developed a theory that air contamination reduced the possibility of rain. He anticipated later work in plate tectonic theory by his study of mountain building and the relationship between mountains and oceanic deeps.

As superintendent of the mechanics and electricity division he developed the idea that earned him the title "father of the nuclear submarine." Uranium fission seemed to Gunn to be the answer to submarine propulsion, a problem upon which the division was then working. On Mar. 20, 1939, he proposed the idea of a fission chamber for a submarine and received $1,500 for the initial research. The main problem concerned separating the lighter U-235 isotopes from heavier uranium isotopes. Gunn and his colleague, Dr. Phillip H. Abelson, had solved the separation problem by the early stages of World War II.

California representative Charles S. Gubser in 1963 introduced a resolution in the United States House of Representatives to honor Gunn and Ableson as the true fathers of the nuclear submarine. The resolution had a lukewarm reception. Many supporters of Admiral Hyman Rickover felt the resolution was intended as a slight to him.

Gunn's awards reflect his wide-ranging interests and accomplishments: the Air Safety Award from the Flight Safety Foundation in 1951; the Robert M. Losey Award of the Institute of the Aeronautical Sciences in 1956; and the United States Department of Commerce Exceptional Service Award in 1957. His contribution to the separation of isotopes of uranium was cited by Secretary of the Navy James V. Forrestal and earned him a Distinguished Civilian Service Award in 1945. Gunn served as a consultant to the Atomic Energy Commission, the National Advisory Committee for Aeronautics, the C. F. Kettering Foundation, and the Geophysical Union.

Gunn contributed to the national security of his country, representing the blend of science and technology with military security that became intensified during and after World War II. He died in Washington, D.C.

[See Norman Polmar and Thomas Allen, *Rickover* (1982); and the obituary in the *New York Times*, Oct. 16, 1966.]

RONALD H. RIDGLEY

GUNTHER, JOHN (Aug. 30, 1901–May 29, 1970), journalist and author, was born in Chicago, the son of Eugene M. Gunther, a traveling businessman, and Lisette Schoeninger, a teacher. Gunther later described his father as a "robust ne'er-do-well," and it was his mother who carried most of the burden of rearing Gunther and his sister. From childhood, Gunther was an omnivorous fact gatherer and, at the age of eleven, started to write an encyclopedia. He was a shy, lonely adolescent when he attended Robert Morris and Lake View high schools in Chicago. He graduated from Lake View in 1918 and, over his father's objections, entered the University of Chicago with the halfhearted objective of becoming a chemist. In his final two years he changed his major to English and enjoyed his first social and professional success when he became literary editor of the campus newspaper.

After earning his bachelor's degree in 1922, Gunther toured Europe briefly and returned to Chicago committed to becoming a journalist. He learned the trade as a cub reporter at the *Chicago Daily News*. Eager to work abroad, he quit his Chicago job in 1924, went to London, and subsisted on part-time assignments. He was hired as a correspondent in the *Daily News* bureau in Paris under Paul Scott Mowrer, who sent Gunther around to the other European bureaus as a roving "swing man." In 1930, Gunther was rewarded with a bureau of his own, in Vienna. These were "the bubbling, blazing days of American foreign correspondence in Europe," Gunther wrote in *A Fragment of Autobiography* (1962), and Gunther was part of a coterie of freewheeling, often opinionated American reporters. He was particularly a friend and student of the older correspondent M. W. Fodor of the *New York Evening Post*, whom he credited with being a major influence on his later work. In 1927, Gunther married Frances Fineman; they had two children.

By the early 1930's, Gunther had published four novels, the first of the string of undistinguished literary efforts that he wrote, he said, "almost as one produces a stick of chocolate by putting a penny in a slot machine." In 1934, Gunther embarked on the project destined to win him fame when he took his wife's suggestion to write a book of reportage on Europe. Cass Canfield of Harper and Brothers raised an advance of $5,000, and Gunther set to work. Midway into the project, Gunther's employer transferred him to London. Despite being much busier, he finished the writing in seven months, and *Inside Europe* was published in February 1936.

A country-by-country survey of the Continent in prewar crisis, *Inside Europe* reflected Gunther's conviction, stated in the preface, "that the accidents of personality play a great role in history." It contained plentiful information on the characteristics and personality traits of Hitler, Mussolini, Stalin, and other political figures. The book, breezy and mildly liberal, was generally welcomed by reviewers. In England, Harold Nicolson praised it as "a serious contribution to contemporary knowledge," but in America, Malcolm Cowley, while praising its range and accuracy, complained that its emphasis on the personal "distorts the author's picture and often weakens his judgment of events." With the public, the work enjoyed success unusual in that day for nonfiction. The Book-of-the-Month Club alone distributed 240,000 copies in seven months in the United States, and it was widely translated and sold abroad.

Gunther and his publisher expended great effort to keep the book current. Nine months after the first edition, a complete revision was published, and further revisions continued into World War II. Richard H. Rovere remarked that Harper had discovered that "books by Gunther can be sold the way dress manufacturers sell dresses and automobile makers sell cars—by changing the model."

Gunther was soon at work on other *Inside* books. He resigned from the *Chicago Daily News* in 1936 and lived thereafter, often tenuously, on the earnings from his books. The success of *Inside Europe* opened doors on other continents. *Inside Asia* was published in 1939, and *Inside Latin America* two years later; both were highly successful.

During World War II, Gunther covered the Allied campaigns in Europe as a radio correspondent, but in 1944 he returned to America and began work on his most demanding project, *Inside U.S.A.* In thirteen months of preparation, he took more than a million words of notes and then spent fourteen months writing 505,000 words. The book, published in 1947, followed the pattern of *Inside Europe*, considering the country state by state and emphasizing the personalities of state political leaders. Depicting America, in the words of the review by Arthur M. Schlesinger, Jr., as a "nation bursting at the seams with vitality," the book was a major success, selling half a million copies in three months. Yet, Gunther was so daunted by the effort that he never completed a projected second volume, to be centered on Washington.

In this same period, Gunther's life was stalked by tragedy. In April 1946, two years after his divorce from Frances Fineman, their one surviving child became ill with a malignant brain tumor. The boy died in June 1947, a month after the publication of *Inside U.S.A.* Gunther wrote a private memoir of his son's illness but, persuaded that it might help other parents, permitted it to be published as *Death Be Not Proud* (1949).

Assisted by his second wife, Jane Perry Vandercook, whom he married in 1948 (they adopted one child), Gunther spent the remaining years of his life turning out books at a factorylike pace. There were more *Inside* books: *Inside Africa* (1955), which he completed despite disabling cataracts; *Inside Russia Today* (1958); and *Inside Australia*, left unfinished at his death but completed by William H. Forbis and published in 1972. There were also books on Franklin D. Roosevelt, Dwight D. Eisenhower, and Douglas MacArthur, as well as novels and juvenile books. In 1957, to meet financial obligations, he wrote an advertisement for a drug company under the title "Inside Pfizer." An international celebrity, he also earned a reputation as a lavish host at his New York apartment. "I've eaten every book," he said, "by the time it's published."

He came to have regrets about introducing the "Inside" usage into the American vernacular. In 1962 he wrote that, with imitation, the term had "come to connote vulgarity and sensationalism, as well as false intimacy." Gunther's own work was seldom criticized on such grounds, however; more often, he was dismissed as superficial. He responded that his purpose was popular education, "to inform substantial numbers of readers on basic facts and themes." In his later years, his reputation, not only as an unprecedentedly successful journalist but as a celebrity on speaking terms with the world's powerful, came to seem a phenomenon of an earlier era. He died in New York City.

[Gunther's papers are at the University of Chicago library; additional papers, mostly radio scripts and lectures, are at the State Historical Society of Wisconsin. For first-person accounts, see Gunther's introduction to M. W. Fodor, *Plot and Counterplot in Central Europe* (1937); "Autobiography in Brief," *Story*, May 1938; and A *Fragment of Autobiography* (1962). See also Malcolm Cowley, "The Personal Element," *New Republic*, Feb. 12, 1936; Richard H. Rovere, "Inside," *New Yorker*, Aug. 23, 1947; "The Insider," *Time*, Apr. 14, 1958; and Marion K.

Sanders, *Dorothy Thompson* (1973). An obituary is in the *New York Times*, May 30, 1970.]

JAMES BOYLAN

GUTHRIE, WOODY (July 14, 1912–Oct. 3, 1967), songwriter and singer, was born Woodrow Wilson Guthrie in Okemah, Okla., the son of Charles Guthrie, who ran a cattle and real estate business, and Nora Belle Sherman, a rural schoolteacher. Although the family endured tragedies in Okemah—a sister was burned to death, three of the family's homes were destroyed, the father's business failed, and the mother began displaying mental symptoms of Huntington's chorea—Woody remained in the town with his older brother, Roy, when the rest of the family moved to Pampa, Tex. He completed his junior year in Okemah High School, serving as the humor editor of the school annual; to raise money for the class treasury, he danced jigs and played harmonica on the streets of the town. He left Okemah in 1927 to rejoin the family in Pampa. It was there that he developed his ability as a guitarist, performing at dances with a trio that included his uncle on fiddle and aunt on accordion, and playing with a country-and-western band.

On Oct. 28, 1933, Guthrie married Mary Jennings; they had three children. In 1937 he suddenly left for California. He soon was performing daily on a sing-and-talk program on radio station KFVD in Los Angeles and became extremely popular for his Will Rogers type of humor. This led to a friendship with newscaster Ed Robbins, through whom he made contact with the progressive left-wing movement of California. In 1939, at the urging of actor Will Geer, Guthrie traveled to New York City, again leaving behind his family. There he acquired admirers in folksinger Pete Seeger and historian Alan Lomax, to whom he was introduced by Geer at a benefit concert for Spanish Loyalist refugees. Lomax presented Guthrie on his CBS network show, "Folk School of the Air"; taped songs and conversations with him for the Library of Congress Archive of American Folksong; and arranged for him to record on Victor. Released early in July 1940 in two volumes (Victor P-27 and P-28), the twelve sides constituting the legendary "Dust Bowl Ballads" were Guthrie's first commercial discs; they brought him renown and remain a landmark in American folk balladry.

In 1941, again through Lomax, Guthrie was hired by the Department of the Interior to write songs and act in a film produced about the Bonneville Power Administration in the Northwest. (In 1968 his contribution was given recognition when a power substation was named after him and Secretary of the Interior Stewart Udall granted him the department's Conservation Service Award.) During World War II Guthrie and folksinger Cisco Houston joined the merchant marine and sailed on three ships that were torpedoed. Guthrie wrote anti-Hitler songs and inscribed his guitar with the legend This Machine Kills Fascists. He was drafted as the war was ending and served almost a year before receiving a dependency discharge. In this period Guthrie's *Bound for Glory* (1943) was published. This portrayal of Guthrie's childhood, family tragedies, and life in Okemah was always referred to by him as his "novel," but others regarded it as an autobiography. (In 1976 the book was filmed, with David Carradine playing Guthrie.)

Having divorced his first wife, Guthrie married Marjorie Greenblatt Mazia soon after World War II. They had four children, one of whom is the singer-songwriter Arlo Guthrie. This marriage also ended in divorce (probably in the mid-1950's), and Guthrie subsequently married Anneke Van Kirk. They had one child. On Guthrie's return to New York after a trek across country in 1952, the symptoms of Huntington's chorea, inherited from his mother, were beginning to manifest themselves. At his wife's urging, Guthrie voluntarily entered a hospital. Finding it difficult to perform and even to write, he remained hospitalized for most of the time until his death at Creedmore State Hospital in Queens, N.Y.

Although Guthrie's father actively fought socialism, Guthrie's own political development was steadily leftward. In the early 1940's he joined the Almanac Singers, formed by Pete Seeger, Lee Hays, and Millard Lampell to promote leftist songs and to perform at factories, union meetings, and antifascist conclaves. "He briefly embraced Communism," the *Rolling Stone Encyclopedia of Rock and Roll* reports, "although he was denied membership in the U.S. Communist party because he refused to renounce his religion, but he did write a column for a Communist newspaper, the *People's Daily World*."

Guthrie is said to have written more than a thousand songs between 1932 and 1952. Many were popularized by the Weavers, the most successful folk group of the 1950's, whose personnel overlapped that of the Almanac Singers. The Guthrie best-sellers in their repertoire included "Hard, Ain't It Hard" and "So Long, It's Been Good to Know You," one of the celebrated "Dust Bowl Ballads." "This Land Is Your Land," also introduced by the Weavers, enjoyed renewed commercial acceptance in 1961, when it was recorded by the New Christy Minstrels. In 1986 the reigning giant of rock music, Bruce Springsteen, included the song in a five-volume best-selling compendium, prefacing his rendition by observing that it was written by Guthrie as a response to Irving Berlin's "God Bless America."

Other popular numbers in the Guthrie oeuvre include "Pastures of Plenty" and "Oklahoma Hills," both extolling the scenic beauty of America; "You've Got to Go Down" and "Union Maid," fervent labor songs; "Blowing Down This Old Dusty Road" and "Do Re Mi," detailing the hardships of migratory workers; "Tom Joad," written after he saw the film *The Grapes of Wrath,* based on the John Steinbeck novel; "Pretty Boy Floyd," a ballad in the Robin Hood tradition; and "Hard Traveling," one of many songs based on his experiences as a hobo. Of this last song, Guthrie wrote, "It's the kind of song you sing after you had been booted off your little place and had lost out, lost everything. . . . It tells about a man who had ridden the flat wheels, kicked up cinders, dumped the red-hot slag, hit the hard-rock traveling."

The novel *Seeds of Man* (published posthumously in 1976) is based on stories Guthrie had written about his search for a silver mine in Texas. His other publications include *American Folksong* (1947) and *Born to Win* (1965).

Guthrie became a major influence on Bob Dylan, who was drawn to his hospital bed. In his debut album (1962), young Dylan not only sang his own "Song to Woody" but imitated Guthrie's singing style. By introducing poetry and protest into rock and roll, Dylan further transmitted Guthrie's message to popular-music audiences in the 1960's.

In the late 1960's Pete Seeger organized a number of memorial concerts for Guthrie. The concerts at Carnegie Hall in 1968 and at the Hollywood Bowl in 1970 were recorded and released as albums, featuring Bob Dylan, Joan Baez, Judy Collins, Richie Havens, Tom Paxton, and Country Joe McDonald, among others. Seeger has also appeared periodically in concert with Arlo Guthrie, who carried his father's folk tradition into the music scene of the 1960's, 1970's, and 1980's.

Guthrie was the poet of the Oklahoma Dust Bowl, of unionization and antifascism, and, above all, of the American hobo and the West. He "sang of the beauty of his homeland," the *New York Times* observed in his obituary, "a beauty seen from the open door of a red-balling freight train or from the degradation of the migrant camps and the Hoovervilles of the Depression years. . . . His vision of America was bursting with image upon image of verdant soil, towering mountains, and the essential goodness and character of its people." In the *New Yorker* in the early 1940's, Clifton Fadiman wrote, "Someday people are going to wake up to the fact that Woody Guthrie and the ten thousand songs that leap and tumble off the strings of his music box are a national possession, like Yellowstone and Yosemite, and part of the best stuff this country has to show the world."

[In addition to the autobiographical books mentioned in the text, see Guthrie's *Woody Sez,* edited by Marjorie Guthrie, with a preface by Studs Terkel and a biography by Guy Logsdon (1975); and Joe Klein, *Woody Guthrie: A Life* (1980). See also Alan Lomax, *Hard-hitting Songs for Hard-hit People* (1967), which contains notes by Guthrie. An obituary is in the *New York Times,* Oct. 4, 1967.]

ARNOLD SHAW

HADAS, MOSES (June 25, 1900–Aug. 17, 1966), classicist, humanist, and translator, was born in Atlanta, Ga., the son of Russian-Jewish immigrant parents, David Hadas and Gertrude Draizen. His father was a shopkeeper and a scholar who published in Hebrew and Latin on the rabbinical exegesis of the Pentateuch. Hadas first studied Greek and Latin at Boys High School in Atlanta. He took his B.A. at Emory University in 1922, having studied classics under E. K. Turner and C. E. Boyd. He received his M.A. (1925) and Ph.D. (1930) in classics at Columbia University and a rabbinical degree at Jewish Theological Seminary (1926).

At Columbia, in classes where he was often the sole pupil, he learned philological and historical method from C. W. Keyes, E. D. Perry, and W. L. Westermann. The teacher to whom he owed, in Hadas' words, "a new conception of the methods, aims, and ideals of scholarship, and of the obligation of teacher to pupil" was Charles Knapp. Hadas' dissertation, published as *Sextus Pompey* (1930), remains the authoritative biography of its subject.

Hadas taught two years (1928–1930) at the University of Cincinnati and then returned to Columbia, where he served in the Department of Greek and Latin until his death. From 1956 to 1966 he was Jay Professor of Greek. During his Columbia years he achieved a fame that transcends narrow boundaries. His lifework divides into scholarship, popularization, and teaching. His most enduring scholarly contributions are his dissertation, his editions of *The Epistle of Aristeas* (1950) and *Third and Fourth Maccabees* (1953), and his own *Hellenistic Culture* (1959). These books display his mastery of Greek and Jewish sources and his consistently sound judgment. His command of German enabled him to translate important secondary works into English: Alfred Körte's *Hellenistic Poetry* (1929), Elias Bickermann's *The Maccabees* (1947), F. A. Gregorovius' *The Ghetto and the Jews of Rome* (1948), Jacob Burckhardt's *The Age of Constantine the Great* (1949), Walter F. Otto's *The Homeric Gods* (1954), and (with James Willis) Hermann Fränkel's *Early Greek Poetry and Philosophy* (1975).

Hadas wrote that anyone who entered classics in the Great Depression was "foolhardy" but "willingness to starve did prove something." As a member of "the generation of the deluge," he watched sorrowfully as the classics were banished from the center of the liberal arts to near oblivion. He was molded by defeat. His first duty became to rescue the classical heritage for democratic America. Hadas long taught extra classes without additional stipend. Concerned because Victorian translations had become an impediment to appreciating the classics almost as formidable as the ancient languages, Hadas saw the desperate need for translations that modern American readers could understand. He began an American tradition of prose translations. He translated Euripides (1936), Xenophon of Ephesus and Longus (1953), Seneca (1956–1958), selections from Roman historians (1956), Plutarch (1957), and Heliodorus (1957). From the Hebrew he translated Joseph Ben Meir Zabara's *Book of Delight* (1932) and the fables of Berechiah ha-Nakdan (1967).

Hadas' greatest single contribution to humane studies in America was his establishment of courses on the classics in translation in the Columbia General Education program, despite the bitter opposition of older classical colleagues. The introduction of these and the required humanities course at Columbia College began what he later called "the American Renascence." His teaching and frequent lecturing extended the popularization of the classics far beyond the Columbia campus. That Sophocles is almost as well known as Shakespeare to so many Americans educated after 1945 is largely due to Hadas. His frequently reprinted histories of Greek (1950) and Latin (1952) literature and his *Ancilla to Classical Reading* (1954) were intended as aids to teachers. Hadas and Gilbert Highet made the Columbia classics department the best known in America.

Hadas was one of the first American Jews to gain tenure in what was then an anti-Semitic profession, but he rejected traditional Judaism and took his religion from Spinoza. He detested official Christianity; indeed, as Norman Podhoretz justly observed in *Making It*, Hadas had a "positively Voltairean hatred of clergymen of any and all denominations." After 1945, Plutarch became one of his favorite authors, a fact that tells us much about Hadas himself. "The amiable and charming sage of Chaeronea," as Hadas referred to Plutarch, resisted the sirens of Christianity and Rome to make of Hellenism a cult whose "prophet and high priest" he became. In such Hellenism, Hadas sought the moral salvation of his own age. To students, he was a revered figure but always accessible. To colleagues, he was an urbane despot, an aristocratic liberal, erudite, elegant, and always ironic. Pretension he could not abide. He began an autobiographical essay, "I am a teacher. Except for wars and holidays I have never been out of the sound of a school bell. I have written books and given public lectures, but these I have regarded as part of my teaching. The life I lead is the most agreeable I can imagine."

Hadas' marriage (1926) to Ethel J. Elkus ended in divorce in 1945, and that year he married Elizabeth M. Chamberlayne. He had two children from each marriage. He died in Aspen, Colo.

[The Hadas papers are deposited in special collections in the Butler Library, Columbia University.

There is no published bibliography. See Hadas, *Old Wine, New Bottles* (1962), an autobiographical essay; and "The Religion of Plutarch," *South Atlantic Quarterly*, XLVI (1947), often autobiographical. See also Gilbert Highet, "Moses Hadas, 1900–1966," *Classical World*, LX (1966–1967); *Commentary*, Sept. 1966; and the obituary in the *New York Times*, Aug. 18, 1966.]

WILLIAM M. CALDER III

HAGEN, WALTER CHARLES (Dec. 21, 1892–Oct. 5, 1969), golfer, was born in Rochester, N.Y., the son of William Hagen, a blacksmith in car shops, and Louise Balko. Hagen wrote in his autobiography that the family "had a simple comfortable home and good plain food but not much left over for extras." When he was seven, Hagen tried to contribute to the family income by offering his mother part of his first week's pay as a caddie at the Country Club of Rochester, but she would not accept it.

One day when Hagen was twelve, he saw through the windows of his schoolroom the golfers at the country club. When the teacher was not looking, Hagen jumped out the window and never went back to school regularly. Later he took courses in car repair, wood finishing (for a piano company), and taxidermy, but his main interests were baseball and golf. Since caddies were not allowed to play on the club course in Rochester, Hagen fashioned his own course in a nearby cow pasture, naming each of the four holes after towns in Florida, where in later years he would win $1,800 to $2,000 per outing. After Hagen won the U.S. Open in 1914 at Midlothian in Chicago, golf claimed him for good.

On Jan. 29, 1917, Hagen married Margaret Johnson. They had one child and in 1921 were divorced. In 1924 Hagen married Edna Strauss; they were divorced in 1934.

In 1919 Hagen won the U.S. Open again, beginning a string of sensational victories that made him the first giant of American and international golf. He was Professional Golfers' Association (PGA) champion in 1921, 1924, 1925, 1926, and 1927, and British Open champion in 1922, 1924, 1928, and 1929. He also won the French Open in 1920, the Belgian in 1924, and the Canadian in 1931.

In addition, Hagen won opens in Massachusetts (1915), Michigan (1921 and 1931), New York (1922), and Texas (1923 and 1929); three Metropolitan Opens (1916, 1919, and 1920); two North and South (1918 and 1923), five Western (1916, 1921, 1926, 1927, and 1932); one Eastern (1926); and the Gasparilla Open in 1935. He was captain of the American Ryder Cup team in 1927, 1929, 1931, 1933, and 1935, and nonplaying captain in 1937. Hagen also played in a number of famous challenge matches. His most cherished victory was over his great rival Bobby Jones, whom he defeated in 1926 by twelve and eleven in seventy-two holes. His most disappointing defeat was his loss to Archie Compston in 1928 by eighteen and seventeen.

In 1922 Hagen toured the United States with Joe Kirkwood, Australian Open champion and trick-shot artist. The pair made a tour of Australia and Japan in 1929, and in 1937–1938 they went around the world, delighting crowds with their show.

It has been estimated that Hagen played over 2,500 exhibitions, often with the rich and famous, including the duke of Windsor and Presidents Warren Harding and Dwight Eisenhower. In 1940 he was named one of the charter members of the PGA Hall of Fame. The following year he retired from competition.

Hagen was one of the most colorful figures ever to play the game of golf. Through his victories, exhibitions, and promotions he made $1 million and, he said, spent $2 million. "I never wanted to be a millionaire," he once said, "just to live like one." He loved fine cars and expensive clothes. "I traveled first-class," he said, "and that included a suite at the Savoy at five pounds a day, the Chez Paris, cocktail hour at the Ritz, the Daimler car with chauffeur and footman, [and] fine silk shirts custom-tailored by A. J. Izod on Conduct Street just off the Strand."

His style of play, like his dress, matched his flamboyant personality. On his tours, as Herbert Warren Wind has written, "Hagen would step shining and unconcerned from the limousine his chauffeur had moved near the first tee—always a little late for his matches." In contrast to Bobby Jones, who wanted every shot to be perfect, Hagen would gamble away a second or third place for a seemingly impossible shot that might bring him in first. He accepted the inevitability of some bad shots and depended on his skill in recovery and putting, for which he was famous. His swing was unorthodox; taking a wide stance, he would start with a sway and end with a lunge, the rhythm evident, according to Ben Hogan, in "the order of procedure." Always conscious of the gallery, he was a master showman in the golden age of sport.

Hagen was the first golf superstar. He was the first, for example, to hire a manager, Robert E. Harlow, and in Hagen's enthusiasm for exhibitions and endorsements, he anticipated the now familiar pattern of the athlete turned celebrity. Hagen's success and showmanship served both to popularize golf worldwide and to elevate the status of the golf professional. He promoted the Reddy tee, which eliminates the need for a pinch of sand or earth for teeing off. He is credited with revolutionizing the dress of golfers by introducing knickerbockers and popularizing the pullover or cardigan sweater and black-and-white shoes. But Hagen's greatest contribution to golf may have been the simple reminder that golf—and life—should be fun. His philosophy was: "You're only here for a short visit. Don't hurry; don't worry—and be sure to smell the flowers along the way." Hagen died in Traverse City, Mich.

[*The Walter Hagen Story* (1956) by Hagen, as told to Margaret Seaton Heck, is the most complete source on his life. Excellent portraits appear in Grantland Rice, *The Tumult and the Shouting* (1954); and in Herbert Warren Wind, *The Story of American Golf* (1956). A summary of his career appears in Will Grimsley, *Golf: Its History, People and Events* (1966). Obituaries are in the *Times* of London and the *New York Times*, both Oct. 7, 1969.]

ROBERT J. HIGGS

HALL, JUANITA ARMETHEA (Nov. 6, 1901–Feb. 28, 1968), actress and singer, was born Juanita Armethea Long in Keyport, N.J., the daughter of Abram Long, an oyster fisherman, and Mary Elizabeth Richardson. Her mother died when Hall was a baby, and so she was raised by her grandmother, whose love of singing had a profound influence on her. She attended public schools in Keyport, sang in the church choir, and in her teens married Clayton King. There is little information about this marriage or about her early years in general, but by most accounts, she moved to New York City in the 1920's to pursue a musical career. Hall, who had a strong mezzo-soprano voice, attended the Juilliard School for a time before abandoning classical studies in favor of the theater.

Hall made her debut in the chorus of an obscure black revue called *Blackbirds of 1926* (not to be confused with the famous *Blackbirds of 1928*), which was produced by Lew Leflies at the Alhambra Theatre in Harlem and starred Florence Mills; it ran for only six weeks. During rehearsals of *Blackbirds*, she met Clement Hall, a singer, whom she soon married in Newark, N.J. The marriage ended in divorce; there were no children.

According to many accounts, Hall went from *Blackbirds* into the chorus of Florenz Ziegfeld's *Showboat* (1927), but this is probably apocryphal, for her name does not appear in the programs and press releases. It is more likely that she spent some time in the late 1920's discovering how difficult it was for a young black woman to work professionally in New York. Black performers were barred from opera (which she loved) and from nearly all theater. Moreover, Hall was short and stocky and thus not a candidate even for the dubious category of "smoky exotics" who occasionally appeared on the Broadway stage of that era.

But Hall could sing, and in the late 1920's she began a long association with the Hall Johnson Choir, which became famous after its appearance on Broadway in *The Green Pastures* (1930). Hall was a soloist with the choir until 1936, when she established her own group. She later estimated that the Juanita Hall Choir had given over 5,000 performances, including concerts at the 1939 New York World's Fair and on the radio with Norman Corwin, Kate Smith, and Rudy Vallee.

In the 1940's Hall set out to establish herself as a singer-actress on Broadway. She played a mango seller—with one line and several crowd appearances—in the Lunts' production of *The Pirate* (1942). In *Sing Out Sweet Land* (1944), a revue of American folk and popular music that starred Alfred Drake, she earned a rave review for her rendition of "Five o'Clock Whistle." She won further critical praise as Leah in *St. Louis Woman* (1946), a Johnny Mercer–Harold Arlen musical about a black jockey. In the role of the jockey's older sister, Hall had several good scenes and a solo number, "Racin' Forms."

In 1948 Richard Rodgers and Oscar Hammerstein II saw her in the revue *Talent '48* and offered her the role of Bloody Mary in their musical *South Pacific* (1949). It was her big break: her portrayal of a barefoot Tonkinese woman who chews betel nuts and sells souvenirs to American sailors delighted audiences and critics, and her singing of "Bali Ha'i" and "Happy Talk" made her a celebrity. She won a Tony and a Donaldson Award for her performance. The *New York Post* columnist Leonard Lyons reported that she was so well known that the post office delivered letters to her addressed "Bloody Mary, N.Y.C." In the second year of the show her salary was raised to $350 per week, and she "switched from whiskey to champagne to enjoy life." She liked to cook, dance, and root for the Brooklyn Dodgers. Suspicious of exercise, she delighted friends with stories of her sedentary habits of reading and watching her cat.

Hall's next Broadway role was the brothel owner Madame Tango in *House of Flowers* (1954), which had book and lyrics by Truman Capote and music by Harold Arlen. On Jan. 25, 1954, she made radio history when she starred in "The Story of Ruby Valentine," the first program broadcast on the National Negro Network. In 1956 she was back on Broadway as an outspoken maid in *The Ponder Heart*. Two years later she completed the film version of *South Pacific*, for which she won a Box Office Award, although—in typical Hollywood style—her songs were dubbed by another singer. Rodgers and Hammerstein then cast her as Madame Liang in *Flower Drum Song* (1958), which she played in New York for 600 performances, on a long road tour, and in the film version (1961).

With the security of *South Pacific*, Hall had resumed her solo singing career. Always a fan of the blues, and especially of Billie Holiday, she appeared as a blues singer in a number of New York clubs, where her fame as Bloody Mary increased her following. For fifteen years, whenever time allowed, Hall sang the blues, and her renditions of "Mean to Me" and "More Than You Know," among others, survive in recordings. In 1966, despite failing health, she presented a tribute to Holiday and Ethel Waters called A *Woman and the Blues*, which played a limited run in New York.

After the success of *Flower Drum Song*, however, Hall's career began to fade. She lost money in a restaurant, the Fortune Cookie, in New York City, and poor health drained her savings. But the same pride and spirit that had pushed her to the top of a very competitive profession made it difficult for her to seek help. Eventually her friends and family moved her to an actors' home in Englewood, N.J., and in December 1967 to the Percy Williams Home for Actors in East Islip, Long Island. Although her eyes were failing, her spirits were always bright, and she would reprise her songs from *South Pacific* if someone needed cheering up. She died in Bayshore, Long Island, remembered most for her haunting rendition of "Bali Ha'i."

[A clipping file on Hall is in the Performing Arts Research Center of the New York Public Library at Lincoln Center. An obituary is in the *New York Times*, Mar. 1, 1968. Richard Rodgers wrote a tribute to Hall in the *New York Times*, Mar. 10, 1968.]

BARRY B. WITHAM

HALPERT, EDITH GREGOR (Apr. 25, 1900–Oct. 6, 1970), art dealer, was born Edith Gregor Fivoosiovitch in Odessa, Russia, the daughter of Gregor Fivoosiovitch, a tailor, and Francis Lucom. In 1906 the family immigrated to New York City, but Halpert did not become a naturalized citizen until 1921. While attending Wadleigh High School, she also studied at the National Academy of Design, taking classes in 1914–1915 with Leon Kroll, Ivan Olinsky, and Frederic A. Bridgman. In 1917 she began writing copy and doing sketches in the advertising department of the Stern Brothers department store.

During these years Halpert found a mentor in Dr. John Weichsel, who founded the People's Art Guild in 1915. Devoted to expanding and improving the knowledge of art, the guild was an artists' cooperative that organized exhibitions in churches, meeting halls, and settlement houses. At a weekly Weichsel soiree she met the painter Samuel Halpert, whom she married in 1918; they had no children.

Edith Halpert worked as personnel manager and head of the correspondence department for the investment bankers S. W. Straus and Company from 1920 to 1925. In 1925 Galerie Lilloises asked her to reorganize its department store in Lille, France. After a year in Europe the Halperts returned to New York resolved to open a gallery for contemporary American artists.

In 1926 the Halperts launched the Downtown Gallery, the first gallery devoted to modern art in New York City's Greenwich Village. It was one of only seven in the city that exhibited modern American art and, along with Alfred Stieglitz' Intimate Gallery and the Charles Daniel Gallery, was one of only three that dealt exclusively in American art. A statement issued at the opening declared, "The Downtown Gallery rises as a new need in the art life of New York. It will present exhibitions from the work of the best artists representing the various tendencies in American art. The Gallery has no special prejudice for any school. Its selection is directed by what is enduring, not what is in vogue." Artists represented in the gallery's inaugural exhibition, now regarded as leading figures of their time, included Mary and William Zorach, Walt Kuhn, John Marin, Niles Spencer, Yasuo Kuniyoshi, Elie Nadelman, Abraham Walkowitz, John Sloan, and Max Weber.

Halpert also began to collect American folk art in 1926, and in 1929, in an upstairs room at the Downtown Gallery, she opened the first gallery devoted to American folk art. Beginning in 1929 she made numerous trips to New England, Pennsylvania, and upper New York State in her black Hupmobile, looking for old portraits, still lifes on velvet, birth certificates with watercolor designs, figureheads, and weather vanes. Always paying cash and never leaving a forwarding address, Halpert amassed in three years a collection of over 1,000 works, many of them masterpieces of pre-twentieth-century American folk art. Among the artists she favored were Edward Hicks and William Michael Harnett, whose once-popular Victorian still-life paintings she rediscovered in the 1930's. Halpert could justify the inclusion of a wide range of artists in her collection because she defined "folk art" broadly. She wrote in 1950, "'Folk' in this country does not denote 'peasant.' Basically American folk art was the art of middle-class kindred folk with a kindred philosophy. Folk art includes the work of professionals as well as amateurs, of adults and minors, of the taught and untaught, produced commercially or as an avocation, in both rural and urban communities."

Buyers were infrequent for Halpert's collection of American folk art until Mrs. John D. Rockefeller, Jr., began making regular purchases. These came to form the bulk of the Abby Aldrich Rockefeller collection of American folk art at the Ludwell-Paradise House in Williamsburg, Va. Halpert wrote the first catalog for the collection in 1939. She became well known for her expertise in the field in the 1940's, lecturing frequently and writing articles for popular magazines.

Although Halpert was widowed suddenly in 1930, her success as a folk-art dealer enabled her to continue supporting contemporary American artists. The painters Jack Levine, Ben Shahn, Louis Guglielmi, George L. K. Morris, and Jacob Lawrence were given their first one-person shows at the Downtown Gallery. Stuart Davis, Bernard Karfiol, and Charles Sheeler were shown frequently. In the late 1930's and early 1940's the gallery held several exhibitions of American social-realist painting and gained a reputation for backing socially and artistically progressive work. The paintings of virtually all the twentieth-century pioneers of modern art in America appeared at the Downtown Gallery.

Halpert organized New York City's first municipal art exhibition, held at Radio City Music Hall in 1934. Later in the 1930's she organized allocation and exhibition programs for the Federal Art Project. In 1941, with the assistance of Alain Locke of Howard University, Halpert mounted one of the first major survey exhibitions of nineteenth- and twentieth-century black American artists, featuring work by Henry O. Tanner, Horace Pippin, Romare Bearden, and Jacob Lawrence.

In the 1940's Halpert moved the Downtown Gallery uptown to East 51st Street and then to East 57th Street, where it continued to operate under the same name. In 1951 she sectioned off a portion of the premises to form the Ground Floor Gallery, where she exhibited young, unknown artists. Throughout the 1950's she continued to show unknown (primarily abstract) artists along with well-established members of the gallery.

Although devoted to the artists she represented, Halpert was also concerned with the social and economic rights of visual artists in general. In the 1950's she established a small but active private foundation that published guidelines concerning the relationship between museums and living artists. A woman who felt a moral obligation to support American art and living American artists, Halpert enjoyed one of the longest and most distinguished careers of any art dealer in New York City. She died there after a long illness.

[Halpert's papers and records of the Downtown Gallery are in the Archives of American Art, New

York City. An obituary is in the *New York Times*, Oct. 7, 1970.]

PATRICIA FAILING

HAMILTON, ALICE (Feb. 27, 1869–Sept. 22, 1970), physician, social reformer, and professor of industrial medicine, was born in New York City, the daughter of Montgomery Hamilton, a wholesale grocer, and Gertrude Pond. Despite her father's business failure, she grew up in the privileged and sheltered atmosphere of her grandmother's estate in Fort Wayne, Ind. Taught by her parents and tutors, she had little formal training except in languages until she entered Miss Porter's School in Farmington, Conn., in 1886.

After leaving Miss Porter's in 1888, Hamilton chose medicine "because as a doctor I could go anywhere I pleased . . . and be quite sure that I could be of use anywhere." She made up for her deficiencies in science at the Fort Wayne College of Medicine and in March 1892 entered the University of Michigan. She received her M.D. the following year and interned at the Northwestern Hospital for Women and Children in Minneapolis and the New England Hospital for Women and Children in Boston. In 1895 she returned to Ann Arbor to work in the bacteriology laboratory of F. G. Novy. That fall she traveled with her elder sister, the classicist Edith Hamilton, to Germany and studied bacteriology and pathology at the universities of Leipzig and Munich. She then spent a final year of training at the Johns Hopkins Medical School before taking a job in 1897 as a professor of pathology at the Woman's Medical School at Northwestern University.

Convinced that "teaching pathology, and carrying on research would never satisfy," Hamilton became a resident of Hull House, where, under the guidance of Jane Addams, Florence Kelley, and Julia Lathrop, she took up the cause of the working class. When the Woman's Medical School closed in 1902, Hamilton accepted a position as bacteriologist at the Memorial Institute for Infectious Diseases. Before taking up her duties there, she studied briefly at the Pasteur Institute in Paris. She returned to Chicago in the autumn to find the city in the midst of a typhoid epidemic that was especially severe in the Hull House area. She gained acclaim for a paper presented to the Chicago Medical Society pinpointing flies as the agents in spreading the disease. She was later chagrined to discover that the major problem had been a break in the local pumping station that allowed sewage to escape into the water pipes. Although the true situation never gained wide publicity, Hamilton herself attempted "for years . . . to lay the ghosts of those flies."

While at Hull House, Hamilton became involved in the labor movement and learned much about the lives of immigrant workers. She was appalled to discover the disease, disability, and premature death common to workers in certain industries. Her interest in these hazardous occupations was stimulated by Sir Thomas Oliver's *Dangerous Trades* (1902). Reading all the materials she could find, she learned that the United States lagged far behind Germany and England in providing for safety in the workplace. The nation lacked occupational safety laws, workmen's compensation laws, and an effective factory-inspection system. In 1908, Hamilton was named to the Illinois Commission of Occupational Diseases by Governor Charles S. Deneen. Its preliminary investigation revealed the need for a larger study, and she resigned from the commission in 1910 to direct that survey. The following year she accepted an appointment as special investigator for the United States Bureau of Labor. These duties led her into field investigations of mines, mills, and smelters. Concentrating at first on lead, the most widely used industrial poison, she compiled statistics dramatically documenting the high mortality and morbidity rates of workers. She later did the same for aniline dyes, picric acid, arsenic, carbon monoxide, and many other industrial poisons. Although she avoided sensationalism, she nevertheless became a crusader for public health and an advocate of such causes as woman suffrage, birth control, a federal child labor law, state health insurance, and workmen's compensation.

During World War I, Hamilton, a pacifist, accompanied Jane Addams to the International Congress of Women at The Hague and on a mission to the war capitals to present the women's peace proposals. In 1919 she visited Germany to investigate the famine there and became involved in the Quaker famine relief effort. That year Hamilton left Hull House and accepted a half-time position as assistant professor of industrial medicine at the Harvard Medical School, a job she held until 1935. Barred from the Harvard Club because of her sex, she suffered many discriminations as the university's first female professor. Her classic textbook *Industrial Poisons in the United States* (1925) established her as one of the world's leading authorities on the subject. Another textbook, *Industrial Toxicology* (1934), was revised in 1949 with Harriet Hardy.

Hamilton served two terms on the Health Committee of the League of Nations (1924–1930), becoming an ardent proponent of the League, which she had earlier opposed. In 1924 she was invited to make a survey of industrial hygiene in the Soviet Union. Concluding "that there was more industrial hygiene in Russia than industry," she found some things to admire in the Bolshevik system but deplored its suppression of free speech. She was far more critical of Nazi Germany, which she visited in 1933. By 1940 she felt that the United States should oppose Hitler.

After retiring from Harvard, Hamilton moved to Hadlyme, Conn., where she and her sister Margaret shared a house they had purchased in 1916. In 1935 she accepted a position as consultant to the Division of Labor Standards in the United States Department of Labor. As a part of her duties, she conducted her last field survey, an investigation of the viscose rayon industry. Her autobiography, *Exploring the Dangerous Trades*, was published in 1943. From 1944 to 1949 she served as president of the National Consumers' League. She retained in old age her interest in politics, withdrawing in 1952 her opposition to the equal-rights amendment and in 1963 calling for an end to American military involvement in Vietnam. She died in Hadlyme.

[Hamilton's papers are in the Schlesinger Library at Radcliffe College and the Connecticut College Library at New London. Important holdings are in the Allen Hamilton Papers at Indiana State Library and in the Edith Hamilton Papers and the Hamilton Family Papers, both at the Schlesinger Library. On her life and work, see Madeline P. Grant, *Alice Hamilton: Pioneer Doctor in Industrial Medicine* (1967), a biography for young readers; Wilma Ruth Slaight, "Alice Hamilton: First Lady of Industrial Medicine" (Ph.D. diss., Case Western Reserve University, 1974), which contains a bibliography of Hamilton's publications; Angela Nugent Young, "Interpreting the Dangerous Trades: Workers' Health in America and the Career of Alice Hamilton, 1910–1935" (Ph.D. diss., Brown University, 1982); and Barbara Sicherman. *Alice Hamilton: A Life in Letters* (1984). An obituary is in the *New York Times*, Sept. 23, 1970.]

MELBA PORTER HAY

HAMMOND, BRAY (Nov. 20, 1886–July 20, 1968), economic historian and banking official, was born in Springfield, Mo., the son of Harry Hammond, a bank cashier, and Lucy Bray. After attending public schools in Iowa and California, he followed his father into banking, first as a bookkeeper and as an assistant cashier in the Iowa State Bank in New Sharon. There, in April 1907, he married Lucille Bennett; they had four children. His wife died in 1927. He married Melitta de Kern on Feb. 3, 1939.

Hammond enrolled at Stanford University in 1909, received his degree within three years, and was elected to Phi Beta Kappa. From 1913 to 1916 he taught English at the State College at Pullman, Wash. During World War I he rose from second lieutenant to captain in the Aviation Section of the Signal Corps of the army and was stationed in Washington, D.C. From 1919 to 1929 he was personnel director of a small manufacturing firm in New Haven, Conn. He then returned to banking, first as a bookkeeper for the Irving Trust Company in New York City and, beginning in 1930, for the Board of Governors of the Federal Reserve System in Washington, D.C. He continued at the board until retiring in 1950, serving as assistant secretary for his last six years there.

From the first the board availed itself of Hammond's talent as writer. Following preparation of the report of a committee on branch, group, and chain banking, he was placed in charge of publications. He wrote speeches and reports, including the first edition of *The Federal Reserve System: Its Functions and Purposes* (1939) and the historical introduction to *Banking Studies* (1941).

While engaged at the Federal Reserve Board, Hammond was preparing for the books that were to make him famous. Many Saturdays found him at the Library of Congress. He wrote articles and reviews in learned journals that anticipated his later works.

After leaving government service Hammond devoted himself to study and writing. A Guggenheim Fellowship (1950–1951) provided for research in the Library of Congress and in the British Museum. On a second Guggenheim grant in 1955 he wrote *Banks and Politics in America from the Revolution to the Civil War,* but publication was delayed by preparation of an account of Eugene Meyer's service as chairman of the Federal Reserve Board. When the book appeared in 1957, it received the Pulitzer Prize in history.

Banks and Politics drew immediate attention because of Hammond's interpretation of President Andrew Jackson's war on the Second Bank of the United States. Reflecting earlier interpretations, Hammond attributed the episode to the explosion of business enterprise. According to him, a remarkable variety of businessmen and speculators demanding easy credit grew impatient with the wise control that the central bank sought to apply. In "a rapidly growing and acquisitive population pressing to exploit immense resources . . . ," he wrote, "the public interest required an extremely powerful restraint upon inflation." The book was much more than the depiction of the destruction of the Second Bank of the United States. The story of banking, set forth in illuminating detail, served also to recount almost a century of American economic history.

Like Alexander Hamilton, Hammond preferred central authority in economy and government. He held that the Constitution, "a document prepared for a small, simple 18th-century economy, mostly agrarian and partly mercantile, had to be made practicable for a vastly greater one complicated by growth and the industrial revolution; and this required a Hamiltonian interpretation." Some critics suggested that Hammond's attitude grew from his long engagement in the Federal Reserve System. But Hammond countered by arguing that the states' rights argument often served as a cover for selfish and shortsighted motives. "The aggrandizement of federal powers has not been brought about by any deliberate purpose pursued by the personnel of the federal government. It is due to the incompetence of the states and municipalities to perform piecemeal the responsibilities required to be performed in an immense homogeneous society."

Hammond settled in Thetford, Vt., and working in the library of nearby Dartmouth College, he wrote *Sovereignty and an Empty Purse* (published posthumously in 1970), which described the financing of the Civil War. In this work he traced "the appalling situation into which a stunted federal government had been pitched by its unreadiness." (The Confederacy was in a worse plight, with not only empty purse but empty sovereignty as well.) The book was a lesser effort than the earlier volume.

Hammond was modest, intensely curious, and able to make quick acquaintance with people in many walks of life because he showed intelligent interest in their concerns. In later years a heart condition did not stop his ardent gardening. He died in Middlebury, Vt., having willed his body to the nearest medical school (at Burlington, as it happened).

[Hammond's papers are in the library of Dartmouth College. See the *Federal Reserve Bulletin*, Jan., Nov., and Dec. 1944. Obituaries are in the *New York Times*, July 23, 1968; and the *Valley News* (West Lebanon, N.H.), July 22, 1968.]

BROADUS MITCHELL

HARRIMAN, FLORENCE JAFFRAY HURST (July 21, 1870–Aug. 30, 1967), socialite, reformer, diplomat, and political activist, was born in New York City, the daughter of Francis W. J. Hurst, a merchant, and Caroline Elise Jaffray, who died in 1873. Known throughout her life as Daisy, she was raised largely by her grandfather, Edward Jaffray, whose friends included many influential men on both sides of the Atlantic. She had what she called a "sketchy" education under Mrs. Lockwood, first in the J. P. Morgan mansion and then in a private school, but she traveled widely. Her lifelong passions for yachting, polo, golf, and riding were legacies of the opulent world of her childhood, as was her fascination with politics. She gradually moved from her grandfather's Republicanism and beyond the society of her own hunting set after her marriage to the banker J. Borden Harriman on Nov. 18, 1889; they had one child.

In 1902, Harriman was among the founders of the Colony Club for women who, like her, needed a place to stay while they were in New York City tending to civic or philanthropic affairs. She held the first presidency of the club, serving until 1916. Her affiliation with the National Civic Federation, whose Women's Department she helped to establish, led her to study industrial working conditions, particularly for women, and to her appointment as head of the federation's Committee on Welfare Work for Industrial Employees.

Named as manager of the state's Reformatory

for Women at Bedford, Harriman was regularly reappointed until 1916. A devoted friend of progressive mayor John Purroy Mitchel, she adopted reform with a vengeance. An antisuffrage rally turned her from a passive to an active supporter of the vote for women, but she never approved of the militancy of what she called "the sex-conscious bloc."

Harriman was an enthusiastic supporter of Woodrow Wilson's presidential aspirations from the time she first met him in Bermuda, although he dismissed her at first as a "fine, uninteresting person." She established and chaired the Women's National Wilson and Marshall Association, which became the Women's Division of the Democratic National Committee. Her energetic efforts gave the cause of woman's suffrage far more visibility in the campaign of 1912 than the candidate's tepid support justified. Wilson appointed Harriman to the Federal Industrial Relations Commission, which was chaired by her close friend Frank P. Walsh. She played a central role in organizing the arbitration that averted a nationwide railroad strike in 1913. While sympathetic to the workers' cause and a friend of the labor leaders John Mitchell and "Mother" Jones, she insisted on a balanced view and ultimately dissented from Walsh's strongly prounion final report. On a fact-finding mission in 1914, while her ailing husband sought a cure, she was at Carlsbad when Austria declared war and in Paris when the socialist Jean Jaurès was assassinated. Her husband died in December 1914.

Wilson personally instructed party leaders not to employ Harriman again as head of the Women's Division in 1916. Her outspoken advocacy of woman's suffrage and perhaps her attempt in 1915 to persuade the president, through Colonel Edward M. House, to support counterrevolution in Mexico, had convinced Wilson that she was "a most difficult woman to handle." Harriman then turned to the campaign for American preparadeness and to work for Allied relief. When the United States entered World War I, Samuel Gompers named her the head of the Committee of Women in Industry of the Advisory Committee of the Council of National Defense. She was in Europe three times during the war, once to inspect industrial conditions and twice as commander of the Red Cross Motor Corps. She was assistant director of transportation in France in 1918 and a delegate to the Inter-Allied Women's Council in Paris during the peace conference.

Eager to keep a Wilsonian in the White House, Harriman supported William G. McAdoo's several bids for the presidency, starting in 1920. During the Republican decade, she began a tradition of Sunday-night dinners at her Washington home. Originally limited to progressive Democrats, by the mid-1920's these were nonpartisan gatherings of influential citizens at which stimulating conversation, scrupulously unreported by attending journalists, was the order of the day. As president of the Woman's National Democratic Club and as the Democratic national committeewoman for the District of Columbia (1924–1936), Harriman participated in every presidential campaign, although she was strictly nonpartisan in New York City's municipal elections. Backing Newton D. Baker in 1932, she remained neutral during the Democratic National Convention that year, and so she was not a member of the New Deal's inner circle. Yet, she was at the hub of Franklin Roosevelt's administration, sharing her estate in Washington with Frances Perkins in 1933. Roosevelt named her minister to Norway in April 1937.

During World War II, hers was the first official report of the German invasion of Norway. She spent several harrowing days under German fire, following the government in its flight from Oslo before she found refuge in Sweden. Unable to rejoin the Norwegian government as it escaped to London, she supervised the evacuation of more than 800 refugees, including the crown princess of Norway and her children, to the United States. With them, she sailed from Petsamo, Finland, in August 1940. Next, she joined Roosevelt's reelection campaign and then served as vice-chairperson of the White Committee to Defend America by Aiding the Allies, which led the anti-isolationist crusade between the fall of France and Pearl Harbor. In 1942 she received the highest honor of Norway, the Great Cross of St. Olav.

Harriman was an avid supporter of postwar international organization, and after 1945, of world disarmament. She also campaigned vigorously for home rule for the District of Columbia. Her Sunday dinners, revived after the war, made her home the capital city's leading salon. She was renowned for her wit, her hospitality, and the erect bearing that her father, a former army officer, had trained her to maintain. In 1963, President John F. Kennedy awarded her the first Citation for Distinguished Service. "I haven't the least illusion . . . that I am an important person," she wrote in 1923. "I have always had through sheer luck . . . a box seat at the America of my times."

[Harriman's personal papers are in the Library of Congress. She wrote two volumes of memoirs, *From Pinafores to Politics* (1923) and *Mission to the North* (1941). Her relationship with Wilson and her role in his campaigns is traceable in Arthur S. Link, ed., *The Papers of Woodrow Wilson*, XXII–XXVIII (1976–1978). Her official reports from Norway are in United States Department of State, *Foreign Relations of the United States, 1940*, I (1955). Recollections of her Sunday salons are in Paul H. Douglas, *In the Fullness of Years* (1972); and David E. Lilienthal, *Journals*, III (1969). An obituary is in the *New York Times*, Sept. 1, 1967.]

RICHARD A. HARRISON

HARTLEY, FRED ALLEN, JR. (Feb. 22, 1903–May 11, 1969), congressman and coauthor of the Taft-Hartley Act, was born in Harrison, N.J., the son of Fred Allen Hartley, a produce merchant and realtor, and Frances Hartley. (Hartley was her maiden name, but she was not related.) He attended public school in Kearny, Rutgers Preparatory School, and Rutgers University for two years. He married Hazel Lorraine Roemer on Jan. 30, 1921; they had three children. He boxed as an amateur welterweight, coached boys' teams, and organized a jazz band at Rutgers, the Hartley Joy Boys, in which he was pianist.

Hartley involved himself in Republican campaigning in New Jersey, winning elections as Kearny's library commissioner in 1923, police and fire commissioner in 1925, and county Republican chairman in 1925. In 1928 he became the youngest man ever elected to Congress and for twenty years served his New Jersey district, which included part of Newark and the affluent suburban areas around Kearny and East Orange. He was a party loyalist, and his political views were in the mainstream of New Jersey Republicanism.

Before 1947, Hartley spoke little on the House floor and introduced few bills. The only bill labeled with his name established a boxing commission for the District of Columbia. He served on the Labor Committee, but lacking sympathy for its strongly prolabor majority, he participated little. Nonetheless, he received endorsements from the American Federation of Labor (AFL) until about 1942, primarily because he voted for legislation to protect craft unions from the Congress of Industrial Organizations (CIO).

Although conservative, Hartley was more pragmatist than ideologue and could make exceptions to his small-government, laissez-faire principles. In 1937 he introduced a bill granting the Federal Trade Commission authority to eliminate abuses in child labor. After the passage of the Wagner Act in 1935, his misgivings about organized labor intensified. He argued that federal regulation of unions was a necessity. During World War II his strong advocacy of antistrike legislation cost him the support of the AFL leadership. After the war, he favored dismantling the Office of Price Administration (OPA) and voted for the tax-reduction bill. He opposed the poll tax and supported the 1953 tidelands oil bills. His speeches extolled free enterprise, states' rights, and strictly limited national government.

Hartley held strong isolationist views throughout the 1920's and 1930's, opposing revision of the neutrality laws, lend-lease, and peacetime conscription. His views changed after Pearl Harbor: he supported the war effort and favored internationalist postwar policies such as United Nations membership, the Marshall Plan, and the Truman Doctrine.

Republican leaders interpreted the party's victory in the congressional elections of 1946 as a mandate to revise New Deal legislation. The House leaders, Joe Martin and Charles Halleck, turned to Hartley to oversee the writing and passing of labor bills. Impressed by his wartime zeal in investigating alleged abuses in the OPA, they persuaded him to take the chairmanship of the reorganized Education and Labor Committee, even though he was second in seniority and possessed little expertise in labor relations. That committee contained a large number of freshman members, including Richard Nixon and John F. Kennedy. Robert Taft became chairman of the Senate Labor Committee, the Republican strategy apparently having been for that committee to draft a series of bills for Hartley to push through the House.

Hartley helped draft and pass the Labor Management Relations Act of 1947, better known as the Taft-Hartley Act. He led in producing a stricter bill than many, including Taft, had favored or thought possible; he insisted on one omnibus bill to include all important points; and he promoted passage by a large bipartisan vote that held together for a record-breaking override of President Truman's veto (331–83) in June 1947, though Hartley exaggerated his role in his book *Our New Labor Policy* (1948). The Hartley bill, drafted by corporation lawyers he selected, outlawed the closed shop, required an anti-Communist oath from labor officials, imposed criminal penalties for corruption, prohibited secondary boycotts and industrywide bargaining, and allowed states to pass right-to-work laws. All except the ban on industrywide bargaining survived.

Hartley's insistence on one bill and his success in presenting it as an attack on corruption and Communist influence in unions, both highly publicized in 2 million words of testimony before his committee, was his greatest contribution. This became a bill that most Democrats and nearly all Republicans felt they could not afford to oppose. Its passage marked the first major revision of the New Deal.

Hartley's hope that the Taft-Hartley Act would prove only a first step in controlling big labor was dashed by Truman's reelection in 1948. Hartley, who had decided as early as 1946 to let the Eightieth Congress be his last, became a lobbyist, business consultant, and defender of the Taft-Hartley Act on the lecture circuit. The defeat of repeated efforts to amend or repeal the law perhaps owes something to his efforts. He strongly supported Taft for president but rallied to Dwight D. Eisenhower in 1952. Hartley broke with the liberal wing of the New Jersey party in 1954 and sought a seat in the United States Senate by a write-in campaign against Clifford Case, but failed. Thereafter, he devoted less time to politics and more to cattle farming. He died in Linwood, N.J.

Hartley was a typical representative of his party, particularly in labor relations. In 1947 a strong bill would have passed with or without his help. Nonetheless, he played a significant role in molding and moving it. He helped lead the first successful Republican revision of the New Deal.

[There is no collection of Hartley papers and no biography. See his articles "Hidden Taxes," *Vital Speeches*, Apr. 6, 1936; "What Hidden Hand Takes Your Money?" *ibid.*, Apr. 1, 1937; "Can Industrial Peace Be Attained?" *ibid.*, June 15, 1937; and "Wage and Hours," *ibid.*, Jan. 1, 1938. R. Alton Lee, *Truman and Taft-Hartley* (1966), is the standard account of Hartley's role in the passage of the act. See also "Joy Boy," *New Yorker*, Jan. 17, 1948; Herbert Mitgang, "Then and Now," *New York Times Magazine*, Nov. 23, 1952; and W. G. Boesser, "Remember When," *Saturday Evening Post*, May 8, 1954. An obituary is in the *New York Times*, May 12, 1966.]

WAYNE C. BARTEE

HASTINGS, DANIEL OREN (Mar. 5, 1874–May 9, 1966), United States senator, was born near Princess Anne, Md., the son of Daniel H. Hastings, a farmer, and Amelia Parsons. Hastings attended a one-room grade school for about five months each year and Princess Anne High School for two winters. In July 1892, he left school to work as an office boy and clerk with the railroad company in Salisbury, Md. Two years later he began working at the Pennsylvania Railroad freight office in Wilmington, Del., and studied shorthand and typewriting at night at Goldey College in Wilmington, Del. Professor Charles Eastman tutored Hastings privately and prepared him for law school in only sixteen months. Hastings married Garrie Lee Saxton on Apr. 19, 1898; they had two children. To enhance his income Hastings worked in the law office of Christopher Ward for sixteen months.

In the fall of 1899 Hastings entered Columbian (George Washington) University Law School, Washington, D.C. He worked in the auditor's office of the Southern Railroad and was a clerk for the chief engineer of the United States War Department until his graduation from law school in 1901. After passing the Delaware bar examination in September 1901 he returned to Wilmington and the next year was admitted to the Delaware bar. He formed a law partnership with Henry Conrad and soon won considerable acclaim as a trial lawyer for securing the acquittal of three clients charged with homicide.

In the fall of 1904 Hastings campaigned for the state Republican party ticket. Although the son of a Democrat, he supported the Republican party because of its high-tariff policy. State Attorney General Robert Richards appointed Hastings as his deputy in January 1905. During the next four years Hastings prosecuted nearly all the criminal cases tried in Delaware, until Governor Simeon Pennewill named him Delaware secretary of state in January 1909. Five months later Hastings was selected associate justice of the Delaware State Supreme Court for a twelve-year period; he was then the youngest state judge in Delaware history. In January 1911 he resigned to resume his law practice and became special counsel for the Delaware General Assembly. From July 1911 to July 1917 he served as city solicitor of Wilmington. In January 1920 Governor John Townsend, Jr., designated Hastings as municipal court judge of Wilmington. Hastings cherished this position, which he held until 1928, because it afforded him great opportunity to help people.

On Dec. 10, 1928, Governor Robert Robinson appointed Hastings to fill the United States Senate vacancy created by the resignation of Thomas Coleman du Pont. Hastings initially aligned himself with the "Young Turks," whose Republican politics rested between the old guard conservatives and the progressives. He was assigned to the Judiciary Committee because of his legal expertise and to the Interstate Commerce Committee because of his widespread grasp of railroad problems. His wife died on Feb. 7, 1930. On Oct. 17, 1931, he married Elsie Saxton, a sister of his first wife. In November 1930, in his first quest for elective political office, Hastings defeated former Democratic senator Thomas Bayard and was elected to a full United States Senate term.

From 1929 to 1933 Hastings consistently supported President Herbert Hoover's domestic and foreign policies. He defended Hoover's positions on Muscle Shoals, veterans' bonuses, farm-debt moratoriums, and the Reconstruction Finance Corporation; on the La Follette–Costigan relief bill and the Glass-Steagall banking bill; and on the revenue and public works bills. Hastings limited his early speeches to legal questions and backed Hoover's nomination of Judge John Parker to the Supreme Court. He sponsored the Bankruptcy Law of 1933 to relieve individuals, farmers, and railroads suffering from debt.

From 1933 to 1936 Hastings criticized President Franklin D. Roosevelt and his New Deal programs. The journalist Arthur Krock called Hastings "the political gadfly of the Administration." Hastings' epithets for New Deal measures included "orgy of spending," "waste," "extravagance," "robbery," "bait for the voter," "revolutionary," and "unconstitutional." During the first New Deal, he opposed Roosevelt's economy, federal emergency relief, agricultural adjustment, and national industrial recovery acts and the Tennessee Valley Authority. He assailed the World Court, the Works Progress Administration, the Wagner national labor relations and social security acts, and the public utilities, wealth tax, and Guffey coal bills during the second New Deal. Hastings, who chaired the Republican Senatorial Campaign Committee, originally did not intend to run for reelection in 1936, but the Republican State Convention renominated him. In November 1936 he lost to Democrat James Hughes.

Hastings resumed his law practice in Wilmington upon leaving the Senate and associated with Ayres Stockly, August Walz, Stewart Lynch, Clarence Taylor, and Russell Willard, Jr. He represented the stockholders of Pennroad Corporation in a $95 million suit against the Pennsylvania Railroad, winning a $22.1 million verdict and earning a fee of nearly $2 million for his firm. In addition to being special trustee of the Standard Gas and Electric Company while it reorganized, he served as special master in the celebrated proceedings of the Midland United and Midland Utilities companies. Hastings, whose firm handled many cases of national importance, was president of the Interstate Amiesite Corporation and was associated with the General Precision Corporation and Twentieth Century–Fox.

Hastings remained influential in local, state, and national Republican party activities, serving on the Republican National Committee from 1928 to 1943 and on the Republican National Convention Credentials Committee in 1952. After World War II he disapproved of the United Nations and of peace talks with the Soviet Union. Hastings, who resided in Centreville, Del., raised purebred Holstein cattle on his summer farm near Dover, Del. In 1964 he wrote *Delaware Politics, 1904–1954*, a memoir on state politics and political leaders. He practiced law until becoming ill several months before his death in Wilmington. Hastings filled more public offices than did any other Delaware politician and reached the top of his profession, as a lawyer and a legal counsel.

[The Hastings papers are at the Delaware Historical Society, Wilmington. See *Wilmington Every Evening*, Dec. 27, 1928; *Wilmington Sunday Morning Star*, July 27, 1930, and Jan. 7, 1934; Roger Pichot, *Delaware*, III (1947); and *Delaware Morning News*, Dec. 30, 1965.]

DAVID L. PORTER

HAYES, GABBY (May 7, 1885–Feb. 9, 1969), actor and comedian, was born George Francis Hayes in Willing, near Wellsville, N.Y., the son of Clark R. Hayes, a prosperous hotelkeeper, and Elizabeth Morrison. At eight Hayes began appearing in school theatricals and as a teenager played professional baseball in Wellsville and Olean, N.Y. Though his parents expected him to enter the family business, Hayes left home at seventeen to work in traveling shows. After performing briefly with a small circus, he joined the Burke-McCann repertory company, touring small towns for one-week engagements and playing multiple roles in some forty productions. "I was never much of an actor," he later said, "but I was loud, and that made up for a lot of things."

About 1904 Hayes entered burlesque as a singer and dancer. He was popular in travesties of popular musical comedies as a comic small-town constable with a false goatee, foreshadowing his later film success in "old codger" character roles. Hayes teamed in 1910 with Alice Hamilton in *The Spirit of '76*, a vaudeville sketch about the reunion of high school sweethearts after sixty years. The act played for several seasons in B. F. Keith theaters and twice at the Palace in New York City. At the age of twenty-five Hayes had embarked on a career of portraying old men.

On Mar. 4, 1914, Hayes married Dorothy Earle (Olive Dorothy Ireland), a musical comedy actress; they had no children. She performed with Hayes in sketches but retired shortly after their marriage. With the decline of vaudeville in the 1920's, Hayes found fewer engagements; and his wife worked as a clerk to supplement their income. In 1928, after seeing a sound film, she advised Hayes to leave the stage, and the couple moved to Los Angeles.

In 1929 Hayes appeared in *The Rainbow Man* and played a small role in *Smiling Irish Eyes*, a silent film with Colleen Moore. With the coming of the Great Depression his career faltered; in 1930 he appeared briefly in *For the Defense*, his only known work for that year. At a party in 1931 Hayes met Trem Carr, a producer of low-budget westerns, who recalled Hayes's vaudeville impersonations of old men. Carr suggested that Hayes play similar parts in Carr's films, on condition that Hayes use his own beard to save time and expense in makeup. As Hayes said later, "It was either that or sell pencils."

At forty-five Hayes had never ridden or handled a horse, but he learned rapidly and made five pictures in 1931, twelve in 1932, and seventeen in 1933, most of them westerns directed by W. P. McCarthy. Hayes was featured not as the irascible but amiable geezer for whom he later became famous but often as the villain. The familiar character began to appear in 1934, particularly in the musical *In Old Santa Fe,* in which Hayes played Ken Maynard's sidekick. Harry Sherman at Paramount saw the film and signed Hayes to appear as Windy Halliday, William Boyd's garrulous companion in the "Hopalong Cassidy" series. The character proved popular, and from 1935 to 1939 Hayes made twenty-two pictures with Boyd.

Late in 1938 Sol Siegel of Republic Pictures signed Hayes to work in Roy Rogers westerns. Because Paramount refused to allow Hayes to use the name Windy, with which he had become identified, he became Gabby at Republic and made twenty-six pictures with Rogers from 1939 to 1942. The studio then reassigned Hayes to help establish a new series starring Wild Bill Elliot; retaining the well-established Gabby character, Hayes made ten pictures with Elliot in 1943 and 1944.

The blend of Hayes's crustiness and Rogers' geniality had worked so well that in 1944 Republic reunited them for fourteen more films. In 1943 he had been named one of the ten most popular western stars, and in 1945 theater owners voted him second only to Rogers. This period is generally considered Hayes's best. He had substantial parts, notably in *Don't Fence Me In* (1945), and displayed his talent not only for comedy but also for light drama.

In 1946 Hayes left Republic Pictures. He subsequently made seven more pictures, most of them with Randolph Scott, and retired from films in 1950, after having appeared in 177 features. From 1946 Hayes performed on the weekly Roy Rogers radio show, and in 1950 he had his own network television program, which featured patriotic stories introduced by Hayes. During the series' two-season run, NBC gave him another program on which he introduced western movies. His last regular television work was in 1954–1955 on the children's program "Howdy Doody."

In retirement Hayes traveled, made public appearances, and devoted himself to gourmet cooking, baseball, and other hobbies. After his wife's death in 1957, he lived in seclusion. He died in Burbank, Calif.

Although his career included a few outstanding films, such as *Mr. Deeds Goes to Town* (1936) and *The Plainsman* (1937), Hayes is best remembered for his ongoing screen character, which personified the Wild West ideal of unpretentious, untutored American virtue enlivened by comic mischief and unruliness. He was so recognizable that in the late 1940's comic books featured his western character's shabby dress and rustic talk. Fans who met him in person were surprised to find him a polished, well-read gentleman of dapper appearance.

[The Academy of Motion Picture Arts and Sciences, Beverly Hills, Calif., maintains a file on Hayes. See also D. Rothel, *Those Great Cowboy Sidekicks* (1984); Buffalo (N.Y.) *Courier-Express*, June 5, 1949; *New York Times*, Mar. 25, 1951; and Fort Wayne (Ind.) *Journal-Gazette*, May 28, 1960. The *New York Times* obituary appeared on Feb. 10, 1969.]

ALAN BUSTER

HAYNES, WILLIAMS (July 29, 1886–Nov. 16, 1970), publisher, historian, and economist, was born Nathan Gallup Williams Haynes in Detroit, Mich., the son of David Oliphant Haynes, a publisher, and Helene Dunham Williams. He studied economics, chemistry, and biology from 1908 to 1911 as a special student at Johns Hopkins but never took a degree. Haynes married Elizabeth Bowen Batchelor on June 10, 1911; they had one child. From 1911 to 1916 he dallied in various journalistic ventures, editing *Field and Fancy* (1911), serving as a special correspondent in Canada and Europe (1911–1916), editing the *Northampton* (Mass.) *Herald* (1914–1915), and publishing books on terriers and dog breeding.

After Haynes brashly told his father that anyone could improve the magazine, he was challenged to try. Thus, in 1916, his father took him into his firm, D. O. Haynes and Company, which published *Drug and Chemical Markets*, as secretary and editorial director. By 1920, Haynes had become publisher. He split the publication in 1926 into *Drugs and Cosmetics Industry* and *Chemical Industries*, remaining publisher of the former until 1926 and of the latter until 1939. In 1928 he founded *Chemical Who's Who* and edited it through five editions. He also founded *Plastic Products*, which later became *Modern Plastics*. After his wife's death, he married Dorothy Farrand on June 5, 1926; they had two children.

Haynes also wrote less-technical books on the chemical industry: *Chemical Economics* (1933), *Men, Money and Molecules* (1935), *Chemistry's Contributions* (1936), *Chemical Pioneers* (1939), *The Stone That Burns* (1942), and *Cellulose, the Chemical That Grows* (1953). During World War II he was the author of several popular books dealing with chemistry and the war effort: *Rationed Rubber* (with Ernest Hauser, 1942), *This Chemical Age* (1942), and *The Chemical Front* (1943).

The attention attracted in chemical circles by Haynes's books and magazines led to his being selected to write *The American Chemical Industry: A History*, published in six volumes between 1945 and 1954. A less massive study had been envisioned in the 1930's by Francis P. Garvan, the founder of the Chemical Foundation, to stimulate the American chemical industry following World War I. Garvan and his associates envisioned a book that would stress the importance of American self-sufficiency in chemicals. Charles H. Herty, a leader of the Farm Chemurgic Council, was expected to write the book. After both Garvan and Herty died in the late 1930's, Haynes was chosen to undertake authorship.

Haynes was unwilling, however, to write propaganda to warn American legislators and entrepreneurs of the dangers of chemical insufficiency. For years he had collected materials relevant to his ambition to write a history of the American chemical industry. On the basis of his intimate association with leading industrialists, he proposed a three-volume treatise not restricted to the coal-tar dye industry, as Garvan and Herty had planned, but a history of the American industry from the colonial period to the onset of World War II.

In 1939, Haynes sold his trade magazines to devote his time to his historical projects. He moved permanently into a farmhouse built in 1750 near Stonington, Conn., which location permitted him to pursue research at the New York Public Library and at the specialized library of the Chemists Club, also in New York City. He was also within easy reach of libraries at Yale, Brown, and Harvard.

Haynes realized that the projected books would be costly to edit and print. He and his backers sought financial help from the chemical industry. Industrial executives were not interested until Willard H. Dow of Dow Chemical and Edgar M. Queeny of Monsanto pledged the backing of their companies. After an advisory committee was created, financial support was forthcoming from nearly all of the major chemical corporations, particularly after a volume of company histories, written by an author within each company, was included.

The project was expanded to five volumes, with a sixth containing the company histories. Two volumes dealing with the 1912–1922 period were published in 1945, with additional volumes appearing at intervals. In 1954 the first volume, covering the years 1606–1911, finally appeared; Haynes was then nearly seventy. Largely as a result of this work, Haynes became the second recipient in 1957 of the Dexter Award for distinguished contributions to the history of chemistry.

Haynes was proud of his descent from colonial families and knowledgeable about the colonial period. He was an expert on Connecticut history and compiled a three-century chronology of Stonington that was published in 1949.

Haynes and his wife wintered in Oaxaca, Mexico, where he developed an enthusiasm for the history of Mexico and its culture. His passion for history transcended research into any one subject, and he became deeply involved in the preservation of historic sites and artifacts in Connecticut and elsewhere, and in the preservation of the environment. He died in Stonington, Conn.

[Many of Haynes's papers are lost, but certain categories are preserved in the historical societies of Stonington and Connecticut. Some of his chemical papers were passed on to the libraries of Stanford and Denison universities. A short sketch of his life is by S. D. Kilpatrick in W. D. Miles, ed., *American Chemists and Chemical Engineers* (1976). An obituary is in *Chemical and Engineering News*, Dec. 10, 1970.]

AARON J. IHDE

HENDERSON, RAY (Dec. 1, 1896–Dec. 31, 1970), composer, was born Raymond Brost in Buffalo, N.Y., the son of William Brost, a merchant, and Margaret Baker, a piano teacher. From his earliest years Henderson was educated to be a musician. His mother gave him piano lessons before he was five. He attended local schools in Buffalo while studying piano, organ, harmony, counterpoint, and music theory with private tutors (1911–1914). By the time he was eight, he was creating melodies for the piano. He also played the organ and sang in the choir of the Episcopal church in Buffalo.

Brost continued his formal training at the Chicago Conservatory of Music. To support himself while at the conservatory, he played the piano in jazz bands, performed songs at parties, and served as an accompanist for an Irish tenor. (He later studied privately with the British composer Benjamin Britten.) The strong rhythms and inventive melodies of jazz, however, ultimately lured Brost from classical music, and during World War I he made his way to New York's Tin Pan Alley. There he found a job with the Leo Feist music publishing company, playing Feist's songs for vaudeville and cabaret singers. He soon became a staff pianist and arranger for the Shapiro-Bernstein Company. He also began to compose tunes on his own. On Oct. 18, 1918, he married Florence Hoffman; they had three children. In 1920, Brost adopted the professional name Ray Henderson.

Henderson met the lyricist Lew Brown in 1922, and they began to work together. One of their songs, "Georgette," was used in the *Greenwich Village Follies* of 1922. During the next three years Henderson collaborated with a number of different lyricists, creating a series of eminently singable and danceable songs that captured the spirit of the post–World War I years. During this period he wrote the music for the sweetly sentimental "That Old Gang of Mine," with lyrics by Billy Rose and Mort Dixon (1923); "Follow the Swallow," with Rose and Dixon (1924); the rollicking "Alabamy Bound," with B. G. ("Buddy") De Sylva and Bud Green (1925), which achieved a million-copy sheet-music sale after Eddie Cantor and Al Jolson took it into their repertoire; the euphonious "I'm Sitting on Top of the World," with Sam M. Lewis and Joe Young (1925), which was also popularized by Jolson; and "Five Foot Two, Eyes of Blue," with Lewis and Young (1925).

Henderson's big break came when George Gershwin, who had written the music for George White's popular *Scandals* revues, bowed out in 1924 to focus on his own musical productions. Henderson, chosen as Gershwin's replacement, was teamed with Buddy De Sylva and Lew Brown, and in 1925 the three began what was to become one of the most successful musical collaborations of the 1920's. The trio's first effort, *George White's Scandals* of 1925, failed to flourish, despite the presence of Helen Morgan in her Broadway debut, but White confidently engaged the team again for the *Scandals* of 1926, and the result was what the *New York World* critic Wells Rout called "the master *Scandal* of the series." Indeed, the revue, the longest-running *Scandals* by far, featured one showstopper after another: "Lucky Day," "The Girl Is You," and two songs destined to become smash hits, "The Birth of the Blues" and "Black Bottom," which inspired one of the most famous dance crazes of the flapper age.

What made the team of De Sylva, Brown, and Henderson unique, observed the music historian David Ewen, "was the way in which they functioned with a unanimity of thought, feeling, purpose, and style, as if they were a single person. More times than one, De Sylva and Brown crossed the line from words to music to suggest to Henderson ways and means of developing a melody. Just as often, Henderson offered ideas for lyrics and contributed valuable suggestions for individual lines or rhymes." Nowhere was the team's affinity with each other and with their era more in evidence than in their first musical comedy, the rousing *Good News!*, which opened on Broadway on Sept. 6, 1927, and ran for 557 performances. Often called the quintessential college musical, *Good News!* focuses on a football hero who will not be able to play in a big game unless he passes astronomy and the lovestruck girl who tutors him despite her suspicion that he loves someone else. The spirited score includes "The Varsity Drag," the title song, and the memorable "The Best Things in Life Are Free."

The De Sylva, Brown, and Henderson songs for *George White's Scandals* of 1928 have passed into history, but their score for *Hold Everything!* (1928), a musical comedy that pokes gentle fun at the world of professional boxing, featured the phenomenally popular "You're the Cream in My Coffee," plus other hits such as "To Know You Is to Love You" and "Too Good to Be True." Equally successful was *Follow Thru* (1929), a lighthearted send-up of golf and swank country clubs. The show's musical highlights are the tender "My Lucky Star," "I Want to Be Bad," and the audience-pleasing "Button Up Your Overcoat." With *Flying High* (1930), the triumvirate turned from sports to another 1920's obsession, air travel. Bert Lahr, the scene-stealing comedian who played a supporting role in *Hold Everything!*, starred as an aviator who sets a world record for time in the air because he does not know how to land his plane. Songs include "Without Love," "Thank Your Father," "Wasn't It Beautiful?" and "Red Hot Chicago," in which the Windy City is celebrated as the birthplace of jazz.

De Sylva, Brown, and Henderson also collaborated on songs for three early sound motion pictures, *The Singing Fool* (1928) and *Say It with Songs* (1929), both starring Al Jolson, and *Sunny Side Up* (1929). For *The Singing Fool*, the team responded to Jolson's request for a tear-jerking ballad by concocting the purposely maudlin "Sonny Boy." To the writers' surprise the song—with its saccharine melody and lyrics like "You're my dearest prize, Sonny boy / Sent out from the skies, Sonny boy"—sold 1.5 million copies of sheet music and became a best-selling Jolson recording. *Sunny Side Up*, a Janet Gaynor–Charles Farrell vehicle, charmed critics and audiences with its Cinderella story and lively score, which included the spirited title number, "Aren't We All," and "If I Had a Talking Picture of You."

The success of their film scores prompted De Sylva, Brown, and Henderson to move to the West Coast in 1930. Within a year, however, the partnership broke up. De Sylva remained in Hollywood, and Brown and Henderson returned to Broadway, where they collaborated on the 1931 *George White's Scandals*. The revue fared well on the strength of a talented cast that included Ethel Merman, Rudy Vallee, and Everett Marshall, and a score highlighted by "Life Is Just a Bowl of Cherries," "This Is the Missus," "My Song," "The Thrill Is Gone," and "That's Why Darkies Were Born," a tribute to the courage of blacks in the face of injustice.

In 1932, Henderson and Brown wrote the score for the Broadway musical *Hot-Cha!*, a spoof of bullfighting, and the next year they collaborated on the irreverent *Strike Me Pink*, an old-fashioned musical revue. Neither show did well in the politically charged atmosphere of the Great Depression. In 1934, when Brown departed for Hollywood, Henderson joined forces with a succession of lyricists, including Ted Koehler and Irving Caesar. The Shirley Temple favorite "Animal Crackers in My

Soup" was one of the highlights of the Henderson-Koehler-Caesar score for the film *Curly Top* (1935). On Broadway, Henderson worked with Koehler on the score of the short-lived *Say When* (1934) and with Jack Yellen on the 1936 edition of *George White's Scandals*, which opened on Christmas Day 1935 and ran for only 110 performances. Henderson, Yellen, and Caesar wrote the songs for the motion-picture musical *George White's Scandals* (1943), which was sparked by Alice Faye's memorable redition of "Oh, You Nasty Man."

Henderson's last theater score, for the 1943 edition of the *Ziegfeld Follies*, flourished as a nostalgia piece. Yellen wrote the lyrics and Henderson the music for songs such as "Love Songs Are Made in the Night," "Come Up and Have a Cup of Coffee," and "Hold That Smile." From 1942 to 1953, Henderson served as director of the American Society of Composers, Authors, and Publishers. He spent the last two decades of his life in semiretirement in his home in Greenwich, Conn., where he died.

The Best Things in Life Are Free, a film depicting the careers of Henderson, De Sylva, and Brown, was released in 1956, with Dan Dailey portraying Henderson. The film, which showcased the team's best-known songs, gave 1950's audiences a taste of the thumping rhythms and devil-may-care spirit that characterized the 1920's and to which Ray Henderson's talents were so well suited.

[The New York Public Library at Lincoln Center has a file on Henderson. See Cecil Smith and Glenn Litton, *Musical Comedy in America* (1950); David Ewen, *Great Men of American Popular Song* (1970); Ethan Mordden, *Better Foot Forward* (1976); and Stanley Green, *The World of Musical Comedy*, 4th ed. (1980). Obituaries are in the *New York Times*, Jan. 2, 1971; and *Variety*, Jan. 13, 1971.]

GAIL GARFINKEL WEISS

HENDRIX, JIMI (Nov. 27, 1942–Sept. 18, 1970), guitarist, singer, and songwriter, was born James Marshall Hendrix in Seattle, Wash., the son of James Allen Ross Hendrix, a landscape gardener, and Lucille Jetters. His father played saxophone and "the spoons," and his mother, who died when Jimi was ten, was an amateur pianist. Hendrix attended elementary school in Vancouver, Wash., where a grandmother lived and where his parents originally came from, but he went to Garfield High School in Seattle. He left school in 1961 to join the 101st Airborne Division. (An unconfirmed story has been widely circulated that Hendrix, who was black, was expelled for holding hands with a white girl.) He was in the paratroopers for twenty-six months until a back injury forced him to accept a medical discharge.

Hendrix received his first guitar when he was eleven years old, and possessed of perfect pitch, he taught himself to play by listening to blues guitarists like "T-Bone" Walker, Muddy Waters, and B. B. King. During 1963 and 1964 a stint in the backup band of the Isley Brothers took him to Nashville, where he joined a touring show starring B. B. King, Sam Cooke, Solomon Burke, and Chuck Jackson. In Atlanta, Hendrix hooked up with a Little Richard tour that took him to the West Coast, where he worked with Ike and Tina Turner's backup band. Drifting back to New York in 1964, he participated in rhythm and blues with the Famous Flames of James Brown and with King Curtis, and even became involved with the twist music of Joey Dee and the Starlighters. Harlem did not prove hospitable to the iconoclastic guitarist and he drifted downtown to the Cafe Wha! in Greenwich Village. He was performing there as Jimmy James, with the Blue Flames, when Bryan ("Chas") Chandler, the former bassist of the British group Eric Burdon and the Animals, persuaded him to leave the group and go to England. Chandler was so impressed by Hendrix' guitar-playing that he paid for his trip.

With Mitch Mitchell on drums and Noel Redding on bass guitar, the Jimi Hendrix Experience, as the new group was called, made its debut at the Olympia in Paris in 1966 and began producing best-selling discs on British charts, among them "Hey Joe" and "Purple Haze." The group's success spread through Europe, so that it drew record-breaking crowds in appearances at the Tivoli in Stockholm and the Sports Arena in Copenhagen. It made its American debut in June 1967 at the Monterey International Pop Festival, where Hendrix was a sensation because of his imaginative and virtuosic manipulation of distortion—and his ploy of dousing his expensive guitar with lighter fluid and setting it on fire. A 1967 tour with the Monkees, a teenage television group, proved a fiasco, although much media coverage was generated by an invented tale that Hendrix' band had been ousted as a result of protests by the Daughters of the American Revolution.

In 1968 Hendrix was named artist of the year by both *Billboard* and *Rolling Stone*, with *Playboy* adding its voice the following year. Of a performance in 1968, *Time* magazine wrote, "He hopped, twisted and rolled over sideways without missing a twang or a moan. He slung the guitar low over swiveling hips, or raised it to pick the strings with his teeth; he thrust it between his legs and did a bump and grind. . . . For a symbolic finish, he lifted the guitar and flung it against the amplifiers." His appearance at the Woodstock Festival in 1969 added to his following. Later that year, reacting to criticisms by black activists regarding his working with racially mixed groups, he formed the all-black Band of Gypsies, which made its debut at the Fillmore East in New York City and produced a single album.

Despite the caliber of the musicians with whom he worked, Hendrix was the superstar, his masterful guitar-playing surpassing the theatrics of his presentation. His magnetic role as an innovator of the improvisatory style known as heavy metal is well described by Eric Barrett, who served as his equipment manager and sound engineer between 1967 and 1970: "Jimi is the master of feedback. He plays both amplifiers full up at volume ten. . . . He destroys at least two speakers whenever he plays. . . . Then there's the wah-wah pedal. Most people just touch it with their foot. Jimi jumps on it with his full weight. . . . He ruins a lot of tremolo bars, too. He bends the strings with the bar, and they get bent way past the distortion level." Behind the ear-shattering thunder was a feeling and a philosophy, as well as a desire to create aural excitement: "Man, the world's a bring-down," Hendrix said. "If we play loud enough, maybe we can drown it out."

Hendrix' major singles include Bob Dylan's "All Along the Watchtower" and "Like a Rolling Stone," and his most popular albums were *Are You Experienced?*, *Electric Ladyland*, and *Axis: Bold as Love*. He was typed at times as "the black Elvis" and "the wild man of pop." His frank sexuality attracted the young as it alienated their elders. Just before his premature death, he opened Electric Lady, his own recording studio in New York City. Early rumors attributed his 1970 death in London to a drug overdose. The coroner attributed death to "the inhalation of vomit due to barbiturate intoxication."

[Two biographies are Chris Welch, *Hendrix* (1972); and Curtis Knight, *Jimi* (1975). See also *Ebony*, May 1968; Arnold Shaw, *The World of Soul* (1970); and the liner notes and article from *Guitar Player Magazine* in *The Essential Jimi Hendrix*, released by Warner Brothers Records (1978). Posthumous albums include *Rainbow Bridge*, *Hendrix in the West*, *Rare Hendrix*, and *War Heroes*. An obituary is in the *New York Times*, Sept. 19, 1970.]

ARNOLD SHAW

HENIE, SONJA (Apr. 8, 1912–Oct. 12, 1969), ice skater and film actress, was born in Oslo, Norway, the daughter of Hans Wilhelm Henie, a prosperous wholesale fur merchant, and Selma Lochman-Nielsen. In her autobiography, *Wings on My Feet* (1940), Henie wrote that the circumstances of her childhood "conspired to make a skater of me." She inherited a love of sports from her father, who competed in winter sports and won two world championships in bicycling. Her mother introduced her to ballet, and she studied with a former teacher of the great ballerina Anna Pavlova, whom she first saw dance in London in 1927.

Henie received her first skis when she was four and a much-desired pair of ice skates two years later. She quickly mastered the basics of figure skating during daily winter outings to Oslo's Frogner Stadium, an outdoor rink, and with assistance from her brother, Leif. She had private skating lessons and tutors when training and competition soon made school attendance impossible. She also traveled throughout Europe. A determined and gifted athlete, she was receptive to instruction and willingly practiced for hours every day. Despite a demanding training schedule, she enjoyed many sports and excelled in several. In 1932, for example, she finished second in the Norwegian national tennis tournament and was runner-up in a Swedish three-day cross-country auto race.

In 1921, Henie won a figure-skating competition for children in Oslo. Two years later, with coaching from Oscar Holte and Martin Stixrud and summer trips to London for ballet classes, she was the senior national champion of Norway. In 1924 she entered the first winter Olympics, held at Chamonix in the French Alps. Although she finished last in a field of eight, the eleven-year-old enjoyed international competition. Within months she and her family set the goal of winning the world championship scheduled for the familiar environs of Frogner Stadium in 1927. Performing before the Norwegian royal family and thousands of her countrymen, she won the first of her ten consecutive world championships at the age of fourteen. Before her retirement from amateur competition a decade later, she won all seven European championships she entered and Olympic gold medals at St. Moritz in 1928, Lake Placid in 1932, and Garmisch-Partenkirchen in 1936. By incorporating music and dance into the free-skating portion of her routine, she revolutionized figure skating. Never again would audiences and judges be satisifed with technically correct but disconnected performances. Figure skating was now an art, and Henie, its most celebrated practitioner.

Following the 1936 Olympics, Henie turned professional, signing with the Chicago promoter Arthur Wirtz for seventeen performances in nine American cities. The tour was a financial success, but failed to bring a coveted movie contract. With the same planning and determination that had marked her competitive efforts, she and her family set out to win her a movie contract. Wilhelm Henie rented Hollywood's Polar Palace for two performances in early May 1936. Through skillful promotion, the Henies drew many celebrities to the shows, which, according to one correspondent, "had the standing, staring, curbstone-sitting look of an old-fashioned Hollywood premiere." Within days, Henie signed a lucrative five-year contract with Darryl F. Zanuck of Twentieth Century–Fox.

Henie's first film, *One in a Million* (1936), was a box-office smash, as were *Thin Ice* (1937), *Happy Landing* (1938), *My Lucky Star* (1938), *Second Fiddle* (1939), *Everything Happens at Night* (1939), and *Sun Valley Serenade* (1941). Generally saccharine and weak of plot, the films were designed to showcase Henie's talent and Nordic beauty. Obviously that sufficed, since by 1939 only Clark Gable and Shirley Temple outranked her as a box-office attraction, despite the prediction of many that she would fade into obscurity following the end of her amateur career. In 1937, King Haakon of Norway made her only the fifth woman and the youngest person ever to be named a Knight First Class of the Order of St. Olav, and a poll taken by an Oslo newspaper that same year ranked her as one of the five greatest Norwegians in history. In the United States she appeared on the covers of many tabloids and magazines, including *Time* (July 17, 1939).

With fame came fortune. By one estimate, Henie earned more than $2 million during the first three years of her professional career. She gained a reputation in business dealings as being as cold and hard as the ice on which she skated and became the wealthiest sportswoman in the world. Although her later films— *Iceland* (1942), *Wintertime* (1943), *It's a Pleasure* (1945), and *The Countess of Monte Cristo* (1948)—were not as popular as her earlier ones, she continued to draw sellout crowds and earn huge profits with her touring *Hollywood Ice Revue*, which she coproduced with Arthur Wirtz from 1937 to 1951. In cooperation with Wirtz, she also produced, but did not appear in, an ice show that ran at New York's Center Theatre from 1940 to 1950. After breaking with Wirtz, she skated in her own production, *Sonja Henie with Her 1952 Ice Revue*. After that production, her performances were largely limited to occasional appearances on television.

After marrying the wealthy sportsman Daniel Reid Topping on July 4, 1940, Henie applied for United States citizenship, which was granted in 1941. She and Topping were divorced in 1946. On Sept. 15, 1949, she married socialite Winthrop Gardiner, Jr. That marriage ended in divorce in 1956. A few weeks later, on June 9, 1956, she married Niels Onstad, a Norwegian shipping magnate she had known since childhood. She had no children.

For years, Henie had invested in art. Onstad was also a patron and during the early 1960's they began planning for a museum to house their collections. The dedication in August 1968 of the Sonja Henie–Niels Onstad Art Center at Høvikodden, near Oslo, was attended by an international contingent of their "gem-studded friends." The Henie-Onstad gift of 250 paintings and a building to exhibit them was reported to be one of the largest private donations ever made to the Norwegian people. Shortly thereafter, Henie was diagnosed as having leukemia. While in Paris a few months later, her condition suddenly worsened. She died on an ambulance plane flying her to Oslo.

[Scrapbooks of clippings about Henie's life are housed at the Henie-Onstad Art Center, Høvikodden, Norway. In addition to her autobiography, see

Leif Henie and Raymond Strait, *Queen of Ice, Queen of Shadows: The Unsuspected Life of Sonja Henie* (1985), which contains a filmography and a partial listing of her skating championships. Lengthy articles about Henie appeared in *Time*, July 17, 1939; *Liberty*, Nov. 1, 1941; and *Skating*, Dec. 1969. Obituaries are in the *New York Times* and the *Los Angeles Times*, both Oct. 13, 1969.]

PETER L. PETERSEN

HERBST, JOSEPHINE FREY (Mar. 5, 1892–Jan. 28, 1969), radical journalist and novelist, was born in Sioux City, Iowa, the daughter of William Benton Herbst, a farm-equipment salesman, and Mary Frey, who were distant cousins. Herbst, called Josie all her life, graduated from high school in 1910, briefly attended Morningside College in Sioux City, and by the fall of 1912 had saved enough to enroll at the University of Iowa, where she determined that she wanted to be a writer.

When her father's business failed in 1913, Herbst taught grade school. In September 1915 she enrolled at the University of Washington at Seattle but withdrew because of illness. At this time, Herbst, who had been raised in genteel poverty, began to read *The Masses*, the radical periodical, which widened her horizons. After doing clerical work in Sioux City, Herbst went to Berkeley, Calif., in the summer of 1917; there she worked on her writing and met members of the radical community of Oakland and San Francisco. She received her B.A. in 1918. After a series of clerical jobs, she went to New York City, where Genevieve Taggard, a friend and fellow radical from Berkeley (later to be a noted poet), was living. Ushered into the radical community by Taggard, Herbst was stimulated by its politics and its heady talk.

Herbst soon fell under the spell of Maxwell Anderson, then a young married newspaperman, by whom she became pregnant. He insisted she have an abortion and then ended the brief affair. The abortion haunted Herbst to the close of her life; of all her friends, only Taggard was told of it. In the fall of 1920, Herbst began to work for H. L. Mencken and George Jean Nathan, as a reader for their magazines, which included the *Smart Set*, to which she sold two stories. In May 1922 she departed for Europe to travel with Max Eastman and Albert Rhys Williams. She remained in Berlin to write a novel that was never published. After resuming her travels, she then moved to Paris in April 1924, where she met John Herrmann, also an aspiring writer. A friend of Ernest Hemingway, Herrmann introduced Herbst to the American expatriate world in Paris, and in the fall the couple returned to the United States, where they wrote and lived together in New Preston, Conn. They were married Sept. 2, 1926, and were separated in 1935 after a turbulent union. They were divorced in 1940.

The couple made friends with Malcolm Cowley, John Dos Passos, Katherine Anne Porter, Robert Penn Warren, Allen Tate, Hart Crane, and many others in literary and left-wing circles. Herbst published her first novel, *Nothing Is Sacred*, in 1928. Strongly autobiographical, it told of her family life up to her mother's death. *Money for Love*, also autobiographical, appeared in 1929. Herbst and Herrmann, meantime, had bought a small farmhouse in Erwinna, Bucks County, Pa., that was to be Herbst's home for the rest of her life.

As the Great Depression began, the politics of Herbst and Herrmann moved leftward, and she began to write political articles for several magazines, including *New Masses*, a magazine close to the Communist party. Over the next several years she contributed vivid and compassionate articles about the oppression of blacks and farm unrest in the Midwest. Herbst never joined the Communist party, although Herrmann did. In 1933, *Pity Is Not Enough*, the first novel in Herbst's trilogy, was published to good reviews. Horace Gregory called her "one of the few American important women novelists." A social history of a family from Reconstruction to 1920, the book centers on the need for change in industrial society. The widely praised second volume, *The Executioner Waits* (1934), depicted the lives of two young women in the 1920's. It told a story of radicalism in contest with conservatism. *Rope of Gold* (1939), the third novel, was a plea for human rights over property rights and a call for revolution. This book, which was judged largely by its politics, did not win critical esteem.

In the 1930's Herbst's journalism put her in the public eye. She covered the underground movement in Cuba, resistance to Hitler inside Germany, and the Spanish Civil War. Her reportage was often hailed by fellow journalists for its accuracy and crispness, and Herbst herself was legendary for working under fire. Spain was the high point of her journalistic career. In 1938 she wrote, with Nathan Asch, *The Spanish Road*, a documentary play that the League of American Writers circulated to raise funds for Loyalist Spain. Her novel *Satan's Sergeants* (1941) is an account of the exploitation of the innocent told in flinty dialogue.

Herbst got a job in Washington, D.C., in 1941 writing daily broadcast scripts in German for the Office of the Coordinator of Information, a propaganda agency. After five months she was rudely ousted on suspicion of being a Communist. Many years later her biographer discovered that the Federal Bureau of Investigation had acted on totally false information supplied by Katherine Anne Porter, a writer who had often professed close friendship for Herbst and had been the recipient of her confidence. No motive for Porter's lies has surfaced.

Herbst returned to writing with *Somewhere the Tempest Fell* (1947), a novel that did not do well commercially or critically. In her final two decades, Herbst began her memoirs, and she published *Hunter of the Doves*, a novella centering on Nathanael West, and *New Green World* (1954), a biography of John and William Bartram, the eighteenth-century American naturalists.

Three segments of Herbst's memoirs were issued in magazines; in 1960 and 1961 *Noble Savage*, a literary journal, published "The Starched Blue Sky of Spain" and "A Year of Disgrace." *New American Review* carried "Yesterday's Road" in 1968. In the mid-1960's she received grants from the Rockefeller Foundation and the National Institute of Arts and Letters. Herbst died in New York City.

Herbst responded to what she perceived as the struggle between the oppressed and the exploiters by taking the side of the downtrodden. Her journalism derived its power from her compassion and from her professionalism. Her trilogy, unfairly neglected, tells an earthy story of family growth and conflict against a background of American history. Her final words, "Tell my friends I do not repent, that I love life unto eternity—love and life," stand as her epitaph.

[Martha Pickering compiled a complete bibliography of Herbst's published work in 1968 with Herbst's cooperation; it is available at the Beinecke Library, Yale. Some Herbst papers and letters are owned by Elinor Langer, Herbst's biographer; others are privately owned. The only biography is Elinor Langer, *Josephine Herbst* (1984).]

ALDEN WHITMAN

HERTER, CHRISTIAN ARCHIBALD (Mar. 28, 1895–Dec. 30, 1966), congressman, governor of Massachusetts, and United States secretary of state, was born in Paris, France, the son of two American artists, Albert Herter and Adele McGinnis. After spending his first eight years in the bohemian art world of Paris, Herter was sent to New York to live with his austere uncle, Christian Archibald Herter, a noted physician and biochemist, and to receive an American education. In 1908, Herter returned to his parents, who had settled in East Hampton on Long Island. He attended the Browning School and Harvard College, where he studied fine arts and Romance languages and received his B.A. in 1915. Following an unsuccessful experience as an architecture student at Columbia, Herter was convinced by a Harvard classmate to join the diplomatic service in 1916 as a clerk in the American embassy in Berlin. In both Germany and Belgium, where he was transferred in 1917, the multilingual Herter performed his duties with distinction. When the United States entered World War I, Herter was judged too tall and underweight for the army; instead, he accepted a desk job in the State Department in Washington, D.C. On Aug. 25, 1917, he married Mary Caroline Pratt of Brooklyn, whose father, Charles Pratt, was a Standard Oil partner of John D. Rockefeller; they had four children.

In the fall of 1918, Herter served with John W. Davis at a German-American conference on prisoners of war in Bern, Switzerland, which hammered out an agreement just as the war ended. Herter remained in Bern until his appointment as secretary to Henry White, one of the five American commissioners at the 1919 Paris Peace Conference. Promoted to secretary to the entire American Commission to Negotiate Peace (under the supervision of Secretary-General Joseph C. Grew), Herter became disheartened by President Woodrow Wilson's capitulation to the Allies on harsh treatment of Germany and other matters. Though he was tempted, Herter did not join William C. Bullitt in resigning his post in protest. Herter subsequently became a State Department expert on the Treaty of Versailles and the League of

Nations. Seeing no future for himself at the State Department after the United States Senate's defeat of the treaty and the League in 1920, Herter angled for, and won, the job of secretary to relief administrator Herbert Hoover. Thus began an association of mutual admiration and respect that lasted until Hoover's death.

When President Warren G. Harding appointed Hoover secretary of commerce in 1921, Herter became the secretary's special assistant. He served as Hoover's press coordinator and liaison to the State Department. In 1922, Hoover dispatched Herter to Soviet Russia to investigate famine conditions and determine whether American Relief Administration (ARA) feeding programs should continue. Despite the prospect of a good Russian harvest, Herter recommended that ARA assistance go on for another year. He feared that Bolshevik authorities would precipitate another famine by selling harvested grain abroad for gold.

In 1924, Herter left government for publishing. With an associate he purchased the *Independent*, a bankrupt New York–based magazine of politics and the arts, and moved it to Boston. The *Independent* catered to elite tastes, lacked popular appeal, and was sold in 1928. After serving as vice-chairman of the Hoover presidential campaign in Massachusetts, Herter sought appointment as an assistant secretary of state in his old chief's new administration. However, Secretary of State Henry L. Stimson had promised to reappoint all incumbent assistant secretaries in 1929 and could only offer Herter a lesser position, which he declined. Herter kept busy helping to establish a new magazine, the *Sportsman*, teaching a course in international relations at Harvard, and involving himself in civic and philanthropic ventures in Boston. In 1930, Herter ran for public office for the first time as the handpicked successor of the patrician political leader Henry Lee Shattuck, who had left his state legislative seat to become the treasurer of Harvard. Herter triumphed easily as a Republican and was reelected five times.

In the Massachusetts House, Herter voted as a moderate conservative on social and economic questions and a liberal on civil liberties. He was also an elite reformer who bitterly opposed the unorthodox methods of the "Kingfish of Massachusetts," Democratic governor James Michael Curley. By the middle of the depression decade, Herter was one of several eastern Republicans seeking a pragmatic accommodation with the policies of President Franklin Roosevelt's New Deal. Herter thus chaired a 1935 commission that designed state unemployment-compensation legislation applauded by labor unions and their supporters. Elected speaker of the Massachusetts House in 1939 and 1941, Herter edged slightly to the left of moderate Republican governor Leverett Saltonstall. He broke with the governor most notably in 1941 by opposing a Saltonstall veto of a bill liberalizing old-age assistance payments.

After Pearl Harbor, Herter was recruited back to Washington as a deputy director of the Office of Facts and Figures, the wartime clearinghouse of government information headed by Archibald MacLeish. An ardent internationalist, Herter returned to Massachusetts in April 1942 to run for Congress against the isolationist Republican George Holden Tinkham. The elderly Tinkham, whose district had been altered severely by the Herter-led legislature's redistricting committee in 1941, stepped aside. Herter narrowly defeated an Irish Catholic Democrat to win the seat. He was reelected by large margins four times.

As a congressman during World War II, Herter criticized the Office of Price Administration and other wartime agencies for bureaucratic excesses and strongly backed the idea of a postwar United Nations organization. After languishing on insignificant committees from 1943 to 1947, Herter got a chance to shine in the Republican Eightieth Congress as the vice-chairman and virtual head of the House Select Committee on Foreign Aid. Under his leadership, the "Herter Committee" toured eighteen wartorn countries, issued a series of detailed reports demonstrating the need for substantial American economic assistance to Europe, and laid the groundwork for congressional passage of the Marshall Plan. Although his was not the bill ultimately passed, Herter received the *Collier's* award for distinguished congressional service in 1948 for his committee's work.

Herter ended his years in Congress as the quintessential "modern Republican." Though steadfastly conservative on labor-management issues, he lined up with other self-styled progressive Republicans in support of civil rights, public works, vigorous antitrust law enforcement, and selected social welfare programs. In

Herter

foreign affairs, Herter accepted the Truman administration's hard-line view of the Soviet Union as an expansionist power in need of containment, and endorsed the economic and military measures proposed for that purpose. Outside of Congress, Herter was a founder of, and a major fund-raiser for, the School of Advanced International Studies, which became part of Johns Hopkins University in 1950.

Along with Senator Henry Cabot Lodge, Jr., Herter took part in the successful effort to draft General Dwight D. Eisenhower as the Republican candidate for president in 1952. Herter was then drafted himself by Massachusetts Republicans to run for governor against two-term Democrat Paul A. Dever. He won by a slim margin on Eisenhower's coattails. (Herter was reelected more decisively in 1954.) As might be expected, the Herter governorship was characterized by careful moderation. He pushed through a Republican legislature a mix of bills to reorganize the state tax-collection department, to create a special commission on Communism, to initiate a public-housing program, and to increase benefits for the elderly and needy. During his second term when Democrats controlled the Massachusetts House, he was somewhat less successful. Still, in four years as governor, Herter won approval for 90 percent of his legislative initiatives. Just prior to the 1956 Republican National Convention, presidential adviser Harold Stassen proposed Herter as a replacement for Vice-President Richard Nixon, whom Stassen saw as a drag on Eisenhower's reelection chances. Upon advice from Republican elders, Herter disavowed the Stassen gambit and nominated Nixon at the convention.

With Eisenhower safely reelected, Herter was made undersecretary of state at the urging of Nixon and White House chief of staff Sherman Adams; Secretary of State John Foster Dulles had wanted Herter at the lower rank of assistant secretary. After two years of doing relatively little, Herter had important duties thrust upon him in early 1959, when Dulles was ailing with cancer. Though his appointment as secretary of state shortly after Dulles' resignation in April 1959 seemed the fulfillment of a dream, Herter's brief tenure proved a disappointing anticlimax to his long career.

Herter never established the close working relationship with Eisenhower that Dulles had developed over time; the president also decided to become more active in designing American foreign policy as his administration drew to a close. Major Herter proposals for disarmament and a "permanent settlement" of cold-war disputes in Europe failed to break the ice in Soviet-American relations. Simmering crises in Cuba, the Congo, and Laos vexed Herter but were left to be resolved by a new administration. The lowest point of Herter's secretaryship came in May 1960 when Soviet Premier Nikita Khrushchev used the downing of an American U-2 reconnaissance plane over the Soviet Union to break up the long-anticipated East-West summit conference. After Herter admitted the U-2 missions and defended them as necessary to American security interests, Khrushchev insisted that the flights cease and demanded an apology from the president, thereby destroying the last hope for détente in the Eisenhower years.

Herter did manage to win high marks from the professional foreign service for his administration of the State Department. He corrected some personnel wrongs committed during the McCarthy era and regularly consulted foreign-service policy experts ignored by his predecessor. In addition, Herter's low-key anti-Communism has been viewed generally as a historical bridge between the stridency of Dulles and the more flexible cold-war diplomacy of President John F. Kennedy.

As if to illustrate the point, Democrat Kennedy appointed Republican Herter as the president's special representative for trade negotiations in 1962 (despite the persistence of crippling arthritis that had plagued Herter throughout his secretaryship). Retained by President Lyndon Johnson, Herter participated in the "Kennedy Round" tariff-reduction negotiations in Geneva from 1964 through 1966. Differences with European Common Market countries prevented Herter from achieving a substantial agreement before he died. Upon his death in Washington, D.C., Congressman Thomas P. O'Neill, Jr., a Massachusetts Democrat, paid Herter a fitting final tribute: "His style was that of the classic diplomat. He was patient, understanding and fair; and beneath his pleasant, polite manner was assurance and strength."

[Herter's papers are at the Houghton Library, Harvard University. The Massachusetts Historical Society has a collection of Herter family papers. Important

Herter manuscripts can be found at the Dwight D. Eisenhower Library; the Herbert Hoover Library; the Hoover Institution on War, Revolution and Peace; the Lyndon B. Johnson Library; and the John F. Kennedy Library.

The *Final Report on Foreign Aid of the House Select Committee on Foreign Aid* (1948) represents Herter's most significant contribution as a member of Congress. *Addresses and Messages to the General Court, Proclamations, Public Addresses, Official Statements and Correspondence of His Excellency Governor Christian A. Herter . . .* (1956) is the official record of Herter's governorship. Herter's books are *Miscellaneous Speeches* (1959–1960) and *Toward An Atlantic Community* (1963). Articles written by Herter include "Capacity to Pay," *Atlantic Monthly*, Jan. 1926; "Looking Back at Kansas City," *Independent*, June 30, 1928; "UNRRA on Balance," *Atlantic Monthly*, Apr. 1946; "Our Most Dangerous Lobby," *Reader's Digest*, Sept. 1947; and "Atlantica," *Foreign Affairs*, Jan. 1963.

Biographical studies of Herter are G. Bernard Noble, "Christian A. Herter," in Robert H. Ferrell, ed., *The American Secretaries of State and Their Diplomacy*, XVIII (1970), an early effort focusing almost exclusively upon the Eisenhower years; and Richard H. Gentile, "Public Service and Politics: Christian A. Herter, 1895–1957" (Ph.D. diss., Boston College, 1988), which covers Herter's life and career prior to his service in the Eisenhower administration. See also Bill Davidson, "Congress' Conscience Is Six Foot Six," *Collier's*, Jan. 10, 1948; Henry F. Pringle, "The Yankee Who Surprised Congress," *Saturday Evening Post*, Feb. 14, 1948; William V. Shannon, "Herter Stands By," *Progressive*, Feb. 1956; Robert C. Bergenheim, "Top GOP Alternate: Herter of Massachusetts," *Nation*, Feb. 11, 1956; E. W. Kenworthy, "Quarterback of State's Team," *New York Times Magazine*, Mar. 29, 1959; "Yankee Internationalist," *Time*, Jan. 13, 1967; *Memorial Addresses and Other Tributes in the Congress of the United States on the Life and Contributions of Christian Archibald Herter* (1967); Townsend Hoopes, *The Devil and John Foster Dulles* (1973); Stephen E. Ambrose, *Eisenhower: The President* (1984); and Michael R. Beschloss, *Mayday* (1986). Obituaries are in the *Boston Globe*, the *Boston Herald*, and the *New York Times*, all Jan. 1, 1967; and the *Times* of London, Jan. 2, 1967.]

RICHARD H. GENTILE

HIGGINS, MARGUERITE (Sept. 3, 1920–Jan. 3, 1966), journalist, war correspondent, and author, was born in Hong Kong, the daughter of Lawrence Daniel Higgins, a businessman and former pilot, and Marguerite de Godard, who were American citizens. From the age of five, Higgins resided with her family in Oakland, Calif., where she attended Anna Head's private high school on a scholarship. In 1941, after graduating cum laude with a B.S. from the University of California and working for one summer for the *Vallejo* (Calif.) *Times-Herald*, Higgins moved to New York City. She attended the Columbia University School of Journalism on a scholarship and received her M.S. in 1942. While at Columbia she worked as campus reporter for the *New York Herald Tribune*, which she joined as a full-time staff member after graduation. In her first year as a reporter, Higgins demonstrated the determination and ingenuity that became her trademark by securing an exclusive interview with Madame Chiang Kai-shek. On July 12, 1942, she married Stanley Moore; they had two children before their divorce in 1948.

Because of her fluency in French, Higgins was assigned to the *Herald Tribune*'s Paris office as a correspondent in 1944. While with the Seventh Army in Europe, she provided first-hand accounts of the capture of Munich and the American entry into the Dachau and Buchenwald concentration camps and Hitler's lair at Berchtesgaden; at the liberation of Dachau, an SS officer tried to surrender to Higgins and a fellow correspondent, who were among the first Americans within its gates. These stories, as well as her special interviews with the wives of high-ranking Nazi officials, brought her worldwide attention and the New York Newspaper Women's Club Award for 1945. In 1947 Higgins was promoted to chief of her paper's Berlin bureau, where she combined exhaustive news coverage with an instinct for being in the right spot at the right time. Her position allowed her to report a dramatic insider's view of the Berlin blockade and airlift.

In 1950, as the *Herald Tribune*'s Far Eastern correspondent, Higgins covered the frontline engagements of the United States Army in Korea. When Lieutenant General Walton H. Walker ordered her out of Korea along with other female correspondents, Higgins appealed to General Douglas MacArthur, who rescinded the order. At a time when women were expected to prefer safer occupations and special treatment, Higgins argued, "I am not working in Korea as a woman. I am there as a war correspondent." Described by her colleagues as "alarmingly brave and extraordinarily durable," Higgins routinely accompanied fighting units into combat. Her complete involvement with the troops, including their retreat from Seoul and their landing at Inchon, won her the highest respect of the combatants as well as numerous awards, including a 1951 Pulitzer Prize for international reporting. Often described as fearless, the slightly built Higgins shared the same hardships as the soldiers and won a regimental commendation for administering plasma to the wounded while under enemy fire. *War in Korea: The Report of a Woman Combat Correspondent* (1951) brought favorable reviews for her objectivity and her epigrammatic style. On Oct. 7, 1952, she married Lieutenant General William E. Hall; they had one child.

Higgins won many more awards and honors, so many that after publication of her semi-autobiographical *News Is a Singular Thing* (1954), she stated that she had "quit counting" them. Although male journalists occasionally accused her of employing her femininity to unfair advantage in securing a story, most agreed that her presence and enormous productivity inspired their own work to higher levels of achievement. Higgins once enumerated the necessary qualities for first-rate war reporting: a capacity for unusual physical endurance, a willingness to take personal risks, exhaustive background work, strong nerves, persistence, and an ability to get to important news sources. She possessed all these talents but candidly admitted that her determination was strengthened by a desire to prove that a female reporter need not be left behind. She considered her story on the landing at Inchon her best, because of the authenticity and excitement with which she could report the events as she pushed ashore under enemy fire in the first wave of landing craft.

In 1958 Higgins returned to the United States to serve as Washington correspondent for the *Herald Tribune*. She remained there until 1963, when the Long Island daily *Newsday* offered her an attractive salary and travel account. Her thrice-weekly column appeared in *Newsday* and ninety-two other American newspapers. Higgins was one of the first to warn of the Russian buildup in Cuba and to criticize American strategy in Vietnam. While agreeing with the American intent to contain the spread of Communism in Asia, she criticized as unrealistic the hopes of American administrations that stable, democratic governments could be set up in nations with no previous experience with democratic institutions. In her book *Our Vietnam Nightmare* (1965), she was particularly critical of "the inglorious role" of the United States in the fall of the Diem regime in 1963. In the autumn of 1965, somewhere between Saigon and Karachi, she contracted a rare tropical disease, leishmaniasis, from the bite of a sandfly. She was hospitalized at Walter Reed Medical Center in Washington, where, despite an intermittent raging fever, she continued to produce her column until a few days before her death.

[Books by Higgins in addition to those already mentioned are *Red Plush and Black Bread* (1956); *Jessie Benton Fremont* (1962); and, with Peter Lisagor, *Tales of the Foreign Service* (1963). Higgins' articles include "Russia's New Look," *National Parent-Teacher*, Oct. 1959; "Our Secret Allies: The Captive People of East Germany," *Reader's Digest*, Oct. 1961; and "Saigon Summary," *America*, Jan. 4, 1964. A biography of Higgins is Antoinette May, *A Witness to War* (1983). For photographs, see "Girl War Correspondent," *Life*, Oct. 2, 1950; "This Time, Korea," *Newsweek*, July 10, 1950; and "Pride of the Regiment," *Time*, Sept. 25, 1950. Obituaries are in the *New York Times*, Jan. 4, 1966; and *Time*, Jan. 14, 1966.]

SUSAN J. CUNNINGHAM

HINDUS, MAURICE GERSCHON (Feb. 27, 1891–July 8, 1969), writer and authority on Soviet affairs, was born in Bolshoye Bikovo, Russia, the son of Jacob Hindus, a kulak, and Sarah Gendeliovitch. After his father's death, the family fell on hard economic times, and Hindus came to the United States with his mother and siblings in 1905, settling in New York City. He took a job as an errand boy, attended night classes, and became a naturalized citizen in 1910 or shortly thereafter. After two years at Stuyvesant High School, he attended Colgate University, graduated with honors in 1915, and earned an M.S. a year later. A year of further graduate study followed at Harvard University.

Confident by now of his mastery of the English language, Hindus plunged into freelance writing, which was to become his career. His first book, *The Russian Peasant and the Revolution*, appeared in 1920. After a visit of several months in 1922 among Russian émigrés in Canada, he sold a number of articles about them to *Century* magazine, whose editor then commissioned Hindus to return to Russia to study the collective farming system. Several books resulted, including *Humanity Uprooted* (1929) and *Red Bread* (1931), both of which were well received. Most of Hindus' works deal with Soviet life and current events, and he revisited his homeland many times. His autobiography, *Green Worlds: An Informal Chronicle* (1938), describes his experiences on an upstate New York farm and draws contrasts with Soviet collective farming.

Hindus spent nearly three years in the Soviet Union during World War II as a war correspondent for the *New York Herald Tribune*, an experience reflected in *Mother Russia* (1943), a sympathetic portrayal of wartime conditions there.

During the cold war, Hindus became highly critical of the Soviet government, although he was always careful to distinguish between the Kremlin and the Russian people, whom he characterized—as in *Crisis in the Kremlin* (1953)—as decent, long-suffering, and peace-loving. "Anyone who has broken bread with them," he wrote, "or has slept in their homes . . . or has heard them talk and laugh and weep, must attest that they are crusaders neither for world revolution nor world conquest." Hindus also wrote four novels during his career: *Moscow Skies* (1936); *Sons and Fathers* (1940); *To Sing with the Angels* (1941), about Czechoslovakia; and *Magda* (1951), the story of a Polish farmer who emigrates to America. In the late 1940's Hindus traveled in Iran, Iraq, Egypt, and Palestine. *In Search of a Future* (1949) chronicled his visits there. In 1957 he married Frances McClernan. He died in New York City.

Hindus was a prolific writer, with twenty books and numerous magazine articles to his credit, and he lectured frequently. Reviewers praised his works for their narrative and descriptive qualities and for his portrayals of Russian peasant life, but they found the analytical skill of some of his work uneven.

Hindus undoubtedly helped to increase American understanding of, and sympathy for, the Soviet Union in the 1920's and 1930's and during its years as an ally in World War II. His disenchantment with Soviet foreign policy during the cold war paralleled that of many of his fellow Americans, and he had no illusions about his native land. In *House Without a Roof* (1961) he wrote that although the Russian Revolution was "the most violent revolution ever engineered by man, it has also been spectacularly creative; else there would have been no sputniks, no cosmonaut, and Russia would not have become the super-power that it is, second only to America. But the creativeness has been achieved in a traditional Russian way, by iron rule from above and in complete disregard of human cost and the freedoms that the West cherishes."

[Besides the works mentioned above, Hindus wrote *Broken Earth* (1926); *The Great Offensive* (1933); *We Shall Live Again* (1939); *Hitler Cannot Conquer Russia* (1941); *Russia and Japan* (1942); *The Cossacks* (1945); *Bright Passage* (1947); and *The Kremlin's Human Dilemma* (1967). See *Wilson Library Bulletin*, Feb. 1931. An obituary is in the *New York Times*, July 9, 1969.]

WILLIAM F. MUGLESTON

HINES, JOHN LEONARD ("BIRDIE") (May 21, 1868–Oct. 13, 1968), army officer, was born in White Sulphur Springs, W.Va., the son of Edward Hines, a merchant and postmaster, and Mary Frances Leonard, both of whom were natives of Ireland. Hines attended the local one-room school and later a normal school near Athens, W.Va., where he was tutored by a dedicated teacher who helped him win a competitive appointment to the United States Military Academy in 1887. The nickname Birdie, conferred on him by his fellow cadets because of his springy step, stuck throughout his forty-one years of active service. Standing well over six feet and weighing some 200 pounds, he was an impressive figure when commissioned a second lieutenant in 1891. (He was retroactively awarded a B.S. in 1933, along with all other living graduates of the academy.)

After initial assignments at posts in the western United States, he volunteered for service in Cuba during the Spanish-American War and won a Silver Star for gallantry under fire at Santiago. Returning to the United States, he married Harriet ("Rita") Schofield Wherry, the daughter of Brigadier General William M. Wherry, his former commanding officer, on Dec. 19, 1898; they had two children.

After serving in the Philippines during the Philippine insurrection, Hines had a succession of broadening assignments, including running a coaling station in Nagasaki, Japan, for army transports, serving as chief quartermaster for an army maneuver in Pennsylvania and for the Jamestown Exposition in Virginia, and serving as adjutant general and sometime chief of staff for General Pershing's expedition into Mexico in pursuit of Pancho Villa. Having won Pershing's respect, Hines was included in the initial group of officers the general took with him to France to form the American Expeditionary Force (AEF) in May 1917.

Never entirely happy serving as a staff officer at a desk, Hines was delighted when, in October 1917, newly promoted to colonel, he was given command of the Sixteenth Infantry Regiment in the First Division and moved to the front. His coolness under fire, his ability to inspire the officers and men under his command, and his skill in developing a competent staff out of inexperienced temporary officers led to his promotion to brigadier general in May 1918 and to command of the First Brigade in thc First Division.

Hines's performance in the heavy fighting in the Montdidier-Cantigny area led to his further promotion to temporary major general in August 1918 and to command of the Fourth Division, as well as a Distinguished Service Cross for extraordinary heroism in action near Soissons. His division was on the offensive continuously for twenty-five days, longer than any other division in the AEF, and yet, he was seemingly imperturbable when subjected to such severe stress. On one occasion his commanding officer found him sleeping peacefully in the front lines among his troops. For his successes in the Meuse-Argonne offensive, he was moved up to command of the Third Army Corps, making him the only officer in the AEF to command successively a regiment, a brigade, a division, and a corps, and the only American to do so in action since Stonewall Jackson.

Back in the United States after the Armistice, Hines held divisional and corps area commands until called to Washington, D.C., by Pershing to be his deputy chief of staff in 1922. Although Hines disliked staff duty, he accepted the call, having made it his practice never to ask for an assignment and never to refuse one. He brought considerable skill to the post even though he had never served in Washington before. He had a gift for solving problems, and his wide-ranging experience in supply, finance, and personnel in his years as a subaltern now paid off. Pershing was often absent in France on American Battle Monuments Commission problems, so Hines frequently served as acting chief of staff. In 1924, upon Pershing's retirement, he became chief of staff but only for two years because, under the prevailing statutes, no officer could serve on the General Staff for more than four years without returning to duty with the troops.

As chief of staff, Hines faced an almost insurmountable challenge. With Congress in a budget-cutting mood, about the best he could do was fight a rearguard action to save what was left and keep some fragments of the army intact. It was, Hines said, the hardest work he ever did. A poor speech-maker, he came off rather badly on ceremonial occasions and in testifying before Congress. He was, however, a social success, for he loved to dance. Once in London, with Pershing, he danced with Nancy Astor and swept her off her feet, leading her to declare him the best thing that ever came out of West Virginia. When he went out on inspection trips as chief of staff, unit commanders knew that the most effective way to handle him was to schedule a military ball.

Because he was only fifty-eight when he stepped down as chief of staff in 1926, Hines continued on active duty as a major general until his retirement in 1932. He died in Washington, D.C. Pershing ranked him "first on the list of generals known to me." While his role as chief of staff could hardly be called distinguished, he was a superb troop leader. A meticulous planner, he insisted on being up on the front, where he could "see for himself." He stressed physical fitness and rode horseback, even when he was chief of staff, at least an hour every day. An amateur botanist especially interested in wildflowers, he was a great favorite with children. Hines was such a taciturn soul that the journalist Frederick Palmer said of him, "He could be silent in more languages than any man I know."

[Hines's manuscripts are in the Library of Congress and the Military History Institute, Army War College, Carlisle, Pa., which also contains a manuscript biographical sketch of Hines in the papers of General Charles L. Bolte, an oral history interview with Bolte, and an Office of Chief of Military History oral history interview with Hines by Harold D. Cater. Brief sketches are also in *Generals of the Army*, Apr. 1953; and United States Congress, *Congressional Record*, 90th Cong., 2d sess., 1968, vol.

114, pt. 3. An obituary is in the *New York Times*, Oct. 14, 1968.]

I. B. HOLLEY, JR.

HIRSCH, MAXIMILIAN JUSTICE (July 30, 1880–Apr. 3, 1969), horse trainer, was born in Fredericksburg, Tex., the son of Jacob Hirsch, a carpenter and postmaster, and his wife, Mary (maiden name unknown). By the age of ten, Hirsch was riding quarter horses on the ranch of John A. Morris. He served his apprenticeship on the half-mile and county-fair tracks of Texas. When Hirsch was twelve, he stowed away in a boxcar that was taking some of Morris' horses to Baltimore. "I just made up my mind I'd go with the horses. I wanted to see the races," he later said. He worked as an exercise boy in Baltimore and became a jockey in 1894. Hirsch had 123 victories before his career was ended when he gained too much weight. He then became a trainer, and the first winner he saddled was a four-year-old, Guatama, at the fairgrounds in New Orleans on Mar. 21, 1902.

Hirsch married Kathryn Claire in 1905; they had five children. He named a colt Beauclere in honor of his wife; it became his first stakes winner and won the Washington Cup in 1907. By 1915, Hirsch-trained horses were winning important races: Norse King won the Dwyer and became his first stakes winner in New York, and Papp (owned by George Loft) won the 1917 Futurity.

The gangster Arnold Rothstein was one of the owners Hirsch trained for. The two men were involved in a famous betting coup on Sidereal, a horse that had not won a race. The trainer knew from his workouts that Sidereal could win and therefore entered him in the last race at Aqueduct. "I saw Rothstein and told him to organize things. Rothstein collected about eight guys and stationed one at each book, ready to bet as soon as he got the word. Sidereal trotted in and Rothstein started betting," he later recalled. Sidereal won by a length and a half, and Rothstein and Hirsch are said to have won $770,000.

The first champion that Hirsch trained was Sarazen, an undefeated two-year-old of 1923 bought by Mrs. Graham Fair Vanderbilt. Sarazen won eight stakes races in 1924, beating Epinard in the third International Special, and at four and five he was the leading handicapper. Hirsch trained for many owners in the 1920's, including Bernard Baruch. In 1928, Hirsch won the Belmont with Vito, owned by A. H. Cosden.

The Hirsch children received a thorough training in horses, and in 1933, Hirsch's daughter, Mary McLennan, became the first woman in the United States to get a thoroughbred trainer's license; two years later she became the first woman licensed to train in New York. Max, Jr., and William ("Buddy") Hirsch were also trainers.

The King Ranch of Texas was Hirsch's largest assignment; its owner, Robert Kleberg, Jr., said Hirsch "showed us how to race." In 1935, Split Second won the Selima Stakes, and in the years thereafter Hirsch would saddle fifty-three more stakes winners for the King Ranch.

Hirsch won the Arlington Classic in 1941 with Attention, and then went on to train what is often considered Hirsch's best horse, Assault. When a yearling, he took a spike through a hoof, and many horsemen considered him hopeless. But Hirsch sent Assault to Columbia, S.C., where he wintered his best stock. He inserted a steel spring on the sole of the injured hoof. Assault won the 1946 Kentucky Derby by eight lengths and completed the Triple Crown with victories in the Preakness and Belmont. After Assault became ill and had a very bad race, Hirsch showed his ability by bringing the horse back; Assault beat his stablemate Stymie in the Pimlico Special, and the year ended with Assault's victory in the Westchester Handicap.

Hirsch showed he could get the best out of a jockey as well as a horse by picking apprentice jockeys who would win. When Bold Venture, another Hirsch-trained horse, won the Kentucky Derby and the Preakness in 1936, it was the first time the Derby was won by an apprentice jockey (Ira Hanford, who had been developed by Mary McLennan). Hirsch displayed courage when he chose an eighteen-year-old apprentice, Bill Boland, to ride Middleground at Churchill Downs in 1950, but Boland gave Hirsch his third Derby.

Hirsch was also a superb judge of yearlings. Among those he bought were Grey Lag, On Watch, Roman Soldier, Dawn Play, Sortie, and High Gun (winner of the 1954 Belmont). Among the Hirsch-trained fillies were But Why Not, One Hour, Good Gamble, Clarify, Hindu Queen, and Ciencia (winner of the Santa Anita Derby). Gallant Bloom was the champion two-year-old filly of 1968.

Hirsch had a reputation for generosity: at

Saratoga his large breakfasts became famous. He could also be blunt with owners. Edward Lasker telephoned Hirsch with advice and received this telegram: "Any damn fool can read a condition book at 3,000 miles. Max Hirsch." Lasker later wrote, "Mr. Hirsch always felt that training owners was one of the most difficult parts of his profession."

In the last sixty years of his career, Hirsch won over 1,900 races and over $12 million. When asked what he had learned about horses, he said, "Not a thing, at least as to how they'll turn out. Horses are a mystery. You can learn how to train a horse and keep improving your methods over the years, like I've done, but you'll never learn how to determine in advance which horse will be good and another bad."

His home, Cottage 1 at Belmont Park, had a library of English and American books on training and breeding that was used by owners and their friends. At the time of his death, horsemen considered him the best. The last horse he ran, Heartland, a four-year-old filly, won the feature race at Aqueduct on Apr. 2, 1969. Hirsch died in New Hyde Park, N.Y.

[See Donald Henderson Clarke, *In the Reign of Rothstein* (1929); John Hervey, *Racing in America: 1922–1936* (1937); Hambla Bauer, "He Trains Horses and Millionaires," *Saturday Evening Post*, June 26, 1948; "Rookie's Ride," *Newsweek*, May 15, 1950; Leo Katcher, *The Big Bankroll* (1958); Bernard Postal, *Encyclopedia of Jews in Sports* (1965); Edward Lasker, "Memories of Max," *Blood-Horse*, May 31, 1969; and *To Absent Friends from Red Smith* (1982). Obituaries are in the *New York Times*, Apr. 3, 1969; and *Blood-Horse*, Apr. 12, 1969.]

RALPH KIRSHNER

HOBART, ALICE NOURSE TISDALE (Jan. 28, 1882–Mar. 14, 1967), writer and novelist, was born in Lockport, N.Y., the daughter of Edwin Henry Nourse, a music teacher, and Harriet Augusta Beaman. She grew up near Chicago. After high school in Downer's Grove, she attended Northwestern University briefly and taught elementary school for one year. From 1904 to 1907 she studied at the University of Chicago, where she became interested in writing in her freshman English class. She suffered from spinal meningitis aggravated by a fall during childhood and never fully recovered; she was unable to complete a degree. During this period she worked for the Young Women's Christian Association, spending two years in organization work at Kansas State University.

In 1908, Nourse visited an older sister who was teaching in Hangchow, China. She stayed there two years and then traveled throughout Russia and Europe before returning to Hangchow to teach. On June 29, 1914, she married Earle Tisdale Hobart, a businessman with Standard Oil, in Tientsin; they had no children. They remained in China, living in frontier villages in Manchuria and Mongolia as well as in larger cities until 1927, when political unrest forced them to leave the country. Their home in Nanking was attacked, and most of their possessions were lost. After a brief period in France, Germany, and New York City, they settled in Virginia near Washington, D.C.

Hobart began writing in 1917. Her first books, based on her life and experiences in China, included *Pioneering Where the World Is Old: Leaves from a Manchurian Note-Book* (1917), *By the City of the Long Sand: A Tale of New China* (1926), *Within the Walls of Nanking* (1928), and her first novel, *Pidgin Cargo* (1929), reissued in 1934 as *River Supreme*. Material for these early books had been previously published as travel essays in the *Atlantic Monthly*.

Hobart's most popular novel, *Oil for the Lamps of China* (1933), was the story of an idealistic oil-company engineer and his wife living in China. The story juxtaposes the power of the corporation with the young couple's idealism. The book also contrasts American ideas of efficiency with China's Confucian philosophy of individual responsibility. In *Yang and Yin* (1936), Hobart presented a picture of Chinese civilization and culture as seen through the eyes of an American doctor; it is regarded as her most philosophical work. *Their Own Country* (1940), a sequel to *Oil for the Lamps of China*, followed the American couple's return to the United States during the Great Depression. It is a realistic examination of American business in conflict with individual morality.

In 1935, Hobart and her husband moved to California, first living in Berkeley, later on a ranch, and finally in Oakland. There she wrote *The Cup and the Sword* (1942), which chronicles three generations of a French immigrant family of winegrowers. *The Cleft Rock* (1948) is also centered around a powerful family, focusing on the conflict between large and small farmers in California and the exploitation of water rights for irrigation.

The Peacock Sheds His Tail (1945), set in Mexico, where the Hobarts lived in 1942 and 1943, traces the tragic decline of a Spanish-Mexican land-holding family under the impact of the revolution and ensuing reforms. Hobart's most controversial novel, *The Serpent-Wreathed Staff* (1951), about a family of doctors, arose out of her lifelong association with the medical profession because of her chronic back condition. In it, she advocated prepaid preventive group health care and attacked conservative elements in medicine. Her later work included *Venture into Darkness* (1955) and her autobiography, *Gusty's Child* (1959). Her last novel, *The Innocent Dreamers* (1963), examines an interracial marriage in China.

Ten of Hobart's novels became best-sellers. Her books sold more than 4 million copies and were translated into a dozen languages. Many of her articles and stories were published in leading magazines and periodicals, including *Century, Harper's, American Geographic, National Geographic*, and *Asia*. Two of her most popular novels were made into motion pictures, *Oil for the Lamps of China* (1935 and, as *Law of the Tropics*, 1941) and *The Cup and the Sword* (1959, under the title *This Earth Is Mine*).

Hobart was optimistic about the future. Summarizing her work, she said, "I'm enormously interested in democracy, in the breaking up of tradition wherever it is. . . . I've felt that a society that crystallizes is in danger." Her novels reflect her commitment to improving the quality of life for ordinary people. While criticized for overly serious handling of some themes and issues, Hobart gained a reputation for skillful storytelling and a genuine concern for humanity. She died in Oakland, Calif.

[There is no collection of Hobart's papers. Her autobiography is the best source of information. See also Ruth Moore, *The Work of Alice Tisdale Hobart* (1940). An obituary is in the *New York Times*, Mar. 15, 1967.]

MARY SUE SCHUSKY

HOCKING, WILLIAM ERNEST (Aug. 10, 1873–June 12, 1966), philosopher and educator, was born in Cleveland, Ohio, the son of William Francis Hocking, a homeopathic physician who migrated to the United States from Canada, and Julia Carpenter Pratt, a descendant of the *Mayflower* passenger Degorie Priest. Hocking and his four younger sisters received a strict Methodist upbringing. Only fifteen when he graduated from high school in Joliet, Ill., Hocking spent four years as a surveyor and civil engineer. In 1893 he attended the University of Chicago for one semester but lacked the money to continue. The next year Hocking entered the Iowa State College of Agriculture and the Mechanic Arts. There he read William James's *Principles of Psychology* and decided to study with James at Harvard University.

Hocking left Iowa State College in 1895 and taught school in Davenport, Iowa, to save for his Harvard studies. Entering the university in 1899, he concentrated on philosophy and psychology, benefiting from a brilliant Harvard faculty that included Josiah Royce, George Santayana, George Herbert Palmer, and Hugo Münsterberg as well as James. Royce's influence on Hocking proved the most decisive.

Hocking received his B.A. in 1901 and remained at Harvard to complete his M.A. the following year. He then studied in German universities at Göttingen, Berlin, and Heidelberg. While at Göttingen, he was one of the first Americans to work with the phenomenologist Edmund Husserl. Hocking received his Ph.D. at Harvard in 1904 and became an instructor in comparative religion at Andover (Mass.) Theological Seminary. He married Agnes Boyle O'Reilly, a schoolteacher, on June 28, 1905. They had three children. They also started the innovative Shady Hill School in 1915. Founded in their Cambridge home, the school became one of the leading educational experiments in the United States.

The Hockings moved west in 1906, and Hocking spent two years in the philosophy department at the University of California at Berkeley. Hocking next accepted a position at Yale University, where he taught for six years, rising to professor of philosophy in 1913. At Yale he published his first major book, *The Meaning of God in Human Experience: A Philosophic Study of Religion* (1912). This work put Hocking in the front rank of American philosophers, and it remains his magnum opus. Exploring the borderland between philosophy and theology, the book interprets James's pragmatism and Royce's idealism to create Hocking's own philosophical system. A version of objective idealism, or "nonmaterialistic realism," as he sometimes called it, this outlook focused on the philosophical issues that concerned Hocking throughout his life: the purpose and destiny of human existence, human awareness of God, and the fundamentally social nature of reality.

Hocking left Yale in 1914 to become professor of philosophy at Harvard University. During World War I he received officers' training and in 1916 became a captain in the army, serving as an instructor in military engineering for the Reserve Officers Training Corps at Harvard. In 1917 the British Foreign Office requested that he visit the British and French fronts to study the psychology of morale. These investigations resulted in *Morale and Its Enemies* (1918). After working as inspector of war-issues courses for the army in 1918, Hocking resumed teaching philosophy at Harvard. Named Alford Professor of Natural Religion, Moral Philosophy, and Civil Polity in 1920, he occupied that chair until 1943, when he retired to the mountaintop home he had built at Madison, N.H.

Hocking had a lifelong interest in art, architecture, farming, carpentry, and painting. He lectured widely at home and abroad and gave the prestigious Gifford Lectures at the University of Glasgow, Scotland, in 1938–1939.

Hocking published some twenty books, including *Human Nature and Its Remaking* (1918; revised 1923), *The Present Status of the Philosophy of Law and of Rights* (1926), and *Man and the State* (1926). The last two linked Hocking's metaphysical and religious perspectives to his persistent concern with the practical realities of social existence. Those concerns expanded when Hocking visited the Middle East in 1928. Reflecting on his experiences in that region, he published *The Spirit of World Politics: With Special Studies of the Near East* (1932), which explored the ethical foundations necessary for international cooperation. He remained especially interested in Middle Eastern politics. Visiting India, China, and Japan in 1932, he also became a staunch advocate of interreligious dialogue.

Hocking studied global affairs and analyzed the personal dimensions of human life. Based on his Terry Lectures at Yale University, *The Self: Its Body and Freedom* (1928) elaborated Hocking's conviction that selfhood entails purposive interaction with others. Later he used concepts from physics to suggest that the self is a "field of fields." His views on selfhood found their most mature expression in *The Meaning of Immortality in Human Experience* (1957), an enlarged and revised version of *Thoughts on Death and Life* (1937). Meanwhile, many college students read his *Types of Philosophy* (1929; revised 1939 and 1959).

Hocking gave the 1936 Powell Lectures at Indiana University, published as *Lasting Elements of Individualism* (1937) and dedicated to John Dewey. Hopes for religious ecumenicity were expressed in *Living Religions and a World Faith* (1940). Derived from his 1936 Hibbert Lectures, this book asserted that the world's religions should replace their sectarian divisiveness with mutual appreciation; religious diversity, he argued, could deepen the spiritual awareness of all persons. *Science and the Idea of God* (1944) was followed by *Experiment in Education* (1954) and *The Coming World Civilization* (1956). Along with *Strength of Men and Nations* (1959), these works suggested that despite international conflicts, Hocking discerned signs pointing toward a more humane and harmonious world.

Hocking was the most important exponent of the philosophical idealism championed by Royce, but even Hocking's impressive efforts could not prevent the eclipse of that tradition by a less speculative, religiously skeptical, and frequently antimetaphysical empiricism. Hocking's writings are no longer studied extensively, yet his influence remains. He pioneered a global perspective in philosophy, facilitating dialogue between East and West and among diverse outlooks.

[See Andrew J. Reck, *Recent American Philosophy* (1964); Daniel Somer Robinson, *Royce and Hocking, American Idealists* (1968); Leroy S. Rouner, *Within Human Experience* (1969), and, as ed., *Philosophy, Religion, and the Coming World Civilization* (1966), which contains an extensive bibliography prepared by Richard C. Gilman. Bruce Kuklick, *The Rise of American Philosophy: Cambridge, Massachusetts, 1860–1930* (1977), discusses Hocking's development in and contributions to the philosophy department at Harvard University. An obituary is in the *New York Times*, June 13, 1966.]

JOHN K. ROTH

HODGES, COURTNEY HICKS (Jan. 5, 1887–Jan. 16, 1966), soldier and military commander, was born in Perry, Ga., the son of John Hicks Hodges, a newspaperman, and

Katherine Norwood. He always wanted to be a soldier and eventually became one of that generation of military officers singled out and nurtured by General George Marshall as Marshall built the American army that fought World War II. Hodges, however, had a career that differed from most of his colleagues'. In 1904, after graduating from high school in Perry, he received an appointment to the United States Military Academy at West Point, but he failed geometry and had to leave after one year. He spent the following year as a grocery clerk in Georgia but refused to abandon his dream of soldiering. In 1906 he enlisted as a private at Fort McPherson, Ga., serving in the Seventeenth Infantry for two and a half years and rising to the rank of sergeant. In 1909 he became a second lieutenant in the infantry through competitive examination, a very rare achievement at that time.

Hodges served successively in peacetime at Fort Leavenworth, Kans., in San Antonio, Tex., and in the Philippine Islands. From March 1916 to February 1917, he served in Mexico with General John Pershing's Punitive Expedition, which tried to capture Pancho Villa. In France during World War I Hodges rose rapidly up the chain of command and led troops in several offensives, most notably the Meuse-Argonne. He led a scouting expedition across the Meuse River and penetrated the main German lines. For more than a day his command held that key bridgehead, which became the lead point of an American advance across the Meuse. For his gallantry and leadership he was awarded the Distinguished Service Cross, the Silver Star, and the Bronze Star with three battle stars.

Between the two world wars Hodges saw his rank reduced as the army contracted in size, but he remained a permanent major from 1920 to 1934. In 1928 he married Mildred Lee Buchner, a widow who, like Hodges, was an expert shot. Hodges had been a crack marksman since childhood and for a long time was the army's leading performer in national rifle matches.

During the interwar period Hodges learned and taught about the use of infantry, artillery, and air support. After brief duty in Germany he graduated from the Field Artillery School at Fort Sill, Okla., in 1920. From 1920 to 1924 he served as an instructor of tactics at West Point, the first nongraduate of the academy to hold that position. While teaching at West Point he met and impressed Omar N. Bradley. Hodges graduated from the Command and General Staff College at Fort Leavenworth in 1925. He served as an instructor at the Infantry School at Fort Benning, Ga., and then taught infantry tactics for three years at the Air Corps Tactical School at Langley Field, Va. In 1929 he became a member of the Infantry Board at Fort Benning, where he served again with Bradley and also won the approval of George Marshall, then assistant commandant of the Infantry School at the fort. In 1933 Hodges and Bradley went to the Army War College, graduating the next year. Hodges served two years with the Seventh Infantry at Vancouver Barracks in the state of Washington, then two years in the Philippines. In 1938 he became assistant commandant and in 1940 commandant of the Infantry School at Fort Benning. Chief of Staff General Marshall promoted Hodges to brigadier general in 1940 and to major general in May 1941, when Marshall named him chief of infantry of the United States Army.

In the wake of the Pearl Harbor disaster of Dec. 7, 1941, the army was reorganized and the position of chief of infantry was abolished. Hodges then organized the Replacement and School Command at Birmingham, Ala. In mid-1942 he activated the X Corps as part of the Third Army and in February 1943, having been promoted to lieutenant general, he took command of the Southern Defense Command (including the Third Army) at Fort Sam Houston, Tex. When the Third Army moved from the United States to England for the projected invasion of Europe, command of the army passed to General George S. Patton, Jr., the premier American army assault commander. The less well known Hodges was named deputy commanding general in Bradley's First Army, which was also in England preparing for the cross-Channel assault on Europe. Eight weeks after the invasion on June 6, 1944, Bradley was named commander of the Twelfth Army Group and Hodges took over the First Army under Bradley's overall command.

Hodges' First Army compiled a record second to none in the European Theater of Operations. It moved quickly across France, helping to liberate Paris on Aug. 25, 1944, then moved into Belgium and Luxembourg. General Hodges' forces were the first Allied troops to penetrate Germany, having reached the German border on September 11. In the autumn of

1944 the army fought long, confusing, and costly battles along the Siegfried Line, especially at Aachen and in the Hürtgen Forest. The battle reached a crisis when, in mid-December, the Germans commenced an offensive from the Ardennes Forest in what came to be known as the Battle of the Bulge. Hodges' First Army absorbed the brunt of the battle, and for two weeks was cut off from Bradley. But Hodges counterattacked and the First Army quickly moved into the Rhineland. In early March 1945 elements of the First Army seized the Remagen Bridge and became the first Allied troops to cross the Rhine. Together with the Ninth Army, the First trapped 300,000 German troops in the Ruhr Valley before achieving another first—the linkup with Soviet forces on the Elbe River. In April 1945, in the final weeks of the campaign, Hodges was promoted to full general.

Hodges and the First Army had their critics. Many argued that Hodges did not properly appreciate the difficulties that the Hürtgen Forest presented for offensive operations, the strategic importance of the Ruhr River dams, and the timing and magnitude of the German counteroffensive. Hodges was almost universally seen as lacking charisma; indeed, as one associate noted, it is telling that he had no nickname. He normally did not visit subordinate headquarters below division level, yet he kept his subordinate commanders on a tight leash, tracking units to the platoon level. Such leadership by management lacked the glamour of a Patton. Hodges did not even publish his memoirs, justifying Bradley's characterization of him as "the most modest man I had ever met." After World War II, Hodges quietly led the First Army in its peacetime defense and training role at Governor's Island in New York Harbor. He retired early in 1949 to San Antonio, Tex., where he died.

When the Supreme Allied Commander in the European Theater, Dwight D. Eisenhower, drew up a confidential evaluation of Hodges on Feb. 1, 1945, immediately after the Battle of the Bulge, he ranked Hodges below army commanders Patton, Truscott, and Patch, and even below Gerow and Collins, two of Hodges' own corps commanders. But two months later, when fuller accounts of battle actions were in, Eisenhower hailed Hodges as the "star" of the drive across the Rhine into the heart of Germany. General Douglas MacArthur, the Supreme Commander in the Pacific, named Hodges as one of two American commanders to undertake the projected invasion of Japan. The fact that the commanders of the two major theaters of World War II agreed that Hodges was an effective leader should afford him a comfortable niche in military annals.

[The Hodges papers are in the Dwight D. Eisenhower Library, Abilene, Kans.; the World War II collections, the National Archives, Washington, D. C.; and the Washington National Records Center, Suitland, Md. See Alfred D. Chandler, ed., *The Papers of Dwight David Eisenhower* (1970); Russell F. Weigley, *Eisenhower's Lieutenants* (1981); and Omar N. Bradley and Clay Blair, *A General's Life* (1983). See also the obituary, *New York Times*, Jan. 17, 1966.]

JOSEPH P. HOBBS

HOFFMAN, CLARE EUGENE (Sept. 10, 1875–Nov. 3, 1967), congressman, was born in Vicksburg, Pa., the son of Samuel D. Hoffman, a wagon and carriage maker, and Mary V. Ritter. While he was still a boy, the family moved to Cass County, Mich., where they settled on a farm near Constantine. Hoffman attended local schools and studied business for one year at Valparaiso University before enrolling at Northwestern University, where he received his LL.B. in 1895. He was admitted to the Illinois bar in that year and the Michigan bar in 1896. For a short time he practiced in Valparaiso, Ind., and in Muskegon, Mich. In 1896 he settled in Allegan, Mich., where he became known as a trial lawyer. On Nov. 22, 1899, he married Florence M. Wason; they had two children.

In 1906 Hoffman was elected district attorney for Allegan. He later served as municipal attorney and was for several decades Republican chairman for the county. In 1934 he was elected to Congress from Michigan's Fourth District. He served fourteen successive terms, priding himself on the fact that his margin of victory grew at each election.

A conservative and an isolationist, as well as a skilled parliamentarian, Hoffman established a reputation in Congress as an individualist who rarely changed an opinion and never straddled an issue. He vehemently opposed New Deal measures, voting against the Social Security Act, the National Labor Relations (Wagner) Act, and measures to provide low-cost housing through government subsidies. Before Pearl Harbor he also voted against lifting the arms embargo, the Lend-Lease Act, the arming of merchant vessels, and the Selective Service Act. A frequent critic of President Franklin D. Roosevelt's prosecution of the war, he warned that it mattered little "whether Hitler gets us and skins us from the top down, or whether our ally, Joe Stalin, gets us and skins us from the heels up." When questioned by a federal grand jury in April 1942 about the distribution by "subversive groups" of an antiadministration speech he had made, Hoffman reportedly testified that he had given out copies of the speech without knowing of any "ulterior purposes" of the groups in question.

Hoffman became noted for his opposition to labor unions during the "Little Steel" strike of 1937. In 1940 he introduced legislation to outlaw strikes in defense industries and to exempt workers from the compulsory payment of union dues. In 1947 he introduced a measure to outlaw the closed shop, work slowdowns, picketing, union-dues deductions from wages, and certain kinds of strikes. Later in the year he supported the Taft-Hartley Act. Referring to Hoffman as a "radical anti-labor congressman," organized labor spent much money in attempts to unseat him.

Hoffman became chairman of the House Committee on Expenditures in the Executive Departments during the Republican-controlled Eightieth Congress. He led it in investigating the disposal of surplus war property, the removal of records by outgoing government officials, federal enforcement of antiracketeering legislation, and the personnel and policy practices of the State Department. In an attempt to stifle criticism of members of Congress, in 1947 he initiated an investigation of a "smear file" that the Civil Service Commission kept on congressional members. He exacted a promise from the commission to destroy the file, but President Harry S Truman upheld the commission's refusal to permit members of Congress to have access to it. In 1948, Hoffman failed to win the support of Congress for a measure penalizing newspaper reporters for divulging information that congressional committees had declared confidential, and in 1952 he failed to persuade Congress to limit the amount of editorial space newspapers could devote to a political candidate.

When an administration bill providing for the reorganization of the army, navy, and air force under a secretary of national defense was introduced in March 1947, it was referred to Hoffman's committee. He opposed attempts to reduce the size and function of the Marine Corps, and he succeeded in having included in the final bill the "roles and missions" paragraphs, which provided a legal guarantee for Marine Corps survival. This act and his work on the Taft-Hartley Act he considered his chief legislative accomplishments. In 1949 he also opposed Truman's government-reorganization plan and attempted unsuccessfully to get a bill passed requiring both houses of Congress to approve the reorganization.

In 1953 Hoffman resumed the chairmanship of his old committee, which had been renamed the Government Operations Committee. His major concern was gangsterism in labor unions, which he described as "twice as dangerous to the country" as Communism. His appointment of twelve special subcommittees and his attempt to cut the staffs and funds of the regular subcommittees led to a revolt in which the committee, by a vote of 23–1, passed a resolution requiring approval of the full committee for the creation of special subcommittees, ending existing special subcommittees within ten days, and giving permanent subcommittee chairmen full power to hire and fire employees, to conduct hearings, and to issue subpoenas. The committee did give Hoffman sixty days to conclude special investigations in Kansas City and Detroit.

A foe of President Dwight D. Eisenhower's New Republicanism, Hoffman opposed the 1957 and 1960 civil rights bills, federal aid to education, a minimum-wage bill, and a measure to permit common-site picketing by construction unions. He opposed the Eisenhower Doctrine for the Middle East and the appointment of Meade Alcorn as Republican national chairman. In 1958 he impugned the budget as too free-spending and internationalist in intent. "I'm for progress, yes," he once told a reporter, "but not at the cost of going deeper in debt. This is the most selfish generation in our history. We buy everything we think we want, whether we need it or not, and charge it off to our kids." During the Kennedy administration he voted against the Peace Corps and other New Frontier programs. The oldest member of Congress, he chose not to run for reelection in 1962. He died in Allegan.

[Hoffman's papers are in the possession of his son, Leo W. Hoffman, in Allegan. For contemporary articles concerning Hoffman's career, see Will Chasin and Esther Jack, "Keep Them Out! Clare E. Hoffman of Michigan," *Nation*, Aug. 15, 1942; "Hoffman's Sleeper," *Newsweek*, May 17, 1948; Richard Tregaskis, "The Marine Corps Fights for Its Life," *Saturday Evening Post*, Feb. 5, 1949; "The Congress: A Committee Revolts," *Time*, Aug. 3, 1953; "Committees," *Newsweek*, Aug. 3, 1953; and Clark Mollenhoff, "How Labor Bosses Get Rich," *Look*, Mar. 9, 1954. The most complete scholarly study is Donald E. Walker, "The Congressional Career of Clare E. Hoffman, 1935–1963" (Ph.D. diss., Michigan State University, 1982). See also the obituaries, *New York Times* and *Detroit News*, both Nov. 5, 1967; and *Chicago Tribune*, Nov. 10, 1967.]

MELBA PORTER HAY

HOFMANN, HANS (Mar. 21, 1880–Feb. 17, 1966), painter, was born in Weissenberg, Bavaria, Germany, the son of Theodor Hofmann and Franciska Manger, the daughter of a brewer and wine grower. The family moved to Munich in 1886 when Theodor Hofmann became government clerk. Hans Hofmann attended the local gymnasium, where he excelled in science and mathematics, and had private instruction in piano, violin, organ, and art. In 1896, with his father's help, he procured a position as assistant to the director of public works of the state of Bavaria, a post he held until 1898. During this time, he devised several electromechanical and electromagnetic inventions. His father rewarded him with 1,000 marks, which enabled him to make painting his profession. Hofmann studied in Moritz Heymann's Munich art school, where he was instructed in the broad, old-master tradition. In 1911 he did a portrait in this style of Maria ("Miz") Wolfegg, whom he married in 1923. His *Self-Portrait* (1902) followed the impressionist, pointillist trend, which he had learned from his teacher Willi Schwarz. Schwarz also introduced him to the art collector Phillip Freudenberg, who provided financial support to Hofmann while he was in Paris from 1904 to 1914.

In Paris Hofmann attended sketch classes at Colarossis and met Henri Matisse at the École de la Grande Chaumière. He came to know Georges Braque and Pablo Picasso, but he was most impressed with Robert Delaunay's color. Hofmann and Delaunay became good friends, and "Miz" designed scarves with Sonja Delaunay. During his Paris sojourn Hofmann absorbed cubo-futurism (which, in his own words, he had "to sweat out" later on), and after 1911 he harbored a lifelong admiration for Piet Mondrian's radical abstractionism (neoplasticism).

Hofmann exhibited with the Neue Sezession in Berlin in 1909. He had his first one-man show at the prestigious Paul Cassirer Gallery there the next year. His painting style followed the school of Paris, especially Cézanne. A sickness in his family took him back to Munich in 1914, and the outbreak of World War I made returning to Paris impossible. A lung condition enabled him to avoid serving in the German army.

Though the early war years had temporarily slowed the abstract movement in Germany, the Hans Hofmann School of Fine Arts opened at 40 Georgenstrasse, Munich, in the spring of 1915. Impressed with Wassily Kandinsky's emphasis on color, Hofmann became one of the leaders of the German abstract movement. After the war ended and the school was firmly established, the freedom of expression permitted by the Weimar Republic encouraged in Hofmann a greater contact with German expressionistic art, evidenced by his portrait drawings of 1926 and 1927. Hofmann took his students to the Bavarian Tegernsee during a summer session in 1922; to Ragusa in 1924; to Capri in 1925, 1926, and 1927; and to St. Tropez in 1928. Among his students were several Americans, including Louise Nevelson, who studied with him in 1931.

In 1930 Hofmann accepted the invitation of Worth Ryder, a former student, to teach at the University of California at Berkeley during the summer. Another former student acted as interpreter. Hofmann returned to America the following spring to teach at the Chouinard School in Los Angeles and then, during the summer, at Berkeley. In 1932 he closed his school in Munich for lack of funds; he remained in America, and his wife stayed in Germany.

Hofmann opened his own art school in 1932 in New York City and the highly successful Hans Hofmann Summer School in 1935 in Provincetown, Mass., where after a long period devoted only to drawing he again took up painting. In the 1940's his manner became increasingly abstract. In 1939 his wife joined him in Provincetown, where they lived until her death in 1961. Three years later he married Renate Schmidt. In 1944 Hofmann became an American citizen. He died in New York City.

In the process of cross-fertilization of the American and, more specifically, the New York City art scene by European emigrants of the 1930's, Hofmann assumed the triple role of creative painter, forceful teacher, and independent writer. He has been cataloged as the father figure and leading theoretician of abstract expressionism. His influence as a teacher was enormous. Such handy Hofmann tenets as "forming with color," "push and pull," and the musical "interval" became part of the argot of young artists. Hofmann had many devoted students—including Robert Motherwell and the sculptor Marisol—but the best did not imitate him, since he always stressed individuality of expression.

Hofmann encouraged the *Entfesselung* ("unchaining") of color from form and line, which he realized in the rapid-gesticulating application of heavy pigment. His brushwork often resembles Jackson Pollock's dripping and flinging action painting.

Line in his paintings exists mainly as an illusion at the meeting of geometric planes of large irregular shapes and contrasting large color-splashes. Real line exists in his masterly drawings, offering the abstracted essence of landscapes, nudes, portraits, and still lifes, with a preference for broad India-ink splashes and colored crayons, often in conjunction with overlaid wiggly lines made with a pointed pen, as in *Provincetown Landscape*. Fractured representational remnants might wander onto the picture plane of his most abstract paintings, such as *Magenta and Blue* (1958).

A collection of his work, numbering forty-five paintings, was opened in 1970 as the Hans Hofmann Wing at the Museum of the University of California at Berkeley. He donated the collection in 1964 because Berkeley had given him his start in America.

[Hofmann's papers are in the archives of the Museum of Modern Art, New York City, and the Smithsonian Institution Archives of American Art. His writings are collected in *Search for the Real, and Other Essays* (1967). See also L. Greenberg, *Hans Hofmann* (1911); Sam Hunter, *Hans Hofmann* (1963); William C. Seitz, *Hans Hofmann* (exhibition catalog, 1963); and John Wilmerding, *American Art* (1976).]

ERNST SCHEYER

HOFSTADTER, RICHARD (Aug. 6, 1916–Oct. 24, 1970), historian and author, was born in Buffalo, N.Y., the son of Emil A. Hofstadter, a Polish-born furrier, and Katherine Hill. He was educated at local schools and in 1937 graduated from the University of Buffalo with a B.A. On Oct. 3, 1936, he married Felice Swados; they had one child. After studying law briefly, Hofstadter undertook graduate studies in history at Columbia University, which awarded him an M.A. in 1938 and a Ph.D. in 1942.

While a graduate student, he taught at Brooklyn College and the College of the City of New York. In 1942 he joined the faculty of the University of Maryland and four years later returned to Columbia as an assistant professor. His first wife died in 1945, and on Jan. 13, 1947, he married Beatrice Kevitt; they had one child.

In conjunction with such honorary positions as Pitt Professor of American History and Institutions at the University of Cambridge in 1958–1959 and Humanities Council Fellow at Princeton University in 1962–1963, Hofstadter maintained his connection with Columbia until his death in New York City. He was promoted to associate professor in 1950 and professor in 1952, then designated DeWitt Clinton Professor of American History in 1959. He was scheduled to serve as president of the Organization of American Historians for 1971–1972.

With few exceptions, Hofstadter's scholarship concentrated on what he variously termed "milieu," "mood," and "mind," especially as these applied to American political life. His major publications were *Social Darwinism in American Thought, 1860–1915* (1944), his doctoral dissertation, which received the Beveridge Award from the American Historical Association in 1942; *The American Political Tradition and the Men Who Made It* (1948); *The Development of Academic Freedom in the United States* (1955), coauthored with Walter P. Metzger and prepared under the auspices of the American Academic Freedom Project; *The Age of Reform: From Bryan to F.D.R.* (1955), which was awarded a Pulitzer Prize; *Anti-intellectualism in American Life* (1963), which won a Pulitzer Prize, the Emerson Award of Phi Beta Kappa, and the Sidney Hillman Award; *The Paranoid Style in American Politics and Other Essays* (1965), pieces completed between 1951 and 1965; *The Progressive Historians: Turner, Beard, Parrington* (1968); *The Idea of a*

Party System: Legitimate Opposition in the United States, 1780–1840 (1969), a revision of his Jefferson Memorial Lectures at the University of California at Berkeley; and *America at 1750: A Social Portrait* (1971), the posthumous publication of materials that were to have been incorporated into the first of three projected volumes on American history from the mid-eighteenth to the late twentieth century.

Social Darwinism established Hofstadter's professional credentials as an intellectual historian. *The American Political Tradition*, with paperback sales of over one million, introduced him to a far wider public. In his second book—a series of scintillating essays that are often bemused, sometimes caustic, but never angry—Hofstadter brought a new cosmopolitan skepticism to bear on the greats and near-greats of a standard schoolbook history. Like other intellectuals who had felt the attractions of student radicalism in the 1930's and then abandoned it, Hofstadter sought to free himself equally from doctrinaire dissent and national piety. What emerged in these essays was an appreciation for the strength of an accommodating American politics and a deflation of its leaders' reputations.

Between 1948 and 1955, Hofstadter's continuing experiments with different points of view led to a second major departure in his writing and to a period of extraordinary productivity in the early 1950's: two book-length histories of the academic world, the most provocative of the essays in *The Paranoid Style*, much of what would become *Anti-intellectualism*, and *The Age of Reform*. Hofstadter was now drawing from a broad range of ideas in many disciplines and benefiting in particular from his colleagues Lionel Trilling and Robert K. Merton at Columbia, from *The Authoritarian Personality* (1950) by T. W. Adorno and associates, and from the writings of Karl Mannheim. By assigning great importance to the independent investigator, Mannheim's work in particular encouraged Hofstadter to adopt the role of clinical observer and commentator. Hofstadter moved easily between the past and the present and between impersonal and personal prose styles. At the same time, he sharpened his commitment to judge, to set ethical standards at the heart of his analysis. The combination of detachment in technique and engagement in values became Hofstadter's hallmark.

The subjects that he addressed were affected above all by the loose amalgam of anti-Communism, antiliberalism, and traditionalism called McCarthyism, which reached its peak of intensity early in the 1950's and shaped Hofstadter's picture of America more fundamentally than anything preceding it, including the Great Depression and World War II. With the repressive effects of McCarthyism in the air, Hofstadter searched out the sources of enmity to independent thought in America. Its twin nemeses, he decided, were sectarianism and provincialism, historically identified with the new democracy of the nineteenth century and geographically concentrated in the Midwest and the South. The triumph of small, scattered denominational colleges, which wreaked havoc on whatever supports for intellectual independence had accumulated by Jefferson's time, dominated Hofstadter's view of higher education after 1800, especially in *Academic Freedom*, where he described a general climate of hostility toward open inquiry. *Anti-intellectualism* contained his fullest account of America's cultural blight in the nineteenth century. Broadening his scope to include politics, business, and religion, he issued a devastating indictment of intellectual leveling, arid popularization, and narrow-minded smugness.

Although Hofstadter saw new hope for independent thought late in the nineteenth century, major obstacles to a cosmopolitan tolerance remained, and these he examined brilliantly in *The Age of Reform*. The first, he argued, was Populism, the culmination of nineteenth-century provincialism that romanticized agrarian virtues and responded to adversity by imagining vast conspiracies against ordinary farmers and townspeople. The second obstacle was Progressivism, urban but not urbane, still the product of a moralistic and individualistic "Yankee-Protestant" political culture, which struck a lower emotional pitch than Populism but expressed a similar impulse to crusade against such unfamiliar modern institutions as national business corporations and urban political machines. In a brief conclusion to the book, Hofstadter located a critical change in political culture with the New Deal, which brought issues down to earth and reckoned with them as practical matters. Hofstadter did not claim the disappearance of a rigid, conspiratorial approach to public policy. In fact, his concern about its revival during McCarthy's time and again during the presidential campaign of Senator Barry Goldwater in 1964 spurred the most imaginative essays in *The Paranoid Style*, particularly the title essay and "The Pseudo-Conservative Revolt." Nevertheless, Hofstadter became increasingly convinced that the norms of modern politics, especially the reliance on bargain and compromise, put the paranoid style on the defensive. In general, Hofstadter gave history a progressive thrust, even though he acknowledged its many dips and twists.

Within this essentially optimistic framework of America's development, Hofstadter often changed his mind. Before publishing *Anti-intellectualism*, he appended introductory and concluding chapters that expressed his growing confidence in the state of American society and softened the book's impression of a sweeping condemnation. At the end of the 1960's, in a particularly striking switch, Hofstadter reversed his assessments of America's revolutionary leaders and their Jacksonian counterparts. As recently as *Anti-intellectualism*, he had praised the former for their rigorous intelligence and deplored the latter's thin, shrill style. In *The Idea of a Party System* he shifted ground, now stressing the inability of the revolutionary leaders to accept a regular political opposition and praising the founders of an institutionalized two-party competition early in the nineteenth century for their service to America's stability. All of his judgments, however, were dominated by the same standards: the importance of reasonableness, moderation, and compromise.

For Hofstadter, the highest purpose of these virtues was their support for the free play of the mind. Wherever he sensed a broad respect for ideas, as he did in contemporary England and in the United States during the presidency of John F. Kennedy, he was particularly warm in his praise. He celebrated the metropolis as the environment that best nourished free inquiry. Nevertheless, the tension between mass democracy and creative thinking normally put intellectuals on the defensive, he concluded, and they needed a secure harbor. That function Hofstadter assigned to the modern university. His attachment to the modern university found its most eloquent expression in 1968, when he became the first faculty member in the history of Columbia University to deliver its commencement address. In the wake of harsh, sometimes violent conflicts between students and authorities at Columbia and other universities, Hofstadter gave voice to the temperate, tolerant quality of "comity," an ideal that he identified with the university.

Inside the centers of free inquiry, moderation was no longer a virtue. There Hofstadter did not merely welcome a spirit of daring; he exemplified it. Although other important historians, including David M. Potter and Oscar Handlin, joined him around midcentury in expanding the range of interdisciplinary history, Hofstadter led the field both in the boldness of his concepts and in the breadth of his audience. With the publication of *The Age of Reform*, a work that incorporated the concepts of myth from anthropology, status from sociology, and modal personality from psychology, and that adapted textual analysis from literary criticism, he stood preeminent among the interdisciplinary pioneers. Why Hofstadter exercised such a powerful influence was not so obvious. Graceful writing helped. To a fluid, accessible prose, he added a genius for phrasing: America's "psychic crisis" in the 1890's, a "paranoid style," the "soft side" and the "hard side" of the agrarian mind, a "status revolution" behind progressive reform. These and the ones he borrowed, such as "agrarian myth" and "anti-intellectualism," he used not to catch the eye as much as to open the mind. Through his phrases he became the gracious yet insistent didact who instructed a wide audience on new ways of understanding.

While Hofstadter led, he also responded. He first championed ideas during an unusual vogue for intellectuals around midcentury. When first Joseph McCarthy and then Barry Goldwater preoccupied his contemporaries, Hofstadter wrote about them. When the subject of violence swept public discussion in the late 1960's, he turned his attention there. Along with Arthur M. Schlesinger, Jr., Hofstadter improved the art of applying history to public commentary. Just as he let current affairs spur his historical inquiries, so he went to the past to illuminate the present. This sensitive interplay between past and present heightened the general interest in Hofstadter's writings.

Hofstadter made his interpretive innovations more acceptable by leaving matters of historical causation flexible. Despite his differences with Charles Beard's history, he rarely failed to give economic motivations their due. In certain studies, notably *The Age of Reform*, he relied heavily on sociological sources (status, occupation, ethnicity) to explain a prevailing mood. In *The Paranoid Style*, on the other hand, he employed a personality type that stood free from an economic or a social context. Hofstadter softened the shock of new ideas by cushioning them with familiar ones. Some of his most striking contributions came disguised as mere adaptations of intellectual history to the study of a popular mind. He treated social movements that arose from fear or anxiety as less substantial than those rooted in motives his readers more readily recognized, such as political ambition and economic interest. In Hofstadter's account, bargain-minded spokesmen for the New Deal had a firmer grip on reality than the status-minded spokesmen for Progressivism. These distinctions also bespoke Hofstadter's beliefs. Under no circumstances, for example, could he accept judgments from the political right and left that the United States government was the "main enemy." Hofstadter's steadfast moderation broadened the audience for his intellectual daring.

Rejecting a fashionable skepticism about ultimate values, Hofstadter held firmly to intellectual freedom as an absolute good. He treated science, which exemplified that freedom in action, as a neutral truth and as a standard for measuring civilization's progress. When critics identified Hofstadter with the consensus school of interpretation, which elevated reasonableness, pragmatism, and accommodation into the American way, they confused his personal convictions with his scholarly conclusions. After 1948, Hofstadter found relatively little in the American tradition that sustained the values of consensus. The more committed he became to moderation's indispensability, the more sensitive he grew to its violations. He never mistook his own creed for the record of America's past.

Hofstadter's looseness about historical causation and his passion for free inquiry contributed to a remarkable openness in intellectual exchanges. Whatever his companion's point of view, Hofstadter asked only that it have substance. Where he found it, his companion became his equal in a common quest, a trait that superior graduate students recalled with great satisfaction. Mediocrity bored Hofstadter, a characteristic that other students recalled less fondly, and his impatience with the limitations of ordinary minds also affected his work. He never achieved a sympathetic understanding of the angry frustration and flawed reasoning of those countless Americans past and present who were stymied or confused by their world. Demagogues in a democracy disturbed him deeply. Why others were less open and adventurous than he became a puzzle which Hofstadter devoted much of his scholarly career to resolving.

[Hofstadter's papers are at Columbia University. Paula S. Fass has contributed a full bibliography to Stanley Elkins and Eric McKitrick, eds., *The Hofstadter Aegis: A Memorial* (1974). The essay in that volume by the editors; Christopher Lasch, "On Richard Hofstadter," *New York Review of Books*, Mar. 8, 1973; and Daniel Joseph Singal, "Beyond Consensus: Richard Hofstadter and American Historiography," *American Historical Review*, Oct. 1984, are important intellectual appraisals. An obituary is in the *New York Times*, Oct. 25, 1970.]

ROBERT WIEBE

HOLMES, JULIUS CECIL (Apr. 24, 1899–July 14, 1968), soldier and diplomat, was born in Pleasanton, Kans., the son of James Reuben Holmes, a businessman, and Loella Jane Friedman. Holmes combined intermittent study at the University of Kansas from 1917 to 1922 with service as an officer in the Kansas National Guard and the army reserve. In 1923 he went into the insurance business but abandoned that activity for the foreign service in April 1925. He served in various posts in Eastern Europe and on Apr. 26, 1932, married Henrietta Allen. They had three children.

In 1934 Holmes was appointed assistant chief of the Division of Protocol and International Conferences, and in 1935 he served as secretary general of the inter-American conference convened to deal with the Chaco War (between Paraguay and Bolivia). He resigned from the State Department in October 1937 to accept a position with the New York World's Fair Corporation (1937–1940), and from 1941 to 1942 he headed the Latin American subsidiary of General Mills. Holmes joined General Dwight D. Eisenhower's staff in 1942 and was involved in planning the invasion of North Africa. He accompanied General Mark W. Clark on his secret mission to meet with French officials to arrange for the entry of Allied troops into neutral French North Africa. Holmes and Robert Murphy later drew up the agreement with Admiral François Darlan that ended Franco-Allied hostilities.

His association with the infamous "Darlan deal" brought Holmes much criticism, although he insisted he did nothing more than carry out the instructions relayed by General

Eisenhower from the Joint Chiefs of Staff. Because of Holmes's diplomatic experience, General Eisenhower made Holmes responsible for developing plans to administer occupied areas in Sicily and Italy. Holmes is thus generally identified as the father of the Allied Military Government of the Occupied Territories. He was later responsible for advising liberated governments on restoring civilian life and devised the code of military laws and ordinances for the occupation of Germany. However, the civilian experts selected to implement Holmes's programs were often inclined to place expediency above ideology, and Holmes was accused of being "soft on fascism." This charge, as well as his involvement with Admiral Darlan, resulted in critical commentary when Holmes was selected as assistant secretary of state for administration and personnel in December 1944.

Although successful in his new post, Holmes was reluctant to continue in government service. In August 1945 he resigned from the State Department to accept a more lucrative position with Transcontinental Western Airways, and in 1946 he became president of Taca Airways. At about the same time, Holmes and others formed the National Tanker Corporation for the purchase of surplus American tankers. The profits from this enterprise were so substantial that Holmes was indicted by a grand jury in Washington, D.C.

Although Holmes returned to the State Department in 1948, the indictment was not dismissed until 1954, and the lingering effects made it difficult for him to secure an appointment requiring senatorial approval. Despite his obvious experience and recognized talents, and the friendship of President Eisenhower, he was deemed too controversial. Obviously disappointed by this restriction, Holmes nonetheless served capably and effectively as minister to the American embassy in London; senior political adviser to the American delegation to the United Nations; minister to Morocco; special assistant to the secretary of state for the North Atlantic Treaty Organization (NATO); and consul general in Hong Kong and Macao.

In 1961 a change of administration allowed Holmes's confirmation as ambassador to Iran. Holmes served in Iran until 1962, a crucial period in Iranian history. For over a decade Shah Mohammed Reza Pahlavi was preoccupied with the defense of Iran against imperialism, particularly Soviet imperialism. Such a policy entailed a substantial commitment in American aid. When Chairman Nikita Khrushchev predicted to President John F. Kennedy in Vienna that the shah would soon be overthrown by an indigenous upheaval, American policy was reevaluated. Holmes strongly supported the decision to curtail American aid until the shah instituted fundamental socio-economic reforms to modernize Iran.

Holmes was not the author of a doctrine or a policy, but he did influence important policies. He died in Washington, D.C.

[The Holmes papers are in the Dwight D. Eisenhower Library in Abilene, Kans. An obituary is in the *New York Times,* July 16, 1968.]

J. K. SWEENEY

HOOVER, HERBERT CLARK, JR. (Aug. 4, 1903–July 9, 1969), engineer, businessman, and undersecretary of state, was born in London, England, the son of Herbert Clark Hoover, thirty-first president of the United States, and Lou Henry. Raised in various countries, the younger Hoover received a B.A. in petroleum geology from Stanford in 1925 and an M.B.A. from Harvard in 1928. On June 25, 1925, he married Margaret Eva Watson; they had three children.

In 1928, Hoover won a Guggenheim grant to conduct aeronautical research. A radio enthusiast since childhood, he became an authority on ground-to-air communication. He worked as the radio communications engineer for Western Air Express and became president of Aeronautical Radio, Inc. In 1930 he contracted tuberculosis. In 1931, following treatment for the disease, he resumed his career, working for Transcontinental and Western Air. That year he also patented an air radio direction finder; he later received patents for electronic, spectrographic, and seismometric devices for the discovery of oil. After serving as a teaching fellow at the California Institute of Technology in 1934–1935, Hoover founded and headed the United Geophysical Company, which employed 1,000 people by the time he entered government service. He was also president from 1936 to 1946 of the Consolidated Engineering Corporation, which contributed significantly to developing devices for testing stress in military aircraft during World War II. From 1942 to 1952, Hoover served as a technical consultant, especially on petroleum matters, to Iran and several Latin American governments.

Hoover avoided exploiting his father's fame, although family connections benefited him and proved a source of controversy in his career. Nevertheless, he was able enough in his own right to become a successful and highly respected figure in engineering and business circles.

In September 1953, Secretary of State John Foster Dulles appointed Hoover a special adviser to help solve the Anglo-Iranian oil dispute. When Iran's nationalization of its petroleum industry in 1951 adversely affected British interests, took Iranian oil off the world market, and impaired the development of America's alliance system, Hoover traveled widely to gather information and develop ideas that would be instrumental in fashioning a solution to the crisis. The resulting highly praised agreement of August 1954 provided for $70 million in compensation to the British and the marketing of Iran's oil by an Anglo-Dutch-French-American consortium. Subsequently, on August 17, President Dwight D. Eisenhower nominated Hoover to be undersecretary of state, to which the Senate consented in less than twenty-four hours.

In October 1954, Hoover assumed his new duties. During his undersecretaryship, he served not only as Dulles' deputy but also as chairman of the Operations Coordinating Board, the executive committee of the National Security Council. In these roles, Hoover was involved in the full range of American foreign-policy development and implementation. He particularly played a significant role in the Egyptian crisis of 1955–1956. Hoover, who was suspicious of British motives and hostile to the regime of Gamal Abdel Nasser in Egypt, helped Secretary of the Treasury George Humphrey to scuttle Dulles' plans to assist Nasser's development of the Aswan Dam. In 1956, Egypt seized control of the Suez Canal, and France, Great Britain, and Israel contemplated taking military action to recover it; but in October, Hoover told Eisenhower of a plan, presumably by the Central Intelligence Agency, to topple Nasser in order to forestall an invasion of Egypt. The president, however, insisted that the dispute should be settled through negotiation. Matters came to a crucial juncture late that month when Israel, soon joined by Britain and France, invaded Egypt, just after Russia had invaded Hungary to suppress revolt there and while an American presidential election was in its final stages.

Affairs were further complicated when Dulles was hospitalized; Hoover then became acting secretary of state. Although the United States successfully pressured Great Britain, France, and Israel to withdraw their forces and Eisenhower handily won reelection, the damage had been done: the Egyptians had blocked the Suez Canal, rendering it useless for months; the North Atlantic Treaty alliance and American relations with Israel had become strained; and the United States had been unable to exploit fully the Soviet repression of Hungary. Although Hoover had acted ably during the worst of the crisis, some criticized him for refusing to give aid to Egypt and comfort to Britain's Prime Minister Anthony Eden after the war.

Hoover, who had considered leaving public life for some time, resigned his office in December 1956. Before he left in February 1957, he thwarted movements to appoint his predecessor, Walter B. Smith, or Vice-President Richard M. Nixon as chairman of the Operations Coordinating Board. Thus, the new undersecretary, Christian A. Herter, also succeeded Hoover as chairman of the board. After returning to California, Hoover worked as a consulting engineer and served on the boards of various corporations; educational institutions; and civic, philanthropic, and radio groups. His only later role in government was as a part-time consultant to the State Department. He died in Pasadena, Calif.

Hoover not only made important contributions as an engineer and a businessman but was also influential in the development of the oil industry. As undersecretary of state, he showed courage and intelligence. Moreover, he was considerably successful in accommodating the interests of conservative and moderate political elements. Eisenhower, in 1954–1955, considered him as his successor as president, but he concluded—probably correctly—that Hoover did not have enough "fire" to win election.

[Hoover's official papers are contained in the Records of the Department of State, Record Group 59, in the National Archives, Washington, D.C. A bit of his personal correspondence is included in the Herbert Hoover Presidential Library, West Branch,

Iowa. Biographical accounts of Hoover are in "Sons of Herbert Hoover," in J. J. Perling, *Presidents' Sons* (1947); and Edward B. Lockett, "Number Two Job in the State Department," *New York Times Magazine*, Oct. 31, 1954. Significant references to him are in Herbert C. Hoover, Sr., *The Memoirs of Herbert Hoover: The Great Depression, 1929–1941* (1952); Leonard Mosley, *Dulles* (1978); and Stephen E. Ambrose, *Eisenhower: The President* (1984). An obituary is in the *New York Times*, July 10, 1969.]

DONALD R. MCCOY

HOPE, CLIFFORD RAGSDALE (June 9, 1893–May 16, 1970), congressman, was born in Birmingham, Iowa, the son of Harry M. Hope, a storekeeper and farmer, and Armitta Ragsdale. In 1901 the family moved to Ripley, Okla., and, in 1906, to a ranch northwest of Garden City, Kans. Hope graduated from Garden City High School in 1913. After attending Nebraska Wesleyan University for one year, he transferred to Washburn University, Topeka, Kans., where he studied law. There Hope became an outstanding debater and, in 1916, the president of the Republican Club. In 1917 he received his LL.B.

Immediately after graduation Hope entered officers' training school at Fort Riley, Kans. Commissioned a second lieutenant, he served in a tank demonstration unit with the Thirty-fifth and Eighty-fifth Infantry Divisions in the United States and France. Following his discharge in April 1919, Hope returned to Garden City to practice law with William Easton Hutchison. He married Pauline Sanders on Jan. 8, 1921; they had three children.

Hope was elected to the Kansas House of Representatives from Finney County in 1920 and was reelected in 1922 and 1924. During his second term, he served as speaker pro tem of the House. He was elected speaker in 1925 as a result of his strong opposition to legalizing the Ku Klux Klan in Kansas.

In 1926 Hope successfully ran for Congress as a Republican in the huge Seventh District of western Kansas. Although he was always opposed in the congressional general elections, he was never in danger of being defeated, for his margin of victory ranged between 9 percent and 41 percent of the vote. When Hope became a member of the United States House of Representatives in 1927, he successfully sought appointment to the Committee on Agriculture because he represented America's largest wheat-growing congressional district. He served thirty consecutive years on this committee, becoming its ranking Republican member in January 1934 and its chairman during the Eightieth and Eighty-third Congresses.

Throughout his congressional career, Hope embraced agrarian values. He called the family farm "one of our fundamental social institutions." He extolled the value of local self-government, free enterprise, fiscal responsibility, and the farmers' collective opinion. The amiable Hope welcomed the close personal contacts and frank discussions with his constituents, and he strove to represent their interests faithfully. He worked for legislation that would stabilize agriculture prices at a fair exchange level and would enable farmers to assume responsibility for planning and executing their operations. Although otherwise a conservative Republican, Hope was often nonpartisan on agricultural legislation. When his party did not follow a sound, sympathetic agricultural policy, he simply parted company with it on that issue.

During the Great Depression, prices for farm products slipped disastrously as a result of overproduction and a decline in demand. To restore balance between production and consumption, Hope endorsed a program of economic planning and control through the voluntary cooperation of farmers under government supervision. In 1932 Hope and Senator Peter Norbeck sponsored the Voluntary Domestic Allotment Plot, which became the basis for the Agricultural Act of 1933. Hope was among those responsible for its successor, the Soil Conservation and Domestic Allotment Act of 1935, which continued farm subsidies. He served as agricultural consultant to the 1936 Republican presidential nominee, Alf Landon, developing a farm program aimed at a better balance of production and consumption. The press often mentioned Hope as the prospective secretary of agriculture, should a Republican be elected president.

From 1937 to 1945 Hope's interest in, if not his influence on, farm legislation remained remarkably high. In 1946 he coauthored the Research and Marketing Act, which encouraged a scientific approach to the production, utilization, and distribution of food.

While chairman of the House Agriculture Committee in 1947–1948, Hope sought to coordinate farm policy with developments elsewhere in the economy. He wanted to initiate a long-range system of commodity price floors in order to cushion declines in farm prices and incomes during recessions. He also moderated Congress's efforts to slash the Agriculture Department's budget for school lunches, soil conservation, and aid to tenant farmers. In 1948 he coauthored the compromise Hope-Aiken price-support law, serving as a champion of high fixed price supports for farmers and less federal control over agricultural production.

As chairman of the House Agriculture Committee in 1953–1954, Hope initiated the Farm Credit Act of 1953, which increased the farmers' control of the federal farm credit system. He was also a coauthor of the Hope-Aiken Watershed Act of 1953, which enabled landowners to use federal aid to conserve water and topsoil. In 1954 Hope was instrumental in securing the passage of the Agricultural Trade Development and Assistance Act, which fostered the overseas sale of surplus farm commodities and provided for the charitable distribution of surpluses to distressed areas in the United States and abroad.

In 1956 Hope decided against running for another term in Congress. Still vigorous, he returned to Garden City. He also founded a company, Great Plains Wheat, to increase markets abroad for American hard winter wheat, and he helped develop watersheds in western Kansas. In addition, Hope was instrumental in building a junior college in Garden City. In 1968 he was elected president of the Kansas State Historical Society. He died in Garden City.

[Hope's papers are located in the Kansas State Historical Society, Topeka. His presidential address to the society is "Kansas in the 1930's," *Kansas Historical Quarterly*, Spring 1970. On Hope's agricultural policies, see James L. Forsythe, "Practical Congressman and Agrarian Idealist," *Agricultural History*, Apr. 1977; and Edward L. Schapsmeier and Frederick H. Schapsmeier, "Farm Policy from FDR to Eisenhower: Southern Democrats and the Politics of Agriculture," *Agricultural History*, Jan. 1979. See also James C. Duram and Eleanor A. Duram, "Congressman Clifford Hope's Correspondence with His Constituents: A Conservative View of the Court-Packing Fight of 1937," *Kansas Historical Quarterly*, Spring 1971; and James L. Forsythe, "Postmortem on the Election of 1948: An Evaluation of Congressman Clifford R. Hope's Views," *ibid.*, Autumn 1972. Obituaries are in the *Garden City Telegram*, May 18, 1970; *Fifty-third Report of the Kansas State Board of Agriculture*, 1970; and the *New York Times*, May 18, 1970.]

SONDRA VAN METER McCOY

HOPPER, EDWARD (July 22, 1882–May 15, 1967), painter, was born in Nyack, N.Y., the son of Garrett Henry Hopper and Elizabeth Griffiths Smith. Described by his son as "an incipient intellectual who never quite made it," Garrett Hopper ran a dry-goods store not far from the family home. The solidly middle-class family attended the Nyack Baptist Church (founded by Hopper's maternal great-grandfather, Joseph W. Griffiths), where his father was a member of the board of trustees. Hopper's mother introduced him to both art and the theater at an early age. He attended a local private school for the early primary grades and graduated from Nyack Union High School in 1899.

Without any special instruction, Hopper drew prolifically from childhood and was a voracious reader. As an adolescent he was already reclusive, preferring solitude to the company of others. When he was about fifteen, his concerned father bought him wood and tools and encouraged him to build a sailboat so that he would get outside and socialize with his contemporaries. By this time, Hopper had developed a fascination with the sea and nautical life, prompted by living only a short walk from the Hudson River. On his New York State Regents Examination, Hopper received honors only in drawing and plane geometry.

Hopper's parents, although supportive of his artistic development, implored him to study commercial illustration rather than to pursue an economically uncertain career in the fine arts. For a year Hopper commuted to New York City to attend the Correspondence School of Illustrating. After another year of studying illustration—this time at the more prestigious New York School of Art, under Arthur Keller and Frank Vincent Du Mond—Hopper took a small studio on Fourteenth Street and began to study painting and drawing at the school. He enrolled in the classes of William Merritt Chase, whose teaching he later disparaged—when he deigned to mention him at all. He studied portraiture and still life under Chase, who was the leading spirit and founder of the school. Hopper preferred the classes he took with Kenneth Hayes Miller and especially those of Robert Henri, the charismatic teacher who came to the school in the fall of 1902.

Hopper took Henri's life-and-portraiture classes, as well as a "special composition class" devoted to pictorial composition and art theory. Later, Hopper acknowledged a great debt to Henri for the latter's belief that "art is life, an expression of life, an expression of the artist and an interpretation of life." Hopper's exceptional facility won him honors and scholarships. In 1905 he was hired to teach the Saturday classes in drawing from life, painting, sketching, and composition. Guy Pène du Bois, Rockwell Kent, and George Bellows were among Hopper's classmates who made names for themselves.

In 1906 Hopper worked part-time as an illustrator for the C. C. Phillips advertising agency, which had been founded by one of his former classmates, the illustrator Coles Phillips. But in the fall he went to Paris to study the works of the great European masters. He did not enroll in any school but, rather, educated himself by visiting museums and exhibitions. The many paintings Hopper produced in Paris were done outdoors, in part because he had no studio space and in part because he was emulating the impressionists. As a result, Hopper's palette lightened remarkably. Hopper was captivated by, and was to be ever mindful of, his French experience.

Leaving Paris in late June 1907, he made a tour of London, Haarlem, Amsterdam, Berlin, and Brussels, and at the end of August he returned to New York, where he attempted to paint while working several days a week as a commercial illustrator. Hopper illustrated for a number of trade magazines, including *System*, *Wells Fargo Messenger*, *Tavern Topics*, *Dry Dock Dial*, and *Hotel Management*. He also illustrated fiction for *Adventure*, *Everybody's*, *Associated Sunday Magazine*, and *Scribner's*. He detested this work and later was loath to discuss it, even to the point of concealing his illustrations from Lloyd Goodrich, who organized his retrospectives in 1950 and 1964.

Hopper first exhibited in March 1908 in a group show organized by some of Henri's former students to protest the conservative taste of the juries at the National Academy. He returned to Paris for four months in 1909 and again briefly in 1910, during which time he also visited Spain. Although Hopper never again went abroad, he continued to read French literature, particularly symbolist poetry, and to admire French painters such as Degas.

Hopper next exhibited in the Independents Exhibition, organized by Henri and John Sloan in 1910, and in nonjuried shows at the MacDowell Club. He spent his summers in rural New England—Gloucester, Mass., on Cape Ann, and Ogunquit and Monhegan Island, Maine. In December 1913 he moved to a studio in Greenwich Village, where, with the addition of two rooms, he lived for the remainder of his life. At the 1913 International Exhibition of Modern Art, popularly known as the Armory Show, he sold his first painting, but he could not sell another for the next ten years.

Hopper took up etching in 1915, teaching himself with technical advice from his friend Martin Lewis, an Australian artist who also worked as an illustrator. With his etchings, Hopper was more successful with both sales and juried exhibitions. Ironically, his first fame as an illustrator came when his four-color poster *Smash the Hun* won top prize in a wartime poster competition sponsored by the United States Shipping Board in 1918. Hopper produced other posters during this period for various movies and for the American Red Cross.

In January 1920 Hopper had his first one-man show of paintings at the Whitney Studio Club. This exhibition was organized by Guy Pène du Bois, and consisted of sixteen oil paintings, ten of which dated from Hopper's years in Paris. Failure to achieve either sales or critical attention with these canvases discouraged Hopper, forcing him to consider the failure of his career as a painter, in contrast to his growing success as an etcher.

Vacationing in Gloucester during the summer of 1923, Hopper encountered Josephine Verstille Nivison, a former art student from the New York School of Art. She encouraged him to take up painting in watercolor, a medium that, except for illustration, he had given up since art school. Hopper painted his first watercolors with an impressive facility, working outdoors and realistically depicting architecture and seascapes. The following autumn Nivison helped arrange for Hopper's watercolors to be included next to her own in a group show at the Brooklyn Museum. His work was singled out for praise by the critics, and the museum purchased his *Mansard Roof*, marking Hopper's first sale of a painting since 1913.

Hopper married Nivison on July 9, 1924, in New York; they spent the summer painting watercolors in Gloucester. Hopper was intolerant of children, and so the couple never had any. Not long after they returned from the summer, Hopper had his second one-man show (his first in a commercial gallery) at the Frank K. M. Rehn Gallery. (Rehn remained his dealer for the rest of his career.) All eleven watercolors exhibited and five additional ones were sold, and the show was a critical success.

With his confidence thus boosted, Hopper happily abandoned working as an illustrator and turned to painting in oil with renewed ambition. He had found in his wife not only a fellow painter but also a readily available model; in fact, she possessively insisted that she should be his only model. She also took upon herself the task of keeping records of Hopper's work and, with his growing fame, intervening when interviewers' questions became too probing.

In 1925 the Pennsylvania Academy of Fine Arts purchased Hopper's oil *Apartment Houses*, becoming the first museum to own one of his oil paintings. That same year Hopper painted *House by the Railroad*, which in 1930 became the first painting acquired for the permanent collection of the Museum of Modern Art. This canvas of a solitary nineteenth-century house standing starkly alone against railroad tracks has become one of the most famous images in American art, evoking the passage of time and the alienation of modern urban life. Nationalistic critics, who had come to view Hopper's work as typically American, also praised his realism and personal content.

Guy Pène du Bois wrote the first monograph on Hopper's work in 1931 for the Whitney Museum of American Art, which, when it opened in November of that year, placed on view Hopper's *Early Sunday Morning* (1930). This deserted urban street scene is now one of his best-known works. In 1933 Alfred Barr organized Hopper's first retrospective for the Museum of Modern Art. At the time Stephen C. Clark, who became Hopper's most important patron, was a member of the museum's board of trustees. A critical debate ensued over whether Hopper was sufficiently modern to be exhibited there.

Beginning in 1930 the Hoppers began to spend their summers painting in Truro on Cape Cod. The view over the bay from their simple three-room house designed by Hopper inspired his *Rooms by the Sea* (1951). During the early 1930's Hopper roamed about Cape Cod, finding ample subjects for both his oils and watercolors, but in time the area became too familiar, prompting him to drive from rural Vermont to Mexico in search of inspiration.

During the 1930's critics categorized Hopper's art as "American scene" painting, linking his work to that of the midwestern regionalists, such as Thomas Hart Benton and Grant Wood. Hopper, who disliked being typecast, decided to show a group of his early works, including eleven scenes of France, at the Rehn Gallery in January 1941, forcing critics to recognize the international roots of his work.

By the 1940's critics had begun to notice that Hopper's painting embodied loneliness. In 1942 he painted his masterpiece, *Nighthawks*, a dramatic canvas depicting people in an all-night diner. Responding to the wartime presence of European artists in exile, particularly the surrealists, critics came to view Hopper's work as poetic. But with the emergence of the American abstract expressionists, Hopper's representational style began to be seen again as "illustrative," a painful reproach for a painter who had disdained illustration. Hopper's second retrospective, organized by Lloyd Goodrich for the Whitney Museum in 1950, was regarded by many as celebrating an obsolete style from the past.

In 1953, in the face of such critical opinion, Hopper, along with Raphael Soyer, Isabel Bishop, Jack Levine, and others, founded a short-lived magazine called *Reality: A Journal of Artists' Opinion*, which demanded that museums give equal consideration to nonabstract art. Hopper's work, while considered unfashionable, continued to be respected by the conservative art establishment. In 1956 *Time* made him the subject of a cover story, pointing out his historical significance and placing him in the American realist tradition of John Singleton Copley and Thomas Eakins.

When Hopper's third retrospective opened at the Whitney Museum in 1964, revisionist critics in a generation of pop artists and photorealists saw him as the forefather of the new avant-garde. Hopper, who had witnessed the partial eclipse of his fame during the heyday of abstract expressionism, viewed the process with cynicism. By then in his eighties, Hopper skeptically watched critics reevaluate his work for their own purposes, confident in the knowledge that he had consistently pursued his own objective: to create realist paintings that expressed personal meaning. William C. Seitz's selection of Hopper's work for a one-man show that would accompany a 1967 exhibition of young pop artists at the São Paulo Biennal became a memorial exhibition when Hopper died in New York City.

[See Gail Levin, *Edward Hopper as Illustrator* (1979); *Edward Hopper: The Complete Prints* (1979); *Edward Hopper: The Art and the Artist* (1980); *Edward Hopper* (1984); and, for a study of his composition and choice of subjects, *Hopper's Places* (1985). For a catalogue raisonné of his prints, see Carl Zigrosser, "The Etchings of Edward Hopper," in Zigrosser, ed., *Prints* (1962). Other useful catalogues and monographs—all, unless otherwise noted, are titled *Edward Hopper* and are by Lloyd Goodrich—include the catalogues of the Whitney Museum of American Art retrospectives of 1950 and 1964; the catalogue of the exhibiton "Selections from the Hopper Bequest to the Whitney Museum" (1971); and an oversize monograph (1971). See also Guy Pène du Bois, *Edward Hopper* (1931); and Alfred H. Barr, Jr., *Edward Hopper: Retrospective Exhibition* (1933), which contains the artist's "Notes on Painting." Revealing interviews with the artist are in Selden Rodman, *Conversations with Artists* (1957); Katharine Kuh, *The Artist's Voice: Talks with Seventeen Artists* (1962); and Brian O'Doherty, *American Masters: The Voice and the Myth* (1973).]

GAIL LEVIN

HOPPER, HEDDA (May 2, 1885–Feb. 1, 1966), newspaper columnist and actress, was born Elda Furry in Hollidaysburg, Pa., the daughter of David E. Furry, a butcher, and Margaret Miller. When Hopper was three, her German Quaker family moved to Altoona, where she went to public school and worked in her father's butcher shop. Hopper's schooling ended with the eighth grade. She determined on a stage career in 1902 after seeing Ethel Barrymore in *Captain Jinks of the Horse Marines*. Then, as later, clothes captivated her more than the content of the play, and to the end of her life she could recall Barrymore's ermine tippet and barrel muff.

Hopper left home in 1903 to attend the Carter Conservatory of Music in Pittsburgh. At the age of twenty-two she moved to New York without her parents' blessing, and with the help of the stagestruck daughter of the director of the Carter Conservatory, she landed a $15-a-week job in the chorus of the Aborn Light Opera Company. Hopper joked about her limited vocal range and never felt that she was pretty, but she was a tall (five feet, seven and a half inches) blonde with green eyes, a peaches-and-cream complexion, and, according to a contemporary, "the most beautiful legs in the New York theater." In 1908 she met DeWolf Hopper, an established actor who was four years older than her father. She became his fifth wife on May 8, 1913. He derided her Altoona accent and taught her to clip her *r*'s so short that she sounded "like an inbred British dowager." He also helped her create the stock character of the brittle, worldly-wise society woman.

In 1915 Hopper had a son, William DeWolf Hopper, Jr. (who later played the detective Paul Drake on the "Perry Mason" television series), and went to Hollywood to make her first film, *The Battle of Hearts* (1916). Returning east, she became a favorite supporting actress in early movies, including *Virtuous Wives* (1919), Louis B. Mayer's first picture, as well as on the Broadway stage. Between 1907 and 1918 she used five different names but, with the help of a numerologist, settled on the name Hedda Hopper. She also changed her date of birth to June 2, 1890. Her success apparently offended her more experienced husband, and they separated in 1920 and divorced in 1922.

The following year Mayer drew Hopper to Hollywood with a ten-year contract for $250 a week. Attracting attention with flashy hats and stylish dresses, she scrambled to work for other studios when Mayer could not provide parts for her. She kept up with inside-Hollywood stories, which she sometimes shared with the gossip columnist Louella Parsons, who gratefully listed Hopper in 1932 as one of the "six reigning favorites."

Ambitious but unable to parlay her assets into better roles, Hopper trod the borderline between success and failure. Although she made most of her 110 movies during these years, she never received top billing. One close friend, Mayer's assistant, Ida Koverman (who had been Herbert Hoover's secretary), encouraged Hopper to try Republican politics. (Hopper's one attempt at electoral politics in 1932 doubled her troubles, for she lost her bid for a Los Angeles County Central Committee seat just when Mayer failed to renew her movie contract.) Another friend was the actress Marion Davies, who was the mistress of newspaper magnate William Randolph Hearst. It was at Hearst's ranch in 1935 that Eleanor Medill ("Cissy") Patterson, intrigued by Hopper's Hollywood talk, asked her to write a letter for Patterson's *Washington Herald*. Aware that Hopper was making fewer films and needed help, Parsons plugged her Hollywood letter, calling it a fashion article.

Hopper dropped her Hollywood letter when the pay shrank from $50 a week to $35. In 1937 she started her first radio gossip program and met Dema Harshbarger, who was working for the National Broadcasting Company. Harshbarger took over Hopper's career and later managed it full-time. Hopper's radio program quickly failed, but Mayer, hoping to diminish Parsons' power, took Koverman's suggestion that Hopper write a rival gossip column. With Metro-Goldwyn-Mayer's publicity department supporting Hopper, the Esquire Features syndicate signed her to do a column.

Hopper's gossip column first appeared on Feb. 15, 1938, in five newspapers, including the *Los Angeles Times*, which was the most important local paper of the movie industry. With Harshbarger's help, Hopper also succeeded in radio. Her radio programs for national networks ran from 1939 to 1951 and featured both gossip and drama.

Writing gently at first, Hopper was scarcely noticed, but when she started ruthlessly reporting on celebrities, her popularity grew by leaps and bounds. In 1940, "Hedda Hopper's Hollywood" was taken over by the *Des Moines Register Tribune* syndicate and two years later by the *Chicago Tribune–New York Daily News* syndicate. She now had some 30 million readers, and her income neared $200,000 annually. Hopper, who often overacted her parts, played the stereotypical newspaperwoman with gusto. With her new fame, she received roles in first-rate films, including *The Women* (1939) and *Sunset Boulevard* (1950).

In three years Hopper raced to a position similar to the one it had taken Parsons thirty years to attain. Despite the two columnists' celebrated feud and tendency to chastise each other's favorites, each thrived on the publicity and competition the other provided. Unable to spell or type, Hopper dictated her chatty column while pacing her office in stocking feet. She unashamedly called herself "a ham trying to be a columnist" and referred to her rival as "a newspaperwoman trying to be a ham." Because Hopper was the more sophisticated of the two, her flaunted prejudices, relentless attacks, and petty snooping were more difficult to forgive. She could be inaccurate and malicious; in 1965 libelous statements cost her $50,000 in an out-of-court settlement with the actor Michael Wilding.

Hopper called her Hollywood home "the house that fear built" and gloried in harassing big stars. Yet, she also helped the careers of newcomers and little-known actors, writers, and directors. She insisted that the war hero Audie Murphy play the lead in the movie version of Stephen Crane's *The Red Badge of Courage* (1951), and she campaigned for better working conditions for film extras. Always a crusader, she attacked sexual license, alleged Communists, and pointed-toed shoes. She joined the ultra-right-wing Motion Picture Alliance for the Preservation of American Ideals, hailed the Hollywood visit of Martin Dies and his House Un-American Activities Committee, and boosted Richard Nixon's career by sticking a "pink" label on the actress Helen Gahagan Douglas, his 1950 rival for the Senate. Disgusted that Charlie Chaplin had never shown any inclination to become a United States citizen, she helped hound him out of Hollywood.

Hopper's gossip column brought her the stardom that had eluded her as an actress: the World War II C-47 ambulance plane was named for her, and she graced Republican conventions, entertained American service personnel abroad with Bob Hope during four Christmas seasons, and made frequent guest appearances on television. She also wrote two best-sellers, her autobiography, *From Under My Hat* (1952), and *The Whole Truth and Nothing But* (1963; written with James Brough), and she appeared on the cover of *Time* magazine. Outrageous hats, many of them sent to her by fans, were her trademark, and each year she purchased about 150 additional ones, for which she received a $5,000 tax deduction. Resisting change in everything but hats, Hopper lamented "the death of glamour," the coming to Hollywood of "the dirty-postcard boys," and the realism that "strangled the dream stuff." Parsons' retirement in 1964 left Hopper the undisputed top Hollywood columnist, but little more than a year later Hopper died in Hollywood.

[Hopper's files, correspondence, and taped transcriptions of interviews are in the Margaret Herrick

Library of the Academy of Motion Picture Arts and Sciences, Beverly Hills, Calif. The best source on Hopper is George Eells, *Hedda and Louella* (1972). Important magazine articles are Francis Sill Wickware, "Hedda Hopper," *Life*, Nov. 20, 1944; Collie Small, "Gossip Is Her Business," *Saturday Evening Post*, Jan. 11, 1947; and the *Time* cover story, July 28, 1947. An obituary is in the *New York Times*, Feb. 2, 1966.]

OLIVE HOOGENBOOM

HORTON, EDWARD EVERETT, JR. (Mar. 18, 1886–Sept. 29, 1970), actor, was born in Brooklyn, N.Y., the son of Edward Everett Horton, a printer and foreman in the *New York Times* composing room, and Isabella Diack. (His paternal grandfather named his six sons after famous Americans and included Edward Everett, the orator and politician, because he preferred his two-hour address at Gettysburg, Pa., on Nov. 19, 1863, to Abraham Lincoln's.) Horton graduated from Boys' High School in Brooklyn and attended Baltimore City College, Oberlin College, Brooklyn Polytechnic Institute, and Columbia College. Despite his parents' desire that he become a teacher, show business appealed to him more than academic pursuits, and he directed and performed in amateur productions at Oberlin and Columbia.

Leaving Columbia in 1907 without a degree, Horton sang and danced in the chorus of several Broadway musicals, eventually joining the Dempsey Light Opera Company on Staten Island, which performed Gilbert and Sullivan operas. In 1908, he joined Louis Mann's Broadway company as a stage manager. Watching the famous actor-impresario from the wings, Horton learned timing and dramatic characterization. Mann gave him bit parts and walk-ons, and in 1910, Horton made his Broadway debut as a butler in Mann's production of *The Cheater*.

Horton worked up to romantic and juvenile leads when in 1912 he joined Philadelphia's Orpheum Players at the Chestnut Street Theatre, reputedly the best stock company of its day. Here and in long engagements with stock and road companies from 1914 to 1919, he perfected an acting style appropriate to drawing-room comedies and farces. In 1919, Thomas Wilkes hired him as a leading man for his production company at the Majestic Theatre in Los Angeles. For forty-four weeks in 1923, he played the title role in his own production of Booth Tarkington's *Clarence*. Horton enjoyed considerable success and was soon earning $1,250 a week.

In the late 1920's he and his brother Winter Davis Horton established a repertory company that presented George Bernard Shaw and Noel Coward comedies, French farces, and Broadway hits to a loyal California following. As a producer and actor, he remained a mainstay of West Coast and regional theaters but never attained success on Broadway.

At the Hollywood Playhouse in 1932, he first played Henry Dewlip, the aging, prissy bachelor roué, in Benn W. Levy's comedy *Springtime for Henry*, which had opened on Broadway in December 1931. Looking for a play to complete his company's season, he had persuaded Levy to let him mount a West Coast production of the hit. His characterization enjoyed great popular success, and Horton made the part his own, performing it nearly 3,000 times in summer stock and touring companies. The role brought him national fame and considerable wealth.

Horton was one of the few actors with the talent to appear in both legitimate theater and movies. His first silent film was Vitagraph's *Too Much Business* (1922), in which he played the proprietor of a day nursery. At Paramount, James Cruze directed him in two roles that won him critical acclaim, an English butler transported to the West in *Ruggles of Red Gap* (1923) and a composer with a rich fantasy life in *Beggar on Horseback* (1925), but all in all, Horton enjoyed only modest success in silent comedies.

Stage experience had given him speaking ability, and so, with the arrival of sound, he was in great demand. Refusing to sign an exclusive contract, he made films for all the major studios as a free lance. His first all-sound feature-length film was Warner Brothers' *The Terror* (1928), in which he portrayed a drunken, half-crazy detective. He gave a finely crafted performance as the daydreaming, fussbudgety feature writer in Lewis Milestone's *The Front Page* (United Artists, 1931). More typical were his appearances in many of the sophisticated, glittering comedies of the 1930's. Ernst Lubitsch directed him in five such films: *Trouble in Paradise* (Paramount, 1932), *Design for Living* (Paramount, 1933), *The Merry Widow* (MGM, 1934), *Angel* (Paramount, 1937), and *Bluebeard's Eighth Wife* (Paramount, 1938). He excelled in three

Fred Astaire–Ginger Rogers dance films, usually playing Astaire's best friend: *The Gay Divorcee* (RKO, 1934), in which he danced with Betty Grable in the showstopper "Let's K-nock K-nees"; *Top Hat* (RKO, 1935); and *Shall We Dance* (RKO, 1937).

Although stardom proved beyond his reach, Horton was a comic mainstay in more than one hundred films over a twenty-year period. With a flawless sense of timing, he employed deadpan seriousness, piercing stares, furtive looks, double or triple takes, raised eyebrows, mischievous grins, pursed lips, and panicky gestures in a manner ideal for light comedies or farces. He became well known for his portrayals of jittery, addlebrained fussbudgets. Horton accurately appraised his career when he confessed to an interviewer, "I have my own little kingdom. I do the scavenger parts no one else wants and I get well paid for it."

Horton never took his film work seriously but regarded it as a profitable sideline. Neither billing nor the size of his part concerned him, but his salary did. At the height of his career in the 1930's, he made nearly $5,000 a week, which, added to his summer-stock and tour earnings, gave him an income equal to that of many stars.

Horton's desire to live like a star necessitated a large income. In 1925 he and his brother George had purchased twenty-two acres of land in California's San Fernando Valley. On the estate, which he called Belleigh Acres, he built an elaborate home of colonial design that grew in size as his film career prospered. Its seventeen rooms housed an extensive collection of antique furniture and books. The estate included dog kennels, a swimming pool, sunken tennis courts, and an extensive garden of rare shrubs and flowers. Here he entertained lavishly; his champagne breakfasts were famous among members of the film colony. Although Horton never married, he enjoyed a close-knit family life on his estate. His two brothers and their families lived in guesthouses, and his mother and, later, his widowed sister lived with him.

Horton's film career virtually ended in the late 1940's, and during the next twenty years, he played cameo roles in only six films, most of them undistinguished. He returned to his first love, the legitimate theater, touring in roles that had been created on Broadway by more famous actors; for example, in 1949 he played the lead in Noel Coward's *Present Laughter*, which Clifton Webb had originated on Broadway. He also toured widely in his summer-stock perennial, *Springtime for Henry*. In the early 1960's, when he was in his mid-seventies, he played the mute king to Imogene Coca's princess in an eighteen-month tour of *Once upon a Mattress*. In a national tour in 1963 of *A Funny Thing Happened on the Way to the Forum*, he took a bit part. In 1965 he played the Star-Keeper in a revival of *Carousel* at the New York State Theatre. It was clear that he wanted to die with his greasepaint on.

He made numerous guest appearances on television situation comedies, and from 1965 to 1967 he played the medicine man Roaring Chicken on "'F' Troop." He was in great demand for talk shows and did offscreen voices for cartoons and commercials. His final television appearance—as a crusty doctor in an episode of "The Governor and J.J."—was broadcast after his death. He died at his home in the San Fernando Valley.

[Horton contributed an oral memoir to Bernard Rosenberg and Harry Silverstein, eds., *The Real Tinsel* (1970). His collection of theater memorabilia is at the American Conservatory Theatre, San Francisco. Clipping files are in the National Film Information Service of the Academy of Motion Picture Arts and Sciences and in the New York Public Library's Performing Arts Research Center at Lincoln Center. See Kyle Crichton, "Comedy—Six Days a Week," *Collier's*, July 18, 1936, for biographical information and a checklist of his screen roles; Jeanne Stein, "'Fusspot' and 'Fortune's Fool': Edward Everett Horton," *Focus on Film*, Jan.–Feb. 1970; and James Robert Parish and William T. Leonard, *The Funsters* (1979).]

G. F. Goodwin

HOWE, MARK DE WOLFE (May 22, 1906–Feb. 28, 1967), legal historian and civil rights activist, was born in Boston, Mass., the son of Mark Antony De Wolfe Howe, the biographer and essayist, and Fanny Huntington Quincy. He attended Phillips Andover Academy and received his B.A. from Harvard in 1928 and his LL.B. from the Harvard Law School in 1933. On Feb. 28, 1935, he married Mary Manning; they had three children.

Upon graduation from law school, Howe served for one year as secretary to Oliver Wendell Holmes, Jr., who by then had retired from the United States Supreme Court. Nonetheless, Howe considered the year well spent, not only for the older man's friendship but for what he learned about the relation of law to society. Years later Howe wrote that Holmes's clerks "learned that professional capacity achieves the highest fruitfulness only when it is combined with energy of character and breadth of learning."

After clerking with Holmes, Howe joined the Boston law firm of Hill, Barlow, Goodale, and Wiswall; but his own inclinations, as well as repeated urgings from Felix Frankfurter and Louis D. Brandeis, led him back to the academy. In 1937 he joined the University of Buffalo Law School as a professor of law and in 1941 became dean. He also edited the correspondence between Holmes and Sir Frederick Pollock (2 vols., 1941). In 1943 he entered the army as a major in the Civilian Affairs Branch and saw service in North Africa, Sicily, and southern France. He received the Legion of Merit and the Distinguished Service Medal and was discharged in 1945 with the rank of colonel.

After the war Howe went to Harvard as a professor of law. Unlike many of his law-school colleagues, Howe taught undergraduates at Harvard College, where he soon became an extremely popular teacher. At Frankfurter's prodding, he continued his study of Holmes's life and work. Over the next several years he produced *Touched with Fire* (Holmes's Civil War letters and diary; 1946), *The Holmes-Laski Letters* (2 vols., 1953), and a definitive annotated edition of *The Common Law* (1963).

Howe also began work on a multivolume biography of Holmes. Only the first two parts, *The Shaping Years* (1957) and *The Proving Years* (1963), were completed before his death. It is this latter volume that has earned the greatest appreciation from legal scholars, because in it Howe managed, with skill and grace, to explore Holmes's intellectual development leading to the seminal Lowell Institute lectures on the common law.

Howe also edited a casebook, *Readings in American Legal History* (1949), and wrote *The Garden and the Wilderness* (1965), in which he argued that the evangelicalism of Roger Williams was as much responsible for the separation of church and state as Thomas Jefferson's political secularism. Williams' concern for the "purity of the church's garden" required that religious and secular activities be totally separate.

Howe was an early opponent of Senator Joseph McCarthy and in 1953 joined with Arthur M. Schlesinger, Sr., and Archibald MacLeish in issuing a letter calling upon liberals to work for McCarthy's defeat. Following the Supreme Court's school desegregation decision in 1954, Howe became a passionate proponent of civil rights, declaring that racial inequality is "the greatest brutality of our time." He signed on as a member of the Legal Defense Fund of the National Association for the Advancement of Colored People, and helped teach scores of southern trial lawyers how to conduct civil rights litigation.

Howe did more than just teach; he also set a personal example. He founded the Lawyers' Constitutional Defense Committee and participated in the March on Washington in 1963. The next year, he challenged Attorney General Robert F. Kennedy's assertion that the federal government lacked jurisdiction to take police action in Mississippi during the racial disturbances. In 1966 he spent weeks in local courts in Mississippi defending civil rights workers. Shortly before his death, he was appointed chairman of the Massachusetts Attorney General's Advisory Committee on Civil Rights and Civil Liberties. He died at his Cambridge, Mass., home.

[The Howe Papers are in the Harvard Law School library. Several memorial articles are in the *Harvard Law Review*, June 1967. An obituary is in the *New York Times*, Mar. 1, 1967.]

MELVIN I. UROFSKY

HUGHES, JAMES LANGSTON (Feb. 1, 1902–May 22, 1967), poet, playwright, and novelist, was born in Joplin, Mo., the son of James Nathaniel Hughes, a stenographer for a mining company, and Carrie Mercer Langston. After his father abandoned the family for a business career in Mexico, Hughes lived in various places but mainly in Lawrence, Kans., in the home of his grandmother Mary Langston, whose first husband had been a member of John Brown's "army" and died at Harpers Ferry. She instilled in her grandson a reverence for social and racial justice. But neither she nor his mother, who was frequently absent from Lawrence in pursuit of work, satisfied the boy's craving for affection, and he grew up a lonely child who sought relief mainly in books.

Hughes excelled at predominantly white schools in Topeka and Lawrence, where he faced prejudice from certain officials. Between 1915 and 1916 he lived in Lincoln, Ill., with his mother, who had remarried after divorcing his father. At the Central School he wrote his first poem and was elected class poet in the eighth grade. In 1916 he moved with his family to Cleveland, Ohio, where he entered Central High School. In a student body dominated by the children of European immigrants, Hughes found a home. Handsome and personable, a leading runner and high-jumper, and the author of verse and short stories published in the school magazine, he was popular and respected. In 1919–1920, his senior year, he was elected class poet and editor of the yearbook; he also decided to be a writer.

In September 1921, after a trying year in Mexico with his father, who thought writing a waste of time, Hughes entered Columbia University. By this point, he had absorbed his early influences in poetry—notably the black poet Paul Laurence Dunbar, Walt Whitman, and above all Carl Sandburg, whom Hughes referred to as "my guiding star." In 1921–1922 he began to lay the foundations of his literary career by publishing free-verse poems such as "The Negro Speaks of Rivers" and "Mother to Son" in W. E. B. Du Bois' *Crisis*, the organ of the National Association for the Advancement of Colored People (NAACP). The poems were inspired mainly, but not exclusively, by Afro-American culture.

Finding the university inhospitable (he was one of perhaps a dozen black students there), Hughes completed most of his freshman courses but then withdrew. For a while he worked in Manhattan as a delivery boy and then on a Staten Island vegetable farm. Seeking an ocean voyage as a messman, he found himself instead on a ship in a sleepy fleet of surplus vessels anchored up the Hudson River. He continued to publish verse, on which his experiences in New York, and especially Harlem, had left its mark. In "The Weary Blues," for example, he showed the creative attentiveness to black music and the fearlessness in drawing inspiration from the most humble aspects of black culture that would distinguish his entire career. He learned more about that culture in the summer and fall of 1923, when he sailed on a freighter down the west coast of Africa. He also saw firsthand the effects of European colonialism, which he abhorred.

Early in 1924, after serving on a vessel bound for Europe, Hughes jumped ship and spent several months as a cook's helper in a Paris nightclub that featured black American performers. Here he experimented further with jazz and blues rhythms in his verse. The following year, spent mainly with his mother in Washington, D.C., was a turning point in his life. In May 1925, "The Weary Blues" won first prize in poetry in a major literary contest run by *Opportunity*, the magazine of the Urban League. He then met Carl Van Vechten, a white writer who encouraged Alfred A. Knopf to publish Hughes's first book of poems, *The Weary Blues* (1926). A second volume, *Fine Clothes to the Jew* (1927), though scathingly reviewed in the black press for its free use of the blues and dialect, confirmed his reputation as by far the most innovative of the younger black poets. Along with writers such as Wallace Thurman, Countee Cullen, and Zora Neale Hurston and artists such as Aaron Douglas, Hughes was a major figure in the movement known as the Harlem Renaissance. His landmark essay "The Negro Artist and the Racial Mountain" (1926), in which he affirmed the determination of young black writers to treat the subject of race without shame or fear, appeared in the *Nation* and became virtually the manifesto of the Harlem Renaissance.

In 1926, Hughes resumed his schooling at predominantly black Lincoln University, in Pennsylvania, from which he graduated in 1929. From 1927 to 1930 he enjoyed the patronage of Mrs. Rufus Osgood Mason, a wealthy, aged widow with a fervent faith in parapsychology. Under her guidance, Hughes wrote his touching first novel, *Not Without Laughter* (1930), about a black boyhood in the Midwest, and visited Cuba, where he met and influenced the poet Nicolás Guillén. In 1930, however, the collapse of his relationship with Mrs. Mason left him in an emotional crisis that lasted several months. With money awarded by the Harmon Foundation as a prize for his novel, he spent several weeks in 1931 recuperating in Haiti.

Still reeling from his disastrous encounter with philanthropy and feeling revulsion at imperialism in the Caribbean, Hughes returned to the United States committed to Marxism, to which he had been introduced in high school by the children of Russian immigrants. He associated with the John Reed Club of New York and published pieces denouncing imperialism in *New Masses*. Then, prompted by the black educator Mary McLeod Bethune, he set out in November 1931 to take his poetry to the people. Touring the South and the West until the following June, he read his poems in scores of black churches and schools. Hughes—who was slight of build at about five feet, four inches and had a somewhat singsong reading voice—often seemed at odds with his courageous poems, but he captivated audiences with an air of youthful innocence and a love of laughter. This tour solidified his commitment to advancing the status of blacks in a democratic and just America.

At the end of the tour, just after publishing *Scottsboro Limited: Four Poems and a Play* (1932) in support of the young black men accused of rape in Alabama, Hughes joined a band of twenty-two young blacks going to the Soviet Union to make a film on race relations in the United States. The film project soon collapsed, but Hughes traveled extensively in Soviet Central Asia, at one time in the company of Arthur Koestler, and spent the winter and spring of 1933 in Moscow. Although he never joined the Communist party, his radicalism was at its height—as reflected in poems such as "Good Morning, Revolution," published during his Soviet stay. Returning home via China and Japan, he accepted the invitation of a wealthy admirer to spend a year in Carmel, Calif. Here, in a community of writers that included Robinson Jeffers and Lincoln Steffens, he finished *The Ways of White Folks* (1934), a collection of tough-minded, even embittered stories of race; he had begun the book in the Soviet Union after he had read several tales by D. H. Lawrence.

Driven from Carmel by right-wing pressure during a period of labor unrest in California, Hughes spent a half-year in Mexico following the death there of his father. He returned to the United States in June 1935. His play *Mulatto*, about the fatal conflict between a white man and one of his mulatto sons, had been written at Jasper Deeter's Hedgerow Theater five years earlier and was about to appear on Broadway. Although the production was panned by the critics—Hughes blamed the producer for adding sensational details—the play ran for a year, becoming the longest-running work by a black on Broadway until Lorraine Hansberry's play *A Raisin in the Sun* (a title taken from a Hughes poem) ran for 530 performances in 1959–1960. But little money reached Hughes, who lived in poverty with his mother mainly in Oberlin, Ohio. There he wrote for Russell and Rowena Jelliffe's Gilpin Players in Cleveland a number of plays, including the comedy *Little Ham* and the historical drama *Emperor of Haiti* (both 1936), that established him as a major Afro-American playwright.

In 1937, Hughes spent several months in Spain, especially in besieged Madrid, reporting on blacks in the civil war for the *Baltimore Afro-American*. He returned home in 1938 and founded the Harlem Suitcase Theatre, which staged his *Don't You Want to Be Free?*, a radical play based on his poems and the blues; in that year, he also published a pamphlet of political verse, *A New Song*, with an introduction by Mike Gold, the editor of *New Masses*. But Hughes's increasing need for money sent him to Hollywood, where he worked with the black actor and singer Clarence Muse on the film *Way Down South* (1939). Its stereotypical portrayal of black life led to severe criticism of Hughes but also enabled him to pay off several debts and to work on his first volume of autobiography, *The Big Sea* (1940).

The Big Sea was overwhelmed by the appearance in the same year of *Native Son* by Richard Wright, who displaced Hughes as the most acclaimed of Afro-American writers. Other setbacks followed. Work on musical revues in Chicago and Los Angeles ended in acrimony and failure, and right-wing religious forces picketed him over his most iconoclastic poem, "Goodbye Christ," written eight years earlier when Hughes was in Russia and published without his approval. When he renounced the poem, elements of the Left denounced him.

After a quiet year in Carmel Valley, Hughes returned east late in 1941. The following spring, working with a black theater group in Chicago, he staged *The Sun Do Move*, a play with poems and music that emphasize racial but also patriotic themes rather than leftist radicalism. The volume of verse *Shakespeare in Harlem* (1942) also avoids Marxism. Moving to Harlem, where he lived the rest of his life, he began a weekly column in the black *Chicago Defender* in 1942. The column's main feature soon became conversations with the comic character Jesse B. Semple, or "Simple." This black Everyman, initially created to bolster support for the war effort among blacks, spoke out humorously but with uncompromising, often paranoid racial feeling on almost every imaginable subject. While the war lasted, Hughes fought segregation, especially in the armed forces, but he also toiled, usually without pay, to write scripts and songs for various government agencies.

Just after the war, Kurt Weill and Elmer Rice hired Hughes as lyricist on their Broadway opera *Street Scene* (1947), based on Rice's 1929 Pulitzer Prize–winning play. With his royalties, he bought a three-story town house in Harlem, where he lived to the end of his life with Emerson and Toy Harper, old friends who virtually adopted him as a son. He devoted himself to a wide variety of projects, although he failed in the next few years to repeat the financial success of *Street Scene*. (*Troubled Island*, an opera with music by William Grant Still and based on his Haitian play, was staged in New York in 1949.) He published volumes of verse: *Fields of Wonder* (1947), which avoids both race and politics; *One-Way Ticket* (1949); and *Montage of a Dream Deferred* (1951), a loving, jazz-based portrait of Harlem as a community both unfairly maligned and in genuine distress.

With his longtime friend and correspondent Arna Bontemps, Hughes edited a number of anthologies, including *The Poetry of the Negro, 1746–1949* (1949). In 1950 he brought out *Simple Speaks His Mind*, the first of five collections of his Simple columns. He wrote about a dozen books for children, almost all on black life and culture, and translated books of verse by Federico García Lorca, Nicolás Guillén (with Ben Carruthers), and Gabriela Mistral, as well as (with Mercer Cook) *Masters of the Dew*, a novel by Jacques Roumain of Haiti. With the German-born composer Jan Meyerowitz, he collaborated on several cantatas and operas, including *The Barrier*, based on the play *Mulatto*, which succeeded at the Columbia University Opera Workshop in 1950 but failed on Broadway. The sheer accumulation of work, as well as its quality, made Hughes again the central figure in Afro-American literature.

In 1953, at the height of Senator Joseph McCarthy's anti-Communist campaign and following damaging attacks on Hughes for his earlier radicalism, he was summoned before McCarthy's committee. Although he named no one as a Communist, he cooperated with McCarthy. His political philosophy had changed, but he also wished to avoid the price for defiance paid by black leftists such as Du Bois and Paul Robeson and to preserve his standing with his most important audience, the black community. Free now to pursue his career, he prospered as never before. In 1956 came his second volume of autobiography, *I Wonder As I Wander*, which treats the period between 1931 and 1938 and features a long, evenhanded account of his year in the Soviet Union. In 1959, Knopf published Hughes's *Selected Poems*. In 1961 came *Ask Your Mama*, a jazz-influenced book-length poem that reflects his prophetic sense of coming racial turmoil in America even as integration was becoming law.

Hughes also returned to musical theater. In *Simply Heavenly* (1957), which centers on Simple, he enjoyed a measure of financial and critical success. But during this period he devoted most of his energy to drama and to pioneer fusions of black gospel music, which he saw as the last vestige of Afro-American folk music. His play *Tambourines to Glory* (1963), which depicts religious hypocrisy, was criticized as demeaning to blacks, but other dramas, such as *Black Nativity* (1961), on the Christmas theme, and *Jericho—Jim Crow* (1964), about the civil rights movement, played successfully in the United States and abroad. These plays are only a part of Hughes's enormous output, which includes the books of short stories *Laughing to Keep from Crying* (1952) and *Something in Common* (1963); *A History of the NAACP* (1962); pictorial volumes, such as *The Sweet Flypaper of Life* (1955), with the photographer Roy De Carava; and two anthologies of new writing by black Africans.

In 1961, at the height of his prestige, Hughes was elected to the National Institute of Arts and Letters. As always, he tried hard to bring the work of younger writers to public attention either by private encouragement or by editing anthologies such as *New Negro Poets, USA* (1964). In spite of these efforts, the end of his life found him on the defensive against the most militant and divisive black-power and black-arts spokesmen. But no black American writer was more admired or beloved by the general Afro-American population or by black artists. In 1966, at the first World Festival of Negro Arts in Dakar, Hughes was honored by the poet

Leopold Sedar Senghor, the president of Senegal, and others for his historic contribution to the evolution of literature by blacks in the twentieth century. He died in New York City.

[Hughes's papers are in the James Weldon Johnson Memorial Collection at the Beinecke Library, Yale University. Additional important material may be found in the Moorland-Spingarn Research Library of Howard University; the Amistad Collection in New Orleans; the Fisk University Library; the Bancroft Library of the University of California at Berkeley; and the Kenneth Spencer Research Library of the University of Kansas. The *Langston Hughes Reader*, selected by Hughes, appeared in 1958. For his plays, see Webster Smalley, ed., *Five Plays of Langston Hughes* (1963). For his correspondence, see Charles H. Nichols, ed., *Arna Bontemps–Langston Hughes Letters, 1925–1967* (1980). Useful studies include James A. Emanuel, *Langston Hughes* (1967); Donald C. Dickinson, *A Bio-bibliography of Langston Hughes* (1972); Onwuchekwa Jemie, *Langston Hughes: An Introduction to the Poetry* (1976); Edward J. Mullen, ed., *Langston Hughes in the Hispanic World and Haiti* (1977); and Arnold Rampersad, *The Life of Langston Hughes*, I (1986). An obituary is in the *New York Times*, May 23, 1967.]

ARNOLD RAMPERSAD

HUMPHREY, GEORGE MAGOFFIN (Mar. 8, 1890–Jan. 20, 1970), lawyer, industrialist, and secretary of the treasury, was born in Cheboygan, Mich., the son of Watts Sherman Humphrey, an attorney, and Caroline Magoffin. Shortly after his birth his family moved to Saginaw, Mich. After attending public schools in Saginaw, where he was a star high school football player, Humphrey entered the University of Michigan in 1908, intending to become a civil engineer. After one year, he transferred to Michigan Law School. There he achieved an academic record that earned for him the editorship of the *Michigan Law Review* and election to the order of the Coif, the national honor society for students of law. Upon receiving his LL.B in 1912, Humphrey returned to Saginaw to become a partner in his father's law firm, which then became Humphrey, Grant, and Humphrey. On May 3, 1913, he married Pamela Stark; they had three children.

Although his law practice grew and he acquired such important clients as the Michigan Central and Grand Trunk railroad companies, Humphrey began to search for new interests. In 1917, when he was considering entry into the banking business in Saginaw, his senior partner, Richard Grant, became general counsel for the M. A. Hanna Company in Cleveland, Ohio, and invited Humphrey to join him as an assistant. (The Hanna Company, an iron-ore and shipping firm, had been founded in 1886 by Marcus A. Hanna, who later served as United States senator from Ohio.) Humphrey's rise in the company was rapid. Within a year, he had succeeded Grant as general counsel; in 1920 he was made a partner in charge of the Hanna iron-ore properties; and soon thereafter, he was named executive vice-president. The Hanna Company was in serious financial difficulties during the post–World War I slump, but Humphrey reorganized the company and eliminated unprofitable operations. By 1924 the company had once again become a leader in iron-ore production and Great Lakes shipping.

As the fortunes of the company improved, the restless Humphrey looked for new enterprises into which to direct his energy and managerial talents. Through his business connections, he had become a close friend of the steel manufacturer Ernest T. Weir. In 1929 Humphrey, the newly chosen president of the Hanna Company, joined forces with Weir to create the National Steel Corporation, with steel mills in Detroit, Mich., and Gary, Ind. One month later, the Wall Street stock market crash heralded the onset of the Great Depression, but National Steel, with its sound financial basis and its expert management, continued to expand while its competitors cut back. It became the sixth-largest steel producer in the nation and was the only steel company to show a profit during each year of the depression.

Humphrey's legal background, conservative economic philosophy, and keen ability to evaluate corporate efficiency were characteristic of the new generation of twentieth-century organization men. His conservatism was deeply ingrained, but it was not inflexible. He liked to think of himself as a practitioner of "imaginative orthodoxy." It was said of him that he would fire his own grandmother if she were not doing a good job—but he would give her a pension. That ameliorating clause distinguished him from such archconservatives as his associate E. T. Weir.

Both the Hanna Company, which Humphrey had transformed into a holding company for several subsidiary enterprises, and National Steel were in a position to profit greatly from the

World War II demand for steel products. In the immediate postwar period, Humphrey further expanded his operations by creating the Pittsburgh Consolidation Coal Company. He regarded the development of the theretofore untapped iron-ore resources of Labrador as his most significant business achievement. At a time when the northern iron ranges of Michigan and Minnesota were being exhausted, the Labrador iron ore was crucial to American steel mills.

In 1948 Humphrey was asked by Paul Hoffman, head of the Economic Cooperation Administration, to serve as his adviser for the coal and steel industries. On a trip to Germany in that year to assess the possibilities of rehabilitating the German steel industry, Humphrey greatly impressed General Lucius D. Clay, administrator of the American occupied zone. It was Clay who urged Dwight D. Eisenhower to name Humphrey as his secretary of the treasury in 1952. Humphrey had long been active in Republican politics, but he had supported Senator Robert Taft for the presidency since 1940. Humphrey and Eisenhower had never met until the president-elect decided to follow Clay's recommendation and asked Humphrey to join his cabinet.

The nomination came as a surprise to both the press and the Senate. Although one of America's leading industrialists, Humphrey had always shunned publicity and had never given an interview. The only time he had come to the attention of the general public was in 1947 when he successfully negotiated a new labor contract for the coal industry with John L. Lewis' United Mine Workers. To their mutual surprise, Lewis and Humphrey had discovered that they could deal successfully. Both men had a deep-seated distrust of big government, and in the interest of negotiating a contract outside of governmental supervision, both had been willing to make concessions.

Humphrey easily won Senate confirmation, and in a matter of weeks after taking office, the press, which had dubbed him Eisenhower's "dark horse," now hailed him as "the strong man of the Cabinet." Humphrey welcomed the public attention he had so long avoided. Of all the Eisenhower team, he enjoyed the best press. His financial program was simple and direct: reduce government expenditures, particularly in the military sector; lower taxes; and balance the budget. Eisenhower took the unprecedented step of inviting him to sit on the National Security Council, and it was Humphrey who became the major architect of the president's "New Look" in national defense—a sharp curtailment of expenditures for conventional weapons and a greater reliance on nuclear arms, which were less expensive.

During his four years as secretary of the treasury, Humphrey was able to implement his major goals: taxes were reduced by some $7.4 billion, inflation was checked, the value of the dollar abroad rose, and for two years the budget was balanced. "When George speaks, all the rest of us listen," Eisenhower said of Humphrey.

At the beginning of his second term, however, Eisenhower, under pressure from the Defense Department, submitted the largest peacetime budget in history. Humphrey's displeasure was apparent, and he warned the nation that unless expenditures were sharply cut and taxes further reduced, "you will have a depression that will curl your hair." Shortly thereafter, Humphrey resigned to return to private business. It was believed at the time that his remark had caused a break between him and the president, but in reality Humphrey was expressing Eisenhower's true philosophy. The two men remained close friends, taking frequent trips together.

In 1962 Humphrey resigned as chairman of National Steel and thereafter devoted much of his time to breeding racehorses on his Georgia estate. He died in Cleveland.

[Humphrey's public papers are in the Western Reserve Historical Society archives. Selected documents from this collection are in *The Basic Papers of George M. Humphrey*, edited by Nathaniel R. Howard (1965). Additional correspondence is at the Dwight D. Eisenhower Library in Abilene, Kans.; the Herbert Hoover Library in West Branch, Iowa; the University of Michigan; the University of Wyoming; and the Minnesota Historical Society in St. Paul. See also the obituary in the *New York Times*, Jan. 21, 1970.]

JOSEPH FRAZIER WALL

HUMPHRIES, GEORGE ROLFE (Nov. 20, 1894–Apr. 22, 1969), poet, translator, and scholar, was born in Philadelphia, Pa., the son of John Henry Humphries, a Latin teacher and school superintendent, and Florence Yost, an English teacher. His father began teaching him Latin at an early age. He was a student at

Stanford University from 1912 to 1913, and he received a B.A. cum laude from Amherst College in 1915. At Amherst he heard William Butler Yeats read his poems and studied the classics with Gilbert Murray and philosophy with Alexander Meiklejohn. During World War I he served in the army from 1917 to 1918, rising to the rank of first lieutenant. On June 26, 1925, he married Helen Ward Spencer; they had one child, a son who predeceased them.

Humphries taught and coached athletics at the Potter School for Boys in San Francisco (1914–1923) and the Browning School for Boys in New York City (1923–1924) and taught Latin at Woodmere Academy on Long Island, N.Y. (1925–1957). He was a professor of Latin at Hunter College in 1957 and a lecturer in English at Amherst College from 1957 to 1965. He also taught briefly at the University of Washington in 1966. He served on the faculties of summer writers' conferences at the University of New Hampshire, Indiana University, the University of Colorado, the University of Utah, and Portland State University.

Humphries was a Guggenheim Fellow in creative writing in 1938–1939, a period he spent traveling in Mexico and Europe. He was a fellow of the Academy of American Poets in 1955. He won the Shelley Memorial Award for Poetry in 1947, the Borestone Mountain Poetry Award in 1951 and 1956, and the Winterfest Poetry Award in 1966.

Humphries published several volumes of poetry: *Europa, and Other Poems and Sonnets* (1929), *Out of the Jewel* (1942), *The Summer Landscape* (1944), *Forbid Thy Ravens* (1947), *The Wind of Time* (1950), *Poems, Collected and New* (1954), *Green Armour on Green Ground* (1956), *Collected Poems of Rolfe Humphries* (1956), and *Coat on a Stick: Late Poems* (1969). Humphries' poems are exuberant. Sometimes rhymed and sometimes not, they speak of nature, passion, sports, travel, and everyday scenes. Some of them are of the essence, others trivial. Always the poems are laced with humor and frequently with classical references.

Although Humphries was usually described as a minor poet, his poems were generally well received, if with reservations about his flamboyant language and contemporary usages. A reviewer of *Europa* complained that the poet failed "to distinguish between the stable diction of art and the smart words and topics which current sophistication employs." Nearly forty years later, a reviewer of *Collected Poems of Rolfe Humphries* described Humphries as "a lion-tamer who will stoop, through sheer exuberance of craft, to train a flea."

Humphries translated the writings of the Spanish poet Federico García Lorca. Among them were *Poet in New York* (1940), *Gypsy Ballads* (1953), and *Five Plays: Comedies and Tragicomedies* (1963). Humphries also edited *New Poems by American Poets* (1953; 2nd ed., 1957) and *Nine Thorny Thickets: Selected Poems of Dafydd Ap Gwilyn* (1970).

Perhaps as notable as his poetry was Humphries' work as a translator of classical literature. Combining his early training in the ancient languages with his poetic skills, he provided able translations of Virgil's *Aeneid* (1951), Ovid's *Metamorphoses* (1955), Juvenal's *Satires* (1958), Ovid's *Art of Love* (1958), Martial's *Selected Epigrams* (1963), and Lucretius' *The Way Things Are* (1968). Humphries died in Redwood City, Calif.

[See *Poetry*, Aug. 1930, Nov. 1937, June 1939, Aug. 1966, and July 1969. An obituary is in the *New York Times*, Apr. 24, 1969.]

DONALD F. TINGLEY

HUNTER, CROIL (Feb. 18, 1893–July 21, 1970), airline executive, was born in Casselton, N.Dak., the son of John Croil Hunter, a wholesale grocer, and Emma Schulze. His father, a Canadian immigrant of Scottish ancestry, built a thriving business in Fargo, N.Dak., where young Croil attended public school. He entered Yale in 1912 and left in 1914 without graduating. He returned home and worked in the credit department of his father's firm until he entered the army in 1917. He served overseas with the 338th Field Artillery, attaining the rank of captain. After his discharge in 1919, he was for nine years treasurer of his father's enterprise. On Feb. 24, 1923, he married Helen Floan; they had two children.

In 1928, Hunter became eastern representative and New York office manager of the First Bancredit Corporation, an installment loan affiliate of a Minnesota-based holding company. Two years later, the business interests with which Hunter had become associated acquired Northwest Airways, an airmail and passenger carrier with a 350-mile route from Minneapolis–St. Paul to Chicago and extensions to such places as Green Bay, Fargo, and Winnipeg. Although Hunter had no experience in aviation, his business acumen and familiarity with the territory in which the airline operated led to his being appointed traffic manager in 1932, followed by promotion to vice-president and general manager in 1933, the year in which the enterprise was reorganized as Northwest Airlines. Four years later he became president and general manager.

From the beginning of his association with Northwest, Hunter pursued an aggressive policy of new route acquisition, fleet expansion, and technological innovation. By the end of 1933, the company's route system stretched to Seattle and Tacoma, Wash. In 1934 it became the first airline to operate the Lockheed L-10A Electra, setting a speed record on the Twin Cities–Chicago route. Still newer, faster, and larger planes were added later in the decade.

Hunter, however, had larger goals in mind, laying plans to connect the American Midwest with a number of Asian destinations by following the "Great Circle Route" via Alaska. In 1939, Northwest applied to the Civil Aeronautics Board (CAB) for a route from Chicago to Calcutta via Seattle, Fairbanks, and points in Siberia and China. Shortly thereafter, having personally taken part in a survey flight to the Far East via the Great Circle, Hunter filed an amended application with the CAB for a route from Seattle to Tokyo via Anchorage and the Aleutian Islands. At the same time, he tried to elevate Northwest to transcontinental status by seeking CAB approval for flights from the Midwest to New York City.

United States entry into World War II temporarily sidetracked Hunter's expansionist efforts but soon brought Northwest opportunities that solidified its claims to postwar preferment. Under a contract with the armed services' Ferrying Command, the airline established military supply routes from Minneapolis–St. Paul and Seattle to various Alaskan destinations. By the end of the war, Northwest pilots had flown approximately 21 million miles transporting military personnel and cargo and had gained indispensable experience coping with adverse weather and difficult terrain. In addition, the company conducted government-sponsored research in high-altitude flying and aircraft deicing, and operated plants at St. Paul and at Vandalia, Ohio, to modify bombers for cold-weather performance. In 1943, Northwest renewed efforts to secure postwar routes to such destinations as Peking, Shanghai, Calcutta, and Manila.

The return of peace brought fulfillment to many of Hunter's visions. Even before the end of the war, the CAB granted Northwest a route from Milwaukee to New York, making it (along with United, Trans-World Airlines, and American) the fourth transcontinental air carrier. In September 1946 the Great Circle Route mapped out by Hunter before the war began to materialize when Northwest inaugurated commercial service from Seattle to Anchorage, followed by flights from Chicago to Anchorage via Edmonton in January 1947. In July 1947, following survey flights in which Hunter personally took part, Northwest began service from the Twin Cities and Seattle to Tokyo, Seoul, Shanghai, and Manila, with stops at Edmonton, Anchorage, and Shemya on the westernmost fringe of the Aleutians. Within the next few years, service began to Okinawa, Honolulu, and Hong Kong, while Taipei on the island of Formosa (Taiwan) was substituted for Shanghai after Communist forces took control of the Chinese mainland. At home, new routes were won to Pittsburgh and Washington, D.C.

While these route accessions took place, Northwest continued to expand and modernize its fleet, adding four-engine Douglas DC-4's in 1946 and Boeing 377 Stratocruisers in 1949. The latter, with a range of 4,600 miles, were particularly well suited to Northwest's transcontinental and Great Circle routes. The company was also the first to use a postwar twin-engine passenger plane, the Martin 2-0-2, though the aircraft proved accident-prone because of a structural deficiency in the wing.

Northwest's experience in flying the Great Circle proved its value after the outbreak of the Korean War in June 1950. The company flew approximately 13 million miles of airlift operations for the Military Air Transport Service, transporting 40,000 military personnel and 12 million pounds of cargo while maintaining its regularly scheduled commercial service. One of Northwest's planes, a Douglas DC-3, was also acquired by the United Nations and gained fame as "UN-99," shuttling wounded servicemen and military cargo between Japan and Korea.

In 1953, Hunter resigned the presidency of

Northwest and became chairman of the board. Hunter retired from the board chairmanship in 1965 but continued to be active in company affairs until his death in St. Paul.

Hunter was described in his prime as "wiry, energetic, as friendly as the dogs he slightly pampers, as casual as the snap-brim hat he wears." *Business Week* commented in 1947 that "the growth of Northwest Airlines from a regional air carrier is strictly the history of Croil Hunter's association with the company." Hunter's enduring legacy is the role he played in the development of the Great Circle Route, which greatly reduced flying time from New York, Chicago, and many other American and Canadian cities to the Far East. It was due to Hunter's tireless efforts that the airline he led became familiarly known by the name that was for many years emblazoned on its distinctively red-tailed planes: Northwest Orient.

[Documentary materials covering his years with Northwest are in the company's records, now in the possession of the Minnesota Historical Society at St. Paul. An article about Hunter is in *Business Week*, July 19, 1947. On the history of Northwest during Hunter's association with the company, see R. E. G. Davies, *A History of the World's Airlines* (1964), *Airlines of the United States Since 1914* (1972), and "Northwest by East: The Story of Northwest Orient Airlines," *Exxon Air World*, 23 (1970); Stephen E. Mills, *More than Meets the Sky* (1972); Kenneth Ruble, *Flight to the Top* (1986); and Bill Yenne, *Northwest Orient* (1986). Obituaries are in the *St. Paul Dispatch*, July 22, 1970; and the *Minneapolis Tribune* and the *New York Times*, both July 23, 1970.]

W. David Lewis

HUNTON, GEORGE KENNETH (Mar. 24, 1888–Nov. 11, 1967), lawyer, editor, and civil rights activist, was born in Claremont, N.H., the son of George P. Hunton, a small businessman, and Elizabeth Dugan. He attended public schools in Claremont until 1904, when his family moved to New York City and his father went into the real estate business. Hunton finished his last two years of high school at Holy Cross Preparatory School and entered Holy Cross College in 1906. After only a year as an undergraduate, he began the study of law at Fordham University. He graduated in 1910 with an LL.B. and soon thereafter was admitted to the New York State bar.

As a part of a tiny Roman Catholic minority in a Protestant town, Hunton felt the sting of religious prejudice at an early age. At Fordham, Hunton came under the influence of Father Terence Shealy, a liberal Jesuit and social scientist, who nudged him toward social action. From 1912 to 1915, Hunton worked for the Legal Aid Society in Harlem, on Manhattan's Lower East Side, and in Brooklyn. This work acquainted him with the most acute problems of the industrial city. In Brooklyn, in 1915, he started a private legal practice, which was interrupted by a brief stint in the army at Scott Field in Illinois during World War I. Discharged in early 1919, Hunton returned to New York. He became an ardent supporter of the League of Nations, and his advocacy of the world organization and his activities for a group called Woodrow Wilson Democracy brought him and several other like-minded individuals an invitation to visit the White House in October 1920 to discuss the League of Nations. Saddened by the failure of the United States Senate to approve membership in the world body, and by the general course of politics in the 1920's, he did not become deeply involved in social action again until the 1930's.

In 1931, Father John La Farge offered Hunton a job as executive secretary of a fund-raising committee for the Cardinal Gibbons Institute, a secondary school for blacks that the priest had founded near Ridge, Md., in 1924. La Farge, an editor of the influential Catholic weekly *America*, became perhaps the foremost Catholic clergyman in the field of civil rights in the era preceding the Supreme Court's decision in *Brown* v. *Board of Education of Topeka* (1954). In 1934, La Farge took the lead in forming the Catholic Interracial Council (CIC) of New York, the first such council of its kind. Hunton became the first executive secretary of the CIC and the editor of its official journal, the *Interracial Review*. For the next three decades Hunton wedded himself to the task of advancing blacks within the Catholic church and in society at large.

As executive secretary of the CIC, Hunton's primary aims were to educate Catholics about the oppression of blacks and to inform his coreligionists about the glaring discrepancy between Catholic theory and Catholic practice toward blacks. This approach was premised on his belief that ignorance about blacks accounted for racial prejudice and that ignorance about the true teachings of the church explained the discontinuity between Catholic ideals and Catholic realities. A rather blunt man with a bit of a temper, Hunton boldly broke the calculated silence of the Roman Catholic church on black-white relations. He pointed out that most Catholic schools, seminaries, hospitals, and social clubs excluded blacks. In defining Catholic doctrine on race relations, Hunton stressed the theological maxim that all men were one in the Mystical Body of Christ; for moral precepts he constantly referred to the papal encyclicals *Rerum Novarum* (1891) and *Quadragesimo Anno* (1931).

The *Interracial Review* served as Hunton's principal weapon. Within a decade it became a kind of national clearinghouse of information for the Roman Catholic church. Numerous Catholic periodicals fed upon it and spread its message widely. In 1944, the Swedish economist Gunnar Myrdal, author of *An American Dilemma* (1944), ranked the *Interracial Review* third in importance among race-relations journals, behind *Crisis* and *Opportunity*.

Hunton's activities went beyond strictly Catholic concerns. In the 1930's he crusaded for a federal antilynching bill. In the 1940's he worked for the creation of a permanent Fair Employment Practices Committee in Congress and testified on the issue before a Senate committee in 1945. During World War II and after, as a member of the Advisory Committee on Human Relations, established by the New York City Board of Education, he was a major force in setting up community-action programs. One of his most valuable contributions was to help foster better relations between the Catholic church and other churches and agencies. He and Father La Farge particularly courted black leaders, many of whom were initially hostile toward, or suspicious of, the church. The CIC established cordial working relations with the National Association for the Advancement of Colored People (NAACP), the Urban League, and the March-on-Washington movement of A. Philip Randolph. In 1955 the NAACP selected Hunton to be a member of its national board of directors.

Hunton and La Farge both retired from the CIC on Feb. 11, 1962. Both men deserve substantial credit for the fact that by this date the Catholic church had become a vital force in the civil rights movement. On June 4, 1962, a large number of notables in the movement honored La Farge and Hunton at a banquet in New York, with Mayor Robert F. Wagner as the featured speaker. For the occasion President John F. Kennedy sent a long telegram that lauded the persistent and selfless work of the "beloved priest and the dedicated lawyer." In August 1963 Hunton mustered enough strength to participate in the famous March on Washington. In 1965 he went suddenly and totally blind. Two years later he died in Brooklyn. He never married.

[Many of Hunton's papers are in the archives of the Catholic Interracial Council of New York; at Catholic University in Washington, D.C.; and among the John La Farge Papers at Georgetown University in Washington, D.C. Hunton's autobiography (as told to Gary McEoin) is *All of Which I Saw, Part of Which I Was* (1967). The autobiography of John La Farge, *The Manner Is Ordinary* (1954), sheds considerable light on Hunton and the CIC.

No scholarly work deals comprehensively with Hunton or the CIC. The best studies available are Marilyn Wenzke Nickels, "The Federated Colored Catholics" (Ph.D. diss., Catholic University, 1975); and Martin A. Zielinski, "The Promotion of Better Race Relations: The Catholic Interracial Council of New York, 1934–1945" (M.A. thesis, Catholic University, 1985). See also Warren G. Bovee, "His Brother's Keeper," *Today*, May 1958; "Bravo George Hunton!" *America*, Feb. 10, 1962; and "George K. Hunton R.I.P.," *America*, Nov. 25, 1967. An obituary is in the *New York Times*, Nov. 13, 1967.]

DAVID SOUTHERN

HURLEY, JOSEPH PATRICK (Jan. 21, 1894–Oct. 30, 1967), Roman Catholic clergyman, was born in Cleveland, Ohio, the son of Michael Hurley, an Irish immigrant steelworker, and Anna Durkin. Hurley attended St. Ignatius College (high school) and John Carroll University, from which he received a B.A. in 1915. He attended St. Bernard Seminary in Rochester, N.Y., from 1915 to 1916 and St. Mary's Seminary in Cleveland from 1916 to 1919, and was ordained a priest on May 29, 1919.

Hurley was an assistant pastor at the churches of St. Columba in Youngstown, Ohio, from 1919 to 1923; St. Philomena in East Cleveland from 1923 to 1925; and the Immaculate Conception in Cleveland from 1925 to 1927. In 1927 a fellow Cleveland priest, Edward A. Mooney (later cardinal archbishop of Detroit), who had been appointed the apostolic delegate to India the year before, asked Hurley to be his secretary. After diplomatic and language studies at the University of Toulouse, France, Hurley served with Mooney in India (1928–1931) and Japan (1931–1933). With Mooney's reassignment, Hurley was named chargé d'affaires of the apostolic delegation in Japan (1933–1934). Next, he served as attaché to the Papal Secretariat of State in Vatican City (1934–1940).

Hurley began another phase of his career on Aug. 19, 1940, when he was appointed the sixth bishop of the Diocese of St. Augustine, Fla.; he was consecrated in Rome on Oct. 6, 1940, and installed in St. Augustine Cathedral on Nov. 26, 1940. Hurley's episcopal motto, Virtus in arduis ("Virtue in the midst of difficulties"), aptly describes his episcopacy, which can be divided into four periods: diocesan reorganization with few resources (1940–1945); papal diplomacy in Yugoslavia and during Florida's postwar boom (1945–1950); the Florida Catholic population explosion (1950–1958); and the diocesan split and the Second Vatican Council (1958–1967).

At first Hurley faced a lack of diocesan organization and a poverty of financial and personnel resources, a situation aggravated by the wartime influx of servicemen into South Florida. Hurley responded with characteristic vigor and imagination by recruiting priests from other regions, by instituting an annual Catholic Charities Drive, and by boldly announcing a $1.5 million fund drive for the construction of Mercy Hospital in Miami.

On Oct. 22, 1945, Hurley was again called to Vatican diplomatic service, this time as regent of the Apostolic Nunciature in Yugoslavia. While carrying on delicate negotiations for the protection of Catholics there, Hurley continued to administer the postwar affairs of his Florida diocese, including the construction of thirteen new churches and twelve new parish schools. Hurley's Yugoslavian experience, especially the 1946 trial of Archbishop (later Cardinal) Aloysius Stepinac for collaboration with the Nazis, strengthened his ecclesiastical sense, his opposition to Communism, and his distaste for priests in religious orders. (Few such priests were admitted into his diocese, even though they and their skills could have been used.) In appreciation of his services in Yugoslavia, Pope Pius XII named Hurley a titular archbishop (an honorary title) in August 1949. When his Vatican diplomatic service ended in 1950, he returned to his diocese.

The third phase of Hurley's episcopacy (1950–1958) was characterized by a 165 percent increase in the Catholic population of his diocese. In response, Hurley established the Diocesan Development Fund (1950) to fuel institutional construction. He promoted Catholic parochial and centralized secondary education, the aggressive recruitment of candidates for the priesthood from Florida (as well as men and women from Ireland), and the erection of twenty-five churches and thirty-nine parochial schools. Hurley's most enduring contribution was his foresighted Florida real estate purchases for future ecclesiastical development.

Hurley was disturbed by the loss of one-third of his jurisdiction with the creation of the Diocese of Miami in 1958. At stake were territory, people, property, assets, and personnel. Hurley and the bishop of Miami, Coleman F. Carroll, wrestled for seven years over the matter, until it was settled by a papal commission in 1965. The Second Vatican Council, which Hurley attended, provided a challenge to his episcopal self-conception. But, as in the case of the interdiocesan controversy, he accepted its authoritative decisions with equanimity. As a result of the limitations imposed by the 1958 split and the changes created by Vatican II, Hurley in the last phase of his episcopacy redirected his energies and rekindled his interest in history. In 1965–1966 he refurbished his cathedral, constructed a new rectory, erected a mission church and a memorial cross at a historic site in St. Augustine, and sponsored a scholarly symposium on the Spanish Borderlands. He died in Orlando, Fla.

Archbishop Hurley was an eloquent public speaker but was uncomfortable around people; the laity rarely saw him. Although jealous of his authority and a hard taskmaster, he earned the respect of his priests by his churchmanship and his loyalty to them as individuals. As a builder, organizer, educator, and visionary who was ever dedicated to the welfare of the church, he left an indelible mark on the character of Florida Catholicism.

[Hurley's official correspondence is in the archives of the Diocese of St. Augustine, Fla. Incidental information on him can be found in the Edward A. Mooney correspondence at the archives of the Archdiocese of Detroit, the Francis P. Keogh and Lawrence J. Shehan correspondence at the Archives of the Archdiocese of Baltimore, as well as in the official records of the Diocese of Cleveland.

There is presently no published work on Hurley, but material about him may be found in Michael J. Hynes, *History of the Diocese of Cleveland* (1953); Richard Pattee, *The Case of Cardinal Aloysius Stepinac* (1953); Bernard Brassard, *Biographical and Heraldic Dictionary of the Catholic Bishops of America*, II (1960); Joseph B. Code, *Dictionary of the American Hierarchy* (1964); Lawrence Cardinal Shehan, *A Blessing of Years* (1982); and Michael J. McNally, *Catholicism in South Florida, 1868–1968* (1984). Obituaries are in the *New York Times*, Oct. 31, 1967; and in the *Catholic Universe Bulletin* and the *Florida Catholic*, both Nov. 3, 1967.]

MICHAEL J. MCNALLY

HURST, FANNIE (Oct. 19, 1889–Feb. 23, 1968), novelist, was born in Hamilton, Ohio, the daughter of Samuel Hurst, the owner of a small shoe factory, and Rose Koppel, both of whom came from German Jewish families. Hurst grew up in St. Louis, Mo. She noticed quite early that no one in her house ever read a book or attended a lecture or concert. She decided that words were "my colored hands, my bright beads, my hummingbirds." A lonely, isolated, fat girl, Hurst knew pity, mercy, and compassion; she was drawn to people en masse, who became her surrogate for family love. In 1901 she was sent to Harperly Hall, a private high school, which she hated; she then transferred to Central High School, graduating in 1905. After graduating in 1909 from Washington University in St. Louis, she fell in love with a young Russian Jewish pianist, Jacques Danielson, and moved to New York City. There she apparently wrote constantly; worked briefly in department stores, restaurants, and the like; and yearned to know New York. "The crowded East Side swarmed through my mind," she recalled. "Silhouettes . . . interiors of tenements . . . people becoming persons." Always she compared what was with what could be.

By chance Hurst met Bob Davis, the managing editor of several Munsey-owned magazines. In 1910 she sold human-interest sketches to the *New York Times* and *Smith's* magazine. She also was given a bit part as a fat girl in David Belasco's *The Music Master*. In 1911 she sold some stories to Davis for $30 each; the next year she sold "Power and Horse Power" for $300 to the *Saturday Evening Post*, which by 1914 had published twenty of her stories. In 1917 she was paid $1,200 for a story by the *Post*, $1,400 by *Metropolitan*, and $5,000 by *Cosmopolitan*. Within a few years Hurst had become a supreme example of the "success story," an inspiration for all young writers; she preached sincerity and sacrifice ("Work, dig, sweat—then you'll get what you want"). Her ability to publicize and dramatize her own writing was matched by hard work, perseverance, and sensitivity.

In May 1920 it was discovered that Hurst and Danielson had been married since May 6, 1914. What was unusual was that they maintained separate names, friends, and apartments, and had to call each other for appointments. (They had no children.) For a while the story caused a sensation and brought her a good deal of notoriety, but she soon won back her audience.

In her later years, Hurst moved from writer to artist, social critic, and reformer, involving herself in issues of war and peace, racial discrimination, poverty in America, and women's rights. She campaigned for Franklin D. Roosevelt, served in the New York Urban League, was a delegate to the World Health Organization in Geneva in 1952, and served as vice-president of the Authors' Guild in 1937, 1944–1946, and 1947. As she told Harry Salpeter in 1931, "I am passionately anxious to awake in people in general a sensitiveness to small people."

Every author knows, Hurst wrote in 1923, that stories that do not appeal to women will not be read. Most of her stories deal with women in nontraditional roles. Her working women, often nineteen or twenty years old, are usually trusting orphans who fall in love with the wrong man. Well-dressed, skilled with a needle, and hardworking, these women are ultimately rewarded, in spite of their choices. Typically there is a heroine, her confidante, and a Mr. Wrong and a Mr. Right. In one variation the heroine chooses marriage over career; in another she chooses a career but is intent on marrying off her daughter. Always the message is, Love is all. On occasion she wrote about exceptional women, as in the short stories "Give This Little Girl a Hand" and "Candy Butcher."

Hurst's novels, from *Star-Dust: The Story of an American Girl* (1921) to *Fool—Be Still* (1964), indicate a measure of experiment and growth. *Star-Dust* features the first of her career woman. *Lummox* (1923), a social melodrama, exposes the hardships confronting domestic workers. *A President Is Born* (1928) deals with the problems of a president, *Five and Ten* (1929) describes the corrosive effects of success, and *Appassionata* (1926) presents a religious heroine faced with the need to choose between an affair and a stable relationship. *Back Street* (1931), filmed three times, describes a woman who is mistress to a married man for over twenty years. *Imitation of Life* (1933), twice made into a film, reverses the situation, choices, and decisions: Bea Pullman, who loses her lover to her daughter, finds solace in work.

In all, Hurst wrote eighteen novels, an autobiography, and more than 400 short stories, plays, movie scripts, and articles. She also had her own radio and television shows. In the 1920's she and F. Scott Fitzgerald were the two most highly paid short-story writers in America. Often derided as the "sob sister" of American fiction, she acknowledged her preoccupation with the theme of women suffering for love. In 1925, asked to state her credo, she replied, "I care passionately about people . . . when I think of my work I like to contemplate it in terms of plowing through the troubled and troubling scenes and getting said some of this sublimity of the human race."

Hurst's novels and stories were passionately attacked and defended. Although into the 1940's all of her books sold well, her status as a writer is uncertain. A formulaic and sentimental writer, Hurst will be remembered for her portrayal of women and their conflicts in the first half of the century, and for the great range of characters who embody those attitudes and struggles. Hurst held her own life up to the mirror and thereby enlarged the range of possibilities for women. She challenged several generations of women to go and do likewise. Hurst died in New York City.

[The Fannie Hurst Collection, in the Humanities Research Center, University of Texas at Austin, is the central and most essential source for all Hurst studies. Also useful, but of limited value, are the Fannie Hurst Papers, in the Olin Library of Washington University, St. Louis, and the Fannie Hurst Danielson Estate, in the Goldfarb Library at Brandeis University.

Hurst's eighteen novels are *Star-Dust* (1921); *Lummox* (1923); *Mannequin* (1926); *Appassionata* (1926); *A President Is Born* (1928); *Five and Ten* (1929); *Back Street* (1931); *Imitation of Life* (1933); *Anitra's Dance* (1934); *Great Laughter* (1936); *Lonely Parade* (1942); *Hallelujah* (1944); *The Hands of Veronica* (1947); *Anywoman* (1950); *The Man with One Head* (1953); *Family!* (1960); *God Must Be Sad* (1961); and *Fool—Be Still* (1964). Her eight short-story collections are *Just Around the Corner* (1914); *Every Soul Hath Its Song* (1916); *Gaslight Sonatas* (1918); *Humoresque* (1919); *The Vertical City* (1922); *Song of Life* (1927); *Procession* (1929); and *We Are Ten* (1937). Many of her stories and almost all her articles and interviews are uncollected.

The best sources for information about Hurst's life and work are Mary Rose Shaughnessy, *Myths About Love and Women: The Fiction of Fannie Hurst* (1980); and Cynthia Brandimarte, "Fannie Hurst and Her Fiction: Prescriptions for America's Working Women" (Ph.D. diss., University of Texas, 1980). Also useful is Hurst's autobiography, *Anatomy of Me* (1958). Bibliographies in both Shaughnessy and Brandimarte are exceedingly helpful; a list of films based on Hurst's novels and stories is included in Shaughnessy. An obituary is in the *New York Times*, Feb. 24, 1968.]

DANIEL WALDEN

JACKSON, CHARLES REGINALD (Apr. 6, 1903–Sept. 21, 1968), novelist and short-story writer, was born in Summit, N.J., the son of Frederick George Jackson, who left the family when the boy was ten, and Sarah Williams. When he was three, his family moved to Newark, Wayne County, N.Y., where Jackson graduated from high school in 1921. Throughout his life Jackson was a voracious reader, with a special fondness for Shakespeare, to whom he grew to bear a striking resemblance.

Jackson attended Syracuse University for one year, probably in 1922. In 1925–1926 he found employment with Krock's bookstore in Chicago and then with the Doubleday bookstores in New York City. After contracting tuberculosis in 1927, he sought treatment in a sanitarium in Allenwood, Pa., and then, from October 1929 through July 1931, in Davos, Switzerland, to which he had been attracted after reading Thomas Mann's *The Magic Mountain*. In 1931, after a year on the Riviera, he returned to the United States.

Jackson's career as an author began in 1936 when he was employed by Max Wylie as a staff writer for the Columbia Broadcasting System (CBS). On Mar. 4, 1938, he married Rhoda Booth, an associate editor for *Fortune* magazine; they had two children. The period from 1939, when he resigned from CBS, to 1944 was especially productive for Jackson. As a freelance writer, he contributed works to the "Columbia Workshop" radio program, among them two original plays, *Dress Rehearsal* and *The Giant's Share*, and several adaptations, including *A Letter from Home*, *The Devil and Daniel Webster*, *Outward Bound*, and *Jane Eyre*. He also wrote for Max Wylie's soap opera "Sweet River," taught scriptwriting at New York University, and had his first short story, "Palm Sunday," published in *Partisan Review* in 1939.

Jackson's first novel, *The Lost Weekend*, was published in January 1944. The story of an alcoholic, Don Birnam, on a five-day binge, the novel gained the attention and praise of reviewers for its sensational subject, precision of detail, and artful presentation. Philip Wylie, in the *New York Times* (Jan. 30, 1944), called it "the most compelling gift to the literature of addiction since De Quincey," and A. C. Spectorsky, in the *Chicago Sun Book Week* (Jan. 30, 1944), praised Jackson's masterful handling of "stream of consciousness, mind wandering, twisted recollection, and alcoholic delirium." With his novel a best-seller, Jackson was able to purchase a spacious house in Orford, N.H., where he lived until 1954, when he moved to Sandy Hook, Conn. In 1945, Paramount released a movie version of *The Lost Weekend*, starring Ray Milland. The film received four Academy Awards, including one for best picture.

Jackson's second novel, *The Fall of Valor* (1946), was the story of an unhappily married professor who develops a homosexual attraction to a marine captain. This novel was less successful than his first—perhaps, as some reviewers noted, because public taste required deleterious compromises in the development of the subject.

From the mid-1940's through the mid-1960's, Jackson struggled with writer's block, recurring lung disease, and alcoholism. His friend Dorothea Straus described his violent mood swings and the existence of "many Charles Jacksons," including "the warm proud father, the occasionally companionable husband, the unbridled alcoholic, the famous author, the clown, the irrepressible homosexual."

Jackson's third novel, *The Outer Edges* (1948), deals with the murder of two girls by a mentally deficient seventeen-year-old boy. During this period Jackson also wrote short fiction for *Mademoiselle*, *Collier's*, the *New Yorker*, *Esquire*, and *McCall's*. These and other stories were collected in two volumes, *The Sunnier Side* (1950) and *Earthly Creatures* (1953). The stories in the first volume are set in Arcadia, a fictional town based on the Newark, N.Y., of the early years, during the youth of Don Birnam. The title story was written as a reply to charges that Jackson neglected the sunnier side of life. Unified by the character of Birnam and by the theme of sexual awakening in a small town, the collection has been favorably compared to Sherwood Anderson's *Winesburg, Ohio*.

In 1965, with an advance from Macmillan, Jackson took an apartment in New York City's Chelsea Hotel, where he completed his last novel, *A Second-Hand Life* (1967). Like his other novels, it was a sensitive treatment of a sensational subject. The story of a sexually compulsive woman and an intimacy-avoiding man who had been friends since their childhoods in Arcadia, the book became a best-seller. In the *Saturday Review* (Aug. 12, 1967), Granville Hicks said that Jackson had written yet "another novel that, without being a literary masterpiece, deserves to be taken seriously." Hicks's view reflects the general critical estimate of Jackson's works. Although Jackson has received little attention from academic critics and literary historians, he is remembered for his frank yet sympathetic portrayals of tormented characters. Jackson died in New York City, apparently from a suicidal overdose of sleeping pills.

[See bibliography by Shirley Leonard, *Bulletin of Bibliography*, 1971; and *Serif*, Fall 1973, which includes recollections by Dorothea Straus and Max Wylie and a bibliography by Leonard. Jackson's books are listed in Dean H. Keller, *First Printings of American Authors* (1978). An obituary is in the *New York Times*, Sept. 22, 1968.]

CRAIG ABBOTT

JACOBS, HIRSCH (Apr. 8, 1904–Feb. 13, 1970), horse trainer and breeder and stable owner, was born in New York City, the son of a poor immigrant tailor and his wife. Shortly after Jacobs' birth, the family moved to the East New York section of Brooklyn. There, at the age of twelve, he began to race pigeons. He showed a remarkable ability to identify and remember racers.

Jacobs graduated from public school at thirteen and worked briefly as a pipe fitter.

Through the brother of his boss, Charlie Ferraro, he received an introduction to the world of horse racing. While still in his teens, he used money saved from wagers on pigeon races to buy his first horse, and on Dec. 29, 1926, he saddled his first winner at Pompano, Fla., a horse named Reveillon. Two years later he formed a partnership with Isidor ("Beebee") Bieber, who had made a fortune gambling. The union, which lasted for some thirty years, grew until the Bieber-Jacobs Stable owned more than 200 horses at locations throughout the country. In 1933, despite the Great Depression, Jacobs married Ethel Dushock, the daughter of a wealthy manufacturer; they had three children.

Jacobs became recognized for his ability to choose little-known, ailing, or otherwise undesirable horses and fashion them into winners. Especially noted for his "voodoo veterinarian" abilities, he used a wide variety of unorthodox remedies to treat injured horses. Jacobs was also renowned for his uncanny ability to take losing horses and make winners of them. Jacobs dismissed his immense success by saying, "Anyone can train a horse. But to win you've got to have a horse that's in shape. That's the only secret there is."

Unlike many of the great racehorse trainers, Jacobs owned and bred his own horses. He believed that horses that competed regularly were less likely to become injured than were horses that trained for extended periods and raced only occasionally. Accordingly, he raced his horses often. He also liked to buy cheap horses and "run them like a fleet of taxicabs." The tactics succeeded, and Jacobs became the winningest trainer in American history. During his forty-three years as an active trainer, he saddled a total of 3,569 winners. His most important horse was Stymie, a puny, awkward-looking animal that he bought for $1,500 and that won stakes totaling $918,485. In 1936, Jacobs' best year, his trainees won 177 of the 632 races entered. In addition to his special training and racing methods, Jacobs was considered in a class by himself when it came to equine psychology. He could rehabilitate losers, calm notoriously skittish animals, and invariably get the best out of horses.

By the time illness forced Jacobs into retirement in 1966, he had become the darling of the $2 bettors. He successfully challenged millionaire scions of the turf at their own game and, in so doing, made a fortune. He enjoyed his wealth, purchasing a Forest Hills mansion and owning a succession of green Cadillacs, one of his many superstitions. He always ran his horses in salmon pink and emerald green silks, and when his horses were on a winning streak, he would wear the same suit for weeks on end. The "reduction" of the Bieber-Jacobs Stable, when the partners sold their holdings in five separate offerings, was what many considered the ultimate testament to his abilities as a trainer. The high prices paid indicated that the public at large recognized that Jacobs was perhaps the finest judge of horseflesh of his day.

Although Jacobs never won America's biggest race, the Kentucky Derby, horses he trained collected purses totaling $15,340,354, according to calculations prepared at the time of his retirement. He died in Miami, Fla.

[Articles on Jacobs' career include "Head of the Horse Factory," *Time*, Apr. 11, 1960; Howard M. Tuckner, "Man with Horse Sense," *New York Times Magazine*, May 21, 1961; and Gerald Holland, "Sex, Slaughter and Smoke!" *Sports Illustrated*, June 26, 1961. See also Frank Litsky, *Superstars* (1975). An obituary is in the *New York Times*, Feb. 14, 1970.]

JAMES A. CASADA

JENSEN, BENTON FRANKLIN ("BEN") (Dec. 16, 1892–Feb. 5, 1970), United States congressman, was born in Marion, Iowa, the son of Martin Jensen, a drainage-tile ditchdigger, and Gertrude Anna Andersen, both emigrants from Denmark. In March 1900 the family moved to a 200-acre farm in Audubon County, Iowa, near the center of the largest rural settlement of Danes in the United States. Here Jensen attended a one-room school and assisted with the farm work. As his father's health deteriorated, responsibility for operating the farm fell to Jensen and his brother Oskar. The work proved too heavy, and when Jensen was fifteen, his father sold the farm and bought a small acreage on the outskirts of the nearby town of Exira, Iowa. After completing the ninth grade, Jensen dropped out of school and worked as a ditchdigger, a store clerk, a farmhand, and a button cutter.

In March 1914 Jensen went to work as a yardman and bookkeeper for the Green Bay Lumber Company in Exira. Two years later he was promoted, and traveled from town to town in the Midwest to fill in for managers who were ill or on vacation. On Dec. 13, 1917, he married Charlotte E. Hadden. They had one child. During World War I Jensen was a second lieutenant in the army and served most of his tour at Camp Pike, Ark. Following his discharge in December 1918 he returned to Exira and the retail lumber business. Appointed manager of the local Green Bay yard in 1919, he held that position for the next nineteen years. He helped organize the local post of the American Legion and later served as county and district commander.

In 1938 Jensen entered the Republican primary for Iowa's Seventh District congressional seat. He finished second in an inconclusive six-man race but won the nomination at the party convention on the thirty-seventh ballot. The popular Democratic incumbent, Otha Wearin, had abandoned the office to make an unsuccessful bid for the Democratic senatorial nomination. Jensen won the general election, the first of thirteen consecutive victories in his congressional career.

To some, Jensen seemed out of place in Congress. He was not a great orator (he had a deep, nasal voice and read his speeches in a monotone) and seemed most comfortable in direct contact with the farmers and small-town residents of his Iowa district. He particularly enjoyed discussing political issues with schoolchildren. "The kids spread the word at home. You can make a lot of political hay that way," he told a reporter.

Although Jensen supported federal programs beneficial to his district—soil conservation and flood control, the farm program (particularly the soil bank), the Rural Electrification Administration (REA), and the establishment of the DeSoto Bend National Wildlife Refuge and Recreation Area along the Missouri River—his legislative philosophy was fiscally conservative. A self-proclaimed watchdog of the treasury, he attacked what he called the "socialistic pattern of excessive government spending." In 1942 he secured a seat on the powerful Appropriations Committee and eventually became its ranking Republican. He served as chairman of the Interior and Government Corporations subcommittees during the Republican-controlled Eightieth Congress (1947–1949) and later as the ranking minority member of four subcommittees—Interior; Deficiencies; Atomic Energy; and Public Works.

Beginning in 1950, Jensen sought, with varying degrees of success, to reduce the number of federal employees by attaching to appropriations bills the so-called Jensen amendment to prohibit the filling of three out of every four routine vacancies until overall federal employment had been cut by 10 percent. A frequent foe of public power, Jensen often criticized the Tennessee Valley Authority and projects such as Hell's Canyon Dam. Although he initially supported the Marshall Plan, his opposition to federal spending eventually turned him against most foreign-aid programs. Nor was he easily swayed by arguments for greatly increased military appropriations.

On Mar. 1, 1954, Jensen was one of five members of the House of Representatives wounded by four Puerto Rican extremists who opened fire upon the chamber from a visitors' gallery. Struck in the shoulder, he was not seriously injured. One of many conservative victims of the 1964 Democratic landslide, Jensen was defeated by John R. Hansen. Although he continued to maintain an apartment in Washington, D.C., he spent his summers in Exira, where he opened a small museum. He died in Washington, D.C.

[The Jensen papers are in the Special Collections Department, University of Iowa Libraries, Iowa City. Obituaries are in the *New York Times* and the *Des Moines Register*, both Feb. 6, 1970.]

PETER L. PETERSEN

JOHNSON, EDWIN CARL (Jan. 1, 1884–May 30, 1970), governor of Colorado and United States senator, was born on a farm near Scandia, Kans., the son of Nels Johnson, a farmer, and Annabelle Lunn. In 1888 his family moved to a cattle ranch in western Nebraska, and in 1903, Johnson graduated from high school in Lincoln. He then worked as a railroad section hand, telegrapher, and train dispatcher. On Feb. 17, 1907, he married Fern Claire Armitage; they had two children.

Seeking a cure for his tuberculosis, Johnson and his wife moved to Colorado in 1909 and lived for six months in a tent colony in Fountain, near Colorado Springs. In 1910 they homesteaded near Craig in northern Colorado. After regaining his health, Johnson taught school, managed a farmers' cooperative milling and elevator company, and operated a trucking firm. In 1922 he was elected as a Democrat to

Johnson

the Colorado House of Representatives, soon becoming a leader of the minority party. He served four terms between 1923 and 1931. From 1931 to 1933 he was lieutenant governor and confidential secretary to Governor William H. ("Billy") Adams.

Johnson was elected governor of Colorado in 1932. In the 1934 Democratic primary he defeated Josephine Roche, who was the manager and part owner of the Rocky Mountain Fuel Company and had the backing of the United Mine Workers, Franklin D. Roosevelt, and Edward P. Costigan, Colorado's liberal senator. He then won the general election.

Johnson's primary concern upon assuming office in 1933 was to reduce government expenses through reorganization and streamlining. He also called for tax reduction, civil service reform, highway construction, unemployment relief, penal reform, and constitutional revision. Although he accepted federal aid for Colorado, Johnson was a states'-rights advocate and resented federal interference. Throughout most of his two terms, he engaged in a bitter struggle with Harry Hopkins, who, as administrator of the Federal Emergency Relief Administration (FERA), refused federal funds for relief until the state legislature appropriated matching money. Johnson resented the fact that FERA spent state funds at its own discretion. He referred to Hopkins and the federal appointees who administered the relief program as "social workers full of theories on humane welfare of the parlor socialist type." Because of delays in getting projects started, Johnson became discontented with the Works Progress Administration (WPA), also headed by Hopkins, and engaged in constant battle with Paul D. Shriver, the man chosen as WPA administrator for Colorado. Johnson claimed that the administrator was filling positions with Costigan people. Although Johnson backed some New Deal programs, including the Civilian Conservation Corps and the National Recovery Administration, in 1944 he labeled the New Deal "the worst fraud ever perpetrated on the American people."

Johnson attracted national attention during the spring of 1936 when he declared martial law and sent the National Guard to the Colorado–New Mexico border to prevent migrant farm laborers from entering the state and competing with Coloradans for jobs. He was forced to lift the embargo a few days later in the face of widespread protest from farmers, sugar companies, and New Mexican officials.

In April 1936, Johnson announced his candidacy for the United States Senate after Costigan became ill and declined to seek reelection. Despite opposition by young liberals in the Democratic party, Johnson easily won the primary and then the general election, campaigning as an independent thinker who was not afraid to criticize the New Deal. "Big Ed," as Coloradans called him, won reelection in 1942 and again in 1948. He later claimed that his political success came from personal contact with constituents. "Principles and issues are fine," he said, "but they don't win elections."

Johnson established a record in the Senate as a maverick and a workhorse, exhibiting consummate political skill, though he rarely made speeches. He voted more than 50 percent of the time against administration programs, opposed a third and a fourth term for the president, and sided with isolationists. He opposed the nomination of both Frank Knox as secretary of the navy and Henry Stimson as secretary of war, calling them warmongering interventionists. Although Johnson voted against the lend-lease bill in 1941, he later called upon Americans to accept lend-lease and to support the president in his foreign policy.

During World War II, Johnson sponsored legislation granting pay raises and benefits to servicemen, supported agricultural programs, and opposed the Smith-Connally antistrike bill. After the war, Johnson voted for a volunteer army, increased benefits to veterans, the United Nations, and Bernard Baruch's plan for international control of atomic development. Nevertheless, he remained largely an isolationist, opposing military aid to foreign powers. He fought against the Truman Doctrine but voted for the Marshall Plan because it involved no military aid. He advocated using atomic weapons to end the war in Korea.

As a member of the Congressional Joint Committee on Atomic Energy, Johnson created a sensation in 1949 when, in a televised plea for tighter security, he revealed that United States scientists were working on a weapon 1,000 times more powerful than the bomb dropped on Nagasaki. This disclosure was considered a violation of security; it also led to a popular outcry against development of the hydrogen bomb. In 1950, Johnson again came to national attention when he introduced a bill requiring federal licensing of actors, actresses, producers, and distributors of films. He called his bill "a practical method whereby the mad dogs of the industry may be put on a leash to protect public morals." In 1954 he once more drew attention when he served as vice-chairman of the special Senate committee that investigated censure charges against Senator Joseph R. McCarthy. Johnson subsequently voted with the Senate majority to censure the Wisconsin senator. Rather than seek reelection to the Senate for a fourth term, Johnson, at his wife's request, returned to Colorado, where he served a third term as governor (1955–1957). He died in Denver.

[Johnson's gubernatorial papers are at the Colorado State Archives and Record Service. The majority of his senatorial papers were destroyed at his request. A small collection covering 1960–1970 is at the University of Colorado, Boulder. The best study of his political career is Patrick F. McCarty, "Big Ed Johnson of Colorado: A Political Portrait" (M.A. thesis, University of Colorado, 1958). See also James F. Wickens, *Colorado in the Great Depression* (1979). An obituary is in the *New York Times*, May 31, 1970.]

DARLIS A. MILLER

JOHNSON, LOUIS ARTHUR (Jan. 10, 1891–Apr. 24, 1966), lawyer and United States secretary of defense, was born in Roanoke, Va., the son of Marcellus A. Johnson, a grocery clerk, and Katherine Leftwich. Although Johnson's father lacked money and education, he pressed his son to work hard and get ahead. Johnson's maternal grandfather, a colonel in the Confederate army, encouraged Johnson to become a lawyer and a Virginia gentleman. After graduation from Roanoke High School, Johnson entered the University of Virginia in 1908 and received his LL.B. in 1912. Enormously ambitious and a natural leader, he cut a large figure on campus as a boxer and wrestler, public speaker, and president of his law class. Admitted to practice law in Clarksburg, W.Va., in 1913, he soon became a partner of Philip P. Steptoe. The firm of Steptoe and Johnson eventually established offices in Clarksburg and Charleston, W.Va., and Washington, D.C.

Johnson was elected in 1917 as a Democratic member of the West Virginia House of Delegates and was chosen as his party's floor leader. He joined the army during World War I and engaged in combat as a captain with the Eightieth Infantry Division; later, in the reserves, he attained the rank of colonel and was widely addressed thereafter as Colonel Johnson. He was discharged from the army in 1919, and in the following year he married Ruth Frances Maxwell, the daughter of a large landowner, cattle raiser, and founder of the Union National Bank of Charleston, W.Va. The couple had two children.

After resuming his law practice, Johnson became increasingly active in politics and in the American Legion. He took a large step forward in both areas when he was elected national commander of the organization for 1932 and 1933. In those days the position generated considerable political influence. It was at American Legion conventions, for example, that Johnson first met Harry S Truman. Johnson was able to help President Franklin D. Roosevelt ride out a storm from veterans' groups opposed to the administration's cut in veterans' pensions.

In 1937 a grateful Roosevelt appointed Johnson assistant secretary of war. Johnson was so hardworking and aggressive that he appeared to clash with Secretary of War Harry H. Woodring over the direction of the War Department. Nevertheless, Johnson was zealous about enlarging and modernizing the army. He was later credited with helping to prepare the army for America's entry into World War II. Johnson aspired to be secretary of war, but when Roosevelt ran for a third term in 1940, with war threatening to engulf the United States, the president wanted to give the administration a more bipartisan character. Thus, Roosevelt replaced Woodring with Henry L. Stimson, a distinguished Republican, who wanted to choose his own assistant secretary. Johnson resigned and became the president of the General Dyestuff Corporation, part of I. G. Farben Industrie, in which position he helped manage alien property. He also served as Roosevelt's personal representative to India, assisting in India's contribution to the Allied war effort.

A dramatic change in Johnson's career occurred in 1948 and 1949. When Truman ran for a full presidential term against Thomas E. Dewey in 1948, the president's chances, as reflected in public opinion polls, seemed so hopeless that he could not find anyone to head the Democratic finance committee. Johnson volunteered and collected enough money to get the president's campaign train from whistle-stop to whistle-stop. Truman astonished everyone by winning and felt deeply indebted to Johnson. Johnson lobbied for appointment as secretary of defense. The position had been created in 1947 when the War and Navy departments and the newly formed Department of the Air Force had been combined into a single establishment. The first and incumbent secretary of defense was James V. Forrestal, a Wall Street Republican. Democrats pressured Truman to replace Forrestal, but the question soon became academic because of Forrestal's deteriorating health. Truman nominated Johnson, who took over on Mar. 28, 1949. The Pentagon rarely knew another quiet moment for the next eighteen months.

When Johnson arrived, bitter interservice rivalries impeded efforts to unify the three main branches of the armed forces. The most pressing issue was the settlement of what mission the navy and the air force should play in air warfare. The navy had recently laid the keel for the supercarrier *United States* to ensure its role in strategic bombing. On the recommendation of the Joint Chiefs of Staff, however, Johnson abruptly canceled the supercarrier. Truman upheld the decision but was irritated by Johnson's abrasive methods. Johnson's support of land-based strategic air power produced an extraordinary reaction by the navy hierarchy—"the revolt of the admirals," it was called. Official documents supporting the navy's views were leaked to the press, and the entire navy high command paraded before stormy sessions of the House Armed Services Committee to denounce Johnson's policies.

Meanwhile, Truman became angry over Johnson's meddling in other departments. "Louis began to show an inordinate egotistical desire to run the whole government," said Truman, who shared a widely held opinion that Johnson was maneuvering for the 1952 Democratic presidential nomination. Johnson also feuded with Secretary of State Dean Acheson, partly because of the latter's Asian policy, which Johnson considered weak in the face of Communist challenges. By the time the Korean War began in 1950, Truman was faced with a situation in which his secretary of state and secretary of defense were barely on speaking terms. When Truman decided to appoint Thomas K. Finletter, a New York City attorney, as secretary of the air force, Johnson threatened to resign. Truman named Finletter and said Johnson could resign if he wished to. Johnson backed off. Truman then learned that Johnson had telephoned the Senate Republican leader, Robert A. Taft of Ohio, to compliment the senator for a speech in which he had demanded that Acheson resign. Truman's patience came to an end, and in September 1950 he insisted that Johnson sign a letter of resignation. "You are ruining me," Johnson protested. Truman named General of the Army George C. Marshall as secretary of defense. Johnson returned to his law practice and a quieter life. He died in Washington, D.C.

[William E. Miller, *You Can't Tell by Looking at 'Em* (1945), is the privately published memoir of the Steptoe and Johnson law firm. See *Time*, Aug. 22, 1938, and June 6, 1949; the diary of Eben A. Ayers, entry of Mar. 27, 1950, Harry S Truman Library, Independence, Mo.; President Truman's Longhand Notes File, Longhand Personal President's Secretary's File, Memoirs 1950, Folder, Box 33, Truman Library; and Robert J. Donovan. *Tumultuous Years* (1982). An obituary is in the *New York Times*, Apr. 25, 1966.]

ROBERT J. DONOVAN

JONES, ROBERT REYNOLDS ("BOB") (Oct. 30, 1883–Jan. 16, 1968), evangelist and college founder, was born in Skipperville in Dale County, Ala., the son of William Alexander Jones, a farmer, and Georgia Creel. His father told of his experiences in the Confederate army, particularly his leg injury at the Battle of Chickamauga Creek, and his involvement in such agricultural-lobby causes as the Farmers' Alliance. He named Bob both for the man who aided him after his war injury, Robert Reynolds, and for Jefferson Davis, but the middle name Davis was later dropped.

Jones's father required that he regularly memorize and recite to family supper guests long passages from the classics and other literature. One of Jones's first public addresses was an 1895 speech in defense of the Populist party. Other early speeches included his talks at the local Methodist church at Brannon's Stand, where the parishioners elected him Sunday-school superintendent when he was only twelve.

Soon Jones sought and received invitations to preach throughout his community in homes, schoolhouses, small country churches, and even "brush arbors." The Mt. Olive church at Brannon's Stand was the site of his first revival, and the twelve-year-old witnessed sixty conversions during the one-week meeting. At thirteen, he led a brush-arbor meeting that resulted in the establishment of a church of fifty-four members where he served as minister for about a year. The rotund youth (he weighed 150 pounds at age thirteen) became known locally as "the boy preacher." He received a license to preach from the Methodist Episcopal Church South when he was fifteen, and the next year, he accepted a call to the Headland Circuit of the Mariana District of the Alabama Conference, which included the church that he had founded and four others. Even as pastor, his emphasis was more that of an evangelist, and during his first year on that circuit, the churches gained more than 400 members by profession of faith.

During Jones's middle teenage years, both his parents died. He received a diploma from Kinsey High School in 1899 and, in 1901, he enrolled in Southern University in Greensboro, Ala. (now Birmingham Southern University), paying for three years of college from earnings as minister of small country churches and as a part-time revival preacher. He was a serious and hardworking student but ordinary in academic accomplishment. While at Southern, he met Bernice Sheffield, a student at nearby Judson College of Marion, Ala. They were married on Oct. 24, 1905, but his wife died from tuberculosis ten months later. They had no children.

Jones's career as a full-time evangelist spanned approximately the first quarter of the twentieth century. By sixteen, he was holding meetings throughout southern Alabama, and he spent his college summer vacations leading revivals in Louisiana. During a campaign in Uniontown, Ala., he met his second wife, Mary Gaston Stollenwerck. They married on June 17, 1908, and shortly thereafter moved to Birmingham, which was to be their home for nearly two decades. They had one child. Gradually he received invitations from larger and more-distant cities. By 1914 he was known as "the Billy Sunday of the South." In that period a typical campaign would be held in a 10,000-to-15,000-seat tabernacle with long pine-board seats, sawdust aisles, and a huge platform to accommodate a choir of up to 1,000 voices. By 1924, he had preached over 12,000 sermons in all the states and 30 foreign countries and counted over 15 million listeners and 300,000 converts. His meetings attracted a broad range of Protestants, but primarily Methodists and Baptists.

Jones preached not only the Christian Gospel but also against liquor, gambling, Catholicism, and Protestant liberalism. His preaching style was direct, dramatic, and self-assured and featured a folksy, down-home delivery. Except for Billy Sunday, he was probably the most significant American evangelist in the period between Dwight L. Moody and Billy Graham.

Jones's early career coincided with the movement toward secularization in higher education. During his revival tours, he became increasingly disturbed by the reports of Christian parents who had sent their children to supposedly trustworthy colleges only to have them lose their faith and/or purity. A solution, he believed, was to found a Christian college with a highly controlled intellectual and social environment. Accordingly, he opened Bob Jones College in St. Andrews, Fla., in 1926. For financial reasons, he moved the school to Cleveland, Tenn., in 1933; and in 1947, to provide for further growth, he relocated the school (renamed Bob Jones University) to its present site in Greenville, S.C.

Jones continued his evangelistic travels, promoting the college as well as the Gospel, and soon delegated much of the internal management of the school to his son, Bob Jones, Jr. When on campus, he spoke regularly in daily chapel to the student body, which grew from 88 in 1927 to 2,500 in 1947 and 4,000 by the 1960's. The chapel talks featured "preachy," even paternalistic, counsel that emphasized the values of hard work, obedience, loyalty, and Christian discipline.

Jones's institution identified itself as "the world's most unusual university," a phrase that reflected its tendency toward promotional overstatement. In certain respects, however, the institution has been unique. Perhaps no modern American college has as strongly opposed racial integration on religious grounds. Jones believed he found support for that belief and practice in Acts 17:26, which says that God "hath made of one blood all nations of men for to dwell on all the face of the earth, and hath determined . . . the bounds of their habitation." No school matched its combination of excellence in the fine arts and fervor in fundamentalism. During Jones's time, the institution was the largest college in America to give major emphasis to the training of students—especially his beloved "preacher boys"—who would seek to duplicate his emphasis upon "soul-saving." He died in Bob Jones University Hospital and is buried on the campus.

[Jones's books include *Comments on Here and Hereafter* (1942); and *Things I Have Learned: Chapel Talks by Bob Jones, Sr.* (1944). The best book on Jones's career is Melton Wright, *Fortress of Faith: The Story of Bob Jones University* (1960), which is much more autobiographical than most college and university histories. More completely focused upon biographical materials, particularly the evangelistic campaigns, is R. K. Johnson, *Builder of Bridges: The Biography of Dr. Bob Jones, Sr.* (1969). An obituary is in the *New York Times*, Jan. 17, 1968.]

WILLIAM C. RINGENBERG

JOPLIN, JANIS LYN (Jan. 19, 1943–Oct. 4, 1970), singer, was born in Port Arthur, Tex., the daughter of Seth Joplin, an engineer, and Dorothy East, the registrar of a Texas business college. Joplin had almost no musical training, although she sang in "a piping soprano" in her junior high school glee club. A voluminous reader interested in art and poetry, she felt alienated from her schoolmates and was attracted to beatniks and folk and blues singers such as Huddie ("Leadbelly") Ledbetter and Odetta.

After graduating from Thomas Jefferson High School in Port Arthur in 1960, Joplin enrolled at Lamar State College of Technology in Beaumont, Tex., and took courses at Port Arthur College. In the summer of 1961, she lived with an aunt in Los Angeles, worked as a keypunch operator for the Los Angeles Telephone Company, and discovered the beatnik community of Venice, Calif. That fall she returned to college in Texas but periodically visited beatnik communities in Houston. By then, she was experimenting with drugs and alcohol.

Joplin's first official singing engagement was at the Halfway House in Beaumont in 1961. She also sang at the Purple Onion in Houston and later at Threadgills in Austin, while she lived at the Ghetto, a run-down apartment house frequented by members of the counterculture. Often accompanying herself on an Autoharp, Joplin, backed by a bluegrass band, the Waller Creek Boys, sang songs popularized by Leadbelly, Bessie Smith, and Jean Ritchie. In 1962 she enrolled as a fine-arts major at the University of Texas at Austin, while deepening her involvement with drugs and music.

Humiliated after being voted "the ugliest man on campus," Joplin left the University of Texas in 1963 and hitchhiked with Chet Helms, a friend, to San Francisco, where she sang at coffeehouses. She spent the summer of 1964 on New York's Lower East Side, "shooting pool and speed," according to her biographer David Dalton, before returning to San Francisco. In June 1965 she registered as a sociology major at Lamar State College and considered marriage and a settled life in Texas. But Chet Helms, by then a successful rock promoter in San Francisco, suggested her as lead singer for a new rock group—later known as Big Brother and the Holding Company—and Joplin made her final break with middle-class respectability. Her first appearance with the group was in June 1966 at the Avalon Ballroom in San Francisco. She later called it "the most thrilling time in my life . . . all that rhythm and power. I got stoned just feeling it, like it was the best dope in the world."

The group signed with Mainstream Records and made an album released after their success in June 1967 at the Monterey International Pop Festival in Monterey, Calif., where Joplin was an enormous success singing "Love Is Like a Ball and Chain." While not primarily a rock singer, Joplin used her blues background and her own personality to explode in performance, roaring, wailing, stomping, and shaking her body. On a nationwide tour that began in the fall of 1967, Joplin and Big Brother played to enthusiastic audiences in Los Angeles, Chicago, Philadelphia, and Boston. Their New York City debut, at the Anderson Theater in February 1968, drew raves, especially for Joplin, whom a *Village Voice* writer saw as a combination of Bessie Smith's soul, Aretha Franklin's finesse, and James Brown's drive. Joplin herself acknowledged her debt to Otis Redding, but her appeal was largely due to her unrestrained energy. Joplin punctuated performances with frequent gulps of Southern Comfort—she claimed that she consumed as much as a pint and a half during each concert—and the distilling company rewarded this free publicity by giving her a fur coat. When interviewers expressed concern that her voice and body might become exhausted, Joplin responded, "I think you can destroy your now worrying about tomorrow."

In July 1968, Joplin and Big Brother triumphed at the Newport Folk Festival. Albert Grossman became their manager, and their album, *Cheap Thrills* (1968), featuring the hit single "Piece of My Heart," sold a million copies during the first month of release. Critics and audiences agreed that Joplin outshone Big Brother, and by December 1968, Joplin had formed her own band, which eventually became known as Kozmic Blues. Backed by the new group, Joplin launched a nationwide tour in February 1969 with a two-night stand at the Fillmore East in New York City. The response to Kozmic Blues was lukewarm, but Joplin continued to electrify audiences. After several television appearances, she left for a European tour, which was capped by a hugely successful appearance at the Albert Hall in London.

In August 1969, Joplin performed at the Woodstock rock and folk music festival in Bethel, N.Y. Her album *I Got Dem Old Kozmic Blues Again Mama* was released in October. The year was marred by Joplin's arrest in November after a concert in Tampa, Fla., for screaming obscenities at policemen who were trying to keep spectators from dancing. She was later fined $200 in absentia. Joplin bounced back, appearing before a near-capacity crowd in New York's huge Madison Square Garden in December 1969. She also bought a new house in Larkspur, Calif., and began forming a new backup group, called the Full-Tilt Boogie Band, when Kozmic Blues disbanded. Her last year was filled with concert perfomances, including a peace festival at Shea Stadium in New York, two appearances on Dick Cavett's television show, a vacation trip to Rio de Janeiro, and recording sessions. She died in Hollywood, Calif., of acute heroin-morphine intoxication. Her album *Pearl* (her nickname), released after her death, featured the songs "Me and Bobby McGee," "O Lord, Won't You Buy Me a Mercedes Benz?" (her own composition), and "Cry Baby." "Bobby McGee," written by Kris Kristofferson, with whom Joplin had a highly publicized love affair, became a hit.

Offstage, Joplin wore huge glasses and an eclectic wardrobe. Her performance costumes were accented by large, psychedelic feathers in her long brown hair, beads, bracelets, bells, and often a long, sequin-studded black velvet cape. Her poor complexion marred her face, but her frenetic, uninhibited performances compensated for these flaws. She never married but was reportedly engaged to Seth Morgan, a Berkeley student, at the time of her death. Although she was sometimes said to be lesbian, she had numerous love affairs with men.

Joplin's public image of raunchy, funky, gutsy rebelliousness made her an avatar of the 1960's spirit, but in private she was introspective, often drawn to touch base in Port Arthur. This need for security was poignantly captured in the interview at her tenth high school reunion two months before her death. Though defiant, she enjoyed her family's acceptance of her life-style and success. Joplin insisted she never wanted stardom or even to be a singer, but she revitalized blues and was considered by many to be the top female vocalist of the late 1960's.

[The New York Library of the Performing Arts at Lincoln Center has a file on Joplin. *Janis: The Way She Was*, a documentary made up of interviews and performance footage, gives viewers the opportunity to appreciate her dynamic stage presence, a dimension not fully revealed by her recordings. Biographies are Myra Friedman, *Buried Alive* (1973); and David Dalton, *Piece of My Heart* (1985). See "Passionate and Sloppy," *Time*, Aug. 9, 1968; Michael Lydon, "Every Moment She Is What She Feels," *New York Times Magazine*, Feb. 23, 1969; "Janis," *Newsweek*, Feb. 24, 1969; and "Rebirth of the Blues," *Newsweek*, May 26, 1969. An obituary is in the *New York Times*, Oct. 5, 1970.]

ELIZABETH NELSON

KAGAN, HENRY ENOCH (Nov. 28, 1906–Aug. 16, 1969), rabbi, psychologist, and promoter of interfaith understanding, was born in Sharpsburg, Pa., the son of Alexander Benjamin Kagan, a designer of men's suits, and Sarah Rivlin Ginsburg, a milliner-designer. His ancestry on the maternal side contains an unbroken line of rabbis dating back four centuries. After spending his childhood in Washington, Pa., Kagan moved to Cincinnati, Ohio, where he graduated in 1924 from Hughes High School and in 1928 from the University of Cincinnati with a B.A. degree and Phi Beta Kappa election. He spent the following year studying theology at Hebrew Union College, also in Cincinnati. Following ordination he held rabbinical positions at Temple Beth Zion in Johnstown, Pa. (1929–1930), Temple Israel in Uniontown, Pa. (1930–1934), and Temple Rodef Shalom in Pittsburgh (1934–1937). While at Uniontown he also earned the M.A.

degree in political science and directed the Hillel Foundation at West Virginia University. In 1937 he accepted what was to become his major lifetime position, rabbi of the Sinai Temple in Mount Vernon, N.Y. This suburban congregation, which numbered 125 families when Kagan arrived, grew to 1,800 members by 1965. Kagan married Esther Ruth Miller, a teacher, librarian, and writer, on July 16, 1939; they had two children.

Kagan became increasingly convinced of the need for clergymen to understand psychology and to emphasize their role in counseling. He was greatly influenced by Freudian thought and even argued that this emphasis was warranted by ancient rabbinical traditions. Kagan maintained that the religious counselors of biblical times, who used healing techniques intuitively similar to those of modern psychotherapists, greatly outnumbered the prophets and priests. He pursued graduate work in psychology at Columbia University for over a decade before completing the Ph.D. degree in 1949.

In many ways, Kagan pioneered in promoting the integration of the rabbinical ministry and psychotherapy. He was the first practicing rabbi to deliver a scientific paper before the American Psychological Association and the first Jewish clergyman to gain official certification as a psychologist by the state of New York. He founded both the Committee on Psychiatry and Religion of the Central Conference of American Rabbis and the Counseling Center of the New York Federation of Reformed Synagogues. He also served on the Committee on the Relations Between Religion and Psychology of the American Psychological Association.

The contribution for which Kagan earned his greatest recognition nationally and internationally was his promotion of Freudian insights and group-therapy techniques to reduce anti-Semitism among Christians. His 1934 M.A. thesis, "The Treatment of Jewish Minorities Under the League of Nations," indicated his developing interest in relations between Jews and non-Jews; however, his most influential writing was his Columbia dissertation, which was later published as *Changing the Attitude of Christian Toward Jew: A Psychological Approach Through Religion* (1952). In this study, Kagan described the results of his work with over 500 Christian youths at Episcopal and Methodist summer church camps in 1946 and 1947. He found that traditional efforts to reduce anti-Semitism by admonition and appeal to religious ideals influenced how a person believed he should feel but not how he actually felt. Kagan, by contrast, achieved much more significant attitudinal changes when he encouraged the young people to discuss openly their feelings while he guided them in evaluating these feelings in the context of the Christian value system. The key ingredients, then, in Kagan's system of group prejudice-reduction included verbal catharsis, a skillful counselor, and an objective evaluation of how the prejudice related to the charitable ideals of the faith accepted by the group.

Kagan's method of combating prejudice became widely influential, especially in the Roman Catholic church, where eventually it was incorporated into the church's educational system. He accepted a perhaps unprecedented role for a rabbi when in the 1950's and 1960's Roman Catholic authorities invited him to serve as a professor of pastoral psychology and counseling for priests at St. John's Abbey in Minnesota and for priests and nuns studying at Iona College in New York.

Especially noteworthy was Kagan's impact on the Second Vatican Council's Declaration "The Attitude of the Church Toward Non-Christians" (1965), which formally redefined the age-old charge of Jewish guilt for the death of Jesus. Two years earlier Kagan had appeared at the Third International Congress of Group Psychotherapy in Milan, Italy, to read a paper on his method for dealing with anti-Semitism resulting specifically from the New Testament account of the Crucifixion of Jesus. As a result Roman Catholic authorities in Italy invited him to the University of Milan to organize a research program studying the relation of the Crucifixion story to anti-Semitism throughout the centuries. The program was linked with the proposed declaration then before the Vatican Council, and Kagan served as a consultant to Augustin Cardinal Bea, who prepared the declaration. Kagan died in Pittsburgh.

[Kagan's books include *Judaism and Psychiatry* (1956); *Six Who Changed the World* (1963); and *Rabbi as Counsellor* (1964). An obituary is in the *New York Times*, Aug. 18, 1969.]

WILLIAM C. RINGENBERG

KAISER, HENRY JOHN (May 9, 1882–Aug. 24, 1967), industrialist, was born in Canajoharie, N.Y., the son of poor German immigrants Frank Kaiser, a cobbler, and Mary Yopps. At thirteen he left school to work in a dry-goods store at $1.50 a week. He supplemented his income by working as a photographer's apprentice. Before he was twenty, he bought the photography business and, at twenty-two, photographed tourists at Lake Placid in the summer and in Florida and Nassau in the Bahamas in the winter. During a sitting he met Bessie Hannah Fosburgh, the daughter of a wealthy Norfolk, Va., lumberman. He wanted to marry her, but when her father objected, Kaiser headed west to Spokane, Wash. A year later he returned as sales manager of a hardware store, married Fosburgh on Apr. 8, 1907, and headed back to the Pacific Northwest to make his fortune. The couple had two children during a marriage that lasted until Bessie's death in 1951. Later in that year Kaiser married Alyce Chester.

Beginning as a salesman for a paving contractor in Spokane, Kaiser spearheaded the business's expansion throughout Washington and into British Columbia. In 1914 he began his own construction company in Vancouver and soon extended it along the Pacific Coast. "Find a need, and fill it," he once said, and over the next three decades he repeatedly did both.

Kaiser had a genius for building government-funded works projects efficiently. Initially he built roads funded by state gasoline-user taxes. He underbid competitors by devising techniques that accelerated work. For instance, he put rubber tires on wheelbarrows and hitched them to tractors, and he replaced ordinary gasoline engines with more-efficient diesel engines in tractors and shovels. No big project fazed him. Moreover, in a business in which contractors were dormant between jobs, before one project was completed he was casting about for another. This enabled him to keep his organization together by assuring engineers and managers steady employment. By the end of the 1920's he had extended his search for projects beyond the West Coast and into other fields. He built a 300-mile stretch of highway through a primitive part of Cuba. In 1931 he organized the Six Companies combine that would build Hoover Dam on the Colorado River, a project so vast that it took seven firms to complete it.

Kaiser and the New Deal were perfectly suited to each other. No construction feat awed Kaiser, who shared President Franklin D. Roosevelt's conviction that man could conquer nature with determination, engineering, and planning. During the 1930's Kaiser built the piers for the Oakland–San Francisco Bay Bridge and headed the companies that constructed Parker, Bonneville, and Grand Coulee dams. Although his combination lost the contract to build Shasta Dam, he supplied the sand and gravel for it by building a conveyor belt that freed the project from a more expensive dependence upon the Southern Pacific Railroad. He once won a contract to furnish cement before he had built the plant at Permanente, Calif., that would produce it. He also built levees on the Mississippi River, pipelines throughout the West and Mexico, naval defense installations on Wake, Guam, and Hawaii, and a thirty-mile aqueduct that supplied New York City's water. Most of the financing came from the federal government's Reconstruction Finance Corporation (RFC) and the Bank of America. With an eye on international markets, he and the Bechtel Corporation created the first multinational construction firm.

The outbreak of World War II in 1939 took Kaiser into other fields. Forming the Seattle-Tacoma Shipbuilding Corporation with A. L. Todd, an experienced shipbuilder, Kaiser negotiated an agreement to build freighters for the British. Other contracts followed and during the war his yards along the West Coast turned out over 1,000 Liberty ships—one-third of United States wartime production—with incredible speed. His desire for an independent source of steel led him to build at Fontana, Calif., the first integrated steel plant west of the Rockies. Rather than wait, as other businessmen did then, for the government's Defense Plants Corporation to build it for him, Kaiser financed it with a loan from the RFC. The loan was guaranteed by the profits from his shipyards, a fortunate arrangement for both the RFC and Kaiser because the steel plant was not profitable.

Lightweight metals for the aircraft industry also attracted his interest. Ever a big risk-taker, he used another RFC loan to enter the magnesium industry. The magnesium plant was no more profitable than was a subsequent airplane-building venture with Howard Hughes. But during the 1930's and World War II he participated in about 1,000 projects totaling $383 million.

Convinced that the postwar era would be one of enormous economic expansion, Kaiser dreamed of manufacturing automobiles for the superhighways that he knew would soon be built throughout the world. At a time when the automobile industry was already dominated by three giant corporations, that was an audacious challenge. Kaiser envisioned a low-cost, lightweight vehicle made of aluminum with front-wheel drive and torsion-bar steering that might go 100 miles per gallon of gasoline. Together with an experienced automobile salesman, Joseph W. Frazer, he leased the government's aircraft plant at Willow Run, Mich., in 1945. At the same time, he bought an aluminum plant from the government. Both enterprises required RFC and Bank of America financing as well as a big public sale of shares in the Kaiser-Frazer Corporation.

Knowledgeable industrialists expected Kaiser to fail, but the dominant corporations in the automobile and aluminum industries, General Motors and the Aluminum Corporation of America, gave him technical and material assistance because they feared antitrust action. Kaiser Aluminum quickly became the second-largest corporation in the industry when an anticipated postwar glut of aluminum did not materialize. However, many of Kaiser's auto innovations were not yet feasible or marketable (the "Henry J," as Kaiser's car was called, anticipated a later small-car market) and Kaiser-Frazer failed in 1955—the company explaining that it had been undercapitalized. In order to salvage the Kaiser reputation, Kaiser-Frazer stockholders were given shares in Kaiser's other companies. Kaiser always boasted that every government loan had been paid back, a point that RFC chairman Jesse Jones later disputed.

Kaiser seemed indefatigable, rising daily at 5:30 for an eighteen-hour working day. He had a knack for finding or developing shrewd administrators. While he drove his executives hard and paid them only average salaries, he kept their loyalty by offering bonuses, delegating great responsibilities, and involving them in some of the most exciting enterprises imaginable. Wearing two watches—one for West Coast time and the other for local time wherever he was—Kaiser was famed for transacting business via transcontinental telephone conferences. While his far-flung industrial empire was based in Oakland, Calif., he maintained an office in Washington, D.C., that coordinated a network of contacts (including President Roosevelt's spokesman, Thomas G. Corcoran) for obtaining government contracts and financing. Kaiser was known as the New Deal's favorite businessman, and Roosevelt encouraged members of his cabinet to consult with Kaiser on economic planning for the postwar era. Kaiser's exploits were legendary and he shrewdly played upon his fame. Although he disclaimed an interest in politics, a wartime Gallup poll found that 8 percent of those Americans who were asked which public figure not in politics might make a good president named Kaiser, ranking him just behind Generals MacArthur and Eisenhower.

Kaiser fostered a reputation as a humanitarian businessman at a time when many industrialists were hostile to anything requiring cooperation with workers and the government. His labor relations were exceptional, a major reason Kaiser could deliver on contracts so quickly. On every project, he made liaison with unions one of his priorities. Thus, the United Auto Workers helped him start Kaiser-Frazer, and in 1965 the American Federation of Labor–Congress of Industrial Organizations made him the first industrialist to receive its award for outstanding service to the labor movement. Concerned with the general welfare of workers, Kaiser founded the country's largest health-maintenance organization, now known as Kaiser Permanente.

In his later years Kaiser moved to Hawaii, where he invested in real estate development. His home, car, boat, and many other possessions were distinctively pink because he believed it a happy color. He died in Hawaii.

[Biographical material is in Frank J. Taylor, "Builder No. 1," *Saturday Evening Post*, June 7, 1941; "The Earth Movers II," *Fortune*, Sept. 1943; "Henry J. Kaiser" and "The Earth Movers III," *Fortune*, Oct. 1943; "Kaiser Integrating," *Business Week*, Dec. 30, 1944; "The Empire Kaiser Is Building," *Newsweek*, Nov. 22, 1948; "Kaiser's Offsprings Settle Down," *Business Week*, Dec. 9, 1950; "The Arrival of Henry Kaiser," *Fortune*, July 1951; "Kaiserdom," *Economist*, Feb. 18, 1956; Robert Sheehan, "Kaiser Aluminum: Henry J.'s Marvelous Mistake," *Fortune*, July 1956; "Kaiser, 'Easing Up' at 75, Makes Hawaii Project Hum," *Business Week*, Sept. 14, 1957; and Mark S. Foster, "Giant of the West: Henry J. Kaiser and Regional Industrialization, 1930–1950," *Business History Review*, Spring 1985.

On Kaiser in Washington, see Alva Johnston, "The Saga of Tommy the Cork," *Saturday Evening Post*, Oct. 20, 1945; Jesse H. Jones, with Edward H. Angly, *Fifty Billion Dollars* (1951); John Morton Blum, ed., *The Price of Vision* (1973); Jonathan Daniels, *White House Witness: 1942–1945* (1975); and "The Disposal of the Aluminum Plants," in Harold Stein, *Public Administration and Policy Development* (1952).

On the Kaiser-Frazer Company, see Richard M. Langworth, *Kaiser-Frazer* (1975); "The Adventures of Henry and Joe in Autoland," *Fortune*, Mar. 1946; and "Kaiser-Frazer: 'The Roughest Thing We Ever Tackled,'" *Fortune*, July 1951. An obituary is in the *New York Times*, Aug. 25, 1967.]

JORDAN A. SCHWARZ

KANE, HELEN (Aug. 4, 1904–Sept. 25, 1966), singer and film actress, was born Helen Schroeder in New York City, the daughter of Louis Schroeder and Ellen Dixon. She attended St. Anselm's School in the Bronx, appearing in school productions. At thirteen she secured her working papers and began a series of jobs to help support her family while she tried to establish a career in show business. Her first important venture came when she was fifteen; spotted by Chico Marx, she was asked to join the Four Marx Brothers as their ingenue-foil in a review opening at the Fordham Theater in the Bronx (Orpheum circuit). The minor success led to further engagements, including several in music halls in London, England.

After she returned to New York, the petite, brown-eyed brunette appeared as a singer in Harry Richmond's club and won a small part in the unfavorably reviewed *A Night in Spain* (1927). An Atlantic City singing engagement won her a part in bandleader Paul Ashe's new review at the Paramount in 1928. At a rehearsal she inserted "boop-boop-a-doop" into her song "That's My Weakness Now," and the phrase was added for the show. "I don't know why I did it," she later remarked. "It just came out that way." She was an instant Broadway success, soon seeing her name in lights for *Good Boy* (1928), in which she introduced "I Want to Be Loved by You." *Vanity Fair* said this musical had "pretty nearly everything, including the originator of the baby-talk school of *bel canto* which threatens to send all the ingenues back to their swaddling days." Personal and radio appearances, as well as a recording contract with Victor, followed. In nightclubs she was famous, as Edward Stumpf said, as "a singer of semi-salacious folk songs . . . voted as the favorite actress of young men in eastern colleges."

Kane began her movie career in *Nothing But the Truth* (1929), with Richard Dix and Madeline Gray. Her other films include *Sweetie* (1929), with Jack Oakie and Nancy Carroll; *Pointed Heels* (1929), with William Powell and Fay Wray; and *Paramount on Parade* (1930), a showcase of Paramount performers, including Maurice Chevalier, William Powell, Clara Bow, and Leon Errol. *Dangerous Nan McGrew* (1930) starred Kane in the title role, "rendering songs in her own original manner" but, in the nonmusical intervals, "acting in a tediously cute manner," according to the *New York Times*. In *Heads Up* (1930) she appeared with Victor Moore and Charles ("Buddy") Rogers. She also appeared in a few shorts, including *The Dentist* and *The Spot on the Rug* (1932), *The Pharmacist* (1933), and *Counsel on the Fence* (1934), and her voice was used on the sound tracks of movie cartoons.

In vaudeville she appeared with Clayton, Jackson and Durante; Bill Robinson; Ruth Etting; and Ken Murray. At the height of her fame, her salary was $8,000 a week. She earned $5,000 for special appearances at private parties, where she sang a few choruses of one of her trademark songs. Helen Kane dolls, toys, games, and look-alike contests became the national rage.

In the early 1930's, her career suddenly waned, despite her successful appearance in *Shady Lady* (1933) on Broadway. Kane reported that she was "tired of it all, . . . I was on a merry-go-round. Money was falling off trees. I was killing myself, but I loved it. . . . For a kid brought up in a poor family in the Bronx, I should have known better." In 1935 she retired. She had a few bookings in the United States, Mexico, and Europe, including a command performance before the king and queen of England in 1935.

Kane's relatively quiet life was disrupted by two lawsuits. Kane sued Max Fleischer and Paramount Pictures for $250,000 in damages and asked for an injunction against the use of her characterization and voice in the popular Betty Boop cartoons. Kane insisted that Betty was a caricature of her own voice and mannerisms, including the notorious "boop-boop-a-doop," which she asked to have declared her exclusive property. The suit dragged on for months, introducing as evidence several Kane look-alikes. In May 1936 the judge declared in favor of Paramount, ruling that Kane had failed to prove the defendants had appropriated her baby way of singing. Kane was also involved in the bankrupt Bond Dress Company suit when its owner, Murray Posner, paid her $50,000 in return for an earlier investment; creditors demanded she return the money plus interest and won the case.

Bad investments and fewer bookings caused Kane to live in virtual poverty during the last quarter of her life. She and her third husband, Daniel Healy (nicknamed "the Night Mayor of New York"), tried unsuccessfully to operate a nightclub. She was able to get a few nostalgia-type engagements on the Orpheum circuit in the Midwest and at the RKO Palace in New York billed as "The Boopa-doop Girl," and she promoted a film biography of the songwriters Bert Kalmar and Harry Ruby, *Three Little Words*, in which she was portrayed by Debbie Reynolds, for whom Kane dubbed the lyrics of her trademark songs. The movie sparked some interest in Kane, and she was signed to make records for Columbia, but it was not until her plight was exposed in Jim Bishop's newspaper column in 1958 that the world remembered Helen Kane. Inspired by the column, Ralph Edwards featured Kane on the television show "This Is Your Life." That led to some nightclub engagements and a few other television offers.

Kane was married three times. Her first marriage (date unknown) to a businessman, Joseph Kane, ended in divorce in 1932. Her second husband was Max Hoffman (date of marriage unknown), the son of the choreographer and dancer Gertrude Hoffman; they divorced in September 1935. She married Daniel Healy around 1939.

Kane, who, as *Variety* said, "represented sex in a perambulator" and "whose baby voice was one of the best-known sounds of the early 30's," died in New York City.

[Clippings and scrapbooks are in the New York Public Library's Performing Arts Research Center at Lincoln Center; in the National Film Information Service, Academy of Motion Picture Arts and Sciences; and in the Harvard Theater Collection. See Stanley Green, *Encyclopedia of Musical Theater* (1976); and Edward Stumpf, *The World of Yesterday* (1979). Listings of her records are in Roger D. Kinkle, *Complete Encyclopedia of Popular Music and Jazz, 1900–1950* (1952); and Brian Rust, *Complete Entertainment Discography* (1973). Obituaries are in the *New York Times* and the *Los Angeles Times*, both Sept. 27, 1966; and *Variety*, Sept. 28, 1966.]

ELIZABETH R. NELSON

KARLOFF, BORIS (Nov. 23, 1887–Feb. 2, 1969), actor, was born William Henry Pratt, at Camberwell, in south London, England, the son of Edward Pratt, a civil servant in the Indian Salt Revenue Service, and Eliza Sara Millard. His parents died while he was young, and he was brought up by his seven brothers, his sister, and his half-sister in Enfield, where he appeared in local theatrical productions. After attending Dr. Starkey's School and the grammar school in Enfield, Pratt entered Merchant Taylor's School in London in 1899. He left in 1903 to attend Uppingham School, Rutland, where he developed a lifelong interest in cricket. In 1906 he enrolled at King's College, London, to complete his education and, in keeping with the wishes of his family, to read for the consular service. Instead, he showed a continual disregard for higher learning and quietly pursued his growing passion for acting.

Determined not to follow most of his brothers into the consular service, Pratt emigrated to Canada in 1909. After working on a farm in Ontario for six months, he wandered westward. Arriving in Vancouver in 1910, he worked as a real estate salesman and then as a laborer. In 1911, after repeated failures to land an acting job, he applied for a job with the Ray Brandon Players in Kamloops, British Columbia. Deciding that Pratt was not a good stage name, he signed his application "Boris Karloff," Karloff being a remote family name. He was hired and stayed with the company for more than a year, quickly becoming a popular villain. When the company went broke in 1912, he joined the repertory company of Harry St. Clair in Saskatchewan. During a fifty-three-week stint in Minot, N.Dak., he played 106 parts.

Karloff left St. Clair in 1916 to join a road company of *The Virginian*. He toured the western United States with this troupe for a year, winding up in Los Angeles in 1917. When the company disbanded he joined a stock company in San Pedro, Calif. and then the Maude Amber Players of Vallejo, Calif. The 1918 influenza epidemic ruined theater business in the West, and the Maude Amber Players disbanded. While working as a day laborer, Karloff, a tall, gaunt man with striking features and a slowness about his movements that could suggest menace, became an extra at Universal studios.

The title of Karloff's first film faded from his memory, but he later recalled being part of a mob scene in a picture directed by Frank Borzage in 1919. Cynthia Lindsay claims he first appeared as an extra in *The Dumb Girl of Portici* (1916). He had a bit part in the Douglas Fairbanks vehicle *His Majesty, the American* (1919), followed by a brief appearance in *The Prince and Betty* (1920). For twelve years Karloff worked in small parts; as films took more of his time he made fewer stage appearances. His foreign-looking face caused him to be cast mainly as villains of exotic ethnic origins.

The record of Karloff's marriages is sketchy. By 1929 he may have been married and divorced three times. He was apparently married to Olive de Wilton. In July 1920 he married Montana Laurena Williams; the date of their divorce is unknown. On Feb 3, 1924, he married Helen Vivian Soule; the date of their divorce is also unknown, though by 1929 Karloff was paying her alimony. In 1930 he married Dorothy Stine; they had one child. Following their divorce in early 1946, he married Evelyn Helmore on April 11.

Karloff's film career took a big step forward when Howard Hawks cast him as the governor's butler in *The Criminal Code* (1931). Good parts followed in *Five-Star Final* (1931), *The Mad Genius* (1931), and *The Yellow Ticket* (1931). When James Whale took over the direction of *Frankenstein* (1931), preferring Karloff to Bela Lugosi for the monster, Karloff was on his way to becoming a household name. Karloff's make-up and interpretation were central to the part. His colossal creature was capable of great destruction, but vulnerable and touched by beauty.

Karloff appeared in such films as *Scarface* (1932), *The Lost Patrol* (1934), *The House of Rothschild* (1934), *The Secret Life of Walter Mitty* (1947), and *Unconquered* (1947). Occasionally he returned to the stage, notably in *Arsenic and Old Lace* on Broadway during the early 1940's. But for the most part he worked in horror films. An actor of intuitive skill, Karloff improved his parts by his presence. He created a gallery of roles in such films as *The Mummy* (1932), *The Mask of Fu Manchu* (1932), *The Old Dark House* (1932), *The Ghoul* (1933), *The Black Cat* (1934), *The Bride of Frankenstein* (1935), *The Raven* (1935), *The Invisible Ray* (1936), *The Walking Dead* (1936), *The Man They Could Not Hang* (1939), *Son of Frankenstein* (1939), *The Tower of London* (1939), *Before I Hang* (1940), *The Devil Commands* (1941), *The House of Frankenstein* (1945), *The Body Snatcher* (1945), *Isle of the Dead* (1945), *Bedlam* (1946), *The Strange Door* (1951), *The Raven* (1962), *The Terror* (1962), *Black Sabbath* (1963), *Comedy of Terrors* (1964), and *Die, Monster, Die* (1965). Peter Bogdanovich rendered an affectionate tribute to the actor in *Targets* (1968), in which Karloff's character, Byron Orlok, a grand old man of horror movies, is a barely disguised portrait of Karloff himself.

Frankenstein launched Karloff on a thirty-eight-year career associated with horror. Although he became the model for numerous imitations and caricatures, he appeared quite content with his position. Having maintained his British citizenship, Karloff made England his home after 1955. He died at Midhurst in Sussex.

[See Peter Underwood, *Karloff: The Life of Boris Karloff* (1972); Denis Gifford, *Karloff: The Man, the Monster, the Movies* (1973); Paul M. Jensen, *Boris Karloff and His Films* (1974); and Cynthia Lindsay, *Dear Boris* (1975), all of which contain filmographies. An obituary is in the *New York Times*, Feb. 4, 1969.]

L. Moody Simms, Jr.

KATCHEN, JULIUS (Aug. 15, 1926–Apr. 29, 1969), concert pianist, was born in Long Branch, N.J., the son of Ira J. Katchen, an attorney and municipal judge, and Lucille Svet. Both his parents were talented musicians and had studied with Katchen's maternal grandparents, who were graduates of the Warsaw Conservatory of Music and proprietors of a music studio in Newark, N.J. When Katchen was five years old, he commenced piano lessons with his grandmother. At eleven he made his public debut performing Mozart's Piano Concerto in D Minor, K. 466, with Eugene Ormandy and the Philadelphia Orchestra on Oct. 21, 1937. On November 22, Katchen played the same work with the New York Philharmonic under John Barbirolli. The critic Lawrence Gilman enthusiastically equated his ability with that of an earlier prodigy, Josef Hofmann.

During the next four years Katchen continued to study with his grandparents and received academic instruction at home from tutors. Concurrently, under the management of Columbia Artists, he performed in community concert series throughout the country and appeared on "The Ford Sunday Evening Hour" radio program.

Katchen's parents suspended his concert career when he was fifteen to enable him to complete his academic education. During his junior and senior years, he attended Long Branch High School, graduating in 1943. He also took weekly piano lessons from David Saperton in New York City.

In 1943, Katchen enrolled at Haverford College in Pennsylvania, where he studied philosophy and English literature, graduating with a B.A. summa cum laude in 1946. He was awarded a French government scholarship for academic study in Paris. Receiving permission to pursue musical studies instead, Katchen enrolled in 1946 in the Paris Conservatoire, where he was the pupil of Lazare Lévy. Later that year Katchen gained instant acclaim when he performed seven programs with the Orchestre National and the Société des Concerts du Conservatoire in an eleven-day span during the first United Nations Educational, Scientific, and Cultural Organization Festival in Paris.

European concert engagements followed, and Katchen signed a recording contract in 1946. He settled in Paris because he believed that Europe offered him "more chances for concert dates and a better climate for growth" than the United States. He toured extensively throughout Europe during the next twenty-two years and was particularly well received in London, which he regarded as the musical center of the world. He gave numerous recitals there, performed regularly with the London Symphony Orchestra, and made forty-seven records for Decca, including the first long-playing record of a solo piano work ever made by a British firm, Brahms's F-Minor Sonata.

Katchen seemed indefatigable in maintaining a performing schedule often in excess of 150 concerts a year. Although it was not until late in his career that he visited the United States with any regularity, he performed continually throughout the world and appeared in numerous international music festivals. On Apr. 10, 1956, Katchen married Arlette Patoux; they had one child.

Katchen was equally in demand as a symphonic soloist and as a recitalist. His early reputation rested upon his dynamic interpretations of large-scale virtuosic works, especially those of Russian composers. His recording of Rachmaninoff's Second Piano Concerto sold over a million copies. Although he habitually eschewed modern works, finding them unmelodic, devoid of emotion, and laced with "ugly sounds," Katchen occasionally played compositions of contemporary composers, including Benjamin Britten, Aaron Copland, Ned Rorem, and Igor Stravinsky. But, as Rorem wrote, Katchen's "musical heart lay generally in Germany," and his many memorable performances of Mozart, Beethoven, Schubert, Mendelssohn, and Schumann revealed his affinity for German music. Katchen is best remembered for his interpretations of Brahms, and particularly for undertaking the monumental task of becoming, in 1964, the first pianist to perform, and subsequently record, the complete solo piano works of Brahms in a cycle of four consecutive recitals.

Katchen had a frank, outgoing personality and was a provocative and stimulating conversationalist. Generous in his support of young musicians, he taught a number of them without remuneration. Pascal Rogé was one of his better-known pupils. Katchen's principal nonmusical activity was collecting objets d'art, and he became an acknowledged expert on Japanese netsukes. He died of cancer in Paris.

[There is no full-length biography of Katchen. His only published work is "The Wand'ring Minstrel," an article describing the life of a concert artist, in the *Concert Goer's Annual* (1957). See C. B. Rees, "Impressions: Julius Katchen," *Musical Events*, Apr. 1965; the tributes by Ray Minshull, *Gramophone*, June 1969, and Ned Rorem, *High Fidelity*, Sept. 1969; and Gary Graffman, *I Really Should Be Practicing* (1981). An obituary is in the *New York Times*, Apr. 30, 1969.]

LOUIS R. THOMAS

KEATON, JOSEPH FRANCIS ("BUSTER"), V (Oct. 4, 1895–Feb. 1, 1966), stage and screen comedian, was born in Picqua, Kans., the son of Joseph Francis Keaton IV, a comic dancer in medicine shows and vaudeville, and Myra Cutler, a musician. From infancy Keaton was known as Buster, a nickname he received from the escape artist Harry Houdini, his father's medicine-show partner. Keaton first appeared in his parents' act at Dockstader's Theater in Wilmington, Del., in 1899, and by the age of five he was the featured member of the Three Keatons.

Child performers were not unusual in vaudeville, but Buster was unique by any standard. He was known on the circuit as the Human Mop because his father would wipe up the stage floor with the boy, whose costume included a suitcase handle mounted between his shoulders, the better to jerk him about with. The success of this stunt led his father to devise other knockabout routines in which Keaton was thrown or kicked about the stage, often to the tune of his mother's saxophone solos. There is no evidence that Keaton suffered serious physical injury from such treatment, for he quickly mastered the art of the pratfall. But Thomas Dardis, his most thorough biographer, maintained that Keaton's peculiar childhood accounted for his subsequent passivity in his relations with women and employers.

Keaton's rough-and-tumble apprenticeship aroused the ire of urban reformers (such as the Gerry Society in New York City) who sought to regulate child labor in show business. Keaton, who received no formal education except for one day in a Jersey City public school, was an excellent test case for the Gerry Society. The Keatons temporarily managed to fend off the reformers, but the society finally succeeded in having them banned from New York City theaters for two years, prompting an unsuccessful tour of England in 1909.

Eventually Keaton grew too large to be easily thrown about, and his father became increasingly unreliable. They were unable to maintain the physical precision necessary to perform their most popular routines. His father's drunkenness and disagreements with promoters marred the final years of the Three Keatons. With the act reduced to playing minor theatrical circuits, Myra Keaton encouraged her son to pursue an independent career.

In February 1917 Keaton signed to do a Broadway review. A chance meeting in New York City with the comedians Lou Anger and Roscoe ("Fatty") Arbuckle, acquaintances from vaudeville, led to Keaton's movie debut. Arbuckle, under the tutelage of the producer Joseph Schenck, had recently formed a movie company specializing in two-reel comedies. He invited Buster to appear in his next picture, *The Butcher Boy* (1917). Moviemaking fascinated Keaton from his first day on the set, and so he promptly abandoned Broadway to work with Arbuckle's Comique Film Corporation. He did six two-reel comedies in New York City, always in support of Arbuckle, and continued in that role when the company moved to California in October 1917. The war in Europe interrupted Keaton's movie career in 1918. He served in France for seven months but was not sent to the front, because the army thought he was more valuable entertaining the troops.

Keaton returned to California in 1919. He did three more pictures with Arbuckle before Schenck decided to launch a series of comedies starring Keaton. The comedian retained artistic control over his pictures, while Schenck handled financial matters. Their business association turned to kinship when Keaton married actress Natalie Talmadge, Schenck's sister-in-law, on May 31, 1921.

During Keaton's first three years of independent production he turned out several memorable two-reel comedies, including *One Week* (1920), *The Boat* (1921), *Cops* (1922), and *The Electric House* (1922). But his most fully realized works, as actor and director, are the feature-length films completed between 1923 and 1927. The cycle began with *Our Hospitality* (1923), in which Keaton used a story of feuding families to deflate the legend of gracious hospitality in the antebellum South. In *Sherlock, Jr.* (1924), Keaton portrayed a motion-picture projectionist who wants to be a detective. The film features an ingenious special-effects sequence in which the hero falls asleep on the job and, in his dream, steps into the screen and participates in the action of a movie within the movie. The comedian's greatest popular success was *The Navigator* (1924), which centers around Keaton's misadventures with an abandoned ship. But, by critical consensus, Keaton's masterpiece is *The General* (1927), an epic comedy-adventure set in the Civil War.

Keaton imprinted his genius on these films. While much of his humor, like that of Charlie Chaplin and Stan Laurel, drew upon vaudeville formulas, Keaton's best gags revealed a fascination with mechanism, the hallmark of his style. And, unlike the other great clowns of his age, Keaton seemed contemptuous of mere sentiment. The stoicism of his characters is the only rational response to a world always slightly out of joint. Keaton's famous deadpan countenance is the outward emblem of his absurd predicament. Amid the chaos of silent comedy, Keaton used his expressionless yet fascinating face to convey, however precariously, a belief in order. And despite the chaos, Keaton's films display a unique pictorial sense and a strong feeling for landscape and structure. He was no mere slapstick artist but one of early Hollywood's most creative directors.

After *The General,* Keaton progressively lost artistic control over his pictures. By then Schenck had joined United Artists, which distributed *The General, College* (1927), and *Steamboat Bill, Jr.* (1928). All failed at the box office. Schenck decided to curtail independent production and arranged for his brother-in-law to join Metro-Goldwyn-Mayer (MGM), the industry's leading studio. This move was the greatest mistake of his career, Keaton later admitted.

Keaton's early films for MGM were profitable, but he soon found himself at odds with the studio. Previously he had been free to improvise or rework gags during production. Now MGM required him to follow detailed scripts with fixed story lines. Keaton never fully adjusted to the studio's methods, though at MGM he successfully managed the transition to talking pictures. Alcoholism and a deteriorating marriage made the dissatisfied comedian even more troublesome on the job. MGM released him in February 1933.

After an abortive return to vaudeville, Keaton was reduced to signing on with Educational Pictures, a studio known for its low-grade, low-budget comedy shorts. When Educational went out of business in 1937, Keaton worked briefly as a gag writer at MGM and Twentieth Century–Fox. Then, in 1939, Columbia Pictures signed him for a series of two-reel comedies. From time to time Keaton landed small roles in minor feature films, but his work during this period was undistinguished and his reputation ruined. As Thomas Dardis wrote, "Buster Keaton had become an anachronism in the Hollywood of the late thirties."

Keaton fared no better offscreen during that decade. His marriage to Natalie Talmadge ended in 1932, separating Keaton from his two sons. On Jan. 8, 1933 (with a second ceremony on Oct. 17, 1933, because his divorce from Talmadge was not yet final at the time of the first ceremony), just before his release from MGM, the comedian married Mae Scribbens, a practical nurse who specialized in caring for alcoholics. During much of their marriage Keaton was broke and drunk, while Scribbens reportedly turned to prostitution. They were divorced in October 1936. During the next four years Keaton began to control his alcoholism. On May 29, 1940, he married Eleanor Norris, an MGM contract dancer who was twenty-three years his junior. She infused their marriage with the stability and sense of direction that the naive and impulsive Keaton evidently needed.

Keaton's professional rehabilitation began a few years after the turnabout in his private life. Between 1947 and 1954 he earned acclaim for appearances at the Cirque Medrano in Paris, which led to successful engagements in Italy, England, and Scotland. In 1949 *Life* published James Agee's influential essay "Comedy's Greatest Era," which stimulated renewed interest in Keaton's early work. A cameo appearance in *Sunset Boulevard* (1950) and his memorable scenes with Charlie Chaplin in *Limelight* (1952) enhanced the Keaton revival.

During the 1950's Keaton appeared regularly on leading television variety programs and starred in his own comedy show for KTTV in Los Angeles. *The Buster Keaton Story* (1957), with Donald O'Connor as the comedian, was a timely tribute but a mediocre movie. Keaton remained busy in feature films and television commercials well into the next decade. In September 1965, a few months before his death, he received an extraordinary ovation at the Venice Film Festival. It was the crowning moment of his later career, which saw his critical reputation eclipse even Chaplin's. Keaton died in Woodland Hills, Calif.

[Keaton, with Charles Samuels, *My Wonderful World of Slapstick* (1960), is a superior Hollywood memoir. Thomas Dardis, *Keaton: The Man Who Wouldn't Lie Down* (1979), is the most complete biography and contains a detailed filmography. See also Rudi Blesh, *Keaton* (1966); Kevin Brownlow, *The Parade's Gone By* (1968); and Penelope Gilliatt, *Unholy Fools* (1973). Studies of Keaton in a broader context are Raymond Durgnat, *The Crazy Mirror* (1969); Gerald Mast, *The Comic Mind* (1973); and Walter Kerr, *The Silent Clowns* (1975). Daniel Moews, *Keaton: The Silent Features Close Up* (1977), contains close analyses of Keaton's major works. An obituary and a lengthy article on his career are in the *New York Times*, Feb. 2, 1966.]

WILLIAM HUGHES

KELLER, HELEN ADAMS (June 27, 1880–June 1, 1968), author and lecturer, was born in Tuscumbia, Ala., the daughter of Arthur H. Keller, a gentleman farmer and former captain in the Confederate army, and Kate Adams. In her nineteenth month, she suffered a high fever (never properly diagnosed) that left her deaf and blind. Until she was seven years old, Keller had no formal instruction. She did not speak, read, or write. She devised a number of manual signs to communicate with her family and developed a large repertoire of antisocial behaviors. Her parents, on learning of Samuel Gridley Howe's success years before with another deaf-blind girl, Laura Bridgman, contacted the Perkins Institution for the Blind. In 1887, Michael Anagnos, who had succeeded Howe as director at Perkins, recommended a recent graduate, Anne Sullivan, to become Keller's tutor.

Sullivan, who arrived at the Keller home in March 1887, applied Howe's methods with her own variations. Like Howe, she communicated by spelling in her pupil's hand; unlike Howe, she used naturally occurring situations in place of invented lessons and, in the beginning, insisted on strict discipline as a prerequisite for instruction. Because Keller made astonishing progress—within a month she learned the manual alphabet and that everything had a name—Sullivan earned the sobriquet "the Miracle Worker."

The enthusiastic writings of Anagnos and of other luminaries such as Alexander Graham Bell and Edward Everett Hale, who claimed distant kinship with her, made Keller a celebrity before she was ten years of age. On a visit to the Northeast in 1888, Keller met President Grover Cleveland, Oliver Wendell Holmes, and John Greenleaf Whittier. She also met Laura Bridgman, Howe's famous pupil, who was over fifty at the time and whom Keller would soon supplant as the best-known deaf-blind person in the world.

An indefatigable letter writer whose list of correspondents ultimately numbered in the hundreds, Keller appeared destined to be an author from childhood. Her earliest letters and diary entries gained wide circulation through the efforts of Anagnos and Bell, who regarded them as splendid proof of the docility of deaf-blind children. Bell predicted that the child would "make her mark in English literature." But her first story, "The Frost King," written when she was ten years old solely for the delectation of Anagnos, aroused controversy. At the time, Keller was taking classes at the Perkins Institute at the invitation of Anagnos. Her story delighted him so much that, as he had done with her letters, he had it published. Later, it was discovered that the story had been taken almost verbatim from a book published in the 1870's. Among the prominent persons who came to Keller's defense was Mark Twain, who argued, in his characteristically sardonic style, that all authors, including himself, plagiarize. Anagnos formed a commission to investigate, and he broke its tie vote with a Scotch verdict, "Not proved." However, the incident, combined with Sullivan's claim in a newspaper interview that Keller was a guest, not a student, of the school and that she only used its special equipment, resulted in Keller's break with Perkins.

From 1894 to 1895, Keller attended the Wright-Humason School in New York City, where she sharpened her lipreading skills (she read lips by placing her hand over the speaker's mouth) and tried to improve her recently acquired speech. From 1896 to 1897, Keller attended the Cambridge School for Young Ladies, to prepare for Radcliffe College. She also studied for two years with a private tutor before passing the admissions examinations in 1899 and entering Radcliffe in 1900. She graduated in 1904 with a B.A. cum laude. Although Sullivan accompanied Keller to every class as an interpreter, she was barred from attending Keller's examinations—a procedure that largely silenced those who scoffed at Keller's achieving the degree on her own merits.

Keller, lacking sight and hearing, depended upon touch to communicate. She read the American one-handed manual alphabet by placing her hand over the speller's. She responded by spelling or speaking. Instruction in speech began when Keller was nine years old, and although she quickly acquired rudimentary speech, throughout her life her vocalizations were characterized by a high-pitched, nasal quality that few persons understood on first encounter and that, in public meetings, was often inaudible. Along with speech and finger spelling, Keller communicated by reading raised letters and braille, which she learned at Perkins, and by typewriting, reserving handwriting for her signature only. She had a remarkable facility for languages, learning French, German, Greek, Italian, and Latin, in addition to English.

In most of her encounters with strangers who did not know the manual alphabet or whom she had difficulty tactually lipreading, Keller depended upon interpreters who finger-spelled in her hand what was said to her and who vocalized her finger-spelled replies. Keller's symbiotic relationship with Sullivan, whom she always addressed as "Teacher," lasted until Sullivan died in 1936. When Sullivan married John Macy in 1905, he, too, interpreted for Keller by means of the manual alphabet. Others in Helen's entourage also learned to finger-spell, including her mother, with whom she exchanged visits until Mrs. Keller died in 1921. From 1914 to 1960, Keller's companion was Polly Thomson, who came as an immigrant from Scotland without special knowledge or skills but who quickly developed those necessary to assist Keller.

In her sophomore year at Radcliffe, Keller assembled *The Story of My Life* (1903). She was assisted by John Macy, a professional editor and Harvard instructor. The book consisted of two accounts, Keller's and Sullivan's, and a collection of letters. While favorably reviewing it, some critics raised questions about authorship, implying that Macy and Sullivan, not Keller, were the authors.

Perhaps Keller's most famous work was *Teacher* (1955), written as a memorial to her beloved instructor and dear friend. In all, Keller published fourteen books. A count of articles printed in journals, newspapers, and magazines would extend into the hundreds. In addition to autobiography, she wrote on political, social, and educational issues. Keller wrote *My Religion* (1927) at the behest of the General Convention of the New Jerusalem but she entrusted it to Doubleday, her regular publisher, which paid welcome royalties. It remained in print for half a century. Keller embraced Swedenborgianism at sixteen years of age, and her faith in it remained strong throughout her life. She found its emphasis on the validity of inner experiences particularly appealing.

In 1909, Keller joined the Socialist party. It suited her desire to bring justice to all people, with special attention to those who were deaf, blind, or mentally retarded. An active party member, she wrote and spoke in favor of Socialist principles and even considered running for office. On the eve of World War I, however, she resigned from the Socialist party, whose methods she regarded as too slow to achieve the changes for which she fought, and joined the Industrial Workers of the World. She also became a leading figure in the suffragist movement, serving that cause with essays, lectures, and personal appeals to politicians. Following World War I and the victory for woman's suffrage, Keller's political activities slowly came to a halt, partly because they interfered with her writing and lecturing. Keller remained outside politics until 1944, when she campaigned for Franklin D. Roosevelt's fourth term.

From her childhood, Keller benefited from donations from various philanthropists, including John D. Rockefeller and Andrew Carnegie. Their generous gifts, however, did not abate her struggle for financial independence. In 1908, two years after she was appointed to the Massachusetts Commission for the Blind, Keller published her second book, *The World I Live In*, which was praised by such scholars as William James. While her writing provided some income, it was not sufficient for the needs of her household. John Macy, Sullivan's husband, did not provide much in the way of income, though he was of unquestioned assistance to Keller as an editor. Faced with the need for money, Keller and Sullivan toured in 1914 on the Chautauqua lecture circuit, drawing large and appreciative crowds and commanding fairly good fees with a demonstration of how Helen had been taught.

In 1919, *Deliverance*, a movie of Keller's life, based on her first book, was released. She played herself as an adult in the film's latter portions. Despite critical acclaim, the film was not a financial success. But it did lead to vaudeville, in which Keller and Sullivan toured successfully from 1919 to 1923. The act began, much as had their Chautauqua performances, with Sullivan recounting her first efforts to instruct Keller, followed by Keller's entrance, a demonstration of methods of teaching deaf people to speak (which accustomed the audience to Keller's voice), and then a talk by Keller. The performance concluded with Keller answering questions from the audience, something that she did with great wit. By 1923, Keller's radical political views caused a general disaffection with her, ending her stage career.

In 1924 the American Foundation for the Blind sought Keller's assistance in raising funds for its information and scientific programs. For the next three years, Keller and Sullivan undertook meetings patterned after their vaudeville turn, generating great enthusiasm, raising considerable funds for the foundation, and providing them with modest recompense. Most of Keller's audiences overlooked her political stance when she was pleading the cause of blind people, an attitude she encouraged by becoming less and less outspoken politically.

The project ended partly because Keller would not agree to the foundation's terms and partly because she wished to get on with her writing. When she completed *Midstream: My Later Life* (1929), she returned to fund-raising for the foundation, a task that occupied her for the remainder of her life. The American Foundation for the Blind established a trust to administer her affairs. While Sullivan lived, she remained in charge of their joint finances, but on her death, Keller turned to the foundation for the support she needed. The trust arrangements also assured her that she would never again need to be concerned about immediate finances.

In 1916, Keller had a brief, notorious love affair with Peter Fagan, who had joined her staff as a secretary. The news that they had applied for a marriage license energized Keller's mother, who barred Fagan's repeated efforts to marry Keller. After several months, Keller ceased to struggle and said that the actions of her family were in her best interests. Six years later, Keller received a proposal of marriage from a widowed insurance executive in Kansas whom she had never met. She firmly rejected his persistent efforts over almost a year and, so far as is known, that episode ended further romantic advances.

In 1953, a film documentary, *The Unconquered*, told Keller's story. It won an Academy Award but made little money. Four years later, William Gibson wrote the television drama "The Miracle Worker," about the initial breakthrough in teaching Keller. In 1959, Gibson's script was adapted for the stage, where it won several awards. A film version, released in 1962, was similarly successful.

Among the many honors Keller received were honorary doctorates from Glasgow, Harvard (its first to a woman), and Temple universities, and decorations from many governments, including one personally given to her by the king of Yugoslavia and another from Britain's Queen Elizabeth II. France made her a chevalier of the Legion of Honor.

Because Sullivan was so often her voice onstage and offstage, skeptics claimed that the wondrous skills and voluminous writings credited to Keller were fabricated by Sullivan. John Macy's role as editor also aroused the same doubts about Keller's capabilities. However, those who could communicate directly with Keller rather than through an interpreter concluded otherwise. Keller died in Easton, Conn.

For her generation and for generations to come, Keller affirmed that life, even for the severely handicapped, could still be worth living. Without exception, those who knew her found most impressive her unfailing enthusiasm for life. Hers was a spectacular achievement against formidable odds.

[Keller's papers and correspondence are at the American Foundation for the Blind, New York City. Works by Keller not mentioned in the text are *The Song of the Stone Wall* (1910), *Optimism: My Key of Life* (1926), *We Bereaved* (1929), *Peace at Eventide* (1932), *Helen Keller in Scotland* (1933), *Helen Keller's Journal: 1936–1937* (1938), *Let Us Have Faith* (1940), and *The Open Door* (1957). See Nella Braddy, *Anne Sullivan Macy* (1933). An obituary is in the *New York Times*, June 2, 1968.]

JEROME D. SCHEIN

KELLER, KAUFMAN THUMA (Nov. 27, 1885–Jan. 21, 1966), automotive executive and president of the Chrysler Corporation, was born in Mount Joy, Pa., the son of Zachariah Keller, a farmer of modest means, and Carrie Thuma. After graduating from the local high school in 1901, he enrolled in a one-year secretarial program at Wade Business College in nearby Lancaster. From 1904 until 1906 he traveled throughout Great Britain as secretary to a Baptist minister who was lecturing for the temperance cause.

On his return, Keller went to work as a secretary at the Westinghouse Machine Company works in East Pittsburgh, Pa. After working in the office for about a year, he accepted a cut in pay in order to take a two-year special apprenticeship as a machinist. He had worked with machinery as a boy and quickly showed an adult talent for the craft at Westinghouse. When the firm won a contract in 1909 to manufacture automobile engines, Keller, although he had just completed machinist training, was named assistant to the superintendent of the auto engine department.

Keller moved in 1910 to the booming automotive center of Detroit to work as chief inspector in the axle factory at Detroit Metal Products. In November 1911, after brief jobs at the Metzger, Hudson, and Maxwell motor car companies, where he deliberately sought to broaden his range of experience in the industry, Keller joined the central staff of General Motors, working chiefly with the Cadillac division. There, he met Walter P. Chrysler, a rising young executive some years his senior. After a few unhappy months with Cole Motors in Indianapolis, Keller was hired by Chrysler in 1916 to work as general master mechanic for the Buick division of General Motors. K. T., as Keller was always called, made his reputation as an efficient plant manager who understood both machinery and personnel, but he was unknown outside the automobile industry.

General Motors assigned Keller to a variety of increasingly responsible positions: he became a member of the central mechanical engineering staff in 1919, vice-president of Chevrolet in 1921, and general manager for all Canadian operations in 1924. On Apr. 1, 1926, Keller accepted his old friend Chrysler's invitation and returned to Detroit as vice-president in charge of manufacturing for the recently established Chrysler Corporation. He joined the board of directors the following year.

Keller achieved wider recognition in 1928 when he returned the troubled Dodge division to profitability within a year of its acquisition. Chrysler telephoned from New York late one afternoon and said, "Go over and take charge of the Dodge plant. We have just taken it over." Keller was on the job within half an hour. His achievement was rewarded with the presidency of the Dodge division in 1929; he was widely regarded as the second-ranking executive of the Chrysler Corporation, where he had the title of general manager from 1930. Although Keller was named president of the corporation in 1935, Chrysler, the chairman of the board, was clearly the chief executive officer. Only when Chrysler's health failed in the late 1930's did Keller take full command, and the change was not official until Chrysler died in August 1940.

World War II brought production problems to which Keller's talents were ideally matched. He had always been a hard-driving manager, never more so than when pushing the massive Detroit tank plant into production in 1941. Keller became an active member of the Army Ordnance Association. He received its gold medal in 1945, and the following year he received the presidential Medal for Merit for his contributions to wartime production. He remained active in defense matters after the war and served as chairman of a special commission to expedite production of guided missiles between 1950 and 1953. At Chrysler, he resigned as president and assumed the revived office of chairman of the board in 1950, continuing in that office until his retirement from the company in April 1956. For several months in 1957 he was a director of Loew's, Inc., but he was not an active participant in the well-publicized struggle for control of the company.

The Chrysler Corporation was consistently profitable during Keller's leadership, and he always demanded a high level of efficiency throughout the company, particularly in manufacturing. He had little interest in automobile styling, and only after his retirement did Chrysler achieve a reputation for innovative car design.

Keller's private life was quiet. He married Adelaide Taylor on Sept. 21, 1911; they had two children. The Kellers never participated in the publicized social whirl of the wealthy Detroit automotive families. Keller took few vacations before 1945; his chief recreation was fishing, either in Florida waters or in nearby Lake St. Clair. Keller quietly played an active role at the Detroit Institute of Arts. He was appointed to the city arts commission and to the museum's fund-raising Founders Society in 1942, and he died in London while traveling with a museum delegation studying British museum administration and seeking works of art to purchase for Detroit.

Keller's special interest, which he shared with his wife, was Chinese ceramics, and several of his gifts are displayed at the Detroit Institute. He also donated funds for expansion of the museum and for the purchase of paintings, furniture, and stained glass. Keller's character was summed up by a Detroit friend on the occasion of his sixty-fifth birthday: "K. T. never went social or got high-and-mighty. He's just plain vanilla."

[Sources for Keller's life are scant. A few items are available from the corporate archives at Chrysler, but the clipping files at the Detroit Public Library, in both the Burton Collection and the National Automotive History Collection, are far richer. There is an additional uncataloged group of manuscripts and scrapbooks in the National Automotive History Collection, and a small body of papers concerning his postwar defense activities in the Harry S Truman Library at Independence, Mo. Keller was the subject of an admiring but not entirely accurate cover story in *Time*, Oct. 16, 1939; and of two extensive stories in *Forbes*, Sept. 1 and Oct. 1, 1939, and June 15, 1948. An obituary is in the *New York Times*, Jan. 22, 1966.]

PATRICK J. FURLONG

KENNEDY, JOSEPH PATRICK (Sept. 6, 1888–Nov. 18, 1969), entrepreneur and government official, was born in Boston, Mass., the son of Patrick Joseph Kennedy and Mary Hickey. His father was a successful saloonkeeper, businessman, and politician who served in both houses of the Massachusetts legislature, and his grandfather had emigrated from Ireland in 1848. Educated among the Brahmin elite at Boston Latin School and Harvard, from which he received his B.A. in 1912, Kennedy began his career as an appointed state bank examiner. By 1914 he had acquired stock in, and become president of, a small bank his father had helped to found, the Columbia Trust Company; at the age of twenty-five he was perhaps the youngest bank president in the state. On Oct. 7, 1914, he married Rose Fitzgerald, the daughter of John Francis ("Honey Fitz") Fitzgerald, an early—but not, as often stated, the first—Irish-American Catholic mayor of Boston and a sometime congressman; they had nine children, four of whom predeceased him. He was a devoted father who insisted that his children excel, but as a husband he freely exercised the double standard: among his extramarital lovers was the actress Gloria Swanson.

In 1917, after the entrance of the United States into World War I, Kennedy became the assistant general manager of Bethlehem Steel's Quincy, Mass., shipyards, which brought him into contact with Assistant Secretary of the Navy Franklin D. Roosevelt. After the war he became manager of the Boston branch of the investment banking firm of Hayden, Stone, a position he kept until 1924. In the fall of 1927 he moved his family to New York; from then on, he lived mostly there and in Palm Beach, Fla.

From 1926 to 1930 Kennedy was chiefly involved in the motion-picture business, first as the head of a syndicate that purchased thirty-one small New England movie houses; then, as chairman of the board of the Keith-Albee-Orpheum Theaters Corporation, he helped arrange the merger that created RKO Pictures. In the course of this merger, he made the kind of insider profits that the Securities and Exchange Commission (SEC) would later regulate. He was also involved in the production of profitable but unmemorable motion pictures. Sometime before the 1929 crash he got out of the stock market. By the time he began to play an important role in politics in the 1930's, he was many times a millionaire. His continued business success was largely dependent on his penchant for seeking and taking good advice and his employment of able managers and advisers. Thus, his wide-ranging enterprises continued to prosper even while he devoted himself largely to public service.

During the 1932 presidential campaign, Kennedy made significant monetary contributions to the Roosevelt war chest and was one of several persons who helped persuade William Randolph Hearst to support Roosevelt. Kennedy served in three government posts during the New Deal and was, after James A. Farley, the most visible Catholic New Dealer, often serving as an intermediary between Roosevelt and certain elements in the Catholic community, including Father Charles E. Coughlin.

He became a member and first chairman of the SEC from 1934 to 1935. Although some purists, including Secretary of the Interior Harold L. Ickes, were shocked at the appointment of an ex-speculator, Kennedy got that important regulatory agency off to a good start. After the 1936 campaign, during which he contributed money and signed his name to a vigorous book, *I'm for Roosevelt*, he served for less than a year (1937) as chairman of the United States Maritime Commission, where he effected reorganization and earned the enmity of labor by his pro-shipowner policies.

In 1938, Kennedy was appointed ambassador to Great Britain. No envoy to the Court of St. James's since John Adams can have felt as much personal satisfaction as this third-generation Boston Irish Catholic. In the early days of his mission, he made a great social success; but with the coming of war, his views, which Roosevelt increasingly felt were tantamount to appeasement, drifted farther and farther from those of his own government. He returned home days before the 1940 election, and after press speculation about a possible break, he gave a radio address endorsing Roosevelt. He never again held a New Deal post and made no public endorsement in 1944. His only other government positions were as a Senate appointee to the Hoover Commission in 1953 and 1957. His political support in those years went largely to right-wingers, including Senator Joseph R. McCarthy.

When his second son, John, began to develop a national political career in the mid-1950's, Kennedy was both an asset and an embarrassment. Money and contacts were what made his son's early career possible, while his own reputation made his son suspect to many liberal Democrats. His son's nomination and election as president in 1960 brought the elder Kennedy back into the public spotlight. The entire Kennedy family took on an almost mythical aura, with some even trying to cast Joseph Kennedy as Merlin to his son's Arthur. The aura could only be heightened by subsequent Kennedy triumphs and tragedies. On Dec. 19, 1961, Joseph Kennedy suffered a coronary thrombosis that left him a helpless invalid. He died at Hyannis, Mass.

[The Kennedy papers are closed. Much Kennedy material may be found at the Franklin D. Roosevelt Library, Hyde Park, N.Y.; and in the National Archives, Washington, D.C. Oral-history interviews are in the John F. Kennedy Library, Boston; and in the Columbia Oral History Collection, N.Y. Kennedy also wrote *The Story of the Films* (1927); and, with James M. Landis, *The Surrender of King Leopold* (1950). The most useful books on Kennedy are Richard J. Whalen, *The Founding Father* (1964); David E. Koskoff, *Joseph P. Kennedy* (1974); and Michael J. Beschloss, *Kennedy and Roosevelt* (1980). Doris Kearns Goodwin, *The Fitzgeralds and the Kennedys* (1987), is a superior family biography. Two relevant monographs are Michael E. Parrish, *Securities Regulation and the New Deal* (1970); and Donald A. Ritchie, *James M. Landis* (1980). Gloria Swanson, *Swanson on Swanson* (1980), gives an account of him as a film producer and lover. An obituary is in the *New York Times*, Nov. 19, 1969.]

ROGER DANIELS

KENNEDY, ROBERT FRANCIS (Nov. 20, 1925–June 6, 1968), attorney general of the United States and senator from New York, was born in Brookline, Mass. His parents, Joseph Patrick Kennedy and Rose Fitzgerald, were second-generation Irish-Americans whose families had risen in Boston business and politics. His father graduated from Harvard, made a fortune in the 1920's in Wall Street and Hollywood, and in the 1930's became Franklin Roosevelt's first chairman of the Securities and Exchange Commission and ambassador to Great Britain.

Robert Kennedy was the seventh child in a closely knit but highly competitive family. He was the smallest of the four boys, the least coordinated physically, the least articulate, the most gentle and dutiful. The contrast with his commanding older brothers Joseph, Jr., and John doubtless increased early feelings of inadequacy. His father was absent during much of his childhood and, when at home, was often impatient with him. "I was the seventh of nine children," Robert once said, "and when you come from that far down you have to struggle to survive."

He went first to public school in Riverdale, N.Y., where the family had moved in 1927, and then to the Gibbs School in London when his father was ambassador. He completed college preparation at Milton Academy in Massachusetts. School was a struggle for survival too, and he concentrated on sports rather than scholarship. Perhaps more important for his education was the Kennedy dinner table. "I can hardly remember a mealtime," Robert Kennedy once recalled, "when the conversation was not dominated by what Franklin D. Roosevelt was doing or what was happening in the world."

In October 1943 he enlisted in the naval reserve. After his discharge in 1946, he went to Harvard, graduating with a B.A. in 1948. His grades were mediocre, and his consuming interest was football. Determined to win his father's respect and love, he had begun to harden his personality. The inner sensitivity and vulnerability remained, but a protective covering now formed over it. He became the Robert Kennedy who burst into public notice in the 1950's: an aggressive young fellow, opinionated, censorious, prickly, rigid, moralistic, inclined to tell people off and to get into fights.

After Harvard he entered the University of Virginia Law School, graduating in 1951 fifty-sixth in a class of 124. On June 17, 1950, he married Ethel Skakel, a lively, mischievous young woman. Her humor and enthusiasm lightened his moodiness, and her lifelong devotion offered him reassurance and security. Hickory Hill, their antebellum mansion in McLean, Va., became celebrated for the profusion of children (eleven in all), dogs, horses, and other pets.

After brief service in the Department of Justice's criminal division, Kennedy made his political debut in 1952 as manager of his brother John's successful campaign for the Senate from Massachusetts. The next year, he went to work for the Senate Subcommittee on Investigations, headed by Joseph McCarthy, the Wisconsin senator already notorious for reckless accusations of Communist infiltration in American society. Kennedy carried out one assignment for McCarthy—an inquiry into the trade between North Atlantic Treaty Organization (NATO) allies and the People's Republic of China during the Korean War. His report was factual and did not, in the McCarthy style, question the loyalty of government officials. Disturbed by McCarthy's hit-and-run tactics, Kennedy resigned in July 1953. In 1954 he became counsel for the Senate Democratic minority. In this capacity he wrote the minority report condemning McCarthy's conduct of the investigation of the army.

The midterm election of 1954 gave Democrats control of the Senate. The Investigations Committee, with Kennedy now chief counsel, concentrated on fraud and mismanagement in government. One of Kennedy's investigations forced the resignation of Secretary of the Air Force Harold Talbott in 1955. In 1957, Kennedy became chief counsel of the Senate Select Committee on Improper Activities in the Labor or Management Field, popularly known as the Rackets Committee. Its target was the penetration of trade unions by organized crime. Kennedy's relentless investigation of the Teamsters led to a famous feud with Jimmy Hoffa, who was eventually sent to prison. One result of the investigation was the Labor Reform Act of 1959, which established new guarantees for union democracy.

John Kennedy drafted his younger brother to run his 1960 campaign for the presidency. As manager, Robert was tireless, intimidating, and effective. Once elected, John persuaded a reluctant Robert to become attorney general. Though nearly nine years separated them in age, the two brothers had grown close in the 1950's and now formed an intimate partnership. Robert began to lose his intolerance and rigidity. He grew more relaxed and rueful, acquired a more ironic view of life, developed a wry, self-mocking humor, and in time displayed a charm against which newspaper editors warned their reporters. The brothers remained, however, different men. John Kennedy was urbane, objective, controlled, a man of reason; Robert Kennedy was brusque, subjective, intense, a man of emotion. John Kennedy was a realist disguised as a romantic, and Robert, a romantic disguised as a realist.

As attorney general, Robert Kennedy assembled a staff of notable lawyers, led by Byron White (followed by Nicholas Katzenbach) as deputy attorney general, Archibal Cox as solicitor general, and Burke Marshall as assistant attorney general for civil rights. He strove especially to bring the imperious J. Edgar Hoover and his long untouchable Federal Bureau of Investigation under control. Hoover was then a national idol obsessed with the pursuit of Communists, but Kennedy forced him to divert budget and agents into two new fields—organized crime and racial justice.

In 1961 the freedom riders, a group of white and black civil rights activists, were assaulted by white mobs during their journey through southern states to assert constitutional rights in interstate travel. Robert Kennedy dispatched federal marshals to protect them and persuaded the Interstate Commerce Commission to issue regulations ending segregation in interstate bus terminals. By 1963 systematic segregation was eliminated in all forms of interstate transport throughout the South. In 1962, when James Meredith, a black student, attempted to register at the University of Mississippi, the state governor defied a federal court ruling ordering his admission, and a violent mob descended on Meredith and the marshals protecting him. The Kennedys sent in federal troops to uphold the Constitution.

Kennedy saw voting rights as the key to improved opportunities for black Americans in education, housing, employment, and public accommodation. Department of Justice lawyers encouraged voter-registration drives and filed suit when voting rights were denied. Civil rights workers meanwhile streamed into the South and often encountered local retaliation. Many were beaten, and some murdered. Constrained by the constitutional doctrine that police power was reserved for local authorities,

Kennedy

Kennedy believed that the national government could intervene only when there was a specific and clear "federal responsibility." This led to bitter criticism by civil rights activists, as did Kennedy's early recommendations of racial conservatives for southern judicial appointments.

The spread of violent defiance across the South in 1963 made civil rights legislation both a political possibility and, in the view of President Kennedy, a moral necessity. Opponents charged that Martin Luther King, Jr., the black civil rights leader, was controlled by Communist agents. Publicly Robert Kennedy defended King. Privately he acceded to Hoover's request that King's telephones be wiretapped, confident that this would disprove the allegations. King did not hold the wiretaps against the Kennedys. He planned to endorse John Kennedy for reelection in 1964 and was preparing, before his own murder, to endorse Robert Kennedy in 1968. The Civil Rights Act of 1964 outlawed discrimination, whether based on race, color, religion, national origin, or (in the case of employment) sex, in public accommodations, employment, voting, and education. It was the most far-reaching civil rights law since Reconstruction.

Robert Kennedy's relationship to the president carried his duties considerably beyond his own department. "Management, in Jack Kennedy's mind," remarked the liberal leader Chester Bowles, "consisted largely of calling Bob on the telephone and saying, 'Here are ten things I want to get done.'" The president especially respected his brother's ability to get to the heart of difficult problems and, after the Bay of Pigs fiasco, brought Robert increasingly into foreign affairs.

Cuba became a particular preoccupation. In 1961 and 1962, Robert Kennedy spurred on the Central Intelligence Agency (CIA) to undertake covert action—infiltration, arms drops, sabotage—against Cuba. There is no evidence, however, that he was aware, except as past history, of the CIA efforts, originating under the Eisenhower administration, to assassinate Fidel Castro. After Castro accepted Soviet nuclear missiles in 1962, Robert Kennedy played a critical role in bringing about a peaceful resolution of the crisis.

When the Joint Chiefs of Staff and eminent civilians like Dean Acheson called for a surprise air attack on Cuba, Robert Kennedy led the fight against the idea, calling it "a Pearl Harbor in reverse" and saying that "all our heritage and ideals would be repugnant to such a sneak military attack." Later, when the president was confronted by two messages from Premier Nikita Khrushchev of the Soviet Union, the second more intransigent than the first, Robert suggested that his brother ignore the truculent letter and respond to the reasonable one. Finally the younger Kennedy, on his brother's instructions, secretly assured the Soviet ambassador that if the Russians removed their missiles from Cuba, the Americans would remove their missiles from Turkey. Khrushchev noted in his memoirs that the Americans were "open and candid with us, especially Robert Kennedy."

His brother's assassination in November 1963 devastated Robert Kennedy. For months he was immobilized by grief. Yet in a sense it liberated him too. He had repressed his inner self since childhood, first to prove himself to his father and then to serve his brother. In 1961 his father had been disabled by a stroke; now his brother was dead. At last Robert Kennedy was free to be himself and to become a leader in his own right.

After Lyndon Johnson rejected him as a running mate in 1964, Kennedy resigned from the cabinet to seek a Senate seat from New York. He defeated the Republican incumbent, Kenneth Keating, in the fall election. As senator, he welcomed the reforms of Johnson's Great Society but found himself in growing disagreement with the president over foreign policy and finally over domestic policy too. The press often refused to accept such disagreement on its merits, presenting it instead as a political maneuver by which "ruthless" Robert Kennedy was out to reclaim the White House. This response depressed and inhibited him.

He spoke out nevertheless. He criticized United States intervention in the Dominican Republic in 1965 and concluded that Johnson had abandoned the reform aims of John Kennedy's Alliance for Progress. In 1966, he warned his countrymen, after returning from a Latin American tour, "If we allow Communism to carry the banner of reform, then the ignored and the dispossessed, the insulted and injured, will turn to it as the only way out of their misery."

As American involvement in Vietnam grew, Kennedy called for bombing pauses and for negotiations. When escalation continued, Kennedy evoked the "horror" of the war in urgent speeches. "Are we," he cried in 1968, "like the God of the Old Testament that we can decide in Washington, D.C., what cities, what towns, what hamlets in Vietnam are going to be destroyed?"

By 1966, with Johnson increasingly absorbed in Vietnam, the promise of his Great Society had faded. The president even dropped the phrase. As black ghettos exploded in riots, Kennedy identified himself increasingly with the insulted and injured of America—Indians on reservations, Chicanos picking grapes in California, hungry blacks in the Mississippi Delta, migrant workers in filthy camps in upstate New York, families in rat-infested tenements in New York City. He argued that the disparities of power and opportunity were acute and becoming intolerable. "Today in America," he said, "we are two worlds."

His critique of Johnson policies pointed toward a challenge to Johnson's renomination in 1968. But when Kennedy hung back, still fearing misconstruction of his motives, dissident Democrats rallied around Senator Eugene McCarthy of Minnesota. After McCarthy's success in the New Hampshire primary, Kennedy belatedly entered the contest. McCarthy adherents denounced him as an opportunist. With Johnson's withdrawal, Vice-President Hubert Humphrey became the administration candidate.

Kennedy's eloquent campaign generated wild enthusiasm as well as deep anger. Though many saw him as a divisive figure, Kennedy saw himself on a mission of reconciliation, seeking to bridge the great schisms in American society—between white and nonwhite, between rich and poor, between age and youth, between order and dissent. After beating McCarthy in Indiana and Nebraska, he lost to McCarthy in Oregon. Then on June 4 he defeated McCarthy in California and Humphrey in South Dakota—"the most urban of any of the states," he told the crowd in the Ambassador Hotel ballroom in Los Angeles late that night, and "the most rural of any of the states. . . . What I think is quite clear is that we can work together in the last analysis." When he left the ballroom, he was shot by Sirhan Sirhan, a Jordanian Arab embittered by Kennedy's pro-Israel sympathies. He died in Los Angeles the following day.

Starting out as a man of the Right, Robert Kennedy ended as the champion of the dispossessed and powerless in American society. His enemies considered him cold and ruthless; his friends found him gentle, considerate, and funny. His rude challenge to the complacencies of American life made many uncomfortable; but his insistence that any individual who "stands up for an ideal, or acts to improve the lot of others, or strikes out against injustice" can make a difference to the world struck a moral nerve, especially among the young. His combination of social idealism with political realism promised much for American life. His murder at the age of forty-two, eight weeks after the murder of Martin Luther King, Jr., and five years after the murder of his own brother, shadowed a turbulent decade in American history.

[Kennedy's papers and oral histories are at the John F. Kennedy Library in Boston. His books include *The Enemy Within* (1960), the story of the Rackets Committee investigations; *Just Friends and Brave Enemies* (1962), reflections on a 1962 trip through the Third World; *The Pursuit of Justice*, edited by Theodore J. Lowi (1964), a discussion of issues confronted as attorney general; *To Seek a Newer World* (1967), his commentary on the United States in the 1960's; and *Thirteen Days* (1969), a memoir of the Cuban missile crisis drawn from his personal diary. Douglas Ross, ed., *Robert F. Kennedy: Apostle of Change* (1968), is the most complete collection of his public utterances.

Arthur M. Schlesinger, Jr., *Robert Kennedy and His Times* (1978), is a full biography based on the Kennedy papers as well as on personal acquaintance. Perceptive contemporaneous accounts are William V. Shannon, *The Heir Apparent: Robert Kennedy and the Struggle for Power* (1967); Jack Newfield, *Robert Kennedy: A Memoir* (1969); and Edwin Guthman, *We Band of Brothers* (1971). Jean Stein and George Plimpton, eds., *American Journey: The Times of Robert Kennedy* (1970), is a valuable compilation of interviews. Victor Lasky, *RFK: The Myth and the Man* (1968), conveniently assembles a vast stock of anti-Kennedy lore.

For sidelights on Robert Kennedy during his brother's presidency, see Arthur M. Schlesinger, Jr., *A Thousand Days* (1965); Theodore C. Sorensen, *Kennedy* (1965); Pierre Salinger, *With Kennedy* (1966); and Kenneth P. O'Donnell and David F. Powers with Joseph W. McCarthy, *Johnny, We Hardly Knew Ye* (1972). Victor Navasky, *Kennedy Justice* (1971), assesses his record as attorney general. For the civil rights struggle, see Carl M. Brauer, *John F. Kennedy and the Second Reconstruction* (1977); Harris Wofford, *Of Kennedys and Kings* (1980); and David J. Garrow, *The FBI and Martin Luther King,*

Kerouac

Jr. (1982). Walter Sheridan, *The Fall and Rise of Jimmy Hoffa* (1972), is a detailed account by a Kennedy associate. William vanden Heuvel and Milton Gwirtzman, *On His Own: Robert Kennedy, 1964–1968* (1970), deals with his senatorial career. Doris Kearns, *Lyndon Johnson and the American Dream* (1976), casts light on the Kennedy-Johnson relationship. For the 1968 campaign, see David Halberstam, *The Unfinished Odyssey of Robert Kennedy* (1968); and Jules Witcover, *85 Days: The Last Campaign of Robert Kennedy* (1969).]

ARTHUR M. SCHLESINGER, JR.

KEROUAC, JACK (Mar. 12, 1922–Oct. 21, 1969), novelist, poet, and essayist, was born Jean Louis Kérouac in Lowell, Mass., the son of Leo Alcide Kérouac (Kéroack), a printer, and Gabrielle Levesque, a shoe skiver. Both parents were French Canadians who had moved early in life to New Hampshire and then to the large textile town on the Merrimack River. Kerouac's mother was a devout Catholic. Kerouac grew up in working-class ethnic neighborhoods with fellow French Canadians and Greeks. Quebecois was his first language, and English, his second. This early sense of the doubleness of language may have contributed to his neologistic, richly pliable treatment of both poetry and prose later in life. When Kerouac was four, his nine-year-old brother, Gerard, died. The loss affected him greatly, and death figured prominently in his life and work. Maternal and fraternal canonization of Gerard intensified Kerouac's lifelong sense of filial insufficiency toward his mother; repeated forays on sea or land, or drunken binges in New York, often ended with a return to his mother. He repeatedly promised his dying father he would care for her.

Kerouac skipped sixth grade and entered Lowell's Bartlett Junior High School in 1933. He became a member of a writers' club sponsored by the school's librarian, whom he greatly impressed with his first piece of description. He wrote prolifically, creating a newspaper in which he reported the results of his own baseball-card games, and he began writing a novel, *Jack Kerouac Explores the Merrimack*.

Kerouac's parents discouraged him from writing, which they found impractical and unpromising. But everyone approved of his zealous involvement in high school athletics. Kerouac enjoyed the heroic aspects of sports, and he thought it might take him out of the mill town and into college. He excelled at baseball, track, and football and was the star of Lowell High's 1938 Thanksgiving Day game. Not long after that game, he received a scholarship to Columbia University.

Kerouac spent the 1939–1940 school year at the Horace Mann preparatory school in New York City. He enrolled at Columbia in September 1940 but left after a year, reenrolling briefly in 1941 and 1942. He served in the merchant marine and the United States Navy but was discharged honorably from the latter after three months for having "an indifferent character." Shortly thereafter, he fell in love with a young art student named Frankie Edith ("Edie") Parker, and they began living together.

At Edie Parker's home Kerouac met the novelist William Burroughs, eight years his senior, and the poet Allen Ginsberg, then a Columbia sophomore. Less than two months later, when another member of their circle was charged with manslaughter, Kerouac was arrested as a material witness. During his brief stay in a cell, he proposed to Parker, and on Aug. 22, 1944, he was let out for their wedding ceremony. Though he and his new wife shared much in common, they quickly drifted apart.

As his marriage deteriorated, Kerouac grew closer to Ginsberg and Burroughs, the latter serving as mentor to the other two. Ginsberg also fell in love with Kerouac. In January 1945 a dean who had been Kerouac's freshman coach found Ginsberg and Kerouac sleeping back to back in Ginsberg's dormitory bed. Although another student confirmed that no sexual encounter had taken place, the dean banned Kerouac from Columbia.

The conflict between the values of postwar American society manifested around the university and those of Kerouac and his friends was by now growing immense. American materialism, the military-industrial state, the atomic bomb, the decorous conformity, and the privatization of American society all reaffirmed the "separateness" of Kerouac and his friends. One of the key points of this separateness was literary. At Columbia and most other universities of the day, as well as in reigning literary circles, the tenets of the New Criticism were held in highest esteem; literature was to be impersonal. For Kerouac, who was committed to writing about what he himself had seen, New Critical literary standards were inadequate to encompass his Whitmanesque expansiveness. Kerouac was enormously productive. He typically wrote every day in small notebooks, and he collaborated with Burroughs and Ginsberg on numerous writing experiments. Nearly a decade would pass while his own methods and standards matured.

Crucial to that maturation was his meeting Neal Cassady in 1946. This car thief and would-be intellectual became for Kerouac "a young Gene Autry . . . a sideburned hero of the snowy West." That year also marked the death of Kerouac's father and the beginning of *The Town and the City* (1950), a bildungsroman rich with the periodic sentences and rhythms of Thomas Wolfe, which contrasted Kerouac's Lowell and early New York City life. But it took the assertive influence of Cassady, who lived life in a mad rush of speech, energy, curiosity, and a restless search for more women and a mystical "it," to catalyze for Kerouac the recognition that his picaresque fiction need not follow a narrative nor contain a "plot."

On Nov. 17, 1950, a year after his marriage to Parker was annulled, Kerouac married Joan Haverty; they had one child, but the marriage lasted only for a few months. In February 1951, Kerouac received a 40,000-word letter Cassady had composed in three days; according to Ginsberg, it read "with spew and rush, without halt, all unified and molten flow . . . breathtaking in speed and brilliance." Approximately six weeks later, Kerouac inserted into his typewriter a continuous stream of Oriental art paper he had taped together in long sheets so as not to disturb his flow of thought and writing, and began *On the Road*, a novel that he completed in three weeks. A single long paragraph, the work was one of several novels he would write about Cassady; it elegiacally recounted the 1946–1951 cross-country hitchhiking, car rides, freight rides, all-night confessional conversations, sexual and comradely escapades, commitments, and failures of Kerouac, Cassady, Ginsberg, Burroughs, and others in their circle. It also contained important statements by Kerouac as writer and prophet. Early on, he expressed his commitment to write about "the mad ones, the ones who are mad to live, mad to talk, mad to be saved, desirous of everything at the same time." This commitment was maintained in a career in which he produced fourteen published novels that he saw as a single Balzacian whole.

On the Road also mentioned "a new beat generation," a phrase Kerouac had coined years earlier. By the time the novel appeared in 1957, after extensive revision by Kerouac and numerous efforts by Ginsberg to place it with a publisher, the nation at last seemed ripe for Kerouac. (Fifteen years of large output and small number of publications had yielded only mixed reviews.) Young people rushed to buy *On the Road*, which eventually sold half a million paperback copies, but critics of many established journals quickly condemned it. The *Saturday Review* called it "infantile, perversely negative," and *Encounter*, which was then receiving funds from the Central Intelligence Agency, dismissed it as "a series of neanderthal grunts." However, Gilbert Millstein, in the *New York Times*, acclaimed *On the Road* as "a major novel" that spoke for a whole new generation, just as *The Sun Also Rises* had for the Lost Generation.

Many critics rejected the plotless and personal nature of Kerouac's fiction, its seeming immorality, and its indulgent depiction of drug taking, sex, and traveling. During the next few years, the daily press, movies, television shows, and even learned journals depicted beats as freaks, fiends, ignoramuses, and juvenile delinquents. In his essay "The Origins of the Beat Generation" (1959), Kerouac explained that "the word 'beat' originally meant poor, down and out, deadbeat, on the bum, sad, sleeping in subways" and added that his own religious experience gave it the added connotation of "beatific."

In 1958, the *Evergreen Review* published Kerouac's "Essentials of Spontaneous Prose," a manifesto that drew upon his devotion to writing, Cassady's 1951 letter, and jazz. He proposed "sketching," much like a visual artist, only with words. Like the jazz musician, the writer was to "blow" to generate a spontaneous, "undisturbed flow," to "tap from yourself the song of yourself." Except for obvious mistakes, writers were not to revise: "Craft *is* craft."

In spite of such efforts, Kerouac found himself increasingly under attack by the turn of the decade; overly enthusiastic fans as well as pejorative critics appalled him, and unlike Ginsberg, who had a gift for manipulating the media, Kerouac was unnerved by the spotlight, even on the infrequent occasions when it was benign or neutral. By the fall of 1961, he had completed *Big Sur* (1962), a painfully honest account of his delirium tremens the previous summer. In 1957, he bought his mother a home in Florida, and in 1958, another on Long Island. Though he continued to travel in later years, he spent more time at home with his mother, writing at a slower pace and drinking to excess. When drunk at bars, he would step beyond social bounds and was beaten several times by strangers, without ever attempting to defend himself. The sanctity of his home was maintained by his mother, who refused to give him telephone messages from old friends such as Ginsberg and barred the door when they appeared in person.

In September 1966, Kerouac's mother suffered a paralyzing stroke; in January of the following year, mother and son moved back to Lowell, at the same time keeping a house in St. Petersburg. Moving with them was Stella Sampas, who had become Kerouac's third wife on Nov. 18, 1966. Stella had cared for Kerouac's mother previously and was the sister of a close friend who was killed in World War II. In 1967, developing a theme and title that had first come to mind twenty-five years earlier, Kerouac wrote an autobiographical novel of his early years, *The Vanity of Duluoz* (1968). In 1969 he completed the novel *Pic* (1971). Shortly before his death in St. Petersburg, Fla., the *Chicago Tribune* and syndicated newspapers published "After Me, the Deluge," a kind of position paper in which Kerouac renounced a popular conception of him as "the great intellectual forebear who spawned a deluge of alienated radicals" and announced, "I'm a Bippie in the middle."

Kerouac contributed a new syncretic approach to the theory and aesthetics of fiction and its composition. His novels anticipate the New Journalism and are valuable as fictionalized chronicles of the Beat Generation; moreover, they constitute an epic hymn to America. Kerouac is known chiefly and popularly for his fiction, but his gift for poetry was equal to, or perhaps greater than, his gift for prose. His use of the vernacular, diction, enunciation, tonal variety, and reading style influenced almost all poets who heard him. He also helped resurrect the oral tradition, which had long since been sacrificed by the New Criticism in its devotion to the printed page. Moreover, much of Kerouac's fiction represents the first major infusion of Buddhism into American fiction and poetry. Virtually none of his novels written after 1953 are without significant reference to Buddhism, which he may have valued above all else. The efforts of this "great rememberer redeeming life from darkness" appear to have been true to his announced intention to write in his own words what he had seen with his own eyes.

[The Ginsberg Special Collection at Butler Library, Columbia University, contains some of his correspondence, as does the Humanities Research Center, University of Texas, Austin; the City Lights Collection, University of California at Berkeley; and the Philip Whalen Collection at Reed College. Some of Kerouac's notebooks are at the Berg Collection of the New York Public Library. The Grove Press Collection at Syracuse University contains archives on *Pull My Daisy* (1959), a film that Kerouac wrote and narrated. The Kerouac estate possesses publishing rights to a considerable volume of unpublished work, including at least one unpublished book of poems, all of Kerouac's journals, numerous letters, and essays.

See Ann Charters, *A Bibliography of Works by Jack Kerouac* (1975); and J. Milewsk, *Jack Kerouac: An Annotated Bibliography* (1981). Important shorter writings by and on Kerouac are collected in Thomas Parkinson, ed., *A Casebook on the Beat* (1961); and Scott Donaldson, ed., *On the Road: Text and Criticism* (1979).

Since Ann Charters' groundbreaking *Kerouac* (1973), a number of biographies and memoirs have appeared, including Allen Ginsberg, *The Visions of the Great Rememberer* (1974); Barry Gifford and Lawrence Lee, *Jack's Book* (1978); Dennis McNally, *Desolate Angel* (1979); Joyce Johnson, *Minor Characters* (1983); Gerald Nicosia, *Memory Babe* (1983); Tom Clark, *Jack Kerouac* (1984); and John Clellon Holmes, *Gone in October* (1985). Critical studies include Frederick Feied, *No Pie in the Sky* (1964); Robert A. Hipkiss, *Jack Kerouac, Prophet of the New Romanticism* (1976); John Tytell, *Naked Angels* (1976); and Tim Hunt, *Kerouac's Crooked Road* (1981). Ginsberg comments on Kerouac's theory, art, and role in Gordon Ball, ed., *Allen Verbatim* (1974). See also George Dardess, "The Logic of Spontaneity," *Boundary* 2, 3, no. 3 (1975).

Recordings by Kerouac include the following LP's: *Readings by Jack Kerouac on the Beat Generation* (1959); *Poetry for the Beat Generation* (with Steve Allen, 1959); and *Blues and Haikus* (1959). *What Happened to Kerouac?*, a videotape documentary produced by Lewis MacAdams and Richard Lerner, was released in 1985. An obituary is in the *New York Times*, Oct. 22, 1969.]

GORDON BALL

KEYES, FRANCES PARKINSON (July 21, 1885–July 3, 1970), writer and editor, was born Frances Parkinson Wheeler in Charlottesville,

Va., the daughter of John Henry Wheeler, a professor of Greek at the University of Virginia, and Louise Johnson. Her mother moved the family to her paternal ancestors' home, the Oxbow, near Newbury, Vt., after her husband died in 1887; she later also established a home on Beacon Street in Boston. Wheeler studied with governesses and attended private schools, among them Miss Winsor's in Boston. She was also educated in Geneva and Berlin and passed the entrance examination for Bryn Mawr. Her marriage on June 4, 1904, to Henry Wilder Keyes (pronounced to rhyme with "skies") of North Haverhill, N.H., a man twenty-two years her senior, precluded her attendance at college, but she was well read and spoke five languages.

Keyes lived at her husband's family home, Pine Grove Farm, N.H. The couple had three children. Henry Keyes was governor of New Hampshire from 1917 to 1919, and he served three terms in the United States Senate from 1919 to 1937. In Washington, Frances Keyes moved in the highest social circles. She became one of the capital's most active hostesses, and she was a frequent guest at the White House and on Embassy Row. She also began writing "Letters from a Senator's Wife" for *Good Housekeeping* in 1920. These monthly columns were delightfully chatty accounts of Washington and incisive cameos of the personalities in that city.

Keyes's career as a writer had a strong financial impetus. Money had always been a problem, for her husband's family possessed little more than social position and Pine Grove Farm. She had had to endure the humiliation of being refused credit for the gown she had chosen for her husband's gubernatorial inauguration because the bill for another garment, purchased years previously at a Boston establishment, had not been paid.

Keyes's first novel, *The Old Gray Homestead*, appeared in 1919, but it was not until the 1930's that she began writing in earnest. In the next four decades she produced a book almost every year, publishing more than fifty. Her association with *Good Housekeeping* was strengthened with her appointment as an associate editor in 1923, a position she held until 1935. Two years later she was named editor of the *Daughters of the American Revolution Magazine*, which she attempted to rejuvenate by renaming it the *National Historical Magazine* and converting it into a forerunner of *American Heritage*. In 1939 she resigned the editorship and her membership in the Daughters of the American Revolution (DAR). The reasons given for the rupture were cryptic, and during her lifetime Keyes refused to discuss the matter. Her eldest son later wrote that her resignation was precipitated by the cancellation of the black contralto Marian Anderson's scheduled concert at Constitution Hall, which was owned by the DAR.

Keyes's research for her novels was extremely thorough. She totally immersed herself in the milieu or locale that she intended to write about, becoming an authority on a wide range of subjects, from how to cheat at poker to the intricacies of chess gambits. In her best-selling novel *Dinner at Antoine's* (1948), a mystery, she skillfully captured the social whirl and exotic atmosphere of mid-twentieth-century New Orleans. Her first drafts were written in longhand and then dictated to secretaries who would prepare typed manuscripts for extensive revisions. However much she enjoyed writing and its financial rewards, Keyes advised her grandchildren not to become writers.

Keyes was an early feminist whose heroines usually save the day when the men in their lives prove inadequate to the situation at hand. This formula may be a reflection of Keyes's own marital situation; she surpassed her husband (who died in 1938) in both fame and earning power. Her fictional world is a narrow one in which the characters are wealthy, well-mannered people from good families who usually have their romantic fantasies gratified by marriage.

Although Keyes never won critical acclaim or prestigious awards—she once told an interviewer, "I am not a reviewer's author. I rarely get a good press"—critics generally accepted her on her own terms. They advised prospective book buyers to enjoy the novel under review, which they did in huge numbers; total sales were in excess of 20 million. In addition to her enormously popular novels, Keyes wrote religiously oriented books, verse, and four autobiographical works, including the posthumously published *All Flags Flying* (1972).

Keyes's family was Congregational, but she was confirmed in the Episcopal church. She became a Roman Catholic in 1939 and took great pride in her selection as the outstanding Catholic woman of the year in 1946. Her health was poor for many years, but she doggedly overcame her infirmities. She walked with two canes, rising and sitting by using her hands, and she displayed great compassion for those with physical disabilities.

Keyes had a strong personality; intimates described her as imperious. In social situations she loved to tell stories and be the center of attention. She died at her winter residence, Beauregard House in New Orleans, once the home of the Confederate General P. T. G. Beauregard, which she had restored and deeded to the Keyes Foundation, a charitable trust to help struggling writers and to preserve historic homes and gardens.

[Some of Keyes's papers are at the Alderman Library of the University of Virginia; others are at Beauregard House. Many of her personal papers and her scrapbooks, which she began filling at an early age, are at the Oxbow, and some of her library is at Pine Grove Farm. See Robert Wernick, "The Queens of Fiction," *Life*, Apr. 6, 1959. An obituary is in the *New York Times*, July 4, 1970.]

MARTIN TORODASH

KIMBALL, DAN ABLE (Mar. 1, 1896–July 30, 1970), business executive and secretary of the navy, was born in St. Louis, Mo., the son of John H. Kimball and Mary Able. Kimball grew up and attended public schools in St. Louis. Accounts differ as to whether he graduated from Soldan High School there or quit to take a job as a mechanic in a garage that repaired electric automobiles. In any case, he furthered his education by studying engineering through correspondence courses.

During World War I, Kimball enlisted in the army to learn aviation. He completed ground school in Berkeley, Calif., and flight training at Rockwell Field in San Diego, where he was a classmate of Jimmy Doolittle. Although Kimball was urged by his superiors to seek a career in army aviation, he preferred to return to civilian life and was discharged in 1919 as a first lieutenant, having done a stint as an engineering test pilot.

Kimball secured a sales job with the General Tire and Rubber Company and soon progressed through the corporation's ranks as Los Angeles area manager and then manager of the eleven-state western region. He married Dorothy Ames on June 22, 1925; they had no children. After his first marriage ended in divorce in 1957, he married Doris Fleeson, a syndicated political columnist, in August 1958.

When World War II came, General Tire and Rubber secured extensive defense contracts, manufacturing life rafts and many other items. Its newly acquired subsidiary, the Aerojet Engineering Corporation of Azusa, Calif., brought into large-scale production the jet-assisted take-off (JATO) apparatus to help boost planes off short runways. Kimball was named both a vice-president of the parent corporation and executive vice-president and general manager of Aerojet. He stayed with Aerojet after the war. The company helped to develop the Aerobee rocket, used for weather research in the early years of the nation's space program.

In addition to his business career, Kimball was active in California politics. A lifelong Democrat, he backed Franklin D. Roosevelt throughout the twelve years of Roosevelt's presidency and helped raise funds for Harry Truman's 1948 campaign. Kimball almost sought the California Democratic party's gubernatorial nomination in 1950 but concluded that no one could defeat the popular Republican Earl Warren and decided not to enter the contest.

Kimball had been named assistant secretary of the navy for air in February 1949. Shortly thereafter Secretary of Defense Louis Johnson halted construction of a supercarrier in order to fund additional B-36 bombers for the air force. Both the secretary and the undersecretary of the navy resigned in protest. Johnson dissuaded Kimball from following their example. Kimball was soon named undersecretary, a position he held until July 1951, when he became secretary of the navy.

The energetic Kimball was the right man for the post, for the continuing feud over the supercarrier and other matters had led to the resignation of the navy's top uniformed officer, Chief of Naval Operations Louis Denfeld, and to ill feelings between Secretary of the Navy Francis Matthews and other high-ranking officers. In contrast to his predecessor Matthews, whose ignorance of naval affairs at the time of his appointment was such that he had been nicknamed "the rowboat secretary," Kimball had become well schooled in naval matters prior to assuming the top civilian office in the Navy Department. A tall, heavyset man, Kimball was hardworking and affable, ideally suited for dealing with admirals, his counterparts in the defense establishment, and influential congressmen.

Due in part to Kimball's skills and in part to the Korean conflict, which made it easier to secure defense appropriations, the navy was able to gain funding for nuclear submarines and for large carriers of the new Forrestal class capable of handling planes that could deliver atomic bombs. The keel for the submarine *Nautilus*, the world's first nuclear-powered vessel, was laid during his tenure, although plans had been made for it before Kimball became secretary. A forceful advocate of modernization, Kimball urged the construction of other nuclear-powered ships, including carriers, and insisted that priority be given to replacing guns with guided missiles as the navy's primary antiaircraft weapon. Kimball also called for enhanced defenses against Soviet submarines. When he left office in January 1953 to return to General Tire, Kimball could claim that his service had been "enjoyable and satisfying"; it certainly strengthened the navy.

In July 1953, Kimball became president of the renamed Aerojet-General Corporation and continued with the company as president and subsequently chairman until his retirement in 1969. His contribution to civic life did not end with his departure from the Navy Department. He was perhaps proudest of his efforts to secure construction of a factory in the Watts neighborhood of Los Angeles after the riots of 1965. Priority in hiring went to those who had not completed high school and/or who had police records. Kimball arranged for management personnel to receive training at Aerojet, hoping to develop a leadership cadre prior to turning over operation of the factory to Watts residents. He died in Washington, D.C.

Rising from the ranks of General Tire, Kimball was with the company and its Aerojet subsidiary for half a century. His chief successes were with Aerojet, where he became one of the most influential figures in the aerospace industry, and in his four years in the Navy Department. A strong but tactful leader, he provided continuity in the navy's civilian hierarchy as undersecretary and in his tenure as secretary helped restore a sense of purpose to a demoralized and dissension-ridden service.

[A small collection of Kimball's papers is in the Harry S Truman Library. See K. Jack Bauer, "Dan Able Kimball," in Paolo E. Coletta, ed., *American Secretaries of the Navy*, II (1980). Of interest are Robert Hotz, "Navy Air Boss Once Army Pilot," *Aviation Week*, Mar. 21, 1949; Paul Y. Hammond, "Super Carriers and B-36 Bombers," in Harold Stein, ed., *American Civil-Military Decisions* (1963); and Dennis J. O'Neill, *A Whale of a Territory* (1966), an account of General Tire. An obituary is in the *New York Times*, July 31, 1970.]

LLOYD J. GRAYBAR

KIMMEL, HUSBAND EDWARD (Feb. 26, 1882–May 14, 1968), naval officer, was born in Henderson, Ky., the son of Manning Marius Kimmel, a civil engineer and businessman, and Sibbella Lambert. His father, a graduate of West Point, served in the Union cavalry at the First Battle of Bull Run, after which he entered the Confederate service. Determined to follow his father into the military, Kimmel tried unsuccessfully to enter West Point. He then spent a year at Central University in Richmond, Ky. In 1900 he obtained an appointment to the United States Naval Academy; among his classmates was William F. Halsey, Jr. He won high standing in the class of 1904, which was graduated early (in February) to fulfill manpower requirements in the new battleship navy.

Kimmel was assigned to the Naval War College at Newport, R.I., for postgraduate instruction in ordnance. He immediately excelled in naval gunnery, thereby placing himself in line for key professional posts and promotions. Brief tours of duty on five ships along the eastern seaboard culminated in his being commissioned an ensign and given additional instruction in ordnance engineering in 1906. Late in 1907 Kimmel was assigned to the battleship *Georgia* of the "Great White Fleet" for its global cruise. He became the fleet's champion officer of the main battery twelve-inch guns and an important staff officer. Between 1909 and 1917 he served twice as assistant to the director of target practice at the Navy Department, on board two more battleships, and as gunnery officer of the Pacific Fleet. He was wounded slightly at the Veracruz intervention in 1914. He married Dorothy Kinkaid, daughter of a future admiral, on Jan. 31, 1912; they had three children. During 1915 he served briefly as aide to Assistant Secretary of the Navy Franklin D. Roosevelt.

Upon the entry of the United States into World War I in 1917, Kimmel was sent to Great Britain; he materially assisted the Royal

Navy in improving its gunfire techniques and participated in a British naval raid on Helgoland in the North Sea. When the American battleship squadron joined the Grand Fleet, he became staff gunnery officer to its commander, Admiral Hugh Rodman. He finished the war as gunnery officer on the *Arkansas*. Promoted to the rank of commander in February 1918, Kimmel served at the Naval Gun Factory from 1920 to 1923, successively commanded two destroyer divisions in the Asiatic Fleet, and spent 1925–1926 as a student at the Naval War College. Advanced to captain, he occupied several prestigious posts. In the office of the chief of naval operations (CNO), he was liaison officer between the navy and State Department during the Nicaragua intervention (1926–1928). He also served as destroyer squadron commander with the Battle Fleet (1928–1930); director of ship movements in the office of the CNO (1930–1933); captain of the battleship *New York* (1933–1934); chief of staff of the fleet's battleship command (1934–1935); and budget officer of the navy (1935–1938). In November 1937 he was advanced to rear admiral.

Assigned to command of a cruiser division, Kimmel made a goodwill tour of South American ports in 1939 and later that year assumed command of all cruisers in the Battle Force, then operating in the Pacific. His bold tactical leadership in this post attracted the notice of Secretary of the Navy Frank Knox. When the United States Fleet was divided into the Atlantic and Pacific fleets on Feb. 1, 1941, Kimmel was named commander in chief of the Pacific Fleet (while retaining the title of commander in chief of the United States Fleet) and given the temporary rank of four-star admiral; he was advanced over forty-six more-senior admirals because the navy was seeking young, dynamic commanders in its preparations for a probable war with Japan. Headquartered at Pearl Harbor, Hawaii, Kimmel labored to maintain the credibility of United States naval deterrence in the Pacific at a time when the navy's resources were being diverted to the Atlantic.

On Dec. 7, 1941, the Japanese launched their devastating surprise attack on Pearl Harbor, sinking or disabling most of the battleships moored there and destroying most of the army and navy aircraft in Hawaii. Along with the senior army commander, Lieutenant General Walter C. Short, Kimmel was relieved of command on December 17, reverting to his permanent rank of rear admiral, but he remained in Hawaii during the initial investigation of the disaster by a commission headed by Supreme Court Justice Owen J. Roberts. When the commission found Kimmel and Short guilty of "dereliction of duty," both men applied for retirement; Kimmel retired on Mar. 1, 1942. A proposed court-martial never materialized. Kimmel was immediately hired by a marine consulting engineering firm in New York under contract to the navy, for which he developed a drydock used in the Pacific war. In the long postwar debate over responsibility for the Pearl Harbor attack, he defended himself in a short book, *Admiral Kimmel's Story* (1955). He died in Groton, Conn.

The heated emotions over assigning blame for America's most ignominious defeat have clouded fair judgment of Kimmel's role. However "guilty" American political, diplomatic, and military leaders may have been in underestimating Japan's capability and intention to attack Pearl Harbor, Kimmel was the man on the spot and thus placed in the position of becoming the scapegoat, no matter what evidence might have surfaced to exonerate him. A keen strategist, he had appreciated full well the possibility of a Japanese attack, though he had shared the general belief that war would commence in the Philippines. Tactically, he had made the unfortunate analysis that any attack on Hawaii, if it came, would be from the southwest rather than the northwest. He had thus concentrated his limited patrol planes in the southwest, allowing the enemy to strike from the unprotected northwest. This was his fundamental military error—his "lack of superior judgment" in the words of Admiral Ernest J. King (quoted in Morison, p. 142)—and the one on which his ultimate performance must be weighed.

[Kimmel's papers are in the Naval Historical Foundation at the Library of Congress and at the University of Wyoming; copies are at the United States Naval Academy library. Kimmel's Naval Academy years are covered in his class's *Lucky Bag* (1904); and his role at Pearl Harbor is covered in the findings of the six commissions and boards compiled in United States Congress, Joint Committee on the Investigation of the Pearl Harbor Attack, *Pearl Harbor Attack: Hearings . . .* , 39 vols. (1946). These are summarized in Samuel Eliot Morison, *History of U.S. Naval Operations in World War II*, vol. III,

5*The Rising Sun in the Pacific* (1948), and are analyzed in Roberta Wohlstetter, *Pearl Harbor: Warning and Decision* (1962). Kimmel's ten days in command of the fleet at war are treated in Edwin P. Hoyt, *How They Won the War in the Pacific* (1970). Kimmel's entire career is traced in a biography at the Naval Historical Center, Washington, D.C. (1956); and in Clark G. Reynolds, *Famous American Admirals* (1978). An obituary is in the *New York Times*, May 15, 1968.]

CLARK G. REYNOLDS

KING, MARTIN LUTHER, JR. (Jan. 15, 1929–Apr. 4, 1968), Baptist minister and civil rights leader, was born in Atlanta, Ga., the son of Martin Luther King, Sr., a Baptist minister, and Alberta Williams. Known as M. L., young King was a gifted child. At five, he could recite biblical passages and sing hymns from memory. His parents and maternal grandmother praised his precocity, inculcating in him a lifelong self-esteem.

Nonetheless, he had his share of hurts and conflicts as a boy. Painfully sensitive, he twice tried to commit suicide by leaping from a second-story window, first when he thought his grandmother had been killed and then after she actually had died. He had a lot of anger in him too. Growing up black in segregated Atlanta, he felt the full range of racial discrimination—the Whites Only signs posted near public accommodations, the constant insults from whites, and the pain and humiliation of being called "nigger." He recalled being "determined to hate every white person."

Forced by law to attend inferior "colored" schools, he sailed through elementary school, skipping grades. At the Booker T. Washington High School he effortlessly achieved a B-plus average. Atlanta's Morehouse College then admitted exceptional high school juniors. In 1944 King passed the college's entrance examinations, graduated from high school after the eleventh grade, and entered Morehouse at age fifteen, thinking he might help his people by becoming a physician or a lawyer. However, largely because of the influence of Benjamin Mays, the president of Morehouse, King elected to become a minister. In 1947 he was ordained and made assistant pastor of Atlanta's Ebenezer Baptist Church, where his father was pastor. By that time, contact with white students on an intercollegiate council had softened King's resentment toward whites, but he hated his segregated world more than ever.

He was a sensuous young man who played the violin, enjoyed opera, and relished "soul food." He joked that food and women were his main weaknesses. Physically he stood five feet, seven inches, with a plump face, almond-shaped eyes, a mahogany complexion, and expressive hands. He claimed that he was an "ambivert," a cross between an extrovert and introvert, and that he had a tender heart as well as a tough mind. The most memorable thing about King was his voice, a rich and resonant baritone that commanded attention.

After graduating from Morehouse in 1948 with a degree in sociology, he attended Crozer Theological Seminary in Pennsylvania. In 1951 he graduated at the top of his class with a B.A. in divinity. King was influenced by the writings of the Social Gospeler Walter Rauschenbusch. He learned that a socially relevant faith must deal with the whole man—his body and soul, his material and spiritual well-being—and must work for the kingdom of God on earth as well as in heaven.

Inspired by Rauschenbusch's denunciation of capitalism's exaltation of profit over brotherhood, King developed distinct "anticapitalist feelings." Yet, as a Christian minister, he abhorred Communism, which he thought fundamentally evil, an atheistic ideology that denied man's spiritual needs and led to "crippling totalitarianism." The best economic system, he decided, was one that synthesized collective and individual enterprise.

At Crozer, King also became an ardent disciple of Gandhi, whose teachings about nonviolent resistance and redemptive love became the foundations of King's own philosophy. Indeed, Gandhi was a personal revelation for King, who had felt considerable hatred in his life, especially toward whites. Gandhi showed him a means of harnessing his anger and channeling it into a positive and creative force for social change.

Assisted by a $1,300 scholarship, King entered Boston University in the fall of 1951 to obtain a Ph.D. in systematic theology. On June 18, 1953, he married Coretta Scott, a student at Boston's New England Conservatory of Music. They had four children.

While serving as pastor of Dexter Avenue Baptist Church in Montgomery, Ala., King completed a Ph.D. thesis entitled "A Comparison of the Conceptions of God in the Thinking of Paul Tillich and Henry Nelson Wieman." He received his doctorate in 1955. His adviser, L. Harold De Wolf, thought him "a scholar's scholar" of great intellectual potential. King was happy in the world of ideas and said he hoped someday to teach theology at a university or seminary.

But that was not to be. In December 1955 Montgomery blacks undertook a boycott of the segregated city buses and chose King as their leader. He was unusually well prepared for this role: drawing on Gandhi's teachings, he directed a nonviolent boycott designed both to end an injustice and to redeem his white adversaries through love. Love, he said, not only avoided the internal violence of the spirit but also severed the external chain of hatred that only produced more hatred. Somebody, he argued, must be willing to break this chain so that "the beloved community" could be restored and true brotherhood could begin.

In sharp contrast, white supremacists threatened King's life and in January 1957 dynamited his home, but luckily no one was hurt. Two months earlier, on Nov. 13, 1956, the boycotters had won a resounding moral victory when the United States Supreme Court nullified the Alabama laws that enforced segregated buses. Although it was not the first bus boycott in the South, the Montgomery protest captured the imagination of progressive people the world over and marked the beginning of a southern black movement that rocked the segregated South to its foundations.

King emerged as an inspiring new moral voice in civil rights. It was during the mass meetings in Montgomery's black churches that King discovered his extraordinary oratorical powers. His rich religious imagery reached deep into the black psyche, for religion had been black people's main source of strength and survival since the days of slavery. A woman journalist named Almena Lomax compared his voice to "a narrative poem," claiming that it had such depths of tenderness and sincerity that it could "charm your heart right out of your body." He could make unlettered people respond to a quotation from Hegel or Thomas Aquinas. "I don't know what that boy talkin' about," said one black woman, "but I sure like the way he sounds."

In August 1957 King and 115 other black leaders met in Montgomery and formed the Southern Christian Leadership Conference (SCLC), with King as its presiding and guiding spirit. Operating through southern churches, the SCLC sought to enlist the black masses in the freedom struggle by expanding "the Montgomery way" across the South.

In 1958 King's *Stride Toward Freedom: The Montgomery Story* was published. It was widely read and acclaimed. When a promotional tour took him to New York City in September, a deranged black woman stabbed him in the chest with a letter opener. After recuperating, he made a pilgrimage to India in February 1959 and rededicated himself to Gandhian principles. Yet he was a man of contradictions. While renouncing material things and trying to emulate Gandhi, he liked to stay in posh hotels and was always immaculately dressed. While caring passionately for the poor, the downtrodden, and the disinherited, he was fascinated by the rich and enjoyed the company of wealthy SCLC benefactors.

In 1960 King moved his family to Atlanta so that he could devote most of his time to the SCLC and civil rights. He served, too, as copastor of his father's Ebenezer Baptist Church. When southern black students launched the sit-in movement that winter and spring, King helped them form the Student Nonviolent Coordinating Committee (SNCC). He raised money for the organization and provided it with a temporary office at the Atlanta headquarters of the SCLC. In October 1960 King joined local college students in a sit-in against the segregated snack bar of an Atlanta department store and was arrested when he refused to leave. He considered it "a badge of honor" to be imprisoned for violating unjust laws. He was put in a cell for hardened criminals at the state prison in Reidsville, Ga. State officials released him when Democratic presidential nominee John F. Kennedy and his brother Robert interceded for King. According to many analysts, the episode ensured the crucial black votes for Kennedy that won him the election in November.

Through 1961 and 1962 King pressured the Kennedy administration to support a tough civil rights bill. King urged the president to issue a second Emancipation Proclamation, one that would employ federal power to wipe out segregation just as Lincoln's decree had used it to vanquish slavery. When Kennedy shied away from a strong civil rights commitment, King and his lieutenants took matters into their own hands. They orchestrated a series of mass demonstrations throughout the South. Their protests resulted in the strongest civil rights legislation in American history to date.

Getting the federal government to act was the purpose of all King's major southern campaigns. He and his staff would single out some notoriously segregated city with officials prone to violence; mobilize the local blacks with songs, Scripture readings, and rousing oratory; and then lead them on protest marches conspicuous for their nonviolent spirit and moral purpose. Then they would increase their demands—even fill up the jails—until they brought about a moment of "creative tension," when white authorities would either agree to negotiate or resort to violence. If the authorities did the latter, the brutality inherent in segregation would be exposed, stabbing the national conscience and causing the federal government to intervene.

The technique failed in the 1962 campaign in Albany, Ga., where white authorities handled King's marchers with unruffled decorum. ("We killed them with kindness," chuckled one city official.) But the next year it succeeded brilliantly in Birmingham, Ala., where Police Commissioner Eugene ("Bull") Connor went berserk at the spectacle of the marching blacks and turned firehoses and police dogs on them—in full view of reporters and television cameras. King thus exposed racist savagery to the court of national and world opinion. Jailed during the demonstrations, King wrote his classic "Letter from Birmingham Jail," perhaps the most eloquent expression of the goals and philosophy of the nonviolent movement. Revolted by the ghastly scenes in Birmingham and stricken by King's eloquence and the bravery of his unarmed followers, the government eventually produced the 1964 Civil Rights Act, which desegregated public facilities—the thing King had demanded all along.

The technique also worked in Selma, Ala., in 1965. King launched a drive in support of a federal voting rights law for blacks. The violence that resulted in Selma—the beating of black marchers by state troopers and deputies, the killing of a young black deacon and a white Unitarian minister—horrified the country. When King asked for help, thousands of ministers, rabbis, priests, nuns, lay leaders, students, and ordinary people—white and black alike—rushed to Selma from all over the nation to stand with King in the name of human liberty. Never in the history of the movement had so many people of all faiths and classes come to the southern battleground. The Selma campaign culminated in a mass march to Montgomery, the state capital. Before the statehouse, a throng of 25,000—the largest civil rights demonstration the South had ever witnessed—sang a new rendition of "We Shall Overcome," the anthem of the black movement. They sang, "Deep in my heart, I do believe, we have overcome—*today*."

The Selma campaign, like those in Birmingham and Albany, underscored King's significance as a civil rights leader: his ability to arouse the spirit of oppressed men and women, helping them "destroy barriers of fear and insecurity that had been hundreds of years in the making," as black leader Cleveland Sellers said. Whereas segregation had taught blacks all their lives that they were nobody, King taught them that they were somebody. Nonviolent resistance furnished blacks with something no other black leader had been able to provide: a way of controlling anger and using it as a constructive force for social change.

Aroused by the events in Alabama, Congress passed the 1965 Voting Rights Act, which outlawed impediments to black voting and empowered the attorney general to supervise federal elections in seven southern states where blacks were kept from the polls. Political analysts almost unanimously gave King's Selma campaign credit for the law. With federal examiners supervising voter registration, blacks were able to get on the rolls. They voted by the hundreds of thousands, permanently altering the pattern of southern and national politics. The civil rights legislation generated by King and his tramping legions ended statutory racism in America and realized at least the social and political promise of emancipation a century before.

The Voting Rights Act was the result of a broad civil rights coalition that included the federal government, various white organizations, the SCLC, and other civil rights organizations. King expressed the coalition's spirit and aspirations when, on Aug. 28, 1963, standing before the Lincoln Memorial, he electrified an interracial crowd of 250,000 with perhaps his greatest speech, "I Have a Dream." Because of his achievements and moral vision, he won the

1964 Nobel Peace Prize. At thirty-five he was the youngest recipient in Nobel history.

However, King paid a high price for his achievement and fame. He suffered from stomachaches and insomnia. Born in relative material comfort and given a superior education, he believed he had not earned the right to lead the impoverished black masses. He complained, too, that he no longer had a personal self and that sometimes he did not recognize the public King. Away from home and his wife for protracted periods, beset with temptation, he slept with other women and often felt guilty about it. In the late summer or early fall of 1963, the director of the Federal Bureau of Investigation (FBI), J. Edgar Hoover, found out about King's sexual indiscretions and claimed that King was a hypocrite and a dangerous subversive under Communist influence. Under Hoover's orders, FBI agents conducted a ruthless secret crusade to discredit King. They not only tapped King's and the SCLC's telephones (which Attorney General Robert Kennedy authorized), but planted unauthorized and illegal microphones in his hotel rooms, distributed to various journalists and political and religious leaders a monograph that accused him of sexual and financial misconduct, and even sent King a composite tape with a note hinting that he should kill himself.

After the August 1965 riot in the Watts section of Los Angeles, King took his movement to the racially troubled urban North. Several members of his staff objected when in 1966 he opened a campaign to end the conditions that led to the formation of black slums and forestall rioting in Chicago. Despite the powerful opposition of Mayor Richard Daley, King extracted concessions from city hall, and the SCLC established Operation Breadbasket, which utilized a network of black churches to pressure local merchants to hire blacks and sell products made by black-owned companies. Nevertheless, the slums remained as wretched as ever.

In 1966 angry young militants in SNCC and the Congress of Racial Equality (CORE) renounced King's teachings and advocated "black power," black separatism, and even violent resistance to racism. King retorted that black separatism was chimerical, if not suicidal, and that nonviolence remained the only workable way. "Darkness cannot drive out darkness," he reasoned; "only light can do that. Hate cannot drive out hate; only love can do that." Despite his efforts, black power fragmented the black movement.

As a champion of world peace, King first condemned the Vietnam War in the summer of 1965, and by 1967 he was devoting entire speeches to denunciations of the conflict. American ghettos across the country, King warned, were likely to explode with riots if funds used for the war were not diverted to antipoverty programs. Because of King's stance against the war, the Johnson administration cooperated with the FBI in its attempts to defame him.

King became increasingly distressed about the plight of the poor. Convinced that America would do nothing about poverty without pressure and confrontation, he devised a bold new project called the Poor People's Campaign. The master plan, worked out by February 1968, called for the SCLC to lead an interracial army of poor people to Washington to dramatize poverty. King was projecting a genuine class movement that he hoped would bring about significant changes in American society—a redistribution of economic and political power, and an end to poverty, racism, and war.

In the midst of his preparations, King went to Memphis, Tenn., to help black sanitation workers who were striking for the right to unionize. An assassin's bullet struck him down at the Lorraine Motel in Memphis' waterfront area. Subsequently, James Earl Ray, a convict who had escaped from the Missouri State Penitentiary, was arrested, convicted, and sentenced to life imprisonment for King's murder. In the late 1970's, evidence compiled by the Select Committee on Assassinations, United States House of Representatives, pointed conclusively to Ray as King's lone assassin and to a link between Ray and two right-wing St. Louis area residents—John Kauffmann and John Sutherland—who had offered substantial sums of money for King's life.

King was a preeminent spokesman for human rights in his time. He had reached more blacks, more Americans, more citizens of the world, than any other American reform leader in the twentieth century. He was one of America's most erudite social and religious activists—a scholarly and yet passionate young minister who forged a world view of profound historical and spiritual insight.

[The largest collection of King materials is in the archives of the Martin Luther King, Jr., Center for

Nonviolent Social Change in Atlanta. Another important collection is in the Mugar Memorial Library at Boston University. Among King's books are *Strength to Love* (1963); *Why We Can't Wait* (1964); *Where Do We Go from Here: Chaos or Community?* (1967); *The Trumpet of Conscience* (1968); and *A Testament of Hope: The Essential Writings of Martin Luther King, Jr.*, James Melvin Washington, ed. (1986).

Memoirs and contemporary assessments include Coretta Scott King, *My Life with Martin Luther King, Jr.* (1969); Charles Eric Lincoln, ed., *Martin Luther King, Jr.: A Profile* (1970); Martin Luther King, Sr., with Clayton Riley, *Daddy King: An Autobiography* (1980); and Harris Wofford, *Of Kennedys and Kings: Making Sense of the Sixties* (1980).

Biographies include L. D. Reddick, *Crusader Without Violence: A Biography of Martin Luther King, Jr.* (1959); David L. Lewis, *King: A Biography* (2nd ed., 1978); Stephen B. Oates, *Let the Trumpet Sound: The Life of Martin Luther King, Jr.* (1982); and David J. Garrow, *Bearing the Cross: Martin Luther King, Jr., and the Southern Christian Leadership Conference, 1955–1968* (1986).]

STEPHEN B. OATES

KIPHUTH, ROBERT JOHN HERMAN (Nov. 17, 1890–Jan. 7, 1967), swimming coach and physical educator, was born in Tonawanda, N.Y., the son of John Kiphuth, a lumber-mill hand, and Mary Benin. He graduated from Tonawanda High School in 1909. The next year, Kiphuth became director of physical education at the Tonawanda Young Men's Christian Association (YMCA). During the summer he studied physical education at Silver Bay, N.Y. (1911), Harvard (1912), and Buffalo (1913–1916). In 1914, Dr. W. G. Anderson, the head of Yale's athletic department, hired the short and heavily muscled Kiphuth as a physical education instructor. Kiphuth also audited undergraduate courses. On June 6, 1917, he married Louise DeLaney, who had introduced him to Anderson; they had one child.

In 1917, Kiphuth was asked to coach Yale's swimming team. Initially reluctant because he had no background in swimming, Kiphuth ultimately agreed, and in 1918 he became the varsity swimming coach. He later said, "I must have read a million books on the subject during the months right after my appointment." As a coach, Kiphuth defied the prevailing convention, which held that bodybuilding was harmful, by developing exercises to make swimmers strong and loose-limbed. His program included calisthenics and the use of pulleys and medicine balls. Swimmers had to churn water for weeks before they were allowed to swim. The emphasis on conditioning resulted in sixty-five straight victories for Yale in dual meets from 1918 to 1924, when the streak ended with losses to the United States Naval Academy and Princeton.

In the 1920's, Kiphuth spent most summers in Sweden and Germany studying physical education and swimming. He coached the United States Olympic women's swimming team in 1928, and his reputation was enhanced when American women won five swimming titles in Amsterdam. In 1932, the year he was promoted to assistant professor at Yale, Kiphuth wrote *The Diagnosis and Treatment of Postural Defects* with Dr. Winthrop Phelps. That same year, Kiphuth was head coach of the United States Olympic swimming team in Los Angeles; the men won three titles and the women six. Kiphuth served as chairman of the Amateur Athletic Union's swimming commission from 1933 to 1935, and he coached the American swimming team competing in Japan in 1931, 1934, and 1935.

Kiphuth kept detailed charts on each swimmer's conditioning. He never cut anyone from his Yale team: cramps did that. In the gym, Kiphuth was tough and demanding. He was no less hard on himself. On the way to Berlin in 1936, Kiphuth ignored his streptococcal fever and continued to direct the United States men's Olympic team, practicing in the ship's pool. John Macionis of Yale was a member of the American squad that won two gold medals that year.

Yale's Timothy Dwight College made Kiphuth a fellow in 1936. From 1924 to 1937, Yale swimming teams won 175 straight dual meets, until upset by Harvard. In 1940, Kiphuth was promoted to associate professor, and he became director of the Payne Whitney Gymnasium, opened eight years earlier and already the site of many world records in swimming. While barking orders during calisthenics, Kiphuth sometimes used dance terms.

Kiphuth was again named head coach of the Olympic swimming team, but there were no games in 1940. The year after the United States entered World War II, Kiphuth wrote *How to Be Fit*. According to the foreword by John Kieran, the book's aim is "to strengthen arms that they may fitly bear arms." Many servicemen learned to swim by using the backstroke instead of the crawl, a stroke that Kiphuth disliked. He noted in his book *Basic Swimming* (1950; written with Harry M. Burke), "The thrashing victim is likely to arrive at the end of the course more dead than alive." The army and navy located officer-training schools at Yale, and Kiphuth directed the physical training of a campus in uniform.

A Yale winning streak ended in 1945, after sixty-three victories, when West Point won a dual meet that went to the final relay. The next year, Kiphuth became Yale's athletic director. His greatest Olympic achievement was the sweep at London in 1948. The United States men's team took first place in all six swimming and both diving events. Seven medals were won by Yale swimmers: Alan Ford (silver), Allan Stack (gold), John Marshall (silver, bronze), and James McLane (two gold, one silver). McLane had belonged to Kiphuth's New Haven Swimming Club.

After a heart attack in 1949, Kiphuth continued to teach and coach but was succeeded as athletic director by his son, DeLaney Kiphuth, a Yale 1941 graduate. Two of Robert Kiphuth's younger brothers, Oscar and Carl, also worked for the Yale athletic department. In 1950, Kiphuth, who had never graduated from college, was promoted to full professor. Kiphuth stressed exercise for women, saying, "Women generally learn to swim more skillfully than men at almost any age." Kiphuth was a member of the boards of trustees of the Boy Scouts, YMCA, and Hotchkiss School. He gave swimming clinics for the United States Army in Europe in 1951, 1952, and 1953, and in 1955 he went to Israel to help train the Israeli Olympic team.

Kiphuth was popular with students and alumni, many of whom admired his collection of first editions, which emphasized American literature. In 1958, John Schiff, the business manager of the 1925 swimming team, donated a book to the Yale Library in honor of his coach: *A Short Introduction for to Learne to Swimme*, printed in 1595.

Kiphuth retired in 1959 with a winning streak of 182 dual meets. In forty-two years, his squads had won 528 dual meets while losing only 12. Yale won 38 Eastern Intercollegiate championships and 14 National Collegiate Athletic Association championships. Although called the greatest swimming coach in history, Kiphuth did not like to swim. His successor at Yale, Philip Moriarty, remarked, "Bob didn't go in the water because he didn't particularly like the water. So he never swam." Kiphuth played handball and squash. Retirement included traveling around the world to give swimming clinics. From Japan, Kiphuth received the Third-Class Order of the Sacred Treasure, and Lyndon B. Johnson awarded him the Presidential Medal of Freedom in December 1963. Kiphuth died in New Haven following an afternoon at the pool watching Yale beat West Point.

[Kiphuth's papers are in Yale's Payne Whitney Gymnasium. He also wrote the book *Swimming* (1942). The brochure *Yale and the Olympics* (1981), issued by the Yale Department of Athletics, has information on Kiphuth and the Kiphuth Fellowship Program. Interviews are in the *New York Times*, Mar. 16, 1931, and Jan. 22, 1955. See Charles Rumford Walker, "Campus Revolution at Yale," *American Mercury*, Feb. 1944; "Alan Ford of Yale, Swimming Champion," *Life*, Mar. 5, 1945; and John Knowles, "How to Make Champions," *Saturday Evening Post*, Mar. 3, 1956. Obituaries are in the *New York Times*, Jan. 9, 1967; *Yale Daily News*, Jan. 9 and 10, 1967; and *Yale Alumni Magazine*, Feb. 1967.]

RALPH KIRSHNER

KIPLINGER, WILLARD MONROE (Jan. 8, 1891–Aug. 6, 1967), journalist and publisher, was born in Bellefontaine, Ohio, the son of Clarence Elmer Kiplinger, a carriage maker, and Cora Miller. He attended public schools in Bellefontaine, Dayton, and Columbus. Kiplinger enrolled in a new program in journalism at Ohio State University and in 1912 was part of its two-man graduating class. The Columbus *Ohio State Journal* hired him as a reporter and assigned him the city hall beat. After two years at the *Journal* he began covering the state capitol for the Associated Press (AP). The news service then transferred him to Washington, D.C., to report on the Treasury Department. There he acquired a knowledge of governmental finance. "I understood what a rediscount rate was," he later explained, "and that made me an expert." From 1916 to 1919 he served in the AP Washington bureau.

Lured away from reporting by New York's National Bank of Commerce in 1920, Kiplinger spent almost three years discovering how much vital news affecting business-government relations was being suppressed by excessively cautious public officials. By 1923 Kiplinger was ready to become his own boss. He tried his hand at free-lance writing for newspapers and magazines and then borrowed $1,000 to begin the *Kiplinger Washington Letter*, a mimeographed, one-page weekly newsletter. The annual subscription price of $10 attracted limited support, and only the income from Kiplinger's free-lance articles prevented the venture's failure. Kiplinger developed a writing style notable for telegraphic brevity. Years later he described his staccato writing: "Brevity, brevity. Essence. Main point. Scant detail. Speed." By 1928 he had expanded the newsletter to four pages and had 3,000 paying customers.

Kiplinger ("Kip" to his friends) profited from the New Deal, which greatly expanded the role of the federal government in all phases of business activity. His staff of one reporter and two secretaries also grew, until the firm had departments for news, sales, accounting, and medical care. Kiplinger acquired two buildings, created a publishing subsidiary, and added his *Tax Letter* (1925), *Agricultural Letter* (1929), *Florida Letter* (1956), and *California Letter* (1965) to his news empire.

In 1947 Kiplinger founded the monthly magazine *Changing Times*. Aimed at a family readership, the magazine provided information on investments, budgeting, home ownership, and credit. No advertising was accepted. Circulation grew steadily, and by 1967 *Changing Times* had almost 1.25 million subscribers. Although he remained editor in chief, Kiplinger increasingly delegated duties to others. He turned the presidency of his publishing corporation over to his son Austin in 1961 and devoted more time to civic affairs, an azalea garden, and a collection of historic prints and paintings of Washington, D.C. He presented to the Smithsonian Institution fifty bronze statuettes (created for him by the sculptor Max Kalish) portraying political and military leaders of the 1930's and 1940's.

Kiplinger wrote four popular books: *Inflation Ahead!* (1935), *Washington Is Like That* (1942), *Kiplinger Looks to the Future* (1958), and *Kiplinger Sees Prosperity Ahead* (1959). Kiplinger also developed an interest in education. He helped establish the Washington educational television station, and in 1965 he organized the Washington Journalism Center, a nonprofit graduate school for aspiring reporters of national and international news.

In 1914 Kiplinger married Irene Austin. They had two children before they were divorced in 1923. He married Leslie Jackson in 1926, and they had one child; that marriage was dissolved in 1931. Then, in 1936, he married LaVerne Colwell; they had one child. Kiplinger died in Bethesda, Md.

[Kiplinger's personal correspondence is in the archives of the Kiplinger Washington Editors, in Washington, D.C. See also *Newsweek*, Jan. 6, 1947; *Saturday Evening Post*, Jan. 25, 1947; and *Nation's Business*, Aug. 1966. An obituary is in the *New York Times*, Aug. 7, 1967.]

ROBERT A. RUTLAND

KISS, MAX (Nov. 9, 1882–June 22, 1967), pharmacist and pharmaceutical manufacturer, was born Miksa Kiss in Kisvárda, Hungary, the son of Illes Kiss, a lumber merchant, and Regina Schwartz. After graduating from high school in 1897, Kiss left home. Borrowing money from a friend of his father, Kiss made his way to Hamburg, Germany, and boarded a ship for New York City. He had heard that "everyone in America shoveled gold right from the streets. I wanted to shovel."

When Kiss arrived in New York City, his only possessions were the clothes he wore. Hungry and unable to speak English, he walked the streets for sixteen hours until a storekeeper directed him to a shelter for immigrants, the Baron de Hirsch Home. There he got free lodging and a lead to a job. His first employment was nailing skins for a furrier at $2.50 a week, and he studied English at night school. A few months later, Kiss began serving an apprenticeship as a druggist. In 1902 he entered the Columbia University College of Pharmacy, from which he received the degree of Ph.G. in 1904. During these two years, he worked in a drugstore without a day off and attended classes at night. In 1904 he also became a United States citizen. On Aug. 23, 1910, Kiss married Minna Cohen; they had two children.

By 1906, Kiss had saved enough money to visit his family in Hungary, and the trip determined his future. Some years before, the German chemist Karl Joseph Bayer, the inventor of aspirin, had also developed phenolphthalein, an odorless and tasteless synthetic organic compound useful as an analytical reagent, and now

Kiss learned that Zoltán von Vamossy, a Hungarian professor, had made an interesting observation about phenolphthalein. Certain wine merchants in Hungary used small amounts of the powder to reveal the presence of adulterants. Professor Vamossy, in verifying the harmlessness of the reagent, accidentally discovered its laxative properties.

From this unexpected circumstance came the world's most widely used laxative ingredient. Experimenting on himself, Kiss took a small dose, which confirmed its effectiveness. As a pharmacist, he knew that children, repelled by the taste, fought against taking castor oil, then the common laxative. He put phenolphthalein into a pleasant-tasting chocolate tablet; it won popular favor among his clientele.

Kiss gave up his job to concentrate on manufacturing, packaging, and marketing the chocolate laxative. It was first offered as Bo-Bo (from *bonbon*) but a claimant with prior rights to the name appeared. The search for a new name ended when Kiss's brother, Adolph, called attention to a report in a Hungarian newspaper that there had been an *ex lax* in the Hungarian parliament, a term meaning that legislation was blocked. Bo-Bo quickly became Ex-Lax, which could be also construed as a contraction of the words *excellent* and *laxative*. To introduce Ex-Lax, Kiss utilized consumer sampling, small space advertisements, and point-of-purchase displays. Later, radio and television advertising were also employed. The Ex-Lax logo also appeared on drugstore windows and became a familiar part of the American scene. (When Edward Hopper painted *Drugstore*, an Ex-Lax sign occupied a prominent place in the composition.)

As a further promotional device Kiss gave store owners shares of stock with their orders, one share with each ten-dollar order. Eventually, these shares were purchased by the General Cigar Company for $500 each. In its early years the business was undercapitalized, but the needed capital was supplied by Israel Matz, a drug wholesaler; Ex-Lax was incorporated in 1908. Ultimately, Ex-Lax became the largest-selling laxative in the world.

In his later years as treasurer and chairman of Ex-Lax, Kiss encouraged an aggressive program of acquisition and product development that transformed Ex-Lax into a diversified pharmaceutical company with plants in Canada and England as well as Brooklyn, N.Y.

Kiss was a zestful man who enjoyed telling stories. One of his publicity ideas, he later recounted, was a commercial film for local theaters. The movie portrayed youngsters climbing into an apple tree, eating apples, and then running home with stomachaches. The mothers prescribed Ex-Lax. "I used my son and all his friends for the cast," Kiss recalled. "There were no apples on the trees so I bought some and tied them on. I found out later that it was an oak tree."

Kiss was active in various philanthropic causes and civic affairs in Brooklyn. He looked upon his charities and public service as a way of repaying the United States for the opportunities it had given him. He died in Atlantic Beach, Long Island, N.Y.

[See typescripts from the Ex-Lax Pharmaceutical Company, "A Brief History of Ex-Lax" and "Obituary of Max Kiss." See also articles in *Drug Trade News*, Aug. 5, 1963; and *Journal of the American Pharmaceutical Association*, Sept. 1967. Obituaries are in the *New York Times*, June 23, 1967; and *Time*, June 30, 1967.]

GERALD CARSON

KNIGHT, GOODWIN JESS ("GOODIE") (Dec. 9, 1896–May 22, 1970), attorney and governor of California, was born in Provo, Utah, the son of Jesse Knight, a lawyer and mining engineer, and Lillie Milner. Shortly after his birth, the family moved to Southern California, where his father participated in developing the mines of the Mojave Desert. Knight spent his childhood in Los Angeles and attended Manual Arts High School.

In 1915, Knight enrolled at Stanford University and soon became involved in all phases of campus life, from debating to amateur theatricals and even tap dancing. One close companion recalled that Knight seemed "the eternal sophomore. Everyone knew he was around." On the eve of his graduation in 1917, Knight enlisted in the United States Navy for service in World War I. He spent a year on a submarine chaser and was discharged in January 1919. Knight then returned to Stanford and collected his B.A. degree. In 1919–1920 he went to Cornell University, where he studied political science. He was admitted to the California bar in March 1921. In 1925, Knight formed a partnership with Thomas Reynolds, a Stanford classmate, and within a decade the firm possessed one of the most important practices in the state.

Knight, a Republican, campaigned on behalf of Hiram Johnson in 1924, but his serious involvement in California politics started ten years later when he went to work for Frank Merriam. As a payment for political services, Governor Merriam appointed Knight to a vacancy on the Los Angeles Superior Court, where he proved a competent judge. Knight used the position to launch his political ambitions. The medium of radio offered him access to a wide audience, and in 1941 he became the moderator of "The Open Forum," a well-known discussion program in Los Angeles. He later boosted his statewide recognition by traveling to San Francisco on weekends to host "The Round Table," a Bay-area radio show. During these years, Knight was twice elected to the superior court.

Knight's efforts to gain statewide elective office commenced in earnest in the mid-1940's. In 1944 he sought a United States Senate seat, but the Republican party leadership endorsed Lieutenant Governor Frederick N. Houser. Two years later, Knight hired the campaign management firm of Whitaker and Baxter to direct his bid for lieutenant governor. In a remarkable display of energy, Knight toured some fifty counties in California, campaigning on the popular postwar platform of economy in government and urging the development of the state's water resources, a long-standing issue in California politics. In the fall election, he won a landslide victory over State Senator John F. Shelley.

As lieutenant governor, Knight worked to broaden the power and visibility of his office. He added assignments to the lieutenant governor's traditional role of presiding in the state senate and was appointed to serve on the state's land commission and disaster council, the University of California Board of Regents, the toll bridge authority, and a committee for interstate cooperation.

A thoroughly political man, Knight often calculated his activities toward future elections. He began to anticipate the retirement of Governor Earl Warren. Knight gave enthusiastic support in 1948 to the presidential ticket of Thomas E. Dewey and Earl Warren, but Truman's surprise victory ended Knight's dream of an easy upward move into Warren's office. By 1950, Knight had begun to distance himself from the liberal governor. He publicly criticized as too liberal Warren's positions on such topics as state health insurance, loyalty oaths, and fiscal matters, and many Republicans felt that he would challenge Warren in 1954.

Early in September 1953, Warren announced that he would not seek another term, and on September 16, Knight proclaimed his own candidacy and forecast a "businesslike administration with emphasis on reduced spending." Knight became California's thirty-first governor on October 5 when President Eisenhower appointed Warren to the United States Supreme Court. Knight commenced a whirlwind tour of the state to ensure his election the next year. He altered his image to appeal to Warren's vast constituency in that while he continued to talk of fiscal conservatism, he emphasized that public services should not be sacrificed.

Knight's first budget, delivered to the state legislature in March 1954, reflected his new outlook. Despite a $6 million reduction in total spending, Knight increased funding for mental hygiene, youth and correctional facilities, state colleges, and the University of California. The governor also recommended a single agency to regulate the control of alcoholic beverages, an increase in unemployment insurance payments, and a bond issue for veterans' farms and homes.

Knight seemed assured of victory in the fall election, despite a new law that required a candidate's party affiliation to be listed on the ballot. Confident of the Republican nomination, Knight also sought the Democratic party's nomination for governor. As Warren had done, he narrowly missed capturing both but went on to a substantial victory in the general election. Democrats welcomed his promise to veto any right-to-work law passed by the state legislature.

During his years as governor, Knight continued his predecessor's agenda. He recommended increases in social spending and even signed into law a bill that created permanent child-care centers. During the recession of 1957, he used the California "rainy day" fund to avoid raising taxes but explained that state responsibilities had grown so great in the last twenty years that a reevaluation of the state tax structure was overdue.

To the public, Knight seemed an amiable,

competent governor, the type of man who would be reelected without opposition. But within Republican ranks, a growing conservative movement, led by Senator William F. Knowland, was disenchanted with the liberal wing of the party. In 1957, rumors began to circulate that Knowland would oppose Knight in the primary contest for governor in 1958. Such an ideological battle within California would have had national consequences. Vice-President Richard Nixon, worried that a liberal-conservative feud would ruin his election prospects for 1960, immersed himself in state politics in an effort to bring party peace. The result was an unusual compromise: Nixon pressured Knight to drop out of the governor's race and permit Knowland to be nominated, and Knight, with Knowland's blessing, would run for the latter's seat in the United States Senate. When Knight refused to support Knowland because of the conservative's endorsement of right-to-work legislation, the old coalition that had controlled California politics for a generation collapsed. Both Knight and Knowland lost their races. The only one to emerge with his political base intact was Richard Nixon. Knight's defeat marked the end of his political career.

Knight spent the remainder of his life preoccupied with domestic concerns. His family life had always been happy. On Sept. 19, 1925, he had married Arvilla Cooley; they had two children. In 1954, two years after the death of his first wife, he married Virginia Carlson.

Goodwin Knight served as governor of California during a period of unusual growth. He felt that his most important contribution was the creation of the state's Department of Water Resources and the completion of such major water-conservation works as the Feather River project, which helped to expand the state's industrial and agricultural base.

[Knight's private papers are at Stanford University; his official papers are in the California State Archives, Sacramento. Additional correspondence may be found in a number of collections at the Bancroft Library of the University of California at Berkeley. See Thomas S. Barclay, "The 1954 Election in California," *Western Political Quarterly*, VII (1954); Ralph Friedman, "The Gay Beaver," *Frontier Magazine*, June 1958; Totton J. Anderson, "The 1958 Election in California," *Western Political Quarterly*, XI (1959); and H. Brett Melendy and Benjamin F. Gilbert, *The Governors of California* (1965). An obituary is in the *New York Times*, May 23, 1970.]

GERALD THOMPSON

KNOPF, BLANCHE WOLF (July 30, 1893–June 4, 1966), editor and publisher, was born in New York City, the daughter of Julius W. Wolf, a wealthy jeweler, and Bertha Samuels. She was tutored by governesses and attended New York City's Gardner School. In 1911 she met Alfred A. Knopf, who was in his senior year at Columbia University. Blanche became Knopf's fiancée and strongly supported his desire to be a book publisher. In 1915, with $5,000 obtained from his father, Knopf started a publishing house in the elder Knopf's Manhattan office. Blanche worked in the business from the outset. The two were married on Apr. 4, 1916; they had one child, Alfred, Jr., who also became a successful publisher.

At first the Knopfs worked on all phases of the operation. They solicited authors, read manuscripts, designed books, wrote advertising copy, and kept an eye on the mechanics of production. When her husband traveled, Blanche Knopf "kept shop." (She sometimes referred to herself as the firm's "charwoman.") She brought to her job a sharp intelligence and an enormous capacity for work. She acquired a sound knowledge of typography, paper, and printing, as well as familiarity with the work of European writers. She is credited with the creation of the noted Borzoi (Russian wolfhound) imprint on Knopf books. In 1921 she became a vice-president and director of the corporation.

The firm first made its reputation by publishing European authors in attractively designed books. W. H. Hudson's *Green Mansions* (1916) was the first big seller; it was followed by works of E. M. Forster, A. A. Milne, Thomas Mann, Knut Hamsun, Robert Bridges, and Walter de la Mare, among others. Russian literature was well represented, with books by Tolstoi, Gogol, Goncharov, Gorki, and Lermontov. Among books by Americans were Joseph Hergesheimer's *The Three Black Pennys* (1917), E. W. Howe's *Ventures in Common Sense* (1919), and Willa Cather's *Youth and the Bright Medusa* (1920). From the first, Knopf's lists were strong in belles lettres, history, and music.

Beginning in 1920, Blanche Knopf made annual trips abroad until World War II restricted travel. She interviewed writers, solicited manuscripts, and arranged for translations. Much of the English and French flavor of Knopf's list was due to her influence. Her alertness to current literary trends bore fruit on a number of occasions. When interest in Sigmund Freud was strong in the mid-1930's, publishers sought his unfinished book on Moses. In September 1938, Blanche Knopf returned from Europe with the manuscript of *Moses and Monotheism*.

Among the French writers she published were André Gide, Jean-Paul Sartre, Jules Roy, Simone de Beauvoir, and Albert Camus. Camus, whom she met in Paris, became a special friend. (Her relationships with Camus, H. L. Mencken, Robert Nathan, Hergesheimer, and Cather were probably her most enduring and satisfying literary associations.) When Camus won the Nobel Prize in 1957, the Knopfs went to Stockholm for the ceremony. When he died in an auto accident in 1960, Blanche Knopf wrote a moving memoir, "Albert Camus in the Sun," for the *Atlantic* (February 1961). In recognition of her support of French literature in the United States, she was named a chevalier of the Legion of Honor in 1948. She spoke French fluently and Italian and Spanish somewhat less well.

During World War II she traveled to Latin America, commissioning books from writers such as Eduardo Mallea, Jorge Amado, Gilberto Freyre, and Germán Arciniegas. The *Saturday Review of Literature* (Apr. 10, 1943) published her account of the tour. ("Lima was exciting," she reported, "full of spies.") She also visited England and wrote "Impressions of British Publishing in Wartime" for *Publishers Weekly* (Dec. 18, 1943), in which she observed that the publishing business was thriving in England despite the scarcity of labor and paper. In 1945 she was named a consultant for the personnel narratives office of the army air force.

Many of Blanche Knopf's favorite authors were intellectuals, but she heartily approved of the hard-boiled fiction of Dashiell Hammett, James M. Cain, and Raymond Chandler. (She called Chandler "one of the best authors we had.") And she supported the publication of popular books by Fannie Hurst, Warwick Deeping, and Kahlil Gibran. Gibran's *Prophet* (1923) was one of the firm's all-time best-sellers (over 2 million copies). Blanche Knopf obtained William L. Shirer's *Berlin Diary* (1941), which was another big seller.

Mencken's *Book of Prefaces* (1917) was one of Knopf's early publications. The firm continued to publish Mencken's work for many years, including the journal *American Mercury* from 1924 to 1933, when he was editor. Blanche Knopf and Mencken were close friends; he thought she was more generous with authors than her husband. At her urging, Mencken enlarged his nostalgic, autobiographical articles for the *New Yorker* into three fine volumes—*Happy Days* (1940), *Newspaper Days* (1941), and *Heathen Days* (1943). When Mencken was mortally ill, Blanche Knopf was the only woman friend allowed to see him.

Blanche Knopf was strong-willed and confident in her judgments of literary matters. Professionally, she insisted on being called Blanche W. Knopf rather than Mrs. Alfred Knopf. She and her husband often failed to see eye to eye. Their tastes differed. "A good deal of the time in editorial meetings was taken up by Alfred's objections to Blanche's ideas," a former employee once said. In 1928, Alfred Knopf built a house in Purchase, N.Y.; evidently, though, Blanche Knopf was not happy there. Later she took an apartment in Manhattan within walking distance of her office. "A man and his wife," she said, "do not become Siamese twins, bent on identical pursuits and craving the same foods, friends, and diversions." The couple, though, did share a fondness for music and numbered among their friends Myra Hess, Jascha Heifetz, and Artur Rubinstein.

In 1960 the firm merged with Random House, with control going to the latter. Knopf preserved considerable autonomy, however, keeping its own writers, editors, and publishing style. Alfred A. Knopf remained chairman of the board, and Blanche Knopf retained the presidency she had held since 1957.

In her 1968 book on Mencken and his friends, Sara Mayfield described Blanche Knopf in the 1920's: "Small and slender . . . , she had great dignity and poise. Elegantly dressed, she was cosmopolitan, sprightly, indefatigable—a dark-haired, green-eyed dynamo of energy and enthusiasm." Harding Lemay, the firm's publicity director at one time, respected the Knopfs but was well aware of their foibles and eccentricities. He described Blanche Knopf in her later years as "shrewd, reticent, witty, a proud, wary, unapproachable lady."

In an article for *House Beautiful* (January 1948), Blanche Knopf wrote, "The world of books is the world I know. I would not change it for any other." In what was clearly a man's field, she not only survived but succeeded remarkably. She asked no quarter and gave none. During her career the firm published more than 5,000 titles. Borzoi imprints won eighteen Pulitzer Prizes and six National Book Awards. Eleven of Knopf's authors were Nobel Prize winners.

Blanche Knopf helped significantly to broaden the perspectives and enrich the content and style of book publishing in America over the span of a half-century. In her last years her health was poor. Her eyesight failed, yet she continued to put in long workdays that both astonished and appalled her associates. She died in New York City.

[Knopf's papers are at the Humanities Research Center at the University of Texas at Austin. There is a biographical sketch in Alden Whitman, *The Obituary Book* (1971). See Alfred A. Knopf, ed., *The Borzoi 1920*; Geoffrey T. Hellman, "Publishers," *New Yorker*, Nov. 20, 27, Dec. 4, 1948; "Borzoi at Random," *Time*, May 9, 1960; Clifton Fadiman, ed., *Fifty Years: Borzoi Books, 1915–1965* (1965); "Golden Anniversary of Excellence," *Life*, July 23, 1965; Charles A. Madison, *Book Publishing in America* (1966); Sara Mayfield, *The Constant Circle* (1968); Carl Bode, *Mencken* (1969), and, as ed., *The New Mencken Letters* (1977); Harding Lemay, *Inside, Looking Out* (1971); and Frank McShane, ed., *Selected Letters of Raymond Chandler* (1981).

Alfred A. Knopf, *Sixty Photographs* (1975), has a portrait of Blanche Knopf with Dorothy Canfield Fisher taken by Knopf. Obituaries are in the *New York Times*, June 5, 1966; *Publishers Weekly*, June 13, 1966; and *Newsweek*, June 20, 1966.]

WILLIAM MCCANN

KÖHLER, WOLFGANG (Jan. 21, 1887—June 11, 1967), psychologist, was born in Reval, Estonia, to German parents, Franz Köhler, an educator and Wilhelmine Girgensohn. When he was six, his family returned to Germany. Köhler attended school in Wolfenbüttel and then went to the universities of Tübingen (1905–1906), Bonn (1906–1907), and Berlin (1907–1909), where he studied under Carl Stumpf, Max Planck, and Walther Nernst. He received his Ph.D. in 1909; his dissertation was based on auditory investigations. In 1909 he also became assistant at the Psychological Institute at Frankfurt am Main. Köhler married his first wife in 1912; they had four children before their divorce. On July 9, 1927, he married Lili Harleman; they had one child.

At the institute Köhler met Max Wertheimer and Kurt Koffka; the collaboration that followed was the beginning of Gestalt psychology. Köhler remained at Frankfurt until 1913. During this period he continued his auditory studies and wrote an important paper, "On Unnoticed Sensations and Errors of Judgment" (1913). This sharp criticism of the elementarism of the prevailing psychology was the first published expression of Gestalt psychology as a protest movement.

In 1913 Köhler became director of the Anthropoid Station of the Prussian Academy of Sciences on the island of Tenerife. Intending to stay for a year, he was unable to return to Germany until 1920 because of World War I. His best-known work of this period, still widely studied, is *Mentality of Apes* (published in German in 1917 and in English in 1925). This book describes experiments on problem-solving in chimpanzees; it is concerned with the question of whether under favorable conditions nonhuman primates behave with insight. The animals found intelligent solutions when they were able to survey all relevant aspects of the situation and thus to behave in terms of its objectively given possibilities and obstacles. Although the focus of this work was observation and experiment, it presented a serious challenge to the then-dominant theories of association and trial and error in problem-solving and offered a new direction for the psychology of thinking.

At Tenerife, Köhler also carried out important work on perceptual functions in chimpanzees and hens. He began to search for new ways of training that would replace the tedious procedures current in studies of animals. As in the problem-solving experiments, when he devised situations that were simple, direct, and fully visible, the ease of learning increased dramatically.

Another major work of this period was his book *Die physischen Gestalten in Ruhe und im stationären Zustand* (1920), which examines the relations between Gestalt psychology and physics. Could a psychology whose fundamental category is gestalt be related to the other sciences? A "gestalt" is a structure that has specific properties as a whole and whose characteristics can therefore not be derived from those of constituent elements. Gestalt properties, as Christian von Ehrenfels had shown in 1890, are transposable; for example, a melody in one key can be recognized in another. Are such structures exclusive to psychology? An affirmative answer would mean an unfortunate isolation of psychology from the other sciences. Köhler found that although physicists might describe them from different points of view, there are physical events that show the same characteristics as gestalts in psychology. Köhler first demonstrated the possibility of physical gestalts in the nervous system, since neural events are the physical facts that correspond most immediately to psychological ones; then he extended his investigation to other physical phenomena.

Having demonstrated in physics specific wholes showing characteristic structural properties, Köhler turned his attention to what he called "the Wertheimer problem," known today as isomorphism. This hypothesis, which Wertheimer had adumbrated in 1912, is that there is a structural identity between organized psychological phenomena and the corresponding events in the nervous system. Köhler worked out the hypothesis more and more specifically over the years, first developing it as a physiological theory of perception and then extending it to memory and to attention. The hypothesis has been much criticized and often distorted; in Köhler's hands it became a powerful heuristic, leading to the discovery of figural aftereffects, a discovery that spurred a great deal of research. Köhler further used figural aftereffects to clarify his perceptual theory. Then he began directly testing his theory that steady cortical currents correspond to organized perceptions. This work again drew much criticism; an almost exclusive interest of researchers in the activity of single cells turned attention away from the more molar phenomena investigated by Köhler. The status of the theory remains unclear because it has not been tested since Köhler's own early explorations. Whatever its ultimate status, it seems clear that a theory of perception must include molar physiological events.

When Köhler returned to Germany in 1920, he was appointed acting director of the Psychological Institute of the University of Berlin. He spent the following year as professor of psychology at the University of Göttingen and in 1922 returned to Berlin as professor of philosophy and director of the Psychological Institute. The institute flourished during the years of Köhler's directorship, becoming what many regarded as the foremost psychological institute of its time. In addition to Köhler, Wertheimer was in Berlin until 1929, and Kurt Lewin until 1932. These three attracted students from many countries. A journal was founded, *Psychologische Forschung*, which contained the work of Gestalt psychology between 1921 and 1938. Köhler's own work of this period extended his experimental contributions to new areas, the most notable of which was, perhaps, his work with Hedwig von Restorff and others on memory and recall; later Köhler became interested in the nature of associations, bringing this central concept of traditional psychology under the category of gestalt. *Psychologische Forschung* also contains Köhler's polemical articles, answering attacks on Gestalt psychology from traditional psychologies.

Köhler taught in the United States as a visiting professor at Clark University in 1925–1926, as William James Lecturer at Harvard in 1934–1935, and as visiting professor at the University of Chicago in 1935. Two of his important books came out of these visits. *Gestalt Psychology* (1929) was written in English, for America; it not only surveys the theories and findings of Gestalt psychology but extends the critique to American behaviorism, which is shown to resemble in important respects the traditional European (and American) introspectionism, against which the polemics had previously been directed. *The Place of Value in a World of Facts* (1938) grew out of his lectures at Harvard. Here values, whose neglect by other psychologies was one of the reasons for the emergence of Gestalt psychology, are shown to be entirely compatible with natural science. Values are treated not as merely subjective but in terms of requiredness, which can be identified in nonphenomenal contexts as well as in phenomenal ones. As in his earlier work, Köhler was concerned with showing the relation of psychology to natural science.

In January 1933 the Nazis came to power in Germany. Very soon Jewish professors and other opponents of the regime were dismissed from the universities. Their colleagues kept silent. On Apr. 28, 1933, after the dismissal of James Franck, a great experimental physicist, Köhler spoke out. He wrote for a newspaper the last anti-Nazi article to be printed openly in Germany under the Nazi regime. In "Gespräche in Deutschland" ("Conversations in Germany") he praised the patriotism of those who had not joined the Nazi party and expressed appreciation of the contributions of Jews. To the surprise of many, he was not arrested.

For Köhler there followed two years of courageous struggle against the regime in an attempt to save the institute. The Nazis staged raids on the institute, dismissed assistants, made an important appointment behind Köhler's back, and failed to live up to agreements. In 1935 Köhler immigrated to the United States, where he became professor of psychology and then research professor of philosophy and psychology at Swarthmore College. He became an American citizen in 1946. He retired from Swarthmore in 1958 and continued his work at Dartmouth College. In that same year, he delivered the Gifford Lectures in Edinburgh. An overview of Gestalt psychology appears in his Herbert Langfeld Lectures at Princeton; these lectures were published posthumously as *The Task of Gestalt Psychology* (1969), which is perhaps the best summary of Gestalt psychology for the beginner.

The contributions of Köhler the natural scientist and philosopher were not confined to psychology. His perceptual theory brought him directly into physiological research. His examination of evolutionary theory brought to the fore an often neglected but essential aspect of the theory, which he called its principle of invariance; in doing so, he again set psychology in its place in the world of nature and broke out of the nativism-empiricism dichotomy. His book *Physischen Gestalten* brought new perspectives to physics itself. Phenomenology was the starting point of his experimental work, and he concerned himself explicitly with philosophical problems so often covered up in psychology. His contributions include a remarkable paper on psychological anthropology, a field virtually untouched at the time (1937). The arts, particularly music, meant much to him. All these fields enriched his psychological thought; as he once remarked, "Trespassing is one of the most successful techniques in science."

Although Gestalt psychology was neither well understood nor accepted in predominantly behavioristic America, Köhler was received with great respect. He lectured widely, both in America and in Europe, and he received the Distinguished Scientific Contribution Award of the American Psychological Association (1956), whose president he became in 1959. He received the Wundt Medal of Die Deutsche Gesellschaft für Psychologie and was elected its honorary president in 1967. He was made an *Ehrenbürger* of the Free University of Berlin, a rare honor for an American, in recognition of his help in establishing its psychological institute.

Köhler's work was done with zest. He never glossed over an error but always acknowledged and corrected it to get on with the scientific matter at hand. He had a passion for clarity, in the formulation of research problems and in thinking and writing. A man of courage, he was one of the very few German professors to stand up against the Nazis. He was revered by his colleagues and students and respected by his opponents. He was also generous with his time, helping younger colleagues, assistants, and students. He was remarkably sensitive, to persons, to art, to nature, to the nuances of language. Distinguished in appearance, dignified, modest, direct in his approach to people and to ideas, he possessed a quiet sense of humor. Köhler has had a lasting impact on psychology. He died in Enfield, N.H.

[The major collection of Köhler's correspondence, unpublished manuscripts, and notes is in the Library of the American Philosophical Society in Philadelphia. Other letters are in the Archives of the History of American Psychology at the University of Akron and in the Harvard University Archives.

His work on figural aftereffects was first presented in *Dynamics in Psychology* (1940); and then in a monograph with Hans Wallach, "Figural Aftereffects: An Investigation of Visual Processes," *Proceedings of the American Philosophical Society* (1944). A number of Köhler's articles are reprinted in M. Henle, ed., *Documents of Gestalt Psychology* (1961); and *The Selected Papers of Wolfgang Köhler* (1971), which contains a bibliography.

An account of his career through 1956 is in *American Psychologist*, 1957. Three appreciations of him, by R. Bergius, H.-L. Teuber, and H. Hörmann, are in *Psychologische Forschung*, 1967. Köhler's struggle against the Nazis is related by M. Henle in *American Psychologist*, 1978.

Obituaries are in the *New York Times*, June 12. 1967; *American Journal of Psychology* (1968); and *Year Book of the American Philosophical Society* (1968).]

Mary Henle

KRACAUER, SIEGFRIED (Feb. 8, 1889–Nov. 26, 1966), social scientist and writer, was born in Frankfurt am Main, Germany, the son of Adolf Kracauer, a successful businessman, and Rosette Oppenheim. From childhood he was afflicted with a severe stammer. His father died while Kracauer was still a child, and the boy subsequently lived with his uncle Isidor K. Kracauer, a well-known historian of the Frankfurt Jewish community. Although brought up in religious surroundings, Kracauer, like many German Jews of the time, was assimilationist. His wife, Elisbeth ("Lili") Ehrenreich, whom he married on Mar. 5, 1930, was Catholic; they had no children.

Kracauer attended the Klinger Oberrealschule in Frankfurt and, from 1908 to 1914, various German universities and polytechnics, where he studied architecture, philosophy, and sociology. Because of his stammer (which he felt closed the academic world to him), as well as for financial reasons, he chose to become an architect. He received his doctorate in engineering from the Berlin-Charlottenburg Technische Hochschule in 1915; his dissertation dealt with wrought-iron decoration in Prussia between the seventeenth and nineteenth centuries.

While Kracauer was working as an architect, a number of German periodicals published his essays on philosophical, sociological, and cultural problems. In 1920 he abandoned architecture and joined the prestigious *Frankfurter Zeitung*. He quickly assumed much of the editorial responsibility for its cultural pages, contributed numerous essays and reviews, and wielded great influence as a cultural critic. In 1930, when the newspaper went national, he assumed the editorship of its Berlin feuilleton page, a task that he performed brilliantly.

Kracauer's writing was influenced by various strands of Marxism. Although radical, he was never a member of any political party, being what one critic has called "an existential leftist." His close associates were part of the coterie of intellectuals who clustered around the Institut für Sozialforschung, first in Frankfurt and then in exile after the Nazis assumed power in 1933.

Between 1922 and 1933, Kracauer published a number of books, including a well-received sociological overview, *Soziologie als Wissenschaft* (*Sociology as a Science*, 1922); a semiautobiographical antiwar novel, *Ginster* (1928), which he published anonymously; and a striking study of German white-collar workers, *Die Angestellten* (*The Employees*, 1930).

On Mar. 3, 1933, shortly after the Nazi takeover, the Kracauers left for France. There Kracauer tried to establish ties with French intellectuals. André Malraux's wife translated *Ginster*, but the French edition (1933), though well reviewed, was not successful.

Like many exiles, Kracauer had a hard time making ends meet. Despite problems, he continued to write, often anonymously or pseudonymously, for French journals, the exile press, and Swiss newspapers. A favorite topic of his was the cultural politics of Nazi Germany. A novel, *Georg*, the story of a newspaper editor just prior to the Nazi takeover of Germany, was finished in 1934, but it was not published until 1977. In 1937 he published a biography of Jacques Offenbach in French, American, and Dutch editions. As with much of Kracauer's work, this biography dealt with a marginal culture, in this instance, operetta.

In 1941, when it finally became possible to leave France, Kracauer immigrated to the United States. He arrived in New York City on Apr. 25, 1941. During his first years there he eked out a limited income with foundation grants and a Guggenheim Fellowship (1943–1945). This support helped finance research for his best-known American work, *From Caligari to Hitler* (1947), a psychological study of German film from 1919 to 1933. In this work, Kracauer argued that there are deep layers of a "collective mentality" that extend to a greater or lesser degree below "the dimensions of conciousness." He saw in almost all pre-Nazi German films protofascist tendencies. Controversy surrounded his concepts for decades, but the book remains seminal and has had an enormous influence on film-content analysis. He also published articles on film in journals such as the *Public Opinion Quarterly* and in magazines such as *Harper's*.

During the 1950's, Kracauer used his expertise in qualitative analysis while working for the Evaluation Branch of the Voice of America (1950–1952) and as a senior staff member of Columbia University's Bureau of Applied Social Research (1953–1958). Much of his work for these organizations remained unpublished. But 1956 saw the publication of *Satellite Mentality* (written with Paul Berkman), an empirical study of Eastern European refugees based on hundreds of interviews; the work, which suffered from its cold-war overtones, lacks the panache of his earlier efforts.

Theory of Film (1960), a complex reworking of Kracauer's ideas, emphasized the importance of what was filmed rather than how it was captured and spliced together. Kracauer insisted that the realistic or documentary tendency of film was more important than the purely cinematic. The book was not well received by critics, who held that Kracauer's theories were inadequate, contradictory, and questionable.

Thereafter, Kracauer turned away from film and became interested in the philosophy of history. He had by the time of his death prepared the bulk of a manuscript, which was published posthumously. *History: The Last Things Before the Last* (1969), the subject of a lawsuit between Kracauer's widow and the person hired to put the manuscript into publishable shape, fared badly. The work emphasized "the heterogeneity of the historical universe" and argued against identifying history as a process. Kracauer's ideas were greeted unsympathetically and the book, as one critic put it, "sank with scarcely a ripple."

In the main, Kracauer's last years were happy ones. His work received new attention in West Germany, where his early journalism was anthologized in *Das Ornament der Masse* and *Ginster* was republished (both 1963). He served as a consultant to various foundations in the United States and in 1965 participated in the University Seminar on Interpretation at Columbia University.

Kracauer was not an unprejudiced observer, albeit he became less radical over the years. But he was shrewd and sensitive. In his journalism, as in his more serious writings, he served as a worthy pioneer, especially in film history, where a subsequent generation of scholars, even those who disagreed with his basic premises, continued to refer to many of his theories.

[A comprehensive collection of Kracauer's papers is in the Schiller National Museum in Marbach am Neckar, Baden-Württemberg, West Germany. The Suhrkamp Verlag (Frankfurt, West Germany) has published his books in new German editions and anthologized much of his journalism (1971–1982). See Theodor W. Adorno, in the *Frankfurter Allgemeine Zeitung*, Dec. 1, 1966; *Text-Kritik*, Oct. 1980, which is dedicated to him; and Martin Jay, "The Extraterritorial Life of Siegfried Kracauer," in *Permanent Exiles: Essays on the Intellectual Migration from Germany to America* (1985). An obituary is in the *New York Times*, Nov. 28, 1966.]

DANIEL J. LEAB

KRESGE, SEBASTIAN SPERING (July 31, 1867–Oct. 18, 1966), merchant and philanthropist, was born in Bald Mount, Pa., the son of Sebastian Kresge and Catherine Kunkle. He attended the Fairview Academy in Brodheadsville, Pa., and the Gilbert (Pa.) Polytechnic Institute. In 1889 he graduated from Eastman Business College in Poughkeepsie, N.Y. His parents were poor during his school years, but they agreed to his proposal to turn his entire salary over to them until he reached the age of twenty-one if they would finance his education. In 1886 he taught at Gower's School and Monroe Academy, and during the years he attended business college he worked as a deliveryman and clerk for Patrick Ward in Scranton, Pa. During 1890–1892 he was a bookkeeper in the Howley Brothers Store, Scranton. He also sold industrial insurance and owned a half-interest in a bakery, which failed.

From 1892 to 1897 Kresge sold tinware and hardware specialties in New England and the north-central states for the W. B. Bertels and Sons Company of Wilkes-Barre, Pa. During this period he met F. W. Woolworth, the dime-store merchant, and determined to follow his business example. During the 1890's, a time of economic depression, Kresge saved $8,000, which he invested in the company of J. G. McCrory, an early chain-store merchant. After learning the business in McCrory's store in Jamestown, N.Y., he joined him as an equal partner in opening stores in Memphis and Detroit. Kresge managed the Memphis store, but in 1899 traded his half of it to McCrory and took full possession of the Detroit store. This was the beginning of the S. S. Kresge Company, which in time became the largest chain-store company in the country.

A large sign on the Detroit store proclaimed: "Nothing Over 10 Cents in Store." Soon after it opened Kresge formed a partnership with his brother-in-law, Charles J. Wilson, and they opened a second store in Port Huron, Mich., in 1900. In 1907, when Kresge bought out Wilson, they also owned stores in Indianapolis, Toledo, Pittsburgh, Cleveland, Columbus, and Chicago. When the company was incorporated as S. S. Kresge in 1912, it then operated eighty-five stores with an annual business of $10 million. When Kresge stepped down as president in 1925 to become chairman of the board, the company was operating over 300 stores, and his personal fortune exceeded $200 million.

In 1920 Kresge acquired the Mt. Clemens Pottery Company in Michigan as a subsidiary; half its production was sold in Kresge stores. He also was president of the Kresge Realty Company, and in the 1920's he acquired other stores—the Palais Royale in Washington, D.C.; the Fair in Chicago; Steinbach-Kresge in Asbury Park, N.J.; Stern Brothers in New York City; and the L. S. Plant Store in Newark, N.J. At this time he had a $30 million brokerage account in Wall Street and was very visible to the public because of the breakup of his first two marriages and his passionate support of the Anti-Saloon League and the National Vigilance Committee for Prohibition Enforcement, which he organized when the Eighteenth Amendment was adopted. His first wife, Anna Emma Harvey, whom he married in 1897 and by whom he had five children, divorced him in 1924. That year he married Doris Mercer, who divorced him in 1928, the year that he married Clara Katherine Zitz. In the next decade he abandoned public crusades and the stock market.

The ten-cent limit was maintained in the Kresge stores until 1920, when the company opened the first of its "green front" stores, which sold items worth up to one dollar; after World War II, Kresge stores were selling a wide range of goods at various prices. Finally in 1961 Kresge approved an $80 million deal for financing a line of discount stores called K-Marts. In 1963 the company transformed unprofitable stores with long leases in deteriorating neighborhoods into Jupiter stores, which sold both variety and discount goods.

By 1966 the Kresge company operated the second-largest chain in the country and employed over 4,200 people in 670 variety stores, 150 K-Mart department stores, and 110 Jupiter discount stores. Annual sales for 1965 totaled $851 million. After Kresge's death the chain passed Woolworth to become the largest in the country. Almost to the end of his life Kresge was involved with his company. When illness forced him to retire four months before his death, he had been chairman of the board for forty-one years, attending every board meeting and studying every monthly report.

Convinced that men of wealth were obliged to return to society the money they amassed, Kresge engaged in many philanthropic enterprises. During World War I he was active in the National War Work Council of the YMCA and the International Methodist Centenary Movement, and he regarded his defense of Prohibition, though it was doomed to failure, as work in the best interest of the public. In 1924, well before income and inheritance taxes were a factor in philanthropy, he established the Kresge Foundation with an initial gift of $1.3 million. During the next thirty-three years his endowments to the foundation totalled over $60 million. "I can get a greater thrill out of serving others," he said, "than anything else on earth. I really want to leave the world a better place than I found it."

The Kresge Foundation made grants to a number of American institutions, including Children's Village near Detroit, a home for dependent children; the Newark Museum; the Massachusetts Institute of Technology; and Harvard, Michigan, Michigan State, Northwestern, Wayne, and Columbia universities. Other gifts aided overseas operations, including a program to train flying doctors in Kenya. At the time of his death Kresge had given the foundation the bulk of his personal fortune, including 2.5 million shares of Kresge stock worth $100 million. The foundation by that time had assets of $175 million and had given away $70 million.

Kresge was noted among his friends, associates, and employees as an eccentrically frugal man. Believing that money should not be wasted on clothing, he wore his suits until they were threadbare and he was known to line his old shoes with paper. The same frugality was expected of his employees, but he was also distinguished for enlightened personnel policies. Early in the century, when absence because of sickness was often grounds for dismissal, he gave his employees sick leave and paid holidays, and earlier than most employers he gave employees profit-sharing bonuses and retirement pensions. Although his first two wives accused him of miserliness, he was generous in his divorce settlements. He reportedly gave $10 million to his first wife and their children and another $3 million to his second wife.

Kresge combined shrewd merchandising methods, an uncanny ability to pick talented subordinates, and a spartan capacity for hard work to create a great chain of stores and a huge personal fortune. At Harvard in 1953 to dedicate Kresge Hall at the university's Graduate School of Business Administration, he was asked to speak. His address was just six words: "I never made a dime talking!" All his life he embodied traditional virtues, often in ways that seemed odd to those who did not understand his personal philosophy. He was a devout Methodist and a staunch Republican who never used alcohol or tobacco, refused to give financial support to any church if he knew the minister used tobacco, considered playing cards a "frivolity," and gave up golf because he claimed he could not afford to lose so many balls. "I think I was successful because I saved and because I heeded good advice," he once said. "I worked . . . sometimes eighteen hours [a day]. When one starts at the bottom and learns to scrape, then everything becomes easy." He died in East Stroudsburg, Pa.

[See Stanley S. Kresge, as told to Steve Spilos, *The S. S. Kresge Story* (1979); *Literary Digest*, June 12, 1926; *Fortune*, June 1940; *Business Week*, Jan. 29, 1966; and *Time*, July 1 and Oct. 28, 1966. An obituary is in the *New York Times*, Oct. 19, 1966.]

ROBERT L. BERNER

KREYMBORG, ALFRED FRANCIS (Dec. 10, 1883–Aug. 14, 1966), poet, editor, dramatist, and literary historian, was born in New York City, the son of Hermann Charles Kreymborg, a cigar maker, and Louisa Nascher. By 1897, Kreymborg had graduated from the Ninety-sixth Street Elementary School with more interest in chess and music than in classes. He had watched his father play chess with friends and had mastered the game by the time he was eight years old. Later he was able to support himself by playing in chess clubs and tournaments or by teaching others. At eleven he taught himself to play the mandolin. After two years at Morris High School, he dropped out of school to look for a job.

By 1900, Kreymborg had tried several clerical positions before going to work in Manhattan at the Aeolian Hall music company, where he played and sold music rolls and sometimes demonstrated them at public performances. Here he met a number of famous musicians and acquired a deep love of classical music. A young coworker poet encouraged him to write. Partly because he lacked musical training, Kreymborg turned to experimental poetry. His attempts "to approximate music with words" brought him on his own to concepts of modern poetry held by T. S. Eliot and Ezra Pound. He immersed himself in the classics, reading Shakespeare, Cervantes, Goethe, Chekhov, Aristophanes, and Whitman. He became friends with artists and writers such as Marsden Hartley, George Luks, Edward Steichen, Joyce Kilmer, and Alfred Stieglitz.

Discouraged with editors' rejection slips, Kreymborg published his first volume of poetry, *Love and Life and Other Studies* (1908), at his own expense. His dream to publish his own magazine was nearly realized in 1909 with the *American Quarterly*. He had already collected manuscript for it when bankers withdrew their support. In 1913 a wealthy eccentric, Franklin Hopkins, the inventor of the mandolute, an instrument designed to replace all string instruments in the symphony orchestra, asked Kreymborg to manage the journal *Musical Advance*. The project failed, but Kreymborg salvaged a mandolute, which he later used in public appearances for poetry readings and puppet-theater productions.

At the suggestion of the artist and photographer Man Ray, Kreymborg made plans for a new magazine, the *Glebe*, which was eventually sponsored by the Boni Brothers Bookshop. The magazine's ten issues—from September 1913 to November 1914—pioneered experimental writing; one contained Kreymborg's novelette "Erna Vitek," the story of a prostitute, written in 1905. The imagist number included poems by Ezra Pound, James Joyce, and William Carlos Williams. When the Bonis urged that more foreign writers in translation be included, Kreymborg resigned as editor. In 1915, two of his early experimental poems appeared in Guido Bruno's *Bruno Chap Books*, "Mushrooms, 16 Rhythms" and "To My Mother, 10 Rhythms." For printing Kreymborg's novelette, retitled "Edna: A Girl of the Streets," Bruno was indicted and tried on charges of obscenity but was acquitted. Recognized finally as a new poet, Kreymborg was asked to give public readings in Bruno's Garret, the Boni Brothers Bookshop, and the Liberal Club.

With financial help first from Walter

Arensberg and later from John Marshall, Kreymborg began publication in July 1915 of *Others: A Magazine of New Verse,* which aimed at printing writers other than those who were appearing in *Poetry* magazine. *Others* quickly gained notoriety for its outlandish offerings and brilliant writers—T. S. Eliot, Wallace Stevens, Marianne Moore—and became one of the most influential little magazines in America. Partly to promote it, Kreymborg made trips to Chicago and the West Coast to meet writers and artists and give public readings. He edited three anthologies of *Others* writers (1916, 1917, 1920). Meanwhile, in July 1915 he had married Gertrude Lord, but the marriage ended in legal separation after only a year. On Oct. 26, 1918, he married Dorothy Bloom, whose devotion to the arts paralleled his own; they had no children.

Interested also in experimental theater, Kreymborg had become a member of the Provincetown Players and founded the short-lived Others Players. With his wife and the puppeteer Remo Buffano, he created his own puppet theater and toured cities throughout the United States. Usually he read the lines and sometimes played the mandolute. He published *Plays for Poem-Mimes* (1918), *Plays for Merry Andrews* (1920), and *Puppet Plays* (1923).

In 1921, Harold Loeb, the Princeton bookseller and novelist, persuaded Kreymborg to become coeditor of yet another "little magazine," *Broom: An International Magazine of the Arts,* to be published in Rome. In Paris the Kreymborgs met well-known artists and writers, gathering manuscripts on their way. The magazine, which first appeared in November 1921, was eminently successful, but the editors became divided over questions of financial and editorial policies; in February 1922, after four issues, Kreymborg resigned. The Kreymborgs traveled extensively on the Continent and in England before returning to New York.

During the 1920's, Kreymborg turned more and more to traditional forms of poetry. In *Less Lonely* (1923) and *The Lost Sail* (1928), he used the sonnet form; in *Scarlet and Mellow* (1926), rhymed couplets; and in *Manhattan Men* (1929), both traditional and free forms. In *Troubadour: An Autobiography* (1925), the personal story he tells is also literary history. In addition to editing a number of anthologies of American poetry, he published *Our Singing Strength* (1929; rev. ed., 1934), a history of American poetry from colonial times to Hart Crane. He taught and lectured at several colleges, including the New School for Social Research, the University of Kansas City, Olivet (Mich.) College, and Oxford University.

In 1935, Kreymborg joined the Federal Theater Project in New York, working as a director in poetic theater. His growing sensitivity to social and economic changes and his concern for peace are evident in *Selected Poems, 1912–1944* (1945); *Man and Shadow: An Allegory* (1946), his long autobiographical study in blank verse; and *No More War, and Other Poems* (1950). His poetic dramatization of Gustav Holst's orchestral suite *The Planets* was broadcast by the National Broadcasting Company (NBC) from the Hayden Planetarium in New York on June 6, 1938. Ten radio plays, produced by NBC in January, February, and March 1939, were published as *The Four Apes, and Other Fables of Our Day* (1939). In 1945 he wrote lyrics for H. E. Heller's cantata *Ode to Our Women: A Ballad of Our Time.* During the 1950's and early 1960's he continued to write and publish. He served as a judge for the Pultizer Prize in poetry. He was elected president of the Poetry Society of Greenwich Village in January 1959. A quiet man, slight of build, fond of good talk, Kreymborg died at a nursing home in Milford, Conn.

[Some of Kreymborg's letters and manuscripts may be found at the American Academy and Institute of Arts and Letters; Buffalo State University; Dartmouth College; Harvard University; the University of Illinois; the University of Pennsylvania; the University of Texas; and Yale University.

No complete bibliography exists; for a fairly complete listing, see Russell Murphy, "Alfred Kreymborg," *Dictionary of Literary Biography,* LIV, *American Poets, 1880–1945.* Selected works include *Apostrophes* (1910); *Mushrooms* (1915); *Blood of Things* (1920); *Rocking Chairs, and Other Comedies* (1925); *The American Caravan,* edited by Kreymborg and others (1927; rev. eds., 1928, 1929, 1931, 1936); *Lyric America: An Anthology of American Poetry,* edited by Kreymborg (1930, 1935; revised as *Lyric America* (1941); *The Little World, 1914 and After* (1932); *How Do You Do, Sir? and Other Short Plays* (1934); and *Ten American Ballads* (1942).

There are no full-length studies of Kreymborg. See Elizabeth Margaret Weist, "Alfred Kreymborg in the Art Theater" (Ph.D. diss., University of Michigan, 1965); and Marie Celeste Miller, "Seeking Similar Fundamentals: The Relationship Between Painting and Poetry of American Early Moderns" (Ph.D.

diss., Emory University, 1983). An obituary is in the *New York Times*, Aug. 15, 1966.]

JOHN E. HART

KRUEGER, WALTER (Jan. 26, 1881–Aug. 20, 1967), army officer, was born in Flatow, West Prussia (now Złotów, Poland), the son of Julius O. H. Krüger, a former officer in the Prussian army and prominent landowner, and Anna Hasse. Brought to the United States by his mother in 1889, four years after his father's death, Krueger grew up in Ohio, Illinois, and Indiana. He was tutored in mathematics and languages by a demanding stepfather and taught to play the piano by his mother.

Krueger was attending Cincinnati Technical High School when, caught up in the patriotic fervor that swept the country at the outbreak of the Spanish-American War, he enlisted in the army in June 1898. He served in Cuba with the Second Volunteer Infantry. Mustered out as a sergeant in February 1899, he decided to become a professional soldier. Eager to see action during the Philippine Insurrection, he joined the regular army as a private in June 1899. During four years in the Far East, he participated in several engagements, securing a commission as second lieutenant of the infantry in 1901. Following his return to the United States, Krueger married Grace Aileen Norvell on Sept. 11, 1904. They had three children.

Krueger spent the years before World War I in a variety of command, staff, and academic assignments. He translated several volumes of German military writings and gained a reputation as an expert in this area. He served overseas during the war as assistant chief of staff of the Twenty-sixth Division and, at the time of the armistice, chief of staff of the tank corps.

The 1920's brought duty with the War Plans Division of the War Department General Staff and tours as student and instructor at both the army and naval war colleges. The next decade saw important command responsibilities. His aggressive leadership of the Third Army during the giant Louisiana maneuvers of 1941 brought widespread recognition but did not lead to an immediate combat assignment.

Krueger concentrated on training following Pearl Harbor, with special attention to preparing junior officers for combat leadership. Although he played a significant role in turning a flood of draftees and volunteers into an effective military force, Krueger yearned for combat duty. By 1943, however, he had become resigned to his fate: "I had just about concluded that being practically sixty-two, I would be thought too old for active overseas command."

Then General Douglas MacArthur's need for a senior commander in the southwest Pacific gave Krueger the opportunity to use on the battlefield the skills that he had developed over a lifetime. Krueger organized and assumed command of the Sixth Army in February 1943. Executing MacArthur's grand design to return to the Philippines, he led his troops in a series of bitterly fought engagements from New Guinea to the Moluccas. The high point of Krueger's career came with the campaigns of Leyte and Luzon. Methodical and prudent, he sometimes caused MacArthur to grow impatient, especially as American forces approached Manila. But MacArthur valued Krueger's conservative leadership, recommending his promotion to four-star rank and selecting him to lead the planned invasion of Kyushu in the autumn of 1945. Japan's surrender in August made the final assault unnecessary, and the Sixth Army assumed occupation duties. Krueger returned to the United States in 1946 and retired. He died at Valley Forge, Pa.

Despite his outstanding combat record, Krueger remained one of the least-known senior commanders of World War II. The southwest Pacific received less publicity than other theaters, and MacArthur was usually the focus of stories that did appear in the press. But lack of attention never bothered Krueger, as it did several of MacArthur's other subordinates; he was content to concentrate on the job at hand.

Krueger's style of leadership gave great latitude to subordinates. He rarely interfered with the details of operational planning; in the field, he kept his orders to a minimum and allowed corps commanders to use their best judgment in achieving objectives. He insisted that his officers concern themselves with the well-being and comfort of their men. "It must never be forgotten," Krueger often pointed out, "that the individual soldier is the most important single factor in this war."

Whether Krueger's military leadership was unduly cautious or properly conservative, his record of accomplishment remains impressive. During the Leyte operation, for example, the Sixth Army inflicted over 56,000 casualties on Japanese units while suffering only 12,700 killed and wounded. As an officer who knew him well remarked, "If I had a campaign to direct in circumstances that called for the greatest prudence, the largest skill, and the utmost employment of all the resources of a single army, I would put it in Krueger's hands."

[Krueger's papers are at the United States Military Academy, West Point, N.Y. His *From Down Under to Nippon* (1953) states his military views. Krueger's major campaigns are in M. Hamlin Cannon, *Leyte* (1954); and Robert Ross Smith, *Triumph in the Philippines* (1963). See also D. Clayton James, *The Years of MacArthur, 1941–1945* (1975). Obituaries are in the *New York Times*, Aug. 21, 1967; and *Newsweek*, Sept. 4, 1967.]

WILLIAM M. LEARY

KRUG, JULIUS ALBERT (Nov. 23, 1907–March 26, 1970), government administrator, was born in Madison, Wis., the son of Julius John Krug, a policeman and prison warden, and Emma Korfmacher. Krug attended the University of Wisconsin and received a B.A. in 1929 and an M.A. in economics and utilities management in 1930. While still an undergraduate, on March 22, 1926, he married Margaret Catherine Dean, a childhood friend. They had two children. As a student he had to work as a laborer to support his family. One of his chief characteristics throughout life was his capacity for hard work.

During the early years of the Great Depression Krug served as a research analyst for the Wisconsin Telephone Company and later for the Wisconsin Public Utilities Commission. He became a close friend of David Lilienthal, later chairman of the Tennessee Valley Authority (TVA).

From 1935 to 1937 Krug worked for the Federal Communications Commission (FCC) in Washington, D.C. He was responsible for convincing the FCC that American Telephone and Telegraph was charging more than was reasonable for long-distance calls. However, he soon tired of the FCC because the agency seemed more interested in social reform than in regulating industry.

After returning briefly to Wisconsin, Krug accepted a position as a kind of troubleshooter for Kentucky governor A. B. Chandler. He reorganized the Kentucky Public Service Commission and supervised the rebuilding of electric power lines after the 1937 Ohio River flood. Krug then joined the TVA as its chief power engineer. In this post he was responsible for negotiating the TVA's purchase of many existing private power installations. He also supervised TVA construction projects. As Lilienthal's chief witness at congressional hearings on the TVA, Krug, who was six feet, three inches tall and weighed 225 pounds, defended the TVA vigorously in front of congressional committees.

During World War II Krug served in Washington, D.C., as power coordinator, deputy director for priorities control, and director of the Office of War Utilities for the War Production Board (WPB). He worked six days and three nights a week with almost no vacations. Considered the "boy genius" of the WPB, he saw his main assignment as guaranteeing a steady flow of raw materials to key industries. He controlled the production and distribution of electrical, gas, and water power. Krug also served on committees that recommended how Europe should reestablish utility services in liberated areas.

In 1944 Krug resigned all of his positions and accepted a commission as a lieutenant commander in the navy. He was assigned to sea duty, but President Roosevelt soon called him back to Washington, D.C., and appointed him chairman of the WPB, a post that had become vacant when Charles E. Wilson resigned after a policy dispute with his deputy, Donald Nelson. Krug presided over the WPB during the last year of World War II and ably charted a reconversion program that was designed to avoid massive unemployment after the war.

In 1946 President Harry S Truman appointed Krug secretary of the interior. As secretary Krug advocated the creation of more utility authorities modeled on the TVA. He also supervised the operation of the nation's coal mines when Truman seized the mines during the United Mine Workers' nationwide strike of 1946. Krug tried to involve the federal government in massive reclamation projects as well as to expand other agencies such as the National Park Service. Truman was unable to persuade Congress of the necessity of these projects, and he finally tired of Krug's aggressiveness. Late in 1949, after the steelworkers' strike, Krug resigned. He then left government service and returned to Tennessee, where for the rest of his life he worked in a variety of consultant positions and as a director in a Tennessee cotton mill. He died in Knoxville, Tenn.

[Archival collections on the career of Krug are in the Roosevelt Library, Hyde Park, N.Y.; the Truman Library, Independence, Mo.; the National Archives, Washington, D.C.; and the Wisconsin Historical Society, Madison, Wis. Obituaries are in the *New York Times*, Mar. 28, 1970; and *Newsweek*, Apr. 6, 1970.]

F. Ross Peterson

KRUTCH, JOSEPH WOOD (Nov. 25, 1893–May 22, 1970), writer, was born in Knoxville, Tenn., the son of Edward Waldemore Krutch, an employee of a wholesale drug firm, and Adelaide Wood. Neither parent was notably committed to the arts, and the education young Krutch enjoyed in the Knoxville public schools was unexceptional. As an undergraduate at the University of Tennessee, which he entered in 1911, Krutch prepared for a career teaching high school mathematics. But several literature courses and his editorship of the university's student magazine persuaded him to pursue graduate study in English at Columbia University, where he enrolled following his graduation from Tennessee in 1915.

Krutch reveled in the cultural opportunities of New York City, and imagined himself an urban sophisticate. His love of the theater, first stimulated by performances of touring companies in Knoxville, was reinforced. He earned his master's degree in 1916 with a thesis on nineteenth-century American drama. In the spring of 1918 he interrupted his doctoral studies to enlist in the Army Psychological Corps. Following the armistice, he returned to Columbia to write a dissertation on English Restoration comedy. He received a fellowship that enabled him to spend the 1919–1920 academic year in Europe along with a fellow graduate student, Mark Van Doren, who had become and would remain his closest friend. In 1924 Krutch's dissertation was published and he was awarded a Ph.D.

Following his return from Europe, Krutch taught English at Brooklyn Polytechnic Institute and contributed book reviews and essays to some of the leading periodicals of the day. On Feb. 10, 1923, he married Marcelle Leguia, who had come to America from her native France shortly before the outbreak of World War I and had been trained in America as a public health nurse. She was an admiring helpmate who patiently accommodated his valetudinarian demands.

Unhappy in the classroom, Krutch resigned his position at Brooklyn Polytechnic in 1924 and became associate editor of the *Nation*, where his responsibilities included drama criticism. During the next quarter-century, he attended some 2,000 Broadway plays and wrote more than 500 reviews. He also contributed book reviews, essays, and unsigned editorials. He was proud to associate himself with the *Nation*'s outspoken liberalism, and in *Edgar Allan Poe: A Study of Genius* (1926) he embraced another of the fashionable literary and intellectual movements of the day by viewing Poe's career in terms of Freudian psychopathology.

Heartened by the critical success of his book on Poe, Krutch wrote a series of long essays, collected as *The Modern Temper* (1929). Examining the origins and consequences of contemporary attitudes and beliefs, the book portrayed man's sense of emotional impoverishment in a world dominated by the debilitating, corrosive reason of science. *The Modern Temper* remains an eloquent synopsis of the modernist thought of the day. Krutch's uneasiness with the radical political thought of the 1930's was reflected in *Was Europe a Success?* (1934), a forceful liberal critique of the attraction Marxism held for many American intellectuals.

Increasingly alienated from the literary and political enthusiasms of his contemporaries, Krutch also distanced himself physically from the urban life he had earlier relished. Since the mid-1920's, he and his wife had summered in rural Connecticut. In 1932 they purchased a home in Redding, Conn., which soon became their primary residence. In Redding, Krutch became an avid student of nature and discovered there a source of spiritual solace from the despair of modernism.

Krutch resigned his editorial position at the *Nation* in 1937, but retained his post as drama critic. That year he became professor of English at Columbia, where his courses on drama were highly popular. Two critical biographies, *Samuel Johnson* (1944) and *Henry David Thoreau* (1948), renewed Krutch's standing as a critic while paying tribute to two quite different writers whose outlooks Krutch was embracing as his own. His writing during the 1950's and 1960's evidenced his debt both to Johnson's commonsense philosophy and respect for the intelligent layperson and to Thoreau's demonstration that science could enhance man's appreciation of the human significance of nature.

The publication of *Thoreau* was soon followed by the first of Krutch's essays about the natural universe in and around his Redding home. *The Twelve Seasons* (1949) marked the beginning of his successful career as a nature writer. Drawing upon his own daily observation, these essays combined scientific explanation of both common and unfamiliar natural phenomena with reflection upon their human significance. During a 1950–1951 sabbatical in Tucson, Ariz., Krutch found material for a second such collection, *The Desert Year* (1952), and decided to make his home in Arizona.

In 1952 Krutch resigned his professorship, relinquished his post as drama critic, and moved to Tucson. Free of academic and other responsibilities, and now dependent wholly upon his earnings as a writer, his literary output was prodigious in quantity though uneven in quality. In addition to several collections of essays on the flora and fauna of the Southwest, he published books on the Grand Canyon and Baja California. That plants and animals could survive—even joyously—amid the heat and aridity of the desert implied for Krutch man's capacity to endure and find meaning in a modern world bereft of traditional beliefs.

In *The Measure of Man*, which received the 1954 National Book Award for nonfiction, Krutch reconsidered issues explored twenty-five years earlier in *The Modern Temper*. His rejection of positivism and mechanistic determinism and his assertion of the reality of consciousness and value announced his new sense of man's potentialities. In numerous essays of social and literary criticism, he offered a humanist's indictment of the materialism, moral relativism, and artistic nihilism he found in contemporary society. First published in journals such as the *Saturday Review* and the *American Scholar*, many of those essays were collected in *Human Nature and the Human Condition* (1959), *If You Don't Mind My Saying So* (1964), and *And Even If You Do* (1967).

Krutch, having abandoned his earlier ambition to be counted among the modernist thinkers of his day, enjoyed the admiration of a large readership along with considerable financial success. In 1967 he received the Emerson-Thoreau Medal of the American Academy of Arts and Sciences for "distinguished achievement in the broad field of literature." He died in Tucson.

[Krutch's papers are available in the Manuscript Division of the Library of Congress. In addition to those cited above, books by Krutch include *Comedy and Conscience After the Restoration* (1924); *Five Masters* (1930); *Experience and Art* (1932); *The American Drama Since 1918* (1939); *"Modernism" in Modern Drama* (1953); *The Best of Two Worlds* (1953); *The Voice of the Desert* (1955); *The Great Chain of Life* (1956); *Grand Canyon* (1958); and *The Forgotten Peninsula* (1961). Krutch's autobiography is *More Lives than One* (1962). Shortly before his death, Krutch prepared two collections of his writings: *The Best Nature Writing of Joseph Wood Krutch* (1969) and *A Krutch Omnibus: Forty Years of Social and Literary Criticism* (1970). John D. Margolis, *Joseph Wood Krutch: A Writer's Life* (1980), includes a bibliographical essay. See the obituary, *New York Times*, May 23, 1970; and the editorial tribute, *ibid.*, May 26, 1970.]

JOHN D. MARGOLIS

LAHR, BERT (Aug. 13, 1895–Dec. 4, 1967), comic actor, was born Irving Lahrheim in the Yorkville section of New York City, the son of German immigrants Jacob Lahrheim, an upholsterer, and his wife, Augusta (her maiden name is unknown). Lahr attended Public School 77. After the family moved to the Bronx, Lahr, who was by his own admission a lazy student, quit school at the age of fifteen after one year at Morris High School (P.S. 40) and worked as an office boy in a jewelry house. In one year he had at least six additional jobs. During these formative years Lahr came to be called "Swedish" after squaring off against a brawny Swede. Despite parental objections, Lahr attended variety theaters frequently and got his first taste of performing for money by singing in blackface in the streets. In 1910 he joined a child vaudeville act, the Seven Frolics, performing in a show called *The Little Red School House*. For the next several years he toured minor vaudeville circuits, appearing in such acts as Nine Crazy Kids, and Boys and Girls of Avenue B. With the Whirly Girly Musical Comedy Success he appeared in skits such as "College Days" and "Garden Belles."

Outgrowing child parts, Lahr was seen at the Olympia Theater in Brooklyn by William K. ("Billy") Wells, a vaudeville monologist and writer for the Columbia Burlesque Circuit. In June 1917, through Wells's influence, Lahr joined Blutch Cooper's *Best Show in Town* as third comedian, opening in Cleveland that September with a troupe called the Roseland

Girls. By perfecting his interpretation of the German-accented "Dutch" dumb-cop character that had fascinated him as a boy, Lahr soon became "the boy wonder of burlesque." In three years his salary increased from $35 to $100 per week. Appearing in this troupe with Lahr was Mercedes Delpino, a dancer who became his vaudeville partner. After brief service in the navy as a seaman second class stationed at Pelham Bay, Lahr expanded one of his burlesque skits into the twelve-minute vaudeville act "Lahr and Mercedes—What's the Idea?" and moved into big-time vaudeville, touring the Keith and Orpheum circuits for four years and earning $350 a week. In this and other acts, he developed the leer, grimace (said to make him look like "a camel with acute gastric disorder"), and wild cry of "gnong-gnong-gnong" (a sound that defies spelling) that were to be his stock-in-trade for years.

Lahr married Delpino in August 1929; they had one child. The relationship, however, was strained irrevocably by Delpino's psychological problems; in April 1930 she was committed to a sanitarium in Connecticut. After a decade of litigation, their marriage was annulled.

Lahr's major break came in 1927 with his Broadway debut in the revue *Harry Delmar's Revels*. This engagement led to his role as Gink Schiner, a punch-drunk fighter, in *Hold Everything* (1928), with Victor Moore. Despite his persistent self-doubts, Lahr was an overnight success. His newfound celebrity status led to three vaudeville engagements at the Palace in six months at $4,500 a week and a series of successful musical appearances, including *Flying High* (1930); *Hot-Cha!* (1932); *Life Begins at 8:30* (1934), featuring "The Woodchopper's Song," a merciless travesty of concert baritones that he reprised often throughout his career, frequently on Ed Sullivan's television variety show; *George White's Scandals* (1935); and *The Show Is On* (1936) with Bea Lillie.

On Dec. 6, 1939, Lahr opened with Ethel Merman in *Du Barry Was a Lady*. He played Louis Blore, a washroom attendant who dreams he is Louis XV. Lahr also appeared that year in his only enduring Hollywood role, that of the Cowardly Lion in the film classic *The Wizard of Oz*. Although Lahr appeared in a score of motion pictures, beginning with the short *Faint Heart* in 1931, his style was generally too broad for film. Other films featuring Lahr included *Flying High* (1931), *Mr. Broadway* (1933), *Hizzoner* (a 1934 short), *Gold Bricks* (a 1936 short), *Merry-Go-Round of 1938* and *Love and Hisses* (1937), *Jossette* and *Just Around the Corner* (1938), *Zaza* (1939), *Du Barry Was a Lady* (1940), *Sing Your Worries Away* and *Ship Ahoy* (1942), *Meet the People* (1944), *Always Leave Them Laughing* (1949), *Mr. Universe* (1951), *Rose Marie* (1954), *The Second Greatest Sex* (1955), *Ten Girls Ago* (1962), *The Sound of Laughter* (a 1963 documentary), and *Big Parade of Comedy* (a 1964 documentary). He also appeared on "The Hallmark Hall of Fame" in *The Fantasticks*, a 1965 television version of the off-Broadway musical hit.

The musical theater of the 1940's, which emphasized operetta-like sound and romantic stories, did not appeal to Lahr, so he played summer stock, performed on radio, appeared in a Billy Rose extravaganza (*Seven Lively Arts*) in 1944, and toured in *Harvey* in 1945. His major stage appearance of the 1940's was in a dramatic role, as Skid in a revival of *Burlesque* (1946), later seen on television. In 1951 he returned to the musical stage in *Two on the Aisle*, a revue in the older tradition and a moderate success, although clearly Lahr's time as a star turn in musical theater, wherein he could dominate and glean most of the laughs, was at an end, as vividly illustrated in his last book musical, *Foxy* (1964), based on Ben Jonson's *Volpone* but set in the Alaska gold rush. Although he received the Antoinette Perry (Tony) Award as Best Actor in a Musical for his performance as a miser who pretends to be dying in order to trick his voracious associates, he gained the recognition essentially by ignoring the poor material and resorting to tricks learned in burlesque and vaudeville.

The 1940's also marked a shift in Lahr's personal life. On Feb. 11, 1940, he married Mildred Schroeder, a former showgirl. They had two children, one of whom, John, became a critic and authored the definitive biography of Bert Lahr, *Notes on a Cowardly Lion* (1969).

Lahr's career experienced an important turning point in 1956 when he appeared as Estragon in Samuel Beckett's *Waiting for Godot*, first in an ill-conceived production directed by Alan Schneider in Florida and then in its New York premiere, directed by Herbert Berghof. Despite his own uncertainty about the role and the play, Lahr was hailed for his performance, called by the *New York Times* critic Brooks Atkinson "Mr. Lahr's hour of triumph." Atkinson added,

"His long experience as a bawling mountebank has equipped Mr. Lahr to represent eloquently the tragic comedy of one of the lost souls of the earth." This association with the avant-garde of the 1950's brought Lahr roles in George Bernard Shaw's *Androcles and the Lion* and Molière's *School for Wives,* both on television in 1956. He toured as Bottom in the American Shakespeare Festival's production of *A Midsummer Night's Dream,* for which he received the Best Shakespearean Actor of the Year Award in 1960; and in 1966 he played Pisthetairos in Aristophanes' *The Birds* at the Ypsilanti (Mich.) Greek Theatre Festival. His last major straight role on Broadway—and a striking demonstration of his protean virtuosity—was in S. J. Perelman's *The Beauty Part* (1962), which Lahr considered one of his best efforts.

Lahr was a hypochondriac and an inveterate worrier. Schneider called him "the saddest of all men." And while Lahr constantly fretted over the vagaries of his profession, he was rarely out of work. He was one of the few of his generation to adapt to the changing times and to expand as a performer, learning how to use his archetypical character to touch a universal nerve. He was able to modulate his broad, exaggerated style, "to put comedy to the challenge of expanding along with the musical rather than containing it," as the critic Ethan Mordden noted, and to move into comic forms far afield from his early training in vaudeville and burlesque. Lahr suggested that he had "developed a technique that might be called a style" and believed that a comedian should be able to make the audience cry as well as laugh. Lahr as a comic actor was also endowed with a look that was comic without speaking; a worried expression was always on his face, enhanced by small eyes set close together, a clown's mouth, and a large nose. One critic noted that "God must have laughed when he invented Mr. Lahr."

Lahr, an indefatigable worker, accepted jobs in his last years primarily for large fees and turned down less than lucrative roles. He gained public recognition for commercials made for Lay's Potato Chips ("Bet you can't eat just one"). In November 1967, while playing the role of Spats in *The Night They Raided Minsky's,* which was being filmed in New York, Lahr was hospitalized for a back ailment; he died shortly thereafter. Brooks Atkinson lamented that "the last of the great buffoons has gone," adding that "he proved that he was not merely a hired fool but a gifted actor." In 1972, in recognition of his varied accomplishments, Lahr was elected to the Theatre Hall of Fame. Dubbed the King of Clowns, Lahr was, with Buster Keaton, W. C. Fields, and Zero Mostel, one of this century's great comic actors.

[No notable collection of Lahr's papers exists, although personal scrapbooks and other memorabilia can be found at the Museum of the City of New York and the Performing Arts Research Center of the New York Public Library at Lincoln Center. Lahr discusses his art in Gilbert Millstein, "A Comic Discourses on Comedy," *New York Times Magazine,* Mar. 31, 1957; and in Lewis Funke and John E. Booth, eds., *Actors Talk About Acting* (1961). The definitive biography, as noted, is by his son. See also *New York Times,* Oct. 21, 1928; Lucius Beebe, "Bert Lahr, Living Contradiction," *New York Herald Tribune,* Jan. 13, 1937; *New York Herald Tribune,* Mar. 31, 1940; Brooks Atkinson, "Bert Lahr: 1895–1967," *New York Times,* Dec. 10, 1967; William C. Young, ed., *Famous Actors and Actresses on the American Stage* (1975); Ethan Mordden, *Broadway Babies* (1983); Stanley Green, *The Great Clowns of Broadway* (1984); and Alan Schneider, *Entrances* (1986). An obituary is in the *New York Times,* Dec. 5, 1967.]

DON B. WILMETH

LANGLIE, ARTHUR BERNARD (July 25, 1900–July 24, 1966), attorney, publisher, and governor of Washington, was born in Lanesboro, Minn., the son of Bjarne Alfred Langlie, a grocer, and Carrie Dahl, both Norwegian immigrants. Langlie attended public schools in Bremerton, Wash. In high school he was active in athletics, drama, and debate, and worked regularly in the family store. In 1919 he was admitted to the University of Washington, where he supported himself by employment at farms, service stations, logging camps, and lumber mills. He excelled in both baseball and tennis, serving as captain of the university's teams in both sports. (He was captain of the baseball team when it toured Japan in 1925.) He received his B.A. in 1923 and his LL.B. in 1926. Later in 1926, Langlie was admitted to the Washington State bar and joined the Seattle firm of Shank, Balt, and Rode, of which he was a member until 1935. On Sept. 15, 1928, he married Evelyn P. Baker; they had two children.

During the Great Depression, Langlie was one of the organizers of the New Order of Cincinnatus, which advocated applying good business-management principles to the government of Seattle. He was one of three members of the New Order elected to the city council in 1935. In 1936 he was an unsuccessful candidate for mayor but won that office in 1938 and 1940. During his first term he fulfilled a campaign promise to rationalize the city's finances and to rehabilitate Seattle's streetcar system.

In the summer of 1940, Langlie became the Republican candidate for governor of Washington. In November he was elected, narrowly defeating former Democratic senator Clarence C. Dill. Dill's supporters contested the result, but the legislature in a joint session voted 97–45 to confirm Langlie's election. Langlie's gubernatorial agenda included an expansion of state services to be financed by vigorous application of business methods to state government, the improvement of social programs, and the introduction of the merit system to the state civil service.

Langlie was active among Republican governors. At a conference on Mackinac Island in 1943, he joined seventeen other governors in proposing substantial revision of the Republican platform. With Governor Earl Warren of California, he drew up a new policy statement on organized labor. He was active in his support of Thomas E. Dewey's presidential aspirations at the 1944 Republican National Convention. In the elections of that year he was defeated in his bid for reelection by former senator Monrad C. Wallgren.

Early in 1945, Langlie began a year of active duty in the navy, in which he held a reserve lieutenant's commission. He served in both the Atlantic and Hawaii. At the end of his year of active duty he joined the Seattle law firm of Langlie, Todd, and Nickel.

In 1948, Langlie was again the Republican nominee for the governorship. Despite a strong Democratic trend nationally, he defeated Wallgren by very nearly the same margin by which he had lost in 1944. At the same time, the Washington electorate approved the Citizens' Security Act, which increased old-age pensions and medical care for pensioners and welfare recipients. Langlie found himself in the difficult position of asking the legislature for new taxes to cover costs that he found excessive; the tax increases were voted down. In 1950 he supported a campaign to reduce the state's welfare expenditures, which he felt to be as extravagant as the British health program.

Although he favored establishment of the Washington State Toll Bridge Authority, he strongly opposed a plan for a Columbia Valley regional scheme modeled after the Tennessee Valley Authority. He was philosophically opposed to public ownership of utilities, his principal objection to the plan being the tremendous influence that it would confer on a three-man federal commission over the economy of the whole Northwest; his opposition played an important role in defeating it. He also fought public construction of the Hell's Canyon Dam on the Snake River, the major tributary of the Columbia. (It was finally built by the Idaho Power Company in 1968.)

Langlie was reelected in November 1952, becoming the state's first three-term governor. He had been a strong supporter of Dwight D. Eisenhower in that year and in 1954 was the American delegate to the International Labor Organization conference in Geneva. He was the keynote speaker at the 1956 Republican National Convention, which nominated Eisenhower for his second term. That year, he was also elected chairman of the Conference of State Governors.

When Langlie's term as governor was drawing to a close in 1956, he was persuaded by the White House to run for the Senate against the veteran Democratic incumbent, Warren G. Magnuson. Langlie was defeated. Although he had been a popular governor, he had been involved during his third term in several controversies. He had incurred the wrath of conservationists when he supported lumber companies with designs on Olympic National Park, and his effort to unseat Magnuson was criticized as a "smear campaign."

In 1957, Norton Simon, whose Hunt Foods and Industries had recently acquired the McCall Corporation, invited Langlie to be president of the firm, principally known for publishing *McCall's Magazine*. Langlie moved to New York City, where he was chief executive officer of McCall until 1961, when he suffered a heart attack. After he left the presidency, he continued as chairman of the board of directors, but failing health caused his retirement from the firm in 1965. He and his wife returned to Seattle, where he died.

[Langlie's papers are in the Library of the University of Washington. He was the author of a small Newcomen Society publication, *The Printed Word*

(1959). Obituaries are in the *New York Times* and the *Seattle Post-Intelligencer*, both July 25, 1966.]

David Winston Heron

LAPCHICK, JOSEPH BOHOMIEL (Apr. 12, 1900–Aug. 10, 1970), basketball player and coach, was born in Yonkers, N.Y., the son of Joseph B. Lapchick, a Czech immigrant who was a hat finisher but later became a policeman, and Frances Kassik. As the oldest of seven children, Lapchick was forced to go to work at an early age; he therefore did not attend high school but worked as a machinist's apprentice.

Lapchick got his first basketball experience with neighborhood teams. At the age of twelve he played for the Trinity Midgets. At sixteen he played for the semiprofessional Hollywood Inn Club in Yonkers. In 1919, Lapchick quit his machinist's job to enter professional sports.

Six feet, five inches tall and possessed of excellent passing and shooting skills, Lapchick began playing center for Holyoke in the old Western Massachusetts League and remained with the team until 1923. At the same time, he played for the Brooklyn Visitations of the Metropolitan League and for Troy in the New York State League. His excellent career with the original New York Celtics began in 1923. In 1927 he joined the Cleveland Rosenblums and was the center for two world-title teams. From 1930 to 1936 he toured the United States with the reorganized New York Celtics, a team financed by the singer Kate Smith. On May 14, 1932, Lapchick married Elizabeth Sarubbi; they had three children.

In 1936, Lapchick accepted the position of coach at St. John's University, which was then located in Brooklyn, N.Y. In that position, he adhered closely to the principles he had learned with the Celtics: a freewheeling offense featuring quick, slick, sure ball handling; five-man movement; extensive individual initiative; and tenacious man-to-man defense. Also characteristic of Lapchick-coached teams were poise and intelligence. In his first tenure at St. John's (1936–1947), his teams never lost more than seven games a season.

In 1947, Lapchick reentered professional basketball as head coach of the New York Knickerbockers of the National Basketball Association (NBA). In his nine seasons with the "Knicks," the team reached the NBA playoffs eight times, and in 1951, 1952, and 1953 it reached the championship finals. His 1954 team is known as the Team of Coaches, because eight members of that team became coaches themselves.

The pressures of a seventy-two-game schedule, constant travel, and tension with the owner of the Knicks, Ned Irish, led to Lapchick's resignation on Jan. 27, 1956. Shortly thereafter, he returned to St. John's, which was in the process of moving to Jamaica in Queens, N.Y. He remained at St. John's until 1965, when he retired from active coaching.

During Lapchick's years as coach, St. John's won over 70 percent of its games and played in a dozen postseason tournaments. His teams captured a record four National Invitational Tournament (NIT) championships—in 1943, 1944, 1959, and 1965. His 1959 and 1965 teams also won the Holiday Festival. Fittingly, his last game as St. John's coach was a 55–51 upset win over Villanova for the NIT title on Mar. 20, 1965.

After his retirement, Lapchick was employed by a New York shoe company as a consultant on athletic footwear. He also served as director of sports at Kutsher's Country Club in Monticello, N.Y. He spent most of his time, however, enjoying his favorite recreational activities—carpentry, golf, and gardening. He died at Kutsher's Country Club after finishing a round of golf.

Despite a persistent problem of referee baiting, Lapchick was referred to affectionately as "the Coach." College players and coaches respected him for his knowledge of the game and concern for his players. Leroy Ellis, a member of the 1965 NIT championship team, recollected, "The thing about playing for Mr. Lapchick is that he cares about you as a person. If you've got a problem you can come to him. He helped me as a player, but he helped me more as a person." Lou Carneseca, who succeeded Lapchick as coach at St. John's, stated, "I learned more about basketball, and life, just by hearing the old Coachie clear his throat than I did at a thousand basketball clinics." Lapchick received numerous awards for his fifty years of service to the game, including national college Coach of the Year (twice) and the National Association Basketball Committee's Metropolitan Award. He was inducted into the Naismith Memorial Basketball Hall of Fame twice, as a member of the original New York Celtics in 1959 and as an individual player in 1966. The Joe Lapchick Award, established in 1971, is presented annually to the nation's top college-senior basketball player. A tournament in his honor initiates the St. John's basketball season.

[Lapchick's scrapbooks and memorabilia are at the Naismith Memorial Basketball Hall of Fame, Springfield, Mass., and at St. John's University, Jamaica, N.Y. His autobiography is *Fifty Years of Basketball* (1968). See Al Hirshberg, *Basketball's Greatest Teams* (1966); Leonard Koppett, *Twenty-four Seconds to Shoot* (1968) and *The Essence of the Game Is Deception* (1973); Sandy Padwe, *Basketball's Hall of Fame* (1970); and Neil D. Isaacs, *All the Moves* (1975). See also *New York Post Magazine*, Oct. 30, 1955; *Sports Illustrated*, Feb. 19, 1962; *New York Post*, Mar. 26, 1962; *New York Herald Tribune*, Jan. 3, 1965; *Look*, Mar. 9, 1965; and *New York World-Telegram*, Mar. 10, 1965. An obituary is in the *New York Times*, Aug. 11, 1970.]

CHARLES F. HOWLETT

LATOURETTE, KENNETH SCOTT (Aug. 9, 1884–Dec. 26, 1968), historian and educator, was born in Oregon City, Oreg., the son of Dewitt Clinton Latourette, a lawyer and banker, and Rhoda Ellen Scott, a graduate of Pacific University, where she and her husband both received their B.A. and M.A. degrees. Books, music, and Christian conviction filled their home. Latourette attended public schools in Oregon City, graduating from high school when he was not quite sixteen. He worked for a year in his father's bank. In 1901 he entered McMinnville (later Linfield) College, Oreg., where he was a member of the debating team and the glee club. He received his B.S. in chemistry in 1904 and was valedictorian of his class.

Latourette had intended to become a lawyer and banker, but his college involvement in the Young Men's Christian Association and the Student Volunteer Movement for Foreign Missions made him decide to become a Christian missionary. In 1905 he entered Yale College as a senior. Shortly before receiving his B.A. in history and membership in Phi Beta Kappa in 1906, Latourette accepted an offer to join the staff of Yale-in-China. Prior to leaving for the Orient he studied history at Yale Graduate School, obtaining his M.A. in 1907 and his Ph.D. in 1909. His dissertation was entitled, "The History of Early Relations Between the United States and China, 1784–1844." He then spent a year as traveling secretary for the Student Volunteer Movement for Foreign Missions.

In the autumn of 1910 Latourette joined the faculty of Yale-in-China at Changsha, the capital of Hunan province. The next summer he became seriously ill from amebic dysentery and appendicitis. When he arrived in the United States in March 1912 to recover his health he planned to return to China, but his convalescence was slow and it was two years before he could do even part-time work.

Reed College hired Latourette as a lecturer in history in 1914, and he was promoted to associate professor the following year. At Reed he wrote *The Development of China* (1917), which became a standard text and appeared in several revised editions. Meanwhile Latourette had gone to Ohio in 1916 to teach at Denison University. He advanced to professor of history the next year. While at Denison he first taught a class on the history of Christian missionary efforts. That course eventually led to *A History of the Expansion of Christianity* (1937–1945), a seven-volume work that explored not only Christianity's geographical expansion but also its encounters with diverse cultures.

Although Latourette formally resigned his Changsha post in 1917 and did not resume his missionary efforts in China, he was ordained a Baptist minister in 1918. In addition to his professorial duties, he was chaplain at Denison until 1921, when he joined the faculty of the Yale University Divinity School as the D. Willis James Professor of Missions. In 1925 he also began to teach Oriental history. Appointed chairman of Yale's Department of Religion in 1938, Latourette became its director of graduate studies in 1946 and then was named Sterling Professor of Missions and Oriental History in 1949. Before officially retiring from the university in 1953, Latourette was elected president of the American Historical Association in 1947 and of the American Baptist Convention and the Japan International Christian University Foundation in 1951. He remained a working scholar until December 26, 1968, when he was accidentally struck and killed by a car in front of the house where he had been raised in Oregon City.

Latourette, a bachelor, was affectionately known to his Yale Divinity School students as "Uncle Ken." He annually organized student groups for Bible study, conversation, and prayer. Dedicated to writing as well as teaching, in his prolific work he focused primarily on the history of Christianity, particularly the history of missions, and secondarily on Far Eastern and especially Chinese history. His hundreds of publications, among them more than thirty books, made him both a respected sinologist and an honored church historian. In particular his *A History of the Expansion of Christianity* made him the best-known American church historian in the mid-twentieth century. Other important books include: *The Development of Japan* (1918, revised six times and retitled *The History of Japan* in 1947); *Anno Domini: Jesus, History, and God* (1940); *A Short History of the Far East* (1946); *A History of Christianity* (1953); *A History of Modern China* (1954); and the five-volume *Christianity in a Revolutionary Age: A History of Christianity in the Nineteenth and Twentieth Centuries* (1958–1962).

As a specialist on Asia, Latourette did much to introduce Asian studies into college and university curricula in the United States. At a time when most church historians were preoccupied with the early Christian era and the West, he pioneered the study of recent decades and Asian Christianity. Detailed verification of facts, careful interpretation of evidence, and illumination provided by his own faith were the hallmarks of Latourette's scholarship. As he combined his concern for historical accuracy and the vitality of Christianity,. Latourette found the worldwide spread of Christian influence to be especially beneficial in raising standards of human decency. Christianity's strength might ebb and flow, he acknowledged, but the faith's reforming spirit and propensity to spawn new movements contained hopeful energy. Latourette contended that the nineteenth century, which gave rise to extensive missionary efforts that made Christianity a truly global faith, was the greatest Christian era. And unlike many who regarded the revolutionary twentieth century as one of recession for Christianity, Latourette remained optimistic. A Christian resurgence, he believed, would follow.

Latourette's passion for Christian mission and expansion produced a more triumphal interpretation of church history than succeeding generations of historians have accepted. Even those who disputed his optimism recognized that Latourette gave valuable service by focusing Western eyes—secular as well as religious—on the East. Latourette's history continues to show how encounters among diverse religions and cultures affect the world.

[Latourette's papers and a bibliography are in the Day Missions Collection, Yale University Divinity School library. His autobiography is *Beyond the Ranges* (1967). See E. Theodore Bachmann, "Kenneth Scott Latourette," in Wilber C. Harr, ed., *Frontiers of the Christian World* (1962). An obituary is in the *New York Times*, Jan. 1, 1969.]

JOHN K. ROTH

LAWRENCE, DAVID LEO (June 18, 1889–Nov. 21, 1966), mayor of Pittsburgh and governor of Pennsylvania, was born in Pittsburgh, the son of Charles B. Lawrence, a teamster and Democratic chairman of Pittsburgh's Third Ward, and Catherine Conwell. Lawrence grew up in the Point, a working-class section of the city, and attended St. Mary's parochial school. He then took a two-year commercial course instead of a high school education. At the age of fourteen he became an office boy for William J. Brennan, who for twenty-five years was Democratic chairman of Allegheny County. Lawrence worked for Brennan for ten years.

In 1912, Lawrence was a page at the Democratic National Convention in Baltimore that nominated Woodrow Wilson for president. "Wilson was the real class," Lawrence recalled years later. After that experience he never lost his interest in national politics. In 1914, Lawrence became a member of the Pittsburgh Registration Commission, a position he held until 1924. Lawrence served in the Office of the Judge Advocate General in Washington, D.C., during World War I. After the armistice he returned to Pittsburgh and sold insurance. Upon Brennan's death in 1920, Lawrence was chosen to replace him as county Democratic chairman. On June 8, 1921, Lawrence married Alice Golden; they had five children.

Franklin D. Roosevelt's election in 1932 marked the first time since 1856 that a Democratic presidential candidate carried Pennsylvania. Roosevelt appointed Lawrence collector of internal revenue for the western part of the state. Lawrence resigned a year later to become chairman of the Democratic State Committee, a position he held, with the exception of one two-year period, until his election as mayor of Pittsburgh in 1945.

In 1935 the businessman George H. Earle swept into the governorship of Pennsylvania. Because Earle turned out to be something of a playboy, during this period, Lawrence, as secretary of the commonwealth, was considered the "real ruler of Pennsylvania." While serving in that appointive position, Lawrence was indicted on charges of awarding illegal contracts and "macing" state employees for political contributions. After a long trial a jury acquitted him on all counts.

In 1939, Lawrence left Harrisburg for Pittsburgh to rebuild his political fortunes and to head the Harris-Lawrence Company, an insurance firm. He continued as Pittsburgh's Democratic leader, and in 1940 he was named Democratic national committeeman. At the 1944 Democratic National Convention in Chicago, he was instrumental in stopping a boom for the renomination of Vice-President Henry A. Wallace. Lawrence demanded, and got, a recess. The following day, the convention passed over Wallace in favor of Harry S Truman, who was Lawrence's close friend and political ally.

After engineering the election of two ineffective Democratic mayors of Pittsburgh, Lawrence decided in 1945 to step out from behind the scenes and run for mayor himself. He was elected, and became the only mayor in the history of the city to serve four terms. When Lawrence took office, Richard K. Mellon of the Mellon National Bank, Gulf Oil, and Alcoa, and a committee of Pittsburgh's top business leaders, were preparing to tear down and rebuild the city. In Mayor Lawrence, Mellon and his colleagues found an eager and willing partner. While Mellon's group, the Allegheny Conference on Community Development, provided the money and plans for the reconstruction of downtown Pittsburgh, Lawrence enforced antipollution and smog-control measures and lobbied at the state capital and in Washington for funds to build roads, bridges, and dams. When asked what he and Mellon had in common, Lawrence replied, "We have the same hobby . . . Pittsburgh." On Nov. 4, 1957, *Time* magazine said of Lawrence, "Like the latter-day apostle of civic progress he has become, he never missed a chance to mention his 'better Pittsburgh,' with its smog-free air, rising skyscrapers, parks, bridges, and elevated highways." In 1958, *Fortune* magazine listed Pittsburgh among the eight best-administered cities in the United States.

Lawrence, a Roman Catholic, felt that members of his faith could not win statewide election in Pennsylvania or be elected to national office. He ran for governor in 1958 only because the Democratic organization could not agree on a candidate. "I am not a candidate of my own choosing. They decided I was the man to make the fight and I was willing to go through with it," he said. He defeated Republican Arthur T. McGonigle of Reading, a wealthy pretzel manufacturer, but his victory, making him Pennsylvania's first Catholic governor, was a narrow one: he defeated McGonigle by only 76,000 votes (50.8 percent) instead of the 200,000 margin he had predicted. He attributed the close race to the religious issue. A Pennsylvania law that prohibits governors from succeeding themselves made this his last try for elected office.

In the early maneuvering for the 1960 presidential nomination, Lawrence made it clear that he would welcome a third presidential bid by Adlai Stevenson. Ironically, he was cool to the candidacy of John F. Kennedy on religious grounds. Lawrence explained, "I am sure that a Catholic running for the presidency must have an issue so big, so strong, so completely overriding that his religion is never thought of. . . . It's got to be something that touches the people's hearts—an appeal to the passions." At the eleventh hour, when Stevenson pulled out of the contest, Lawrence backed Kennedy. The *New York Times* wrote on Aug. 24, 1964, that Lawrence's move was decisive in assuring Kennedy's nomination on the first ballot. Lawrence also nominated Senator Lyndon Johnson for the vice-presidency.

When Lawrence's term as governor ended in 1962, he returned to Pittsburgh and to his role of party leader. Soon after, Kennedy appointed him chairman of the President's Committee on Equal Opportunity for Housing. That same year, Lawrence saw one of his favorites, Philadelphia's Mayor Richardson Dilworth, defeated for governor of Pennsylvania by Republican William Scranton. Two years later, Lawrence's choice for the United States Senate was beaten in a primary. In 1966, Lawrence's candidate for governor lost in the primary to millionaire Milton Shapp, who had berated Lawrence during the campaign as a "political boss." Lawrence nevertheless campaigned vigorously for Shapp in the general election; he suffered a cardiac arrest while speaking at a rally on Shapp's behalf. Seventeen days later, Lawrence died in Pittsburgh, never to learn that Shapp had lost decisively and that the political organization he had crafted over the years was in disarray.

[For journalistic accounts of Lawrence's career, see *Time*, June 1, 1942, Nov. 15, 1954, June 18, 1956, Nov. 4, 1957, Dec. 2, 1957, Apr. 21, 1958, Nov. 2, 1959, Nov. 30, 1959, July 25, 1960, and Oct. 19, 1962; *Life*, Nov. 28, 1955; *New York Herald Tribune*, June 5, 1958, and Oct. 14, 1960; *Christian Science Monitor*, Sept. 5, 1958; *Saturday Evening Post*, March 14, 1959; *New York Post*, Sept. 2, 1960; and *New York Times*, Nov. 5, 1962, and Aug. 24, 1964. An obituary is in the *New York Times*, Nov. 22, 1966.]

JOHN T. GALVIN

LEAR, BEN (May 12, 1879–Nov. 1, 1966), army officer, was born in Hamilton, Ontario, Canada, the son of Ben Lear, a printer, and Hannah Senden. When he was two years old, the family moved to Pueblo, Colo., where his father became shop foreman for the *Pueblo Evening Press*. Following his graduation from high school, Lear worked as a printer's devil for his father and, at the age of sixteen, was selected as secretary-treasurer by the employee-owned newspaper. He continued to work with his father until the Spanish-American War broke out in the spring of 1898. He enlisted in the First Colorado Infantry, a volunteer unit, at the beginning of May 1898 and immediately became a first sergeant.

In June 1898, Lear's unit was sent to the Philippines. Lear's father was among the first batch of new recruits sent to join the unit, and he seems to have accepted orders from his sergeant son with few complaints. On one occasion, the father, a private, observed that he was being assigned to too many kitchen-police details. Lear lectured his father on the importance of performing one's military duties, and the matter was closed. Lear fought in several campaigns and received a battlefield commission as a second lieutenant of volunteers on Apr. 1, 1899. Promotion to first lieutenant followed in July of that year. He continued to serve in the Philippines until 1902, receiving regular army appointments as second lieutenant in February 1901 and first lieutenant in December 1901.

On Oct. 6, 1906, Lear married Grace Russel; they had one child, who was born in an army tent during one of Lear's assignments in Cuba. Lear graduated from the army's Mounted Service School in 1911 and subsequently participated as an equestrian in the 1912 Olympic Games in Stockholm. He later fought on the Mexican border against Pancho Villa's border raiders as part of Brigadier General John J. Pershing's command.

During World War I, Lear was a member of the army general staff in Washington. After the war, he completed courses at the School of the Line (1922), the General Staff School (1923), and the Army War College (1926). In 1936, following assignments as an instructor and cavalry unit commander at various army posts, Lear was named a brigadier general. By 1940 he was a lieutenant general and commander of the Second Army. This command, with headquarters soon established by Lear in Memphis, Tenn., was the army's principal training element.

Lear was an uncompromising disciplinarian. In June 1941 several subordinate headquarters within the Second Army noted that complaints had been received concerning insulting comments made to civilians, particularly women, by soldiers in passing trucks and convoys. Lear was determined to curb this behavior. On Sunday, July 6, 1941, Lear and some friends were playing golf at a country club in Memphis when a truck convoy of the Thirty-fifth Division, a National Guard unit, passed by the course. Many of the troops waved and shouted "Yoo-hoo" and other comments at several groups playing golf, including some "appreciative girls clad in shorts," who "gaily waved back." An angry Lear called to the men to be quiet. He was not recognized in his civilian clothes and was told to shut up. Infuriated, he returned to his headquarters and directed that the offending troops be returned to Memphis. This accomplished, the 325 officers and men were ordered to march back to their post at Camp Robinson, Ark., a distance of forty-five miles. He specified that the shuttle method, entailing five miles of marching for every five miles of truck riding, was to be used.

The press picked up the story and implied that the men had been compelled to walk the entire distance under a broiling sun. Although the march was not severe for men who had been on maneuvers for many weeks, Lear was excoriated in hundreds of letters for his alleged brutality. A comparative few commended Lear for what they considered his forthright and necessary action, but the incident clouded his remaining years in the army. Some pressure was brought to bear on the War Department to discipline Lear, but the matter was dropped following American entry into World War II.

Lear led the Second Army in several major maneuvers in Louisiana in 1941 and 1942. The 1941 maneuvers, which also brought generals Dwight D. Eisenhower and George S. Patton, Jr., to public attention, were the largest known in American history to that time. They involved some 400,000 troops, 1,000 planes, and unprecedented numbers of armored and parachute troops.

Lear retired in 1943, having reached the statutory retirement age, but was immediately recalled to active duty. When the commander of army ground forces, Lieutenant General Leslie J. McNair, was killed in France in July 1944, Lear was named to succeed him. In January 1945, General Eisenhower, who confronted a manpower shortage in the European theater of operations, asked General George C. Marshall, the army chief of staff, to send him a senior officer to deal with the problem. Marshall sent Lear, who was promptly appointed deputy commander of the European theater and directed to identify for frontline duty infantrymen then serving in noncombat billets. Lear and his staff were able in part to fill the urgent need for combat soldiers and for infantry officer replacements. Lear did not, however, have sufficient control over the replacement process to institute all the reforms he desired. The pressure of time compelled them to use patchwork solutions, and there were complaints concerning the quality of officers and men sent to the frontline units.

When Lear returned to the United States following the end of the European war in July 1945, hundreds of GI's called out, "Yoo-hoo," as the general walked down the gangplank of his transport ship in Boston. Following his retirement in 1945, he continued with his interest in horsemanship, marksmanship, and golf. His last two years were spent as a patient in a Veterans Administration hospital in Murfreesboro, Tenn., where he died.

[There is no biography of Lear. His tenure as commander of the Second Army is discussed in Bell I. Wiley and William P. Govan, *History of the Second Army* (1946). His activities in the period from 1940 to 1945 are discussed in Forrest C. Pogue, *George C. Marshall*, II (1966) and III (1973); and Russell Weigley, *Eisenhower's Lieutenants* (1981). Obituaries are in the *New York Times* and the *Washington Post*, both Nov. 2, 1966.]

KEIR B. STERLING

LEE, GYPSY ROSE (Jan. 9, 1914?–Apr. 26, 1970), entertainer and writer, was born Rose Louise Hovick, probably in Seattle, Wash. (although it is impossible to verify either her birthdate or her birthplace), the daughter of John Olaf Hovick, a newspaperman, and Rose Thompson, whom Lee in her 1957 autobiography described as the archetypal stage mother. In 1960 Lee added that "Mother was rougher and more ruthless than I have portrayed her. She ran roughshod over the world."

When Louise (as she was called by family members) was about four her parents divorced, and the family went to live with Mrs. Hovick's parents in Seattle. About 1918 she and her sister Ellen Evangeline (later known as June Havoc) made their singing and dancing debut at a Knights of Pythias lodge. They were successful, especially June, who was cute and talented. Louise, large for her age, settled into a supporting role. Soon Mrs. Hovick took her daughters to California, where the girls performed in an act called Dainty June, the Hollywood Baby, and Her Newsboys, with Louise as the Doll Girl. In 1922 they were on the Pantages Circuit as Baby June and Her Pals. Their first long contract was on the Keith-Orpheum Circuit, in an act most often known as Dainty June and Her Newsboy Songsters. Louise appeared on stage, and often off, in boy's clothes, in order not to detract from the femininity of her sister. Until 1928 they toured the country, and at the height of their vaudeville careers earned as much as $1,250 to $1,500 a week. Louise's schooling was minimal. When complaints of child-labor violations surfaced, Mrs. Hovick would hire a tutor on the road. Still, Louise in her early teens developed a love for books that continued into adulthood.

At the age of thirteen June eloped with one of the "newsboys." The act then became Rose Louise and Her Newsboy Songsters until revamped into an all-girl act called Madame Rose's Dancing Daughters. In 1929, stranded in Kansas City, the act changed to Rose Louise and Her Hollywood Blondes and was booked for the first time in a burlesque house. Louise was about fifteen when she first stepped into a solo strip spot at the Gaiety in Toledo, Ohio. Working under various names, she finally settled on the cognomen Gypsy Rose Lee and developed her trademarks as a stripper: peeling off her garments by removing strategically placed straight pins, tossing a garter with a rose attached into the audience, and winning the audience with her wit as much as with her sensuality.

Though not a classic beauty, Lee was tall (five feet, nine inches) and statuesque (130 pounds), with hazel eyes, auburn hair, a subtle overbite, and a throaty voice. Although not the first burlesque queen, she was the best-known of her era and probably the most remembered. H. L. Mencken coined the term "ecdysiast" to describe her; the French, to emphasize the sophistication of her strip, called her *une déshabilleuse*. Lee had little talent, but, as Leonard Spigelgass noted, "she glowed. She stepped upon a stage, and she filled it, because she was a presence." Billy Minsky claimed that she transformed the crass striptease into "seven minutes of sheer art"; Burns Mantle commented that "Miss Lee is very careful not to take off more than she has on." In 1942 *Life* termed her "a classic paradox: an intellectual strip-teaser." Lee often stated that she actually spent no more than fifty weeks as a stripper and coasted for years with a fake strip. Believing that sex onstage should be played for laughs, she set her act by the mid-1930's and made few changes thereafter.

Lee's big break came in April 1931 in New York City at Minsky's Republic Theater. By 1935, at the Irving Place Theater, she made as much as $1,000 a week. She became a friend of such intellectuals and artists as Mark Van Doren, e.e. cummings, Deems Taylor, Carson McCullers, Janet Flanner, Max Ernst, and Christopher Isherwood. In 1932, as Rose Louise, she appeared in *Hot-Cha*, the beginning of her career outside of burlesque. Using the name Gypsy Rose Lee, she appeared in 1936 with Fannie Brice and Bobby Clark in Florenz Ziegfeld's *Follies*.

Lee went to Hollywood in 1937. In response to demands from church organizations, the Hays Office, which was known as the guardian of morality in the motion-picture industry, insisted that she be billed as Louise Hovick and that her career as a striptease artist not be mentioned. Without her stage name, the studio lost interest in her and pushed her into five "B" films over the next two years. Although her film career was never very successful, she returned in 1943 to make *Stage Door Canteen*, featuring a spoof on the striptease, and the following year *Belle of the Yukon*. In 1945 she appeared in a version of her own play, *The Naked Genius*, called *Doll Face*. She was in two unsuccessful films in 1958, appeared in *The Stripper* in 1963, and made her final film, *The Trouble with Angels*, in 1966.

Lee's first stage role in a straight comedy, *I Must Love Someone* (1939), was followed in 1940 by Michael Todd's *The Streets of Paris* at the New York World's Fair at $4,000 a week. During this engagement her affair with Todd began. The same year she appeared in *Gay New Orleans* at Todd's Theatre-Café in Chicago.

Lee was unsuccessful with men, from her first passion, the burlesque comic Rags Ragland, to Billy Rose, with whom she had a platonic relationship in the 1960's. She was married and divorced three times. She first married Arnold R. Mizzy, a New York dental-supply manufacturer on Aug. 13, 1937, and divorced him in 1941; her second marriage, to the actor William Alexander Kirkland, began on Aug. 31, 1942, and was dissolved three months later (they were formally divorced in 1944). Lee's final marriage, to artist Julio de Diego, lasted from Mar. 19, 1948 to 1955. Her son, Erik Lee, born in December 1944, was thought to have been fathered by her second husband. In 1971, however, Otto Preminger acknowledged that Erik was his son and adopted him. Lee told her son that she chose Preminger to be his father intentionally. "It was right after Mike [Todd] left me. I felt so alone that I decided to have something no one would ever be able to take away from me."

In 1940 Walter Winchell asked Lee to write a guest column. This experience led to a serious interest in writing and to the publication of two mystery novels, *The G-String Murders* (1941) and *Mother Finds a Body* (1942), followed by an unsuccessful play, *The Naked Genius* (1943). In the 1940's and 1950's articles by her appeared in the *New Yorker*, *American Mercury*, *Mademoiselle*, *Harper's*, *Collier's*, *Variety*, *Cosmopolitan*, and *Flair*. She recommended to other writers, "*You* write it, so that it sounds like you and won't get slicked up; let someone else punctuate it."

Her most significant stage appearance in the 1940's was in *Star and Garter* (1942), a burlesque for the carriage trade, for which she was paid $3,000 a week. During World War II she played in numerous military camp shows with the United Service Organizations (USO). After touring carnivals in 1949 and earning a minimum guarantee of $10,000 a week plus a percentage of the gross, she was fond of saying,

"I'm probably the highest-paid outdoor entertainer since Cleopatra." In the mid-1950's she decided that she was too old to strip and began to seek other sources of income. In 1956 she performed in Las Vegas and first appeared on television, in an episode of "The U.S. Steel Hour" called "Sauce for the Goose." In 1958 she tried her first televised talk and variety show, which led to a syndicated talk show, starting in 1966. She appeared on numerous dramatic shows in the 1960's and was a regular on the situation comedy "The Pruitts of Southampton" in 1966–1967.

Her major accomplishment in this period was *Gypsy: A Memoir* (1957), a somewhat fanciful account of her early career. The book was more a celebration of her mother and her mother's ruthlessness, and of vaudeville and burlesque in the 1920's and 1930's, than an autobiography. Its success allowed Lee to exploit more fully her passion for collecting Victorian antiques. *Gypsy*, the musical based on her memoirs, opened on Broadway in 1959, followed by a film version in 1962.

Lee's last major creative effort was a one-woman show called *A Curious Evening with Gypsy Rose Lee*. Its first performance, in January 1958 in Palm Beach, was followed in 1961 by a brief run in New York City at the Mayfair Theater, with disappointing results. In 1961 she took her show to Los Angeles, moving permanently to Beverly Hills the same year. In the late 1960's she toured Vietnam for the USO, distributing Gypsy's Kosher Fortune Cookies, with bawdy, humorous fortunes inside. She died in Los Angeles.

Although Lee could be difficult, demanding, maddeningly self-assured, and astonishingly frugal, she was, as her son notes, "a woman of taste, intelligence, and style—an intellectual in the best sense of the word." Her sister remembers her as "many people, all of them vivid and powerful." As an entertainer and self-publicist, she was tireless. She was also something of an anomaly, quite modest, and almost Victorian in private life. Toward the end of her life she issued occasional admonitory statements about theatrical nudity that were both shrewd and an explanation of her success as a sex symbol. "Bare flesh bores men," she often warned, and added, "I'm really a little prudish."

[Lee's collection of scrapbooks and home movies is in the possession of her son, Erik Preminger, in San Francisco. A clipping file is in the Billy Rose Theatre Collection of the New York Public Library at Lincoln Center. Her publications include "My Burlesque Customers," *American Mercury*, Nov. 1942; "Shades of Paul Moss," *Variety*, Jan. 3, 1943; "Mother and the Man Named Gordon," "Mother and the Knights of Pythias," and "Just Like Children Leading Normal Lives," all in *New Yorker*, Nov. 20, Apr. 10, and July 3, 1943, respectively; and "Stranded in Kansas City, or, a Fate Worse than Vaudeville" and "Up the Runway to Minsky's," both in *Harper's*, Apr. and May 1957, respectively. See her mother's remembrances, "A Stage Mother Tells of the Trials and Tribulations of Guiding Two Talented Daughters Along the Road to Success," *New York Journal-American*, July 1944; June Havoc, *Early Havoc* (1959); and Erik Lee Preminger, *Gypsy and Me* (1984). Articles about her include Kyle Crichton, "Strip to Fame," *Collier's*, Dec. 19, 1936; John Richmond, "Gypsy Rose Lee, Striptease Intellectual," *American Mercury*, Jan. 1941; J. P. McEvoy, "More Tease than Strip," *Variety*, June 4, 1941; "Gypsy Rose and Muse," *Cue*, July 12, 1943; Bass Yarling, "An Ecdysiast's Memoir," *New Republic*, May 27, 1957; Stanley Richards, "A Visit with Gypsy Rose Lee," *Theatre*, Jan. 1960; and Jack Hamilton, "Gypsy Rose Lee," *Look*, Feb. 22, 1966. See also the obituaries, *Los Angeles Times*, Apr. 27, 1970, and *New York Times*, Apr. 28, 1970; and the eulogy, *New York Times*, May 10, 1970.]

DON B. WILMETH

LEEDOM, BOYD STEWART (Sept 28, 1906–Aug. 11, 1969), chairman of the National Labor Relations Board (NLRB), was born in Alvord, Iowa, the son of Chester Nevius Leedom, a farmer, and Gertrude Emmaline Stewart. In 1907 Leedom moved to western South Dakota, where his parents' interest in politics, religion, and temperance causes deeply influenced his later career. He attended public schools and Black Hills Teachers College before earning his LL.B. at the University of South Dakota in 1929. In 1927 he married Irene Cecil Robertson; they had three children.

Leedom began to practice law in Rapid City, S.D., in 1929. After stateside duty in the navy in World War II, he returned to his law practice and to civic and religious activities. Leedom served for two years in the South Dakota state senate and in 1950 unsuccessfully sought the Republican nomination for governor. In 1951 he was appointed to the South Dakota Supreme Court.

While on the state supreme court, Leedom was drawn into a series of labor disputes that brought him to the attention of Secretary of Labor James P. Mitchell. Assigned to serve as a referee on the National Railroad Adjustment Board, Leedom ruled in about forty labor cases. While his decisions were attacked by the railroad brotherhoods as promanagement, his detached approach brought him favorable comment within the Eisenhower administration. Secretary Mitchell then advised President Eisenhower to nominate Leedom to the NLRB in February 1955. Leedom's relatively noncontroversial record reduced liberal opposition to his appointment, while his personal ties to South Dakota's congressional delegation, especially to conservative Senator Karl Mundt, blunted right-wing criticism. In November 1955 the president appointed Leedom chairman of the NLRB.

With a Republican majority, the Eisenhower NLRB issued rulings more to the liking of businessmen than had the Truman board. It expanded the right of employers to communicate with their employees during labor disputes, and it tightened the rules on permissible picketing and the secondary boycott. The NLRB under the previous Eisenhower chairman had restricted its jurisdiction to larger employers. Then, in 1957, the Supreme Court ruled that state courts could not assume labor cases governed by federal law, even if they had been rejected by the NLRB. The Leedom board subsequently tried to redefine its jurisdiction, but not until the Landrum-Griffin Act of 1959 were cases effectively parceled out between the states and the NLRB.

Leedom emerged as a moderate within the NLRB. As chairman, he devoted about half of his time to administrative problems, including budgetary and public relations questions. Possibly as a way of forestalling further congressional investigation, he announced in 1955 that some 300 additional field jobs with the NLRB would be labled "sensitive" and hence open to personnel review by the FBI. As presiding member, Leedom sought to avoid prolonged discussion and acrimony and to create a professional, judicial atmosphere within the NLRB. By the late 1950's, however, he warned against a breakdown of collective bargaining machinery and called for mutual restraint by labor and management.

Charging the Leedom board with an antilabor bias, Democratic politicians frequently drew upon a lengthy 1956 indictment by Chicago labor lawyer Mozart Ratner, who had been associated with the NLRB during the Truman administration. Defenders of the board, including Leedom, responded that the appointees of a new administration were often accused of bias and that the Eisenhower board was merely correcting the excessively prolabor stance of the Truman administration. Although the publication of a letter written by Leedom in 1960 endorsing Senator Mundt (a frequent critic of labor leaders) brought some embarrassment, Leedom generally avoided open political activity.

Confronted with a mounting caseload and increasing delays, the Leedom board hired a consulting firm to conduct a confidential efficiency study of the agency. The resulting McKinsey Report urged the board to delegate greater authority to regional offices and to stop dilatory behavior by labor and management representatives. Concerned about due process, Leedom and the board moved slowly in implementing the McKinsey recommendations, even after the Landrum-Griffin Act empowered the NLRB to delegate some of its powers. Meanwhile, Democratic congressman Roman Pucinski leaked the McKinsey Report to the press and began an attack upon Leedom and the board both for its delays and its alleged antilabor bias. In 1961 Pucinski chaired highly critical hearings on the Eisenhower board, but by then he had moderated his personal attacks on Leedom, who had endorsed a Kennedy-administration proposal for additional reforms of the NLRB.

Leedom's role with the NLRB changed during the Kennedy and Johnson administrations. Although Leedom remained a member, Kennedy named a new chairman in 1961 and quickly transformed the board with other appointments. The Kennedy NLRB reversed Eisenhower board decisions on picketing, secondary boycotts, and employer "free speech" rights during labor disputes. Leedom dissented in each of these rulings as well as in a 1961 decision (later upheld by the Supreme Court) approving the agency shop, a form of union security agreement whereby nonunion workers are required to pay the equivalent of union dues. While arguing that reversals of earlier decisions would contribute to instability in labor-management relations, Leedom stressed that the overall pattern of the 1960's rulings was not as antibusiness as critics suggested. Although Leedom had Senator Mundt's support for a third five-year term in 1964, President Johnson did not reappoint him. Instead, Leedom became a trial examiner for the board. In 1967 he held that the J.P. Stevens Company had blatantly violated the law when it fired southern textile workers for unionizing.

Leedom thought of his attempts at harmonizing labor-management relations as an extension of his activities as a Christian layman. A devout Methodist Sunday-school teacher, Leedom promoted the Billy Graham Evangelistic Crusade. He also served as president of International Christian Leadership, a lay organization best known for initiating the prayer-breakfast tradition. He died in Arlington, Va.

[References to Leedom are in the Karl E. Mundt Archival Library, Madison, S.D.; and in the Eisenhower Presidential Library, Abilene, Kans. The McKinsey Report is in *Reports of the House Committee on Education and Labor* (1961). See Frank W. McCulloch and Tim Bornstein, *The National Labor Relations Board* (1974). Obituaries are in the *New York Times* and the *Washington Post*, both Aug. 12, 1969.]

William Howard Moore

LEHMAN, ROBERT (Sept. 29, 1891–Aug. 9, 1969), investment banker, was born in New York City, the son of Philip Lehman, a banker, and Carrie Lauer. His father ran Lehman Brothers, the banking firm founded by his father and uncles. Lehman attended the Hotchkiss School (1905–1909), and received a B.A. in 1913 from Yale University. He then devoted himself to his father's art collection until 1917, when he enlisted in the army, where he served as a captain with the 318th Field Artillery in France. In 1919 Lehman joined his father's firm. By 1921 he had become a partner, and by 1925 he was functioning as the bank's principal partner, a position he held for forty-three years. On Oct. 26, 1923, he married Ruth Rumsey, whom he divorced in 1931. They had no children. He married Ruth Owen Meeker on Jan. 29, 1932. They had one child. On July 12, 1952, he married Lee Anz Lynn.

Early on, Lehman initiated the recruitment of the firm's first nonfamily partners, and he involved the bank increasingly with retail businesses rather than producers, the traditional Wall Street investments. Retail merchandising soon became the firm's forte. It provided financial services for Federated Department Stores, W. T. Grant, F. W. Woolworth, Interstate Department Stores, Gimbels, Macy's, and the Allied Stores Corporation.

Lehman was also interested in the entertainment industry. In 1928 he created the nation's largest vaudeville circuit, comprising more than 700 theaters, through a consolidation of the Keith-Albee and Orpheum theaters. This inevitably led to his interest in the motion picture industry, and he provided funding to RKO, Paramount Pictures, and Twentieth Century–Fox. He also pioneered in television financing. In the late 1930's his firm sponsored the first public underwriting of a television company, Allan B. DuMont Laboratories.

In 1929, Lehman Brothers began a long involvement with the air transportation industry. That year Lehman was named to the board of directors of Pan American Airways and assisted it in funding its early expansion in South America. Also in 1929, Lehman Brothers helped underwrite the creation of the Aviation Corporation, of whose executive committee Lehman became chairman. The corporation soon acquired many airlines and related companies and had approximately eighty subsidiaries when the airlines were consolidated as American Airways (later American Airlines) in 1933. That year Lehman lost control of the Aviation Corporation in a stock battle. In 1934 Lehman Brothers gained a controlling interest in Transcontinental and Western Airlines later Trans World Airlines), which it held until 1939. Lehman also helped finance Capital, Continental, and National airlines.

During the Great Depression, when many investors lacked either the capital or the inclination to acquire corporate securities, Lehman creatively funded his clients through the capital resources of insurance companies and pension funds.

In the 1940's Lehman became intrigued by Thoroughbred horse racing. During the next quarter-century, he purchased, bred, and raced dozens of horses. By the late 1960's he had more than sixty horses in Kentucky and New York racetracks.

In the early 1950's Lehman underwrote the initial offerings of the conglomerates Litton Industries, Inc., and Ling-Temco-Vought, Inc. Reportedly, Lehman Brothers accepted shares of Litton then worth less than one dollar each; those shares later rose to $150 each.

The Lehman art collection, one of the finest

private collections in the United States, included approximately 1,000 paintings, including works by great European masters. In 1957 a selection of 293 works was exhibited at the Louvre. Lehman also collected Gothic tapestries, Renaissance furniture and jewelry, Venetian glass, Persian and Chinese ceramics, and bronzes. The collection was maintained in a private museum in New York City until it was donated to the Metropolitan Museum of Art in 1969. In 1963 Lehman established a $500,000 endowed chair in art history at Yale University and in 1967 he gave $1 million to the Institute of Fine Arts, New York University. In 1967 Lehman was made chairman of the board of trustees of the Metropolitan Museum of Art. At his death his art collection was valued at between $50 and $100 million.

Lehman had the rare capacity to accurately anticipate economic trends and the wisdom to support industries in their vanguard. Although he invited all to call him "Bobbie," few could bring themselves to so address the patrician financier. Lehman died at Sands Point, Long Island, N.Y.

[Lehman's role within Lehman Brothers is in the in-house publication, *A Centennial* (1950). See also Stephen Birmingham, *Our Crowd* (1967). An obituary is in the *New York Times*, Aug. 10, 1969.]

STEPHEN D. BODAYLA

LEIGH, VIVIEN (Nov. 5, 1913–July 7, 1967), actress, was born Vivian Mary Hartley in Darjeeling, India, the daughter of Ernest Richard Hartley, a junior partner in an English brokerage firm, and Gertrude Robinson Yackje. When she was six her parents sent her to a convent school at Roehampton, England. The youngest child in the convent, she was not to see either parent for two years. She showed an immediate talent for drama and music. Her Indian childhood, added to her exotic looks, gave her a charisma and precocity not usually found in a child her age. She attended convent schools in Paris and San Remo from 1927, when she left Roehampton, until 1931, when her parents requested that she return to India. Instead she enrolled at the Royal Academy of Dramatic Art in London. She married Herbert Leigh Holman, a barrister, on Dec. 20, 1932. She was presented to King George V and Queen Mary on June 13, 1933, and shortly thereafter returned to the Royal Academy to continue her preparation for a stage career.

The birth of a daughter in 1933 interrupted her studies but did not end her acting aspirations. Her spectacular beauty brought her to the attention of film producers. She made her professional acting debut in 1934 in the motion picture *Things Are Looking Up*, in which she played a schoolgirl and was listed in the credits as Vivian Holman. Leading roles in two more inauspicious British films, *The Village Squire* and *Gentleman's Agreement*, followed the same year. For her moderately successful stage debut in *The Green Sash* on Feb. 25, 1935, she changed her name to Vivian Leigh (the surname being the name her husband used as his first name). In her next theater appearance as the lead in *The Mask of Virtue* her name went on the marquee as Vivien Leigh. The morning after the play's premiere on May 15, 1935, she was a star.

Now known as "the fame-in-one-night girl," she signed a contract with Alexander Korda, one of the leading British film producers. She also entered into a romantic liaison with England's young matinee idol Laurence Olivier, who was married to actress Jill Esmond and the father of a young son. Korda cast them as lovers in *Fire Over England* in 1937, the year that David O. Selznick launched his well-publicized search for an actress to play Scarlett O'Hara in the screen adaptation of Margaret Mitchell's *Gone with the Wind*. Selznick saw a print of *Fire Over England*, in which Leigh portrayed a lady-in-waiting to Queen Elizabeth I, and decided against her. Two years later, when she accompanied Olivier to Hollywood, where he was cast as Heathcliff in the film version of *Wuthering Heights*, Selznick changed his mind. *Gone with the Wind* (1939) won her an Academy Award and made her an international star. She divorced Leigh Holman on Feb. 19, 1940, and married Olivier on Aug. 31. Almost immediately they became known as "the golden couple," perhaps the most romantic and famous twosome of the 1940's. Appropriately, they toured onstage in *Romeo and Juliet*.

With the outbreak of World War II the Oliviers returned to Great Britain. Shortly thereafter, Leigh contracted tuberculosis. Although the disease continued to plague her, as did severe mental depression, she continued to star onstage, frequently with Olivier, and in films. In 1952 she won her second Academy

Award for her portrayal of Blanche DuBois in the film adaptation of Tennessee Williams' *A Streetcar Named Desire*, which was released in 1951. Olivier had been knighted in 1947 and Leigh was now privately and socially Lady Olivier.

After her divorce from Olivier on Dec. 2, 1960, Leigh's health and mental condition deteriorated. She lived to make two more films, *The Roman Spring of Mrs. Stone* (1961) and *Ship of Fools* (1965); to tour with the Old Vic in Australia in 1962, portraying Viola in *Twelfth Night*, Paola in *Duel of Angels*, and Marguerite in *La Dame aux Camellias;* and to star on Broadway in the musical *Tovarich* (1963), for which she received an Antoinette Perry Award, and in Chekhov's *Ivanov* (1966). She died in London of tuberculosis. Her death was almost a replay of *La Dame aux Camellias*, for she tried to conceal her critical condition from those closest to her. Having often been close to death during her long illness, she had a fearlessness, almost an insolent attitude, toward death, along with a tender regard for the living. She is best remembered as a southern belle in *Gone with the Wind* and *A Streetcar Named Desire*, but she was a fine stage performer and appeared in many Shakespearean roles.

[See Felix Barker, *The Oliviers* (1953); Anne Edwards, *Vivien Leigh* (1977); and material at the Academy of Motion Picture Arts and Sciences, Los Angeles, Calif., and the Harvard University Theatre Archives. An obituary is in the *New York Times*, July 9, 1967.]

ANNE EDWARDS

LELAND, WALDO GIFFORD (July 17, 1879–Oct. 19, 1966), historian and archival theorist, was born in Newton, Mass., the son of Luther Erving Leland and Ellen Gifford, both public school teachers. Upon graduating from Newton High School in 1896, Leland went to Brown University, where one of his history professors was J. Franklin Jameson. After receiving his B.A. in 1900, Leland enrolled at Harvard, where he switched from sociology to history, earning his M.A. in 1901. While in later life he would often be addressed as Dr. Leland, his doctorates all were honorary.

In 1903, Harvard professor Albert Bushnell Hart offered Leland, then a teaching assistant, the opportunity to assist Claude H. Van Tyne in a survey sponsored by the newly founded Carnegie Institution of Washington. A six-month temporary assignment became the basis of Leland's twenty-four-year association with the institution. The *Guide to the Archives of the Government of the United States in Washington* (1904), coauthored by Leland and Van Tyne, was followed in 1907 by an edition revised and expanded by Leland. Those works established Leland as the nation's leading authority on federal archives. This period also marked the beginning of Leland's close relationship with the Library of Congress. On Apr. 26, 1904, Leland married Gertrude Dennis, a Canadian-born violinist; they had no children. Both Leland and his wife were active members of the Literary Society of Washington.

Three organizations played prominent roles in Leland's career: the Carnegie Institution, the American Historical Association (AHA), and the American Council of Learned Societies (ACLS). When Jameson joined the Carnegie Institution in 1905, he promoted assistance to the AHA. With Jameson's encouragement, Leland served as AHA general secretary, a position he held from 1909 to 1920.

Leland's primary assignments were with the Carnegie Institution. After completing the *Guide*, he traveled to repositories throughout the eastern United States to collect letters of Continental Congress delegates. He then began work on his multivolume *Guide to Materials for American History in the Libraries and Archives of Paris*. For extended periods from 1907 to 1914 and then again from 1922 to 1927, he served as the institution's principal representative in France. The first two volumes, on libraries and on the archives of the Ministry of Foreign Affairs, were published in 1932 and 1943, respectively. Drafts for an additional three volumes are among the Leland Papers at the Library of Congress. In an associated activity, he directed the foreign copying program of the Library of Congress for French manuscripts relating to the United States. He also initiated work on what became the institution's two-volume *Calendar of Manuscripts in Paris Archives and Libraries Relating to the History of the Mississippi Valley to 1803*.

While Leland was in Europe he edited the AHA annual reports and prize essays, with many of his routine secretarial responsibilities being performed in the United States by Patty W. Washington of the AHA staff. On return trips to America, Leland involved himself in archival matters. He delivered the 1909 keynote paper at the first Conference of Archivists, a forum proposed by Leland that was the forerunner of the Society of American Archivists (SAA). He also presented papers at archives-oriented gatherings in 1910, 1912, 1915, and 1917.

In his best-known archival-related activity he provided documentation and backup assistance for Jameson's campaign to establish the National Archives. In 1926, Congress voted funds for the building's construction.

During World War I, Leland served as secretary-treasurer of the Jameson-sponsored National Board for Historical Service and was the board's major stabilizing force. Leland and Newton D. Mereness coauthored *Introduction to American Official Sources for the Economic and Social History of the War* (1926).

Leland had been an official American delegate to the International Congress of Historical Sciences (ICHS) in 1908 and 1913. As plans were being made for the group's first postwar gathering Leland noted two deficiencies: the exclusion of Germans as a national body and the lack of a follow-through mechanism for activities from congress to congress. In 1923 the ICHS appointed a committee that, under Leland's guidance, led to the formation in 1926 of the International Committee of Historical Sciences. Leland initially served as the new group's treasurer and in 1938 became its president, a position he held for ten years. During much of that period he also served as president of the International Union of Academies, or Union Académique International (UAI).

In 1919, Leland acted as organizing secretary for a meeting of representatives from leading American scholarly societies in the social sciences and the humanities that led to the formation of the ACLS, a step taken to create an American organization eligible for membership in the newly reorganized UAI. In 1927 the ACLS received a major grant from the Rockefeller Foundation, enabling it to secure the services of a full-time administrative officer. Leland left the Carnegie Institution to take the position. Leland, a bit formal, witty, and thoroughly professional, served as ACLS secretary from 1927 to 1939 and as director from 1939 until his retirement in 1946.

Leland oversaw both the ACLS's international cooperative activities and its domestic programs, including publication of the *Dictionary of American Biography* (1927–1936) and the annual *Handbook of Latin American Studies*, begun in 1935. Through Leland's efforts, the ACLS distributed money to individual scholars to support research and publications. Also, through fellowships and the sponsorship of scholarly conferences, the ACLS was able to encourage the development of area studies in the United States for Chinese, Japanese, Indian, Iranian, Slavic, Near Eastern, and Latin American culture and civilization.

During his term as director of the ACLS, Leland maintained an active involvement in archival matters. He served two terms in the early 1940's as president of the SAA.

During World War II, Leland served on numerous advisory committees. Even after his retirement he continued to be a part of the Brown University Board of Fellows, the chairman of the Advisory Board of the National Park Service, and, for one term, thc president of the Cosmos Club. International intellectual cooperation remained an abiding interest. During the interwar years he worked with the League of Nations and served as a delegate to the 1945 London conference that led to the establishment of the United Nations Educational, Scientific, and Cultural Organization (UNESCO) and to the 1948 UNESCO General Conference in Beirut. From 1946 to 1949 he served as vice-chairman (under Milton Eisenhower) of the United States National Commission for UNESCO. He died in Washington, D.C.

[The Library of Congress holds the Leland Papers and other collections that contain significant materials, including those for Jameson, the AHA, the ACLS, and the Carnegie Institution. A bibliography of Leland's works up to 1941 appears in the ACLS-compiled tribute volume *Studies in the History of Culture* (1942). Leland discussed the beginnings of his professional career in "Some Early Recollections of an Itinerant Historian," *Proceedings of the American Antiquarian Society*, Oct. 1951. The National Archives' Staff Information Paper 20, "Archival Principles," excerpts Leland's writings. On May 24, 1955, Leland recorded his reminiscences for the Columbia University Oral History Project. See also Rodney A. Ross, "Waldo Gifford Leland: Archivist by Association," *American Archivist*, Summer 1983; and "Waldo Gifford Leland and Preservation of Documentary Resources," *Federalist*, Summer 1986. A *Washington Post* editorial marking his death appeared on Oct. 23, 1966. An obituary is in the *New York Times*, Oct. 20, 1966.]

RODNEY A. ROSS

LEWIS, ED ("STRANGLER") (1890?–Aug. 7, 1966), wrestler, was born Robert H. Friedrich to a farm family. Almost nothing is known of his origins and early life. As a brawny, 200-pound farm boy at the age of fourteen, he left his Wisconsin farm home and entered his first professional wrestling match in Madison. He won the match and took the name Ed Lewis so that his parents, who did not approve of wrestling, would not know that was what he was doing. Two years later, in 1906, he was given the nickname Strangler by a reporter for the *Chicago Tribune* who thought Lewis resembled an earlier wrestler who went by that name.

Lewis, commonly referred to as "the Kentuckian" (he may have been born in the Bluegrass State), steadily worked his way up into the top rank of heavyweights until he was one of the four wrestlers picked to compete in a tournament to select the new champion after World War I. In a group with Earl Caddock, Joe Stecher, and Wladek Zbyszko, a Pole, Lewis had his first chance at the heavyweight title, but he lost to Stecher on Nov. 3, 1919. This highly publicized match was a replay of an earlier battle between them on July 4, 1916, in Omaha, Nebr., when Lewis and Stecher, the inventor of the scissors hold, lasted five and a half hours in the ring, perhaps the longest professional wrestling match on record.

Lewis, whose forte was a nasty headlock that was so dangerous it was banned at one time by the Illinois Athletic Commission, met Stecher again at the Seventy-first Regiment Armory in New York City on Dec. 13, 1920, and Lewis prevailed by pinning Stecher. Lewis successfully defended his title against other opponents until May 6, 1921, when he was pinned by Stanislaus Zbyszko, the son of the great Wladek Zbyszko, at the Twenty-second Regiment Armory in New York City. They next faced one another in Wichita, Kans., on Mar. 3, 1922, when Lewis regained his title by winning two of three falls (two pins out of three). This time, Lewis kept the title for nearly three years, a remarkable feat considering the frequency with which he wrestled.

In the early 1920's, professional wrestling was considered just a notch below professional boxing in its interest to fans and in the skills involved. Large crowds assembled in such places as Fenway Park in Boston, Wrigley Field in Chicago, and Madison Square Garden in New York to watch the top matches. Lewis appreciated the entertainment value of his sport as well as anyone did. His nickname, his willingness to be "the bad guy" for using the headlock (which was usually applied by getting his opponent's head in a viselike grip in the crook of his elbow), and his sheer size (between 230 and 260 pounds then) and strength made him a natural drawing card. Lewis inspired greater enmity in the crowds than any other wrestler of his time. Some observers thought the headlock was a form of torture that must be banned, like the stranglehold, to save the sport. Cries of "Kill the murderer" filled the air after victories won by use of the headlock, and Lewis sometimes needed police protection to leave an arena safely. As the object of so much emotion, Lewis could earn large guarantees while champion, sometimes as much as $125,000 for a big match, and his career earnings were estimated at more than $4 million, most of which he squandered.

In July 1922, Lewis tried to capitalize on his title and drawing power by challenging the heavyweight boxing champion Jack Dempsey to a "mixed match." The rules, as explained by the would-be promoter, Lou Cutler of Wichita, would have put Dempsey with boxing gloves in the ring with Lewis, who could use his wrestling moves but could not punch. The match would have been of normal length for a boxing match (thirty minutes), but many of Lewis' bouts went over two hours. Despite a brief spurt of publicity, the proposed "mixed match" never was held.

Lewis remained a major sports figure throughout the decade, and periodically his exploits out of the ring would receive coverage. In March 1924, Lewis made front-page news when he locked his manager, Billy Sandow, in a Chicago hotel room while he married Bessie McNear. Sandow was reportedly opposed to having his star wrestler marry anyone while his career was going so well, and he had broken up an engagement the year before between Lewis and a Russian princess named Marie Travasiki. Lewis had been married earlier to a physician from San Jose, Calif., Dr. Ada Morton Lewis, but they divorced in 1923 or early 1924.

On Jan. 8, 1925, Lewis lost his title in an upset when Wayne ("Big") Munn, a former star football player from Nebraska, won two falls out of three in Wichita. Lewis claimed he was fouled in the match and proved himself the true champion by defeating Munn in a rematch four months later in Michigan City, Ind. Again, Lewis dominated the opposition while holding the title for three years. Stecher, whom Lewis had not faced since winning his first title in 1920, provided the opposition for a memorable match in St. Louis in early 1928, but Lewis kept his crown in a match lasting over two and a half hours.

In 1928, Lewis announced that he would sail to Europe for a three-month tour, including exhibition matches, before returning for a farewell tour of the United States. When he returned late in the year, there was a new man atop the wrestling world, Gus Sonnenberg, a former football star from Dartmouth who introduced the flying tackle into the wrestling repertoire. Sonnenberg, who is credited with beginning the change of professional wrestling from serious feats of skill, strength, and agility into showmanship, beat Lewis in July 1929 before a packed house at Fenway Park, but Lewis did not make 1929 his farewell year. He continued to wrestle regularly, and by late 1932 he was again declared champion when titleholder Jim Londos failed to agree to Lewis' challenge for a championship match.

In January 1933, Lewis retained his title by easily beating Jim Browning in Madison Square Garden, but just a month later at the same site, Browning upset Lewis. It was then noted that in the previous twenty years Lewis had lost only six times. Never again would Lewis be champion. He was still enough of a draw to earn two title matches in 1934—in a Mexico City bull ring against Browning and in front of 35,000 fans in Wrigley Field against Jim Londos—but he was forty-four years old and unable to keep up with his younger opponents. In 1937, Lewis returned from a world tour, called a press conference, and announced his retirement with some stinging commentary on what he termed the new style of "slambang wrestling." Despite that farewell, he continued to appear in the ring from time to time until his final match in 1947 in Honolulu.

Lewis appeared in a few movies in Hollywood, such as *That Nazty Nuisance* (1943) and *Bodyhold* (1950). He also tried his hand at ranching, operating a restaurant, and running a health club. Before his death in Muskogee, Okla., he was blind and poor, yet content with his lot after becoming deeply religious.

During his prime in the 1920's, Lewis was the top draw and often the undisputed champion. His career spanned over forty years and an estimated 6,200 matches, of which, by his own account, he lost only 33. His place in sports history is minor because professional wrestling ceased to be a truly competitive sport, not because his achievements were ever surpassed.

[Serious studies of professional wrestling have yet to be written. The only coverage readily available today comes from the newspapers of that era, especially the *New York Times*, which regularly mentioned Lewis' matches. An obituary is in the *New York Times*, Aug. 8, 1966.]

ALFRED L. MORGAN

LEWIS, FULTON, JR. (Apr. 30, 1903–Aug. 20, 1966), radio commentator and newspaper columnist, was born in Washington, D.C., the son of Fulton Lewis, Sr., a wealthy attorney, and Elizabeth Saville. His maternal grandfather, James Hamilton Saville, had served as United States treasurer. Lewis grew up in the Georgetown section of the capital, studied music as a youth, and graduated from Western High School in 1920. He matriculated in the 1920–1921 and 1922–1924 academic years at the University of Virginia, writing the Cavaliers' football fighting song and playing a theater organ in Charlottesville, but he did not receive a degree.

In the fall of 1924, Lewis briefly attended George Washington University School of Law. At about this time he joined the *Washington Herald* as an industrious, self-assured reporter for $18 a week and became city editor within three years. William Randolph Hearst's Universal News Service hired Lewis as assistant chief of its Washington bureau in 1928; he served as bureau chief from 1929 to 1937. On June 28, 1930, he married Alice Huston; they had two children, one adopted.

In 1930 and 1931, Lewis gathered enormous data indicating collusion between Postmaster General Walter Brown and large airlines in the awarding of government airmail contracts. Although Hearst refused to publish the story, Lewis persuaded Congress to investigate airmail contracts. Another Lewis investigation helped convict Lieutenant John Farnsworth in 1936 of selling naval secrets to the Japanese.

From 1933 to 1936, Lewis wrote a syndicated column, "The Washington Sideshow," which included gossipy information about the Washington political scene. In October 1937, Lewis began making regular news commentaries on radio station WOL in Washington for $25 a week. His fifteen-minute program, "The Top of the News," was broadcast five evenings a week and gradually appeared on other Mutual Broadcasting System affiliates, making Lewis the first Washington-based national news commentator. His program initially enjoyed a very limited audience, subscribed to no news service, and had no sponsor. By 1939 many congressmen were listening to his news commentary regularly because he had cultivated their friendship and frequently defended their activities. In July 1939, Lewis persuaded Congress to have radio newsmen admitted to the Senate and House press galleries on the same basis as journalists. According to a 1939 survey, 39 percent of the congressmen (mostly Republicans) considered Lewis the best national news commentator. Lewis, however, had not attracted a comparable national following, as *Fortune* (1939) and *Radio Daily* (1940) polls did not mention Lewis among the nation's most popular newscasters. Lewis founded the Radio Correspondents' Association and served as its first president.

During World War II, Lewis utilized his news commentaries consistently to advance his isolationist views and criticize President Franklin D. Roosevelt's foreign policy. Lewis and news commentator Boake Carter both protested that Roosevelt had involved the United States too much in European affairs. In September 1939 the aviator Charles Lindbergh, who was then an isolationist, appeared on Lewis' radio program; this increased Lewis' following among isolationists opposing American entry into World War II. Lewis constantly downplayed the importance of German military activity in Europe and considered a strong national defense the best way to keep the United States out of war. He also claimed that the United States Army was not properly equipped, uncovering military and government bungling. His disclosures included army contracts with a German alien, Hans Rohl, for the installation of radar around Pearl Harbor and with other private builders for construction of an oil pipeline linking Canada and Alaska.

Lewis' commentaries reflected his conservative Republican views, assailed New Deal programs, and defended the free-enterprise system. Lewis criticized wage and price controls, farm cooperatives and subsidies, wartime taxes, organized labor, and the American Youth Congress. Besides lauding National Association of Manufacturing policies, he praised the contributions of big business to the defense effort and launched private investigations of official bungling and boondoggling. He exposed synthetic-rubber production problems and urged termination of the wartime Office of Price Administration. By 1942 his commentaries were carried by 160 Mutual affiliates. The strident tone, righteous air, and controversial positions of Lewis' commentaries enhanced his public recognition. His program eventually drew the largest audience (an estimated 10 million listeners) of any news commentary, earning Lewis at least $250,000 annually. In 1943 he received the Alfred I. du Pont Prize, the Sigma Delta Chi Award, and the Florida National Group of Banking Institutions Award as the year's best commentator. During the next two years, he also wrote a syndicated column, "Fulton Lewis, Jr., Says," and a weekly editorial column, "Washington Report."

Following World War II, Lewis intensified his praise of conservative political activities and beliefs. He made sweeping generalizations attacking government centralization and President Harry Truman's Fair Deal, using salty language, slang, and clichés to describe liberal programs, politicians, and columnists. Liberal writers and commentators criticized Lewis for his divisive views and intolerant attitudes. Lewis increasingly employed sarcasm by chuckling or lingering over a syllable. Words sometimes came out so quickly that his diction was not always clear. Lewis erroneously accused the Roosevelt aides Henry A. Wallace and Harry Hopkins of having conspired in 1944 to pass uranium and atomic secrets to the Soviet Union. In the early 1950's, Lewis used his nightly program to publicize the anti-Communist activities of Senator Joseph McCarthy and let the Wisconsin Republican appear on one program to rebut the television commentator Edward R. Murrow.

After the army-McCarthy hearings and the subsequent Senate censure of McCarthy, Lewis' influence and radio audience diminished to mainly devout right-wing Republicans and retired conservative businessmen. His extreme political views and wholehearted backing of McCarthy had made it increasingly difficult for him to secure sponsors but won for him the American Jewish League Against Communism Award in 1958 and the Fourth Estate Award of the American Legion in 1962. Lewis edited a weekly newsletter, *Exclusive;* lectured widely across the nation; and conducted television commentaries, although the serious-minded Lewis, who had a drooping mouth and slicked-down hair, did not adapt well to the medium of television. In 1964 he vigorously backed Republican Barry Goldwater for the presidency. Lewis continued his radio news commentary until succumbing in Washington. His son, Fulton III, took over his radio news commentary and produced several film documentaries.

[The Lewis Papers are at the Syracuse University Library. On his life and work, see Sidney Reisberg, "Fulton Lewis, Jr.: Analysis of News Commentary" (Ph.D. diss., New York University, 1952); Booton Herndon, *Praised and Damned: The Story of Fulton Lewis, Jr.* (1954); David Culbert, *News for Everyman* (1976); and Irving E. Fang, *Those Radio Commentators* (1977). An obituary is in the *New York Times,* Aug. 22, 1966.]

DAVID L. PORTER

LEWIS, JOHN LLEWELLYN (Feb. 12, 1880–June 11, 1969), labor leader, was born in the coal-mining hamlet of Cleveland, Iowa, the son of Welsh immigrants Thomas H. Lewis, a farm laborer and coal miner, and Ann Louisa Watkins. During Lewis' childhood his family moved repeatedly from one small central Iowa mine and farm town to another, his father apparently working both as a farm laborer and a coal miner. In the early 1890's the family settled in Des Moines, Iowa, where Thomas Lewis worked on the city police force and John completed all but the final year of high school. In 1897 the family returned to Lucas County, the place of John's birth, where they rented a farm. John went to work in local coal mines, and by 1901 he had been elected secretary of a local of the United Mine Workers of America (UMW). From 1901 to 1905 he mined coal and metals in the West, worked on construction projects, and tried his hand at business. Many myths have accumulated concerning the impact of his years in the West on Lewis' convictions, but few can be authenticated.

In 1905 Lewis returned to Lucas, where he joined the Masons, courted the local doctor's daughter, opened a grain and feed business, and ran for political office. He was a success in fraternal and personal affairs, a failure in business and politics. The panic of 1907 wiped out his grain enterprise. That same year the voters of Lucas rejected his mayoralty bid. But the Masons elected him a lodge officer and the doctor's daughter, Myrta Edith Bell, married him on June 5, 1907. They had three children.

After his marriage Lewis settled down to a career in trade unionism. In 1908 he, his wife, his parents, five brothers, and a sister all moved to Panama, Ill., a newly developed coal-mining village in the south-central part of the state. The men worked in the mines, and Lewis built a union machine that elected him to the presidency of one of the ten largest locals in the state. He quickly ingratiated himself with Illinois District Twelve (UMW) leaders and won appointment as a union lobbyist in Springfield, Ill. By 1911 Lewis had inveigled an appointment from Samuel Gompers as an organizer for the American Federation of Labor (AFL).

Over the next six years (1911–1917) Lewis was rarely at home. He traveled to all parts of the country seeking to organize workers and developing contacts with leading trade unionists. His most intensive organizing efforts involved industrial workers in western Pennsylvania, Ohio, and West Virginia, especially steel workers, with whom he had little success. He also carried out political assignments for the AFL, campaigning in 1912 for Woodrow Wilson and clearing presidential appointments after Wilson's election.

Lewis' union career began to flourish during World War I, coinciding with organized labor's rapid growth and rising influence in that era. In 1917 he became UMW statistician and editor of its journal. He represented the union on government commissions and in major collective bargaining negotiations. A year later he was made an acting vice-president of the UMW, and in 1919 he became acting president. Without ever standing as a candidate for election to office, Lewis had risen from obscurity to the leadership of the nation's largest trade union.

In 1919 the UMW claimed over 400,000 members. Immediately after he became acting president Lewis led a national coal strike that pitted the UMW against the federal government and tested Lewis' talents as a labor leader. He steered a safe course between the demands of union militants and the threats of federal officials. Having arranged a compromise, Lewis called the strike off, declaring that "I will not fight my government, the greatest government on earth." A year after the strike UMW members elected Lewis their president, a position he held until his retirement in 1960.

The 1920's, a decade of prosperity for most Americans, were filled with paradox and irony for Lewis. The coal industry and its workers did not share in the general prosperity. Too many miners working in too many mines produced too much coal. As unemployment spread UMW membership declined. There was little Lewis could do, and almost everything he tried failed. In 1921 he challenged Gompers for the presidency of the AFL, but lost. In 1922 he led the largest national coal strike in American history, one that he proclaimed a victory but that in fact weakened the UMW considerably. Hoping to stabilize the coal industry, he negotiated the Jacksonville agreement of 1924 with mine operators, which provided a three-year period of no strikes. The pact brought neither stability to the industry nor safety to the union.

Coal production continued to increase in the nonunion southern Appalachian fields while northern operators discharged UMW members and broke their contracts with the union. Although he was the best-known Republican labor leader of the 1920's (several prominent party members recommended him as secretary of labor or as a potential vice-presidential candidate), Lewis' political contacts scarcely helped him accomplish his union goals. He wrote a book, *The Miners' Fight for American Standards* (1925), in which he sought to enlist public opinion and the Republican administration on the side of his union. The book, which inconsistently mixed praise of laissez-faire principles, Americanism, and scientific management with demands for the federal regulation of coal mining and government promotion of unionism, had little impact on political leaders or the public.

Nevertheless, Lewis tightened his grip on the UMW, becoming its virtual dictator by 1930. He defeated every challenge to his authority and expelled his most bitter critics. But the union grew ever weaker. By 1929, even before the Great Depression, the UMW numbered less than 100,000 members, and probably had even fewer legitimate dues payers. When the Depression struck, Lewis became even more inconsistent, endorsing Herbert Hoover's bid for reelection in 1932 while working behind the scenes for Franklin D. Roosevelt. As the historian David Brody wrote, Lewis seemed "merely a labor boss of the most conventional kind, and a largely discredited one at that." One of Lewis' later associates, the radical labor journalist Len DeCaux, described the Lewis of this period in even more scathing terms: "A big-bellied old-time labor leader. . . . An autocrat, per capita counter, egotist, power seeker. . . . He was a man who had bowed the knee to capitalism, who had been merciless against the red and the rebellious."

Then, in a most unexpected development, the conventional and discredited labor boss of the 1920's became an imaginative and creative labor leader. Lewis used the reforms of the New Deal not only to rebuild the UMW but also to organize millions of workers in the mass-production industries. By the end of 1933 the UMW numbered more than 350,000 members and had won contracts in every part of the nation, even in the heretofore nonunion South. In 1934 he was elected a vice-president of the AFL, earning a position on its executive council. The next year, when other union leaders refused to join his crusade to organize the less skilled, Lewis stopped attending AFL executive council meetings. Realizing that the New Deal provided a once-in-a-lifetime opportunity to organize the mass of blue-collar workers, Lewis gambled all his own union's strength and financial resources on the campaign. In November 1935 he created the Committee for Industrial Organization (CIO), which in November 1938 became the Congress of Industrial Organizations. He resigned his AFL vice-presidency and invited his former UMW critics and many of the "red and rebellious," including scores of Communist party members, to join his crusade.

Lewis' gamble paid off. Between January and March 1937, CIO affiliates obtained collective-bargaining contracts with two of the most powerful antiunion corporations in the nation, General Motors and United States Steel. General Motors surrendered as a result of the great Flint (Michigan) sit-down strike, during which Lewis negotiated with company executives, Governor Frank Murphy of Michigan, and President Roosevelt. U.S. Steel conceded without a strike; Lewis and Myron Taylor, chairman of the U.S. Steel Corporation, secretly negotiated an agreement between the Steelworkers Organizing Committee–CIO and the company. By November 1937 the CIO claimed more members than the AFL; it had accomplished in less than two years what the federation had failed to win in half a century. "Around mammoth modern mills and bleak old factories, on ships and on piers, at offices and in public gathering-places," wrote a contemporary journalist, "men and women roared, 'CIO! CIO!' Labor was on the march as it had never been before in the history of the Republic." Lewis had risen to the apex of his career. As another journalist noted, "In the second half of this decade the most significant leader in American society will be John Lewis."

Lewis' fame and power were linked to his leadership of millions of CIO-affiliated industrial workers. He also benefited from the part he played in Roosevelt's landslide reelection victory of 1936. Lewis had contributed over $500,000 of the UMW's funds to the Democratic campaign and had formed Labor's Nonpartisan League (LNPL) to help Roosevelt. Lewis was so taken with his own power in 1936–1937 that one hostile reporter noted that "Lewis had come to believe that his own birthday should be celebrated instead of Christmas." Lewis' likeness confronted Americans at movie theaters, on magazine covers, and in newspaper political cartoons. His physical appearance seemed to embody the spirit of the movement he led. His ample frame, made more imposing by a carefully tailored wardrobe, communicated power and strength. His large leonine head, forestlike eyebrows, firmly set jaw, and ever-present scowl suggested the anger, determination, and militancy of the workers for whom he spoke. In January 1937, the *Nation* magazine placed Lewis on its honor role for 1936 "for continuing to give strength and backbone to the American labor movement." And the journalist Heywood Hale Broun, bringing to mind another famous John L., the boxer John L. Sullivan, quipped, "I think that Lewis is the greatest heavyweight of our day."

Alliance with Roosevelt had helped Lewis achieve his goals and gain influence; an evolving rift with the president undermined Lewis' power in the labor movement. First, the so-called Roosevelt recession of 1937–1938 caused the CIO to lose momentum. Rising unemployment cost many of the new industrial unions members and caused firmer resistance by employers. Lewis began to economize, cutting CIO staff and expenditures. By the end of 1938 the AFL again had many more members than the CIO. Simultaneously, in 1938 Roosevelt began to lose his ardor for domestic reform. Yet Lewis demanded an expanded welfare state and more power for labor. As the president drew the nation toward involvement in World War II, the labor leader allied himself with America's leading anti-interventionists. By 1940 a split between Lewis and Roosevelt was inevitable, and in the election of that year Lewis endorsed the Republican candidate, Wendell Willkie. Lewis also pledged to resign as president of the CIO if Roosevelt was reelected. At the CIO convention on Nov. 18, 1940, Lewis kept his pledge and stepped down as president. With that act he relinquished much of his power. Less than two years later, in May 1942, he ordered all UMW affiliates and officials to withdraw from the CIO. Thereafter, except for a short time in 1946–1947, the UMW functioned as an unaffiliated union.

For the remainder of his career Lewis engaged in incessant guerrilla warfare against other labor leaders, Congress, and the White House. In 1943, in the midst of World War II, he led his coal miners in a national strike that caused many Americans to "damn his coal-black soul," but which brought coal miners substantial material benefits. The strike fueled the antiunion campaign of business and congressional conservatives. Still later, in 1945, 1946, 1948, and 1949–1950, he led strikes that President Truman condemned as threats to national security and for which Lewis was twice cited for and convicted of contempt. But the strikes won for UMW members wages, hours, and fringe benefits then enjoyed by no other industrial workers. In 1946 he had returned his union to the AFL. A year later he led the UMW back out because the federation refused to join him in noncompliance with the Taft-Hartley Act. Thereafter the UMW remained independent of both the AFL and CIO. Lewis played no part in the merger of the two federations in 1955. He led his last strike in 1949–1950, and subsequently transformed himself into a "labor statesman" much admired by coal operators and other entrepreneurs. Meantime, as had happened in the 1920's, coal production again outstripped demand, cleaner fuels competed successfully for the market, fewer miners found work, and the UMW steadily lost dues-paying members.

This time, however, employed union miners earned high wages and retired ones received good pensions. Miners and their families also enjoyed the benefits of a generous medical and dental plan which Lewis had won for them through collective bargaining. In those facts, Lewis took great pride. He also took pride in the new system of collective bargaining in the coal industry, in which negotiations occurred secretly, contract lengths became flexible, and settlements were made without much participation of the union's rank and file. All these tactics were aimed at eliminating costly strikes, winning better contracts, and reducing the government's role in the coal industry, for Lewis had become by the mid-1950's again an apostle of "cooperative capitalism." He even called for the repeal of the Wagner Act as well as the Taft-Hartley Act. He joined with mine owners to form the National Coal Policy Conference, invested UMW funds in the American Coal Shipping Company, and lent funds from the UMW's National Bank of Washington (the third largest in the District of Columbia) to coal firms that used the loans to replace miners with machinery. All these maneuvers turned the union into a friendly collaborator of the mine owners. Indeed, Herbert Hoover complimented Lewis for his industrial statesmanship.

When Lewis finally retired in January 1960 he left his successors a financially healthy, stable union, but one that was rapidly losing members and influence. For a man who had once been so controversial and influential, his retirement occasioned scarcely a ripple. The same might be said of his death in Washington, D.C. Twenty years earlier, in 1949, one of his biographers, Saul Alinsky, had prophesied, "His passing will mean the end of an era. It will be greeted with curses and feelings of deliverance from a life-long plague." Alinsky was wrong. Most Americans reacted with mild indifference.

Lewis' life is an impressive personal success story, the tale of a man who rose from obscure and impecunious origins to great national influence and substantial material comfort. As a public figure, however, his career was erratic. In the 1920's he benefited himself but not most of the coal miners he claimed to lead. In the 1950's he became a friend to some of the country's leading industrialists precisely when more and more miners lost jobs. In between, he proved an innovative labor leader who won great gains for coal miners and brought millions of other workers into the labor movement. For those workers, Lewis was "the great emancipator." More than any other labor leader of his generation, he enlisted state power to unionize mass-production workers and to assure "an American standard of living" for all. Yet he always deeply distrusted the state for its probusiness bias and its stifling of private initiative. He was a man whose life centered around accumulating power, yet he stood alone among major American labor leaders as one who relinquished authority voluntarily. He was a man of firm loyalties and strong dislikes. "I never forget a friend," he once wrote, "and I find it increasingly difficult to forget an enemy." Lewis served America well during the Great Depression and he always acted as, in his own words, "something of a man."

[Lewis' papers are at the State Historical Society of Wisconsin at Madison. For samples of his speeches and correspondence see *United Mine Workers' Journal* and *United Mine Workers' Convention Proceedings*, wherein such documents are reprinted. The most extensive biography is Melvyn Dubofsky and Warren Van Tine, *John L. Lewis* (1977). See McAlister Coleman, *Men and Coal* (1943); and Saul Alinsky, *John L. Lewis* (1949). For the 1920's see Irving Bernstein, *The Lean Years* (1960); and Robert Zieger, *Republicans and Labor, 1919–1929* (1969). For the Great Depression and the New Deal, see Matthew Josephson, *Sidney Hillman* (1952); Art Preis, *Labor's Giant Step: Twenty Years of the CIO* (1964); Sidney Fine, *Sit-Down: The General Motors Strike of 1936–1937* (1969); Irving Bernstein, *Turbulent Years* (1970); and Len DeCaux, *Labor Radical* (1970). For World War II and after, see David Brody, *Workers in Industrial America* (1980); and Nelson Lichtenstein, *Labor's War at Home* (1982).]

MELVYN DUBOFSKY

LEWIS, OSCAR (Dec. 25, 1914–Dec. 16, 1970), educator and anthropologist, was born in New York City, the son of Herman Lewis, a Polish immigrant who was a rabbi and cantor, and Bertha Biblow. He grew up in a small town in upstate New York. As a youth and into adulthood, Lewis enjoyed both music and athletics. He possessed a fine voice and continued to take voice lessons until late in his life. At the City College of New York (CCNY) he studied history and was influenced by the philosopher Morris R. Cohen. Twin interests in history and Marxist thought carried over into his work as an anthropologist. While an undergraduate he met Ruth Maslow. The couple married in 1937; they had two children.

After graduating from CCNY in 1936, Lewis

enrolled at Columbia University to do graduate study in history. Dissatisfied with the graduate program, he followed the advice of his brother-in-law, Abraham H. Maslow, a well-known psychologist, and spoke to Ruth Benedict about graduate study in anthropology. His discussions with Benedict convinced Lewis of the intellectual challenge of that field and influenced him to do research in culture and personality. At Columbia, Lewis also studied with Franz Boas, Ralph Linton, Margaret Mead, Abram Kardiner, and Alexander Lesser.

In 1939 Lewis and his wife did fieldwork among a Blackfoot Indian tribe in Alberta, Canada. The resulting dissertation, which examined the behavior of a group of women of the tribe, reflected Lewis' concern with the problem of personality and its relationship to culture. Lewis earned his Ph.D. the following year.

Because of his work with North American Indians, Lewis visited Mexico in 1943 as a representative of the Inter-American Indian Institute. During this visit Lewis restudied the peasant village of Tepoztlán, first analyzed by Robert Redfield in 1926. Lewis planned to use Redfield's ethnography as the starting point of personality and culture study. But Lewis came to differ with Redfield's interpretations of the life-style and outlook of Tepoztecans. The disagreement illustrates how different research strategies and approaches can affect results. Lewis used conflict theory and Redfield used consensus theory to interpret the lives of the villagers.

In spite of the controversy, Lewis' *Life in a Mexican Village: Tepoztlán Restudied* (1951) became a classic case study of a Mexican peasant village and is considered his most important contribution to anthropology. Since many Tepoztecans migrated to Mexico City, Lewis became involved in urban studies and in the second major controversy of his career. He noted that Tepoztecans who migrated to the city lived in culturally similar slum neighborhoods, much like small villages. This prompted him to advance the theory of "the culture of poverty." The theory, as Lewis initially expressed it, views the poor as living in a separate subculture within the national culture. Lewis held that the characteristics of this subculture are perpetuated through the family and have "distinctive social and psychological consequences for its members." The application of Lewis' theory to the poor in the United States sparked considerable debate. According to critics, the theory became the basis for blaming the poor for their situation, and thus undermined efforts to improve their living conditions. Looking at the poor from a cultural perspective allowed researchers to ignore the social and economic conditions that caused poverty. Clearly this was not Lewis' intention, but because of the dissension his concept was discredited.

During the controversy over the culture of poverty Lewis wrote and published two family studies. These works—*Five Families* (1959) and *The Children of Sánchez* (1961)—documented the role of the family in placing an individual within a culture. In Lewis' words, the family "bridge[s] the gap between . . . culture at one pole and the individual at the other." *The Children of Sánchez* provided an inside view of one poor family living in a slum neighborhood of a rapidly changing city. *Five Familes* showed the variation in family life resulting from differences in socioeconomic class. Both books were based on extensive recorded interviews. They were written in a slice-of-life style using dialogue and actual events to give the descriptions greater verisimilitude. In 1966 Lewis published a similar study of Puerto Rican family life, *La Vida*, which won the National Book Award. Although he cautioned readers not to generalize from his cases, some scholars criticized his choice of families and questioned whether they were representative of Mexican and Puerto Rican families.

In 1969–1970 Lewis went to Cuba to test his thesis that the culture of poverty did not exist in socialist countries. He suffered a fatal heart attack in New York City before he was able to report his results. Throughout Lewis' career, his wife collaborated in his research and writing. After his death, she and Susan Rigdon used his oral history data from Cuba to trace the lives of eight Cubans—four men and four women—in their two-volume work, *Living the Revolution: An Oral History of Contemporary Cuba* (1977).

As an educator at the University of Illinois, where he founded the anthropology department in 1948, and as an anthropologist working in Mexico, the United States, and Cuba, Lewis strove to expose the roots of poverty. His writings on Mexico, Puerto Rico, and Cuba helped bring the plight of the poor to public attention.

[Scholarly papers by Lewis include "An Anthropological Approach to Family Studies," *American Journal of Sociology*, Mar. 1950; and "The Culture of the *Vecindad* in Mexico City," *Actas de XXXIII Congreso de Americanistas*, July 1958. See also his *Pedro Martínez: A Mexican Peasant and His Family* (1964). Obituaries are in the *New York Times*, Dec. 18, 1970; *Publishers Weekly*, *Newsweek*, and *Time*, all Dec. 28, 1970; and *Trans-Action*, Feb. 1971.]

CHARLES WAGLEY

LEY, WILLY (Oct. 2, 1906–June 24, 1969), writer and rocket scientist, was born in Berlin, Germany, the son of Julius Otto Ley, a wine merchant, and Frida May, whose family was prominent in the hierarchy of the German Lutheran church. Ley attended public schools in Berlin and, in high school, developed a lifelong interest in science and its history. Intermittently between 1920 and 1926, he satisfied this interest by attending the University of Berlin and the University of Königsberg, specializing in paleontology, astronomy, zoology, and physics.

The inflation that followed World War I in Germany and the impact of Hermann Oberth's work on space travel combined to prompt Ley to abandon the university and his plans for a career in geology and embark instead on investigations into space travel. He submitted articles on scientific subjects regularly to German magazines and, in 1926, published his first book, *Die Fahrt ins Weltall* ("Trip to Space"), which dealt with rocket ships. In 1927 he became a founding member of the Verein für Raumschiffahrt (Society for Space Travel), which came to include Reinhold Tiling, the inventor of the winged rocket, and Wernher von Braun, who headed the project that created the German V-2 rocket and who later assisted in American rocket programs.

Ley was vice-president of the Society for Space Travel from 1928 until the society's dissolution by the Nazis in 1933. During this period Ley collaborated with the motion-picture director Fritz Lang on several science-fiction films, including *Frau im Mond* (*Woman in the Moon*, 1928), edited *Die Möglichkeit der Weltraumfahrt* (*The Possibility of Interplanetary Travel*, 1928), and published a biography of the sixteenth-century naturalist Konrad Gesner, *Konrad Gesner: Leben und Werk* (1929), and an outline history of rockets, *Grundriss einer Geschichte der Rakete* (1932).

In 1935, suspecting that he was in trouble with the Gestapo, Ley left Germany for England. On February 21, at the invitation of the American Interplanetary Society, which had put up his entry bond, he arrived in New York City and for the next six months lived with G. Edward Pendray, who headed the newly renamed American Rocket Society. Finding America uninterested in rocket theory, Ley began writing articles on zoology and other subjects for *Coronet*, *Natural History*, *Frontiers*, *Zoo*, *Fauna*, and *Esquire*. In May 1940 he joined the New York newspaper *PM* as a science editor and was encouraged to publish his first book in English, *Bombs and Bombing: What Every Civilian Should Know* (1941).

While working on *PM*, Ley met a Russian-born ballet dancer, Olga Feldman, who wrote the newspaper's column on physical fitness. On Dec. 24, 1941, they were married; they had two children. Also in 1941 he published *The Days of Creation* and his first American popular success, *The Lungfish and the Unicorn*. The latter became a Scientific Book Club selection and subsequently underwent revision and reprintings as *The Lungfish, the Dodo, and the Unicorn* (1948). Well researched and written in a readable journalistic style, the book blends accounts and drawings of mythological and extinct animals with "living fossils" based on sound zoological principles. *Shells and Shooting* followed in 1942, and in May 1944, Ley issued *Rockets: The Future of Travel Beyond the Stratosphere*, dealing with Russian and German developments. It underwent revision and reprinting as *Rockets and Space Travel* (1948), *Rockets, Missiles, and Space Travel* (1951), and *Rockets, Missiles, and Men in Space* (1968). In March 1944, Ley became an American citizen, and later that year he left *PM* for the Burke Aircraft Corporation in Atlanta, Ga. When Burke Aircraft reorganized into the Washington Institute of Technology at College Park, Md., Ley remained director of engineering. The assault of the first V-2 rockets on London in November 1944 had created a demand for Ley's knowledge by arms manufacturers as well as the reading public.

In 1945 the American Museum of Natural History issued Ley's *Inside the Atom*, to satisfy an interest in atoms generated by the first atomic bombs. By the end of 1947, Ley had left the Washington Institute of Technology to become a consultant to the office of technical services of the United States Department of Commerce. Believing that the average reader should understand the ideas, achievements, and future of space science, Ley published *The Conquest of Space* (1949), which earned him the prize for nonfiction in the First International Fantasy Fiction Awards. In the early 1950's, Ley also began public lectures on space travel at New York's Hayden Planetarium, and from 1950 to 1955 he served as technical adviser on the television program "Tom Corbett, Space Cadet." Later he served the same role for two Walt Disney programs, "Man in Space" (1955) and "Man and the Moon" (1956). Ley also embarked on a new series of science books, *Dragons in Amber: Further Adventures of a Romantic Naturalist* (1951), *Engineers' Dreams* (1954), *Salamanders and Other Wonders* (1955), *Satellites, Rockets, and Outer Space* (1958), and *Exotic Zoology* (1959). He collaborated with Wernher von Braun and others on *Conquest of the Moon* (1953); with von Braun on *The Exploration of Mars* (1956) and *Start in dem Weltraum* (*Takeoff into Outer Space*, 1958); and with others on such projects as *Across the Space Frontier* (1952), *Mystery of Other Worlds, Revealed* (1953), and *The Complete Book of Satellites and Outer Space* (1957).

During the 1950's, Ley completed the Adventures in Space series for children: *Man-Made Satellites* (1957), *Space Pilots* (1958), *Space Stations* (1958), and *Space Travel* (1958). In the next decade, he wrote *Rockets* (1960), *Planets* (1961), *Watchers of the Skies* (1963), *Ballistics* (1964), *Beyond the Solar System* (1964), *Missiles, Moonprobes, and Megaparsecs* (1964), *Our Work in Space* (1964), *Ranger to the Moon* (1965), *Fire* (1966), and *Mariner IV to Mars* (1966). These were followed by *The Borders of Mathematics* (1967), *For Your Information: On Earth and in the Sky* (1967), *Dawn of Zoology* (1968), *The Discovery of the Elements* (1968), *Inside the Orbit of the Earth* (1968), *The Meteorite Craters* (1968), *Another Look at Atlantis, and Fifteen Other Essays* (1969), *Events in Space* (1969), *Visitors from Afar: The Comets* (1969), and *The Drifting of the Continents* (1969). *Gas Giants: The Largest Planets* (1970) and *Worlds of the Past* (1971) appeared after his death in New York City.

Ley's aim was to stimulate the imagination by presenting mysteries and oddities whose explanations also provided possibilities and sound approaches. He believed that scientific knowledge would ultimately be used for good, that ignorance was the real villain. Ley is credited with devising the basic principles that led to the development of the liquid-fuel rocket and for accurately predicting space travel. He contributed to such magazines as *Astounding Science Fiction*, *Thrilling Worlds*, *Startling Stories*, and *Super Science Stories* under his own name and under the pseudonym Robert Willey. He enjoyed classical music, and from 1959 to 1961 he was a part-time professor of science at Fairleigh Dickinson University in Rutherford, N.J.

[Biographical information may be culled from his obituaries in the *New York Times*, June 25, 1969; and the *Times* (London), June 26, 1969.]

JEROME MAZZARO

LIEBLING, ESTELLE (Apr. 21, 1880–Sept. 25, 1970), soprano, voice teacher, and composer, was born in New York City, the daughter of Max Liebling, a pianist and accompanist, and Matilde de Perkiewicz. The Lieblings were a German-American family of well-known professional musicians. Her father immigrated to America in the mid-1860's; his brothers Emil, Saul ("Solly"), and George were pianists who had studied with Franz Liszt. Liebling's brothers, Otto, James (a cellist), and Leonard, were also musical. Leonard was a pianist, critic, and writer, and the editor in chief of the *Musical Courier* from 1911 until his death in 1945.

Liebling went to Europe to study voice as a young girl. First she studied with Selma Nicklass-Kempner in Berlin. Dame Nellie Melba, the great soprano, advised Liebling to study with Melba's own teacher, Mathilde Marchesi, one of the most famous of all singing teachers. At eighteen, Liebling made her operatic debut in Dresden as Lucia di Lammermoor and then appeared with the Dresden company in *The Barber of Seville* and *The Magic Flute*. She also appeared during this period with the Stuttgart company and with the Opéra-Comique in Paris.

Liebling returned to the United States and became active as a concert singer. Her manager, Henry Wolfson, brought her back from a concert tour to make an appearance at the Metropolitan Opera on Feb. 24, 1902, as a last-minute substitute, without rehearsal, for Suzanne Adams in the fiendishly difficult role of Marguerite in Meyerbeer's *Les Huguenots*.

Having learned the role only in German, she sang in this language while the rest of the cast sang in French. Her next appearance, her "official" debut, was also made with short notice as Musetta in *La bohème* on the afternoon of Dec. 5, 1903, when Enrico Caruso was singing his first Rodolfo with the company. Liebling had not sung the role before, and it is not a very rewarding one for a coloratura soprano. The reviews were mixed, with the critics seeming to vie with one another to praise or fault her voice and her acting. She appeared only one more time with the company, as the First Genie in *The Magic Flute* on Feb. 18, 1904.

Liebling returned to her first love, the concert stage, and established herself there as a popular recitalist. "I always liked concert work more than opera," she told Harold C. Schonberg of the *New York Times* in 1968. She concertized throughout the United States, France, and Germany with great success and frequently appeared with great orchestras such as the Berlin Philharmonic, the New York Philharmonic, the Boston Symphony, and the Philadelphia Orchestra. She was often referred to in the press as "the fair singer," and photographs taken during the early years of the century show her as petite, fashionably gowned, and attractive.

Liebling probably reached the largest audiences of her career as soloist with John Philip Sousa's band. She toured with it for several years, including trips to Europe. On Christmas Day of 1904, she made her one-thousandth appearance with the band at Carnegie Hall. She appeared with it a total of 1,600 times. On Sept. 17, 1905, Liebling married a distant relative, Arthur Rembrandt Mosler, a mechanical engineer and a member of the Mosler Safe family; they had one child.

Liebling continued her singing career for several years, but the *New York Times* review of her Town Hall recital on Apr. 19, 1921, mentions that she had been "for some years absent from the local stage." Her programs were then of unusual interest, being made up of neglected works of the past and contemporary songs by European and American composers. The *New York Times* critic Richard Aldrich, who had severely criticized her Musetta years before, noted in 1921 that she sang with "ripe musical intelligence, with full round tone, and with evident pleasure to her audience."

Although Liebling continued to sing up to her fiftieth birthday, it was as a teacher that she became most renowned. In 1921 she opened a private voice studio at 145 West Fifty-fifth Street in Manhattan; she and her husband lived in the penthouse. Many of the world's greatest singers, including Maria Jeritza, Titta Ruffo, Frieda Hempel, Maria Müller, and Max Lorenz, studied with her. She also worked with nonoperatic performers, including Gertrude Lawrence, Adele Astaire, Joan Crawford, and Vivienne Segal. She claimed that seventy-eight Metropolitan artists had studied or coached with her at one time or another. The coloratura Amelita Galli-Curci, who claimed to have been self-taught, studied with Liebling when established as a great star, and when the young singer Jessica Dragonette wrote to Galli-Curci asking for advice in the choice of a teacher, the singer wrote back, "In my opinion, the outstanding teacher in New York is unquestionably Estelle Liebling." Dragonette followed this advice and soon became one of the most popular radio singers in the early days of broadcasting. Margaret Truman, the president's daughter, and Doris Duke, the tobacco heiress, also took lessons from Liebling.

One of Liebling's gifts was her early recognition of the need for singers to study radio technique, and she scheduled special radio classes for her students. Elisabeth Rethberg and many other famous singers went to Liebling especially to learn this approach. As early as 1937, Liebling reported that she had been working with her students on television techniques for the past five or six years and was looking forward to the day when technical problems would be solved and "engineers have passed the experimental stages." Liebling was on the faculty of the Curtis Institute of Music In Philadelphia from 1936 to 1938.

One of Liebling's most famous students was Beverly Sills, who began lessons with her at the age of seven and who continued to work with her for more than thirty years. In addition to voice lessons, Liebling took an interest in what Sills read and wore, and introduced her as a guest at her frequent dinner parties to give Sills a chance to develop social skills. Sills wrote, "Three-quarters of who I am came from my family; the other 25 percent came from Miss Liebling. She was funny, attractive, and knew everybody in opera." Many of Liebling's students reported this same interest in their behavior and appearance and cited her important connections.

Liebling continued to teach into her eighties, giving classes at her apartment on Central Park South. Following a heart attack in 1964, she was forced to cut the teaching schedule she had maintained for years (from 9:30 A.M. to 6:30 P.M.) to four half-hour lessons in the morning and four in the afternoon. In addition to her singing and teaching, Liebling collected and published cadenzas, many of which she got from Marchesi and famous singers of the past and some of which she composed herself. She also composed some songs and edited separate arias and collections. She died in New York.

[Liebling's correspondence with Mathilde Marchesi (in the Marchesi Collection) and the manuscript to a song for two sopranos based on Schubert waltzes are in the Special Collections of the Music Division of the New York Public Library at Lincoln Center. Her published works include *The Estelle Liebling Coloratura Digest* (1943); *The Estelle Liebling Book of Coloratura Cadenzas* (1943); *Fifteen Arias for Coloratura Soprano* (1944); and *The Estelle Liebling Vocal Course*, 4 vols. (1956), edited by Bernard Whitefield. See "Heeding Musical 'Handwriting on the Wall,' " *Musical Courier*, Oct. 1, 1937; Harold C. Schonberg, "Estelle Liebling, 84, Eases Off to 8 Pupils a Day," *New York Times*, Dec. 28, 1968; and Quaintance Eaton, "First Lady of Voice," *Opera News*, Mar. 1, 1969. Some characteristic reviews of her singing are in the *New York Times*, Dec. 6, 1903, Apr. 20, 1921, and Oct. 26, 1921; the *Musical Courier*, Dec. 9, 1903, and *Musical America*, Nov. 5, 1921. Descriptions of her as a teacher are in Jessica Dragonette, *Faith Is a Song* (1951); and Beverly Sills, *Bubbles: An Encore* (1981) and *Beverly* (1987). An obituary is in the *New York Times*, Sept. 26, 1970.]

GEORGE LOUIS MAYER

LINDSAY, HOWARD (Mar. 29, 1889–Feb. 11, 1968), playwright, actor, and director, was born Herman Nelke in Waterford, N.Y. His stage name was taken from a grandmother. His father, whose first name is unknown, was a German immigrant who was unable to support his family on his income as a traveling salesman. Lindsay's mother, whose name is unknown, divorced his father and took her children to Atlantic City, N.J., where she worked as a compositor on her brother's newspaper. As a child, Lindsay sold newspapers on the street and took elocution lessons from a teacher who had failed to pay her bill for advertising in his uncle's newspaper. When Lindsay was twelve his family moved to Dorchester, now part of Boston, Mass., where his mother had found more regular employment. He attended the Boston Latin School, graduating in 1907, and then enrolled at Harvard University, intending to become a Unitarian minister. This resolve did not last past his first infatuation with the theater, and he dropped out of college in 1908 to take a six-month course at the American Academy of Dramatic Arts in New York City.

Lindsay's first professional acting job was with a touring company of *Polly of the Circus* in 1909. During several months of one-night stands, he played bit parts and served as assistant stage manager. Later he toured with other companies and worked briefly in movies. His education in the theater came when he toured from 1913 to 1918 with Margaret Anglin's company. Anglin, a distinguished actress, was known for her extensive repertory of classical and modern drama. Lindsay performed bit parts, substituted for actors who were ill, and served as stage manager. In 1918 Lindsay joined the army and was assigned to army headquarters in Brest, France, where he directed comic plays to entertain the troops.

After the war, Lindsay returned to New York City, where he worked as stage manager, director, and sometime actor for theatrical producer George C. Tyler. Lindsay directed *Dulcy* (1921), a play that secured the reputation of Marc Connelly and George S. Kaufman as playwrights and Lynn Fontanne as an actress. In the early 1920's Lindsay doctored a few plays and longed to write a full-length drama. He teamed with Bertrand Robinson, and together they wrote three successful plays, *Tommy* (1927), *Your Uncle Dudley* (1929), and *Oh Promise Me* (1930), all of which Lindsay also directed.

On Apr. 29, 1920, Lindsay married Virginia Fralick; they divorced in 1925. On Aug. 13, 1927, he married actress Dorothy Stickney. They had met in New York and courted while in summer stock in Skowhegan, Maine. They had no children. During their long marriage Lindsay and Stickney entertained their friends in style, acted together on the stage, and shared an imposing townhouse on East Ninety-fourth Street in Manhattan.

Even though he wrote the popular *A Slight Case of Murder* (1935) with Damon Runyon,

Lindsay's most important collaboration was with Russel Crouse. In 1934 he and Crouse began what was to become the longest and most successful joint effort of American playwrights. Their collaboration began after Lindsay wrote the book for a musical comedy about a fire aboard an ocean liner. Just as he completed it a genuine fire aboard the *Morro Castle* took many lives and, of course, made Lindsay's comedy inappropriate. He sought a collaborator to help him revise the play quickly and happened upon Crouse. They hurriedly composed *Anything Goes* (1934), and its success assured the continuation of their partnership. Their personalities meshed perfectly. They spent months—even years on occasion—discussing ideas for new plays. One would offer a line; the other would accept or reject it without offending, as though they had only one ego between them. Once the concept was clear, they would begin the actual writing. Crouse sat at the typewriter (a habit left over from his days as a journalist) while Lindsay paced the room. The result was the complete blending of ideas and lines; they claimed that once a play was finished they could not distinguish their contributions.

In 1936 they wrote the book for *Red, Hot, and Blue*, a Cole Porter musical starring Ethel Merman. This modestly successful play was directed by Lindsay. The team followed with *Hooray for What!* (1937), also directed by Lindsay. In 1939 Lindsay and Crouse collaborated on the play with which they are most associated, *Life with Father*. Based on Clarence Day's stories of his Victorian boyhood in New York, which Lindsay had read in the *New Yorker*, the play took two years to plot and write; the production required the Lindsays to mortgage their house and furniture. Lindsay also played the role of the father, and in the mind of a generation of theatergoers Lindsay was the blustery, hot-tempered, but lovable Victorian. Stickney took the role of his stage wife, Vinnie, and the couple played opposite each other on Broadway for over five years. The play, the longest running nonmusical in Broadway history, ran for over seven years. During the run of *Life with Father*, Lindsay and Crouse produced *Arsenic and Old Lace* (1941), which starred Josephine Hull and Jean Adair as two eccentric old ladies who murder lonely gentlemen. It ran for over three years in New York and did well in London.

Following *Strip for Action* (1942), which failed, Lindsay and Crouse wrote *State of the Union* (1945), a political satire. Ralph Bellamy headed the cast as the idealistic man who runs for president. An important characteristic of the play was its timely dialogue, which was constantly updated during the play's run to reflect current events. *Life with Mother* (1948), the sequel to *Life with Father*, again starred Lindsay and Stickney, but the play's run was short. Lindsay and Crouse, however, quickly recovered with *Call Me Madam* (1950), with music by Irving Berlin. After several plays that were not as well received, the team wrote the book for *The Sound of Music* (1959), with music by Richard Rodgers and Oscar Hammerstein, which became a major hit on both stage and film. The team's last play was *Mr. President* (1962). During their collaboration they wrote fifteen plays, produced numerous others, and won a Pulitzer Prize for *State of the Union* and a joint Tony Award in 1959 for their "distinguished achievement in the theater."

Lindsay was a man of considerable humor and generosity. His well-developed sense of the comic was evident in his private life as well as in his plays, and he was widely respected for never refusing to assist a friend financially. For a decade he served as president of the Players, a theatrical club, where he enjoyed pool, bridge, and comradeship. He was active in the Dramatists Guild and the Authors League, and he helped establish the New Dramatist Committee, which assisted many young playwrights. As an advocate for the arts, he lobbied in Washington, D.C., on behalf of the establishment of a national endowment for the arts and humanities. He also served as an officer of the Committee for Modern Courts, a group of citizens dedicated to improving the grand jury system. He died in New York City.

[A clipping file on Lindsay is at the Performing Arts Library, Lincoln Center, New York City. See Lincoln Barnett, *Writing on Life* (1951); Gilbert Millstein, "First Twenty-five Years of Lindsay and Crouse," *New York Times*, VI, Nov. 22, 1959; Jean Gould, *Modern American Playwrights* (1966); and Cornelia Otis Skinner, *Life with Lindsay and Crouse* (1976).]

ROBERT ARMOUR

LITTLE, WILLIAM LAWSON, JR. (June 23, 1910–Feb. 1, 1968), professional golfer, was born at Fort Adams in Newport, R.I., the son of William Lawson Little, a colonel in the United States Army Medical Corps, and Evelyn Baldwin Ryall. He spent his early life at a succession of army bases in the United States, the Philippines, and China. Little became adept at golf as a young man, practicing and occasionally caddying for his father when he was stationed in San Antonio, Tex., in 1918–1919. He shot his first nine holes in Manila, scoring an impressive 53 strokes. He entered a number of junior tournaments in California but did not win any of them. He won his first amateur championship, the North California tournament, in 1928.

In 1929, Little entered Stanford, where he was coached by Eddie Twiggs, but left to play golf. That same year, he won the United States Open Championship at Muirfield, defeating Walter Hagen. He won the Pacific Coast interchampionships in 1931 and 1933. In 1934 he defeated David Goldman to win the United States Amateur Championship at the Brookline Country Club in Massachusetts. Also in 1934 he won the British amateur championship by defeating James Wallace. Those two victories qualified him for the American Walker Cup team.

Little repeated his sweep of amateur titles in 1935 by winning the United States and British championships, defeating Walter Emery and William Tweddle, respectively. He is the only player to have won both titles in the same year twice in succession. In all, Little won thirty-one consecutive amateur tournaments. In 1935, sportswriters considered him the outstanding athlete of the year, and he was awarded the James E. Sullivan Memorial Award for amateur athletes. In 1936, Little married Dorothy Hurd and became a professional golfer. In that year he also set a new course record at St. Andrews, the site of the Canadian Open, where he shot a 271, which was 8 strokes under the old course record.

The most exciting point of Little's professional golf career was in 1940, when he qualified for the United States Open by shooting 134 on thirty-six holes at Chicago's Olympia Fields Golf Club. That was the lowest score of the 1,100 qualifiers for the open. During Open play, Little tied with Gene Sarazen, both scoring 287 strokes at the end of the regulation seventy-two holes. In the tie-breaking round, Little won, 70–73.

During World War II, Little twice ran second to Ben Hogan at the Asheville, N.C., Land of the Big Sky Open. In 1946 and 1947 he qualified for the British Open. Little's last major tournament win was in 1948 at the St. Petersburg (Fla.) Open, held at the Lakewood Country Club.

Bernard Darwin described Little as "intimidating. Not very tall, but enormously broad and enormously strong, capable of a daunting pugnacity of expression, he was as a bull in the long game, and yet no dove could be gentler near the hole." Little ascribed his success to always thinking out his play on each hole before addressing the ball. However, his powerful hitting and long drives down the fairway contributed to his wins and earned him the nickname Cannonball.

Little was honored by the Professional Golfers Association in 1951 and 1952 by being named national tournament cochairman. He was inducted into the Professional Golfers Association Hall of Fame in 1961. He died in Pebble Beach, Calif.

[See L. Atkinson, "William Lawson Little: The Greatest Athlete of 1935," in Atkinson et al., *Famous American Athletes of Today* (1937). Articles on Little appear in *Time*, Sept. 23, 1935; and *Christian Science Monitor Magazine*, June 29, 1940.]

MICHAEL R. BRADLEY

LOCKHEED, ALLAN HAINES (Jan. 20, 1889–May 26, 1969), airplane manufacturer, was born Allan Loughead in Niles, Calif., the son of John Loughead and Flora Haines. An older stepbrother spelled the family name Lougheed, but it was pronounced "Lockheed," spelled that way in the 1920's, and legally changed in 1934. Little is known of John Loughead, but his wife was a professional writer who tutored Allan when ill health limited his schooling. All the Loughead brothers had mechanical skill. Malcolm, two years older than Allan, became an automobile mechanic in San Francisco in 1906 and Allan followed him in 1908.

In 1909 James E. Plew, a Chicago automobile distributor interested in aviation, hired Allan as a mechanic for his Curtiss biplane and took him to Chicago. Lockheed made his first flight there in 1910 with George Gates, the builder of a pusher biplane. Lockheed then worked for a year as a flight instructor for the International Aviation Company of Chicago.

In 1912 he returned to San Francisco and joined with Malcolm to build a seaplane, called Model G, financed by Max Mamlock, head of the Alco Cab Company of San Francisco. This plane flew exhibition flights at the Panama-Pacific International Exposition in 1915.

In 1916 the brothers established the Loughead Aircraft Manufacturing Company in Santa Barbara, Calif., and hired John K. Northrop as engineer. During World War I the company built a twin-engine flying boat, the F-1, and received orders for two others. It later built a monocoque high-wing airplane, the S-1.

Business declined after World War I. Malcolm left the firm in 1919 to develop a hydraulic four-wheel brake system for automobiles. In 1921 the company was liquidated. Allan Lockheed went into real estate, but his heart remained in aviation. In 1926 he and Northrop founded the Lockheed Aircraft Company; Fred S. Keeler, a brick and tile manufacturer, put up $25,000 for 51 percent of the company's stock. The first factory was located in Hollywood, Calif. There Lockheed and Northrop designed and built the Vega, based on the S-1.

With a capacity of ten passengers, the Vega was an important step in the development of air transport. The first Vega was bought by George Hearst, son of William Randolph Hearst, the publisher, for $12,500. Further favorable publicity came when Sir Hubert Wilkins flew in a Vega across the North Pole from Barrow Point, Alaska, to Spitsbergen, Norway, in 1928 and used it for Antarctic exploration a year later. Famous pilots who flew the Vega included Amelia Earhart and Charles and Anne Lindbergh. Business boomed, and in 1928 Lockheed Aircraft moved to more spacious quarters in Burbank, Calif., where its headquarters has remained.

The aviation boom of the late 1920's, stimulated by Lindbergh's flight from New York to Paris and by rapid technical developments in air transport, led to the emergence of several ambitious combinations of aviation companies. The Detroit Aircraft Corporation, formed by prominent automobile men, including Ransom E. Olds, Charles F. Kettering, Roy D. Chapin, and Charles S. Mott, aspired to become "the General Motors of the air." In July 1929 this organization acquired 87 pecent of Lockheed by an exchange of stock. Allan Lockheed left the company and predicted that the deal would lead to disaster. He was right. With the coming of the Great Depression the Detroit Aircraft Corporation collapsed, dragging the Lockheed Aircraft Company into bankruptcy with it. Lockheed was sold at a receiver's sale in 1932 for $40,000 to a small group of businessmen who managed to rehabilitate it.

Although he retained no further connection with the company bearing his name, Allan Lockheed remained associated with aviation. He became a consultant, and in 1937 he organized the Alcor Aircraft Corporation in San Francisco and designed a twin-engine, high-wing cantilever monoplane. But the company survived for only two years. During World War II he worked for two furniture companies in Grand Rapids, Mich., that had been converted to making aircraft components. He served as vice-president and manager of the aviation division of Berkey and Gay in 1941 and as general manager of the Aircraft Division of the Grand Rapids Store Equipment Company from November 1942 until the end of the war. From August 1941 to January 1942 he was also a member of the Cargo Plane Commission of the Reconstruction Finance Corporation.

After World War II Lockheed withdrew from aviation. He returned to California and resumed his real estate activities. He retired to Arizona and died in Tucson. He married Dorothy Watts in Chicago in June 1911. They had two children. Dorothy Lockheed died in 1922, and on June 5, 1938, Lockheed married Helen M. Kundert. They had one son.

[*Of Men and Stars* (1957), published by the Lockheed Aircraft Corporation, is the most detailed study of Lockheed's career until 1929. See also John B. Rae, *Climb to Greatness*, (1968). For Lockheed's later career, see the obituaries in the *Los Angeles Times* and the *New York Times*, both May 28, 1969.]

JOHN B. RAE

LOESSER, FRANK (June 29, 1910–July 28, 1969), composer and lyricist, was born Francis Henry Loesser in New York City, the son of Henry Loesser, a pianist, and Julia Ehrlich. His father, who had been an accompanist for the soprano Lilli Lehmann, gave his children a strong musical upbringing. (Frank's older brother, Arthur, became a pianist, critic, and educator.) But even as a child Frank was aggressively lowbrow: his first lyrics were set to the rhythms of the elevated trains, and he took pride in winning third prize in a citywide harmonica contest. Years later, the Loesser family would remark that Frank's songs were "very nice, but of course they're not music."

Bored with formal education (he flunked out of the City College of New York in 1925, his first year), Loesser tried newspaper work, cartooning, advertising, press agentry, and radio writing. His great pleasure, though, was writing verses for others' music, a few of them performed in Lions Clubs and other inauspicious places. These were difficult years. Loesser occasionally sold songs, but his first show, the *Illustrators' Revue* (1936), closed in four nights. For a time he resorted to such jobs as screwing the tops onto insecticide bottles.

In 1935, Loesser performed in a club with a singer called Lynn Garland (born Mary Alice Blankenbaker). They were married on Oct. 19, 1936; they had two children. In 1936, Loesser signed a contract with Universal Films and left for Hollywood, a year later switching to Paramount. He remained in Hollywood until World War II, his reputation as a fine lyricist (at least for novelty numbers) rising very quickly. Among the dozens of songs for which Loesser provided the words in those years were "Two Sleepy People" and "Heart and Soul," with Hoagy Carmichael; "Blue Nightfall," "Dancing on a Dime," and "The Lady's in Love with You," with Burton Lane; and such others as "Snug as a Bug in a Rug," "Sand in My Shoes," "Jingle, Jangle, Jingle," and "The Boys in the Back Room."

During World War II, Loesser served in the army air force but continued to contribute timely lyrics (such as the winsome "They're Either Too Young or Too Old") for films and for isolated songs expressive of the new wartime sensibility. Seizing on the watchcry of Pearl Harbor, Loesser wrote "Praise the Lord and Pass the Ammunition," which came to be to World War II what "Over There" had been to World War I. Shortly thereafter came the moving "Ballad of Rodger Young" and the characteristic Loesser "gripe" song "What Do You Do in the Infantry?" Not only was Loesser suiting his lyrics to the mood of the times, but he was now doing so to his own music, following Jerome Kern's advice: "Your lyrics make the writing of melody a cinch."

After the war, Loesser returned to writing for films and for Tin Pan Alley, now exclusively his own collaborator. Among his songs from those years are "What Are You Doing New Year's Eve?", "On a Slow Boat to China," and, for the film *Neptune's Daughter*, "Baby, It's Cold Outside," which won him the 1949 Academy Award for best song. In *Red, Hot, and Blue* (1949) he made his only screen appearance. Despite these successes, Loesser wanted "to create situations" rather than songs: "Songwriting is a little thing and I settled for a big thing." The "big thing" was the Broadway musical, and Loesser never again wrote single songs. His *Where's Charley?* (1948), which ran over two years, surprised those who had doubted Loesser's ability to craft an integrated musical score on his first try. But *Where's Charley?* paled in comparison to his *Guys and Dolls* (1950), universally recognized as among the greatest of all Broadway musicals. Loesser found the eccentric idioms of the Damon Runyon characters (in Abe Burrows' script) ideal for his colloquial lyrical style, but the great accomplishment was suiting each song to the character who performs it; the songs here are as important as the book in depicting character and propelling plot.

Loesser never doubted that he could amuse, but he felt that touching an audience required more dexterity. His next endeavors moved him in that direction. In 1952 came his only complete film score, composed for Samuel Goldwyn's *Hans Christian Andersen;* its romantic ballads and children's songs have the ardor and Old World charm of the film. Then, returning to Broadway, he created his most ambitious work, *The Most Happy Fella* (1956). This musical, for which Loesser wrote the book (based on Sidney Howard's play *They Knew What They Wanted*) and more than forty musical numbers, is an unparalleled mixture of Puccinean aria, folk song, and Broadway show tune. "Mr. Loesser has now come about as close to opera as the rules of Broadway permit," was Brooks Atkinson's verdict in the *New York Times*. "He has told everything of vital importance in terms of dramatic music." In 1957, Loesser and his wife were divorced. On Apr. 30, 1959, he married Jo Sullivan (born Elizabeth Josephine Sullivan), who had played the female lead in *Most Happy Fella;* they had two children.

Loesser was proud of having surpassed his status as "songwriter," and he had considerable affection for his next musical, the gentle *Greenwillow* (1960), though its commercial failure distressed him sorely. In fact, he had but one more success, *How to Succeed in Business Without Really Trying* (1961), which marked a return to the wisecracking idiom of *Guys and Dolls*. It was his first attempt at light satire. Though decidedly not in the lyrical vein that Loesser craved, the show suited his knack for parody and character song, and it suited the 1960's: it became the longest-running of any of Loesser's shows and only the fourth musical to win a Pulitzer Prize.

It was also his last work to reach Broadway: *Pleasures and Palaces* (1965) closed out of town, while *Señor Indiscretion*, barely completed at the time of Loesser's death, has not yet had a professional production. Loesser devoted much of his last years to publishing and production, introducing several new talents to Broadway. He died in New York City.

Unquestionably Frank Loesser achieved what every artist most covets: the esteem of his colleagues. Richard Rodgers called him "a man for all theater seasons," while Bob Fosse regarded *Guys and Dolls* as simply "the greatest American musical of all time." Nonprofessionals are likely to remember Loesser as the composer-lyricist of hundreds of enduring songs and five full scores, music with a trademark combination of tenderness, toughness, and fun. Paddy Chayefsky remarked that "he introduced reality and sanity into the musical comedy," but he never forgot that he was foremost an entertainer.

[The Billy Rose Theatre Collection of the New York Public Library at Lincoln Center contains manuscripts and an extensive clipping file. The music and lyrics for fifty-one Loesser songs are in *The Frank Loesser Song Book* (1971). See Goddard Lieberson, "*Guys and Dolls* and Frank Loesser," *Saturday Review*, Dec. 30, 1950; David Ewen, "He Passes the Ammunition for Hits," *Theatre Arts*, May 1956, and *Great Men of American Popular Song* (1972); and Martin Gottfried, *Broadway Musicals* (1979). An obituary is in the *New York Times*, July 29, 1969.]

J. D. SHOUT

LOMAX, LOUIS EMANUEL (Aug. 16, 1922–July 30, 1970), journalist and author, was born and raised in Valdosta, Ga., where his family had lived for four generations. His father's name and occupation are unknown. His mother, Sarah, died shortly after his birth, and he spent his first eleven years with his maternal grandmother, Rozena Lomax, who was well known locally as an author of religious plays. Following her death, Lomax lived with his uncle and aunt, James L. and Fannie Hardon Lomax. Both were teachers in local public schools, and they encouraged and fostered his interest in learning and writing. The J. L. Lomax Junior High School was later named for James Lomax, who was also minister of the Macedonia First African Baptist Church in Valdosta and president of the Georgia Baptist Training Union Convention. The Lomax family's strong religious roots and social consciousness led to friendship with the family of Martin Luther King, Jr. Lomax first met King when the former was in college and the latter was in junior high school.

Although Lomax was raised in a prominent middle-class family that he later described as part of the black bourgeoisie, he was still conscious of blatant segregation. He did not know any whites well. He recalled hearing his white employer recite, with obvious relish, vivid accounts of black lynchings. Later, putting an arm on Lomax' shoulder, the man claimed that he would not hurt *him*. Such experiences had a profound and lasting impact.

Lomax graduated from Dasher High School in Valdosta and received his B.A. from Paine College in Augusta, Ga., in 1942. He was editor of the college newspaper, the *Painette*. He received his M.A. from American University, Washington, D.C., in 1944 and a master's degree in philosophy from Yale University in 1947.

Lomax began his professional career as a reporter on the *Afro-American* and as assistant professor of philosophy at Georgia State University in 1942. He became a staff feature writer for the *Chicago American* in 1947, and he went to Montgomery, Ala., to cover the bus boycott in 1956. Two years later he moved to New York City, where he was employed by WNTA-TV, as the first black television newsman, and he worked as a newswriter for "The Mike Wallace Show." He became a news analyst for KTTV and for Metropolitan Broadcasting in Los Angeles, Calif., in 1964, and hosted a television program, "Louis Lomax," in 1967. He was a syndicated columnist for the North American Newspaper Alliance during the same interval.

During the 1960's Lomax' articles, which appeared in national journals, were varied and showed objective reporting. He traveled to Africa and to the Caribbean. In 1966 he was the first American newspaper correspondent invited to visit North Vietnam. However, the invitation was withdrawn at the last minute and he visited Thailand instead. Lomax reported on the Duvalier regime in Haiti, on the tension between blacks and whites in Africa, and on the bitterness of African blacks toward American blacks.

Lomax claimed that the National Association for the Advancement of Colored People (NAACP) was obsolete, since it refused to organize demonstrations against segregation. He added that the NAACP gave tacit support to demonstrations only because it was forced to do so. He described the emergence of young black leadership and felt that more militant groups such as the Congress of Racial Equality (CORE), the Southern Christian Leadership Conference (SCLC), and the Student Nonviolent Coordinating Committee (SNCC) would produce change. Lomax wrote of dissension among young black leaders and believed that their strong individualism and lack of unified leadership hindered the black community in its struggle for equality.

As a writer and producer, Lomax used television and other media to arouse northern white interest in Jim Crow laws and in segregationist policies of the South and North. He organized and produced a telethon that raised $50,000 for CORE's Freedom Ride into the Deep South to test segregation laws in July 1961, and in 1963 he covered the CORE demonstrations against Harlem Hospital, which had not hired a sufficient number of blacks to construct a new hospital annex. He was the associate producer of an ABC-TV award-winning documentary "Walk in My Shoes," and, with Mike Wallace, wrote and produced "The Hate That Hate Produced," a documentary on the Black Muslims.

Lomax met Malcolm X in Harlem in 1959, and they became close friends. Lomax helped edit and write the first few issues of the *Islamic News*, later known as *Mr. Muhammed Speaks*. He held a debate with Malcolm X at the Chicago Opera House on May 23, 1964. Lomax did not share Malcolm's bitterness toward whites, and Lomax insisted that the ancestors of American blacks were not Muslims. He did not advocate a separate independent nation for American blacks. He also believed that the federal government supported civil rights for blacks, that changes had come and that more would follow. Lomax felt that blacks should assert themselves and work boldly toward both integration and black pride.

Lomax' first book, *The Reluctant African* (1960), won the Anisfield-Wolf Saturday Review Award as the best book on racial problems. *The Negro Revolt* (1962) dealt with emergent black leadership and the failures of the NAACP. *When the Word Is Given* (1964) studied the Black Muslim movement under the leadership of Malcolm X. *Thailand: The War That Is, the War That Will Be* (1967) was a devastating exposé of American action in one theater of the Vietnam War. *To Kill a Black Man* (1968) examined the conspiracy that led to the murder of Malcolm X.

Critics such as August Meier questioned the accuracy of Lomax' black history and his antagonism toward the NAACP. They argued that his work reflected a bias against the NAACP and in favor of younger organizations such as CORE and SNCC, and that by describing black political movements as revolutionary and radical or conservative and ineffectual Lomax provided ammunition for white racists.

On Sept. 19, 1961, Lomax married radio personality Betty Frank. His fourth marriage, which took place on Mar. 1, 1968, was to Robinette Kirk. He died in an automobile accident near Santa Rosa, N.Mex. At the time of his death he was a writer in residence at Hofstra University in Hempstead, N.Y., having joined the faculty as professor of humanities and social science in 1969.

Lomax left an unfinished three-volume history of American black people. His writing style has been compared to the narrative and rhetoric of Baptist preachers. His reportorial skills and unbiased observation of human affairs brought a new focus to the study of racism. His critics included partisans from every quarter, and he experienced threats of assassination from both black and white extremists. His early death ended the evolution of a gifted intellect that was grappling with the basic problems of human relationships in worldwide contexts.

[Lomax' major articles include "Eight-Man Invasion," *Nation*, Aug. 30, 1958; "Negro Revolt Against the Negro Leaders," *Harper's*, June and Aug. 1960; "Voices in Dialogue," *Saturday Review of Literature*, May 20, 1961; "White and Black Views of the African," *New Leader*, May 22, 1961; "The Unpredictable Negro," *New Leader*, June 5, 1961;

"The American Negro's New Comedy Act," *Harper's*, June 1961; "Meeting Racism in Reverse, W. Chapman," *New Republic*, Dec. 9, 1961; "The Kennedys Move in on Dixie," *Harper's*, May 1962; "Tomorrow's Leaders," *Ebony*, July 1963; "Lead or Get Out of the Way," *Negro Digest*, July 1963; "Georgia Boy Goes Home," *Harper's*, Apr. 1965; "White Liberal," *Ebony*, Aug. 1965; "The Dying Beast of Racism," *Negro Digest*, Jan.–Feb. 1967; "Memo from Amman," *Look*, May 14, 1968; and "Mississippi Eyewitness," *Ramparts*, Jan. 25, 1969. See J. A. Morsell, "Revolt of Louis E. Lomax," *Crisis*, October 1962; Ernest Kaiser, "The Literature of Negro Revolt," *Freedomways*, Winter 1963; August Meier, "The Revolution Against the NAACP," *Journal of Negro Education*, Spring 1963. See also the obituaries in the *New York Times*, Aug. 1, 1970; and *Negro History Bulletin*, Nov. 1970.]

BONITA FREEMAN-WITTHOFT

LOMBARDI, VINCENT THOMAS (June 11, 1913–Sept. 3, 1970), professional football coach, was born in Brooklyn, N.Y., the son of Henry Lombardi, an immigrant wholesale meat dealer, and Matilda Izzo. Raised in the Sheepshead Bay section of Brooklyn, Lombardi attended Cathedral High School, planning to enter the priesthood. But he soon changed his plans (his father said, "The Greek [language] got him") and transferred to St. Francis Preparatory School, where he played basketball and baseball, and starred as a fullback in football.

Lombardi entered Fordham University in 1933 and graduated magna cum laude in 1937 with a B.S. in business administration. At Fordham, which then had one of the best teams in the country, he played guard on the famed line called "the Seven Blocks of Granite." At less than five feet ten inches tall and under 175 pounds, Lombardi was small even by the standards of that day. But his fierce charge and durability helped the team to win all but two games in 1935 and 1936.

After graduation Lombardi worked as an insurance investigator while attending Fordham University Law School at night. In 1939 he was hired by his former Fordham teammate Andy Palau to be line coach at St. Cecilia's, a small Catholic preparatory school in Englewood, N.J. He was also to be basketball coach, baseball assistant, and teacher of physics, chemistry, algebra, and Latin, at a salary of only $1,700 per year. Lombardi later said he took the job in order to marry (on Aug. 31, 1940) Marie Planitz. They had two children. By 1942 he was head coach of football, basketball, and baseball, and in eight years led his teams to six state football titles and one New Jersey parochial school basketball championship.

Lombardi also worked at various odd jobs in construction and at a du Pont research laboratory in Wilmington, Del., and he took education courses at Seton Hall University. On weekends he played semiprofessional football in Springfield, Mass., Brooklyn, and Wilmington. But his ambition was to be a head football coach at a major university. In this quest he accepted the position of freshman coach at Fordham in 1947 and moved up to coach the varsity offense in 1948.

From 1949 to 1954 he worked at the United States Military Academy, West Point, N.Y., under the famous coach Earl H. ("Red") Blaik. Army was in those days one of the dominant football teams in the country, and Lombardi was in charge of the successful, fast-striking T-formation offensive attack. He later credited Blaik with teaching him the importance of organization in the football program, of meticulous preparation and motivation of the players, and of controlling his volatile temper.

Lombardi became offensive coach of the New York Giants professional team in 1954. By his own admission he had paid little attention to the professional game. His lack of experience and emotional style of coaching, along with his introduction of new techniques, brought him into conflict with his players. But he helped transform the Giants into a major National Football League (NFL) contender. Although he was soon mentioned as a possible head coach at both the collegiate and professional levels, he received no offers. He later speculated that his Italian-American heritage was held against him.

His chance finally came in 1959 when he was recommended to the Green Bay Packers by former army colleague Sid Gillman, then a successful professional coach. With only five years in professional football and with little experience as a head coach, Lombardi, the inveterate New Yorker, moved his family to northern Wisconsin to take over the Packers, a team that had won only two games the previous season. At his insistence he was appointed both head coach and general manager, and placed in charge of all phases of the team's operation.

After carefully evaluating his personnel, Lombardi began to rebuild the Packers by disciplining and motivating the players. His rigid control and exhausting training camps became legendary. Using the Giants' brand of power football, he quickly made Green Bay competitive in the league. The team also began to make money, and Lombardi soon upgraded the stadium and training facilities.

In the first year the Packers won seven games and lost five, and Lombardi was named the league's Coach of the Year. In 1960 the team won the Western Conference title before losing the league championship to the Philadelphia Eagles. In 1961 and 1962 Green Bay won the NFL championship, but in 1963 and 1964 it failed to make the playoffs. Lombardi then rebuilt his aging team, and Green Bay won an unprecedented three consecutive league championships, in 1965, 1966, and 1967.

Lombardi faced a new challenge in 1960 with the formation of the competing American Football League (AFL). In what Lombardi and others saw as a crucial test of the credibility of the older NFL, Green Bay easily defeated the new league's champions, Kansas City and Oakland, in the first two Super Bowls in 1967 and 1968. In nine seasons with Lombardi at the helm the Packers had become a symbol of strength, precision, and excellence in football and Lombardi a folk hero. However, exhausted by the tensions of coaching and claiming that the demands of two jobs were too great, Lombardi resigned as head coach in 1968. He planned to concentrate on his duties as general manager and to give more time to league matters, including the still-in-progress merger of the two football leagues. But he found that he missed "the fire on Sunday" and the close camaraderie of the team. Soon there were rumors that he would sign as coach with any one of seven different professional teams. In early 1969 he accepted an offer from the Washington Redskins to become head coach and executive president with complete control of the organization; as an added bonus he was given 5 percent ownership of the team.

The Green Bay corporation was reluctant to let Lombardi go and complained that Washington had violated league rules by approaching him directly. They also reminded Lombardi that his contract did not permit him to coach elsewhere until 1974. But ultimately they released him, and he moved to Washington, D.C., to attempt to repeat the miracle of Green Bay. With full media coverage, Lombardi began to transform a weak Redskins program, and the team won seven, lost five, and tied two games in 1969. But in the late spring and summer of 1970 Lombardi became ill during preseason drills. Exploratory surgery revealed he had intestinal cancer. He died in Georgetown University Hospital. Along with other honors and tributes he was posthumously given the National Football League Distinguished Service Award in 1970, and the following year he was elected to the NFL Hall of Fame.

Lombardi's reputation rested on his accomplishments as a coach and on his being a symbol of authority and discipline. His record of 135 victories, forty-one defeats, and eleven ties in fifteen years of coaching was exceptional in that day. Yet he was hardly an innovator in football tactics. While he rejected the standard professional "slot T," his "close-end" offensive system owed much to an older single-wing formation, and he clearly preferred a running attack to the forward pass. His offensive game was best illustrated by the famed Green Bay "end sweep," with guards pulling out to lead the formation. Yet he delighted in variations such as the halfback option pass perfected first with the Giants' Frank Gifford and later with Lombardi's favorite player, the Packers' Paul Hornung. He also popularized the idea of "running to daylight," or permitting the runner to choose his own route according to the actions of his blockers. Football to Lombardi was a simple game. If you blocked and tackled better than your opponent and got the breaks, you won.

His system of coaching was an amalgam of his memories of his loving, perfectionist father, his years at St. Cecilia's, his belief in the hierarchical system of the Catholic church, and the lessons he learned from Blaik at West Point. He said coaching was teaching, and he worked to achieve excellence by endless repetition and by motivating each of his players. A stern disciplinarian who set rigid rules to govern his player's personal lives, he was blunt, direct, and not above verbal abuse of his players and staff. He liked to speak in terse epigrams such as "Winning isn't everything, it's the only thing," which became part of the popular rhetoric of his day. Lombardi once said that "a university without football is in danger of deteriorating into a medieval study hall." Yet he came to question some aspects of the professional game. He called it a game for madmen, and worried over the insatiable demands of success.

With the help of television, professional football had become the major spectator sport of the 1960's, and Lombardi symbolized its success. But he also represented order and stability in a troubled time. He spoke of the older values of hard work, discipline, loyalty to family and team, duty to God, and respect for authority. He was openly critical of individualism that lacked personal responsibility. He condemned his players' long hair, sideburns, and mustaches. He also attempted to direct their outside interests. He had little time for player agents and he sided with professional football's management in its developing quarrels with players over rights and benefits.

Lombardi always struggled to separate his private and professional lives. Devoted to his family and close friends, he was a committed Roman Catholic who attended mass daily. He was shy, wary of the press, and difficult to approach. But many of his players spoke of him with affection as well as respect. He was active in community affairs in the Green Bay area. Always concerned with financial security, he reportedly left an estate worth more than $1 million.

[See Vincent Lombardi with W. C. Heinz, *Run to Daylight!* (1963); Jerry Kramer, *Instant Replay* (1968), *Farewell to Football* (1969), and *Lombardi* (1970; rev. ed., 1976); and J. May, *Vince Lombardi* (1975). Among many articles on Lombardi are those in *Look*, Sept. 5 and Sept. 19, 1967; *Life*, Sept. 12, 1968; *Newsweek*, Jan. 29, 1968, and Feb. 17, 1969; and *Sports Illustrated*, Mar. 3, 1969. Obituaries are in the *New York Times*, Sept. 4, 1970; *Time*, Sept. 14, 1970; and *National Review*, Sept. 22, 1970.]

DANIEL R. GILBERT

LUCAS, SCOTT WIKE (Feb. 19, 1892–Feb. 22, 1968), attorney, United States congressman, and senator, was born Scott Wyke Lucas in Cass County, Ill., the son of William Douglas Lucas, a tenant farmer, and Sarah Catherine Underbrink. His father was a poor provider, so Lucas financed his own education by playing semiprofessional baseball, teaching school (while in high school himself), and stoking furnaces, sometimes saving money by cooking his meals on top of the furnace. The greatest influence during his youth was his oldest brother, Thurman, who encouraged him to study law and helped him to get started in the legal profession. Lucas attended public schools in Bath, Ill., and graduated from Virginia (Ill.) High School in 1911. Having already acquired some college credits, he entered Illinois Wesleyan University, majored in law, and graduated in 1914 with an LL.B. After passing the bar exam on his second try, he began to practice law in Havana, Ill., in 1915.

During World War I Lucas entered the service as a private, leaving in 1918 as a lieutenant. In subsequent years he was active in the American Legion, serving as state commander and, from 1928 to 1932, as national judge advocate. He entered elective politics as state's attorney for Mason County, Ill., in 1920. On Jan. 21, 1923, he married Edith Biggs; they adopted one child. In 1932 he sought the Democratic nomination for the United States Senate, but he did not have the support of the powerful Kelly-Nash political machine in Chicago and lost the primary by a large margin. Nevertheless, Governor Henry Horner appointed him chairman of the Illinois State Tax Commission in 1933 and urged him to run for the vacant Twentieth District congressional seat in 1934. He did so successfully, entering Congress as a loyal supporter of the New Deal. He was reelected in 1936. He also served as a delegate to the Democratic National Convention every four years from 1932 to 1964, except for 1936.

Occasionally Lucas demonstrated an independent streak that strengthened his position in Illinois. He not only opposed but denounced President Franklin D. Roosevelt's plan to pack the Supreme Court. On July 15, 1937, he rose in the House to ask, "Is there a single Democrat in this historic hall who believes that continuation of this fight will accomplish a single constructive thing?"

With the support of downstate political forces, Lucas again took on the Kelly-Nash machine with a bid for the United States Senate in 1938. Upon winning the nomination, he reconciled with the machine, thereafter receiving its complete support. As a senator he supported President Roosevelt's attempts to strengthen defense, and he served on the Joint Committee on Pearl Harbor, fully endorsing its conclusions in the assignment of responsibility for the disastrous events of Dec. 7, 1941.

Strongly representing the interests of farmers and businessmen, Lucas garnered increasing political support in Illinois. He was proposed for vice-president by the Kelly-Nash machine at the Democratic conventions of 1940, 1944, and 1948, with his name actually voted upon in 1944. He was elected Democratic whip of the Senate in 1946, and following Alben Barkley's elevation to the vice-presidency in 1949, Lucas was unanimously elected majority leader.

Despite his popularity, Lucas could count on only forty of the fifty-four Democratic senators to support the Truman administration's domestic proposals. Indeed, a coalition of Republicans and southern Democrats was able to block the enactment of civil rights legislation, federal aid to education and housing, national health insurance (opposed by Lucas himself), and the nomination of Leland Olds to the Federal Power Commission. Although Lucas and Truman got along well, there were some instances when the president's behavior left Lucas at a disadvantage. For example, in 1950 Truman indicated that he would support a particular version of the natural gas bill; then, when it passed, he bowed to liberal opposition and vetoed the measure.

Lucas, like most liberals, had difficulty grappling with the issue of domestic Communism. During his tenure as majority leader, a Republican proposal for registration of Communists, anathema to liberals, was countered by a Lucas-sponsored substitute plan to place Communists in detention camps in the event of a national security emergency. This measure was put forth as tougher than mere registration, but was believed less likely to be implemented. In the end Lucas and the other liberals outmaneuvered themselves; both provisions found their way into the Internal Security Act of 1950. Also, when Senator Joseph McCarthy aired his claim that card-carrying Communists were on the staff of the State Department, neither Lucas nor an investigating committee set up by Lucas and headed by Senator Millard E. Tydings of Maryland was able to obtain from McCarthy any substantiation of his charges. By successfully ducking the issue, McCarthy was able to remain viable.

These occurrences coincided with an effort by McCarthy to target his opponents for defeat in 1950. When Lucas, who had been tied up until September by Senate duties, began to campaign for reelection he found that his political base in Illinois had eroded. Republican Everett McKinley Dirksen wrested the seat from him. Many political observers attributed Lucas' defeat to his support of an unpopular administration and to a public reaction against the brutal Chinese offensive begun in October in the Korean War. Afterward, Lucas' physician observed that his defeat probably saved his life. While leader of the Senate he had suffered two heart attacks that were not revealed to the press; one, in fact, was reported as an ulcer. He spent the next eighteen years practicing law in Washington, Springfield, and Havana, and serving as a lobbyist.

Lucas was a storyteller in the Lincoln tradition, nearly always captivating his listeners. A flamboyant dresser who favored double-breasted suits and a homburg, he was charming to women; Capitol Hill secretaries named him the congressman they would most like to see in a leopard-skin suit. He hunted regularly, and was renowned for having dispatched three ducks with one shot—a feat that was reported in Ripley's "Believe It or Not." A dedicated golfer, he served as president of Washington's prestigious Burning Tree Golf Club. He enjoyed a weekly high-stakes poker game attended frequently by Chief Justice Earl Warren. He also wrote verse as a form of self-expression and he read constantly.

Unable to accept the Primitive Baptist beliefs of his parents, Lucas confided to his daughter-in-law, "I am an agnostic. I don't believe in a supreme being, but I do believe in a supreme power. There is an order that governs the universe." Complications from diabetes led to the amputation of his leg in 1966 and to a fatal stroke on a train from Washington, D.C., to Florida. He died in Rocky Mount, N.C.

[Lucas' papers are at the Illinois State Historical Society in Springfield. See William S. White, "Rugged Days for the Majority Leader," *New York Times Magazine*, July 3, 1949; and Edward L. Schapsmeier and Frederick H. Schapsmeier, "Scott W. Lucas of Havana," *Journal of the Illinois State Historical Society*, Nov. 1977. An obituary is in the *New York Times*, Feb. 23, 1968.]

JOSEPH MAY

LUCE, HENRY ROBINSON (Apr. 3, 1898–Feb. 28, 1967), editor and publisher, was born in Tengchow, China, the son of Henry Winters Luce, a Presbyterian missionary, and Elizabeth Middleton Root, a former social worker. Like most American children raised in China at the turn of the century, Luce was relatively isolated from the Chinese, and he absorbed his father's nationalism and admiration for the diplomacy of Theodore Roosevelt. From 1908 to 1913 he attended the British-run Chefoo School. In 1913 a family benefactor, Mrs. Cyrus H. McCormick, sent Luce to the Hotchkiss School in Lakeville, Conn. There he took up journalism and became friends with Briton Hadden, editor of a student publication. Together they enrolled at Yale in 1916 and joined the staff of the *Yale Daily News*. After serving in the army in 1918–1919, Luce received his B.A. in 1920. With financial help from Mrs. McCormick, he spent a year after graduation studying history at Oxford.

On his return from England, Luce became a reporter on the *Chicago Daily News*. After two months he joined Hadden at the *Baltimore News*. Together they plotted a new journalistic enterprise. Daily newspapers, Hadden had concluded at Hotchkiss, inundated readers with information, but none offered, even once a week, a comprehensive news summary and analysis. Luce proposed a weekly news magazine, *Time*, to synthesize and evaluate the most important events; *Time* was to speak its own mind and convey omniscience. "*Time* gives both sides," Luce and Hadden wrote in the magazine's prospectus, "but clearly indicates which side it believes to have the stronger position." The news, organized in different departments, was to be presented concisely: no one entry was to run more than 400 words.

With no money of their own to invest, Hadden and Luce spent the summer of 1922 persuading college friends, relatives, and Mrs. William Harkness to put up the $86,000 to bring out *Time*. Through a preferred stock formula the two retained control of the magazine. The first issue appeared in late February 1923. On Dec. 22, 1923, Luce married Lila Hotz. They had two children.

Hadden edited the magazine, with Luce handling business transactions and different *Time* departments. In *Time*'s first years, they had to struggle to keep the magazine afloat; circulation and advertising grew slowly. Yet operating costs were not high, in part because until the late 1930's the magazine did little reporting. Entries were based on newsclips and research. Old news was made fresh by being told as stories—unlike conventional newspaper accounts—usually with a beginning, middle, and end, and laced with often insignificant facts (such as a newsmaker's physical appearance) to give each entry a documentary quality. *Time* began to achieve a distinctive language of sentences in reverse of normal order and neologisms. Lacking an editorial page, Hadden and Luce's publication usually favored a moderate Republicanism, although the party's continued endorsement of Prohibition—which Luce regarded as hypocritical—drove him to vote for the Democratic nominee, Al Smith, in 1928.

As Time Incorporated, the concern acquired other properties. In 1924 Luce and Hadden became publishers of the *Saturday Review of Literature*, which had been the weekly book supplement to the *New York Post*, but they gave up their interest in it two years later. In 1928 Time Inc. began publishing *Tide*, an advertising trade journal; *Tide* was sold in 1930. Two years later, Luce approved the acquisition of *Architectural Forum*, which Time Inc. operated until 1964, when it ceased publication.

After Hadden's death on Feb. 28, 1929, Luce obtained majority control of Time Inc. and named John S. Martin, Hadden's cousin, managing editor of *Time*. Under Martin, *Time* realized the tone of omniscience and emphasis on colorful description that Hadden had sought. The magazine's circulation also started to rise, from 300,000 in 1930 to 700,000 in 1936.

At Luce's insistence, Time Inc. launched a business monthly, *Fortune*, in Feburary 1930. *Fortune*, especially in the early 1930's, covered far more than business and finance; unlike *Time*, individual stories were detailed. No expense was spared on illustrations; leading photographers like Margaret Bourke-White worked for *Fortune*. The magazine also pioneered, beginning with the *Fortune* Survey in 1935, in the reporting of polling results. Yet, because *Fortune* was too expensive even for many business executives, its circulation remained relatively modest.

Many Americans were exposed to Luce's radio and newsreel services of the 1930's. First produced on the radio in 1931 at the suggestion of circulation manager Roy E. Larsen, *The March of Time* resembled *Time* magazine in its highly structured, directed form. The *March of Time* producers reenacted important events of the week. A newsreel version, appearing once a month beginning in 1935, occasionally staged news events, what Luce described as "fakery in allegiance to the truth." Although widely attacked later, the reenacted portions of both the radio and newsreel *March of Time* drew few protests at the outset. However, Luce cared only for the printed page and rarely interested himself in *The March of Time*. The radio version left the air in 1945; the newsreel ceased production six years later.

Luce was far more intrigued by the possibilities of a picture magazine. Since the 1920's, developments in photography and photoengraving had made a popularly priced, generously illustrated magazine possible. *Time* and *Fortune* used photographs extensively and creatively, being among the first to offer the new "candid" camera work of Erich Salomon and others. Late in 1933 Luce asked several aides to begin planning a picture weekly. Among those subsequently encouraging Luce to produce the magazine was Clare Boothe Brokaw, a playwright and former editor of *Vanity Fair*.

Luce fell in love with Brokaw and, after much agonizing, asked her to marry him. She agreed, but divorcing Lila precipitated an emotional crisis in Luce. Moreover, his parents deeply disapproved. Lila Luce reluctantly consented to a divorce (Oct. 5, 1935), and Harry and Clare married on Nov. 23, 1935. Despite Clare's talents as a writer, staff resentment kept Luce from giving his new wife an editorial post at Time Inc., but she frequently advised Luce.

Luce's picture magazine, *Life*, appeared in November 1936. Unlike established low-priced magazines, *Life* relied mostly on photographs, many of them arranged in the "photoessay," an innovation of German photographers advising *Life*. All told, *Life* tried to use pictures as *Time* did words, granting photographers new status as they sought to offer what one critic of the magazine called a visual "finality" to reporting.

Partly because *Life* came out before rivals such as *Look*, Luce's magazine immediately won substantial consumer favor. The mass demand for photographs, long thought great, had been confirmed. After four weeks, *Life*'s circulation topped 500,000; by late 1937, it had reached 1.7 million. Never had a new magazine commanded such a large circulation. Yet that popularity almost bankrupted Time Inc. The first-year contracts for advertisers were formulated on a circulation base of 250,000; as a result, the magazine's advertising subsidy was cut and Time Inc. had to make up the difference. Then, too, other advertisers waited before buying space in the magazine, despite its popularity. Not until early 1939, when its circulation had passed the 2-million mark, did *Life* begin to earn money.

With *Life*'s difficulties resolved, Luce began to devote himself to public issues. Some aides later attributed his newfound interest in politics to *Life*'s vast circulation, which inflated Luce's sense of his own importance. Some weeks, up to one-fourth of the adult population read at least one Luce publication; *Business Week* reported in 1948 that only the chewing-gum manufacturer William Wrigley, Jr., had his name printed on more pieces of paper.

Luce took an active interest in politics. Although contemptuous of the Republican party's more conservative wing, Luce believed that the Roosevelt administration's hostility toward business had hampered economic recovery. Together with other members of the nation's business and banking elite, Luce worked to formulate an alternative to both the New Deal and its reactionary critics.

Luce's public phase was also spurred by events in Europe. By 1939 Luce had come to regard Hitler as a grave threat to America and the West. Earlier, both *Time* and *Fortune* had run pieces relatively uncritical of fascism in Europe. Now Luce chose to use news services to warn readers about events in Europe. Once war broke out late in that year, he supported American intervention. He and his magazine, in step with the internationalist Republican press, promoted Wendell Willkie, the most interventionist of the possible 1940 Republican presidential nominees; *Fortune* editor Russell Davenport served as Willkie campaign manager, and Luce, as an adviser.

Roosevelt's reelection did not lessen Luce's urge to influence American policy-making. For *Life* in February 1941, the publisher wrote a widely discussed essay, "The American Century," admonishing Americans to recognize that America had replaced Great Britain as "the most powerful and vital nation in the world." At the conclusion of the war, America, like Britain in the nineteenth century, could bring stability to the world, all the while promoting democratic capitalism.

Sometime between late 1943 and 1944, Luce began to regard the Soviet Union as the great obstacle to a postwar American hegemony. Until 1944 his magazines had, like other American news services, cast Russia in the most favorable light, but Luce had become concerned over Russia's intentions in Eastern Europe and elsewhere. He moved cautiously at first. A few anti-Communist articles in *Life* and *Time* in late 1944 angered his predominantly progressive writers. But as the Truman administration began to criticize the Soviet Union, Luce's magazines applauded. In the late 1940's, Luce offered his own solutions to the East-West crisis. In *Fortune* essays and speeches, he urged businesses to invest abroad to stabilize non-Communist economies, and he decried trade barriers and cumbersome currency exchanges. Assailing the "containment" strategy of the Truman administration as too defensive, Luce embraced what Republican foreign-policy adviser John Foster Dulles in *Life* called "a foreign policy of boldness."

Although Luce's magazines were widely read in Washington, Luce personally enjoyed little influence in either the Roosevelt or the Truman administration. At White House meetings, Roosevelt tended to patronize him and ignored his advice; Truman dismissed Luce as another Republican publisher.

In no area did Luce enjoy less sway than China policy. In the late 1930's, he had rediscovered his native China, becoming deeply involved in raising relief funds for China during its war with Japan. Long a supporter of the Nationalist Chinese leader Generalissimo Chiang Kai-shek, Luce watched helplessly as Chiang steadily lost battles to the Chinese Communists in 1947–1949. Earlier, Luce had ignored his own correspondent, who had warned him of Chiang's deteriorating position. Visits to China in 1941, 1945, and 1946 had convinced him of Chiang's greatness. Yet the Truman administration ignored Luce's pleas and *Life* editorials on behalf of American military aid.

Despite his preoccupation with public affairs in the late 1940's, Luce oversaw a major "rethinking" of his magazines. He ordered *Fortune* to narrow its agenda and concern itself exclusively with business; each issue of *Life*, he insisted, must run at least one "serious offering" on the great art, religion, and ideas of Western civilization.

Luce involved himself in politics even to the extent of considering running for the United States Senate from Connecticut in 1950, but friends dissuaded him from making the race. In 1952 both he and Clare (who had become involved in Republican politics as a member of the House of Representatives from Connecticut, in 1943–1947) were early supporters of Dwight D. Eisenhower for the Republican presidential nomination. Winning the nomination, Eisenhower received *Life*'s endorsement; *Time* promoted him indirectly in its coverage of his campaign and its hostility to the Democratic candidate, Adlai E. Stevenson. After Eisenhower's election Luce frequently met and corresponded with the president but never commanded great influence within the administration.

Eisenhower did name Clare Luce ambassador to Italy in April 1953. Luce lived in Rome with his wife for four years, traveling to New York frequently to plan another magazine, *Sports Illustrated*. First published in 1954, the magazine aimed at a young, affluent consumer of sports news. Although the magazine incurred losses for over a decade, it eventually proved profitable.

Luce's magazines came under increasing attack in the 1950's. Although Luce had wide-ranging intellectual interests, his magazines tended to be "middle-brow," critical of most American intellectuals and avant-garde movements in the arts. Detractors also assailed his publications' favorable opinion of Eisenhower. Although most writers were well to the left of Luce, every editor after the departure of T. S. Matthews at *Time* in 1953 shared Luce's politics. And because *Time* entries were heavily edited, the magazine came under increasing attack for its biases. Luce publicly dismissed such comments. Privately he expressed disappointment in both Eisenhower and Secretary of State Dulles; the administration had failed to adopt a more aggressive foreign policy. Yet, out of personal loyalty to both men, Luce refused to voice his displeasure.

Although cheered by the economic expansion of the 1950's, Luce worried that America lacked a mission. Following the Soviet Union's successful launch of the world's first artificial satellite in October 1957, *Life* immediately and loudly championed a space "race" with Russia and eventually gained exclusive rights to the stories of the original American astronauts. In 1959 and 1960 various contributors to *Life* attempted to define the "national purpose."

In 1959, Eisenhower named Clare Luce ambassador to Brazil. During her confirmation hearing, Senator Wayne Morse of Oregon attacked her partisan speeches and *Time*'s condescending treatment of Latin America. Although the Senate overwhelmingly approved her nomination, Clare Luce issued a statement insulting Morse and causing a furor; Luce persuaded her to resign.

In the presidential election the following year, Luce and his publications restrained their partisanship. *Life* did endorse Republican nominee Richard M. Nixon, but Luce was less outspoken, for he had known Democratic candidate John F. Kennedy and his father, Joseph P. Kennedy, since the 1930's; indeed, Luce had written the introduction to the young Kennedy's first book, *Why England Slept* (1940). Once elected, Kennedy treated Luce respectfully but complained vigorously when he regarded a *Time* entry as unfair to his administration.

For its part, *Time* treated Kennedy roughly on occasion. It urged a tougher American policy toward Communist Cuba. Luce and his publications supported America's growing involvement in Vietnam. *Time* heavily edited its Vietnam correspondents' dispatches to reflect a more positive, interventionist stance.

Luce stepped down as editor in chief in 1964. He traveled, lectured, studied theology, and promoted the peace-through-law movement. He died in Phoenix, Ariz.

Even before his death, Luce had come under attack for his inflexible views on the cold war and China. Most critics, however, failed to note the extent to which Luce's views were to be found in other news services. Moreover, most of Luce's readers—middle- or upper-middle-class Americans—were likely to share his world view.

Luce was perhaps the most innovative publisher in twentieth-century America. Although most of his creations owed much to the work of others, especially Hadden, Luce had the organizational ability to carry out the ideas of friends and aides. His magazines did not necessarily inform: often his journalism stressed nonessential information or overstated personality. Yet, by succeeding, Luce helped to reshape the news, to make a complicated world seem comprehensible. Although most Americans did not regularly read his magazines, other, more popular news media often imitated *Time, Life,* and *The March of Time.*

[Luce's papers are in the Time Inc. archives and the Library of Congress. John K. Jessup, ed., *The Ideas of Henry Luce* (1969), is a collection of some of Luce's more important speeches and writings. An invaluable collection is the John Shaw Billings papers at the University of South Carolina; Billings, a writer, editor, and chief aide to Luce from 1928 to 1955, kept a diary, an annotated scrapbook, and much office memoranda.

Biographies include John Kobler, *Luce: His Time, Life, and Fortune* (1968); W. A. Swanberg, *Luce and His Empire* (1972); and James L. Baughman, *Minister of Information* (1987). See Robert A. Elson, *Time Inc., 1923–1941* (1968), and *The World of Time Inc., 1941–1960* (1973); David Halberstam, *The Powers That Be* (1979); and Curtis D. Prendergast, *The World of Time Inc, 1960–1980* (1986).

See also Joseph Epstein, "Henry Luce and His Time," *Commentary*, Nov. 1967; and Daniel Bell, "Henry Luce's Half Century," *New Leader*, Dec. 11, 1972. Wolcott Gibbs wrote a classic profile of Luce in *Time* argot in the *New Yorker*, Nov. 28, 1936. Obituaries are in the *New York Times*, Mar. 1, 1967; *Time*, Mar. 10, 1967; and *Newsweek*, Mar. 13, 1967.]

JAMES L. BAUGHMAN

LUCHESE, THOMAS (1899?–July 13, 1967), organized crime leader, was born Gaetano Luchese (sometimes spelled Lucchese) in Palermo, Sicily. In 1911 he immigrated to the United States, and by 1919 he had employment as a plumber's helper and machinist in the East Harlem section of New York City. That year he lost his right index finger in a machine-shop accident, which led to his being nicknamed Three-Finger Brown—a reference to a famous baseball player of the early twentieth century, Mordecai ("Three-Finger") Brown—by a policeman who arrested him two years later. Luchese hated the nickname and would not allow anyone to call him that to his face. However, he did go by the name Tommy Brown in his dealings as a garment manufacturer.

Luchese's accident was the catalyst in turning him from honest labor to working with the New York City underworld. In 1921 he was arrested for car theft, and he spent three years in jail, the only time he was ever convicted of a crime, although he was later arrested twice in homicide investigations. Luchese's first membership in a "Mafia family" was in that of Gaetano Reina, whose death set off the "Castellammare war" between leading crime organizations in 1930–1931. Luchese was next put under Gaetano Gagliano, one of Salvatore Maranzano's top loyalists and head of one of the "five families" of New York.

Maranzano's forces prevailed over those of Joe ("The Boss") Masseria in the Castellammare war, but Maranzano's reign was shortlived. He was assassinated on Sept. 11, 1931, and Charles ("Lucky") Luciano became the top boss of the New York families. Gagliano and Luchese, his second in command, had aided Luciano's plots; in fact, Luchese may have been the insider who tipped off Maranzano's movements the day of his death. The position of Luchese was secure within the overall organization, and for over twenty years he loyally served Gagliano and a series of top bosses—Luciano, Frank Costello, and Vito Genovese.

Although Luchese did not succeed to the head of the family until 1953, when Gagliano died a natural death, his power and influence within the organization grew steadily. Unlike some of his cohorts, Luchese moved easily with the political powers in New York, and he had significant friends in high places, including Congressman Vito Marcantonio, Congressman Louis Cappozzoli, United States attorney Myles Lane, and Thomas Murphy, the prosecutor of the Alger Hiss case. Luchese arranged key political support for his friends and received various forms of protection for his own activities, which used legitimate businesses as a cover. Among Luchese's operations as "legitimate businessman" was principal ownership of Braunell, Ltd., a ladies' garments manufacturer on Seventh Avenue; he was also involved in real estate, sand and gravel supplies, a hoist company, and several service firms.

Before Luchese became one of the five family heads in New York, he was instrumental in picking the mayor of New York City. In 1950, Mayor William O'Dwyer resigned his office, and Vincent R. Impellitteri, the president of the City Council, became mayor. Impellitteri had been selected for City Council president at the insistence of Marcantonio, who was returning a favor for Luchese. In spite of press revelations about Luchese's role as the power behind the mayor, Impellitteri won election to a full term in November 1950, running as an independent when Tammany boss Carmine De Sapio refused him the Democratic nomination.

The full range of Luchese's activities will never be known, but he was accused at various times of involvement in narcotics distribution, gambling, numbers running, and racketeering. When called on to testify before the New York State Crime Commission in 1952, he portrayed himself as a falsely accused businessman. "The only thing I belong to is the Knights of Columbus," he later claimed. And when confronted with allegations of controlling the narcotics vendors in the city, he reacted with injured pride. "Any man who got a family should die before he goes into any of that kind of business," Luchese said.

From 1953 until his death, Luchese was a leading member of the "Commission," the top bosses who decided the group's policies and tried to iron out differences. Although his role was generally well known to law enforcement officials, he escaped the indignity of harassment and jailings that other organized-crime leaders of that time faced. When sixty-five crime bosses from around the nation converged at the home of Joseph Barbara in Apalachin, N.Y., in November 1957, the police apprehended a large number of them. Luchese escaped detection, however, by heading into the woods as he approached the Barbara house and saw police cars.

According to Joseph Bonanno, Luchese faced his most dangerous moment in the mid-1950's when Frank Costello accused Luchese of plotting to kill Costello's top ally, Albert Anastasia. The Commission held what became known as the Luchese Tribunal, to judge whether Luchese should die. Luchese used his wits to save his life, by refusing to say if the charges were true and then appealing directly to the honor of Anastasia: "You, Albert, only you have the right to say if I should die." With the support of Bonanno and the reluctance of Anastasia to openly call for the death of a longtime colleague, Luchese survived.

Of the five families in New York, Luchese's was the smallest. Estimated figures for 1963 listed his at 150 members, out of a total of 2,350 for all five. But Luchese's influence, while never as well publicized as that of his fellow bosses, was substantial, in large part because of his political contacts. Indeed, it was his political connections that enabled him to be naturalized in 1943, thirty-two years after his arrival, and that allowed him to receive a certificate of good conduct from the New York State Parole Board on Apr. 18, 1950, allowing him, as an ex-convict, to vote.

Luchese's last years were spent in seclusion at his luxurious home on Long Island. He was ill for over a year before his death at Lido Beach,

Long Island. His control of the family passed to Carmine Tramunti.

[There are numerous accounts of organized crime, most of which mention Luchese only in passing. See Virgil Peterson, *The Mob* (1983), for extended discussion of the Luchese family. See also Joseph Bonanno, *A Man of Honor* (1983), which gives many personal anecdotes involving Luchese. David Leon Chandler, *Brothers in Blood* (1975), is a good background source and refers to Luchese at some length. Peter Maas, *The Valachi Papers* (1968), gives some details about Valachi and his relationship to Luchese. An obituary is in the *New York Times*, July 14, 1967.]

ALFRED L. MORGAN

LYND, ROBERT STAUGHTON (Sept. 26, 1892–Nov. 1, 1970), sociologist and author, was born in New Albany, Ind., the son of Staughton Lynd, a banker, and Cornelia Day. Lynd was raised in Louisville, Ky., and attended local schools. He graduated from Princeton University—whose atmosphere he found snobbish and uncongenial—in 1914, becoming the first of his family to go to college.

Lynd was managing editor of *Publishers Weekly* for four years after leaving college. He was wounded during one year of service in the field artillery in World War I. During his convalescence he read John A. Hobson's *Work and Wealth*, a book he considered seminal to his growing awareness of the conflict between haves and have-nots. He also worked with the men on his hospital ward, writing letters, helping with personal problems, and advising on social and financial matters. There he had his first taste of being involved and directly useful—a combination that appealed to his social conscience.

After the war Lynd worked for the publishers Charles Scribner's Sons and was briefly on the editorial staff of the *Freeman Magazine*. On Sept. 3, 1922, he married Helen Merrell. (They had two children, one of whom, Staughton Lynd, became a noted historian, lawyer, and civil rights activist.) Lynd then abandoned publishing and enrolled at Union Theological Seminary, from which he received the D.D. in 1923. Shortly thereafter he became a missionary preacher in Elk Basin, Mont., an experience that vividly focused his attention on the plight of the oil workers, with whom he quickly identified, seeing them as exploited, powerless, disfranchised, and deprived of the knowledge or means to effect change. That summer radically altered the course of his intellectual development.

Immediately following Elk Basin, Lynd directed the "Small City" studies of the Institute for Religious and Social Studies. Two of his essays, "Crude Oil Religion" (*Harper's*, September 1922) and "Done in Oil" (*Survey Graphics*, November 1922), mark his shift in interest and career drive from religion to sociology. The first is a vivid, sometimes humorous and earthy, anecdotal account of his Elk Basin ministry; the second is an academic analysis and critical discussion of the Rockefeller interests in the Elk Basin oil fields, showing the inferiority of the pay, hours, and working conditions as compared to those of other oil fields, along with a program for change.

On the basis of these articles, Lynd and his wife were invited to do the study that would make them famous. The Lynds soon found the assignment—to study religion in its social context—was too confining and opted for a study of all facets of an urban society, believing that it was impossible to examine one aspect, like religion, in isolation. Because the sponsoring committee refused to publish the result, the Lynds published *Middletown* (1929) on their own, and the book was immediately recognized as a landmark in American sociology.

Middletown is a factual sociological description of life in Muncie, Ind. Muncie was chosen in part for what it was not (not southern, not western, not eastern), as well for what it was (middle-sized, Middle American). According to Lynd, it was "as representative as possible of contemporary American life." The Lynds examined the ordinary daily life of Muncie inhabitants of all classes in various spheres: how they made their money and spent it, what they did for amusement, how they brought up their children, how they interacted in the family, what they thought about each other. It was the first objective examination of an American city in its totality, and its emphasis was (at least theoretically) on description, not on value judgment. Nevertheless, the values of the authors permeate the study. The citizens of Muncie regarded *Middletown* as critical and disparaging, and the book was denounced from the pulpit and in the press. One critic suggested that the study confirmed the cynical views of Sinclair Lewis and H. L. Mencken on the intellectual and moral limitations of the elites in Middle America. Mencken himself entitled his review of Middle America "A City in Moronia."

Middletown in Transition (1937), written during the New Deal, is a more dynamic study of social change. The Lynds emphasized the effects of increasing industrialization on the city and its growing class differentiation. The power structure is here more clearly identified and delineated and its ubiquitous character described, extending beyond economic control to the institutions governing the flow of information, often resulting in discrepancies between the accepted myth of success as the reward for hard work and the reality of the individual's inability to break out of his particular position in the web of power and status.

The Lynd Middletown studies derived intellectually from a number of sources: the philosophical positivism of Auguste Comte; early empirical studies in Europe, such as those of Émile Durkheim in France; statistical studies of urban communities by Charles Booth and by Sidney and Beatrice Webb in England; and the new application of the anthropological approach to contemporary society. Robert and Helen Lynd were frequently compared to the Webbs, primarily because of their empirical approach to contemporary culture but also because both couples were sympathetic to socialism and, not least, because each couple consisted of married working partners.

Robert Lynd's work as teacher, researcher, and writer reflected his passionate concern about inequality in American society, and his search for leverage for change. On the strength of *Middletown*, he was named Giddings Professor of Sociology at Columbia in 1931 (the year in which he received his Ph.D. from the university) and held the chair until his retirement in 1960. He was considered a somewhat dry and less than charismatic lecturer but was stimulating and involved in small groups and one-to-one interaction with his students.

Lynd's delight in the outdoors made him an enthusiastic hiker, and he was famous for his folk-song repertoire. The Lynds were core members of the Holderness New Hampshire intellectual summer community, with the psychologists Gardner and Lois Murphy, the anthropologists Margaret Mead and Gregory Bateson, and others. Under the aegis of Lawrence Frank, a brilliant and original mind who was the catalyst of the community and provided access to important foundation resources, this group did much to shape the social thinking of the time.

Sociology at Columbia in Lynd's time was represented by Robert MacIver, a traditionalist, at one end of the spectrum, and by C. Wright Mills, a Marxist, at the other, with Lynd somewhere between them, though ideologically closer to Mill. Lynd became a lively participant in struggles to define and invigorate his field, and his last book, *Knowledge for What?* (1939), is an attack on what he believed to be the feckless accumulation of facts for their own sake rather than the analysis of data pertinent to the problems of contemporary society and to the advance of egalitarian political goals.

Over his professional lifetime Lynd came increasingly to focus on the inequalities and injustices of American society, and especially on the differences in class power. On a trip to England during World War II, he became friends with the left-wing Labour leaders Aneurin Bevan and Jennie Lee. The exhilaration and sense of effective participation gained from his activities during this period may have been as close as he ever came to the activist role he so believed in. His work always had an intense moralistic flavor, perhaps deriving from, or expressing in academic terms, the religious and social zeal of his youth. He was politically engaged but was never a Communist, although he was often in step with Communists on social goals while disagreeing on politics and strategy. When he died, he had been at work on a book on power for a number of years and had written several preliminary articles questioning whether technology could be socially neutral. An intellectual and academic, with his work he advanced the tradition of liberal social activism.

[Lynd's papers are in the Library of Congress, and his files are at the University of California at Santa Cruz. See C. Wright Mills, *The Power Elite* (1956); John H. Magde, "Life in a Small Town," in *The Origins of Scientific Sociology* (1962); Robert B. Downs, *Books That Changed America* (1970); and Charles H. Page, *Fifty Years in the Sociological Enterprise* (1982). An obituary is in the *New York Times*, Nov. 3, 1970.]

EDNA LERNER

McCULLERS, CARSON (Feb. 19, 1917–Sept. 29, 1967), novelist, short-story writer, and playwright, was born Lula Carson Smith in Columbus, Ga., the daughter of Lamar Smith, a jeweler, and Marguerite Waters. She attended the Sixteenth Street School and in 1933 graduated from Columbus High School. At the age of ten she began serious piano study. She developed a close friendship with Mary Tucker, who became her piano teacher in 1931. In 1932 she contracted rheumatic fever and was extremely ill; although she recovered completely, she never was really strong and healthy. Late in the year she gave up her goal of becoming a concert pianist and decided instead to become a writer, but she nevertheless continued her musical studies. At about this time she also began to read voraciously, especially the nineteenth-century Russian novelists, and to write plays and short fiction.

In 1934 McCullers moved to New York City, where she worked at odd jobs and studied at Columbia University. At the end of the academic year she returned to Georgia, but the following September found her once again in New York to take courses at New York University. In November 1936, while studying with Whit Burnett, the editor of *Story*, McCullers became so ill (due in part to not eating and to smoking three packs of cigarettes a day) that she had to return to Columbus. She spent the winter recuperating and writing. "Wunderkind," her first publication, came out in *Story* late in the year. After another stay in New York, illness, and a return to Columbus, she married Reeves McCullers on Sept. 20, 1937, and moved to Charlotte, N.C. The following year they moved on to Fayetteville, N.C., from where McCullers submitted part of her first novel to Houghton Mifflin. The publisher presented her with a contract and promised a $500 advance, money that the couple badly needed. *The Heart Is a Lonely Hunter* was published in June 1940 and was hailed in extremely positive reviews.

The summer of 1940 found McCullers and her husband in New York, where she basked in her achievement. She complicated her personal life by falling in love with Annemarie Clarac-Schwarzenbach, but escaped from the tense situation in mid-August by attending the Bread Loaf Conference, where she and Louis Untermeyer became good friends. In September she decided to leave Reeves and move into February House, a communal building at 7 Middagh Street in Brooklyn; an astonishing array of creative people lived there, including Richard Wright, W. H. Auden, Benjamin Britten, and Paul Bowles. But her sojourn was cut short because of sickness, including a February 1941 stroke, which resulted in a temporary loss of sight. Throughout all of this, McCullers continued to write and to publish short pieces as well as a serialization of her second novel, *Reflections in a Golden Eye* (1941), in magazines like *Vogue* and *Harper's Bazaar*. In April she was back with Reeves in their old New York apartment. Here they spent much time drinking with their new friend, the composer David Diamond, and then in mid-June Carson left to spend the summer at the writers' colony Yaddo in Saratoga Springs, N.Y. There she met Katherine Anne Porter, Newton Arvin, and Granville Hicks and renewed her acquaintance with Eudora Welty. On Aug. 23, 1941, the *New Yorker* published her story "The Jockey," for which she received about $400.

Her relationship with Reeves degenerated to such an extent that she filed for an uncontested divorce, which was granted in 1941, while she was once again recuperating in Columbus. She thrived briefly but then in December double pneumonia, pleurisy, severe chest pains, and delirium resulted in her hospitalization. In March 1942 she was awarded a Guggenheim Fellowship, and four months later she returned to Yaddo. Her story "A Tree. A Rock. A Cloud." was published in the November issue of *Harper's Bazaar* and was subsequently chosen for *O. Henry Prize Stories of 1942*. The news of the death of her friend Clarac-Schwarzenbach, which reached her in early December, threw her into turmoil, and she left Yaddo and returned to February House, where she immediately came down with influenza.

As usual, the negative aspects in her life were counterbalanced, this time by an Arts and Letters grant; she also sold *The Ballad of the Sad Café* to *Harper's Bazaar*, which published the novella in August. She spent more time at Yaddo and at home in Columbus, and following her father's death in August 1944, she and her mother moved to Nyack, N.Y. *The Ballad of the Sad Café* was chosen for inclusion in *Best American Short Stories* for 1944.

On Mar. 19, 1945, Carson and Reeves McCullers were remarried. At the end of August she completed the seventh and final version of her novel *The Member of the Wedding*, which was published in March 1946. After another brief respite at Yaddo, during which she learned that she had been awarded another Guggenheim Fellowship, she went to Nantucket to spend some time with Tennessee Williams. In November McCullers and her husband left for Paris, where they had some enjoyable experiences but also bickered and drank heavily. Her health degenerated, and in August 1947 she suffered a second stroke, which resulted in a partial loss of sight and paralysis; a third followed soon thereafter. On December 1, both extremely ill, the McCullerses returned to New York, and the following February they separated.

Distraught and physically incapacitated, Carson McCullers attempted suicide in March and was briefly institutionalized. Her condition fluctuated during the rest of the year. By January 1949 she and Reeves had reunited. On Dec. 22, 1949, *The Member of the Wedding*, reworked into dramatic form, opened in Philadelphia; in New York it premiered on Jan. 5, 1950, to virtually unanimous acclaim, and it later won many honors, including the New York Drama Critics' Circle Award for best play. Financially secure at last, McCullers went alone to Ireland in the spring and stayed with Elizabeth Bowen. Then she moved on to Paris with Reeves. In early August they returned to New York, and for a while they went their separate ways. At the end of October she met Edith Sitwell, and they became good friends.

May 1951 saw the publication of an omnibus volume that contained McCullers' four novels as well as six short stories. Thereafter she and Reeves repeated their cycle: they drank excessively, and on July 28 McCullers fled to England. But this time there was a twist: Reeves, without money or passport, traveled on the same ship as a stowaway. Three months later McCullers was back in Nyack, sick but working on her poetry. Early in 1952 she and Reeves left for Rome, where they stayed until April, when they moved on to France and purchased a farm, and McCullers settled down to a long period of work on *Clock Without Hands*. Soon thereafter she was honored with a lifetime membership in the National Institute of Arts and Letters.

In the summer of 1953 Reeves attempted suicide, and a few months later he tried to convince McCullers that a double suicide would solve their problems. She returned to the United States and never again saw Reeves, who, on Nov. 19, 1953, finally succeeded in killing himself.

McCullers began a series of lectures in early 1954. Later in the spring, and again during the summer, she paid her last visits to Yaddo. Then, less than two years after Reeves's suicide, McCullers suffered the severe emotional trauma of losing her mother, upon whom she had always depended for solace and inspiration. Her play *The Square Root of Wonderful* opened in New York on Oct. 30, 1957, to less than enthusiastic reviews. It closed after only forty-five performances, which sent McCullers into a deep depression. Beginning in 1958 she underwent a series of operations to relieve her paralysis and pain. In January 1959 she met Isak Dinesen, whom she had long admired, and they became good friends. In September 1961, *Clock Without Hands*, a novel on which she had worked for fourteen years, finally appeared, but to mixed reviews. The last years of McCullers' life were filled with pain and many operations for her atrophied limbs, cancer, a broken hip, and a shattered elbow. Her great internal strength and will to live carried her through, and she continued to travel and write until her final stroke; after forty-seven days in a coma, she died in Nyack.

Despite the rigorous discipline that her early musical training required, McCullers developed in a somewhat haphazard fashion, primarily because of her nurturing and imaginative mother. By stressing her daughter's putative precocity, her mother also isolated her. McCullers' eccentricities, including peculiar dress habits, stubbornness, bisexuality, and, later, a difficult personality, as well as the loneliness, violence, grotesqueness, and imagined worlds that inform her writings, all derived in part from her early family life and from her ongoing bouts with sickness and pain. Toward the end of her life, as Virginia Spencer Carr puts it, "she had become her own fiction."

Frequently criticized for her emphasis on the negative and bizarre aspects of life, McCullers reaped high praise from diverse reviewers and influential critics. *The Heart Is a Lonely Hunter* has been called astounding, extraordinary, and remarkable. Gore Vidal characterized her as the greatest and most enduring of the southern writers. More recently, critics have tempered their appraisals, agreeing that although the long fiction is outstanding, the other writings are less successful. As Margaret B. McDowell observed, "Her achievement is substantial and undeniable, but . . . we are continually haunted by the sense of what might have been had she lived long enough to consolidate her powers and to mature even more richly her artistry and her insights into human nature."

[McCullers' manuscripts, correspondence, and other documents are deposited in almost twenty collections. The most important of these are at Duke, Emory, and Indiana universities; the universities of Georgia, Iowa, and Texas; the New York Public Library; and the Ford Foundation. Her publications not mentioned in the text include *Sweet as a Pickle and Clean as a Pig* (1964) and a posthumous volume, *The Mortgaged Heart* (1971).

The major biography is Virginia Spencer Carr, *The Lonely Hunter: A Biography of Carson McCullers* (1975). See also Oliver Evans, *The Ballad of Carson McCullers* (1965). Bibliographical material can be located in Robert F. Kiernan, *Katherine Anne Porter and Carson McCullers: A Reference Guide* (1976); and Adrian M. Shapiro, Jackson R. Bryer, and Kathleen Field, *Carson McCullers: A Descriptive Listing and Annotated Bibliography of Criticism* (1980). Two critical works are Richard M. Cook, *Carson McCullers* (1975); and Margaret B. McDowell, *Carson McCullers* (1980).]

ROBERT HAUPTMAN

MCFEE, WILLIAM (June 15, 1881–July 2, 1966), writer, was the son of John Henry McFee, an English sea captain from a seagoing family, and Hilda Wallace, a Canadian whose Tory ancestors had fled north during the American Revolution. McFee was born at sea on the *Erin's Isle*, a three-masted square-rigger that his father had designed, built, and owned and that was homeward bound to England from India and Canada; the birth was registered in Islington, London. In 1881, after three years of sailing, the family settled in New Southgate, a suburb of North London, where McFee grew up.

McFee attended a series of "slow sardonic schools," where, he recalled later, "nothing grew." He was mostly unhappy. Slow at learning to read, he soon became addicted to books. He struggled to learn Latin declensions; he had no passion for games. From 1894 to 1897 he attended East Anglia School (now Culford School) at Bury St. Edmunds, Suffolk, where he "found refuge from home life and suburban suppression." What he liked best was life in the dormitory after eight, when he often entertained his classmates with improvised stories from remembered readings. He loved ideas and wanted to write, but he had the notion that in order to become a writer, a person "should loaf at a university." "Fortunately," he said, "nothing came of it." Rather, in 1897 he went to work. Later he thought that the "form and contour of this world comes to us through our hands."

At the age of seventeen McFee was apprenticed in mechanical engineering to Richard Moreland and Sons in McMuirland's Engineering Shops, Aldergate, at £100 a year. "At the end of the three years," he wrote, ". . . I was fired." He worked briefly at a waterworks pumping job at Tring and thereafter joined a large Yorkshire firm that manufactured laundry machinery. He then worked in London as an assistant to Thomas George Nelson, a consulting engineer, and learned selling and designing; later he traveled for the firm in the south of England. He had the opportunity to read and even to write; he remembered this period as his "university training." He spent Saturday afternoons at the British Museum and evenings at Northampton Institute. The artist Arthur Elder persuaded McFee to live in Chelsea, where he met artists and writers, including Oliver Onions and Hilaire Belloc. McFee became interested in socialism, and he lectured on Rudyard Kipling. After four years as a commercial traveler, McFee was consumed with the ambition to write, read, travel, talk, and "achieve distinction." In 1906, with the help of his uncle, a marine superintendent in London, McFee became a junior marine engineer on a tramp steamer bound for Genoa.

In September 1907, back in London, McFee passed the Board of Trade examination (with a grade of 98 percent); by November he had shipped on the SS *Burrsfield* as third engineer. His first book, *Letters from an Ocean Tramp* (1908), records the impressions of a third engineer on a trading steamer. The letters are filled with moral philosophy and literary allusions. Inspired in part by the writings of the Fabian socialists Beatrice and Sidney Webb, McFee began work on *Casuals of the Sea* (1916), the story of a middle-class family struggling against the laws of economics. This novel established his literary reputation.

By 1912, McFee had come to America to write. After a farewell walking tour from Glasgow to London, he sailed to Wilmington,

N.C., and then joined his artist friend Arthur Elder and his wife, who lived in New Jersey. While trying to have his novels published, McFee worked as a copywriter for J. Fischer and Brothers, the New York music publishers.

In 1913 he obtained a chief's license in the American merchant marine and joined the United Fruit Company, first in New York and then in New Orleans, as a member of its port engineering staff. Two months after the outbreak of World War I, he returned to England to enlist in the armed forces. Refused by the army, he was appointed an engineer on a British transport and later became a sublieutenant in the British naval reserve, serving mostly in the Mediterranean. When the war ended, he returned to the United States, living with the Elders again and writing.

In 1920, McFee married Pauline Khondoff, a Bulgarian refugee whom he had met during the war. They settled in Westport, Conn., the home of his maternal ancestors, but for two years he returned to the United Fruit Company as chief engineer, commuting between New York City and the Spanish Main, on ships carrying both passengers and bananas. During each voyage, he read classical and modern writers and wrote. In 1922 he quit the sea to devote all his time to writing. In the next three decades he produced more than thirty volumes, including novels, essays, memoirs, articles, letters, and book reviews. For a while he also wrote a weekly column on shipping for the *New York Sun*.

McFee became an American citizen on May 6, 1925. In 1932, after divorcing his first wife, he married Beatrice Allender, a novelist. After her death in 1952, McFee published little but continued to write. On July 24, 1965, he married Dorothy North, whom he had known since the 1920's and who had served as his housekeeper since 1963. He died in New Milford, Conn.

Although the sea is central to McFee's writing, his major theme is "the problem of human folly." His writing, lucid and colorful, reflects his vast reading and his seafaring experiences. Reviewers saw him as a first-rate storyteller, a master of characterization, and a good craftsman. He often used a narrator to tell his story. Notable is his creation of an alter ego, the garrulous and ironic chief engineer Spenlove, who is introduced in *Captain Macedoine's Daughter* (1920) and appears in *The Harbourmaster* (1931), *The Beachcomber* (1935), *Derelicts* (1938), *Spenlove in Arcady* (1941), and *Family Trouble* (1949). In these and other works, McFee left a nostalgic account of seafaring life in the early twentieth century.

[McFee's papers are in Yale's Beinecke Library; his autobiography, "The City and the Sea," and his diary remain unpublished. His autobiographical works include *Harbours of Memory* (1920; essays); *An Engineer's Note Book: Essays on Life and Letters* (1921); *The Gates of the Caribbean* (1922); *The Reflections of Marsyas* (1933); *Watch Below* (1940); and *In the First Watch* (1946). His other writings are *Aliens* (1914); *Command* (1922); *Race* (1924); *Swallowing the Anchor* (1925); *Sunlight in New Grenada* (1925); *Guatemala* (1926); *The Life of Sir Martin Frobisher* (1928); *Pilgrims of Adversity* (1928); *Sailors of Fortune* (1929); *Born to Be Hanged* (1930); *No Castle in Spain* (1933); *David Stanley Livingstone* (1936); *Ship to Shore* (1944); *The Law of the Sea* (1941); and *Port of Lonely Men* (1953). McFee also contributed the "Introduction and Notes" to James T. Babb, *A Bibliography of the Writings of William McFee;* and comments by him are in Harry Edward Maule, *William McFee, with Bibliography* (1928).

On McFee, see the piece by Lucille Gulliver in the *Boston Evening Transcript*, July 3, 1925; H. R. Warfel, *American Novelists of Today* (1951); and Donald M. Martin, "The Sea Novels of William McFee" (Ph.D. diss., University of Michigan, 1958). An obituary is in the *New York Times*, July 4, 1966.]

JOHN E. HART

McGILL, RALPH EMERSON (Feb. 5, 1898–Feb. 3, 1969), journalist, was born on a farm at Igou's Ferry, Tenn., the son of Benjamin Franklin McGill and Mary Lou Skillern. The family moved to the coal town of Soddy, where his father took a miner's job, and then to Chattanooga, where he became a clerk. McGill's father's middle name had been changed, and the boy's name chosen, with a bow to literary culture, and the education of this only son was a key concern of the family. McGill's health did not permit him to begin school until he was eight. He enrolled at Vanderbilt University in 1917, dropped out to enter the marines, and then returned for three years to study. In college he was interested in a circle of "fugitive" writers and in the football team, on which he played guard. McGill was expelled from Vanderbilt in 1922 for a prank played on a rival fraternity, and so he did not receive a degree. He wrote for the *Nashville Banner* while in school and became a full-time reporter soon after leaving the university.

McGill rose rapidly in journalism, for he wrote lucidly and quickly and was drawn to stories with broad appeal. A ruminative man, he found reporting to be a tonic. He made his mark in the profession through his coverage of Floyd Collins, who was trapped in a cave, one of the biggest newspaper stories of the 1920's. McGill's folksy "I'm the Gink" column was syndicated and his sports reporting was widely admired. Unlike many other reporters, he remained in, and loved, the South and had a brooding concern with racial issues.

McGill was hired by the *Atlanta Constitution* in 1929 as an assistant sports editor. (On September 4 of that year, he married Mary Elizabeth Leonard in Atlanta; they had three children.) McGill was a leading editorial voice of the *Constitution* by thc end of the decade, and in 1942 he became editor in chief, a position that made him a spokesman for the South. After the Civil War, Henry Grady, the publisher, had used this paper as a pulpit for his "New South" creed. Clark Howell followed with an editorial policy of moderation on racial issues and encouragement for modern industry and agriculture. McGill worked at Grady's rolltop desk under Howell's protecting hand.

McGill was an effervescent Democratic partisan. When he returned from the 1936 Democratic National Convention, he attempted to urinate on members of the Georgia delegation who made the mistake of ridiculing the New Deal in the bar car of their train. At the 1952 convention McGill jumped on his desk to cheer the nomination of Adlai E. Stevenson, bringing 220 pounds down on the hand of a fellow reporter. In his daily column on the front page of the *Constitution*, McGill struck the expected notes of regional celebration. He had a fine ear for country dialogue, and he took readers with him across the rural South; hunting dogs, football teams, and agricultural agents often appeared in his column. In the face of Atlanta's growth and the lure of urban life, McGill's columns were daily assurance that the intoxicating landscape, plain talk, and rhythms of the King James Bible had survived.

Slowly, but even more eloquently, McGill went beyond the New South creed and told Georgians that segregation and all forms of discrimination must cease. McGill recalled that he had not seen a black person before he was six years old and that in East Tennessee, with its small farms and Unionist heritage, the subjugation of blacks was not covered with glorious memories of the plantation and the lost cause. McGill welcomed blacks to his home in Atlanta, often repaying their social visits. Many Georgians in positions of authority heard McGill on their phone arguing for generosity or simple fairness for blacks.

Before the 1950's, McGill spoke out against lynchings but opposed federal intervention in such cases. The *Constitution* also opposed fair-employment-practices legislation. McGill opposed Jim Crow regulations only when the separate facilities for blacks were not equal. He initially opposed integrated schools. After the Supreme Court ruled against segregated schools in *Brown* v. *Board of Education* (1954), McGill, in the face of broad resistance to the court order, argued that the law must be obeyed and that integration was a positive good. McGill also defended the subsequent "freedom rides" and sit-ins against segregation in public facilities, and he supported court orders and the use of federal troops to open southern universities to blacks, as well as the marches and legal actions that gave blacks the power of the ballot.

McGill was reviled and threatened for his crusading and some readers and advertising revenue were lost; he was protected by his friendship with Robert W. Woodruff, the president of the Coca-Cola Company. And the Cox newspaper organization had bought the *Constitution* in 1949, placing McGill in the employ of Governor James M. Cox of Ohio, an important liberal Democrat who did not follow the business logic of restraining McGill's challenge to racial mores. As in many news organizations, McGill's effort to mold public opinion in a period of controversy made for caution in other aspects of journalism. The *Constitution* made little effort to cover the civil rights revolution in its own backyard.

McGill's courage brought him a shower of honors in the last fifteen years of his life. He became a fixture on foundation boards and State Department tours. McGill was loved for the enemies he had made and for the sympathies he shared with the broad coalition in favor of civil rights. All his life, for example, McGill had reported on developing countries. He published *Israel Revisited* (1950), on his travels in that nation, and he won a Pulitzer Prize in 1959 for an editorial on the bombing of an Atlanta synagogue.

McGill did not believe himself to be, as some of his enemies and admirers said, a southern man with northern principles. The North was not his model. He claimed to know nothing more than what every southerner could see: blacks haunted whites in a segregated society, and integration freed whites as much as blacks. McGill closely followed historians, such as C. Vann Woodward, who argued that there had always been flexibility in southern racial mores. Thus, McGill's journalism was more closely keyed to southern notions of guilt and tradition than to northern ideas of justice. McGill's defense of the American role in Vietnam was also loud and confident. Patriotism, anti-Communism, and national service seemed all the more important to cling to because they had also been challenged.

His first wife died in 1962; he married Mary Lynn Morgan, a dentist, on Apr. 20, 1967. He died in Atlanta.

[McGill's papers are in the Woodruff Library, Emory University. His book *The South and the Southerner* (1963) is largely autobiographical. The editorial honored by a Pulitzer is in *A Church, a School* (1959). *The Fleas Come with the Dog* (1954) is the only other collection of his columns about the American scene. Calvin M. Logue, ed., *No Place to Hide*, 2 vols. (1984), is a comprehensive collection of McGill's work. Harold M. Martin, *Ralph McGill, Reporter* (1973), is by a colleague on the *Constitution*. See also the memoir by Eugene C. Patterson in the *Washington Post*, May 18, 1976. Paul Gaston, *The New South Creed* (1970), sets the stage for McGill's career. Obituaries are in the *New York Times* and the *Atlanta Constitution*, both Feb. 4, 1969.]

THOMAS C. LEONARD

McGRATH, JAMES HOWARD (Nov. 28, 1903–Sept. 2, 1966), governor of Rhode Island and United States senator and attorney general, was born in Woonsocket, R.I., the son of James J. McGrath, an Irish immigrant who owned a real estate and insurance business, and Ida Eleanor May. McGrath graduated from Providence's La Salle Academy in 1922; he received his Ph.B. from Providence College in 1926 and his LL.B from Boston University Law School in 1929. He was admitted to the Rhode Island bar and began practice the same year, specializing in labor law. He married Estelle Arnette Cadorette on Nov. 28, 1929; they had one child.

McGrath worked for the Democratic party while at Providence College. In 1924 he helped found the Young Men's Democratic League of Rhode Island and served as its first president. He became vice-chairman of the Rhode Island Democratic State Committee in 1928 and chairman from 1930 to 1934. He was chairman of the Rhode Island delegation to the 1932 Democratic National Convention; he served as a delegate in 1936 and to all of the national conventions from 1944 to 1960.

McGrath began his political career in 1930 as the city solicitor of Central Falls, R.I., a position he held until 1934, when he was appointed United States attorney for the district of Rhode Island. In 1940 he won the Democratic gubernatorial nomination. He defeated the incumbent, William H. Vanderbilt, and was reelected in 1942 and 1944. As governor, he effected revision of the state tax structure, as well as legislation establishing a state labor-relations board and a sickness compensation fund. He promoted state aid to cities, revised the juvenile-court system, and presided at a state constitutional convention. In October 1945, President Truman appointed him solicitor general of the United States. In this position McGrath successfully defended the constitutionality of the Public Holding Company Act and the conviction of Japan's General Tomoyuki Yamashita for war crimes. In 1946, McGrath was elected United States senator from Rhode Island.

As senator, McGrath was known as a liberal who consistently supported administration policies. He opposed the Taft-Hartley Act, the removal of wartime economic controls, and the reduction of income taxes; supported a loan to Britain; advocated wider social security measures; and cosponsored bills for national health insurance and federal aid to education.

In October 1947, McGrath was elected chairman of the Democratic National Committee. He did not give up his senatorial post but refused any financial compensation for his work as chairman. Despite widespread pessimism within the party, he felt that the Democrats could win the 1948 presidential election and set out to unite the party in support of Truman. His management of the campaign helped produce Truman's upset of Thomas Dewey in November. In the same year, his book, *The Power of the People*, was published. At his suggestion the staff at the Democratic headquarters was desegregated, and he introduced the administration's civil rights bill in the Senate on Apr. 28, 1949.

McGrath left the Senate to assume the office of United States attorney general on Aug. 24, 1949. In this post he was a strong advocate of civil rights. The Justice Department for the first time challenged the constitutionality of racial segregation, with McGrath arguing three landmark cases before the Supreme Court in April 1950. In one of these cases, the Court outlawed discriminatory dining arrangements in railroad cars. McGrath was a strong defender of the administration's loyalty program, recommending that Truman refuse Senator Joseph McCarthy's request that the government disclose the contents of its loyalty files to his committee. Overall, however, McGrath was not considered a particularly effective attorney general because he reportedly left much of the administration of the Justice Department to subordinates, supplying little or no supervision.

In late 1951, a House Ways and Means subcommittee uncovered evidence of corruption in the Bureau of Internal Revenue and the Tax Division of the Justice Department. In January 1952, Truman announced that the Justice Department would investigate and clean up any corruption in the government, but critics pointed out that the Justice Department was itself suspect. On February 1, Truman appointed Newbold Morris, an independent New York Republican, as special assistant to the attorney general to investigate the charges. When Morris began his probe, McGrath promised his full support and cooperation, but he had second thoughts in March when Morris asked that McGrath and over 500 top Justice officials each fill out a detailed financial questionnaire. At first McGrath indicated his willingness to complete the form, but on March 31, while testifying before a House Judiciary subcommittee, McGrath said that the questionnaire was a violation of individual rights and an invasion of privacy. He indicated that he had not decided whether to fill out his form or require his subordinates to do so. Three days later, apparently without presidential mandate, McGrath fired Morris; and later that day, Truman asked for, and received, the attorney general's resignation. McGrath's sense of humor came to the fore when he sent his successor a wire saying, "My heartiest congratulations and I suggest you bring a pair of asbestos trousers with you." In 1960 he made public a letter from Truman, dated Apr. 18, 1955, which he considered an apology. It said in part, "The happenings in the Newbold Morris case were very disturbing to me. I want you to know that my fondness for you has not changed one bit. Political situations sometimes cause me much pain."

After leaving government service, McGrath returned to the practice of law and the management of his many business interests. He made two more sorties into the political arena. In 1956 he was campaign manager for Senator Estes Kefauver's unsuccessful bid for the Democratic presidential nomination and remained to manage Kefauver's vice-presidential campaign. In 1960 he lost a Democratic primary race for the United States Senate. He died in Narragansett, R.I.

[McGrath's papers are in the Truman Library in Independence, Mo. See Milton Mackaze, "He'll Sink or Swim with Harry," *Saturday Evening Post*, May 29, 1948; "National Affairs," *Time*, Aug. 8, 1949, and Apr. 14, 1952; Richard H. Rovere, "A Reporter at Large," *New Yorker*, Apr. 19, 1952; Cabell Phillips, *The Truman Presidency* (1966); Irwin Ross, *The Loneliest Campaign* (1968); Harold F. Gosnell, *Truman's Crisis* (1980); and Robert J. Donovan, *Tumultuous Years* (1982). An obituary is in the *New York Times*, Sept. 3, 1966.]

ANNA B. PERRY

MACIVER, ROBERT MORRISON (Apr. 17, 1882–June 15, 1970), political philosopher and sociologist, was born in Stornoway, Isle of Lewis, Scotland, the son of Donald Morrison MacIver, a middle-class clothing merchant, and Christine Morrison (or Morison). The parochial and fundamentalist environment of the island people impressed upon him the importance of community and social values. MacIver attended Nicolson Institute on the island until the age of sixteen, learning the classics in a disciplined environment. He continued classical studies at Edinburgh University, from which he graduated in 1903. He then attended Oxford and obtained his graduate degree in 1907. He earned a Ph.D. from Edinburgh in 1915. His classroom work was in the classics and philosophy, but in informal sessions he learned political science and was introduced to sociology.

In 1907, MacIver began teaching at Kings

College, Aberdeen. He first taught the classics but then added political science and inaugurated the teaching of sociology there. On Aug. 14, 1911, he married Ethel Marion Peterkin; they had three children.

In 1915, distressed with European politics and troubled by a misunderstanding with a colleague at Aberdeen, MacIver accepted a professorship of political science at the University of Toronto. His new life in Canada was only a brief reprieve from the war; he joined the Canadian war effort, serving on the War Labor Board while still teaching. He described the experience in *Labor in the Changing World* (1919). His first book, and one of his best-known works, was *Community* (1917), which describes the social evolution of humans as a liberating experience whereby the socialization of community life contributes to individualism.

The variety of immigrants in Canada made MacIver aware of ethnic groups and their problems. He became active in social-work training, encountering problems of academic freedom when he was forced, for political reasons, to cancel a lecture by Jane Addams, whom he had invited to the campus. Both experiences influenced later work. In *The Modern State* (1926) he distinguished government from society and introduced sociological perspective into political science.

In 1927, MacIver was invited to head Barnard College's Department of Economics and Sociology and to teach political theory in the graduate school at Columbia University. (He became an American citizen at about this date.) He was amazed at the variety of students he met in the United States and spent much time with them while writing *The Contribution of Sociology to Social Work* (1931). During the Great Depression, the president of Columbia University asked him to head a commission of economists and others to make recommendations to revive the economy. Out of the conference, he produced the report *Economic Reconstruction* (1934), which seemed of little value to him initially but parts of which were adopted by the Roosevelt administration, in particular, those relating to banking and monetary policy.

A major task was to rebuild the sociology department at Columbia, which he described as an "agonizingly long process." He attracted Robert Lynd to the department with the intent of promoting study of the community, but Lynd's shift of interest from community studies to national issues, such as education, took the department in new directions. MacIver assumed duties with the American Council of Learned Societies, the American Academy of Arts and Sciences, and community-oriented organizations such as the American Civil Liberties Union and the Russell Sage Foundation. He developed close relations with the New School for Social Research and its president, Alvin Johnson. Before his final service as head of the sociology department, he wrote *Society* (1931), in which he sought to clarify basic concepts in sociology and introduced his theories of social class and social change. In *Leviathan and the People* (1939) he warned about dictatorships and emphasized the necessity of protecting democracy.

When Columbia added Robert Merton and Paul Lazarsfeld to the sociology department, MacIver, freed from administrative duties, was able to buy a country home and spend time collecting mushrooms, a favorite hobby. He wrote numerous articles on the impending war and undertook various summer assignments, one of which introduced him to Eleanor Roosevelt, and in the summer of 1943 the State Department sent him to Mexico to promote relations with Mexican scholars and writers. (He also taught a few social science classes at the Colegio de México.) He wrote what he considered his most serious work in sociology, *Social Causation* (1942), but was disappointed by its reception among sociologists. It was followed by *Towards an Abiding Peace* (1943), which warned against stereotyping Germans and Japanese.

MacIver turned again to political philosophy at the end of the war to write his most prized book in the field, *The Web of Government* (1947). He set the forms and functions of government against a background of theory extending from Hobbes down to the present. The book stresses the importance he gave to incorporating a humanist perspective into political science. He followed that work with a call for the application of theory to the solution of the problems of minorities in the United States. He raised the subject in the Institute for Religious and Social Studies, an outlet that allowed him to edit books on a variety of subjects, and published his own thinking in *The More Perfect Union* (1948), where he clarified the workings of the "vicious circle" of discrimination. He included discrimination among the problems of democracy in outlining its strengths and weaknesses in *The Ramparts We Guard* (1956).

The protection of individual liberty and personal freedom was a constant concern for MacIver. He understood that Americans confused individualism with laissez-faire capitalism but continually encountered opposition in showing the necessity of distinguishing between them. His concern with the protection of individual rights is expressed throughout his work and exemplified in *Academic Freedom in Our Time* (1955).

Although MacIver had to retire from Columbia in 1950, he continued to lecture as a visiting professor, to write, and to serve on various commissions. His lectures at the University of Michigan Law School were published as *Democracy and the Economic Challenge* (1952), and he wrote what he described as "my first book of untrammelled reflections," *The Pursuit of Happiness* (1955). The Carnegie Foundation gave him the assignment of summarizing and evaluating the reports of the signatory countries of the United Nations on their experience with the international body in preparation for a revised organization. The project spanned several years because of delays by members in reporting, but its findings appeared as *The Nations and the United Nations* (1959). During this time Mayor Robert Wagner asked MacIver to undertake a study of juvenile delinquency in New York City. His criticism of the public schools and other city agencies led to years of conflict, but eventual reforms were instituted because of his recommendations.

While in retirement, MacIver also served on the Board of Directors of the New School for Social Research; in 1963 he became its president and, later, chancellor until 1966. Despite administrative and fund-raising duties, he continued to direct research projects and never ceased writing. Two years before his death in New York, he published his autobiography, *As a Tale That Is Told*.

[See Robert Bierstedt, *American Sociological Theory* (1981). Obituaries are in the *New York Times*, June 16, 1970; and *Political Science Quarterly*, Sept. 1971.]

ERNEST L. SCHUSKY

McKAY, DAVID OMAN (Sept. 8, 1873–Jan. 18, 1970), missionary and ninth president of the Church of Jesus Christ of Latter-Day Saints (LDS), was born in Huntsville, Utah, the son of David McKay, a farmer, and Jennette Eveline Evans. His father was a native of Scotland, and his mother, of Wales. They supported their family on a subsistence farm in the Mormon village of Huntsville, three miles east of Ogden, Utah. The father, bishop of the Huntsville LDS Ward for twenty years, served three terms in the Utah State Senate and was one of the founders of Weber State College.

McKay was educated at the Huntsville Ward grade school and Weber Stake Academy (high school) and was installed as principal of the grade school when he was twenty. In 1897 he graduated from the University of Utah with a B.A. in pedagogy. He played on the university's first football team, was elected president of his class, and gave the valedictory address.

McKay was then called to serve a proselytizing mission for the LDS Church in Scotland, where he remained for two years. During most of that period he served as president of the Scottish Conference. After returning to Utah, he became an instructor and later principal at Weber Stake Academy (now Weber State College) in Ogden. On Jan. 2, 1901, he married Emma Ray Riggs; they had seven children.

In 1906 McKay was sustained as a member of the Council of the Twelve Apostles of the Church of Jesus Christ of Latter-day Saints, and he held that position until 1934, when he became a member of the First Presidency of the church. McKay's assignments as a full-time church official included service as a member of the General Superintendency of the Sunday Schools (1906–1934) and as church commissioner of education (1919–1922); and an official tour of all the foreign missions of the church (1920–1921) that took him to the South Seas, Australia, Egypt, Jerusalem, Europe, and Great Britain. He was president of the European Mission from 1922 to 1924.

McKay subsequently filled several civic assignments. He was chairman of the Utah State Advisory Committee of the American Red Cross, chairman of the Utah Council for Child Health and Protection, chairman of the Utah Centennial Commission, regent of the University of Utah, and member of the board of trustees of Utah State University and Brigham Young University. He was also a director of Zion's Savings Bank and Trust Company, the Utah First National Bank, the Heber J. Grant Insurance Company, the Utah Home Fire

Insurance Company, the Beneficial Life Insurance Company, Zion's Securities Corporation, and Zion's Co-operative Mercantile Institution.

Beginning in 1934, McKay helped to establish the Church Welfare Program, designed to provide work and welfare assistance for those suffering from depression-caused privation and want. During World War II he helped to direct special programs designed to benefit the church and its members.

In 1950 David O. McKay became the senior apostle of the church, and on Apr. 9, 1951, he was sustained as president of the church. He retained this office until his death, in Salt Lake City, Utah.

Tall, with wavy white hair (black when he was younger) and hazel-brown eyes characterized by one newsman as "fiercely tender," McKay looked like the prophet that the Latter-day Saints believed him to be. He was a popular and forceful personality and an effective speaker who flavored his talks with quotations from Robert Burns, Shakespeare, Sir Walter Scott, Charles Dickens, and others.

As president of the church, McKay supported the growth of Brigham Young University, stepped up foreign missionary activity, actively recruited new industries to communities where Mormons settled, and sought to improve the status of church auxiliaries. From 1951 to 1970 the number of Latter-day Saints rose from 1.1 million to 2.9 million, the number of stakes (dioceses) increased from 184 to 500, and the missionary force expanded from 2,000 to 13,000. Under McKay's leadership more than 3,750 chapels, seminaries, and other buildings were constructed, including temples in Switzerland, England, New Zealand, and California. He dedicated the huge record vault in a granite mountain near Salt Lake City.

Traveling more widely than any earlier president, McKay visited church members and dedicated chapels in South Africa, South America, Central America, the South Sea Islands, and Great Britain. He directed the organization of student wards and stakes on the campuses of many universities attended by LDS students. He also supervised the completion of the $10 million David O. McKay Hospital in Ogden and the Visitors Center and Salt Lake Temple Annex in Salt Lake City, and he initiated the construction of the twenty-six-story Church Office Building completed in 1972 in Salt Lake City. His approach was personal rather than doctrinal, and he encouraged freedom of opinion and speech. He took a strong stand against Communism and issued official statements supporting civil rights for blacks and other minorities. His public relations program included sermons on the CBS "Church of the Air" and the establishment of the Mormon Pavilion at the New York World's Fair in 1964.

McKay's sixty-four-year service as a general authority of the church is the longest in Mormon history, and his thirty-six years in the First Presidency was exceeded only by Joseph F. Smith. Asked to describe his greatest accomplishment, McKay said, "Making the church a worldwide organization." He is also remembered for his emphasis on the family, and for his statement: "No other success can compensate for failure in the home."

[McKay's diary and papers are in the possession of David Lawrence McKay, his son, in Salt Lake City; there is also a substantial body of papers in the archives of the LDS Historical Department, Salt Lake City. Compilations of his sermons and writings include Clare Middlemiss, comp., *Cherished Experiences from the Writings of President David O. McKay* (1955); and David O. McKay, *Treasures of Life* (1963). There are numerous articles by and about McKay in *The Improvement Era*, 1906–1970. Biographies include Llewelyn R. McKay, *Home Memories of President David O. McKay* (1956); Jeanette McKay Morrell, *Highlights in the Life of President David O. McKay* (1956); and Francis M. Gibbons, *David O. McKay* (1986). See also James B. Allen, "David O. McKay," in *The Presidents of the Church*, Leonard J. Arrington, ed. (1986); and the obituary in the *New York Times*, Jan. 19, 1970.]

LEONARD J. ARRINGTON

MACNIDER, HANFORD (Oct. 2, 1889–Feb. 17, 1968), businessman and army officer, was born in Mason City, Iowa, the son of Charles Henry McNider, a banker, and May Elizabeth Hanford. Until his teenage years he used the name McNider. When it was discovered that his grandfather had dropped the "a," his father, who was unable to change his own name because of legal complications, insisted that Hanford return to the original spelling.

The son of Mason City's most prominent citizen, MacNider spent summers sailing and fishing, and learned to use his fists at an early age to defend himself from local toughs.

In 1907 MacNider graduated from Milton Academy, in Massachusetts, and he received a B.A. from Harvard in 1911. Following a round-the-world trip (a graduation present from his father), he returned to Mason City and joined the First National Bank as an apprentice bookkeeper.

As MacNider rose rapidly through the ranks in his father's bank, he grew increasingly restless with the fixed direction of his life. In 1916, after leading a drive to build a new armory for the local infantry company, he was elected a second lieutenant in the Iowa National Guard. When his company was called into federal service and sent to the Mexican border, he quickly developed a deep affection for the comradeship of military life.

After the United States entered World War I in 1917, MacNider gave up his commission and enlisted in the regular army. He completed the officers' training course and joined the Ninth Regiment of the Second (Indianhead) Division. He arrived in France and was assigned as an instructor at the Army Candidate School at Langres. Impatient for action, he left the school without permission and rejoined his unit as it prepared for combat.

MacNider was adjutant of the Ninth Regiment when it went into battle on Sept. 12, 1918, the first day of the St. Mihiel offensive. Carrying instructions to the front, he found the advance being held up by machine-gun fire. He led an attack that captured the gun, receiving the first of three Distinguished Service Crosses. He was discharged in 1919, a much-decorated lieutenant colonel.

Following the war MacNider became active in veterans' affairs. In 1920–1921 he served as Iowa state commander of the newly organized American Legion. Elected to a one-year term as national commander in 1921, MacNider led the fight for an adjusted compensation, or bonus, for veterans. As chairman of the Republican Service League in 1924 he organized veterans in support of Republican regional and national candidates. He played a similar role during the presidential campaigns of 1928 and 1932. MacNider married Margaret Elizabeth McAuley on Feb. 20, 1925; they had three children.

MacNider's increasing public prominence led to governmental appointments during the administrations of Calvin Coolidge and Herbert Hoover. From 1925 to 1928 he served as assistant secretary of war. In charge of procurement, MacNider was especially interested in developing plans to mobilize industry in the event of war. Although budgetary restraints prevented full implementation of his ideas, they later were used by the War Department on the eve of American entry into World War II.

In 1930 MacNider was named American minister to Canada. The *New York Times* hailed the appointment, characterizing him as a man of wide contacts and boundless energy who had "a gift of speaking his mind in vigorous Anglo-Saxon soldier talk without making enemies." Canadians appreciated his forthright, friendly manner, and he became a popular figure in Ottawa. Charged with facilitating negotiation of a treaty for the development of a Great Lakes–St. Lawrence River waterway, he was successful in his efforts, although the agreement became bogged down in the Senate and was not approved until 1953. He resigned in June 1932 to campaign for President Hoover's reelection.

MacNider devoted most of his time and attention during the 1930's to business enterprises in Mason City. He reorganized his family's major holding, the Northwestern States Portland Cement Company, and nurtured its growth into one of America's largest producers. Adamantly against unions, MacNider in 1936 pioneered employee profit sharing.

A strong critic of the New Deal, MacNider accused President Franklin D. Roosevelt of conducting socialistic experiments and undermining the Constitution. He was equally unhappy with Roosevelt's foreign policy. An isolationist, MacNider became prominent in the America First movement, serving as the organization's national vice-chairman in 1941. However, when the United States entered World War II, he sought and obtained recall to active duty.

MacNider saw extensive action in the southwest Pacific. Promoted to brigadier general in 1942, he commanded a task force (the Warren Force) of the 128th Infantry Regiment during an assault against Japanese positions at Buna, on the northern coast of New Guinea. MacNider won his third Distinguished Service Cross in this battle. Severely wounded by an enemy grenade on Nov. 23, 1942, he was evacuated to Australia. Although he later required medical treatment in the United States, MacNider returned in time to command the

158th Regimental Combat Team during the fighting on Luzon in the Philippines.

MacNider returned to Mason City after the war. He rose to the rank of major general in the reserves and commanded the 103rd Infantry (Reserve) Division before retiring in 1951. He continued in business and in local philanthropy until his death in Sarasota, Fla.

[The MacNider papers are in the Herbert Hoover Presidential Library, West Branch, Iowa. "The Many Lives of Hanford MacNider," *Iowan*, Spring 1965, is the best summary of his life. See Richard S. Jones, *A History of the American Legion* (1946); and Wayne S. Cole, *Roosevelt and the Isolationists, 1932–45* (1983).]

WILLIAM M. LEARY

MALLINCKRODT, EDWARD, JR. (Nov. 17, 1878–Jan. 19, 1967), chemist, chemical manufacturer, and philanthropist, was born in St. Louis, Mo., the son of Edward Mallinckrodt, the owner of a family chemical manufacturing firm founded in 1867, and Jennie Anderson. The rapidly growing Mallinckrodt Chemical Works produced chloroform, carbolic acid, and refined chemical salts in an easy-to-use granular form. Mallinckrodt attended Smith Academy, a preparatory school for boys allied with Washington University in St. Louis. He then studied at Harvard University, where he was awarded a B.A. cum laude in 1900. His interest in chemistry led him to remain for graduate study in a department that included Theodore W. Richards, who in 1914 would become the first American to win the Nobel Prize in chemistry. Mallinckrodt received his M.A. in 1901. Although he expressed an interest in an academic career, his father persuaded him to return to St. Louis to use his talents in the family firm, a decision he never regretted.

Mallinckrodt spent much of his early career in the laboratory studying the properties of ether as an anesthetic. He developed the first continuous distillation equipment for the production of ether, which eliminated impurities such as peroxides, aldehydes, and acids and exceeded the standards established by the United States Pharmacopeia. The packaging of ether was also improved to eliminate the dangerous deterioration that occurred during storage. His study of the interaction of ether with various materials continued for many years. He published several papers and was awarded sixteen patents as a result of his research. On June 3, 1911, Mallinckrodt married Elizabeth Baker Elliot, the daughter of a prominent St. Louis family; they had three children.

Mallinckrodt was primarily responsible for the technical activities of the firm until 1928, when, following the death of his father, he became chairman of the board. Mallinckrodt Chemical had become one of the three leading firms in its field, and throughout the 1930's it remained a leader of the fine-chemical industry. He remained active in the supervision of laboratory research at the company and in the development of new products and processes, including products for photoengraving plates, contrast media for X-ray diagnosis, radiopharmaceuticals, and a process for separation of columbium and tantalum from their ores.

In April 1942, Arthur H. Compton of the Manhattan Project proposed that Mallinckrodt Chemical manufacture the purified uranium salts necessary for the construction of the atomic pile at the University of Chicago. The first self-sustaining nuclear reaction took place on Dec. 2, 1942, using uranium dioxide and uranium metal prepared from Mallinckrodt products. The company continued to process uranium throughout World War II and to produce nuclear fuels for military use and power plants until 1961.

Although Mallinckrodt preferred that the company remain a small family-owned concern, he yielded to the advice of his managers to further expand and to offer stock in the company to the public. By 1966, the Mallinckrodt Chemical Works was producing sales of $59 million and earnings of $3.6 million. Mallinckrodt retired as chairman of the board in December 1965 and was named honorary chairman.

An avid admirer of Theodore Roosevelt, Mallinckrodt shared the president's enthusiasm for big-game hunting, mountain climbing, and photography. His own expeditions took him to Alaska and eastern Africa. In the 1920's, using a lightweight, spring-driven movie camera mounted on a gunstock, he was able to make some of the earliest films of wildlife and of mountain climbers. He was also interested in conservation and worked for the preservation of tracts of land in the Adirondacks and at the site of Dinosaur National Monument in Colorado and Utah.

Mallinckrodt's generous gifts to education and medicine totaled many millions of dollars. A large endowment was given to establish the Mallinckrodt Institute of Radiology in St. Louis in memory of his father. Chairs in anesthesiology were established at Harvard and at Washington University in memory of his middle son, who died of a heart ailment in 1945. His gifts to the Harvard Divinity School helped it become a major center for religious studies. He contributed to Washington University's Louderman Chemistry Building, its engineering development fund, and its fluid science research, as well as to the Shields Radiation Research Laboratory in Boston. He endowed Ward 4 at Massachusetts General Hospital for the study of baffling diseases, and his will included large bequests to Harvard and Washington universities. Described as a shy and retiring man who seldom gave speeches, his philanthropies were often anonymous. In 1952 he was given the gold medal of the Midwest Award by the St. Louis Section of the American Chemical Society for his research and activities as a scientist and industry leader. In 1962 he received the Horace Marden Albright Medal for leadership in the field of scientific preservation and the St. Louis Humanistic Award for his works, which "have shown an enduring love and compassion for mankind." He was killed in New York in the explosion of a private plane.

[Material on Mallinckrodt is in the archives of Mallinckrodt, Inc., Washington University; Christ Church Cathedral, St. Louis; and the University of Missouri–St. Louis. See also Williams Haynes, *The American Chemical Industry: A History* (1945–1954); and Wyndham D. Miles, ed., *American Chemists and Chemical Engineers* (1976). Obituaries are in the *New York Times*, Jan. 20, 1967; and *Chemical and Engineering News*, 45, no. 6 (1967).]

JANE A. MILLER

MANSFIELD, JAYNE (Apr. 19, 1933–June 29, 1967), actress and entertainer, was born Vera Jayne Palmer in Bryn Mawr, Pa., the daughter of Herbert Palmer, an attorney and politician, and Vera Jeffrey, a kindergarten teacher. Her father died when Mansfield was three, and three years later her mother remarried and moved the family to Dallas. Mansfield attended Highland Park High School, and on May 6, 1950, married Paul Mansfield, a teenage boyfriend. Following the birth of a daughter in November, she enrolled with her husband at the University of Texas. After her husband was drafted in 1952, Mansfield accompanied him to Camp Gordon, Ga., where she appeared in army shows and created a sensation offstage by appearing in bikinis and leotards.

When her husband left for Korea, Mansfield returned to Dallas, where she studied drama and appeared in local television plays. There she became "Miss Photoflash," the first in a long series of glamour titles that she was to hold. Determined to become a star, she persuaded her husband in April 1954 that they should set out for Hollywood. After six months, he returned to Dallas, but Mansfield stayed on to win small parts on the television program "Lux Video Theatre" and in the film *The Female Jungle* (also titled *Hangover*; 1956), in which she played a nymphomaniac. She also hired an agent who established her long and cordial relationship with the press, generating publicity that became an end in itself. In January 1955 her agent got her aboard a plane carrying press people to a film premiere in Florida. She made a spectacular bikini appearance and courted the reporters. Overnight she became a starlet and was sought by several studios. At Warner Brothers in 1955 she had parts in *Pete Kelly's Blues*, with Jack Webb; *Illegal*, with Edward G. Robinson; and *Hell on Frisco Bay*, with Robinson and Alan Ladd. She then starred in an independent comedy, *The Burglar* (1956).

Though the studio dropped her contract, Mansfield went on to bigger success in New York as the dizzy blond heroine of George Axelrod's play *Will Success Spoil Rock Hunter?* (1955–1956) *Life* magazine featured her as "Broadway's smartest dumb blonde." In February 1955, Mansfield appeared nude in *Playboy* magazine, as she did at intervals until 1964. *Playboy*'s photos in 1956 prompted her husband to sue for custody of their daughter, but she won the suit and obtained a divorce. Later that year she met the bodybuilder Mickey Hargitay, and their romance became a staple of the press. They were married on Jan. 13, 1958, and remained close even after their divorce in 1964; they had three children.

In August 1956, under contract to Twentieth Century–Fox, Mansfield made *The Girl Can't Help It* (1956); *The Wayward Bus* (1957), in which she gave what some consider her best performance; *Will Success Spoil Rock Hunter?* (1957); and *Kiss Them for Me* (1957), with Cary Grant. Though the films were mediocre, they added to Mansfield's celebrity as a busty, sexy naïf. In 1958, following her spectacular glass-chapel wedding to Hargitay, Mansfield appeared in the British comedy *The Sheriff of Fractured Jaw* (1959). The studio then loaned her out for two low-budget British underworld melodramas, *Too Hot to Handle* (1959) and *The Challenge* (1960; American title, *It Takes a Thief*).

Toward the end of the decade, Mansfield's exaggerated figure became less fashionable, and the tastelessness of her publicity drew criticism. In Italy she played a near-caricature double role in *The Loves of Hercules* (1960), and her studio contract ended with the romantic comedy *It Happened in Athens* (1962). She did more nightclub work and began to drink excessively. In 1962, apparently because of a publicity stunt gone wrong, she and Hargitay were lost at sea overnight; this news helped promote her work in *The George Raft Story* (1961). Later that year, while working in Rome on *Panic Button* (1964), Mansfield began a raucous affair with the producer Enrico Bomba; others followed, notably with the Brazilian singer Nelson Sardelli. Although her personal life became more disordered, she continued a heavy schedule of appearances and films and was even named the most popular screen actress in Italy for 1962. She made a sex farce called *Promises! Promises!* (1963) and acted and sang in a German musical, *Heimweh nach St. Paul* (*Homesick for St. Paul*, 1963). She also starred with Cameron Mitchell in the German-Italian crime film *Einer Frisst den Anderen* (1964; American title, *Dog Eat Dog*, 1966); and in the quasi-pornographic *L'amore primitivo* (1964), parts of which were released posthumously in *The Wild, Wild World of Jayne Mansfield* (1968).

In May 1964, while acting in Yonkers, N.Y., Mansfield met the director Matt Cimber (Thomas Vitale Ottaviano), whom she married on Sept. 24, 1964; they had one child. Under Cimber's direction Mansfield appeared on talk shows, and in January 1966 she attracted large audiences at a New York City nightclub. She made a cameo appearance opposite Terry-Thomas in *A Guide for the Married Man* (1967) and appeared in a Las Vegas travelogue called *Spree* (1967). In an effort to gain artistic acclaim, she made *Single Room Furnished* (1968; directed by Cimber and released posthumously), an improbable film about a woman embittered by faithless men. Less ambitious were her small roles in *The Fat Spy* (1966) and *The Las Vegas Hillbillys* (1966).

After quarreling with Cimber in 1966, Mansfield met Sam Brody, a prominent trial lawyer, who became her attorney and lover. Brody proved to be unstable and violent, and seriously disrupted Mansfield's public appearances. When in December her son Zoltan was mauled by a lion, Mansfield and Brody were excluded from the hospital because of a violent argument. Early in 1967, Mansfield's daughter Jayne Marie complained to juvenile authorities that Brody had beaten her. Soon after, near New Orleans, Mansfield, Brody, and a teenage chauffeur died in a grotesque auto accident widely exploited in the press.

Though Mansfield performed in twenty-five films, her accomplishment as an actress is negligible compared to her fame as a "sex goddess." To some, she symbolized the self-destructive sex object who tried to conform to fantasies. To others, she was an ironic parody of sexuality, an exploiter of, and commentator on, sexual mores. She had a gift for light comedy, but her remarks suggest that she was unaware of any irony in her popular image. She clearly aspired to be a movie star in the flamboyant, witty tradition of Mae West, but she also tried for the ingenuousness of her early idol, Shirley Temple.

[The Academy of Motion Picture Arts and Sciences, Beverly Hills, Calif., maintains a file on Mansfield. See also *Life*, Apr. 23, 1956; May Mann, *Jayne Mansfield* (1973); Raymond Strait, *The Tragic Secret Life of Jayne Mansfield* (1974); and Martha Saxton, *Jayne Mansfield and the American Fifties* (1975). An obituary is in the *New York Times*, June 30, 1967.]

Alan Buster

MANSHIP, PAUL HOWARD (Dec. 24, 1885–Jan. 31, 1966), sculptor, was born in St. Paul, Minn., the son of Charles Henry Manship, a merchant, and Mary Etta Friend. (Most accounts cite Manship's birthdate as Dec. 25, but the Manship family Bible records it as Dec. 24, 1885.) Manship attended school in St. Paul from 1892 to 1903. He took art courses at the

Mechanical Arts High School and the St. Paul Institute School of Art, an evening school. As a child, Manship wanted to become a painter, but he began to realize his talent as a sculptor by the age of fifteen. He especially enjoyed modeling clay masks of family members.

Manship, uninterested in academic studies, left school in 1903 to work at an engraving company in St. Paul but quit after a year in order to become an independent designer and illustrator. By the spring of 1905 he had realized that he would have greater career opportunities outside St. Paul. He moved to New York City, where he attended the Art Students League and assisted the sculptor Solon Borglum. While Manship helped Borglum with his large equestrian monuments, he began to appreciate the importance of anatomical knowledge to the sculptor. He dissected animals in Borglum's studio, and the following year he attended Charles Grafly's life classes at the Pennsylvania Academy of Fine Arts in Philadelphia. Manship studied at the academy until 1908. He also assisted the sculptor Isidore Konti, who helped Manship improve his modeling techniques and encouraged him to enter the competition for the American Prix de Rome, which Manship won in 1909. This coveted prize in sculpture gained Manship a scholarship to the American Academy of Rome, where he studied from 1909 to 1912, and enabled him to travel in Europe. Manship returned to New York in the fall of 1912 and married Isabel McIlwaine on Jan. 1, 1913; they had four children.

By the time of his marriage, Manship had gained recognition as a sculptor whose works demonstrated both technical excellence and simplicity of execution. The city architects Charles A. Platt and Welles Bosworth promoted Manship's work, and he began to create garden sculpture for the estate homes of Harold McCormick, Charles Schwab, and Herbert Pratt, among others. Manship also executed in 1914 the exterior and interior relief sculptures for the Western Union Building in New York City. Besides life-size bronze figures and monumental pieces, Manship continued to produce small bronze figures similar to those he had executed as a student at the American Academy. A selection of these bronzes were shown at the National Academy of Design's 1914 exhibition and evoked the praise of Herbert Adams, the president of the National Sculpture Society. Adams noted Manship's "great technical address, backed by a sound knowledge of form," and asserted that "some of his little bronzes seem to be absolutely complete—real objets d'art in the best sense." Thirty-eight of Manship's bronze figures went on a national museum tour in 1915–1916. At the time of Manship's first one-man show in New York, directed by Martin Birnbaum in February 1916, Manship had a reputation as an American sculptor who incorporated both classical and modern elements.

Manship joined the American Red Cross in Italy during the fall of 1918, and he returned again to Europe after World War I had ended. He resided in Paris from 1922 to 1926, where he executed several portrait busts. He regarded portrait work as a lesser art form, yet he continued to do it throughout his career, executing about forty in the 1920's. Some of his most noted portrait busts are those of John D. Rockefeller (1918) and John Barrymore (1918). Although some critics complained that his portraits were too stylized and formal, his portrait work was noted for its natural blending of realistic detail with design elements. He completed the Soldiers Monument at Thiaucourt, France, in 1926, and in 1927 he returned to America. He established a studio in Manhattan, where he continued to execute portraits, reliefs, small figures, medals, and large monumental works.

Many of Manship's best-known monuments were commissioned during the 1930's. For his *Abraham Lincoln, the Hoosier Youth* (Fort Wayne, Ind., 1932), he wanted to emphasize Lincoln's personal characteristics—"his kindness, his strength of body and of spirit, and his wisdom." He designed the statue to be both realistic and inspirational, a balance of movement and form that was aesthetically pleasing and emotionally elevating. He adhered to authentic representational detail (Lincoln's rustic costume, his hound by his side, his ax), which underscores the symbolic dimensions of the work. His *Prometheus Fountain* at Rockefeller Plaza in New York (1934) is more typical of his attempt to integrate mythical and classical themes and modes with a modern setting and style. This resulted in a work that, like *Prometheus*, is "more decorative" and "less monumental" and even lighthearted. Manship spent two years designing the *Paul J. Rainey Memorial Gateway* at the New York Zoological Park (1934). The gateway is forty-two feet wide and thirty-six feet high, "with ten gilded bronze birds and ten other animals placed in the foliated structure." For the 1939–1940 New York World's Fair, he created three sculpture groups: *The Moods of Time* and *Time and the Fates of Man* (a sundial) on Constitution Mall, and *Celestial Sphere* in the Court of States. *The Moods of Time,* which comprised four groups of large plaster figures representing the times of day, was destroyed after the fair, although smaller bronze casts of the figures survive. He also created the *Woodrow Wilson Memorial Celestial Sphere* for the League of Nations in Geneva, Switzerland (1939).

During the 1940's and 1950's, Manship continued to do portraits and medals, as well as official corporate and government sculpture. The range of his work continued to be varied in scope, yet it received less recognition than that of his prolific output during the 1930's. In 1958 the Smithsonian Institution sponsored a retrospective exhibition of his work. In 1960 he was commissioned to do the inaugural medal for John F. Kennedy, having produced one for Franklin D. Roosevelt in 1933.

Throughout the 1940's and 1950's, Manship lectured extensively, sometimes highlighting his lectures on sculpture history and techniques with demonstrations. Booth Tarkington remarked, "Other men could do some painting or modelling and do an accompanying 'patter,' of course, but no other even rumored to me could simultaneously produce a real 'object of art' and a gayly highlighted history of sculpture—the essentials of that history—all in human terms and as if from the mouth, not of Sir Oracle, but of a customary friend and crony talking intimately."

Friends commented on Manship's sense of humor as well as his seriousness and powers of concentration. One visitor to his studio in the 1930's noted how Manship worked "cheerfully despite the noise made by the three young Manship children racing around the modelling stands on their tricycles." Throughout his career he adhered to the idea that form and emotional content in art must be conjoined. "Sculpture is but a part of the greater scheme of art," he said. "Dissociated from Nature, it still must find its rhythms in the organization of natural forms. . . . But more important than formalities and geometrical considerations is the feeling for human qualities and harmony and movement of life." His work is largely representational, reflecting an eclectic blend of several artistic influences. He was inspired by the formal classicism of Greek and Roman sculpture (which he came to appreciate during his years of study in Italy and travels to Greece), and he admired the linear grace of Eastern art. Some critics attributed the decorative qualities of his earlier work, such as *Dancer and Gazelles* (1916), to East Indian influences. Overall, what critics recognized as "the Manship style" reflected his ability, as one critic expressed it, to "project himself into another culture, extract its essence, and make it his own."

Not all critics have praised Manship's work. Some have felt that he did not live up to his early promise, that his works lack depth and are all form and no substance. Some have believed that he remained tied to an academic tradition that encouraged representation rather than experimentation in sculpture. One critic in the early 1920's summarized the persistent critical trend when he noted the "provocative quality" of Manship's art, which "has been the more interesting because it has excited admiration and doubt in pretty nearly equal measure." Manship's work can be seen in public and private buildings, as well as museums, throughout America. He died in New York City.

[Manship's one-page statement of his "Credo" begins his book *Paul Manship* (1947). On his life and work, see Royal Cortissoz, "Paul Manship," in *American Artists* (1923); Edwin Murtha, *Paul Manship* (1957), the most complete source on Manship and his works and their locations; and the catalog of the Smithsonian Institution, *A Retrospective Exhibition of Sculpture by Paul Manship, February 23–March 16, 1958.* An obituary is in the *New York Times*, Feb. 1, 1966.]

LINDA PATTERSON MILLER

MANVILLE, THOMAS FRANKLYN ("TOMMY"), JR. (Apr. 9, 1894–Oct. 8, 1967), a wealthy eccentric and playboy, was born in Milwaukee, Wis., the son of Thomas Franklyn Manville, who developed a regional business manufacturing insulation materials into the international Johns-Manville Corporation, and Clara Coleman. His parents were divorced in 1909. Tommy, as Manville became known to the press and public, matured early. He began smoking at eleven, took his first drink in London at the same age, shaved when he was twelve, and at seventeen was wearing his fourth mustache. Astutely, he played his parents off against each other. This was not difficult to do, since their interests lay in directions other than parenting. His father lived at luxury hotels or in one of his clubs and concentrated upon his career as a multimillionaire and industrialist. Manville's mother traveled extensively in Europe and lived from 1927 until her death in 1941 in a hotel suite in New York City, busy with her collection of porcelains, 200 exotic birds, and, at one time, twenty-one dogs who occupied individual kennels.

So far as Manville was concerned, the situation was, a psychiatrist said later, "precisely the right environment to develop something spectacular." At any early age Manville became an object of journalistic interest as the heir of "the asbestos king" and as one given to precocious adventures—eight runaways from school by the time he was fifteen and random employment during his teenage years as an elevator boy, night clerk, baker, chauffeur, crewman on a cattle boat, and common laborer nailing up boxes in an asbestos factory. His relationship with his father was stormy, oscillating between disinheritance and reconciliation.

When he was seventeen years old Manville found his career—marriage. In the decades that followed, he was married thirteen times to eleven comely young women, most of them blondes and most recruited from Broadway chorus lines. The discrepancy in the marriage figures results from the fact that he married two of his wives twice. The longest marriage lasted seven years, the shortest seven hours and forty-five minutes, while reported engagements that fell short of the altar ranged between 27 and 529, according to conflicting scores compiled by reporters, columnists, and the wire services.

Newspaper editors scoffed at Manville yet found the combination of money, beauty, and outrageous behavior irresistible and cooperated in making him a public figure. Manville, in turn, developed a flair for giving the newspapers the story they wanted. He met his first wife, he told the press, under the marquee of a Broadway theater. "I like your looks," he told her. "And I like yours," she replied. Two days later they were married. Often, during the marital difficulties that followed each wedding, the brides contributed statements that served to brighten up a story. "What is it that you have that Mr. Manville's other chorus-girl wives lacked?" a reporter asked the fourth wife, Marcelle Edwards, who had been Miss Broadway of 1933. "I don't know," snapped Marcelle, "unless it's this cold in my head."

Following the death of his father in 1925, Manville inherited a fortune of approximately $10 million. The next year he developed a lavish property on Long Island Sound between New Rochelle and Mamaroneck, N.Y. The twenty-eight-room residence and environs were known as Bon Repos. Among the unusual features of the house were a radio and record player in every room, a telephone switchboard in the master bedroom, a motion-picture theater, and a completely equipped guesthouse, to which Manville retired when pandemonium reigned. Security was well maintained. Watchtowers were staffed by armed guards, supplemented by loudspeakers and giant floodlights in the treetops. A siren and red light were installed on the roof for summoning the police when there was a domestic contretemps, such as the time when Manville's angry eighth wife heaved a hot plate of cheese dreams at him.

New Yorkers, the *London Daily Mirror* assured its readers, paid a dollar a head to stand outside the palisade surrounding Bon Repos just to listen to one of Manville's quarrels with his wife-of-the-year or his blonde secretary. These bouts, which were often refereed by what the Mamaroneck Police Department came to call "the bedroom detail," sometimes ended in charges of second-degree assault.

In 1955, describing himself as "really retired," Manville acquired a more modest property in Chappaqua, N.Y., which he called Bon Repos No. 2. It was while living there that his thirteenth and last marriage was, as he informed the United Press International, "kaput." Most of the divorce settlements Manville negotiated were comparatively modest though their total ran to an estimated $2.5 million. This figure does not include the costs of courtship—limousines, orchids, nightclubbing, diamonds, wedding rings, lawyers, liquor, furs, and aspirin.

On several occasions Manville took large display space in New York City newspapers to advertise for a lawyer or a secretary. Press agents in his employ kept in touch with the newspapers and Manville himself often issued communiqués on his marital situation from the Stork Club, then a center of New York City night life. Seen in perspective, the marriages and divorces were devices to attract the notice Manville craved and constituted his only claim to public attention. Happy to be called "the marrying Manville," he was simply, in Daniel Boorstin's felicitous phrase defining celebrity, "well known for his well-knownness." Manville was of medium height, dapper, sunlamp ruddy, soft-spoken except when bored or aroused, and distinguished by a crest of wavy, prematurely white hair. He died in Chappaqua.

[The *New York Herald Tribune* files, now in the Queens Borough Public Library, Jamaica, N.Y., cover Manville's life and explain his notoriety. Obituaries are in the *Milwaukee Journal*, the *Milwaukee Sentinel*, and the *New York Times*, all Oct. 9, 1967.]

GERALD CARSON

MARCIANO, ROCKY (Sept. 1, 1923–Aug. 31, 1969), heavyweight boxer, was born Rocco Francis Marchegiano in Brockton, Mass., the son of Piero Marchegiano and Pasquelena Picciuto (or Piccento). His father, an Italian immigrant shoe-factory worker, was slight of build, and Marciano, who weighed over thirteen pounds at birth, inherited his size and strength from his mother's side of the family.

Marciano was a good high school athlete. He played linebacker for the Brockton High football team, and he once returned an intercepted pass sixty-seven yards for a touchdown. But he dreamed of becoming a major-league baseball player and trained assiduously to that end. An indifferent student, he quit school at sixteen, worked at a variety of laboring jobs, and played sandlot baseball before being drafted into the army in 1943. He served with the 150th Combat Engineers in Wales, in English Channel operations, and at Ft. Lewis, Wash. Marciano had had some experience as a street fighter, but it was during his years in the army that he first became involved in organized boxing.

Upon his discharge from the service in 1947, Marciano worked again at a variety of laboring jobs and failed a tryout as a catcher and first baseman with the Chicago Cubs. He then returned to boxing and soon gained a reputation as a hard-punching, awkward amateur. Although considered "old" by some, he turned professional in the spring of 1947 (some wrongly say 1948). He was managed briefly by a Brockton mechanic, Gene Caggiano, but ambitious to move ahead, he soon put himself under the direction of the well-known New York manager and promoter Al Weill. The latter brought Marciano under the tutelage of the famed trainer Charlie Goldman, who perfected Rocky's crouching, right-handed punching style and developed his left hook.

On Dec. 20, 1949, Marciano, with a record of sixteen straight knockouts, gained national attention with his brutal knockout of, and serious injury to, Carmine Vingo. He became a major contender for the heavyweight title with his close decision over Roland La Starza in ten rounds on Mar. 24, 1950, and with his knockout of Rex Layne (six rounds, July 12, 1951) and of the aging former champion, Joe Louis (eight rounds, Oct. 26, 1951). He finally won the heavyweight title from "Jersey Joe" Walcott in Philadelphia on Sept. 23, 1952. His rigorous training for this title bout is legendary. It paid off when he was able to overcome a first-round knockdown, severe facial cuts, and the superior boxing skills of the champion to knock Walcott out in the thirteenth round. Marciano, the idol of the new television boxing audience and the first white heavyweight champion since 1937, had reached the pinnacle of his career.

Marciano defended his title six times over the next four years. He knocked out Walcott again in one round (May 15, 1953) and La Starza in eleven rounds (Sept. 24, 1953), and he won a decision over former champion Ezzard Charles in fifteen rounds (June 17, 1954) before knocking him out in eight rounds in a return bout (Sept. 17, 1954). He then knocked out Don Cockell in nine rounds (May 16, 1955) and, in his last fight, the venerable former light-heavyweight champion Archie Moore in nine rounds (Sept. 21, 1955). While he was never seriously challenged in any of these bouts, he did suffer major injuries, including serious facial cuts in the two fights with Charles. This tendency to injury, along with wearying training, contributed to his decision to retire in April 1956. But his friends also noted a growing tension with Al Weill, with whom he had frequently quarreled over the years about his personal life and the division of his earnings. Marciano briefly considered a comeback in 1959, but after a month of training in secret, he abandoned the attempt.

Marciano retired with a record of forty-nine victories (forty-three knockouts) and no defeats. He was named Fighter of the Year by *Ring* magazine in 1952 and 1954, received the Chicago boxing writers' Packy McFarland Memorial Trophy in 1951, and in 1952 was voted the prestigious Edward Neil Memorial Plaque by the New York boxing writers. Marciano married Barbara M. Cousens, his childhood sweetheart, on Dec. 31, 1950; they had two children, one of them adopted. Marciano, whose fortune was estimated to be as high as $4 million, spent his retirement years in restless pursuit of business opportunities, with a wide circle of friends, and in travel with his family. He died in the crash of a light plane while on his way from Chicago to Des Moines, Iowa.

At five feet, eleven inches and about 185 pounds, and with the shortest reach of any modern heavyweight champion (sixty-seven inches), Marciano perfected a crouching style marked by relentless, aggressive pursuit, a good left hook, and an awkward but powerful overhand right punch. He was always willing to absorb punishment with full confidence that he could knock out any of his opponents. While durable, he suffered broken hands, back injuries, and facial cuts in his fights. He was often compared to Jack Dempsey because of his aggressive style, his left hook (actually Marciano's right hand was his better punch), and his record of knockouts.

Marciano was close to his family and friends, including his boyhood friend and trainer Allie Colombo. Those close to Marciano described him as warm and affable. But he was also somewhat vain about his appearance, secretive in his business dealings, and suspicious of established ways of doing business. He died without a will and left a mystery as to where he had placed his considerable fortune.

Marciano came to prominence in a transitional era. The Depression-period boxers such as Joe Louis, Joe Walcott, and Archie Moore were past their prime and the legendary Muhammad Ali was yet to come on the scene. It was also a time of declining box-office revenues, the emergence of a new television audience, and, for many, unsettling racial change in the ring. Marciano became a public idol through his ethnic background, his brawling style and knockouts, and his convincing victories over black boxers.

[See Everett M. Skehan, *Rocky Marciano* (1977; written with the assistance of the family); and Bill Libby, *Rocky* (1971). An obituary is in the *New York Times*, Sept. 1, 1969.]

DANIEL R. GILBERT

MARTIN, WARREN HOMER (Aug. 15, 1901–Jan. 22, 1968), clergyman and first elected president of the United Automobile Workers (UAW), was born in Goreville, Ill., the son of W. H. Martin, a farmer, and Sidney F. Smith. He received his early education in Goreville but finished high school at Southern Illinois Normal College in Carbondale in 1920. During his high school years he worked on a farm and as a railroad section hand; he also began preaching and, in 1922, was ordained a Baptist minister and appointed pastor of the Goreville Baptist Church. After graduating from high school he became a teacher and attended Ewing College in Ewing, Ill. He was very athletic, and in 1924 and 1925 was national Amateur Athletic Union champion in the hop, skip, and jump.

Martin married Norma May Graves on Mar. 19, 1922; they had two children. In 1926 the "Leaping Parson" moved his family to Liberty, Mo. There he was appointed pastor of the William Jewell Baptist Church and attended William Jewell College, from which he graduated in 1928. In 1932 he moved to Leeds, Mo., to assume the pastorate of its Baptist church. While there, he did postgraduate work at the Kansas City (Kans.) Baptist Theological Seminary.

A good part of his new congregation was made up of workers from the Kansas City, Mo., Chevrolet plant. Their poverty prompted him to encourage them, from the pulpit, to unionize, but Martin's deacons objected, removing him from his position in 1934. He then went to work at the Chevrolet plant, where he became an active union organizer. He was made president of the American Federation of Labor (AFL) local he helped form there, and in June 1934 went to Detroit as a delegate to the first national AFL-sponsored conference of automobile workers. Shortly thereafter Martin was discharged from the plant for his union activities.

In 1935 he moved to Detroit, where in August the AFL called the first convention of the United Automobile Workers. The federation granted a charter to the UAW but chose the officers of the new union itself—Francis J. Dillon as president and Homer Martin as vice-president. The next year, at the UAW convention in South Bend, Ind., the "probationary control" of the UAW by the AFL was lifted, and on the third day of the proceedings, Apr. 29, 1936, Martin was elected the first president of the UAW.

At first Martin seemed adequate as the new union head. All his contemporaries agreed that, based on his experience in the pulpit, he was a good speaker. The trouble was, one associate noted, that he had only one speech, which he used over and over again. Others claimed he tried to be all things to all people. "He always says yes to the last man who talks to him."

These weaknesses were soon apparent, and many of Martin's colleagues came to regard him as incompetent and even unstable. Unfortunately, he fell under the spell of Jay Lovestone, a man who had been expelled from the Communist party leadership in 1928. Lovestone apparently exerted an entirely negative influence on Martin. When Martin began to replace early UAW activitists with "Lovestonites," bitter divisions appeared within the union.

Meanwhile, the UAW began increasing its organizing activities, especially at General Motors. In late 1936 and early 1937 the UAW workers staged their sit-down strikes. To the dismay of Martin's UAW officers and the Congress of Industrial Organizations (CIO), which the UAW had joined in 1936, Martin seemed willing to negotiate settlements on a plant-by-plant basis, thereby undercutting the power of the union to obtain one blanket settlement with the company. Finally, his frustrated colleagues encouraged him to go on a speaking tour, and the first contract with General Motors was signed without him.

By August 1937, at the time of the third UAW convention, the split in the union was intense. Nevertheless, Martin remained popular among the workers, especially those outside Detroit, whom he continued to dazzle with his oratory. Moreover, despite the dissension, the union's membership had grown remarkably. The CIO leadership, fully aware of the divisions in the UAW, counseled compromise at the convention to prevent an irrevocable split. Largely as a result of these factors, Martin was reelected president. But the dissension grew. Martin, increasingly dominated by Lovestone, ironically began to accuse those who opposed him of Communism. This seemed to corroborate the charge that Martin was incapable of making "common cause with opponents" and therefore had to "destroy them."

When the UAW tried to organize the Ford Motor Company from 1937 through 1939, Martin's behavior was erratic. On one occasion, he stated that Henry Ford was "sincere and honest in his efforts to give his men the best possible working conditions"; on another, he declared Ford "America's outstanding lawbreaker." This ambivalence, his increasing accusations of Communism, and the certainty by many that he was actually in Ford's pay alienated him from the rest of the union leadership. In January 1939 Martin suspended fifteen members of the executive board. In March he called a union convention in Detroit. At the same time the suspended officers, who had in turn expelled Martin from the union forever, met at a convention in Cleveland. These officers had set up separate union headquarters in Detroit, to which per capita taxes from the UAW locals continued to be sent and which had the support of the CIO. It was from this nucleus that the future union sprang.

Martin's convention, however, had little support. He took his group out of the CIO to rejoin the AFL, but by August it was clear that the majority of auto workers had repudiated the Martin UAW-AFL. He "retired" from the labor movement in April 1940.

Martin remained in Michigan for most of the rest of his life. In 1942 he formed the United Investors of America, and from 1951 through 1955 he operated a storm-window and awning business. He was president of Lite Thru Products in 1952 and 1954. As organizational director of the Dairy Farmers Cooperative Association, he led an unsuccessful milk strike in 1957 and resigned the following spring.

In the fall of 1958 Martin entered the Democratic primary for senator against Philip Hart, stating that "the Democratic party because it is a captive of [Walter] Reuther is getting the blame . . . for building the worst unemployment situation in the nation." Reuther had been elected president of the UAW in 1948 and became head of the CIO in 1952. Martin lost the primary, and in 1961 he and his second wife, Vivian, moved to Los Angeles, where he became a labor counselor for the Tulare and Kings County Employers Council. He died in Los Angeles.

Homer Martin was a man of energy, imagination, and ambition. His talents, however, were limited, and his weaknesses, especially his inability to work with others, were considerable. It was probably unfortunate for him that he rose so far so quickly in a movement he neither came from nor really understood. In a sense he was more the tool of circumstances than their master.

[Martin's papers are in the Archives of Labor and Urban Affairs at Wayne State University in Detroit. There is no complete biography of Martin. See the UAW publicity department and oral histories of Martin's contemporaries in the Wayne State archives; Irving Howe and B. J. Widick, *The UAW and Walter Reuther* (1949); George Douglas Blackwood, "The United Automobile Workers of America, 1935–1951" (Ph.D. diss., University of Chicago, 1951); Sidney Fine, *Sit-Down: The General Motors Strike of 1936–1937* (1969); Warner Pflug, *The UAW in Pictures* (1971); and Victor G. Reuther, *The Brothers Reuther and the Story of the UAW* (1976).]

SANDRA SHAFFER VAN DOREN

MARTIN, JOSEPH WILLIAM, JR. (Nov. 3, 1884–Mar. 7, 1968), Speaker of the House of Representatives, was born in North Attleboro, Mass., the son of Joseph William Martin, a blacksmith, and Catherine Katon. As a youth, Martin worked in his father's shop and as a newspaper delivery boy. He later worked at a local jewelry store and at the North Attleboro telephone exchange as the night operator. An outstanding athlete, Martin was captain of his high school baseball team and was offered an athletic scholarship to Dartmouth College. But instead of continuing his education, Martin joined the *North Attleboro Evening Leader* as a reporter, copyboy, and printer's apprentice. When the *Leader* closed down, Martin was hired by the competing *Sun* and also worked as a local correspondent for the *Boston Globe* and the *Providence Journal*. In 1908 he and a group of local citizens bought the *North Attleboro Evening Chronicle*, and Martin became editor and publisher. He later bought out the shares of his partners and became full owner of the newspaper. Under his management, the newspaper's circulation rose from eight hundred to four thousand. Martin also acquired the weekly *Franklin Sentinel*.

As the politically active editor of a Republican newspaper, Martin was a natural choice to run for the Massachusetts House of Representatives; he was elected in 1911 and served three one-year terms. In the 1912 presidential race, Martin supported the regular Republican, William Howard Taft, over the Bull Moose Republican, Theodore Roosevelt. In the Massachusetts House, Martin was a floor leader and a key strategist in the 1912 election of John W. Weeks to the United States Senate. (The Seventeenth Amendment to the Constitution, which requires direct election of senators, did not go into effect until the following year.)

In 1914, Martin was elected to the Massachusetts Senate and was later reelected to two more one-year terms. During this period, he was secretary of the Joint Rules Committee, headed by State Senator Calvin Coolidge, who became Martin's friend and political ally. Martin also served as chairman of the Republican Legislative Campaign Committee. He did not seek reelection in 1917, but he remained politically involved. He was a Republican presidential elector in the 1920 election and managed Senator Henry Cabot Lodge's 1922 campaign for reelection. Martin unsuccessfully challenged seventy-three-year-old Congressman William Greene in the 1924 Republican congressional primary. Greene, who had been the district's congressman since 1898, died in September 1924, and Martin won a special election to replace him.

Martin represented his congressional district for the next forty-two years and became among the most influential legislators of his generation, the only Republican Speaker of the House in the middle third of the twentieth century. Beginning as a confidant of President Coolidge, Martin had considerable influence from his earliest days in Congress. He also became a protégé of Nicholas Longworth, who was Speaker during Martin's first three terms, and was a member of the prestigious Foreign Affairs and Rules committees. A conservative protectionist, he voted for the Smoot-Hawley tariff bill and opposed recriprocal trade agreements. Although a teetotaler, Martin thought that Republican-imposed Prohibition was politically unwise and urged President Herbert Hoover to support its repeal during the 1932 presidential campaign. "More than anything else, it was the wet issue that crushed the Republican party during this period," Martin wrote in his memoirs.

Selected as assistant floor leader to House minority leader Bertrand Snell in 1933, Martin gained recognition as one of the Republican party's shrewdest and most effective legislators. Martin supported some of President Franklin D. Roosevelt's New Deal reforms, including the National Recovery Act, social security, and the federal guarantee of bank deposits. He helped shape the Hatch Act, which prohibited federal employees from participating in political campaigns. Martin opposed the Agricultural Adjustment Act and the Tennessee Valley Authority. "Many of the experiments of the New Deal," Martin later observed, "seemed to us to undermine and destroy this society." In 1936, at the Republican National Convention, Martin was the floor manager of Alfred M. Landon's successful bid for the Republican nomination for the presidency and was later his eastern campaign manager; the only two states that Landon carried were in Martin's region.

Martin's political reputation peaked in 1938, when he served as chairman of the Republican Congressional Campaign Committee and his party gained eighty seats in the midterm elections. He had accurately targeted many of the "swing" districts (those in which Republicans were thought to have a 50–50 chance of winning congressional seats) and had personally recruited candidates and raised funds for a national campaign effort. He also survived a strong challenge in his district from Lawrence J. Bresnahan, who had been director of the Works Progress Administration (WPA) in Massachusetts. With Snell's retirement in January 1939, Martin was elected House Republican leader.

Martin expanded the party's leadership and the Republican Steering Committee and established a research office to study and help draft legislation and speeches for Republican congressmen. Because his party was still in the minority, Martin often urged restraint over blatant partisanship and picked his battles carefully. By forging coalitions with conservative Democrats, Martin was able to help pass the Arms Embargo Act and to place restrictions on the WPA. In 1939 a *Life* magazine poll of fifty-two Washington correspondents designated Martin as the most able member of Congress.

Although not an active candidate, Martin received prominent mention as a possible Republican presidential contender in 1940 and was the favorite-son candidate of the Massachusetts delegation to that year's Republican National Convention, of which he was the permanent chairman. When the convention deadlocked, another dark-horse contender, Wendell L. Willkie, was nominated for the presidency. Willkie later persuaded Martin to become Republican national chairman, a post he held until November 1942. Even though Martin pleaded with Willkie not to endorse the peacetime draft in 1940, because it was too controversial, Martin voted for it when Willkie indicated that he strongly favored the selective service. Like Willkie, Martin also supported lend-lease aid to the Allies in the winter of 1941.

When the Republicans gained control of the House in 1946, Martin was elected Speaker. In retaliation for Roosevelt's defiance of the two-term tradition, Martin used his influence to pass the Twenty-second Amendment, which officially limits presidents to two terms. The Republican-controlled Eightieth Congress passed the Labor-Management Relations (Taft-Hartley) Act (and overrode Truman's veto of it) and established the Hoover Commission on the Organization of the Executive Branch of the Government. Martin supported a $4.8 billion tax cut that President Harry Truman vetoed, but the Republican majorities in both houses of Congress overrode the veto. In foreign policy, Martin supported Truman's Greek-Turkish aid program and the Marshall Plan, although he backed the Appropriations Committee's $1.5 billion reduction of Marshall Plan funds. After the House Rules Committee blocked consideration of a bill to permit United States participation in the World Health Organization, Martin forced it to a floor vote and the measure was passed. When Truman asked for federal aid to elementary and secondary schools, Martin charged that it was a political ploy, and the administration proposal never got beyond the House Education and Labor Committee.

During the 1948 presidential campaign, it rankled Martin that Truman went on the attack against the "do-nothing" Eightieth Congress. But the silence of the Republican presidential nominee, Thomas E. Dewey, on that Congress troubled Martin even more. With Truman winning the election in an upset, the Republicans also lost control of both houses of Congress, and Martin returned to his old position as minority leader.

Martin, who had been critical of the Truman administration's refusal to make use of Chiang Kai-shek's Nationalist Chinese forces in the Korean War, touched off a political firestorm on Apr. 5, 1951, by reading a letter from General Douglas MacArthur, supreme commander in Korea, that concurred with Martin's criticism of the administration's foreign policy. Four days later, Truman fired MacArthur from his command. "I was appalled that I should have contributed to a chain of circumstances that had deprived the United States of its greatest general," Martin wrote in his memoirs. On MacArthur's return to the United States, Martin offered to support him for the presidency in 1952. While plainly interested, MacArthur did not formally seek the nomination. Martin was the chairman and MacArthur the keynote speaker of the 1952 Republican National Convention, which nominated Dwight D. Eisenhower.

In the 1952 Eisenhower landslide, the Republicans regained control of both houses of Congress, and Martin was elected to a second term as Speaker. Overshadowed by the new president of his own party, Martin acknowledged that his role had been somewhat diminished. Even so, Martin was an administration loyalist who took the House floor to speak in behalf of Eisenhower's foreign-aid and farm bills. Martin also outmaneuvered Daniel Reed, the conservative chairman of the Ways and Means Committee, in forcing legislation to a floor vote that extended the excess-profits tax. "I had to loyally follow President Eisenhower," Martin said. "As leader, my loyalty was to him." Because of concern about its impact on the New England economy, Martin opposed Eisenhower on construction of the St. Lawrence Seaway.

Martin lost the speakership in 1954 when the Democrats recaptured Congress. Following a Democratic sweep in the 1958 midterm elections, Martin was ousted as Republican floor leader, in a close vote, by Charles Halleck of Indiana, his longtime assistant leader. Martin blamed Eisenhower and his White House staff for his defeat. While Eisenhower did not intervene in the House election, he did not discourage Halleck's challenge. Six years later, Martin voted for Gerald R. Ford when he edged out Halleck for the minority leadership. In 1966, Martin was defeated for renomination in the Republican primary by Margaret Heckler. He died in Hollywood, Fla.

[Martin's *My First Fifty Years in Politics* (1960), as told to Robert J. Donovan, is a readable and informative memoir, See also Robert J. Donovan, *Conflict and Crisis: The Presidency of Harry Truman, 1945–48* (1977); Steve Neal, *Dark Horse: A Biography of Wendell Willkie* (1953); and Gary W. Reichard, *The Reaffirmation of Republicanism* (1975). Obituaries are in the *New York Times*, the *Boston Globe*, and the *Washington Post*, all Mar. 8, 1968.]

STEVE NEAL

MARTINELLI, GIOVANNI (Oct. 22, 1885–Feb. 2, 1969), tenor, was born in Montagnana, Italy, the son of Antonio Martinelli, a cabinetmaker, and Lucia Bellini. Though in his boyhood Martinelli sang in the church choir and played the clarinet in the town band, he received no formal musical instruction until comparatively late. "I never thought of myself as especially gifted," he once told an interviewer. His elementary schooling took place in his native town, following which he was apprenticed to a cabinetmaker.

In 1905, while fulfilling the required military service, Martinelli played the clarinet in the regimental band. His bandmaster, overhearing him sing one day, encouraged him to perform for prominent families in Piedmont, who then raised a fund to send him to Rome to study voice (with Mandolini) when his military service ended. On Dec. 3, 1910, Martinelli made his debut in a concert performance of Rossini's *Stabat Mater* in Milan, and on December 29 of that year he made his opera debut at Milan's Teatro dal Verme in the title role of *Ernani*. He soon attracted the interest of Giacomo Puccini, who selected him to sing the role of Dick Johnson in the first European performance of *The Girl of the Golden West*, at La Scala in 1911. There followed successful appearances in opera houses in Budapest, Monte Carlo, Brussels, and London. On Aug. 7, 1913, Martinelli married Adele Previtali; they had three children.

Martinelli first appeared in the United States on Nov. 3, 1913, as Cavaradossi in *Tosca*, in Philadelphia with the Chicago-Philadelphia Opera Company. His debut at the Metropolitan Opera, in New York City, as Rodolfo in *La bohème*, followed on Nov. 20, 1913. He remained with the Metropolitan Opera for thirty-two seasons (the second-longest period of service there by any singer, that of Giuseppe De Luca exceeding his by two seasons). At the Metropolitan Opera, Martinelli made about a thousand appearances in thirty-six roles, including the principal tenor parts in the basic Italian and French repertory. In 1937, in London and New York City, he assumed for the first time, and scored a striking success in, the title role in Verdi's *Otello*. The roles in which he was most often heard at the Metropolitan Opera were Radames (*Aida*), Don José (*Carmen*), Canio (*Pagliacci*), Manrico (*Il trovatore*).

The purity of texture and beauty of his voice, coupled with his discerning musicianship, placed Martinelli among the world's foremost tenors and made him the one most often singled out as Caruso's successor. He was equally celebrated for an uncommon stamina that enabled him to perform demanding roles at an advanced age and for a versatility that allowed him to appear in several operas in the Russian, German, and Spanish repertories and in a number of world premieres (Granados' *Goyescas*, Giordano's *Madame Sans-Gêne*, Respighi's *The Sunken Bell*).

Martinelli also sang regularly at the San Francisco Opera, the Chicago Civic Opera, and major European opera houses, as well as in the concert hall. In Chicago, in 1939, singing opposite Kirsten Flagstad, he became one of the few notable Italian tenors to undertake the lead in Wagner's *Tristan und Isolde*. His last appearance at the Metropolitan in a complete opera took place on Mar. 8, 1945, as Pollione in *Norma*. On the fiftieth anniversary of his Metropolitan Opera debut, the company's principal artists were heard in arias for which Martinelli had become most famous. He was last heard on the opera stage in Seattle, Wash., in his eighty-third year, on Jan. 31, 1968, as Emperor Altoum in *Turandot*.

Between 1953 and 1956, Martinelli was a member of the opera department at the Benedetto Marcello Conservatory in Venice. He subsequently headed the voice department and was chief consultant in the opera workshop at the Music School Settlement in New York City. Martinelli was named Knight Commander of the Order of Merit by the Republic of Italy, and the opera house in his native city bears his name. He lived his last years at the Buckingham Hotel, opposite Carnegie Hall. He died in New York City.

[See the *New York Times*, Nov. 13, 1960, and Jan. 9, 1969; *Opera News*, Oct. 19, 1963; and David Ewen, *Musicians Since 1900* (1978).]

DAVID EWEN

MASLOW, ABRAHAM H. (Apr. 1, 1908–June 8, 1970), founder of humanistic psychology, was born in Brooklyn, N.Y., the son of Samuel Maslow, a Russian-born cooper, and Rose Schlosky. While a student at Brooklyn Borough High School he was editor of its Latin and physics magazines, and for the latter wrote an article predicting atom-powered submarines. He enrolled in the College of the City of New York, but transferred to the University of Wisconsin, where he received his B.A. in 1930. He married Bertha Goodman, an artist, on Dec. 31, 1928. They had two children.

Maslow received his M.A. from the University of Wisconsin in 1931, and his Ph.D. in 1934. He was an assistant instructor there from 1930 to 1935. From 1935 to 1937 he was the Carnegie Fellow at Columbia Teachers College. He became an instructor in psychology at Brooklyn College in 1937. When he left in 1951 to head the psychology department at Brandeis University, he was an associate professor. He remained at Brandeis until 1961.

Under the influence of Harry Harlow at Wisconsin, his first research interests were in the field of animal psychology, notably the emotion of disgust in dogs, delayed reactions of the lemur and the orangutan, food preferences of primates, and the role of dominance in the social and sexual behavior of infrahuman primates. His interests moved steadily away from behavioristic animal experiments toward intuitive studies of human potential.

His article "Dominance-Feeling, Personality, and Social Behavior in Women" (1939) applied his interest in primate dominance to humans. He concluded that highly dominant women, regardless of their sex drives, are more likely to be sexually active and to experiment sexually than are less dominant women. In 1941, with Bela Mittelman, he published the textbook *Principles of Abnormal Psychology*, wherein he stated that his final shift to a humanistic view occurred as he cried while watching a parade soon after Pearl Harbor: "Since that moment in 1941 I've devoted myself to developing a theory of human nature that could be tested by experiment and research."

In his most important work, *Motivation and Personality* (1954), Maslow did not repudiate classical psychology; rather, he attempted to enlarge upon its conception of personality by stressing man's higher nature. In contrast to "the analytic-dissecting-atomistic-Newtonian approach" of behaviorism and Freudian psychoanalysis, it emphasized the holistic character of human nature. It defined and explained "the need hierarchy," "self-actualization," and "peak experiences," phrases that have become part of the vocabulary of psychologists.

Maslow asserted that the genetic blueprint of humans includes a hierarchy of "instinctoid" needs: physiological, safety, belonging, self-esteem, and self-actualization. The first four of these Maslow called D (deficit) needs. Once the physiological needs are satisfied, the safety needs take over. When these are satisfied, the belonging needs become dominant, and then, in turn, the need for self-esteem. Once the D needs are met, the B (becoming) needs come into play. These ideas stimulated research in business organizations. The resultant studies showed that the typical job is unlikely to satisfy the higher needs, executives are motivated by these needs more than workers, and conferences dominated by these needs are more task-oriented and productive.

In Maslow's view, "self-actualized" people are those whose lives are dominated by the desire for B-need satisfaction. Maslow came to believe that only people over fifty years of age can achieve full self-actualization. In an effort to describe the common qualities of the self-actualized, he studied contemporary and historical figures, among them Albert Einstein, Thomas Jefferson, Eleanor Roosevelt, William James, and Aldous Huxley. The qualities he identified were deep interpersonal interests, a feeling of kinship with all people, a strong need for privacy and solitude, independence, integrity, naturalness, humor, and a high level of creativity. Maslow then tried to measure differences in degrees of self-actualization.

Maslow believed that the self-actualized are also "peakers"; that is, they have intense experiences in which there is a loss of self or a transcendence of it. He thought that most people probably have mild experiences of this type and some may have them almost daily. In *Religions, Values, and Peak-Experiences* (1964) and *The Farther Reaches of Human Nature* (1971), Maslow argued that the study of peak experiences, which occur in both religious and nonreligious forms, provide a way of closing the unproductive gap between religion and science.

In 1967, Maslow was named humanist of the year by the American Humanist Association. That same year he was elected president of the American Psychological Association. He also played a major role in organizing both the *Journal of Humanistic Psychology* and the *Journal of Transpersonal Psychology*. At the time of his death he was a resident fellow at the Laughlin Foundation in California. Like the early humanists, he emphasized the inherent goodness in people. Maslow viewed humans as exercising a high degree of conscious control over their lives and as having a high resistance to pressures from the environment. He viewed personality development as the process of breaking the chains binding an individual to the animal world and building a more human world.

Many of his wide circle of admiring friends considered his views of human nature too optimistic. He wrote about his own utopia, called Eupsychia, whose inhabitants were permissive, wish-respecting, and wish-gratifying whenever possible. Under such conditions, he believed the deepest layers of human nature could show themselves with ease. He died in Menlo Park, Calif.

Maslow's theories have had a major impact upon practicing psychologists because of his ideas' direct, personal, and subjective plausibility. Synanon, the drug-addiction rehabilitation center, and the Esalen Institute, one of the best-known centers for practicing group-encounter psychotherapy, make use of Maslow's ideas, but the need hierarchy and other popular conceptions have had little influence on psychological research. Maslow was a global theorist who tested his ideas imprecisely and nonquantitatively. He believed that his theories could never be tested in an animal laboratory or test tube but that they required "a life situation of the total human being in his social environment."

[See *Abraham Maslow: A Memorial Volume* (1972), which includes eulogies, previously unpublished notes, and a bibliography; and *The Journals of A. H. Maslow*, edited by R. J. Lowry (1979). *Psychologia*, Sept. 1970, has a tribute to Maslow by Misako Miyamoto. An obituary is in the *New York Times*, June 9, 1970.]

HENRY CLAY SMITH

MATTHEWS, JOSEPH BROWN (June 28, 1894–July 16, 1966), author and reformer, was born in Hopkinsville, Ky., the son of Burrell Jones Matthews, a businessman and member of the Kentucky legislature, and Fanny Wellborn Brown, a former schoolteacher. In 1915, Matthews graduated from Asbury College in

Wilmore, Ky., where he majored in Greek and Latin. After ordination as a Methodist minister that same year, he went to Java to do missionary work and to teach at a Chinese school.

To facilitate the teaching of native preachers, Matthews learned Malay. Within a few years, he was sufficiently fluent to edit a paper, translate over 200 Methodist hymns, and author numerous books in the language. In 1917 he married Grace Doswell Ison, a fellow Kentuckian and missionary in Java; they had four children. Sympathetic to Malay nationalistic aspirations, he criticized Dutch colonial rule, which prompted church officials to recall him in 1921.

For the next three years, Matthews supported his family with grants from church foundations and part-time ministerial work while he earned a B.D. from Drew University, an S.T.M. from Union Theological Seminary, and an M.A. from Columbia University. He was greatly influenced by Social Gospel teachings. In 1924 he was appointed to teach at Scarritt College, a Methodist training school in Nashville, Tenn. He advocated pacifism and the abolition of child labor, campaigned for Robert La Follette in 1924, and shocked college officials with his attacks on racial segregation. In 1927 he resigned his teaching position and left the Methodist church. For two years, Matthews held short-term appointments, chiefly at two black universities, Fisk in Nashville and Howard in Washington, D.C.

In June 1929, Matthews was appointed executive secretary of the Fellowship of Reconciliation (FOR), an organization dedicated to Christian pacifism, social reform, and better race relations. He proved to be an energetic administrator. Many of his associates were socialists, and in November 1929, Matthews, who had concluded that a new economic order was needed to achieve real reform, joined the Socialist party. He also questioned whether a Christian pacifist approach could be effective. He urged the FOR to abandon its insistence on pacifism and permit members to support class warfare. After a lengthy debate, the executive council accepted his resignation in December 1933.

For several years, Matthews had worked to create a solid "united front" of left-wing groups to achieve peace and economic and social equality. He later claimed membership in twenty-eight front organizations and official positions in fifteen. The best known was the American League Against War and Fascism, organized in October 1933, ostensibly to stop fascist aggression. The league was also the Communist party's most ambitious effort to influence public opinion through a united front. With the approval of Earl Browder, the party's chairman, league members chose Matthews as their first national chairman, although he always denied that he was a party member. He resigned in February 1934, following the disruption by Communists of a Socialist meeting at Madison Square Garden in New York City. Still committed to a united front, he remained a league member until September 1935.

In early 1934, Matthews' friend Fred J. Schlink hired him as vice-president and member of the Board of Directors of Consumers' Research, an organization that sought to counter the effects of advertising by making product evaluations available to consumers. In 1935 he coauthored *Partners in Plunder* with Ruth Enalda Shallcross, whom he married on Dec. 15, 1936, following the termination of his first marriage in 1934. That book and *Guinea Pigs No More* (1936) exposed the ways in which advertising misled consumers, but Matthews concluded that the real culprit was capitalism itself.

In September 1935 a group of Consumers' Research employees went on strike after Schlink refused to recognize their union or improve salaries and working conditions. Matthews sided with Schlink, calling the strikers traitors and eventually denouncing the strike as a Communist conspiracy to seize control of the organization. Assailed by the *Daily Worker* and convicted at a mock trial in New York City of anti–working-class activities, Matthews soon found himself blacklisted by every left-wing organization that had once welcomed him. Increasingly, he began to view himself as the innocent victim of a Communist conspiracy, and he resigned in June 1938.

In August 1938, before the House Un-American Activities Committee (HUAC), chaired by Martin Dies, Matthews testified about the existence of united-front organizations, secretly organized and controlled by the Communist party, and named ninety-four. As an insider who had seen the light, Matthews was a real find for HUAC. The following month, Dies appointed him chief investigator and staff director, a post he held until 1945. Within a year, HUAC began to concentrate on those organizations and their members. Matthews and his staff began to pore over organizational letterheads, mailing lists, meeting programs, public statements, and back issues of the *Daily Worker*, compiling thousands of names. The Federal Bureau of Investigation supplied others from its confidential files. Initially, Matthews recognized that some participants were not Communists or fellow travelers, but he quickly became convinced that all were subversives. The investigations culminated in a seven-volume report, *Communist Front Organizations with Special Reference to the National Citizens Political Action Committee* (1944), one of whose appendices contained 22,000 names identified as likely Communist subversives.

To many contemporary observers, Matthews was the driving force behind Dies's chairmanship. He prepared most of HUAC's reports, often without benefit of public hearings or comment from other committee members. He wrote many of Dies's speeches and magazine articles, and most likely Dies's book *The Trojan Horse in America* (1940). It was under their joint direction that HUAC pioneered the technique of "guilt by association," later popularized as "McCarthyism," by which individuals were judged subversive because of their friends or relatives or the organizations they belonged to.

After leaving HUAC, Matthews remained active in the anti-Communist cause. The Hearst newspaper chain hired him as a consultant on Communism, and he continued to maintain his files, which by the late 1940's contained 500,000 names linked in some fashion to left-wing organizations. For a fee, he would provide names of alleged subversives to state boards investigating Communism. In 1947 the American Legion hired him to compile a list of film-industry figures who had "Communist" associations. In New York City he presided over what one of his admirers called "the nearest thing to an anti-Communist salon" that ever existed there.

Senator Joseph R. McCarthy's rise to prominence occasioned a brief return to the limelight for Matthews. McCarthy needed evidence to support the reckless charges he had made about Communist subversion in the State Department. With his bulging files and numerous contacts, Matthews became the central figure in a clique of anti-Communists who provided McCarthy with names and support. McCarthy had raised the issue in hopes of gaining political advantage, but Matthews' group convinced him that Communist subversives were a threat to the United States. In turn, McCarthy recognized his debt to Matthews, calling him a "star-spangled American."

In June 1953, to no one's surprise, McCarthy appointed Matthews executive director of the Senate Permanent Subcommittee on Investigations, which he chaired. However, the publication of Matthews' article "Reds and Our Churches" in the July 1953 issue of the *American Mercury* created a storm of protest. Opening with the startling assertion that "the largest single group supporting the Communist apparatus in the United States today is composed of Protestant clergymen," the article proclaimed a widespread clerical conspiracy. Although Matthews qualified his remarks by admitting that the vast majority of clergymen were loyal, he insisted that 7,000 supported the Communist party. McCarthy's adversaries saw an opportunity to discredit him and organized a public rebuke by President Dwight D. Eisenhower and national religious leaders. Recognizing the damage that had been done, McCarthy reluctantly accepted Matthews' resignation on July 19, 1953.

Throughout the 1950's, Matthews was a regular contributor to the *American Mercury*, by then a right-wing periodical, and in the 1960's he wrote for *American Opinion*, the organ of the John Birch Society. His name appeared on the masthead of the conservative *National Review* until his death in New York City. His last years were spent as research director of the Church League of America, which was founded to combat Communism among the Protestant clergy but quickly expanded its scope and became a private dossier service that checked the backgrounds of suspected leftists for businesses and organizations.

Matthews needed causes to which he could commit himself with the zealousness of the true believer. The greater part of his intellectual journey—from evangelical Protestantism to left-wing socialism—was one made by many of his generation. But it was his final destination, militant and obsessive anti-Communism, that made him appear erratic and led to charges of opportunism, though he was sincerely fearful of the threat posed by Communist subversion.

[Matthews' files and papers are at the J. B. Matthews Memorial Library of the Church League of America, Wheaton, Ill. In addition to writings mentioned in the text, his most notable work is *Traffic in Death* (1934), an exposé of the arms industry. His autobiography, *Odyssey of a Fellow Traveler* (1938), recounts his life up to his testimony before HUAC. On Matthews' intellectual conversions, see Richard Rovere, "J. B. Matthews: The Informer," *Nation*, Oct. 3, 1942; Matthew Josephson and Russell Maloney, "The Testimony of a Sinner," *New Yorker*, Apr. 22, 1944; Paul Hutchinson, "The J. B. Matthews Story," *Christian Century*, July 29, 1953; and Murray Kempton, *Part of Our Time: Some Monuments and Ruins of the Thirties* (1955). An obituary is in the *New York Times*, July 17, 1966.]

G. F. Goodwin

MAY, MORTON JAY (July 13, 1881–May 17, 1968), merchant, was born in Denver, Colo., the son of David May, a merchant, and Rosa Schoenberg. His father was a German immigrant who had gone to Colorado for his health in 1877 and had stayed to start a dry-goods store in Leadville during the silver strike. In the year of Morton May's birth, his father owned six stores in Colorado, but in 1888 he shifted his headquarters to Denver when he and his brother-in-law, Louis Schoenberg, acquired a bankrupt store there and made it a success.

May attended preparatory schools in Denver and entered the University of Colorado in 1899. During summer vacations he learned the clothing business by unloading freight and clerking in the Denver store. In the summer of 1901 he toured Europe with his parents, and when they returned home too late for the fall semester, he decided to leave college and enter his father's business. He went to the May Company store in Cleveland and learned the department-store business from the ground up, beginning as a stock boy and working up through all the menial jobs to salesman and floorman. In 1903, when his father moved his headquarters to St. Louis, May went there to work in the May-owned Famous store. In 1909 he married Florence Goldman; they had two children.

In 1910, David May's partnership with his brothers-in-law was dissolved and the company was incorporated, with Morton May as a member of its board of directors. The company then began a vigorous program of store acquisition. In 1912 the May firm purchased the William Barr Dry Goods Company in St. Louis and merged it with the Famous store; the Famous-Barr Company became the biggest department store west of the Mississippi. Later the May Department Stores Company acquired Boggs and Buhl in Pittsburgh and M. O'Neil and Company in Akron, and in 1923 it bought A. Hamburger and Sons in Los Angeles. In 1926, sales of the May group passed $100 million. During the Great Depression the company attracted shoppers by maintaining large stocks of merchandise and thus consistently showed profits and paid dividends.

May became president in 1917 when his father retired to the chairmanship of the board. When his father died in 1927, May became chief executive officer. He served as president until 1951 and as chief executive officer until 1957, when he surrendered the former office to his son, Morton David May. He remained chairman of the board until 1967.

During the thirty-four years May was president, the chain grew to twenty-five stores. In 1939 the company acquired control of the William Taylor, Son and Company store in Cleveland and built the company's Wilshire Boulevard store in Los Angeles. The May stores, which featured a tremendous assortment of goods and large inventories, had always appealed to lower- and middle-income groups. The Wilshire store was the first designed to appeal to upper- and middle-income shoppers. In 1946, May acquired Kaufman's in Pittsburgh, and in 1948, the Strouss-Hirshberg Company in Youngstown, Ohio. In 1958, May acquired the Hecht Company stores in Baltimore and Washington, and in 1965, the G. Fox store in Hartford, Conn., and Meier and Frank in Portland, Oreg.

Under May's management, the May Company was conservative in business but daring in merchandising. Because the company operated stores in various parts of the country under a variety of names, May preferred not to employ a system of central purchasing. Rather, he gave each store autonomy and let local buyers run the stores.

By 1968 the May chain, with eighty stores in nine states and the District of Columbia and sales of $1 billion, was the fourth-largest chain in the United States. There were fifteen May Company stores in Los Angeles, seven in Cleveland, four Kaufman stores in Pittsburgh, six Famous-Barr stores in St. Louis, fourteen

Hecht stores in Baltimore and Washington, and twelve O'Neil stores in Akron, among others.

May was quiet, unassuming, and apparently indifferent to fame. (He made it a practice, for example, to throw his *Who's Who* questionnaire into the wastebasket.) He surrounded himself with capable subordinates, to whom he delegated considerable responsibility; he never let his wealth or success keep him from taking their advice. He was attuned to his customers and made a habit of walking the floors of his stores to be sure that their needs were being served. Until the end of his life he appeared at his office in St. Louis almost every day.

With little publicity, May engaged in a variety of philanthropic enterprises. He was an active supporter of various St. Louis cultural and philanthropic institutions and bestowed large benefactions on St. Louis, Washington, Brandeis, and Fisk universities. Although May was Jewish, his fund-raising work on behalf of the St. Louis University library prompted Pope John XXIII to award him the Knighthood in the Order of Pope St. Sylvester, the oldest of papal orders. In 1959, May founded the Morton J. May Foundation. He died in Clayton, Mo.

[See "May Stores: Watch Them Grow," *Fortune*, Dec. 1948; "May Company Lets Out Its Belt—Again," *Business Week*, June 5, 1954; "Humanities Award to Morton May," *St. Louis Globe-Democrat*, Dec. 24, 1966; and Forbes Parkhill, *The May Story* (n.d.). An obituary is in the *New York Times*, May 18, 1968.]

ROBERT L. BERNER

MENDELSOHN, SAMUEL (Mar. 3, 1895–Feb. 3, 1966), inventor and manufacturer, was born in Chicago, Ill., the son of Gedalah Mendelsohn, a physician and rabbi, and Rebecca Pearl Lustgarten. The family moved to Roanoke, Va., and he graduated from Roanoke High School in 1912. Mendelsohn married Hannah Block on May 23, 1925; they had one child.

For a time Mendelsohn and his brother sold and manufactured radio tubes. They sold the company in 1930. Mendelsohn then had a flashlight and battery concession in a Times Square drugstore in New York City. During this period, he invented a three-cell, dry-battery-powered flashgun that replaced the manganese-powder devices then used by photographers. When press photographers complained about the lack of synchronization between the flashgun and camera shutter, Mendelsohn developed a flashbulb that could be delayed to synchronize with the opening of the shutter. He called the invention the Mendelsohn Speedgun and founded the Mendelsohn Speedgun Company in 1932, opening a plant in Bloomfield, N.J.

The first significant news photo taken with the Speedgun was that of Chicago's Mayor Anton Cermak on Feb. 13, 1933, shortly after his assassination while riding in Miami with President-elect Franklin D. Roosevelt. The photo resulted in a great deal of publicity for the Speedgun. Mendelsohn operated the Speedgun plant until the state took it for a highway right-of-way in 1951. He sold the business to the Micro Laboratory of Livingston, N.J.

During World War II and the Korean War, Mendelsohn developed microwave components and coaxial connections for the military and the United States Office of Scientific Research. He also developed a number of devices for aircraft and target controls as well as for radar systems. He held nearly thirty patents and served as a consultant for universities and industry. Mendelsohn emerged from retirement in 1961 to manage the Line Electric Company of Orange, N.J. He was active in civic and community affairs in Bloomfield, N.J., and was a life member of the National Press Photographers Association. He died in Glen Ridge, N.J.

[An obituary is in the *New York Times*, Feb. 4, 1966.]

RONALD RIDGLEY

MENNINGER, WILLIAM CLAIRE (Oct. 15, 1899–Sept. 6, 1966), psychiatrist, was born in Topeka, Kans., the son of Charles Frederick Menninger, a pioneering physician, and Flora Vesta Knisely, a former teacher. His father encouraged his sons to become involved in civic activities and to take up medicine. William enrolled at Washburn College and in 1918 interrupted his education to enlist in the United States Army. He completed his B.A. at Washburn College the following year. He did graduate work in medicine and obtained an M.A. in 1922 from Columbia University and an M.D. in 1924 from Cornell University Medical School. From 1924 to 1926 he was an intern in medicine and surgery at Bellevue Hospital in New York City. In 1925, during his residency, he met Catharine Louisa Wright, and they were married on Dec. 11, 1925; they had three children.

Menninger returned to Topeka in 1926. There he entered into general practice and served as a specialist in internal medicine on the staff of the Menninger Clinic, a cooperative medical institution founded by his father and older brother, Karl, in 1919. Influenced by his brother, who was interested in psychiatry, Menninger became convinced of the significance of emotional problems in medicine generally and returned to school in 1927 for training in psychiatry. He began postgraduate work in the subject at St. Elizabeths Hospital in Washington, D.C. He gained additional experience working at Queen's Square Hospital, London, in 1933 and the Chicago Psychoanalytic Institute in 1934–1935. From 1930 to 1945 he served as the director of the Menninger Sanitarium and, following the expansion of the Menninger Foundation and educational facilities for psychiatry in Topeka, became a professor of psychiatry at the Menninger School of Psychiatry in 1946, a position he held until his death.

Much of Menninger's early medical research focused on the study of the nervous system and neurological diseases. In 1923, while spending the summer working in the laboratory of the Menninger Clinic, he witnessed an outbreak of poliomyelitis and published his first scientific paper on that subject. He became interested in the study and treatment of other disorders, including paralysis, Alzheimer's disease, and brain tumors, and became recognized locally for his work as a neurologist.

Another neurological disease, syphilis, became a primary interest because in the early 1920's many of the patients who came to the Menninger Clinic were suffering from the disease. He focused his attention on juvenile paresis, an inherited form of syphilis found among teenage children. That work, summed up in his classic study *Juvenile Paresis* (1936), demonstrated the growing importance of psychiatry in his research. While Menninger's analysis of juvenile paresis indicated that the physical and mental deterioration associated with the disease were caused in part by the physical destruction of the organic brain, more important was the fact that individuals with the disease manifested a series of regressions in psychological and sexual development. Applying the basic tenets of the Freudian theory of psychoanalysis to juvenile paresis, Menninger interpreted the disease as a progressive retrogression caused primarily by the underdevelopment of the individual's ego and libido, a condition that ultimately leads to the withdrawal of any concern with the external environment, a total fixation on self, and complete helplessness.

Convinced of the importance of emotional and psychological factors in disease, Menninger became increasingly committed to disseminating information on psychiatry. In numerous papers published in the late 1930's, he examined the role of psychological factors in heart disease, gastrointestinal problems, and pregnancy. A series of articles in the *Journal of the Kansas Medical Society* led to the publication of *Fundamentals of Psychiatry* (1943). On another front, Menninger examined the many needs of psychiatry: the various kinds of therapy; the function of psychiatric hospitals; and the role of psychiatrists, psychiatric nurses, and others in providing individualized patient care. Concerned with establishing rational, well-defined means for treating the mentally ill, Menninger gradually moved away from research in clinical and experimental medicine, becoming a spokesman and educator for psychiatry.

World War II accelerated and considerably expanded Menninger's work on behalf of psychiatry. He reentered the army in 1942 and the next year was appointed to the position of neuropsychiatric consultant for the Fourth Service Command. He was promoted in 1944 to the rank of lieutenant colonel and the position of chief psychiatrist for the army. In that capacity, Menninger played a pivotal role in promoting the importance of that branch of medicine. He identified for army psychiatrists, selective service boards, and military personnel in general the important reasons for conducting neuropsychiatric examinations of inductees and developed examinations for that purpose. In contrast to earlier conditions, when there were few army psychiatrists and soldiers with psychological problems were discharged, Menninger administered and coordinated a psychiatric division and inaugurated programs to treat and rehabilitate psychiatric cases. He also sought to define the wide variety of emotional and psychological problems posed by the war. In 1945, by which time he had become a brigadier general, he compiled a nomenclature of psychiatric disorders and reactions that was considerably more comprehensive than previous classifications. World War II thus provided Menninger with the opportunity to spread basic knowledge and a message about the importance of psychiatry to physicians, military personnel, and eventually the general public. His book *Psychiatry in a Troubled World* (1948) was an examination not only of the stresses and psychological problems experienced during the war but also of the role that psychiatry could play in reducing tensions in everyday life. He was awarded the Distinguished Service Medal, the French Legion of Honor, and the Albert and Mary Lasker Award.

After the war, Menninger became one of the nation's leading figures in the fight against mental illness. Within the medical community, he helped to establish the Group for the Advancement of Psychiatry in 1946 and the following year was elected president of the American Psychiatric Association. He also became a popular author and lecturer. Believing that psychiatry offered the means for dealing with a host of psychological and sociological problems, he became a salesman for psychiatry in a wide variety of forums in the 1950's and 1960's. Through public presentations and books such as *You and Psychiatry* (1948), *Making and Keeping Friends* (1952), and *Human Understanding in Industry* (1956), Menninger applied the lessons of psychiatry to issues in family relations, business and public relations, and virtually any problem in personal development or social interaction. In 1957 he became president of the Menninger Foundation. He died in Topeka.

[Menninger's manuscripts and correspondence are housed at the Menninger Foundation, Topeka. During his lifetime, he published more than 200 articles on psychiatry and related topics. A complete bibliography of his published works and reprints of many of his papers are in Bernard H. Hall, ed., *A Psychiatrist for a Troubled World: Selected Papers of William C. Menninger, M.D.* (1967). The cover story of *Time*, Oct. 25, 1948, focuses on psychiatry with an emphasis on Menninger and his work. Personal reminiscences include memorial articles by Walter E. Barton, Henry W. Brosin, and Malcolm J. Farrell, *American Journal of Psychiatry*, 123 (1966); Jeannetta L. Menninger, *Bulletin of the Menninger Clinic*, 30 (1966); L. Rangell, *Journal of the American Psychiatric Association*, 15 (1967); and Henry W. Brosin, "A Biographical Sketch," in Hall, which also includes several laudatory but informative synopses of various aspects of Menninger's work. An obituary is in the *New York Times*, Sept. 7, 1966.]

RONALD RAINGER

MERTON, THOMAS (Jan. 31, 1915–Dec. 10, 1968), clergyman and writer, was born in Prades, France, the son of Owen Merton, a landscape painter from New Zealand, and Ruth Jenkins, a citizen of the United States. Soon after his birth, the family moved to his maternal grandparents' home on Long Island, N.Y. His mother died in 1921, and four years later he returned to France with his father, living in St. Antonin and attending the Lycée de Montauban from 1926 to 1928. He and his father then moved to England, where he studied at the Oakham School during 1929–1932. During this period his father died, leaving him in the guardianship of his godfather, Tom Bennett. He was at Clare College, Cambridge, in 1933 and 1934, but his escapades there prompted his guardian to insist that he return to America.

In January 1935, Merton began studies at Columbia University. The search for meaning and purpose in life, which he had managed to stifle, surfaced at last. Briefly, he became a Communist. Mark Van Doren, his English professor, and Daniel Walsh, his philosophy instructor, kindled his religious sensibilities and sharpened his search for truth. In 1938, the year he completed undergraduate studies at Columbia, he was baptized into the Roman Catholic church. In 1939 he received an M.A. from Columbia, writing a dissertation on William Blake. While studying for his degree, he did volunteer work at Friendship House in Harlem.

In the fall of 1939, Merton began teaching English at St. Bonaventure University. During the year and a half he taught there, he struggled with his vocation. A Holy Week retreat at the Trappist monastery of Our Lady of Gethsemani in Kentucky impressed him deeply. He grappled with two possible callings: working at Friendship House or giving up everything and going into the Trappist order. He decided that he could better serve God in the monastery. On Dec. 10, 1941, he entered the Gethsemani monastery and received the religious name Louis. On Mar. 19, 1944, he made simple vows; on Mar. 19, 1947, he made solemn vows; and on May 26, 1949, he was ordained a priest. In 1951 he became a naturalized American citizen. From 1951 to 1955 he served as master of scholastics (students for the priesthood), and from 1955 to 1965, as master of novices.

A jovial man of cheerful disposition, Merton lived happily in the monastery, but not without struggle. At first, he struggled over what seemed to him to be a conflict between writing and contemplation. He struggled, too, with a strong desire for deeper solitude and the possibility that this might mean that he had a vocation to the Carthusian order. But his greatest struggle was with the meaning of the monastic "flight from the world." Initially it meant to him leaving the world in order to seek God in solitude. While he never lost his commitment to that quest, his understanding of monastic life underwent profound changes. He came to realize that "leaving the world" is at best a metaphor that, if pushed too far, becomes an illusion. Monks, he concluded, also had responsibilities to the world. In his later writings, he attempted to determine his responsibilities. Contemplation, he made clear, is not a compartment of life but the deep experience in which one finds God, one's own true self, and one's brothers and sisters.

Merton's contemplative experience explains his involvement with social issues and his dialogue with other religious traditions in the East and West. During the 1960's he became, from behind his monastery walls, a recognized leader for many in the struggle for racial justice, for world peace, and for nonviolence as a way of life. He expanded his involvement in interreligious dialogue, eager to enrich his own faith by contact with other Christian traditions as well as with Judaism and the religions of Asia. His interest in religious dialogue was not primarily ecumenical; his concern lay not so much in resolving differences in religious formulations as in discovering the fundamental unity underlying different religious traditions—namely, the unity of the religious experience.

Merton's literary output was enormous: at least ten books of poetry (all contained in *Collected Poems,* 1970) and more than forty books in all. Moreover, his works have been translated into more than twenty foreign languages. Besides the published works, there are unpublished journals, talks, and essays, as well as some 4,000 letters.

Merton's writings, as witness to his personal growth, may be divided into three periods. The first would be from the time of his conversion in 1938 to the publication of *The Seven Storey Mountain* in 1948. The writings from this period tend to be ascetic, unworldly, intransigent, presupposing a sharp separation between God and the world. They include *Thirty Poems* (1944), *Man in a Divided Sea* (1946), and *Seeds of Contemplation* (1949).

In the second period, roughly from 1950 to 1960, Merton, much affected by the best-seller popularity of *The Seven Storey Mountain*, gradually opened up to the world. He was influenced by his contact with young monks and by psychoanalysis, Zen, and existentialism. In the books of these years, such as *The Ascent to Truth* (1951), *The Sign of Jonas* (1953), and *No Man Is an Island* (1955), Merton did not express a truly new perspective but, rather, seemed to be straddling the monastic wall.

The first of Merton's many articles on war and peace appeared in the *Catholic Worker* in the fall of 1961 and mark the beginning of his last period. By the spring of 1962 he had been forbidden by his highest superiors to write on the subject. He went underground, sending various bits of unpublished mimeographed writings to friends. He became even more intensely interested in Eastern religions, especially Zen, Taoism, and Sufism. He began to write experimental and satirical prose and poetry. His works from this period include *New Seeds of Contemplation* (1962), *Emblems of a Season of Fury* (1963), *Seeds of Destruction* (1964), *Gandhi and Non-violence* (1965), *The Way of Chuang Tzu* (1965), *Conjectures of a Guilty Bystander* (1966), *Raids on the Unspeakable* (1966), *Mystics and Zen Masters* (1967), *Zen and the Birds of Appetite* (1968), *Cables to the Ace* (1968), and *Geography of Lograire* (1969).

From 1965 to 1968, Merton lived as a hermit. In 1968 he was invited to speak at a meeting of monks and sisters in Bangkok, Thailand. On this trip he visited India, met three times with the Dalai Lama, and arrived on December 7 at Bangkok for the meeting at which he was to speak. His extensive plans to visit other countries were abruptly terminated by his accidental death by electrocution (caused by a defective wire on a fan), exactly twenty-seven years to the day of his entrance into the monastery. His body was flown back to the United States in a military plane and buried in the cemetery at Gethsemani.

[Merton's papers are in the Thomas Merton Studies Center, Bellarmine College, Louisville, Ky. There are also Merton collections at Columbia University, the University of Kentucky in Lexington, and the University of Syracuse. The first of a projected five volumes of his letters was published as *The Hidden Ground of Love* (1985), edited by William H. Shannon. Biographies of Merton include Edward Rice, *The Man in the Sycamore Tree* (1970); Monica Furlong, *Merton* (1980); and James Forest, *Thomas Merton: A Pictorial Biography* (1980). Studies of his thought include George Woodcock, *Thomas Merton, Monk and Poet* (1978); James Finley, *Merton's Palace of Nowhere* (1978); Ross Labrie, *The Art of Thomas Merton* (1979); William H. Shannon, *Thomas Merton's Dark Path* (1981); Anthony Padavano, *The Human Journey* (1982); Victor Kramer, *Thomas Merton, Monk and Artist* (1984); Alexander Lipski, *Thomas Merton and Asia* (1984); and Michael Mott, *The Seven Mountains of Thomas Merton* (1984). A documentary, *Merton: A Film Biography* (1984), was produced by Paul Wilkes and Audrey Glynn. An obituary is in the *New York Times*, Dec. 11, 1968.]

WILLIAM H. SHANNON

MEYER, AGNES ELIZABETH ERNST (Jan. 2, 1887–Sept. 1, 1970), journalist, writer, and philanthropist, was born in New York City, the daughter of Frederick H. Ernst, a lawyer, and Lucie Schmidt. A daily ritual of "icy baths" thought necessary to build a strong moral character supplemented a strict Lutheran upbringing by her parents, immigrants from northern Germany. Her three brothers treated her as one of the boys, and she once described herself as a "tomboy," unafraid to stand up for the underdog. Her most intense relationship was with her father, with whom she strongly identified. Her autobiography, *Out of These Roots* (1953), makes repeated reference to that relationship. She described her "extraordinary Oedipus complex" and wrote that she "was always unconsciously looking for father substitutes." An infatuation with male luminaries such as Paul Claudel, Thomas Mann, and Ignace Jan Paderewski continued throughout her life.

During her early childhood Ernst's father developed a successful law practice in rural Pelham Heights, N.Y., but moved the family to New York City in 1899. By the time she was an adolescent, her father had begun to write books and plays, neglecting the family and his law practice. She was devastated by her father's opposition to her pursuit of a college education, a dream he had inspired in her. After attending Morris High School she won a scholarship to Barnard College and enrolled in 1903. Bored with, and inattentive to, her math classes, she was branded "irresponsible." She lost her scholarship and had to work at a variety of jobs to continue her education. She also changed her field of specialization from mathematics to philosophy and literature. Although she did not meet John Dewey until her senior year, she credited him with planting the seeds of her social conscience and commitment to public service. After graduating from Barnard in 1907, she became the first female reporter for the *New York Morning Sun*, a job that brought her into contact with people such as Alfred Stieglitz, Edward Steichen, and Elizabeth Gurley Flynn. Although she was impressed by the innovative photography of the first two, Flynn's orations left her with a lifelong "contempt for American radicalism."

Ernst traveled to Paris in 1908 to study at the Sorbonne, yet her memories were more of people than of schooling. She met the Romanian sculptor Constantin Brancusi, the French composer Darius Milhaud, and the French sculptor Auguste Rodin. She also developed a friendship with Leo Stein, but she had "an immediate antipathy" for his sister, Gertrude Stein, whose appearance and demeanor "offended" her "aesthetic sense." One woman who did impress Ernst during her stay in Paris was the scientist Marie Curie.

On Feb. 12, 1910, exactly two years after first meeting him, she married Eugene Meyer, a financier eleven years her senior. Soon pregnant with the first of her five children, she resisted traditional female roles and returned to graduate school. She was especially unprepared for motherhood and often forgot to go home to nurse her baby.

Meyer neverthless continued to write professionally. Her first book, *Chinese Painting as Reflected in the Thought and Art of Li Lung-mien* (1923), followed years of study of Chinese art, literature, and philosophy at Columbia University and a close friendship with the collector Charles L. Freer. The work tried to capture the wisdom of the Chinese sages and urged Western peoples to distrust philosophical ideals not used to improve human relations.

Meyer received an education in politics after being recruited by William Lukens ("Boss") Ward in 1921 to get out the female voters for Republicans in Westchester County. She turned down an opportunity to run for office herself, saying that she must put her family first. Yet, she accepted when Ward appointed her chairman of the Recreation Commission of Westchester County, a post she held from 1923 to 1941. Meyer and the commission promoted festivals, concerts, athletic events, workshops, and summer camp for disadvantaged children. This position marked the beginning of her lifelong commitment to social reform.

The Meyers maintained two places of residence and entertained lavishly in both. They often spent the summers at Seven Springs Farm in Mount Kisco, N.Y., and the rest of the year they lived at Crescent Place in Washington, D.C. Eugene Meyer held a number of public-service positions in Washington from the 1920's on. In 1932 he became chairman of the board of the Reconstruction Finance Corporation (RFC). In 1933 he resigned from the RFC, and following his wife's suggestion, he bought the *Washington Post*. (Philip L. Graham, who was married to the Meyers' daughter Katharine, became publisher of the *Post* in 1946. After his suicide in 1963, Katharine Meyer Graham took over the newspaper.)

Agnes Meyer often wrote for the *Post*, but even though she was a legal partner at the paper, she did not share in its management. In fact, the news department had orders not to print any writings of Meyer family members or anything written about them without Eugene Meyer's approval. In the late 1930's the *Post* did publish Agnes Meyer's review of Thomas Mann's *Joseph in Egypt*. Mann was pleased with the review and granted Meyer an interview; thus began their twenty-year friendship. She later translated his *Coming Victory of Democracy* and other works.

During World War II, Meyer's son, Eugene Meyer III, and Philip Graham urged Meyer to put aside her literary project, a comparison of the works of Mann, Tolstoy, and Dostoevski, to write about the war effort. She flew to Britain in September 1942 and wrote a series of Associated Press articles about the British people's brave efforts to cope with the ravages of war. The success of that series led her to travel around the United States to assess conditions on the home front. She documented problems of war centers throughout the country, such as child labor, delinquency, racial discrimination, and the disintegration of family life and moral character. She pleaded for improving community life and moral education. These pessimistic reports were published as *Journey Through Chaos* (1944). She also covered postwar progress and publicized community-center projects such as the Chicago Back of the Yards movement.

In the 1940's, Meyer began to press for a cabinet-status department of health, education, and security, an organ of the federal government that would promote human welfare. She also launched a campaign for federal aid to public education. During the 1950's she spared no words in denouncing Senator Joseph McCarthy and his red-baiting allies as a threat to academic freedom. In *Education for a New Morality* (1957) she reacted to the devastating possibilities of an atomic world and challenged Americans to become "global citizens" by developing a creative system of public education to bridge the gap between science and humanism. Quoting Dewey, she argued that education could use the scientific method for social well-being. She hoped that the American child would grow up to be "a composite of citizen and scientist." Women as dedicated mothers, she declared, were vital to this goal. Her observations of the home front during the war had led her to an indictment of American women as "more selfish and more material" than American men. Meyer bitterly criticized the "disastrous" influence of postwar feminists who competed with men. In Meyer's view, woman's natural expertise was in "co-operative living," her greatest asset was "humility," and her "proper role" was found in the family. Meyer, who had recognized her own inadequacies in adjusting to traditional roles in raising her children, called the American woman back to the home, and to motherhood in particular, for, to her, it was only woman as mother who could "close the tragic gap between emotion and reason."

Despite illnesses and an alcohol problem, Meyer lectured widely, contributed articles to a number of publications, and carried out philanthropic work for public education and social reform. In December 1944 she and her husband created the Eugene and Agnes E. Meyer Foundation, to fund community service, the arts and humanities, and projects in physical and mental health and education. In her later years she worked for improvements in public education through the Urban Service Corps and the National Committee for Support of the Public Schools. Meyer remained active until her death at Seven Springs Farm.

[Meyer's papers are in the Library of Congress; they include extensive correspondence, speeches, writings, and diaries for several years (1909 to circa 1960), as well as her unpublished manuscipt of "Chance and Destiny." Meyer's works not already cited in the text include a long interview with John Dewey, "Significance of the Trotsky Trial," *International Conciliation*, Feb. 1938; and "A Challenge to American Women," *Collier's*, May 11, 1946. Information about Meyer can be found in her husband's papers at the Library of Congress and in interviews with him in the Columbia University Oral History Project. Merlo J. Pusey, *Eugene Meyer* (1974), contains much valuable information. Deborah Davis, *Katharine the Great: Katharine Graham and the Washington Post* (1979), provides much family history. Two previously unpublished letters of Thomas Mann to Agnes Meyer are printed in *Books Abroad*, Autumn 1971. See also Josephine Ripley, "Agnes Meyer, Practicing Citizen," *Christian Science Monitor*, June 10, 1967. Obituaries are in the *Washington Post* and the *New York Times*, both Sept. 2, 1970; and *Time*, Sept. 14, 1970.]

SARA ALPERN

MICHAUX, LIGHTFOOT SOLOMON (1885?–Oct. 20, 1968), clergyman, social activist, radio personality, and real estate developer, was born in Buckroe Beach, Va. His parents' names are unknown. He attended public schools in nearby Newport News until the fourth grade, when he began working full-time for his father selling crabs and oysters. Michaux (pronounced "Me-shaw") eventually expanded his father's small operation into a profitable business, selling to army and defense establishments in the area. He married Mary Eliza Pauline in 1906; they had no children.

In 1917, Michaux moved his business to Hopewell, a boomtown that was rife with crime and corruption. Pauline Michaux, an evangelist who remained her husband's closest associate throughout his life, inspired him to turn his enormous energies from business to evangelism. On her own, Pauline organized girls' groups called Purity Clubs, for which she coined the motto Be a Peach Out of Reach.

As a preacher, Michaux, who was black, stressed interracial social and political action to battle immorality and poverty. He took full advantage of technology to spread his message. Soon after he opened a church in Newport News, he began preaching over the radio and quickly gained a large interracial following. Despite strong objections from local authorities, his church meetings were integrated. In 1922, segregationist authorities put him on trial but he was acquitted.

In 1929, inspired by what he said was "a voice out of the void," Michaux moved to Washington, D.C., and established what was to become the headquarters for his Church of God and its social arm, the Gospel Spreading Association. From a former pool hall across from Griffith Stadium, Michaux began broadcasting daily over commercial radio station WSJV. (The call letters, he insisted, stood for "Willingly Suffered Jesus for Victory over the grave.") Beginning in 1931, he was heard on network radio every Saturday evening, and from 1936 to 1938, his sermons were also broadcast by the British Broadcasting Company. "The Happy Am I Preacher and His Famous Choir" program, with its 156-member choir (at one time including Mahalia Jackson and Clara Ward), made him a celebrity and helped inspire the establishment of at least seven churches in various cities.

Michaux was noted for his spectacular baptisms. Until 1938 he conducted a yearly Potomac River ceremony, baptizing hundreds of black and white believers while thousands watched from the banks. In 1938, because of his friendship with Clark Griffith, he switched this ceremony to Griffith Stadium, where, in a canvas tank often filled with water imported from the river Jordan, he baptized hundreds more each year. A gifted orator with a flair for the dramatic, one year he staged the second coming of Christ; another time, he officiated at the devil's funeral; on another occasion, he presided while an electrical heart of Jesus splattered blood on white-robed penitents.

During the Great Depression, Michaux expanded his social-welfare work. When a branch luncheonette failed, he convinced its owner to turn the building over to him. Michaux renamed it the Happy News Café and employed jobless poor to operate it. He also operated a free employment service and had his followers repair an old building to house forty evicted black families.

Michaux was deeply involved in politics. Like most blacks, he had been a staunch Republican all his life, but after President Herbert Hoover evicted the Bonus Army, to which Michaux was ministering, he became a supporter of the New Deal. (Franklin D. Roosevelt, he said, was an instrument of God and the emancipator from social injustice.) He later supported President Truman's civil rights program but switched back to the Republicans when Eisenhower became president. Like numerous other prominent whites, Eisenhower was an honorary deacon of Michaux's church, having begun this association in 1944.

As a result of his friendship with government officials, Michaux received a Reconstruction Finance Corporation loan of $3.5 million to complete, in 1946, a 594-unit housing development called Mayfair Mansions, for which he had been able to purchase land. In 1964 the Gospel Spreading Association received an additional $6 million loan to construct an adjoining 672-unit apartment project called Paradise Manor on his acquired land. Later there were unproven accusations that Michaux was guilty of bribe taking in these two ventures.

Michaux was not enthusiastic about the civil rights movement of the 1960's. He openly criticized Martin Luther King, Jr., for his attack on J. Edgar Hoover and the Federal Bureau of Investigation and for his use of the boycott to force implementation of the 1965 Voting Rights Act. Since Michaux had long conducted integrated religious and social functions, he was shocked at the confrontational tactics of King and other civil rights advocates. He seemed determined to show his white patrons that he did not support such activities.

Michaux is a prominent example of the so-called storefront religious leader. His mixture of fundamentalist religion and social welfare had wide appeal among the destitute, although middle-class blacks were not as widely attracted. But Michaux's effective use of radio; his monthly newspaper, *Happy News*, which had a circulation of 8,000; his residence in the nation's capital; and his ability to attract prominent white supporters gave him an influence that few such preachers ever gained. Michaux died in Washington, D.C.

[The most detailed accounts of Michaux's life are Chancellor Williams, "The Socio-economic Significance of the Store-Front Church Movement in the U.S. Since 1920" (Ph.D. diss., American University, 1949); and James D. Tyms, "A Study of Four Religious Cults Operating Among Negroes" (M.A. thesis, Howard University, 1938). See also E. F. Lark, *Presenting a Pictorial Review of Elder Solomon Michaux* (1941); C. M. Green, *Washington, 1800–1950*, II (1962–1963); E. Franklin Frazier, *The Negro Church in America* (1964); and Patricia W. Romero, *In Black America: 1968, the Year of Awakening* (1969). A collection of his music is Lightfoot Solomon Michaux, ed., *Spiritual Happiness–Making Songs* (n.d.). Obituaries are in the *New York Times*, the *Washington Post*, and the *Washington Evening Star*, all Oct. 21, 1968.]

JOHN F. MARSZALEK

MIES VAN DER ROHE, LUDWIG (Mar. 27, 1886–Aug. 17, 1969), architect, was born Maria Ludwig Michael Mies in Aachen, Germany, the son of Michael Mies, a master mason, and Amalie Rohe. He attended local schools, including the Cathedral School (1897–1900) and a craft school, where he studied in 1900 and 1901 before going to work as a contractor's apprentice. He became a journeyman brickmason, a skill he later referred to with pride, and also worked in architects' offices in Aachen. In 1905 he moved to Berlin, where he joined the office of Bruno Paul, an architect of quality and sophistication who was also well regarded for his furniture design. Although Mies produced no furniture until the 1920's, it is likely that he began to consider the problems of such design, especially the chair, at this time. In 1907, with his first independent commission, he showed skills that offered promise of greater success in the future. His client was Alois Riehl, the Nietzsche scholar. In Riehl, Mies found a mentor able to satisfy his increasing appetite for philosophy and the purpose of architecture.

The next year, Mies began to work for Peter Behrens, the most important figure in German progressive architecture prior to World War I. An indication of Behrens' stature at the time is that his students also included Walter Gropius, who was a studio head, and Le Corbusier. In 1910, the Berlin exhibition of the work of Frank Lloyd Wright impressed Behrens so much that he led his entire staff on frequent lunchtime visits to the gallery. Mies later wrote of the profound impact of Wright's work on his own ideas. Mies was also influenced by Hendrick Petrus Berlage and Karl Friedrich Schinkel. Behrens gave Mies increasing responsibility, ultimately making him a construction supervisor for the German embassy in St. Petersburg in 1911–1912.

Mies left Behrens' office in 1912, when he

received the commission for the Kröller-Müller House, in the Netherlands. Although the house was never built, the full-scale model that Mies erected on the actual site illustrates the great importance he attached to scale, proportion, and composition and to the study of architecture through the model.

On Apr. 10, 1913, Mies married Adele Auguste Bruhn; they had three children. Their marriage was not a success, and although they never divorced, they lived apart after 1921. During World War I, Mies was not drafted until late 1915 and saw no action.

Resuming his practice after the war, Mies first attempted a continuation of his work of the prewar years. Then, in the ferment of the Weimar era, he began to rethink the role of architecture, and in a series of projects from 1919 to 1924 he advanced the most consistent and coherent summary of the claims for a modern architecture that had yet been made in Europe. Five projects, two for glass-enclosed, steel-framed skyscrapers, one for an office building of reinforced concrete, and two for country houses, one of reinforced concrete and the other of brick, presented to Europeans ideas that had become part of the scene in America, where the suburban dwelling and the skyscraper were the major modern architectural innovations.

Mies also became active in professional architectural associations and developed an interest in architectural education. He viewed himself as the inheritor of an ancient system of apprenticeship and sought to incorporate that quality into architectural education when he began to give public lectures around 1923. Following the disastrous inflation of the early 1920's in Germany, Mies began to build more toward the end of the decade, culminating his individual work with the luxurious Tugendhat House, Brno, Czechoslovakia, in 1928–1930 and the regal Barcelona Pavilion for the international exposition there in 1929. The Tugendhat House survives, and in 1986 the city of Barcelona rebuilt the pavilion on its original site. Also during the 1920's, Mies established a professional and personal relationship with the designer Lilly Reich. Their collaboration, by which designs were simplified and refined, continued until the summer of 1939, when she joined him in the United States to develop the campus plan for the Illinois Institute of Technology (IIT).

As an administrator, Mies organized and directed the Weissenhofsiedlung project in 1927, wherein he invited leading architects from throughout Europe to design a model community of modern architecture outside Stuttgart. His interest in education culminated in his acceptance of the directorship of the Bauhaus in 1930, moving it as a private school to Berlin in 1932, when the city of Dessau ceased to fund it, and then closing it after interference by the Nazis in 1933.

In the 1930's, after the closing of the Bauhaus and because of the Great Depression, Mies built little. Nonetheless, he suffered no persecution, and in 1933 he entered and won a competition for the new Reichsbank in Berlin. In his studio he did some private teaching and prepared a series of projects that addressed the problem of the house and its environment, united by the development of a set of linked courts. Some of these projects focused on the problem of the plan; others considered structure or explored form. Throughout, the definition of space, both interior and exterior, attracted his attention and served as a focus for his work in the future. His principal source of income in this period was the royalties he received from his various designs for furniture, the most famous of which is the Barcelona chair.

In 1938, Mies immigrated to the United States to become director of the Armour Institute of Technology school of architecture in Chicago, a position he would hold until his retirement in 1958. He became an American citizen in 1944. His American career began in the winter of 1937–1938, mostly spent in New York, with the development of a unique architectural curriculum that stressed a precise progression of professional training from the simplest of tasks to the most complex, building on the mastery of craft, until, as Mies liked to say, it transcended into art. In presenting his educational ideas to Henry Heald, the president of Armour, Mies stressed that he had studied carefully the character and needs of American architecture and architectural education. His aim, he said, was not to graft imported ideas onto native stock but to nurture a program in the fertility of American ideas and practices. Armour (since 1940 the Illinois Institute of Technology) also gave him his first American commission, the design of the school's new campus, which gave Mies the opportunity to draw on his exploratory work of the 1930's and embark on an architectural system of expression that led to personal success and immense influence.

Throughout Mies's American career, his office completed about one building per year. He purposely kept the office small so that he could retain direct control of all its aspects, thus assuring the quality and attention to detail for which he was so respected. At the same time, he usually had in his office or at the school a project to which he could devote more abstract thought. As earlier with Lilly Reich, he usually had one person in his office—Myron Goldsmith, Gene Summers, and his grandson Dirk Lohan, among them—whose contribution was nearly a collaboration. His practice focused on two building types: tall, repetitive buildings and low, large-span, special-use buildings. Of the tall buildings, the 860–880 Lake Shore Drive apartment houses in Chicago, built in 1951, and the Seagram Building in New York, completed in 1958, are the most famous, although other complexes in Toronto, Montreal, Baltimore, and Chicago also demonstrate his ideas and their refinement. Of the low buildings, the Farnsworth House (1950) in Plano, Ill.; Crown Hall (1956) on the IIT campus; and the New National Gallery (1968) in West Berlin are the most highly regarded. He died in Chicago.

Known as Ludwig Mies van der Rohe from the 1920's, he achieved renown, admiration, respect, and influence as an architect through the spare beauty and elegance of his buildings, the force and clarity of his visionary projects, and the coherence and rigor of his architectural curriculum. Among the great architects, he focused his attention on the expression of modern architectural materials (steel and glass), modern architectural problems (tall buildings and vast buildings), and modern architectural aesthetics (space and light). In his practice he combined the arrogance to attempt definitive solutions and the doubt that led him always to rethink what he had done.

Mies's dictum that "less is more" summarizes his point of view and indicates why his work has become an acquired taste. In seeking to express structure and space, the most tangible and intangible of problems an architect can address, he placed issues of use, comfort, and accessibility in a secondary position. Work of simplification, refinement, and focus was purposely directed at the solution of some, but not all, the problems an architect might address. Further, his method of showing precisely how his buildings were put together meant that he assumed the observer would take the time to study carefully what he had done. Once, in responding to a question about the challenges his museum in Berlin would present to those who would mount exhibitions there, he acknowledged the difficulty and then said, "But what a wonderful opportunity."

[Mies's correspondence, including much from his German career, is in the Manuscript Division of the Library of Congress. The drawings and correspondence associated with them are in New York's Museum of Modern Art. Smaller collections of Mies's drawings are at the Bauhaus Archive in Berlin, the Canadian Center of Architecture in Montreal, and the Art Institute of Chicago. His personal library was given to the Rare Book Collection of the Library of the University of Illinois at Chicago.

Franz Schulze, *Mies van der Rohe: A Critical Biography* (1985), is excellent and offers a good analysis of his art. Peter Carter, *Mies van der Rohe at Work* (1974), is a clear guide to design method and practice. Philip Johnson, *Mies van der Rohe* (1947; minimally updated, 1978), is a good summary of formal more than intellectual influences on Mies's work. Fritz Neumeyer, "Mies as Self-Educator," in *Mies van der Rohe: Architect as Educator* (1986), a good introduction to that subject, also contains a discussion of Mies's ideas on architectural education by Kevin Harrington, "Order, Space, Proportion: Mies's Curriculum at IIT." David Spaeth, *Ludwig Mies van der Rohe: An Annotated Bibliography and Chronology* (1979), is the best source for further reading. Films about Mies include Michael Blackwood, *Mies van der Rohe* (1986). Mies's daughter Dorothea, known professionally as Georgia van der Rohe, made a film in 1980, and in 1965, Norman Ross made a film for public television in Chicago. An obituary is in the *New York Times*, Aug. 19, 1969.]

KEVIN HARRINGTON

MILLER, GILBERT HERON (July 3, 1884–Jan. 2, 1969), theatrical producer and director, was born in New York City, the son of Henry Miller, an actor-manager, and Helene Stoepel, an actress whose stage name was Bijou Heron. He attended De La Salle Institute in New York City until he was twelve, when his mother took him to Europe. There he attended Catholic schools in France, Germany, and England. He became fluent in Italian, German, Spanish, French, and Hungarian. In 1904 he joined the

United States Marines and was stationed for two years in Haiti.

In 1906 Miller began his stage career in *Julie Bon-Bon* in London, but lacking his father's enthusiasm for acting he quickly turned his attention to theatrical managing. In 1907 he was appointed manager of his father's touring company of *The Great Divide*, and between 1910 and 1915 he was manager for all Henry Miller productions. He made his debut as a producer in London in 1916 with *Daddy Long-Legs*, beginning a career that included perhaps 200 productions in New York and London. In his early years his biggest hit was his only musical, *Monsieur Beaucaire*, which he brought to New York in 1919 as his first Broadway show.

During World War I, Miller served as a lieutenant in United States Army Intelligence. In 1922 he became producing director of the movie production company Famous Players–Lasky, which had a subsidiary that imported plays. He continued as an officer in that corporation until 1932.

Having been married to, and divorced from, Jessie Glendenning, with whom he had one child, and Margaret Allen (the dates of these marriages are missing from all published sources), on July 16, 1927, he married Kathryn Bache, the daughter of art collector and banker Jules S. Bache. During the 1927–1928 theatrical season Miller produced four Broadway hits, *The Captive, The Play's the Thing, The Constant Wife*, and *Her Cardboard Lover*.

In 1929 Miller announced that he was leaving New York for London because he could no longer deal with the numerous demands placed on producers by unions representing stagehands and musicians. But he had a change of heart and soon was again busy in New York, despite financial setbacks in the stock market. He found considerable success with the antiwar play *Journey's End* (1929).

In 1936, after a string of plays that did not fare well, he produced and directed *Victoria Regina* on Broadway. This portrait of Queen Victoria, with Helen Hayes in the title role, later toured forty-three cities and broke box-office records. During World War II, Miller returned to military service. In 1944–1945 he served as a civilian aviation technician aboard the aircraft carrier *Shangri-La*.

In 1950 he brought T. S. Eliot's *The Cocktail Party* to Broadway, and the next year he discovered Audrey Hepburn and starred her in *Gigi*. In 1951 he also arranged with Laurence Olivier and Vivien Leigh to bring to New York their productions of Shaw's *Caesar and Cleopatra* and Shakespeare's *Antony and Cleopatra*. During the latter part of the decade he brought to the stage *Witness for the Prosecution* (1954), *The Caine Mutiny Court-Martial* (1956), and *The Rope Dancers* (1957), among other plays. His last Broadway play was *Diamond Orchid* in 1965, which was a failure. He died in New York City.

Physically Miller was a large man. A lover of good food, he was constantly fighting his weight. He had a famous temper, and his quick rages were widely known. His interests were wide-ranging, as indicated by Ward Morehouse: "He's a linguist, a raconteur, a gourmet, an art collector, a crack shot, an estate owner, and part owner of an airline." In his younger days he piloted his own plane and was known as an expert hunter.

In his later years he spent a good deal of time in England, where he owned a home in London and a seventeenth-century country house in Sussex. He was an enthusiastic art collector; his New York home had paintings by Renoir, Dufy, Rowlandson, and Goya. He also owned the Henry Miller Theater (named for his father) in New York and the St. James and Lyric theaters in London.

Miller recognized the value of stars and claimed that he never haggled over the fee for an actor. As a result, his career was studded with successes featuring Broadway's leading players. He introduced Charles Laughton, Alec Guinness, Leslie Howard, and Robert Morley to New York audiences. Helen Hayes, Ruth Gordon, Katharine Cornell, Gertrude Lawrence, Ethel Barrymore, and Herbert Marshall were others representative of the quality of the actors and actresses who graced his productions.

Even though he usually avoided plays with heavy social significance, his productions showed him to be a man of unusual courage. He introduced American audiences to numerous French plays noted for their elegance. Ten years after World War I he brought *Journey's End* to both New York and London. Despite the grim images of war depicted and the absence of women from the cast, critics and audiences supported the play.

He was known for selecting plays with literate dialogue. Playwrights he produced included

Somerset Maugham, Philip Barry, Dylan Thomas, T. S. Eliot, and Sherwood Anderson. He richly deserved his reputation for fine performances that generally met critical and financial success. His trademark, according to *Look*, was the combination of "top stars, superb acting, and good taste." His obituary in the *New York Times* summarized his career: "Gilbert Heron Miller was born into show business, which was not of his doing; he made a success out of it, which was."

[A clipping and photograph file is in the Performing Arts Research Center of the New York Public Library. Articles include Ward Morehouse, "Portrait of a Producer: Gilbert Miller," *Theatre Arts*, July 1956. See also the obituary in the *New York Times*, Jan. 3, 1969.]

ROBERT A. ARMOUR

MILLIKAN, CLARK BLANCHARD (Aug. 23, 1903–Jan. 2, 1966), physicist and aerodynamicist, was born in Chicago, Ill., the son of Robert Andrews Millikan, a physicist, and Greta Irvin Blanchard. He attended the elementary and high schools of the University of Chicago, where his father was professor of physics. His graduation from high school coincided with his father's winter assignment at Throop Institute of Technology (now California Institute of Technology, or Caltech) in Pasadena; Millikan spent a year at the University of California at Berkeley and Throop Institute before entering Yale University in 1920.

Upon graduating from Yale in 1924 with majors in physics and mathematics, Millikan pursued graduate studies in the same subjects at Caltech, obtaining his Ph.D. in 1928 with the thesis "The Steady Motion of Viscous Incompressible Fluids." Millikan's interest in airplanes and aeronautics began in childhood, when he started to build model airplanes and flourished under the guidance of his mentor Harry Bateman. He and fellow students Arthur L. Klein and Albert Merrill demonstrated their aeronautical prowess by designing, building, and flying a biplane of unique design, capable of taking off and landing with a minimum of pilot control.

Millikan's interest in everything aeronautical made his choice of Caltech, in the heart of Southern California's burgeoning aircraft industry, a logical place for him to seek employment and settle down with his new bride, Helen Staats, whom he married on June 9, 1928. (They had three children.) Millikan spent his entire professional career there, as assistant professor (1928–1934), associate professor (1934–1940), and professor of aeronautics (1940 until his death). His tenure at Caltech spanned, and to a considerable extent was responsible for, that institution's rise to a position of world leadership in aeronautical education and research.

In 1925 the Daniel Guggenheim Foundation for the Promotion of Aeronautics was founded, and three years later Caltech received funds from it to establish a graduate school of aeronautics and to erect an aeronautical laboratory. Theodore von Kármán was brought from Germany to supervise the project, and Millikan and Klein performed much of the actual design work, especially for the wind tunnel, which, by employing the modifications and improvements suggested by von Kármán, became one of the most advanced and efficient in the world. It was the availability of this wind tunnel and its associated support facilities and personnel that enabled several American commercial aircraft companies (Douglas, Boeing, North American, Northrop, Lockheed, and Consolidated) to become leaders in the aircraft industry.

Millikan, as supervisor of all testing and research in the wind tunnel, was directly involved in all phases of the work; he seemed happiest when he was actually in the wind tunnel itself, taking measurements or suggesting improvements. One of his projects pointed to the advantages of high-altitude flying and the development of multiengine pressurized aircraft for commercial use. Following von Kármán's departure in 1944, Millikan served as acting director, and after 1949 as director, of the entire laboratory (GALCIT, as it was commonly called, standing for Guggenheim Aeronautical Laboratory, California Institute of Technology). In 1958, Millikan was divorced, and on Feb. 19, 1959, he married Edith Nussbaum Parry.

Besides his great interest in aeronautical research and development, Millikan took his teaching responsibilities very seriously. He prepared meticulously for his classes at Caltech, teaching both basic courses in aerodynamics and advanced courses in the theory of fluids. In 1945, Millikan and Frank Malina established the nation's first academic course in jet propulsion. Millikan published forty papers on a wide range of topics, and his textbook *Aerodynamics of the Airplane* (1941) was the first volume of the GALCIT series of textbooks. He took an active part in professional societies such as the Institute of Aeronautical Sciences, which he served as president in 1937, and the National Academy of Engineering, which he helped found in 1964.

Millikan was constantly challenged by, and contributed to, new developments in aeronautics. For example, immediately after World War II, Millikan became director of a new project shared by five Southern California aircraft companies. Called the Southern California Cooperative Wind Tunnel, the project was designed specifically to test aircraft at supersonic speeds. This was one of the first large supersonic wind tunnels anywhere, and it achieved worldwide fame for its efficiency, flexibility, and accuracy. It had immense influence on all postwar commercial and military aircraft, including developments such as swept-wing designs that Millikan's assistant, Ernest Robischon, had helped uncover among the tons of documents that were supposedly destroyed by the Germans at the close of the war.

Millikan was initially skeptical regarding the value of rocket propulsion for aircraft and spacecraft, and he even advised one graduate student, Frank Malina, to "get a good job in the aircraft industry" instead of wasting time on rockets. But, by 1938, Millikan had changed his mind, and he then took the lead in championing both rockets and jet engines as propulsion systems; in 1941 he showed that rocket-assisted takeoff could shorten takeoff distances by as much as 50 percent. In 1949, Millikan and his father were jointly awarded the Presidential Medal of Merit "for exceptionally outstanding conduct" in the field of rocket and jet propulsion development during World War II. Millikan was cofounder, along with von Kármán and others, of the Jet Propulsion Laboratory; he helped to form the Aerojet General Corporation; and he served as a member of the board of directors of the National Engineering Science Company of Pasadena.

Millikan was in great demand as a consultant in both military and civilian affairs because of his wide knowledge of the field of avionics and his vast circle of friends, colleagues, and former students. In early 1946, in an era when many academicians were becoming extremely skeptical of the propriety of close ties between academic institutions and research laboratories funded by the military, Millikan was instrumental in convincing the trustees of Caltech that its international reputation in aeronautics would be seriously jeopardized if it lost the unique facilities of the Jet Propulsion Laboratory to other institutions. In the early 1950's, Millikan foresaw, and helped promote, the role of long-range missiles and satellites in both military and civilian affairs, particularly through his membership on the Air Force's Scientific Advisory Board and as an adviser to the National Aeronautics and Space Administration.

Millikan was an enthusiastic, outgoing, engaging person who played a major role in the worldwide development of aeronautical and space programs. His vigorous approach to his profession was carried over into his private life, where he enjoyed music (especially singing with friends around the piano while he played), outdoor recreation (particularly hiking and camping in remote areas), social clubs and gatherings, and keeping in touch with his vast circle of friends the world over. He died in Pasadena.

[Millikan's papers are in the Institute Archives, California Institute of Technology, Pasadena, Calif. Additional papers are in the collections of Robert Andrews Millikan (his father) and Theodore von Kármán at the same location. A complete list of Millikan's published works follows the biographical sketch by E. E. Sechler in *Biographical Memoirs of the National Academy of Sciences* (1969). See also Theodore von Kármán, *The Wind and Beyond* (1967); and Clayton R. Koppes, *JPL and the American Space Program* (1982). An obituary is in the *New York Times*, Jan. 3, 1966.]

RICHARD K. GEHRENBECK

MILLIS, WALTER (Mar. 16, 1899–Mar. 17, 1968), writer, was born in Atlanta, Ga., the son of John Millis, a career army officer, and Mary Raoul. Like many other children of military professionals, Millis could call no single place home; in addition to Atlanta, he lived in Willets Point, N.Y.; Seattle; Cleveland; Savannah; and Manila, in the Philippine Islands.

Millis prepared for college at the Moses Brown School in Providence, R.I., and then entered Yale, where he was active in debate and fencing and earned selection to Phi Beta Kappa. At Yale he participated in officers' training and was commissioned a second lieutenant in the field artillery in September 1918. He saw no overseas duty and was discharged in December.

After his graduation from Yale in 1920, Millis spent four years as an editorial writer with the *Baltimore News* and then the *New York Sun*. In 1924 he joined the *New York Herald Tribune*. He was with this paper for thirty years, doing brief stretches as a reporter and correspondent in London and winning distinction as a gifted writer for one of American journalism's finest editorial pages. On Apr. 11, 1929, he married Nora Thompson of London; they had two children. The marriage was subsequently annulled. On May 6, 1944, Millis married Eugenia Benbow Sheppard, a fashion writer and columnist for the *Herald Tribune*.

For a time, Millis aspired to try his hand at fiction in addition to his newspaper work. He wrote some short stories during the 1920's and the novel *Sand Castle* (1929). He thereafter undertook several historical studies of international affairs, beginning with the much-praised *The Martial Spirit* (1931), a gracefully written examination of America's war with Spain that stressed the senselessness of the conflict and of the expansionism that followed it.

Millis next completed an even more important study, *Road to War: America, 1914–1917*. A Book-of-the-Month Club selection, *Road to War* was published early in 1935 while the Munitions Investigating Committee of the United States Senate was holding hearings on the role of the arms trade in ensnaring the United States in World War I. Debate on the legislation that culminated in the passage of the Neutrality Act of 1935, the first of several laws based on the assumption that the United States had been duped into going to war in 1917 by profiteers and Allied propaganda and should avoid entry into another European war, added to the relevance of Millis' book, which held that the United States had drifted toward war between 1914 and 1917 in the absence of any properly informed policy. "Read it and beware!" was emblazoned on the dust jacket, and Millis, along with C. Hartley Grattan, Charles Tansill, and others, won celebrity as one of the so-called revisionists, a group that pointed out the needlessness and futility of America's entry into World War I.

Grattan and Tansill joined other scholars and writers in efforts to keep the United States from becoming involved in another world war, but Millis, who had a much higher opinion of former president Woodrow Wilson than most of the other revisionists and who also subtly qualified his thesis in other ways, evidently became embarrassed by the partisan uses to which his work was put. In his statements on international relations, he soon began to distance himself from the unconditional revisionists. As late as 1937, however, Millis still believed it likely that no major war would break out in the foreseeable future. When war did begin in Europe in 1939, he made clear that his sympathies were with England and France, a subject that he discussed in *Why Europe Fights* (1940). By 1940 he was urging Americans to be prepared to intervene on the Allied side. In one of his most memorable editorials, "Dover Beach," he pointed out that while there were logical reasons to anticipate why England might be defeated, at bottom England's ability to continue the war effort against Nazism was a matter of the human spirit.

During the war years, Millis did some writing and consulting for the Office of War Information in addition to his duties on the *Herald Tribune*. Thereafter, he undertook one of the earliest book-length studies of Pearl Harbor, *This Is Pearl!* (1947), finding that the blame for the debacle lay with the American commanders in Hawaii. Despite his reputation and obvious qualifications for the position, Millis was passed over in 1952 when a vacancy opened at the top of the editorial staff of the *Herald Tribune*. Millis, a Democrat and an outspoken member of the American Civil Liberties Union, might have been considered somewhat too liberal in his domestic politics by the paper's proprietors. He was given his own column, "Arms and Men," as a sop. His vigorous opposition to McCarthyism and his personal abrasiveness toward the paper's owners probably contributed to his dismissal from the *Herald Tribune* in 1954.

Millis remained occupied with many endeavors. He contributed frequently to the *Saturday Review* and other journals of opinion and became a staff member of the Fund for the Republic as well as a consultant, from its founding in 1959, to the Center for the Study of Democratic Institutions, where he conducted an ongoing assessment of the relationship between military developments and the future of democracy. He also wrote articles for the group's journal, the *Center Magazine*. Although Millis continued to reside in the New

York area rather than at the center's headquarters in Santa Barbara, he took part in roundtable conferences at the center and wrote several articles and booklets under the center's auspices.

A critic of American policies in Vietnam, Millis nevertheless supported the draft as the most equitable means of raising the manpower necessary for the American armed forces during the cold war. He did not believe that world disarmament would soon be achieved, but in some of his final writings he argued that such steps as the partial nuclear test-ban treaty of 1963 were necessary preludes to any overall improvement in international relations. Peace, he held, would precede general disarmament. He died in New York City.

[In addition to his column and his unsigned editorials, Millis wrote dozens of articles and many books on international affairs. Besides those titles mentioned in the text, these include "Will We Stay Out of the Next War?" *New Republic*, July 31, 1935; *Viewed Without Alarm: Europe Today* (1937); "1939 Is Not 1914," *Life*, Nov. 6, 1939; "Faith of an American," in Stephen Vincent Benét et al., *Zero Hour* (1940); *Arms and Men* (1956); *An End to Arms* (1965); "On Disarmament," *Center Magazine*, Jan. 1968; and "The Call to Arms," *Center Magazine*, Mar. 1968. Millis, with Eugene S. Duffield, edited *The Forrestal Diaries* (1951). See also Warren I. Cohen, *The American Revisionists* (1967); and Richard Kluger, *The Paper: The Life and Death of the New York Herald Tribune* (1986). An obituary is in the *New York Times*, Mar. 18, 1968.]

LLOYD J. GRAYBAR

MITCHELL, LUCY SPRAGUE (July 2, 1878—Oct. 15, 1967), educator, was born in Chicago, Ill., the daughter of Otho Sprague, a wholesale grocer, and Lucia Atwood. Her father had contracted tuberculosis while serving in the Union army. The illness had a profound effect on the entire family but particularly on Lucy, the youngest daughter, who was increasingly charged with his care. Her mother seldom expressed her emotions, and her autocratic father rarely displayed affection toward his wife or children. The children learned to associate guilt with religious belief, because each had to keep a conduct book in which, she later recalled, they were to paste a star every night—"gold for perfect righteousness, silver for a small sin, red for a big sin."

Into this introspective and lonely world came governesses to tutor the children, and dinner guests from business and academic circles. Sprague thus became acquainted with John Dewey and his Laboratory School, with Jane Addams and Hull House, and with Alice Freeman Palmer, a former president of Wellesley College, who introduced her to women such as Marion Talbot and Sophinisba Breckenridge. Efforts to continue Sprague's formal education in private schools after age twelve failed because of her extreme nervousness and seeming inability to adjust to a school environment. Her father's extensive library became her school; her notebooks, filled with poems and stories of her own composition, became her chief mode of reflection and expression. She began to develop a sense of social responsibility and sensitivity to human suffering, perceptions that were heightened by the death of two younger brothers from contagious diseases, the mental illness of a favorite older sister, her father's invalidism, and her friendship with Jane Addams. (During the Pullman strike of 1894, her father withdrew support from Addams, who sympathized with the workers.) Her growing desire for independence ran headlong into increased pressure to nurse her father, especially after her family moved in 1893 to Southern California, which was considered favorable for the treatment of tuberculosis.

In 1896, Sprague entered Radcliffe College. While in Cambridge, she lived with Alice Palmer and her husband, George. She graduated with honors in philosophy, having studied with Josiah Royce, George Santayana, and William James. In 1904 she accepted the invitation of Benjamin Wheeler, the president of the University of California at Berkeley, to become the first dean of women there.

Demeaning attitudes toward women at Berkeley had a profound effect on Sprague. "It came as a shock," she later wrote, "when I realized most of the faculty thought of women frankly as inferior beings." She made full use of her mandate from Wheeler to develop the dean's office, addressing herself successfully during her six-year tenure to strengthening women's organizations on campus and to what would later become known as career counseling, using a four-month leave to apprentice herself to a variety of professional women in teaching and social work in New York City. Her New York contacts, particularly with Julia Richman, the principal of a Manhattan high school, helped Sprague to embrace teaching as a vocation. Despite a lifelong struggle to overcome her lack of formal training in a specialized field and the strictly domestic expectations society and her family seemed to have for her, Sprague established herself as an educational experimenter who endeavored to relate learning research to the classroom. She was greatly aided in this work by the economist Wesley Clair ("Robin") Mitchell, whom she met at Berkeley and who shared her interest in social and educational reform. They were married on May 8, 1912; they had four children, two of them adopted. Their relationship transformed her life, there being absent the authoritarian attitude of her father toward her mother.

Mitchell took up residence in New York City in 1913, when her husband became a professor at Columbia. She took courses at Columbia Teachers College under John Dewey. From 1915 on, she taught young children and became an educational adviser in twelve of New York City's early experimental schools. In 1916 a financial pledge from a first cousin, Elizabeth Sprague Coolidge, enabled her to found the Bureau of Educational Experiments to carry out her ideas of progressive education. She guided the bureau (incorporated in 1950 as the Bank Street College of Education) for forty years.

During a period of enforced rest in 1920 while recuperating from pneumonia, Mitchell wrote *Here and Now Story Book* (1921). The book is notable because in it Mitchell anticipated Jean Piaget's theories on how children use language.

Mitchell's interests gradually moved from teaching and educational research to the training of teachers and writers for children. In 1931 she helped found the Cooperative School for Teachers. Writers' workshops originated by her in 1938 influenced many authors; she herself wrote and coauthored numerous stories for children and several texts on the teaching of social studies. She also wrote *Our Children and Our Schools* (1950), an influential work on curriculum.

Mitchell's husband's death in 1948 left her lonely and unsure about her ability to continue guiding the Bank Street College enterprise. She relinquished its presidency in 1950 and retired from its board in 1956. But she gradually regained her sense of self-possession and pleasure in writing. *Two Lives: The Story of Wesley Clair Mitchell and Myself* (1953) began as a biography of her husband but ended as an account of both their lives. In an era of remarkable advances in the knowledge of children and how they learn, Mitchell strove with considerable success to unite theory and practice. Her organizational talents brought educators and researchers together in the common enterprise of teaching and learning more about how children learn. Her own dark childhood gave her an esteem for the child as a person and a devotion to education as "the most constructive attack on social problems," dealing, as she saw it, "with children and the future." She died in Palo Alto, Calif.

[The Mitchell papers are at Columbia University. The Bank Street College of Education has most of Mitchell's publications. The Bancroft Library at the University of California at Berkeley has materials relating to her work as dean. An oral history of Mitchell was produced in 1964 by the Regional Oral History Office, University of California at Berkeley.

Works by Mitchell not cited in the text are *North America: The Land They Live in for the Children Who Live There* (1931); *Young Geographers* (1934); and *My Country, 'Tis of Thee: The Use and Abuse of Natural Resources* (1940), written with Eleanor Bowman and Mary Phelps. She coauthored stories for children that appeared in the Our Growing World series (1944–1945) and the Bank Street Golden Books series (1946–1951).

A biography is Joyce Antler, *Lucy Sprague Mitchell* (1984). Recollections of Mitchell appear in Bank Street College, *Lucy Sprague Mitchell: An Hour of Remembrance* (1967) and *Lucy Sprague Mitchell Memorial Dedication Ceremony* (1971). See Mary Phelps and Margaret Wise Brown, *Horn Book Magazine*, May–June, 1937; and *Time*, Aug. 28, 1950. Obituaries are in the *New York Times*, Oct. 17, 1967; and *Publishers Weekly*, Oct. 30, 1967.]

KAREN M. KENNELLY

MOREHOUSE, WARD (Nov. 24, 1899–Dec. 8, 1966), theater critic, newspaper columnist, and playwright, was born in Savannah, Ga., the son of Augustus Ward Morehouse, a writer, and Sara McIntosh. His interest in the theater began in his teens, when he organized a stock company to produce plays that he wrote, directed, and acted in. He attended North Georgia College in 1916. His first experience as a newspaperman came early, when he joined the *Savannah Press* as a reporter. He left in 1916 to work for the *Atlanta Journal*, where he was assigned to the city room until 1919. One of his fellow staff members on the *Journal* was the future playwright Laurence Stallings.

In the fall of 1919, Morehouse went to New York City, even though the city terrified him. By the next year, he was writing about the theater for the *New York Tribune* and, later, the *New York Herald-Tribune*. In 1926 he commenced a twenty-five-year association with the *New York Sun*, for which he wrote "Broadway After Dark," a lively and entertaining column that included theatrical interviews, anecdotes, reminiscences, and comments on current shows. His sprightly style attracted a wide readership. His pungent personality sketches became renowned, and his acquaintances in the theater seemed numberless. One of his favorite places for conducting interviews was the 21 Club. A short, somewhat stout man, he was witty, energetic, and a skillful raconteur.

Morehouse also served as a drama critic for the *Sun* and, as such, came to have a profound respect for Maude Adams, Jeanne Eagels, and Laurette Taylor, among others. In his theater memoir *Matinee Tomorrow: Fifty Years of Our Theater* (1949), he described the legendary performance of Eagels as Sadie Thompson in Somerset Maugham's *Rain:* "I occupied a seat in the rear of the balcony on that opening night [in 1922] and experienced one of the most genuinely stirring moments in all my theatergoing years in the final scene of the third act when Sadie's long-silent phonograph broke into the haunting strains of 'Wabash Blues,' her gesture of complete disgust with all mankind." In the 1930's and 1940's he was particularly impressed by the work of Richard Harrison as De Lawd in *The Green Pastures* (1930), Alfred Lunt and Lynn Fontanne in *Reunion in Vienna* (1931), and Laurette Taylor in *The Glass Menagerie* (1945). Although Morehouse was influential as a critic, he believed that the power of theater critics was frequently overrated and that they themselves were never above criticism. Morehouse was often kind and generous in his critical comments about performers, and when he noticed a spark of talent in a young player, he did his best to be helpful.

In 1928, Morehouse wrote the play *Gentlemen of the Press,* which ran for 128 performances on Broadway, but unfortunately it had to compete with the classic newspaper drama *The Front Page.* Later, his play was adapted for motion pictures (1929). During the late 1920's and early 1930's, Morehouse worked in Hollywood as a scenarist for Universal, Warner Brothers, and Paramount Pictures, but he had a strong preference for the legitimate theater. He wrote that Hollywood devoured actors and actresses and robbed the stage of exciting players. He also thought that the work of playwrights suffered when they became involved with the business of writing for motion pictures. His other plays were *Miss Quis* (1937) and *U.S. 90* (1941), which met with only modest success. A prolific writer, he was the author of *Forty-five Minutes Past Eight* (1939), which the New York theater critic John Anderson said was "full of grease paint and lobby smoke"; *George M. Cohan: Prince of the American Theater* (1943); *Just the Other Day* (1953); and other books. They established him as a theater historian as well as a critic.

Morehouse was an inveterate traveler, and he sometimes served as a roving correspondent for the *Sun*. He crossed the United States twenty-three times, writing about obscure as well as famous people and places that he encountered along the way. In three trips around the world he visited about eighty countries. His travels gave him an opportunity to broaden his interest in wild animals; he once bought a bear in Thailand and lion cubs in South Africa. During World War II, he crossed the Atlantic on a United States Navy destroyer escort and wrote about his experiences in a column called "Atlantic After Dark."

When Morehouse reached London and Paris during and immediately after World War II his columns were known as "London After Dark" and "Paris After Dark," and his treatment of personality stories was in the same style as his Broadway column. In 1946 he traveled across the United States and interviewed such people as "Alfalfa Bill" Murray, a former governor of Oklahoma; Sergeant Alvin York, the World War I hero; and "Shoeless Joe" Jackson, the baseball player. His column for this trip, "Report on America," received an award from the Society of Silurians, an organization of veteran New York City newspapermen, for the best editorial achievement of the year.

When the *Sun* ceased publication in 1950, Morehouse continued to write "Broadway After Dark" for the *New York World-Telegram and Sun*. By this time, he was of the opinion that the theater was a victim of prohibitive costs and that there was a grave need to develop young playwrights and players. In 1956 he joined the

S. I. Newhouse newspaper chain as a Broadway critic and columnist. He usually produced two pieces each week, one a theatrical interview and the other a brief review of a new play or a miscellany of anecdotes. He also wrote for the General Features Syndicate until his death in New York City.

Morehouse was married four times. He and his first wife, Ruth Nisbet, divorced in 1925. He next married Jean Dalrymple, but the union ended in 1937. On Jan. 24, 1941, he wed Joan Marlowe. That marriage ended, and he married Rebecca Franklin on Aug. 13, 1949. In all, he had two children.

[Morehouse' papers and scrapbooks are in the New York Public Library's Performing Arts Research Center at Lincoln Center. Obituaries are in the *New York Times,* Dec. 9, 1966; and *Variety,* Dec. 14, 1966. The playwright Sidney Kingsley wrote an appreciation of Morehouse in the *New York Times,* Jan. 22, 1967.]

ERNEST MCKAY

MORGENTHAU, HENRY, JR. (May 11, 1891–Feb. 6, 1967), secretary of the Treasury, was born in New York City, the son of Henry Morgenthau, a German immigrant who prospered in real estate, and Josephine Sykes. Morgenthau grew up in a wealthy Jewish family that was dominated by his strong-willed father. He attended private schools in New York, Phillips Exeter Academy, and Cornell University. An indifferent student, he left Cornell after three semesters and served an apprenticeship at the Henry Street Settlement. In 1913, to escape the authority of his father, he purchased several hundred acres, much of it orchard, in East Fishkill, Dutchess County, N.Y., and became a farmer. On Apr. 17, 1916, he married Elinor Fatman, whose mother was a member of the wealthy Lehman family. They had three children. From 1922 to 1933 Morgenthau published the *American Agriculturalist,* a farm weekly, which sought to influence agriculture throughout the state.

The Morgenthaus took an active part in the political affairs of Dutchess County. They became friends with their neighbors Franklin and Eleanor Roosevelt, and after his election as governor of New York in 1928, Roosevelt appointed Morgenthau chairman of the new Agricultural Advisory Commission. In 1930 Roosevelt made him state conservation commissioner. In both posts Morgenthau managed innovative programs for land reclamation, reforestation, and conservation. He received the kind of reward he most desired when Roosevelt, as president-elect, named him chairman of the Federal Farm Board and, in May 1933, governor of its successor agency, the Farm Credit Administration (FCA).

By 1933, Morgenthau had developed distinctive personal and administrative characteristics. He was tall, bald, and near-sighted (he squinted through pince-nez), an appearance accentuated by his often lugubrious mood. Roosevelt, in a teasing but affectionate phrase, called him "Henry the Morgue." Yet the president sometimes resented Morgenthau's voice when it functioned, in Eleanor Roosevelt's words, as "Franklin's conscience." As an administrator, Morgenthau compensated for his limited understanding of finance, economics, and law by surrounding himself with able experts in these fields whose judgment he trusted. Still, when he disagreed with them in matters of large policy, he trusted his own intuition—"my educated elbow," as he called it.

On the Federal Farm Board and as governor of the FCA, Morgenthau presided over new programs that provided farmers strapped by the Great Depression with low-interest long-term loans to refinance their mortgages and with easy credit for purchasing machinery and seed. In saving thousands of farms from foreclosure, the FCA also restored liquidity to hundreds of banks and insurance companies that exchanged mortgages they could not collect for instantly negotiable federal securities.

In 1933 Roosevelt asked Morgenthau to help negotiate recognition of the Soviet Union. The president also directed Morgenthau to arrange large purchases and sales of grain to squeeze out speculators. That effort constituted a precedent for the program, executed by Morgenthau in 1933, to buy gold for the purpose of raising commodity prices, then depressed far more than industrial prices. The policy rested on the fallacious hypothesis of George F. Warren, a Cornell agricultural economist whom Morgenthau knew. Contrary to Warren's predictions, buying gold at increasing prices did not lift commodity prices, but it did satisfy much of the strong congressional demand for currency inflation.

Roosevelt made Morgenthau undersecretary and acting secretary of the Treasury in November 1933, and secretary in January 1934. In the latter month Roosevelt stabilized the price of gold at $35 an ounce, 59.01 percent of the metal's pre-1933 value. Since gold had been nationalized the previous April, much of that profit went to the federal government. It was placed in a stabilization fund that the Treasury used to manage the international exchange value of the dollar, an awkward venture at best, and to sustain the value of federal bonds and notes at low interest rates. In performing this function, Morgenthau became the chief agent of the administration's easy-money policy.

In exercising his new authority, Morgenthau continually came into conflict with other New Dealers who were jealous of their prerogatives, especially Secretary of State Cordell Hull; the Federal Reserve governor, Marriner Eccles; and the director of economic stabilization, James F. Byrnes. Eccles particularly objected to Morgenthau's fiscal conservatism. Morgenthau's advocacy of restraint in federal spending did exempt funds for relief and for humanitarian purposes. He also supported tax reform both to increase revenue and to shift the burden of taxation to the wealthy. The Treasury drafted the "soak the rich" revenue bill of 1935, which Congress weakened by reducing proposed rates on individual and corporate income taxes and on estates. In the absence of a deliberate countercyclical spending policy, the Revenue Act of 1935 (as supplemented in 1936 and 1937) retarded recovery, but once the economy returned to full employment during World War II, it helped redistribute income.

Morgenthau acquired his reputation as a conservative because of his resistance to Keynesian economic theory. He was dismayed when Keynesians persuaded Roosevelt in 1938 to embark on a spending program to counter the deepening recession. Yet Morgenthau soon advocated spending for defense, which restored full employment and gave Keynesian theory the primacy it enjoyed for two decades. For his part, he continued to believe that a balanced budget would also have achieved recovery.

The international responsibilities of the Treasury and the extra duties imposed by the president brought Morgenthau into foreign and military policy. Convinced of the threat to America posed by the Nazis, he tried continually to make common cause with Great Britain and France and to devise obstacles to Germany and its allies. To that end he negotiated, with Roosevelt's approval, the Tripartite Stabilization Pact of 1936. In that pact, the American, British, and French treasuries agreed to cooperate in the management of their currencies, a decision that permitted France's anti-Nazi Socialist government of Léon Blum to devalue the franc without fear of reprisals. Morgenthau also combated German export subsidies through his use of the Tariff Act of 1930, and he proposed economic sanctions against Japan after the *Panay* episode of 1937 and against Germany after the dismemberment of Czechoslovakia in 1938. But the Tripartite Pact represented the inadequate best that the administration could achieve, given public and congressional opposition to American involvement abroad. The pact set a precedent for postwar international monetary policy.

Morgenthau undertook crucial assignments that Roosevelt could not entrust to the War Department until Henry L. Stimson put it on an effective footing in the summer of 1940. In 1939 Morgenthau assisted the French and British in their attempt to procure the modern American military aircraft necessary to balance superior German air power. The resulting increase in investment in American productivity greatly benefited national defense. After the fall of France in 1940 Morgenthau managed the administration's program to sell surplus war matériel to the British. In 1941 he oversaw the drafting of the Lend-Lease Act and later expedited lend-lease aid to Russia.

During World War II, Morgenthau, with Roosevelt's support, devised and defended a Treasury program to finance the war partly by the sale of small-denomination bonds to private citizens, which he thought would improve civilian morale. His related hope to stem inflation by large tax increases foundered for the most part on congressional resistance. His most enduring wartime achievements were the agreements reached in 1944 at Bretton Woods to establish the International Monetary Fund and the World Bank. In that year Morgenthau also persuaded Roosevelt to set up the War Refugee Board, the only American public endeavor to assist European Jews.

Morgenthau was best known for his plan to convert postwar Germany into a pastoral country, a plan that Roosevelt and Churchill embraced. His belief in the benefits of rural life partly explained this otherwise vindictive and economically impractical scheme.

Roosevelt's death in April 1945 cost Morgenthau his mentor and closest friend and ended his interest in further public service. In July he resigned and returned to his farm. For several years he raised funds for the United Jewish Appeal and Bonds for Israel. The death of his father in 1946 and his wife in 1949 left him lonely and depressed, but his second marriage, to Marcel Puthon on Nov. 21, 1951, provided him with companionship during the extensive travels he undertook between harvest seasons. He died in Poughkeepsie, N.Y.

[The "Morgenthau Diary," almost 900 volumes of bound typescripts covering his years as secretary of the Treasury, is located, with Morgenthau's other manuscripts, in the Franklin D. Roosevelt Library in Hyde Park, N.Y. Morgenthau's "Farm Credit Diary" is indispensable for the period it covers, as is his intimate "Presidential Diary." The Franklin D. Roosevelt Papers and the diary of Henry L. Stimson in the Yale University Library are also useful. Morgenthau's only book was *Germany Is Our Problem* (1945). He supervised articles written under his name by Arthur Schlesinger, Jr., "Morgenthau Diaries," *Collier's*, Sept. 27–Nov. 1, 1947.

The authorized biography is John M. Blum, *From the Morgenthau Diaries* (1951–1967), condensed and revised as *Roosevelt and Morgenthau* (1970). See also Allen S. Everest, *Morgenthau, the New Deal, and Silver* (1950); Paul Y. Hammond, "Directives for the Occupation of Germany," in Harold Stein, ed., *American Civil-Military Decisions* (1963); and Warren Kimball, *Swords and Plowshares?* (1976).]

JOHN MORTON BLUM

MORTON, CHARLES WALTER (Feb. 10, 1899–Sept. 23, 1967), author and editor, was born in Omaha, Nebr., the son of James Charles Morton and Cynthia Ann Edwards. His family had a prosperous hardware business that enabled Morton to enjoy upper-middle-class life. He was educated in Omaha public schools and after 1912 at the Morristown (N.J.) School.

Morton was expected to learn the family business. Instead, he wandered through two enrollments at Williams College in 1916 and 1919, one matriculation at the University of Chicago in 1917, five months as a tractor driver on a ranch in Pitchfork, Wyo., and eight years working for his father. Morton finally began to write fiction in 1926. On Aug. 16, 1920, he married Mildred Wadleigh Penick; they had two children.

Morton's first article went to the *Haldeman-Julius Monthly*. Success there prompted him first to develop a series, "Peter Profit's Partner," for *Hardware Age* and then to try eastern literary magazines. In 1928 he moved to Boston in order to write for the *Independent*. When that journal got into financial difficulties, Morton went to work for the *Boston Herald*. Although he lacked journalistic experience, he quickly showed great skill as a reporter for the *Herald* and then for the *Boston Evening Transcript*.

The *Evening Transcript* proved to be a most unusual newspaper. The chapters of Morton's autobiography describing that newspaper are the best part of the book. The *Evening Transcript* was an unread, unsold, and unloved newspaper that specialized in obituaries. Its city room was disreputable, its journalistic techniques nonexistent, and its employees barely surviving at a newspaper that itself suffered severe financial problems. Yet, Morton not only had no regrets about working there for six and a half years but even enjoyed the experience. However, his salary kept shrinking, and in August 1936 he left to head the new information service of the Boston office of the new United States Social Security Board.

Morton's continuing success in writing articles for the *New Yorker* gained him a trial on the magazine's editorial staff in 1933. His inability to meet the high standards of Harold Ross, the editor in chief, proved both traumatic and enlightening. He learned that he was suited for short, light pieces, not for the lengthy essays favored by Ross. For the rest of his life, he continued to write for Ross and his successors but from outside the *New Yorker* staff.

Morton turned enthusiastically to the task of publicizing the work of the Boston social security office. An ardent New Dealer, he remained in that post until he felt that the social security concept was permanently established. Morton accepted an editorial position with the *Atlantic Monthly* in 1941. It was a position that matched man and job perfectly for the first time in Morton's life. In 1966 he looked back over twenty-five years of association with the *Atlantic* and declared himself content.

In 1943, Morton began the *Atlantic* feature "Accent on Living," a monthly essay interpreting the American scene in a light, dry, but frequently sharp style. In 1948 he was elected to the *Atlantic* board of directors. His friend and colleague Robert Manning, the editor of the magazine, explained that he "meant more to the *Atlantic* than his modest spot on the masthead could have made clear. He added to our editorial deliberations, and to our pages, a profound distaste for the bogus, the pedantic, and the self-interested argument. He forced us to look sharply at our world's congenital foolishness, he made us laugh, and he long ago made us realize that he won't be replaceable. He was one of a kind."

As important as was Morton's work on the *Atlantic*, it was as an essayist, satirist, and autobiographer that Morton made his greatest contribution. He collaborated with Francis Dahl, a *Boston Herald* cartoonist, on *Dahl's Boston* (1946) and *Dahl's Brave New World* (1947). *How to Protect Yourself Against Women and Other Vicissitudes* (1951) and *A Slight Sense of Outrage* (1955) collected his best *Atlantic*, *New Yorker*, and *Punch* essays. *Frankly, George* (1957) collected his humorous comments and advice to his first book's publisher, J. B. Lippincott. In his autobiography, *It Has Its Charms . . .* (1966), Morton wittily but lovingly described his childhood in Omaha, his experiences on the *Evening Transcript*, and his failures and successes prior to 1941.

Morton was a perceptive observer of the American scene, which he approached with a less imperious and arrogant manner than many contemporary essayists. Modest and self-deprecating, he could not single out individuals or specific groups for criticism. His humor could be quiet and lightly placed or suddenly sharp and biting, but never malicious, angry, or belligerent. *A Slight Sense of Outrage* summed up his philosophy for dealing with a world filled with the outrageous behavior of women, public speakers, drivers, scholars, and the haughty rich.

Only rarely did Morton, who loved President Roosevelt and his policies, believed fervently in social justice, and suffered through the Great Depression, even hint at his political leanings. On one such occasion, he began by lamenting the rise in prices before recalling the low prices of the 1930's, noting that it did not require much money to live well then. Even Park Avenue restaurants trumpeted the "dollar dinner," he mused. "But there were too many people who couldn't buy a dollar dinner. On the whole I prefer higher prices," concluded Morton.

Morton lived near Harvard for many years, and as an ex-journalist and editor of the *Atlantic*, he associated closely with Harvard's Nieman Fellows. His list of friends among journalists was formidable, and his counsel and understanding always remained available to them. But his books earned better reviews outside the cultural centers of the East. He died in London, England.

[See the interview by Harvey Breit, *New York Times*, Oct. 7, 1951; *New York Times*, Sept. 23, 1951, and May 8, 1955; and *San Francisco Chronicle*, Sept. 27, 1951, and May 13, 1955. Obituaries are in the *Boston Globe* and the *New York Times*, both Sept. 24, 1967.]

WILLIAM F. STEINER, JR.

MULLER, HERMANN JOSEPH (Dec. 21, 1890–Apr. 5, 1967), founder of radiation genetics, was born in New York City, the son of Hermann Joseph Muller, Sr., a partner in a bronze-artworks shop, and Frances Lyons. Muller's father died when Muller was ten years old. Muller excelled at Morris High School and entered Columbia College in 1907 on a Cooper Hewitt scholarship. There he developed an interest in heredity and evolution, particularly through the courses of Edmund Beecher Wilson. He received his B.A. in 1910 and then attended Cornell Medical School, receiving an M.A. in physiology in 1911. During this time he discussed and debated the new findings in *Drosophila* (fruit fly) genetics initiated by Thomas Hunt Morgan.

In 1912 Muller returned to Columbia as a graduate student and member of Morgan's *Drosophila* group. With Alfred Henry Sturtevant and Calvin Blackman Bridges, Morgan and Muller constituted the major figures in a laboratory that introduced X-linked inheritance, crossing-over, chromosome rearrangements, nondisjunction, chromosome mapping, and the proofs of the chromosome theory of heredity. Although Muller contributed to many interpretations in the period from 1910 to 1912, he received no formal credit and became embittered and later estranged from Morgan and Sturtevant. This competitive attitude and his later emphasis on his priority of discovery for some of these ideas impaired Muller's reputation. Muller's anger over what he perceived to be a personal injustice was complemented by an intense sense of social justice that led him to socialism and sympathy with the Bolshevik revolution. He spent the period from 1933 to 1937 in the Soviet Union as a guest investigator and corresponding member of the Soviet Academy of Sciences.

In 1915 Muller completed his Ph.D. dissertation on coincidence and interference in crossing-over and was recruited by Julian Huxley to join the recently created Department of Biology at Rice Institute. There Muller began a series of experimental and theoretical papers on the gene, which led to his definition of mutation as a change in the individual gene and demonstrated the genetic basis of variable or inconstant traits. That analysis was important in bringing back to Darwin's theory of evolution by natural selection a mechanism that permitted character-trait evolution and relied on classical genetics as the basis for the observed fluctuations of a trait in a population.

Muller returned to Columbia in 1918 and stayed until Morgan returned from sabbatical leave in 1920. He then joined the staff of the University of Texas at Austin from 1921 to 1932. In this period he proposed his theoretical interpretation of the gene as a molecule that reproduces or copies its errors. This theory gave Muller the confidence in 1926 to proclaim the gene as the basis of life. During these years he demonstrated that mutation rates could be obtained and that they changed with temperature. In the fall of 1926, after overcoming many theoretical and practical difficulties, Muller proved decisively that X rays induce mutations at a frequency 150 times their spontaneous rate. Muller's findings, announced without data in *Science* and with full technical detail at the Congress of Genetics in Berlin in 1927, created a sensation. Many laboratories confirmed Muller's major results.

Muller and his students established that X rays induce gene mutations in direct proportion to the dose received and that they also induce chromosome breakage that leads to structural rearrangements. He demonstrated that these rearrangements increase with a power of dose greater than 1 and less than 2. Using radiation as a tool for the study of gene and chromosome organization, Muller and his students demonstrated that the genetic map constructed through crossing-over corresponded to the map constructed by utilizing chromosome fragments bearing individual genes. He demonstrated that genes have boundaries, that their size can be estimated, and that the number of genes in an organism can be calculated. He also noted that genes have a double structure, that they are linear, and that their mutations usually lead to a substantial or complete loss of their functions rather than to gains or only modest losses of functions.

Muller's studies of mutation and the gene led him to an intense defense of Darwinian evolution by natural selection. He analyzed the role of chromosomal changes in species formation and in the evolution of separate sexes. He also studied hybrids of *Drosophila* species and concluded that their infertility and abnormalities were the result of chromosome gene differences rather than of physiological incompatibilities.

Later in his career Muller applied his ideas of mutation and gene function to human genetics. He proposed a theory of genetic load based on the constant production of new spontaneous mutations, with natural selection eliminating equivalent numbers of mutations through sterility, early death, or reduced survival. Muller calculated long-term increases in genetic load under conditions of modern medicine, which, he felt, should be compensated by differential reproduction. This eugenic position was extended beyond maintenance of the present genetic load for humanity. In his later years Muller proposed a positive eugenic philosophy of germinal choice, in which brighter, healthier, and more cooperative individuals would contribute semen to sperm banks. He hoped the semen would be used to increase these attributes in future generations.

Muller had rejected the American eugenics movement in the 1920's and 1930's as racist and its programs as based on unproven hereditary claims and spurious values, but he hoped to introduce a modern eugenics program in the Soviet Union. Both his eugenic ideas and classical genetics itself were denounced in the Soviet Union by a growing movement that interpreted hereditary change as a consequence of directed environmental influence. This neo-Lamarckian theory was championed by Trofim D. Lysenko, and Muller was drawn into debate with him in 1936. By 1937 Muller managed to leave the Soviet Union by volunteering for service in the Spanish Civil War.

On June 11, 1923, Muller married Jessie Marie Jacobs, from whom he was divorced in 1934; they had one child. During 1938–1940 he was guest investigator at the University of Edinburgh. There, on May 20, 1939, he married Dorothea Kantorowicz; they had one child. He returned to the United States in 1940 for an ad interim post at Amherst, and in 1945 he received a permanent appointment at Indiana University. He was awarded the Nobel Prize in physiology and medicine in 1946.

Muller's return to the United States was accompanied by numerous public controversies. He became a leading critic of the Soviet attack on genetics; he advocated protection from medical and industrial exposure to ionizing radiation; he became concerned over widespread atmospheric testing of nuclear weapons; and he fought for an evolutionary perspective in the teaching of secondary school biology.

Muller was raised as a Unitarian but considered himself an atheist. He was president of the American Humanist Association and believed in the potential of individuals to act rationally and improve their well-being. In temperament he was intense, easily excited, critical, and outspoken, but witty and eager to share his views. He was short (five feet, one inch) and athletic. He died in Indianapolis, Ind.

Muller was the author of some 370 published papers. His popular writings were frequently graceful and compelling in style, but his technical papers were weighted with numerous phrases that made his sentences lengthy and difficult to read. Muller's emphasis on the gene as the basis of life greatly influenced later geneticists, who applied that view to molecular biology. His ideas were especially appreciated by Max Delbrück, J. D. Watson, and Salvador Luria. The extent of Muller's contribution can be understood only when one is cognizant of how much effort and research were required to convince biologists in the first half of the twentieth century that the chromosomal genes provide the basis for other cell components and for the variability of expression of character traits.

[The bulk of Muller's correspondence (more than 30,000 letters), manuscripts, photographs, and notebooks are at the Lilly Library, Indiana University at Bloomington; additional correspondence (from his early years) is in the American Philosophical Library in Philadelphia. Muller's complete bibliography is in G. Pontecorvo, ed., *Biographical Memoirs of Fellows of the Royal Society*, XIV (1968). His books include *Out of the Night* (1936); and three collections of articles and essays: *Studies in Genetics* (1962), edited by Muller; and *The Modern Concept of Nature* (1973) and *Man's Future Birthright* (1973), both edited by Elof Axel Carlson. For a full-length biography, see Elof Axel Carlson, *Genes, Radiation, and Society: The Life and Work of H. J. Muller* (1981).]

ELOF AXEL CARLSON

MUNCH, CHARLES (Sept. 26, 1891–Nov. 6, 1968), conductor, was born in Strasbourg, Alsace (then part of Germany), the son of Ernest Münch, a musician, and Célestine Simon. While studying at the Gymnase Protestant from 1898 to 1912, he also specialized in the violin at the Strasbourg Conservatory, which was directed by Hans Pfitzner. In addition, he played the church organ and he was a second violinist in his father's orchestra. After receiving his conservatory diploma in 1912, he pursued advanced violin studies with Carl Flesch in Berlin and Lucien Capet at the Paris Conservatory. He also began medical studies in Paris.

During World War I Munch served as a sergeant gunner in the German army. He was gassed at Péronne and wounded at Verdun. In 1919 he returned to Strasbourg (Alsace had been restored to France by the Versailles Treaty) and briefly worked as a translator for an insurance company before becoming assistant concertmaster of the Strasbourg Orchestra under Guy Ropartz, director of the conservatory. In 1920 he was appointed violin professor at the conservatory. In the early 1920's he also was concertmaster of Hermann Abendroth's Gürzenich concerts in Cologne, where he coached with Joseph Szigeti. Munch was concertmaster from 1926 to 1932 of Leipzig's Gewandhaus Orchestra, directed by Wilhelm Furtwängler. Munch's first conducting opportunities came in Leipzig, with the Gewandhaus Orchestra and with the chamber orchestra at Bach's Thomaskirche, where he usually played on Sunday. It was at this time that Munch resolved to become a conductor.

Munch relinquished his German citizenship, left the Gewandhaus Orchestra, and settled in Paris, where he and his fiancée, Geneviève Maury, granddaughter of a founder of the Nestlé Chocolate Company, rented a hall and hired the Straram Orchestra. Munch made his professional conducting debut on Nov. 1, 1932. This successful performance earned him engagements in Paris with the Concerts Siohan and the Lamoureux Orchestra and at the Biarritz Orchestra's 1933 summer season. He also coached with Paul Bastide and the Hungarian

Alfred Szendrei. On Jan. 31, 1933, he married Geneviève Maury.

Munch was principal conductor from 1935 to 1938 of the Société Philharmonique de Paris. Already established as a leading interpreter of Berlioz, Munch soon identified himself with contemporary music, especially that of his friends Arthur Honegger, Albert Roussel, and Francis Poulenc. Upon Philippe Gaubert's resignation in 1938, Munch became director and principal conductor of the Société des Concerts du Conservatoire de Paris, one of France's oldest and most respected orchestras. He became professor of violin at the École Normale de Musique in 1936 and taught conducting at the Paris Conservatory from 1937 to 1945.

Believing that wartime performances would help maintain French morale, Munch remained with the Paris Conservatory Orchestra after Paris was occupied by the Germans in World War II, though he would not direct the Paris Opera. He avoided presenting official concerts for the Nazis and refused to conduct contemporary German music. He was able to protect members of the orchestra and other musicians from the Gestapo and reportedly contributed all of his wartime music earnings to the resistance. For this he was awarded the French Legion of Honor with the red ribbon in 1945 and the title of commander in 1952. After the war he was the first French conductor to perform in England, where he conducted the British Broadcasting Company (BBC) Symphony. He was the first foreigner after the war to conduct the London Philharmonic (1944–1945 season).

Munch resigned from the Paris Conservatory Orchestra in 1946 when asked to perform fewer modern works. On Dec. 27, 1946, he made his North American debut with the Boston Symphony Orchestra, as part of his first American tour. In 1948 he led the Orchestre National de la Radiodiffusion Française on its first American tour, the first American tour by any French orchestra in thirty years. Performances were given at Carnegie Hall and in over thirty American and Canadian cities. The next year he was appointed conductor of the Boston Symphony Orchestra. (Years before in Paris, the *New York Tribune* music critic Virgil Thomson had observed that Munch would be an ideal conductor for the Boston Symphony.)

Munch gave the first performance of his thirteen-year tenure (the second-longest uninterrupted term with the orchestra after Serge Koussevitzky's twenty-five years) on Oct. 7, 1949, the fiftieth anniversary of Symphony Hall. His modesty and graciousness contrasted sharply with Koussevitzky's more autocratic and theatrical personality; for example, Munch had more relaxed, less disciplinarian rehearsals. The orchestra produced a different sound, especially from the strings, under his direction. Some critics complained about his excessively accelerated tempi, especially in the German classics, but most admired his intensity as well as his mastery of rhythm and clarity of phrasing. In March 1952, when he returned to the podium after an extended illness, he received a standing ovation from both orchestra and audience.

Upon Koussevitzky's sudden death in 1951, Munch assumed sole directorship of the Berkshire Music Center and the Tanglewood Music Festival (July–August concerts) in Lenox, Mass., though he still returned each summer to Paris. In May 1952 he took the orchestra to the Paris Festival of Twentieth-Century Music as part of its first European tour. Assisted by Pierre Monteux, Munch led another tour of Europe in 1956. In September the Boston Symphony became the first American orchestra to play in the Soviet Union. It performed before enthusiastic audiences at the Leningrad Conservatory and in Moscow. Munch's wife died on Aug. 21, 1956.

Munch, assisted by Aaron Copland and Richard Burgin, conducted the orchestra on a tour of Japan, Korea, the Philippines, Australia, and New Zealand in 1960. Munch retired in 1962. During his tenure in Boston Munch offered 39 world premieres, 17 American first performances, and 13 Boston premieres. He presented 168 (including 36 American) contemporary works, and he appointed the first woman soloist to the orchestra. After his retirement Munch returned to Paris.

In 1963 Munch became president of the École Normale de Musique, and in 1964 he conducted the inaugural concert for the auditorium of the Maison de la Radio in Paris. He was named president of the Guilde Française des Artistes Solistes in 1966. As part of the plans proposed by André Malraux, minister of cultural affairs, and Marcel Landowski, general inspector of culture, to establish and subsidize France's first full-time salaried orchestra, Munch became the permanent director of the Orchestre de Paris, which made its debut in

Paris on Nov. 14, 1967. While on a tour of North America with the orchestra, he died in Richmond, Va.

[Munch wrote *Je suis chef d'orchestre* (1954), translated as *I Am a Conductor* (1955; repr., 1978) by Leonard Burkat. He discussed the study of music in *Étude*, May 1948; and commented upon contemporary music in a symposium with six other conductors in *Musical America*, Feb. 15, 1954; and in an article for *Music Journal Annual*, 1964.

Musical tributes and analyses include Harold C. Schonberg, *New York Times*, Nov. 7 and 17, 1968; and Joseph Szigeti, *High Fidelity/Musical America*, Mar. 1969. Georges Collard, *Audio and Record Review*, May 1963, includes a discography; and record reviews are in *Saturday Review*, Aug. 29, 1953; and two articles in *American Record Guide*, Feb. 1969.

See also David Ewen, *Dictators of the Baton*, 2nd ed. (1948); Roland Gelatt, *Music Makers* (1953); Hope Stoddard, *Symphony Conductors of the U.S.A.* (1957); Harold C. Schonberg, *The Great Conductors* (1967); and Nicolas Slonimsky, *Music Since 1900*, 4th ed. (1971). Information about Munch and his family is in *Boston Symphony Concert Bulletin*, Apr. 27, 1951; and in *High Fidelity/Musical America*, Dec. 1965. A "Charles Munch Scrapbook," compiled by the music department staff of the Boston Public Library, forms part of its Allen A. Brown Collection.]

MADELINE SAPIENZA

MUNI, PAUL (Sept. 22, 1895–Aug. 25, 1967), actor, was born Mehilem ("Muni") Weisenfreund, in Lemberg, Austria (now Lvov, U.S.S.R.), the son of Nachum Favel Weisenfreund and his wife, Salche, itinerant entertainers. As a child he traveled in Austria-Hungary with his parents, who performed brief plays, songs, and dances for Yiddish-speaking villagers.

When Muni was four the family moved to London, where his father played bit parts at a Yiddish theater in Whitechapel. He then opened his own variety theater, which prospered until customers were frightened away by the street wars of neighborhood gangs. In 1901 the family resettled in New York City, on the Lower East Side, where Muni attended public school.

Unable to find work in Yiddish theater companies, Muni's father moved the family to Cleveland in 1904. There Muni attended Case-Woodland Elementary School and made his first stage appearance at the Perry Theatre in the summer of 1908, as a last-minute replacement for the character man. His performance as an old man in *Two Corpses at Breakfast* so impressed his parents that they kept him in the cast.

Muni was thirteen when the family moved to Chicago, where they opened Weisenfreund's Pavilion Theatre on 12th Street, and he became a full-time actor, specializing in portraying old men. From the start his characterizations depended heavily upon his skill with makeup. He later said, "I thought I was going to revolutionize the whole art of makeup. I thought if we could only use putty and completely cover my face and so mold it that no part of the real face or expression could be seen by the audience, a great step forward would be taken in character impersonation." The Wiesenfreund troupe disbanded when Muni's father died in 1913, and Muni peddled wick trimmers and read gas meters between stints with regional Yiddish theater groups. During World War I he worked at Yiddish theaters in Boston and Philadelphia.

In 1919 Maurice Schwartz, founder of the Yiddish Art Theatre, invited Muni to join his newly formed company in New York City. Muni's first role was Zazulye, a comic postal clerk, in Sholom Aleichem's *Tevye, the Dairyman*. He then played the grandfather in *The Blacksmith's Daughter*. Despite his youth Muni saw himself as a character actor specializing in comic old men. Others saw in him, even in such limited roles, a budding genius of the American stage. In October 1920 Schwartz gave him the leading role in Aleichem's *Schver tzu sein a Yid*; his performance made him a major star of the Yiddish theater. During rehearsals Muni met the actress Bella Finkel, niece of the actor Boris Tomashefsky. They were married on May 8, 1921. They had no children. Two years later Muni became an American citizen.

Muni remained on the Yiddish stage until 1926, when Sam Harris hired him to replace Edward G. Robinson in *We Americans*, billing him as Muni Wisenfrend. His transition to the English-speaking theater came as the great age of the Yiddish theater was ending. Many of its finest actors were leaving for Broadway or Hollywood, and with immigration restrictions and assimilation, the audience for Yiddish productions was dwindling. Again billed as Muni Wisenfrend, he starred as an ex-convict in *Four Walls* (1927). He was uncharacteristically cast as a young man, but nevertheless the *New York Post* devoted an editorial to his performance.

Rechristened Paul Muni, he appeared in *The Valiant* (1929), an early sound film, for which he received an Academy Award nomination. The studio exploited Muni's penchant for makeup by dubbing him "the new Lon Chaney" and assigning him to *Seven Faces* (1929), a mediocre film in which he portrayed the aged caretaker of a wax museum and six of his charges who come to life.

Muni returned to Broadway in Sidney Buchman's *This One Man* (1930). Although the *New York Times* called his acting "overpowering and magnificent" and named him "one of the giants of his profession," after two flops in 1931 he was ready for Hollywood again. In *Scarface* (1932) Muni's riveting portrayal of the murderous gangster Tony Camonte made him a major Hollywood star. Prior to its release, Muni had opened to great success in *Counsellor-at-Law* (1931), by Elmer Rice. It remained a popular vehicle for him; he revived it for the stage in 1942–1943 and 1947, and on television for "The Philco Playhouse" in 1948.

In 1932 Muni signed a three-picture contract with Warner Brothers. *I Am a Fugitive from a Chain Gang* (1932) triggered a succession of social-consciousness films by the studio. Based on an actual case, it dramatized the plight of an unemployed veteran unjustly convicted of robbery and sentenced to a chain gang. Muni, as the tragic James Allen, earned another Academy Award nomination. After *The World Changes* (1933) and *Hi, Nellie!* (1934), Muni's new contract with Warner Brothers gave him final approval of his film projects and freed him to return to the stage each year. Such authority was unprecedented for an actor in Hollywood's studio system of the 1930's.

His next series of roles made him one of the most respected American actors of the day. As Johnny Ramirez in *Bordertown* (1935) and Joe Radek in *Black Fury* (1935), he portrayed noble but misused ethnic figures in two hard-hitting social melodramas. In the title role of *The Story of Louis Pasteur* (1936) Muni won an Academy Award. He was a long-suffering Chinese peasant in *The Good Earth* (1937), a prestigious production by Irving Thalberg. He won the New York Film Critics' best-actor award for *The Life of Emile Zola* (1937). In a cover article *Time* (Aug. 16, 1937) proclaimed him the "first actor of the American screen." *Juarez* (1939), in which he portrayed the Mexican patriot, further enhanced his reputation. His final picture for Warner Brothers was *We Are Not Alone* (1939), a romantic melodrama.

Despite his remarkable talents, Muni was an unlikely film star. Neither handsome nor athletic, he seldom played romantic leads. Instead, his starring roles were enhanced character parts. Most Hollywood stars projected the same image from one picture to the next; Muni transformed himself for each role. Bette Davis, who was in *Bordertown* and *Juarez*, recalled that Muni "seemed intent on submerging himself so completely that he disappeared." Mary Astor, another early costar, described his method as involving "total attention to externals, makeup, hair, clothing, manner of walking, gesturing." Muni's stature derived almost entirely from the completeness and integrity of his impersonations. According to Nick Roddick, he became a star only because Warner Brothers "found a formula in which the entire weight of the film could be made to hinge on the impersonation." That these dramas also captured the spirit of New Deal liberalism certainly enhanced Muni's box-office appeal during the 1930's.

Muni's association with Warner Brothers ended in 1940 when, after a season on Broadway in Maxwell Anderson's *Key Largo*, he refused to star in *High Sierra*. After leaving the studio, he made only eight more films, most of them undistinguished. During the 1940's he was on the radio sporadically, narrated pro-Israel pageants, revived *Counsellor-at-Law* for stage and television, and starred in an unsuccessful Broadway revival of Sidney Howard's *They Knew What They Wanted* (1949). He gave an inspired performance as Willy Loman in the London company of Arthur Miller's *Death of a Salesman* (1949). *Stranger on the Prowl* (1952), an ill-fated Italian film, and a negligible role on television's "Ford Theatre" (1953) seemed to mark the end of his career.

In 1955 Muni made a comeback in *Inherit the Wind*, a play based on the Scopes trial. As Henry Drummond he won every major Broadway acting award, including the Antoinette Perry (Tony) Award, Donaldson Award, Variety Critics Poll, Outer Circle Award, and Newspaper Guild Page One Award. His subsequent television work earned him an Emmy nomination for his role as an aging lawyer in *Last Clear Chance* (1958) on "Playhouse 90." His final film appearance was as the star of *The Last*

Angry Man (1958), for which he received an Academy Award nomination.

Poor health and failing vision ended Muni's career, after twenty-three films, twelve Broadway plays, and more than 300 roles in the Yiddish theater. He spent his final years with his wife in Montecita, Calif., where he died.

[The Billy Rose Theatre Collection, New York Public Library, Lincoln Center, has a collection of Muni materials, including annotated scripts and a scrapbook compiled by his wife.

See Jerome Lawrence, *Actor: The Life and Times of Paul Muni* (1974). Lewis Funke and John E. Booth, *Actors Talk About Acting* (1961), includes a lengthy Muni interview. The Yiddish theater is detailed in Nahma Sandrow, *Vagabond Stars* (1977). The best treatment of Warner Brothers in the 1930's is Nick Roddick, *A New Deal in Entertainment* (1983); and see Rudy Behlmer, *Inside Warner Brothers, 1935–1951* (1985), which reproduces studio memoranda.

See also David Shipman, *The Great Movie Stars* (1970); *The New York Times Film Reviews* (1970); *The Film Criticism of Otis Ferguson* (1971); and Graham Greene, *The Pleasure Dome* (1972). Alexander Walker, *Stardom* (1970), briefly analyzes Muni's screen persona. An obituary is in the *New York Times*, Aug. 26, 1967.]

WILLIAM HUGHES

MURCHISON, CLINTON WILLIAMS (Oct. 17, 1895–June 20, 1969), oilman and industrialist, was born in Athens, Tex., the son of John Murchison, a bank president, and Clara Williams. He attended public schools in Athens and then Trinity University in Waxahachie, Tex., for a few months. In 1916 he worked as a teller at his father's bank.

With the outbreak of World War I, Murchison enlisted in the United States Army, attended officers' training school at Camp Pike, Ark., and served his tour in the United States. After the war, Murchison entered an informal partnership with Sid W. Richardson at Wichita Falls, Tex., in the trading of oil leases; the recession of 1921 forced them to abandon their business. On Apr. 21, 1920, Murchison married Anne Morris; they had three children.

In 1921, Murchison formed Fain and Murchison, a partnership, to drill wildcat oil wells in northwestern Texas. After some of the oil properties were sold to Magnolia Petroleum Company in 1926, Murchison temporarily retired with a $1.6 million profit, but he soon resumed developing oil and natural-gas deposits. In 1928 he organized the Murchison Oil Company in Dallas, and in 1929 he founded the Southwest Drilling Company. When many of the wells produced natural gas, Murchison formed the Southern Union Gas Company to pipe the gas to cities in several southern and western states.

Murchison wanted to use Southern Union to exploit the discovery of oil in eastern Texas in 1930, but his partners were reluctant. He left the company (while maintaining his stock interest) and formed Golding and Murchison Production (later the American Liberty Oil Company). To fund the new operation, Murchison introduced an innovative approach to financing the cost of well drilling: he bought properties in exchange for oil payments to be made after oil had been found and production had begun. Frequently, the costs of drilling wells were similarly financed.

During this period Murchison was in the vanguard of opposition to Texas oil-proration laws, which limited the amount of oil that could be removed from the ground. His contention that the law violated his liberties was rejected by the courts. He also introduced the concept of reversionary interest to the oil industry. He would sell oil properties at reasonable prices with the understanding that once the property had earned enough to repay the new owner for his investment (plus interest), a half-interest in all additional production would revert to Murchison. During World War II the demand for oil skyrocketed, and Murchison's reversionary-interest plan brought him huge dividends, since the war reduced significantly the time required for investors to recoup their funds and begin paying him his 50 percent.

In the late 1930's, Murchison began to diversify his holdings. In 1936 he acquired the Reserve Loan Life Company of Indiana, which grew into Life Companies, with assets in excess of $130 million in 1955. In 1944 he acquired a Dallas bus line that became the Transcontinental Bus Company, with assets of $23 million in 1955. His first wife having died in 1926, Murchison married Virginia Long on Jan. 21, 1942; they had no children.

In 1947, with some properties spun off by Southern Union, Murchison organized, and became the president of, the Delhi Oil Corporation. Delhi began developing oil fields in western Canada and then transferred those interests to Canadian Delhi Petroleum. In

1949, Murchison sold his interest in American Liberty to his partner. In 1950 he sold his holdings in Southern Union. In 1955, Delhi Oil was merged with the Taylor Oil and Gas Company to form the Delhi-Taylor Oil Corporation, a wholly integrated oil company, with assets in excess of $71 million.

In 1952 he and associates began to develop oil fields in Venezuela in association with the Pantepec Oil Company. In 1955 those operations were merged with the Venezuela Syndicate, an oil royalty company. Murchison's diversification continued when he purchased the Consumers Company, a Chicago building-materials company, in 1951; the Frontier Chemical Company in 1952; and the Easy Washing Machine Corporation in 1953. He then formed the Union Chemical and Materials Corporation in 1954 by merging these companies with the Follansbee Steel Corporation.

Altogether Murchison owned as many as 115 companies simultaneously. He owned, or had controlling interest in, companies in a wide range of fields, such as textbook and magazine publishing and the manufacturing of fishing tackle, candy, and office systems, as well as banking and steamship lines. In 1952 he united all his investments, excluding oil, under the Investments Management Corporation, which was directed by his two sons.

In 1953, Boys, Inc., established by Murchison and Sid Richardson, acquired the Del Mar Turf Club in California and, through an operating company, used its revenues for the rehabilitation of delinquent youths. All proceeds above the cost of operations plus 10 percent went to various programs to assist delinquents. The scheme eventually was abandoned after several years of success when the Internal Revenue Service refused to issue a favorable tax ruling on the charity.

Murchison's politics were conservative, but his business ventures were decidedly daring. His early wildcat oil-drilling efforts coincided with the rapid growth in popularity of petroleum-dependent automobiles in the 1920's, and later he profited from the increased reliance on oil as a home heating fuel. His entrepreneurial skills, ability to anticipate future needs, and natural cunning served him well throughout his life. In Murchison's later years he devoted himself to farming and raising cattle. His personal fortune at the time of his death has been estimated at $500 million, placing him among the world's wealthiest persons. He died at Athens, Tex.

[There are no Murchison papers. The *New York Times* reported on Murchison's primary business transactions. An obituary appeared in that paper, June 21, 1969.]

STEPHEN D. BODAYLA

MUSMANNO, MICHAEL ANGELO (Apr. 7, 1897–Oct. 12, 1968), judge and writer, was born in McKees Rocks, Pa., the son of Italian immigrants, Antonio Musmanno, a coal miner, and Maddelena Castellucci. Although his family was poor, Musmanno wanted to be a lawyer from the time he was twelve. While working in the day, he took evening high school courses and eventually enrolled at Georgetown University, where he earned a B.A. and an M.A. and began work toward his law degree. He served in World War I as an infantryman and was slightly wounded; after the war he completed law school. In all, Musmanno earned seven degrees, including doctorates from American University and the University of Rome.

Musmanno found it difficult to join an established law firm but finally found a job after responding to an anonymous advertisement for a legal assistant. He proceeded to win his first forty-two cases. He wore a brown suit to the first of these cases and soon developed a superstitious attachment to the color. When a colleague argued that it was skill, not the color of the suit, that won cases, Musmanno agreed to wear a different color and promptly lost the next case. Although he won sixty of his first sixty-five cases, he took the losses with such anguish that he decided he was not cut out to be a lawyer. He went to Europe but could not stay away from the law and therefore enrolled at the University of Rome to study Roman law. While there, he worked as an English tutor, as a newspaper stringer, and even as an extra in the silent film version of *Ben-Hur*.

Musmanno returned to Pittsburgh in 1925 and again had trouble developing a private practice. Then he defended a man who had drunkenly assaulted him and slowly his reputation began to spread. Musmanno took on numerous indigent clients and acquired a reputation as a defender of the underprivileged. As such, he became interested in the most notorious case of the 1920's, that of the anarchists

Nicola Sacco and Bartolomeo Vanzetti. Believing they had been tried not for murder but for their political views, Musmanno joined the battery of lawyers trying to reverse their conviction. Following their execution, Musmanno continued to believe in Sacco and Vanzetti's innocence and wrote a vindication of the two men, *After Twelve Years* (1939).

In 1926 Musmanno lost an election bid for the Pennsylvania General Assembly, but two years later won by a narrow margin to become the youngest member of the Pennsylvania House of Representatives. He was reelected in 1930 and began a campaign to repeal the Coal and Iron Police Laws, which allowed private companies to maintain their own police forces to break strikes and forcibly discourage other "undesirable" activity. Although he got the bill through the legislature, the governor vetoed it. Musmanno continued his attack, however, by publishing "Jan Volkanik," the story of a miner beaten to death by private police. He then convinced Paul Muni to star in *Black Fury*, a movie based on the story. Musmanno toured with the film in 1935, urging audiences to demand repeal of the police laws, and he credited the film with doing much to accomplish that goal. Among his other achievements as a legislator were laws permitting Sunday baseball and movies, election reform, and lower taxes for small wage earners.

In 1932 Musmanno successfully ran for judge of the Allegheny County court, and two years later was elected, with 94 percent of the vote, to the Court of Common Pleas, a position he held for the next sixteen years. His terms on that bench were marked by colorful and often controversial behavior. He led a crusade against drunken drivers, imposing sentences of up to six months in jail for serious offenders. At the same time, he took a paternalistic attitude toward women defendants, sentencing them to only two-thirds of the penalties he imposed upon men, because he believed they were "finer and more delicate." He attracted national attention in 1936 when he sentenced himself to a three-day prison sentence "to find out what it really feels like" to be incarcerated. He mingled freely with the inmates, some of whom he had sentenced, and did not conceal his identity. Afterward he told a reporter that just as a doctor should study inside a hospital, lawyers and judges should also study inside the institutions of the law.

When the United States entered World War II, Musmanno joined the navy as a lieutenant commander. His ship was sunk in the Adriatic, and he was then assigned to General Mark Clark's staff for the invasion of Italy. His knowledge of Italian language and customs led to his appointment as governor of the Sorrento Peninsula for six months. At the end of the war he held a number of decorations as well as the rank of rear admiral. President Truman then named him to head the Board of Forcible Repatriation in Austria, where he prevented thousands of refugees from being sent back to Russia to face either firing squads or exile in Siberia. Musmanno was also a member of the team sent to determine whether Adolf Hitler had actually died, and in his investigations Musmanno interviewed dozens of the dictator's staff members, from generals to cooks and butlers. In 1950 he published a book based on his findings, *Ten Days to Die*, which was made into a movie, *The Last Ten Days* (1956).

Musmanno's most important task, however, was as a judge in the Nuremberg trials of Nazi war criminals. He sat on three of the tribunals, including the *Einsatzgruppen* (death squads) case, in which twenty-one defendants were charged with the responsibility for nearly 2 million deaths. At the time, Musmanno called for a world court to be established to try such criminals, and a number of years later he defended the Israeli trial of Adolf Eichmann on the ground that no other forum existed. In 1961, because of his extensive knowledge, Musmanno became a key witness for the prosecution against Eichmann; he later wrote, "If my testimony could make any contribution toward upholding the dignity and sanctity of human life, I could not, in conscience, refuse the invitation from Jerusalem."

Upon returning to the United States after Nuremberg, Musmanno again sat on the Court of Common Pleas until 1951, when, without Democratic-party support, he won a twenty-one-year term on the Pennsylvania Supreme Court. He had lost a bid the previous year for lieutenant governor and in 1964 made his last attempt to enter national politics, losing a bitter primary fight for the United States Senate. In 1961 President Kennedy appointed him to the Commission on International Rules of Judicial Procedure.

Musmanno never developed any particular stature in jurisprudential thought; his decisions were noted for their common sense, sympathy for the underprivileged, and forceful language rather than for doctrinal brilliance or innovation. He dissented often, especially when he felt his fellow judges applied the formulas of law too rigidly without reference to the facts of the case or the persons involved. Roscoe Pound, in an introduction to a collection of Musmanno's dissenting opinions in 1956, noted that the justice spoke more as an advocate but "his strong sense of justice, zeal for individual rights, and lively style of expression make application of legal principles to particular states of fact vivid and appealing."

Off the bench Musmanno was greatly in demand as an orator, and he continued to write on a variety of subjects. Ever proud of his Italian heritage, he praised his ancestors' accomplishments in *The Story of the Italians in America* (1965). When Yale scholars claimed, on the basis of the Vinland Map, that Scandinavian explorer Leif Ericsson had been the first European to discover America, Musmanno jumped into the fray. He studied the map and declared it to be spurious evidence that would never hold up in a court of law. He presented a full-scale attack on the Ericsson claim, as well as a defense of Christopher Columbus, in *Columbus Was First* (1966). Musmanno was an avid anti-Communist, and once declared that all Communists should be sentenced to twenty years in prison. He was a coauthor of the 1954 Communist Control Act.

Musmanno's devotion to the law and to writing took all his energies, and he often put in a sixteen-hour day. He never married and recalled that as a young lawyer he never attended social functions. "Being a lawyer was not only my occupation—it was my avocation, diversion, and entertainment. It was my wife, children, and grandchildren!" He died in McKees Rocks.

[Musmanno's autobiography is *Verdict!* (1958). See his *Justice Musmanno Dissents* (1955) and *That's My Opinion* (1966). See also *New York Times*, May 16, 1961, and the obituary therein, Oct. 13, 1968.]

MELVIN I. UROFSKY

MUSTE, ABRAHAM JOHANNES (Jan. 8, 1885–Feb. 11, 1967), clergyman, labor leader and educator, and peace activist, was born in Zierikzee, the Netherlands, the son of Martin Muste, a coachman, and Adriana Jonker. In 1891 the family emigrated to Grand Rapids, Mich., where they had relatives. Muste and his family were naturalized in 1896. Dutch Calvinism suffused Muste's upbringing. His father was a deacon and later an elder of the local Dutch Reformed church. Muste became a full member of the church at the unusually young age of thirteen, and his family and church expected him to become a minister. With that goal in mind, Muste left the Grand Rapids public schools for the church-connected Hope Preparatory School in Holland, Mich., in 1898. Seven years later he graduated as valedictorian from Hope College. After a year teaching in Iowa, Muste entered his church's official seminary, the New Brunswick Theological Seminary in New Jersey.

On June 21, 1909, shortly after his seminary graduation, Muste married Anna Huizenga. They had three children. Also in 1909 he received ordination and became minister of the Fort Washington Collegiate Church in New York City. Muste proved popular with his affluent parishioners, yet he also began to drift away from Calvinist dogma, particularly under the influence of his studies at the liberal Union Theological Seminary, where he earned a B.D. in 1913. Two years later he broke with the Dutch Reformed church and became minister of the Central Congregational Church in Newtonville, Mass. Readings in Tolstoy, the Christian mystics, and the Quaker scholar Rufus Jones led Muste to pacifism. World War I thrust him into an active role in the antiwar movement and out of the Congregational church. In 1918 he became minister of the Providence Friends' Meeting in Rhode Island.

Later that year Muste took up residence in Boston with a group of pacifists who called themselves the Comradeship. Just as Muste's theological views were becoming less and less orthodox, so were his political views. When a textile strike broke out in Lawrence, Mass., Muste and other members of the Comradeship went to investigate the workers' conditions. Almost immediately Muste found himself head of the strike committee. The workers won a moderate victory, and Muste emerged as a national labor leader. In October 1919 he was chosen as general secretary of the newly formed Amalgamated Textile Workers Union. When that union foundered in the midst of the textile depression of the early 1920's, Muste accepted a position as chairman of the faculty at

Brookwood Labor College in Katonah, N.Y. With characteristic energy and dedication, Muste fashioned Brookwood into America's leading labor school as well as one of the chief centers for trade union progressivism and opposition to the conservative leadership of the American Federation of Labor (AFL).

In 1929, as Muste's differences with the AFL grew, he helped found the Conference on Progressive Labor Action (CPLA), which advocated industrial unionism and a labor party. Muste, who chaired the new group, and his followers (often known as Musteites) played an energetic, if not always successful, role in union struggles in the textile, coal, and steel industries. Their greatest triumphs came as leaders of the 1934 Toledo Auto-Lite strike and as organizers of the midwestern jobless, whom they enlisted in Unemployed Leagues. Increasingly radicalized by the conditions of the Great Depression, Muste moved further toward the political Left and away from Christian pacifism. In 1933 he quit Brookwood and transformed the CPLA into the American Workers Party (AWP), an avowedly Marxist and revolutionary party. Just one year later the AWP merged with the American Trotskyist Communist League of America to form the Workers Party.

Muste's involvement with Marxist-Leninism ended abruptly in 1936 when he experienced a revelation (one of several religious experiences he reported during his lifetime) and returned to Christian pacifism, a faith that guided him for the rest of his life. In keeping with these convictions, Muste accepted a staff position with the Fellowship of Reconciliation (FOR), a nondenominational peace organization. The following year he became director of the Presbyterian Labor Temple in New York City. But with the outbreak of World War II Muste returned to antiwar work as FOR executive secretary. As a nonviolent revolutionary, Muste was part of the FOR's radical wing, and he supported those who refused all cooperation with the Selective Service System.

After the war, Muste campaigned for disarmament, refused to pay taxes, spoke out against McCarthyism, and urged draft resistance. His peace activism grew rather than diminished after his retirement from the FOR in 1953. One of his biographers noted in the early 1960's that "Muste's name is on the letterhead of nearly every American peace organization." In the 1950's and 1960's Muste sought converts to radical pacifism among scientists, academics, and especially Christians in America and abroad, through such groups as the Society for Social Responsibility in Science and the Church Peace Mission and through publications like *Liberation*, which he helped found in 1956. Muste also organized, raised funds, and joined marches and acts of civil disobedience against civil defense drills, the building of missile bases, and nuclear weapons testing.

In 1959 Muste led members of the Committee for Nonviolent Action, a group he chaired, in protesting at an Omaha, Nebr., missile base. After he climbed over a fence into Mead Air Force Base, the frail, seventy-four-year-old Muste spent eight days in jail for trespassing. Muste was instrumental in infusing the civil rights movement with the philosophy of nonviolent direct action. The Congress of Racial Equality emerged directly out of the FOR in 1942, with Muste as "a kind of grandfather." Martin Luther King, Jr., credited Muste as an important inspiration.

Muste was a forerunner of the anti–Vietnam War movement that began to emerge in the mid-1960's. He helped organize some of the first protests against that war, and characteristically it was respect for "A. J.," as Muste was always called, that allowed politically divergent groups to unite in the Fifth Avenue Peace Parade Committee, the first broad-based antiwar coalition of the 1960's. During the year before his death in New York City, Muste dedicated himself to the antiwar movement, speaking, writing, organizing, and even traveling to Saigon and Hanoi.

One coworker, noting Muste's reserve and aversion to small talk, called him not "the sort of man you'd slap on the back," and Edmund Wilson similarly described him as a "lean Netherlander who resembles a country schoolmaster and stands in the posture of a preacher." Yet he inspired love and respect from even his political opponents. "For many thousands of Americans," Paul Goodman wrote, "Muste is an Authentic Great Man." Most Americans rejected or never heard his message of radical pacifism, but they felt its force through the civil rights and antiwar movements that he helped to lead and inspire.

[Muste's papers are in the Swarthmore Peace Collection in Swarthmore, Pa., which also contains the papers of the FOR; the Brookwood Labor College papers at Wayne State University in Detroit; the Socialist Workers papers at the Wisconsin State Historical Society; and the Labor Temple Collection at the Presbyterian Historical Society in Philadelphia. A memoir is included in the Columbia University Oral History Project.

Muste wrote *Nonviolence in an Aggressive World* (1940) and *Not by Might* (1947). A selection of his writings, edited by Nat Hentoff, is *The Essays of A. J. Muste* (1970), which includes Muste's "Sketches for an Autobiography." Muste published his recollections of one decade in Rita J. Simon, ed., *As We Saw the Thirties* (1967).

Biographies of Muste are Nat Hentoff, *Peace Agitator* (1963); and Jo Ann Robinson, *Abraham Went Out* (1981). See also James O. Morris, *The Conflict Within the AFL* (1958); Roy Rosenzweig, "Radicals and the Jobless: The Musteites and the Unemployed Leagues, 1932–1936," *Labor History*, Winter 1975; and Lawrence S. Wittner, *Rebels Against War: The American Peace Movement, 1941–1960* (1969). Firsthand recollections of Muste are in Paul Goodman, "On A. J. Muste," *New York Review of Books*, Nov. 28, 1963; John Nevin Sayre, "Fighting Reconciler: A. J. Muste as I Knew Him," *Fellowship*, Mar. 1967; Nat Hentoff, "A. J. Muste, 1885–1967," *Saturday Review*, Apr. 8, 1967; and *Liberation*, Sept.–Oct. 1967. Obituaries are in the *Village Voice*, Feb. 23, 1967; and the *New York Times*, Feb. 12, 1967.]

ROY ROSENZWEIG

NAGEL, CONRAD (Mar. 16, 1897–Feb. 24, 1970), film, stage, radio, and television actor and director, was born in Keokuk, Iowa, the son of Frank Nagel and Frances Murphy, both musicians. Frank Nagel, a pianist, composer, and teacher, became dean of music at Highland Park College in Des Moines, Iowa, when his son was two. Conrad Nagel exhibited acting talent while in public school, where his first role was Scrooge in *A Christmas Carol*. At the age of fifteen he was admitted to his father's college, from which he graduated in 1914 with a bachelor of oratory. Immediately after graduation he went to work for a local stock company, where in his first year he acted in forty-five plays.

In 1916 Nagel went to New York City and quickly found employment in bit roles in vaudeville. He was spotted and given a position with the touring company of *Experience*, a modern version of the morality play *Everyman*. In 1918 he opened on Broadway in *Forever After*, which established his reputation as an actor. Near the end of World War I he enlisted in the navy, but he was stationed in the New York area and able to continue performing in the play.

Forever After was produced by William Brady, whose daughter, Alice, was a stage and film star. Brady, pleased with the success of the play, cast Nagel opposite his daughter in a film version of Louisa May Alcott's *Little Women* (1919), which was shot on location at Alcott's home. Nagel continued to perform in *Forever After* at night and in films during the day. On June 24, 1919, he married Ruth E. Helms, whose father had been a colleague of the elder Nagel. The couple had one child. In the same year he joined the Actors' Equity Association, which had been trying to unionize Broadway actors. He believed strongly in its cause and devoted much of his energy for the next decade and a half to actors' interests.

In 1919 Nagel went to Hollywood to make the film *The Fighting Chance* for Famous Players–Lasky. Its success prompted Lasky to offer him a five-year contract at a salary large enough to persuade him to settle in California. In 1921 Cecil B. DeMille cast him in *Fool's Paradise*. He appeared in another of Cecil DeMille's films and in three directed by William DeMille, experiences that greatly enhanced his reputation. While popular with both fans and the Hollywood community, Nagel avoided the sensational life of film stars; he even was an usher each week at services of the Christian Science church.

Early in 1927 Nagel joined with L. B. Mayer and Fred Niblo in forming the Academy of Motion Picture Arts and Sciences, which brought into one organization all who worked in motion pictures. This new group soon came into conflict with Actors' Equity, with which Nagel was also still affiliated. Mayer and the Producers' Association dropped a proposed pay cut, which the actors had opposed; but they made it appear that they had done so at the request of the academy, not Equity. Equity's prestige was hurt and Nagel was blamed for the failure, causing the national office of Equity to dissolve the Hollywood office. Nagel was then free to devote his time to the activities of the academy.

Nagel claimed that Mayer was angry over his role in the dispute and to punish him lent him to the struggling Warner Brothers studio. He was working on *Glorious Betsy* (1928) at the time Warner Brothers released *The Jazz Singer*, starring Al Jolson. This latter film was the first widely released movie with sound, but the sound was limited to Jolson's musical numbers. Warner executives, pleased with the public response to sound pictures, quickly inserted talking scenes into *Glorious Betsy*, giving Nagel the distinction of starring in the first movie with spoken dialogue. He became one of the most popular actors in America, averaging over 3,000 fan letters every week. In the early 1930's he made thirty-one movies in twenty-four months.

In 1932, despite his heavy acting schedule, he accepted the presidency of the academy. When the Great Depression caused motion picture producers to propose that all employees take a 50 percent pay cut to keep the studios in operation, the academy and its president found a compromise by which the brunt of the burden would fall on highly paid employees, and then only for a few weeks. When, at the end of the period, two studios refused to return all employees to full salary, the split between the producers and the rest of the academy was complete. Nagel was caught in the middle and could find no solution that would hold the academy together as a political force. On Apr. 20, 1933, he resigned as president. The academy never recovered and soon became little more than a society for awarding Oscars.

Nagel's life and career were seriously damaged by the controversy. Mayer was unhappy with him, and in 1935 his wife divorced him. He married Lynn Merrick in 1945 and Michael Coulson Smith in 1955; both marriages were short-lived.

Nagel left Hollywood in 1933 to devote himself again to the theater. He returned to New York City in *The First Apple* (1933) and then took such plays as *The Petrified Forest* and *The Male Animal* on tour.

From 1937 to 1949, Nagel was also director and host for the Columbia Broadcasting System's radio drama series "Silver Theater." In 1940 he was presented with an Oscar for his work in behalf of actors for the Motion Picture Relief Fund. He became host for the American Broadcasting Company's television show "Celebrity Time" in 1948. During the next several years he appeared often on television. He continued to take time from his stage and television activity to act in the movies until the late 1950's, but he thought of New York as home during the latter part of his life; he died in New York City.

Nagel appeared in at least 111 movies and in more than twenty theatrical productions. His popularity was widespread, although he never achieved superstar status. He was a handsome man with an extraordinary voice, but his success was due primarily to his acting ability. His major contribution, however, lay in his unflagging service to his fellow actors.

[A clipping and photograph file is in the Performing Arts Research Center of the New York Public Library. Nagel provided an autobiography in Bernard Rosenberg and Harry Silverstein, eds., *The Real Tinsel* (1970). A survey of his career is in Larry Lee Holland, "Conrad Nagel," *Films in Review*, 1979. An obituary is in the *New York Times*, Feb. 25, 1970.]

ROBERT A. ARMOUR

NESBIT, EVELYN FLORENCE (Dec. 25, 1884–Jan. 17, 1967), entertainer, was born in Tarentum, Pa., near Pittsburgh. Her father was Winfield Scott Nesbit, a lawyer, and her mother, Elizabeth F. Nesbit, had been a clothing designer. Nesbit's father died when she was eight years old, leaving Nesbit, her younger brother, and her mother with little financial support. The family then moved to Pittsburgh, where her mother ran a boardinghouse and Nesbit attended grammar school.

In 1899, Nesbit's mother moved the family to Philadelphia, where she found work for them all at Wanamaker's department store, Evelyn as a stockgirl. Evelyn was quite beautiful, with thick, curly, copper-colored hair and hazel eyes, and so she began to pose as an artist's model. After a year, Nesbit and her mother moved to New York City, where Elizabeth Nesbit looked unsuccessfully for work as a clothing designer. Evelyn began to model again, posing for Carroll Beckwith, Frederick S. Church, and others. George Grey Barnard sculptured her as "Innocence," now in the Metropolitan Museum of Art, and Charles Dana Gibson drew her in his famous sketch "The Eternal Question."

Photographs of Nesbit in newspaper advertisements brought her a part in the musical *Floradora* in 1901. As a featured dancer, she was noticed by many wealthy men and showered with gifts and invitations. In August she was taken to a private luncheon by a showgirl friend. There, in a hideaway apartment, Nesbit met the architect Stanford White. He praised her beauty, introduced her to champagne, and playfully pushed her in a red velvet swing. White shortly won the confidence of Nesbit's mother and began supporting them both financially. He persuaded Mrs. Nesbit to leave Evelyn in his care while she visited Pittsburgh, and a few days after her departure White and Nesbit dined alone in his apartment. He gave her abundant champagne and a yellow kimono to model for him. Nesbit's story of this night varied with the telling, but her usual description was of waking in terror to find herself naked and no longer a virgin. She continued to see White, however, joining the extravagant parties he frequently gave in his tower studio at Madison Square Garden, which he had designed. He supported her in lavish style.

In December Nesbit was introduced to Harry K. Thaw, a thirty-five-year-old railroad millionaire from Pittsburgh. Though Nesbit disliked him intensely, he courted her and impressed her mother.

Floradora closed in the summer of 1902, and Nesbit joined the company of George Lederer's *Wild Rose.* She began an affair with John Barrymore, then twenty-two years old. White and her mother disapproved, and when the show closed in the fall, they sent her to the DeMille School in Pompton Lakes, N.J. In April 1903 she was hospitalized with acute abdominal pains and underwent surgery for what appeared to be appendicitis, though it was rumored she had been pregnant. She convalesced in New York, where she was attended continually by Thaw and White.

Upon her release, Thaw persuaded Nesbit to accompany him to Europe to recover, and in May she and her mother arrived in Paris to share Thaw's apartment and indulge in a spree of shopping, dining, and theatergoing. Thaw proposed several times, and Nesbit put him off by telling him she was not worthy of him because of her seduction by White. Elizabeth Nesbit returned home while Thaw and Evelyn continued their tour. During this time Thaw, apparently under the influence of cocaine, beat Nesbit severely with a dog whip. In spite of her professed terror of him, she stayed with him on their tour of Europe.

Nesbit returned to New York in October 1903, a few weeks ahead of Thaw. When White visited her and she told him of the beatings, he arranged for her to meet with lawyer Abe Hummel, who recorded her statements in an affidavit. Thaw's lawyers were notified, and they advised him not to see Nesbit until Christmas Day, when they supposed she would reach her majority, which at that time was age eighteen (but it would in fact be her nineteenth birthday). The pair celebrated their reunion at dinner together that night and resumed their affair, traveling to Europe again in the summer of 1904. Thaw continued to beat Nesbit; but she increased her power over him each time he begged her forgiveness, and she purposely enraged him by mentioning White's name.

On Apr. 5, 1905, Nesbit and Thaw were married in the Third Presbyterian Church in Pittsburgh and, after a honeymoon in the western United States, went to live at Lyndhurst, the home of Thaw's widowed mother. Nesbit became fairly comfortable with her mother-in-law and new home. Thaw, however, resumed frequent "business" trips to New York by that fall, and by the following spring his fits of rage were increasing.

During a trip to New York together, the Thaws had tickets to the opening of *Mamzelle Champagne* at the Madison Square Garden roof theater, on June 25, 1906. Thaw wore an overcoat in spite of the hot weather as he and Evelyn had dinner and then went on to the theater. Nesbit became bored with the show, and their party got up to leave. However, Thaw lagged behind them, approaching Stanford White, who sat alone near the front of the room. Thaw drew a gold-plated revolver from beneath his coat and shot White three times in the head. As he entered the elevator with Nesbit he told her, "My dear, I have probably saved your life."

Thaw was incarcerated immediately in the Tombs Prison, where Nesbit visited him faithfully. His mother and family came at once to New York and arranged for legal counsel. The trial began on Jan. 23, 1907, and was sensationalized by the press. Thaw's defense depended on proof of his temporary insanity as a result of White's seduction of his wife and thus centered on Evelyn's testimony regarding her relationships with the two men. In April the jury declared it could reach no verdict, and a second trial began in January 1908. The following month Thaw was found not guilty on the ground of his insanity and sentenced to the Asylum for the Criminal Insane at Matteawan.

During the second trial Nesbit's relationship with Thaw and his family deteriorated. She was given a financial settlement but went through the money quickly. In early 1910 she went to Europe supported by a male friend, and in Berlin on October 25 she gave birth to a son, who, she said, was fathered by Thaw during a visit to his rooms at Matteawan. She came back to New York with the infant.

Nesbit returned to Europe in May 1913 and appeared that summer in *Hello Ragtime* in London with dancer Jack Clifford (born Virgil Montani). The show opened in New York in August and then went on the vaudeville circuit. When Thaw was released from Matteawan in June 1915, he divorced Nesbit immediately and she married Clifford, touring with him throughout the war years. She also appeared in a number of films, including *Threads of Destiny* (1914); *Judge Not* (1915); *Redemption* (1917); and *Woman, Woman; I Want to Forget; Her Mistake; My Little Sister; The Woman Who Gave;* and *Thou Shalt Not* (all 1919).

When Nesbit and Clifford divorced in 1919, she continued performing for a short time with a new partner. She became addicted to heroin and had difficulty finding work as her beauty and ability diminished. In 1921 she opened a tearoom near Broadway to support herself but moved in 1924 to Atlantic City. There she appeared at Martin's and the Palais Royale and then opened her own short-lived club called El Prinkipo. In 1925 she appeared at the Moulin Rouge in Chicago and, the following year, returned to Atlantic City. She opened a number of speakeasies in New York and Atlantic City, but all closed very quickly as a result of raids or badly chosen business partners.

Nesbit continued to work in burlesque through the 1930's, and her second volume of autobiography, *Prodigal Days*, was published in 1934. By the 1940's she was living in a Hollywood rooming house. She was supported by her son, although Harry Thaw left her $10,000 when he died in 1947. She said she had become a theosophist and spent her time in religious study, painting, and modeling in clay. In 1955 she acted as technical adviser for the producers of a motion picture based on her life called *The Girl in the Red Velvet Swing*, starring Joan Collins, Ray Milland, and Farley Granger. Early in the 1960's she was moved to a nursing home. Interviewed there, she said, "Stanny White was killed, but my fate was worse. I lived." She died in Santa Monica, Calif.

[Nesbit's autobiographies, *The Story of My Life* (1914) and *Prodigal Days* (1934), are important sources of information, despite their vagueness and questionable credibility. See also Harry K. Thaw, *The Traitor* (1926); F. A. MacKenzie, *The Trial of Harry K. Thaw* (1928); Michael MacDonald Mooney, *Evelyn Nesbit and Stanford White* (1976); and R. M. Ketchum, "Faces from the Past, XXIII," *American Heritage*, June 1969. Obituaries are in the *New York Times*, Jan. 19, 1967; and *Newsweek*, Jan. 30, 1967.]

PATRICIA SCOLLARD PAINTER

NEUTRA, RICHARD JOSEPH (Apr. 8, 1892–Apr. 15, 1970), architect, was born in Vienna, Austria, the son of Samuel Neutra, a metallurgist, and Elizabeth Glaser. He attended a local primary school and the Sophiengymnasium (1902–1910). He commenced study at Vienna's Technischehochschule in 1911, but the coming of war was to interrupt his education. Though his parents lived a quiet, middle-class life, his sister and brothers moved in sophisticated Viennese cultural circles, and through them he came into contact with Arnold Schoenberg, Sigmund Freud, and Gustav Klimt.

The architecture of Neutra's birthplace left a lasting imprint on him. "The entire plan of Vienna," he wrote years later, "is still in my blood when I talk of city planning. The Baroque palaces are still in my blood too. . . . I love it, I may write about it with a lusty pencil, but I shrink from seeing it imitated. We live too late for that."

Neutra was impressed at an early age by the architecture of Otto Wagner, particularly the Vienna subway stations he had designed in the 1890's and his Postal Savings Bank of 1905, which was the first "modern" building on the city's historic Ringstrasse. Neutra was more directly influenced by the spare facades and simple interiors of Adolf Loos, whose crusade against traditional ornament culminated in the Kaertner Bar (1907) and the Steiner House (1910).

During World War I, Neutra served as an artillery officer in the Balkans. While on duty in Trebinje, Serbia, he designed and constructed his first building, an officers' teahouse, an early expression of his penchant for post-and-beam pavilions. Stricken with malaria, he returned to Vienna during the war and graduated cum laude from the Technischehochschule in 1918.

In 1919, Neutra worked briefly in Switzerland for Gustav Amman, a well-known landscape architect; from him Neutra learned site planning and landscaping. In 1920, Neutra served as the city architect of Luckenwalde, Germany. There he designed a housing project and cemetery gatehouse, fusing official building styles with modernist ideas.

He joined the Berlin architect Eric Mendelsohn in 1921 just as Mendelsohn was completing the Einstein Tower in Potsdam. With Mendelsohn, he worked on the remodeling of the Berliner Tageblatt Building and the Zehlendorf housing project. On Dec. 23, 1922, he married a Swiss musician, Dione Niedermann; they had three children.

Neutra immigrated to the United States in 1923. (He was naturalized in 1929.) Like many young European architects, Neutra had been greatly moved by the German publication of Frank Lloyd Wright's designs in 1910. Encouraged by Loos, Neutra became convinced that America, particularly Chicago, had become the capital of modern architecture. He worked briefly in New York, which he described as possessing a "wild, accidental beauty." He then went to Chicago and joined the firm of Holabird and Roche, where he gained insights into American building technology. There he also met one of his first American heroes, Louis Sullivan, who was dying in poverty and neglect. At Sullivan's funeral in 1924, he met Frank Lloyd Wright, Sullivan's disciple. Wright invited Neutra to Taliesin, his Wisconsin home and studio, to work and study through the fall and winter of 1924.

Wright's meager practice was centered in Los Angeles, where he had built the Barnsdall Hollyhock House in 1920 and a significant group of concrete-block houses in 1923 and 1924. Attracted by the possibilities of the area's climate and landscape, Neutra decided to migrate to Los Angeles. With the encouragement of Wright and the help of Rudolph Schindler, a Viennese school friend and former Wright disciple then in California, Neutra set up a Los Angeles practice in 1926. Ultimately, his architecture would become as important to the West Coast as Wright's and Sullivan's had been to the Middle West. Gregory Ain and Harwell Harris were among the first of the numerous talented architects who were influenced by Neutra.

Neutra's basic structure was the timeless post-and-beam with cantilevered roof slabs extending into space. His favorite early materials were concrete, steel, stucco, and wood. He also valued glass for both its transparent and reflecting qualities. His architecture stressed above all the interpenetration of inner and outer space. As a student of Wright and of the new architecture of Europe, Neutra bridged, perhaps better than anyone, the frequently polarized worlds of Taliesin and Bauhaus. Neutra was especially concerned that good design be available to people of modest means; he therefore translated his most expensive architecture into less-costly forms.

Of twentieth-century architects, Neutra was perhaps the most interested and knowledgeable in the biological and behavioral sciences. He wrote and lectured extensively on what he called "bio-realism"—that is, the psychological, physiological, and ecological dimensions of architecture. His best-known book, *Survival Through Design* (1954), had an especially wide influence.

Neutra's first independent design was for the Jardinette Apartments (Hollywood, 1927), one of the earliest buildings in what would come to be called the international style. In 1929 he became internationally famous with his prefabricated steel-framed Lovell (Health) House, built for a physician who stressed preventive medicine. Resting on a light steel frame perched over a canyon in the Hollywood Hills, the three-story house of concrete, glass, and metal panels epitomized the aesthetic of mechanical assemblage. A terrace led from the street to an entry hall and to bedrooms on the top floor. The hall also functioned as a balcony, framing and overlooking one of the finest stairways in all modern architecture; the stair lights beneath the railing were headlights from a Model-T Ford. Neutra designed the furniture of the living room and library. Both the Jardinette and the Lovell House were featured in the 1932 Museum of Modern Art exhibition that gave the international style its name.

In the 1930's, Neutra was especially noted for his modern California houses of stucco, glass, and metal and for innovative ideas in school and apartment design. The house built in 1934 in Santa Monica for the film actress Anna Sten epitomized his larger single-family houses of the 1930's. It had white stucco walls, a curving front bay, and silver-gray trim. A smaller, more modest variant of his 1930's aesthetic was the

Miller House (1937) in Palm Springs, with its reflecting pool, soffit lighting, and built-in furniture. The Corona Avenue School (1935) in the Bell district of Los Angeles had sliding glass walls opening to outdoor classrooms. It was nicknamed the "test-tube school."

The scarcity of metal and glass during World War II forced Neutra to use the warmer, more available materials of brick, stone, and redwood in such works as the 1942 house in Los Angeles for the radio broadcaster John Nesbitt. A gently pitched shed roof folded over the rear glass wall with a down-turning overhang. Board and batten redwood covered the exterior. The floors and fireplace wall were brick. A lily pool outside the front entrance extended beneath the glass into the interior hall. A broadly cantilevered overhang on the front protected the western exposure and connected the main house with the guesthouse and garage. For the rest of his life, Neutra would continue to use natural materials in tandem with industrial products.

Conscious of the broader obligations of his profession, Neutra served in the 1930's and 1940's as a member and chairman of the California State Planning Board. In 1939 he became a consultant to the United States Housing Authority and the National Youth Administration.

Following the war, Neutra's most-celebrated buildings continued to be his California houses. The Kaufmann House in Palm Springs (1946) updated his elegant pavilions of the 1930's, while the Tremaine House in Montecito (1948) adumbrated his more relaxed style of the 1950's and 1960's.

In the 1940's and 1950's, Neutra and his partner, Robert Alexander, designed large public and commercial projects throughout the world, including the Los Angeles County Hall of Records and the American embassy in Karachi, Pakistan. He also designed the Channel Heights housing project (1942) for California shipyard workers. The Alexander partnership ended in the late 1950's, and Neutra's son Dion, a longtime associate, became his partner in the mid-1960's. They redesigned Neutra's own studio-home, the Van der Leeuw Research House, to reflect their changing ideas after a fire in 1963 had destroyed the more austere 1932 original.

Neutra was a tall, handsome man with a fine voice and a commanding presence whose personal charm and humane concerns were frequently countered by an egocentric arrogance. Throughout his life, he also suffered from neurotic manifestations of the manic-depressive syndrome. He died in Wuppertal, West Germany.

In the late 1960's and 1970's, Neutra's work, and modern architecture generally, came increasingly under attack from the new generation of "postmodern" architects, who called for an architecture that alluded to the past and featured ornament. But postmodernists such as Robert Venturi and Denise Scott-Brown have acknowledged their intense admiration of modernists such as Neutra. Celebrating the machine and its place in the modern world, Neutra was ever the romantic engineer, searching for the nexus of art, technology, and life.

[Most of Neutra's papers and drawings are in the Neutra Archive, Special Collections, University of California at Los Angeles. His other major published works are *How America Builds (Wie baut Amerika?* 1927); and his autobiography, *Life and Shape* (1962). See Esther McCoy, *Two Journeys: From Vienna to Los Angeles* (1979); Thomas S. Hines, *Richard Neutra and the Search for Modern Architecture* (1982); and Arthur Drexler and Thomas S. Hines, *The Architecture of Richard Neutra: From International Style to California Modern*, a catalog of the exhibition at the Museum of Modern Art, New York (1982). The most nearly complete catalog of Neutra's work is Willy Boesiger, ed., *Richard Neutra: Buildings and Projects*, 3 vols. (1950–1966). An obituary is in the *New York Times*, Apr. 18, 1970.]

THOMAS S. HINES

NEWMAN, ALFRED (Mar. 17, 1900–Feb. 17, 1970), film music director, composer, and conductor, was born in New Haven, Conn., the son of Russian immigrants Michael Newman (né Nemirovsky?), an unprosperous produce dealer, and Luba Koskoff, the daughter of a cantor, and a devoted but untutored music lover who soon recognized her son's talent and was an active force in promulgating his musical career. Newman began as a piano prodigy, making his first public appearance (in New Haven, where he attended public schools) at the age of eight. His first teachers were Guido Hocke Caselotti and Edward A. Parsons. One of his most enthusiastic supporters was the well-known poet and society leader Ella Wheeler Wilcox. Through her connections in the New Haven musical and social worlds, Newman won a scholarship with the eminent pianist and composer Sigismond Stojowski, who was teaching at the Von Ende School of Music in New York City. Despite the hardship of commuting twice a week to New York for his lessons, Newman progressed quickly under Stojowski's tutelage. He won the school's silver medal for piano in 1915 and the gold medal in 1916. He also acquired more boosters, the most important of whom was John Christian Freund, the founder and editor of *Musical America*. His talent was praised by Stojowski, Ferruccio Busoni, Frank Damrosch, and Ignace Paderewski (whom he met in 1916 but who never sponsored any of his concerts, contrary to the assertion in some Newman biographies). His debut recital took place on Nov. 5, 1916.

Family financial and domestic troubles forced Newman to abandon the concert world for that of show business. His first commercial jobs were in vaudeville and as accompanist to the popular comedienne Grace La Rue in the 1917 and 1918 runs of the revue *Hitchy-Koo*. He was befriended by the show's music director, William M. Daly, who later became influential in the career of George Gershwin. Daly encouraged the young pianist to take up conducting and taught him the fundamentals of baton technique. In 1919, Newman began conducting musical comedy on his own, receiving attention as "the youngest musical director in the country," but none of his shows made it to Broadway. His breakthrough to success occurred when George Gershwin recommended him to the producer George White for the *Scandals* of 1920. That show was a substantial hit, and Newman became one of the theater's most sought-after music directors. His Broadway credits include *The Greenwich Village Follies* and musical comedies by the Gershwins, Otto Harbach, Jerome Kern, and Rodgers and Hart. He made his first appearance as a symphony conductor in 1926, when he was invited by Fritz Reiner to conduct a concert with the Cincinnati Symphony Orchestra.

Newman's Broadway work ended in February 1930, when, at the request of Irving Berlin, he was invited to Hollywood by United Artists (UA) to take over as music director for Berlin's forthcoming film, *Reaching for the Moon*. Upon his arrival, Newman was told that production had been delayed; he was then assigned to UA member Samuel Goldwyn, who was producing his first musical film, *Whoopee*, starring Eddie Cantor. The film was a success, and he was appointed music director of UA, a post he held for almost nine years. Of the many producers with whom he was involved at UA, the two who were most significant in shaping Newman's Hollywood career were Samuel Goldwyn and Darryl F. Zanuck. Newman composed the music for all of Goldwyn's prestige pictures, including *Street Scene* (1931), *Beloved Enemy* (1936), *Stella Dallas* (1937), *Dead End* (1937), *The Hurricane* (1937), and *Wuthering Heights* (1939), in addition to serving as music director for the rest of the Eddie Cantor musicals and for *The Goldwyn Follies*, the film that Gershwin was working on at the time of his death. He scored all of Zanuck's pictures at UA (1933–1935), three of which are classics of the first decade of talking pictures: *The House of Rothschild* (1934), *Clive of India* (1935), and *Les Miserables* (1935). With the UA music editor Charles Dunworth, he devised the "Newman System" for film music synchronization, still much in use today. In 1936 he sponsored and produced the first complete recordings of Arnold Schoenberg's string quartets, with the Kolisch Quartet. He left UA in December 1938, and the following year he scored on a free-lance basis the enduring classics *Gunga Din*, *The Hunchback of Notre Dame*, *Wuthering Heights*, *Beau Geste*, and *Drums Along the Mohawk*.

In 1940, Newman signed with Zanuck as general music director of Twentieth Century–Fox (TCF). Under Newman's direction, the TCF staff orchestra gained a reputation as the finest in Hollywood. He wrote music for most of the large-scale pictures produced during his tenure at TCF, notably *Brigham Young* (1940), *How Green Was My Valley* (1941), *The Song of Bernadette* (1943), *The Keys of the Kingdom* (1944), *The Razor's Edge* (1946), *Captain from Castile* (1947), *The Snake Pit* (1948), *All About Eve* (1950), and *The Robe* (1953). His name appears on TCF's most lavish musicals, including those starring Alice Faye and Betty Grable and the adaptations of *Call Me Madam* (1953), *Carousel* (1956), *The King and I* (1956), and *South Pacific* (1958). As head of the music department, he was obligated to oversee the work of other composers assigned to TCF films, to confer with them, and often to conduct the recordings of their scores. In 1943 he recorded the first commercial multiside album of a film score, his score for *The Song of Bernadette*. In the programs he conducted at the Hollywood

Bowl and elsewhere, he habitually included film music by himself and others.

As the power of the major studios began to decline in the mid-1950's, TCF's output gradually decreased, studio expenses were cut back, and staffs were greatly reduced. Zanuck resigned in 1956, the musicians' strike in 1958 signaled the end of studio staff orchestras, and Newman's music department soon was decimated. He left TCF in 1960 to become a free-lancer once more. His film work during his remaining years included more big pictures, such as *The Counterfeit Traitor* (1962), *How the West Was Won* (1962), *The Greatest Story Ever Told* (1965), and the musicals *Flower Drum Song* (1961) and *Camelot* (1967). His last film score was *Airport* (1970), for which he was posthumously nominated for an Academy Award.

Newman scored and conducted more than 230 films and was the most honored of all screen composers; he received forty-five Academy nominations and won nine Academy Awards: for *Alexander's Ragtime Band* (1938), *Tin Pan Alley* (1940), *The Song of Bernadette* (1943), *Mother Wore Tights* (1947), *With a Song in My Heart* (1952), *Call Me Madam* (1953), *Love Is a Many-Splendored Thing* (1955), *The King and I* (1956), and *Camelot* (1967). More important, he had a profound and lasting effect on the style and sound of America's film music. With Max Steiner and Erich Wolfgang Korngold, he was one of the three pioneer composers who evolved the grand symphonic style of movie music that prevailed in Hollywood from the mid-1930's to the mid-1950's. In contrast to them, Newman had little or no preparation as a composer. Some biographies state that he studied composition in New York City with Rubin Goldmark and George Wedge, but no documentary evidence of such instruction has been found; the few sporadic private lessons he took with Schoenberg between 1936 and 1938 had no discernible effect on his musical style. He became a composer of film music simply by learning on the job and because of his innate musicality. As a studio music executive, he used his authority to experiment with new, improved recording methods and to give opportunities to composers other studios would not hire because their music was considered to be out of the Hollywood mainstream.

Newman was married three times, and all of his wives were showgirls. His first wife was Beth Meakins, whom he married on Feb. 14, 1931, and divorced in 1940; they had one child. His second wife was Mary Lou Dix, whom he married on Dec. 13, 1940; they, too, had one child, and were divorced in 1943. He married Martha Montgomery on Nov. 6, 1947; they had five children. He died in Los Angeles.

[Some of Newman's music, interviews, writings, and memorabilia are in the Alfred Newman Memorial Library at the University of Southern California. The text (slightly edited) of a Newman lecture on the problems of adapting stage musicals to the screen is in Tony Thomas, *Film Score: The View from the Podium* (1979). Thomas also has some useful Newman material in *Music for the Movies* (1973). An interesting, if not entirely accurate, TCF studio biography (c. 1959) was reprinted, under the name of Ken Darby, in *Film Music Notebook*, 2, no. 2 (1976). The only full-length study is Frederick Steiner, "The Making of an American Film Composer: A Study of Alfred Newman's Music in the First Decade of the Sound Era" (Ph.D. diss., University of Southern California, 1981), which includes a list of Newman's Broadway work and a complete filmography. An obituary is in the *New York Times*, Feb. 19, 1970.]

FRED STEINER

NEWMAN, BARNETT (Jan. 29, 1905–July 4, 1970), painter and sculptor, was born in New York City, the son of Polish immigrants Abraham Newman, a prosperous garment manufacturer, and Anna Steinberg. He grew up in the Bronx, where he attended grammar school and the National Hebrew School, of which his father, an ardent Zionist, was a founding trustee. He enjoyed drawing and frequently cut classes at De Witt Clinton High School to visit the Metropolitan Museum of Art. By the age of sixteen, he had decided to become an artist.

In 1922, while a senior in high school, Newman obtained permission from his mother to attend classes at the Art Students League, where he studied part-time from 1922 to 1926. He enrolled at the City College of New York at his father's insistence in 1923 and received a B.A. in 1927. Intending to become a full-time artist after graduation, he accepted his father's proposal to work in the family's merchant tailoring establishment, the A. Newman Company, until he saved enough money to underwrite his new career. Just as Newman was about to launch himself as a painter, the 1929 stock-market crash ruined the family business. He took charge of the nearly bankrupt clothing enterprise, which he ran until his father retired in 1937. He then liquidated the company.

During the 1930's, Newman also supported himself by working as a substitute high school teacher. At a teachers' meeting in 1934 he met Annalee Greenhouse, who became his wife and inseparable companion on June 30, 1936; they had no children. Despite Newman's sympathies for anarchism during the depression years, he became involved in municipal politics and ran for mayor of New York in 1933. Appealing to the "cultural write-in vote," Newman's last-minute campaign called for a clean-air department, casinos in the parks, sidewalk cafés, free music and art schools, and a municipal opera.

Newman continued to draw and paint in the 1930's, although with increasing dissatisfaction. "Everything around bored me stiff," he recalled. "I was interested in serious questions. What *is* painting? Is it really *circles*? Is it really *nature*? What are we going to paint? Surrealism? Cubism? I was drifting along and casting about, involved in a search for myself and for my subject." In 1939 he decided to stop painting and review the entire discipline systematically. He began a series of essays, written initially for himself. In these monologues, he reexamined past and present presuppositions of art history, seeking basic premises and turning repeatedly to the question of the proper subject matter for great art.

Several of Newman's artist friends, among them the painters Adolph Gottlieb and Mark Rothko, agreed that American painting was at a crossroads in the early 1940's. Neither representationalism nor European abstract styles, they believed, were adequate to express the timeless, heroic, and tragic content of modern life. Stimulated by Carl Jung's theory of the collective unconscious and French surrealist investigations of nonrational modes of creativity, Newman and his friends turned to the abstract symbols of primitive and tribal artists as new models for artistic communication. With Newman's editorial assistance, Gottlieb and Rothko summarized these ideas in a polemical letter to *New York Times* art critic Edwin Alden Jewell on June 13, 1943. "There is no such thing as a good painting about nothing," the letter states. "We assert that the subject is crucial and only that subject matter is valid which is tragic and timeless. This is why we profess spiritual kinship with primitive and archaic art."

Newman's ideas were further elaborated in his catalog essays for exhibitions of pre-Columbian stone sculpture at the Wakefield Gallery in 1944 and Northwest Coast Indian art at the Betty Parsons Gallery in 1946. In the Parsons catalog, he lauded primitive artists for their ability to create visual forms that embody feelings and ideas instead of referring to them indirectly through illustration. "Among these simple peoples, abstract art was the normal, well-understood, dominant tradition," he observed. "Shall we say that modern man has lost the ability to think on so high a level?"

In 1944, Newman began to paint and draw again, and by the summer of 1945 he was experimenting enthusiastically with the surrealist technique of automatic drawing. In 1946–1947 he created several paintings with a circular void or simple vertical rays of color as major compositional elements; they were dedicated to epic themes, as in *The Command* (1946) and *Death of Euclid* (1947). Like his friends Jackson Pollock, Mark Rothko, and Clyfford Still, each of whom achieved a major breakthrough during the years 1947–1949, Newman's painting reached a turning point in 1948 with *Onement I*. This stark composition consisted of a vertical field of dark, earthy red pigment traversed in the center with a brushy strip of lighter red. After studying the composition for eight months, Newman concluded that he had found his way to a new kind of painting.

Between October 1948 and December 1949, Newman completed twenty large paintings, several of which he exhibited at his first one-man show at the Betty Parsons Gallery in 1950. These expansive canvases (the largest, *Be I*, was ninety-four by seventy-six inches) were characterized by an almost uninflected expanse of a single color, traversed from top to bottom by one or more narrow stripes of contrasting hues. Newman urged viewers to stand close to the pictures, to immerse themselves in what was, in effect, a color environment.

The show was a critical disaster, as was his second one-man exhibition in 1951. Newman was most dismayed by the reaction of artists associated with abstract expressionism, some of whom saw in his minimal compositions an implied criticism of their own brushy, passionate paintings. He withdrew from the art world and rarely exhibited his work again until 1958, when he was given a major retrospective at

Bennington College in Vermont. Many younger artists reacted favorably to his subsequent shows, seeing in Newman's work a precedent for their interest in cool, disciplined, reductivist compositions. Newman was careful to insist that his own work was concerned not primarily with formal issues, but with the employment of line and color to evoke the sublime and tragic profundities of human life. For Newman, minimizing the number and range of the physical forms in painting was a means of intensifying spiritual meanings: in his *Stations of the Cross* series of 1966, for example, he sought to express the despair and suffering of Christ in fourteen compositions consisting of wide and thin strips of black and white paint on raw canvas.

During the 1960's, Newman's work was exhibited in major American and European galleries and museums and acquired by important private collectors. In thc mid-1960's he also created a number of freestanding sculptures related to his paintings, the most well known, *Broken Obelisk* (1967), dedicated to Martin Luther King, Jr. At the height of his prestige he suffered a fatal heart attack in New York.

[Newman's paintings are included in the collections of the Whitney Museum of Modern Art and the Museum of Modern Art, New York. Casts of *Broken Obelisk* have been installed at the University of Washington, Seattle, and at the Institute of Religion and Human Development, Houston. The major study of Newman's life and work is Thomas Hess, *Barnett Newman* (1971). Other important references include Lawrence Alloway, *Barnett Newman: The Stations of the Cross* (1966); and Harold Rosenberg, "The Art World: Icon Maker," *New Yorker*, Apr. 19, 1969. An obituary is in the *New York Times*, July 5, 1970.]

PATRICIA FAILING

NEWSOM, HERSCHEL DAVID (May 1, 1905–July 2, 1970), agricultural leader, was born on a farm near Columbus, Ind., the son of Jesse R. Newsom and Nellie Davis, both Quaker farmers. After attending Columbus High School, he entered Indiana University in 1921, graduating in 1925. He returned to the family farm until Oct. 26, 1929, when he married Blanche Hill, whom he had met in college; they had two children.

Newsom continued farming in the Columbus area. A member of the Indiana Grange, he promoted scientific farming and soil conservation during a period of declining farm prices. As the economic problems of farmers worsened with the onset of the Great Depression in 1929, Newsom became a spokesman for more-effective government aid programs. In 1937 he was elected master of the Indiana Grange and later served on its executive board, consistently calling for policies to increase farm income. In 1950 his ability as a spokesman led to his being elected master of the National Grange.

Operating from the organization's office in Washington, D.C., Newsom became even more effective in lobbying for agricultural causes, earning the respect, if not always the support, of Presidents Truman, Eisenhower, Kennedy, and Johnson. Newsom advocated American agricultural involvement in foreign trade and argued that foreign sales of American commodities could help make up for the low farm income caused by a domestic "cheap food" policy. He was particularly effective during the Johnson administration, which often consulted the National Grange in formulating policy.

In 1964, Newsom supported the payment of $600 million in support to wheat and cotton farmers. Newsom also favored using surplus American food in foreign aid in a fashion analogous to the Food for Peace program. This use would, he felt, reduce the surpluses of wheat, corn, and sorghum. Newsom joined with Secretary of Agriculture Orville Freeman to work out the 1965 Food and Agriculture Act, with its production controls, high levels of price supports, pesticide labeling, and government payments to producers. In 1967, Newsom lobbied Congress to advance additional foreign aid to India, to meet the critical food shortage caused by the 1966 drought. This aid was to amount to 1.8 million tons of grain.

In 1967, Newsom voiced strong disagreement with the plan to eliminate the school milk program, which made milk available to all school children at reduced prices. Congress agreed with his views and retained the program.

Newsom always favored reducing surplus food stockpiles to improve farm prices and advocated strong price supports for farmers. In October 1968, President Johnson appointed Newsom to the Tariff Commission. Newsom expressed his hope that in this position he could affect trade policies that had a direct impact on farm prices and income. He died in Washington, D.C.

[Newsom's papers are at Cornell University and Indiana University. An obituary is in the *New York Times*, July 3, 1970.]

MICHAEL BRADLEY

NIMITZ, CHESTER WILLIAM (Feb. 24, 1885–Feb. 20, 1966), naval officer, the son of Chester Bernard Nimitz, a cattle drover, and Anna Henke, was born in Fredericksburg, Tex. He grew up in Kerrville, Tex., where his mother and stepfather, William Nimitz, managed a hotel. The child's father died of chronic health problems a few months before the birth of his son; after six years of widowhood Anna married her late husband's younger brother William.

Working part-time from the age of eight to supplement the family's meager income, Nimitz got high grades in school and hoped to enter West Point. There were no vacancies. Instead Nimitz secured an appointment to the United States Naval Academy in 1901. He graduated seventh in the class of 1905. He then saw sea duty in the Far East, serving in succession on the battleship *Ohio*, on the cruiser *Baltimore*, and as commander of the gunboat *Panay* and the destroyer *Decatur*.

Nimitz returned to the United States in 1909 and began many years of service in the submarine force, where he became an authority on diesel engines. Although his expertise in this field brought him civilian job offers at many times his lieutenant's pay, his commitment to the navy remained firm. On Apr. 9, 1913, he married Catherine Freeman; they had four children.

During World War I, Nimitz served on the staff of Rear Admiral Samuel Robison, the chief of the Submarine Force, Atlantic Fleet. This was a step forward, because Nimitz escaped stereotyping as an engineering specialist and returned to a normal career progression for line officers. Robison, with whom Nimitz served again in 1923–1926, was one of the ablest officers of his generation and exerted a positive influence on Nimitz' views of command and on the course of Nimitz' career.

In the two decades after World War I, Nimitz' career continued to advance. He was promoted to commander in 1921, captain in 1927, and rear admiral in 1938. During these years, he held a variety of staff and command positions, studied at the Naval War College, and served in the Office of Naval Operations and in the Bureau of Navigation in Washington. He went to sea in such capacities as executive officer of the battleship *South Carolina* (1919–1920), captain of the cruiser *Augusta* (1934–1935), and commander of Battleship Division One (1938–1939).

In 1939, Nimitz was named to head the Bureau of Navigation. The responsibilities of the post were large and increasing, for it required him to handle such personnel matters as recruiting, training, promotion, and assignment at a time when the service was expanding in response to the outbreak of World War II. Nimitz' work so impressed Secretary of the Navy Frank Knox that after the Japanese attack on Pearl Harbor he was given command of the battered Pacific Fleet. "Tell Nimitz to get the hell out to Pearl and stay there till the war is won," President Roosevelt told Knox.

Nimitz took command of a fleet in shambles and an officer corps beset with doubt and indecision. Familiar with their records from his work in the Bureau of Navigation, he reassured Pacific Fleet staff officers that he had faith in their abilities and wanted them to remain with him. This did much to dispel the gloom and restore the morale of the Pacific Fleet.

Early in 1942, Nimitz was given the additional assignment of commander in chief of the Pacific Ocean Area. He now wore two hats: he commanded the vast Pacific Ocean Area (CinCPOA) and, within that area, commanded both the Pacific Fleet (CinCPac) and designated army ground and air units. As commander of the Pacific Ocean Area, Nimitz was the equal in responsibility, if not always in public acclaim, of the two other Americans who commanded major theaters in World War II, General Dwight Eisenhower in Europe and General Douglas MacArthur in the Southwest Pacific. The magnitude and complexity of his duties required that he maintain his headquarters ashore—at Pearl Harbor for most of the war and, after late 1944, at Guam. Despite the demands on his time, he remained approachable and concerned with the morale of the men under him.

Throughout 1942 the Pacific Fleet operated on the proverbial shoestring but nevertheless halted Japanese momentum with strategic victories in the Coral Sea and at Midway. In early 1943, after the protracted Guadalcanal campaign, more-ambitious plans could be made because manpower, ships, planes, and the other necessities of war were becoming available in increasing numbers. Nimitz' immediate superior in Washington, Admiral Ernest J. King, the chief of naval operations (CNO), conferred with him regularly about future moves and strategic priorities and learned to respect Nimitz' judgment. The soft-spoken Nimitz had an inner resolve that enabled him to mold the many able but often contentious officers under his command into a superb group. Planning sessions were often stormy, but at critical moments Nimitz displayed a Lincolnesque talent for telling a humorous anecdote to ease tensions and steer the debate back into constructive channels. Once a strategic decision had been made, Nimitz would give such able subordinates as Admirals William Halsey and Raymond Spruance general directions, trusting them to prepare detailed operating plans and to control their forces in combat.

In November 1943, Nimitz' forces initiated the legendary Central Pacific offensive. Employing a combination of devastating carrier attacks, amphibious assaults, and the leapfrogging of certain enemy strongholds such as Truk, they advanced in only nine months thousands of miles from Tarawa on Japan's defensive perimeter to Saipan and other islands in the Marianas from which Japan itself could be bombed by air force B-29's. After cooperating with MacArthur's Southwest Pacific command in the reconquest of the Philippines, CinCPOA forces in 1945 seized Iwo Jima and Okinawa, the latter only a few hundred miles from Japan. By the war's end in August, the Pacific Fleet was operating off Japanese shores.

In 1944, Nimitz was promoted to the five-star rank of fleet admiral. He succeeded King as CNO on Dec. 16, 1945. In the two years he held that position, he successfully dealt with the problems attendant upon demobilization and peacetime retrenchment. Under his leadership the navy developed a strategy to deal with the perceived Soviet threat. Assuming that any new global conflict would begin with a Soviet attack on Western Europe and the Middle East, Nimitz and his planners argued that the navy would have to hold the line while the other services mobilized.

Nimitz' long experience in engineering made him alert to the potential of atomic power, and while he envisioned maintaining a balanced fleet emphasizing powerful carrier task forces of the type that had evolved during World War II but now armed with nuclear bombs, he also favored the development of nuclear-powered submarines capable of firing missiles with atomic warheads. Subsequent developments in these areas, however, caused him concern; in retirement he confided to family members that he disliked what the military had become. He had little use for technocrats and a defense strategy that placed ever-increasing reliance on weapons of mass destruction.

At the end of his tour as CNO, Nimitz retired to Berkeley, Calif., where he had established and headed the Naval Reserve Officers Training Corps at the University of California from 1926 to 1929. Adjusting to civilian life was more difficult than he had anticipated. He refused many offers to enter private industry, on the ground that to do so would undermine respect for the navy. But he accepted positions with the United Nations and as a regent of the University of California. A resolute foe of McCarthyism, he tried in vain to prevent the imposition of a loyalty oath upon faculty of that institution. With the United Nations (1949–1952) he served as a roving goodwill ambassador and was to have administered a plebiscite to determine a disputed border between India and Pakistan, but the plebiscite was not held.

Nimitz died on Yerba Buena Island, Calif. As he had wished, he is buried with his wife and three of their friends, Charles Lockwood, Raymond Spruance, and Kelly Turner, all Pacific Fleet admirals, in the Golden Gate National Cemetery in San Bruno, Calif.

[Nimitz' own letters and World War II documents, especially the CinCPac Command Summary (Gray Book), are in the Operational Archives, Naval Historical Center, Washington, D.C. Other materials are in the National Archives, Washington, D.C. With E. B. Potter, Nimitz wrote *Sea Power* (1960) and *Triumph in the Pacific* (1963). Published sources include Samuel Eliot Morison, *The Two-Ocean War* (1963); E. B. Potter, *Nimitz* (1976); Stephen T. Ross, "Chester William Nimitz," in Robert William Love, Jr., ed., *The Chiefs of Naval Operations* (1980); and Frank A. Driskill and Dede W. Casad, *Chester W. Nimitz, Admiral of the Hills* (1983). See also Foster Hailey, "Master of the Pacific Chessboard," *New York Times Magazine*, Feb. 27, 1944; Joseph Driscoll, "Admiral of the Reopened Sea," *Saturday Evening Post*, Apr. 8, 1944; and Fletcher Pratt, "Nimitz and His Admirals," *Harper's*, Feb. 1945. Oral history interviews about Nimitz are at the United States Naval Institute in Annapolis. An obituary is in the *New York Times*, Feb. 21, 1966.]

LLOYD J. GRAYBAR

NORRIS, KATHLEEN THOMPSON (July 16, 1880–Jan. 18, 1966), novelist, was born in San Francisco, Calif., the daughter of James Alden Thompson, a bank manager, and Josephine E. Moroney. Her childhood home was at Mill Valley near Muir Woods, across the Golden Gate from San Francisco. A sickly child who for a time was sent to a slaughterhouse for a daily glass of warm blood, Thompson alternated between attending a country school and being taught at home and also briefly stayed at a Dominican convent school in San Rafael. Her parents took an apartment in San Francisco to better their children's educational opportunities, but Thompson, who was the oldest of three daughters and the second of six children, stayed home to help her mother care for the younger ones, whom she often entertained with stories. Her main education came from reading Dickens and other authors in the library of her father, who had, she later wrote, a "sharp eye for the misuse of words."

When Thompson was nineteen, her parents died within a month of each other, leaving her and her siblings to support themselves and their father's unmarried sister, who lived with them. During these difficult years, Thompson worked primarily in a hardware store and in a library. In 1903 she spent a few exhilarating months at the University of California at Berkeley, where, she recalled, her "heart leaped with sheer joy" when her composition professor praised one paper after another. Over the next few years, she wrote society columns for three San Francisco newspapers, published a bit of fiction, and met Charles Gilman Norris, whom she married on Apr. 30, 1909; they had three children.

The couple settled in New York, where Charles Norris had become an editor for the *American Magazine*. Like his brother Frank, Charles Norris became a novelist dealing with controversial social problems. Kathleen Norris credited New York with making her a writer and her husband with making her a success. Impressed by the established novelists and short-story writers she met through her husband, Norris determined to be one of them. She had no trouble publishing three stories in the *New York Telegram*, but her husband, who was her literary agent, sent another story, "The Tide-Marsh," to twenty-six publishers before it was printed in the *Atlantic Monthly*, which earlier had rejected it. During the next half century, Norris, who has been called the "grandmother of the American sentimental novel," published eighty-eight books, which sold 10 million copies and, along with her other writing, earned $9 million, making her the highest-paid writer of her day.

Eighty-one of her books are novels. Her protagonists are generally young women who get into—and then out of—considerable trouble. In her autobiography *Family Gathering* (1959), Norris wrote that her novels often detail "the fearful power of money upon human lives." (An earlier autobiography, *Noon*, was published in 1925.) Before typing a synopsis of a new story and discussing it with her husband, Norris worked out its plots and scenes while playing solitaire. She then sat down at her typewriter and words came, according to her husband, "as water flowing from a pitcher." She seldom changed more than a word or two on each page, and once a story was in progress she could write on a makeshift table in a boardinghouse parlor or in her own milieu, surrounded by her children and their numerous cousins.

Norris wrote of the people and things that she knew best. Her writing was characterized by honesty, directness, and clear-cut issues. Her first big money-maker was *Mother* (1911), a warm, fairy-tale-like story based on her own family and friends. It was followed by scores of books blending sentiment and romance, with sharply drawn and alluring characters. She portrayed life so carefully and rendered it so truthfully that many of her characters assumed, in the words of one reviewer, "proportions of flesh and blood." She was especially good at telling Irish anecdotes and used to advantage the gross overstatements and the mild understatements of second-generation Irish-Americans. Always able to envelop her narrative in a family atmosphere, Norris, as a critic declared, rendered domestic interiors that matched those of Dutch artists.

In 1922, Norris turned from her usual formula to write *Certain People of Importance*, a sprawling family chronicle that sparkled with period detail and spanned more than a century. Most critics, who had often called her earlier books slight, conventional, and sentimental, applauded. But Norris' usual readers were disappointed, and she went back to writing the romantic novels they appreciated.

Though Norris never won an award or an

honorary degree, her novels were almost always best-sellers and were consistently among the best-circulating library books. Because she always got her heroines out of their scrapes, readers sought her help in solving real-life problems. She answered many of their queries in *Hands Full of Living: Talks with American Women* (1931), which a reviewer pronounced "likely to put sense into the head of the average American girl."

So popular was Norris' writing that when a magazine ran one of her stories or articles, the issue sold 100,000 additional copies. One month her work appeared in five magazines simultaneously. For years, she would begin serializing a novel in the *Woman's Home Companion* in April, another in *Collier's* in July, and a third in the *American Magazine* in October. In 1945, Norris wrote scripts for a radio soap opera called "Bright Horizon." For more than twenty-five years she also worked for the Bell Newspaper Syndicate, covering the 1952 Republican National Convention in Chicago and writing articles of interest to women and often answering their queries. She covered the trial of Bruno Richard Hauptmann, the accused kidnapper of the Lindbergh baby, for the North American Newspaper Alliance and the *New York Times*.

Alexander Woollcott called Norris "the ideal lady president of all the women's clubs in the world," and another friend described her as "a gracious hostess, tall, striking, carefully tailored—a woman with rare charm and a . . . racy Irish love of the ridiculous." She was a feminist, a pacifist, and a prohibitionist, and she campaigned in small California towns and in Madison Square Garden for her causes, which included the America First Committee, abolition of the death penalty, and a nuclear-weapons test ban. Her novels give hints of her pacifism and feminism, but they avoid controversy.

Norris crowded her home with children and visitors, just as her childhood home had been. She had a son (twin daughters died in infancy) and adopted a second son, and after her sister Teresa, who had married William Rose Benét, died during the 1918–1919 influenza epidemic, Norris added two nieces and a nephew to her household. At their 200-acre summer ranch near Saratoga, Calif., the Norrises and their guests put on amateur plays and fostered endless croquet games, continued into the night under locomotive lights. They had camping facilities for their many nieces and nephews and twelve guest cabins for their numerous friends, who included Theodore Roosevelt, Jr., Charles A. Lindbergh, Noel Coward, and Harpo Marx. The Norrises traveled a great deal but were most at home in San Francisco and New York. In later years, their main home was their large Spanish-style house in Palo Alto. Despite crippling arthritis, Norris continued her writing into her eighties. She died in San Francisco.

[The papers of Norris and her husband are at Stanford University and the Bancroft Library at the University of California. Information on her life and writing is in Joyce Kilmer, *Literature in the Making* (1917); Alexander Woollcott, *While Rome Burns* (1934); Charles Norris' introduction to *Mother* (1935); and Isabella Taves, *Successful Women* (1943). See also *Time*, Jan. 28, 1935; and the *New York Times Book Review*, Feb. 6, 1955. Obituaries are in the *New York Times*, Jan. 19, 1966; *Time*, Jan. 28, 1966; and *Newsweek*, Jan. 31, 1966.]

OLIVE HOOGENBOOM

NOTESTEIN, WALLACE (Dec. 16, 1878–Feb. 2, 1969), historian and educator, was born in Wooster, Ohio, the son of Jonas O. Notestein, a professor of Latin and literature, and Margaret Wallace. Educated at the preparatory department of the College of Wooster, where his father taught for more than fifty years, he entered the college itself in 1896 and received his B.A. summa cum laude four years later. Notestein pursued his graduate education at Yale, earning his M.A. in 1903 and Ph.D. in history in 1908.

Notestein devoted his academic career to studying Elizabethan and Stuart England. His doctoral dissertation, "A History of Witchcraft in England from 1558 to 1718," was awarded the Herbert Adams Prize and published as a prize essay by the American Historical Association in 1911. He further demonstrated wide knowledge of his subject when he issued a volume of edited documents, *Source Problems in English History*, in 1915.

Notestein began his long teaching career as an assistant professor at the University of Kansas in 1905. During World War I he left the classroom to serve as a research assistant for the Committee on Public Information. In this capacity he produced *Conquest and Kultur: Aims of the Germans in Their Own Words* (1917), a brochure that sought to discredit Prussian militarism and imperialism. He was later attached to the State Department and then the American Commission to Negotiate the Peace, doing special research on the tangled problem of Alsace-Lorraine for the Treaty of Versailles in 1919. In 1917 he became a full professor at the University of Minnesota. Three years later Notestein moved to Cornell, before becoming Sterling Professor of English History at Yale, where he remained from 1928 to 1947.

Notestein made more than forty trips to England to consult original manuscripts not only in the major London depositories but also in rural parishes throughout the country. He taught his graduate students that a cache of unexplored documents was the "finest gold" a scholar could hope to discover. His patient research enabled him to publish a series of important studies in English legislative history. *Commons Debates for 1629* (1921) pieced together an account of debates derived from the letters and diaries of members of Parliament. Notestein edited rough notes taken by a member of the Long Parliament to produce *The Journal of Sir Simonds D'Ewes* (1923), a reconstruction of the proceedings of the House of Commons for 1640–1641. The following year, he presented the annual Sir Walter Raleigh lecture to the British Academy, the first American ever to do so. Published as "The Winning of the Initiative by the House of Commons," this short essay closely analyzes a crucial episode in Parliamentary history preceding the English Civil War.

In 1929, the British prime minister recognized Notestein's contributions to English history by appointing him to the Treasury Committee on the House of Commons Records. Notestein's research helped produce a seven-volume edition of *Commons Debates, 1621* (1935), a work that critically examines the notes and records of speeches delivered in Parliament and reproduces numerous scarce documents.

Notestein wrote *English Folk: A Book of Characters* (1938), a collection of vivid portraits of thirteen individuals who lived between the sixteenth and nineteenth centuries. *The Scot in History* (1946), a subject that deeply interested him because his mother was of Scottish ancestry, briskly surveyed Scotland's national character. Notestein's most enduring work, *The English People on the Eve of Colonization, 1603–1630* (1954), part of the New American Nation series, synthesizes decades of research on social, political, and cultural conditions in Stuart England. *Four Worthies* (1956), the last work that Notestein published during his lifetime, detailed the biographies of some seventeenth-century figures whose careers illustrated conditions in their era.

Besides writing numerous books, Notestein contributed some 100 articles, reviews, and commentaries to scholarly journals that appeared on both sides of the Atlantic. His style displayed not only great erudition but also literary skill and personal charm. Students found him a warm and enthusiastic teacher and referred to him affectionately as "Note." He married Ada Louise Comstock, the president of Radcliffe College, on June 14, 1943; they had no children. Notestein died in New Haven, Conn.

Of average height and slight of build, Notestein remained agile well into his later years by taking long walks and playing golf. One observer at Yale later recalled of Notestein, "A hurrying scuffle of footsteps, a cheery hel-lo, and there he would come, with a great load of books under his arm. Bent a little sideways and forward, he seemed, but more out of eagerness than from his burden—felt hat all crushed and askew on his head—a cigarette half swallowed between his lips."

[Notestein's papers are at Yale and the College of Wooster, where his large collection of rare books and pamphlets is also preserved. A work left unfinished at his death, *The House of Commons, 1604–1610*, was published in 1971. William A. Aiken and Basil D. Henning, eds., *Essays in Honour of Wallace Notestein* (1960), provides a complete bibliography of his writings. Information about Notestein's family is given in Lucy L. Notestein, *Wooster of the Middle West*, 2 vols. (1971). His personality is evoked in George W. Pierson, *Yale: The University College, 1921–1937* (1955). For his contributions to the Committee on Public Information, see James R. Mock and Cedric Larson, *Words That Won the War* (1939); for his role on the American Commission to Negotiate Peace, see Lawrence E. Gelfand, *The Inquiry* (1963). Appreciations of Notestein appeared in *American Historical Review*, June 1969; and *American Philosophical Year Book*, 1969. Obituaries are in the *New York Times* and the *Times* of London, both Feb. 3, 1969.]

JAMES FRIGUGLIETTI

NOVARRO, RAMON (Feb. 6, 1899–Oct. 31, 1968), motion-picture actor, was born José Ramón Gil Samaniegos, in Durango, Mexico, the son of Luis Gil Samaniegos, a dentist, and Consuela Gavilán. By his own account, he enjoyed an idyllic childhood on the family ranch. He attended Catholic schools and received additional instruction from private tutors. Even as a boy, he dreamed of acting in movies. In 1916, while visiting relatives in El Paso, Tex., he and a brother decided to set out for Los Angeles. They arrived on Thanksgiving Day with $10 and no prospects. While trying to get into films, Ramón worked as a grocery clerk, theater usher, piano teacher, and café singer. In 1917 he began to appear regularly in movies as an extra. Between film jobs he was with the Los Angeles Theatre Stock Company as stage manager and actor.

At the end of 1918, Samaniegos joined a dance troupe headed by Marion Morgan for a six-month tour of Canada and the northern United States. Although he left the troupe when it returned to Los Angeles in June 1919, Marion Morgan was instrumental in getting him dance roles in films. He was appearing at the California Theatre, for $35 a week, in live prologues to films when Morgan recommended him for a dance scene in *Man, Woman, Marriage* (1921). Years later the actor reminisced about the experience, which marked his transition from an extra to a featured player, "It was a marvelous stage dance. We came . . . practically naked in a swing over a mirrored table. It took about a week and they paid us $25 a day and we had private dressing rooms and we had our lunches served to us. Oh, I was feeling grand." He did prominent dance scenes in *A Small Town Idol* (1921) and *The Concert* (1921), as well.

Although he was regularly cast as a dancer, Samaniegos always reminded his directors that he wanted to act. He got his first opportunity in 1922, playing a minor role in *Mr. Barnes of New York*. In the same year, he played the lead in an independent production of *The Rubaiyat of Omar Khayyam* (released in 1925 as *A Lover's Oath*). He continued to do stage work, appearing in pantomimes at the Hollywood Community Theatre. The director Rex Ingram saw him onstage in *The Spanish Fandango* and, at the urging of writer June Mathis, cast him as Rupert of Hentzau in *The Prisoner of Zenda* (1922).

Ingram signed Samaniegos to a personal contract at $125 per week, gave him his film name, and cast him in the Latin-lover mold of Rudolph Valentino. Appearing for the first time as Ramon Novarro in *Trifling Woman* (1922), the actor then costarred in three films with Ingram's wife, Alice Terry. Novarro portrayed a native who fell in love with a missionary's daughter in *Where the Pavement Ends* (1923), the swashbuckling hero in *Scaramouche* (1923), and a Valentino-type lover in *The Arab* (1924).

Novarro's rising popularity led to a lucrative contract with Metro-Goldwyn-Mayer (MGM). He completed two undistinguished films for the studio prior to replacing George Walsh in the coveted title role of *Ben-Hur* (1926). That film enjoyed worldwide success and made Novarro an international star. Yet, he was unable to sustain his popularity. Even when typecast, the wide-faced, dreamy-eyed Novarro lacked the intensity and chiseled features of Hollywood's other romantic Latins. Nor was he entirely convincing in roles requiring machismo. When the vogue for exotic leading men waned in the late 1920's, MGM was unable to develop a successful formula for Novarro.

Talking films did nothing to boost Novarro's fading popularity, although he continued in leading roles well into the 1930's. But, except for *Mata Hari* (1932), in which he played opposite Greta Garbo, Novarro no longer appeared in MGM's major productions. The studio twice cast him as a Spanish troubadour to take advantage of his musical talents and Latin background. MGM released several of his pictures in Spanish-language versions, evidently hoping the actor might appeal to Latin American audiences. However, the studio blurred Novarro's screen identity, successively casting him as a Yale undergraduate, an Oriental prince, and an Indian brave. An attempt to resurrect his early persona with *The Barbarian* (1933), a remake of *The Arab*, proved futile.

MGM dropped Novarro in 1934. By then he was financially secure and disenchanted with film acting. Instead of trying to associate himself immediately with another studio, Novarro went to London as a singer and musician. In 1936 he wrote, produced, and directed (but did not appear in) *Contra la corriente*, a Spanish feature film. Upon his return to Hollywood, he signed with Republic, a low-budget studio that sought to capitalize on Novarro's former stature. After two mediocre pictures he asked to be released from his contract.

Semiretired, Novarro bought a small ranch near San Diego. In 1940 he appeared in a

French film, *La comédie de bonheur*, written by Jean Cocteau. During World War II he moved to Mexico and quixotically volunteered for the Mexican army. While there, Novarro starred in *La virgen que forjo una patria* (1942), a patriotic picture. During the 1940's he also acted in road-company musicals and plays.

In 1949, Novarro successfully returned to Hollywood feature films with supporting roles in *We Were Strangers* and *The Big Steal.* The next year, he earned plaudits for his work in *The Outriders*, an MGM western. Notwithstanding his newly won acceptance as a character actor, Novarro virtually withdrew from feature films after *Crisis* (1950). Thereafter he confined his work to television dramas and a final movie, *Heller in Pink Tights* (1959), for director George Cukor.

Novarro, who was homosexual, never married. He spent his later years in Hollywood Hills, Calif. His chief avocations were music, painting, and landscape gardening. In addition, he wrote stories and worked on a memoir. His health was failing, and his driving record attested to a problem with alcohol. Several days after Novarro was found dead at his home, police charged two male prostitutes with his murder.

[Novarro's memoir was unfinished at his death. The fullest accounts of his career are De Witt Bodeen, *Films in Review*, Nov. 1967; and David Shipman, *The Great Movie Stars: The Golden Years* (1970). Novarro's 1958 interview with George Pratt, in *Image*, Dec. 1973, differs from Bodeen and Shipman on his early career. Information on *Ben-Hur* is in Bosley Crowther, *The Lion's Share* (1957). For a description of Novarro's home and life-style, see *Ramon Novarro Fan Club News*, Autumn 1966. The library of the Academy of Motion Picture Arts and Sciences maintains a file of news items. An obituary is in *Variety*, Nov. 1, 1968. The circumstances of his death are reported in the *New York Times*, Nov. 1, 2, 4, and 7, 1968.]

WILLIAM HUGHES

O'BRIEN, JUSTIN (Nov. 26, 1906–Dec. 7, 1968), translator and scholar, was born in Chicago, the son of Quin O'Brien and Ellen McCortney. He graduated from Phillips Exeter Academy in 1924 and the University of Chicago in 1927. He then studied French literature at Harvard, concentrating on adolescence in the French novel. After receiving his M.A. from Harvard in 1928, he taught French there from 1929 to 1931 before moving to Columbia, where he was to spend the rest of his career. On Jan. 24, 1931, he married Isabel Ireland; they had no children. O'Brien received his Ph.D. from Harvard in 1936. He served in the United States Army during World War II and was decorated in 1945 with the Légion d'Honneur and the Croix de Guerre for his services in the French campaign and for his work as a liaison officer.

O'Brien's scholarship was based on a close reading of original texts and a firm sense of the moral and psychological issues raised by the authors. His translation of the *Journals of André Gide*, published in four volumes between 1947 and 1951, helped create a remarkably large English-speaking readership for this quintessentially French and occasionally elusive author. In 1953, the same year that his *Index des oeuvres complètes d'André Gide* came out, O'Brien published his *Portrait of André Gide.* The latter work perhaps best illustrates O'Brien's ability to combine analysis with a sympathetic and intuitive understanding of a subtle and controversial writer.

O'Brien's object in his *Portrait* was to do what Aristaeus does in one version of the myth of Proteus: oblige the wily old deity to reveal his true nature. If this endeavor was not entirely successful, it was because of the problems confronting any biographer of a subject who, in the last analysis, did not even know what he really thought or felt and could not anticipate what new changes might come over him. There was nevertheless a pleasing contrast between O'Brien's slightly dry, analytical approach and Gide's subtle personality. The book was thus a perfect introduction to two styles of writing: on the one hand, the style of the elusive artist and, on the other, that of the sharp-minded critic anxious to solve the questions of whether Gide was a Christian or a pagan, a mystic or a sensualist, an anguished puritan or a self-justifying homosexual. O'Brien's own moral concerns shone through and made his Gide, to some extent, a man of whom the New England Puritan tradition would not finally have disapproved.

O'Brien had the greatest impact on English-language readers through his translation of the essays and fiction of Albert Camus. While O'Brien was not invited to translate *L'Étranger* (*The Stranger*) or *La Peste* (*The Plague*)—to the detriment of both of these classic novels—his renderings of *Le Mythe de Sisyphe* (*The Myth of Sisyphus*, 1955), *La Chute* (*The Fall*, 1957), and *L'Exil et le royaume* (*Exile and the Kingdom*, 1958) reveal a mastery of both languages and cultures. O'Brien knew Camus personally and had the good fortune of being able to discuss his translations with him. In 1958, O'Brien also selected and translated what he called *From the N.R.F.*—an anthology of works from the most influential literary magazine in France (*Nouvelle Revue Française*)—and here again the qualities of this perspicacious but slightly self-effacing man came out clearly in his readiness to let the authors speak for themselves.

O'Brien's contribution to the intellectual life of mid-twentieth-century America was not limited to his books and translations. At Columbia, he chaired the Department of French from 1958 to 1963, and he was a member of the board of trustees. From 1954 to 1961 he was the general editor of the *Romanic Review*, after having previously served as reviews editor. He received the Médaille d'Or du Rayonnement Français in 1965. Less than a week after he was named Blanche W. Knopf Professor of French Literature at Columbia, he died in New York City.

[An obituary is in the *New York Times*, Dec. 8, 1968.]

P. M. W. Thody

O'CONNOR, EDWIN GREENE (July 29, 1918–Mar. 23, 1968), novelist, was born in Providence, R.I., the son of John Vincent O'Connor, a doctor, and Mary Greene. He grew up in Woonsocket, R.I., where he attended elementary school. In 1931 he entered La Salle Academy in Providence. Run by the Christian Brothers, the academy followed a classical curriculum. In 1935 he entered the University of Notre Dame, intending to study for a career in journalism or perhaps the priesthood. Frank O'Malley, a young professor of English, inspired him to study literature, and O'Connor then began to write. O'Connor also became an announcer at the college radio station. In 1939 he received the B.A. cum laude, and in the autumn he returned for graduate study, but after one term gave it up.

O'Connor then joined station WPRO in Providence as a radio announcer, and he later worked at stations in Palm Beach, Fla.; Buffalo, N.Y.; and Hartford, Conn. In September 1942, having been rejected by the army because of his poor vision, he enlisted in the United States Coast Guard. For two years he served as information officer at district headquarters in Boston under Louis J. Brems, a former vaudeville performer and once Boston's official greeter, whose stories about politicians O'Connor always treasured.

In the Coast Guard, O'Connor began writing about his experiences but soon came to believe that a writer of fiction must finally rely on his imagination, not on events in his own life. Discharged from the service in September 1945, he joined station WHAC in Boston and the Yankee network as a writer and announcer, but by October 1946 he had concluded that "if you want to write, you should do it for yourself, alone." He left radio to become a free-lance writer.

O'Connor settled down in Boston, living in various boardinghouses and always in need of funds. Under the name Roger Swift, he wrote a radio and television review column for the *Boston Herald* and a few short pieces for the *Atlantic Monthly*. His first short story appeared as an *Atlantic* "first" in September 1947. During 1948–1949 he worked with the *Atlantic* editor Edward Weeks, who had a weekly radio program. O'Connor's job was to listen to the rehearsal and criticize Weeks's delivery. Weeks said later that writing and producing radio shows had taught O'Connor "to write with his ears." In 1949, O'Connor taught a night course in writing at Boston College. Acquaintance with the *Atlantic* staff grew into a long association. A genial companion with a merry wit and deep resonant voice, O'Connor loved talk, stories, and ideas; his near-perfect ear caught the lilt and cadence of Irish-American speech and enriched his natural gift for mimicry and dialect.

In 1951, O'Connor published his first novel, *The Oracle*, about a radio newscaster who uses pompous phrasing and careful conniving to achieve success. The novel, well received in England but not in the United States, shows O'Connor's gift for satire, his comedic insight into human folly, and the grace and humor of his objective style.

O'Connor had made several attempts on a second novel when in January 1953 he suffered a severe hemorrhaging ulcer. In March 1954, to recuperate and work at a more leisurely pace, he made his first trip to Ireland. On his return, Edward Weeks introduced him to Fred Allen, the radio comedian, who needed help editing his radio scripts into a book, and a lasting friendship developed. In the autumn of 1954, O'Connor made a second trip to Ireland, this time with Allen and Portland Hoffa, Allen's wife. In January 1955 he finished a new novel in time to meet the deadline for the $5,000 award offered by Atlantic Monthly Press. First readers were critical, but Esther Yntema, also a staff reader, perceived its worth. *The Last Hurrah* (1956) won the award and became a best-seller; it was selected by five book clubs and later became a successful movie starring Spencer Tracy. It has been called the best American novel on urban politics.

O'Connor aimed, he said, "to do for the Irish in America what Faulkner did for the South." Writing about a nameless city in an imaginary commonwealth, he analyzed ordinary individuals who have achieved power and authority in church, government, or family but who have found difficulty in coping with change and with their obligations to others. In *The Last Hurrah*, Frank Skeffington is defeated for reelection as mayor of an eastern city and dies; he is a "tribal chieftain" who is defeated, not through corruption, but through a failure to recognize new centers of power.

In *The Edge of Sadness* (1961), which won a 1962 Pulitzer Prize, Father Hugh Kennedy loses his faith and turns to alcohol. The vitality of a family friend who probes the past keeps him from the edge of sadness and enables him to regain a sense of duty. In *I Was Dancing* (1964), both a play and a novel, O'Connor portrayed an aging and scheming vaudeville performer. *All in the Family* (1966) examines the erosion of family relations that are beset by death, political chicanery, and shifts in personal loyalties. Some reviewers thought that O'Connor's novels portray real people; O'Connor said that they did not. In depicting the ordeal of change in his imaginary Irish-Catholic community, O'Connor, a devout Catholic himself, had written not only about the Irish but about people everywhere.

Success as a writer brought great changes in O'Connor's style of living. He bought a car, built a summer house, and rented a large house in Boston. After his father died in September 1956, he took his mother to Atlantic City to help her recover from her loss; there he wrote most of *Benjy: A Ferocious Fairy Tale* (1957). Although friends thought him a confirmed bachelor, on Sept. 2, 1962, he married Veniette Caswell Weil. O'Connor died in Boston.

[No biography exists. The Atlantic Monthly Press and Little, Brown have "immense files on O'Connor." Useful comments by those who knew him appear in *The Best and the Last of Edwin O'Connor* (1970), edited by Arthur M. Schlesinger, Jr., which includes excerpts from O'Connor's published novels and several of his unpublished writings. The most complete guide to his works is Hugh Rank, *Edwin O'Connor* (1974). See also Howard Mumford Jones, "Politics, Mr. O'Connor and the Family Novel," *Atlantic Monthly*, May 1968. An obituary is in the *New York Times*, Mar. 24, 1968.]

JOHN E. HART

O'DANIEL, WILBERT LEE ("PAPPY") (Mar. 11, 1890–May 11, 1969), businessman, radio musician, governor of Texas, and United States senator, was born in Malta, Ohio, the son of William O'Daniel and Alice Ann Thompson Earich. His father, a Union veteran, was a farmer, factory worker, and construction crewman; his mother, a widow when she married William O'Daniel, was a housewife, but after her second husband's early death, she worked as a seamstress and washerwoman. Her children remembered her as firm, strong, industrious, and religious. In 1895, when his mother married an old classmate, Charles H. Baker, O'Daniel moved with his family to Baker's farm near Arlington, Kans., about twenty miles southwest of Hutchinson.

After completing public school in Arlington in 1906, O'Daniel opened a small restaurant there and in a year earned enough for tuition at a business college in Hutchinson. He finished the two-year course in eight months even though he was holding two part-time jobs. Hired by a milling company upon graduation, O'Daniel advanced from stenographer to bookkeeper and then sales manager, moving from Arlington to a larger milling company in Kingman, Kans., in 1912. Four years later he organized his own business, the Independent Milling Company, and expanded his marketing into Texas. On June 30, 1917, he married Merle Estella Butcher; they had three children. In 1919 his firm merged with a Kansas City company, and O'Daniel left the organization. In 1921, in the midst of the postwar recession, O'Daniel established the United States Flour

Mills Company in New Orleans in order to facilitate export marketing. In 1925 the family moved to Fort Worth, Tex., where O'Daniel began a ten-year association with Burrus Mill and Elevator Company, an extensive northern Texas and Oklahoma concern. While he rose to the position of president of the Fort Worth mill, O'Daniel also introduced laboratory and experimental operations into milling and began to advertise on radio.

In 1930, O'Daniel joined with Bob Wills to create a radio program, "Light Crust Doughboys" (later "Hillbilly Boys"). O'Daniel himself wrote over 150 songs and programs on religion, education, families, thrift, morals, heritage, politics, and Americanism. The income from such songs as "Beautiful Texas," "Texas Rose," "Bluebonnet Waltz," "Alamo Waltz," and "Them Hillbillies Are Politicians Now" helped O'Daniel launch his new Hillbilly Flour Company and resulted in a grass-roots letter campaign that encouraged him to enter—and easily win—a hotly contested Democratic gubernatorial nomination in 1938 over twelve opponents. O'Daniel could vote in neither the primary nor the election, as he had refused to pay the poll tax, but his "Pass the Biscuits, Pappy" platform (based on a radio advertising slogan from which his nickname was derived), which lauded the Ten Commandments, the Golden Rule, pensions, family life, mother love, schools, commerce, and simple government, attracted mass sing-along rallies throughout Texas. O'Daniel garnered nearly 52 percent of the primary vote in the one-party state, obviating the need for a runoff.

Before the runoff primaries for other races, O'Daniel unprecedentedly endorsed candidates for the Democratic nomination and state supreme court and thus divided the party before the Democratic convention. He advocated "more smokestacks and businessmen, and less Johnson grass and politicians," and called for advances in education, labor relations, agriculture, conservation, and law and order.

O'Daniel governed Texas much as he had presided over his own businesses and the Fort Worth Chamber of Commerce, which he had headed in 1933. His cabinet functioned like a board of directors of a business corporation, an approach that blurred distinctions between the three branches of government and alienated an entrenched bureaucracy. Despite his inexperience and failure to repeal the poll tax, to institute a "transactions tax," and to increase old-age pensions, O'Daniel was reelected in 1940, the first candidate for governor of Texas to secure more than a million votes. In 1941, halfway through his second term, he campaigned to fill a vacated seat in the United States Senate and defeated twenty-five other candidates, ranging from veteran politicians to a relatively new congressman named Lyndon B. Johnson. O'Daniel was reelected to a full term in the Senate in 1942. For the next six years, he served without distinction. He identified increasingly with the conservative, isolationist Republican bloc. In 1948 he retired from the Senate and sold real estate in Washington, D.C. He then moved to a home in Dallas and started an insurance company that he headed until his death. He twice again sought the Democratic nomination for governor—in 1956 and 1958—but was defeated. He died in Dallas eleven years after his last attempt to reenter politics.

O'Daniel's election successes are often attributed to showmanship and radio. But contemporary newspaper accounts suggest that voters responded to his sincerity and proindustry position. By demonstrating the value of public relations and mass media, O'Daniel changed the nature of electioneering in Texas. Most historians hold that O'Daniel was a better campaigner than administrator of the offices to which he was elected.

[See Seth Shepard McKay, *W. Lee O'Daniel and Texas Politics, 1938–1942* (1944); John E. Ferling, "The First Administration of Governor W. Lee O'Daniel" (M.A. thesis, Baylor University, 1962); and T. R. Fehrenbach, *Lone Star: A History of Texas and the Texans* (1985). A biographical sketch of O'Daniel appears in *The Handbook of Texas*, III (1976). Obituaries are in the *New York Times* and the *Dallas Morning News*, both May 12, 1969.]

GLEN E. LICH

O'DOUL, FRANCIS JOSEPH ("LEFTY") (Mar. 4, 1897–Dec. 7, 1969), baseball player and manager, was born in San Francisco, Calif. He grew up in the rough Irish neighborhood called Butchertown (near present-day Candlestick Park), where he attended Bay View School. In 1912, Rosie Stoltz, one of his teachers, taught him the fundamentals of baseball. O'Doul later asserted, "I'll tell you this: Miss Stoltz alone is responsible for my success in baseball." Under Stoltz's coaching, O'Doul led Bay View to the grammar school city championship. The following year, he pitched two semiprofessional clubs to city championships in the Native Sons League and the Mish-Taylors. Besides baseball, he learned little during his seven years at school before his father, who believed that young people should learn a trade, insisted he leave and take a job in a slaughterhouse.

O'Doul's professional baseball career began in 1917 when he was signed by the San Francisco Seals of the Pacific Coast League. Just twenty years old, he had no idea how good a player he was until he got to training camp. The manager sent all fifty players to center field and then placed a $5 gold piece on home plate. O'Doul slid into home first to claim the money. Despite his speed, the team farmed him out to gain experience. He went to Des Moines, Iowa, where he pitched three or four games before a line drive hit him and knocked off the tip of one finger. The injury ended his first professional season. He returned to San Francisco in 1918 to pitch for the Seals, but when the United States entered World War I, he enlisted in the navy.

In 1919, O'Doul joined the New York Yankees. This was his first major-league stop in a career that saw him optioned or traded thirteen times by different professional clubs. He went from the Yankees to the Boston Red Sox in 1922 and then, in 1924, was sent to the Pacific Coast League club in Salt Lake City. He had been a pitcher, but Utah's high altitude favored batters. He told his manager that from that time on he was an outfielder, because "you could hit a ball with one hand and hit it out of the ball park." As a hitter, he developed rapidly, leading the Pacific Coast League in 1924 with a .392 average. The following year he set a Pacific Coast League record of 309 hits. His team moved to Hollywood in 1926, and O'Doul's batting average dropped to .338, which resulted in his being traded back to the Seals. Hitting .378, he won the batting crown, was voted the league's most-valuable player, and was drafted for the 1928 season by the New York Giants.

Back in the major leagues, O'Doul again found himself traveling from team to team. During his one year with the Giants, an injury to his leg slowed him down, and he was traded to the Philadelphia Phillies. In 1929, O'Doul had his greatest year. He won the National League batting crown, hitting .398. On the last day of the season, in a doubleheader, he went 4 for 4 in the first game to break Rogers Hornsby's National League record of 250 hits in a season. He got 2 more hits in the second game to establish the new league record at 254 hits. (Bill Terry tied O'Doul's record in 1930; George Sisler of the St. Louis Browns set the major-league record in 1920 with 257 hits.)

O'Doul played one more season for Philadelphia, two years for Brooklyn (again winning the batting title in 1932 with .368), and then played for the Giants from mid-1933 until the end of the 1934 season. Thus, he was one of only a handful of men who had played for all three New York City teams. His career batting average was .349; he twice won the batting crown, played in the first all-star game (1933), and appeared in the 1933 World Series, where his pinch hit started a six-run rally that won the second game for the Giants.

After leaving the major leagues, O'Doul managed in the Pacific Coast League in San Francisco (1935–1951), San Diego (1952–1954), Oakland (1955), Vancouver (1956), and Seattle (1957). He also worked as a batting coach for the Giants when they moved to San Francisco. Among his protégés were Joe DiMaggio, who played under him for two years on the Seals, and Willie McCovey, the Giants all-star first baseman. He refused credit for developing DiMaggio, saying, "Nobody taught Joe DiMaggio how to hit. . . . I was just smart enough to leave him alone."

O'Doul made at least twenty trips to Japan to promote baseball, the first in 1931. He usually led all-star teams in games against Japanese squads, and he coached the Japanese University League teams. His lasting contribution was the organization of the first Japanese professional team, the Tokyo Giants. During his lifetime, he was the best-known and most popular American ballplayer in Japan.

In 1958, O'Doul opened a restaurant in San Francisco that became a popular gathering spot for sports fans. His business interests and his many close friends reportedly prompted him to decline offers to manage the major-league Pittsburgh Pirates. He had become a popular character in San Francisco during his minor-league career by stuffing baseballs in his pockets before going into the field and then tossing them to the children in the stands. He was also active in the local Catholic Youth Organization. His bright personality was accentuated by his eye-catching wardrobe, which at one time included more than 200 ties and an equal number of suits, most of which were green. He was called "the Man in the Green Suit" until late in his career, when he entered business and adopted more conservative dress.

Many baseball writers and fans have observed that O'Doul probably would have been named to the Baseball Hall of Fame if he had come up to the majors as an outfielder. Yankees manager Miller Huggins thought he should pitch, thus delaying his success in the big leagues until 1928. O'Doul was married twice: in 1924 to Abigail Lacey and in 1953 to Jean Goodman. He died without issue in San Francisco.

[The National Baseball Hall of Fame in Cooperstown, N.Y., has a file on O'Doul that includes an undated interview probably done in 1960 and numerous newspaper clippings. An obituary is in the *New York Times*, Dec. 8, 1969.]

WILLIAM H. BEEZLEY

O'HARA, JOHN HENRY (Jan. 31, 1905–Apr. 11, 1970), novelist and short-story writer, was born in Pottsville, Pa., the son of Patrick Henry O'Hara, a physician, and Katharine Delaney. His father was a notable figure in Schuylkill County; and despite prejudice against Irish Catholics, his family enjoyed an affluent life. Tension between O'Hara and his father was exacerbated by O'Hara's dismissal from three schools—Fordham Preparatory School, Keystone State Normal School, and Niagara Preparatory School—and by his drinking. O'Hara's ambition was to attend Yale, but after he was denied graduation from Niagara in 1924 because of an alcoholic spree, his father arranged for him to work as a reporter on the *Pottsville Journal* until he had proved his seriousness. The death of his father in March 1925 terminated O'Hara's plans to attend Yale and reduced the family to genteel poverty.

In March 1928, O'Hara went to work as a reporter for the *New York Herald Tribune*, and in May his first story appeared in the *New Yorker*, to which he became a steady contributor. After he was fired by the *Herald Tribune*, he had a series of journalistic jobs, most of which he quickly lost because of drinking. Although he formed friendships with Dorothy Parker, Robert Benchley, Wolcott Gibbs, and other *New Yorker* writers, his extreme sensitivity and ungovernable temper made him a difficult friend. On Feb. 28, 1931, he married Helen Ritchie Petit, an actress; they had no children. On their delayed Bermuda honeymoon that summer he wrote a short novel, "The Hofman Estate" (unpublished), set in the anthracite region of Pennsylvania. It was followed in the fall by "The Doctor's Son," the first long story in which the autobiographical character James Malloy appears. From these works developed his Gibbsville–Lantenengo County cycle of novels and stories, based on what O'Hara referred to as "the Region" and "my Pennsylvania protectorate." The depth of the Gibbsville material has led to the generalization that most of O'Hara's fiction is set there or in the surrounding territory, but in fact much is set in New York, Hollywood, or other Pennsylvania locales.

After his divorce in 1933, O'Hara renounced alcohol to write *Appointment in Samarra*, which focuses on three days in the life of Julian English, a hard-drinking Gibbsville Cadillac dealer, from the time he throws a drink at a creditor to his suicide. Published on Aug. 16, 1934, this novel established O'Hara as a literary figure. His realism—particularly his selection of meaningful details and his accuracy in rendering speech—was praised, but some reviewers and readers objected to his callousness and what was then regarded as sexual frankness. The influence of Ernest Hemingway, F. Scott Fitzgerald, and Sinclair Lewis was detected; although O'Hara admired these writers, he did not imitate them.

Beginning with his first novel, O'Hara was incorrectly perceived as a have-not using fiction to avenge himself on the haves. His work was social history, not revenge. Although he began publishing novels in the 1930's, O'Hara was never a proletarian writer or writer of protest fiction. He practiced the novel of manners, observing the operation of the American social system in terms of the customs, language, and appurtenances of his characters. Nor was his material limited to the upper classes: his characters include workers, shopkeepers, and racketeers. Although he maintained an objective point of view, his work expresses sentimentality—often as nostalgia—and conveys pity for his defeated characters. O'Hara's principal themes were the cruelty of human conduct and the pain of loneliness.

In 1935, O'Hara published *The Doctor's Son*,

his first short-story collection. The stories were distinguished by economy of treatment and close observation of human behavior—which led detractors to complain that they were too elliptical—and he has been credited with perfecting a subgenre that became known as "the *New Yorker* story." But O'Hara did not restrict himself to formula fiction; his later stories are longer and more fully developed. Among the strongest of them are "It Must Have Been Spring," "Over the River and Through the Wood," "Price's Always Open," "A Respectable Place," "Graven Image," "The Decision," "A Family Party," "The Cellar Domain," "The Bucket of Blood," "Pat Collins," and "Fatimas and Kisses."

His second novel, *Butterfield 8*, based on the Starr Faithfull murder case, also appeared in 1935. O'Hara's novels brought him employment in Hollywood as a script polisher, but he did not take that work seriously. He did not work on the screenplays for *Butterfield 8*, *From the Terrace*, *Ten North Frederick*, and *Pal Joey*. On Dec. 3, 1937, he married Belle Mulford Wylie; they had one child. A novel about Hollywood, *Hope of Heaven* (1938), was not well received; it was followed by a short-story collection, *Files on Parade* (1939).

O'Hara's stories about "Pal Joey," written in the form of letters from a reprehensible nightclub entertainer, began appearing in the *New Yorker* in 1938. They were collected in 1940, the year in which the Richard Rodgers and Lorenz Hart musical *Pal Joey*, for which O'Hara wrote the book, opened on Broadway. *Pal Joey* has been described as the first American musical in which the plot and songs were integrated; it became one of the standards of the American musical stage. O'Hara continued to write plays but never achieved another production on Broadway.

During the 1940's, O'Hara published stories in the *New Yorker*, commuted to Hollywood, and wrote a column for *Newsweek*. Two more short-story collections appeared, *Pipe Night* (1945) and *Hellbox* (1947); the latter was his first book for Random House, where he remained for the rest of his career with the publisher Bennett Cerf and the editor Albert Erskine.

A Rage to Live was published in 1949 and became a best-seller. O'Hara's first major work since *Appointment in Samarra*, it examines the life of Grace Caldwell Tate, a wealthy Pennsylvanian. Because of a disrespectful review of this novel in the *New Yorker*, O'Hara abandoned the short-story form—and thus the *New Yorker*—for a decade. *The Farmers Hotel* (1951), a play set in the Region, was rewritten as a short novel. In the summer of 1953, O'Hara permanently stopped drinking after suffering a stomach hemorrhage. Belle O'Hara died in January 1954, and on Jan. 31, 1955, O'Hara married Katharine Barnes Bryan.

The year of his remarriage also marks the commencement of his most productive period. *Ten North Frederick*, a novel about Joseph Chapin, a Gibbsville aristocrat with a secret ambition to become president, appeared in 1955 on Thanksgiving Day (which became O'Hara's preferred publication date). *From the Terrace*, which O'Hara regarded as his best novel, was published in 1958. At 897 pages his longest novel, it chronicles the career and marriages of Alfred Eaton, a Wall Street and government figure who ends as a man with nothing to do. *Ourselves to Know* (1960), O'Hara's third major novel in five years, studies the life of a middle-aged man in the Region who murders his promiscuous young wife.

O'Hara returned to the *New Yorker* with "Imagine Kissing Pete" in 1960 and began a prolific output of short stories and novellas. At this time he wrote, "I want to get it all down on paper while I can. I am now fifty-five years old and I have lived with as well as in the Twentieth Century from its earliest days. The United States in this Century is what I know, and it is my business to write about it to the best of my ability, with the sometimes special knowledge I have. The Twenties, the Thirties, and the Forties are already history, but I cannot be content to leave their story in the hands of the historians and the editors of picture books. I want to record the way people talked and thought and felt, and to do it with complete honesty and variety." During the next decade O'Hara published thirteen volumes of fiction: *Sermons and Soda-Water* (three novellas, 1960), *Five Plays* (1961), *Assembly* (stories, 1961), *The Big Laugh* (novel, 1962), *The Cape Cod Lighter* (stories, 1962), *Elizabeth Appleton* (novel, 1963), *The Hat on the Bed* (stories, 1963), *The Horse Knows the Way* (stories, 1964), *The Lockwood Concern* (novel, 1965), *Waiting for Winter* (stories, 1966), *The Instrument* (novel, 1967), *And Other Stories* (stories, 1968), and *Lovey Childs* (novel, 1969). Three more volumes were published posthumously.

None of the late novels is a major work, but the stories, novellas, and novelettes substantiate O'Hara's position as the greatest American master of short fiction.

During the 1960's, O'Hara was probably America's best-selling serious writer, but he was embittered by the denial of critical respect. Although O'Hara yearned for the badges of recognition—especially the Nobel Prize—he was openly scornful of the literary establishment, which disparaged his unfashionable material and later political conservatism.

When O'Hara died at his Princeton home, he left a body of fiction unsurpassed in its scope and fidelity to American life. His epitaph was selected by his wife from his own self-assessment: "Better than anyone else, he told the truth about his time, the first half of the twentieth century. He was a professional. He wrote honestly and well."

[O'Hara's papers are in the Pennsylvania State University Library. Posthumous publications include *The Ewings* (novel, 1972); *The Time Element and Other Stories* (1972); *Good Samaritan and Other Stories* (1974); *"An Artist Is His Own Fault": John O'Hara on Writers and Writing*, edited by Matthew J. Bruccoli (1977); *The Second Ewings* (unfinished novel, 1977); *Selected Letters of John O'Hara*, edited by Bruccoli (1978); and *Two by O'Hara* (play and screen story, 1979). The principal biography is Matthew J. Bruccoli, *The O'Hara Concern* (1975). See also Finis Farr, *O'Hara* (1973); and Frank MacShane, *The Life of John O'Hara* (1980). The standard bibliography is Matthew J. Bruccoli, *John O'Hara: A Descriptive Bibliography* (1978). Among critical studies are Edwin Russell Carson, *The Fiction of John O'Hara* (1961); Sheldon Norman Grebstein, *John O'Hara* (1966); Charles C. Walcutt, *John O'Hara* (1969); and Robert Emmet Long, *John O'Hara* (1983). An obituary is in the *New York Times*, Apr. 12, 1970.]

MATTHEW J. BRUCCOLI

OPPENHEIMER, JULIUS ROBERT (Apr. 22, 1904–Feb. 18, 1967), theoretical physicist, was born in New York City, the son of Julius Oppenheimer, a prosperous textile importer, and Ella Friedman, an artist. (Although the name Julius appears on his birth certificate, he said that the initial J stood "for nothing"; his brother thought that the initial was a nod to the tradition of naming a firstborn son after his father.) He graduated from the Ethical Culture School in New York in 1921, having been a precocious student in all subjects, with special aptitude in chemistry and English. The following summer, on a visit to relatives in Germany, he contracted dysentery while collecting geological specimens in old mines in Bohemia, and so, instead of going to Harvard, he spent the winter recuperating in New York. In the summer of 1922, Oppenheimer explored the trails and plateaus of New Mexico with his English teacher, Herbert W. Smith. Over the next few years, as his commitment to science became clear, he corresponded with the future writers and scholars Francis Fergusson, Paul Horgan, and Herbert Smith. Oppenheimer's love of books and command of language are revealed in these letters.

In September 1922, Oppenheimer entered Harvard. Carrying the maximum load of credit courses, auditing others, and indulging a catholic curiosity in the stacks of Widener Library, he quickly acquired advanced standing. In his second year he was elected to Phi Beta Kappa and in 1925 received the B.A. summa cum laude. Although his degree was in chemistry, Oppenheimer's real interest had shifted to physics, and he spent much of his final year in the laboratory of Percy W. Bridgman.

Oppenheimer did not develop Bridgman's experimental skills; indeed, during his time as a graduate student at the Cavendish Laboratory in Cambridge, England (1925–1926), his ineptitude in experiment was a principal cause of a depression that lifted only as he learned about the exciting developments in quantum theory in Germany. He accepted Max Born's invitation to work at the University of Göttingen, where he received his Ph.D. in March 1927 for the thesis "Zur Quantenmechanik der Richtungsentartung." His paper with Born on the quantum theory of molecules described what is known as the Born-Oppenheimer approximation.

Oppenheimer spent the year 1927–1928 as a National Research Council Fellow at Harvard and the California Institute of Technology (Caltech). During a second postdoctoral year he worked with Paul Ehrenfest in Leiden and H. A. Kramers in Utrecht and then with Wolfgang Pauli at the Eidgenössische Hochschule in Zurich. Pauli, who had a gift for asking provocative questions, greatly influenced Oppenheimer's teaching and research.

In August 1929, Oppenheimer began a joint appointment as assistant professor at the University of California and at Caltech. From August through March he taught graduate courses at Berkeley and spent occasional weekends at Caltech discussing research; during the spring term he held informal seminars at Caltech. He was promoted to associate professor in 1931 and to professor in 1936.

Oppenheimer's lectures were always stimulating, and he and his students often talked physics late into the evening. "The work is fine," Oppenheimer wrote his brother Frank in 1932, "not fine in the fruits but in the doing. There are lots of eager students, and we are busy studying nuclei and neutrons and disintegrations, trying to make some peace between the inadequate theory and the absurd revolutionary experiments."

By 1929, Oppenheimer had published fifteen papers on quantum physics. His subsequent research in quantum mechanics, nuclear physics, and cosmic rays resulted in fifty-two papers and abstracts published between 1930 and 1941. Over half were written jointly with students or postdoctoral fellows. Others reflected his collaboration with Ernest O. Lawrence and the Berkeley experimentalists or with his Caltech colleagues Richard C. Tolman, Charles C. Lauritsen, and William A. Fowler.

Oppenheimer played a major role in the emergence of an American school of physics by training outstanding members of a new generation. His own place in theoretical physics is less clear. Hans Bethe cites Oppenheimer's 1929 work on continuing spectra as leading to a better understanding of opacity and hence of stellar interiors, and he cites a 1930 paper of Oppenheimer's on the theory of electrons and protons as "essentially predicting" the positron (discovered in 1932). In 1936, Oppenheimer explained why electron-positron showers required a new cosmic-ray particle; the meson was found the following year. Two important discoveries in astrophysics rest in part on his 1939 papers on neutron stars (with G. M. Volkoff) and black holes (with Hartland Snyder), but no major breakthrough bears Oppenheimer's name.

Although absorbed in physics, Oppenheimer found time to study Sanskrit, read poetry, and enjoy music. He spent his holidays at the simple cabin in the Pecos Valley in New Mexico that he and his brother Frank acquired in 1929.

Like many of his generation, Oppenheimer reacted to the Great Depression, the rise of Nazism, and the Spanish Civil War by supporting liberal and left-wing causes. He did not join the Communist party, but his association with some who did, including a former fiancée, dramatically affected his life in later years. On Nov. 1, 1940, he married Katherine Puening Harrison; they had two children.

Oppenheimer participated in the surge of nuclear research that followed news of uranium fission in early 1939. He became involved in atomic bomb development in October 1941, when Lawrence urged that Oppenheimer be consulted about fast-neutron reactions. In May 1942 he was put in charge of all fast-neutron research sponsored by the United States Office of Scientific Research and Development. That autumn General Leslie R. Groves, the head of the Army Corps of Engineers' newly formed Manhattan District, appointed Oppenheimer director of the central laboratory for bomb design and development to be established at Los Alamos, N.Mex. Using arguments about a possible German atomic bomb and the eventual nonmilitary applications of atomic energy, Oppenheimer recruited a distinguished staff, the nucleus of which assembled at Los Alamos in April 1943.

Some elements in Oppenheimer's now legendary wartime leadership were predictable: his prodigious ability to absorb information was extended to ballistics engineering and the behavior of metals, and his thoughtfulness for people he cared about, to the welfare of a large and diverse community. Newly apparent was the self-discipline with which he controlled a tendency to what critics called arrogance and the tact with which he mediated the incongruent needs of scientists for openness and the army for secrecy. Oppenheimer did not direct from the head office, recalled the physicist Victor Weisskopf. "He was present in the laboratory or in the seminar rooms when a new effect was measured, when a new idea was conceived."

By early 1944, Allied successes in Europe removed the threat of a German atomic bomb, but Oppenheimer focused on completing a weapon to end the Pacific war. Under the influence of Niels Bohr, who served as a Los Alamos consultant, Oppenheimer began to hope that by making war unacceptably destructive the bomb might force nations to live in peace.

Exhausted and deeply troubled in the aftermath of the atomic bombings of Hiroshima and

Nagasaki in August 1945, Oppenheimer resigned as director of Los Alamos to accept a professorship at Caltech. In August 1946 he rejoined the Berkeley faculty but was constantly called to Washington for consultation, and therefore a return to the old ways of teaching and research proved impossible. In October 1947 he became director of the Institute for Advanced Study in Princeton, N.J.

Under Oppenheimer's leadership, Princeton succeeded prewar Copenhagen as the world center of theoretical physics. Young people gravitated to the institute as postdoctoral fellows or joined its nonteaching faculty, of which Albert Einstein was already a member. Visitors included Bohr, Pauli, and other molders of modern physics. Seminars in Oppenheimer's office, at which each new clue to particle physics was examined, were enlivened by his probing questions, his expert summaries, and his sense of continuing excitement. Oppenheimer's interest in literature and philosophy also helped to develop the institute's high repute in humanistic studies. Aided by his prestige as institute director, Oppenheimer became the principal spokesman for those who believed that the atomic age demanded a broader public understanding of science and technology. At first his articles and lectures emphasized the impact of the bomb upon international relations. Later he explored more subtle links between science and other aspects of Western culture.

In early 1946, as consultant to the State Department committee charged with drafting a proposal for the international control of atomic energy, Oppenheimer was largely responsible for the tone and substance of the Acheson-Lilienthal plan. This plan, with modifications, was presented to the United Nations Atomic Energy Commission and accepted as a basis for negotiation. In September, Oppenheimer joined Soviet-bloc scientists on a subcommittee that concluded that international control was technically feasible.

In 1947 the civilian United States Atomic Energy Commission (AEC) replaced the army's Manhattan District. Of numerous committees on which Oppenheimer served thereafter, the most important was the AEC's nine-member General Advisory Committee (GAC), of which he was chairman. In October 1949, three months after the first Soviet atomic bomb test, the GAC was asked to consider whether the United States should undertake a crash program to develop a thermonuclear weapon. Its negative recommendation was not accepted by President Truman and was not made public. The episode emphasized the growing cleavage between advocates of large offensive nuclear weapons and advocates of more varied weaponry and tactics, as represented by Oppenheimer and the GAC. Oppenheimer's less than enthusiastic support of the hydrogen bomb program failed to mollify those who regarded him as leader of the opposition.

When Oppenheimer's GAC term expired in July 1952, he remained an AEC consultant but without specific duties. With Senator Joseph McCarthy's campaign against Communists in government in full swing, Oppenheimer's critics successfully urged that his security clearance be withdrawn on the grounds that Soviet sympathies might account for his position on nuclear weapons.

In December 1953, Oppenheimer was notified by the AEC's general manager that his clearance, due for routine review in July 1954, had been suspended. Rather than accept the implication of disloyalty, Oppenheimer chose the option of a secret hearing before a special appeals board. During the hearing, which lasted from April 12 to May 6, 1954, distinguished scientists and public servants testified unequivocally on Oppenheimer's behalf, but the board recommended against continuation of his clearance. On June 16 the AEC released the printed transcript of the hearing and on June 28 delivered its conclusion that although Oppenheimer's loyalty was not in doubt, his left-wing associations of the 1930's made it unwise to trust him with official secrets.

The decision was denounced by a large segment of the scientific community. Oppenheimer never commented on it publicly. He continued to direct the Institute for Advanced Study and to entertain old friends and official guests at Olden Manor, the director's residence. A house in the Virgin Islands, where Oppenheimer could indulge his lifelong love of sailing, replaced his New Mexico cabin as a retreat. With his wife he traveled abroad to lecture, attend conferences, and accept honors. In December 1963 he received the AEC's Enrico Fermi Award for outstanding contributions to atomic energy. For reasons of health Oppenheimer resigned as institute director in June 1966. He died in Princeton.

[Oppenheimer's personal papers are in the Library of Congress. Other repositories of source material are the Center for History of Physics of the American Institute of Physics, in New York; Bancroft Library at the University of California at Berkeley; the California Institute of Technology Archives; the Harvard University Archives; the Los Alamos National Laboratory, Records Division; and the National Archives, in Washington, D.C. Oppenheimer's scientific papers are listed in Smith and Weiner, cited below. Lectures and articles (1946–1966) are published in *Science and the Common Understanding* (1954); *The Open Mind* (1955); and *Uncommon Sense* (1984).

See United States Atomic Energy Commission, *In the Matter of J. Robert Oppenheimer: Transcript of Hearing Before Personnel Security Board* (1954); Hans A. Bethe, "J. Robert Oppenheimer, 1904–1967," *Biographical Memoirs of Fellows of the Royal Society*, 14 (1968); I. I. Rabi et al., *Oppenheimer* (1969); Philip M. Stern, with Harold P. Green, *The Oppenheimer Case: Security on Trial* (1969); and Alice Kimball Smith and Charles Weiner, eds., *Robert Oppenheimer: Letters and Recollections* (1980). Transcribed interviews with Oppenheimer and many who knew him are in the Archive for History of Quantum Physics and the Center for History of Physics (American Institute of Physics) and in the Archives and Special Collections of the Massachusetts Institute of Technology. An obituary is in the *New York Times*, Feb. 19, 1967.]

ALICE KIMBALL SMITH

OSBORN, HENRY FAIRFIELD (Jan. 15, 1887–Sept. 16, 1969), naturalist and conservationist, was born in Princeton, N.J., the son of Henry Fairfield Osborn, a biology professor and president of the American Museum of Natural History, and Lucretia Perry. He grew up in a family of considerable wealth and social standing, for his paternal grandfather, William Henry Osborn, had made a fortune in the railroad business, and by marriage the Osborn family had ties to J. Pierpont Morgan and Cleveland Dodge. Drawing upon those powerful social and economic connections, Osborn's father had forged a career as a leading organizer and administrator for science in New York City: in the early 1890's he founded the departments of biology at Columbia University and vertebrate paleontology at the American Museum of Natural History, he was a founder and the first president of the Bronx Zoo (1896), he helped to reorganize the New York Aquarium (1902), and he became president of the American Museum of Natural History (1908).

Osborn's father's enthusiasm for science had a profound impact on him. As a child, Osborn developed a private collection of animals, and on several occasions he accompanied his father on museum expeditions for fossil vertebrates, trips that took him to dinosaur beds in the western United States and prehistoric elephant deposits in Egypt. Similarly, he followed his father's footsteps in his formal education: after graduating from the Groton School in 1905, Osborn attended Princeton University for four years, graduating with a B.A. in 1909. He spent the next year studying at Trinity College, Cambridge. His education included several courses in the natural sciences, though he consciously avoided becoming a specialist.

After college Osborn held a number of jobs. He worked first in the freight yards of San Francisco and later as a member of a railroad crew in Nevada. Eventually he returned to New York and, on Sept. 8, 1914, married Marjorie M. Lamont; they had three children. In order to support his family, Osborn sought a career in business. He became treasurer of the Union Oil Company and from 1914 to 1917 served as treasurer of a business that manufactured labels. After serving as a captain in the army during World War I, he became a partner in Redmond and Company, a New York investment banking firm. In 1935 he joined the banking firm of Maynard, Oakland, and Lawrence, but he quit the same year and retired from a business world that he now considered artificial.

Osborn's retirement from business enabled him to devote all his time and energy to his passion for animals. Since 1923 he had served as a trustee and member of the executive board of the New York Zoological Society, and in 1935 he became the secretary and in 1940 the president of the organization. In those positions Osborn made his most important contributions to science and society. As president of the Zoological Society, Osborn had responsibility for the Bronx Zoo, and during his twenty-eight years in office, he instituted a number of changes. Interested in exhibiting animals in their natural habitat, Osborn played a central role in developing the African Plains exhibit, a bird house that allowed tropical birds to fly freely in native surroundings, and new buildings for penguins, apes, and nocturnal animals. Osborn's efforts were not revolutionary, but under his direction the Bronx Zoo and the New

York Aquarium developed new facilities for animals and viewers, thereby promoting better opportunities for public education and scientific research.

Osborn's work in conservation broadened the interests of the Zoological Society and made his reputation. In a 1945 editorial in the zoo's bulletin, *Animal Kingdom*, he warned of a depletion of forests, soils, and water resources that would threaten human existence. He further developed that argument in *Our Plundered Planet* (1948) and *The Limits of the Earth* (1953). The former described how humans had misused the land and called for the conservation of natural resources to ensure the continuation of civilization. The latter defined the explosive increase in world population and its impact on food, water, and other natural resources. Both books were nontechnical expositions, and their popularity established Osborn as a leading advocate for conservation and intelligent use of the earth's resources.

Within the Zoological Society, Osborn and others soon established the Conservation Foundation, an organization that produced books, films, and special studies on water resources, flood control, and endangered species. He and Laurance Rockefeller, a vice-president of the Zoological Society, helped to create the Jackson Hole Wildlife Park at Moran, Wyo., a preserve where naturalists could investigate the biology of the Rocky Mountains. Throughout the 1950's and 1960's, Osborn lectured on conservation and wrote articles on the impending ecological crisis for *Science*, the *Atlantic Monthly*, and other periodicals. From 1950 to 1957 he served on the Conservation Advisory Committee of the United States Department of the Interior and on the Planning Committee of the Economic and Social Council of the United Nations. He died in New York City. Not a scientist himself, Osborn popularized the concerns of scientists and helped to mobilize public and government support for a nascent ecology movement that a decade later became a major scientific and public-policy issue.

[Manuscript sources on Osborn include records, correspondence, and other materials at the Bronx Zoo and his father's papers at the New-York Historical Society. Osborn edited *The Pacific World* (1944) and *Our Crowded Planet* (1962).

On Osborn's work as president of the New York Zoological Society, see William Bridges, *A Gathering of Animals* (1974). See also the interview with Osborn in the *New Yorker*, Mar. 9, 1957; and Laurance Rockefeller, "My Most Unforgettable Character," *Reader's Digest*, Oct. 1972. An obituary is in the *New York Times*, Sept. 17, 1969.]

RONALD RAINGER

OUIMET, FRANCIS DESALES (May 8, 1893–Sept. 2, 1967), golfer and stockbroker, was born in Brookline, Mass., the son of Arthur Ouimet, a gardener from Canada, and Mary Ellen Burke. Whenever his older brother, Wilfred, worked as a caddy, Ouimet borrowed his club. He played in the cow pasture behind their house, where there were swamps, brooks, and a gravel pit. He called it the most difficult course he ever played.

Ouimet started working as a caddy at the age of eleven. He often played golf at 5 A.M., until chased away by the greenskeepers. Samuel Carr, who was kind to the boys who carried his clubs, gave him a driver, a lofter, a midiron, and a putter. In 1908, Ouimet graduated from Heath Grammar School. He attended Brookline High School, where he organized the golf team, but he did not graduate. In 1909 he won the Greater Boston Interscholastic Championship. He failed to qualify for the National Amateur Championship by one stroke in 1910, 1911, and 1912. But in 1913, at Wollaston, he won the Massachusetts State Amateur Championship.

While working as a clerk at the Wright and Ditson Sporting Goods Company, Ouimet joined the Woodland Golf Club. The president of the United States Golf Association, Robert Watson, persuaded him to enter the United States Open at the Brookline Country Club. The 1913 Open was one of the most publicized tournaments in the United States, and it helped change the image of golf, which, until that time, did not have mass appeal in the United States or players who could compete with the best Europeans. Harry Vardon, five-time Open champion of Great Britain, and the long hitter Edward ("Ted") Ray were favored to win at Brookline. On September 19, after fifty-four holes in the rain, Ouimet was tied with Vardon and Ray at 225. Both Englishmen finished the seventy-two holes with 304. Ouimet needed to play the last six holes in 2 under par to tie. At the seventeenth hole, Ouimet needed a 3. Ray recalled, "Ouimet's ball finished twelve feet or so from the tin, leaving him with the most difficult kind of putt in the world, with a down-slope and a side-slope to negotiate at the same time. Only perfect judgment of both line and strength would get the ball in. . . . The ball took the slope down in a gentle curve, and hit the very centre of the cup." Ouimet finished in a three-way tie with Vardon and Ray.

In the playoff the next day, Ouimet was steady, while the Englishmen beat themselves. His caddy and lifelong friend, Eddie Lowery, was a serious ten-year-old. Ouimet said, "Eddie kept telling me to keep my eye on the ball. He cautioned me to take my time. He encouraged me in any number of different ways." Ouimet took the lead on the tenth hole and never lost it, finishing with a score of 72, beating Vardon by 5 strokes and Ray by 6. The unexpected victory made him the first major American golf hero. Ten years later the number of American golfers had increased from 350,000 to 2 million.

Ouimet won the United States Amateur Championship in 1914, at the Ekwanok Country Club in Manchester, Vt. He won the French Amateur and the Massachusetts Amateur championships that same year. In 1915 he formed a sporting-goods partnership with his friend Jack Sullivan. After he won the Western Amateur Championship in 1917, he entered the United States Army and was stationed at Camp Devens during World War I. On Sept. 11, 1918, he married Stella Mary Sullivan (whose brother had eliminated him in the first round of the Boston Interscholastic in 1908); they had two children.

Ouimet was the winner of the Massachusetts Amateur in 1919. The next year he won the North and South Amateur Championship and was runner-up in the United States Amateur. In 1922 he won the Houston Invitational and the Massachusetts Amateur and was a member of the United States Walker Cup Team. He played on, or captained, every Walker team sent to Britain until 1949. He won the St. George's Challenge Cup in 1923, the Crump Memorial in 1924, the Massachusetts Amateur and the Gold Mashie Tournament in 1925 (the year he lost the United States Open by one stroke), and the Crump Memorial again in 1927.

In 1931, Ouimet once again won the United States Amateur Championship, saying that one of the factors in his favor was that Bobby Jones did not play in that tournament. In 1932 he won the Massachusetts Open.

Ouimet became a stockbroker in 1919. From 1932 he worked in the Boston office of White, Weld and was active in sports businesses. He said that if he had not been a golfer, he would have been a baseball player. In 1942 and 1943 he was vice-president of the Boston Braves baseball team. The Francis Ouimet Caddie Scholarship Fund was founded in 1949 to help former caddies.

In 1951, Ouimet became the first American elected captain of the Royal and Ancient Golf Club of St. Andrews. In 1954, President Dwight D. Eisenhower painted a portrait of him (from a sketch by Thomas Stephens), which the president gave to Bobby Jones, who presented it to the Royal and Ancient Golf Club of St. Andrews, Fife, Scotland, the most prestigious golf club and the world's last arbiter of golf rules. Ouimet played golf with Eisenhower on Sept. 16 and 17, 1955, at the Cherry Hills Country Club, in Denver, Colo.

In 1954, Ouimet joined the Boston office of Brown Brothers, Harriman, where he worked as a stockbroker until his death. Modest and low-keyed, he considered "a clear head" the best asset in golf and was usually the calmest man on a course. He was admired by fellow golfers for both his temperament and ability. He died in Newton, Mass.

[Ouimet's papers are at the Ouimet Museum, Weston, Mass. The United States Golf Association Museum and Library (Golf House) in Far Hills, N.J., has a Ouimet Room with objects from the 1913 Open. He wrote *Golf Facts for Young People* (1914) and *A Game of Golf: A Book of Reminiscence* (1932). On his role in golf history, see Herbert W. Wind, *The Story of American Golf* (1948); Robert Browning, *A History of Golf* (1955); and Marshall Smith, "Old Man Brings Back a Great Day," *Life*, June 21, 1963. An obituary is in the *New York Times*, Sept. 3, 1967.]

RALPH KIRSHNER

OVERSTREET, HARRY ALLEN (Oct. 25, 1875–Aug. 17, 1970), philosopher, social psychologist, and adult educator, was born in San Francisco, Calif., the son of William Franklin Overstreet, a printer who had fought in the Civil War, and Julia Maria Pauline Detje, a German immigrant. As a boy, Overstreet worked at odd menial jobs and helped his father in the composing room of the *San Francisco Bulletin*. When his father was stricken with paralysis during Overstreet's sophomore year at the University of California, Overstreet became the sole support of his family, working six hours a day in the college recorder's office. As a consequence, he needed five years to complete his requirements for the B.A. degree, granted in 1899. He was elected to Phi Beta Kappa and Beta Theta Phi and received the Carnot Medal for excellence as an intercollegiate debater and the Mills Traveling Fellowship to the University of Oxford (1899–1901). While still a freshman, he was strongly influenced by his professor of philosophy, George Holmes Howison, whom he served as secretary during the summer in Europe before taking up residence at Balliol College. Overstreet's dissertation, "The Theory of Knowledge in Aristotle and Hegel," earned him the B.S. degree in 1901.

Overstreet's childhood memories of listening to street orators and observing the activities associated with the city jail, located in his neighborhood, influenced his philosophical outlook and his career. His early inclination was to study literature, for he was an avid reader of such authors as Herbert Spencer, Ralph Waldo Emerson, Charles Darwin, and Mrs. Humphry Ward (author of the socialist novel *Robert Elsmere*), but under Howison's influence abandoned literature and the study of law in favor of philosophy. Ideologically, he was interested in the working poor; in the 1920's he took a year's leave from his academic job and worked in a shoe factory in Connecticut, polished bearings in California, made sacks for the Hawaiian Sugar Company, and spent some time as a traveling salesman. Problems in industrial relations, he concluded, were endemic not to the division of capital and labor but to the differences between the intelligent and the unintelligent. It followed that industrial conflict could be avoided by lifelong education. Overstreet began his career as an educator as an instructor in philosophy at the University of California at Berkeley in 1901; he was promoted to associate professor early in 1911. He married Elsie Burr of San Francisco, the daughter of the chemist and financier Edmund Coffin Burr, on May 18, 1907; they had three children.

While at Berkeley, Overstreet published *The American College Course* (1904) and *The Dialectic of Plotinus* (1909). In the autumn of 1911, he left Berkeley to chair the Department of Philosophy and Psychology at the City College of New York, a position he held until his retirement in 1939. From 1924 to 1936 he also taught in the continuing-education program of the New School for Social Research, as well as adult-education courses for the International Ladies' Garment Workers Union; at the Labor Temple; and at the People's Institute. He was by midlife one of the nation's leading adult educators. Overstreet's marriage ended in divorce in 1932. Bonaro Wilkinson, the daughter of a farmer, became his second wife in New York City on Aug. 23, 1932; they had no children.

In 1938, Overstreet lectured at Town Hall and was instrumental in the development of its educational radio program "America's Town Meeting of the Air." This program is described in the book written by him and his wife Bonaro, *Town Meeting Comes to Town* (1938). With Bonaro, he directed Town Hall's Leadership School in 1940–1941 and served as one of its trustees from 1940 to 1950.

Overstreet's abiding interest in adult education, shared by Bonaro, is easily traced through his activities, publications, and associations. The need to develop one's individual mental capacities to cope with societal problems was the main thread of his philosophical-educational orientation. His concern for the industrial worker was later supplemented by a solicitude for black Americans, the victims of world hunger, and underprivileged children, among others. Because of this "liberal" orientation, his name, along with sixty-two others, including Jane Addams and Charles Beard, was listed by the Military Intelligence Service in a 1919 report to the Senate Judiciary Committee Investigating German Propaganda among those "who did not help the United States when the country was fighting the Central Powers." The list was called a "Who's Who in Pacifism and Radicalism." Overstreet denied that he was a pacifist, although he belonged to the Emergency Peace Federation, the Collegiate Anti-Militarism League, the Intercollegiate Socialist Society, and the League of Free Nations Association. Some twenty years later, at the outbreak of World War II, he publicly declared farewell to his "old self" and pledged "to help win the war and build a new world."

By the end of the 1950's, the Overstreets had become preoccupied with Communism as a domestic and foreign menace to American society and were writing persistently on the subject. Nevertheless, their fear of Communism did not prevent them from recognizing the threat posed by the radical Right. As if captured by their subject, extremism in the United States, they wrote a defense of the Federal Bureau of Investigation, albeit, in one reviewer's words, "not an unsophisticated apologia."

Overstreet was a prolific author, alone and with Bonaro, and in general received favorable reviews. His first book, *Influencing Human Behavior* (1925, the first of twenty-six printings), described as "a brilliant exposition of behaviorist philosophy," attempted to explain, in response to requests by his students at the New School, "how human behavior can actually be changed, in light of the new knowledge gained through psychology." This edited compendium of class lectures covers such topics as how to speak and write more effectively, how to mold personality, and how to control the public. In *About Ourselves* (1927), he described in layman's terms concepts from the field of abnormal psychology as a guide for normal people who might be tempted to avoid everyday responsibilities. Overstreet followed his discussion of human frailties with an analysis of the positive contributions the arts can make to our personalities. Aimed at popular audiences, the book was designed to make the reader reflect on his or her own personal development. By 1941 he had changed his emphasis from a concern with the individual to an emphasis on the social context. In *Our Free Minds* (1941), he argued that there are two threats to the American way of life—namely, the threat from without (such as totalitarianism) and the threat from within (social injustice, anti-Semitism, and the like). He then proceeded to explore the second. The pinnacle of his success was reached with *The Mature Mind* (1949), which was chosen as a Book-of-the-Month Club offering and within a year went through eighteen printings. Much praised, it also had its critics, professionals who thought the subject matter oversimplified. Overstreet used psychology and psychiatry as vehicles for the exploration of personal interrelationships. Those forces shaping us, according to him, include politics, economics, family life, and religion; how the mature individual copes with these forces is the theme of the book.

In response to questions regarding his politics and religion, he responded, "A free American," but it is alleged that he was a Democrat and attended the Congregational church. He enjoyed swimming and tennis at his two residences, at Mt. Tamalpais, Calif., and a farm in Vermont. He died at Falls Church, Va.

[Overstreet's publications are *Principles of Truth Evaluation* (1904); *The Enduring Quest* (1931); *We Move in New Directions* (1933); *Civilized Loafing* (1934; reprinted as *Books for Libraries*, 1969); *A Declaration of Interdependence* (1937); *Let Me Think* (1939); and *The Great Enterprise* (1952). Books coauthored with Bonaro Overstreet are *Town Meeting Comes to Town* (1938); *Leaders for Adult Education* (1941); *Where Children Come First* (1949); *The Mind Alive* (1954); *The Mind Goes Forth* (1956); *What We Must Know About Communism* (1958); *The War Called Peace* (1961); *The Iron Curtain* (1963); *The Strange Tactics of Extremism* (1964); *The FBI in Our Open Society* (1969). There is no book-length biography of Overstreet. See *California Monthly*, Oct. 1929; *Town Crier*, Nov. 1933; *Book-of-the-Month Club Notes*, Midsummer 1949; and *Saturday Review of Literature*, Aug. 13, 1949. An obituary is in the *New York Times*, Aug. 18, 1970.]

HAROLD L. WATTEL

PANOFSKY, ERWIN (Mar. 30, 1892–Mar. 14, 1968), art historian, was born in Hannover, Germany, the son of independently wealthy parents, Arnold Panofsky and Caecilie Solling. He began his education at the Joachimsthalsches Gymnasium in Berlin and attended the universities of Freiburg, Berlin, and Munich before receiving his Ph.D. from the University of Freiburg in 1914 under the tutelage of Wilhelm Vöge and Adolf Goldschmidt. On Apr. 9, 1916, he married art historian Dorothea (Dora) Mosse; they had two children.

Panofsky was forced to seek employment after the fall of the German mark at the end of World War I. Appointed privatdocent at the newly founded University of Hamburg in 1921, he became a professor in 1926 and held the position of *Ordinarius* during the Weimar Republic. He soon established a productive intellectual relationship with several scholars from the Warburg library of cultural studies in Hamburg, including Aby Warburg, Edgar Wind, Gertrud Bing, Fritz Saxl, Rudolf Wittkower, and Ernst Cassirer. When he was dismissed from Hamburg by the Nazi regime in 1933, he was well known for his theoretical and historical studies of medieval and Renaissance art, having published a number of acclaimed essays, such as "Dürers Stellung zur Antike" (1922), "Dürers 'Melencolia I'" (with Fritz Saxl, 1923), "Die deutsche Plastik des 11. bis 13. Jahrhunderts" (1924), "Idea" (1924), and "Hercules am Scheidewege" (1931).

Compelled to leave Germany, Panofsky immigrated to New York City in 1934 and took a position as visiting professor of fine arts at New York University. Since 1931 he had periodically lectured in the basement of New York's Metropolitan Museum of Art under the auspices of what would soon become the Institute of Fine Arts. In 1934 he went to Princeton University as a visiting lecturer and became a professor at the Institute for Advanced Study in 1935. With colleagues such as Albert Einstein, Jacques Maritain, Thomas Mann, and J. Robert Oppenheimer, he claimed that he suffered an "expulsion into Paradise," at a place "where members do their research openly and their teaching surreptitiously." In 1947–1948 he held the Charles Eliot Norton lectureship, previously occupied by Igor Stravinsky and Robert Frost, at Harvard University.

Panofsky returned to Princeton and taught and wrote there until his death. His wife, with whom he wrote *Pandora's Box: The Changing Aspects of a Mystical Symbol* (1956), died in 1965, and the following year, he married Gerda Sörgel, also an art historian. During his thirty-five years in America, he received many honors and academic prizes, including honorary degrees from Utrecht, Princeton, Oberlin, Rutgers, Bard, Upsala, Harvard, New York University, Columbia, and Bonn; awards from the Mediaeval Academy of America and the National Gallery of Art; the Jungius Medal from Hamburg; and the Ordre pour le Mérite for arts and sciences from West Germany.

In addition to his publications, Panofsky's great legacy was his students. He trained many art historians whose fame would come close to rivaling his own. His disciples in Germany included Hugo Buchtal, Adolf Katzenellenbogen, Lise Lotte Moller, H. W. Janson, Hans Swarzenski, Walter Horn, Lotte Brand Philip, P. H. van Blanckenhagen, and William Heckscher. His American students initiated the study of art history as a serious humanistic pursuit.

Panofsky has been called the most influential art historian of the twentieth century, but his impact on scholarship far exceeds the boundaries of one discipline. Literary critics, intellectual historians, and philosophers of science, among others, have turned both to his practical studies of medieval and Renaissance imagery and to his theoretical inquiries into the relationship between works of art and the culture that generates them. In the former category, most of his essays and books attest to his devotion to a subject and method of research associated with many Warburg Institute scholars: the investigation of the *Nachleben* ("afterlife") of classical images and themes, the ways in which certain antique forms and myths become invested with new meanings across time.

Among Panofsky's most frequently cited practical studies are *Albrecht Dürer* (1943; entitled *The Life and Art of Albrecht Dürer* after the fourth edition, 1955), *Early Netherlandish Painting* (1947–1948), *Renaissance and Renascences in Western Art* (1960), and *Problems in Titian, Mostly Iconographic* (1969). He is best remembered as the deviser of a method or approach to analyzing works of visual art that depends upon a well-thought-out theory of the relation of mind to world. In this sense, he was a philosopher of art rather than a traditional art historian.

Trained in neo-Kantian epistemology and much influenced by the teaching and writing of Ernst Cassirer, Panofsky abhorred the simple-minded "appreciationism" of his fellow art historians, a stance that "deprives naiveté of its charm without correcting its errors." When he first began writing, he openly challenged the formal analyses and connoisseurship of his predecessors and even confronted the formidable stylistic criticism of Heinrich Wölfflin and Alois Riegl. His 1924–1925 essay "Eine Perspektive als 'symbolische Form'" set the stage for later investigations into the ways in which visual imagery can both reflect and be generated by larger cultural and philosophical predispositions.

The preface to *Studies in Iconology* (1939) systematizes Panofsky's iconological method. He distinguished between three levels of investigation and employed Leonardo da Vinci's *Last Supper* as an example. The preiconographic level depends upon practical experience and interprets primary subject matter apart from its historical embodiment (for example, the universal recognition of thirteen men seated at a table laden with food). The iconographic stage "reads" this information according to its textual precedents; that is, it identifies its subject matter by recourse to the Gospel story. An iconological analysis, the third stage, represents "iconography turned interpretive." Here the art historian deciphers the work of art as a cultural document, expressive of the "essential tendencies of the human mind" as they are crystallized into a particular historical, personal, and cultural moment. In this regard, the *Last Supper* is not only a testimony to the artist's idiosyncratic genius but also a supreme confirmation of Renaissance ideas and ideals. Two other noted examples of Panofsky's method are *Gothic Architecture and Scholasticism* (1951) and "The History of the Theory of Human Proportions as a Reflection of the History of Styles" (1921).

Panofsky also wrote several essays in film criticism. His collection of essays *Meaning in the Visual Arts* (1955) provides the most succinct statement of his wide-ranging intellectual interests. The essay "Three Decades of Art History in the United States" traces the course of his scholarly career as it reflects changing perspectives in the evolution of the discipline of art history. "The History of Art as a Humanistic Discipline" is an eloquent testimony to his cherished intellectual values.

Late in his life, Panofsky began a lecture on the subject of one of his last books, *Tomb Sculpture* (1964), with words to the effect that he had "reached an age when one could take pleasure in being able to look at the grave from the outside." He died in Princeton.

[Panofsky's correspondence and papers are with William Heckscher in Princeton, N.J., and the Institute for Advanced Study. For a complete listing of Panofsky's works, see H. Oberer and E. Verheyen, eds., *Erwin Panofsky: Aufsätze zu Grundfragen der Kunstwissenschaft* (1964). On his life and work, see *A Commemorative Gathering for Erwin Panofsky at the Institute of Fine Arts* (1968); C. Eisler, "Kunstgeschichte American Style," in D. Fleming and B. Bailyn, eds., *The Intellectual Migration* (1969); G. Hermeren, *Representation and Meaning in the Visual Arts* (1969); J. Białostocki, "Erwin Panofsky (1892–1968)," *Simiolus kunsthistorisch tijdschrift*, 4 (1970); G. C. Argan, "Ideology and Iconology," *Critical Inquiry*, 2 (1975); S. Alpers, "Is Art History?" *Daedalus*, 106 (1977); R. Heidt, *Erwin Panofsky: Kunsttheorie und Einzelwerk* (1977); C. Hasenmueller, "*Panofsky, Iconography, and Semiotics*," *Journal of Aesthetics and Art Criticism*, 36 (1978); Michael Podro, *The Critical Historians of Art* (1982); J. Bonnet, ed., *Erwin Panofsky* (1983); M. Holly, *Panofsky and the Foundations of Art History* (1984); and K. Moxey, "Panofsky's Concept of 'Iconology' and Art," *New Literary History*, 17 (1985–1986). An obituary is in the *New York Times*, Mar. 16, 1968.]

MICHAEL ANN HOLLY

PARKER, DOROTHY ROTHSCHILD (Aug. 22, 1893–June 7, 1967), short-story writer, poet, dramatist, and critic, was born in West End, N.J., the daughter of J. Henry Rothschild and Eliza A. Marston. Her father was a prosperous businessman in the garment industry in New York City, as well as a Talmudic scholar. Her mother, a Scot, died shortly after Dorothy's birth. A pious Catholic stepmother, who considered Parker Jewish, raised her and sought to "reform" her through severe indoctrination. When Parker was about seven, she was sent to the Blessed Sacrament Convent School in New York, where she remained until age fourteen, a lonely child estranged from her father. About 1907 she entered Miss Dana's School in Morristown, N.J., a prestigious and progressive boarding school where she spent four more unhappy years but did receive rigorous and ultimately valuable training in Latin, French, and English.

Upon graduation in 1911, Parker took up residence in a Manhattan boardinghouse, supporting herself by playing piano in a dancing school, composing light verse (her first acceptance was in 1913), and writing captions for fashion illustrations at *Vogue*. Frank Crowninshield, the editor of *Vanity Fair*, arranged for her transfer to his magazine (another Condé Nast publication) in 1916, by which time she was publishing verse, captions, satiric sketches, and essays. Crowninshield, who was making *Vanity Fair* into a witty and fashionable review of literature, thought her satiric touch was exactly what the magazine needed. In June 1917 she married Edwin Pond Parker II of Hartford, Conn., a Wall Street broker. She kept her writing career going in New York after he enlisted in the army and was sent overseas.

Parker became drama critic of *Vanity Fair* in 1918, and the following year befriended Robert Benchley and Robert E. Sherwood, two young staff writers recently hired by Crowninshield. Soon "the three wits of *Vanity Fair*" began lunching at the Algonquin Hotel with the critic Alexander Woollcott, the columnist Franklin P. Adams (F.P.A.), and Harold Ross, later the founding editor of the *New Yorker*. The six formed the nucleus of a group called the Algonquin Wits, who were notorious for their puns, gibes, gossip, and bons mots. Recording their best remarks in his newspaper column, F.P.A. helped to make Dorothy Parker famous for her lively repartee.

Fired from *Vanity Fair* for an acerbic theater review in 1920, Parker promptly found a job at *Ainslee's Magazine*, writing a monthly column titled "In Broadway's Playhouses" and contributing humorous squibs and satiric verse to *Life* (not Henry Luce's magazine but an American counterpart of the British *Punch*). She also published essays and character sketches in the *Saturday Evening Post*, *Ladies' Home Journal*, and *Everybody's*. Her separation from Eddie Parker in 1922 and an unhappy love affair set in motion a period of depression climaxed by an abortion and a suicide attempt. One acquaintance described her as "a masochist whose passion for unhappiness knew no bounds." Characteristically, she took much of her unhappiness out on others.

Parker's first published short story, "Such a Pretty Little Picture," about a suburban husband caught in a failed marriage, appeared in *Smart Set* in December 1922. That same year she issued satiric verse in *Men I'm Not Married To* (bound with F.P.A.'s *Women I'm Not Married To*); wrote a song for the Broadway musical *No, Siree!* and played a part in it; collaborated with Elmer Rice on the play *Close Harmony, or The Lady Next Door* (produced in 1924) and collaborated with Benchley on the one-act play *Nero*. Periods of intense productivity alternated with fits of depression. In 1925 she collaborated with nineteen other writers on a novel, *Bobbed Hair*, and wrote (with George S. Kaufman) her first film script, *Business Is Business*. She also drank heavily and attempted suicide a second time. Her famous sardonic poem on the subject of suicide, "Résumé," was closer to autobiography than most people knew. It concludes, "Guns aren't lawful,/Nooses give;/Gas smells awful;/You might as well live." She collected all her poems in this vein in *Enough Rope* (1926), and it became a national best-seller. The following year she marched in sympathy with Sacco and Vanzetti in Boston.

Parker had contributed occasionally to the *New Yorker* during its fledgling years, but in October 1927 she began a weekly book-review column that continued, with interruptions, through 1931. Signing the column "Constant Reader," she began to demonstrate more critical depth than her public had seen before. A second collection of poems, *Sunset Gun* (1928), and her first collection of stories, *Laments for the Living* (1930), were both popular and critical successes. One reviewer said she "has become the giantess of American letters"; another wrote that her verse had "a Horatian lightness, with an exquisite certainty of technique"; and a third found her stories "as individual and unmistakable as Ring Lardner's or Hemingway's." Yet in private life she continued to suffer depression, attempting suicide again in 1927, divorcing Eddie Parker in 1928, and turning away many an old friend with her nasty tongue. Drinking more heavily, she began missing magazine deadlines and putting off her editors, a habit that would continue for the rest of her life.

Parker met Alan Campbell, a young actor, in 1933; they married and went to Hollywood in 1934 to write filmscripts. (In which of these years they married remains unclear; 1934 is the year given in their 1947 divorce papers.) Over the next sixteen years they collaborated on twenty-two scripts, ten of them written for Paramount between 1934 and 1936.

Parker helped organize the Screen Actors' Guild in 1934 and the Anti-Nazi League in 1936; she went to Spain in 1937 to report on the Loyalist cause for *New Masses*. Meanwhile her collected poetry appeared in *Not So Deep as a Well* (1936) and her collected stories in *Here Lies* (1939), but her production in both genres had fallen off sharply. With the onset of world war in 1939, her radical leftist activities ceased, but she devoted herself to a variety of causes in the war years: European Jews, the United Service Organizations (USO), the United Nations, American-Soviet friendship, the Spanish Refugee Appeal.

After Parker and Campbell were divorced in 1947, she returned to Hollywood to write filmscripts and plays. Collaborating with Ross Evans, she wrote *The Coast of Illyria* (1949), a play about Charles and Mary Lamb. She was blacklisted for "un-American activities" in California in June 1949, accused of Communist-front activities in House Un-American Activities Committee hearings of 1951, subpoenaed by Senator Joseph McCarthy in 1953, and criticized for her supposed Communist sympathies by the New York State Legislature in 1955. She remarried Campbell on Aug. 17, 1950, but they separated again when both were blacklisted. Her best play was produced during this difficult era—*The Ladies of the Corridor* (1953), written with Arnaud D'Usseau. Parker herself called it "the only thing I have ever done in which I had great pride." The play concerns the fate of lonely women, living in side-street New York hotels, victims of boredom, self-pity, and despair.

In her later years Parker wrote occasional sketches for the *New Yorker*, adapted three of her stories for television, was a distinguished visiting professor of English at California State College at Los Angeles, and wrote lyrics for the Leonard Bernstein musical *Candide* (1958). Her finest achievement in the years 1957–1963 was her monthly book-review column for *Esquire*, where her shrewdness and pungent skepticism were once more at their best. She died unhappy and alone in her rented room at the Volney Hotel in Manhattan.

Parker's achievements in American literature remain unquestionably important. Her voice helped to define what was most daring and skeptical in the 1920's; she not only was the best epigrammatic poet of the century but, in her laconic short stories, was at least the equal of Hemingway and Lardner. Using scorn and bitterness and acerbic wit, Parker devised a profoundly moving art out of her lifelong unhappiness.

[Parker's extensive papers were willed to the National Association for the Advancement of Colored People. The largest holding of her letters is at the Houghton Library of Harvard University. Her other major publications include *Death and Taxes* (poems, 1931); *After Such Pleasures* (stories, 1933); *Collected Stories* (1942); *Collected Poetry* (1944); *The Portable Dorothy Parker*, edited by W. Somerset Maugham (1944); and *Constant Reader* (her *New Yorker* criticism, 1970). For a full-length biography, see John Keats, *You Might as Well Live* (1970). For further biographical material, see Alexander Woollcott, *While Rome Burns* (1934); Marion Capron, "Dorothy Parker" (an interview), in Malcolm Cowley, ed., *Writers at Work* (1957); Wyatt Cooper, *Esquire*, July 1968; Lillian Hellman, *An Unfinished Woman* (1969); and Arthur F. Kinney, *Dorothy Parker* (1978). An obituary is in the *New York Times*, June 8, 1967.]

DEAN FLOWER

PARRISH, MAXFIELD (July 25, 1870–Mar. 30, 1966), artist, was born Frederick Parrish in Philadelphia, Pa., the son of Stephen Parrish, a businessman and artist, and Elizabeth Bancroft. The only child in an affluent Quaker household, Parrish received instruction in art from his father, whom he later credited with being his most influential teacher. While still a young man, Parrish adopted as his middle name his paternal grandmother's maiden name, Maxfield, and it was as Maxfield Parrish that he became known professionally.

Until 1884, Parrish attended school in Philadelphia. He then accompanied his parents on an extended visit to Europe and continued his education in France and England. In 1888 he entered Haverford College in Philadelphia, intent on becoming an architect. But his interests and energies turned increasingly to art, and he left Haverford in his junior year to study under the painters Robert Vonnoh and Thomas Anschutz at the Pennsylvania Academy of Fine Arts. He also sought instruction at the Drexel Institute from the illustrator Howard Pyle, with whom he shared an enthusiasm for medieval themes and historic European imagery.

In 1894, Parrish was commissioned to paint a mural and other wall decorations on the theme of Old King Cole for the Mask and Wig Club of the University of Pennsylvania. In that year he opened his own studio in Philadelphia to pursue commercial illustration. A cover design for *Harper's Weekly* in 1895 brought Parrish national recognition as an illustrator. He also established himself as a poster designer by winning a national contest sponsored by the Pope Bicycle Company. For the next several decades his work appeared constantly before the public. He designed over sixty covers for *Collier's*, as well as illustrations for *Century Magazine, Scribner's Magazine, Ladies' Home Journal*, and the *National Weekly*. On June 1, 1895, Parrish married Lydia Austin, a painting instructor at the Drexel Institute who later became an authority on black American folk music; they had four children.

So successful were Parrish's whimsical paintings for L. Frank Baum's *Mother Goose in Prose* (1897) that he soon found himself in demand as a book illustrator. He illustrated an edition of Washington Irving's *Knickerbocker's History of New York* (1900) and Kenneth Grahame's *Golden Age* and *Dream Days* (both 1902).

Parrish left Philadelphia in 1898 and settled in Plainfield, N.H., near the colony of prominent artists and writers established at Cornish by the sculptor Augustus Saint-Gaudens. Here Parrish designed and built the Oaks, an estate frequently featured in architectural magazines.

During the early twentieth century, Parrish became America's most popular and successful commercial artist. He took full advantage of the new technology of color reproduction and became one of the very best designers of the "golden age of illustration," when print media were the only mass media. Edith Wharton's *Italian Villas and Their Gardens* (1903) was the first book in which his paintings were reproduced in color.

Parrish's book illustrations for such children's classics as Eugene Field's *Poems of Childhood* (1904), the *Arabian Nights* (1909), Nathaniel Hawthorne's *Wonder Book and Tanglewood Tales* (1910), and Louise Saunders' *Knave of Hearts* (1925) firmly established him as a master of fantasy and romance. His paintings of gnomelike characters in fairytale settings captured the imagination of a vast public that was both charmed and intrigued by his unorthodox use of color (especially "Parrish blue," which became his trademark), his preoccupation with medievalism, and his wit and sentimentality.

In addition to his poster art and magazine illustrations, Parrish designed dozens of advertisements that established the public image of products such as Edison-Mazda light bulbs, Fisk tires, and Jell-O. He also became widely recognized as a muralist. His best-known work was the Old King Cole mural commissioned in 1906 for New York City's Knickerbocker Hotel (now in the St. Regis Hotel). He also painted murals for the Sheraton Palace Hotel in San Francisco, the Hotel Sherman in Chicago, the Broadmoor Hotel in Colorado Springs, the University of Rochester (N.Y.) School of Music, and the Curtis Publishing Company in Philadelphia.

Parrish probably became best known for his color prints, which were hung over mantels in millions of middle-class homes across the nation. Typical of these prints were *The Garden of Allah* (1919) and *Daybreak* (1920), which featured lounging maidens in semiclassical settings with romantic natural backgrounds. From 1918 to 1934 the General Electric Company published seventeen of these prints on a variety of its promotional materials, including calendars, playing cards, and blotters.

Parrish entered a period of relative obscurity in the mid-1930's as romanticism and representational art increasingly lost favor. He retired from illustration and devoted the next thirty years to painting rural landscapes. After 1934 most of these works, designed for reproduction on calendars and greeting cards, were widely distributed by the Brown and Bigelow Publishing Company. The artist was forced by arthritis to put away his brushes forever in 1962.

With the advent of the pop-art movement of the early 1960's, which was inspired in part by the imagery of commercial art, Parrish's work enjoyed a revival; major exhibitions of his paintings and drawings were organized in 1964 and 1966. He died at the Oaks.

[Most of Parrish's personal papers and correspondence are in the Library of Dartmouth College. Scrapbooks, correspondence, and photographs are also in the Smithsonian Institution's Archives of American Art, Washington, D.C., and in the Haverford College Library.

For his biography, see Coy Ludwig, *Maxfield Parrish* (1973), which contains a catalog of his works. Other catalogs include Harold Knox, *Collectors Guide to Maxfield Parrish* (1972); and Marian S. Sweeney, *Maxfield Parrish Prints* (1974). See also Irene P. Norell, *Maxfield Parrish: New Hampshire Artist* (1971); Paul W. Skeeters, *Maxfield Parrish: The Early Years, 1893–1930* (1973); *The Maxfield Parrish Poster Book* (1974), with an introduction by Maurice Sendak; and Virginia Hunt Reed, *In the Beginning: 25 Maxfield Parrish Drawings from the Pennsylvania Academy of Fine Arts* (1976). Syracuse University has produced a film on Parrish entitled *Parrish Blue*. An obituary is in the *New York Times*, Mar. 31, 1966.]

MICHAEL L. LAWSON

PATTERSON, RICHARD CUNNINGHAM, JR. (Jan. 31, 1886–Sept. 30, 1966), engineer, ambassador, and corporate executive, was born in Omaha, Nebr., the son of Richard Cunningham Patterson, an attorney with land and mining interests, and Martha Belle Neiswanger. After graduating from high school he worked as a laborer in a gold mine in South Dakota, and for many years he maintained his membership in the Western Federation of Miners.

Patterson attended the University of Nebraska for a year (1905–1906) but left to enroll at Columbia University, from which he received the degree of engineer of mines in 1912. At Columbia he was a member of the swimming team and president (1909–1910) of the Intercollegiate Swimming Association. After graduating he worked briefly for Brown Brothers in Manhattan as a runner and then was employed by the city of New York as an engineering inspector in the construction of the Catskill Aqueduct.

Early in 1916 Patterson volunteered as a private in the cavalry and went with Pershing's expedition to Mexico in pursuit of Pancho Villa. After returning from Mexico, Patterson was appointed secretary of the New York City Fire Department.

In November 1917 he rejoined the army, this time as a captain of engineers. While serving in France he was promoted to the rank of major and in 1918 was chosen by Colonel Edward M. House, President Woodrow Wilson's representative to the Paris Peace Conference, to be administrative officer of the American Commission. Patterson later described this assignment, from December 1918 to July 1919, as the most important job of his career. He reported to Joseph C. Grew and "ran the business end of the conference." While in Paris he became one of the founders of the American Legion and a member of its first executive committee. He was discharged from the army in 1919 with the reserve rank of lieutenant colonel.

Returning to the United States in 1920, Patterson became assistant to Gano Dunn, president of the J. G. White Engineering Corporation. The following year he accepted a position with E. I. du Pont de Nemours and Company as an engineer. Between 1922 and 1927 he made four trips to China to investigate construction prospects for du Pont. He lived in Shanghai and Peking, explored a number of remote interior towns, and learned Chinese. In May 1924 he was married to Shelley McCutcheon Rodes; they had one child.

During his residence in China, Patterson became interested in Chinese motion pictures and in the export to China of American films. Early in 1927 he wrote a substantive article for the *New York Times*, "The Cinema in China," in which he compared Chinese and American films and audiences. He also acquired a 44 percent interest in the Peacock Motion Picture Company, of which he became president.

In August 1927 Mayor James J. Walker appointed Patterson New York City's commissioner of corrections and commissioner of the city's parole board. During his five-year tenure Patterson improved conditions in the city's eighteen prisons, particularly in the principal city prison, the Tombs, which he referred to as a "crime college." A newspaper report described him as "rather short, of broad build, [with] black hair and brown eyes. He is a dynamic type, talks very directly, and sartorially ranks with the Mayor himself." The reporter also mentioned that Patterson played squash and golf, and that he was the donor of the Patterson Cup for intercollegiate swimming.

Although he had become active in Democratic politics as a student, Patterson had avoided being closely linked with Tammany Hall. Because of this and his success as commissioner of corrections, he was invited, a few months after Mayor Walker's resignation, to run as a Republican and Fusion-party candidate for mayor. Patterson had resigned a month after Walker's resignation to become executive vice-president of the National Broadcasting Company. Frank Polk, whom he had known at the Paris Peace Conference, Arthur Sulzberger of the *New York Times*, and his wife all advised him not to run.

In 1938 and 1939 Patterson was assistant secretary of commerce. From 1939 to 1945 he was chairman of the board of R.K.O., an active member of several other boards, and a trustee of the Import-Export Bank. From 1941 to 1943 he was also head of the United States War Savings Bond program for the state of New York.

In November 1944 President Franklin D. Roosevelt appointed Patterson ambassador to Yugoslavia's government in exile in London. The following September he went to Belgrade when the United States granted provisional recognition to Marshal Tito, whom Patterson described as "a great personality, easy to like." Their relationship initially was cordial but deteriorated in 1946. In October of that year the United States Information Agency library in Belgrade was forced to close, and Patterson held a press conference at the embassy, forthrightly criticizing Tito's government for this and for human-rights violations. Shortly thereafter he took home leave, and in March 1947 he resigned as ambassador, though he continued as a State Department consultant.

In September 1948 President Harry S Truman appointed Patterson ambassador to Guatemala to study means of improving relations with President Juan José Arevalo, whose attitude toward foreign business interests had been consistently unfriendly since his election in March 1945. During Patterson's fifteen months in Guatemala City he tried to counteract the strong leftist influence on Arevalo's government. In March 1950 he returned to Washington after threats against his life. In April 1951 Truman appointed him minister to Switzerland, and he served until President Dwight D. Eisenhower took office in 1953.

Robert F. Wagner, mayor-elect of New York City, designated Patterson chairman of the Mayor's Reception Committee, in which capacity he presided over Wagner's inauguration on New Year's Day 1954. During his first year in office Wagner appointed Patterson head of the new Department of Commerce, charged with "attracting more business life to our city." He continued in this post and with similar responsibilities until 1966, when he became commissioner of public events and chief of protocol. He died in New York City.

[Patterson's papers, including correspondence, notes, speeches, and published material covering the period 1918–1966, are in the Harry S Truman Library; access is restricted. His publications include a small monograph, *Responsibilities of Directors* (1940). An article about him is in the *New Yorker*, Aug. 21, 1954; and an obituary is in the *New York Times*, Oct. 1, 1966.]

DAVID W. HERON

PEARSON, DREW (Dec. 13, 1897–Sept. 1, 1969), journalist, was born Andrew Russell Pearson in Evanston, Ill., the son of Paul Martin Pearson, a professor of speech and English at Northwestern University, and Edna Wolfe. When Pearson was six years old, his father accepted a position in Pennsylvania at Swarthmore College, a Quaker institution, and the entire family became Quakers. Pearson attended preparatory school in Swarthmore, with a final year (1914–1915) at Phillips Exeter Academy in New Hampshire. From 1915 to 1919 he attended Swarthmore College, graduating with a B.A. For the next two years he worked with the British Red Cross in the Balkans. He then briefly taught geography at the University of Pennsylvania and Columbia University and toured Asia and Europe extensively as a foreign correspondent for several newspapers.

On Mar. 12, 1925, Pearson married Felicia Gizycka, the daughter of the imperious Eleanor Medill ("Cissy") Patterson, a scion of the McCormick family, which owned the *Chicago Tribune* and the *Washington Times-Herald*; they had one child before the marriage ended in divorce three years later. Pearson and his former mother-in-law maintained a journalistic and social relationship, sometimes tempestuous, for some years.

In 1926, Pearson became foreign editor of the *United States Daily*, the predecessor of *U.S. News and World Report* magazine. His duties were to cover international conferences, and he witnessed the signing of the Kellogg-Briand Pact in 1928. A year later he became diplomatic correspondent for the *Baltimore Sun*.

In 1931, Pearson and Robert S. Allen, the Washington bureau chief of the *Christian Science Monitor*, coauthored anonymously *Washington Merry-Go-Round*, a book containing Washington social gossip and attacks on President Herbert Hoover and Congress. A best-seller, the book was followed by *More Merry-Go-Round* (1932), with indictments of General Douglas MacArthur and the Supreme Court and accounts of the risqué social life of Cissy Patterson. These books displayed for the first time Pearson's unique style of slashing and partisan political observation mixed with titillating revelations about the private lives of Washington higher-ups. Pearson and Allen were fired when their respective employers learned they had written the books. In 1932 they began "Washington Merry-Go-Round," which became the most widely read daily newspaper column in the United States. By 1942, when Allen left to join the military, the column was syndicated in 350 newspapers. Thereafter, Pearson continued the column alone, and by the time of his death, 650 papers carried it. From 1938 until 1955 Pearson had a weekly radio program on the American Broadcasting Company.

After the staid political journalism of the 1920's, Pearson's aggressive and irreverent reportorial style captured the loyalty of millions of readers and roused the intense hatred of others, usually his targets. He was aided by a staff of dedicated, if underpaid and overworked, associates and by information and confidential tips from hundreds of sources in and out of government. In July 1936, Pearson married Luvie Moore Abell, who had a son by a previous marriage.

Pearson's politics were liberal and left of center, although he was far from uncritical of Democratic administrations. He attacked racism, militarism, the House Un-American Activities Committee, religious intolerance, and oppression of the poor, and supported welfare programs, Medicare, civil rights, and foreign aid. He also encouraged closer relations with the Soviet Union; thus, after he interviewed

Soviet premier Nikita Khrushchev in 1961 and 1963, his subsequent columns, unlike those of many in the establishment press, stressed Khrushchev's overtures for peaceful coexistence.

Pearson's major efforts were aimed at exposing corruption and incompetence in government and the private lives of public figures. He was the first to reveal that Germany was about to invade Russia in 1941, that General George Patton had slapped a soldier, and that advisers to President Franklin Roosevelt believed Great Britain would have to give up India following World War II. He broke the story of Igor Gouzenko, the Russian code clerk who had defected and revealed the existence of Soviet spy rings in the United States and Canada. Pearson attacked corruption in the Truman administration and reported that President Dwight Eisenhower's aide Sherman Adams had accepted a vicuña coat from the Boston financier Bernard Goldfine. Pearson's muckraking in the area of fiscal corruption led to the retirement of numerous public officials, including Congressman Adam Clayton Powell of New York and Senator Thomas J. Dodd of Connecticut, and to the jailing of others.

Two of Pearson's major targets were General Douglas MacArthur and Senator Joseph R. McCarthy. Pearson criticized MacArthur's heavy-handed dispersal of the 1932 "Bonus Army" of unemployed veterans in Washington, revealed his disobedience of orders during the Korean War, and disclosed his secret 1950 Wake Island conference with President Truman, at which MacArthur erroneously predicted American victory in the war within two months. Pearson exposed Senator McCarthy's unimpressive war record, his income tax evasion, and his unsubstantiated charges of Communism against government employees.

Pearson was sued for libel scores of times and took great pride in having lost only one lawsuit. Indeed, he carefully cultivated a reputation for legal invincibility. One of the largest suits against him, by General MacArthur for $1.75 million, was dropped in 1934, because Pearson threatened to make public the existence of MacArthur's mistress.

After Pearson died in Washington, D.C., his column was continued by his longtime associate Jack Anderson. Pearson's Quaker background had instilled in him the desire to do good in the world, and to his mind, his column did just that. While some of his charges were reckless and unsubstantiated, his exposés undoubtedly kept the federal government cleaner than it otherwise would have been. As he once said, "It is the job of a newspaperman to spur the lazy, watch the weak, expose the corrupt. He must be the eyes, ears, and nose of the American people." At Pearson's death, a journalistic colleague, Chalmers Roberts, wrote, "Drew Pearson was a muckraker with a Quaker conscience. In print he sounded fierce; in life he was gentle, even courtly. For thirty-eight years he did more than any man to keep the national capital honest."

[Besides the two *Merry-Go-Round* books, Pearson wrote five books of varying quality: *Nine Old Men* (1936) and *Nine Old Men at the Crossroads* (1937), with Robert S. Allen, muckraking attacks on the Supreme Court; *U.S.A.: Second-Class Power?* (1958), with Jack Anderson, an alarmist charge of American military weakness; *The Senator* (1968), a novel, written largely by Gerald Green; and *The Case Against Congress* (1968), with Jack Anderson. Writings about Pearson include Charles Fisher, *The Columnists* (1944); Herman Klurfeld, *Behind the Lines: The World of Drew Pearson* (1968); Oliver Pilat, *Drew Pearson: An Unauthorized Biography* (1973); and Jack Anderson and James Boyd, *Confessions of a Muckraker* (1979). An obituary is in the *New York Times*, Sept. 2, 1969.]

WILLIAM F. MUGLESTON

PEGLER, WESTBROOK (Aug. 2, 1894–June 24, 1969), journalist, originally named Francis Westbrook Pegler but later called James Westbrook Pegler, was born in Minneapolis, Minn., the son of Arthur James Pegler, a journalist, and Frances Nicholson. He spent his early years in St. Paul, Minn., and in 1904 his family moved to Chicago, where his father worked for William Randolph Hearst's *Chicago American*. In Chicago, Pegler completed his elementary schooling but attended Lane Technical High School for only a year before dropping out. He then worked at various odd jobs, including one as office boy for the United Press, and attended a Jesuit preparatory school, Loyola Academy, for eighteen months. In 1912 he returned permanently to newspaper work.

After a stint with the International News Service, Pegler returned to the United Press, where he covered a variety of human-interest stories and won a byline for a daily sports squib. His bachelor status made him available for assignments outside Chicago, chiefly in the Middle West. In 1916, Roy Howard, the president of the United Press, offered him a post on the staff in London. After the United States entered World War I, Pegler was transferred to Queenstown, Ireland, a major port used by American warships. When he prematurely filed a news story about an American destroyer firing on a German submarine, he was reprimanded by Admiral William Sims. The altercation led the United Press to conclude that it would be wise to assign Pegler to France. There Pegler offended General John J. Pershing by making critical comments on army censorship and efficiency. At Pershing's request, Pegler's status as an accredited correspondent was revoked. Although Pegler was not discharged by the United Press, he decided to return to London, where he volunteered for service in the American navy in March 1918. He served as a yeoman second class, doing desk work in Liverpool until the end of the war.

In 1919, Pegler settled in New York City, which became his professional base for the next four decades. In 1921 he received a byline for a full-length sports column for the United Press, and in 1925 he was appointed eastern sports editor for the *Chicago Tribune*. A rather shy and lonely bachelor, Pegler brightened his personal life by his marriage to Julia Harpman on Aug. 29, 1922. Although his wife was in poor health through most of the thirty-three years of their childless marriage, there is no reason to doubt Pegler's unabashedly sentimental comments to his friends that it was a loving union.

In his sports columns, Pegler showed traits that later characterized his political columns—a cynical pose, a sustained irreverence toward national heroes and institutions, and a sure instinct for uncovering hypocrisy in the righteous. His use of sports as a vehicle for making sardonic comments on Prohibition, gambling, and national politics prompted Howard to offer him a contract as a general columnist. Although Pegler initially professed to be uncertain about his qualifications, the appearance of his column, "Fair Enough," in the Scripps-Howard newspapers in 1933 was the turning point in his career. The only change in his position as a nationally recognized journalist was his move to the Hearst chain in 1944, where his growing conservatism was more congenial to the views of the publisher. The title of the column became "As Pegler Sees It." Pegler stayed with the Hearst organization until 1962.

Pegler's strength as a columnist lay in his abilities as a parodist, an investigative reporter, and a polemicist. His spoof of Eleanor Roosevelt's newspaper column, "My Day," while uncharacteristically gentle, reveals his talent as a parodist. As an investigative reporter, he was particularly effective in uncovering the criminal backgrounds and activities of labor-union officials. His greatest coup was winning a Pulitzer prize in 1941 for his articles on labor racketeers in the International Alliance of Theatrical Stage Employees and Motion Picture Operators.

Pegler's polemics were aimed at personalities as much as at issues. He was remembered after his death for hurling tirades and vituperative epithets at Franklin D. Roosevelt ("the feeble-minded Fuehrer"), Eleanor Roosevelt ("La Boca Grande"), Henry A. Wallace ("Old Bubblehead") and Dwight Eisenhower ("a picnic pitcher in a World Series"). Pegler consistently criticized the New Deal and the Fair Deal for paving the way for Communism. He became an ardent supporter and personal friend of Senator Joseph McCarthy and regularly endorsed the idea that the Roosevelt and Truman administrations constituted "twenty years of treason." By the mid-1950's, Pegler's biases increasingly distorted his perspective. In several columns in 1954, for example, he asserted that Colonel Edward House's novel *Philip Dru, Administrator* (1912) was an actual blueprint for an ongoing conspiracy to establish a police state in the United States.

In 1954 the Hearst organization had to pay a libel award of $175,000 to the journalist Quentin Reynolds for charges against, and innuendoes about, him in Pegler's columns, which had questioned Reynolds' bravery and sexual morals. During the next eight years, Pegler attacked federal judges and Presidents Eisenhower and Kennedy, and not only opposed American support for Israel but insisted on referring to the original Jewish names of persons who had changed them. When his increasingly restive employers changed or suppressed entire columns, Pegler protested this censorship with characteristic vehemence. When some of his private comments about the Hearst hierarchy were leaked to the press, a continuing relationship became impossible, and thus, his contract was bought up in 1962.

Pegler's correspondence of his last fifteen years reflects personal bitterness and professional frustration. In 1955, Julia Pegler died, and on May 11, 1959, he married Pearl Wiley Doane. A separation followed in 1960, and divorce, in 1961. After his break with Hearst, he published only sporadically, chiefly in right-wing journals. On Nov. 22, 1961, he married his longtime secretary and assistant, Maude Towart; they had no children. He died in Tucson, Ariz.

[The Pegler papers in the Herbert Hoover Presidential Library in West Branch, Iowa, include an extensive correspondence topically arranged as well as drafts of columns that were never published. Anthologies of Pegler's columns are *'T Aint Right* (1936); *The Dissenting Opinions of Mr. Westbrook Pegler* (1939); and *George Spelvin, American, and Fireside Chats* (1942). See Oliver Pilat, *Pegler* (1963); and Finis Farr, *Fair Enough* (1975).]

CHARLES E. LARSEN

PEREZ, LEANDER HENRY (July 16, 1891–Mar. 19, 1969), politician and segregationist leader, was born in Plaquemines Parish, La., the son of Roselius E. ("Fice") Perez, a planter, and Gertrude Solis. He grew up in an isolated, swampy parish south of New Orleans and attended a one-room schoolhouse run by his sister. Perez attended Holy Cross College, a secondary academy for boys in New Orleans, but he dropped out in 1906 without receiving a diploma. In 1912 he graduated from Louisiana State University. While there, he began his lifelong habit of attending sessions of the state legislature and, in 1912, was appointed secretary of its House appropriations committee. Following his graduation from Tulane University Law School, which he attended from 1912 to 1914, he set up practice in New Orleans.

In 1916, Perez ran unsuccessfully for the state legislature on a reform ticket. He married Agnes Chalin on May 12, 1917; they had four children. Appointed judge of the Twenty-ninth Judicial District, which comprised Plaquemines and St. Bernard parishes, in 1919, Judge Perez, as he was called forever after, earned a lasting reputation as a flamboyant, ruthless partisan willing to mete out stern punishment to his political enemies and dismiss charges against his supporters. The revolver that he kept in plain sight on the bench warned all of his resolve. Efforts to impeach him bogged down in the courts and ultimately were dropped.

In 1924, Perez was elected district attorney for the two parishes. During the next thirty-six years, he used this post to enrich himself, intimidate his enemies, manipulate election returns, and perpetuate segregation. An early ally of Huey Long, Perez campaigned strenuously for him and, in 1929, was a chief defense strategist in Long's successful effort to avoid impeachment. In return, Perez associates were appointed to key local positions overseeing the disposition of valuable oil and sulfur properties. Although his official salary never exceeded several thousand dollars a year, Perez amassed a fortune estimated at $100 million, much of it from the sale of mineral leases. As the dominant political power in his parish, Perez rarely bothered to hide election fraud. It was common to see in the records that entire precincts had "voted" in alphabetical order or that such names as Babe Ruth and Charlie Chaplin were listed among those registered to vote in Plaquemines Parish. In at least one election a Perez candidate received more votes than the number of registered voters.

Perez gained national notoriety in 1943 during a tense confrontation with the reform governor Sam Jones. A crime commission established by Jones condemned Perez for creating "a dynasty saturated with crime and corruption" and ordered him to produce certain documents. Perez was able to delay the matter in the courts, and ultimately the commission was abolished before reaching Perez. That same year, Jones appointed a reformer to serve as sheriff of Plaquemines Parish. When Perez vowed not to let the reformer take office, Jones declared martial law and sent in the National Guard. Preparing for armed resistance, Perez erected wooden barricades around the courthouse. In the midst of World War II, Perez, fitted out in hunting clothes and pith helmet, was scorned for mobilizing local residents in defiance of state authority, only to slip out of town just ahead of an advancing armed convoy. Perez was vindicated in 1944, however, when a court struck down the governor's declaration of martial law as unconstitutional and a Perez candidate was elected sheriff.

Staunchly conservative, Perez denounced as socialism the domestic programs of the Truman administration and in 1948 broke permanently with the Democratic party to help found the Dixiecrat party, led by Senator Strom Thurmond of South Carolina. Although Perez lost a bid to keep Truman's name off the ballot in Louisiana, he was instrumental in carrying the state for Thurmond. In 1952, Perez delivered 93 percent of Plaquemines Parish to the Republican presidential candidate, Dwight D. Eisenhower, by the greatest majority of any county in the nation that year.

In the wake of the Supreme Court's school desegregation decision in 1954, Perez helped found the White Citizens Council and worked feverishly to thwart integration. He spent so much time in Baton Rouge helping to draft anti–civil rights bills that he became known as "the third house of the Louisiana legislature." In testimony before congressional committees and in speeches throughout the South, Perez blamed racial unrest on Communists and Zionist Jews. He barred blacks from parish libraries and ordered the removal of all books inimical to segregation. As New Orleans public schools prepared to desegregate under court order in 1960, Perez inflamed a crowd of 5,000 in that city: "Don't wait for your daughters to be raped by these Congolese. Don't wait until the burrheads are forced into your schools. Do something about it now." Gangs of whites left the rally to stone passing cars driven by blacks, seriously injuring several.

In 1960, Perez resigned as district attorney (he was succeeded by his son Leander Perez, Jr.) but remained political boss of the parish. In a political reorganization of the parish the following year, he was elected president of the newly created Commission Council. Perez continued to battle the civil rights movement as it gained momentum in the 1960's. In 1962 he was excommunicated from the Roman Catholic church for leading the effort to thwart Archbishop Joseph Rummel's order to desegregate parochial schools in the archdiocese of New Orleans. When, in 1963, Defense Secretary Robert McNamara ordered military commanders to promote racial equality in and around their bases, Perez retaliated by barring personnel of the Naval Air Station at Belle Chasse from nearby night spots. In 1964, Perez converted Fort St. Philip, a 200-year-old Spanish fortress in the Mississippi River, into a prison ready to house, he warned, any civil rights organizers foolish enough to stray into his parish.

In 1965, Perez again became the object of ridicule for his remarks before the Senate Judiciary Committee, which was considering the voting rights bill. He claimed that the dismal 3 percent black voter registration in his parish was due not to discrimination but to an innate lack of ambition and interest in government among blacks. His charge that the bill was Communist-inspired was dismissed as "stupid" by Senator Everett Dirksen. In 1966, when Plaquemines Parish was placed under court order to desegregate its public schools, Perez led the drive to establish a private school system for whites.

Perez resigned from the Commission Council in 1967 and was succeeded by his other son, Chalin Perez. The following year, he campaigned extensively for George Wallace for president. He died at his home. Catholic funeral services were permitted because his excommunication order had been quietly removed the previous year.

Perez epitomized the bigotry, demagoguery, and arrogance of the political bosses of the Old South. He was among the last of a dying breed of archsegregationists to battle black civil rights on blatantly racist terms without benefit of the code words and euphemisms used so effectively by younger politicians. His enduring appeal among southern whites lay in his flamboyant defiance of central government, both in Baton Rouge and in Washington.

[The definitive biography is Glen Jeansonne, *Leander Perez: Boss of the Delta* (1977). See also James Conaway, *The Life and Times of Leander Perez* (1973). An obituary is in the *New York Times*, Mar. 20, 1969.]

William A. DeGregorio

PHILLIPS, WILLIAM (May 30, 1878–Feb. 23, 1968), diplomat, was born in Beverly, Mass., the son of John Charles Phillips and Anna Tucker. Descended from a family of some wealth and considerable distinction, Phillips had the means and the connections to forge a distinguished public career without undue concern about compensation. After attending Milton Academy and Noble and Greenough's School in Boston, Phillips enrolled at Harvard in 1896. After receiving his B.A. in 1900, he attended Harvard Law School for two and a half years.

In 1903, Phillips joined Joseph Choate, the

United States ambassador to the Court of St. James's, as an unpaid private secretary; here he dressed in striped pants and a morning coat and sat at a desk in front of the ambassador, with his back to him. Phillips' first real appointment came in 1905, as second secretary of the United States legation in Peking. From then on, Phillips served in the diplomatic service under every president from Theodore Roosevelt to Harry Truman.

In 1907, Phillips went to Washington, D.C., to work at what was literally the Far Eastern Desk. He also served as the first chief of the Division of Far Eastern Affairs. In 1910 he returned to London to serve as first secretary to the embassy and Ambassador Whitelaw Reid. On Feb. 10, 1910, Phillips married Caroline Astor Drayton, a granddaughter of William Astor and a second cousin to Franklin D. Roosevelt, with whom the young couple became very close and under whom Phillips had some important assignments, even though he was a Republican all his life. (They had six children, one of whom, Christopher Hallowell Phillips, served in ambassadorial posts for the United States at the United Nations.) When not on station, he and his family lived in North Beverly, Mass.

During his career of forty-four years (with brief stand-downs), Phillips alternated between appointments in the foreign service and the State Department. From 1912 to 1914 he was secretary of the Corporation of Harvard College. He was assigned to Washington (1914–1920), achieving rank as first assistant secretary of state; the Lowlands (1920–1922), as envoy extraordinary and minister plenipotentiary; Washington (1922–1924), as undersecretary of state; Belgium and Luxembourg (1924–1927), as ambassador and minister, respectively; Canada, (1927–1929), as first minister ever; Washington (1933), as undersecretary of state; and Italy (1936–1940), as ambassador. While in Italy he repeatedly tried to persuade Mussolini to not enter the war against the Allies. He was then assigned to India as personal representative of the president of the United States and ambassador (1942–1944) and to London as resident director of the Office of Strategic Services and then ambassador to Supreme Headquarters, Allied Expeditionary Force (SHAEF), where he worked closely with General Dwight D. Eisenhower (1943–1944). Phillips held his highest rank very briefly, when, in the absence of Cordell Hull from the United States, he served as acting secretary of state and, at the demise of the Eighteenth Amendment, had the "privilege to take part in the interment ceremonies of this singularly ill-advised piece of legislation."

That Phillips was able to serve under so many presidents suggests that he was not only a shrewd career officer but also, as P. H. Reuter, his closest student, suggests, not one who "rocked the boat." Yet, he also proved himself willing to take unpopular stands.

As wartime ambassador to India (and special envoy of the president), Phillips had the difficult task of representing the United States without antagonizing the British over the issue of an end to colonialism. The Indians expected much of him, but he could not antagonize the British. For example, he was not allowed to meet with Gandhi. In the process, he changed from Anglophile to Anglophobe and represented his views strongly in the only place he could—in reports to the president. One letter, dated May 14, 1943, was leaked by Drew Pearson to the *Washington Post*, on July 25, 1944. It was uncomplimentary toward Winston Churchill and his views on Indian independence and his disregard for the Atlantic Charter. By then, Phillips was at SHAEF, and the letter made him unpopular with the British. He officially retired in 1944.

In 1946, President Harry Truman assigned Phillips to a committee with the thankless task of pulling the British chestnuts out of the Palestinian fire. Phillips became a member of the twelve-man Anglo-American Committee on Palestine, which reviewed the problem of Jewish refugees still detained in Europe, more than a year after the war had ended. Phillips' tact and diplomacy were often the only things that kept the committee functioning. After hearings in Europe and the Middle East, the committee unanimously issued a ten-point plan recommending that 100,000 Jewish refugees should be allowed to proceed in an orderly manner from Europe to Palestine, that Palestine should not be divided and should become neither a Jewish nor an Arab state, and that controlled immigration should be accompanied by aid to the Palestinian economy so that the Arabs could close the gap between themselves and the Jews. Tragically, only the first recommendation was adopted. The worst fears of the committee were realized: all doors, except those in the Holy Land, remained closed to the Jews, who overran Palestine, and the Jewish state established in 1948 resulted in civil strife that, as predicted, would "threaten the peace of the world."

In 1947, Phillips headed a commission established to help settle the boundary between Siam and French Indochina. Because the French were intransigent, arrogantly holding on to an empire they had morally lost, the mission failed.

During his long retirement in Beverly, Phillips composed his memoirs, *Ventures in Diplomacy* (1952), a period piece from an age and a way of life now long gone. He retained his interests in foreign affairs, participating in various international conferences and publishing pieces on his career with, for example, the Massachusetts Historical Society, of which he was a valued member. He died while on vacation in Sarasota, Fla.

[Phillips' papers are in the Houghton Library at Harvard, and his wife's diaries are at Harvard's Schlesinger Library. His reminiscences are available at the Columbia University Oral History Project (1951). See also the Harvard Class of 1900, *Reports*, 1910 et seq.; and Paul Henry Reuter, Jr., "William Phillips and the Development of American Foreign Policy, 1933–1947" (Ph.D. diss., University of Southern Mississippi, 1979). An obituary is in the *New York Times*, Feb. 24, 1968.]

LAWRENCE W. TOWNER

PINCUS, GREGORY GOODWIN ("GOODY") (Apr. 9, 1903–Aug. 22, 1967), biologist and scientific entrepreneur, was born in Woodbine, N.J., the son of Joseph W. Pincus, a teacher, editor, and agricultural consultant, and Elizabeth Florence Lipman. His father was a leader of the community of Russian Jews established in the late nineteenth century by philanthropists who hoped to turn refugees from the czar's pogroms into American yeomen. The coastal scrublands of southern New Jersey proved a challenging habitat for commercial agriculture, but Joseph Pincus and his brother-in-law Jacob Lipman, who became dean of the College of Agriculture at Rutgers University, devoted their careers to spreading the gospel of scientific farming. After Joseph moved his family to the Bronx and became an editor of the *Jewish Farmer*, "Goody" Pincus attended Morris High School and dreamed of becoming a farmer, but he was discouraged by his father, who believed that farming did not pay; instead, Pincus pursued his interest in nature by majoring in biology at Cornell (B.S., 1924), where his Uncle Jake had obtained a Ph.D.

Pincus continued his study of nature at Harvard under the direction of the geneticist William Castle. On Dec. 2, 1924, during his first year of graduate study, he married Elizabeth Notkin, a social worker whom he had met while she boarded in his parents' home; they had two children. Pincus received his M.S. and Sc.D. degrees in 1927 for his study of the inheritance of coat coloring in rats.

During his last year as a graduate student at Harvard, Pincus was greatly influenced by the physiologist William Crozier, who championed the scientific style of Jacques Loeb. Loeb had proclaimed that living things could be understood as "chemical machines" whose behavior was best explained by the laws of physical science and that man ought to improve upon nature through biological engineering. Pincus knew firsthand from his father and uncle that nature was often inadequate to human needs, and he joined their struggle to engineer a better order by moving into Crozier's laboratory and devoting the rest of his life to developing techniques for controlling mammalian physiology. With a postdoctoral fellowship from the National Research Council, Pincus began to study the effects of pH on mammalian sperm. In 1929 he continued his research at Cambridge University and the Kaiser Wilhelm Institute in Berlin and set for himself the problems of developing in vitro fertilization and artificial parthenogenesis in mammals, in imitation of Loeb's famous experiment with the artificial reproduction of sea urchins. By 1930, Pincus was claiming privately to have initiated parthenogenetic development in rabbits. He returned to Harvard as an instructor in the fall of 1930 and became assistant professor of general physiology in 1931.

In early 1934, Pincus announced that he had fertilized rabbit eggs in vitro, transplanted them into a host mother, and brought them to term. Two years later he claimed to have successfully initiated parthenogenetic development in rabbits and to have reinserted the eggs into the mother. He had also begun practicing manipulation of human ova, but his research program was interrupted when he was denied tenure in 1937. After James B. Conant became the president of Harvard in 1933, he reorganized the biological sciences, in part because of his lack of confidence in Crozier. As one of Crozier's most visible protégés, whose controversial attempts to create life in a test tube drew widespread media attention, Pincus was vulnerable to criticism by academic competitors who claimed that he could not fully explain his experiments in terms of well-delineated theory.

Since the 1950's a consensus has developed among specialists in mammalian reproduction that Pincus was mistaken in most, if not all, of his claims to have developed rabbits through in vitro fertilization or artificial parthenogenesis. In the late 1930's, however, Crozier, Pincus, and their circle of experimenters believed that Pincus was the victim of scientific conservatism, anti-Semitism, and dislike of sex research. Pincus spent the academic year of 1937–1938 on a research fellowship at the Cambridge University School of Agriculture, but his failure to find a regular academic position in the United States embittered him.

At this nadir in Pincus' life, fellow Crozier protégé Hudson Hoagland, who was head of the small biology department at Clark University, raised funds from Jewish philanthropists to support Pincus and provided a courtesy appointment at Clark. After joining Hoagland, Pincus continued to publish studies of ovum activation and growth, moving beyond his early emphasis on the mechanism of fertilization to the study of the role of hormones in embryonic maintenance. By 1943, Hoagland and Pincus had assembled a fifteen-member research team that was supported by grants from private foundations and industry. The team constituted an informal institute for the study of mammalian neural and hormonal messenger systems, a field that was attracting increasing attention from large pharmaceutical corporations as the therapeutic potential of such drugs as cortisone became apparent.

Pincus and Hoagland were confident that they could flourish outside of academic science, and so, in 1944 they founded the Worcester Foundation for Experimental Biology, a research institute dedicated to biological engineering. Pincus became a scientific entrepreneur par excellence, serving as liaison between academic scientists and commercial interests who needed independent evaluation of new drugs and techniques for control of such biological processes as the insemination of livestock.

Pincus' most important achievement as a pioneer in biotechnology was the development of the first oral contraceptive. In 1951, Margaret Sanger, the charismatic leader of the American birth-control movement, convinced Pincus that there was need for an entirely new method of contraception because of the problems posed by world population growth. In addition, Sanger introduced Pincus to Katharine Dexter McCormick, an heir to the International Harvester fortune, women's rights activist, and longtime supporter of Sanger's efforts to promote reproductive autonomy for women. With the social justification and generous subsidies provided by Sanger and McCormick, Pincus began a major effort to translate recent advances in endocrinology and steroid chemistry into a pill that would induce a reversible state of "pseudopregnancy" in fertile women and thus suppress ovulation.

Pincus' success depended upon the recent synthesis of orally active analogues of progesterone, the primary female sex hormone, by Carl Djerassi, a chemist associated with the Syntex Corporation. Djerassi's new molecule provided a model drug for Pincus and his associates at G. D. Searle and Company, who recognized the contraceptive potential of the drug that Djerassi developed for other purposes. With the support of McCormick and Searle, Pincus organized animal studies of a range of synthetic hormones, enlisted the aid of Harvard gynecologist John Rock in the testing of the effects of these drugs on women in Massachusetts and Puerto Rico, and helped Searle orchestrate the marketing of the first birth-control pill in 1960. As "the father of the pill," Pincus achieved international fame and such scientific honors as election to the National Academy of Sciences in 1965. When Pincus died in Boston, he had been recognized as a pioneer in the social role of scientific entrepreneur.

[Pincus' papers are in the Library of Congress. Accounts of his career are provided in James Reed, *The Birth Control Movement and American Society* (1983); and Philip J. Pauly, *Controlling Life: Jacques Loeb and the Engineering Ideal in Biology* (1987). An excellent Pincus bibliography is in Dwight J. Ingle, "Gregory Goodwin Pincus," *Biographical Memoirs of the National Academy of Sciences*, 42 (1969). An obituary is in the *New York Times*, Aug. 23, 1967.]

JAMES REED

PIPER, WILLIAM THOMAS (Jan. 8, 1881–Jan. 15, 1970), oil company executive and airplane manufacturer, was born in Knapp Creek, N.Y., the son of Thomas Piper, a farmer who entered the oil business in Bradford, Pa., and Sarah Elizabeth Maltby. He attended public school in Bradford and at home received a strict Methodist upbringing. In 1899, after serving in a volunteer unit during the Spanish-American War, he entered Harvard, where he played football and threw the hammer. He graduated in 1903 with a B.S. in mechanical engineering.

Piper then worked for the United States Steel Corporation in Loraine, Ohio, and for construction firms in several cities. In 1914, Piper returned to Bradford and founded the Dallas Oil Company, which operated several wells. During World War I he was commissioned a captain in the Corps of Engineers. Piper was married on Apr. 14, 1910, to Marie Van de Water, who died in 1937, and then, on Aug. 10, 1943, to Clara Taber. He had five children by his first marriage.

In 1931, Piper bought the C. G. Taylor aircraft company to prevent its bankruptcy. Dedicated to the idea of an inexpensive airplane for the average person, Piper encouraged design changes in the Taylor aircraft. The first new plane, called the Cub, was licensed on June 15, 1931. During the next few years, the company produced several hundred planes but continued to lose money, but Piper made up the losses from his oil business. In 1936, Piper purchased Taylor's remaining interest, cut the selling price of the new-model Cub to $1,270, and made a small profit.

After the Bradford factory burned in 1937, Piper reopened the Piper Aircraft Corporation in an abandoned silk mill in Lock Haven, Pa. He soon began to dominate the private-airplane industry. Pilots were hired to promote the Cub by acrobatic flying at air shows and by setting endurance and distance records. The "Cub Convoy" of several hundred planes began flying each New Year's Day to Orlando, Fla., to dramatize the air age. By 1939, when he sold 1,806 Cubs, Piper was marketing more private planes than all his competitors combined.

Piper attracted skilled workers by offering them flying lessons at $1.10 an hour in company planes. By 1940 he had over a thousand employees, whose average age was twenty-three and whose average wage was forty-four cents an hour. Dealers, backed by the Aviation Funding Corporation, were able to advertise a Cub for a down payment of $333, including free flying lessons. During World War II, Piper sold 7,000 L-4's (called "Grasshoppers," "puddle jumpers," "flying jeeps," or "putt-putts") to the army. They were used for observation, medical evacuation, communication, and aerial photography. With a slow landing speed of thirty-eight miles an hour, they were able to take off and land in less than a hundred yards. Even before the end of the war, Piper predicted a boom in private flying and urged the federal government and local communities to build airports and landing fields.

Although orders for new planes went up in 1946, they fell drastically in early 1947, forcing many companies to close and causing Piper's creditors to reorganize his company with William Craig Shriver as chief executive. Shriver cut the payroll, closed some plants, and reorganized the board of directors. In less than a year, most of the loans were repaid, and despite Piper's objections, the company purchased the Stinson division of the Consolidated-Vultee Aircraft Company.

Amid growing conflicts on the board, Piper Aircraft began producing the Super Cub and the Pacer in 1948 and planning a twin-engine plane. The twin-engine Apache, the first all-metal Piper airplane, went on the market in 1954, selling for $32,500—more than Piper wanted but below the prices of the Beech Twin Bonanza and the Cessna 310. Piper produced 2,000 Apaches in seven years, and the plane became the cornerstone of Piper Aircraft's prosperity.

The Apache and later models were promoted through long-distance flights: Max Conrad flew nonstop from New York City to Paris in an Apache in 1954; in 1959 he flew from Casablanca to El Paso in a Comanche; and Sheila Scott flew around the world in a Comanche in thirty-three days in 1966. With the addition of several new models such as the Pawnee, an agricultural plane, and the nine-passenger Navajo, Piper Aircraft was producing 12,000 to 15,000 planes a year by 1970. The company that Piper built was continued by his sons until 1971, when the Piper Aircraft Corporation was taken over by Bangor-Punta. In 1984 the company closed the Lock Haven headquarters and moved to Vero Beach, Fla.

Piper, who died in Lock Haven, Pa., made a lasting contribution to private flying by developing a safe and relatively inexpensive airplane that was fun to fly. It has been estimated that four of five American pilots in World War II received their initial instruction in a Piper Cub; this helped to make the Cub virtually synonymous with its form of transportation.

[Piper wrote *What Your Town Needs for the Coming Air Age* (1944). See "Count the Cubs," *Fortune*, June 1940; Lincoln Barnett, "Mr. Piper of Cub-Haven," *Life*, Oct. 29, 1954; and Devon Francis, *Mr. Piper and His Cubs* (1973). An obituary is in the *New York Times*, Jan. 17, 1970.]

BERNARD MERGEN

POLING, DANIEL ALFRED (Nov. 30, 1884– Feb. 7, 1968), Protestant minister and author, was born in Portland, Oreg., the son of Charles Cupp Poling and Savilla Ann Kring. Both parents were United Evangelical ministers; indeed, his mother was the first woman the denomination ordained. Poling grew up in a series of parsonages in the Willamette Valley. In 1904, after receiving his B.A. from Oregon's Dallas College, which had been founded by his father, he was licensed to preach by the United Evangelical Church and was assigned to a church in Canton, Ohio, where his parents had once lived. On Sept. 25, 1906, he married Susan Jane Vandersall; they had four children, two of whom became ministers. His wife died in 1918, and on Aug. 11, 1919, Poling married a widow, Lillian Diebold Heingartner. They had one child and adopted another, and Poling adopted her two children.

Poling's evangelical faith led him to social reform. A staunch prohibitionist, he became active in the temperance movement after accepting a church in Columbus, Ohio, in 1907. Five years later the Prohibition party nominated him for governor. Barnstorming the state in a red automobile, he drew a record "dry" vote that caused the defeat of the Republican candidate and thereby pushed that party toward Prohibition. In 1914–1915, Poling and his wife were part of the Flying Squadron of America, which crisscrossed the country to gather support for Prohibition. A pragmatist within the Prohibition party, Poling negotiated among party leaders, the Woman's Christian Temperance Union, and the Anti-Saloon League in efforts to obtain a constitutional amendment banning liquor. After repeal of Prohibition, Poling came to believe that persuasion was more important than compulsion in dealing with alcohol. He was also active in Christian Endeavor, a youth movement to build peace and understanding through individual commitment to Christian values, including abstinence from alcohol. After Poling became the leader of the International Society of Christian Endeavor in 1915, he moved his family to Boston.

Poling always rejected pacifism, and after the United States entered World War I, he took a leading role by organizing a frontline Chaplain Corps in France. His wartime experiences, including his accidental gassing, became the basis for *Huts in Hell* (1918), his first popular book. After the Armistice he returned to Europe to survey religious needs. In 1919 he participated in the Interchurch World Movement's investigation of the American steel strike; he was shocked by the strong-arm tactics used by the steel corporations to break the strike. A year later he accepted an associate pastorate at the New York Marble Collegiate Reformed Church, the oldest congregation in the city. He was the church's minister from 1923 to 1930, when other duties led him to resign. His ministry was noted for such innovations as street preaching in front of the church. During the 1920's, Poling also gave a series of radio talks to youths on the National Broadcasting Company; they were published in three volumes.

From 1926 to 1965, Poling edited the *Christian Herald*, a Protestant interdenominational monthly that sponsored a children's home, a summer camp, the Bowery Mission, and orphanages in China and Korea. These activities were subsidized by Poling's friend J. C. Penney and, later, by Poling's wife's family, owners of the Diebold Safe and Lock Company. Poling's energy seemed boundless, and in 1927 he became head of the World's Christian Endeavor Union. He and his wife traveled in the United States, to Europe, and in 1935–1936 and 1938 around the world. They met world leaders, carried peace messages, and visited Christian orphanages in the Far East. In 1936, with world tensions rising, Poling accepted the pastorate of the Baptist Temple, associated with Temple University, in Philadelphia. There he sought to instill in youth a moral toughness that would be useful in the coming world crisis.

In 1941, following the attack on Pearl Harbor, Poling's son Clark, who had been ordained, considered volunteering for the regular army. Poling persuaded him to join the Chaplain Corps, which, far from being a haven, had a higher fatality rate than other branches of service. In 1943, Clark Poling was one of four chaplains aboard the troop ship *Dorchester* when it was torpedoed off Greenland. Many of the men were not wearing life jackets, and the four chaplains handed theirs to the troops. As the ship sank, the chaplains stood together on the bridge and prayed. Daniel Poling publicized the incident in *Your Daddy Did Not Die* (1944), the most popular of his twenty-nine books. In 1951, President Harry Truman dedicated an interdenominational chapel to the four chaplains at the Baptist Temple.

Poling had always considered himself an independent Republican. An early admirer of Theodore Roosevelt, he favored the prohibitionist Herbert Hoover over the "wet" Alfred E. Smith in 1928. During the 1930's he opposed President Franklin D. Roosevelt and the New Deal, and he backed Wendell Willkie in 1940. However, during World War II he became acquainted with Roosevelt, whom he came to see as a compassionate, Christian statesman. In 1944 he endorsed Roosevelt, and he offered to resign from his pulpit; his offer was refused, and he continued at the Baptist Temple until 1948. He also liked and respected Truman, whom he knew personally. In the postwar period Poling's major interest was anti-Communism. He advocated universal military training and admired such men as General Douglas MacArthur. Poling was an important part of the "China lobby," supporting Chiang Kai-shek's Chinese Nationalist government in exile on Taiwan. He continued to be a reformer and in 1951 even ran for mayor of Philadelphia as an anti-machine Republican, but he lost to Joseph S. Clark, a reform Democrat. A few years later the Polings moved to New York City. He died in Philadelphia.

[Poling's autobiography, *Mine Eyes Have Seen* (1959), includes a list of his publications. An obituary is in the *New York Times*, Feb. 8, 1968.]

W. J. Rorabaugh

POOL, JOE RICHARD (Feb. 18, 1911–July 14, 1968), attorney, state legislator, and United States congressman, was born in Fort Worth, Tex., the son of William Wesley Pool, a mattress manufacturer, and Bonnie Jean King. Pool grew up in Dallas and attended Oak Cliff High School from 1925 to 1929. He then enrolled at the University of Texas, where he pursued business and prelaw studies until 1933. In college he was called "Porky" Pool for his round face and rounder figure: he stood five feet, six inches tall and weighed more than 200 pounds. Pool won a campus election as chairman of the Judicial Council before financial problems made him leave college.

Two years later Pool entered Southern Methodist University in Dallas and earned his LL.B. in 1937. On Apr. 1, 1940, he married Elizabeth Chambless; they had four children. Pool practiced law with J. Frank Wilson, a former congressman, until 1943, when he entered the Army Air Corps as an intelligence investigator. After returning to civilian life in 1945, he practiced law again, did some farming, and opened Alden Mills, a mattress and bedding business, in Plano, Tex.

Pool first participated in state politics in 1952 as a Democratic candidate for the Texas House of Representatives. During the campaign he handed out fans bearing the slogan "Keep Cool with Pool." He won the election, and in six years as a state legislator he chaired several committees but attracted most attention when he proposed a law banning comic books that depicted sex and horror. Pool also introduced a measure to shift the state primary election to May so that Senator Lyndon Johnson could run simultaneously for reelection and for the Democratic presidential nomination in 1960.

Pool lost races for the United States House of Representatives in 1958 and 1960. Then in 1962 he ran for congressman-at-large when Texas became entitled to an additional congressman after the 1960 census. Distributing his fans, shaking hands across the state, and opposing federal aid to education and socialized medicine, Pool won the Democratic runoff primary when his principal opponent was indicted for tax evasion.

In the House of Representatives, Pool was given a place on the House Un-American Activities Committee (HUAC) and on the Post Office and Civil Service Committee. On most votes, he opposed the programs of Presidents Kennedy and Johnson. While his was the only vote against the 1964 bill establishing the National Wilderness Preservation System, he advocated the acquisition of parkland in Texas and in 1960 recommended the creation of a lake near Dallas that would control Mountain Creek. (Joe Pool Lake, created after his death, resulted from this proposal.) Pool was reelected in 1964 and continued to oppose Johnson's Great Society measures. He also said that he would vote to declare war on North Vietnam, stating, "I think we should accelerate and get it over with as fast as possible." Early in 1966, Pool served as acting chairman of HUAC when it conducted hearings on the Ku Klux Klan. He became a national figure later that year when he chaired a subcommittee that held hearings on his bill to make it a federal crime to aid anyone engaged in an armed conflict against the United States. He subpoenaed the leaders of organizations that had resisted the Vietnam War by collecting money for North Vietnam or by blocking troop trains. The American Civil Liberties Union sought to stop the hearings as an infringement of free speech. A federal judge issued a restraining order, but Pool said he would hold the hearings anyway. Finally, an appeals court dissolved the order, and the hearings began on Aug. 16, 1966.

The proceedings were tumultuous. Hundreds of people filled the hearing room, and supporters of the antiwar movement heckled the subcommittee and its chairman. When Pool directed one witness, Stuart McRae, to answer a question put to him about the Medical Aid Committee at Stanford University, McRae responded, "I will not answer this question, on the grounds that it nauseates me and I am liable to vomit all over this table." Impatient with delaying tactics and personal abuse, Pool had more than fifty spectators and witnesses removed. Fifty-four people were arrested. Arthur Kinoy, one of the lawyers for the protesters, began a heated exchange with Pool that ended with the attorney being dragged from the room shouting, "Don't touch a lawyer." Other attorneys for the witnesses then left in protest. When the hearings concluded, the full committee sent Pool's bill to the House, where it passed in October 1966. The Johnson administration, which had debated whether the president should "publicly lower the boom on the Joe Pool bill," was not disappointed when the Senate adjourned without acting on the measure.

Pool's constituents cheered him when he returned to Dallas. "Most Americans live for the day when they can do something that will go down in history," he told them. "I feel like I did exactly that last week." The *New York Times*, on the other hand, called the hearings an "unseemly spectacle," and *Time* said that they set a new standard for "sheer summer madness." In the fall elections Pool ran from the newly apportioned Third Congressional District of Dallas County, where he faced strong Republican opposition. He narrowly defeated James M. Collins, his Republican challenger, with 34,890 votes to 30,186. The last years of his life were marked by minor legal troubles (such as arrests for reckless driving) and little of the public attention that had surrounded him in 1966. Pool died of a heart attack in the Houston airport. His wife was defeated in a special election to fill out his unexpired term. Pool's hearings exemplified the tensions that the Vietnam War produced in the 1960's and gave him a moment of celebrity in an undistinguished career. Joe Pool Lake is the most important legacy of his public service.

[Pool's papers are in the possession of his family. A clipping file is at the Dallas Public Library. The Lyndon B. Johnson Library also has documents relating to his career in Congress. See also University of Texas, *The Cactus* (yearbook; 1929–1933); "The Congress," *Time*, Aug. 26, 1966; Larry L. King, "Joe Pool of HUAC: McCarthy in the Round," *Harper's*, Nov. 1966; United States House of Representatives, *Hearings on H.R. 12047 . . . Bills to Make Punishable Assistance to Enemies of U.S. in Time of Undeclared War*, 89th Cong., 2d sess., 1967; United States House of Representatives, *Joe Richard Pool: Late a Representative from Texas* (1968); and Arthur Kinoy, *Rights on Trial* (1983). Obituaries are in the *New York Times* and the *San Antonio Express*, both July 15, 1968.]

LEWIS L. GOULD

POPE, JAMES PINCKNEY (Mar. 31, 1884–Jan. 23, 1966), lawyer, United States senator, and director of the Tennessee Valley Authority, was born in Vernon, La., the son of Jesse T. Pope, a farmer, and Lou McBride. There were thirteen children in his poor family, and he grew up accustomed to hard work. He became the Jackson Parish cotton-picking champion before leaving home to attend the Louisiana Polytechnic Institute, where he earned a bachelor of industry degree in 1906. He then worked his way through law school at the University of Chicago, where he received an LL.B. degree in 1909.

After graduation Pope set out for Europe on a cattle boat and toured the Continent on a bicycle. Upon his return to the United States, he decided to seek opportunity in the West. He apparently ran out of money in Boise, Idaho, and decided to settle there. In 1909 he joined the law firm of Morrison and Pence, but the following year he formed his own firm, Pope and Barnes. On June 26, 1913, he married Pauline Ruth Horn, whom he had met when they were both students at the University of Chicago; they had two children.

Pope quickly aligned himself with the Democratic party, which was in a minority in Idaho. He served as secretary of the Democratic Central Committee from 1914 to 1916 and as its chairman from 1920 to 1922. In addition, he was the Boise city attorney for 1916–1917 and in 1916 was deputy collector of internal revenue. From 1917 to 1919 he served as assistant attorney general for Idaho. He was a member of the Boise board of education from 1924 until 1929, when he won the office of mayor of Boise. He was reelected in 1931 without opposition.

By the time he was chosen mayor, Pope was recognized as a leader of the progressive, "dry" segment of the state's highly factionalized Democratic party. In 1928 he supported the unsuccessful bid of C. Ben Ross for the Idaho governorship, and in 1930, although mentioned as a possible gubernatorial candidate himself, he again endorsed Ross. In this campaign, effective organization of the dissident sections of the party brought the Democrats success, and two years later Pope's party loyalty was rewarded when he was given the Democratic nomination for the United States Senate. He had the advantage of running in 1932 on a platform he had personally written, deftly sidestepping the issue of repeal of Prohibition, which sharply divided Idaho Democrats, and focusing instead on the economic distress of the depression. He defeated Republican incumbent John Thomas by a vote of 103,020 to 78,225 in a state Democratic landslide.

In the Senate, Pope became one of the most ardent supporters of Franklin D. Roosevelt's New Deal. An internationalist in foreign affairs, he frequently found himself opposing Idaho's senior senator, the Republican isolationist William Borah. Trips to Europe in 1934 and 1935 convinced Pope more firmly of the need for American membership in the World Court. He was a consistent critic of neutrality legislation, and in 1935 he introduced a resolution in the Senate calling for United States participation in the League of Nations. As his reputation as an internationalist grew, his political fortunes declined in his home state, where he was sometimes referred to as "ambassador to Europe from Idaho."

Pope's support of the New Deal angered many of his constituents. He spoke out against the "strict" interpretation of the Constitution by which the Supreme Court declared unconstitutional many of the early New Deal acts. He also supported Roosevelt's "Court-packing" plan, as well as the administration plan for reorganization of the executive departments. In 1938 he cosponsored the second Agricultural Adjustment Act. He sought to balance the development of natural resouces and the preservation of the environment through the creation of national parks. He also advocated a Columbia Valley authority modeled after the Tennessee Valley Authority, another idea attacked by his political opponents in Idaho.

Pope also convinced the administration to appoint a presidential committee to study whether the development of power resources would promote the development of phosphate resources in Idaho. The committee, headed by Pope, began hearings on July 29, 1938, on the eve of Idaho's primary election. Pope's opponent in the 1938 Democratic primary was D. Worth Clark, a conservative, isolationist congressman who was supported by Governor Ross, from whom Pope had become increasingly alienated after 1933. National attention focused on the election as a test of New Deal popularity. Roosevelt and the Democratic party's national chairman, James Farley, strongly endorsed Pope, but to no avail. Clark won the primary by a vote of 43,736 to 40,726. Pope's defeat could be attributed not only to his internationalist, pro–New Deal stance but also to the fact that many Republicans crossed party lines to vote for Clark, apparently thinking he would be easier to defeat in the general election. Briefly considering a write-in campaign as an independent in the general election, Pope visited Roosevelt at Hyde Park, where he was apparently dissuaded from such an attempt. On September 4, Pope announced that he would support Clark and the entire Democratic ticket.

Pope was rewarded in 1939 when Roosevelt named him one of the three directors of the Tennessee Valley Authority (TVA). His tenure on the board brought a period of relative harmony in the TVA administration, where he was in the forefront in defending the agency from the attacks of conservatives and private industry. After his resignation from the TVA in May 1951, Pope practiced law in Knoxville, Tenn. In 1963 he moved to Alexandria, Va., where he died.

[Pope's papers are at the Idaho Historical Society, Boise, and the University of Tennessee, Knoxville. On his career, see "Persons and Personalities," *Literary Digest*, Sept. 7, 1935; "Political Phosphate," *Business Week*, Mar. 12, 1938; David E. Lilienthal, *The Journals of David E. Lilienthal*, I–II (1964); Michael P. Malone, C. *Ben Ross and the New Deal in Idaho* (1970); Robert C. Sims, "James P. Pope, Senator from Idaho," *Idaho Yesterdays*, Fall 1971; F. Ross Peterson, *Idaho: A Bicentennial History* (1976); and Paul K. Conklin and Edwin C. Hargrove, eds., *TVA: Fifty Years of Grass-Roots Bureaucracy* (1983). An obituary is in the *New York Times*, Jan. 24, 1966.]

MELBA PORTER HAY

POWDERMAKER, HORTENSE (Dec. 24, 1896–June 15, 1970), anthropologist, was born in Philadelphia, Pa., the daughter of Louis Powdermaker, a middle-class businessman, and Minnie Jacoby. Her father's success fluctuated, making her family aware of fine social distinctions. This experience contributed to her sensitivity to social facts. Her family settled in Baltimore about the time Powdermaker started school. She attended Western High School and graduated from Goucher College in 1919, having majored in history. Her first conscious encounter with anti-Semitism occurred when she tried to join a sorority; in reaction, she turned to the labor movement and socialism. Upon graduation, she accepted a position with the Amalgamated Clothing Workers and spent time in Cleveland as a union organizer. Although Powdermaker looked back on this work with nostalgia, she never felt fully accepted in the union hierarchy.

Powdermaker reentered intellectual life in 1925, enrolling at the London School of Economics to study geography and anthropology. After a class with Bronislaw Malinowski, she knew anthropology would be her lifework. (Her fellow students Raymond Firth and Isaac Shapera became major figures in British anthropology.) This was a time when Malinowski was combining Freudian psychology with anthropology and, above all, developing functional theory. With this theoretical background, Powdermaker settled in the New Ireland (Bismarck Archipelago) village of Lesu after completing her Ph.D. in 1928.

Powdermaker spent ten months in Lesu, becoming a pioneer among women anthropologists who did fieldwork alone in exotic places. Her data helped update and further the ethnography of Melanesia. She also extended the evidence for functional theory. After returning to the United States, she secured funding at the Institute of Human Relations at Yale University to write *Life in Lesu* (1933), which found an important place in anthropological literature, and to continue research.

At Yale, Powdermaker met Edward Sapir, whose interest in personality and culture further shaped her thinking. With his aid, she received a grant from the Social Science Research Council that allowed her to spend twelve months early in the Great Depression in Indianola, Miss. Fieldwork conditions were more difficult there than in Lesu. Powdermaker had to exert much tact to gain rapport with both blacks and whites. Introduced as a "visiting teacher," she found that her contacts were limited largely to women. The resulting work concentrated on education, religion, and the family, but her theoretical position demanded attention to all parts of culture. She managed this synthesis so well that she contributed much of the data used by John Dollard in *Caste and Class in a Southern Town* (1937), but she felt he failed to give her the credit she deserved.

Powdermaker's *After Freedom* (1939) was widely read by social scientists and read again after the White Citizens Council originated in Indianola. She concluded this phase of research with an influential article, "The Channeling of Negro Aggression by the Cultural Process" (*American Journal of Sociology*, 1943), which reflects her interest in a combination of psychology and anthropology.

Powdermaker's career as teacher began in 1938, when she became an instructor at Queens College in New York City, remaining until her retirement. There she soon established the Department of Sociology and Anthropology, which she sometimes chaired, and was notably successful as a professor; she also lectured at other universities as a visiting professor. She published *Probing Our Prejudices* (1944), which served as a high school text. After World War II she taught at the William Alanson White Institute of Psychiatry, Psychoanalysis, and Psychology.

During her Mississippi fieldwork Powdermaker attended movies to escape the stress of a biracial community, but even in this diversion she found data. Blacks and whites significantly differed in their interpretation of films. This interest led to a meeting with the director of the Viking Fund, Paul Fejos, a film director turned anthropologist. With his encouragement and aid in securing funding, Powdermaker went to Hollywood in 1946–1947. This fieldwork was even more untraditional than that done at Indianola. She spent most of her time interviewing rather than participating, and found herself frustrated with the values and practices of the film industry. In *Hollywood, the Dream Factory* (1950), Powdermaker showed that the values were a reflection of the community's social structure and that this structure determined the content of American films and restricted innovation and experiment. This work brought her recognition far beyond the field of anthropology.

Although discouraged by her Hollywood experience, Powdermaker maintained her interest in the relationship between society and mass communication. On sabbatical in 1953–1954, she went to Zambia (then Northern Rhodesia) to study culture change and the media. By gathering responses to film viewings, she found that respondents were readily grouped into traditionalists and modernists. Among teenagers, females continued to hold traditional values and the old outlook on life, but the young men who worked in new occupations and spent more time in cities were developing cosmopolitan life-styles. The results, reported in *Copper Town and Changing Africa: The Human Situation on the Rhodesian Copperbelt* (1962), show that Powdermaker found that functionalism was of less use in studying change than was theory derived from culture and personality.

Reflecting upon her lifework in *Stranger and Friend: The Way of an Anthropologist* (1966), which became her best-known book, Powdermaker emphasized how fieldwork is done. The book reveals how Powdermaker learned from psychoanalysis what motivated her selection of problems and their solutions. Her empathy with others clearly emerges, and it was a characteristic that inspired many of her students, who often saw her as a surrogate mother.

She enjoyed hosting parties for students as well as colleagues and developed a reputation as a charming, witty, and warm person who lent a helping hand in time of need. These attitudes were reflected in her care for her foster son, Won Mo Kim. When she retired from teaching in 1968, she became a research associate at the University of California at Berkeley, where she died.

[The Bancroft Library at Berkeley has a few letters of Powdermaker's in the A. L. Kroeber collection, but her will called for destruction of her papers. Eric R. Wolf wrote her obituary for the *American Anthropologist*, 73 (1971), which is accompanied by a bibliography and a tribute by George L. Trager. An obituary is in the *New York Times*, June 17, 1970.]

ERNEST L. SCHUSKY

PRESSMAN, LEE (July 1, 1906–Nov. 19, 1969), lawyer, was born in New York City, the son of Harry Pressman, a millinery manufacturer, and Clara Rich, both Russian immigrants. After graduating at sixteen from Stuyvesant High School, he enrolled at New York University and then Cornell. Aided by scholarships, he earned election to Phi Beta Kappa and graduated from Cornell in 1926. He then attended Harvard Law School and served on the law review. After graduation in 1929, he joined the New York law firm of Chadbourne, Stanchfield, and Levy; he specialized in cases involving corporate reorganization and pursued an interest in labor law by participating in the International Juridical Association. On June 28, 1931, he married Sophia Platnik; they had three children.

Soon after Franklin Roosevelt became president in 1933, Pressman was recruited by Jerome Frank, a member of his law firm, to serve as an assistant general counsel for the Agricultural Adjustment Administration (AAA). Clashing with the leaders of the AAA, he was fired in the "purge" of February 1935 and then became general counsel for relief programs and the Resettlement Administration. While serving the New Deal, Pressman joined the Communist party. Drawn in by Harold Ware, he was influenced apparently by concern about Hitler, the Great Depression, and what he perceived to be the defects of capitalism and the inadequacy of the New Deal. Although he left the party when he returned to private law practice in the winter of 1935–1936, he did not reject its ideology.

In 1936, John L. Lewis hired Pressman as general counsel for the Steelworkers Organizing

Committee and later for the Congress of Industrial Organizations (CIO). Pressman became one of Lewis' most important lieutenants and greatest admirers during a period of rapid growth in the American labor movement. The young lawyer impressed associates with his intellectual ability, his coolness and smoothness, his hard work, eloquence, and persuasiveness, and his athletic and well-dressed appearance. He also often seemed ambitious, hard, arrogant, eager for (and impressed by) power, cynical, and concerned more with means than ends. He saw himself as a creative, aggressive lawyer capable of representing labor effectively and in essential ways and as a man of strong convictions.

Pressman met frequently with American Communists in the CIO and tried to promote cooperation between them and non-Communists. He did not tell Lewis that he had belonged to the party, and Lewis did not ask, even though some people accused Pressman of being a Communist. Pressman saw Lewis, who had confidence that he could use Communists for his own purposes, as the dominant person in the labor organization.

From 1939 to 1941 the Communist presence was a hot issue in the CIO. At the organization's 1940 convention, Pressman, as secretary of its resolutions committee, dutifully moved adoption of a resolution denouncing both Communism and fascism. At the same time, his most important ally, Lewis, stepped down as president and was succeeded by Philip Murray, a devout Catholic with a negative attitude toward Communists. Murray, eager to avoid a split in the organization and convinced that Pressman was an able and reliable man, retained him as general counsel and relied heavily on him. After Germany invaded the Soviet Union in June 1941, Pressman became an active supporter of American participation in the war and strengthened his position. He pressed for labor policies designed to maximize the contributions of industrial workers to the war effort. Although anti-Communists continued to complain about Pressman, his non-Communist admirers insisted that he did not inject ideology into his work as a lawyer.

After World War II and with the onset of the cold war, Pressman's involvement with Communism again became an issue. Murray continued to admire him and to fear a weakening of the CIO, but the pressures on him to fire Pressman grew. Pressman, meanwhile, focused on the battle against the antiunion sentiment that culminated in the Taft-Hartley Act of 1947 and on drafting resolutions designed to hold rival CIO factions together. He also became interested in the third-party movement that centered around Henry A. Wallace, an outspoken critic of the Truman administration, especially its anti-Soviet foreign policy. Following Truman's veto of Taft-Hartley and the introduction of the Marshall Plan, the CIO executive board denounced Wallace's candidacy, and Murray felt compelled to force Pressman to resign in February 1948. Convinced that Wallace would attract millions of votes, Pressman became a leader of the Progressive party and ran for Congress from Brooklyn's Fourteenth District. Some of Wallace's foes used Pressman's participation as evidence of Communist control of the party.

In August 1948, Whittaker Chambers and Louis Budenz testified before the House Un-American Activities Committee (HUAC) that Pressman had been a Communist; Pressman himself refused to answer questions from the committee and the Federal Bureau of Investigation (FBI) about his affiliations. In November the Progressive party—and Pressman—suffered a crushing defeat.

Two years later, Pressman publicly broke with Communism, citing its support of "aggressive war" by the North Koreans and his desire to support the United Nations and his country. He discussed his past with HUAC on August 28 and with the FBI. Perhaps he hoped confession would revive his career, but he never reestablished himself in the labor movement or regained stature as a public figure. He died in Mount Vernon, N.Y. Pressman made some contributions to the New Deal and especially to the labor movement, but his opportunities to do more had been destroyed by his involvement with Communists and Communism in the 1930's and 1940's and the rise of a "red scare" in the United States after World War II.

[Pressman's life is surveyed in Murray Kempton, *Part of Our Time: Some Monuments and Ruins of the Thirties* (1955); and Eleanora W. Schoenebaum, ed., *Political Profiles: The Truman Years* (1978). The best discussion of Pressman's involvement in the New Deal is in Peter H. Irons, *The New Deal Lawyers* (1982). On Pressman's participation in the "Ware cell," see Herbert L. Packer, *Ex-Communist Witness* (1962); Earl Latham, *The Communist Con-*

troversy in Washington (1969); and Allen Weinstein, *Perjury: The Hiss-Chambers Case* (1978). Evidence on Pressman's activities in the labor movement is in Sidney Fine, *Sit-Down: The General Motors Strike of 1936–1937* (1969); Irving Bernstein, *Turbulent Years* (1970); Bert Cochran, *Labor and Communism* (1977); Melvin Dubofsky and Warren Van Tyne, *John L. Lewis* (1977); Harvey A. Levenstein, *Communism, Anticommunism and the CIO* (1981); Maurice Isserman, *Which Side Were You On? The American Communist Party During the Second World War* (1982); Nelson Lichtenstein, *Labor's War at Home* (1982); and Peter L. Steinberg, *The Great "Red Menace"* (1984). On Pressman and the Progressive party, see David A. Shannon, *The Decline of American Communism* (1959); and Curtis D. MacDougall, *Gideon's Army* (1965). Pressman's break with Communism is discussed in Robert K. Carr, *The House Committee on Un-American Activities, 1945–1950* (1952); and Walter Goodman, *The Committee* (1964). Pressman gave an interview to the Columbia Oral History Project, but it should be compared with the United States Congress, House Committee on Un-American Activities, *Hearings Regarding Communism in the United States Government*, 81st Cong., 2nd Sess. (1950). An obituary is in the *New York Times*, Nov. 21, 1969.]

RICHARD S. KIRKENDALL

QUILL, MICHAEL JOSEPH (Sept. 18, 1905–Jan. 28, 1966), labor leader, was born on a mountain farm, Gourtloughera, near Kilgarvan, County Kerry, Ireland, the son of John Daniel Quill, a farmer, and Margaret Lynch. He attended the Kilgarvan National School from 1910 to 1916. Quill's family actively supported the Irish Republican Army (IRA) during the Irish Rebellion and subsequent civil war. Quill belonged to Fianna Eireann, the Republican Boy Scout movement. In 1920 he joined the IRA and until 1923 saw sporadic service near his home. In 1926 he immigrated to New York, where he found work as a gateman for the Interborough Rapid Transit Company. Two years later he was promoted to ticket agent. Quill became a naturalized citizen in 1931. On Dec. 26, 1937, he married Maria Theresa O'Neill; they had one child.

In 1933, Quill belonged to a group of former IRA members that began exploring the possibility of forming a transit workers union. They soon joined forces with a Communist-led organizing drive. Quill was a charter member of the Transport Workers Union (TWU) when it was founded in April 1934. He was elected TWU president in December 1935, replacing Thomas O'Shea, who had been appointed to the office a year earlier. Quill held this post for the remainder of his life. In May 1937 the TWU received an international charter from the Committee for Industrial Organization (later the Congress of Industrial Organizations, or CIO). Shortly thereafter it won a series of recognition elections on the major New York mass-transit lines and signed contracts covering 30,000 workers. By the end of World War II, the TWU had gained another 15,000 members, including transit workers in Philadelphia and Chicago and utility workers in Brooklyn.

Until 1948, the TWU was politically aligned with the Communist party. The TWU leadership was unusually collective, but Quill was the union's most influential officer. He generally supported the Communist party position on labor and political issues and was active in several Communist-led organizations. It is not clear if he ever joined the Communist party; several former Communists claimed that he did, but Quill repeatedly denied this. Although the TWU was only a moderate-sized union, Quill, a member of the CIO executive board, developed a national reputation as a left-wing unionist and advocate of Irish causes.

In 1937, Quill was elected to the New York City Council as a candidate of the American Labor party (ALP). The ALP refused to endorse him for reelection in 1939 because he would not condemn the nonaggression pact between the Soviet Union and Germany. He narrowly lost the election but was returned to the council in 1943 as an independent. Two years later he was reelected with ALP backing and served until 1949.

In 1947, Quill succeeded Joseph Curran as president of the CIO's Greater New York City Industrial Union Council, a left-wing stronghold. In March 1948, Quill resigned from this position, signaling a break with the Communist party. He opposed the Communist party's decision to back Henry Wallace's presidential candidacy and the party's fight against Mayor William O'Dwyer's effort to raise the New York City transit fare. Other factors behind his political shift included domestic anti-Communism, internal changes in the Communist party, raids on the TWU by other unions, and pressure from O'Dwyer. Aided by O'Dwyer and the national CIO, Quill won a bitter struggle against TWU officials who remained allied with the Communist party.

Quill, after being reelected TWU president in December 1948, purged the union leadership of Communists and Communist sympathizers. Nonetheless, within the narrowed political spectrum of the labor movement of the 1950's and 1960's, Quill remained on the left. He generally supported liberal Democratic candidates but advocated the creation of a labor party. He endorsed the civil rights movement, opposed the Vietnam War, and called for the nationalization of major industry. In 1949 he was elected president of the reorganized New York City CIO Council and the following year became a vice-president of the CIO. He also served as a CIO delegate to the International Confederation of Free Trade Unions. Quill was the only head of a major CIO union to oppose the merger with the American Federation of Labor (AFL) in 1955. He criticized the AFL for tolerating racial discrimination, raiding, and racketeering. In 1961, two years after the death of his first wife, he married Shirley Garry, his administrative assistant. Also in 1961, he led an unsuccessful campaign to readmit the International Brotherhood of Teamsters to the AFL-CIO. During these years Quill traveled widely, returning often to Ireland.

Under Quill's leadership, the TWU reached a membership of 135,000 in 1966. In addition to transit workers, the TWU organized workers in the airline industry and in 1954 absorbed the United Railroad Workers Union (CIO). Quill helped lead transit strikes in several cities as well as a twelve-day strike against the Pennsylvania Railroad in 1960. In New York City he directed a successful campaign to win back the collective-bargaining rights the TWU had lost when the private subway and elevated lines were taken over by the city in 1940. In the process he helped establish important precedents for public-sector unionism.

Quill's public image was that of a militant unionist prone to theatrical gestures and extravagant rhetoric. Known for his sharp wit and use of ridicule, he was considered one of the best orators in the labor movement. Throughout his career he repeatedly threatened to call a general transit strike in New York City. In practice, however, after 1948 he worked closely with New York officials to maintain orderly labor relations. In the mid-1950's, Quill's conciliatory policies led to a proliferation of dissident groups and wildcat strikes. Finally, in January 1966, faced with widespread worker unrest and a hostile new mayor, John V. Lindsay, Quill called a strike against the New York City transit system. The walkout, which lasted twelve days, virtually paralyzed the city. On its fourth day, Quill, who had a history of heart disease, collapsed after being jailed for defying a court injunction. He remained hospitalized while the strike was settled on terms favorable to the union. He died shortly thereafter.

[Relevant union records and some of Quill's personal papers are in the Transport Workers Union Collection at the Robert Wagner Archives, New York University. Quill wrote a column for the *Transport Workers Bulletin* and the *TWU Express*. Several oral history interviews that discuss Quill, as well as films in which he is featured, are available at the Robert Wagner Archives. On his life and career, see L. H. Whittemore, *The Man Who Ran the Subways* (1968); and Shirley Quill, *Mike Quill—Himself* (1985). See also *Report of Proceedings, Transport Workers Union of America* (1937–1965); and *New York Times Magazine*, Mar. 5, 1950. An obituary is in the *New York Times*, Jan. 29, 1966.]

JOSHUA B. FREEMAN

RADEMACHER, HANS (Apr. 3, 1892–Feb. 7, 1969), mathematician and educator, was born in Wandsbeck, near Hamburg, Germany, the son of Adolph H. Rademacher, a merchant, and Emma Weinhöver. He attended the Hamburger Volksschule, the Eilbecker Realschule, and the Uhlenhorst Oberrealschule, completing his schooling by Easter 1911. He then entered the University of Göttingen, where he spent nine semesters studying mathematics, physics, and philosophy. Because his interests were broad and the lectures of the famous but aging Felix Klein were disappointing, Rademacher temporarily abandoned his mathematical pursuits in order to study philosophy with Leonhard Nelson. The influence of Richard Courant brought him back to mathematics, however, and Rademacher completed a dissertation on single-valued mappings and mensurability under Constantin Carathéodory, obtaining his doctorate in 1917. His studies were temporarily interrupted by military service in the German army during World War I.

Upon graduation from Göttingen, Rademacher obtained a position as mathematics teacher at a school with rather modern educational ideas in the idyllic hamlet of Wickersdorf, near Saalfeld. During his two years there he published five papers that extended his work on mapping and differentiability, including a long two-part paper that introduced the term "total differentiability," now in common use. In 1919 he left Wickersdorf for Berlin, becoming privatdocent under Carathéodory, who had left Göttingen and relocated at the University of Berlin. There he continued publishing in the areas of mensurability, real variables, convergence factors, and Euler summability of series, culminating his work in 1922 with a paper that introduced a type of orthogonal functions now generally known as Rademacher functions. While in Berlin he married Suzanne Gaspary in 1921; they had one child before their divorce in 1929.

In 1922, Rademacher was appointed assistant professor of mathematics at the recently created University of Hamburg. There, under the influence of Erich Hecke, Rademacher turned his attention to number theory, a subject that was to occupy much of his energy for the rest of his life and in which he made his most-outstanding contributions. In 1925, after writing two long papers extending Viggo Brun's methods in number theory, he was offered, and accepted, a position as full professor at the University of Breslau.

During his nine-year career at Breslau, Rademacher produced numerous studies in analytic number theory (particularly additive problems), functions of complex variables, Goldbach's problem, the Riemann zeta function, modular functions, and Dedekind sums. He also entered briefly the fields of theoretical physics and biology, writing two papers on Schrödinger's wave mechanics and one on certain mathematical aspects of genetics. He also produced, in collaboration with Otto Toeplitz of the University of Bonn, a book on number theory addressed to a wide, nonspecialized audience. This book, *Von Zahlen und Figuren* (1930), was eventually translated into nine languages and enjoyed numerous editions; in English it was known as *The Enjoyment of Mathematics* (1957). Rademacher's final work at Breslau was an excursion into geometry: he edited the posthumous manuscript of Ernst Steinitz on the theory of polyhedra, which was published as *Vorlesungen über die Theorie der Polyeder, unter Einschluss der Elemente der Topologie* (1934).

Rademacher's stay at Breslau ended in 1934 when he was forced out of his position by the Nazis for having participated in the International League for the Rights of Man and having served as chairman of the Breslau chapter of the Deutsche Friedensgesellschaft (German Society for Peace). He relocated to the small town of Nienhagen in Mecklenburg, on the Baltic coast. While there under less-than-ideal circumstances, he managed to write two mathematical papers on prime numbers in a real quadratic field. He also met and married Olga Frey; they had one child.

In late 1934, Rademacher accepted an invitation to spend two years at the University of Pennsylvania in Philadelphia as a Rockefeller Fellow. He returned to Germany briefly in the summer of 1935 but then resumed his association with the University of Pennsylvania. In spite of his full professorship in Germany and his international reputation, the university instated him as an assistant professor, a situation that was not remedied until 1939, when he was again made full professor.

Despite the disappointment at his initial demotion, Rademacher's work flourished in his new surroundings and his new language. He found professional stimulation from colleagues such as Antoni Zygmund and Isaac Jacob Schoenberg of the University of Pennsylvania, Arnold Dresden of nearby Swarthmore College, and his numerous graduate students, many of whom soon became productive mathematicians in their own right. Rademacher founded a departmental "problems seminar" that enjoyed widespread fame for over two decades.

It was during this period that Rademacher achieved, among numerous other accomplishments, his most singular result: an expression for, and a means of calculating, the partition function $p(n)$, which enables one to determine in how many ways integers can be added together to yield a given integer. This result had eluded mathematicians since Leonhard Euler had called attention to it two centuries earlier. Building on the work of Godfrey Harold Hardy and Srinivasa Ramanujan, Rademacher published the long-sought result in *Proceedings of the National Academy of Science*, 23 (1937). As an example of the application of his result, Rademacher showed that the partition function for the number 721 is a number containing twenty-seven digits.

In 1943, Rademacher became a naturalized citizen. His second marriage ended in divorce in 1947, and two years later he married Irma

Wolpe, the sister of his colleague Schoenberg and an accomplished pianist. The Rademacher home served as a meeting place for mathematicians, musicians, and other interesting personalities. Rademacher's interest in peace issues found an outlet in his association with the Society of Friends, with whom he remained active to the end of his life.

Rademacher enjoyed several leaves during his later years at institutions such as Haverford College, the Institute for Advanced Study in Princeton, the University of Oregon, the Tata Institute in Bombay, and his alma mater in Göttingen; numerous papers and four monographs resulted from these leaves. To honor him upon his retirement in 1962, the University of Pennsylvania organized the year-long Institute in the Theory of Numbers. After his retirement, Rademacher taught for two years at New York University and then at the Rockefeller Institute until a cerebral hemorrhage left him paralyzed from 1967 to the end of his life. He died in Haverford, Pa.

[Rademacher's papers are in the Rockefeller Archive Center at Pocantico Hills, North Tarrytown, N.Y. Emil Grosswald, ed., *Collected Papers of Hans Rademacher*, 2 vols. (1974), includes a biographical sketch, a portrait of Rademacher, and a list of his other works. Two other volumes of Rademacher's work are Emil Grosswald, ed., *Dedekind Sums* (1972); and Emil Grosswald, Joseph Lehner, and Morris Newman, eds., *Topics in Analytic Number Theory* (1973). Rademacher's Haverford lectures appeared as *Lectures on Elementary Number Theory* (1964). A brief autobiographical sketch of Rademacher's early years is in *German Mathematical Dissertations*, 29 (1915–1917). An obituary is in the *New York Times*, Feb. 9, 1969.]

RICHARD K. GEHRENBECK

RAINS, CLAUDE (Nov. 10, 1889–May 30, 1967), actor, was born William Claude Rains, in London, England, the son of Frederick William Rains, an actor, director, and producer of early silent films, and Emily Eliza Cox. Rains was sent at the age of nine to live with his grandparents in Kent. He subsequently ran away from school and, through a choirboy he met on the London streets, gained a place in a London choir. In 1900 he was one of a group of boy singers in a crowd scene in the Haymarket Theatre production of *Sweet Nell of Old Drury*; at the age of eleven he determined never to return to school. He later said that the only money he ever made apart from theatrical work was from his army service and from his farm in Pennsylvania.

Rains began as a callboy at His Majesty's Theatre, where he also trained in set building and in theatrical lighting. Soon he was holding the prompt book, and then moved up to assistant stage manager, with the aid of Sir Herbert Beerbohm Tree. At eighteen, now a stage manager, he was determined on an acting career. He had to overcome a lisp and other severe speech defects related to what he later called his "wrong side of the Thames" Cockney accent. The actors and directors at the theater gave him exercises at which he worked diligently.

In 1911, in a small role in Dunsany's *Gods of the Mountain*, Rains made his adult acting debut. He then toured Australia as actor–stage manager for a company of *The Bluebird*. Back in London in 1913, he became general manager, assistant director, and an actor in the repertory company of director-critic Harley Granville-Barker. Repertory gave Rains opportunities to play character roles in the classics, and he received good notices when the company toured the United States in 1913. During this tour Rains married the leading lady, Isabel Jeans, on May 4, 1913; they divorced in 1915, before the company returned to England. Rains enlisted in the London Scottish Regiment as a private, drawn, he said later, to the "gorgeous tartan" of the kilts. Gassed at Vimy Ridge, France, and transferred to a regiment from Bedford, Rains became a captain in 1919. Within a year of his return to the London stage he was acclaimed for his Casca in *Julius Caesar* and for his Khlestakov in *The Government Inspector*. On Feb. 3, 1920, he married the actress Marie Hemingway; they were divorced the same year. Rains had also begun to teach acting at the Royal Academy of Dramatic Art; John Gielgud, then one of his students, later recalled that Rains was "an enormous favorite" of the students, and that "most of the girls were in love with him." He next married Beatrix Thomson, the "most talented student" of 1922 at the academy, on Oct. 28, 1924. They were divorced in 1935.

Rains played leading roles, especially in George Bernard Shaw's plays at the Everyman Theatre; but in 1926, when his wife was offered the lead in the American company of *The Constant Nymph*, he accepted the role of the butler in order to be with her. His success on Broadway quickly surpassed hers. Rains starred as Samuel Pepys in *And So to Bed* (1927), played Napoleon in *Napoleon's Barber* (1927), and toured for the Theatre Guild as Volpone in the fall of 1928, after which he signed a contract with the Theatre Guild's repertory company. His wife, homesick and disappointed, left him to return to her own London career. Rains continued playing leads and character roles with the guild until the repertory company was disbanded in 1932. During the Great Depression, he became discouraged by lack of work in the theater and invested his savings in a farm in New Jersey, intending to live by farming. Lightning soon destroyed the farmhouse.

RKO invited him to do a screen test for the role of the mad father in *A Bill of Divorcement*, but he did not get the part. He then bought another farm, in Bucks County, Pa. The film director James Whale, who had known Rains in England, saw his test while searching for a lead for *The Invisible Man* and offered Rains the part and a contract with Universal Pictures. Almost entirely unseen in the film, Rains created the character through his voice, which was credited by critics with adding urbanity to the film. Rains, expecting disaster, had returned to Broadway in *They Shall Not Die* (1934) as the defense attorney; the play, which ran for eight weeks, was his last stage appearance for sixteen years.

As a character actor Rains tended to be cast as villains and madmen in Hollywood films. His first five films involved insanity, and two-thirds of his fifty-five roles were unsympathetic. His speciality was playing charming, likable villains or rogues, such as the prefect of police in *Casablanca* (1942).

Rains married Frances Propper on Apr. 9, 1935, having known her since touring in *Marco Millions* (1933) for the Theatre Guild. They had one child. He became an American citizen in 1938 and enlarged his farm to 350 acres, living there when not in Hollywood.

Rains had signed a long-term contract with Warner Brothers in 1936 and kept busy playing starring and supporting parts in a variety of films, from costume epics like *Anthony Adverse* (1936) and *The Adventures of Robin Hood* (1938) to the classic Frank Capra film *Mr. Smith Goes to Washington* (1939). In 1946, with four films starring Rains playing on Broadway at the same time (*Notorious*, *Angel on My Shoulder*, *Deception*, and *Caesar and Cleopatra*), film critic Bosley Crowther quipped, "It never rains but what it pours."

Rains was nominated four times for an Academy Award, for *Mr. Smith*, *Casablanca*, *Mr. Skeffington* (1944), and *Notorious* (1946). His fee for *Caesar and Cleopatra*, for which Shaw had personally chosen him, was reportedly the highest paid a British actor for a single role until that time; the *New York Times* gave it as $1 million, but in 1949 his agent said the net payment to Rains had been $100,000.

Rains returned to the stage in 1950–1951, at the playwright Sidney Kingsley's suggestion, in a dramatization of Arthur Koestler's *Darkness at Noon*. His performance as the imprisoned Bolshevik won six stage awards, including a best-actor citation from the Critics' Circle and the Antoinette Perry Award. He also received a gold medal from the American Academy of Arts and Letters for stage speech. His next Broadway appearance, in T. S. Eliot's *The Confidential Clerk* (1954) was also highly praised, but his last was in Arch Oboler's *Night of the Auk* (1959), which ran only one week.

He divorced Frances Propper in 1956; on June 14, 1959, he married the Hungarian pianist Agi Jambor, only to be divorced six months later. He married Rosemary Clark on Mar. 28, 1960, later selling his farm to move with her and her three children to Sandwich, N.H.

His last film appearances were in *Lawrence of Arabia* (1962), *Twilight of Honor* (1963), and *The Greatest Story Ever Told* (1965). A planned return to the stage in 1964 was prevented by his illness and by the death of his wife, who had been helping him with his autobiography. In later years he played numerous roles on television and made a number of dramatic recordings. One noteworthy example was Richard Strauss's *Enoch Arden*, with the pianist Glenn Gould. Rains had also won praise for his narration in Aaron Copland's *A Lincoln Portrait*, at the closing concert of the Philadelphia Orchestra season on Apr. 19, 1949. He died at the Lakes Region Hospital, near his Sandwich home.

Rains was one of that small cadre of character actors who, without ever becoming objects of cult worship, performed major and even starring roles in many dramatic films of Hollywood's studio era.

[The best source on Rains, Jeanne Stein, "Claude Rains," *Films in Review*, Nov. 1963, includes a complete filmography, a portrait, and photos of scenes from his major roles. An obituary notice is in the *New York Times*, May 31, 1967.]

DANIEL S. KREMPEL

RANDALL, CLARENCE BELDEN (Mar. 5, 1891–Aug 4, 1967), industrialist, was born in Newark Valley, N.Y., the son of Oscar Smith Randall, who ran a general store, and Esther Clara Belden. In 1906, Randall graduated as valedictorian of his five-member high school class. His mother, determined that Randall should be well educated, persuaded his father to move the family to Kingston, Pa., where Randall could attend Wyoming Seminary, a Methodist preparatory school. In 1908 she wrote to Charles Eliot, the president of Harvard, urging that a scholarship be awarded to Randall, which the university agreed to. The family moved to Cambridge, Mass., where his father worked as a coal salesman and Randall attended Harvard. Randall was elected to Phi Beta Kappa and received his B.A. in 1912 and his LL.B. from the Harvard Law School in 1915.

Declining a position with the prestigious firm of Cadwalader, Wickersham, and Taft in New York City, Randall moved to Ishpeming, Mich., to work in the law office of his cousin William P. Belden. Randall was admitted to the Michigan bar in 1915. In May 1917 he enlisted in the army officers' training program, was commissioned a first lieutenant in August, and was posted to Camp Custer, Mich., where he trained enlistees. On Aug. 18, 1917, he married Emily Fitch Phelps; they had two children. Ordered to France in July 1918, Randall served at the headquarters of the Thirty-fifth Division of the Allied Expeditionary Force. He was promoted to captain in February 1919 and was discharged that April.

Returning to Ishpeming, Randall became a partner in the firm of Berg, Clancey and Randall. In 1925 the Inland Steel Company invited Randall to become assistant vice-president in charge of their iron mines, ore fleet, and coal properties. For one year he also managed a steel-rolling mill for the company in Milwaukee. From 1930 until 1948 he was a vice-president and, from 1935 on, a member of Inland Steel's board of directors. Following a year's service as assistant to the president, Randall became president in 1949, and from 1953 to 1956 he served as chairman of the board and chief executive officer of the firm. Under his leadership, Inland Steel expanded its basic resources by acquiring extensive limestone, iron ore, and coal deposits. In the same period, Inland's capacity ranking among American steel firms went from eighth to seventh. From 1946 to 1956, Randall sat as a member of the Industrial Conference Board.

In the area of labor relations, Randall believed in corporate responsibility and collective bargaining. Critics dubbed the company's worker-welfare schemes "paternalism." In dealing with the United Steelworkers of America, Randall believed it unfair for the federal government to intervene in the process so as to prevent strikes, particularly when federal fact finders came down on the side of the workers. When President Harry Truman seized most of the nation's steel plants to forestall a strike during the Korean War, industry leaders asked Randall to address the nation by radio on their behalf. The address, characteristically composed without the help of speech writers or public relations experts, was blunt and to the point: he described the president's action as simple repayment of a political debt to the unions. The speech briefly made Randall a national celebrity.

Randall's public service began in 1948 as a steel consultant to the Economic Cooperation Administration in Paris. From 1951 to 1957 he was a member of the Department of Commerce's Business Advisory Council. With the advent of the Eisenhower administration in 1953, Randall was repeatedly pressed into service because he championed freer world trade. He was sent on special economic missions to Turkey in 1953 and 1956, he chaired the Commission on Foreign Economic Policy from 1954 to 1956, and he served as special assistant to the president on foreign economic policy from 1956 to 1961. President John F. Kennedy appointed Randall special emissary to Ghana in connection with the Volta River project in 1961 and chair of the panel that reviewed federal pay schedules in 1962–1963. In 1963, Randall was awarded the Presidential Medal of Freedom.

A conservative Republican in politics, Randall became an Eisenhower Republican after 1953. In the business world he was regarded as moderately liberal, for he criticized business leaders as frequently as he did labor unions. He believed in the value of a liberal education rather than in specialized training, especially for business executives. Randall sat on the board of trustees of the University of Chicago from 1936 to 1961 and was a member of the Harvard Board of Overseers from 1947 to 1953. Articulate and forceful with both the spoken and written word, and calm in debate, Randall was an effective spokesman for the causes in which he believed. Although Randall made his home in Winnetka, Ill., after 1925, he maintained a summer cottage near Ishpeming, where he died.

[Randall's papers are in the Seeley G. Mudd Manuscript Library at Princeton University. He wrote numerous articles and books, of which the most notable are *Civil Liberties and Industrial Conflict* (1938), with Roger N. Baldwin; *A Creed for Free Enterprise* (1952); *Freedom's Faith* (1953); *Over My Shoulder* (1956), a memoir; *The Folklore of Management* (1961); *Sixty-five Plus* (1963), a memoir; and *Making Good in Management* (1964). An obituary is in the *New York Times*, Aug. 6, 1967.]

GERALD G. EGGERT

RATHBONE, BASIL (June 13, 1892–July 21, 1967), actor, was born Philip St. John Basil Rathbone in Johannesburg, South Africa, the son of Edgar Philip Rathbone, a mining engineer, and Anne Barbara George. After spending his early years in the Transvaal, Rathbone was sent to England for his education. He attended the Repton School, where he was active in sports, debating, and music, although the classroom did not appeal to him. He worked briefly for an insurance company and then, in 1911, joined a theatrical company operated by a cousin, Sir Frank Benson. Rathbone's first appearance was as Hortensio in *The Taming of the Shrew* at the Theatre Royal in Ipswich. The following year he traveled with Benson's troupe throughout the United States. Among the parts he played were Fenton in *The Merry Wives of Windsor* and Paris in *Romeo and Juliet*, as well as other Shakespearean roles. In 1914 he performed in London for the first time, as Finch in *The Sin of David*.

During World War I, Rathbone enlisted as a private in the British army and rose to captain in the Liverpool Scottish Regiment. He fought at the front and received the Military Cross for gaining information about the enemy. After the war, he returned to the stage and appeared in a British film, *The Fruitful Vine* (1921). He married Ethel Marian Forman on Mar. 4, 1920; they had one child. In 1922 he played Count Alexei in *The Czarina*, starring Doris Keane, at the Empire Theater in New York City. When he appeared with Elsie Ferguson in *The Dark* (1925), a psychological drama, a Boston critic wrote that his portrayal of the tortured husband was "so true as to be almost painful."

Rathbone's long film career in Hollywood, mainly as a contract player for Metro-Goldwyn-Mayer and for Universal Pictures, began with *Trouping with Ellen* (1924). Tall, dark, and handsome, with finely chiseled features and an excellent profile, he made a vivid impression on the screen in a variety of productions that ranged from classics to low-grade horror films. His first marriage ended in divorce in 1925, and on Apr. 18, 1926, he married Ouida Bergere, a motion-picture scenario writer and actress; they had one child. He became a naturalized citizen in 1930.

The arrival of talking pictures was a boon to Rathbone, for he had fine diction, a resonant voice, and spoke with authority. His first talking picture was *The Last of Mrs. Cheyney* (1929). He was often cast as a swashbuckling villain in such parts as the pirate Levasseur in *Captain Blood* (1935), Sir Guy of Gisbourne in *The Adventures of Robin Hood* (1938), the unprincipled King Louis XI in *If I Were King* (1938), and the haughty Captain Esteban Pasquale in *The Mark of Zorro* (1940). His theatrical swordplay was brilliant; unlike many actors, he had taken fencing lessons as a young man and was highly skilled. He also created memorable roles as villains of a different sort: Mr. Murdstone in *David Copperfield* (1935), the self-righteous Karenin in *Anna Karenina* (1935), Pontius Pilate in *The Last Days of Pompeii* (1935), and the evil Marquis de St. Evremonde in *A Tale of Two Cities* (1935). During the 1930's he also exuded a sense of evil in horror films. Among them were *Tower of London* (1939), in which he was Richard III, with Boris Karloff as Mord the executioner. In *Son of Frankenstein* (1939), with Boris Karloff and Bela Lugosi, Rathbone was Dr. Frankenstein.

Despite a busy film schedule during these years, Rathbone retained his interest in the stage. He was coauthor, with Walter Ferris, of *Judas* (1929), in which he also starred; the play was not a success. In 1934 he made a 17,000-mile tour of the United States as Katharine Cornell's leading man in *Romeo and*

Juliet, *The Barretts of Wimpole Street*, and *Candida*.

Rathbone is best remembered for his portrayal of Sherlock Holmes in a series of films and on the radio, with Nigel Bruce playing Dr. Watson in both media. This role was not particularly to his liking, since he preferred the classics. Although he did not appear to take pride in his Holmes, he admitted that the famous detective had universal appeal. He had previously played Philo Vance in *The Bishop Murder Case* (1930), but even that renowned detective did not have the popularity of Holmes. Rathbone defined Holmes clearly as the scientific and logical detective with a sense of his own superiority. He fixed the part so indelibly in the minds of his audiences that they were ready to believe that he was the only authentic Holmes. The first of the Holmes films was *The Hound of the Baskervilles* (1939), and this was followed by thirteen others. "The Adventures of Sherlock Holmes," equally successful, began on the radio in 1939 and continued for six seasons.

World War II gave Rathbone the opportunity to play a sinister Nazi in both *Paris Calling* (1941) and *Above Suspicion* (1943), with Joan Crawford and Fred MacMurray. On Broadway, among other roles, he was the severe father, Dr. Sloper, in *The Heiress* (1947). During the 1950's and the early 1960's he again appeared in horror films. Although most of these were B-pictures, two of better quality were *Tales of Terror* (1962), with Vincent Price and Peter Lorre, and a spoof, *Comedy of Terrors* (1963), with Vincent Price, Boris Karloff, Peter Lorre, and Joe E. Brown. In contrast, he was a Boston aristocrat in *The Last Hurrah* (1958).

Rathbone worked steadily, appearing in about 150 films. His last stage appearance on Broadway was as Mr. Nickles, the devil, in Archibald MacLeish's *J.B.* (1959). During the latter part of his career he also visited colleges and gave readings from the works of Shakespeare, Browning, and other poets. He also recorded classics for Caedmon Records. He lived in New York City in his later years and continued to act until nearly the end of his life. In 1966 he appeared on the "Hallmark Hall of Fame" television show as the Duke of York in "Soldier of Love." He died in New York City.

[Material on Rathbone is in the New York Public Library's Performing Arts Research Center at Lincoln Center. His autobiography is *In and Out of Character* (1962). See also Charles Higham and Joel Greenberg, *Hollywood in the Forties* (1968); John Brosnan, *The Horror People* (1976); Jeffrey Richards, *Swordsmen of the Screen* (1977); and J. Fred MacDonald, *Don't Touch That Dial* (1979). An obituary is in the *New York Times*, July 22, 1967.]

ERNEST MCKAY

REID, HELEN MILES ROGERS (Nov. 23, 1882–July 27, 1970), newspaper executive, was born in Appleton, Wisc., the daughter of Benjamin Talbot Rogers, a hotel operator and owner of mining interests in Wisconsin and Michigan, and Louise Johnson. Business difficulties and the death of her father in 1885 irreversibly depleted the family's resources. She received encouragement from one of her older brothers, who in 1892, as headmaster of Grafton Hall, an Episcopal seminary for girls in Fond du Lac, secured a scholarship for his sister. In 1899 she enrolled at Barnard College in New York City. She managed and acted in school plays, sang in the chorus, turned a profit for the yearbook, and volunteered at the Henry Street Settlement. She chose zoology as her major, influenced by Henry Crampton, for whom she wrote a senior thesis called "The General Physiology of Minute Crustacea." Money from home completely disappeared in the middle of her college years, and she therefore took on clerical work in the bursar's office, tutoring, and dormitory housekeeping.

Rogers received her B.A. in 1903 and, with her mother as chaperone, was hired as social secretary to Elisabeth Mills Reid, who was the daughter of the financier Darius Ogden Mills and the wife of Whitelaw Reid, the owner of the *New York Tribune*. Elisabeth Reid admired Rogers' better education and her articulate decisiveness. For the next eight years, Rogers made the most of her knack for detail, an unfrivolous nature, and a determination to escape her family's genteel poverty. She started at $100 a month, twice the salary she was offered to teach school in the Midwest, and proved a good companion and increasingly indispensable manager for the lavish Reid households in Westchester, New York City, and London, where, from 1905 until his death in 1912, Whitelaw Reid was ambassador to the Court of St. James's.

Feeling burdened by "the almighty struggle for adjusting and manipulating everything for myself," Rogers became engaged in 1910 to Francis Nash, a Princeton graduate whose background resembled her own. Rogers' interest in Nash paled quickly, however, when she assessed his limited prospects as a small-town lawyer. She broke the engagement within a few months, much to the relief of Elisabeth Reid and her only son, Ogden Mills Reid, who had casually entertained Rogers for years. Attracted to Ogden Reid's sunny personality, though dubious of his intellectual abilities and flippant attitude toward work, Rogers married him in Appleton on Mar. 14, 1911; they had three children. Elisabeth Reid gave her daughter-in-law a generous monthly allowance and substantial cash gifts on each anniversary, effectively foreclosing Helen's dependence on her husband and permitting her to help her family.

Helen Reid began to study her husband's pursuits. As she had learned to use the *Social Register* and *Burke's Peerage* for Elisabeth Reid, she now made herself competent at shooting, golf, tennis, swimming, canoeing, and sailing. She took little interest in the *Tribune*, her husband's property after his father's death, until 1918, when her sister Florence moved east to help with the children and housekeeping, freeing Reid to become the *Tribune*'s advertising director. Her first two years with the paper were especially productive, with gross revenues increasing from $1.7 million to $4.3 million. The newspaper's historian, Richard Kluger, credits her with securing 90 percent of the increase. She personally interviewed and persuaded leading retailers to buy advertising space in the *Tribune*. She was made a vice-president in 1922 and helped arrange Elisabeth Reid's purchase of the *New York Herald* in 1924. The expanded paper, the *Herald Tribune*, returned a profit of over $1 million by 1928 and became one of the nation's best newspapers.

Reid bitterly blamed herself and her busy schedule for her daughter's death in 1924 from typhoid fever. A healthy child was born the next year, and she entrusted him to a nanny and returned to the newspaper. Her husband's ill health, a result of alcoholism, began to curtail his role at the paper and in Republican politics. She tried to fill the void, earning a reputation as "Queen Helen." At dinner parties, she combined prestige and politics, and illustrious guests were known to rise and answer her questions as if addressing a public meeting.

Although Reid was generally kept to the advertising side of the newspaper by her choice and her husband's design until his death in January 1947, when she succeeded him as president, her influence extended to editorial content. She brought the columnists Walter Lippmann and Dorothy Thompson to the paper and appointed Marie Mattingly Meloney director of the annual Forum of Current Events, which in the 1930's and 1940's served as the political agenda for an estimated 50,000 women's clubs. She helped establish the paper's Home Institute, a demonstration kitchen, and hired Clementine Paddleford as a food writer. She hired Dorothy Dunbar Bromley to write on social issues and her close friend Irita Van Doren, Wendell Willkie's companion, as the well-regarded editor of a Sunday literary section. She brought in the fashion arbiter Eugenia Sheppard and sent to Europe and the Far East the reporter Marguerite Higgins, one of the first women to cover a war and the first to win a Pulitzer Prize for doing so, for her coverage of the Korean War. The *Herald Tribune* is credited with having had more women staff members in the 1940's than any other American daily newspaper.

Reid traced her feminism to her Barnard years, noting that "working my way through, the necessity for complete independence of women was borne in upon me." She rallied to woman's suffrage as state treasurer for New York's successful 1917 campaign, helping to raise a half-million dollars. She was a trustee of Barnard from 1914 to 1956 and chairman from 1947 until her death. She instituted a liberal maternity leave policy at the college and solicited donations that enhanced its budget. She regularly endorsed educational advancement and economic independence for women, greater contributions by men to daily family life, and military service for women.

A liberal Republican all her life, Reid met with President-elect Warren Harding to influence his cabinet choices. She also advised the presidential campaigns of Wendell Willkie and Dwight D. Eisenhower. The latter appointed her in 1953 to the Committee on Government Contracts, investigating discrimination in the awarding of federal funds. Clare Boothe Luce said of Reid's influence in New York, "In those years, New York Republicanism was Helen Reid." Since a great deal of local and state politics was controlled by Democrats, Reid was not always in touch with decision-makers. Her preference for the social elite often inhibited, rather than fostered, her influence.

Similarly, at the *Herald Tribune* many associates thought she refused to promote capable Jewish staff members, some of whom left to pursue brilliant careers at the rival *New York Times*. In 1937 poor judgment led her to accept the Cuban Red Cross's Comendador Order of Honor and Merit in October and, the next month, to publish a forty-page supplement extolling Cuba's Fulgencio Batista, an essay purchased for $32,000 and not identified to the reader as an advertisement. She also lost irretrievable advertising and circulation to the *Times* because of her higher advertising prices, based on the assumption that the bulk of her newspaper's readers were, and should remain, well-to-do consumers.

In 1953, Reid became chairman of the *Tribune*'s board and relinquished the presidency to her son Whitelaw, retaining controlling stock ownership. In 1955 she eased Whitelaw out of the presidency to make way for her younger son, Ogden, who became president, publisher, and editor. Neither son succeeded at the editorial or business tasks of the paper, and in 1958 the *Herald Tribune* was sold to John Hay Whitney, who also was unable to reverse the decline. Renamed the *World Journal Tribune*, the paper closed in 1967, though offspring such as the *International Herald Tribune* and *New York* magazine continued to maintain independent publication. She died in New York City.

[Reid's papers are in the Library of Congress, but some letters remain in the family's possession, especially correspondence with her sister, Florence Rogers Ferguson. The Barnard College Archives contain material on her undergraduate and trustee activities and all honorary degrees and awards. See also Don Wharton, "The Girl Who Made Good," *Today*, July 11, 1936; Mona Gardner, "Queen Helen," *Saturday Evening Post*, May 6 and 13, 1944; "Recollections of Helen Rogers Reid '03," *Barnard Alumnae*, Fall 1970; and Richard Kluger, *The Paper: The Life and Death of the New York Herald Tribune* (1986). An obituary is in the *New York Times*, July 28, 1970.]

CAROLINE NIEMCZYK

REID, IRA DE AUGUSTINE (July 2, 1901–Aug. 15, 1968), sociologist and educator, was born in Clifton Forge, Va., the eldest son of Daniel Augustine Reid, a Baptist minister, and Willie Robertha James. Reid grew up in comfortable circumstances in Harrisburg, Pa., and Germantown, a Philadelphia suburb, where he attended public schools. The family moved to Savannah, Ga., when his father accepted a pastorate there in 1915. Recruited in 1917 by President John Hope of Morehouse College in Atlanta, Reid completed the college preparatory course at Morehouse Academy in 1918 and received his B.A. from Morehouse College in 1922.

From 1922 to 1923, Reid taught sociology and history and directed the high school at Texas College in Tyler, Tex. After graduate study in sociology at the University of Chicago during the 1923 summer session, he spent the following year as instructor of social science at Douglass High School in Huntington, W.Va. He was selected as a National Urban League Fellow for 1924–1925, and he earned an M.A. in social economics at the University of Pittsburgh in 1925. He was then appointed industrial secretary of the New York Urban League, a position he held until 1928. Reid married Gladys Russell Scott of Xenia, Ohio, on Oct. 15, 1925; they had one adopted child. From 1926 to 1928 he served as a first lieutenant in the New York National Guard.

During Reid's tenure with the New York Urban League, he surveyed the living conditions of low-income black families in Harlem, conducted an ambitious study that was published as *The Negro Population of Albany, New York* (1928), and worked as Charles S. Johnson's research assistant in a National Urban League survey of blacks in the trade unions. He also served as Johnson's research assistant in gathering data for the National Interracial Conference of 1928 in Washington, D.C. The conference yielded the landmark volume *The Negro in American Civilization: A Study of Negro Life and Race Relations in the Light of Social Research* (1930).

In 1928, Reid succeeded Johnson as director of research and investigations for the National Urban League. As part of the league's efforts to establish local branches, he conducted surveys of seven black communities in the United States. The most important studies are *Social Conditions of the Negro in the Hill District of Pittsburgh* (1930) and *The Negro Community of Baltimore: Its Social and Economic Conditions* (1935). Drawing on earlier league research, he also published one of the first reliable studies of blacks in the work force, *Negro Membership in American Labor Unions* (1930). From 1928 to 1934, he was enrolled as a graduate student in sociology at Columbia University, where he began research on West Indian immigration.

In 1934, John Hope, the president of Atlanta University, encouraged W. E. B. Du Bois, the chairman of the Department of Sociology, to recruit Reid. Du Bois, who in 1937 described Reid as "the best-trained young Negro in sociology today," worked closely with him until 1944. In that year Du Bois was forced to retire, and Reid succeeded him as chairman of the department. Having also served under Du Bois as managing editor of *Phylon: The Atlanta University Review of Race and Culture* since its founding in 1940, Reid succeeded Du Bois as the journal's editor in chief.

In 1936, under the auspices of the Office of the Adviser on Negro Affairs of the Department of the Interior, Reid directed a survey published as the first volume of *The Urban Negro Worker in the United States, 1925–1936* (1938), an undertaking financed by the Works Progress Administration. In 1939 he published *The Negro Immigrant: His Background, Characteristics and Social Adjustment, 1899–1937*, which was based on his dissertation. He earned his Ph.D. from Columbia University in that year. In 1940, Reid prepared *In a Minor Key: Negro Youth in Story and Fact*, the first volume of the American Youth Commission's study of black youth. He also drafted "The Negro in the American Economic System," a research memorandum used by Gunnar Myrdal in *An American Dilemma* (1944). He collaborated with the sociologist Arthur F. Raper on *Sharecroppers All* (1941), a study of the feudal political economy of the South.

After the death of Hope in 1936, Reid grew restless at Atlanta University. From 1945 to 1947 he was visiting professor of sociology at the New York University School of Education, the first full-time black professor at the university. Sponsored by the American Friends Service Committee, he also was visiting professor of sociology at Haverford College in Pennsylvania from 1946 to 1947. In 1948 he became professor of sociology and chairman of the Haverford Department of Sociology and Anthropology, a position he held until his retirement in 1966.

On Dec. 21, 1950, Reid and his wife joined the Society of Friends, and over the next fifteen years he was increasingly involved in the educational activities of the American Friends Service Committee. Although his scholarly output diminished during this period, his earlier professional contributions were fully acknowledged. He was assistant editor of the *American Sociological Review* from 1947 to 1950, vice-president and president of the Eastern Sociological Society from 1953 to 1955, and second vice-president of the American Sociological Society from 1954 to 1955. Despite the approval of his peers, the State Department suspended Reid's passport from 1952 to 1953 for suspected Communist sympathies. When he challenged that action, his passport was returned.

In the wake of the 1954 Supreme Court decision in *Brown* v. *Board of Education*, Reid was invited to edit "Racial Desegregation and Integration," a special issue of the *Annals of the American Academy of Political and Social Science* (March 1956). His first wife died a short time later, and on Aug. 12, 1958, he married Anne M. Cooke of Gary, Ind.

Late in his career Reid appeared more frequently in the public eye. He served on the Pennsylvania Governor's Commission on Higher Education and was a participant in the 1960 White House Conference on Children and Youth. In 1962 he was visiting director of the Department of Extramural Studies at University College in Ibadan, Nigeria, and from 1962 to 1963 he was Danforth Foundation Distinguished Visiting Professor at the International Christian University in Tokyo. He retired as professor of sociology at Haverford on June 30, 1966, and died in Bryn Mawr, Pa.

[No comprehensive collection of Reid manuscript materials exists; his personal papers are with his family. A bibliography of his writings from 1925 to 1959, prepared by Reid in 1960, is available in the Ira De A. Reid File, Office of College Relations, Haverford College, Pa. Information about Reid and his work, as well as relevant memoranda and correspondence, can be found among the papers and records of W. E. B. Du Bois; Haverford College Office of College Relations and the Haverford College Library's Quaker Collection, Haverford, Pa.; John Hope Presidential Papers, Special Collections/Archives, Robert W. Woodruff Library, Atlanta University, Atlanta, Ga.; Charles S. Johnson Papers, Special Collections, Fisk University Library, Nashville, Tenn.; National Urban League records, Library of Congress, Washington, D.C.; *Phylon* editorial correspondence, Atlanta University; Race Relations Department of the United Church Board for Homeland Ministries, Amistad Research Center, Tulane University, New Orleans, La.; Julius Rosenwald Fund Archives, Special Collections, Fisk University Library, Nashville; and Urban League of Philadelphia records, Urban Archives, Temple University, Philadelphia, Pa. The biographical sketch in James E. Blackwell and Morris Janowitz, eds., *Black Sociologists: Historical and Contemporary Perspectives* (1974), is untrustworthy. Obituaries are in the *New York Times*, Aug. 17, 1968; and the *Philadelphia Evening Bulletin*, Sept. 19, 1968.

PAUL JEFFERSON

REIK, THEODOR (May 12, 1888–Dec. 31, 1969), psychoanalyst and writer, was born in Vienna, Austria, the son of Max Reik, a civil servant, and Caroline Trebitsch. His family lived in genteel semipoverty. Reik's father died in 1906, the year that Reik entered the University of Vienna to study literature and psychology. Reik supported himself throughout his years at the university by tutoring and doing odd jobs.

In 1910 Reik met Sigmund Freud and began a professional and personal relationship that survived Reik's later theoretical deviations from Freud's teachings. Reik became Freud's pupil and protégé. Freud contributed to Reik's financial support, advised against a medical degree in favor of research and writing, and arranged for Reik's analysis with Karl Abraham, who waived his fee.

Reik earned his Ph.D. in psychology in 1912. His doctoral thesis, a psychoanalytic study of Gustave Flaubert's *Temptation of St. Anthony*, was the first dissertation in the field of psychoanalysis to be accepted by the university. In 1914 Reik married a woman who is referred to as "Ellie O" in his autobiographical writings; they had one child. The next year Freud presented Reik with the First International Prize for his essay in applied psychoanalysis, "The Puberty Ritual of Primitives."

Reik served in the German army for three years during World War I. In 1919 he published his first book, *Das Werk Richard Beer-Hofmanns*. From 1918 to 1928 he lived and practiced in Vienna, and was a participant in Freud's famous pedagogical Wednesday evenings. In 1928 Reik moved to Berlin, where he taught at the Berlin Psychoanalytic Institute. In 1933, with the growth of Nazi power, he fled to The Hague. That year his wife died. He then married Marija Cubelik; they had two children. The family immigrated to the United States in 1938.

Reik arrived in New York City penniless, with a pregnant wife and two children, but with twenty-five years of experience in psychoanalysis and fifteen books to his credit. He was disappointed by his reception in the psychoanalytic community and embittered by the refusal of the New York Psychoanalytic Institute to grant him full membership because he lacked an M.D. Nevertheless, he soon established a thriving private practice, and he set up a clinic for people who could not afford the high fees of most psychoanalysts. In 1946 he established the National Psychological Association for Psychoanalysis, an organization that accepted both physicians and nonphysicians. Reik was naturalized as an American citizen in 1944. He died in New York City.

Reik was a cultivated man with a wide range of interests. He was a prolific and vivid writer who frequently drew on his own experiences as well as those of his patients. His work was liberally sprinkled with references to history, literature, and music. He was an exploratory thinker who questioned established psychoanalytic ideas and suggested innovations in theory and practice. Yet he apparently did not arouse the hostility of his colleagues. His style was lively, colloquial, and anecdotal. He wrote fifty books and innumerable articles on myth, ritual, religion, crime and punishment, love, sex, and the problems of psychoanalytic practice. His writings about Freud often focused on his own experiences with the founder of psychoanalysis.

Several major themes stand out in Reik's work. In *Listening with the Third Ear* (1948), his fullest exploration of the practice of psychoanalysis, he discussed the crucial importance of intuition in psychoanalysis and the unconscious "duet" of patient and therapist, with "surprises" arising from this underground communication leading to therapeutic progress. He believed that therapists should rely primarily on their own unconscious in their responses to their patients, and that theoretical assumptions often only stood in the way.

In what he considered his most significant work, *Masochism in Modern Man* (1941), Reik analyzed the role of masochism in human relations. He saw the masochist as "a pleasure seeker" willing to endure pain and humiliation in order to be loved. Reik disagreed with some orthodox Freudian emphases and criticized what he called the "grotesquely sexual" nature of the psychoanalytic view of human nature. Reik denied both the theory that all neuroses had a sexual base and the idea of the sublimation of sex. He believed that neurosis was primarily due to a weakness of ego and the resultant inability to handle inner conflict.

Reik perhaps was not in the first rank of creative practitioners and theorists, but he was a stimulating and provocative writer and personality who permitted himself to wonder and speculate freely in a substantial body of work. His contribution was as much in his sanction of divergence and free thinking in psychoanalytic theory as in the specific content of his ideas.

[Reik's works include *Ritual* (1931); *Masochism in Modern Man* (1941); *Listening with the Third Ear* (1948); *From Thirty Years with Freud* (1949); *Fragments of a Great Confession: A Psychoanalytic Autobiography* (1949); *Myth and Guilt* (1957); and *Pagan Rites in Judaism* (1964). See Robert Fleiss, *The Psychoanalytic Reader* (1948); Robert Lindner, *Explorations in Psychoanalysis* (1953); Frederick Redlich and Daniel Freedman, *Theory and Practice of Psychiatry* (1966); and Erika Freeman, *Insights* (1971). An obituary is in the *New York Times*, Jan. 1, 1970.]

EDNA A. LERNER

REINHARDT, AD (Dec. 24, 1913–Aug. 30, 1967), painter, was born Adolf D. Frederick Reinhardt in Buffalo, N.Y., the son of Frank Reinhardt, a Lithuanian socialist of German extraction who emigrated to the United States in 1907 and became a tailor, and Olga Melitat, who emigrated to America in 1909. Reinhardt was raised in New York City's boroughs of Brooklyn and Queens. As a student at the Merton High School in Elmhurst, Queens, he did commercial art for Columbia Pictures, illustrated the books *Voice* and *Speech Problems*, and took summer jobs with newspaper agencies.

After rejecting scholarships to art schools, Reinhardt entered Columbia University in 1931 and graduated with a B.A. in 1935. In the summer of 1932 he worked in Warner Brothers' art department. At college he was an intramural wrestling champion but was thrown off the team for not staying in training. He was elected to the university's student board on the promise to abolish fraternities. He studied painting at Teachers College, where he made menus for the cafeteria. In one of his papers he praised the international style in architecture because it was "intelligent and cold, calm and impersonally happy," a forecast of his own reductivist style in art.

In 1936, Reinhardt began to study art history at Columbia University's Graduate School of Fine Arts. He also studied painting with Karl Anderson and John Martin at the National Academy of Design and in 1936–1937 with Carl Holty and Francis Criss at the American Artists School. In 1937 he joined the Artists' Union and the American Abstract Artists and was hired by Burgoyne Diller for the Federal Art Project, from which he was fired in 1941 for sending a painting to the Moscow Art Festival. In 1939 eight of his paintings were shown at the New York World's Fair. He was doing paintings and collages, a few of which were of rectangular facades punctuated by rows of windows but many of which were nonobjective combinations of rectangular, trapezoidal, and curvilinear planes. He also combined stances on art with art-making; thus, he designed the broadside handed out by those picketing the Museum of Modern Art in April 1940 against that museum's reluctance to exhibit work by current American modernist artists.

Consistently nonobjective in his painting after 1940, Reinhardt is usually grouped with the New York school of abstract expressionism, but he was a gadfly within the group. He became known as "the black monk" of abstract expressionism, partly because he painted at night but mainly because he adopted a position in his work that was more ascetic, less personal, and less emotive than that of Jackson Pollock, Mark Rothko, Willem de Kooning, and others within the group. Although his painting in 1949–1950 was gestural and painterly, by 1952 he was revolting against cubism and the expression of the personality in art. His canvases appeared as monochrome color fields. Only on close examination could one discern that there were a number of rectangles very close in tone to that of the total field. In this apparently featureless painting he anticipated the minimalist approach of postpainterly abstraction, or nonobjective painting, after 1960.

Reinhardt set himself up as an aesthetic, even moral, arbiter within art. He urged an art with "no lines or imaginings, no shapes or composings or representings, no visions or sensations or impulses, no symbols or signs or impastos, no decoratings or colorings or picturings, no pleasures or pains, no accidents or readymades, no things, no ideas, no relations, no attributes, no qualities—nothing that is not of the essence." He insisted that "the one thing to say about art and life is that art is not life and life is not art." Reinhardt could be specific and vitriolic in his condemnations: he called Rothko "a *Vogue* magazine cold-water-flat-Fauve"; Pollock, "the *Harper's Bazaar* bum"; and Barnett Newman, whose canvases were somewhat like his in featuring broad, consistently painted rectangles, "the avant-garde huckster-handicraftsman and educational shopkeeper." Nor did he trust the cultural establishment, as seen in his reference to the Museum of Modern Art as "the Museum of Middlebrow Art." At the same time, Reinhardt often remained within the mainstream, as when he designed baseball magazines for the New York Yankees and Brooklyn Dodgers in 1942.

In April 1944 he entered the United States Navy, was assigned to photography school in Pensacola, Fla., and served as a photographer's mate on the SS *Salerno*. He was hospitalized as an "anxiety case" in San Diego, Calif., and was given an honorable discharge. Under the GI Bill, he studied Asian art history at New York University's Institute of Fine Arts for six years, beginning in 1946. In 1945 he married Elizabeth Armand Decker; they had no children before their divorce in 1949. He had his first one-man gallery exhibition in 1944 at New York's Artists Gallery, and in November 1946 he was given the first of his many exhibitions at the Betty Parsons Gallery.

Reinhardt taught at Brooklyn College from 1947 to 1967 (he was made a full professor in 1965), the California School of Fine Arts in San Francisco in 1950, the University of Wyoming in 1951, the School of Fine Arts at Yale in 1952–1953, and Syracuse University in 1957. His students appreciated and sometimes venerated him, describing him as "spiritual." On Feb. 17, 1953, he married Rita Ziprokowski; they had one child. He traveled to Europe for the first time in 1952 and visited Japan, India, Iran, and Egypt in 1958 (there is a hermetic side to his art, suggesting the influence of Eastern religions) and Turkey, Syria, and India in 1961. In 1967 he received a Guggenheim Fellowship. He died in New York City.

[The Reinhardt Archive, Archives of American Art, New York and Washington, D.C., contains his elaborate charts on the history of art on microfilm-illustrated notes. Reinhardt coedited with Robert Motherwell *Modern Artists in America* (1950). See also Barbara Rose, ed., *Art-as-Art: Selected Writings of Ad Reinhardt* (1975). On his life and work, see Bruce Glaser, "Interview with Ad Reinhardt," *Art International*, Dec. 10, 1966; Irving Sandler, *The Triumph of American Painting* (1970); Düsseldorf Kunsthalle, *Ad Reinhardt* (1972); Marlborough Gallery, *Ad Reinhardt: A Selection from 1937 to 1952* (1974); Margit Rowell, *Ad Reinhardt and Color* (1980); Lucy R. Lippard, *Ad Reinhardt* (1981); Corcoran Gallery of Art, *Ad Reinhardt: Seventeen Works* (1984). An obituary is in the *New York Times*, Sept. 1, 1967.]

ABRAHAM A. DAVIDSON

REUTHER, WALTER PHILIP (Sept. 1, 1907–May 9, 1970), labor leader, was born in Wheeling, W.Va., the son of Valentine Reuther, a brewery-wagon driver, and Anna Stocker. Both of Reuther's parents had emigrated as children from Germany. His father, who became an insurance agent in 1914, was an ardent trade unionist and Socialist, and was active locally in both spheres. Reuther's future career, as well as those of his younger brothers, Roy and Victor, was rooted in the working-class identification and social-justice idealism inculcated by Valentine Reuther. At the age of sixteen, Reuther left high school and became an apprentice die maker at the Wheeling Steel Company. In 1927 he moved to Detroit, found work at the Ford automobile plant, and swiftly acquired a high rating as a supervising die maker. While working full-time, Reuther resumed his schooling, finishing high school and in 1930 enrolling at Detroit City College (later Wayne State University).

As the Great Depression deepened Reuther became increasingly active in politics both on campus and in the presidential campaign of the Socialist Norman Thomas in 1932. He also joined the small Auto Workers Union, an affiliate of the Communist Trade Union Unity League. Laid off at Ford (he suspected it was because of his union activity), Reuther set off in February 1933 with his brother Victor on a long-contemplated trip to Europe. In Germany they witnessed the Nazi seizure of power and acted briefly as couriers in the underground resistance. They left Berlin on Nov. 15, 1933, for their ultimate destination in the Soviet

Union: they had signed on for jobs at the Gorki auto works, which had acquired Ford equipment and desperately needed experienced auto workers. Although troubled by the increasingly repressive Stalin regime, Reuther had not lost his basic sympathy for the Soviet experiment when he left after nearly two years. His own place, however, was within the democratic socialist Left.

Reuther and his brother returned to the United States, via Siberia and Japan, at an auspicious moment in the history of the American labor movement. The unionization of the mass-production sector, after a false start in 1933–1934, was about to commence in earnest. In automobile manufacturing, as elsewhere, the membership gains of the National Recovery Administration (NRA) period had mostly disappeared, but the United Automobile Workers (UAW) of America, part of the American Federation of Labor (AFL), contained the nucleus for the reorganization of the auto workers. In October 1935, Reuther attended the AFL convention in Atlantic City, at which the labor movement split over the industrial-union issue. With the launching of John L. Lewis' Committee for Industrial Organization (after 1938, the Congress of Industrial Organizations, or CIO), Reuther moved single-mindedly to establish himself within the reviving UAW. Although he was jobless, he gained a card in early 1936 in the tiny left-wing UAW Local 86 at the General Motors (GM) Ternstedt plant on Detroit's West Side, and on March 15, he married May Wolf (they were to have two children). A month later, he went as the local's delegate to the South Bend, Ind., convention, at which the UAW for the first time elected a president from its own ranks and effectively declared its independence from the AFL; soon after, it would affiliate with the CIO. The South Bend convention was made for a brash young fellow with well-honed debating skills and solid left-wing credentials. Reuther, never at a loss for words or self-confidence, played a prominent part in the proceedings and was elected to the general executive board.

Reuther was quick to prove himself. He became president of the amalgamated Local 174, whose jurisdiction covered the entire Detroit West Side. The potential membership, scattered in many parts factories and several major assembly plants, numbered 100,000; the actual membership was less than 100. In December 1936, Reuther and his brothers engineered a strike at the Kelsey-Hayes Corporation, a supplier of brakes and wheels for Ford; this started an influx of recruits into Local 174. From that point onward, the West Side provided Reuther with a secure base of support. A week after the Kelsey-Hayes settlement, there broke out the sit-down strike at Flint, Mich., that led to GM recognition of the UAW. Although Reuther provided timely support, he was not centrally involved at Flint, but his brothers, Victor and Roy, were, and the great victory thereby redounded to the Reuther name. On May 26, 1937, Reuther and other UAW organizers were brutally assaulted by Ford goons in the "Battle of the Overpass" in front of the Ford River Rouge plant. Vivid news photographs strengthened Reuther's standing: he had shed blood for the auto workers.

Factional strife over the next two years tested Reuther's capacity for survival. The UAW divided into two great coalitions roughly along ideological lines. The left-wing Unity Caucus included the Reuther and Communist groups but also many others who had lost patience with the weak leadership of the union president, Homer Martin. In 1938 the uneasy standoff ended. The Communists abandoned Reuther for the sake of an alliance with the most powerful faction of the conservative Progressive Caucus, the Chrysler locals led by the union vice-president, Richard Frankensteen. Instead of linking up with Reuther, the equally isolated Martin tried to use his presidential powers to crush the opposition. The effect was to split the UAW apart, with Martin leading his remnant following into the AFL in March 1939. Under CIO supervision, the political situation inside the UAW was stabilized, and a popular but neutral figure, R. J. Thomas, was installed as president.

One of Thomas' first moves was to appoint Reuther director of the General Motors Department, which had become virtually a paper organization by mid-1939. As on the Detroit West Side three years earlier, Reuther showed himself to be a brilliant tactician. He focused on the GM tool and die makers, pulling out the few militant shops and, as these strikes succeeded, extending the walkout to the tool and die makers in other GM plants. With retooling for the 1940 models thus stymied, GM gave in and recognized the UAW as the bargaining agent for the company's tool and die makers.

The reorganization of the GM production workers quickly followed, succeeded by victories elsewhere in the industry and finally at Ford in 1941. Since Reuther emerged as the preeminent bloc leader, he became the focus against which rival factions coalesced. These included the Communists, by now implacably opposed by Reuther; their sympathizer at the top of the union hierarchy, the secretary-treasurer, George Addes; and the president, Thomas, along with his diverse following.

The coming of World War II offered Reuther a wider stage. As the nation struggled to rearm in 1940, he put forward a bold plan for reaching the defense goal of "500 planes a day." Drawing on his tool-and-die-making expertise, he argued that auto plants could be converted to aircraft production. His plan also called for granting labor an equal voice with management in the direction of the reconstructed industry. Company opposition doomed the plan, although its technical feasibility was amply demonstrated once the country actually entered the war. A succession of other proposals established Reuther's reputation as the ablest of a new generation of trade-union leaders. He was clearly seeking to exploit the wartime emergency to bring about reforms that would guarantee a full-employment economy and enlarge labor's voice in industrial and national affairs.

This progressive campaign culminated in his battle against GM in the reconversion period. Reuther made company pricing a bargaining issue. When GM responded that it could not give a wage increase (the union was demanding 30 percent) without a price increase, Reuther proposed that the company "open the books." No other union, not even the other UAW units, followed Reuther's lead. While striking GM workers held out for 113 days in 1945–1946, the rest of the labor movement settled for substantial increases with no restraint on pricing. Thus undercut, Reuther's effort at reforming collective bargaining failed.

Reuther was more successful in advancing his trade-union career. In 1946 he narrowly defeated Thomas for the UAW presidency. It required another year of furious politicking to seize the other national offices from the Thomas-Addes caucus. Reuther then mercilessly purged the union hierarchy of his opponents and established himself unassailably at the helm of the UAW. On Apr. 20, 1948, Reuther barely survived a shotgun attack that crippled his right arm, and a year later, his brother Victor was similarly assaulted and lost an eye; neither crime was ever solved. For Reuther, one of the burdens of success became a lifetime of confining security arrangements.

Once he had consolidated his position within the union, Reuther went on the offensive against the Communists elsewhere in the CIO. The issue, Reuther argued, was over priorities: Were the Communists first of all trade unionists or party adherents? Their support of the Progressive party in 1948, despite CIO endorsement of the Democratic ticket, provided Reuther with the ammunition he needed. He took the lead in the expulsion of eleven Communist-dominated unions from the CIO in 1949. He became a prominent figure in the anti-Communist Left. He was a founder of the Americans for Democratic Action in 1947 and two years later led the CIO delegation to the London conference that set up the International Confederation of Free Trade Unions. Reuther never adopted the hard-line stance of AFL leaders, however. He was not one to boycott Communist unions abroad or to accept reactionary regimes as legitimate allies against Communist subversion.

Within American politics, Reuther moved toward the center. In 1939, after a decade of activity (including a run for the Detroit City Council in 1937), he left the Socialist party. Although reluctant to join the Democrats, he became a consistent supporter of Franklin Roosevelt and other New Deal candidates. After Harry Truman's unexpected victory in 1948, Reuther came to accept the fact that the Democratic party was the only viable instrument for labor politics in America. His desire, never fully realized, was to help bring about a restructuring of the party system along class lines so that the Democratic party would take on the role that labor and social democratic parties played in European politics. He became a major force within the Democratic party: he was instrumental in John F. Kennedy's campaign for the presidency in 1960 and in the shaping of the civil rights and welfare legislation of Lyndon Johnson's administration.

Thwarted in his hopes for a broader industrial role for the UAW, Reuther became a brilliant practitioner of collective bargaining. He was a supremely skilled tactician. Exploiting the automakers' competition, his strategy was to single out one firm for strike action and then to extend the gains achieved there to the rest of the industry. Innovative in the bargaining goals he set for the UAW, he aimed above all at extracting from employers the security protections not forthcoming from the state—adequate, employer-funded pensions (beginning in 1950 at Chrysler), medical insurance (beginning at GM in 1950), and supplementary unemployment benefits (beginning at Ford in 1955). Productivity gains and cost-of-living allowances also were forthcoming, although initially at the suggestion of GM in 1948. In an era of economic expansion, Reuther in effect collaborated with the industry in the exchange of monetary and security benefits for labor peace and shop-floor discipline.

The UAW was the largest union in the CIO, and Reuther was, by common consent, the most gifted of its leaders. When CIO president Philip Murray died in 1952, Reuther succeeded him. An advocate of labor unity, Reuther played a crucial part in the negotiations that led to the merged AFL-CIO in 1955, but labor unity never fulfilled Reuther's hopes for a revival of labor's flagging organizing zeal or for a renewal of the social vision of earlier CIO days. Reuther found himself increasingly at odds with AFL-CIO president George Meany, who was a product of labor's conservative craft traditions. Their differences crystallized around foreign-policy issues. Although striving to remain loyal to the Johnson administration, Reuther grew disillusioned with the Vietnam War and clashed repeatedly with the hard-line Meany. Even more fundamental was Reuther's conviction that organized labor was out of step with the emergent reform movements concerned with the environment, peace, and minority rights. In early 1968 the UAW left the AFL-CIO. No other unions followed, and the Alliance for Labor Action that Reuther founded in 1969 was a strange marriage of opposites, for it included only the UAW and the powerful Teamsters' Brotherhood, which Reuther had helped expel from the AFL-CIO in 1957 for corruption.

Reuther and his wife were killed in a plane crash at Pellston, Mich., near where the UAW was completing a favored project of Reuther's, the Black Lake recreation and education center. The isolation in which Reuther found himself at the time of his death suggests that, had he lived, he would not have been able to materially alter the future course of the labor movement.

[The Archives of Labor History and Urban Affairs at Wayne State University serve as the depository for UAW records and contain Reuther's papers. A collection of Reuther's writings is Henry P. Christman, ed., *Walter P. Reuther: Selected Papers* (1960). Reuther's speeches and views are in the convention proceedings of the UAW, CIO, and AFL-CIO. The best biography is John Barnard, *Walter Reuther and the Rise of the Auto Workers* (1983), which includes a bibliographical essay. Victor G. Reuther, *The Brothers Reuther and the Story of the UAW* (1976), is the most revealing biographical memoir. See also Irving Howe and B. J. Widick, *The UAW and Walter Reuther* (1949). An obituary is in the *New York Times*, May 11, 1970.]

DAVID BRODY

RICE, ELMER (Sept. 28, 1892–May 8, 1967), playwright, producer, director, and novelist, was born Elmer Leopold Reizenstein in New York City, the son of Jacob Reizenstein, a bookkeeper and traveling salesman, and Fanny Lion. Family financial problems caused by his father's ill health forced Rice to quit high school at age fourteen and go to work as an office boy in a law firm. However, he continued to study and passed an examination that certified him a high school graduate. In 1910 he entered New York Law School and two years later graduated cum laude. He was admitted to the bar in 1913. Bored by legal routine, Rice soon announced his intention to become a writer, particularly a playwright. His first publication was a story in the pulp magazine *Argosy* (May 1913), for which he was paid $20.

In 1914, using the name Elmer Rice for the first time, he wrote *On Trial*, a murder mystery. The play, which opened at the Candler Theatre on Aug. 14, 1914, was a sensation and ran for nearly a year. For the first time in the theater the film technique of the flashback was used. Despite the play's favorable reception and the fact that it earned him nearly $100,000, Rice declined to regard it as more than a "shrewd piece of stage carpentry."

On June 16, 1915, Rice married Hazel Levy; they had two children. After *On Trial*, Rice was largely associated with amateur groups around Columbia University and staged a number of productions. In 1918 he was lured to Hollywood, where he spent two unhappy years under contract to Samuel Goldwyn's production company. Following his return to New York, he collaborated with Hatcher Hughes, a teacher of dramatic composition at Columbia, on *Wake*

Up, Jonathan, a successful comedy that opened in 1921 at Henry Miller's Theatre and ran for 105 performances.

In 1923 the Theatre Guild staged *The Adding Machine*, which became one of Rice's most famous plays. However, it was not a popular success and ran only nine weeks, probably because it poignantly conveyed a negative view of life. The protagonist, Mr. Zero, is a "little man" who is repressed and colorless but possesses dignity and courage. He kills his employer, who had coldly replaced him with an adding machine after he had worked twenty-five years as a bookkeeper. Many critics and historians of the drama regard it as one of the truly original plays of the American stage. Rice was accused of liberal borrowing from the German expressionists, but he stoutly maintained that while he had heard of expressionism, he had not read a German play until after his own was written.

Rice's next play, *Close Harmony* (1924), a comedy about a henpecked man who tries to flee the roost, was written in collaboration with Dorothy Parker. Praised by the critics, it met with little box-office success and closed in three weeks. Parker wired her Round Table group at the Algonquin Hotel, "*Close Harmony* did a cool ninety dollars at the matinee. Ask the boys in the back room what they will have."

Street Scene (1929), Rice's most notable success, a tragedy depicting seamy New York tenement life, ran for more than a year and was awarded the Pulitzer Prize in 1929. The play had been rejected by practically every manager in New York before it was produced by William A. Brady, who gave Rice the chance to direct it. The critic Joseph Wood Krutch thought that Rice never again wrote so good a play. In 1947 Kurt Weill collaborated with Rice and the poet Langston Hughes on a highly successful musical version.

Rice returned to his legal background for the subject matter of *Counsellor-at-Law* (1931). Paul Muni had the starring role in this tightly developed, realistic melodrama about a lawyer accused of unethical conduct. In the 1930's Rice turned to political and sociological topics. "Justice was the subject to which he was passionately devoted," Brooks Atkinson wrote, "and he believed in taking sides and making statements." Rice said he had been converted to socialism by the writings of George Bernard Shaw, especially *Plays Pleasant and Unpleasant*, but he never joined the Socialist party. He belonged to the American Civil Liberties Union and numerous other liberal social and professional groups. Because of his left-wing political views, he was eventually named on everyone's "Red" and "front" lists, distinctions that Rice received with notable equanimity. His socialism was idealistic, not practical; he said he was never able to read Karl Marx. His plays with social and political messages were not very successful. Critics generally agreed with George Jean Nathan's judgment that Rice's preoccupation with headlines converted his plays into mere editorial comment.

Rice, together with Maxwell Anderson, Robert E. Sherwood, Sidney Howard, and S. N. Behrman, formed the Playwrights' Producing Company to produce and direct their own plays. One of their first productions was Sherwood's *Abe Lincoln in Illinois* (1938), which Rice directed. Behrman wrote in his memoirs that he found Rice "socially charming and humorous but apt to be strident when arguing for his plays."

On Jan. 10, 1942, Rice and Hazel Levy were divorced. Two days later he married Betty Field, an accomplished actress who had performed in some of his plays; they had three children. It was for his wife that Rice wrote *Dream Girl* (1945). A lighthearted, exuberant play that dramatizes the romantic fantasies of a quiet salesgirl, it was a popular and financial success. In 1955 Rice and Field were divorced. In 1966 he married Barbara Marshall.

Rice's three novels—*A Voyage to Purilia* (1930), a satire on motion pictures; *Imperial City* (1937), a depiction of New York life; and *The Show Must Go On* (1949), a story of theater life and lore—all received mixed reviews. V. S. Pritchett's criticism of the last novel may be applied not unfairly to all three of them: "His sense of scene is considerably stronger than his sense of character, which is summary and cinematic. . . . He is a victim of the old pitfall of social realists and cameramen, and his prose is too dull to save him."

In a career that extended over half a century Rice wrote three novels, numerous essays and short stories, and more than fifty plays, twenty-four of which were produced on Broadway. His plays were innovative and experimental, consisting of tragedies, comedies, mysteries, melodramas, and ideological and psychological dramas. Some were written, Rice said, with "no nobler impulse than a realistic desire to make a comfortable living."

Rice was essentially a modest, unpretentious person who did not have an excessively high regard for his own writing skill, although he was confident of his stagecraft and dramaturgy. He was one of the first dramatists to employ the American stage as a vehicle for social criticism, but he had little impact on the American theater after World War II. He was a protester to the end of his life, persistently criticizing the American bombing of North Vietnam in the 1960's.

In the spring of 1967 Rice and his wife boarded an ocean liner for Europe. He was stricken at sea with a series of heart attacks and died in a hospital at Southampton, England.

[Rice's papers, including manuscripts and correspondence, are at the Humanities Research Center, University of Texas, Austin. His autobiography, *Minority Report* (1963), is candid and informative. See also Meyer Levin, "Elmer Rice," *Theatre Arts*, Jan. 1932; Alan S. Downer, *Fifty Years of American Drama* (1951); John Gassner, *Masters of the Drama* (1954); Gerald Rabkin, *Drama and Commitment* (1964); Robert Hogan, *The Independence of Elmer Rice* (1965); Frank Durham, *Elmer Rice* (1970); S. N. Behrman, *People in a Diary* (1972); Anthony F. R. Palmieri, *Elmer Rice* (1980); and Fred Behringer, "Elmer Rice," in John MacNicholas, ed., *American Dramatists*, VII (1981). Obituaries are in the *New York Times*, May 9, 1967; and *Time*, May 19, 1967.]

WILLIAM McCANN

RICE, JOHN ANDREW (Feb. 1, 1888–Nov. 17, 1968), founder of Black Mountain College, was born in Lynchburg, S.C., the son of John Andrew Rice, a Methodist minister, and Anna Bell Smith. His autobiographical *I Came Out of the Eighteenth Century* (1942) is especially revealing of his childhood. Rice resented his father's peripatetic existence and craving for success, and early on, Rice developed a profound appreciation for what he saw as the tranquil, present-oriented, communitarian, satisfied way of life of southern rural blacks.

At Webb School in Bellbuckle, Tenn., from about 1903 to 1908, Rice learned to question the authority of books and to admire the "inner discipline" of his teacher John Webb. He entered Tulane University in 1908 and graduated with a B.A. in 1911, convinced that he had wasted his time in an institution that insisted on quantifying knowledge into hours and credits. Following a brief term as a New Orleans tenement-house inspector that crystallized his skepticism of social reformism, Rice was selected to serve as Rhodes Scholar from Louisiana to Oxford University (B.A., 1914). He found Oxford laudable in its devotion to free inquiry but excessively concerned with status and success.

Following graduation, Rice returned to Webb School as an instructor and on Dec. 28, 1914, married Nell Aydelotte; they had two children. He studied at the University of Chicago (1916–1918) and served with the Military Intelligence Division of the United States Army (1918–1919). In 1919, he joined the Department of Classics at the University of Nebraska, remaining there as associate professor and chairman through the spring of 1928. From 1928 through 1930, Rice was professor of classics at Rutgers University and head of the Department of Classics at the New Jersey College for Women.

In July 1930, after fifteen uncongenial months as a Guggenheim Fellow, Rice took a position as professor of classics at Rollins College in Winter Park, Fla. It was at Rollins that Rice's talent for sarcasm, biting honesty, and style of sardonic confrontation first got him into serious trouble. He made apparent his belief that Rollins' "Conference Plan" system of curriculum, under which students were required to spend six hours each day in three two-hour classes called "conferences," was just another example of the stultifying character of most higher education. "Two hours with bores," he said, "was at least an hour too much." He was fired in 1933 by Rollins' president, Hamilton Holt. When Holt asked Rice why people hated him so, Rice replied, "I think I know the answer. They know that if I had the making of a world, they would not be in it."

Unemployed and seemingly unemployable, Rice made his own world and, in the process, launched the great experiment of his life. With a few colleagues and little money, he founded Black Mountain College in rented facilities in rural North Carolina. The school opened its doors in the fall of 1933 with four faculty members and twenty-two students. When it closed in 1956, Black Mountain was not much larger, but a steady stream of innovative faculty, including Josef Albers, John Cage, Merce Cunningham, Walter Gropius, Paul Goodman, and Charles Olson, had given the school an unsurpassed reputation for creative work in literature and the arts.

The Rice era at Black Mountain (he served four terms as rector, from 1934 through 1939) was characterized by conflict over the purposes of the college. Some participants wanted Black Mountain to be a utopian community in the tradition of Brook Farm and New Harmony. Others, Rice among them, conceived of it more as a teaching and learning enterprise, a pristine expression of John Dewey's progressive education. Most agreed that Black Mountain should be democratic, and from the beginning, the school's structure gave the faculty a great deal of power and provided for student participation. In addition, Rice believed that "democratic man" must be competitive only within himself—hence, Black Mountain's emphasis on the creative, artistic act, perhaps the school's most important contribution to twentieth-century educational theory.

If his charisma and vision were essential to Black Mountain, Rice also had deficiencies as a leader. In an era of depression, he was no fund-raiser. His abrasive personality wore poorly in the intense emotional climate brought about by students and faculty living and working at close quarters. Rice's advocacy of the primacy of individual self-development alienated those who wished for a cohesive group experience, and his definition of democracy—he believed in governance by a majority of the "intelligent"—did not sit well with many colleagues and students. Yet, one may also interpret the schisms that appeared at Black Mountain in the 1930's as reflections of profoundly different ideas about the nature of thought and inquiry. According to this view, Rice's contempt for the social sciences and the scientific method and his desire to fuse thought with intuition, spontaneity, and emotion came into conflict with a more mechanistic worldview represented by the Bauhaus-educated Albers.

In March 1938, Rice was forced to take a leave of absence from Black Mountain but even then was ostracized until he resigned in early 1940. Although he sorely missed teaching, he reconciled himself to a career as a writer. His short stories appeared in the *New Yorker* and the *Saturday Evening Post* and a column in *PM's Weekly*. His autobiography was cowinner of the Harper 125th Anniversary Award. After being divorced from his wife, he married Caroline Dikka Moen in 1942; they had two children. He died in Silver Spring, Md.

[Rice's tribulations at Rollins are documented in the Rollins College Archives, Winter Park, Fla. Superb primary materials on Black Mountain College are available in the State Archives of North Carolina at Raleigh. Some of Rice's short stories have been collected in *Local Color* (1947). See Martin Duberman, *Black Mountain: An Exploration in Community* (1972); JoAnn C. Ellert, "The Bauhaus and Black Mountain College," *Journal of General Education*, Oct. 1972; Edward Hagerman, "Black Mountain Breakdown," *Canadian Review of American Studies*, Fall 1976; and Charles Martin Garren, "The Educational Program at Black Mountain College, 1933–1943" (Ph.D. diss., University of North Carolina, Chapel Hill, 1980). An obituary with several inaccuracies is in the *New York Times*, Nov. 28, 1968.]

WILLIAM GRAEBNER

RICH, ROBERT (June 23, 1883–Apr. 28, 1968), businessman and United States congressman, was born in Woolrich, Pa., the son of Michael Bond Rich, a businessman, and Ida Shaw. After attending local public schools, he graduated from Mercersburg (Pa.) Academy in 1902. From 1903 to 1905 he studied at Pennsylvania's Williamsport Commercial College and Dickinson College but did not graduate. On June 10, 1910, he married Julia Trump; they had four children. His wife died in 1951, and on July 12, 1956, Rich married Pattie Holmes Wideman.

In 1896, Rich began working summers at Woolrich Woolen Mills, the family business. He became a partner in the company in 1906 and its general manager by 1930 and thus carried on a family involvement begun by his great-grandfather John Rich, who founded the company in 1830. Rich also managed businesses in neighboring communities, including the State Bank of Avis, which he founded in 1910, and the Chatham Water Company, which his father started.

Rich entered the political arena when he became a delegate to the Republican National Convention in 1924. In 1930 the governor of Pennsylvania appointed him to complete the term of the late Edgar H. Kiess of the Sixteenth Congressional District, including Clinton and Lycoming counties, where Rich lived and conducted business. This district was predominantly Republican and rural. Rich was elected from this district for the next six congresses. Throughout this period, he generally carried district elections by substantial margins.

Few in Congress opposed the New Deal as consistently and vociferously as Rich. He alone among House Republicans voted against extending the National Industrial Recovery Act in 1935. On another occasion, he proposed an amendment to cut appropriations for the Tennessee Valley Authority to two cents. He also called for the eradication of such New Deal agencies as the National Labor Relations Board, the Rural Electrification Administration, the Public Works Administration, and the Federal Emergency Relief Administration. "Where are you going to get the money?" Rich often asked in Congress. Besides objecting to deficit spending, he opposed the "excessive" power of the Roosevelt administration, which he believed threatened constitutional government. (Rich once exclaimed that financial extravagance was to be expected from a president who "never did a day's work in his life.") Like most conservatives, Rich put his faith in the doctrines of individual initiative and free enterprise. His solution to the Great Depression was to return to Republican policies of the past.

Rich was more willing to use the federal government in responding to his district's needs. He fought for the funding of the West Branch Dam at Lock Haven, the fish hatchery at Lamar, and other projects. Throughout the 1930's his constituency, for the most part, viewed him as one who responded conscientiously to individual requests, stayed close to the district, and sought to use the private sector to promote employment. At the same time, Woolrich Woolen Mills survived by reducing its labor force and wages.

After the outbreak of World War II, Rich again challenged Roosevelt. Rich was an archisolationist, opposing the American defense buildup and foreign assistance, including the increase of the army to 2 million men in 1941 and the Lend-Lease Act of 1941. He spent the 1943–1944 period outside of Congress, however, following a redistricting fight. After his reelection in 1944, he fought President Harry Truman's foreign-policy initiatives, including the Marshall Plan and the Truman Doctrine. He just as strongly opposed Truman's domestic reform commitments. His anti-Democratic bias and emphasis on economy in government also caused him to vote against granting a $5,000 pension to Roosevelt's widow in 1946 and an increase in Truman's salary in 1949. In 1951, Rich retired from Congress.

In Congress, Rich was known for strong convictions and conscientious service on the Rules, Appropriations, Government Operations, and other committees. Rich was no orator and sponsored little legislation. He focused his greatest attention on trying to reduce the the cost of government. That single-minded concern put him out of step with the times as the federal government sought to overcome the problems of economic recovery and the threat of totalitarianism abroad.

After retiring from Congress, Rich served as treasurer, general manager, and president of Woolrich Woolen Mills. He was chariman of the board from 1964 to 1966; by then the company had expanded and modernized operations. Besides specializing in woolen cloth, it manufactured other fabrics. Its sportswear and outerwear went to retail establishments nationwide. In 1966, Woolrich Woolen Mills had annual sales of $8,325,000 and 650 employees. Rich also served as president of the board of Lycoming College and a trustee of Dickinson College. Both institutions benefited from his financial contributions. Rich died in Jersey Shore, Pa.

[Rich's papers are in the possession of his daughter, Mrs. Roswell Brayton, of Woolrich, Pa. Obituaries are in the *Williamsport* (Pa.) *Sun-Gazette* and *Lock Haven* (Pa.) *Express*, both Apr. 29, 1968; and the *New York Times*, Apr. 30, 1968.]

JAMES N. GIGLIO

RICHTER, CONRAD MICHAEL (Oct. 13, 1890–Oct. 30, 1968), writer, was born in Pine Grove, Pa., the son of John Absalom Richter, a general merchant, and Charlotte Esther Henry, the daughter of a Lutheran minister. In 1899, Richter's father himself decided to become a Lutheran minister. This association with the Lutheran ministry was to strongly influence Richter's writing. The ministry figures directly in two of his best novels, the National Book Award–winning *The Waters of Kronos* (1960), in which the author's fictional counterpart undertakes a spiritual quest miraculously cutting across the present and the past, and *A Simple Honorable Man* (1962), the story of a minister resembling the author's father; it figures indirectly in Richter's other novels and stories.

After graduating in 1906 from the Tremont, Pa., high school, Richter worked as a teamster, farm laborer, bank clerk, timberman, subscription salesman, and private secretary. His work as a newspaper reporter and editor had the most pervasive influence on his writing, teaching him concision of expression: most of his fourteen novels are fewer than 200 pages long.

Richter published his first short story, "How Tuck Went Home," in the Sept. 6, 1913, issue of *Cavalier*. His first acclaimed story, "Brothers of No Kin," appeared in the April 1914 issue of *Forum* and was reprinted in *Reedy's Mirror*, *Illustrated Sunday Magazine*, and *The Best Short Stories of 1915* (edited by Edward J. O'Brien). This became the title piece of Richter's first collection of stories, published in 1924; many of the other pieces had appeared in such magazines as *American*, *Ladies' Home Journal*, and the *Saturday Evening Post*. Set mainly in the twentieth-century eastern United States, the stories were tailored to popular fictional modes and featured idealistic themes.

Later collections of Richter's stories—*Early Americana* (1936), *Smoke Over the Prairie and Other Stories* (1947), and *The Rawhide Knot and Other Stories* (1978)—are set in the nineteenth-century American Southwest and celebrate pioneer virtues. *Over the Blue Mountain* (1967), set in twentieth-century Pennsylvania, is woven of themes appealing to children. *Early Americana*, *Smoke Over the Prairie*, and *The Rawhide Knot* display an artistic sophistication that is minimal in the other collections.

On Mar. 24, 1915, Richter married Harvena Achenbach. (Their only child, Harvena, became a story-writer and poet.) From 1922 to 1928, Richter and his family resided on a Clarks Valley, Pa., farm, where he wrote, in addition to short stories, two book-length philosophical essays, *Human Vibration* (1926) and *Principles in Bio-Physics* (1927). These espouse abstruse theories of human physical and psychological energy supply and expenditure. A third essayistic volume, *The Mountain on the Desert* (1955), employs a novelistic framework in support of those theories. The theories pervade all of Richter's novels and stories.

His wife's illness compelled the Richters to move in 1928 from Pennsylvania to Albuquerque, N.Mex., where he turned to new subjects. Over the next twenty-two years, he wrote seven novels. *The Sea of Grass* (1937), a nineteenth-century southwestern American tragedy about ranchers' feuds with farmers and the resulting demise of free rangeland, won a gold medal for literature from the Society of Libraries of New York University. It became the first of six of Richter's novels adapted for either motion pictures or television. *Tacey Cromwell* (1942) concerns an Arizona mining-town prostitute turned respectable foster mother.

The deftly executed trilogy comprising *The Trees* (1940), *The Fields* (1946), and the Pulitzer Prize–winning *The Town* (1950)—later collected as *The Awakening Land* (1966)—traces the life of a pioneer woman in Pennsylvania and Ohio in the late eighteenth and early nineteenth centuries. *The Free Man* (1943) deals with personal and political freedom in Pennsylvania during the American Revolution. *Always Young and Fair* (1947), a recipient of an Ohioana Library medal, is set in the years between the Spanish-American War and World War I and depicts a Pennsylvania woman's obsessive devotion to a dead lover.

In 1950, Richter returned with his family to Pine Grove, where he lived until his death. There he wrote—in addition to *The Waters of Kronos* and *A Simple Honorable Man*—his final southwestern novel, *The Lady* (1957), a story about an aristocratic woman who avenges the murder of her husband and son, and four novels set in and around Pennsylvania: *The Light in the Forest* (1953), about a boy's Indian captivity, and its sequel, *A Country of Strangers* (1966); *The Grandfathers* (1964), a folkloric story of modern domestic confusion; and *The Aristocrat* (1968), concerning a spinster's warfare on modernity and mediocrity.

Richter died in Pottsville, Pa. Soft-spoken but not reticent, Richter had lived quietly and refrained from the personal excesses characteristic of many writers. In his works, Richter employed restrained realism, quiet humor, and clarity and economy of expression to depict what he called the "small authenticities" of daily life. Even when subjects and themes derived from places and times unknown to him, his meticulous research involved him so personally that the final effect was as though he had experienced them. So cognizant was he of style that, with reference to his habit of repeated rewriting, he remarked, "I probably turn the broom handle too much."

In his best works, Richter produced notable historical and modern fiction. He created two epic fictional characters, James Brewton, a stoic rancher in *The Sea of Grass,* and Sayward Luckett Wheeler, the quintessential pioneer woman in the *Awakening Land* trilogy. Here and elsewhere, he transcended sentiment and simplicity to elevate to high art the theme of simple goodness.

[Some of Richter's manuscripts and galley proofs are in the Princeton University Library. The most comprehensive biographical-analytical study is Edwin W. Gaston, Jr., *Conrad Richter* (1965). See Robert J. Barnes, *Conrad Richter* (1968); Clifford Duane Edwards, *Conrad Richter's Ohio Trilogy* (1971); and John Marvin La Hood, *Conrad Richter's America* (1975).]

EDWIN W. GASTON, JR.

RIIS, MARY PHILLIPS (Apr. 29, 1877–Aug. 4, 1967), second wife of Jacob Riis and one of the first women stockbrokers in New York City, was born in Memphis, Tenn., the daughter of Richard F. Phillips, a cotton broker who emigrated from England and eventually became president of the St. Louis Cotton Exchange, and Lina Rensch. She attended primary and secondary schools in England and France and compensated for her lack of a formal college education by attending evening classes at New York University and by reading heavily in economics. While in her midtwenties and during a two-year stint as an actress, she met the journalist and social reformer Jacob Riis. Rather than return to St. Louis and her family, she accepted Riis's offer to become his secretary and stay in New York. After working for Riis for two years, she married him on July 29, 1907; they had one child. They bought a farm in Barre, Mass., to which state her family had moved. Six years after the marriage, Jacob Riis entered a sanitarium. He died on May 26, 1914, leaving all that remained of his estate to his wife, having previously set up a trust fund for his children by his first wife. In his will, Jacob Riis also named an advisory board to provide support for the Jacob A. Riis Neighborhood House; among its members were his wife, his friend Theodore Roosevelt, and several prominent early social workers. Jacob Riis could spare no money for the settlement house, but support of Jacob Riis House became a lifelong project of his widow.

Within three years of her husband's death, Riis decided to find a job to support herself and her young son. After some difficulty, due in part to the fact that she was a woman, she obtained a position selling bonds for $75 per month at Bonbright and Company. Initially, finding customers was not easy, but she made resourceful use of the telephone book and learned the business well. Two years after starting, she headed a Bonbright branch that employed ten other women and specialized in serving women customers. In spite of her feminist outlook, Riis found men on the average somewhat more reasonable customers.

In 1923, Riis taught an extension class at Columbia University on the principles of investing. The course sought to familiarize women with stocks and bonds; the respective merits of municipal, foreign, railroad, utility, and industrial investments; financial cycles; and procedures for making buy-and-sell decisions.

Riis attributed her own success in the securities business to her ability to evaluate facts unemotionally. Early in 1929 she began urging customers to either sell out or exercise caution. However, she herself had made an ill-considered loan and therefore suffered from the Great Depression. In 1931, speaking to the Scarsdale (N.Y.) Women's Club, she sought an explanation for the nation's financial crisis by drawing a parallel between the frenzied speculation in tulip bulbs that precipitated the depression of 1630 and the excessive speculation on Wall Street in 1929.

The depression evoked a political response in Riis. A lifelong Republican—in part because of her husband's friendship with Theodore Roosevelt—Riis switched her political affiliation in 1936. She endorsed Franklin Roosevelt, praising the lifesaving nature of his relief programs and defending his financial policies.

Riis remained in the brokerage business, working for McQuoid and Coady and then Shearson Hammill. Still active as a broker when eighty years old, she had evolved an investment philosophy that stressed patience and a formula that consisted of investing 20 percent of available funds in safe, income-oriented instruments, 60 percent in major stocks with growth potential, and 20 percent in more-speculative capital gains. Her personal investments were successful as well. She owned a mansion with twenty-two rooms, stables, and a six-car garage, and was a member of the Cosmopolitan Club.

Riis, who never remarried, devoted much effort to the Jacob A. Riis Neighborhood

House. She believed that settlement houses could foster a sense of responsibility for others, enhance democracy, and help immigrants to assimilate. Her fund-raising efforts on behalf of Riis House included annual letters to the *New York Times* appealing for such items as an automobile for the settlement's summer camp, contributions to an ice-cream fund, new playground apparatus, and awnings. She saw organized recreation as a safety valve for children in an explosive slum. She was president of the Riis House board in the 1920's and 1930's. In 1941, Riis House began running a branch operation in school facilities in the Bedford-Stuyvesant neighborhood in Brooklyn, and two years later, Riis recommended more educational and recreational facilities to curb disorder in this black ghetto. In 1952, Riis House sold its Lower East Side building to Trinity Church and moved its settlement-house program entirely into public housing facilities. Riis continued as honorary chairman of the board. She died in New York City.

[Riis's articles on investing include "Model Investment Program," *Woman Citizen*, Mar. 1927; "How to Watch Your Investments," *Woman's Journal*, Apr. 1929; and "Is It Safe to Buy on Margin?" *Woman's Journal*, Feb. 1929. See Elizabeth M. Fowler, "Social Reformer Also Sells Stocks," *New York Times*, Sept. 29, 1957; and "Mrs. Riis Deserts Republican Ticket," *ibid.*, July 20, 1936. An obituary is in the *New York Times*, Aug. 5, 1967.]

JUDITH ANN TROLANDER

RINEHART, STANLEY MARSHALL, JR. (Aug. 18, 1897–Apr. 26, 1969), publisher, was born in Pittsburgh, Pa., the son of Stanley Marshall Rinehart, a physician, and Mary Ella Roberts, a former nurse who, as Mary Roberts Rinehart, became a best-selling author. Rinehart's early boyhood home in Allegheny, Pa., was solidly middle-class. In 1911, thanks to his mother's literary successes, the family moved to an estate in the Pittsburgh suburb of Sewickley. As a teenager he traveled in Europe.

Rinehart attended the Morristown (N.J.) School, a private institution, and entered Harvard University in 1915. Except for his performance in mathematics, his college record was undistinguished, and he even failed an English course. He did, however, impress the literature professor Charles Townsend Copeland with his writing ability. When the United States entered World War I, Rinehart dropped out of Harvard to enlist in the army. Initially denied a commission, he was sent to France with the Eighty-second Infantry Division. Later, having been promoted to second lieutenant, he trained officers and served as an aide-de-camp. Nonetheless, he regretted not being stationed at the front. Just before demobilization, he won 11,000 francs shooting craps and used the money to buy an engagement ring for Mary Noble Doran, the daughter of George H. Doran, his mother's publisher. They were married on May 24, 1919, and had two children.

Instead of returning to Harvard, Rinehart took a job in the advertising department of the George H. Doran Company, where his responsibilities included selling space in the house's publication *The Bookman*. His mother bought him a financial interest in the concern, and Doran welcomed his leadership and business acumen. Within the next few years, he served successively as advertising manager, secretary, and a director of the company. In those capacities, he worked closely with John Farrar, who had become the *Bookman*'s editor in 1920 and editor in chief of the publishing house in 1925. Rinehart's brother Frederick also became a Doran employee in 1924.

Interested in relinquishing control of the firm to his young associates, the aging Doran tendered the stock to the Rinehart family, but they refused his terms. In 1927, Doran accepted a merger offer from Doubleday, Page, forming Doubleday, Doran and Company. The partnership appeared promising, for both were respected houses with strong lists. The Rinehart brothers and Farrar were to manage the firm together with Nelson Doubleday. Yet, because all of the parties involved were outspoken individualists, the combination proved unworkable. On June 4, 1929, Rinehart, his brother, and Farrar left to form their own publishing house, Farrar and Rinehart. The following year, Rinehart and his wife were divorced.

Rinehart and his partners sold their first list, which included novels by Mary Roberts Rinehart and DuBose Heyward, by traveling from bookshop to bookshop. The first month's sales totaled $26, but by September they had reached $46,000; in less than two years the firm required larger quarters. The company's only disastrous venture was a game book called *Speculation* (coincidentally issued the day of the 1929 stock market crash), which sold no copies. In 1931, Farrar and Rinehart bought the Cosmopolitan

Book Corporation, thereby acquiring such writers as Faith Baldwin, Rex Beach, and Ruth Suckow. Some of the firm's other authors in the 1930's were Philip Wylie, Upton Sinclair, Floyd Dell, and Stephen Vincent Benét. The house's greatest success came with Hervey Allen's long historical novel *Anthony Adverse* (1933), which sold over a million copies by the mid-1930's. In general, Farrar and Rinehart became known as a specialist in light fiction, although the reputation was not entirely deserved; for example, the prizewinning Rivers of America series, inaugurated in 1937, indicated the house's wider interests. The company also added a college textbook department in 1934.

In his role as president of the firm, Rinehart exemplified the willingness of new, young publishers in the interwar period to abandon the genteel restraint of their predecessors in favor of an unabashed treatment of books as commodities. He explained, "The publishing office of today is no den of graybeards solemnly reading and conferring"; quoting one of his authors, he described it as more like "a boiler factory." Rinehart's unprecedentedly aggressive promotion of *Anthony Adverse* revealed his acceptance of commercialism. He sent letters to the trade almost three months before publication, tantalized potential readers with an advance syllabus for the book, and kept up a barrage of advertising after it appeared. In addition, he priced the book at a low $3 per copy, gambling that sales would offset the high cost of printing such a lengthy volume. In 1930, Farrar and Rinehart participated in the then-controversial practice of price-cutting, entering the dollar fiction market. The firm also ran manuscript contests, courted reviewers, and held special events to publicize its offerings.

Rinehart married Frances Alice Yeatman on July 28, 1933; they had one child. Rinehart was, at six feet, two inches tall, with black hair and brown eyes, what a writer in the *Saturday Review of Literature* called "a casting director's dream of a handsome, sophisticated publisher." He and Farrar hired attractive Harvard and Yale graduates from literary families who gave the office a glamorous, cosmopolitan tinge. Allen and Benét served as close advisers, the latter considering himself virtually a member of the firm.

During World War II, Farrar took a leave to work for the Office of War Information. Rinehart, who resented Farrar's preoccupation with outside interests, bought him out and dissolved the firm. On Jan. 1, 1946, he and Frederick Rinehart established Rinehart and Company, which in the late 1940's published Norman Mailer's *The Naked and the Dead*, Frederic Wakeman's *The Hucksters*, and Charles Jackson's *The Lost Weekend*. In 1948 the firm started Rinehart Editions, a paperback reprint series for college students. In the 1950's the quality of the house's trade list deteriorated. Having grown tired of the business and skeptical of its future, Rinehart sold it in 1960 to Henry Holt and Company, which then became Holt, Rinehart and Winston. He stayed on as senior vice-president and director of the new firm until his retirement in 1963. He died in South Miami, Fla.

[The Rinehart Collection at the Hillman Library of the University of Pittsburgh, while primarily devoted to the papers of Mary Roberts Rinehart, contains a few documents pertaining to Stanley M. Rinehart, Jr. His own writings include "The Publisher, the Author, and the Reading Public," *New York Times Book Review*, Oct. 25, 1936, and "Boyhood Recollection," *Good Housekeeping*, June 1942.

See "Rinehart and Farrar Announce a New Publishing House," *Publishers' Weekly*, June 8, 1929; George H. Doran, *Chronicles of Barabbas, 1884–1934* (1935); Edith M. Stern, "Farrar and Rinehart," *Saturday Review of Literature*, Mar. 21, 1942; "Take a Bow," *Publishers Weekly*, Mar. 24, 1944; Charles Madison, *Book Publishing in America* (1966); and John Tebbel, *A History of Book Publishing in the United States* (1978; rev. ed., 1981). Works about Mary Roberts Rinehart—her *My Story* (1931) and Jan Cohn's *Improbable Fiction: The Life of Mary Roberts Rinehart* (1980)—also contain glimpses of her son. An obituary is in the *New York Times*, Apr. 27, 1969.]

JOAN SHELLEY RUBIN

RITTER, JOSEPH ELMER (July 20, 1892–June 10, 1967), Roman Catholic cardinal and reform leader, was born in New Albany, Ind., the son of Nicholas Ritter, a baker, and Bertha Luette. Ritter was raised in a liberal German Catholic environment and especially enjoyed the religious services and activities at St. Mary's Church in New Albany, where he later celebrated his first mass. He graduated from St. Mary's Grammar School in 1906. While in the seventh grade he decided to become a priest, and he subsequently enrolled at St. Meinrad's, a Benedictine seminary in Indiana, where he completed his high school, collegiate, and theological studies, graduating in 1917.

Ritter

Ordained on May 30, 1917, Ritter served for six months as assistant pastor at St. Patrick's Church in Indianapolis before going to the Cathedral of Saint Peter and Paul in the same city. Here he began a lifelong career as diocesan administrator and leader. Ritter had an excellent academic record and would have preferred to continue study in Rome, but Bishop Joseph Chartrand of Indianapolis had come to depend on him; the papacy in 1922 awarded Ritter an honorary S.T.D. Chartrand increasingly relied upon Ritter and in 1933 secured for him a papal appointment as auxiliary bishop of Indianapolis. In 1934, after Chartrand's death, Ritter succeeded him, becoming one of the youngest bishops in America.

Ritter headed the see of Indianapolis until 1946, serving the last two years as the city's first archbishop. He proved a capable administrator, managing diocesan finances effectively during the Great Depression and completing construction of the cathedral. He demonstrated special interest in the welfare of blacks, opening five catechetical centers for black children, ordering full integration of parochial schools, and crusading against the Ku Klux Klan.

In 1946, after Pope Pius XII named Ritter archbishop of St. Louis, Ritter created a national stir by ordering the integration of the Catholic schools. When segregationist parents threatened legal action, he reminded them that church law forbade Catholics—under penalty of excommunication—from instituting legal action against their lawful religious superiors. He won the battle. Ritter called racial injustice a sin and argued that Catholics practicing it should not receive communion until confessing.

If Ritter's integration order anticipated the 1954 Supreme Court decision forbidding continued public-school segregation, his proposals during the early 1960's anticipated the federal affirmative action programs of the 1970's. In 1963 he urged Catholics to go beyond mere compliance with integration decrees and actively promote integration. He urged parishes to invite blacks to move into their districts and advised Catholic organizations without black members to recruit them.

Ritter was a champion of the needy even beyond his diocese. He redistributed diocesan wealth by asking affluent parishes to tithe their income to poorer parishes. Alarmed at the extent of physical and spiritual poverty in Latin America, he founded the first mission from an American diocese to a foreign country when, in the 1950's, he sent three priests from St. Louis to La Paz, Bolivia. "The church must be the champion of the active virtues, not just define them," he proclaimed. "It must especially through its priests practice them."

The climax of Ritter's career came in 1961 with his appointment by Pope John XXIII as the seventeenth United States cardinal and with his major role at the Second Vatican Council (1962–1965). At Vatican II he promoted liturgical reform (vernacular masses, greater emphasis upon preaching, and fuller participation by the laity in church worship), expanded participation by the bishops in church governance, increased harmony between Christians and Jews (including specifically the call to exonerate the Jews from guilt in the Crucifixion of Jesus), and ecumenicity. Speaking strongly for the council's ecumenical plan at the 1963 session, he declared, "The presentation of this text marks the end of the Counter Reformation. . . . Separation and division in the ranks of Christians are a scandal to the world." Ritter had become the most respected American Catholic cleric abroad.

Returning home between council sessions, Ritter sought to implement Vatican II. In June 1964 he arranged a wedding in which for the first time in the United States an Episcopal groom and a Catholic bride participated in an authorized wedding, officiated at by both Episcopal and Catholic priests in a Catholic church. Ritter authorized the first English mass, which was held at a liturgical conference in Kiel Auditorium, St. Louis, on August 24, 1965. The next day he celebrated an English mass at the conference, after singing Martin Luther's "A Mighty Fortress Is Our God." Ritter's influence was not due to an imposing stature or spellbinding oratorical skills. Rather, he combined warmth, directness, conviction, and determination with organizational skills to achieve his goals. He died in St. Louis.

[Ritter's papers are in the archdiocesan archives, St. Louis, Mo. For a biographical sketch see Francis Thornton, "Joseph Cardinal Ritter," in *Our American Princes* (1963). See also Donald J. Kemper, "Catholic Integration in St. Louis, 1935–1947," *Missouri Historical Review*, 87 (1978), and obituary notices in the *St. Louis Post-Dispatch* and *New York Times*, both June 11, 1967.]

WILLIAM C. RINGENBERG

RIVERS, LUCIUS MENDEL (Sept. 28, 1905–Dec. 28, 1970), United States congressman, was born in Gumville, N.C., the son of Lucius Hampton Rivers, a farmer and turpentine-still operator, and Henrietta Marion McCoy. Lucius died when his son was about eight years old, leaving the family in precarious economic circumstances. Rivers delivered newspapers, worked at odd jobs, and played professional baseball in the minor leagues. He was educated in the public schools and attended the College of Charleston from 1926 to 1929 and the University of South Carolina School of Law from 1929 to 1931, but he graduated from neither. In 1932 he was admitted to the bar of South Carolina and briefly practiced law. He was elected as a Democrat to the South Carolina legislature in 1933 and served for three years. From 1936 to 1940 he worked for the United States Department of Justice. On Sept. 1, 1938, Rivers married Margaret Middleton; they had three children.

In 1940, Rivers was elected to Congress from South Carolina's First District, and he was reelected fifteen times. He had no serious challenge from within the Democratic party or from the Republicans; indeed, he often ran unopposed. Rivers fitted the stereotype of the hardworking, hard-drinking, flamboyant southern politician whose speeches were heavily laced with poetry and biblical references.

Rivers claimed some credit as a populist, supporting programs such as food stamps, antipoverty legislation, public housing, and mass-transit subsidies. It was, however, his unquestioning and unswerving support of the military that brought him power and attention. Throughout his career, he pressed for more-sophisticated weapons and an expansion of the armed forces. He believed that Congress had the responsibility for, and oversight of, the military, an attitude that brought him into regular conflict with the executive branch, especially the secretary of defense, whose authority Rivers worked to undermine.

One consequence of Rivers' power was the proliferation of military installations in his congressional district around Charleston. Among these facilities were a naval shipyard, a Polaris-submarine base, two naval hospitals, the Parris Island Marine Corps training station, a Coast Guard station, a mine-warfare facility, a Marine Corps air station, an army supply depot, an air force base, and a naval weapons station. Carl Vinson, a Georgia congressman, was quoted as saying, "You put anything else down there in your district, Mendel, it's gonna sink."

As Rivers' power grew, many defense-related industries found it prudent to locate plants in the Charleston area. Among these were the Lockheed Aircraft Corporation, McDonnell-Douglas, J. P. Stevens and Company, Avco, and General Electric. It was estimated that 55 percent of the payrolls of the district came from defense-related operations, and Rivers claimed that he was personally responsible for 90 percent of this.

Rivers, who never served in the armed forces, believed that not only should the nation be strong militarily but the military should be used on any provocation. During the Kennedy administration, he advocated a full-scale invasion of Cuba, and he wanted to use nuclear weapons in Korea and Vietnam. When the North Koreans captured the United States intelligence ship *Pueblo* in 1968, Rivers pressed for severe retaliation. In general, the professional military establishment was more restrained than Rivers. "If Mendel was running things, we'd be in World War V," one of his colleagues remarked.

Rivers liked to be thought of as a friend of the common soldier. Enlisted personnel frequently wrote to him with problems, and he sometimes intervened with the Pentagon or interfered with the military justice system on their behalf. He vigorously opposed the army's prosecution of American soldiers implicated in the massacre at My Lai, Vietnam. He also prevented the prosecution of Green Beret soldiers accused of murdering a Vietnamese double agent. An opponent of an all-volunteer army, Rivers supported the draft and sponsored bills for better pay for military personnel. Rivers died in Birmingham, Ala.

In many ways, L. Mendel Rivers represented the worst of congressional politics: the pork barrel, militarism, and the seniority system. His advocacy of unrestrained growth and indiscriminate use of military force, including nuclear weapons, made him a natural target to antimilitary and antiwar groups. To some degree, his death marked the end of an era: that of the safe district for the bourbon Democrat of the South.

[Obituaries are in the *Washington Post* and the *New York Times*, both Dec. 29, 1970.]

DONALD F. TINGLEY

ROBINSON, RUBY DORIS SMITH (Apr. 25, 1942–Oct. 7, 1967), civil rights activist, was born in Atlanta, Ga., the daughter of John Thomas Smith, an independent mover and Baptist minister, and Alice Banks, a beautician. She grew up in the working-class neighborhood of Summerhill, which was changing racially from white to black. Her parents valued education highly and enrolled her at age three in a church-run kindergarten. She entered the first grade a year later. Smith was involved primarily in the social life of her church and school but was conscious of the racial segregation that engulfed her. At thirteen, she watched news reports of the Montgomery bus boycott. She then realized that something could be done about segregation, that it could be fought.

In 1958, Smith enrolled at Atlanta's Spelman College. When word of the sit-ins in Greensboro, N.C., on Feb. 1, 1960, reached her, she rushed home to see the televised accounts. Later she was among the first wave of Atlanta students to engage in sit-ins to desegregate the city's restaurants. She attended the April 1960 meeting at Shaw University in Raleigh, N.C., that led to the formation of the Student Nonviolent Coordinating Committee (SNCC).

On the eve of the first anniversary of the Greensboro sit-ins, student protesters in Rock Hill, S.C., who sat at a segregated lunch counter were arrested and jailed. They issued a call for other students throughout the South to join them in demonstrations and in jail. Smith and three other SNCC volunteers traveled to Rock Hill, where they were arrested for seeking service at a lunch counter and sentenced to jail. They participated in the first "jail, no bail" stratagem and spent a month in jail. Smith reflected later that during her prison term, "I came to think of myself as an individual, as opposed to what whites might have thought of me as a person."

In May 1961 the "freedom riders," organized by the Congress of Racial Equality (CORE), requested reinforcements to test the federal ban on segregation in interstate transportation. SNCC volunteers, including Smith, continued the freedom rides from Birmingham to Jackson, Miss. There they were arrested for trying to use the white rest room and were given a two-month suspended sentence and a $200 fine. Rather than pay the fine, they elected to go to jail. Smith shared a four-bunk cell in the Hinds County Jail with as many as twenty-three others. After two weeks, they were transferred to the maximum-security unit of Parchman State Penitentiary, where conditions were worse, and there spent forty-five days.

Upon her release, Smith returned to school and was elected to the SNCC Executive Committee. She turned her attention increasingly to SNCC and attended classes sporadically. In the fall of 1962, she became administrative secretary of SNCC, one of the youngest full-time staff members in the Atlanta national headquarters. An office worker later recalled that she "maintained a strong nationalist line but insisted that staff members demonstrate a willingness to work rather than sit around and talk about white people."

In April 1963, Smith coordinated the third annual SNCC Conference in Atlanta. She later became the organization's personnel officer and made a concerted effort to recruit southern blacks for the 1964 Mississippi Freedom Summer Project. In September 1964, with ten other SNCC leaders, she visited Guinea for its independence-day observance. The SNCC contingent was impressed by the sight of black people governing themselves. Under the tutelage of Guinea's president, Sékou Touré, they began to appreciate the economic as well as the racial dimensions of exploitation. Smith already had developed reservations about the civil rights movement, which had accomplished little for poor blacks.

In November 1964, Smith married Clifford Robinson, a mailing clerk in the Atlanta SNCC office. After SNCC's transportation officer was arrested and imprisoned in Mississippi, she took on additional responsibilities as manager of the Sojourner Motor Fleet. The fleet owned and leased cars and light trucks that were essential for SNCC workers in southern rural areas; it also operated a garage in Atlanta for which her husband was chief mechanic.

In May 1965, despite her work with SNCC and the demands of married life, Robinson received a B.S. from Spelman College. Two months later, she gave birth to a son, whom she named after the president of Guinea. At its May 1966 meeting, SNCC elected her executive secretary. She endorsed the call for "black power" in June 1966, during the James Meredith march through Mississippi, although some SNCC veterans voiced strong reservations. For her, there was a crying need to empower poor black people and to move from civil rights legislation to fundamental socioeconomic change.

A fiercely proud woman, Robinson resented the male chauvinism within SNCC. She insisted that black women historically had to play strong roles for the very survival of their families. In 1964 she formally protested the limited roles allotted to women in SNCC. She yearned for the day when a just society would no longer make her own role necessary. Wiry, talented, hardworking, efficient, courageous, determined but soft-spoken, Robinson was "the heartbeat" of SNCC, according to Sara Evans. The writer Alice Walker noted in 1976 that Robinson's life inspired her novel of the civil rights era, *Meridian*. The journalist Charlayne Hunter-Gault designated her banquet address at the Spelman College centennial "For Ruby Doris, Hopefully." Hunter-Gault revealed that Robinson was a standard by which she measured her own impulses as a journalist and a black woman. Robinson died in Atlanta after a ten-month bout with cancer.

[Much of Robinson's work with SNCC is covered in the *Student Nonviolent Coordinating Committee Papers, 1959–1972*, microfilm edition (1982). Phyl Garland, "Builders of a New South: Negro Heroines of Dixie," *Ebony*, Aug. 1966, includes excerpts from his interview with her. See also Howard Zinn, *SNCC: The New Abolitionists* (1964); James Forman, *The Making of Black Revolutionaries* (1972); Cleveland Sellers, *The River of No Return* (1973); *Essence*, July 1976; Sara Evans, *Personal Politics* (1979); and Clayborne Carson, *In Struggle* (1981). Obituaries are in the *New York Times*, Oct. 10, 1967; and *Jet*, Oct. 26, 1967.]

ROBERT L. HARRIS, JR.

ROCKWELL, GEORGE LINCOLN (Mar. 9, 1918–Aug. 25, 1967), organizer and leader of the American Nazi party, was born in Bloomington, Ill., the son of George ("Doc") Rockwell and Claire Schade, vaudeville comedians. Rockwell spent much of his early life on tour with his parents until their divorce in 1924. He attended Atlantic City (N.J.) High School for nearly four years, complaining in his autobiography that the students in the school were primarily Jewish and black. Because he refused to complete certain required assignments, he was not able to graduate from that school, but he did graduate from Central High School in Providence, R.I., in 1937.

From 1938 to 1940, Rockwell attended Brown University, boasting the lowest grades of anyone ever admitted to that school. He studied philosophy and did artwork for the college humor magazine, *Sir Brown*, imitating, so he claimed, the style of the cartoonist Charles Addams. Some psychiatrists later said that his drawings reflected preoccupations with death, cannibalism, blood, and bombing. In his autobiography he again complained that left-wing Jews and blacks seemed to be in control and in favor everywhere in the administration and among the students.

Rockwell left Brown to become a pilot in the navy. After World War II he attended Pratt Institute in New York City on the GI bill. He left without graduating, although in 1948 he won $1,000 in a contest sponsored by the National Society of Illustrators. He again commented disparagingly on the predominance of Jews, blacks, and Communists on campus, referring to them as the dregs of society.

Rockwell founded and managed, with a modicum of success, a small advertising agency in Portland, Maine. During the Korean War he was called back to service in the navy, in which he attained the rank of commander. While stationed in San Diego he was introduced to the works of anti-Semite Gerald L. K. Smith. Thereafter he became an avid reader of racist and, in particular, anti-Jewish literature. Following his study of *Mein Kampf*, which by his reckoning he read a dozen times, he declared himself a disciple of Adolf Hitler. In November 1958, while still in the navy, he founded in Arlington, Va., a fascist group known as the American Nazi party.

On Apr. 24, 1943, Rockwell married Judith Aultman; they had three children. Rockwell later complained that his wife's extreme commitment to feminism prevented her from being a true woman. His writings are full of personal criticisms of her. While stationed in Iceland during the Korean War, Rockwell fell in love with Thora Hallgrimsson, a divorcée with one child. Rockwell quickly divorced his wife, and he and Hallgrimsson were married on Oct. 3, 1953. Fittingly, they spent their honeymoon in Berchtesgaden, the German town in which Hitler and other Nazi leaders once lived. They had four children. In 1958, Thora's parents called her home to Iceland; after a year there, she divorced Rockwell.

Rockwell was a white supremacist who advocated the sterilization or extermination of all Jews. It was they, he insisted, who were responsible for the worldwide Communist movement. He professed to like certain individual Jews, saying on one occasion, "I like Jews. I'll be very sorry when we've killed the last of them." He also called for the deportation of all blacks to Africa and for the hanging of all "traitors," including former presidents Harry Truman and Dwight D. Eisenhower and Chief Justice Earl Warren. Rockwell's followers, whom he himself once described as criminals, psychotics, and social misfits, probably never numbered more than 100, but the American Nazi party under his direction staged numerous provocative demonstrations. His "storm troopers" were provided with Nazi SA uniforms and swastika armbands, as well as gorilla suits and pro–civil rights placards, the last two as taunts to blacks (whom they envisioned as gorillas) and to civil rights advocates.

In May 1960, New York City parks commissioner Newbold Morris denied Rockwell a speaking permit on the grounds that his preaching might incite crowds to riot, but in February 1961 the Appellate Division of the New York State Supreme Court affirmed Rockwell's right to speak in public, regardless of his message and its possible results. In November of the same year the Supreme Court of the United States upheld this decision. Despite his legal right to proclaim his racist doctrines, Rockwell's attempts to hold public crusades were generally unsuccessful, and his public demonstrations often generated hostility even from other right-wing political groups. In February 1960 the navy discharged Rockwell because of his repeated attempts to propagate his racist doctrines. His explanation for his unceremonious, albeit honorable, discharge was that he was caught in a general cutback program and that his former wife Judith had complained about him to his commanding officer.

In January 1961, Rockwell was stoned while trying to picket the pro-Zionist film *Exodus*, and later that year he was arrested in New Orleans for disorderly conduct while picketing the same movie. In 1962 the state of Virginia, in which the American Nazi party had established its headquarters, revoked the party's charter, but in August 1963, Rockwell and a small band of followers were permitted to hold a counterdemonstration during a civil rights march on the nation's capitol. Rockwell's presence at rallies often led to violence and arrests. In January 1965 he was arrested in Selma, Ala., for disturbing the peace outside a church in which a civil rights meeting was being held.

Late in 1965, Rockwell entered the Virginia gubernatorial race, polling 5,730 votes out of 562,789 cast, and he announced that he would run for the presidency. In November he and some of his followers had a run-in with people carrying a National Liberation Front flag at an anti–Vietnam War demonstration in Washington, D.C.

Rockwell's greatest success came in the summer of 1966 during open-housing demonstrations in Chicago, when a number of protesting whites carried swastikas that he had distributed. Rockwell announced in December that he was changing the name of the American Nazi party to the National Socialist White People's party and that he was going to replace its slogan of "Sieg heil" with "White power." Despite this, his Nazis were singularly unsuccessful in identifying themselves with the white backlash against the civil rights movement. In October 1966 the student union at Brown University, at the request of the university president, withdrew an invitation to Rockwell to speak, and in March 1967 the Idaho Board of Education vetoed an invitation from students at the University of Idaho.

Rockwell was shot to death in Arlington, Va., by John Patler, a dark-skinned former member of the American Nazi party who had been expelled a few months earlier for allegedly denouncing his more Nordic-looking colleagues as "blue-eyed devils." Rockwell was succeeded by Matt Koehl as leader of the party.

[See George Lincoln Rockwell, *This Time the World*, 2nd ed. (1963); Fred C. Shapiro, "The Last Word (We Hope) on George Lincoln Rockwell," *Esquire*, July 1967; and Dotson Rader, "The Deadly Friendship," *New Republic*, Sept. 23, 1967. An obituary is in the *New York Times*, Aug. 26, 1967.]

NORMAN E. TUTOROW

ROLFE, ROBERT ABIAL ("RED") (Oct. 17, 1908–July 8, 1969), baseball player, manager, and coach, was born in Penacook, N.H., the son of Herbert Wilson Rolfe, the manager of a prosperous sash, door, and blind business, and Lucy Estelle Huff. After graduating from Phillips Exeter Academy in 1927, Rolfe entered Dartmouth College, where he excelled in basketball and baseball and became one of the school's most celebrated athletes. In his sophomore year he caught the eye of the New York Yankees scout Gene McCann, and when Rolfe graduated in June 1931, he left Dartmouth with a B.A. in one hand and a Yankees contract in the other.

Within a month, Rolfe appeared in a Yankees uniform, but only as a pinch runner against Cleveland. He was farmed out to the Albany Senators of the Eastern League, for whom he hit a respectable .333 in fifty-eight games at shortstop. He was moved up to the Newark Bears of the International League, the Yankees' top minor-league operation, the following year and spent the 1932 and 1933 seasons there. Still playing shortstop, he batted .330 in 1932, and although his average slipped to .326 the following year, his all-around performance earned him the league's most-valuable-player award and advancement to the parent club. On Oct. 12, 1934, after his first full year with New York, he married Maude Isabel Africa; they had no children.

The 1934 season marked the beginning of Rolfe's nine-year career with the Yankees, during which he established himself as one of the top third basemen in all of baseball. (He was shifted from shortstop to third base by manager Joe McCarthy.) Not necessarily a colorful or spectacular performer, he was noted for his steady, consistent play, both in the field and at the plate. Despite a quiet and serious manner, Rolfe was a fierce competitor. His best year was 1939, when he batted .329 and led the American League in runs scored (139), base hits (213), and doubles (46). He batted .300 or better in three other seasons and compiled a lifetime average of .289. In 1936 he tied for the league lead in triples (15). He was also a fine bunter and expert in hitting behind the runner. Usually batting either first or second in the Yankees powerhouse lineup and followed by such sluggers as Lou Gehrig, Joe DiMaggio, and Bill Dickey, he scored more than 100 runs in seven consecutive seasons. An excellent fielder, he topped American League third basemen in fielding percentages in 1935 and 1936. He was selected for the American League all-star team in 1937 and 1939. The *Sporting News* named him to its major-league all-star team in 1937, 1938, and 1939.

When Rolfe moved up to the Yankees in 1934, he began keeping a "black book," in which he recorded detailed information on pitches thrown to him, and under what circumstances, by all the pitchers in the league. He also recorded data on opposing batters on how frequently, and under what conditions, they would bat the ball in his direction. While such recordkeeping is commonplace today, it was then somewhat original.

Throughout his life, Rolfe was plagued with a variety of ailments, but he did not miss many games. In one stretch, he played in 300 straight games, which prompted frivolous comparisons with "Iron Man" Lou Gehrig. In spring training of his rookie year, an attack of boils limited his playing time. An osteoma (a growth on the muscles of his right thigh) developed in 1937, which helps explain a .276 batting average, the lowest of his career. Immediately following that year's World Series, he underwent surgery for the removal of the growth. His play improved sharply after the operation, and he enjoyed his best seasons in 1938 and 1939. In 1941 and 1942 he was troubled by colitis, which brought down his playing time and batting average and hastened his retirement from baseball at the close of the 1942 season. Rolfe was rejected for military service in 1943 because of stomach ulcers, an old problem. His death was due to a chronic kidney ailment. The sportswriter "Red" Smith wondered how great Rolfe might have become if he had enjoyed good health.

After leaving professional baseball, Rolfe worked as a college coach and administrator and a professional coach and manager. One of few Ivy Leaguers to achieve success in baseball, he launched his coaching career at Yale. He coached the Bulldog basketball and baseball teams from the fall of 1943 through the spring of 1946, compiling win-loss records of 48–28 in basketball and 56–17 in baseball. In 1946 he returned to the Yankees as a coach, but left in the fall to coach the Toronto Huskies of the infant Basketball Association of America (later merged with the National Basketball League to form the National Basketball Association). The Huskies lasted only one year, and in 1947, Rolfe joined the Detroit Tigers as supervisor of scouting. He became director of the farm system in 1948 and field manager in 1949.

Rolfe had a meteoric managerial career with the Tigers. The team finished fourth in 1949, and in 1950 it led the American League for most of the season, only to lose out at the end to the Yankees. But he was voted manager of the year, received a lucrative $42,500 contract for 1951, and appeared to be on his way to a distinguished career as a baseball manager. Things began to come apart in 1951, when the Tigers finished fourth, and in mid-July 1952, with the team in last place, Rolfe was fired. Stories of dissension among the players were no doubt true, and resistance to Rolfe's demanding standards disrupted the team's performance. As one player complained, "He still thinks he's with the Yankees. He wants you to do things you can't do. He drives you crazy. He's a perfectionist."

Although Rolfe hoped for another chance to manage in major-league baseball, he returned to the tranquil environment of Dartmouth, where he was athletic director from 1954 until ill health forced his retirement in 1967. As director, he substantially broadened and strengthened the Dartmouth athletic program. Just prior to his death in Gilford, N.H., fans voted him all-time third baseman for the New York Yankees, and Dartmouth renamed its baseball facility Red Rolfe Field.

[Dartmouth's sports information office has a thick file of material on Rolfe. His complete batting and fielding statistics are in *The Baseball Register* and annual baseball guides. *The Baseball Encyclopedia* gives only his major-league batting statistics. Articles touching on different aspects of Rolfe's career are in *Baseball Magazine*, June 1936, Dec. 1938, July 1942, and Oct. 1942; *Sporting News*, Oct. 19, Nov. 9 and 16, 1933, and Jan. 11, 1934; *Literary Digest*, June 30, 1934; *Collier's*, Aug. 17, 1940; and *New York Times*, Oct. 7, 1934, Oct. 15, 16, 19, and 25, 1937, Aug. 7, 1943, Feb. 18, 1954, and Jan. 15, 1967. Obituaries are in the *New York Times*, July 9, 1969; and the *Sporting News*, July 26, 1969.]

EUGENE C. MURDOCK

ROMMEL, EDWIN AMERICUS ("EDDIE") (Sept. 13, 1897–Aug. 26, 1970), baseball pitcher and umpire, was born in Baltimore, Md., the son of Frederick A. Rommel, who ran a pet shop, and his wife, Louisa (her maiden name is unknown). His formal education ended in the fifth grade when he left school to work for his father. Rommel's connection with professional baseball, which lasted nearly fifty years, began when Jack Dunn of the Baltimore Orioles of the International League gave him a job as batboy.

Rommel, a right-handed thrower and batter, began his playing career in 1916 as a pitcher with Seaford, Del., in the Peninsula League. He pitched well and was taken south by the Orioles in 1917 for spring training but was later released. During the winter of 1917–1918, Rommel scalded his hands while working as a steamfitter's helper, and it was feared that his hopes for a baseball career were dashed. But he was signed again by the Orioles in the spring of 1918. This time he was traded to Newark of the International League, where he won twelve games and lost fifteen. At the end of the season he was purchased by the New York Giants. Manager John J. McGraw of the Giants failed to see Rommel's potential as a pitcher, a mistake McGraw seldom made, and released him. After returning to Newark for the 1919 season, Rommel won twenty-two games.

Earle Mack, Connie Mack's son, managed Newark in 1919 and told his father that Rommel was a good prospect. The elder Mack scouted him in a doubleheader with Toronto and saw him knocked out of both games but nevertheless signed him for the Philadelphia Athletics. When the surprised Rommel asked Mack later why he did so, Mack said, "Because you threw curves on the inside." Rommel, who was six feet two inches tall and weighed 195 pounds, joined the Athletics in the spring of 1920. In his first year he won seven games and lost seven. Rommel married Emma Elizabeth Fahey on Sept. 13, 1922; they had two children.

During his minor-league days Rommel had effectively used the spitball in tight pitching situations. When the spitball was outlawed in 1920, Rommel took up the knuckle ball, a pitch he had learned from a minor-league player, Charles Druery, who is credited by some with inventing it. To throw a knuckle ball, the pitcher grasps the ball firmly with the tips of his fingers and fingernails, and throws it in such a way that it rotates little on the way to the plate. It "wobbles and dances," as Rommel put it, making it extremely hard for the batter to hit solidly. Jimmie Foxx of the Athletics, an excellent hitter who faced Rommel often in batting practice, found his knuckler nearly impossible to hit squarely. Another teammate, the pitcher Lefty Grove, thought Rommel had the best control of the knuckler he had ever seen, but the pitch was difficult for the catcher to handle. Fortunately, during his years in the major leagues, Rommel worked with two very able catchers, Cy Perkins (until 1925) and then the great Mickey Cochrane.

Rommel spent his entire major-league career (1920–1932) with the Athletics under Connie Mack, who considered him one of the smartest pitchers he ever managed. Rommel won 171 games and lost 119, with an earned-run average of 3.54. His best years were in 1922, when he won 27 games to lead the league in wins, and in 1925, when he won 21. In 1922 the Athletics, a weak-hitting team, won only 65 games, so that Rommel was credited with an amazing 42 percent of their victories. Rommel's best years came while the Athletics were a struggling ball club. By the time Mack put together his great teams of 1929, 1930, and 1931, Rommel was in the twilight of his career, although he still pitched effectively. From 1927 on, Mack often used Rommel and Jack Quinn in relief, a role Rommel disliked, and relied on Grove, George Earnshaw, Rube Walberg, and Howard Ehmke as starters. In his final four years with the Athletics, Rommel won 29 games and lost 13. During his career, he won 51 games in relief and was credited with 29 saves.

In 1929 the Athletics won the World Series, defeating the Chicago Cubs, and won again in 1930, defeating the St. Louis Cardinals. They won the American League pennant in 1931 but lost the Series to the Cardinals. The 1929 team, with its great pitching staff, and hitters such as Al Simmons, Bing Miller, Mule Haas, Jimmie Foxx, and Cochrane, is considered to be one of the best American League teams of all time. In the 1929 Series, Rommel, who pitched only briefly in two World Series games, one in 1929 and the other in 1931, figured in one of the most unusual games in Series history. In game four at Philadelphia on October 12, the Chicago Cubs, with Charlie Root pitching strongly, hammered Philadelphia's pitchers Walberg and Quinn for six innings. In the top of the seventh, Rommel came in and allowed two hits and one run. The Cubs led 8–0. But in the bottom of the seventh, with an incredible barrage of hits, the Athletics scored ten runs. Mack sent in Lefty Grove, his ace, who pitched two hitless innings. Rommel, probably to his dazed surprise, was credited with the win.

In one of baseball's great pitching duels, Rommel faced Walter Johnson on opening day in 1926 in a game at Griffith Stadium in Washington, D.C., against the Senators. Vice-President Charles G. Dawes tossed out the first ball. In the bottom of the fifteenth inning, with the score tied at 0–0, Joe Harris of the Senators singled off Rommel, scoring Bucky Harris with the winning run, a great victory for "the Big Train" and a tough loss for Rommel.

At the end of the 1932 season, Connie Mack released Rommel as an active player but kept him on as a coach and batting-practice pitcher. In 1935, Rommel managed Richmond, a Philadelphia farm team. He was not notably successful as a manager, had a dispute with Mack over his salary, and with Mack's encouragement turned to umpiring. After two seasons of promising performance in the New York–Penn State League and the International League, he was hired by the American League in 1938. For the next twenty-one years he was a highly respected major-league umpire. He worked in the 1943 World Series between the New York Yankees and the St. Louis Cardinals and the 1947 Series between the Yankees and the Brooklyn Dodgers. He also worked in five All-Star games. Rommel greatly disliked the unnecessary prolongation of games, stalling or dawdling pitchers in particular, having himself once pitched a two-hit shutout in fifty-six minutes. In 1956 he became the first American League umpire to wear glasses on the job.

Rommel retired from baseball in 1959, finding he did not miss the game as much as he thought he might. Governor J. Millard Tawes of Maryland appointed him a senior clerk, a job he held for seven years. Rommel died in Baltimore.

[The statistics of Rommel's career are in Joseph L. Reichler, ed., *The Baseball Encyclopedia* (1985). See also Joseph L. Reichler, *Baseball's Unforgettable Games* (1960); Fred Lieb, *Baseball as I Have Known It* (1977); and Bill James, *Historical Baseball Abstract* (1986). A file of clippings and additional information is at the Baseball Hall of Fame Library, Cooperstown, N.Y. Obituaries are in the *Baltimore Sun* and the *New York Times*, both Aug. 28, 1970.]

WILLIAM MCCANN

RORIMER, JAMES JOSEPH (Sept. 7, 1905–May 11, 1966), art scholar and museum administrator, was born in Cleveland, Ohio, the son of Louis Rorimer, an interior designer and decorator, and Edith Joseph. He absorbed his father's interest in the fine arts early. "I was a woodcarver before I was a Boy Scout," he told a reporter, and at age nine, he enrolled in a course on medieval armor. With his father's encouragement, Rorimer learned the rudiments of architectural design and drawing.

Rorimer received most of his basic education at Cleveland's University School. In 1921 he went to Europe with his parents for a two-year stay. He attended the École Gory in Paris and toured historic buildings and museums. The fourteenth-century Apocalypse tapestries at the Château d'Angers inspired him to make the study of medieval art his vocation. He also became a knowledgeable collector of candlesticks.

Rorimer returned to the United States in 1922 to resume courses at the University School. From 1923 to 1927 he attended Harvard University, from which he graduated cum laude. In the summer of 1927, he joined the staff of New York's Metropolitan Museum of Art as an assistant in its Decorative Arts Department. With a well-trained eye and dedication to his work, Rorimer became a central figure in planning the Cloisters, a facility to house a large portion of the Metropolitan's medieval collections. Working closely with that project's benefactor, John D. Rockefeller, Jr., he eventually revised the original conception of this building and undertook the daily supervision of its construction. Completed in 1938, the Cloisters owed its authentically medieval architectural character to Rorimer.

Rorimer also explored the application of ultraviolet light to the problems of art authentication and conservation. His *Ultraviolet Rays and Their Use in the Examination of Works of Art* (1931) was for many years a definitive reference on the subject.

Rorimer was promoted to the position of full curator in the Department of Medieval Art in 1934. An adept fund-raiser and a discerning and aggressive collector, he caused the medieval collections to make enormous strides in quality and quantity, and the Cloisters became one of the most distinguished museums of its kind in the world. Numbered among Rorimer's greatest acquisitions were the Unicorn and Nine Heroes tapestries, a monastery chapter house, and a Romanesque chapel. In the early 1950's, Rorimer also influenced John D. Rockefeller, Jr., to endow the Cloisters with a $10 million fund. On Nov. 26, 1942, he married Katherine Serrell; they had two children.

In 1943, Rorimer enlisted in the army as a private. He was soon detailed to a division in Europe charged with protecting art treasures and archives from the ravages of World War II. By 1945, he had risen to captain's rank and was serving as chief of the American Seventh Army's Monuments, Fine Arts, and Archives Section, which uncovered art that had been confiscated by the Germans. His memoir *Survival: The Salvage and Protection of Art in War* (1950) relates his efforts to track down lost masterpieces.

In 1946, Rorimer resumed his duties at the Metropolitan, where in 1949 he became director of the Cloisters while still retaining his position as chief curator of medieval collections. In 1955 he succeeded Francis Henry Taylor in the Metropolitan's directorship. Physical facilities underwent extensive renovation and expansion, exhibitions felt the impact of Rorimer's flair for highlighting objects and his eye for detail, endowments grew substantially, and major acquisitions became frequent. Among the most notable additions to the Metropolitan's collections during Rorimer's directorship were Raphael's *Madonna of the Meadows*, Robert Campin's *Annunciation* altarpiece, and Rembrandt's *Aristotle Contemplating the Bust of Homer*.

By the time he died in New York City, Rorimer had nearly doubled the Metropolitan's annual visitorship and increased its exhibition space by 40 percent. A showman who relished the spotlight, a dogged collector, and a perfectionist, he influenced all phases of the Metropolitan's endeavors.

[Rorimer's personal papers are in the possession of his family, but a portion of them, mainly those dealing with his army service, are in the Archives of American Art of the Smithsonian Institution. Rorimer's publications include *The Cloisters* (1938); *Medieval Monuments at the Cloisters* (1941); and articles in the *Metropolitan Museum of Art Bulletin*. See Calvin Tomkins, *Merchants and Masterpieces* (1970). An obituary is in the *New York Times*, May 12, 1966.]

FREDERICK S. VOSS

ROSE, BILLY (Sept. 6, 1899–Feb. 10, 1966), producer, songwriter, and theater and nightclub owner, was born Samuel Wolf Rosenberg on New York City's Lower East Side, but in school he gave William Samuel Rosenberg as his name. His Russian-born parents, David Rosenberg, a button salesman, and Fannie Rosenthal, moved about with Rose and his two younger sisters in low-income neighborhoods in Brooklyn, the Bronx, and Manhattan, where bigger boys taunted him with ethnic slurs. His mother, who "set the pattern" for his "dreams and ambitions," regularly rescued him from his enemies and encouraged him to cadge meals from friends when her pantry was empty.

While attending David G. Farragut Junior High School in the Bronx, Rose won the gold medal for eighty-five-pound sprinters in a Madison Square Garden competition, after putting himself through months of agonizing training. From Farragut, he went to the High School of Commerce, where he played the piano (by ear) with the school orchestra and became the most adept student of the shorthand method developed by John Robert Gregg, who was using the High School of Commerce as a showcase for his system. Rose, whom Gregg declared "the greatest natural writer in the history of shorthand," won the amateur title (with a net speed of 178 words a minute) in the 1918 Metropolitan Open Shorthand Contest, even though a broken thumb forced him to write with his pen thrust through a potato. Having found through part-time jobs that his skill paid well, he had left high school for full employment the year before, a few weeks before he would have graduated.

From the start, Rose was a showman. Demonstrating shorthand while in Gregg's employ, he took rapid-fire dictation, writing on a blackboard with both hands simultaneously. Before World War I ended, he was in Washington, where he worked for Bernard Baruch, as head of the Reports Division of the War Industries Board. On one occasion he met President Woodrow Wilson, who tested his legendary speed by dictating to him from the morning paper.

After the war, Rose, who always maintained that "money" was "the Supreme Court," determined to get rich by writing popular songs. Meanwhile, he went to work for Gregg, who trained him for the 1919 National Shorthand Championship in Detroit. Although favored to win, he fainted while transcribing his notes. Humiliated by his failure, probably caused by drinking the night before, Rose vowed not to return home, never to drink again, and to abandon stenography. He mixed with songwriters, lived for a time at a church mission on Forty-sixth Street in New York City, and spent hours in the public library studying popular lyrics. In 1921 he published his first song, "Ain't Nature Grand," and in 1923 had his first hit, "Barney Google," based on a popular comic-strip character. Of the nearly 400 songs for which Rose helped write the lyrics, 41 were hits, earning him an AA rating from the American Society of Composers, Authors, and Publishers. His songs include "Me and My Shadow," "Without a Song," "It's Only a Paper Moon," and "I Found a Million-Dollar Baby in a Five-and-Ten-Cent Store." To increase the earnings of songwriters, Rose, George Meyer, and Edgar Leslie founded the Songwriters Protective Association in 1931, and Rose became its first president.

Rose invested some of his song earnings in his Back Stage Club, where Helen Morgan first sang sitting on a piano to make more room for cramped customers. Among these was the comedienne Fanny Brice, with whom he fell in love, and he inaugurated the Broadway-to-Hollywood run by flying in the open cockpit of a postal plane in order to see her. Mayor Jimmy Walker officiated at their New York City Hall marriage on Feb. 8, 1929.

Rose's club also attracted underworld figures during the Prohibition era. He at first refused their demands but surrendered after they arranged a series of police raids. He found it lucrative to work with mobsters even after the repeal of Prohibition: Rose received $1,000 a week from them to manage the Casino de Paree. For this first theater-restaurant, he attracted a thousand customers nightly by giving them an eight-course dinner, dancing, and a ninety-minute musical revue for $2.50 a head. Rose worked with mobsters in a second venture, the Billy Rose Music Hall, a lavish nightclub where he developed nostalgia-oriented, panorama-type spectaculars, but he stopped being a front in 1934. When Rose's employers threatened him after he demanded back pay, he became afraid to leave his apartment. For help, he called Baruch, who had become his friend and idol. Federal Bureau of Investigation agents soon interviewed Rose's tormentors, who agreed not to harm him but refused to pay his back wages.

Although it was later believed that everything Rose touched turned to gold, he did have his failures. His first vehicle for Fanny Brice, *Corned Beef and Roses* (1930), failed before reaching New York; a revamped version called *Sweet and Low* (1930) survived six months on

Broadway; and after more tinkering, it was rechristened *Crazy Quilt* (1931) and made $240,000 in nine months on the road, despite the Great Depression. "Too big to make money," *Jumbo* (1935) lost $150,000, but not before nearly a million people saw this giant production, which brought the circus, including the eponymous elephant, to Broadway, along with the comedian Jimmy Durante, songs by Richard Rodgers and Lorenz Hart, and a book by Ben Hecht and Charles MacArthur.

Rose staged regional spectaculars that were as innovative as his Broadway ventures. Helping Fort Worth surpass Dallas' 1936 Texas Centennial celebration, he proved himself well worth the $1,000-a-day salary he demanded. He coined the slogan "Dallas for Education, Fort Worth for Entertainment" and presented *The Last Frontier*, a colossal musical folktale and rodeo complete with covered wagons and buffalo. Combining routines pioneered by P. T. Barnum and Florenz Ziegfeld, Rose also featured the fan dancer Sally Rand and scores of giant Texas beauties in his Casa Mañana, a popular-priced theater-restaurant that seated 4,000. The next year, at the Great Lakes Exposition in Cleveland, he coined the word "aquacade" for his first aquatic musical revue, featuring Eleanor Holm, an Olympic champion backstroke swimmer. On Nov. 14, 1939, she became Rose's second wife, his marriage to Fanny Brice having ended in divorce more than a year earlier.

Rose's drive, organizational genius, and ability to coordinate the talents of others made his New York aquacade the most memorable event of the 1939 World's Fair. Adhering to his dictum that show business must cater to "sex, sentiment, and curiosity," the aquacade put "all other spectacles into eclipse." It had a cast of 350 and attracted one-quarter of all fairgoers. This "gorgeous, streamlined peepshow" took place in a block-long stage filled with purple water before an amphitheater packed with 10,000 delighted spectators. Among the 1,400 people employed to execute this giant show were the members of two full orchestras, a rhythmic chorus line of 72 swimmers, Holm, Johnny Weissmuller, and the English Channel swimmer Gertrude Ederle.

Rose, who also staged the San Francisco aquacade at the Golden Gate Exposition (1940), became known as a tough bargainer who kept labor costs down. Even though he had founded a union to protect songwriters, he extracted free rehearsals from swimmers and performers in his other productions until his actions spawned unions to protect them. It was said of this "headman of mass entertainment," who sold over 100 million tickets, that he got rich by paying five cents for an act and selling it for a dollar.

In the public mind, Rose came to personify Broadway. His second Casa Mañana, a huge Manhattan cabaret that he closed rather than meet a salary increase demanded by the waiters' union, was followed by his most renowned nightclub, the Diamond Horseshoe, which lasted thirteen years (1939–1952) and became a top New York tourist attraction.

Of the eleven Broadway shows that Rose produced, *Carmen Jones* (1943) was his most memorable. Oscar Hammerstein II could find no producer for his all-black version of Bizet's opera *Carmen*, set in a World War II parachute factory, until he contacted Rose. Together they found a reservoir of black talent, and the success of their production, which grossed more than any show had since the onset of the Great Depression, proved that American audiences would accept both opera and black singers. Rose also produced *The Seven Lively Arts* (1944), but despite the contributions of Salvador Dali, Igor Stravinsky, Cole Porter, Benny Goodman, Bert Lahr, and Beatrice Lillie, it merely broke even after a run of seven months.

Signed newspaper advertisements by Rose, starting with one for *Carmen Jones*, evolved into his triweekly, syndicated newspaper column, "Pitching Horseshoes," which at its peak appeared in 467 daily papers and 1,800 weeklies. This lively column, running from 1947 through 1950, was filled with "show-biz, snappy sayings, and schmalz." It paved the way for Rose's triumphant 1948 world junket, during which he and Eleanor Holm dined with world leaders and were front-page copy at every stop. Rose reprinted some of his columns in his book *Wine, Women and Words* (1956), which Dali illustrated.

The fact that Eleanor Holm was often the heroine of Rose's column made their 1954 divorce and the "War of the Roses" that preceded it especially newsworthy. After their divorce, Rose twice married (on June 2, 1956, and Dec. 30, 1961) and twice divorced (in 1959 and 1963) Joyce Mathews, an actress who had slashed her wrists in his apartment before their first marriage. She had previously been married, also twice, to Milton Berle. Rose's last marriage, to Doris Warner Vidor on Mar. 3, 1964, lasted only six months.

Besides a series of marriages, Rose's restlessness produced a series of what he called "toy careers." Wall Street, real estate, and art collecting occupied his last decade. In the late 1950's and early 1960's he became "a one-man stock exchange," and between October 1963 and February 1964 he earned $8,733 for every hour the New York Stock Exchange was open. Besides two theaters, Rose owned an acre in midtown Manhattan and various homes in which he lived and entertained lavishly. In his forty-five-room Manhattan palace, filled with antiques, oil paintings, and sculptures, he regularly slept in Napoleon's field bed, with half-foot-high helmeted heads of classical warriors topping its posts.

In 1958 he organized the Billy Rose Foundation, to which he bequeathed almost his entire estate, estimated at $54 million. Its grants to institutions have furthered education and research, especially in the arts and medicine. The foundation funded, for example, the Billy Rose Theatre Collection of the New York Public Library. Always "conscious of himself as a Jew," Rose announced in 1960 that he would give to Israel his sculpture collection, which included more than a hundred works. To display this gift properly, he retained Isamu Noguchi to design the five-acre Billy Rose Art Garden, part of the National Museum in Jerusalem. "In this clip-clap, rag-tag life," Rose proudly maintained, "this is the most heartwarming thing I have ever done." Rose, who was a heavy smoker, died at Montego Bay, Jamaica, while recuperating from cardiovascular surgery.

Rose, who in life stood only five feet, three inches in what he termed "a five nine world," constantly compensated for his half-foot handicap. In time, he also learned to capitalize on it. He became "the Bantam Barnum" who produced gargantuan entertainments; he became "the runt-sized Runyon" whose newspaper column reached 20 million people; he became "the mighty midget" who surrounded himself with women and objects that towered above him—from giant showgirls, known as long-stemmed roses, to oversized statues in his sculpture collection. He was also the little guy who quarreled with unions and managed to make money in the Great Depression, when bigger and better-established theatrical producers failed. He utilized his "sensational memory," his "gift for concentration," his shrewd bargaining ability, and what Fanny Brice called his "seven-track mind" to succeed in many diverse areas. These varied careers are depicted on the stained-glass windows of the mausoleum housing his sarcophagus in Ardsley, N.Y.

[Rose's papers are in the Billy Rose Theatre Collection of the New York Public Library at Lincoln Center; they include the manuscript and notes for an unpublished biography by Maurice Zolotow. See also Polly Rose Gottlieb, *The Nine Lives of Billy Rose* (1968); Earl Conrad, *Billy Rose: Manhattan Primitive* (1968); and Stephen C. Nelson, "Only a Paper Moon: The Theatre of Billy Rose" (Ph.D. diss., New York University, 1985). For contemporary accounts of his achievements, see *Newsweek*, Dec. 18, 1944, May 27, 1963, Feb. 5, 1968; *New York Times*, Nov. 15, 1931, Aug. 11, 1935, July 26, 1936, June 8, 1941, Sept. 16, 1961, Feb. 12, 1966; *New York Times Magazine*, Apr. 23, 1939, Mar. 26, 1944; *Saturday Review*, May 21, 1949; *Theatre Arts*, Jan. 1945; and *Time*, Oct. 28, 1935, Aug. 21, 1939, Dec. 18, 1944, June 2, 1947, Aug. 18, 1952, Feb. 8, 1960, Mar. 26, 1965, Feb. 18 and Aug. 19, 1966. An obituary is in the *New York Times*, Feb. 11, 1966.]

OLIVE HOOGENBOOM

ROSENBLATT, BERNARD ABRAHAM (June 15, 1886–Oct. 14, 1969), Zionist leader, was born in Grodek, Poland, the son of Louis Rosenblatt, a prosperous Bialystok woolen factory owner, and Mary Hachnochi, whose family had been woolen mill owners for more than a generation. The Rosenblatts' home attracted Jewish nationalists and intellectuals.

The depression of 1890 prompted Louis Rosenblatt to visit a cousin in America in 1891. Two months after he reached Philadelphia, he sent for his wife and children, who arrived in 1892. The family settled in a large house on Philadelphia's South Side, near the center of the emerging immigrant Jewish neighborhood. Rosenblatt attended public school and Jewish religious school. In his autobiography, *Two Generations of Zionism* (1967), he recalled his first passionate pronouncement on Zionism at a lively Sabbath-afternoon discussion about the first Zionist Congress.

In 1900 the family moved to Pittsburgh,

where Rosenblatt attended Central High School. He organized his first Zionist group in 1902, the Zion Literary Society, for high school students. In 1903 he attended his first American Zionist convention, in Pittsburgh. The steel strike that year spurred the Rosenblatts' move to New York City, where they lived in the Jewish neighborhood of Harlem in 1904. Rosenblatt entered Columbia College and by December 1904 had established the first Columbia University Zionist Society, despite the efforts of E. R. A. Seligman and Felix Adler, both professors at Columbia, to discourage him. In a bid to legitimate Zionism on campus, Rosenblatt competed during his senior year for the Curtis Medal. His prizewinning oration, "Palestine: The Future Hebrew State," described the Zionist pioneers as Jewish Puritans laying the foundations for the Jewish state in cooperative agricultural colonies; it articulated themes that he later pursued as a Zionist leader.

In 1908, Rosenblatt completed an M.A. in sociology, and the following year, he received a law degree from Columbia University Law School. In 1911 he went to Tannersville, N.Y., to recuperate from an appendicitis attack. There he attended the Zionist convention as a delegate of the Collegiate Zionist League, which he had helped to organize. He agreed to serve as honorary secretary of the Federation of American Zionists, thus moving into the inner circle of the small American Zionist movement. At one of the weekly administrative meetings, he was delegated to assist a group of women to organize a Zionist society. His efforts helped establish the nucleus of Hadassah, the American women's Zionist organization. At the meetings he met Gertrude Goldsmith, who became a fervent Zionist after attending the World Zionist Congress in 1911 as the American delegate and was one of the principal organizers of Hadassah. On June 3, 1914, they were married; they had two children.

In 1914, Rosenblatt published his first book, *The Social Commonwealth*, in which he combined socialist ideals of cooperation and the regulation of economic life with the benefits of competition and a voluntary democracy. He focused on agricultural labor as a solution to mass unemployment and on the nationalization of land to protect the public as consumers. He consistently tried to implement the latter in Palestine. In 1915 he incorporated the American Zion Commonwealth to purchase land in Palestine for Jewish settlement. The organization adopted his land policy by reserving 10 percent of all lands for communal purposes, including industrial development, and spreading the profit from renting these urban lands throughout the community.

Rosenblatt made a brief, unsuccessful foray into American politics in 1916 as the Democratic candidate in Harlem's Twentieth Congressional District against Morris Hillquit, a Socialist, and Isaac Siegel, the Republican incumbent. The fiercely contested race attracted attention, with Rosenblatt running as the Jewish nationalist candidate who championed President Woodrow Wilson's progressive domestic program.

At the American Zionists' 1918 Pittsburgh convention, Rosenblatt helped draft the two platform articles that advocated the public ownership of land in Palestine. He introduced to the American Jewish Congress platform his concept of a Jewish commonwealth modeled upon the commonwealths of Massachusetts and Pennsylvania but "Hebraic in character and culture." He saw this idea as an American contribution to Zionism. American Jews, however, did not support a Jewish commonwealth until 1942. In 1919, at Louis Brandeis' behest, Rosenblatt traveled to Versailles to urge Felix Frankfurter, the American Zionist representative at the peace conference, to adopt his land-ownership program. But the British refused to incorporate the program into their Palestine mandate. In 1920, Rosenblatt attended the first World Zionist Convention since World War I and fell under the spell of Chaim Weizmann's oratory. He agreed to champion the Keren Hayesod, or Foundation Fund, in the United States.

In 1921, Rosenblatt received a judicial appointment to the New York City Magistrate's Court. He rallied behind the Weizmann group, against the prominent American Zionist leaders identified with Brandeis. Rosenblatt, an exceptionally persuasive speaker who supported Weizmann's program of colonization in Palestine, rather than Brandeis' plan of controlled capitalist development, sounded the opening salvos against Stephen Wise at the bitter Cleveland Zionist convention in 1921. The Brandeis group walked out, leaving the leadership to Rosenblatt and his colleagues. Rosenblatt was elected the first American delegate to the World Zionist Executive. Returning to America in

1922 from the Executive's Jerusalem meeting, he successfully floated the first Jewish municipal bond issue.

Rosenblatt's family's first visit to Palestine in 1925 led his wife to decide to settle in Haifa. For the next thirty years, he divided his time between Haifa and New York City, where he maintained his law practice and home. During the 1920's he acted as mediator between two factions of American Zionism. He also invested in a large number of business enterprises in Palestine, reflecting his belief in the importance of the migration of capital, and oversaw major land purchases, including those leading to the establishment of Herzlia, the industrial region of Haifa Bay, and several agricultural colonies. He served as director of the Israel Land Development Company, the Migdal Insurance Company, and Tiberias Hot Springs.

In the late 1930's, when the British were considering partitioning Palestine, Rosenblatt organized a Haifa committee to advocate partition and federation, adopting the American federal model. He spent the war years in New York engaged in Democratic and Jewish politics. He wrote widely on his vision of a Jewish commonwealth, federated with an Arab one, in Palestine. After the war he returned to Haifa and, as an American citizen, challenged the British ban on land sales in the courts. The issue, however, became academic when the United Nations voted for partition in 1947.

The establishment of the state of Israel, the central dream of Rosenblatt's life, brought to an end his Zionist activity. His vision of a social Zionism guiding a Jewish commonwealth reflected an American perspective that few Israeli leaders understood. After his wife's death in 1955, he returned to New York City, where he died.

[The main source for information on Rosenblatt's life is his autobiography and his oral history in the collection of the Institute of Contemporary Jewry at the Hebrew University of Jerusalem. His articles and books include *Social Zionism* (1919), *Federated Palestine and the Jewish Commonwealth* (1941), and *The American Bridge to the Israel Commonwealth* (1959). Melvin Urofsky discusses him briefly in *American Zionism from Herzl to the Holocaust* (1975). An obituary is in the *New York Times*, Oct. 15, 1969.]

DEBORAH DASH MOORE

ROSSEN, ROBERT (Mar. 16, 1908–Feb. 18, 1966), film writer, director, and producer, was born Robert Rosen, in New York City, the son of Russian immigrants who had settled on the Lower East Side, a crowded section of New York City. The Rosens were poor, and life was combative—in a literal sense for young Rosen, who in the process of growing up had a few bouts as a professional boxer.

Rosen enrolled at New York University for several semesters but left without taking a degree, having been lured away by the possibility of a career in the theater. As Robert Rossen, from 1930 to 1935 he acted in, stage-managed, and directed off-Broadway and summer-stock companies. In 1933 he staged Richard Maibaum's *Birthright*, one of the earliest anti-Nazi plays, on Broadway. Rossen's own play, *The Body Beautiful*, was produced on Broadway in 1935. It closed after only four performances but nevertheless attracted the attention of Hollywood. On Nov. 5, 1935, he married Sue Siegal; they had three children.

Offered a writer's contract by Warner Brothers in 1936, Rossen moved to California. Warner's, more consistently than any other studio, offered films with social content as strong as the mass audience was prepared to take. Its roster included tough-guy actors such as James Cagney and provocative "dames" such as Bette Davis. Settling into the studio system with apparent ease, though later chafing under it, Rossen remained at Warner's until 1943. His first films were *Marked Woman* (1937), a tense, sharp underworld melodrama, and, in the same year, *They Won't Forget*, a forceful examination of racial prejudice and xenophobia in the Deep South. Of his Warner's scripts, this was his favorite. Among other notable Rossen pictures for Warner's were *Dust Be My Destiny* (1939), with John Garfield; *The Roaring Twenties* (1939), with James Cagney; *The Sea Wolf* (1941), with Edward G. Robinson; and *Edge of Darkness* (1943), his last for the studio, with Errol Flynn, Ann Sheridan, and a host of Broadway actors. All were based on actual events or on published material.

At the outset of his Hollywood career Rossen joined the Communist party. He remained in it until 1947 but was not long happy in it. Like many other writers, he could not tolerate the party's attempts to control or censor his work.

In 1943, tired of Communist agitation and of the pressure of writing under contract, Rossen returned to New York City. Within a year he was back in Hollywood, working on scripts for the director Lewis Milestone, of which the first and arguably the best was a war picture, *A Walk in the Sun* (1946). His first opportunity as a film director came in 1947, when Dick Powell, the star of *Johnny O'Clock*, for which Rossen wrote the script, insisted that Rossen direct as well. Rossen then directed *Body and Soul* (1947), for which he is best remembered. Starring John Garfield as a boxer who slugs his way out of poverty only to find material success meaningless, it was a work that owed not a little to Clifford Odets' *Golden Boy*.

Rossen's success made it possible for him to establish his own film-producing unit, under an arrangement with Columbia Pictures. Coinciding with this step was the onset of his problem with the House Un-American Activities Committee (HUAC), which in 1947 began investigating alleged subversive activity in Hollywood. Rossen was among the first wave of Hollywood professionals to be subpoenaed but was not called to testify. At Columbia, where his declaration that he was no longer a party member was sufficient to keep him at his job, he produced, directed, and wrote *All the King's Men* (1949), based on the novel by Robert Penn Warren. After the release of his next film, *The Brave Bulls* (1951), which he produced and directed, Rossen, having been named as a Communist by other witnesses before HUAC, was subpoenaed again. He discussed his own party membership candidly but would not divulge the names of others. Consequently, he was no longer employable in Hollywood. After two years of idleness he requested another hearing. Reasoning that every name he could mention was already in HUAC's files, he provided a list of onetime party associates and then resumed his career.

Of Rossen's late pictures, the most memorable are the final two, *The Hustler* (1961), with Paul Newman, and *Lilith* (1964), with Warren Beatty; each was based on a novel that Rossen admired. In 1960 Rossen was represented on Broadway for the second time, again unsuccessfully, with *The Cool World*, a collaboration with Warren Miller based on Miller's novel of Harlem street life. Ill for many years with diabetes and other ailments, Rossen died in New York City.

Rossen received fewer honors than his work deserved. He received an Academy Award for *All the King's Men*, as best picture of the year, and the New York Film Critics Award for *The Hustler*, again as best picture.

[Rossen's reviews and clippings are in the Library for the Performing Arts at Lincoln Center, New York City. An outline of Rossen's career is in Alan Casty, *The Films of Robert Rossen* (1969). Victor S. Navasky, *Naming Names* (1980), offers insight into Rossen and HUAC. An obituary is in the *New York Times*, Feb. 19, 1966.]

MALCOLM GOLDSTEIN

ROSSITER, CLINTON LAWRENCE, III (Sept. 18, 1917–July 10, 1970), political scientist, historian, lecturer, and writer, was born in Philadelphia, Pa., the son of William Winton Goodrich Rossiter, a stockbroker and partner in the firm of Oliphant and Company, and Dorothy Shaw. When Rossiter was two his family moved to Bronxville, N.Y., where he attended primary school. He received his secondary education at Westminster School in Simsbury, Conn.

In 1935 Rossiter entered Cornell University, where his academic distinction admitted him to Phi Beta Kappa. He graduated in 1939 and received a graduate fellowship to Princeton University, where he studied with the distinguished McCormick Professor of Jurisprudence Edward S. Corwin. Rossiter received his M.A. in 1941 and his Ph.D. in 1942, writing a thesis that was to bring him wide professional acclaim when it was published in revised form as *Constitutional Dictatorship: Crisis Government in the Modern Democracies* (1948). No form of government, he argued, could survive without transforming itself into a dictatorship when the nation's existence was threatened.

For the next three years, until the end of World War II, Rossiter served as an officer in the naval reserve, rising to the rank of lieutenant. In 1946 he began his teaching career as an instructor in political science at the University of Michigan. Before the end of the year he joined the faculty of Cornell as an instructor.

On Sept. 5, 1947, Rossiter married Mary Ellen Crane. They had three children. At Cornell, Rossiter advanced rapidly in the political science department; he became a professor in 1954 and was department chairman from 1956 to 1959. In 1959 he was appointed to the John L. Senior Chair in American Institutions, a position he held until his death.

Although Rossiter wrote or edited more than

a dozen books and a large number of articles and gave many lectures, his reputation as a political scientist and historian was established by his early work. In 1951 he published *The Supreme Court and the Commander in Chief*, in which he examined the scope of presidential power in wartime. It was a continuation of his interest in crisis management in constitutional systems. *Seedtime of the Republic; The Origin of the American Tradition of Political Liberty* (1953) established Rossiter's reputation as a diligent and meticulous scholar who wrote about colonial political ideas with commanding skill. The American Political Science Association gave it the Woodrow Wilson Foundation Award for the best publication of the year in the field of government and democracy; the American Historical Association awarded it the Bancroft Prize for distinguished writing in American history; and the Institute of Early American History and Culture gave it the prize for the best book in the field of early American history.

Rossiter's next book was *Conservatism in America* (1955), which even before publication was awarded the Charles Austin Beard Memorial Prize in 1954. The scope of conservatism in this work included most of the major figures in American political thought. In 1956 Rossiter gave the Walgreen Foundation lectures at the University of Chicago, and in revised form these were published that year as *The American Presidency*. This comprehensive and lucid book met with enormous success both in the scholarly world and in the popular paperback market, where it was translated into more than thirty languages and sold over one million copies. In it Rossiter examined the presidential office, particularly as held by Franklin D. Roosevelt, Harry S Truman, and Dwight D. Eisenhower, and the necessary augmentation of executive power that had occurred under their leadership. In 1960 he gave a series of lectures at Cornell that became the basis for his *Parties and Politics in America*. Even though as the John L. Senior Professor he had no required teaching duties at Cornell, Rossiter continued to teach both undergraduate and graduate courses. In 1960–1961 he was Pitt Professor of American History at Cambridge University, England. Before his career ended he had lectured or given seminars at fifty colleges or universities on every continent. During the 1960's he continued to publish significant work, most notably *Marxism: The View from America* (1960), a book sponsored by the Fund for the Republic as part of a broad study of Communism in American life.

Rossiter left as testimony to his broad erudition a body of work that encompassed most of the major branches and functions of American national government from colonial America to the 1960's, and commentary on topics ranging from Marxism to conservatism. His strength was in his successful merging of political science and history. Throughout the postwar years political science moved away from an historical orientation, so that Rossiter's accomplishments, so notable in the 1950's, received less attention in the next decade. In all of his writing Rossiter testified to his faith in American institutions, the Constitution, the courts, and the fundamental soundness of public opinion. He was ill and depressed at a time when he felt that the political and social institutions he believed in were failing, and he took his own life in Ithaca, N.Y. While he left no new or distinctive interpretations of American politics, he was a careful scholar, an enthusiastic teacher, and a graceful writer. In his books, as in his political beliefs, he was a cautious critic and a constructive conservative.

[Rossiter also wrote *Alexander Hamilton and the Constitution* (1964); *1787: The Grand Convention* (1966); and *The American Quest, 1780–1860*, completed by Mary E. Rossiter (1971). See Edward Cain, *They'd Rather Be Right* (1963); and Theodore J. Lowi, "Clinton Rossiter Remembered," *Cornell Arts and Science Newsletter*, Spring 1982. Obituaries are in the *American Historical Review*, June 1971; and *PS*, Winter 1971.]

ALAN P. GRIMES

ROTHKO, MARK (Sept. 25, 1903–Feb. 25, 1970), painter, was born Marcus Rothkowitz in Dvinsk, Russia, the son of Jacob Rothkowitz and Anna Goldin. Although Jacob was a successful pharmacist in czarist Russia, as a Jew he saw greater opportunity in the United States, and in 1910 he immigrated to Portland, Oreg. Once he found work, Jacob was joined by his family over the next three years, and in 1913 the youngest of his four children, Marcus, came to America.

Rothko attended Hebrew school in Russia and, from 1913 to 1921, Shattuck Grade School and then Lincoln High School in Portland. He excelled in his academic courses and took painting and drawing classes at a nearby art school. Having completed high school in three years, in 1921 he accepted a scholarship to Yale University. During his college years he sketched frequently, but there was still no indication that painting would be his lifework.

In 1923, Rothko left Yale without completing his studies and moved to New York City, where he settled permanently in 1925. Having taken an anatomy course at the Arts Students League in 1923, he returned to the school in 1925 to study painting with Max Weber. His courses with Weber in 1925 and 1926 comprised his only formal training. From Weber he learned about the avant-garde art that had emerged from Europe, particularly the work of Cézanne and the cubists. Rothko's work during the middle to late 1920's consisted primarily of representational landscapes, still lifes, and nudes. These heavily painted works in somber colors with distorted figures and skewed perspective showed the strong influence of Weber's own expressionist style.

In 1928, Rothko participated in his first exhibition, a group show at the Opportunity Galleries in New York that included works by Milton Avery. Rothko regularly visited Avery's studio and began to emulate Avery's Matisse-inspired style of simplified elements and composition, as well as his purity of color. During the following decade, Rothko's subjects expanded to include cityscapes, in addition to the bathers and genre scenes typical of Avery's work.

The 1930's brought Rothko a number of important personal and professional alliances. On Nov. 10, 1932, he married Edith Sachar, a jewelry designer. During these early years, despite regular shows in New York galleries, Rothko's primary source of income was his work as an art teacher for children at Center Academy, Brooklyn Jewish Center, where he taught from 1929 to 1952. In 1936 and 1937, Rothko's livelihood was supplemented by his participation in the Works Progress Administration (WPA) Federal Art Project. In 1935, Rothko, Adolph Gottlieb, and several other artists showing at Gallery Secession in New York, many of whom were employed by the WPA, which had been established in that year, formed "the Ten." The members of this group rebelled against the regional style that prevailed in contemporary American art and admired the innovative works of Avery and the European modernists. Until 1940 the Ten met monthly and exhibited as a group.

Rothko's work of the late 1930's reflects the social and political climate of the decade. Working from numerous preparatory sketches, he painted tortured figures sealed into cramped interiors and a number of subway scenes showing ethereal figures alienated within their urban environment. A disquieting mood prevails in these works, coupled with a simplicity of composition and a lyrical use of light and color.

In 1938, Rothko became a United States citizen. Although he did not legally change his name from Marcus Rothkowitz until 1959, in 1940 he began to sign his works Mark Rothko. From 1938 until 1943 he worked closely with Gottlieb, as both artists began to explore ancient and Christian myths as subject matter for their work. For Rothko, myths provided a more universal expression of the human condition than his earlier subjects of contemporary urban life. Rothko's mythical works combined archaic symbols with fragmented images of humans, animals, and plants. When titles to some of these works made direct reference to specific myths, it was the essence of the myth that Rothko and Gottlieb sought to express.

In 1944, Rothko became interested in the surrealists, many of whom were then living in New York. He was fascinated by their attention to myth and to the world of the unconscious. Rothko painted Miró-like fantasies, populated by flat, biomorphic forms. His oils began to show the same kind of spontaneity, ethereal lightness, and subtlety of color that he achieved in his watercolors. Although the figure still remained evident, these paintings were the link between Rothko's early, realist style and his mature, abstract works.

In early 1945, Rothko divorced his first wife, and on March 31 he married Mary Alice Beistle Mell, a children's book illustrator; they had two children. That year also saw Rothko's major one-man exhibition at Peggy Guggenheim's gallery, Art of This Century. The works he exhibited reflected his developing interest in the surrealists.

By the mid-1940's Rothko's work was frequently included in major museum exhibitions, and in 1947 he started showing at the Betty Parsons Gallery in New York, where he was given one-man exhibitions during each of the following five years. It was in 1947 that Rothko began painting in a purely abstract style. His early abstractions may well have been inspired by the dramatic abstract works of Clyfford Still, who was then living in New York. Throughout his life Rothko maintained that his work was about human drama, but by the late 1940's he realized that the adopted ancient myth, with the presence of an identifiable figure, was no longer his most effective vehicle for expressing psychological states. By 1948 the free-floating, brightly colored rectangles that would constitute his new pictorial vocabulary had emerged in his paintings. During this time Rothko allied himself closely with the artists of the New York school, who soon became known as abstract expressionists. Nonetheless, Rothko never considered himself a colorist or an abstract artist; he saw color and abstract forms as merely ways to suffuse his paintings with what he called "basic human emotions—tragedy, ecstasy, doom."

By 1950, Rothko was painting in the style for which he is best known. His brilliantly colored, vertical canvases usually bore two or three frontally situated rectangles balanced one above the other. These works, primarily in red, orange, yellow, and violet, have a luminous quality. The stained background radiates through and around the thin washes of color that comprise the upper rectangles; this makes the painterly shapes appear to hover over the picture plane. Clearing his work of all extraneous elements, Rothko created the desired mood by manipulating color, light, and proportion. Painting on an increasingly large scale, Rothko intended to allow the viewer to be drawn into the spiritual experience of the painting.

In 1958, Rothko was commissioned to paint murals for the Four Seasons, a restaurant in New York. At the time of the commission, Rothko was represented by the Sidney Janis Gallery, which he had joined in 1955. Working for the first time on a series, Rothko produced three cycles of murals rather than one. By the second series, he had attempted a new format: working on horizontal canvases, he left the central area of the rectangles open, creating a portal through which the background color is revealed. His palette became much darker, and by the third series, he used only maroon and black, colors that rarely appear in his early work. Finding the restaurant an inappropriate setting for his paintings, Rothko withdrew the commission. In 1969 he contributed a number of the works from the third series to the Tate Gallery in London, insisting that they be exhibited as a group.

The environment in which his works were displayed was of paramount importance to Rothko. To achieve greater clarity between the idea of the work and the observer, he preferred that his works be isolated from those of other artists. He was therefore pleased that the Phillips Collection in Washington, D.C., decided in 1960 to devote a room to his works. Rothko was also involved in the installation of his retrospective exhibition at New York's Museum of Modern Art in 1961. He was as concerned with the lighting and how works related to one another within the context of the given setting as he was with the light and proportion within the works themselves.

It was also in 1961 that Rothko received a second mural commission for Holyoke Center at Harvard University. For Harvard, Rothko painted five canvases—a central triptych and two individual panels. These works, painted in red, yellow, orange, black, and purple, were reminiscent of the composition he employed for the Four Seasons murals. Yet, here the outer rectangles bore smaller rectangular forms that pierced the central void.

In 1963, the year following Rothko's completion of the Harvard murals, he joined the Marlborough Galleries in New York. This is the year in which Rothko met Dominique and John de Menil, who in the following year commissioned him to paint murals for an interdenominational chapel in Houston. From 1964 to 1967, Rothko devoted himself to this project. For the octagonal chapel he painted triptychs with five flanking panels. Half of the works bore single black rectangles floating in a color field, while the other half were painted entirely in black and softened only by a maroon color wash. He painted his contemporary vision of the passion of Christ in black, deep reds, and purples. Religious imagery had already appeared in his early representational work, but here Rothko created a spiritual mood with abstract forms.

In 1968, Rothko began producing a large number of works on paper, limiting his colors to browns and grays and, in the following year, to blacks and grays. Despite having suffered an aneurysm of the aorta in the spring of 1968, Rothko did not allow his creativity to become daunted. With an enormously reduced palette and highly simplified forms, he created a dynamic and diverse body of work. Working in a new medium, acrylic, Rothko experimented as well with new ideas about composition. In these works, he divided the paper into two horizontal, rectangular forms anchored by the white border of the paper. Unlike his earlier works, where the viewer is drawn into the painting, here both the composition and the opacity of the acrylic create a shallow picture plane. These late paintings on paper were done with greater ease than any of his earlier works. At this late stage of his career, Rothko could compose spontaneously without revisions.

During the late 1950's and 1960's, Rothko worked primarily in a dark or muted palette, perhaps believing that his earlier, brightly colored paintings would be mistaken for decorative objects. Nonetheless, during the last two years of his life, in addition to doing the brown, black, and gray paintings, he reintroduced the brilliant colors of the late 1950's. Paintings of this kind comprised his final works.

Having not fully recovered from his illness and drinking heavily, Rothko sank into an increasingly deep depression that led to his suicide in his New York studio. At the time of his death, Rothko was already considered to be among the great pioneers who brought American art to international acclaim.

A year after Rothko's death, his children engaged in a prolonged legal battle over the disposition of their father's will. The trial revealed that the three executors, Bernard J. Reis, Theodoros Stamos, and Morton Levine, had conspired with Francis K. Lloyd, the owner of the Marlborough Galleries, in a corrupt handling of the paintings that comprised the bulk of the Rothko estate. In December 1975 a New York surrogate's court ruled in favor of Rothko's heirs. As a result of the decision, the majority of the works were restored to the Rothko children and to the Mark Rothko Foundation, established by the artist in 1969. According to Rothko's wishes, the foundation donated groups of his paintings to museums worldwide.

[For a survey of the artist's life and work, see Diane Waldman, *Mark Rothko, 1903–1970: A Retrospective* (1978); and Dore Ashton, *About Rothko* (1983). For a greater understanding of the significance of the artist's paintings on paper, see Bonnie Clearwater, *Mark Rothko: Works on Paper* (1984). A discussion of Rothko's subject matter appears in Anna Chave, *Mark Rothko Subjects* (1983). Information on Rothko installations is in Bonnie Clearwater, "How Rothko Looked at Rothko," *Artnews*, Nov. 1985. The artist's position on the use of mythological themes is clarified in a letter written by Rothko and Gottlieb to the art critic Edward Alden Jewell of the *New York Times* (June 13, 1943). A discussion of his surrealist works is the subject of Robert Rosenblum, *Mark Rothko: Notes on Rothko's Surrealist Years* (1981), as well as a statement by the artist entitled "The Romantics Were Prompted," *Possibilities I*, Winter 1947–1948. See also Lee Seldes, *The Legacy of Mark Rothko* (1979). An interview with the artist appears in Selden Rodman, *Conversations with Artists* (1957). An obituary is in the *New York Times*, Feb. 26, 1970.]

JULIA BLAUT

ROUS, FRANCIS PEYTON (Oct. 5, 1879–Feb. 16, 1970), medical researcher, was born in Baltimore, Md., the son of Charles Rous, a grain broker, and Frances Anderson Wood. When Rous was eleven years old, his father died. Rous attended public schools in Baltimore and won a scholarship to Johns Hopkins University. His early ambition was to be a naturalist, and while an undergraduate, he earned money by writing articles on flowers for a Baltimore newspaper. He entered the Johns Hopkins Medical School in 1900, but his medical training was interrupted by tuberculous lymphadenitis, which he contracted during an autopsy. In 1903 he went to Texas and worked for a year as a cowboy on a ranch to regain his health. Thereafter, he returned to Baltimore and received his M.D. in 1905.

Rous served his medical internship at Johns Hopkins. During this time, he apparently realized that clinical medicine was not his chief interest, and so, he obtained an assistantship in pathology under A. S. Warthin at the University of Michigan. There he began his lifelong preoccupation with the application of the methods of experimental pathology to the study of disease. His pathological training was further refined by a year of study in Dresden, Germany. After his return home he developed pulmonary tuberculosis and was sent to the Adirondack Mountains of New York to recover. He apparently suffered no further ill effects from the disease.

Rous joined the staff of the Rockefeller Institute for Medical Research (subsequently Rockefeller University) in 1909 and soon began investigations of the pathogenesis of cancer, despite the now-famous advice of his mentor William H. Welch: "Whatever you do, don't commit yourself to the cancer problem." In 1920, Rous was made a full member of the institute, and in 1945, a member emeritus. After his ostensible retirement, he continued laboratory work and published about 60 of his 300 or so papers.

The discovery for which Rous is most famous—that a virus is the causative agent of a chicken sarcoma—occurred soon after he joined the Rockefeller Institute. He published his initial findings in 1911. For forty years this great discovery had little impact, because scientists were unprepared to consider viruses as a cause of cancer. The Rous sarcoma was regarded as a curiosity among tumors rather than as a significant clue to the cause of cancer. In 1966, some fifty-five years after the publication of his original findings, Rous received the Nobel Prize in medicine for his discovery of tumor-inducing viruses.

At the beginning of World War I, Rous, under the pressure of wartime medical needs, gave up his work with chicken tumor virus and for the next twenty years devoted himself to other research interests. A turning point for him occurred in 1933 when a junior colleague, Richard Shope, found that a mammalian tumor, the papilloma of cottontail rabbits, was transmitted by a viruslike agent. Rous then returned to cancer research. Study of the biology of the agent and the Shope papilloma occupied him for the next two decades.

Although his sarcoma virus studies and his later work with the Shope papilloma virus were of great importance, Rous also made many significant contributions in other areas. He used indicator dyes to study tissue pH, magnets to isolate phagocytic cells after ingestion of a metallic compound, and trypsin to separate individual cells from fixed tissues. This last procedure has found wide applicability. Prior to World War I, he conducted pioneer studies on the preservation of whole blood that greatly influenced the feasibility of transfusion and the establishment of blood banks. His extensive experiments on the physiology and pathology of the liver clarified the function of the gallbladder. He also studied aspects of cellular function and vascular permeability. In the 1940's and 1950's, Rous shifted his cancer research to chemical carcinogens. He demonstrated that certain chemical agents and viruses have a cooperative neoplastic action.

In addition to his experimental work, Rous had an absorbing interest in the *Journal of Experimental Medicine*. Soon after Simon Flexner arrived at the Rockefeller Institute, he called upon Rous to be his assistant in editing the journal. Rous was appointed coeditor in 1921 and served as editor for almost fifty years. For most of that time, he read every word submitted for publication. He was in large part responsible for the style and the high standards that have characterized the journal. He had a deep and abiding interest in written English and a true talent for scientific exposition. Many contributors to the journal experienced his uncompromising demand for clarity and precision. Just as his laboratory was active to the end, so he was meeting regularly with his fellow editors of the journal until the onset of his final illness in December 1969.

On Jan. 7, 1915, Rous married Marion Eckford de Kay; they had three children. He routinely took a two-month holiday in thc summer; fishing was a favorite hobby. After World War II, he acquired a summer home at West Cornwall, Conn.

Rous was elected to the National Academy of Sciences in 1927 and subsequently received its Kovalenko Medal. He was an honorary member of the Royal Society of Medicine of London and was a recipient of its gold medal. In 1958 he received the Albert Lasker Award, in 1962 the United Nations' Prize of the World Health Organization, and in 1966 several prestigious awards from West Germany. In 1966 he was presented with the National Medal of Science by President Lyndon B. Johnson. Most of his awards were made in recognition of his research on cancer. His other work was also honored; for example, he received the Landsteiner Award from the American Association of Blood Banks in 1958. No less than twelve universities conferred honorary degrees on Rous between 1938 and 1966. Rous died in New York City.

[See Maclyn McCarthy, "Peyton Rous, 1879–1970," *Transactions of the Association of American Physicians*, 83 (1970); C. H. Andrews, "Francis Peyton Rous, 1879–1970," *Biographical Memoirs of the Fellows of the Royal Society*, 17 (1971); Rockefeller University, A *Notable Career in Finding Out* (1971); and Renato Dulbecco, "Francis Peyton Rous," *Biographical Memoirs of the National Academy of Science*, 48 (1976). An obituary is in the *New York Times*, Feb. 17, 1970.]

HARRIS D. RILEY, JR.

RUBY, JACK L. (Mar. 25, 1911–Jan. 3, 1967), assassin of Lee Harvey Oswald, was born Jacob Rubenstein, in Chicago, Ill., the son of Joseph Rubenstein, a Polish immigrant carpenter, and Fannie Turek Rutkowski. School reports and official records list Ruby's birth on various dates in the spring of 1911; Ruby most frequently used Mar. 25, 1911. Ruby grew up in lower-class Jewish neighborhoods in Chicago. Yiddish was the primary language in his home, a scene of constant strife between his parents. His father was frequently arrested for disorderly conduct, assault, and battery. In the spring of 1921 Ruby's parents separated.

Family discord had adversely affected Ruby's behavior. On June 6, 1922, he was referred to the Institute for Juvenile Research by the Jewish Social Service Bureau because of truancy and for being incorrigible at home. The institute's psychiatric report indicated that Ruby was quick-tempered and disobedient. In the 1920's Ruby and several of his brothers and sisters lived in foster homes in Chicago. His school attendance was erratic, and his highest academic achievement probably was the completion of the eighth grade in 1927.

Ruby engaged in commercial ventures on the Chicago streets. He scalped tickets to sporting events and sold novelty items and knickknacks. Although hot-tempered and quick to fight, Ruby had few difficulties with the police. According to his brother Hyman, his only arrest during this period resulted from an altercation with a policeman concerning ticket scalping. In 1933 Ruby and several friends went to Los Angeles and later to San Francisco. In California he sold handicappers' tip sheets for horse races and became a door-to-door salesman for subscriptions to San Francisco newspapers. After returning to Chicago in 1937, Ruby worked in the Scrap Iron and Junk Handlers Union. He also helped organize the Spartan Novelty Company, which sold small items, including gambling devices known as punchboards. Before American involvement in World War II, Ruby and his friends frequently attempted to break up rallies of the German-American Bund.

After efforts to gain deferment Ruby was inducted into the air force on May 21, 1943. He spent most of his service at air bases in the South and established an excellent record. He attained the rank of private first class and received the Good Conduct Medal before being honorably discharged on Feb. 21, 1946. He returned to Chicago and joined his three brothers in the Earl Products Company, a firm specializing in novelty items. In late 1947 Ruby's brothers Earl and Sam purchased his interest in the firm. Ruby moved to Dallas, Tex., to help his sister, Eva Grant, run the Singapore Supper Club, in which he had an investment. On Dec. 30, 1947, he legally changed his name to Jack L. Ruby by securing a decree from the 68th Judicial District Court of Dallas.

From 1947 until the shooting of Oswald on Nov. 24, 1963, Ruby's main interest—and source of income—was the operation of nightclubs and dance halls in Dallas. In 1953 he managed the Ervay movie theater. Ruby also engaged in speculative economic schemes, including the sale of pizza crust; stainless steel razor blades; and the twistboard, an exercise device. In 1959 he became interested in a venture to sell jeeps to Cuba.

By 1963 Ruby owned interests in two Dallas nightclubs, the Vegas Club and the Carousel Club, both of which featured striptease acts. Ruby had a violent temper and frequently was physically abusive toward customers and employees. He was a fancy dresser and considered himself a ladies' man, although he never married. As a club owner, Ruby had a number of disputes with the American Guild of Variety Artists, the union that represented his entertainers. Between 1949 and Nov. 24, 1963, Ruby was arrested eight times on minor charges in Dallas. He was, however, very interested in police work and had acquaintances on the Dallas police force. By November 1963 Ruby also had serious difficulties with taxes owed to state and federal authorities.

On Sunday Nov. 24, 1963, two days after the assassination of President Kennedy, Ruby entered the Dallas Police Department basement through an auto ramp and shot Oswald, who was being held for the murder of the president. A national television audience witnessed the event. Ruby maintained that he shot Oswald to spare Mrs. Kennedy the ordeal of returning to Dallas to testify in the trial of the president's alleged assassin. Two days later, he was indicted for murder. After a sensational trial in Dallas, Ruby was convicted of murder on Mar. 14, 1964, and was sentenced to death. During the trial Ruby's lawyers offered a defense of insanity, and a psychiatrist testified that Ruby was a "psychotic depressive." Ruby asserted his sanity, a contention upheld in a Texas state court on June 13, 1966. The Texas Court of Criminal Appeals reversed the conviction on Oct. 5, 1966, claiming that trial judge Joe B. Brown had allowed illegal testimony. A second trial was scheduled to take place in Wichita Falls, Tex. While the trial was pending, Ruby became ill and was admitted to Parkland Memorial Hospital on Dec. 9, 1966. Doctors diagnosed his illness as cancer; he died in Dallas of a blood clot in his lungs. Ruby was buried in Chicago.

After the murder of Oswald, various conspiracy theories attempted to link Ruby to a plot to kill President Kennedy. Some writers made much of Ruby's one or more visits to Cuba in 1959; others alleged that Ruby had been involved with organized crime through his dealings with the American Guild of Variety Artists. The Warren Commission report of 1964 found no evidence that Ruby was part of any conspiracy. In 1975 the Rockefeller Commission, set up to investigate Central Intelligence Agency (CIA) activities within the United States, concluded that neither Oswald nor Ruby had ties with the CIA, a charge made by several conspiracy theorists. Despite these investigations, theories and rumors continue to allege that Ruby was part of a conspiracy.

[The records of the Warren Commission are in the National Archives, Washington, D.C. Other related official publications are *Report of the President's Commission on the Assassination of President Kennedy* (1964); *Hearings Before the President's Commission on the Assassination of President Kennedy* (1964); *Report of the Commission on CIA Activities Within the United States* (1975); and *Findings of the Select Committee on Assassinations in the Assassination of President John F. Kennedy* (1979). Writings on the conspiracy theory include Peter Dale Scott et al., *The Assassinations* (1976); and G. Robert Blakey and Richard N. Billings, *The Plot to Kill the President* (1981). Biographies of Ruby include Gary Wills and Ovid Demaris, *Jack Ruby* (1967); and Seth Kantor, *Who Was Jack Ruby?* (1978). For legal proceedings against Ruby, see John Kaplan and Jon R. Waltz, *The Trial of Jack Ruby* (1965); and Elmer Gertz, *Moments of Madness* (1968). See also Renatus Hartogs and Lucy Freeman, *The Two Assassins* (1965); and David W. Belin, "The Case Against a Conspiracy," *New York Times Magazine*, July 15, 1979. An obituary is in the *New York Times*, Jan. 4, 1967.]

JOHN M. CARROLL

RUCKER, GEORGE ("NAP") (Sept. 30, 1884–Dec. 19, 1970), major-league baseball player, was born in Crabapple, in the Georgia piedmont, the son of John Rucker, a farmer, and Sara Hembree. Rucker attended the community's elementary school, completing its eight grades. Then, while learning the printing trade, he turned to baseball and became the pitcher for the local Crabapple team, which played against neighboring communities north of Atlanta. Rucker was left-handed but would upset opponents by occasionally pitching right-handed. (He batted right-handed throughout his career.) Success in these games earned him a tryout at the age of twenty with the professional team in Atlanta. He was cut from the Crackers in spring training, but in September 1904 the Atlanta team signed him when injuries depleted its pitching staff. He first played professionally on Sept. 2, 1904, winning a decision in relief against Birmingham. His real debut came three days later, when 5,000 fans watched him lose to Nashville, 8–2. The Atlanta manager then sent him back to his father's farm in Crabapple.

The next year, Rucker joined Augusta's South Atlantic League team, for which he pitched two seasons, winning forty games and losing twenty. He earned $125 a month during the season. Although he pitched well and was supported by the future major-league players Ty Cobb, Eddie Cicotte, and Ducky Holmes, Augusta regularly finished last in its league. Nonetheless, his record attracted the attention of the Brooklyn team, officially called the Superbas but known as the Dodgers, who signed him in 1907 at a salary of $1,900 for the season.

In his rookie year, Rucker quickly established himself as the best left-handed pitcher in the big leagues, with an outstanding fast ball and a crackling curve. After an injury, he altered his pitching form, and the resulting pitches were, according to one reporter, "the widest curves and slowest balls in the history of the majors." Arm trouble forced him to retire at thirty-one. Several years later he discovered that some of his difficulties resulted from tooth and tonsil infections. He later told reporters he would have lasted longer if he had played in an era when teams had trainers and doctors.

During Rucker's years in the National League, the Dodgers were a rather weak team. His career record—134 wins and 134 losses—

reflects the poor fielding and poor hitting of his teammates more than it does his pitching. Because he refused to give up any game, Rucker was well liked by his teammates and coaches. Chief Meyers and others regarded him as one of the most underrated players of the pre–World War I era. Casey Stengel credited Rucker with keeping him in baseball when he was having a rough stretch with the Dodgers.

Rucker had some outstanding seasons, despite the weakness of the Dodgers. In the 1911 season he had twenty-two wins; in 1912 he won eighteen games; and in both 1908 and 1910 he won seventeen. He pitched a perfect game, striking out fourteen, against the Boston Braves in 1908 and had a remarkable thirty-eight shutouts during his major-league career. Rucker always declared that his sixteen strikeouts against the Cardinals in 1909 was his greatest performance as a pitcher. This gave him the National League's single-game strikeout record until 1933, when Dizzy Dean struck out seventeen Chicago Cubs. Rucker played in one World Series game in 1916, when the Dodgers lost the series 4–2 to the Boston Red Sox. Rucker worked two innings, striking out three, without gaining a decision.

Rucker had the nickname "Nap," short for Napoleon. One anecdote claimed that he got the sobriquet from his fondness for ice cream, especially the confection known as napoleon. Rucker reported that the name was "a gift from Grantland Rice," the dean of American sportswriters, who wrote for the *Atlanta Constitution* while Rucker was in Augusta and moved to New York about the time Rucker went to Brooklyn. The nickname became so widely known that Rucker adopted it as his unofficial middle name.

After leaving the player ranks, Rucker maintained his link to baseball by serving as the Dodgers scout in the South. Back home in Georgia, he worked the family farm and operated a wheat and corn mill with the father of his wife, Edith Wing Wood, whom he married on Oct. 1, 1911; they had one child. In 1934, Rucker was elected mayor of Roswell, the town next to Crabapple. He served for a salary of $100 a year for two years. Later, he continued his public service as the town's water commissioner and umpire for community ball games. He died at his home in Crabapple.

Rucker's career epitomized the pattern of early baseball professionals. He never attended college (where football was the gentleman's amateur sport). His salary never reached above $4,500 a year, and it averaged just a shade under $3,400 a year for his major-league career. He did receive one loser's share of the World Series money, enough to purchase a second farm in his neighborhood of Georgia. Rucker remained the property of the Dodgers, whose owner, Charles Ebbets, refused offers of $25,000 to purchase his contract. Rucker and other professional baseball players had no choice but to play for the team holding their contracts. (Baseball's free agents did not appear until after World War II.) When his career ended, Rucker, like other ballplayers of the era, went home without a pension or retirement fund.

[Information on Rucker is in the files of the National Baseball Hall of Fame and Museum at Cooperstown, N.Y.; and the Roswell (Ga.) Historical Society. See Harry Grayson, *They Played the Game* (1946); and Lawrence S. Ritter, *The Glory of Their Times* (1966). An obituary is in the *New York Times*, Dec. 21, 1970.]

WILLIAM H. BEEZLEY

RUDKIN, MARGARET FOGARTY (Sept. 14, 1897–June 1, 1967), business executive, was born in New York City, the daughter of Joseph J. Fogarty, an Irish-born truckman, and Margaret Healy. When she was twelve, the Fogarty family moved to Flushing, N.Y., where she graduated from high school in 1915. During the next four years she worked at a bank in Flushing, first as a bookkeeper and then as a teller. In 1919 she became a customer's representative with the brokerage firm of McClure, Jones and Company, and on Apr. 8, 1923, she married Henry Albert Rudkin, a partner in the brokerage house; they had three children.

Between 1923 and 1929 the Rudkins lived a prosperous life in New York City. Then they moved to Fairfield, Conn., where they had bought 125 acres of farmland and constructed a Tudor-style mansion. Dubbing their estate Pepperidge Farm after the pepperidge, or black gum, trees on the property, the Rudkins enjoyed a comfortable country life while also experimenting with ways to make money from their estate, beginning with homegrown apples and turkeys.

In the summer of 1937, Margaret Rudkin accidentally launched a new enterprise. After a doctor suggested that her youngest son's asthmatic condition was being aggravated by the chemical additives in commercially baked goods, she developed a special diet for him built upon natural foods. Although lacking any baking experience, Rudkin began to bake her own whole-wheat bread from stone-ground flour, grinding the wheat in a kitchen coffee mill and devising her own recipe, which made generous use of butter, whole milk, honey, and molasses. Before long she was turning out good-tasting bread for her family and friends. When her son's condition seemed to improve after eating the bread, his allergist asked her to make bread for several other of his patients, and this generated a sizable mail-order business.

In August 1937, Rudkin sold her first batch of loaves wholesale to a grocer in Fairfield, and soon after, she persuaded the manager of Charles and Company, a specialty grocer in New York City, to order twenty-four loaves a day. By this time Rudkin had hired some neighbor women to assist her, had converted the estate's stable and part of the garage into her bakery, and was also baking white bread made from unbleached flour for people who could not tolerate much roughage in their diet.

From this beginning, Pepperidge Farm, as Rudkin christened her business, emerged, providing bakery products for people who wanted the quality of homemade food and were willing to pay for it. Despite the high price she charged for her bread (twenty-five cents a loaf compared to ten cents a loaf for commercially baked bread) because of the use of expensive ingredients, she was selling 4,000 loaves a week within a year. Word of mouth prompted many orders, as did the favorable publicity Rudkin received in the New York press, especially an article in the *New York Journal and American* (Nov. 20, 1937). Similar articles in national magazines followed, leading to a number of standing orders from customers throughout the United States and in foreign countries.

As her business mushroomed, Rudkin acquired a fleet of trucks to keep stores stocked with her products, contracted with two old water-powered gristmills to grind the top-grade wheat she bought, and added melba toast and pound cake to her roster of products. In 1940 she transferred her operations to rented buildings in nearby Norwalk, giving her the capacity to bake 50,000 loaves a week. Determined to keep the firm under family control, Rudkin financed most of the expansion from earnings and kept its management in her and her husband's hands. Gradually, her husband, who served as chairman of the board, relinquished his Wall Street connections to direct Pepperidge Farm's finances and marketing activities, while Rudkin, as president, oversaw the personnel and production side of the business.

After World War II, Pepperidge Farm continued to grow. In 1947, Rudkin moved her bakery into a new plant in Norwalk that she had designed herself. It initially had the capacity to produce 4,000 loaves an hour. In 1949 she opened a second bakery in Pennsylvania, and in 1953, a third in Illinois. At the same time, Rudkin deftly utilized television to sell her bread. Often she appeared in homespun commercials herself as "Maggie" Rudkin, basing her sales appeal on the nation's nostalgic yearning for "homey" and nutritious food. She also added new products, including a line of delicate luxury cookies, a frozen pastry line, and brown-and-serve rolls.

Notwithstanding the growth of Pepperidge Farm and the mass production of her bread, Rudkin remained committed to the high-quality baking ingredients and the practices she had first adopted in 1937. She still used only stone-ground wheat, eschewed commmercial shortenings, mixed the dough in small batches, and cut and kneaded it by hand. To ensure freshness, Rudkin decreed that bread not sold after two days on a store shelf must be returned and then solved the problem of what to do with the returned bread by making it into poultry stuffing and selling it at a good profit.

By the late 1950's, Pepperidge Farm employed 1,000 workers, the majority of whom were women, owing to Rudkin's belief that women were more adept than men at baking bread. A stern perfectionist, Rudkin closely supervised all aspects of her bakery to see that everything was done according to her exacting standards, and she demanded a full day's work from her employees. In return, she paid higher wages than the industry level and instituted bonus and insurance plans.

In 1960, with profits totaling $1.3 million on annual sales of $32 million, Rudkin sold Pepperidge Farm to the Campbell Soup Company for Campbell stock worth $28 million. She became a director of Campbell Soup while continuing to run Pepperidge Farm as an independent subsidiary. Two years later Rudkin turned over the presidency of the company to one of her sons and replaced her husband as chairman. She held this position until her retirement in September 1966.

An unassuming and gregarious woman, Rudkin excelled in business because of her unwavering commitment to the high quality of her products and her gift for promotion. She stands out as one of the most successful and nationally prominent businesswomen of her generation. Rudkin died in New Haven, Conn.

[Rudkin's major writing is *The Margaret Rudkin Pepperidge Farm Cookbook* (1963), which contains some autobiographical material. On Rudkin and her career, see J. D. Ratcliff, "Bread, de Luxe," *Reader's Digest*, Dec. 1939; "Rudkin of Pepperidge," *Time*, July 14, 1947; John Bainbridge, "Striking a Blow for Grandma," *New Yorker*, May 22, 1948; "Champion of the Old-Fashioned," *Time*, Mar. 21, 1960; and "Mrs. Rudkin Revisited," *New Yorker*, Nov. 16, 1963. An obituary is in the *New York Times*, June 2, 1967.]

JOHN KENNEDY OHL

RUSSELL, CHARLES ELLSWORTH ("PEE WEE") (Mar. 27, 1906–Feb. 15, 1969), jazz musician, was born in Maple Wood, Mo., the son of Charles Ellsworth Russell and Ella Mary Ballard. When Russell was very young, the family moved to Muskogee, Okla., where his father managed a department store and had oil investments. During his childhood, Russell became proficient at playing a variety of musical instruments, the violin first and then piano and drums, but after hearing the legendary New Orleans clarinetist Alcide ("Yellow") Nuñez play at a local dance, he settled on the clarinet as his favored instrument. He was only twelve years old when he started playing professionally during the summer at a nearby lakeside resort.

After the young Russell tried to join a riverboat orchestra, his family enrolled him at Western Military Academy in Alton, Ill., in an attempt to discipline his rebellious proclivities. As a result, he not only prospered academically but, more important, received thorough musical training, even though he remained only a year. Later he acquired further formal instruction during a semester at the University of Missouri and from Tony Sarli of the St. Louis Symphony Orchestra. In 1922, Russell became a full-time professional musician.

For the next five years, Russell worked as an itinerant player of a music that was increasingly beginning to be called "jazz." His apprenticeship in the new music was with bands that included instrumentalists of major reputation among knowledgeable proponents of the burgeoning art form, among them the pianist Peck Kelley, the clarinetist Leon Rapollo of the New Orleans Rhythm Kings (often considered the first major white jazz musician), and the trombonist Jack Teagarden, who became one of Russell's frequent collaborators in later years and a lifelong friend.

Beginning in 1925, Russell often worked with Bix Beiderbecke and the groups normally associated with Beiderbecke during this period and with Frankie Trumbauer and Jean Goldkette. During this brief period, he fell strongly under the influence of what was later to be called the Chicago style of jazz. Critics of the music often like to point out, correctly, that Russell spent little time in Chicago; but it is also true that the Chicago style indelibly marked his playing for the remainder of his life. Although the Chicago repertoire is largely the same as that of the New Orleans school, the Chicago approach is far more self-consciously excited and angular than the older form: the rhythm shuffles, the brass blares, the reeds rasp. Russell's principal inspiration was Frank Teschemaker, a Chicago clarinetist and alto saxophonist who was killed in an auto crash in 1931. One critic has said that Teschemaker's tone, which Russell emulated, sounded "incredibly strained, and was all the better for it."

The Teschemaker influence is enormously evident on Russell's first recording, "Ida," made in New York with Red Nichols and His Five Pennies in 1927. Very quickly, however, Russell found his individual sound, and his musical ideas started to depart dramatically from Teschemaker's, but his solos, no matter what the musical context, remained imbued with what is sometimes called "Chicago sour." The pianist Dick Wellstood has described this quality as "a crabbed, choked, knotted tangle of squawks with which he could create . . . an enormously roomy private universe." It should also be pointed out that Russell's playing is pervaded by a melancholic strain but is also filled with humor, creating an emotional tone that is paradoxically exhilarating and withdrawn at the same time.

Russell free-lanced in New York for the next six years with such orchestras as those led by

Paul Specht, Cass Hagen, Don Vorhees, Austin Wylie, and Ben Pollack, playing clarinet and doubling on the tenor saxophone. The recordings of "Hello, Lola" and "One Hour" by Red McKenzie's Mound City Blue Blowers feature Russell and the tenor player Coleman Hawkins as soloists, marking one of the earliest interracial phonograph collaborations.

Much of Russell's best work preserved on record from this period is included in the series of discs cut in 1932, usually made under some variation of the name The Rhythmmakers. By this time his tone and the development of his musical ideas had reached full maturity. They did not alter much until the 1960's, even though the inventiveness of his improvisations remained remarkably fresh throughout his career.

After working in Massachusetts in the mid-1930's with the cornetist Bobby Hackett, Russell joined the part-jazz, part-vaudeville band of Louis Prima, with whom he remained for two years, when illness forced him to withdraw from the road. On Mar. 11, 1943, he married Mary S. Chaloff.

The years 1938–1950 mark the period of his work for which Russell is best remembered. A nightclub in Greenwich Village named Nick's had become host to the music of what was called "the Condon mob." Led by Eddie Condon (who later owned a similar club of his own), the music—and, indeed, the musicians—represented the most assertive and even aggressive since the Chicago style. Nicknamed "Nicksieland," the band included variously such Chicago-related musicians as Bud Freeman, Muggsy Spanier, Dave Tough, and Joe Sullivan. Condon was at least three deep at every position; that is, he could draw on the talents of at least three major performers for each chair in the band. Unquestionably, Russell not only played for Condon more than anyone else but was also Condon's most popular soloist. The many titles recorded under a variety of names (but mostly under Condon's) on Milt Gabler's Commodore label during this time are among those most cherished by devotees of this style.

Russell was an alcoholic, and in 1950 he suffered a near-fatal attack of a liver ailment. At one point his death was thought to be imminent, but only seven months after his hospitalization, he was sitting in again at Condon's club. Three months after that, for the first time, he organized his own regular group, which played a particularly impressive engagement at Boston's Storyville club, owned by the jazz impresario George Wein. Russell worked for Wein many times through the rest of his career.

Tiring of the routine of heading a band, Russell rejoined Condon in 1955, remaining with him until 1961, except for his annual trek to the Newport Jazz Festival. Toward the end of this period, a most surprising thing happened: the modern-jazz audience discovered Russell's work. Though he had won the *Downbeat* readers' poll for clarinet in the years 1942–1944, the postwar modern-jazz audience often expressed a rather parochial dislike for anything that smacked of Dixieland. Even so, he captured the *Downbeat* critics' poll award for each of the years from 1962 to 1968. The rough-hewn quality of his playing had become even more intense by this time, though his famous squawking had largely ceased, and his repertoire included works by such modernists as Ornette Coleman, John Coltrane, and Thelonious Monk. For one year, he and the valve trombonist Marshall Brown together led a working quartet.

Russell's wife convinced him to try oil painting in 1965, and he became quite proficient, producing a number of abstract works of excellent quality. After playing for Richard Nixon's inaugural ball on Jan. 21, 1969, he became ill again from his recurring problem of cirrhosis. He died quietly in his sleep in Alexandria, Va., three weeks later.

[No full-length biography of Russell has been published; further information can be obtained from the *New York Times* obituary by John S. Wilson, published Feb. 16, 1969.]

ARTHUR P. LIVINGSTON

SANDBURG, CARL AUGUST (Jan. 6, 1878–July 22, 1967), poet, biographer, journalist, and folklorist, was born in Galesburg, Ill., the son of August Sandburg, a railroad blacksmith who had changed his surname from Johnson, and Clara Mathilda Anderson, devout Lutherans who had come from northern Sweden in the early 1870's. By the time Sandburg was six, he wanted to become an author, but he left school after the eighth grade in 1891 to work at various jobs—washing dishes, shining shoes, selling newspapers. At seventeen he rode freight

Sandburg

trains to Iowa, Kansas, and Nebraska, working as a farmhand and as a gandy dancer. He returned to Galesburg in 1898 and enlisted in Company C of the Sixth Illinois Infantry. During the Spanish-American War he served as a private for six months in Puerto Rico but saw no combat.

After the war, Sandburg returned to Galesburg and enrolled at Lombard College. His congressional appointment to the United States Military Academy was canceled because he failed his entrance examinations in grammar and mathematics. He continued at Lombard, serving in the Galesburg fire department to support himself. In 1902 he left college without graduating. Sandburg then wandered over the country as a salesman and even spent time in a Pennsylvania jail for riding the rails. He returned to Galesburg and briefly wrote a column for the *Evening Mail*, thus starting a journalistic career that continued off and on for more than twenty-five years.

In 1904, Sandburg published his first book of poems, *In Reckless Ecstasy*, signing himself Charles A. Sandburg, a name he was to use for several years. For this Sandburg was indebted to a Lombard professor, Philip Green Wright, who had long encouraged his writing and paid for the publication. Wright was one of the three persons, according to Sandburg, who most deeply influenced his life, the others being his wife and her brother.

In 1905, Sandburg moved to Chicago to be the assistant editor of a little magazine, *Tomorrow*, in which he published poems and sketches; he also lectured on Walt Whitman, whose poetry he admired. Sandburg soon was drawn into the city's radical circles. His latent radicalism had first been aroused in 1893: when Governor John Altgeld of Illinois courageously pardoned the four surviving Haymarket rioters, Sandburg studied the events that preceded the pardon and decided that even rioters and anarchists deserve fair trials. The intervening years had only strengthened his concern for social justice, and so, when Winfield R. Gaylord invited him in 1907 to join the Socialist party and become a professional organizer, making speeches and soliciting memberships, Sandburg accepted. In 1908, Sandburg campaigned for the Socialist Eugene V. Debs in his presidential campaign. On June 15 of that year, Sandburg married Lilian Steichen, a Socialist and schoolteacher, whose brother Edward had achieved distinction as a photographer; they had three children.

From 1910 to 1912, Sandburg was private secretary to Emil Seidel, the Socialist mayor of Milwaukee, and contributed articles to *La Follette's Weekly* and Victor Berger's Socialist *Leader*. In September 1912, Sandburg moved to Chicago to become a full-time newspaperman, writing poetry and free-lancing on the side. He wrote for a variety of periodicals, sometimes under pseudonyms. Harriet Monroe, who had launched *Poetry: A Magazine of Verse* in 1912, liked Sandburg's poems and encouraged his writing, which was in a loose romantic style, full of homely speech and lyrical passages. In the March 1914 issue she printed a number of his poems, including "Chicago," and they won the Helen Haire Levinson Prize of $200. Sandburg's free verse in vigorous colloquial rhythms stimulated controversy and established him as an outstanding figure among Chicago writers. However, the prestigious literary magazine *The Dial* called "Chicago" an "impudent affront to the poetry-loving public."

By 1916, Sandburg had written enough verse to make a book, which was published as *Chicago Poems*. It contained the vivid impressionistic poems "Fog," "Grass," "Nocturne in a Deserted Backyard," and "To a Contemporary Bunk Shooter," which proclaimed the poet's radical views. "Chicago," the lead poem, celebrated "the City of the Big Shoulders," and became an anthology piece, as did "Fog."

Sandburg wrote more than a thousand free-verse poems, but none had a stronger and more memorable impact than the early ones in *Chicago Poems* (1916), *Cornhuskers* (1918), *Smoke and Steel* (1920), and *Slabs of the Sunburnt West* (1922). His sympathy for the oppressed and his quick perception of beauty in unlikely places were everywhere present in the four books. Two moods recur: indignation at the conditions under which humble people often must live, and elation arising from love of life, laughter, and natural beauty. One of Sandburg's definitions of poetry is "the successful synthesis of hyacinths and biscuits."

In the *Chicago Daily News*, Sandburg did a series of articles on the July 1919 race riots, later collected as *The Chicago Race Riots* (1919), with a foreword by Walter Lippmann. Before joining the *Daily News*, he worked on E. W. Scripps's *Day Book*, a daily tabloid, and briefly for William Randolph Hearst's *Chicago American*. As a working Chicago journalist, he rubbed shoulders with a remarkable assemblage of talented writers—Ben Hecht, Charles MacArthur, Harry Hansen, Floyd Dell, Vincent Starrett, Keith Preston, Burton Rascoe, and Lloyd Lewis, who became Sandburg's close friend.

In 1918, Sandburg left the *Daily News* for a year to go to Stockholm, Sweden, to report on the Finnish revolution for the Newspaper Enterprise Association. He had broken with the Socialist party in 1917 because he supported United States entry into World War I, but in Stockholm he had a meeting with Michael Borodin, a Bolshevik whom Lenin had given the mission of smuggling propaganda and money into the United States. The historian Theodore Draper, in *The Roots of American Communism* (1957), recounts the Sandburg-Borodin relationship and Sandburg's smuggling of Lenin's "Letter to American Workingmen" into the United States.

Sandburg's first book for children, *Rootabaga Stories*, originally written for his own children, was published in 1922. It was well received and was followed by *Rootabaga Pigeons* (1923). In the 1920's, Sandburg also made frequent public appearances before college groups and literary audiences, reciting his poems and singing folk songs. (He had long collected ballads and folk songs and had a good singing voice.) His platform appearances increased his popularity and the sale of his books. He became a successful reader and chanter of verse, accompanying himself on the guitar. In *The American Songbag* (1927) he brought together nearly 300 songs and ballads, with annotations, and later supplemented this work with *The New American Songbag* (1950). In 1936 he published *The People, Yes*, an episodic, panoramic glorification of the common people and a stirring defense of democratic idealism. It was a work of great variety, written in dozens of styles, in prose and in poetry. Many consider it his greatest work.

For years in his spare time at home and in his travels, Sandburg searched for material on Abraham Lincoln with the aim of writing a biography, a project he was encouraged to carry out by his mentor Philip Green Wright. His years of research and writing bore fruit when the two-volume *Abraham Lincoln: The Prairie Years* (1926) was received with great popular and critical acclaim. With his earnings, he bought property in Harbert, Mich., on the southern shore of Lake Michigan, and moved there in 1928. He continued to write for the *Daily News* until 1932, but most of his creative energy was directed to his Lincoln biography. The four-volume *Abraham Lincoln: The War Years* (1939), his crowning achievement, won a Pulitzer Prize, and most readers and reviewers greeted it with undiluted praise. With only minor reservations, it was lauded by H. L. Mencken, Robert Sherwood, and the historians Allan Nevins and Charles A. Beard, the latter calling the work "a noble monument."

There were a few detractors, however, who pointed to the work's historical inaccuracies and other defects. Edmund Wilson, for one, thought "the cruellest thing that has happened to Lincoln since he was shot by Booth has been to fall into the hands of Carl Sandburg; . . . the result was a long, sprawling book that eventually had Lincoln sprawling." In the thirteen years between his two Lincoln works, Sandburg produced two lesser biographies, *Steichen the Photographer* (1929) and *Mary Lincoln: Wife and Widow* (1932), the latter with Paul Angle.

Sandburg's one novel, *Remembrance Rock* (1948), about America's greatness and mystique, has an involved plot and is packed with details, songs, anecdotes, and folklore. It was not viewed with favor by serious critics. Diana Trilling thought *Remembrance Rock* was not worth reviewing, a judgment that angered the author. The intellectual historian Perry Miller saw the book as a "movie spectacular," probably not aware that Sandburg had in fact signed a contract with Metro-Goldwyn-Mayer to film the novel.

In 1945, Sandburg moved from Michigan to a new home in a milder climate at Flat Rock, N.C. Here he lived contentedly the rest of his life on Connemara Farm, where he wrote and raised goats. Many honors and awards came to him, including a Pulitzer Prize for his *Complete Poems* (1950) and, in 1964, the Presidential Medal of Freedom. He continued to work on revisions and editions of his books, and, on occasion, new writing, notably an excellent account of his youth, *Always the Young Strangers* (1953). He died quietly at Connemara Farm.

[A large collection of Sandburg's books, manuscripts, letters, and other papers is at the University of

Illinois, Urbana-Champaign, and extensive additional material is at the Library of Congress. Correspondence is in Herbert Mitgang, ed., *The Letters of Carl Sandburg* (1968). Works by Sandburg not cited in the text are *Good Morning, America* (1928), *Home Front Memo* (1943), *Lincoln Collector: The Story of Oliver Barrett's Great Private Collection* (1949), *Harvest Poems* (1960), and *Honey and Salt* (1963). Bibliographies include *The Sandburg Range: An Exhibit of Materials . . . Placed on Display in the University of Illinois on Jan. 6, 1958* (1958); and Mark Van Doren, *Carl Sandburg* (1961).

On Sandburg's life and work, see Harriet Monroe, "Carl Sandburg," *Poetry*, Sept. 1924; Newton Arvin, "Carl Sandburg," *New Republic*, Sept. 9, 1936; Karl Detzer, *Carl Sandburg: A Study in Personality and Background* (1941); Perry Miller, "Sandburg and the American Dream," *New York Times Book Review*, Oct. 10, 1948; William Carlos Williams, "Carl Sandburg's *Complete Poems*," *Poetry*, Sept. 1951; Allan Nevins, "Sandburg as Historian," *Illinois Historical Society Journal*, 45 (1952); Gay Wilson Allen, "Carl Sandburg: Fire and Smoke," *South Atlantic Quarterly*, Summer 1960; Harry Golden, *Carl Sandburg* (1961); Richard Crowder, *Carl Sandburg* (1964); Hazel Durnell, *The America of Carl Sandburg* (1965); North Callahan, *Carl Sandburg: Lincoln of Our Time* (1970); Herbert Mitgang, "Carl Sandburg," *New Republic*, Jan. 14, 1978; and Helga Sandburg, *A Great and Glorious Romance* (1978). See also Edward Steichen, ed., *Sandburg: Photographers View Carl Sandburg* (1966). An obituary is in the *New York Times*, July 23, 1967.]

WILLIAM MCCANN

SANDE, EARL (Nov. 13, 1898–Aug. 20, 1968), jockey and horse trainer, was born in Groton, S.Dak., the son of John C. Sande, a railroad worker (mother's name unknown). Sande attended public school locally and in American Falls, Idaho, where the family moved when he was eight. By the age of thirteen, Sande had his own horse, and at seventeen he left high school to work around local tracks and to race at fairs and on small-town main streets from Idaho to Arizona.

Sande began his professional career in January 1918 in New Orleans and rode 158 winners that first season. He was very quickly at the top of his profession and widely regarded as America's top jockey. His fame was confirmed by Damon Runyon's poetic tribute, the last lines of each stanza being "a handy guy like Sande, bootin' them babies in."

Sande signed with the Canadian sportsman Commander J. K. L. Ross, for whom he rode until 1920. He then signed for a rumored $15,000 a year with Sam Hildreth, the trainer for Harry Sinclair's Rancocas Stable. On Sept. 15, 1921, Sande married Hildreth's niece, Marian Casey; they had no children. He was the leading money-winning jockey in 1921, in 1923 (with a then record of $569,394), and in 1927. A notable victory in 1927 was in the Kentucky Derby, on Zev. Later that year at Belmont, before 40,000 fans and the Prince of Wales, Sande rode Zev to a victory over Papyrus, winner of the English Derby.

Sande's riding career seemed to be over when he suffered serious injuries in a fall at Saratoga on Aug. 7, 1924. Among the spectators was Admiral Cary T. Grayson, who examined Sande on the track and sent him to the hospital immediately with a leg, ribs, and a collarbone badly broken. During sixteen weeks in the hospital, Sande enjoyed the concern of many prominent visitors from the turf and social worlds. Will Rogers even wrote a tribute in the *New York Times* in which he compared Sande's honesty with that of Lincoln.

Sande was ready to resume racing by April 1925. He severed his five-year connection with the Rancocas Stable and said that he would ride free-lance, although he was soon riding mainly for J. E. Widener. Sande showed that he had fully recovered by winning several important races, including the 1925 Kentucky Derby, on Flying Ebony.

The glow of success dimmed badly for Sande in 1927: his wife died on September 3, and two months later, he was suspended for a "serious and flagrant" foul at Pimlico. He was ordered from the grounds, his jockey's license was revoked, and he was barred from accepting a mount at any racecourse in the United States. This was by no means his first suspension, but it was the most serious. Sande denied any fault and appealed for reinstatement; he was finally reinstated by the Maryland Racing Commission in April 1928.

Sande, who at five feet, six inches was rather tall for a jockey, had great difficulty keeping his weight near 112 pounds. Therefore, having accumulated a small fortune, he retired in 1928 with the intention of becoming an owner and trainer. He purchased his own string of horses but soon suffered financial losses. He was obliged to sell his small string and return as a jockey in 1930. This turned out to be one of his greatest years, for he rode Gallant Fox to what was later known as the Triple Crown of racing for three-year-olds. He retired again in 1931. He sang publicly, having taken singing lessons for three years, and he signed a motion-picture contract, hoping for a film career. Nothing came of it, and he returned to ride thirteen winners in 1932. Weight problems continued to plague Sande, and so, he retired for the third time in 1932. On Feb. 17, 1932, he married Marian Kummer, a jockey's widow. (They had no children before they were divorced in 1946.)

Sande next became a trainer for Colonel Maxwell Howard, with whom he remained until the latter's death in 1944. Sande then took over the Howard stable and also trained for Clifford Mooers until 1949. In May 1948 he was accused of doping one of his horses at Jamaica, and although a grand jury refused to indict him, the Jockey Club banned him from the track for sixty days.

Financial problems led Sande to attempt a comeback as a jockey in 1953, after a twenty-one-year absence. Although he did win one race in a stretch drive against Eddie Arcaro, it was clear that he had little left. By 1957, he had been forced to sell his few remaining horses. He was offered several jobs around racetracks but refused them. These were sad years for Sande; he had been a model of courtesy and civility in his earlier years, but he became a bitter, quarrelsome old man, alienating even those inclined to help him. For several years he was a virtual recluse in a room over a restaurant in Westbury, Long Island, where the proprietor permitted him to live and eat for free. Occasionally he would sing for the guests; sometimes he would ask the manager to get rid of them. In 1964 he borrowed his fare to go to Oregon and live with his father. He died in Jacksonville, Oreg.

During his relatively brief riding career, Sande was certainly the most famous and probably the best jockey in America. He rode most of the great horses of his day; he won with the best, and he won with those far from the best. He is one of only eleven jockeys to have won the Triple Crown. Sande's total of 968 victories represents an extraordinary 26 percent victory average. With his 717 second places and 551 third places, out of 3,673 horses ridden, more than 60 percent of Sande's rides finished in the money. Sande was a member of the Jockeys' Hall of Fame and was cited by the Jockeys' Community Fund in 1941 as the jockey who had done the most to honor his profession. He is a part, albeit minor, of the sporting lore and legend of the 1920's.

[See Horace Wade in *Horseman's Journal*, Feb. 1979. Obituaries are in the *New York Times*, Aug. 20, 1968; and *Blood-Horse*, Aug. 31, 1968.]

HORTON W. EMERSON, JR.

SANDOZ, MARI (May 11, 1896–Mar. 10, 1966), historian and novelist, was born Mary Susette Sandoz, in Sheridan County, Nebr., the daughter of Jules Ami Sandoz, a rancher and horticulturist, and Mary Elizabeth Fehr, both Swiss immigrants. Her father, the most important influence on her life, was a champion of small farmers, but he was also an egomaniac and a domestic tyrant whose intellectual gifts and social achievements were marred by an almost constant round of lawsuits against his neighbors and violent rages against his wife and children. All her life one of Sandoz's hands was partially crippled because her enraged father had broken a bone in it. Her entire early life was dangerous even by frontier standards; sent out at the age of twelve to bring in the cattle during a blizzard, Sandoz suffered an attack of snow blindness and never recovered her sight in one eye.

Sandoz received only four and one-half years of often interrupted formal schooling, but at an early age she discovered the novels of Joseph Conrad and knew that she wanted to be a writer. Her career as an artist and scholar was a struggle for which her childhood deprivation and suffering had prepared her.

In 1913 Sandoz passed a qualifying examination for rural teachers. On May 27, 1914, she married Wray Macumber; she divorced him in 1919. For several years she taught in rural schools in western Nebraska, and periodically after 1922 she attended the University of Nebraska as a special student, without taking a degree. During these years she worked in a drug laboratory, as a proofreader, as an assistant in the university's English department, and as a researcher for the Nebraska State Historical Society. Her father told her that he considered artists and writers "the maggots of society," but before his death in 1928 he asked her to write his biography. She had planned to do so for many years, but such was his power over her that she had feared to begin until he suggested it.

It took Sandoz seven years to write *Old Jules* (1935), which was rejected by fourteen publishers before it was awarded the Atlantic Monthly Prize for nonfiction. Written first as a novel, it eventually became an almost anomalous work: too thoroughly researched and grounded in historical actuality to be considered a novel, but too dramatic and even too lurid to be only a work of history. Sandoz fought for the integrity of her literary style, a kind of rough prose that, she believed, was too raw and real for the taste of provincial eastern editors and publishers unfamiliar with western reality.

Old Jules was the first in a series of works that Sandoz had planned early in her life, the Trans-Missouri Series, which recounts the history of the Great Plains from the Stone Age to modern times. Other books in this series are *Crazy Horse* (1942), *Cheyenne Autumn* (1953), *The Buffalo Hunters* (1954), *The Cattlemen* (1958), and *The Beaver Men* (1964). (A seventh work was to have dealt with the history of the petroleum industry.)

In 1943 she moved to New York City to be near research libraries and publishing houses, and she spent the rest of her life there except for research trips to the West and summers from 1947 to 1955, teaching fiction writing at the University of Wisconsin. Her life in New York City was almost monastic in its devotion to research and writing, but it was filled with the people she sought to capture in her writing—the Indians, ranchers, and homesteaders who haunted her memory.

Sandoz showed a deep and lifelong sense of social responsibility. During World War II she attempted to enlist in the Women's Army Corps, and she always helped young writers. Her social conscience probably kept her from critical success as a novelist because reviewers considered much of her fiction moralistic in tone. Two early novels, *Slogum House* (1937) and *Capital City* (1939), reflect her apprehension about native American fascism. But she also wrote two highly regarded short novels on Indian themes, *The Horsecatcher* (1956) and *The Story Catcher* (1962). The best, and least allegorical, of her other novels, *Miss Morissa* (1955), concerns a woman doctor on the frontier but rises above its social messages.

Sandoz struggled with cancer in her last years. Working to complete her last book, *The Battle of the Little Big Horn* (1966), she spent her final days virtually alone, with the courage and stoicism that she had learned as a child. She died in New York City.

Although a minor novelist, Sandoz is certainly a major writer. *Old Jules*, *Crazy Horse*, and *Cheyenne Autumn* will be read long after the American West has ceased to grip the imagination. In the two latter works she entered the psyche of her subjects, convincing the reader that the Indians would have used precisely her language had they been able to tell their story in English. And in *Old Jules*, the beauty of which is heightened by almost unbearable flashes of terror, she produced a great work of American literature.

Her other works include *The Tom-Walker* (1947), *Winter Thunder* (1951), *Hostiles and Friendlies* (1959), *Son of the Gamblin' Man* (1960), *These Were the Sioux* (1961), *Love Song to the Plains* (1961), and *Sandhills Sundays and Other Recollections* (1970).

[Sandoz' papers are at the University of Nebraska; and at the Mari Sandoz Corporation, Gordon, Nebr. See also Stanley Kunitz and Howard Haycraft, *Twentieth-Century Authors* (1942); Scott L. Greenwell, "The Literary Apprenticeship of Mari Sandoz," *Nebraska History*, Summer 1976; Gail Baker, "Mari Sandoz," in *Notable American Women: The Modern Period* (1980); and Helen W. Stauffer, *Mari Sandoz* (1982).]

ROBERT L. BERNER

SANGER, MARGARET HIGGINS (Sept. 14, 1879–Sept. 6, 1966), birth control advocate, was born in Corning, N.Y., the daughter of Michael Hennessy Higgins, a stonemason who had emigrated from Ireland in the 1860's, and Anne Purcell. An outspoken atheist and freethinker, her father earned much official enmity and only a modest income in heavily Catholic Corning. Her older sisters' financial support made it possible for her to attend Claverack College and Hudson River Institute, a private boarding school, from 1897 to 1899. In the latter year she began to study nursing at a hospital in White Plains, N.Y., but her education was cut short when she married William Sanger, an architect and aspiring painter, on Aug. 18, 1902; they had three children, one of whom died in infancy, and were divorced in 1921.

The Sangers spent ten years of what she later called "tame domesticity" in Hastings-on-Hudson, N.Y., but in 1912 moved to New York City, where she experienced her self-described "great awakening." New York was then athrob with young intellectuals airing radical ideas about art, politics, and sex. Sanger, who had an absorbent, eclectic mind, eagerly drank in all these ideas. At Mabel Dodge's salon and in evening classes at the liberal Ferrer School, she heard the radical unionist "Big Bill" Haywood describe the program of the Industrial Workers of the World (IWW), the journalist Walter Lippmann explain Freud, the philosopher Will Durant analyze the sexual theories of Havelock Ellis, and the feminist-anarchist Emma Goldman advocate artificial contraception. She was drawn especially to notions of erotic fulfillment popularized by sexual romantics like the Swedish feminist Ellen Key and the English writer Edward Carpenter. "I love being swayed by emotions by romances," she confided to her journal in 1914. "Emotion . . . urges from within, without consciousness of fear or consequences." Professing the twin goals of sexual and political revolution, she joined the Socialist party, wrote articles for the Socialist *Call*, and participated in IWW strikes in the textile mills of Lawrence, Mass., in 1912 and Paterson, N.J., in 1913.

Sanger also worked as a visiting nurse on Manhattan's Lower East Side. There she encountered many women whose health had been broken by excessive childbearing or botched abortions. As she recalled in her autobiography, the death of one such woman in 1912 made her resolve "to do something to change the destiny of mothers whose miseries were as vast as the sky."

Precisely what she might do, however, was not then clear to her. She traveled to Glasgow and Paris in 1913, a trip she later described as necessary to discover contraceptive information unavailable in the United States. In fact, American medical literature then contained abundant discussion of methods for preventing conception, and indeed, the birthrate in America had been falling for at least a century.

In March 1914, Sanger began to publish the *Woman Rebel*, a belligerently radical sheet that attacked the Rockefellers as rapacious capitalists, denounced marriage, and defended assassination. The publication's postal privileges were almost immediately suspended, and Sanger was indicted for violating federal anti-obscenity statutes. The journal never did fulfill its aim of testing the laws against disseminating information about birth control—a term Sanger coined in early 1914. To avoid prosecution, she fled in October 1914 to Europe, where she stayed until September 1915.

In Europe, Sanger fell deeply under the influence of Havelock Ellis, who advised her to abandon splenetic, broadside attacks on capitalism and marriage and to focus on the single issue of birth control. He encouraged her to visit the Dutch clinic of Dr. Johannes Rutgers, who argued that effective contraception required the involvement of medical professionals—an approach quite different from the self-administered lay methods that Sanger had described in her pamphlet *Family Limitation*, published in large quantities in late 1914.

Ellis also counseled Sanger to temper her shrill style, dress conservatively, and speak softly, a manner she thereafter cultivated. Mabel Dodge called her "the Madonna type of woman." One associate described her as "a rather slight woman, very beautiful, with wide-apart gray eyes and a crown of auburn hair, combining a radiant feminine appeal with an impression of serenity, calm, and graciousness of voice and manner." These attributes won for Margaret Sanger many supporters, friends, and lovers; but at times they masked only imperfectly a powerfully assertive personality that combined dedication to humanitarian ideals with bitter resentment of anyone who challenged her paramount role in the birth control movement.

The federal government dropped the charges against Sanger on Feb. 18, 1916. That October, at 46 Amboy Street in the Brownsville section of Brooklyn, she opened the first birth control clinic in the United States. Within weeks she was arrested, and she served a thirty-day sentence in February and March 1917. The New York Court of Appeals eventually upheld her conviction but handed her a substantial victory when, in January 1918, it greatly broadened its definition of the circumstances under which physicians could legally prescribe contraceptives.

Sanger continued to publicize birth control, especially in the pages of the *Birth Control Review*, which she launched in January 1917. The *Review* served not only as a platform for Sanger's pronouncements but as a communications link for the birth control organizations that were springing up around the country.

Sanger often made a feminist case for birth control, though one at odds with the feminism of such contemporaries as Charlotte Perkins Gilman and Elsie Clews Parsons, who sought to deemphasize sexual differences. Sanger, in contrast, promoted birth control for its role in enhancing women's erotic experiences, which would lead, she argued somewhat mystically, to the release of the "feminine spirit" and the cultivation of the distinctively feminine elements of women's personalities.

After 1917, Sanger increasingly stressed the eugenic benefits of contraception. The *Birth Control Review*'s motto was To Breed a Race of Thoroughbreds. This emphasis on eugenics marked a significant shift in Sanger's attitude and in the groups that supported her. She had at first envisioned birth control as a way to deny abundant and docile labor to exploitative capitalists. But by the 1920's she had abandoned her radical associates and fallen in with upper-class women reformers, well endowed with both the money and the organizational talent she needed. She now referred to "overbreeding among the working class" as the source of "all our problems" and promoted birth control as a means to stop the proliferation of the "unfit" and reduce the menacing differential between immigrant and old-stock American birthrates. With these arguments, her evolution from a socialist to a social Darwinist in her rationale for birth control was complete.

By the early 1920's, Sanger had clearly emerged as the world's foremost champion of artificial contraception. In November 1921 she organized the first American Birth Control Conference, in New York. There she announced the formation of the American Birth Control League, over which she presided until 1928. League members, some 37,000 strong by 1926, tended to be well-to-do native white Protestant Republican women.

On Sept. 18, 1922, Sanger married James Noah Henry Slee, eighteen years her senior and the wealthy president of the Three-in-One Oil Company. His fortune facilitated Sanger's birth control activities, giving the American Birth Control League in the 1920's more the character of a private philanthropy than a broadly based social movement.

In 1923, Sanger opened the Clinical Research Bureau in New York, the first facility regularly to dispense contraceptive services in the United States since the closure of her short-lived Brooklyn clinic seven years earlier. The new clinic at first prescribed German diaphragms smuggled into the country in Slee's Three-in-One oil drums. For the rest of the decade, Sanger tried in vain to reach agreement with the prominent gynecologist Robert Latou Dickinson to place the clinic under the control of physicians. Her efforts were hampered by the acute consciousness among physicians of the fragility of their recent success in establishing themselves as a recognized profession. Fearing to jeopardize that achievement, they resisted prescribing treatment for other than pathological causes, they worried about the unreliability and even the danger of current contraceptive techniques, and they objected heatedly to what they considered Sanger's sensationalism and propagandistic approach. For her part, Sanger repeatedly frustrated Dickinson's offers of cooperation when she reneged on assurances that she would relinquish her personal control over the clinic.

The doctors' anxieties and Sanger's obstructions may well have slowed the pace of medical involvement with birth control. Yet, Sanger successfully prodded the American Medical Association in 1937 to declare its support for prescribing contraception even in the absence of strictly pathological indications and for conducting research into improved contraceptive techniques. That research led, with Sanger's continuing encouragement and quiet financial backing, to the development of the hormonal anovulant pill in the 1950's.

In 1929, having resigned from both the American Birth Control League and the *Birth Control Review*, Sanger established the National Committee on Federal Legislation for Birth Control. Its efforts to change the federal antiobscenity laws became redundant after a series of pro–birth control federal court decisions—notably *United States* v. *One Package of Japanese Pessaries*, 86 F. 2d 737 (1936)—and it was therefore disbanded in 1937. The following year the American Birth Control League and Sanger's Clinical Research Bureau joined to form the Birth Control Federation of America, later the Planned Parenthood Federation of America.

Public opinion, once scandalized by Sanger's broad assaults on sexual conventions, strongly favored birth control by the 1930's. Many Protestant churches gave official approval to the practice of contraception by married couples. Margaret Sanger had begun as a radical iconoclast, challenging old sexual values; she ended her career, heavy with honors, as the respected champion of new ones. Her life spanned a period of striking changes in American attitudes about the family, the role of woman, and sexual standards. All of those changes she helped to catalyze. She can be faulted, perhaps, for the essentially libertarian approach she took to birth control, an approach that assumed all women intuitively knew the benefits of contraception and would practice it effectively if only official obstacles were removed. That premise energized Sanger's successful attacks against the antiobscenity laws, against religious taboos, and against the cautious conservatism of the medical profession, attacks that fitted well with Sanger's deeply combative character. But her character suited her less well when her adversary was neither prudery nor prudence but ignorance or indifference. She was at her best in facilitating sexual liberation and family planning for the middle class; ironically, she was vastly less successful in carrying her campaign for birth control to poor and disadvantaged women, who had professedly been her original concern.

Sanger continued to lobby for federal support of contraceptive services during and after World War II, even though in the late 1930's she had written that she had "left the front." She lived in retirement until her death in Tucson, Ariz.

[The Library of Congress holds a major collection of Sanger's papers, dealing mostly with the official activities of the American Birth Control League and the National Committee on Federal Legislation for Birth Control. An equally rich collection, emphasizing Sanger's personal life, is held by the Sophia Smith Collection (Women's History Archive) at Smith College. Sanger's *Autobiography* (1938) is a highly selective and not always reliable account. Her principal works on behalf of birth control are *Woman and the New Race* (1920) and *The Pivot of Civilization* (1922). Secondary works include David M. Kennedy, *Birth Control in America: The Career of Margaret Sanger* (1970); Linda Gordon, *Woman's Body, Woman's Right* (1973); James Reed, *From Private Vice to Public Virtue* (1978); and Madeline Gray, *Margaret Sanger* (1979). An obituary is in the *New York Times*, Sept. 7, 1966.]

DAVID M. KENNEDY

SARDI, MELCHIORRE PIO VENCENZO ("VINCENT") (Dec. 23, 1885–Nov. 19, 1969), restaurateur, was born in San Marzano Oliveto, a village in Piedmont, Italy, the son of Giovanni Sardi, a college-educated estate overseer, and Anna Gilardino. Reared in a warm, though demanding, family atmosphere, he was a rebellious, adventurous boy who earned the nickname "Il Vagabondo" as well as the exasperation of his parents. In 1896, when he refused to remain at Don Bosco, a school run by the Jesuits, his parents sent him to work as a hand on a coastal schooner. After two years at sea he returned home, only to leave once more to accompany an uncle to England. Left to fend for himself in London, he drifted into his lifework in kitchens and dining rooms. After numerous menial jobs, he became a valet-houseboy in the home of the eminent surgeon George Newton Pitt. There he polished his English and manners and cultivated a country-gentleman style that allowed him to work as a waiter in the restaurants of plush London hotels such as the Savoy, St. James, and Carlton. He also exhibited a love for the stage, attending the city's music halls and theaters at every opportunity. In 1905 he went back to Italy and was conscripted into the army. After serving two years, mostly in the officers' mess, he immigrated to the United States with his younger brother Eduardo, arriving in New York on Nov. 21, 1907.

Sardi quickly found a job as a waiter in one of New York's finest restaurants, Louis Sherry's. There, under the guidance of Charles Pierre, the captain, who later built the Hotel Pierre, he received further training in the art of food service. He refined his skills in numerous other establishments, including Bustanoby's, where Sigmund Romberg played the piano; the Café Martin, a gathering place for wealthy men and their mistresses; the Santa Lucia, in Coney Island, an area famed more for its amusement parks and gambling dens than fine food; and Reisenweber's, in Brighton Beach, a popular summer resort. He also worked at Murray's, a raffish Irish restaurant partially decorated by Stanford White, and the Montmartre, a lavish supper club located on the roof of the Winter Garden Theater. In these and subsequent positions, especially as a captain in the dining room of the Knickerbocker Hotel and as a waiter at the elegant Palais Royale and at the Bartholdi Inn, a theatrical hotel on Broadway, he met scores of show-business people, writers, and politicians. Many, like Paul Whiteman, the bandleader, became lifelong friends. At the Bartholdi Inn, too, he met Eugenia ("Jenny")

Pallera, the chief housekeeper. They married on June 19, 1911, and had two children.

After his marriage and the birth of his children, Sardi sometimes held three jobs at once, working the lunch hour at the Lord and Taylor restaurant, serving dinner at the Yale Club and after-theater supper at the Montmartre. When, in 1921, the year he became an American citizen, a friend offered to sell him on generous terms a small, forty-seat restaurant at 246 West Forty-fourth Street, in the heart of the theater district, Sardi needed little persuasion to accept. Originally called the Little Restaurant, it was renamed Sardi's several months after it opened. At first, the Sardis handled virtually every chore themselves. Jenny Sardi and one assistant did all the cooking and shopping, and Vincent Sardi and one waiter looked after the front. Sardi's soon began to attract a steady stream of actors, producers, and writers, partly because of its location but mainly because of the grace and warmth of the proprietors and their honest, hearty Italian fare. As its reputation spread, Sardi's became a mailing address for dozens of actors, a prop room for shows, and a virtual annex to the Lambs, the men's theatrical club nearby.

Sardi possessed a hard set of convictions about running a restaurant. He insisted upon its having a homey atmosphere where regulars were regarded not merely as customers but as members of an extended family. Very early, unemployed theater people discovered they could count on Sardi for free meals or money to pay the rent. He carried some actors "on the cuff" for years. If they were successful and paid him back, fine; if not, he never brought the subject up. Sardi's insistence on maintaining a familylike setting also meant that during the Prohibition years he refused to sell liquor or wine. Ever accommodating, however, he allowed customers to bring their own libations, provided they were discreet; he supplied the paper cups.

By 1926, Sardi oversaw a staff of eighteen, six in the kitchen crew and twelve waiters, when he was forced to close to make way for the St. James Theater. New quarters took over a year to materialize in the form of a building Lee Shubert, a Sardi admirer, constructed at 234 West Forty-fourth Street. Originally designed as a three-story structure with a roof garden to meet Sardi's specifications, it grew into an eleven-story office tower containing a penthouse apartment for one of the producer's brothers, J. J. Shubert. The area set aside for the restaurant on the first two stories lacked adequate kitchen and storage space as well as easy access between the floors, greatly disappointing Sardi. His unhappiness with the layout was assuaged, however, by his ability to furnish the rooms in a style reminiscent of the elegant hotel restaurants of London: paneled walls, deep carpets, solid mahogany chairs and tables, fine linen, silver, and china.

The new Sardi's opened on Mar. 5, 1927, but customers were slow in returning. Ward Morehouse, a regular who wrote his theater columns there, helped out by mentioning the restaurant four or five times a week; others returned Sardi's friendship and hospitality by lending him money to keep going. Casting about for a way to stimulate business, Sardi remembered Zelli's restaurant in Paris, a popular theater hangout where caricatures of the rich and famous who congregated there plastered the walls. Convinced that the satirical portraits were the secret of Zelli's success, Sardi hired Alex Gard, a Russian émigré, to draw celebrities who came into his establishment. Gard's striking caricatures, eventually covering the walls by the hundreds from floor to ceiling, soon became a Sardi's trademark.

Whether Sardi's idea was responsible for it or not, by the 1930's his restaurant was more popular than ever. With the end of Prohibition, Sardi reluctantly put in a bar—called the Little Bar—which attracted a steady clientele of theater people who turned it into an informal club. Syndicated gossip columnists like Walter Winchell made the dining room their home base, pursuing stories, carrying on interviews, and publicizing the restaurant in the process. In Sardi's, established actors and actresses mingled with aspiring composers; writers rubbed shoulders with politicians; and agents paraded their latest finds before directors and producers. Plays were conceived, partially written, financed, sometimes even cast there. Following opening-night performances, it became a tradition for the cast, directors, and producers to gather at Sardi's and, amid popping corks and platters heaped high with canneloni and crab meat Dewey, await the reviews, which were rushed over by special messenger before they hit the newsstands. Sardi's had become the ultimate place for celebrities to be and to be seen. And affably presiding over it all through lunch, dinner, and supper was "Mr. Sardi," as he was addressed, even by his oldest customers. Always polite and attentive, ramrod straight and commanding in his dark London-cut suits and navy blue bow ties, with his aquiline nose and high forehead, he looked every inch the Noel Coward version of an English gentleman's gentleman.

Sardi's continued to flourish during the 1940's. Nothing—World War II, the decline of Broadway, the migration of many of the faithful to Hollywood—could dim its luster. One observer remarked, "During a typical dinner at Sardi's you are likely to have canapés with Marlene Dietrich, soup with Ethel Merman, your meat served next to Rex Harrison, and salad elbow-rubbed by Marilyn Monroe." Nothing seemed to change, except perhaps the food, which evolved over the years from its simple Italian beginnings into a consistent Sardi's style, best described by the host as "Italian-French-American." But if the fare lost most of its original accents and never reached an exalted level, it was usually creditable and always abundant. It was hardly a gastronomic temple, but most people came to Sardi's to gawk, not to eat.

In 1946 the restaurant became the setting for "Luncheon at Sardi's," a daily radio program featuring interviews with well-known personalities. The program helped to further popularize the place, causing out-of-towners to flock to it in hopes of glimpsing celebrities. A year later, Sardi retired, turning the restaurant over to his son, Vincent Sardi, Jr., who had recently returned from wartime service in the marines. Sardi's wanderlust took him throughout the United States and especially to California to renew old friendships. Always an avid theater- and operagoer, he now rarely missed an opening. The establishment of a Sardi's branch on New York's East Side often brought him there greeting guests. When Sardi's East closed, he could be seen almost daily in the original restaurant, chatting away with the regulars. He died in Saranac Lake, N.Y.

[Letters, memorabilia, and scrapbooks are in the possession of Vincent Sardi, Jr., New York City. Sardi's autobiography, *Sardi's: The Story of a Famous Restaurant* (1953), written with Richard Gehman, is the best published source on his life. The Museum of the Performing Arts of the New York Public Library at Lincoln Center contains material touching on Sardi's and the theater world. Recipes and other information about Sardi's cuisine can be found in Vincent Sardi, Jr., and Helen Bryson, *Curtain Up at Sardi's* (1957). An obituary is in the *New York Times*, Nov. 20, 1969.]

JEROME L. STERNSTEIN

SAVAGE, JOHN LUCIAN ("JACK") (Dec. 25, 1879–Dec. 28, 1967), civil engineer, was born near Cooksville, Wis., the son of Edwin Parker Savage, a farmer, and Mary Therese Stebbins. As a boy he worked on the family farm. Except for two years at a private school in Spring Green, Wis., he attended local public schools and graduated from Madison High School. Savage spent the summers of 1901 and 1902 working on topographical surveys for the United States Geological Survey in Ohio. He received his B.S. in civil engineering from the University of Wisconsin at Madison in 1903.

Upon graduation, Savage was offered a teaching position at Purdue University but chose instead to accept a job with the newly created United States Reclamation Service (renamed the Bureau of Reclamation in 1923). His first assignment was as an engineering aide in the Idaho Division, where he was involved with survey work on the Minidoka Dam project on the Snake River. In December 1903 he was appointed assistant engineer and was transferred to the division headquarters in Boise, Idaho, where he was assigned to investigations, designs, and construction. In July 1905 he was promoted to engineer in charge of designs and supervision of work under construction within the Idaho Division.

Savage left the Reclamation Service in 1908 to join Andrew J. Wiley's engineering consulting practice in Boise. This was a period of rapid growth in the construction of irrigation and hydroelectric projects in the American West, and Wiley's practice flourished. During the eight years Savage was associated with this company, he designed several important projects, including the Salmon River Dam, the Swan Falls Power Plant on the Snake River, the Barber Power Plant on the Boise River, and the Oakley Reservoir Dam. The Reclamation Service also retained Savage as a special consultant on the design of the gates for the Arrowrock Dam on the Boise River, then the world's highest concrete dam.

In 1916, Savage rejoined the Reclamation Service as a designing engineer in charge of all civil engineering design in the service's new office of the chief engineer in Denver, Colo. On June 1, 1918, he married Jessie Burdick Sexsmith. (Savage was widowed in July 1940, and on Jan. 14, 1950, he married Olga Lacher Miner. Both marriages were childless.) He was promoted in 1924 to chief designing engineer and made responsible for all civil, electrical, and mechanical design. He remained in this position until he retired from government work in 1945, thereafter serving as the Bureau of Reclamation's chief consulting engineer. His tenure as chief designing engineer coincided with the era of big federally funded multiple-purpose water projects, and he headed the design work on such massive and well-known dams as Hoover, Grand Coulee, Shasta, Parker, and Imperial. In all, Savage designed nearly sixty major dams in the United States, as well as hundreds of smaller engineering works. His association with this unprecedented number of large engineering projects led to his becoming known as America's first "billion-dollar engineer."

Of all the projects designed and built under Savage's supervision, none posed greater challenges than Hoover Dam on the Colorado River. And none so captured the attention of the world. Built between 1931 and 1935, Hoover was by far the largest dam ever constructed. Its enormous size presented Savage and his engineering staff with numerous problems. One of the principal concerns was the prevention of severe cracking during the setting of the mass concrete. The problem was that in the curing process, concrete heats and expands and then cools and contracts. In a dam the size of Hoover, temperatures were expected to rise as much as fifty degrees Fahrenheit and require nearly a hundred years to cool completely. If not taken into account, the expansion and contraction accompanying this process could result in cracking of the dam. To overcome this problem, Savage designed the dam to be built in a series of huge blocks. When cured, the concrete blocks were to be joined together to form a solid mass by grouting the spaces between them. To reduce the heating and hasten the cooling, 582 miles of piping were embedded throughout the structure, and through the piping, refrigerated water was circulated. So successful were these measures that they became the standard construction techniques for nearly all subsequent high dams.

Savage established a reputation as the nation's premier designer of high dams, and agencies and governments from around the world sought his services. Beginning in 1922, Savage worked as a consulting engineer in the investigation, design, and construction of various projects outside the Bureau of Reclamation. He was retained by the Tennessee Valley Authority to help with the designing of such major dams as Norris, Wheeler, and Pickwick. He assisted in the design of the Madden Dam for the Panama Canal Zone. Prior to World War II, he did consulting work for the island of Puerto Rico; the Dominican Republic, Mexico, and Australia; the state of California; and the cities of Tacoma, Seattle, and Los Angeles. Savage formed an international engineering consulting firm after his retirement in 1945 and was actively involved in postwar reconstruction projects throughout the world. His most noted design was for a dam (never built) on China's Yangtze River that would have far surpassed any dam yet constructed. In 1951 he was made a member of the International Development Advisory Board of President Truman's Point Four program.

Savage continued to work as a consulting engineer into his eighties. Throughout his career he was noted for his indefatigability, rigorous work habits, and commitment to public service. Despite his fame and success, he remained modest and reserved. He died in Englewood, Colo.

[Savage's papers are at the American Heritage Center, University of Wyoming. Related material is at the Rock County Historical Society in Janesville, Wis., and in the records of the Bureau of Reclamation (Record Group 115) at the National Archives. Savage's technical writings include *High-Pressure Reservoir Outlets* (1923), with J. M. Gaylord, and *Special Cements for Mass Concrete* (1936). An obituary is in the *New York Times*, Dec. 29, 1967.]

JEFFREY K. STINE

SCHALK, RAYMOND WILLIAM ("CRACKER") (Aug. 12, 1892–May 19, 1970), baseball player, was born in Harvel, Ill., the son of Herman Schalk, a farmer, and his wife. In 1898 the Schalk family moved to Litchfield, Ill., where Schalk worked on the family farm, lugged coal, and delivered newspapers. At the age of sixteen he earned $3 per week catching for local semiprofessional baseball teams.

Schalk left high school in 1910 to enter an apprentice program as a linotype operator in Brooklyn, N.Y., but after ten weeks, he returned home.

Schalk began his baseball career in 1911, earning $65 a month with nearby Taylorville in the class-D Illinois-Missouri League. The young catcher batted .398. Before the season ended, the Milwaukee Brewers of the American Association purchased Schalk for $750. He began 1912 with the Brewers and caught eighty games into early August. Schalk's career in the major leagues began on August 10, when the Chicago White Sox acquired him. On the next day, one day short of his twentieth birthday, Schalk played his first major-league game as starting catcher for Sox pitcher "Doc" White in a 9–6 loss to the Philadelphia Athletics. On Oct. 25, 1916, he married Lavinia Graham; they had two children.

Offensively, Schalk's career statistics in the majors were average: .253 batting average, with 12 home runs, 596 runs batted in, 579 runs scored, and 1,345 career hits, including 199 doubles and 48 triples. Schalk batted .282 in 1919 and .281 in 1922, his best seasons.

In a baseball era when low scoring and defensive skills were hallmarks of the game, Schalk's forte was defense. He revolutionized the art of major-league catching. Before his time, most catchers were big and slow, but Schalk, at five feet nine inches and 160 pounds, was fast and agile. His 176 career stolen bases included 30 in 1916, a record for catchers that stood for sixty-five years. He was the first catcher to back up first and third base on infield ground balls. When a hit went past first base, Schalk followed the runner to first for a possible play. During his career, Schalk recorded putouts at all four bases, and he still holds five major-league fielding records for his position: most years (eight) leading league in fielding average; most years (nine) leading league in putouts; most career assists (1,810); most career chances accepted (8,965); most years (eight) leading league in chances accepted; and most double plays (217).

Schalk complemented his defensive skills with a keen ability to handle a variety of pitchers. Urban ("Red") Faber, the White Sox Hall of Fame pitcher and, with Schalk, the most successful battery in Sox history, credited his catcher for his pitching success. Schalk claimed that during his 1,760 games behind the plate, he caught more spitters, shine balls, emory balls, and knucklers than any other receiver. He caught four no-hitters, the most by a catcher. One of these pitching gems was a perfect game by Charley Robertson of the White Sox against the Detroit Tigers on Apr. 30, 1922.

Schalk was a confident and energetic ballplayer who loved the game. Early in his career Schalk was nicknamed "Cracker," supposedly after a teammate commented on how "that squirt cracked that ball down to second base." Some insist the name was the result of Schalk's "whiplike manner." On game days Schalk would often arrive at the ballpark hours before the other players, sit in the sunshine, and playfully criticize his teammates upon their late arrival. In 1925, Schalk participated in a remarkable stunt. Before a large crowd and wearing a dress suit and hat, he caught a ball dropped from the top of the 460-foot Chicago Tribune Tower. Schalk's skills were appreciated by his contemporaries. Both Ty Cobb and "Babe" Ruth picked "the durable little iron man" for their all-time all-star teams.

Schalk played in the World Series of 1917 and 1919, batting .286 in fourteen games. In the first Series, Schalk's Chicago White Sox defeated the New York Giants four games to two, with Red Faber winning three contests. On the eve of the 1919 Series, the White Sox were considered far superior to the Cincinnati Reds. However, the Sox were split into two cliques. One group included Schalk and his friends Faber and the second baseman Eddie Collins, whose high salary, double that of anyone else on the team, was the cause of considerable resentment. The second faction, which was to become known as the Black Sox, included the outfield stars Joe Jackson and Happy Felsch, the pitching stalwarts Ed Cicotte and Lefty Williams, and the first baseman Chick Gandil. Gambling interests were a constant presence in the baseball world of the time, and Gandil had contact with gamblers intent on fixing the Series. Before the Series, rumors of a fix were in the air, but nothing was substantiated. The early betting line was 3–1 in favor of the Sox. On the eve of the first game, the spread had dropped to 8–5.

Apparently Schalk suspected something from the first inning of the first game, when Cicotte, the team's best pitcher, hit the first Cincinnati batter and repeatedly ignored Schalk's signals.

The hit batsman was the Black Sox signal to the gamblers that the fix was on. Observers noted Schalk's glaring eyes as he fired the ball back to his uncharacteristically wild pitcher. The Sox lost 9–1. At the subsequent trial Cicotte testified, "It's easy to throw a game. . . . I did it by giving the Cincinnati batters easy balls [to hit]. . . . Ray Schalk was wise the moment I started pitching. I double-crossed him on the signals."

Cicotte was also the losing pitcher in the fourth game, making the two errors that decided the outcome. Lefty Williams, also ignoring Schalk's signals, was the losing hurler in the second, fifth, and eighth games. (In 1919–1921 the World Series had a best-of-nine format.) Following the second game, under the stadium grandstand, Schalk physically attacked Williams because of his suspect play. Schalk's frustration was evident in the fifth game, when he was ejected by the plate umpire for protesting the safe call of a runner at home. The play had begun when outfielder Felsch had misplayed a routine fly ball into a double. The Sox lost the Series, five games to three.

In the December following this upset, suspicions of a fix were fueled by Hugh Fullerton's press reports in the *New York World*. In response to these stories, Schalk declared that he knew of seven White Sox players who would not be back in 1920. Trying to keep a lid on the affair, Charles Comisky, the club owner, spoke with Schalk, who was then quoted as saying that the team had played to the best of its ability. "There was not a single moment of all the games in which we did not try," Schalk said.

As the 1920 season ended, a grand jury convened to investigate the 1919 Series. Cicotte and Jackson confessed, and the trial lasted from July 18 through Aug. 2, 1921. The indictment included the charge of a conspiracy "to defraud Ray Schalk out of $1,760," the difference between the winners' and losers' shares. Schalk testified to the suspicious behavior of the defendants, none of whom took the stand in his own defense. Mysteriously, the grand jury confessions were "lost." The trial judge's narrow definition of the law and his directions to the jury resulted in the acquittal of the Black Sox, but the baseball commissioner, Kenesaw Mountain Landis, banned the fixers from organized baseball. Schalk maintained a public silence about the scandal for the rest of his life, repeatedly spurning lucrative offers to tell his side of the story. He emerged from the episode unscathed and continued his high level of performance.

Following the 1926 season, Comisky hired Schalk as player-manager for the 1927 campaign. Schalk's major-league managerial career was unsuccessful: he lasted less than two seasons, and the team finished no higher than fifth place, with 102 wins and 125 losses. Having been dismissed as manager halfway through the 1928 schedule, Schalk wanted to remain with the White Sox as a backup catcher at $15,000 per year. Comisky offered $6,000, far below the $25,000 managerial salary. Despite their sixteen-year relationship, Schalk and Comisky were unable to resolve their differences. Schalk resigned.

In 1929, Schalk caught five games as player-coach with the National League's New York Giants, managed by John McGraw. For the next two seasons, the Chicago Cubs, the crosstown rivals of the White Sox, hired Schalk as a coach and scout, his last major-league assignment. Schalk then began an extensive minor-league managerial career: from 1932 to 1937 he was with Buffalo of the International League; from 1938 to 1939, at Indianapolis; and in 1940, with Milwaukee of the American Association. In 1950 he returned to manage Buffalo for one year.

In 1921, Schalk cofounded Baseball Anonymous, a Chicago-based organization that distributed charity to needy retirees and helped unemployed ex-players find jobs. It held yearly dinners to honor retired players and to present awards to high school baseball prospects from the Chicago area.

At the end of his playing days, Schalk opened a successful bowling alley in Chicago that became a meeting place for ex-players. In 1947, Schalk began an eighteen-year term as assistant baseball coach at Purdue University in Lafayette, Ind. In 1963 he succeeded Rogers Hornsby as baseball adviser on Mayor Richard Daley's Chicago Youth Foundation.

In 1955, Schalk's career was capped by his election to the Baseball Hall of Fame. At the induction ceremony on July 25 in Cooperstown, N.Y., Schalk reminded the assemblage that he had begun his professional career in Milwaukee forty-four years before to the day. In 1969, Schalk was elected to the all-time White Sox team. He died in Chicago.

[Short biographical sketches of Schalk are in James T. Farrell, *My Baseball Diary* (1957); Martin Appel and Burt Goldblatt, *Baseball's Best: The Hall of Fame Gallery* (1977); and Richard Lindberg, *Who's On Third? The Chicago White Sox Story* (1983). The Black Sox scandal is reviewed in Joseph L. Reichler, ed., *The World Series* (1978); and Eliot Asinof, *Eight Men Out* (1979). An obituary is in the *New York Times*, Oct. 20, 1970.]

DAVID BERNSTEIN

SCHENCK, NICHOLAS MICHAEL (Nov. 14, 1881–Mar. 3, 1969), motion-picture and theater executive, was born in Rybinsk, Russia, the son of Hyman Schenck, a laborer, and Elizabeth Schenck. His father earned a meager income by supplying wood fuel for steamers engaged in commerce on the Volga River. In the early 1890's the family immigrated to the United States, settling first in a tenement on New York City's Lower East Side and later in Harlem. Schenck and his older brother Joseph Michael exhibited the kind of resourcefulness and energy they would later display in their adult business careers. They sold newspapers to supplement the family income and later worked in a drugstore in Manhattan's Chinatown. Within two years they became owners of the store (1901).

Schenck and his brother moved into the entertainment business by obtaining a beer concession and offering vaudeville shows at Fort George in northern Manhattan. There they established Paradise Park, an amusement center catering to holiday crowds, around 1908. Their enterprise attracted the attention of Marcus Loew, who set up a "scenic railway" concession at the park. Impressed by the brothers' business acumen, Loew offered them partnerships in some of his theatrical ventures, beginning with the acquisition of the Lyric Theater in Hoboken, N.J. In 1912 the Schencks established the Palisades Amusement Park in Fort Lee, N.J., which they owned until 1935.

When his brother moved to California in the mid-1910's and launched a career in motion pictures (he became the chairman of United Artists in 1924 and the president of Twentieth Century–Fox nine years later), Schenck remained in New York, where he became Loew's right-hand man in his varied business enterprises, including ventures into the motion-picture industry. Though Schenck was only peripherally involved in the purchase of Metro Pictures in 1920, he played an important role in the acquisition of Goldwyn Pictures in 1924 and in the arrangement made with Louis B. Mayer, Robert Rubin, and Irving Thalberg to supply movies for the nationwide chain of Loew's theaters. When Loew died in 1927, Schenck succeeded him as president of Loew's, Inc., and its motion-picture subsidiary, by this time known as Metro-Goldwyn-Mayer (MGM). On Aug. 1, 1927, following a divorce from his first wife, Annie (about whom little is known), Schenck married Pansy Wilcox; they had three children.

Schenck, who chose to run his theatrical enterprises from Loew's Broadway offices, was less famous than many of his subordinates in Hollywood, notably Mayer, who resented the interference of the New York office in the operation of the studio. His relations with Mayer were further strained when Schenck made an arrangement in early 1929 to sell what was thought to be a controlling interest in Loew's to a rival entrepreneur, William Fox. The stock-market crash of 1929 and a federal antitrust suit intervened to block the sale. Schenck continued to serve as president of Loew's and MGM for another quarter of a century.

In operating his theater and film empire, Schenck, who was called "the general," was instinctively and consistently cautious. The Loew's theaters were slow to convert to sound in the late 1920's and lagged behind in the adaptation to the wide screen in the early 1950's. Schenck's conservatism served him well during the Great Depression, because Loew's, unlike other such companies, did not race to acquire new theater holdings; it thus avoided bankruptcy. Although the company suffered a decline in income during the 1930's, it was Schenck's boast that his was the only such corporation to pay dividends throughout the decade.

The popularity of MGM during the 1930's was in large measure a result of the box-office appeal of its many stars, including Clark Gable, Jean Harlow, and Spencer Tracy. As long as the company maintained its position of leadership in the industry. Schenck rarely intervened in Mayer's operation of the studio, except to mediate between Mayer and Thalberg, the gifted but temperamental vice-president in charge of production.

After World War II the fortunes of Loew's

and MGM declined. Rising studio costs, attributable in part to the expensive long-term contracts of its major stars, led to an abrupt decrease in profits. In 1948, despite the largest gross revenue in its history, the company reported its lowest net income since 1933. That year, at Schenck's insistence, Mayer hired a new vice-president in charge of production, Dore Schary. Once again Schenck attempted to act as peacemaker between Mayer and his new deputy. In 1951, Schenck accepted Mayer's resignation and appointed Schary head of the studio. Despite greatly publicized economy measures in 1952, the financial problems of the studio persisted.

Schenck's conservatism was evident in his last years at Loew's and MGM. For almost a decade, he succeeded in delaying compliance with a 1946 court order requiring the division of Loew's into separate theatrical and motion-picture production firms. (The division was accomplished in 1959, more than three years after Schenck resigned from the presidency.) He also attempted to ignore the rising competition from television, refusing to sell or lease old movies to the new medium or enter into the production of programs designed for that market.

Of greater consequence, Schenck steadfastly resisted the industrywide trend toward making profit-sharing deals with independent production units. His insistence that all films be made by studio personnel required the maintenance of an expensive production plant and a high-salaried stable of actors, directors, and writers that drained the company's resources, while talented people within the company tended to leave MGM at the first opportunity.

As the unrest of the stockholders increased, Schenck was persuaded to resign the presidency in 1955 in favor of Arthur Loew, the son of the founder of the firm. One year later, following the surprise resignation of Loew, Schenck was made honorary chairman. A month later he relinquished his seat on the board and severed his connection with the management of the firm. During his last years he divided his time between his estates on Long Island and in Miami Beach, where he died.

[Schenck's career as head of Loew's and MGM is described in Bosley Crowther, *The Lion's Share* (1957). See also "Loew's, Inc., the World's Most Profitable Picture Trust," *Fortune*, Aug. 1939; and Emmet J. Hughes, "MGM: War Among the Lion Tamers," ibid., Aug. 1957. An obituary is in the *New York Times*, Mar. 5, 1969.]

EDWIN A. MILES

SCHERMAN, HARRY (Feb. 1, 1887–Nov. 12, 1969), publishing entrepreneur, was born in Montreal, Canada, the son of Jacob Scherman, a laborer, and Katharine Harris. The family moved to Philadelphia in 1889, and four years later Scherman's father abandoned the family to return to his native England. Thereafter, Scherman's mother was forced to find employment. Scherman graduated from Central High School in Philadelphia and then enrolled at the University of Pennsylvania, where he attended classes at the Wharton School of Finance. After two years Scherman left college to support his family and worked in the New York area at newspaper jobs and at various advertising agencies, including J. Walter Thompson. He married Bernardine Kielty on July 12, 1914; they had two children.

Scherman specialized in writing advertising copy for book publishers. While working with Max Sackheim, he met the brothers Albert and Charles Boni, and in 1916 the four formed a partnership that began publishing inexpensive leather-bound literary classics. Priced at ten cents, 48 million of their books sold over an eight-year span until the market was glutted. The partnership broke up in 1924, and for two years Scherman operated a book-of-the-week club that offered subscribers low-cost classics at the rate of fifty-two books annually.

Convinced that a vast market for inexpensive books existed outside the metropolitan areas, Scherman decided to launch a subscription bookselling service based on the premise that most Americans lacked access to well-stocked book stores, "but everybody has a mailbox." With two partners and $40,000 in capital, Scherman began the Book-of-the-Month Club (BOMC) in 1926 as a marketing concept involving a prestigious board of editors to select the books, discounts on popular titles, bonuses for present purchases that could be applied to future purchases, free books as enticements for new subscribers, and a total reliance on the United States Post Office's parcel delivery system. Scherman wrote the club's advertisements and placed them in major magazines with a national circulation, so that 4,750 subscribers were in the fold initially. By the year's end, the number had increased tenfold.

The initials BOMC soon were well known in New York publishing circles, particularly after the Great Depression forced even the major firms to retrench drastically. By 1931, Scherman was BOMC president, signing checks that helped hard-pressed publishers meet their payrolls, as well as writing copy for advertisements and preparing the monthly newsletter. In an era when the leisure time of many Americans was divided between viewing motion pictures and light reading, Scherman sensed the public's desire for an association with a cultural stratum above that represented by Hollywood offerings or the popular five-cent magazines. Scherman's advertising stressed the BOMC selection board, made up of several post–World War I literati—including Henry Seidel Canby, Heywood Broun, and William Allen White—and thus helped focus attention on their recommendations of such writers as Sinclair Lewis and Thornton Wilder.

Almost addicted to his work, Scherman went to his office early and stayed late. He became chairman of the board in 1950 and watched BOMC membership rolls reach the million mark in that decade. Meanwhile, although the company became publicly owned in 1947, Scherman and his family retained the majority interest. From his boardroom Scherman was able to boast that he had seen his idea grow until the club distributed $400 million in book dividends to subscribers and $60 million in royalties to publishers and authors.

Aware of the BOMC power in the marketplace, Scherman knew dozens of publishers but was friendly with only a few. Basically a shy person, Scherman avoided luncheons and dinners where writers congregated and preferred quiet private clubs or his own family circle. An abiding personal interest in economics led in 1938 to the publication of his first book, *The Promises Men Live By: A New Approach to Economics*, which for a brief time sold briskly. Scherman's other outside interest was music, which he supported generously. With his son, Thomas, he founded, and was a director of, the Little Orchestra Society of New York.

As a Jew, Scherman became an active friend of refugees from Nazi Germany, helping them with cash gifts and assistance in finding jobs in the publishing industry. As is often the case with people of intense personal drive, Scherman was notoriously absentminded; to compensate for this, he wrote postcards and mailed them to his home to act as reminders. Until ten days before his death he insisted on a regular workday at his office and took pride in his speaking acquaintance with most of the 1,000 BOMC employees. He died in New York.

[Papers retained in the BOMC offices are of a business nature, and the only correspondence retained by the family has little relevance to Scherman's professional life. An interview with Scherman is in the Columbia University Oral History Project. Obituaries are in the *New York Times*, Nov. 13, 1969; and *Publishers Weekly*, Nov. 24, 1969.]

ROBERT A. RUTLAND

SCHUSTER, MAX LINCOLN (Mar. 2, 1897–Dec. 20, 1970), editor and publisher, was born in Kalusz, Austria, the son of Barnet Schuster, who ran a stationery and cigar store in New York City, and Minnie Stieglitz, United States citizens who brought Schuster to New York City when he was several weeks old. He attended De Witt Clinton High School in Washington Heights, where he acquired a strong interest in Abraham Lincoln and adopted Lincoln as his middle name. After high school he became a copyboy at Joseph Pulitzer's *New York Evening World*. In 1913 he entered the Pulitzer School of Journalism at Columbia University and received a B.Litt in 1917. While at Columbia, he edited the radical undergraduate magazine *Challenge*, wrote magazine articles, and served as college correspondent for the *Boston Evening Transcript*.

After graduation Schuster became Washington correspondent for the New Republic News Service (later the United Press). With the entrance of the United States into World War I, he became chief of the publication service of the United States Treasury Department's Bureau of War Risk Insurance. He was later named publicity director for the Navy Liberty Loan and Victory Loan campaigns. After demobilization, Schuster became an assistant to philosophy professor Walter B. Pitkin at Columbia. He also edited the trade journal of the Motor and Equipment Manufacturers Association.

In 1921, Schuster met Richard L. Simon, a piano salesman who had stopped by his office for a potential sale. While in the office, Simon noted a book by Romain Rolland on Schuster's desk and a common interest in the publication grew into a discussion about the author and initiated a friendship that lasted until Simon's death in 1960. Simon and Schuster continued on separate career paths until late 1923, when, with a capitalization of $4,000 each, they decided to start a publishing business. In January 1924, the partners opened a one-room office on West Fifty-seventh Street. Their first publication project was a crossword puzzle book, which by the end of the year had sold 375,000 copies and left the new firm of Simon and Schuster with a handsome profit.

In 1926, Schuster contacted Will Durant, a Columbia University professor, and convinced him to write a book entitled *The Story of Philosophy*. The volume sold over a half million copies. That book was followed a year later by Ethelreda Lewis' *Trader Horn*, recommended by Clifton Fadiman, one of their editors; it sold 170,000 copies. The partnership continued to succeed, with the publication of self-help books and publications directed at bringing cultural works to the general public, many of which sold in the millions, such as Dale Carnegie's *How to Win Friends and Influence People* (1938).

Schuster was the "idea" man for the firm and took part in manuscript selection and rejection. While serving variously as president, editor in chief, and chairman of the board for the firm over the years, Schuster found time to write several books. His first, *Eyes on the World* (1935), was a photographic record of the year 1934. It was a critical success, but sales were modest. In 1940 he compiled *A Treasury of the World's Greatest Letters, from Ancient Days to Our Own Time*, an anthology of characteristic and crucial communications. The volume was a best-seller and was chosen as a book dividend by the Book-of-the-Month Club. In May of that year, Schuster married Ray Haskell; they had no children. In 1941 a second volume of the *Treasury* was published.

In 1939, Schuster, Simon, and Leon Shimkin joined Robert Fair De Graff in establishing Pocket Books, a company specializing in the publication of paperbound books. The first ten titles included classics, mysteries, self-help books, poetry, and a Pulitzer Prize–winner, Thornton Wilder's *Bridge of San Luis Rey*. Pocket Books soon became an outstanding success in the publishing industry. The books, priced at twenty-five cents in those early years, revolutionized American reading habits by making books available to millions of readers. Begun with a capitalization of $30,000, Pocket Books was sold in 1944 to Field Enterprises for $3 million. On October 1 of the same year, Simon and Schuster was also sold to Field Enterprises, headed by Marshall Field III, a millionaire department-store magnate. From 1944 to 1957, Schuster and Simon alternated as president and board chairman of the firm.

In 1957, Simon left the firm, and Shimkin and Schuster bought back the firm from Field Enterprises. With a 50 percent interest in the company, Schuster acted jointly with Shimkin as chief executive officer. Nine years later, Schuster sold his interest to Shimkin for a reputed $2 million. Barred by an agreement at the time of sale from publishing for two years, Schuster bided his time. In 1968 he began an editorial partnership with his wife, named M. Lincoln Schuster and Ray Schuster Publishing and Editorial Research Associates, which was in operation until his death.

Schuster was active in civic affairs and served on the board of trustees of the Montefiore and New York Jewish hospitals. He was a member of the Bibliographic Society of America, the Book Table, the Society for the Prevention of Cruelty to Newspaper Readers, the Wednesday Culture Club That Meets on Fridays, and the Shakespeare Fellowship. He died in New York City.

[On Schuster's publishing career, see John Tebbel, *A History of Book Publishing in the United States* (1978); and Kenneth C. Davis, *Two-Bit Culture: The Paperbacking of America* (1984). Obituaries are in the *New York Times*, Dec. 21, 1970; and *Publishers Weekly*, Jan. 4, 1971.]

Frank R. Levstik

SCHUYLER, ROBERT LIVINGSTON (Feb. 26, 1883–Aug. 15, 1966), historian, educator, and editor, was born in New York City, the son of Montgomery Schuyler, a journalist and architectural writer, and Katherine Beeckman Livingston, a gifted amateur artist and singer. Schuyler studied the violin, which he is reported as playing in the orchestra at a Columbia varsity show, but he decided against a musical career.

Schuyler began his undergraduate studies in 1899, only three years after the formal establishment of a department of history within the School (later Faculty) of Political Science at Columbia. Among his teachers were some of the principal founders and shapers of the historical profession in the United States—John W. Burgess, William A. Dunning, Herbert L. Osgood, and James Harvey Robinson. From them, Schuyler derived his lifelong interest in constitutional history and an impressive capacity for exploiting documentary materials. He graduated from Columbia College in 1903.

In 1904, while working as a reporter for the *New York Times*, Schuyler received the M.A. from Columbia. Two years later, he became an instructor in history at Yale University, where a senior colleague was George Burton Adams, whose celebrated textbook on English constitutional history Schuyler revised in 1934. He married Sara Keller Brooks on Oct. 19, 1907. Schuyler took his Ph.D. from Columbia in 1909 and returned there the next year as lecturer; he was promoted to assistant professor in 1911, to associate professor in 1919, and to professor in 1924, with the title of Gouverneur Morris Professor from 1942.

Schuyler drew up the syllabus for the Columbia College course in American history (1913) and, with Carlton J. H. Hayes, the syllabus in modern European history (1912), the latter notable for its attention to economic and cultural history. But Schuyler's service as a first lieutenant in the Twenty-second Engineers, New York National Guard, in 1918–1921 and perhaps his own academic and scholarly bent kept him apart from the postwar innovations in general education through which Columbia had so profound an effect on American undergraduate curricula. He concentrated instead on training graduate students, offering lecture courses in English constitutional history and the history of the British Empire.

Like his teaching, Schuyler's published work was rooted in both sides of the Atlantic. His dissertation, *The Transition in Illinois from British to American Government* (1909), was followed in 1923 by *The Constitution of the United States*, which grew out of lectures on the formation of the Constitution given two years earlier at Cambridge University and the London School of Economics. In his formidably learned *Parliament and the British Empire* (1929), Schuyler demolished the old contention—which had been recently revived by C. H. McIlwain of Harvard—that the acts against which American colonists had protested in the middle of the eighteenth century were without legal authority. Schuyler was thus one of a remarkable group of American historians who, rejecting the nationalistic bias endemic to much American history-writing, attempted to explain how the old British Empire had really worked. He was also fascinated by the relaxation of the imperial grip in the nineteenth century, anticipated in the eighteenth century in the arguments of Josiah Tucker, the dean of Gloucester. In *Josiah Tucker: A Selection from His Economic and Political Writing* (1931), with its long, perceptive introduction, Schuyler rescued that idiosyncratic economist from near-oblivion. Schuyler's last major book, *The Fall of the Old Colonial System* (1945), traced the victory of free trade over monopolies and preferences, and although subsequent scholarship has somewhat modified the sharp distinction Schuyler saw between imperial and anti-imperial phases in British policy, the case studies in the book are models of close analysis.

Nearly all the chapters of Schuyler's books had been previously published. It was natural that one so expert at small-scale distillation of extensive research should also have had a distinguished career as an editor—of *Political Science Quarterly* (1919–1921), *Columbia Studies in History, Economics, and Public Law* (1923–1929; 1944–1948), and *American Historical Review* (1936–1941). After his retirement from Columbia in 1951 and brief stints of teaching at the University of Denver and Hobart College, he became editor of the second supplement (1958) of the *Dictionary of American Biography*.

Schuyler had an abiding interest in his great English predecessors Macaulay, J. R. Green, and, above all, F. W. Maitland, to whom he devoted his presidential address to the American Historical Association in 1951, describing him as "the historical spirit incarnate." It was therefore appropriate that his students should honor him in 1957 with a festschrift on historians of Britain. In his later years at Columbia, he was in charge of the historiography course required of graduate students, and anyone who heard his opening lectures was permanently inoculated against the dangers of present-mindedness.

Schuyler's exacting standards and scrupulous craftsmanship were reflected in lectures untouched by drama, sweeping speculation, or modish controversy. "Funny," wrote one former student, "he was dull *and* good." But his lectures, like his conversation, were enlivened by a subtle and charming wit that came naturally to the son of parents famous for their repartee: "You must congratulate me," he said to a colleague, "I have been named Gouverneur Morris Professor at no decrease in salary." The pleasure of his conversation belied an appearance that frequently impressed strangers as gloomy—but not entirely. In 1945, Schuyler remarked on the passing of an era symbolized by the retirement of Nicholas Murray Butler after nearly half a century as president of Columbia. "One who was born in the Horse and Buggy Age," he wrote to Butler, "may live a few years into the Atomic Age, but he can never really belong to it"; Butler's successor would preside over a very different order, "in which I am too old to feel thoroughly at home." Schuyler died in Rochester, N.Y.

[See the Nicholas Murray Butler Papers, Columbia University; *New York Times*, Oct. 20, 1907, and July 8 and 17, 1914; Lionel Trilling, "The Van Amringe and Keppel Eras," in *A History of Columbia College on Morningside* (1954); Richard Hofstadter, "The Department of History," in R. Gordon Hoxie et al., *A History of the Faculty of Political Science, Columbia University* (1955); and Herman Ausubel, John Bartlet Brebner, and Erling M. Hunt, *Some Modern Historians of Britain: Essays in Honor of Robert Livingston Schuyler* (1957). Obituaries are in the *New York Times*, Aug. 16, 1966; and *American Historical Review*, Jan. 1967.]

R. K. WEBB

SCHWARTZ, DELMORE DAVID (Dec. 8, 1913–July 11, 1966), writer, was born in Brooklyn, N.Y., the son of Harry Schwartz, who made a fortune in real estate, and Rose Nathanson. When Schwartz was young, his parents were divorced. Soon after the onset of the Great Depression, Harry Schwartz died, and the bank named trustee of his estate allowed his fortune to dwindle through indifference or mismanagement. Young Schwartz, who had assumed he would be heir to a fortune, came of age in poverty. (In later life he engaged in endless litigation in a futile attempt to regain the family fortune. His stories are filled with frustrated characters whose poverty ruined their lives.)

After graduating from George Washington High School in Manhattan, Schwartz enrolled at the University of Wisconsin in 1933. He transferred to New York University, from which he graduated with a B.A. degree in philosophy in 1935. From 1935 to 1937 he did graduate work in philosophy at Harvard University, where he studied with Alfred North Whitehead. Although he received excellent grades, he left Harvard in 1937 without completing his degree to pursue a literary life in Manhattan.

Memoirs about this period tend to emphasize Schwartz's good looks, his noble features, large head, and dignified gait. Later in life, drink and drugs coarsened his features, thickened his frame, and made his gait a shuffle. Throughout his life, however, he was known as a wit and raconteur. It was he who observed, "Even paranoids have real enemies."

On June 14, 1938, Schwartz married his high school sweetheart, Gertrude Buckman, who held various editorial jobs. The marriage ended in divorce in 1943. A reading of Schwartz's letters of the period indicates that the paranoia that was to rule his life for more than twenty years had begun. On June 10, 1949, Schwartz married the novelist Elizabeth Pollet. He constantly accused her of infidelity and "grand larceny" (a reference to her withdrawal of funds from their joint account). She obtained a divorce in 1957. During the last months of the marriage, in 1956, Schwartz kept company with Eleanor Goff, a dancer who lived in Greenwich Village. From this romance, it appears, Schwartz fathered his only child, a daughter, who was raised by Goff and the man who married her after Schwartz broke with her, Walter Doerfler. Doerfler was never told the name of the natural father of the baby, nor was the daughter told until she was sixteen.

Despite his marital and mental difficulties, Schwartz wrote prolifically almost all of his adult life. His masterpiece, "In Dreams Begin Responsibilities," appeared in *New Directions in Prose and Poetry* in 1937. The following year he published his first book, a collection of poetry and prose, under that title; it brought instant critical attention and fame. Allen Tate praised the book as "the first real innovation that we'd had since Eliot and Pound." But Schwartz was never able to equal this bravura performance, and he came to be haunted by his early success.

Schwartz's critical reception was uneven. In 1939 he published his translation of Rimbaud's

Saison en enfer. It was savaged by reviewers, who pointed out errors in Schwartz's understanding of French. (A second, corrected edition was issued the following year.) In 1940 he received a Guggenheim Fellowship and the next year published *Shenandoah*, an autobiographical play in verse and prose, which was well received. But the ambitious, introspective first volume of a projected two-volume poem, *Genesis: Book One* (1943), received mixed reviews.

In 1948 the best of Schwartz's short stories were collected in *The World Is a Wedding*. The book did much to reestablish his reputation and psychic equilibrium. But *Vaudeville for a Princess* (1950), combining poetry and prose, again brought him severe criticism. Schwartz bounced back with a large selection of poems, *Summer Knowledge* (1959), which contains the best of his early work with a large number of later, long-line poems. The book won both the prestigious Bollingen Prize (Schwartz was the youngest poet ever to win it) and the Shelley Memorial Prize in 1960. The last book published in his lifetime was *Successful Love* (1961), six stories, which received respectful reviews.

During the last five years of his life, Schwartz published little. Despite erratic mental health, he managed throughout his career to hold teaching jobs at Harvard (1940–1947), Princeton (1949–1950), Kenyon College (1950), Indiana University (1951), the University of Chicago (1954), and Syracuse University (1962–1965). He was editor (1943–1947) and associate editor (1947–1955) of the *Partisan Review* and poetry editor and film critic for the *New Republic* (1955–1957).

Schwartz died in New York City, where he had been living in a seedy Times Square hotel. His body lay unclaimed in the city morgue for several days until an obituary appeared in the *New York Times*. Since his death, his reputation has enjoyed a renaissance, the result of strong posthumously published works and of depictions of his life in Saul Bellow's novel *Humboldt's Gift* (1975) and in James Atlas' biography *Delmore Schwartz: The Life of an American Poet* (1977).

Although he was gifted as a fiction writer and critic, it is for his poetry that Schwartz is best remembered. From his early Yeatsian lyrics to his later Whitmanesque catalogs, his was a poetry of major conflicts and changes, of the individual in conflict with time and the times. His best poems include "The Ballad of the Children of the Czar," "In the Naked Bed, in Plato's Cave," "The Heavy Bear Who Goes with Me," "Starlight Like Intuition Pierced the Twelve," "Seurat's Sunday Afternoon Along the Seine," and the sequence "Coriolanus and His Mother." Perhaps no poet of his period so skillfully depicted the threat of change in humankind and what he termed "the wound of consciousness."

[Schwartz's papers are in the Beinecke Rare Book and Manuscript Library, Yale University. Additional manuscripts are in the Bird Library, Syracuse University. Bibliographies may be found in Donald A. Dike and David H. Zucker, eds., *Selected Essays of Delmore Schwartz* (1970); and Richard McDougall, *Delmore Schwartz* (1974). Posthumous volumes include Robert Phillips, ed., *Last and Lost Poems* (1979); James Atlas, ed., *In Dreams Begin Responsibilities* (1978), a new selection of short stories; Robert Phillips, ed., *Letters of Delmore Schwartz* (1984); Elizabeth Pollet, ed., *Portrait of Delmore: Journals and Notes* (1986); and Robert Phillips, ed., *The Ego Is Always at the Wheel: Bagatelles* (1986).

See also Philip Rahv, *Essays on Literature and Politics, 1932–1972* (1978); William Barrett, *The Truants* (1982); Eileen Simpson, *Poets in Their Youth* (1982); William Phillips, A *Partisan View* (1983); Lionel Abel, *The Intellectual Follies* (1984); and Bruce Bawer, *The Middle Generation* (1986). Several recordings of Schwartz reading are at the Library of Congress in Washington, D.C. An obituary is in the *New York Times*, July 14, 1966.]

ROBERT PHILLIPS

SCOPES, JOHN THOMAS (Aug. 3, 1900–Oct. 21, 1970), teacher and geologist, was born in Paducah, Ky., the son of Thomas Scopes, a railroad machinist, and Mary Alva Brown. He attended public schools in Kentucky and Illinois and later the University of Illinois and the University of Kentucky, from which he received a B.A. in 1924. That year Scopes became an athletic coach and teacher of algebra, physics, and chemistry at Central High School in Dayton, Tenn.

Local circumstances conspired in 1925 to make Scopes a symbol of academic freedom: In March the Tennessee legislature enacted a law making it a misdemeanor to teach evolution in the state's public schools. In April, when the principal of his school became ill, Scopes substituted for him in a biology course. In May the American Civil Liberties Union (ACLU) advertised that it would pay the expenses of anyone who would test the law's constitutionality. Some of Dayton's worthies, primarily motivated by the hope of benefiting local business, decided to exploit the opportunity. They asked Scopes if evolution was integral to the teaching of biology. When he answered that it was, they pressed him to be the defendant in a test case, which he agreed to do.

Scopes was arrested for teaching evolution, and the ACLU committed itself to his defense. The case developed into the nation's biggest news story when William Jennings Bryan and Clarence Darrow volunteered to oppose each other in trying the case. Not only was Bryan a former Democratic presidential nominee and Darrow America's most famous defense lawyer, but they had become the champions, respectively, of fundamentalist Christians and of freethinkers.

Scopes was, he said, merely "the center of the storm." Yet, he was the vital center. His courage and independence led him to become the defendant in the case, for he believed that neither politics nor religion should dictate what knowledge people should have. He also made important decisions regarding his trial: he accepted as his local defense counsel John R. Neal, an able Tennessee lawyer who was a dedicated defender of intellectual freedom, and he insisted that the ACLU, despite its reluctance, accept Darrow's services, asserting that the trial was going to be a free-for-all fight and would thus demand a roughhouse lawyer. In addition, Scopes comported himself circumspectly during his trial, so he neither embarrassed his defenders nor antagonized the prosecution or the court.

The state indicted Scopes hurriedly so that the trial could begin promptly. Even before the trial started on July 10, Dayton had taken on a circus atmosphere as fundamentalists, tourists, and reporters arrived in town. Prosecution and defense counsel also arrived early to deal with the legal preliminaries. Bryan was assisted by his son and four Tennessee lawyers; Darrow and Neal were joined by two New York attorneys, Dudley Field Malone and Arthur Garfield Hays. The judge was John T. Raulston, who did little to restrain the circus atmosphere surrounding the trial.

During the trial, there was no question that Scopes had violated Tennessee's antievolution statute. At issue were the rights of religion and government to decide what should or should not be taught. Bryan declared that a victory for evolution would strike "at the root not only of Christianity but of civilization." Darrow countered that the prosecution was paving the way for a reign of "bigotry and ignorance and hatred." The tactics and oratory of opposing counsel, the maneuverings of Judge Raulston, and the antics of people in the courtroom and Dayton gave color and life to these issues, and some 200 journalists and photographers were on hand to report it all.

The jury found Scopes guilty on July 21. He was able to take satisfaction in the fact that his defense had clearly enunciated the principles of free inquiry. He contributed to this by telling the court before he was sentenced, "I feel that I have been convicted of violating an unjust statute. I will continue . . . to oppose this law in any way I can. Any other action would be in violation of my ideals of academic freedom—that is, to teach the truth as guaranteed in our Constitution—of personal and religious freedom." Judge Raulston fined him $100.

The case was not over, for the decision was appealed. The ACLU wanted other counsel to continue the case, but Scopes demanded that Darrow argue the appeal. This was done before the Tennessee Supreme Court in June 1926; the court overturned the sentence on the ground that the jury, not the judge, should have set the fine. Thus, technically Scopes had won, and Tennessee was relieved of having to rule on the merits of the antievolution law. The statute was in effect dead, although it was not repealed until 1967.

After his trial, Scopes left teaching. He decided not to exploit his prominence, choosing instead to study geology at the University of Chicago. In 1927 he took a job with the Gulf Oil Company. He worked in Venezuela until 1930, when the company discharged him for refusing to conduct an illegal survey. In February 1930 he married Mildred Walker; they had two children. He pursued doctoral studies at Chicago, but he ran out of funds in 1932 before completing the degree. In 1933, Scopes took a job with the United Gas Corporation, in whose employ he remained in Texas and Louisiana until he retired in 1964. He did not emerge from his relative obscurity until 1960, when he helped to promote the film version of the play *Inherit the Wind*, which was based on his trial.

In 1967, Scopes published his autobiography. He died in Shreveport, La.

The year of his death, Scope spoke at the George Peabody College for Teachers in Nashville, declaring, "It is the teacher's business to decide what to teach. It is not the business of the federal courts nor of the states." Thus, toward the end of his life, Scopes reinforced the idea of academic freedom, of which he had been an outstanding symbol for forty-five years.

[On Scopes's life, see John T. Scopes and James Presley, *Center of the Storm: Memoirs of John T. Scopes* (1967); and D. C. Ipsen, *Eye of the Whirlwind: The Story of John Scopes* (1973). See also the trial record, published as *The World's Most Famous Court Trial* (1925); Ray Ginger, *Six Days or Forever?* (1958); Scopes, "The Trial That Rocked the Nation," *Reader's Digest*, Mar. 1961; and L. Sprague DeCamp, *The Great Monkey Trial* (1968). Accounts of the trial are also found in the biographies of some of the other principals, including Clarence Darrow, *The Story of My Life* (1932); Irving Stone, *Clarence Darrow for the Defense* (1941); Arthur Garfield Hays, *City Lawyer* (1942); Lawrence W. Levine, *Defender of the Faith, William Jennings Bryan: The Last Decade, 1915–1925* (1965); and Arthur Weinberg and Lila Weinberg, *Clarence Darrow: A Sentimental Rebel* (1980). An obituary is in the *New York Times*, Oct. 23, 1970.]

DONALD R. MCCOY

SELDES, GILBERT VIVIAN (Jan. 3, 1893–Sept. 29, 1970), journalist and critic, was born in Alliance, N.J., the son of George Sergius Seldes, a pharmacist, and Anna Saphro, both Russian-Jewish immigrants. Seldes graduated from Central High School in Philadelphia in 1910 and enrolled at Harvard, where he gravitated toward the literary set, joined the staff of the *Harvard Monthly*, and became active in the Harvard Dramatic Club, which in 1926 produced his play *The Wise-Crackers*. He graduated, Phi Beta Kappa, in 1914.

Seldes worked briefly as a reporter on the *Pittsburgh Sun* and as a music critic and editorial writer for the *Philadelphia Evening Ledger* from 1914 to 1916, when he left for England as a free-lance war correspondent. After America's entry into World War I he served briefly in the army and then became American political correspondent of *L'echo de Paris* in Washington, D.C.

Seldes' first book, *The United States and the War* (1917), written earlier but published in England just as America entered the war, sought to explain "the heartbreaking delay" and predicted, as well as urged, an Anglo-Franco-American entente. This work, along with his other journalistic activities, suggests that he might have remained in journalism, but his style betrayed more aesthetic inclinations, and after serving in 1919 as associate editor of *Collier's Weekly*, he became a managing editor—"chief cook and bottle washer"—of the recently reformulated *Dial* magazine, enlisted by its two new owners, Scofield Thayer and James Sibley Watson, Jr., two of his Harvard associates. The new post placed Seldes at the center of a lively endeavor to bring a new aesthetic distinction to American literary life.

As managing editor (1919–1923) and regular dramatic critic (1923–1929), Seldes gained an intimate knowledge of, and often friendship with, such leading literary figures of the 1920's as Edmund Wilson, F. Scott Fitzgerald, and Ring Lardner. He also contributed reviews and critical essays to the *New Republic* and the *Freeman* and wrote one of the first reviews (in the *Nation*) of James Joyce's *Ulysses* when it was published in 1922. That same year, he was instrumental in arranging for the first American publication, in the *Dial*, of T. S. Eliot's *The Waste Land*. His review of Fitzgerald's *The Great Gatsby* (1925) pronounced it "a brilliant work."

Seldes married Alice Wadhams Hall on June 21, 1924. They had two children, one of whom, Marian Seldes, became a noted actress.

Gorham B. Munson, reviewing the critical scene of the 1920's at decade's end, described Seldes as one of the brightest, most "sharply intelligent" of the young critics. Seldes differed, however, from others of the *Dial* set in being lighter and more agile, "a roving critic," Munson said, who had become "expert in making discriminations in the arts of levity and diversion, so much less charted and therefore so much more risky to the critical taste than the serious arts."

Seldes paid his dues to the "serious arts," but he also regularly gave notice to art forms not generally considered serious—the movies, vaudeville, and the popular theater of song and dance. He often tucked such notices into his theater reviews, panning a production of Somerset Maugham's play *The Circle*, or even Eugene O'Neill's *Anna Christie*, by contrasting its effect upon an audience to that of Chaplin's film *The Kid* or a performance of Al Jolson. The latter, he said, is "all we have of the *commedia dell'arte*."

In 1923, Seldes took a year's leave from the *Dial* and went to Paris, where he wrote *The Seven Lively Arts* (1924). A brisk, critical survey of nearly all the then-popular entertainment arts—from vaudeville and burlesque to comic strips, the movies, and the circus—it established him as America's premier critic of art forms previously unacknowledged as such.

Edmund Wilson, writing in the *Dial*, declared the book "a genuine contribution to America's new orientation in the arts which was inaugurated by [Van Wyck Brooks's] *America's Coming of Age*, in 1915, and more violently promoted in 1917 by [H. L. Mencken's] *A Book of Prefaces*"—a judgment from which hindsight need not demur. Others professed to be shocked by Seldes' celebration of the lowbrow arts, particularly by his high ranking, as significant artists, of Al Jolson, Ring Lardner, Mr. Dooley, the comic-strip artist George Herriman (*Krazy Kat*), Florenz Ziegfeld, Mack Sennett, Charlie Chaplin, Irene Castle, and vaudeville and circus performers. The book was reissued in 1957 without changes in the original text, but he provided a brief account of its origin and subsequent reception, in which he acknowledged earlier shortsightedness, particularly regarding radio, but reaffirmed his original thesis.

Seldes continued to demonstrate his independence as a critic and his agility and versatility as a writer. Under the pseudonym Foster Johns, he published two mystery novels, *The Victory Murders* (1927) and *The Square Emerald* (1928), and a "serious" novel, *The Wings and the Eagle* (1929). In 1930 he published an adaptation of *Lysistrata* that was produced on Broadway in 1946. Heeding the changing social and political scene of the 1930's, he published a little book, *The Future of Drinking* (1930); a tract, *Against Revolution* (1932); and *The Years of the Locust: America, 1929–1932* (1933). His most ambitious social criticism of these despairing years was *Mainland* (1936). Seldes suggested that America avoid the twin absolutes of Communism and fascism and hold steadfast to the principles of "national independence, civil freedom, and private prosperity."

Returning to the claim he had staked out in *The Seven Lively Arts*, Seldes wrote *The Movies and the Talkies* (1929) and *The Movies Come from America* (1937). In *The Great Audience* (1950) he still stoutly asserted that "our mass entertainments are . . . the great creative arts of our time" but acknowledged that he had not originally understood or foreseen that their creative effect was upon the audience, "making people over," creating "the climate of feeling in which all of us live." In *The Public Arts* (1956) he returned to his theme that popular forms of entertainment, while still "lively" and ever-changing (television was now central to his concerns), had to assume a responsibility commensurate with the power they wielded.

The steady outpouring of books was accompanied by continuing activity as a columnist for the *New York Journal* (1931–1937) and, in the late 1950's, for the *Village Voice;* as a script writer for radio and television (he published *Writing for Television: A Writer's Handbook* in 1952); as program director in the early days of television (1937–1945) for the Columbia Broadcasting System (he and a secretary constituted the whole department); as editor of the documentary film *This Is America* (1933); and as a teacher and dean of the Annenberg School of Communications at the University of Pennsylvania from 1959 to 1963, when he retired.

As a person, Seldes was as lively as the arts to which he was devoted; this was evident in his literary style and in his talk. "I've been carrying on a lover's quarrel with the popular arts for years," he said. "It's been fun. Nothing like them." He died in New York City.

[No single repository holds correspondence, manuscripts, or related materials as a Seldes collection. The records of the *Dial*, on deposit at Yale University, contain some of his correspondence and typescripts. The Rare Book Room of the University of Pennsylvania Library has clippings and typescripts of radio and television appearances but no correspondence.

There is no full-length biography. An interview with Seldes in the *New York Times Book Review*, July 8, 1956, provides some biographical matter. Edmund Wilson's review of *The Seven Lively Arts* appeared in the *Dial*, Sept. 1924, and was republished, with his review of *The Great Audience*, in his *Shores of Light* (1952). Scattered references to Seldes in Wilson's published notebooks, *The Twenties* (1975) and *The Thirties* (1980), and in *Letters on Literature and Politics* (1977; one letter to Seldes) testify to their long friendship. Gorham Munson's review of "The Young Critics" appeared in the *Book-Man*, Dec. 1929. William Wasserstrom, *The Time of the Dial* (1963), discusses Seldes' *Dial* years.

An obituary is in the *New York Times*, Sept. 30, 1970.]

JAMES R. VITELLI

SHAHN, BENJAMIN ("BEN") (Sept. 12, 1898–Mar. 14, 1969), painter and graphic artist, was born in Kovno (Kaunas), Lithuania, a province of czarist Russia, the son of Hessel Shahn, a woodcarver and furniture-maker, and Gittel Lieberman, a potter. When Shahn immigrated to America with his parents in 1906, settling in Brooklyn, he had already begun to draw. He was taken out of school in 1913 to serve an apprenticeship at $1 a week in Hessenberg's Lithography Shop on Beekman Street in Manhattan. It was a hard apprenticeship: the artist told how he had been made to draw a single letter hundreds of times. Shahn became a naturalized citizen in 1918. He attended school at night and in 1919 enrolled at New York University. In 1922 he transferred to the City College of New York and then studied at the National Academy of Design and the Art Students League. Shahn married Mathilda Goldstein in 1922; they had two children.

Shahn and his wife went abroad in 1924–1925. He studied at the Sorbonne and at the Académie de la Grande Chaumière and traveled in North Africa, Spain, Italy, Austria, Germany, and the Netherlands. On a second trip to Paris in 1927, he was deeply impressed by demonstrations on behalf of the imprisoned anarchists Nicola Sacco and Bartolomeo Vanzetti.

When Shahn returned to New York, he shared a studio with the photographer Walker Evans, who, like Shahn, expressed his concern with social and political issues in his art. Injustices of all kinds animated Shahn. Indeed, his first one-man show in 1930 at New York's Downtown Gallery included African subjects as well as gouaches dealing with the Dreyfus case. Shahn considered the Sacco-Vanzetti case "another crucifixion," and in 1932 he created a series of twenty-three paintings and two large panels showing protest marches, the prisoners manacled, and the corpses in their coffins after the execution. These paintings won Shahn wide acclaim and captured the attention of the Mexican artist Diego Rivera, who in 1933 invited Shahn to assist him with his murals for Rockefeller Center. (The murals were subsequently destroyed because Rivera included a prominent portrait of Lenin.) That year Shahn painted a series of fifteen gouaches illustrating the trial and conviction of Thomas J. Mooney, a labor leader charged with a bombing. Shahn and his wife divorced in 1932, and in 1935 he married the artist-journalist Bernarda Bryson; they had three children.

In 1934, Shahn enrolled in the government's Public Works of Art Project. From 1934 to 1935 he worked with the artist Louis Bloch on a mural that contrasted old and modern penal methods for Rikers Island Penitentiary in New York; although the sketches were approved by the prisoners and Mayor La Guardia, the project was rejected by the Municipal Art Commission. From 1935 to 1938, Shahn was employed by the Farm Security Administration as an artist and photographer. Many of the 6,000 photographs he made for the agency portray rural hardship, showing the homeless and hungry victims of the Great Depression. Shahn's photographs sometimes served as studies for his paintings, as with *Handball* (1939). In 1938 he completed a fresco for the Community Center of the Jersey Homesteads (later named Roosevelt, N.J.), a federally funded housing development near Princeton inhabited mostly by immigrant Jewish garment workers. America is depicted as a land of freedom and opportunity occasionally marred by injustice. In one scene Albert Einstein leads a group of immigrants at Ellis Island as they pass the caskets of Sacco and Vanzetti; in another, a forceful labor organizer is haranguing the masses. From 1938 to 1940, Shahn and his wife executed thirteen large tempera panels picturing urban and farm life across America for the Bronx Central Annex Post Office in New York, which were commissioned by the Public Buildings Administration. From 1940 to 1943, Shahn painted murals for the Social Security Building in Washington, D.C., a commission awarded in a competition from the Treasury Department. Despite his leftist political leanings and his depictions of America's shortcomings, he chose to work within the system, and during the Great Depression and World War II he was often employed by the government. Moreover, his condemnation of poverty and injustice did not offend conservatives, since he seldom focused on specific causes.

Although the liberal slant of Shahn's art did not change after 1940, he frequently replaced his stark posterlike format with subtler modulations of color and a rich calligraphic treatment.

He sometimes used English or Hebrew letters with the image. Contemporary allusions gained force through elements of fantasy. In *Allegory* (1948) a great wolf whose head is wrapped in spurts of fire stands menacingly over the corpses of children, a commemoration of the Chicago tenement fire that prompted a black man who had lost his four children to kill the landlord, whom he suspected of having set the blaze. During World War II some of Shahn's art took account of Nazi brutality. His painting *Lidice* (1942) depicted the Nazi destruction of an entire village, Lidice in Czechoslovakia. In 1942 and 1943 he designed posters for the Office of War Information.

From 1947 to 1950, Shahn taught at the Museum of Fine Arts in Boston, the Brooklyn Museum Art School, and one summer session at the University of Colorado (1950). In 1956 he was named Charles Eliot Norton Professor of Poetry at Harvard University; his lectures there were published as *The Shape of Content* (1957).

The Museum of Modern Art gave Shahn a major retrospective in 1947; he also had one-man shows at the Museum of Fine Arts in Boston and the Phillips Collection in Washington, D.C. In 1954 he was one of the two artists (with Willem de Kooning) chosen to represent the United States at the Venice Biennale exhibition. His thirty-four paintings hung at the United States pavilion won him international recognition.

Shahn designed sets and posters in 1958 for Jerome Robbins' ballet *New York Export—Opus Jazz* and, in 1961, sets for the play *Him* by e. e. cummings and Robbins' ballet *Events*. In 1959 he was called before the House Un-American Activities Committee, with which he declined to discuss his politics. He avoided political commentary in the mosaic murals he executed for Israel's SS *Shalom* (1963–1964), but he chose champions of liberalism such as Dag Hammarskjöld (1962) and Martin Luther King, Jr. (1966), for his portraits. He died in New York.

Shahn is best remembered for his overtly polemical work of the 1930's and 1940's, when he used art as a weapon for political and social change. He was foremost among the social-realist artists.

[Some of Shahn's papers are on microfilm at the Archives of American Art in Washington, D.C., and New York City. His writings on a variety of subjects are contained in John D. Morse, ed., *Ben Shahn* (1973). For his own views on his artistic intentions, see Ben Shahn, *Biography of a Painting* (1966). See also Selden Rodman, *Portrait of the Artist as an American* (1951); Alistair Reid, *Ounce, Dice, Trice: Drawings by Ben Shahn* (1958); James Thrall Soby, *Ben Shahn: Paintings* (1963); Martin H. Bush, *Ben Shahn: The Passion of Sacco and Vanzetti* (1968); Bernarda Bryson Shahn, *Ben Shahn* (1972); David Shapiro, ed., *Social Realism: Art as a Weapon* (1973); Kenneth Wade Prescott, *The Complete Graphic Works of Ben Shahn* (1973); and Davis Pratt, ed., *The Photographic Eye of Ben Shahn* (1975). An obituary is in the *New York Times*, Mar. 15, 1969.]

ABRAHAM A. DAVIDSON

SHAUGHNESSY, CLARK DANIEL (Mar. 6, 1892–May 15, 1970), football coach, was born in St. Cloud, Minn., the son of Edward Shaughnessy and Lucy Ann Foster. In 1908 he entered the University of Minnesota, where he watched the Minnesota football team host the Carlisle Indians, coached by the legendary "Pop" Warner. In 1909 he tried out for the team, but he received little attention from the coaches that year and in 1910. For a time he dropped out of school, apparently for financial reasons, but his devotion to football never flagged. An injury prevented him from playing in 1911, but in 1912, Shaughnessy came into his own as an athlete. In that year he was named an alternate on Walter Camp's all-American team, and in 1913, his final year of college competition, he received accolades as both an offensive fullback and a defensive end. At six feet and almost 200 pounds, he was big for a player of his time. His collegiate experiences convinced "Shag," as he came to be known, that his future lay in the sport.

After receiving his B.A. in 1914, Clark worked as a high school coach. Within a year he was head coach at Tulane University. This was the first of a number of faltering programs he would build to the point of national recognition. During his years at Tulane he compiled a record of 58–27–6. On Dec. 5, 1917, he married Louvania Mae Hamilton; they had three children.

In 1928, Shaughnessy moved to Loyola of the South in New Orleans, where he coached until 1932 with a record of 38–16–2. In 1933 he succeeded Amos Alonzo Stagg, one of the most famous names in the annals of football, at the University of Chicago. His tenure there was not a happy one. The school's president had decided to deemphasize football, and working with few talented players, Shaughnessy's record was an inferior 17–34–4. After the 1939 season the school abandoned its program and he found himself without a coaching job, although he had ample job security as a tenured full professor of physical education.

Within months Shaughnessy accepted a coaching position at Stanford, where he accomplished what many consider his greatest achievement. The Stanford Indians, which had been winless the previous season, went 10–0 and defeated Nebraska in the 1941 Rose Bowl. Shaughnessy was named the Scripps-Howard national coach of the year by an overwhelming margin. Most of his success was predicated on the use of the T formation, which emphasizes flankers and men-in-motion. This innovation resulted in a high-scoring Stanford team, and fans loved it. Shaughnessy remained in California one more year before moving east, where he coached at the University of Pittsburgh until 1946 and then the University of Maryland for one year. His overall record as a college coach was an impressive 149–106–14. In 1946, Shaughnessy took a coaching position with the Washington Redskins. The following year he went to the Los Angeles Rams and guided that team to a divisional championship in 1949. He left the Rams in 1951, when he joined the Chicago Bears as a technical adviser and vice-president. He was never entirely happy in professional football. Roger Treat said that "the jovial thuggery of pro football, where every man has a little assassin in him," troubled Shaughnessy.

Shaughnessy was noted as a hardworking man totally devoted to football. His day regularly began at 3:30 A.M., and he was known to have as many as 20,000 play diagrams. He worked his players hard, but they respected him and liked his emphasis on offense. He had a rigid policy that a team member with even a minor injury could not play.

Shaughnessy, "father of the modern T," revolutionized football. "The object in football," he often said, "is not to annihilate the other team, but to advance the ball." The T formation as he coached it had three key elements: psychology, deception, and personnel. After retiring from football, he had an active interest in his son's publishing business. He died in Santa Monica, Calif.

[Shaughnessy's own books, *Football in War and Peace* (1943) and *The Modern T Formation with Man-in-Motion* (1941, written with Ralph Jones and George Halas), give considerable insight into his coaching philosophy. For detailed coverage of his coaching attributes, see G. Dunscomb, "Shaughnessy Behind the Eight Ball: The Story of the T Formation," *Saturday Evening Post*, Nov. 1, 1941. Edwin Pope, *Football's Greatest Coaches* (1956), devotes a useful chapter to Shaughnessy. An obituary is in the *New York Times*, May 16, 1970.]

JAMES A. CASADA

SHEIL, BERNARD JAMES (Feb. 18, 1886–Sept. 13, 1969), Roman Catholic auxiliary bishop of Chicago and titular archbishop of Selge, was born in Chicago, Ill., the son of James Bernard Sheil, an Irish dealer in coal and real estate and the local Democratic party ward leader, and Rosella Barclay. He received his primary and secondary education at St. Columbkille's Parochial School and in 1904 entered St. Viator's College, Bourbonnais, Ill., where he excelled in debate and public speaking and as a baseball pitcher. His no-hit, no-run performance against the University of Illinois championship team led to trial offers from the Cincinnati Reds and the Chicago White Sox. Sheil rejected them in order to prepare for the priesthood at St. Viator's Seminary, where he completed his theological studies. He was ordained in May 1910.

After serving at Chicago's Holy Name Cathedral, Sheil was named curate at St. Mel's Roman Catholic Church in that city. Following a chaplaincy at the Great Lakes Naval Training Station in 1918 and 1919, he rejoined the cathedral staff, where his duties included the chaplaincy at the Cook County Jail. Asked by a "mad-dog killer" whom he was accompanying to the gallows, "Father, why do they wait until now before they start to care?" Sheil took up the cause of underprivileged youth. After he joined the staff of the chancery office in 1923, Sheil rose rapidly in the administration of the Chicago archdiocese. Named chancellor in 1924, he was consecrated as auxiliary bishop of Chicago and titular bishop of Pege by George Cardinal Mundelein and was named vicar-general of the archdiocese in 1928.

Sheil became a leader in liberal Catholic social action, opposing the regime of Franco in Spain and the rantings of Father Charles Coughlin. Disturbed by the moral influence of gangsters upon the city's youth, in 1930 he founded the Catholic Youth Organization (CYO), which established hundreds of centers across the United States, Canada, Latin America, and Italy.

Despite criticism by wealthy contributors to the archdiocese, he supported Chicago's non-Communist labor organizers in the 1930's. In 1939 his powerful speech helped the CIO to unionize packinghouse workers in the Chicago stockyards. Sheil joined Saul Alinsky in 1939 to found the Back of the Yards Council, which transformed the stockyard slums into a model working-class community, and in 1940, to form the Industrial Areas Foundation, which organized poor communities across the United States for social action. Despite Sheil's close relationship to Archbishop Mundelein and the support of the Roosevelt administration, Pope Pius XII named Samuel Cardinal Stritch of Milwaukee to succeed Mundelein in 1939, and in the new administration, Sheil lost his position as vicar-general of the archdiocese.

While his power in the archdiocese declined, Bishop Sheil continued to champion liberal causes, including the United Nations, Zionism, and racial justice, and the CYO and his other social projects grew and multiplied. He transformed Lewis College, an aeronautical school that he had founded in 1930 at Lockport, Ill., into a four-year coeducational liberal arts college; and he established the Sheil School of Social Studies, an adult education center in Chicago. He established a radio station, WFJL-FM, in Chicago, and a radio news bureau in Brussels, Belgium. Joining the National Committee Against the Persecution of the Jews in 1944, he repeatedly attacked anti-Semitism. At a forum on Jewish-Christian relations, he was attacked for his liberal position by a representative of the Christian Front. "You're not a Catholic . . . you're a nigger lover and a Jew lover," she cried, as she spat in his face. "You're not a bishop. You're a rabbi!" "I thank you, Madam, for the compliment," replied the Bishop. "Rabbi? That is what they called our Lord."

In a speech before an international educational conference of the United Automobile Workers in April 1954 Sheil attacked the tactics of Senator Joseph McCarthy's anti-Communist crusade. Arguing that "you cannot effectively fight tyranny with tyranny," Sheil insisted that Communism presented no serious threat to a society where "justice and charity prevail." Four months later, under attack from those who called him "Judas Iscariot Sheil," the bishop defended his right to address moral issues. "The clergyman at times *must* . . . throw all his energy into the struggle for a God-centered world," he argued. "There may be times also when . . . silence would be a shameful thing."

By September 1954, conservative churchmen's withdrawal of financial support had combined with Sheil's ill health to force his resignation as director of the Chicago CYO. Thereafter, most of his programs were dismantled or decentralized. In 1959 Sheil was appointed titular archbishop of Selge. He continued to serve as pastor of St. Andrew's Roman Catholic parish in Chicago from 1935 to 1966, when he was removed after a dispute with Archbishop John P. Cody over parish finances. Sheil died in Tucson, Ariz.

Sheil was a transitional figure from the "bricks and mortar" Irish-American prelates who led the American church in the early twentieth century to the socially activist clergymen who prodded it in midcentury. A colorful churchman, popular with Chicago newsmen, he was characteristically described as "a stubby, balding, firm-faced Friar Tuck." "I have taken my stand," he once said, "uncompromisingly on the side of the poor, the disinherited, and the dispossessed."

[Sheil's papers are at the Chicago Historical Society and in the Chicago archdiocesan archives, St. Mary of the Lake Seminary, Mundelein, Ill. See Roger L. Treat, *Bishop Sheil and the CYO* (1951); *Chicago's Tribute to His Excellency, Most Rev. Bernard J. Sheil, D.D., on the Twenty-fifth Anniversary of His Consecration* (1953); "The Bishop's 25th," *Time*, May 11, 1953; "Defeat in Chicago," *Time*, Dec. 20, 1954; Mary Elizabeth Carroll, "Bishop Sheil," *Harper's*, Dec. 1958; Edward R. Kantowicz, *Corporation Sole* (1983); and Henry C. Koenig, "Most Rev. Bernard J. Sheil: A Titular Archbishop," an unpublished paper given at the American Catholic Historical Society convention in Chicago, Dec. 30, 1984. An obituary is in the *New York Times*, Sept. 14, 1969.]

RALPH E. LUKER

SHIPLEY, RUTH BIELASKI (1885–Nov. 3, 1966), career civil servant, was born in Montgomery County, Md., the daughter of Alexander Bielaski, a Methodist minister, and Roselle Woodward. After spending her early childhood on the Maryland farm of her paternal grandfather, a Polish immigrant, Bielaski moved with her family to Washington, D.C. The largely Protestant, middle-class, politically neutral community of civil servants in the nation's capital proved congenial to her and her siblings, A. Bruce, who became director of the Bureau of Investigation; Alice, who worked for the army's G-2 Division and the Central Intelligence Agency; and Frank, who became an agent of the Office of Strategic Services. Following her graduation from Western High School and a short stay at business school, Bielaski passed a competitive civil service examination and was hired as a clerk in the United States Patent Office in 1903. In 1909 she married Frederick William van Dorn Shipley, an administrative assistant with the Panama Canal Commission, and went to live in the Canal Zone; they had one child.

When Shipley's husband became ill in 1914, the family returned to Washington. In order to support her child and invalid husband, Shipley took a position in the Records Division of the State Department, where one of her duties was to keep an index of American citizens living abroad. Her husband died in 1919, and the following year Shipley was made special assistant to Alvey Augustus Adee, the second assistant secretary of state, a legendary figure who disposed of the formal and routine business at the State Department for more than three decades. Under Adee's tutelage, Shipley became one of the most able of her generation of bureaucrats. Accordingly, in 1921 she was promoted to drafting officer and three years later to assistant chief of the Office of Coordination and Review, which checked and corrected all outgoing State Department correspondence. In 1928, Shipley was appointed chief of the Passport Division by Secretary of State Frank B. Kellogg. Applauded by feminists as an ideal career woman, Shipley was the first woman to head a major division of the State Department. In 1930 she became the first American woman plenipotentiary as a delegate to the Conference on the Codification of International Law at The Hague.

Though the secretary of state was technically responsible for issuing passports, all secretaries from Kellogg to John Foster Dulles came to rely upon Shipley, the acknowledged department expert on matters of citizenship. Mildly progressive, Shipley turned the division into a model of efficiency. She upgraded passport fraud investigations by employing new detection techniques and obtaining cooperation from other government agencies. Among those caught by Shipley operatives were the American Communist party leaders Earl Browder and Nicholas Dozenberg in 1939 and the Nazi spy Günther Gustav Maria Rumrich in 1943.

The outbreak of war in Europe complicated Shipley's work. She was charged with preventing foreign travel instead of facilitating it. Shipley invalidated all old passports in 1939, designed a lengthy set of application procedures, saw that all applicants were fingerprinted, and decreed that new passports be issued only on special counterfeit-proof paper. With few exceptions, Shipley denied citizens passports to belligerent countries and the combat zone demarcated by the Neutrality Act. After the Japanese attack on Pearl Harbor, she ordered that Japanese-American fishermen on the west coast be blocked from fishing offshore without passports. Although she had no authority to give the order, it was allowed to stand. Even the powerful publishers Roy Howard and Ogden Reid ran afoul of Shipley dicta and were detained for a time in 1944 after returning from a navy-sponsored tour of the South Atlantic without passports. Queried about restrictive administration passport policies at a wartime press conference, President Franklin D. Roosevelt said admiringly, "Mrs. Shipley is a wonderful ogre."

By the end of the 1940's, travel was nearly back to normal and Shipley was at the peak of her power. Her influence reached to the granting of visas and immigration. Her office kept voluminous files that, by 1953, contained detailed information on some 12 million individuals. She also was highly respected in Congress because her division, unlike most federal agencies, made money.

Shipley's last years in office were the most difficult and controversial of her long career. A staunch anti-Communist, she assisted in the preparation of the McCarran Internal Security Act of 1950, which gave the secretary of state the authority to deny passports to members of alleged Communist organizations listed by the attorney general. The task of dealing with such cases then naturally fell to Shipley, who made the decisions, informed unsuccessful applicants that their travel abroad "would be prejudicial to the interests of the United States," and directed an in-house appeals process that usually ratified the original denial. She seemed to crack down even harder on left-wing travelers after 1951, when a United States Senate Internal Security Subcommittee report criticized the Passport Division for allowing eighteen alleged subversives to obtain passports and travel to Moscow. By 1952, liberal critics were accusing Shipley of blatant political bias and of denying passports without due process. When the chemist Linus Pauling was refused a passport to attend a scientific conference in London, Senator Wayne Morse launched a verbal assault on Shipley and the Passport Division on the floor of the United States Senate. Railing against "government by a woman rather than by law," Morse labeled Shipley's methods "tyrannical and capricious" and her appeals process a "star-chamber court." In response, Secretary of State Dean Acheson had new regulations drawn up refining passport-denial procedures and set up an appeals board within the State Department. Observers soon pronounced the new measures ineffectual, and Shipley and the Passport Division were thought to be operating much as before. Though Pauling and Lillian Hellman received passports, Paul Robeson, W. E. B. Du Bois, Arthur Miller, Rockwell Kent, and other notable applicants failed to, and the controversy raged on. Kent, who had refused to sign an affidavit stating he had never been a Communist, sued and finally won his passport by a 5–4 vote of the Supreme Court in 1958, three years after Shipley's retirement. The Kent decision and other court decisions in the 1950's and 1960's called for substantive due process and increased judicial overview of State Department passport decisions, thereby lessening the power of Shipley's successors.

Saying she was "tired in a way I have never experienced before," Shipley politely rejected the plea of Secretary of State Dulles that she stay on and retired from her post on Apr. 30, 1955. She died in Washington, D.C.

[Many of the records relating to Shipley's career in the State Department are in the diplomatic branch of the National Archives. Articles on Shipley include Maxine Davis, "Mrs. Shipley Says No," *Saturday Evening Post*, May 11, 1940; Harold B. Hinton, "Guardian of American Passports," *New York Times Magazine*, Apr. 27, 1941; "If You Were the Chief of the Passport Division," *Good Housekeeping*, Apr. 1944; "Ogre," *Newsweek*, May 29, 1944; "Lady of Passports," *Fortune*, Nov. 1945; André Visson, "Watchdog of the State Department," *Independent Woman*, Aug. 1951; Helen Worden Erskine, "You Don't Go If She Says No," *Collier's*, July 11, 1953; "Mrs. Ruth B. Shipley Retires After Forty-seven Years with Government," *Foreign Service News Letter*, Apr. 15, 1955. See also "Answer to Attack on Passport Operations," *Department of State Bulletin*, Jan. 21, 1952; "Passport Refusals for Political Reasons: Constitutional Issues and Judicial Review," *Yale Law Journal*, Feb. 1952; "Leaving America Is Easy—for Most," *U.S. News and World Report*, July 4, 1952; Dorothy Fosdick, "The Passport—and the Right to Travel," *New York Times Magazine*, July 17, 1955; Lillian Hellman, *Scoundrel Time* (1976); David Caute, *The Great Fear* (1978); Alan Rogers, "Passports and Politics: The Courts and the Cold War," *Historian*, Aug. 1985. An obituary is in the *New York Times*, Nov. 5, 1966.]

RICHARD H. GENTILE

SHOUSE, JOUETT (Dec. 10, 1879–June 2, 1968), United States congressman, was born in Woodford County, Ky., near the village of Midway, the son of John Samuel Shouse, a Disciples of Christ minister, and Anna Armstrong. In 1892 his father accepted a pastorate at Mexico, Mo., where Jouett attended high school. He entered the University of Missouri in 1895, and while there, he worked for the *Mexico Ledger* and the *Columbia Herald*, a country weekly. He left the school at the end of his junior year.

In 1898, Shouse returned to Kentucky, where he served on the staff of the *Lexington Herald*. In Lexington he helped organize the Fayette Home Telephone Company, in protest against the inferior service furnished by the existing Bell company. He also edited the *Kentucky Farmer and Breeder*, a weekly devoted to livestock, especially Thoroughbred horses.

On Oct. 18, 1911, Shouse married Marion Edwards. (They had two children before being divorced in 1932.) In December of that year, he left Lexington for what he thought would be a brief stay in Kinsley, Kans., to help his father-in-law resolve some business affairs. Instead, he became involved in local politics and in 1912 became a Democratic candidate for the state senate. He defeated a longtime resident and former mayor of the largest community in the district. In the legislature he chaired the Committee on Ways and Means. In 1914 he became a candidate for Congress when he won a Democratic primary by carrying thirty of the thirty-two counties in the Seventh Congressional District, the largest wheat-growing area in Kansas. He won the election by 1,559 votes.

Before taking his seat in Congress, Shouse completed his term in the state senate, where in 1915 he waged a battle with the Republican governor, Arthur Capper, who was seeking to slash appropriations for educational institutions. Shouse, supported by a large portion of the Kansas press and many Republicans in the legislature, led the successful fight in favor of the appropriations. In December 1915, Shouse entered Congress. He became a member of the Banking and Currency Committee; formed a close friendship with its chairman, Carter Glass; and was active in developing the Federal Farm Loan Act of 1916.

That year Shouse was reelected by the largest majority (7,500 votes) received up to that time by a congressional candidate in the Seventh District. In the Sixty-fifth Congress he endorsed President Wilson's war measures even when the House leadership opposed a measure, as was the case with the Selective Service Act. In 1918, in reaction to the president's plea for a Democratic Congress to help him in peacemaking, Shouse was defeated for reelection to Congress by a landslide. Instead of returning to his business affairs in Kansas, Shouse became assistant secretary of the Treasury, at the invitation of Carter Glass, who had replaced William Gibbs McAdoo as secretary.

At the Treasury, Shouse devoted his attention to the War Risk Bureau, the agency responsible for the allotments and allowances of military personnel, compensation for wounded soldiers, and the government insurance policy urged upon all new recruits. The bureau, which employed about 18,000 people, was scattered in twenty-seven buildings throughout Washington. When Shouse resigned from the department in November 1920, the personnel of the bureau had been reduced to about 6,000 and was housed in one building. Criticism of its performance had all but disappeared in Congress and among the public.

Following his resignation, Shouse became a director of several corporations and formed a tax-counseling partnership with another former Kansas congressman, Dudley Doolittle. They established offices in Kansas City, Mo., and Washington. Shouse remained active in Kansas Democratic politics and led the Kansas delegation to the 1920 and 1924 Democratic National Conventions. At the latter convention in New York City, he originally supported McAdoo but later shifted the Kansas delegation to John W. Davis. In 1928 he was able to convince the Kansas delegation to join him in endorsing Alfred E. Smith.

Though Shouse twice refused to become a Democratic national committeeman, during the 1928 campaign he served in the Smith campaign on the Executive and Advisory Committee, where John J. Raskob, the chairman of the Democratic National Committee, leaned heavily upon him for advice. Following Smith's defeat, Raskob asked Shouse to take charge of the newly created party headquarters in Washington. Shouse accepted with the understanding that he would have no responsibility for fundraising. In May 1929 he became chairman of the Executive Committee of the Democratic National Committee, with responsibility for resuscitating his badly defeated and demoralized party. He began a continual barrage of publicity against the program and policies of the Hoover administration, charging it with responsibility for the economic collapse evident since the autumn of 1929. Shouse traveled throughout the country speaking against the Hoover administration, particularly against the inequities he found in the Smoot-Hawley tariff. At the same time, he endorsed Democratic candidates for Congress, and in 1930 his party regained control of the House of Representatives.

In 1932, Shouse married Catherine Filene Dodd, the daughter of the Boston department-store owner. In that year he was defeated by Senator Thomas J. Walsh (who was favored by Franklin D. Roosevelt) for the post of permanent chairman of the Democratic National Convention. He was also thwarted in his desire to deliver the keynote address. In August 1932, at the request of Pierre du Pont, he became the president of the Association Against the Prohibition Amendment. During the campaign he delivered but one radio address for the Democratic ticket and in November voted for Roosevelt. He acknowledged that thereafter he never again voted the Democratic ticket. This ended Shouse's connection with the Democratic party.

Shouse opposed the New Deal in all of its aspects, and as he grew older he became more and more conservative, believing the Democratic party had abandoned its traditional tenets and teachings by ignoring states' rights and by succumbing to privileged groups and big-city machines. In 1934, with the endorsement of such friends as Raskob and du Pont, Shouse became the president of the American Liberty League, an isolationist organization that opposed Roosevelt and drew much support from anti–New Deal Democrats. He called the administration's social program "the attempt in America to set up a totalitarian government, one which recognizes no sphere of individual or business life as immune from government authority and which submerges the welfare of the individual to that of government." Shouse served as the president of the league until its dissolution in 1940.

After leaving this post, Shouse maintained a Washington office, maintained his numerous business connections, and vigorously endorsed Republican presidential candidates, most notably Thomas E. Dewey in 1948 and Richard M. Nixon in 1960. He continued his interest in Thoroughbred horses and developed one in boxer dogs. From 1915 until a few years before his death, he owned one or more Thoroughbreds, which he bred or raced, either under his own name or in association with others, and won a number of stakes. He also took an active interest in racing matters and endorsed legislation that legalized pari-mutuel betting at Kentucky tracks. Shouse died in Washington on the day on which it was announced that the Wolf Trap cultural center in Vienna, Va., would be constructed on land donated to the nation by Shouse and his wife.

[Shouse's papers are housed in the Margaret I. King Library at the University of Kentucky. See Charles Michelson, *The Ghost Talks* (1944); and George Wolfskill, *The Revolt of the Conservatives* (1962). An obituary is in the *New York Times*, June 3, 1968.]

RICHARD LOWITT

SINCLAIR, UPTON BEALL, JR. (Sept. 20, 1878–Nov. 25, 1968), journalist and novelist, was born in Baltimore, Md., the son of Upton Beall Sinclair, a wholesale liquor salesman, and Priscilla Augusta Harden, the daughter of a well-to-do Maryland railroad official. His father came from a southern family whose fortunes sank with the defeat of the Confederacy. When Sinclair was ten years old, the family moved to New York City, where he attended an East Side grammar school for three years. At fourteen he entered the College of the City of New York, graduating in 1897 with a B.A.

In college Sinclair wrote juvenile stories for pulp magazines and novels of adventure for young readers to support himself and pay for graduate study at Columbia University. He intended to study law but, instead, became interested in literature and contemporary politics. He did not earn a graduate degree. He was especially interested in Shelley, whom he studied under George Edward Woodberry. Shelley was one of a trio of Sinclair's professed heroes, the others being Jesus and Hamlet.

On Oct. 18, 1900, Sinclair married Meta H. Fuller; they had one child before their marriage ended in divorce in 1913. On Apr. 21, 1913, Sinclair married Mary Craig Kimbrough, a poet; she died in 1961. On Oct. 15, 1961, he married Mary Elizabeth Hard Willis.

In his earliest writings Sinclair exhibited the fluency of pen that enabled him to become one of the most prolific and widely read authors in American literary history. But he also exhibited the weakness of characterization and other flaws that blemished his novels and plays. He wrote more than eighty books, including social and economic studies, and numerous pamphlets, some of which he published himself.

The first of Sinclair's books to cause a stir was *The Journal of Arthur Stirling* (1903), which purported to be the diary of a poet who died because of his failure to be recognized and published. To Sinclair's embarrassment, the work was shown to be a hoax, and interest in it quickly waned. Other early works of fiction—*King Midas* (1901) and *Prince Hagen* (1903)—were immature and unsuccessful. "They brought me less than one thousand dollars altogether," said Sinclair.

During this period, Sinclair became interested in socialism. George D. Herron, a Socialist writer and lecturer, acquainted him with the socialist movement and urged him to join the Socialist party. "Yet what brought me to socialism more than anything else was Christianity," Sinclair later wrote. He took the words of Jesus seriously and considered himself a follower of "the rebel carpenter, the friend of the poor and lowly." He joined the party in 1902 and moved shortly thereafter to Princeton, N.J.

In 1905, Sinclair and Jack London helped found the Intercollegiate Socialist Society. Sinclair ran unsuccessfully as a Socialist candidate for Congress from New Jersey in 1906. A dissenter, a visionary, and a crusader for social justice, he was not a Marxist. "His radicalism is older than Marx's," wrote the journalist John Chamberlain, who called Sinclair the most effective propagandist in the Progressive movement. "His is the radicalism of the eighteenth century, which derives from the belief that man is perfectible."

Herron advanced Sinclair the money to live on while he wrote *Manassas* (1904), a Civil War story in which the son of a plantation owner becomes an abolitionist. The book, the best of his early novels, suggests that he had broken with his roots and adopted a radical stance on social problems, as indeed he had. Sinclair did a great amount of research for the book and demonstrated a prodigious capacity for the accumulation of facts, which proved of great value in his extensive journalistic writing. The literary historian Walter B. Rideout called him "one of the great information centers in American literature." In a letter to Sinclair, George Bernard Shaw wrote, "When people ask me what has happened in my lifetime I do not refer to the newspapers but to your novels."

A scandal over "spoiled beef" during the Spanish-American War prompted J. A. Wayland, the editor of the Socialist weekly *Appeal to Reason*, to offer Sinclair a $500 advance to write a novel about the lives of packinghouse workers and the unsanitary conditions in the meat-processing industry. Sinclair spent seven weeks in Chicago investigating the subject. The result was *The Jungle*, which was printed serially in the *Appeal to Reason*, and aroused great interest. Several book publishers declined the novel, but Doubleday, Page and Company published *The Jungle* in February 1906 after the company's own investigation substantiated most of Sinclair's findings. The book became an immediate and sensational best-seller and was eventually translated into seventeen languages. President Theodore Roosevelt, responding to pressure generated by *The Jungle*, sent a commission to Chicago to investigate. As a consequence, a number of pure-food laws were enacted.

The book's effect was not quite what Sinclair had hoped for. He had wanted to arouse public indignation over the wretched working conditions and mean lives of the workers. Instead, his vivid descriptions of unsanitary food handling, contaminated meat, and generally dirty conditions absorbed the attention of most readers. The author's Socialist propaganda was largely ignored. "I aimed at the public's heart," Sinclair said, "and by accident hit it in the stomach." However, the book strongly affected, one way or another, countless readers. Seven editions were in print eighty years after the book was written. The labor leader Walter Reuther said it was among those books that most influenced him in his youth.

With the $30,000 earned from *The Jungle*, Sinclair established a cooperative residence, Helicon Hall, in Englewood, N.J. William James and John Dewey visited, and Sinclair Lewis worked there for a while as a janitor. But the place burned down in March 1907 (arson was suspected but not proved), and Sinclair's life savings were lost. Afterward Sinclair lived for a time in a Delaware single-tax colony and then traveled in Europe (1912–1913). In Amsterdam he divorced his first wife, who had fallen in love with Sinclair's friend Harry Kemp, the poet.

With the writing of *The Jungle*, Sinclair had become a "muckraker," joining Ida Tarbell, Lincoln Steffens, Frank Norris, Jack London, and others. After *The Jungle* he wrote a number of other muckraking books, some of them novels, some nonfiction. Among the novels were *The Metropolis* (1908), about upper-class New York society and its financial manipulations; *The Moneychangers* (1908), dealing with high finance and the panic of 1907; *King Coal* (1917), a strong indictment of labor conditions in the nation's coal mines; *Oil!* (1927), a novel inspired by the Teapot Dome scandal; and *Boston* (2 vols., 1928), dealing with the Sacco-Vanzetti case. In these books the author's good intentions were sometimes weakened by hasty, negligent composition. But Sinclair always had the good storyteller's knack of making readers want to turn to the next page.

With *Profits of Religion* (1918), Sinclair began a series of nonfiction works on the effects of capitalism in America seen from the socialist standpoint. He examined such areas of American culture as schools in *The Goose Step* (1923) and *The Goslings* (1924), journalism in *The Brass Check* (1919), and the lack of integrity in artists and writers in *Mammonart* (1925), a book that was mildly praised by the critic Edmund Wilson, who seldom had anything good to say about Sinclair's writings.

Sinclair left the Socialist party in 1917, disagreeing with its antiwar stand. However, he returned when he became displeased with President Wilson's postwar policies. In 1920 he ran as a Socialist for the House of Representatives from California, where he resided after 1915. He ran there also for the United States Senate in 1922 and for the governor in 1926 and 1930, unsuccessfully in each case. He left the party once more in 1934 to become the Democratic candidate for governor. In a bitter campaign in which he was denounced as a "Red," a "bloody revolutionary," and a "man who writes books," Sinclair ran on a platform summed up in the slogan End Poverty in California (popularly called EPIC), which advocated, among other things, government-owned factories. He lost to the Republican incumbent, Frank Merriam (1,138,000 to 879,000).

In 1940, Sinclair published the first volume of the eleven-volume Lanny Budd series. He considered it his most important literary production. The story of Lanny Budd, who has socialist leanings and wants to right the world's wrongs, begins when he is a boy, the son of an American munitions tycoon, and ends when he is a middle-aged agent for President Franklin Roosevelt. The narrative unfolds against a historical backdrop that includes the stock-market crash of 1929, the Spanish civil war, and Nazi concentration camps. The third volume in the series, *Dragon's Teeth* (1942), won a Pulitzer Prize.

What Didymus Did (1954), a fantasy, was Sinclair's farewell to fiction writing. He was then in his eighth decade, in partial retirement, and perhaps more skeptical about the limits of political reform. His autobiography was published in 1962. It is an important source of information on the Progressive era and reveals Sinclair's puritan nature and his enormous egotism, always oddly impersonal and somehow inoffensive. He died in Bound Brook, N.J.

Sinclair's books have been translated and published in thirty-nine countries, and it is doubtful if any American writer, save possibly Jack London, has been more widely read abroad. In 1942, Alfred Kazin wrote a prophetic appraisal: "He will remain a touching and curious symbol of a certain old-fashioned idealism and quaint personal romanticism that have vanished from American writing forever. Something more than a 'mere' writer and something less than a serious novelist, he must always seem one of the original missionaries of the modern spirit."

[Sinclair's papers, letters, and manuscripts are in the Lilly Library, University of Indiana at Bloomington. Autobiographical material is found in *The Brass Check* (1920); *American Outpost* (1932); *My Lifetime in Letters* (1960); and *The Autobiography of Upton Sinclair* (1962). See also his foreword to May Craig Sinclair, *Southern Belle* (1957). Bibliographical sources are Ronald Gottesman, *A Catalogue of Books, Manuscripts, and Other Materials from the Upton Sinclair Archives* (1963) and *Upton Sinclair: An Annotated Checklist* (1973).

Biographical-critical studies include Floyd Dell, *Upton Sinclair: A Study in Social Protest* (1927); James L. Harte, *This Is Upton Sinclair* (1938); Leon Harris, *Upton Sinclair: American Rebel* (1975); Jon A. Yoder, *Upton Sinclair* (1975); and William A. Bloodsworth, *Upton Sinclair* (1977). On Sinclair and his writings, see also Carl Van Doren, *Contemporary American Novelists, 1900–1920* (1922); Van Wyck Brooks, *Emerson and Others* (1927); John Chamberlain, *Farewell to Reform* (1932); Granville Hicks, *The Great Tradition* (1933); Carey McWilliams, "Upton Sinclair and His E.P.I.C.," *New Republic*, Aug. 22, 1934; Harlan Hatcher, *Creating the Modern American Novel* (1935); Louis Filler, *Crusaders for American Liberalism* (1939); Alfred Kazin, *On Native Grounds* (1942); Leo Gurko, *The Angry Decade* (1947); Walter B. Rideout, *The Radical Novel in the United States, 1900–1954* (1956); and Daniel Aaron, *Writers on the Left* (1961). An obituary is in the *New York Times*, Nov. 26, 1968.]

WILLIAM MCCANN

SINNOTT, EDMUND WARE (Feb. 5, 1888–Jan. 6, 1968), botanist and geneticist, was born in Cambridge, Mass., the son of Charles Peter Sinnott and Jessie Elvira Smith, both of whom were teachers. After graduating from high school in Bridgewater, Mass., in 1904, he attended Harvard University. Originally interested in becoming a writer, he was soon fascinated by biology and in that field completed a B.A. in 1908, and M.A. in 1910, and a Ph.D. in 1913. Sinnott spent the next two years as an instructor at the Harvard Forestry School and the Bussey Institution. From 1915 to 1928 he was professor of botany and genetics at Connecticut Agricultural College. On June 24, 1916, he married Mabel H. Shaw; they had three children.

In 1928, Sinnott became professor of botany at Barnard College and, in 1939, at Columbia University. He joined the faculty of Yale University the next year. There he was not only Sterling Professor of Botany but also director of the Osborn Botanical Laboratory, the March Botanical Gardens, and, from 1946 to 1956, the Sheffield Scientific School. Under his leadership, Yale's faculty and graduate program in botany increased substantially.

Although a botanist, Sinnott approached the study of plants as a morphologist, a scientist concerned with organic structure and the processes of variation, development, and inheritance. Sinnott's earliest papers were traditional studies of issues pertaining to evolution, notably the evolutionary history and geographical distribution of plants. Beginning in 1916, however, Sinnott focused on organic form and the biological mechanisms that control form. In the 1920's and 1930's he published a series of articles that define how genes affect the shape of fruit, particularly squash. He demonstrated that organic shape is controlled by genes and inherited according to the laws of Mendelian genetics and explained how genes exercise control differently in different species of squash. Using mathematics and biometric techniques, Sinnott was able to define differences in the dimensions and development of shape and to correlate growth rates among organisms.

Sinnott's work drew upon the advances and enthusiasm for genetics and mathematical techniques that then characterized American biology. As such, he played a prominent role in changing morphology's traditional approach, which had emphasized the description and classification of specimens, to one that relied upon experimentation and mathematics to determine the physiological and genetic bases of organic form. Applying those new questions and techniques to botany, Sinnott became one of the leading plant geneticists in the United States and in 1925 coauthored a book that immediately became a standard work in its field, *Principles of Genetics*. He also served as editor of the *American Journal of Botany*.

Sinnott's interest in genetics never overrode his ultimate concern with understanding the growth and development of form. While his work helped to define how genes actually control development, it was the process of individual development that particularly occupied Sinnott. In papers written throughout the 1930's and early 1940's, he concentrated on the study of cellular and tissue development among plants, always emphasizing the need for more-refined description and more-precise quantitative measurements. Sinnott's preoccupation with the development of the size and form of individual cells, tissues, and organs led him to recognize that analysis—the breakdown of development into its smallest components, whether genes or biochemicals—could not fully explain morphogenesis. Specifically, analysis could not explain the problem of organization—that is, how individual bodily units are molded into the higher patterns of synthesis and system that make up an organism. For Sinnott, the problem of organization was the fundamental issue for biology, and in numerous addresses and papers, he called on scientists not merely to draw upon, but to move beyond, the analytical work done in genetics and biochemistry and to address synthetic questions concerning morphology and organization.

Sinnott's concern with the problem of biological organization eventually led him to apply his views to much broader issues. He had never embraced mechanical explanations, which sought to reduce biological processes to physics and chemistry, and in fact, the study of development seemed to demonstrate purpose among even the lowliest organisms. For Sinnott, both bodily development and mental activity were rooted in the self-regulating and goal-seeking nature of protoplasm. Thus, in a number of popular books, including *Cell and Psyche* (1950), *The Biology of the Spirit* (1956), and *Matter, Mind and Man* (1957), he argued that human motives, goals, and even religion had a biological basis. In effect, Sinnott's biological work led him to define the broader consequences of scientific work, to establish biology as the means for reconciling science with philosophy and religion. Moreover, in his role as dean of the Sheffield Scientific School he sought to establish the relation of science to other fields of human activity. Articles such as "The Biological Basis of Democracy" (*Yale Review*, 35 [1945]) or "Plants and the Material Basis of Civilization" (*American Naturalist*, 79 [1945]) defined the role that science played in American social, political, and economic life.

Following a successful career in plant development and genetics, Sinnott in his later years became an advocate of science as a humanistic activity that offered important insights into religion and philosophy and reinforced American political and social objectives. He died in New Haven, Conn.

[Sinnott's correspondence and manuscript materials are housed in the Archives and Manuscripts Division of the Sterling Memorial Library, Yale

University. In addition to writing well over one hundred scientific papers, Sinnott published several books, the most important of which include, along with those cited in the text, *Botany: Principles and Problems* (1923), *Laboratory Manual for Elementary Botany* (1927), *Plant Morphogenesis* (1960), *The Problem of Organic Form* (1963), and *The Bridge of Life: From Matter to Spirit* (1966). A complete bibliography of Sinnott's work accompanies the obituary by George S. Avery in the *Bulletin of the Torrey Botanical Club*, 95 (1968). A short interview by S. J. Woolf is in *American Scientist*, 36 (1948). An obituary is in the *New York Times*, Jan. 7, 1968.]

RONALD RAINGER

SLIPHER, VESTO MELVIN (Nov. 11, 1875–Nov. 8, 1969), astronomer, was born near Mulberry, Ind., the son of Daniel Slipher, a farmer, and Hannah App. After graduating from Frankfurt (Ind.) High School, Slipher taught at a small country school nearby until the fall of 1897. He then entered Indiana University, where he studied astronomy with Wilbur Cogshall, who had served as an assistant at the Lowell Observatory from 1896 to 1897. Slipher received a B.A. in mechanics and astronomy in 1901.

Cogshall persuaded Percival Lowell to hire Slipher as a temporary assistant at the observatory in Flagstaff, Ariz. He returned to Indiana on several occasions for graduate study, earning an M.A. in 1903 and a Ph.D. in 1909. During one of those trips, Slipher married Emma Rosalie Munger on Jan. 1, 1904; they had two children.

Slipher's first task at the Lowell Observatory was to install a new spectrograph made by the famous Pittsburgh instrument-maker John A. Brashear. Lowell had ordered this instrument for research on extraterrestrial life. Slipher obtained estimates of planetary rotation periods and of the atmospheric composition of Mars and Venus, and also investigated stellar and nebular phenomena; this led in 1909 to the detection of interstellar gas and its absorption of light. He discovered that the diffuse nebula in the Pleiades shone solely by reflected starlight, indicating the existence of interstellar dust.

Slipher's most significant work involved the study of spiral nebulae, about which astronomers then knew little. He began his investigations at the direction of Lowell, who thought that these bodies might represent evolving planetary systems. Lowell told Slipher to obtain spectral data from the nebulae to compare with those of the solar system. Although restricted to the observatory's twenty-four-inch refractor (Lowell's new forty-inch reflector was earmarked for Martian work and the continuing search for a trans-Neptunian planet) and forced to construct a suitable spectrograph from available parts, Slipher by 1912 had obtained several exposures of the Andromeda nebula (M31). These spectrograms convinced Slipher that the radial velocity of this nebula (now known to be a galaxy) could be calculated by comparing the position of spectral lines from M31 with the position of the same lines in a laboratory spectrogram. The Doppler shift of these lines would indicate the velocity and direction of the nebula's motion. After four months of observation and calculation, Slipher announced in February 1913 that the Andromeda nebula was approaching the earth at 300 kilometers per second, a velocity three times greater than that of any previously measured astronomical object. Over the next eighteen months, he calculated the radical velocities of fourteen other nebulae, finding that most were receding from the earth at velocities as great as 1,000 kilometers per second. These discoveries provided crucial support for the work of the Dutch astronomer Willem de Sitter, who suggested in 1917 that the universe was expanding.

For the next decade Slipher continued to dominate research into nebular velocities. Although increasingly involved with administrative matters after Lowell's death in 1916, Slipher had obtained the velocities of more than forty nebulae by the mid-1920's. His calculations were an important contribution to the work of Edwin Hubble, who used the measurements to develop his famous velocity-distance law ($v = Hd$), which describes the relationship between a nebula's radial velocity and its distance from the earth. However, Slipher's work on the spiral nebulae soon ended. The Lowell Observatory's equipment could not record the details of the more distant and fainter nebulae, and such research passed to the Mt. Wilson Observatory with its 100-inch reflector.

While measuring the radial velocities of nebulae, Slipher also examined their rotation. By 1917 he had concluded that the spiral nebulae usually rotated in a manner similar to the winding of a spring. Slipher's theory challenged the earlier work of Adriaan van Maanen at Mt. Wilson, who had examined comparative photographs of spiral nebulae taken at short intervals and concluded that these nebulae were actually unwinding. Van Maanen's work was generally accepted by astronomers because of Mt. Wilson's superior reputation and Slipher's unwillingness to involve himself in controversies. By the mid-1930's, however, astronomers (including van Maanen) had rejected the Mt. Wilson measurements as inaccurate and accepted the idea that angular rotation could not be measured with short-interval photographs because of the great distances involved. Not only did this discovery confirm Slipher's initial conclusions, but it also eliminated one of the last remaining arguments against the island universe theory of the spiral nebulae.

Although he remained a major figure in astronomy, Slipher was largely devoted to the administration of the Lowell Observatory after he assumed the directorship in 1926. He continued the observatory's planetary studies, including the work of his brother, Earl, who joined the staff in 1906. He directed the search for a trans-Neptunian planet that culminated in Clyde Tombaugh's discovery of Pluto in 1930. After his retirement in 1954 Slipher worked in observatory and community affairs but pursued no further astronomical research. He died in Flagstaff.

[Slipher's papers are in the Lowell Observatory Archives, Flagstaff, Ariz. His published works include articles in *Lowell Observatory Bulletin* (1904, 1908, and 1913); *Astrophysical Journal* (1908, 1919, and 1922); *Popular Astronomy* (1914 and 1915); *Proceedings of the American Philosophical Society* (1917 and 1938); and *Monthly Notices of the Royal Astronomical Society* (1933). An overview of Slipher's career, with a complete bibliography, is William Graves Hoyt, "Vesto Melvin Slipher," *National Academy of Sciences Biographical Memoirs* (1980). See also Norriss S. Hetherington, "The Simultaneous 'Discovery' of Internal Motions in Spiral Nebulae," *Journal for the History of Astronomy* (1975); Richard Berendzen et al., *Man Discovers the Galaxies* (1976); R. W. Smith, "The Origins of the Velocity-Distance Relation," *Journal for the History of Astronomy* (1979); and Robert W. Smith, *The Expanding Universe* (1982).]

GEORGE E. WEBB

SLOAN, ALFRED PRITCHARD, JR. (May 23, 1875–Feb. 17, 1966), industrialist and philanthropist, was born in New Haven, Conn., the son of Alfred Pritchard Sloan, a well-to-do tea and coffee importer, and Katherine Mead. After the family moved to Brooklyn, N.Y., Sloan attended public school and then Brooklyn Polytechnic Institute, where he demonstrated exceptional ability in mathematics and engineering. At the Massachusetts Institute of Technology (MIT) these talents permitted him to complete the difficult electrical engineering course in three years. He graduated in June 1895, the youngest in his class. On Sept. 27, 1897, he married Irene Jackson of Boston; they had no children.

After graduation Sloan worked briefly for the Hyatt Roller Bearing Company, which produced a newly invented antifriction bearing. He then took a job as an engineer in a firm developing electrical refrigeration for households. In 1898 his father and an associate purchased the Hyatt Roller Bearing Company for $5,000 and put Sloan in charge. Aware of the potential need for the new bearing in the still-experimental horseless carriage, Sloan convinced Henry Ford and Henry Leyland of the Olds Motor Company to use his bearings. Hyatt grew with the industry. By 1916, when Sloan sold the enterprise for $13.5 million to William C. Durant, the founder of General Motors (GM), the company had annual sales of over $20 million, with profits of $4 million.

Sloan received his share of the purchase price in stock of a new holding company, United Motors, a collection of parts and accessories firms that Durant acquired to supply GM's several companies. Durant then placed Sloan in charge of United Motors. When that subsidiary was incorporated into GM in 1918, Sloan became the vice-president in charge of parts and accessories and a member of the GM Executive Committee.

Disturbed by Durant's highly personal and haphazard management, Sloan was ready to resign in the summer of 1920. At that moment the sudden collapse of demand for automobiles brought GM to the verge of bankruptcy and saddled Durant with personal losses of over $30 million. This caused the senior management at the du Pont Company, the explosives maker that in 1917 had invested $25 million in GM common stock, to increase its holdings (by taking over Durant's debt). It removed Durant and appointed Pierre S. du Pont as president and chairman. Sloan quickly became du Pont's right-hand man. In 1923, du Pont turned over the presidency to Sloan, who retained that post until 1937, when he became chairman. Sloan continued as chief executive officer until 1946.

As GM's senior operating executive, Sloan created and carried out policies that transformed the company, the industry, and, in many ways, American management in general. His first contribution was to build the organization necessary to administer the sprawling, uncoordinated enterprise Durant had collected. The resulting administrative structure became a model for the management of large-scale industrial enterprise in the United States and Europe. Working closely with Pierre du Pont, he set up an office to coordinate, monitor, plan for, and allocate resources to the more than forty car, truck, parts, and accessories divisions, many of which operated their own factories, assembly plants, and nationwide sales organizations. The new corporate office included a team of general executives (the president, the vice-president in charge of groups of divisions, and the chief financial officers) who had no day-to-day operating responsibilities and who formed the executive committee of the board of directors. It also included a large advisory staff of functional offices—such as sales, manufacturing, purchasing, public relations, and auditing and accounting—that provided specialized information and advice to both the general executives at the corporate office and the heads of the autonomous operating divisions.

The divisions became integrated business units; that is, they were given the resources necessary to design, produce, sell, and distribute a single line of products. The division managers remained responsible for all the activities of their units and for their profits and losses. The capstone of Sloan's multidivisional administrative structure was the Interdivisional Relations Committees, including those for general sales, works managers, operations, general purchasing, general technical, and power and maintenance, in which senior divisional executives, the general executives, and staff personnel met regularly to review and coordinate their activities. To ensure the effective operation of this structure, Sloan, assisted by John Lee Pratt, developed a sophisticated system of statistical controls by which basic requirements—the purchasing of inventory, the hiring of labor, the provision of short-term and even long-term credit and pricing—were based on the annual forecast, which in turn was constantly adjusted to market demand as established by reports of cars sold submitted by dealers every ten days, supplemented by monthly reports of new car registrations.

Next, Sloan turned his attention to marketing and distribution. Again working closely with du Pont, he first defined the strategy of producing motor vehicles "for every purse and purpose." For example, the automobile divisions were assigned to noncompeting price markets. In this "pyramid of demand," Cadillac, with the smallest volume, sold in the highest price bracket, while Chevrolet, with the largest price volume, sold in the lowest. Convinced of the importance of styling and product improvement as a means of increasing a division's share of its price market, Sloan set up the Art and Color Section and enlarged the technical and research staffs. Realizing that the marketing challenge was no longer to sell a customer his first car but, rather, to replace one he already had, Sloan developed the industry's first systematic trade-in policies. In the 1920's he also paid close attention to developing ways to improve the selection and financing of dealers, to systematize dealer accounting, and to provide incentives and bonus plans for dealers.

Under Sloan, this sales organization quickly expanded abroad. Then came the construction of assembly plants in Canada, Germany, Britain, and France. In order to surmount tariff barriers and to be in closer touch with local European markets, Sloan in 1925 purchased Vauxhall, a small British car maker, and in 1929 he bought Opel, the largest automobile maker in Germany. In 1937, GM manufactured 188,000 vehicles in Europe and sold another 180,000 there.

Sloan's policies and management methods were highly successful. In 1921, Ford dominated the industry, producing 55.7 percent of the passenger cars made in the United States. GM's share that year was only 12.7 percent. By 1929, GM surpassed Ford, and by 1940 it had become by far the largest manufacturer of motor vehicles in the world, producing 47.5 percent of the passenger cars in the United States, as compared to Ford's 18.9 percent. The profit record was comparable. In the decade between 1927 and 1937, when Ford registered losses of nearly $200 million, GM's profits after taxes were more than $1.9 billion.

To remain profitable during the depressed 1930's, Sloan modified, but did not basically change, his policies. Because the low-price market came to provide close to 90 percent of the volume and profit, Sloan decided in January 1934 to have Buick, Oldsmobile, and Pontiac compete with Chevrolet for that market. To keep the dealers, already hit hard by the depression, from becoming further demoralized by this move, Sloan created the company's Dealer Council, the first in the industry. Sloan, as its chairman, met regularly with dealers in different parts of the country to review their problems and those of the company. To allow top management to adjust more quickly to internal and external challenges, Sloan transformed the Interdivisional Relations Committees into policy groups that included general and staff executives but not the representatives of the operating divisions. Because the demand for automobiles remained far below that of the 1920's, Sloan embarked on a strategy of diversification, investing retained earnings in the production and distribution of appliances, aircraft bodies and engines, and diesel-powered locomotives. GM's success in mass-producing diesel locomotives made the steam locomotive obsolete in less than two decades.

Only in labor relations did Sloan fail, at least in his own terms, to meet a new challenge. Unable to resolve the unexpected series of sit-down strikes in early 1937 to the company's satisfaction, Sloan, under pressure from state and federal officials, agreed to recognize the recently formed United Automobile Workers Union as the sole bargaining agent for most of the company's plants.

World War II brought Sloan his final set of challenges as the company's chief executive officer. However, the mammoth conversion of plants to the making of tanks, tank destroyers, armored cars, amphibious vehicles, and marine diesel engines (primarily for landing craft) and then the comparably swift reconversion to peacetime products required only minor modifications of GM's administrative framework.

After Sloan retired as chief executive officer in 1946 (he remained chairman of the board until 1956 and honorary chairman until his death), he concentrated increasingly on philanthropy—a philanthropy of a very practical sort. In 1937, after being accused of tax avoidance, albeit through legal means, he set up the Alfred P. Sloan, Jr., Foundation with headquarters in New York City. In the postwar years, that foundation and MIT received nearly all of Sloan's benefactions. In 1945 the foundation financed the Sloan-Kettering Institute for Cancer Research, which came to have a staff of 1,500. His first major gift to his alma mater, a laboratory for the study of automobile and aircraft engines, came before the war, and in 1949 he gave $1 million for a metals-processing laboratory. Then came $5 million for the Center for Advanced Engineering Study. In 1964, Sloan presented MIT with $10 million for the Fund for Basic Research in the Physical Sciences, a gift that was followed by a similar, somewhat smaller one to the California Institute of Technology. After endowing a chair in industrial management, in 1950 he donated $5.25 million for a school of industrial management that was later given his name. At the time of his death in New York City, he and his wife had given away over $300 million. In his will, $30 million more went to cancer research and to MIT.

Sloan's autobiography, *My Years with General Motors* (1964), provides an authentic picture of how this tall, taciturn (his associates referred to him as "Silent Sloan") engineer pioneered in the methods of modern production, distribution, and, above all, management. He rarely issued orders; instead, he listened attentively, collected the essential information, analyzed it carefully, evaluated the options and their implications, and saw that decisions were implemented with speed. His analytical mind permitted him to create and manage one of the world's largest managerial hierarchies through consensus rather than through authoritative command. Sloan had no children, had no hobbies, collected little art, and rarely read or traveled for pleasure. GM was his life, his love.

[In addition to *My Years with General Motors*, which was edited by John McDonald and Catharine Stevens and became a best-seller, see Boyden Sparkes, ed., *Adventures of the White-Collar Men: Alfred P. Sloan, Jr.* (1941); and Alfred D. Chandler, Jr., "General Motors Creating the General Office," in *Strategy and Structure* (1962). An obituary is in the *New York Times*, Feb. 18, 1966.]

ALFRED D. CHANDLER, JR.

SMITH, COURTNEY CRAIG (Dec. 20, 1916–Jan. 16, 1969), educator, was born in Winterset, Iowa, the son of Samuel Craig Smith, a lawyer and banker, and Myrtle Dabney. He graduated from Roosevelt High School in Des Moines and won a scholarship to

Harvard, from which he received his B.A. magna cum laude in English, in 1938. He was a Rhodes Scholar at Merton College, Oxford, in 1938–1939 and then, until 1943, was a teaching fellow and graduate student in English at Harvard, specializing in seventeenth-century and American literature. He received his M.A. in 1941 and his Ph.D. in 1944. On Oct. 12, 1939, he married Elizabeth Bowden Proctor; they had three children.

Smith served in the United States Navy from 1943 to 1946, most of the time at Pensacola, Fla. As liaison officer for black personnel, he worked with energy and understanding to improve the treatment of blacks in that southern community. From 1946 to 1953 he was an instructor and assistant professor of English at Princeton University. With a penchant and talent for administration, he served as national director of the Woodrow Wilson Fellowship Program in 1952–1953. In the latter year, he was appointed president of Swarthmore College; upon his inauguration, he became one of the youngest college presidents in the United States. In the same year, he was also named American secretary of the Rhodes Scholarships, a post that had been held by Frank Aydelotte and John Nason, his two immediate predecessors as president of Swarthmore. He held both posts until his death.

Aydelotte had made Swarthmore an academically demanding institution, though at the cost of some disaffection among older alumni. The disruptions of the World War II years had also contributed to a loss of momentum for the college. A fund-raising campaign in the 1940's had proved abortive, and it was not clear that the college could continue to recruit first-class faculty or withstand raids from major universities that offered large salaries, light teaching loads, generous leave policies, and the presence of many colleagues. But Smith had an unshakable optimism that Swarthmore could combine the strengths of an exemplary liberal arts college and a university. He himself worked prodigiously long hours. A strong president, he was confident that he knew, and could articulate, not only the goals but the manners of an ideal college. Committed to reasoned discourse, he never doubted that all persons of goodwill would rally to the same standard. He admired, and in some respects resembled, Woodrow Wilson.

Smith wanted a first-class faculty, and he personally interviewed all candidates, seeking to appoint persons not only of intellectual power but also of "character." He worked closely with department chairmen, scrutinizing promotion and tenure decisions. Partly because of these preoccupations, he was perceived as rather remote by many faculty, but he was markedly successful in raising salaries, reducing teaching loads, supporting a generous leave policy, building a modern science center, and securing an excellent library.

Smith challenged Swarthmore students to reach his standards of intellect, character, and deportment. When students sought to opt out from college assemblies, he met with each one in an attempt to show him his shortsightedness. A fastidious man, he tried to persuade students to dress in a seemly manner and conform to Swarthmore's avowedly "conservative" social code. He saw little merit in the cries for student power, though he always listened to students' arguments and reasons. He helped provide a much better dining hall, a number of modern dormitories, an improved social center, and superior athletic facilities.

From the outset Smith was strikingly successful in his relations with the world beyond the campus: he raised a great deal of money from alumni and from foundations, and he helped lead a successful campaign to remove from the National Defense Education Act of 1958 the requirement that applicants file a "disclaimer" of belief in the overthrow of the United States government by violence, regarding such efforts as "mind control." Near the end of his presidency, Smith supported a thorough reconsideration of Swarthmore's educational and administrative practices. He was committed to rational change and even endorsed the appointment of a provost, who would take on many of the responsibilities that Smith had himself assumed.

Smith believed that a college was not a "democracy" of competing interest groups but a "corporation," in which administrators, faculty, and students had distinctive obligations. This traditional view was challenged in many colleges in the 1960's. Many Swarthmore faculty members, increasingly mobile and "professional," were sometimes unwilling to believe that the president appreciated their concerns. Many students were unwilling to presume that the president really understood their passion about the war in Vietnam or the rightful expectations of American blacks.

In the spring of 1968, Smith announced that in June 1969 he would resign from the presidency of Swarthmore to become president of the John and Mary Markle Foundation, of which he had been a trustee for fifteen years. In the winter of 1968–1969, he was confronted with increasingly importunate demands from black students that the college admit more black students and hire more black faculty and administrators. Although Smith had been responsible for an increase in the number of black students, he was strongly committed to a system of merit; probably even more deeply, he resented the decision of the black students to occupy the college admissions office and the willingness of some faculty members to urge capitulation—as it seemed to him—to power, not to reason. He poignantly deplored Swarthmore's decline, even as he worked, skillfully and hard, to resolve the crisis. He died of a heart attack in the midst of that crisis. This sad coda should not obscure his remarkable success in giving immeasurably greater strength to the college.

[Smith's presidential papers are in the Swarthmore College Library, which also contains a number of oral histories dealing with the recent history of the college. Smith's commitment is evidenced in his essay "The Liberal Arts College in the History and Philosophy of Higher Education," in Henry Chauncey, ed., *Talks on American Education* (1962). An obituary is in the *New York Times*, Jan. 17, 1969.]

ROBERT D. CROSS

SMITH, HOLLAND McTYEIRE (Apr. 20, 1882–Jan. 12, 1967), Marine Corps officer, was born in Hatchechubbee, Ala., the son of John Wesley Smith, Jr., an attorney and court solicitor for the state of Alabama, and Cornelia Caroline McTyeire. He was descended on his father's side from Patrick Henry, and both of his grandfathers were Confederate army veterans. The family moved to nearby Seale, Ala., the county seat, when Smith was three. There he attended the public schools for ten years (1888–1898). Until his eighteenth year, he was strongly influenced by a former slave and jockey named "Uncle John" Milby, who lived on the family property. Smith later said of Milby, "I have never loved anyone more."

In 1898, Smith entered Alabama Polytechnic Institute (later Auburn University), a military school in Auburn, Ala., as a sophomore. During his three years there, he did well in history, and especially liked to read about military leaders of the past, and was a sprinter on the track team. Upon graduation in 1901, Smith was offered an appointment to the United States Naval Academy at Annapolis, but he declined because of his parents' opposition, based on their fear that he might "surrender to Yankee ideology." He entered the University of Alabama Law School in 1901 and graduated in 1903. He joined his father's law firm, and they practiced as Smith and Smith for several years, but the younger Smith did not prosper. His congressman, a Spanish-American War veteran, introduced Smith to Secretary of the Navy William H. Moody, with a view to his entering the Marine Corps. Following study at a private school in Washington for officer candidates, Smith took, and passed, the marine officer examinations. Commissioned a second lieutenant in February 1905, he spent the next year in the School of Application at the marine barracks at Annapolis. In April 1906, Smith was assigned to the first of several posts in the Philippines. For a time, he was engaged in emplacing long-range guns at Subic Bay to defend against Japanese attack.

Smith contracted malaria and was invalided home in 1908. He married Ada Wilkinson in Phoenixville, Pa., on Apr. 12, 1909; they had one child. A series of assignments followed: Nicaragua, Puget Sound, California, Central America again, the Philippines, China, and the Pacific. In 1916, in the Dominican Republic, he experimented with amphibious landings. He reportedly won his nickname of "Howlin' Mad" in the Philippines when some marines did not sufficiently grasp Smith's ideas about such efforts. He went to France as a captain in June 1917, was the first marine officer to complete the Army General Staff College at Langres, and was named adjutant of the newly formed Marine Brigade, part of the army's Second Division. In June 1918 he became assistant operations officer with I Corps, First Army, in the Aisne-Marne Sector. He won the Croix de Guerre for maintaining vital communications during the Battle of Belleau Wood. Promoted to major, he served with the occupation army in Koblenz, Germany, until March 1919.

Following a year and a half as commander of the Officers' School for Service Afloat at Norfolk, Va., Smith attended the Naval War

College at Newport, R.I., where he found naval doctrinal teaching obsolescent. He concluded that the commandant of the school, Rear Admiral William S. Sims, held "an unflattering opinion of the Marine Corps." From 1921 to 1923, Smith served on the staff of the chief of naval operations. He was the only marine officer on the Joint Army-Navy Planning Committee, which formulated long-term war plans. He completed the field officers' course at Quantico, Va., in 1926 and then completed assignments as post quartermaster at the Philadelphia Navy Yard, as battle force marine officer at Long Beach, Calif., and as chief of staff for the Marine Corps Department of the Pacific. He was promoted to lieutenant colonel in 1931 and to colonel in 1934, when a new selection system replaced the old seniority system.

By 1937, Smith was assistant to the Marine Corps commandant and director of operations and training. He demanded speed and efficiency in all operations. In 1939 he was named assistant commandant of the Marine Corps and, in August of that year, was promoted to brigadier general. In the spring of 1940, Smith was named commander of the First Marine Brigade, Fleet Marine Force. This, the striking element of the Marine Corps, had been created in 1934. He immediately took his new command to Culebra Island, east of Puerto Rico, for training. Later exercises were conducted at Guantánamo Bay, Cuba. In this new assignment, Smith gradually worked out much of the doctrine and many of the procedures that were to be crucial to American success in the Pacific during World War II.

In 1941, Smith was given command of the First Marine Division. He conducted landing exercises on the New River in North Carolina in August 1941, and in October of that year, he received his second star. Smith became increasingly concerned with the planning of landing operations and stressed the utility of a landing vessel, the Eureka boat, originally designed by the New Orleans shipbuilder Andrew Jackson Higgins in 1926. While the marines, especially Smith, continued to champion Higgins' boat, navy brass resisted it until the eve of World War II. Smith also pressed for the adoption of an amphibious tractor. (Both were to be crucial to his later success in the Pacific.) Late in 1941, Smith was named commander of I Corps, consisting of his division and an army unit, at the instance of Admiral Ernest J. King, the new chief of naval operations. Though originally planned as an attack force, Smith's command was utilized for training purposes. He was impatient to get into the fighting but continued to improve his amphibious warfare methods.

Transferred to command of the joint Army-Marine V Amphibious Corps, Smith was next placed in command of all Marine Corps forces in the Central Pacific in June 1943. He spent much of that fall supervising naval gunfire support on Kahoolawe Island, southeast of Pearl Harbor. No naval vessel could be sent into combat until Smith and his staff were satisfied with the proficiency of its crew. At the same time, navy and army pilots were trained in close air support at a nearby bombing range.

While Smith's forces successfully invaded Makin and Tarawa in November 1943, Smith later argued that the latter operation was unnecessary and "a futile sacrifice of Marines." Operations on Kwajalein and Eniwetok followed in the early months of 1944. The invasion of Saipan in June 1944 precipitated a dispute that was to dog Smith for the remainder of his life. Newly promoted to lieutenant general and operational commander of the invasion, he felt compelled to relieve the commander of the army's Twenty-seventh Division for failure to attack aggressively. Some army leaders excoriated him for this unprecedented action, and other critics asserted that he had been profligate with his manpower resources during the battle. The incident was thoroughly aired in the press, and Smith resented what he regarded as uninformed criticism of his role. While most students of the Pacific war concluded that he was justified in taking the action he did, the controversy impeded interservice cooperation.

In August 1944, Smith was made commander of the Fleet Marine Force, Pacific, and in early 1945, he led successful operations at Tinian and Iwo Jima. In the latter operation, he called for ten days' intensive bombardment before the landings but was granted only three. He later contended that this decision was responsible in large part for the very high number of casualties there. During his two years in the Pacific, Smith commanded more marines in battle than any other marine general.

In July 1945, Smith was named commanding general of the Marine Training and Replacement Command in San Diego, and he remained there until relieved on May 15, 1946. On Aug. 7, 1946, newly promoted to full general, he retired. Settling in La Jolla, Calif., he was primarily concerned about the future of the Marine Corps and his own reputation. Stung by new attacks on his handling of the Saipan operation, he wrote (with Percy Finch) an autobiography, *Coral and Brass* (1948). In it, Smith roundly criticized some former colleagues and aired old controversies and mistakes. Some reviewers consequently treated Smith roughly, and his reputation never fully recovered. He died in San Diego. The headquarters of the Fleet Marine Force, Pacific, Pearl Harbor, was named in his honor in 1956.

[Smith's papers are at the Marine Corps Museum, Quantico, Va., and at Auburn University. His biographical file is maintained at the Reference Branch Historical Division, United States Marine Corps Headquarters, Washington, D.C. Reports of World War II Ground Combat Operations are in Record Group 407, National Archives, Washington. On his World War II contributions, see Norman Varnell Cooper, "The Military Career of General Holland M. Smith, USMC" (Ph.D. diss., University of Alabama, 1974). See also the obituary in the *New York Times*, Jan. 13, 1967.]

KEIR B. STERLING

SMITH, LILLIAN EUGENIA (Dec. 12, 1897–Sept. 28, 1966), writer, editor, and civil rights advocate, was born in Jasper, Fla., the daughter of Calvin Warren Smith, a prosperous businessman, and Anne Hester Simpson. Smith's early years in Jasper influenced her later writing. She witnessed racial segregation and class division, in one instance being forced to separate from a childhood playmate when her parents discovered the girl was a mulatto. From her parents she received the advantages of social class, an appreciation of literature and music, respect for manners, and a strong evangelical Methodism. In 1915 her father's naval-stores and sawmill businesses failed, and the Smiths moved permanently to their summer cottage, on Old Screamer Mountain, Clayton, Ga., where her father ran a girls' camp. In the same year, Smith enrolled at Piedmont College in nearby Demorest, Ga., but after one year she quit school to help run the camp and a Daytona Beach, Fla., hotel that her father leased and operated.

In 1917, Smith entered Baltimore's Peabody Conservatory to study piano, but she left in 1918 to join the Student Nursing Corps. After the Armistice she served as both principal and teacher of a rural school in Tiger, Ga. In the fall of 1919 she resumed her musical studies at the Peabody Conservatory. In Baltimore she fell in love with a fellow musician but decided against marriage because she was reluctant to make promises that extended too far into the future. She never married.

In 1922, Smith accepted a position as music director at the Virginia School, an American Methodist mission school for Chinese girls in Huchow, China. She spent three years in China and was transformed by the experience. Western imperialism shocked her, and she immediately drew comparisons to racism and segregation in the American South. She embraced Chinese concepts of respect for common humanity and human dignity, and she began to read in subjects that would interest her thereafter—psychology (especially Freudian literature), racism, pacifism, and children. Like so many others who became southern "liberals" by living outside the South for a time, Smith's experiences in China and even earlier in Baltimore had given her new critical perspectives on the South's social system.

In 1925 the failing health of Smith's parents called her back to Clayton. She assumed management of Laurel Falls Camp for Girls, the family's major source of income and Smith's passion for the next twenty-four years. With the assistance of Paula Snelling, who would remain her lifelong partner, Smith converted the exclusive girls' camp into a nationally renowned educational institution. Smith and Snelling introduced programs in the arts and in exercise to encourage the campers, who were almost wholly drawn from the white South's prominent and wealthy families, to deal forthrightly with the problems of growing up and becoming socially and emotionally responsible.

With the death of her father in 1930, Smith assumed care of her invalid mother, which, along with other responsibilities for family members, tied her to Clayton. Except for 1928, when she went to New York to study at Columbia Teachers College and taught music to blacks, Jews, and Italians in Harlem, Smith remained confined by circumstances to the South. In the months when camp was out, she turned to writing. Between 1930 and 1935 she drafted three manuscripts—"And the Waters Flow On" (a novel on racism and sexual attitudes set in China), "Tom Harris and Family" (a novel about the South), and "Every Branch in Me" (a novella)—but none was ever published. The three works, along with other papers, were lost in a 1944 fire at Smith's Clayton home. In 1938, after her mother's death, Smith traveled to Brazil. There she observed a pattern of race relations more open than that of the South, and she completed much of the work on a novel, later published as *Strange Fruit* (1944).

As her thinking about racism, sex, child development, and other subjects deepened, Smith sought an outlet for her concerns. In late 1935 she and Paula Snelling launched a little magazine devoted to southern issues. The magazine appeared in spring 1936 as *Pseudopodia* but was renamed *The North Georgia Review* in 1937 and *The South Today* in 1942. The magazine, which reflected Smith's evangelical conception of the artist as social critic, used literary, cultural, and psychological criticism to indict caste and class in the South. The magazine was particularly outspoken in its condemnations of racial segregation. Smith pitched her arguments to middle- and upper-class whites. She appealed to white self-interest, rather than playing on guilt, by suggesting how racism hurt the region's social and economic prospects. In her magazine Smith also regularly published the work of black artists and scholars and encouraged women writers, all in an effort to stimulate creative writing about the South. The quarterly was never on a firm financial footing. Even though it acquired a reputation as an important journal of interdisciplinary thought and commanded a circulation of 10,000, *The South Today* ceased publication in 1945. Smith had sought help from the Julius Rosenwald Fund to expand the magazine's scope and frequency of publication. The Rosenwald Fund declined to underwrite the magazine but did award Smith fellowships in 1939 and 1940 to pursue her own writing.

Smith's writing eventually freed her from dependence on the girls' camp for income and the magazine for a voice. In 1944 her novel *Strange Fruit* finally appeared (it had been completed since 1941). The book's title betrayed its contents, for Smith believed that both southern whites and blacks were the "strange fruit" of white supremacy. Set in an imaginary Georgia town much like her hometown of Jasper, *Strange Fruit* depicts an ill-fated interracial love affair and the pathologies of sexual and racial role expectations in the South. White southerners are portrayed as paranoid, a view she had already advanced in her magazine. The book was an immediate best-seller, no doubt partly because of its controversial subject matter and a sexuality explicit for its time. The book was banned in Boston, which led to a landmark free-speech case ending in victory for the censors. Declaring the book obscene, the United States Post Office refused to allow *Strange Fruit* through the mails, but Eleanor Roosevelt intervened and got a White House order lifting the ban. Smith and her sister Esther adapted the novel for the stage, and it played in Canada but failed on Broadway.

The book gave Smith national prominence as an advocate of racial justice. Her royalties and fame also allowed her an autonomy other southern liberals lacked. She was not constrained by any institutional ties, and as the daughter of a prominent southern family, she had license to criticize the region. More important, her sex gave her freedom to speak out. Smith understood that southern women had special claim to being the region's conscience because they were removed from the corruptions of economic and political life.

Between 1944 and 1947, Smith enlarged her audience by writing for national magazines and by joining the Congress of Racial Equality (CORE), becoming the most prominent white southerner to do so. In 1946 she traveled to India (to which she would return with Paula Snelling in 1955), where she observed the arrogance of caste in a new setting and became imbued with the spirit of Gandhism. In America she continued to chide southern liberals for being cautious in attacking segregation. From October 1948 to September 1949 she wrote a regular column for the *Chicago Defender*, in which she called for world peace, pressed for the abolition of segregation, and revealed her own increasingly mystical religious beliefs.

Smith's second book, *Killers of the Dream* (1949), blends autobiography, history, and psychology to denounce segregation and to label racists as morally and psychologically unbalanced. She sought to understand the separation of humans—black and white, male and female, old and young, rich and poor—from one another. The book evoked strong criticism from white southerners. The controversies surrounding *Killers of the Dream*, in combination with her ill health and financial losses, led to the closing of her camp in 1949. The constant demands of lecturing and contributing to magazines compensated somewhat, but she felt her life and work were being "smothered" by hostile critics.

In 1953, after Smith underwent surgery for breast cancer, she completed *The Journey* (1954), the companion volume to *Killers of the Dream*. A spiritual autobiography, the book profiles two couples—one, paranoic McCarthyites, and the other, morally and intellectually sensitive to southern social problems—in order to explore "the meaning of ordeal" and to grapple with her own mortality. In *Now Is the Time* (1955), Smith urged the South to accept the Supreme Court decision on school desegregation, in part to demonstrate to emerging nations that America opposed racial discrimination. In 1955 a fire set by young whites destroyed much of her private correspondence and papers, several manuscripts, and notes for books (including two autobiographical novellas). Arsonists struck again in 1958. *One Hour* (1959), a novel about people bending to hysteria, speaks to the hostility she witnessed and the repression of the McCarthy era. In 1962 she brought out a family reminiscence, *Memory of a Large Christmas*, but like all her autobiographical works, the book reveals much about Smith's intellectual development but little about her personal relationships.

Her last book, *Our Faces, Our Words* (1964), is a pictorial essay on the nonviolent civil rights movement, with which she had been aligned for many years. Martin Luther King, Jr., and John Lewis, among other black leaders, credited her with influencing their own work. Until the 1960's, Smith had largely eschewed endorsement of mass action by blacks to achieve civil rights, preferring instead to rely on appeals to white self-interest. She did support such agencies as the Southern Regional Council, the Student Nonviolent Coordinating Committee, and CORE but resigned from the executive board of CORE in 1966 when it adopted a militant black-power stance. In all her work, Smith had sought a humane world free of alienation and separation, so that she interpreted the emergence of a black-power philosophy as divisive.

At the time of her death in Atlanta, Smith was working on a collection of essays, a novel, a book on contemporary youth, and an autobiography focusing on the subject of gender. Her body is buried on Old Screamer Mountain, where she had lived and worked and where she had dared to dream that an entire people in a "new South," indeed a new world, could be bound together by Christian love.

[Smith's personal and business papers, including some MSS, are at the University of Georgia, Athens. Smith items also survive in the Julius Rosenwald Fund Papers at Dillard University, New Orleans. Papers relating to *The South Today* are at the University of Florida, Gainesville. An important collection of Smith's writings, introduced by Paula Snelling's reminiscence "In Re Lillian Smith," was published posthumously as *The Winner Names the Age* (1978), edited by Michelle Cliff. An anthology drawn from *The South Today* appeared as *From the Mountain* (1972), edited by Helen White and Redding Sugg, Jr. See also Margaret Sullivan, *A Bibliography of Lillian Smith and Paula Snelling with an Index to The South Today* (1971).

The most substantial biography is Anne C. Loveland, *Lillian Smith: A Southerner Confronting the South* (1986); a shorter biography is Louise Blackwell and Frances Clay, *Lillian Smith* (1971). Important interpretive chapters on Smith and her work are in Morton Sosna, *In Search of the Silent South* (1977); Richard H. King, *A Southern Renaissance* (1980); and Fred Hobson, *Tell About the South* (1983). An obituary is in the *New York Times*, Sept. 29, 1966.]

Randall M. Miller

SMITH, ALBERT MERRIMAN (Feb. 10, 1913–Apr. 13, 1970), journalist, was born in Savannah, Ga., the son of Albert Clinton Smith, who engaged in farming, insurance, shipping, and the automobile business, and Juliet Worth Merriman. Smith attended elementary and secondary schools in Savannah. He displayed an early interest in journalism, working as a newspaper carrier and want-ad collector and serving as editor of the high school newspaper. "It never occurred to me to do anything else," he said later.

In 1931, following graduation from Savannah High School, Smith entered Oglethorpe University in Atlanta, where he majored in English and was managing editor of the school newspaper. While in college he worked as a sportswriter for the *Atlanta Georgia-American*. He left Oglethorpe in 1934 without receiving a degree, to begin full-time newspaper work.

Smith then joined the staff of the *Atlanta Journal Sunday Magazine*. In 1935–1936, Smith was managing editor of the *Athens* (Ga.)

Daily Times, and in the latter year he became a staff correspondent for the United Press (UP, later United Press International, or UPI) and covered various assignments in the South. In 1937, Smith married Eleanor Doyle Brill, a social worker; they had three children before their divorce in 1966. (Shortly after the divorce, he married Gailey L. Johnson; they had one child.)

In 1941, Smith was transferred to the UP Washington bureau to report on White House affairs. As a White House correspondent from then until 1970, he covered six presidents and became the senior press-association reporter at the White House. He was known to millions of Americans as the man who closed presidential press conferences with the words "Thank you, Mr. President." He also wrote a column for UPI, "Backstairs at the White House," covering personal aspects of White House life.

Smith accompanied presidents on many domestic and overseas trips, including Roosevelt's wartime conferences, the Potsdam Conference, the 1960 Eisenhower-Khrushchev summit, and Kennedy's meetings with Charles de Gaulle and Khrushchev. He won the 1946 National Headliners Award for his coverage of Roosevelt's death.

Besides his newspaper work, Smith appeared frequently on radio and television news and talk shows and wrote dozens of articles in national magazines. He was also the author of five books on the presidency. The first, *Thank You, Mr. President* (1946), gave his impressions of Roosevelt and Truman. *A President Is Many Men* (1948) examined daily life in the White House. *Meet Mr. Eisenhower* (1955) dwelt on the general's transition from soldier to politician. *A President's Odyssey* (1961) recounted Eisenhower's 100,000 miles of world travel, on which Smith had accompanied him. In *The Good New Days: A Not Entirely Reverent Study of Native Habits and Customs in Modern Washington* (1962), Smith portrayed the early Kennedy years in Washington in satirical and anecdotal style. Smith's books were generally well received by critics. Making no effort at analysis or profundity, Smith dwelt on the personal, the informal, the anecdotal, sometimes even the trivial, in an attempt to humanize the office of the American presidency. *The Good New Days*, with its somewhat caustic assessment of the New Frontier, drew more divided reviews than any of the previous books.

Smith could be ruthlessly aggressive in his quest for a story. He cultivated the friendship of secretaries, Secret Service men, and other White House staff to get inside information. At the Truman-MacArthur meeting on Wake Island in 1950, he broke an agreement with other correspondents to send a joint first dispatch on a single radio teletypewriter to Honolulu; Smith sent his own communiqué forty minutes early. On Nov. 22, 1963, he was sitting in the front seat of the wire-service car two cars behind President Kennedy in his fateful Dallas motorcade. One of the first to realize the president had been shot, Smith commandeered the car phone and dictated his bulletins during the race to the hospital, with an Associated Press correspondent trying in vain to wrestle the phone from him. For his reporting of the Kennedy assassination, Smith won the 1964 Pulitzer Prize for distinguished service in journalism. He also received journalism awards from the University of Missouri (1963) and the University of California at Los Angeles (1964). In 1969, President Lyndon Johnson awarded him the Presidential Medal of Freedom, the highest civilian award for meritorious achievement.

Smith was plagued by a serious drinking problem during the last several years of his life. In and out of hospitals, he grew increasingly depressed over his inability to overcome the problem and finally shot himself to death in Alexandria, Va.

Smith, an aggressive and tireless reporter and a facile writer, saw himself as a reporter of both the public and private sides of presidents, not as a political analyst. He was rarely critical of his subjects in print, but on television talk shows he could be blunt. The Republicans under Nixon, he charged, had failed to close the "credibility gap" of the Johnson years. "The trouble starts," he explained, "when we refuse to accept as gospel some of the rubbish a government spews out in the name of news." He criticized Nixon for "high-sounding goals and lavish promises compared with a somewhat lower rate of achievement." His friend the talk-show host Merv Griffin said, "Most of the presidents tuned in when Smitty was on. They were scared he'd say something nasty."

Smith was respected by his colleagues, despite his sometimes abrasive tactics in getting scoops. The veteran White House correspondent Carroll Kilpatrick said that Smith "was never bored by his beat." "Nor was he ever boring," added *Newsweek*, "which is a considerable statement to make about any man."

[There is no biography. The Pulitzer award is covered in the *New York Times*, May 5, 1964. Obituaries are in the *New York Times*, Apr. 14, 1970; and *Newsweek*, Apr. 27, 1970.]

WILLIAM F. MUGLESTON

SNYDER, HOWARD McCRUM (Feb. 7, 1881–Sept. 22, 1970), army physician, was born in Cheyenne, Wyo., the son of Albert C. Snyder, a Western Union telegrapher and office manager and subsequently a meat dealer, and Priscilla McClelland McCrum. Snyder, whose father died in 1891, was raised in comfortable circumstances. He attended local schools, the University of Colorado (1899–1901), and Jefferson Medical College in Philadelphia, where he received his M.D. in 1905. He interned at Presbyterian Hospital in Philadelphia.

Snyder returned west to practice medicine and to work as an army contract surgeon at Fort Douglas, Utah. Told by one of his Jefferson College professors that he was "throwing away a brilliant career," he nevertheless enrolled at the Army Medical School in Washington, D.C., in 1907. He graduated with the highest honors in 1908 and was commissioned a first lieutenant in the Medical Corps of the regular army.

For the next two years Snyder was stationed with the Research Board for Tropical Medicine in the Philippines, where he met Alice Elizabeth Concklin. They were married July 12, 1910, and had two sons. Between 1911 and 1917 Snyder held various assignments in the United States. Promoted to captain in 1911 and to major in May 1917, Snyder was an instructor at training camps for medical officers during World War I and in July 1918 was assigned to command a Medical Corps school for noncommissioned officers at Camp Greenleaf, Ga.

During the 1920's Snyder served at Fort Leavenworth, Kans., and at the U.S. Military Academy at West Point, and pursued advanced studies at the Mayo Clinic. He was promoted to lieutenant colonel in 1928 and to colonel six years later. A pioneer in cartilage surgery for the treatment of football injuries, Snyder undertook more studies at the Medical Field Service School and at New York University. Assigned as an instructor with the medical detachments of the New York National Guard in the mid-1930's, Snyder subsequently served from 1936 to 1940 as medical adviser with the National Guard Bureau, Washington, D.C. In this position he supervised on behalf of the army the training and facilities of National Guard medical personnel throughout the United States.

Snyder was promoted to brigadier general in October 1940 and in December of that year was named assistant inspector general. The first member of the inspector general's staff to be specifically charged with overseeing army medicine, he traveled extensively, compiling reports on the health problems of draftees, the care of battle casualties, and evacuation and hospitalization. He was promoted to major general in 1943. On Mar. 1, 1945, he was technically retired for age but was at once recalled to active duty to serve as General Dwight D. Eisenhower's personal physician. He remained with Eisenhower until 1948 while the latter was army chief of staff.

When Eisenhower retired from the army to become president of Columbia University in 1948, Snyder too moved to New York City. One of Eisenhower's greatest interests while at Columbia was the Conservation of Human Resources Project. During his many years in the army Eisenhower had become familiar with the alarming data about illiteracy among young American males and established this project under the direction of Eli Ginzberg, a distinguished economist. Snyder was named senior adviser to the project and took a close interest in it.

Snyder was recalled to active duty in 1951 to join Eisenhower at the North Atlantic Treaty Organization (NATO) headquarters in Europe. Snyder remained with Eisenhower as special adviser and physician until September 1952, when Snyder again retired. By this time Eisenhower's presidential campaign was underway, and Snyder was constantly at Eisenhower's side. Snyder again returned to active status in January 1953 as physician to the president and a member of the White House staff. The relationship between Snyder and Eisenhower was one of close friendship and esteem. Even though Snyder never played golf, he became in his seventies a familiar figure on the links as he jogged alongside the presidential golf cart.

During Eisenhower's two terms in the White House, Snyder made headlines when the president suffered a heart attack in September 1955, a serious attack of ileitis (a gastrointestinal ailment) in 1956, and a minor stroke in 1957. Eisenhower's heart attack occurred when the president and his wife were at her mother's home in Denver, Colo. Snyder, who was at Eisenhower's side within minutes, gave the president a sedative to allow him to get some sleep and the next morning permitted him to walk from the house to his car for the drive to the hospital. At a press conference Snyder's handling of the case attracted several pointed questions, but the famed heart specialist Dr. Paul Dudley White, called in to consult, supported Snyder's initial decisions, saying that they contributed to the president's peace of mind and subsequent recovery.

In retirement Snyder sought to write a narrative medical history of Eisenhower, who had been the first president to have a heart attack or ileitis surgery while in office. Snyder gathered the necessary materials but had written only three draft chapters when his own ill health forced him to stop work in 1966. He died at Walter Reed Hospital, Washington, D.C.

In a medical career that spanned more than half a century, Snyder will probably be remembered chiefly for his eight years as White House physician. His most enduring contribution, however, occurred during World War II when he became the first medical doctor in the army's Office of the Inspector General. He used his unprecedented influence to help remedy shortcomings in the practice of medicine under conditions of total war.

[The Snyder papers are at the University of Wyoming. Copies of a segment of them are in the Dwight D. Eisenhower Library, Abilene, Kans. Consult the Wyoming State Archives; the Museum and Historical Department, Cheyenne, Wyo.; and the U.S. Army Military Institute, Carlisle Barracks, Pa. See also Maxine Davis, "He's the President's Personal Physician," *Good Housekeeping*, August 1954; "When Ike's Heart Faltered," *U.S. News and World Report*, Oct. 7, 1955; "Heart Specialist's Comments After Seeing the President," ibid.; Earl Mazo, "Doctor to the President," *Senior Scholastic*, Apr. 26, 1956; and Fletcher Knebel, "The President's Doctor," *Look*, Sept. 18, 1956. Snyder is mentioned in Eli Ginzberg and Douglas W. Bray, *The Uneducated* (1953); Blanche B. Armfield, *Medical Department, United States Army: Organization and Administration in World War II* (1963); Forrest C. Pogue, *George C. Marshall* (1973); and Stephen E. Ambrose, *Eisenhower* (1983–1984). An obituary is in the *New York Times*, Sept. 23, 1970.]

LLOYD J. GRAYBAR

SORENSEN, CHARLES (Sept. 27, 1881–Aug. 13, 1968), automobile executive, was born in Copenhagen, Denmark, the son of Soren Sorensen, a modelmaker, and Eva Christine Abrahamsen. In 1883, Soren Sorensen immigrated to the United States, and his family joined him a year later. Charles Sorensen finished high school in Buffalo, N.Y., in 1896 and became an apprentice in the pattern shop at the Jewett Stove Works there. When his father moved to Milwaukee in 1898, Sorensen went with him and worked under him, meanwhile taking correspondence courses in drafting, including algebra, geometry, and trigonometry. A year later the family moved to Detroit. There Sorensen met Henry Ford and went to work in the pattern department of the Ford Motor Company in 1904. In the same year, he married Helen E. Mitchell; they had one child.

In his first years at Ford, Sorensen did experimental work as a patternmaker and foundryman. He claimed that his skill in the foundry led Henry Ford to call him "Cast-Iron Charlie." The cognomen stuck for the rest of his career because of his unrelenting harshness as an executive toward the people who had to work with or under him. An instance of this followed upon Ford's purchase of the bankrupt Lincoln Motor Company in 1921, with a verbal agreement that its founder, Henry M. Leland, would remain in charge of it. Sorensen was sent to the Lincoln plant, ostensibly to inspect it for Ford, but he simply took charge, ignored Leland's protests, and in a few months ordered him out.

Because of Henry Ford's dislike of formal organization and job titles, it is difficult to say just when Sorensen became an executive of the Ford Motor Company. In 1908 he became assistant to P. E. Martin, the plant superintendent, an ironhanded driver much like Sorensen himself. He succeeded Martin about 1925; he designated 1925 to 1944 as "the Sorensen period" in the Ford Motor Company, when he was in complete charge of Ford production. In 1941 he became vice-president and a member of the board of directors.

Sorensen's technical skill enhanced his talent for production. He was one of the group that worked out the system of the moving assembly line at Ford between 1909 and 1913. He was a party to the spectacular rise of the Model T, and when it finally went out of production, he assisted Henry Ford and others to design its successor, the Model A of 1928. Sorensen's foundry skills were evident in 1932, when the Ford V-8 engine was made possible by an innovative foundry technique that permitted the entire engine block and crankcase to be cast as a single unit. The same method was used to cast crankshafts.

Throughout his unique tenure of forty years with the Ford Motor Company, Sorensen saw himself as "Henry Ford's man"; he regarded it as his function to take Ford's ideas and make them operative. But Ford encouraged competition among his subordinates to improve their efficiency, and Sorensen came to regard his fellow executives as rivals. He constantly worked to get rid of real or supposed threats to his position. One of his successes, inducing William S. Knudsen to resign, was hardly beneficial to the Ford Motor Company, for Knudsen went on to help Chevrolet overtake Ford in sales.

Early in the 1930's, Sorensen became involved in a bitter power struggle with Harry Bennett, who was in charge of Ford security and had gained a commanding influence with the aging Henry Ford. Sorensen claimed that he sought to heal the widening breach between Ford and his son Edsel, for which he held Bennett largely responsible, and worked to preserve the company so that it could be handed over to the Ford family when its founder died.

The one point on which Sorensen and Bennett were in agreement, in common with Henry Ford, was implacable hostility to labor unions. Sorensen was probably not responsible for the "Battle of the Overpass" in 1937, when union organizers, including the Reuther brothers, were attacked and beaten by Ford security men, but it was certainly with his consent that Ford was the last automobile manufacturer to come to an agreement with the United Automobile Workers (UAW)—and then only after a long and bitter strike in 1941.

During World War II the Ford Motor Company was in confusion. The elder Ford was sinking into senility, and Edsel's sudden death in 1943 meant that his oldest son, the young and untried Henry Ford II, had to be brought back from the navy to take charge. Sorensen was fully occupied with wartime production, in particular with building and operating the gigantic airplane plant at Willow Run for the manufacture of B-24 Liberators. This project fell so far behind schedule that it was referred to as "Will-it Run?" The plant was poorly located in relation to the labor supply, and the labor shortage was exacerbated by the efforts of Sorensen and Bennett to keep the UAW out. Moreover, the automobile and aircraft industries had different philosophies of production, and Sorensen was unable to handle delicate relationships with a company in another industry. He became the scapegoat for Willow Run's disappointments, and in March 1944, Cast-Iron Charlie went the way that he had compelled so many other Ford executives to take. Officially he resigned.

In July of the same year, he became president and vice-chairman of the board of the Willys-Overland Company, a small auto-manufacturing firm. When Willys-Overland was absorbed by Kaiser-Fraser in 1953, Sorensen retired and thereafter spent much of his time on St. Croix in the Virgin Islands. Having been widowed, he married Edith Thompson Montgomery in 1960. He died at his summer home in Bethesda, Md.

"Of all the men who served Henry Ford," the historians Allan Nevins and Frank E. Hill concluded, "Sorensen was the most powerful, and stands alone as the most dynamically ruthless." It seems a fair and accurate appraisal.

[Sorensen's autobiography, *My Forty Years with Ford* (1956), written with Samuel T. Williamson, is revealing of the man and the workings of the Ford Motor Company. Allan Nevins and Frank E. Hill, *Ford: The Times, the Man, the Company* (1954), *Ford: Expansion and Challenge, 1915–1933* (1957), and *Ford: Decline and Rebirth, 1933–1962* (1962), are detailed and authoritative. See also J. B. Rae, *American Automobile Manufacturers: The First Forty Years* (1959) and *The American Automobile Industry* (1984). An obituary is in the *New York Times*, Aug. 14, 1968.]

JOHN B. RAE

SPARGO, JOHN (Jan. 31, 1876–Aug. 17, 1966), socialist, reformer, museum director, and historian, was born in Stithians, Cornwall, England, the son of Thomas Spargo, a stonemason, and Jane Hocking. At the age of ten Spargo entered the tin mines as a "half-timer," dividing his day between the workplace and the elementary schools. At fourteen he left school and worked full-time in a foundry.

In the 1890's, Spargo worked as a stonecutter and Methodist lay preacher, and continued his studies through extension courses at Cambridge and at Oxford. He left the ministry for the labor movement and served on the executive council of the Social Democratic Federation from 1896 to 1901. He also helped found the Federation of Trades and Labour Councils and was president of the Barry Council of South Wales, where he also founded the *Barry Herald*. By 1899, when he publicly opposed the Boer War, Spargo was a well-regarded socialist intellectual, known especially for his prodigious memory and oratorical prowess. On Jan. 24, 1901, he married Prudence Edwards; they had one child.

Spargo immigrated to the United States in February 1901 and settled in the New York City area. He worked on a Jewish encyclopedia, edited an artistic socialist monthly, *The Comrade* (1901–1904), lectured and published widely on socialism, and helped found the Socialist party and the Prospect House Social Settlement in Yonkers. His wife having died in 1904, he married Mary Amelia Rose Bennetts on Mar. 30, 1905; they had three children. Spargo became a United States citizen in 1907.

Robert Hunter's controversial *Poverty* (1904) prompted Spargo to subject the evidence to "strict scientific scrutiny." The result was the best-selling *The Bitter Cry of the Children* (1906), in which Spargo argued that child poverty was not only widespread but a basic source of malnutrition, disease, crime, despair, and deterioration in the quality of the national population stock. Spargo was especially critical of child labor and the employment of women outside the home, and the book was influential in the passage of child-labor and widows' pension laws. Although Spargo did not shrink from advocacy of state intervention ("The child," he wrote, "belongs to society rather than to its parents"), the program of government measures advocated in *The Bitter Cry* was essentially social-justice progressivism rather than doctrinaire socialism.

In 1909, Spargo took up residence in Bennington Center (later Old Bennington), Vermont. There he wrote seven more books on socialism, most notably *Karl Marx: His Life and Work* (1909). He also served on the Executive Committee of the Socialist party. The Socialism he espoused during these years was that of the party's center and right wing: it was evolutionary, grounded in a faith in universal suffrage and democratic politics, and remarkably tolerant of capitalist reforms.

Spargo's Socialism, weakened by Wilsonian liberalism and child-labor reforms, was further undermined by World War I and the Russian Revolution. In 1916, convinced that Socialist opposition to the war confounded an opportunity to extend collectivism, Spargo joined a select group of party intellectuals, including Algie Simons and Upton Sinclair, in resigning from the Socialist party. The next year, with Samuel Gompers and George Creel, he helped organize the American Alliance for Labor and Democracy to counter antiwar propaganda. He traveled to England, France, and Italy to persuade socialist movements there to support the conflict, and he served in Rome as a member of the United States Committee on Public Information.

The ascendancy of the Bolsheviks, moreover, confirmed Spargo's deep-seated anxiety that a Socialist state and individual liberty would be incompatible. Pressing his views through the State Department, Spargo became a major architect of the Wilson administration's anti-Bolshevik policy.

But Spargo's conversion was neither just a reaction to Bolshevism nor the outgrowth of a pragmatic effort to build Socialism on a foundation of wartime collectivism. The wartime performance of the American economy and the boom of the 1920's convinced Spargo that a just and unified society could best be achieved through a largely unfettered, highly productive industrialism—not, he insisted, capitalism. This perspective was apparent in 1919, when Spargo served as a delegate to the First Industrial Conference, called to revive wartime labor-management cooperation. By the mid-1920's, Spargo had repudiated socialism and become a Republican, and a decade later he was speaking out against the New Deal.

Having shed a philosophy that had sustained him for decades, Spargo built a new life around the community and the past. He now wrote of the history of the flag, of the potteries of Bennington (he was an avid collector), and of Vermont's settlers and folkways. Once filled with the cause of social justice, Spargo's public life was now spent as a caretaker and celebrator of American history. In 1926 he founded the Bennington Historical Museum and became president of the Vermont Historical Society, serving until 1938. He headed the Vermont Sesquicentennial Commission (1925–1927) and the George Washington Bicentennial

Commission (1931). He also held several offices in the Old Bennington government and was active in the Episcopal diocese of Vermont. In 1954, Spargo retired as director and curator of the Bennington Historical Museum and from all other diocesan and civic offices, though he continued to write and to tend an elaborate garden. He died in Old Bennington.

[Spargo's papers are in the Wilbur Collection of the Bailey-Howe Library at the University of Vermont, Burlington. His other writings include *The Common Sense of the Milk Question* (1908); *Social Democracy Explained* (1918); *Bolshevism: The Enemy of Political and Industrial Democracy* (1919); *The Jew and American Ideals* (1921); *The Potters and Potteries of Bennington* (1926); and *The Stars and Stripes of 1777* (1928). Walter Trattner's introduction to the 1968 edition of *The Bitter Cry* is the only full account of Spargo's life. Spargo's retreat from Socialism and his influence on Wilson's Russian policy are treated in Ronald Radosh, "John Spargo and Wilson's Foreign Policy, 1920," *Journal of American History*, Dec. 1965. Obituaries are in the *New York Times*, Aug. 18, 1966; and the *Bennington Banner*, Aug. 17, 1966. An oral history memoir is in the Oral History Collection at Columbia University.]

WILLIAM GRAEBNER

SPELLMAN, FRANCIS JOSEPH (May 4, 1889–Dec. 2, 1967), Roman Catholic clergyman, was born in Whitman, Mass., the son of William Spellman, the owner of a grocery store he inherited from his Irish immigrant father, and Ellen Mary Conway, the daughter of Irish immigrants. (Spellman made a point of his parents' American birth and resented being designated an Irishman.) He attended public schools in Whitman and graduated from high school in 1907. He enrolled at Fordham College in New York City and graduated in 1911. He then entered the seminary for the Archdiocese of Boston and was sent to the North American College in Rome, where he received a doctorate in sacred theology from the Urban College of Propaganda and was ordained a priest on May 14, 1916. Upon his return to Boston, Spellman was assigned by the archbishop, Cardinal William Henry O'Connell, first to parish work (1916–1918) at All Saints' Church in Roxbury, Mass., and then to the staff of the *Pilot*, the diocesan weekly newspaper, where he was charged with increasing the paper's circulation. In 1922 he was assigned to the chancery staff, the archbishop's curia, on which he served until 1925. During this period, he and O'Connell, for reasons unclear, developed a strong mutual antagonism. In 1924, O'Connell named him the archivist of the archdiocese and a part-time staff member of the *Pilot*, positions of little authority and even less honor.

Spellman was not put off. He translated into English two books by Monsignor Francesco Borgongini-Duca, one of his professors in Rome, and received the praise of Archbishop Giovanni Bonzano, the apostolic delegate to the United States hierarchy. Borgongini-Duca recommended that O'Connell name Spellman a monsignor—a proposal which brought the cardinal's blunt reply that Spellman did "not yet have a position to be raised to the purple." Spellman then sought to gain such a position through his Roman connections, which eventually led him out of the oppressive atmosphere of Boston.

In 1925, Spellman accompanied a group of Boston pilgrims to Rome—nominally, as secretary to Bishop Joseph Anderson, the auxiliary of Boston. While in Rome, he arranged to be appointed director of the Knights of Columbus playgrounds in Rome, subject to the Extraordinary Affairs of the Vatican Secretariat of State. His diary records his growing friendship with a number of prominent people. Among them were Nicholas and Genevieve Brady, American Catholic millionaires living in Rome; Enrico Galeazzi, a Vatican engineer; and Eugenio Pacelli, who in 1929 became acting papal secretary of state. Later that year, Pacelli was named the cardinal secretary of state.

In 1931, Pope Pius XI issued *Non Abbiamo Besogno*, a condemnation of fascism, but because of the fascist suppression of the church press, Spellman smuggled the letter out of Italy to Paris, where it was printed and distributed by the Associated Press. In 1932 he was consecrated titular bishop of Sila and named auxiliary bishop of Boston; he was consecrated by Cardinal Pacelli on Sept. 8, 1932, in St. Peter's Basilica in Rome.

Spellman's years as auxiliary bishop of Boston, from 1932 to 1939, were difficult ones. O'Connell had not asked for an auxiliary bishop and made it publicly clear that Spellman was not being considered as his successor. Spellman's diary recounts his strained relations with the cardinal on a series of issues: the cardinal would not publish his confirmation schedule;

he publicly opposed Governor James Michael Curley, with whom Spellman was on cordial terms; and he opposed an amendment to the Constitution prohibiting child labor, while Spellman was drafting such an amendment.

In the fall of 1936, Pacelli visited the United States, ostensibly as the personal guest of Genevieve Brady, by then a widow. One of Pacelli's real purposes was to meet President Franklin D. Roosevelt, whom Spellman had met through his friendship with Joseph P. Kennedy. Spellman arranged a meeting at the president's mother's home at Hyde Park, N.Y., on Nov. 5, 1936, two days after Roosevelt was elected to a second term. Spellman was present while the president and cardinal discussed the establishment of formal relations between the United States and the Holy See.

In the fall of 1938, Cardinal Patrick Hayes, the archbishop of New York, died. Several candidates were rumored as the new archbishop, but Spellman's name was not prominent. On Feb. 10, 1939, Pius XI died, and Pacelli was elected pope and took the name Pius XII. During Pacelli's visit in 1936, Spellman had antagonized some officials of the Archdiocese of New York, but on Apr. 15, 1939, Spellman, though little known to many American bishops, was named archbishop of New York. Soon after his appointment, James Francis McIntyre, the chancellor of the New York Archdiocese, offered his resignation to Spellman, who responded that "retaliation is a luxury I have never been able to afford." That began a long-standing relationship between Spellman and McIntyre, who was named auxiliary bishop of New York in 1939.

With the prospect of war in Europe, Spellman worked to establish diplomatic relations between the United States and the Holy See. Spellman had been making overtures since 1935, principally through Kennedy, and, later, James Roosevelt, the president's son. The president, however, was negotiating with Cardinal George Mundelein of Chicago, whom he regarded as a close friend and supporter. When Mundelein died in the fall of 1939, Spellman assumed the mantle of leadership with Roosevelt. On December 24, through Spellman's influence, Roosevelt named Myron C. Taylor as his personal representative to Pius XII, in lieu of establishing official diplomatic relations.

At the same time, Spellman was named the vicar for the armed forces of the United States, and he immediately appointed John O'Hara, C.S.C., the president of the University of Notre Dame, as his auxiliary bishop. He used his dual position as archbishop of New York and military vicar to gain national influence. Learning that Roosevelt had reservations about Archbishop Samuel Stritch, who had succeeded Mundelein in Chicago, Spellman telephoned Stritch and then forwarded to the president a private letter from Stritch describing his attitude toward the White House. In May 1941, Spellman reported to Pius XII that he had completed all the tasks assigned to him when he had been appointed archbishop.

During World War II, Spellman mobilized the Catholic war effort and became a symbol of Catholic patriotism. His novel, *The Risen Soldier* (1944), closely identified the Allied cause and Christian salvation. In the spring of 1943, he visited American armed forces in Spain, Rome, England, North Africa, and the Middle East. In Spain he met with Generalissimo Francisco Franco and explained American war intentions in an effort, made at Roosevelt's request, to persuade the Spanish leader to remain neutral. Traveling to Rome under an Italian safe conduct, he met with the pope but never disclosed the exact nature of their conversations either in his diary or to his authorized biographer, Robert I. Gannon, S.J. The journey introduced him to political and ecclesiastical leaders throughout the world. He befriended Winston Churchill in London and met Archbishop Angelo Roncalli, then apostolic delegate to Turkey, who became Pope John XXIII in 1958. After the liberation of Rome in June 1944, he again visited the pope and offered his advice on American church matters, including the naming of Richard J. Cushing as archbishop of Boston, since O'Connell had died earlier that year. Pius XII also offered to make him the Vatican's secretary of state.

Spellman did not become the secretary of state, but he was named a cardinal in 1946 in Pius XII's first consistory. Three other Americans were named at the same time: John Joseph Glennon, archbishop of St. Louis, who died before returning to the United States; Archbishop Stritch of Chicago; and Edward Mooney, Archbishop of Detroit. Although Spellman was frequently seen as the most powerful American prelate, he never quite dominated the American hierarchy. Mooney,

Stritch, and Archbishop John T. McNicholas, O.P., of Cincinnati resisted his influence both in the administration of the National Catholic Welfare Conference, the organization of the American bishops, and in the appointment of bishops. He was, however, influential in the appointment of key archbishops in the eastern United States, notably Patrick J. O'Boyle to Washington, D.C., in 1947 and O'Hara to Philadelphia in 1950. Outside that region he succeeded in gaining only the appointment of McIntyre as the second archbishop of Los Angeles in 1947.

Spellman emerged as a strong opponent of Communism in the postwar years. His anti-Communism was one of the factors in his opposition in 1949 to the union of gravediggers in Catholic cemeteries, who were affiliated with the Congress of Industrial Organizations (CIO). Publicly accusing the union's leaders of being affiliated with Communists, he refused to give in to their demands when they went on strike. After six weeks, he brought in seminarians to dig graves. The issue ended only when the union voted to sever its relationship with the CIO and join the American Federation of Labor. His anti-Communist stance also led him to side with Senator Joseph McCarthy.

On the political front, Spellman never had the same access to the White House under President Harry Truman that he had under Roosevelt. After Taylor resigned as Truman's personal representative to Pius XII in 1950, Spellman continued to work for the establishment of full diplomatic relations between the United States and the Holy See. Truman nominated General Mark Clark as ambassador to the Vatican in the fall of 1951 but made no new nomination after Clark withdrew. In 1953, Spellman reported to Pius XII that Senate opposition was so intense that confirmation of any ambassador would be impossible. This report led to a controversy with Giovanni Battista Montini, then the pope's substitute secretary of state and later Pope Paul VI, over whether American Catholics were defending the Holy See in the controversy over diplomatic relations, against the strong criticism of the church being leveled by Paul Blanshard.

Spellman was frequently involved in public controversy. In 1949, Eleanor Roosevelt, the president's widow, wrote a series of articles opposing aid to parochial schools, in the context of a bill prohibiting such aid then pending in the House of Representatives. He issued a statement accusing her of anti-Catholicism and of "discrimination unworthy of an American mother." The press reported the controversy, which ended only when he paid Mrs. Roosevelt a visit at Hyde Park. He also strongly opposed the decreasing lack of censorship of American films. In a rare address from the pulpit of his cathedral in 1956, he struck out against the release of *Baby Doll*. His call for Catholic boycotts of this and other films may, in fact, have increased their popularity. Nevertheless, he continued to influence the motion-picture industry.

Throughout the 1950's, Spellman still hoped to see the United States establish diplomatic relations with the Holy See. In 1958, however, Catholic senator John F. Kennedy declared his candidacy for the presidency. Protestants and Other Americans United for the Separation of Church and State, influenced by Blanshard, demanded that every presidential candidate declare himself on diplomatic relations with the Vatican and aid to parochial schools. On the latter, Kennedy said he would be sworn to uphold the Constitution, and he opposed diplomatic relations with the Vatican because the public opposition would undermine any ambassador's effectiveness. Spellman reacted strongly to what he considered to be a betrayal of the work he and Joseph Kennedy, the senator's father, had begun over twenty years before.

Theologically Spellman was a conservative. In the 1950's, the Catholic church was in the process of change that would lead to Vatican II. In the American controversies on such issues as church-state relations, he initially remained aloof. In 1958, Pope Pius XII died, and Spellman attended the conclave that elected John XXIII. Soon after, the new pope elevated Archbishop Cicognani to the cardinalate and replaced him as apostolic delegate with Archbishop Egidio Vagnozzi. Gradually, the new delegate began inserting himself into the domestic affairs of the American bishops. When both Stritch and Mooney died in 1958, Spellman became the senior cardinal and resisted Vagnozzi's efforts, becoming in the process an agent for progress in the church.

In 1961, Spellman defended biblical scholars against Vagnozzi's attacks. In 1962, when Vatican II opened, he discovered that John Courtney Murray, a progressive Jesuit theologian, had been excluded because of the opposition of Vagnozzi and other Roman officials. He had Murray made an official theologian of the council. Spellman was elected to the presidency of the council and made more interventions than any other American prelate. In the summer of 1963 he participated in the conclave that elected Montini pope. He used his power to have religious liberty placed back on the agenda of the council later that year. On Dec. 8, 1965, the council officially promulgated the declaration on religious liberty.

After the council, Spellman became the object of increasing criticism for his stance in favor of United States involvement in the Vietnam War. In the fall of 1965, Pope Paul VI made the first papal visit to the United States and addressed the United Nations. In a ringing plea for peace, he declared, "No more war, never again war." The following Christmas, Spellman made his traditional visit to American troops, this time in Vietnam, where he paraphrased Stephen Decatur's dictum: "My country, may it always be right. Right or wrong, my country!" Despite strong American Catholic opposition to the war, his statement was taken to be a blind paean to American patriotism.

Spellman was perhaps the most powerful American Catholic churchman in the nation's history. Coming into prominence at a time when Catholicism was still a minority religion, he sought to gain acceptance for Catholicism through political influence. Socially and politically, as well as theologically, conservative, he defended priests and nuns who marched in defense of civil rights in Selma, Ala., against Vagnozzi's attacks. An efficient administrator of the nation's principal dioceses, he also had a reputation for standing by his priests and even promoting experimentation. He died in New York City and is buried there in St. Patrick's Cathedral.

[Spellman's papers, which include correspondence, his diary, and newspaper clippings, are in the Archives of the Archdiocese of New York, St. Joseph's Seminary, Dunwoodie, N.Y. His books include *The Road to Victory* (1942), *Action This Day* (1943), *No Greater Love* (1945), *Prayers and Poems* (1946), *Heavenly Father of Children* (1947), *The Foundling* (1951), *Cardinal Spellman's Prayer Book* (1952), and *What America Means to Me and Other Poems and Prayers* (1953). On his life and work, see Robert I. Gannon, S.J., *The Cardinal Spellman Story* (1962), an authorized study that is surprisingly honest in regard to Spellman's relationship with O'Connell; Gerald P. Fogarty, S.J., *The Vatican and the American Hierarchy from 1870 to 1965* (1965), which concentrates on his role in national and international affairs; and John Cooney, *The American Pope* (1984), a highly negative evaluation but based on interviews with many people who were close to Spellman. An obituary is in the *New York Times*, Dec. 3, 1967.]

GERALD P. FOGARTY, S.J.

SPENCE, BRENT (Dec. 24, 1874–Sept. 18, 1967), congressman, was born in Newport, Ky., the son of Philip Brent Spence, a commission merchant, Confederate army colonel, and postmaster, and Virginia Berry. He attended the University of Cincinnati, where he received an LL.B. in 1895, and he was admitted to the Kentucky bar in that year. In 1904 he was elected as a Democrat to the Kentucky State Senate, where he served until 1908. From 1916 to 1924 he served as city solicitor of Newport, representing the city in suits against utility companies. He married Ida Billerman on Sept. 6, 1919; they had no children.

In 1926 he was defeated for the Democratic nomination for the House of Representatives. He received that nomination in 1928 but lost in the Hoover landslide. He was elected to the Seventy-second Congress in 1930 from the Sixth Kentucky District and was reelected as an at-large representative in the next election. In 1934 he was elected from the Fifth District, which was more divided between urban and rural interests than any other in the state, and he was returned to the thirteen succeeding Congresses, serving until Jan. 3, 1963. His closest contest was during the Republican sweep in 1946, when he won by 1,200 votes.

At his retirement, at the age of eighty-eight, he was the chairman of the Committee on Banking and Currency, a powerful position that he had achieved through seniority in 1943 and retained except in the Republican-led Eightieth and Eighty-third Congresses. Spence was the oldest man to have served in the House of Representatives, and he had a longer congressional career than any other Kentuckian. As chairman of the Committee on Banking and Currency he advocated requiring banks to divest themselves of real estate, insurance, and all nonbanking interests. In a farewell interview he insisted that the gold standard was the only way to keep the dollar strong.

Spence was an advocate of almost all New

Deal and Fair Deal measures, including public housing, full payment of the bonus to veterans of World War I, the Reconstruction Finance Corporation, Philippine independence, the Social Security Act, and price controls. He also supported the International Monetary Fund and the International Bank for Reconstruction and Development, organizations that were of special interest to him. Spence had served as a delegate to the multinational conference in Bretton Woods, N.H., in July 1944 and was largely responsible, along with Senator Robert F. Wagner of New York, for the Bretton Woods Agreements Act (1945) providing for American participation in the two bodies.

Spence made no claim to banking expertise, having merely been vice-president of a local Kentucky bank. He maintained that he simply applied common sense to the arcane and specialized issues before his committee. Other major legislation in which he played a key role included the Housing Act (1949), the Export Control Act (1949), the Defense Production Act (1950), the Defense Housing and Community Facilities and Services Act (1951), the Bank Holding Company Act (1956), the Savings and Loan Holding Company Act (1959), and the Area Redevelopment Act (1961). His committee also established the Small Business Administration and was responsible for the later legislative revisions that made it a permanent agency.

Spence sponsored legislation chartering the Export-Import Bank and revising the Federal Deposit Insurance Act to double insurance coverage of bank deposits from $5,000 to $10,000. He was an environmentalist long before the word became fashionable and was largely responsible for the Water Pollution Control Act (1948) and for securing funds for a pollution-control laboratory in Cincinnati, across the Ohio River from his district. His interests also included flood control and electric-power development.

Spence had a poor speaking voice and did not possess the great oratorical skills common among southern politicians, and his vision and hearing were severely impaired after the 1940's. Nevertheless, he was an effective legislative leader who secured much federal largesse for his district and was almost universally praised for his firm control and fairness during committee hearings. Spence died in Fort Thomas, Ky.

[The Spence papers are at the Library of the University of Kentucky, at Lexington. See Richard Hedlund, "Brent Spence and the Bretton Woods Legislation," *Register of the Kentucky Historical Society*, Winter 1981. An obituary notice is in the *New York Times*, Sept. 19, 1967.]

MARTIN TORODASH

SPRAGUE, CHARLES ARTHUR (Nov. 12, 1887–Mar. 13, 1969), newspaper editor and governor of Oregon, was born in Lawrence, Kans., the son of Charles Allen Sprague, a grain-elevator operator, and Caroline Glasgow. The family very soon moved to Columbus Junction, Iowa, where he attended public school and worked for his father. At Monmouth College, a liberal arts school in Illinois, he paid his expenses by reporting part-time for regional newspapers. When his income proved inadequate, Sprague took a leave at the end of his sophomore year and spent two years as a high school principal and teacher in Ainsworth, Iowa. On his return to Monmouth, Sprague earned varsity letters in football and debate, and served as editor of the student newspaper. From then on, he had aspirations to go into journalism. Following his graduation with honors in 1910, Sprague became superintendent of schools in Waitsburg, Wash. Two years later, he married Blanche Chamberlain, the principal of a local grade school; they had two child-children. Sprague was soon named assistant superintendent of public instruction for the state of Washington.

By 1915, Sprague had saved enough to resign his state position and purchase the weekly *Journal-Times* in Ritzville, a small town in eastern Washington. While Sprague made the newspaper profitable and enjoyed his work, he was anxious to move into daily journalism. In 1925 he bought a one-third interest in the *Corvallis* (Oreg.) *Gazette-Times* and became business manager. Sprague increased circulation and advertising revenues and presided over the construction of a new plant. Yet, he found the job confining and less stimulating than writing editorials and reporting the news.

Sprague's ambitions were fulfilled in 1929 when he acquired a two-thirds interest in the *Oregon Statesman*, long the most influential newspaper in the capital city of Salem. For the next forty years, he was editor and publisher of the *Statesman*, and his lucid, terse, direct editorials were frequently reprinted in some of America's largest newspapers. Sprague gained a national reputation as an articulate spokesman for small-town values, fiscal conservatism, and internationalism.

In 1938, Sprague ran for the Oregon governorship and got the Republican nomination by default when party leaders were hesitant to challenge Charles H. Martin, the conservative Democratic incumbent, who commanded strong Republican business support. As it turned out, Martin, a New Deal critic, was upset in the primary by the Roosevelt administration's choice, State Senator Henry Hess. Taking advantage of the split among the Democrats, Sprague made the administration's invervention a major campaign theme, urging voters to "repudiate outside interference in local affairs." Martin and his allies campaigned for Sprague, who defeated Hess by winning all but four of the state's thirty-six counties.

As governor, Sprague was an innovative progressive. Enlisting the support of labor and industry, he moved quickly to improve the state's employment services and launched vocational-training programs to aid the jobless in efforts to lift Oregon out of the Great Depression. He modernized the state school system by pushing through legislation that provided for the consolidation of rural school districts. He reduced the state debt by $12 million and balanced the budget while increasing social welfare services. Sprague helped maintain peace in labor disputes by his forthright opposition to an antipicketing law that was later held to be unconstitutional by the Oregon Supreme Court. He lost the political backing of organized labor, though, as a result of his policy of awarding state contracts to the lowest bidder, whether or not they were union firms.

Sprague was an early conservationist. Under his direction, Oregon became the first state to set up regulation over logging operations, to ensure sustained-yield management of its forests. He also established a forestry research program and obtained authority for the state to acquire abandoned cutover land for replanting. "Wise handling of natural forest lands," he declared, "calls for their consolidation under public ownership except for those lands in the hands of strong private interests capable of carrying them through long growing periods."

In 1940, Sprague chaired the favorite-son presidential bid of Senator Charles L. McNary, but when the Republican National Convention deadlocked in Philadelphia, Sprague helped nominate Wendell L. Willkie by delivering Oregon's votes on the sixth ballot. He encouraged McNary's selection as Willkie's running mate, and that fall he campaigned in nine western states for the Republican ticket.

In the months before World War II, Sprague cautioned against isolationism and was among the few Republican governors who consistently supported Roosevelt's foreign policy. He endorsed lend-lease aid to Britain early in 1941 and, later that year, called for the repeal of the Neutrality Act. While the nation's attention was focused on the hostilities in Europe, Sprague alerted Americans to the threat of imperial Japan. Speaking in Boston at the National Governors Conference in July 1941, he noted that the United States was vulnerable to Japanese aggression. When the Japanese bombed Pearl Harbor five months later, Oregon's aircraft-warning system was already in place. Sprague mobilized the state's war effort, organizing civilian defense units and increasing the size of the National Guard to accommodate local defense battalions. He was defeated for renomination in the 1942 Republican primary by Secretary of State Earl Snell. "Governor Sprague worked so hard on state problems and had so little time for the small amenities—or perhaps was distrustful of them," the *Oregonian* observed, "that the result was political defeat."

As a private citizen, Sprague remained active in state and civic affairs, serving as president of the Oregon War Chest, which raised more than $1 million for war agencies in 1943. He narrowly lost a special election in 1944 for the United States Senate and never sought another public office. On leaving the governorship, Sprague returned to the *Statesman* and began writing a daily front-page column called *It Seems to Me*, as well as most of the newspaper's editorials on state and national issues.

Described by Richard L. Neuberger as "the conscience of Oregon," Sprague was an outspoken defender of civil liberties, using his column as a forum to denounce the wartime internment of Japanese-Americans and the red-baiting tactics of Senator Joseph McCarthy. In 1951 he led the opposition that killed a state loyalty oath for teachers. While he maintained a Republican editorial policy, Sprague often crossed party lines to support Democrats. He gave strong editorial support to President Harry Truman in his unpopular firing of General Douglas MacArthur for insubordination in the

Korean War. In 1952, Truman appointed Sprague as an alternate delegate to the United Nations General Assembly. President Dwight D. Eisenhower named him in 1954 to a three-member national emergency railroad board and in 1955 to a committee on labor relations in nuclear power plants.

Sprague's natural aloofness and reserve were disadvantages in his political career, but he mellowed in later years and was gracious and often witty. A lifelong Presbyterian with what friends referred to as a stern sense of Calvinism, he neither smoked nor drank, and his newspaper would not accept advertising for hard liquor. An avid outdoorsman, he climbed the highest mountains of the Pacific Northwest and, in his seventies, shot the rapids of the Colorado River. He died in Salem.

[Sprague's gubernatorial papers are in the Oregon State Archives in Salem. His personal correspondence is in the Oregon Historical Society's library in Salem. Articles by and about Sprague are in the Oregon State Library. See also George Turnbull, *Governors of Oregon* (1962); and profiles by Richard L. Neuberger in the *Sunday Oregonian*, Mar. 18, 1951, and the *Nation*, Jan. 26, 1952; and by Malcolm Bauer in the *New York Herald-Tribune*, Dec. 11, 1960. An obituary is in the *New York Times*, Mar. 14, 1969.]

STEVE NEAL

SPRUANCE, RAYMOND AMES (July 3, 1886–Dec. 13, 1969), naval officer, was born in Baltimore, Md., the son of Alexander P. Spruance, an unsuccessful businessman, and Annie Ames Hiss, an editor for a book publisher. Unloved by his parents, he was raised mostly by his maternal grandparents and three spinster aunts in East Orange, N.J. After attending the Stevens Preparatory School in Hoboken for one year, he entered the United States Naval Academy in 1903. He graduated a year early, in September 1906.

Spruance was assigned immediately to the battleships then at the center of the navy and circled the globe aboard the *Minnesota* as part of the "Great White Fleet" (1907–1909). After being trained in electrical engineering at the General Electric Company, he served in the Asiatic Fleet, first as chief engineer of the cruiser *Cincinnati*, then as captain of the destroyer *Bainbridge*, and as first electrical officer on the new "superdreadnought" *Pennsylvania*.

With America's entry into World War I in 1917, Spruance achieved the rank of lieutenant commander. He was sent to Great Britain to study fire-control techniques while serving as electrical officer at the New York Navy Yard. He married Margaret Vance Dean on Dec. 30, 1914; they had two children.

Spruance's career was unremarkable up to the end of the war, but in the interwar period he proved to be a superior ship commander and student of strategy and tactics. He brought two destroyers into commission, leading the first, the *Aaron Ward*, as part of the patrol line for the transatlantic flight of the NC flying boats in 1919. He next headed the Electrical Division of the Bureau of Engineering for three years and then served in European waters on staff duty and in command of the destroyer *Osborne*.

In 1926–1927, Spruance attended the senior course at the Naval War College and then spent two years with the Office of Naval Intelligence. He was executive officer of the battleship *Mississippi* in the Pacific in 1929–1931. (In April 1938 he became the ship's commanding officer.) Promoted to captain, he returned to the Naval War College in 1931 to direct its correspondence course for two years, followed by two as chief of staff to Rear Admiral A. E. Watson, Scouting Force destroyer commander on the west coast. In 1935 he was assigned to the Naval War College for the third time, an unprecedented move, but one in which his considerable intellectual powers were utilized as he headed three departments there for one year each: the junior course, Senior Class Tactics, and Operations.

After being advanced to rear admiral, Spruance assumed command of the newly created Tenth Naval District at San Juan, Puerto Rico, in February 1940. The Caribbean region took on increased importance as the Battle of the Atlantic between the Allies and Germany threatened to spread into the western hemisphere. This duty lasted until August 1941, when he was transferred to the Pacific to command a division of heavy cruisers. Aboard his flagship, *Northampton*, he participated in the first aircraft carrier raids of the Pacific war (February to April 1942) against the Marshall Islands, Wake, Marcus, and then Tokyo as part of the Doolittle-Halsey expedition. In May of that year Spruance was selected to relieve Vice-Admiral William F. Halsey, Jr., who had become ill, as commander of one of two carrier task forces assigned to stop the Japanese fleet and invasion force approaching Midway in the Hawaiian group. Though he was not an aviator and had never served on a carrier, he reported aboard the *Enterprise* and retained Halsey's carrier staff for the impending battle. Despite the fact that he was junior to the other task-force commander, Rear Admiral Frank Jack Fletcher, Spruance masterfully handled the two carriers of his force and emerged as the major victor in the epic Battle of Midway (June 4, 1942), in which four Japanese carriers were sunk and the invasion armada turned back. It was the crowning achievement of his career.

World War II was just beginning, however, and Spruance was immediately made chief of staff and then deputy commander in chief of the Pacific Fleet under Admiral Chester W. Nimitz. He was promoted to vice-admiral in May 1943 while helping to plan the Central Pacific offensive against Japan, and that August he took command of the Central Pacific Force, later designated the Fifth Fleet. From the heavy cruiser *Indianapolis*, he directed the capture of the Gilbert Islands in November and the Marshalls in January and February 1944, in the latter month raiding the Japanese fleet base at Truk in the Carolines. He was promoted to full admiral in March, and in June he led the Fifth Fleet in the invasion of the Marianas and the Battle of the Philippine Sea. Though successful, he was criticized by his carrier admirals for failing to attack and destroy the Japanese fleet, a decision he defended by arguing that his primary mission was to defend the amphibious forces at Saipan. His biographers have defended him, too, but other historians have been critical, observing that he failed to realize his flexible carriers could have performed both missions simultaneously.

None could dispute his genius at overall fleet command, however, and after completing the conquest of the Marianas during the summer of 1944, he returned to Hawaii to plan subsequent operations while Halsey took the fleet to the Philippines. Resuming command in February 1945, Spruance led the Fifth Fleet as it captured Iwo Jima and Okinawa. It was a costly campaign; in April a kamikaze plane struck the *Indianapolis*, forcing him to transfer his flag to the battleship *New Mexico*. Relieved by Halsey in May, he spent the summer of 1945 at Guam planning the invasion of Japan, and when that nation surrendered in September, he participated in the occupation. In November he assumed command of the Pacific Fleet. The following February, tired from his long combat service, he stepped down to become president of the Naval War College, a post he occupied until July 1948, when he retired. In 1952–1955, Spruance served as ambassador to the Philippines. He died at his home in Pebble Beach, Calif.

By any measure, Spruance was the most able American fleet commander of World War II. Aside from his debatable failure to destroy the Japanese fleet during the Battle of the Philippine Sea, he had no peer in orchestrating and leading the many amphibious, battle-line, support, and air forces in the counteroffensive that defeated the Japanese navy. He was never excited or emotional in battle, and instead of worrying, he preferred listening to classical music and taking long walks on the beach or around the decks of his flagship. In contrast to the flamboyant Halsey, Spruance was an exceptionally quiet, publicity-shy leader who defied many observers' attempts to characterize him. His most intimate colleague and adviser, Rear Admiral Charles J. Moore, knew him as warm and pleasant but so preoccupied in thought that he appeared discourteous toward his staff and cold to strangers. Lazy in the sense that he hated paperwork, he never drove his staff officers but simply relied upon them to carry out the details of his decisions. Indeed, Spruance was arguably the most intellectual senior officer of the Pacific war, a thinker whose personal reticence deprived him of the public acclaim he richly deserved—and of the rank of fleet admiral, which was conferred instead upon the popular but less able Halsey.

[The Spruance papers, along with those of his two biographers, are at the Naval War College at Newport, R.I. The two biographies are E. P. Forrestel, *Admiral Raymond A. Spruance* (1963); and Thomas B. Buell, *The Quiet Warrior* (1974). See also Samuel Eliot Morison, *History of U.S. Naval Operations in World War II*, III (1948), IV (1950), VII (1951), VIII (1953), and XIV (1960); Walter Lord, *Incredible Victory* (1967); Clark G. Reynolds, *The Fast Carriers* (1968) and *Famous American Admirals* (1978); and William T. Y'Blood, *Red Setting Sun* (1981). The insights of Charles J. Moore are available in his five-volume Columbia University Oral History transcript. An obituary is in the *New York Times*, Dec. 14, 1969.]

CLARK G. REYNOLDS

ST. DENIS, RUTH (Jan. 20, 1879–July 21, 1968), modern-dance pioneer, was born Ruth Dennis in New Jersey, the daughter of Thomas Laban Dennis, a machinist and amateur inventor, and Ruth Emma Hull, who was the second female graduate of the University of Michigan Medical School but was prevented from practicing medicine by a nervous ailment. Her parents met at an artists' colony near Perth Amboy, N.J., and after Dennis divorced his first wife in 1878, they entered into a "marriage by contract," without benefit of clergy or license. One month later, their daughter was born, a circumstance that caused St. Denis to alter her birthdate.

The family settled on a farm near Somerville, N.J., and St. Denis attended the nearby Adamsville School and Somerville High School. She took classes in ballroom and skirt dance from a local teacher, and her mother drilled her in exercises based on the Delsarte theory of expression. After a brief stay at the Dwight Moody Northfield Seminary in Massachusetts, St. Denis went with her mother to New York City, where in early 1894 she obtained her first professional job as a skirt dancer at Worth's Family Theatre and Museum. As "Ruth" and "The Only Ruth," she danced in variety theaters and musical plays. During 1896–1897 she attended the Packer Collegiate Institute in Brooklyn.

From 1900 to 1904, St. Denis appeared with David Belasco's theatrical company in plays such as *Zaza* and *Madame Du Barry*. While touring abroad with the Belasco company, she visited the Paris World's Exposition of 1900 and was deeply affected by the Oriental exhibitions, the art-nouveau–influenced dance of Loie Fuller, and the mime of the Japanese artist Sada Yacco. She also began a lifelong study of Oriental philosophies, particularly Vedanta, and during this period became a Christian Scientist.

Still touring with the Belasco company in 1904, St. Denis spied in a drugstore window in Buffalo, N.Y., a poster depicting an Egyptian goddess. The poster became a catalyst in the creation of her solo dance career. She left the Belasco company, assembled a company of East Indian immigrants, and choreographed a dance, *Radha*, which was performed at the New York Theatre in January 1906. For subsequent performances at the Hudson Theatre, she added "St." to her surname.

Radha made St. Denis famous. A blend of exotic spectacle and morality tale, the dance depicted a Hindu goddess who wrestles with, but overcomes, the temptations of the flesh. The dance established the basic form, theme, and exotic trappings of St. Denis' choreography for the next fifty years. With the success of *Radha*, from 1906 to 1909 she toured Europe, where she danced for King Edward VII of England and was lionized by artists and intellectuals, including the Austrian poet Hugo von Hofmannsthal. Returning to America, St. Denis toured as a solo artist until World War I, pioneering a place for dance on the legitimate concert stage. In 1914 she hired a partner, the young dancer Edwin Myers ("Ted") Shawn.

On Aug. 13, 1914, St. Denis and Shawn were married, despite the protests of St. Denis' mother, who jealously guarded her daughter's career. With Shawn assuming charge, St. Denis found her art institutionalized. In the summer of 1915 the couple opened the Ruth St. Denis School of Dancing and Related Arts in Los Angeles. Denishawn, as the school became known, catered to silent-film actresses and aspiring dancers, including Martha Graham and Doris Humphrey. The Denishawn company toured the United States from 1915 through 1929, creating an American audience for dance and pioneering a modern dance style under the direction of "Miss Ruth" and "Papa Shawn." In the summer of 1925 the company embarked on a fifteen-month tour of the Far East, where its pseudo-Oriental dances were performed to great acclaim.

Denishawn became the focus of the central conflict in St. Denis' career. Though her roots were in variety and vaudeville, she thought of herself as an artist with a spiritual mission. In 1919 she formed the Ruth St. Denis Concert Dancers to experiment with "music visualization," but financial difficulties soon forced her back into the more popular and financially secure Denishawn fold.

This conflict ultimately destroyed St. Denis' marriage. In 1929, as the stock-market crash signaled financial ruin for Denishawn, the Shawns separated, though they never divorced. St. Denis, now middle-aged, found her art eclipsed by her own students, among them Martha Graham. She spent the 1930's impoverished, trying to resurrect her career. Founding the Rhythmic Choir, she devoted herself to liturgical dance, choreographing such works as

The Masque of Mary at Riverside Church in New York City in 1934. She also published a volume of poems, *Lotus Light*. In 1938 she became director of dance at Adelphi College in Garden City, N.Y., and she also briefly joined with the ethnic dancer La Meri in establishing the School of Natya in New York City.

With the publication of her autobiography, *An Unfinished Life* (1939), and the revival of her historic dances, St. Denis created for herself a new role as matriarch of American modern dance. With the onset of World War II, she moved to Hollywood, where her brother built her a studio. In April 1945 she appeared with Ted Shawn at Carnegie Hall, their first joint concert in fifteen years. In 1964, despite their long separation, the couple celebrated with great fanfare their golden wedding anniversary at Shawn's summer dance festival at Jacob's Pillow, Mass.

In 1966, at the age of eighty-seven, St. Denis made her last public dance appearance at Orange Coast College in California. She died in Hollywood. On her vault at Forest Lawn Cemetery are the lines of a St. Denis poem that begins, "The Gods have meant/That I should dance/And by the Gods/I will!"

[St. Denis' diaries and papers are in the Ruth St. Denis Collection at the University of California at Los Angeles. Major manuscript sources include the Ruth St. Denis Collection and the Denishawn Collection, both in the Dance Collection of the New York Public Library at Lincoln Center. On her life and work, see Ted Shawn, *Ruth St. Denis: Pioneer and Prophet* (1920); Christena L. Schlundt, *The Professional Appearances of Ruth St. Denis and Ted Shawn* (1962); Walter Terry, *Miss Ruth* (1969); Christena L. Schlundt, "Into the Mystic with Miss Ruth," *Dance Perspectives*, 46 (1971); Jane Sherman, *Soaring* (1976); Suzanne Shelton, "The Influence of Genevieve Stebbins on the Early Career of Ruth St. Denis," *Dance Research Annual* 9 (1978); Elizabeth Kendall, *Where She Danced* (1979); Suzanne Shelton, "Ruth St. Denis: Dance Popularizer with 'High Art' Pretensions," in Myron Matlaw, ed., *American Popular Entertainment* (1979); and Suzanne Shelton, *Divine Dancer* (1981). Oral-history materials and films of St. Denis' dances are in the Dance Collection at Lincoln Center. An obituary is in the *New York Times*, July 22, 1968.]

SUZANNE SHELTON

STALLINGS, LAURENCE TUCKER (Nov. 24, 1894–Feb. 28, 1968), writer, was born in Macon, Ga., the son of Larkin Tucker Stallings, a bank teller, and Aurora Brooks. As a child, Stallings was steeped in Civil War history and enjoyed attending Confederate Memorial Day and Fourth of July parades, which are described in his later fiction. He read avidly throughout his life, but in his youth he was unaware that the history he learned was romanticized. Later, the impact of this awareness would contribute heavily to his disillusionment about war and be reflected in his writing.

After graduation from Gresham High School in 1911, Stallings moved with his family to Atlanta, where his father became treasurer of a wholesale drug company. In 1912, Stallings enrolled at Wake Forest College, where he majored in classics and biology. He completed his studies in 1915 and got his first job as a reporter at the *Atlanta Journal*. His B.A. was awarded in 1916.

When the United States entered World War I, Stallings joined the Marine Corps Reserve. In October 1917, he was commissioned a second lieutenant in the Fifth Marines. He trained at Parris Island, S.C. Already enchanted with uniforms and parades, Stallings was particularly proud of his handsome appearance in his uniform and anxious for overseas action. In 1918, he sailed to France. He saw heavy action at Château-Thierry and at Belleau Wood, where on the last day of battle, June 26, he was wounded in the right knee. The wound was serious and greatly affected his life, his work, and his determination to tell the truth about war. He spent eight months in a French hospital undergoing several operations to save his leg. The hospital experience is the background for his short story "Vale of Tears" (1932), anthologized by Ernest Hemingway in *Men at War* (1942). He returned to America a captain in February 1919. On March 6 he married Helen Poteat, the daughter of Wake Forest's president; they had two children.

Stallings and his wife settled in Washington, D.C., so that Stallings could continue treatment at Walter Reed Hospital. During this time, he worked at odd reporting jobs for the *Washington Times*. In 1922, after a bad fall on ice that tore the surgeon's repair work on his leg, he returned to Walter Reed for amputation of the leg.

During his recuperation Stallings worked on the autobiographical novel *Plumes* (1924). He then traveled to Europe with his wife and finally settled in New York, where he became the book reviewer for the *New York World*. Among his colleagues at the *World* were Heywood Broun, Franklin P. Adams, Alexander Woollcott, and Maxwell Anderson, all of whom became charter members of the Algonquin Round Table. Stallings was the only member who had been seriously hurt by the war and was therefore revered as a hero. He loved telling stories even more than writing them.

Stallings' constant talk about the war led Maxwell Anderson to sketch a play based on Stallings' experiences. Stallings rewrote the play in an effort to instill it with realism as well as his newly learned philosophy that the hell of war was the same for men on all sides. *What Price Glory?* was an instant success on stage in 1924. Other collaborations with Anderson followed, such as *First Flight* and *The Buccaneer* (1925), but none was nearly so successful.

Hollywood sought the suddenly famous war hero, and with the director King Vidor, Stallings achieved additional success with the film *The Big Parade* (1925), based on one of his short stories. The film ran for two years on Broadway. Stallings then collaborated with Oscar Hammerstein and Vincent Youmans on the musical *Rainbow*, produced in 1928 and filmed in 1930 as *Song of the West*.

Always restless and easily bored, Stallings went to work for the *New York Sun* in 1931 while also doing editorial work on magazines. In 1932 he adapted Ernest Hemingway's *A Farewell to Arms* to the screen. At the same time, he began writing more short stories and working on *The First World War: A Pictorial History* (1933).

Despite the pain caused by numerous falls that injured his remaining leg, Stallings longed for action. In August 1935, sponsored by Fox Movietone News and the North American Newspaper Alliance, he led an expedition to Ethiopia to cover the expected Italian attack; he returned to America in February 1936. Stallings and his wife were divorced in December of that year, and on Mar. 19, 1937, he married Louise St. Leger Vance, a New York debutante who worked as his secretary at Fox. They settled in Santa Barbara, Calif., and had two children. In this period, Stallings worked on such films as *Too Hot to Handle* (1938) and *Northwest Passage* (1940).

Stallings returned to active military duty in April 1942. Much of the time, he was stationed at the Pentagon, but he also spent time in Africa, Europe, and England as an adviser on public relations. Stallings retired in June 1943, a lieutenant-colonel, and settled in Whittier, Calif. Thereafter, he worked on such films as *A Miracle Can Happen* (1948) and *She Wore a Yellow Ribbon* (1949). He also wrote a play, *The Streets Are Guarded* (1944), set in World War II; it closed after twenty-four performances.

In 1963, Stallings published *The Doughboys*, a widely read history of American participation in World War I. In that same year, his remaining leg had to be amputated.

Before he died in Whittier, he was honored at home, where he lay legless for the last five years of his life, for his service to his country.

Stallings was possessed of an exceptional memory, a great sense of humor, and an insatiable appetite for games of chance. He never tired of telling stories about the war. According to the novelist James M. Cain, Stallings' greatest emotional satisfaction came from his "military side." Yet, Stallings maintained a sardonic attitude toward his wounds and refused to claim credit for being heroic.

[Stallings' correspondence with Arthur Krock is in the Firestone Library at Princeton University. See Joan T. Brittain, *Laurence Stallings* (1975). An obituary is in the *New York Times*, Feb. 29, 1968.]

JOAN T. BRITTAIN

STEELE, WILBUR DANIEL (Mar. 17, 1886–May 26, 1970), writer, was born in Greensboro, N.C., the son of Wilbur Fletcher, a Methodist minister, and Rose Wood. His father was principal of Greensboro's Bennett Seminary, now Bennett College. In 1889, while his father studied at the University of Berlin, Steele attended kindergarten, taught by the niece of the German educator Friedrich Froebel. In 1892 the family moved to Denver when Steele's father became professor of Bible at the University of Denver. In Colorado, Steele delighted in adventures, sports, and cartoons. Romantic, athletic, and witty, he entered the University of Denver Preparatory School in 1900 and the University of Denver in 1903. After receiving his B.A. in 1907, he enrolled at the Boston Museum School of Fine Arts. As an art student in Paris (at the Académie Julien) and in Italy in 1908–1909, he wavered between painting and writing. Even at the Provincetown summer art colony he vacillated between a pictorial and a literary career. At the

Art Students League in New York he devoted his days to drawing and his nights to writing.

Success Magazine published Steele's first story, "On the Ebb Tide," in 1910. For a few months he worked in Boston as a reporter and illustrator for *National Magazine* but preferred to spend his winters in Greenwich Village and his summers in Provincetown. In April 1912 his story "White Horse Winter" appeared in the *Atlantic Monthly*. That summer he shared a Provincetown shack with a volatile young writer named Sinclair Lewis. On Feb. 17, 1913, in Brookline, Mass., Steele married Margaret Orinda Thurston, a painter whom he had first met at the Boston Museum School; they had two children. During the summer of 1914 (the year Steele's first adventure novel, *Storm*, was published) his grim and intricate stories graced the pages of *Scribner's Magazine*, the *Atlantic Monthly*, and *Harper's Magazine*. To the budding Provincetown Players he contributed one-act dramas, *Contemporaries* in 1915 and *Not Smart* in 1916. He became friends with Eugene O'Neill and later with *Pictorial Review* editor Arthur T. Vance. For two months in 1917, Steele sailed the Caribbean, writing articles for *Harper's* Magazine and gathering material for his monthly stories the following year. In 1918 he also described the war in Europe for *Cosmopolitan* magazine. Reviewers praised the uncanny dramatic economy of his first story collection, *Land's End* (1918).

From 1915 to 1926 nine Steele stories reappeared in Edward J. O'Brien's annual *Best Stories* volumes: "The Yellow Cat" (1915), "Down on Their Knees" (1916), "Ching, Ching, Chinaman" (1917), "The Dark Hour" (1918), "Out of Exile" (1920), "The Shame Dance" (1921), "From the Other Side of the South" (1922), "Six Dollars" (1925), and "Out of the Wind" (1926). Time and again the anthologist praised Steele's technical ingenuity. So routinely did the O. Henry Memorial Award go to Steele each year that cognoscenti referred to it as the Wilbur Daniel Steele Memorial Award: "For They Know Not What They Do" (1919), "Footfalls" (1920), "Out of Exile" (1921), "The Anglo-Saxon" (1922), "What Do You Mean—Americans?" (1924), "The Man Who Saw Through Heaven" (1925), "Bubbles" (1926), "Lightning" (1928), "The Silver Sword" (1929), "Conjuh" (1930), and "Can't Cross Jordan by Myself" (1931). By 1920, Steele had lived in Bermuda, North Africa, the French Riviera, and Nantucket, places graphically evoked in his second collection, *The Shame Dance* (1923). Wintering in Cannes in 1923–1924, he wrote stories for the *Pictorial Review* and worked on his second novel, *Isles of the Blest* (1924), exotica less successful than his one-act mystery *The Giant's Stair*. Performed in Provincetown in 1924, this play appears with *Ropes* and the early *Not Smart* in his readable, actable volume *The Terrible Woman and Other One-Act Plays* (1925). Steele's third novel, *Taboo* (1925), treats the theme of incest without the quiet solidity of "When Hell Froze," a family story that deservedly won first prize in Harper's 1925 Short Story Contest. Convinced of his wife's infidelity, a farmer commands her to wash her hands in lye water. Not "till hell freezes over," she declares and moves into town. But out of love for her family, she returns to the farmhouse and dips her hands into the lye water. The relaxed plot, luminous motivation, and clean prose make this story of rural mores seem closer to life than most of Steele's ingenious melodramas. Depressed during his 1925–1926 winter in Switzerland, Steele recovered with the publication of *Urkey Island* (1926), eight improbable tales linked by an atmospheric New England fishing village. His best novel, *Meat* (1928), is about a mother's fanatical protection of her defective child at the expense of her other children. The stories of his finest years as a writer appear in his next collection, the stunning *Man Who Saw Through Heaven* (1927). The title story, about the bizarre odyssey of a naive missionary in Africa after he peers through an enormous telescope, allegorizes the history of human evolution. In a tour de force of Euclidean plot, stylized histrionics, and ironic indirection, ontogeny assumes phylogeny.

But by this time the reaction against jigsaw-puzzle plots and heavy-handed chance had destroyed many literary reputations. Still, the O. Henry Committee—O. Henry, too, had been born in Greensboro—favored Steele's jeweled shockers, but O'Brien now preferred stories less contrived, the realism of Anderson, Fitzgerald, and Hemingway. Forced to sell his summer home in Nantucket, Steele, low-spirited, wintered in Charleston, S.C., in 1928–1929. Critics rightly found Steele's sixth collection, *Tower of Sand* (1929), highly strained and only temporarily satisfying. In 1929 he moved to Chapel Hill, N.C., where he and playwright Paul Green became friends. In his Nobel Prize address (1930), Sinclair Lewis generously cited Steele among those "original" writers who, if isolated, might be driven to commercialism. As the quality magazines turned to the "new" story, Steele turned to the popular weeklies and women's magazines. To add to his troubles, his wife died in 1931.

In London, on Jan. 14, 1932, Steele married a family friend, actress Norma Mitchell, divorced from Hayden Talbot; they had no children. They settled in her home in Hamburg, Conn., but spent the winters working in Hollywood. Unable to resist the wild romantic irony of "How Beautiful with Shoes," O'Brien included this classic Steele tale in *Best Short Stories* (1933). Through Appalachian atmosphere, subtle point of view, and powerful symbolism, this enduring piece of hillbilly fiction in the "sick-story" genre depicts an asylum escapee whose abduction of a cloddish Carolina milkmaid awakens her to ideal beauty. With his wife, Steele wrote a hit Broadway mystery-comedy, *Post Road* (1935), but had less success with his and Anthony's Brown's three-act stage adaptation of "How Beautiful with Shoes." From 1938, when he published his psychological detective novel *Sound of Rowlocks*, to 1945, only a trickle of Steele's mechanical efforts sold to mass-market magazines. In 1945, Doubleday published *That Girl from Memphis*, the first of Steele's increasingly tedious quasi-romantic novels set in the American West. Capitalizing on Steele's early fame, Doubleday published the central collection, *The Best Stories of Wilbur Daniel Steele* (1945). Following the poor reception of Steele's second western novel, *Diamond Wedding* (1950), Doubleday anticlimactically published *Full Cargo: More Stories by Wilbur Daniel Steele* (1951). After his third western novel, the involuted *Their Town* (1952), Steele had a nervous breakdown and wintered in 1953–1954 in Florida. Unable to complete his last novel to Doubleday's satisfaction, he resented editorial alterations in *The Way to the Gold* (1955) and refused even to see the film version. Retiring to Old Lyme, Conn., in 1956, he underwent several operations and hospitalizations before he and his wife entered a rest home in Essex, Conn., in April 1964. He died in Essex.

[Steele's papers are in the Stanford University Library. Martin Bucco, *Wilbur Daniel Steele* (1972), the only full-length critical biography, contains a full bibliography as well as articles about Steele. See also Blanche Colton Williams, *Our Short Story Writers* (1926); Frank B. Elser, "Oh, Yes . . . Mr. Steele," *Bookman*, Feb. 1926; Harvey Breit, "Talk with Mr. Steele," *New York Times Book Review*, Aug. 6, 1950; and Martin Bucco, review of *Diamond Wedding*, *Western American Literature*, Spring-Summer, 1973. An obituary is in the *New York Times*, May 27, 1970.]

MARTIN BUCCO

STEINBECK, JOHN ERNST, JR. (Feb. 27, 1902–Dec. 20, 1968), writer, was born in Salinas, Calif., the son of John Ernst Steinbeck, the treasurer of Monterey County, and Olive Hamilton, a former teacher. The Steinbecks had a comfortable income and were highly respected in their community, and John, the only son among four children, was somewhat spoiled. Nevertheless, the young Steinbeck was very shy and developed into something of a loner. He began, at age fifteen, to spend much of his time in his bedroom writing short stories that, in his bashfulness, he would submit to magazines under a pen name and with no return address.

At seventeen Steinbeck graduated from Salinas High School and went on to Stanford University, where he decided not to pursue a degree but to take only those courses that would help him toward his goal of becoming a writer. From 1919 to 1925 he alternated college study with employment for the Spreckels Sugar Company, working either in the beet fields or at the company's processing plant near Salinas.

If the first part of his apprenticeship was associated with Stanford and Spreckels, the second was associated with the Lake Tahoe area. From the summer of 1925 to mid-1929 (interrupted only by an unfortunate few months during the winter of 1925–1926 when he nearly starved in New York), Steinbeck worked as a handyman at a resort, caretaker of a large estate, and assistant at the Tahoe City fish hatchery. In the summer of 1929, while working at the hatchery, Steinbeck met and fell in love with Carol Henning. A few weeks later he quit his job and moved to San Francisco, where she was working. They went to live in Eagle Rock, near Los Angeles, and on Jan. 14, 1930, they were married. Witty, fun-loving, and outspoken, Carol seemed to be the perfect counterbalance to her shy, intense husband; and her typing, proofreading, and suggestions contributed much to his eventual literary success.

With the publication of *The Pastures of Heaven* (1932), *To a God Unknown* (1933), and the stories that were later collected in *The Long Valley* (1938), Steinbeck defined his primary subject matter—farm life in an enclosed California valley. But all of his early publishers went bankrupt, and he remained largely unknown until, after a dozen rejections, *Tortilla Flat* (1935) was published and became a success.

The previous year, Steinbeck had met and interviewed a farm labor organizer, Cecil McKiddy, who was hiding from the law after having assisted in the California cotton strike of 1933. This interview led Steinbeck to the subject of the three great novels of his early midcareer—the migrant worker and the lives of the dispossessed in rural America during the Great Depression. The direct result of the interview was *In Dubious Battle* (1936). This work was followed by *Of Mice and Men* (1937), the tragic story of two bindle stiffs, based on events witnessed by Steinbeck while he was a ranch hand on a Spreckels farm fifteen years earlier. With the help of George S. Kaufman, the novelette was made into a Broadway play that won the Drama Critics Circle Award of 1937.

For most of the period 1933–1936, Steinbeck and his wife lived at his parents' vacation house in Pacific Grove and were frequent visitors at the marine biologist Edward F. Ricketts' laboratory on Cannery Row, which had become a gathering place for local writers and artists. Steinbeck often accompanied Ricketts on collecting trips and helped him prepare the marine specimens that he sold to schools; in this way, Steinbeck received an informal education in marine biology even as he stored up impressions of life on the Row for future work.

After publication of *In Dubious Battle,* Steinbeck was asked by George West, the chief editorial writer for the *San Francisco News,* to go to California's Central Valley and investigate the plight of the Dust Bowl emigrants who for several years had been moving by the thousands into a California farm labor market already bloated by a surplus of workers. In the seven-part series "The Harvest Gypsies," Steinbeck described the inhuman living conditions suffered by the "Okies." This and two other trips to the valley provided the material for his masterpiece, *The Grapes of Wrath* (1939).

The novel won the Pulitzer Prize, among several others, and established Steinbeck's reputation as a major American writer. But the price he paid was high: the furious work schedule had damaged his and his wife's health; the long and often vitriolic controversy over the novel's truth and its "Communistic" message of support for the dispossessed took a severe psychological toll on its author; and the resulting celebrity, which he hated, seemed to make it impossible for him to pass unrecognized as an observer in public places. To escape the furor, Steinbeck, his wife, Ricketts, and a captain and crew of three sailed to the Gulf of California aboard the *Western Flyer* to collect specimens. This expedition resulted in *Sea of Cortez* (1941), coauthored with Ricketts.

In the meantime, Steinbeck had been spending time in Hollywood in connection with the filming of his novels and met a young singer, Gwyndolyn Conger. They saw each other frequently for more than a year prior to his separation from his wife in 1940; once divorce proceedings were initiated in late 1941, Steinbeck and Conger moved to New York City, where, despite two later attempts to reestablish a home in California, he resided for the rest of his life.

Following America's entry into World War II, Steinbeck went to work, without pay, for several government information agencies, writing the novel *The Moon Is Down* (1942) and, for the Army Air Corps, the nonfictional *Bombs Away* (1942). On Mar. 29, 1943, he married Conger; they had two children. Blocked from entering the Air Corps by false charges that he was a Communist, he became a correspondent for the *New York Herald-Tribune* and in 1943 was sent to the Mediterranean, where he joined a secret, commandolike outfit headed by Lieutenant Douglas Fairbanks, Jr.

Steinbeck returned to the United States in 1944 in some shock over his experiences in Europe. This state of mind induced a nostalgia embodied in *Cannery Row* (1945), which was seen as sentimental and irrelevant by critics, many of whom, with Marxist sympathies, had previously lauded his work as making a contribution to "the class struggle." After completing the novel, Steinbeck spent most of 1945 in Mexico writing the script and preparing for the filming of *The Pearl* (1948); when the film was nearly completed, he returned to New York and wrote a novelette based on his script (1947).

Steinbeck's next novel was *The Wayward Bus* (1947), an allegory roughly patterned on Chaucer's *Canterbury Tales* and set in a California valley. In 1948, Ed Ricketts was killed when his car was hit by a train, and shortly after this blow, Steinbeck's wife announced that she had never loved him and had been unfaithful for years. Overcome by shock and grief, Steinbeck suffered a serious nervous breakdown.

Ultimately, Steinbeck's salvation came, first, from meeting another woman, Elaine Scott, the wife of the movie actor Zachary Scott, and, second, from writing out his emotions in regard to what he felt was the betrayal by his wife and the loss of his children to a woman whom he now considered thoroughly evil. The resulting works were the novelette *Burning Bright* (1950) and the epic-length novel *East of Eden* (1952), which had been in his mind for many years.

Following her divorce, Elaine Scott became Steinbeck's wife on Dec. 28, 1950. Despite this generally happy marriage, Steinbeck entered a long period of frustration and uncertainty in regard to his writing. His hope was to turn from the novel and become a playwright, but with the failure of his dramatization of *Burning Bright* (1950) and of *Pipe Dream* (1955; a Rodgers-Hammerstein musical based on *Sweet Thursday*, his 1954 sequel to *Cannery Row*), he began to devote more and more time to travel and journalism.

Near the end of the 1950's he moved in yet another direction, to a project that he had had in the back of his mind for many years—the rewriting in modern English of Malory's *Morte d'Arthur*, the favorite book of his childhood. But he was unable to find a language equal to the magic of the original, and so, he left the project incomplete. However, his feeling that the age of Malory had its counterpart in the confused America of his own time led to the writing of two of his last three books: his last novel, *The Winter of Our Discontent* (1961), an examination of modern, middle-class values, and *America and Americans* (1966), a word-and-picture book, which sought, again in moralistic terms, to examine the lives and values of ordinary citizens. A similar quest for the pulse of America led him on a journey around the country in a camper with his dog in 1960, chronicled in *Travels with Charley* (1962).

Because of his own sense of recent failure and the decline of his reputation, which his latest books had done little to stem, Steinbeck was stunned when in 1962 he was awarded the Nobel Prize for literature. Even if one agrees with his assessment that he did not deserve the prize, the abuse that he suffered in the wake of the announcement, particularly at the hands of the "Eastern literary establishment," must seem tasteless and mean-spiritied. He was so deeply wounded that although he wrote many thousands of words in the years following, he never wrote another word of fiction.

The last years of Steinbeck's life were again given over to travel and journalism. In 1963 he went with his wife and the playwright Edward Albee on a State Department–sponsored trip to the Soviet Union and other Eastern-bloc countries. After Lyndon B. Johnson became president, Steinbeck became one of his friends and informal advisers. This friendship and Steinbeck's hawkish views on the Vietnam War further alienated him from the intellectual community.

In late 1966, Steinbeck went to Vietnam as a correspondent for *Newsday*. He praised the troops (among whom were his two sons) and expressed scorn for the draft-card burners at home. On the way back from the Far East, while in Hong Kong, he stopped to help an elderly Chinese haul a handtruck up a set of stairs and badly injured his back. An operation was successful, but his health went into a decline. He died in New York City.

Few American writers have been the source of as much controversy as Steinbeck. His early books are still denounced by those on the political right, and more of his works are on lists of books banned by schools and libraries than any other writer. On the other hand, many academics dismiss him as merely a "popular" author, and the liberal-intellectual community has not yet forgiven him for his support for the Vietnam War. Nevertheless, many of his novels are commonly taught in schools and colleges, and *The Grapes of Wrath* remains one of the major American novels of the twentieth century.

[The major collections of Steinbeck's papers are in the Stanford University Libraries; the Bancroft Library at the University of California at Berkeley; the Humanities Research Center of the University of Texas at Austin; the Pierpont Morgan Library, New York; the John Steinbeck Library, Salinas; and the John Steinbeck Research Center, San Jose State

University. *The Journal of a Novel* (1969) is a journal kept by the author during the composition of *East of Eden*. For his correspondence, see *Steinbeck: A Life in Letters* (1975), edited by Elaine Steinbeck and Robert Wallsten.

Important works by Steinbeck not mentioned in the text are *The Red Pony* (1945); *A Russian Journal* (1947), with photographer Robert Capa; *The Log* (1951), which comprises the narrative portion of the *Sea of Cortez;* and *Once There Was a War* (1958), a collection of wartime dispatches. Two movie scripts of note are *The Forgotten Village* (film made, and abridged version of script published, in 1941) and *Viva Zapata!* (filmed in 1950 and published in 1975). *The Acts of King Arthur and His Noble Knights* (1976), edited by Chase Horton, is his incomplete Malory project.

The standard biography is Jackson J. Benson, *The True Adventures of John Steinbeck, Writer* (1984). See also Richard Astro, *John Steinbeck and Edward F. Ricketts: The Shaping of a Novelist* (1973). The major bibliography of secondary materials is Tetsumaro Hayashi, *A New Steinbeck Bibliography: 1929–1971* (1973) and *A New Steinbeck Bibliography: 1971–1981* (1983).

Important critical studies include Peter Lisca, *The Wide World of John Steinbeck* (1958); Warren G. French, *John Steinbeck* (1961); Joseph E. Fontenrose, *John Steinbeck: An Introduction and Interpretation* (1963); and Howard Levant, *The Novels of John Steinbeck* (1974). Oral histories are in the John Steinbeck Library, Salinas, and the Stanford University Libraries. An obituary is in the *New York Times*, Dec. 21, 1968.]

JACKSON J. BENSON

STERN, OTTO (Feb. 17, 1888–Aug. 17, 1969, physicist and physical chemist, was born in Sohrau, Upper Silesia, Germany (now Zory, Poland), the son of Oskar Stern, a grain merchant and flour miller, and Eugenie Rosenthal. In 1892 the family moved to Breslau (now Wrocław, Poland), where Stern attended the local schools, graduating from the Johannes Gymnasium in 1906. Following the German custom of that time, he attended lectures at a number of universities, including Freiburg, Munich, and Breslau, where he concentrated on physical chemistry. Although he had studied with several outstanding physicists and mathematicians, such as Arnold Sommerfeld, Jakob Rosanes, Otto Lummer, and Ernst Pringsheim, his interest was stimulated most by his own private study of the works of Ludwig Boltzmann in statistical mechanics and Rudolf Clausius and Walther Nernst in thermodynamics. He wrote his doctoral dissertation under Otto Sackur at Breslau on the osmotic pressure of carbon dioxide in concentrated solutions. The development of both theory and experiment in this study were to typify his research throughout his life.

Upon receiving his doctorate from Breslau in 1912 and taking advantage of his family's financial support, Stern obtained a position as unpaid assistant to Albert Einstein in Prague. Stern was greatly interested in Einstein's work on statistical mechanics and quantum physics, and in 1913 they published a joint paper on the zero-point energy of the harmonic oscillator. In that year, Stern also published a paper of his own on the entropy constant of a perfect monatomic gas, which represented a new combination of classical and quantum approaches and had considerable influence on later workers, particularly Enrico Fermi, who eventually developed the new particle statistics that bear his name. When Einstein left Prague for Zurich in 1913, Stern accompanied him, obtaining his first official academic position, as an unsalaried lecturer at the Eidgenössische Technische Hochschule. He credited Einstein with having taught him how to "sniff out" the really important problems of physics. While at Zurich, Stern also benefited from contact with other leading physicists of the day, notably Karl Herzfeld, Peter Debye, Paul Ehrenfest, and Max von Laue.

In 1914, Stern had his lectureship transferred to the University of Frankfurt under von Laue, but with the outbreak of World War I, Stern was drafted into the German army. He served in 1916 as a meteorological officer in Lomsha, Poland, and his minimal duties allowed him the time to produce a detailed study of the third law of thermodynamics and a lengthy calculation of the energy of a system of coupled mass points. Late in the war Nernst, who was greatly impressed by Stern's work in thermodynamics, had him transferred to the War Department in Berlin, where Stern was able to pursue his scientific work with men such as Max Born, Alfred Landé, Rudolf Ladenburg, and Max Volmer. As a result of work done during this period, Stern and Volmer published papers on the decay time of fluorescence and an attempt to separate heavy hydrogen from ordinary hydrogen.

When the war ended and Stern was able to resume his post at Frankfurt, he began a series of investigations based on a dormant molecular-beam method that had been introduced by the Frenchman Louis Dunoyer in 1911. Stern felt that this method, in which a narrow stream of atoms or molecules is "boiled out" of an oven through a narrow slit into an evacuated chamber, held the potential of answering many of the fundamental questions of atomic and molecular physics in a very direct and straightforward way. He was later fully justified in this assumption, and he went on to develop the technique into one of the most powerful research tools of modern physics, a method that not only confirmed many of the then-current ideas about atomic systems but also revealed many unsuspected ones as well. It was for the results of the series of experiments performed with the technique that Stern was awarded the Nobel Prize for physics in 1943.

Stern's first experiment at Frankfurt was the direct measurement of the distribution of the velocities in a gas at low pressure. The excellent match between his experimental results and the predictions put forward by James Clerk Maxwell sixty years earlier were both a direct confirmation of that theory (the first ever obtained) and an indication of the power of the new experimental technique as an investigative tool. The next result was of a vastly different sort: it showed that a beam of silver atoms, when passed through an inhomogeneous magnetic field, was split into two distinct halves instead of being merely broadened, as was expected according to classical theory. This result, suspected by Niels Bohr and Sommerfeld as one of the surprising consequences of the newly emerging quantum theory, was one of the crucial bits of information that contributed to the fundamental change in viewpoint that physicists reluctantly came to accept during the 1920's. It showed that individual atoms behave in a discontinuous or "jerky" manner instead of smoothly or continuously, as seems to be the case for gross matter.

In the second experiment, Stern was assisted in the laboratory by Walther Gerlach, who had come to Frankfurt in 1920, and the experiment became known among physicists as the Stern-Gerlach experiment. When Stern left Frankfurt to accept an appointment as associate professor of theoretical physics at the University of Rostock in 1921, Gerlach remained at Frankfurt, but Stern commuted to Frankfurt on his vacations to monitor the progress of the experiments still under way. They published a series of three papers during 1921 and 1922 that described all aspects of this remarkable result.

In December 1922, Stern was offered a full professorship in physical chemistry at the University of Hamburg and the opportunity to develop a special laboratory devoted entirely to molecular-beam research. Although it took a few years to ready the laboratory, by 1926 he had initiated a broad program of research that led to numerous fundamental results in molecular and atomic physics. During the next seven years thirty papers were written by him and his collaborators describing the results of this work. The papers cover all aspects of the technique as well as specific results, such as the determination of the magnetic moments of various molecules, atoms, and nuclei; the investigation of the electric dipole moment of certain molecules; the measurement of the de Broglie wavelengths of hydrogen and helium beams; studies of the reflection of molecular beams from various surfaces; and the "flipping" of space-quantized atoms from one orientation to another.

In 1933, Stern discovered, with the help of Immanuel Estermann and Otto Frisch, that the magnetic moment of the proton is approximately two and a half times what the theoreticians had predicted. It was one of his most startling results and is still not clearly understood. In all this work, his keen sense of knowing what fundamental questions to ask, his thorough mastery of both theoretical and experimental issues, and his unswerving attention to detail set the pattern for its remarkable success. Many young physicists who worked with him at Hamburg went on to develop major molecular-beam laboratories of their own; one of the most notable was Isidor Rabi, who won the 1944 Nobel Prize in physics for his development and use of the molecular-beam resonance technique.

In the late summer of 1933 the Nazis dismissed Stern's Jewish colleague Estermann and ordered Stern to remove the portrait of Einstein from his office. Stern, also Jewish, immediately resigned, instead of being forced to leave, and thus, the work of his institute at Hamburg ceased. He obtained positions for himself and Estermann at Carnegie Institute of Technology in Pittsburgh that fall, and together they established a molecular-beam laboratory there, but they were never able to attain the level of achievement they had reached at Hamburg. Stern was naturalized in 1939 and served as a consultant to the United States War Department during World War II. He retired in 1945 and moved to Berkeley, Calif., where he lived with two of his sisters. He never married. In Berkeley he attended regularly the physics colloquium of the University of California and developed an interest in particle physics and astrophysics. He visited Europe regularly but never Germany, maintaining contact with his many friends and previous colleagues at international meetings and conferences. He died in Berkeley.

[A list of interview notes, letters, and a transcript of a tape-recorded interview with Stern is in Thomas S. Kuhn et al., *Sources for History of Quantum Physics* (1967). Additional material is in the Archives of the American Physical Society, New York City. A complete list of his published works follows the biographical sketch by Emilio Segrè in *Biographical Memoirs of the National Academy of Sciences*, 43 (1973). A list of the scientific proceedings issuing from his Hamburg laboratory, the Untersuchungen zur Molekularstrahlmethode, or U.M., series, follows Immanuel Estermann, "Molecular Beam Research in Hamburg, 1922–1933," in *Recent Research in Molecular Beams* (1959), a festschrift celebrating Stern's seventieth birthday. The Stern-Gerlach papers are in *Zeitschrift für Physik*, 7 (1921), 8 (1921), and 9 (1922); and in *Annalen der Physik*, 4th ser., 74 (1924). Stern's Nobel Prize lecture is in *Nobel Lectures, 1942–1962 (Physics)* (1964). Obituaries are in the *New York Times*, Aug. 19, 1969; and *Physics Today*, Oct. 1969.]

RICHARD K. GEHRENBECK

STEWART, JOHN GEORGE (June 2, 1890–May 24, 1970), architect of the United States Capitol, was born in Wilmington, Del., the son of Hamilton Stewart, the president of a construction company, and Marie Schaefer. Educated in the Wilmington public schools, Stewart studied civil engineering at the University of Delaware and left in 1911 during his junior year. (He received an honorary B.S. from the university in 1958.)

He married Helen Tabor Ferry of Norristown, Pa., on Oct. 7, 1911; they had two children. Stewart's wife died in 1936, and in October 1937 he married Rae (Dickerson) Lauritsen. His second marriage was unsuccessful, and so the couple separated.

Stewart's father had founded a heavy construction company, Stewart and Donohue, in 1902, and Stewart joined it in 1911, working in a variety of capacities and rising to partner in 1919 and president in 1929. The firm became one of the largest in the Middle Atlantic region and built highways, bridges, factories, and residences. Stewart developed close ties with both local politicians and the du Pont family. Under his supervision, the firm restored the original du Pont black powder plant at Hagley, Del., and constructed the museum house for Henry F. du Pont at Winterthur, Del., and the extensive classical garden extensions for the Alfred I. du Pont estate, Nemours, near Wilmington, Del. During this period, Stewart came into contact with leading architects from Philadelphia and New York City, and his architectural tastes were formulated in the classical and traditional styles, not in modernism.

The political stage of Stewart's life began in 1931 with his appointment for a year as a member of the Governor of Delaware's Emergency Relief Commission. In 1934 he was elected on the Republican ticket as a representative to the Seventy-fifth Congress. After he was defeated for reelection in 1937, he returned to his construction business, which he sold in 1942. During the war he worked for the Hercules Powder Company of Wilmington as a salesman to the United States Army Corps of Engineers. After the war he worked as a salesman for the Pennsylvania Engineering Company. In 1947 he returned to Washington, D.C., as chief clerk of the Senate Committee on the District of Columbia. He continued as a professional staff member under the Democratic majority during 1949–1951. He remained active in Republican politics during the elections of 1944, 1948, and 1952, and he served as director of the Republican Speakers' Bureau for 1953–1954. In recognition of these services, President Dwight D. Eisenhower named Stewart architect of the Capitol on Oct. 1, 1954.

The eighth person to occupy the position of architect of the Capitol since it was created in 1793, Stewart was in charge of the operation, maintenance, and construction of all buildings and grounds in the Capitol Hill compound of approximately 131 acres. The architect of the Capitol is immune to all local building laws, zoning, and planning commissions, especially the Commission of Fine Arts, which oversees Washington's architecture. (Although appointed by the president, the architect in effect serves at the pleasure of the leaders of Congress.)

Under Stewart's direction, the new Senate

(subsequently named the Dirksen) Office Building was constructed (1955–1958), the Rayburn House Office Building was designed and built (1955–1965), the east front of the Capitol was extended (1958–1960), the Longworth Office Building was remodeled (1966–1968), and preliminary plans for the James Madison Memorial Library were begun (completed in 1982). Beginning in 1963, Stewart advanced ideas for the extension of the west front of the Capitol. This extension, which would have removed the last external vestige of the original Capitol building, was controversial. (After considerable study and argument, the extension schemes were shelved in 1983, and plans were drawn up for the restoration of the west front.)

Stewart's reign on Capitol Hill was controversial, and the criticism of him frequently vituperative. Writers in the professional architectural press and critics for newspapers and magazines bemoaned his impact. He was called "the Emperor of Capitol Hill" and "the Monster Builder," and his work was labeled "Mussolini modern," "Early Rameses and Late Nieman-Marcus," "King-Sized Howard Johnson's," "Texas Penitentiary," and "hard, grotesque, vulgar." The American Institute of Architects issued several formal criticisms of his Capitol Hill work and projects. Stewart, a short round man with a courtly demeanor, appeared unmoved by the various attacks and would simply reply, "No comment." Close friends, however, reported that the criticisms did sting. Sensitive to the charge that he was not an architect, Stewart would proudly point to the honorary membership the American Institute of Architects gave him in 1957.

While roasted in the press, Stewart found only a few congressional critics; most were either pleased with his performance or simply oblivious to the charges of philistinism. Senator Everett Dirksen labeled Stewart's critics "that aesthetic group" and claimed Congress would not be told by anybody what to build or how to build it. Stewart's secret was to please Congress by offering members office space and facilities such as swimming pools and to appeal to the edifice complex of the leaders of both the Senate and the House. Although a Republican, he got on well with Democrats and found his strongest supporters among their ranks. Speaker of the House Sam Rayburn viewed the extension of the east front of the Capitol as a personal memorial and, together with the Senate majority leader, Lyndon Baines Johnson, pushed it through. To critics, it was known as "the Texas front." The House (Rayburn) Office Building was entirely Rayburn's creation, since he arranged for Congress to fund the project, the cost of which rose from $50 million to nearly $150 million. Rayburn convinced President John F. Kennedy to keep Stewart on the job in 1961 after Kennedy had vowed to fire him. Rayburn's successor as Speaker, John McCormack, saw Stewart as a barometer of his political power and viewed the west-front extension as a personal memorial.

The controversy around Stewart's work, especially among professional architects, must be viewed from a historical perspective. Stewart represented the old order, his architectural aesthetics—and those of his congressional sponsors as well—were classical and traditional. With minor exceptions, all American governmental buildings—and especially those in Washington, D.C.—were classically derived; Stewart saw it as his duty to continue this image. However, by the 1950's many American architects, the architectural press, and the architectural schools had converted to modernism. Modern architecture, with its abstract, ahistorical posture, was seen as the wave of the future. In contrast, Stewart surrounded himself with a board of eminent architectural advisers (the committee in 1965 consisted of John Harbeson of Philadelphia; Gilmore Clarke, Alfred E. Poor, and Albert H. Swanke of New York City; Jessie Shelton of Atlanta; Roscoe de Witt of Dallas; and Paul Thiry of Seattle) who represented the old order and were adamantly opposed to modernism. They upheld Stewart's classicism and, not surprisingly, did much of the design work for the Capitol Hill projects.

Some of the design work done under Stewart has a banal touch; fineness of detail is lost and broad, blank, immense Georgia-marble surfaces dominate. In the Rayburn Building, grand staircases lead nowhere and massive muscular Valkyries gaze down on the passerby. Yet Stewart's buildings did continue the classical tradition in Washington. Not really an architect, Stewart proved to be adroit in managing the wishes of Congress. He died in Washington.

[Manuscripts relating to Stewart's tenure as architect can be found in the archives of the architect of the Capitol. For criticism of his work, see Douglas Haskell, "Saying Nothing, Going Nowhere," *Archi-*

tectural Forum, Aug. 1959; Harold B. Myers, "A Monument to Power," *Fortune*, Mar. 1965; Hunter Lewis, "Capitol Hill's Ugliness Club," *Atlantic Monthly*, Feb. 1967; and Rasa Gustaitis, "The Emperor of Capitol Hill," *Architectural Forum*, Sept. 1968. Obituaries are in the *Washington Post* and the *New York Times*, both May 25, 1970.]

RICHARD GUY WILSON

STOKES, MAURICE (June 17, 1933–Apr. 6, 1970), basketball player, was born in Pittsburgh, Pa., the son of Tero Stokes, a steelworker, and Myrtle Stokes (maiden name unknown). Stokes attended Westinghouse High School, graduating in 1951. A highly recruited basketball player, he entered St. Francis College in Loretto, Pa., where he majored in teacher education. He received a B.A. in 1955.

In college Stokes achieved stardom on the basketball court. Although he stood six feet, seven inches and weighed 240 pounds, Stokes possessed the speed and agility of a small man. He could shoot, drive, and pass off the ball. He was considered the greatest all-around college player of his time. In his first two college seasons, Stokes scored 922 points, including a freshman school record of 505. After Stokes scored 32 points against Villanova, Al Severance, the Villanova coach, commented, "He's the best freshman player I've ever seen." During the 1953–1954 season, Stokes established a school record in the highest rebound average for a single season (26.5). The following year, as a senior, he established numerous school records—most field goals scored (302), most free throws (156), most rebounds (733), most points scored in a season (760), and highest scoring average for a season (27.1). Between 1951 and 1955 he scored a total of 2,282 points while holding eleven of the thirteen individual records for a St. Francis College basketball player; eight of those records still stood in 1987. He was named to the All-American Basketball Team from his sophomore year through his senior year.

In 1955, Stokes led the St. Francis team to a fourth-place finish in the National Invitation Tournament. Against Dayton University, on March 17, Stokes scored 43 points and grabbed 19 rebounds. In the tournament he scored a record 124 points in four games. Walter McLaughlin, the St. John's University athletic director and chairman of the tournament's selection committee, said, "This is the greatest performance I have ever seen. There have been other great players here but what they did pales by comparison." Stokes received the most-valuable-player trophy for his performance. His college career ended with his selection to the starting lineup of the All-American Team.

Stokes was a first-round draft choice of the Rochester Royals in the National Basketball Association (NBA) in 1955. (He turned down an offer from the Harlem Globetrotters.) In his first season with the Royals, he averaged 16.1 points a game and was second in the league in rebounds. "Stokes is no rookie," stated Red Auerbach, the Boston Celtic coach and later Hall of Famer. "He was ready for this league when he was in college. Nothing will stop him." He was chosen NBA Rookie of the Year. In his second season, after the franchise moved to Cincinnati, Stokes set a league record by pulling down 38 rebounds in one game. That same year, he led the NBA in rebounds, averaging 17.4 a game. In his final season, Stokes was second in the league in rebounds (18.1 a game), third in assists (6.4), and among the top fifteen scorers with an average of 16.9 points a game.

Near the end of his third NBA season, while at the top of his game, Stokes fell and struck his head while scrambling for a rebound against the Minneapolis Lakers. The fall knocked him unconscious, but he revived and continued playing. Three days later, on Mar. 15, 1958, after an opening-round game against the Detroit Pistons in the Western Division playoffs, he collapsed. He was in a coma for six months and thereafter was paralyzed.

Confined to a wheelchair and with only partial speech, Stokes fought back courageously against his handicap. The rehabilitation process was slow and painful. His mind remained clear and sharp, and he worked continuously at physical-therapy exercises and never lost hope that one day he would walk. When he learned to use an electric typewriter, he wrote, "I always tried to bear down in competition, but I never had to put out quite as hard as I do in this exercising."

Stokes was assisted in his rehabilitation by his former professional teammate Jack Twyman, who became his legal guardian and constant companion. Twyman visited Stokes daily in the hospital and arranged for paying the enormous medical costs. As the "No. 1 Brother's Keeper," Twyman, in 1959, established at Kutsher's

Country Club in Monticello, N.Y., the annual Maurice Stokes Benefit Game, which attracts numerous professional basketball stars.

Stokes died of a heart attack at Good Samaritan Hospital in Cincinnati, where he had been hospitalized since March 1958. His personal battle to overcome his physical handicap became a symbol of one man's courage and determination to restore himself to full health.

[See Neil Amdur, "Maurice Stokes," in Zander Hollander, ed., *Great Rookies of Pro Basketball* (1969); Zander Hollander, *The Modern Encyclopedia of Basketball* (1973); and Neil D. Isaacs, *All the Moves: A History of College Basketball* (1975). Press clippings and biographical sketches are available at the Office of Public Relations of St. Francis College and at the Naismith Memorial Basketball Hall of Fame at Springfield, Mass. Newspaper accounts of Stokes are in the *Cleveland Plain Dealer*, May 16, 1965; the *New York Post*, Aug. 5, 1980; and the *Morning Union* (Monticello, N.Y.), Aug. 9, 1983. An obituary is in the *New York Times*, Apr. 7, 1970.]

CHARLES F. HOWLETT

STRATEMEYER, GEORGE EDWARD (Nov. 24, 1890–Aug. 9, 1969), United States Army and Air Force officer, was born in Cincinnati, Ohio, the son of George Stratemeyer, an army officer, and Belle Rettig. He spent most of his boyhood in Peru, Ind., where he attended high school. In June 1915 he graduated from the United States Military Academy in the class that included Dwight D. Eisenhower and Omar N. Bradley. He married Annalee Rix in August 1916. After earning his wings in 1917 at Rockwell Field, San Diego, Calif., he served successively at Kelly Field, Tex., Chanute Field, Ill., and Luke Field, Hawaii. In 1920 he transferred to the Army Air Service. In 1924 he returned to West Point as an instructor in tactics; six years later he graduated from the Air Corps Tactical School at Langley Field, Va., and in 1932 from the Command and General Staff School, Fort Leavenworth, Kans., where he stayed until 1936 as an instructor.

Promoted to lieutenant colonel in June 1936, he took command of the Seventh Bombardment Group at Hamilton Field, Calif. In 1939 he graduated from the Army War College; in 1941 he became executive officer for the Chief of Air Corps in Washington, D.C. He briefly commanded the Southeast Air Corps Training Center at Maxwell Field, Ala., in 1942, returning to Washington, D.C., in June of that year to become chief of the Air Staff. He became a colonel in March 1940, a brigadier general in 1941, a major general in 1942, and a lieutenant general in 1945.

After the beginning of World War II, Stratemeyer's assignment in August 1943 to the China-Burma-India Theater challenged his considerable diplomatic and administrative skills. Originally intended to be theater air commander, he was assigned instead to the India-Burma sector because of Generalissimo Chiang Kai-shek's objection to any change in the independent status of Major General Claire L. Chennault, then commander of the Fourteenth Air Force in China. Stratemeyer's responsibilities included command of the Tenth Air Force in India-Burma and the theater Air Service Command, supply and maintenance of the Fourteenth Air Force, protection of the Hump air route to China, and coordination of the Air Transport Command's theaterwide operations. He was also air adviser to the China-Burma-India theater commander, Lieutenant General Joseph W. Stilwell. After the establishment of the allied Southeast Asia Command (SEAC) under Vice-Admiral Lord Louis Mountbatten late in 1943, Stratemeyer also became deputy commander (under a British air marshal) of the American and British air forces. By December he exercised operational control of all SEAC air forces.

For the remainder of World War II Stratemeyer directed air operations, first in Burma, later in China. In Burma, the first half of 1944 saw the emergence of a new mode of warfare: extended ground operations sustained by air supply and transportation. Its most novel features were long-range penetration and commando operations behind enemy lines, using transports and gliders in unescorted night landings on jungle air strips. In April, to stem the Japanese encirclement of Imphal, India, two British divisions were flown from the Arakan (Burma) hundreds of miles to the south. Stratemeyer's allied Troop Carrier Command enabled 28,000 British and 30,000 Indian troops to sustain combat for three months entirely by air supply.

Stratemeyer proposed a plan in September 1943 for using the new, long-range B-29s to bomb Japan. It provided for basing the bombers in India and staging them through smaller advanced bases in eastern China, thus minimizing the burden on air supply over the

Hump. This feature was embodied in the plan (known as Matterhorn) approved by President Franklin D. Roosevelt in November, and Stratemeyer was briefly considered to command the operation. Ultimately B-29 operations were directed from Washington, D.C., Matterhorn was overtaken by the swift pace of American advances in the Pacific, and most B-29 raids were launched from the Marianas.

After the collapse of Japanese resistance in Burma in the spring of 1945, Stratemeyer prepared to redeploy his U.S. air forces to China (now a separate theater), where the Japanese had captured most of the East China bases. In July, promoted to lieutenant general, Stratemeyer was given command of all American air forces in that theater, including the Fourteenth Air Force following Chennault's resignation. Stratemeyer directed the air support of the summer offensives that ended with Japan's surrender in August. After supervising the massive eastward air redeployment of some 200,000 Chinese Nationalist troops, Stratemeyer returned to the United States in March 1946, where he was assigned to command the Air Defense Command (renamed the Continental Air Command in 1948). In April 1949 he went to Tokyo to command the Far East Air Forces of the United States (FEAF).

When the North Korean army invaded South Korea on June 25, 1950, Stratemeyer was high above the Pacific returning from conferences in Washington, D.C. By the time he landed, South Korean (ROK) forces were in full retreat, American residents were being evacuated, and President Harry S Truman had ordered United States naval and air forces into action south of the thirty-eighth parallel. On June 29 Stratemeyer persuaded General Douglas MacArthur, the Far East commander, to extend United States air operations into North Korea as a prerequisite to gaining control of the air. The president subsequently confirmed the order and also directed United States ground forces to support ROK troops. By the end of July, Stratemeyer's air forces, together with navy carriers and Marine Corps aviation, had driven the North Korean air force from the skies. During the fighting on the upper Naktong River in mid-August, almost 100 of Stratemeyer's heavy bombers, under MacArthur's orders, carpet-bombed a twenty-seven-square-mile area where 40,000 Communist troops were believed to be concentrated, dropping 1,000 tons of bombs in twenty-six minutes. It was the most massive operation of its kind since the Normandy invasion, but the results were inconclusive. Stratemeyer recommended that no similar effort be undertaken in the future except as a measure of desperation.

Following the successful landings at Inchon behind enemy lines in mid-September 1950, MacArthur's forces drove northward toward the Yalu River. During the advance, Chinese armies, beginning in mid-October, moved into North Korea on MacArthur's left flank, escaping detection by American air reconnaissance through expert camouflage, bad weather, and cover of darkness. MacArthur's final offensive in late November was halted, and United Nations forces retreated pell-mell southward across the thirty-eighth parallel, suffering very heavy losses.

A major threat posed by China's entry into the war was the Soviet swept-wing jet fighter, the MIG-15, which in 1950 and 1951 was supplied to China in unprecedented numbers. It quickly proved superior to all its American counterparts except the F-86 (Sabre). Operating from bases just across the Yalu in Manchuria and later south of it as well, the MIG's challenged American air superiority over northwestern Korea, especially in "MIG Alley" along the Yalu north of the Chongchon River. For several weeks after the long retreat south, Stratemeyer's Sabres were based too far away to escort bombing missions to the far north. Through superior pilot skill, tactics, and coordination, however, FEAF was able to check the buildup of Chinese air power over North Korea, so that Communist ground offensives in May and June received little help from the air. Stratemeyer's air forces were, however, unsuccessful in their efforts to cripple the superb Chinese logistical support system.

Stratemeyer was not involved in the dispute over war strategy that led to MacArthur's dismissal by President Truman in April 1951. He was, however, intensely loyal to MacArthur, whom he regarded as one of history's greatest commanders, and he believed MacArthur's recall was a capitulation to Communist influences in Washington, D.C. But Stratemeyer never questioned the political authority of the president; in March 1951 he stated in a press release, "A decision to extend [our operations] beyond the confines of Korea is not one that should be made by the field commander." On

May 20, 1951, Stratemeyer suffered a severe heart attack, and the following November retired from military service.

Stratemeyer retained some bitter memories of Korea. "We were required to lose the war," he told the Senate Subcommittee on Internal Security in 1954. An ardent anti-Communist, he also served that year as chairman of Ten Million Americans Mobilizing for Justice, a group formed to oppose the censure of Senator Joseph R. McCarthy. Stratemeyer died in Orlando, Fla.

[See Wesley F. Craven and James L. Cate, eds., *The Army Air Forces in World War II*, IV (1950) and V (1953); Charles F. Romanus and Riley Sunderland, volumes on China-Burma-India (1953, 1956, and 1959) in Kent R. Greenfield, gen. ed., *U.S. Army in World War II;* and Robert F. Futrell, *The United States Air Force in Korea: 1950–1953* (1983). An obituary is in the *New York Times*, Aug. 11, 1969.]

RICHARD N. LEIGHTON

STRONG, ANNA LOUISE (Nov. 24, 1885–Mar. 29, 1970), radical journalist and lecturer, was born in Friend, Nebr., the daughter of Sydney Dix Strong, a Congregational clergyman, and Ruth Maria Tracy. Strong was able to read and write by four and to write verse by six. In 1887 the family moved to Mt. Vernon, Ohio, and in 1891, to Cincinnati, where she attended public and then private schools. She completed elementary school at eleven, when the family moved to Oak Park, Ill. There she attended high school for four years, graduating in 1900. On trips to Europe in 1897 and 1898, she acquired a modest fluency in French. Because of schooling abroad, she entered Oberlin in 1902 as a sophomore. After a year she transferred to Bryn Mawr. In 1904 she returned to Oberlin and received her B.A. the following June, graduating magna cum laude and Phi Beta Kappa.

Strong's first job, which lasted seven months, was as an all-purpose writer on the *Advance*, a Protestant weekly in Chicago. In April 1906 she entered the University of Chicago graduate school. After the death of Strong's mother, her father moved to Seattle, leaving Strong alone for the first time. She then experienced the workers' world for the first time by getting a job in a fruit and vegetable canning plant in Chicago and by taking part in the work of Jane Addams' Hull House. Addams became her role model even as she was enjoying academic success that culminated in a Ph.D. Strong's dissertation is entitled "A Consideration of Prayer from the Standpoint of Social Psychology."

Strong, who then considered herself a social activist and writer, moved to New York City in 1909 and got a job through Florence Kelley, a socialist, with Luther Gulick, the head of the Russell Sage Foundation's Child Hygiene Department. Strong's circle of radical and bohemian friends widened to include most of the city's left-wing intellectuals. She soon left to join the National Child Labor Committee, for which she organized several traveling exhibits. After a brief trip to Ireland (1913) to organize a child welfare exhibit, Strong worked for the United States Children's Bureau and again for the Child Labor Committee before resigning in 1916 to live with her father in Seattle.

Seattle, then one of the country's most progressive cities, proved ideal for Strong's talents. She was quickly elected to the school board and made friends with unionists and members of the Industrial Workers of the World (IWW, or "Wobblies"). For the *New York Post*, Strong reported the 1917 murder trial of Wobbly leaders that resulted from the Everett, Wash., "Bloody Sunday" in November 1916, in which eleven Wobblies and two deputies were killed by police at a free-speech rally. During World War I she was active in the anticonscription movement, and United States entry into the European war sealed her disaffection with the American political system.

Strong began to write for the IWW's *Seattle Daily Call* and to defend a woman friend who had circulated an antidraft pamphlet. As a result, Strong was recalled from the school board by a narrow margin in 1918. When a gang of "patriotic" thugs destroyed the *Call*'s presses, Strong wrote for the *Seattle Union Record*, a weekly (soon a daily) run by the Seattle branch of the American Federation of Labor. In it she printed Lenin's speech to the 1918 Congress of Soviets, the only American journalist to do so. At the time, worsening labor relations in the shipyards led to a general strike in February 1919, for which Strong was an ardent propagandist and reporter. When the strike failed after a few days, she arranged through Lincoln Steffens to visit the Soviet Union, doing publicity for the American

Friends Service Committee, then engaged in relief work.

In 1921, with press credentials, including one from *Hearst's International* magazine, then a prestigious organ, Strong traveled via Germany to Moscow to report on the Soviet famine. This was the start of Strong's long and close relationship with the Soviet Union. In her initial stay, which lasted until 1923, she met Leon Trotsky and other leading Soviet figures, and wrote about them for *Hearst's* and other American periodicals. She then returned to the United States and lectured across the country.

In the fall of 1925, Strong made her first visit to China. She fell "in love" with Beijing and traveled to other cities in the strife-torn country. Again in the United States, she lectured and wrote about both China and the Soviet Union, to which she was now wholly committed, though not a member of the Communist party.

In 1927, Strong witnessed the bloody battles between the Kuomintang and the Communists, escaping with Mikhail Borodin, the Soviet adviser, by way of Mongolia. She recounted these events in *China's Millions* (1928). In Moscow in late 1927, she prudently sided with Stalin in his climactic struggle with Trotsky, yet, like many other foreigners, she was isolated from Soviet society, and her friendships were confined to such American correspondents as Walter Duranty, Vincent Sheean, and Eugene Lyons. Shortly, however, she resumed her Soviet travels, venturing to Central Asia, before returning to the United States. A further Soviet trip took her to the Pamirs; on one to the Ukraine she studied farm collectivization, which she defended in *The Soviets Conquer Wheat* (1931). In 1930, Strong became founding editor of the *Moscow Daily News*, an English-language paper designed specifically for Americans working in the Soviet Union but more generally for anyone seeking information about developments there. Strong, never notable for a calm temper, often railed against the bureaucracy the paper faced. A Russian to whom she turned for advice, Joel Shubin, became her husband in 1931. After many crises, the paper folded in 1946. Meantime, Strong had written an autobiography, *I Change Worlds: The Remaking of an American* (1935), which became a best-seller.

Strong attended, and wrote about, the Moscow purge trials of 1936, but held her tongue, explaining to a friend in 1950, "I told no lies, but I didn't tell all the truth." In mid-1940 she left Moscow for the United States via China, interviewing Chou En-lai and Chiang Kai-shek en route. She spent the war years in the United States restively lecturing, writing, and trying to return to Moscow; in 1942 she was badly shaken by her husband's death. Finally, in 1944, despite opposition from the Federal Bureau of Investigation, she managed to go back to Moscow. She returned once more to the United States to lecture in 1946. She then went to China, where, in Yenan, Mao Tse-tung told her in a notable interview that "American reactionaries are merely a paper tiger." Her reportage from Yenan was widely published in the United States, and its tone reflected Strong's mounting enchantment with the Chinese Communists. Typically, she recited her experiences in a book, *Dawn Over China* (1948).

Strong's relationship with Moscow, never smooth, rapidly worsened in 1948. In February 1949 she was arrested and expelled "for spying activities." That action was publicly reversed in 1955, and two years later she obtained a passport from a reluctant United States and went by way of Moscow to China. She lived there the remainder of her life, much cosseted by the Chinese leaders. Her chief activity was in writing *Letters from China*, seventy newsletters that appeared from 1961 to 1970, reporting on events in China and constituting one of the few reasonably reliable sources of information for its 40,000 English-speaking readers.

A middle-class utopian, Strong strove through her prolific writing to persuade Americans of the human potential for a socialist society. Her powerful journalism depicted Soviet and Chinese life with enthusiasm, if not total fidelity. She died in Beijing and was buried there.

[Major collections of Strong's papers are in the archives of the Beijing Library and the Suzzallo Library, University of Washington, Seattle, Washington. The Hoover Library at Stanford University holds a good collection of her published material. *I Change Worlds*, Strong's autobiography, is not entirely reliable. A biography is Tracy B. Strong and Helene Keyssar, *Right in Her Soul* (1984), which contains a bibliography of Strong's principal writings and a full listing of available secondary sources. An obituary is in the *New York Times*, Mar. 30, 1970.]

ALDEN WHITMAN

SULZBERGER, ARTHUR HAYS (Sept. 12, 1891–Dec. 11, 1968), newspaper publisher, was born in New York City, the son of Cyrus Lindauer Sulzberger, a well-to-do importer, and Rachel Peixotto Hays. Sulzberger attended New York City public schools and the Horace Mann School and in 1909 entered Columbia University to study engineering. After receiving a B.S. in 1913, he worked at N. Erlanger, Blumgart and Company, the textile manufacturing and importing firm of which his father was president and later chairman of the board. In 1917, Sulzberger was commissioned a second lieutenant in the Army Reserve and trained as an artillery officer. He married Iphigene Bertha Ochs, the daughter of the *New York Times* publisher Adolph S. Ochs, on Nov. 17, 1917; they had four children.

In later years, Sulzberger often remarked that his "system" for getting to be publisher of a great newspaper was this: "You work very hard, you never watch the clock, you polish up the handle of the big front door. And you marry the boss's daughter." This bothered his wife, who wrote that "the success Arthur made of himself at the *Times* was wholly his own."

Sulzberger's work at the *Times* began in December 1918, shortly after his discharge from the army. He was given the title assistant to the executive manager, with unspecified duties. It was suggested he take on whatever came his way. Sulzberger used this as an opportunity to familiarize himself with all phases of the business. By the late 1920's, he had worked his way up to a vice-presidency.

Sulzberger's role in managing the newspaper grew in the 1930's as Adolph Ochs's health deteriorated. When Ochs died on Apr. 8, 1935, he left controlling interest in the *Times* in trust to Sulzberger's children, with Iphigene and Arthur Sulzberger and Julius Ochs Adler, Ochs's nephew, as trustees and executors of the estate. They chose Sulzberger to succeed Ochs, and on May 7, 1935, the company's board of directors elected Sulzberger president of the company and publisher of the newspaper. Taking note of his new position, *Literary Digest* commented that his acquaintances "characterize him as possessing an unusual sense of humor and an excellent ability to relax. He combines a gift for writing light verse with an aptitude for poker."

On May 8, 1935, in an editorial-page statement, Sulzberger wrote that he prayed "that I may never depart from the principles of honest and impersonal journalism which [Ochs], with such force and courage, impressed upon our land." He pledged himself to Ochs's commitment "to give the news impartially, without fear or favor."

In speeches and articles, Sulzberger often emphasized the importance in a democracy of responsible, accurate, and impartial journalism and the journalist's obligation to present news honestly, fully, and intelligently. Later, he called for more interpretation in the news to supplement the factual report. In 1945 he stated that the newspaper's "chief responsibility lies in reporting accurately that which happens. Whichever way the cat should jump, we should record it, and we should not allow our excitement about the direction which it takes, or plans to take, to interfere with our primary mission."

His commitment to the ideal of impartiality in news presentation moved him vigorously to oppose a closed union shop for news and editorial employees and to bar Communist-party members from employment in what he considered sensitive departments of the newspaper. Sulzberger masked his own expressions of opinion in letters to the editor by using the pseudonym A. Aitchess (A.H.S.).

When he took over as publisher, Sulzberger decided major changes at the *Times* would be put off for at least a year because he did not want it thought he had been waiting until Ochs died to make changes. Under Sulzberger's leadership, the *Times* experienced gradual and steady change and improvement in news coverage and newspaper content, continued financial strength, and technical progress. He expanded the newspaper's production facilities, purchased radio station WQXR in New York in 1944, and created an international edition in 1949. In April 1958 the company issued its first annual public statement of finances. It showed a profit for the sixtieth consecutive year. In his twenty-five years as publisher (1935–1961), the number of *Times* employees more than doubled; advertising linage more than tripled; daily circulation increased by 40 percent, and Sunday circulation nearly doubled; and gross income increased by about $100 million.

During World War II, Sulzberger decided to provide comprehensive war coverage by restricting advertising and thereby making sufficient space available for news in a time of newsprint restriction. This temporary loss of advertising revenue was offset after the war when circulation, which had grown during the war, continued to climb as advertising revenue came back and increased.

As publisher, Sulzberger delegated authority but paid close attention to details. He defined his role as working in harmony with carefully chosen associates, "talking things out and, on occasion, being willing to give way rather than to give orders." Turner Catledge, the executive editor under Sulzberger, described him as "extremely urbane, self-confident, and intelligent, one of the easiest men to deal with I've ever known." After his death, the *Times* wrote of Sulzberger that "the square set of his shoulders and his trim physique" conveyed the impression that he was "a tall and dominating man, although he was of average height—5 feet, 9 inches."

In November 1957 in Burma, while traveling around the world with his wife, Sulzberger suffered the first of a series of strokes that increasingly invalided him during the last eleven years of his life. He retired as publisher on Apr. 25, 1961, and was succeeded by Orvil E. Dryfoos, the husband of his eldest daughter, Marian. Dryfoos, who had apprenticed under Sulzberger as Sulzberger had under Ochs, had been named president of the company in April 1957. On June 20, 1963, Sulzberger's son, Arthur Ochs Sulzberger, was named publisher after Dryfoos died following the strain of a newspaper strike that lasted from December 1962 to March 1963. The elder Sulzberger remained as chairman of the board. He died in New York City, four days after having marked his fiftieth anniversary at the *Times*.

[Sulzberger's papers are in the *New York Times* archives. Issues of the *Times* from 1935 through 1968 contain many articles chronicling Sulzberger's activities, including his speeches, most of which are reported at length. See also "Sulzberger Heads the Times," *Literary Digest*, May 18, 1935; Meyer Berger, *The Story of the New York Times, 1851–1951* (1951); Charles Merz, "An Appreciation: Arthur Hays Sulzberger," *New York Times*, Dec. 13, 1968; Brooks Atkinson, "Arthur Hays Sulzberger," *New York Times*, Dec. 15, 1968; Gay Talese, *The Kingdom and the Power* (1969); Turner Catledge, *My Life and the Times* (1971); Harrison Salisbury, *Without Fear or Favor* (1980); and Iphigene Ochs Sulzberger, *Iphigene* (1981), written with Susan W. Dryfoos. Obituaries are in the *New York Times* and the *Times* of London, both Dec. 12, 1968; and *Newsweek*, Dec. 23, 1968.]

RONALD S. MARMARELLI

SUTHERLAND, RICHARD KERENS (Nov. 27, 1893–June 25, 1966), army officer, was born in Hancock, Md., the son of Howard Sutherland, later United States senator from West Virginia, and Effie Harris. After graduating from high school in Elkins, W.Va., in 1912, he entered Yale University, earning a B.A. in 1916. That summer he served on the Mexican border in a federalized National Guard unit. In November he became a second lieutenant of infantry in the regular army. During the ensuing thirteen months, he first studied at the Army Service Schools in Fort Leavenworth, Kans., and then was in the Eleventh Infantry Regiment at posts in Arizona and Georgia; he gained his first company command and promotions to first lieutenant and captain.

Sutherland joined the Second Infantry Division in France in January 1918 and subsequently saw action in several sectors, including Château-Thierry. After the Armistice he was in the Rhine occupation. He returned to the United States in July 1919, and on October 1 he married Josephine Whiteside; they had one child.

His tours of duty from 1919 to 1937 included various school, troop, and staff assignments. He graduated from the advanced course of the Infantry School in Fort Benning, Ga. (1923); the Command and General Staff School at Fort Leavenworth (1928); the École Supérieure de Guerre in Paris (1930); and the Army War College in Washington, D.C. (1933). He served with the Sixty-third and Twenty-ninth Infantry regiments in New York and Georgia; on the Infantry School faculty; and on the War Department General Staff during General Douglas MacArthur's final three years as army chief of staff.

Sutherland took command of a battalion of the Fifteenth Infantry Regiment at Tientsin, China, four days prior to the outbreak of the Sino-Japanese War in July 1937. Although not attacked by the Japanese army that soon captured Beijing and Tientsin, the Fifteenth Infantry faced months of high tension.

In March 1938, Sutherland was promoted to major and assigned to the Manila staff of MacArthur, military adviser to the Philippine Commonwealth since late 1935. At first, his job was advising the fledgling Philippine army on procurement and budgetary matters. Inadequate funding by the American and Philippine governments had sorely handicapped MacArthur's development of Filipino defense forces. Sutherland demonstrated unusual efficiency and drive, prompting MacArthur to remark that autumn, "Concise, energetic, and able, he has been invaluable." Promoted to lieutenant colonel in mid-1938, he became MacArthur's chief of staff in December 1939, when Lieutenant Colonel Dwight D. Eisenhower was transferred to the United States.

With Japanese relations worsening, President Franklin D. Roosevelt appointed MacArthur as commander of United States Army Forces, Far East (USAFFE), in July 1941. MacArthur, in turn, selected Sutherland as USAFFE chief of staff with the rank of brigadier general (major general in December).

USAFFE headquarters knew of the Pearl Harbor attack nine hours before Japanese aircraft hit Iba and Clark fields on Luzon, destroying most American bombers and fighters there. Major General Lewis H. Brereton, MacArthur's air commander, later blamed Sutherland for the situation that produced the destruction of so many planes on the ground. But the USAFFE chief of staff countered that Brereton was at fault. The controversy remains unsettled, for no official investigation of the fiasco was made.

From late December 1941 onward, MacArthur's headquarters was located on Corregidor Island at the mouth of Manila Bay. As the Japanese invaders pushed the American and Filipino troops down Bataan Peninsula, Corregidor came under mounting air and artillery bombardment. Sutherland performed well under the intense pressure, capably overseeing staff activities, advising MacArthur, and acting as liaison between him and senior field officers. He was awarded a number of decorations for his conduct under combat conditions during the Bataan-Corregidor operations as well as in other situations under fire later in the war against Japan. When MacArthur finally obeyed Roosevelt's order to leave Corregidor, Sutherland was one of the fifteen army officers that he took with him to Australia in March 1942.

MacArthur became commander of a new Allied theater that April, the Southwest Pacific Area (SWPA), and he promptly announced Sutherland as the SWPA chief of staff. In the next few months at Melbourne and later Brisbane, Sutherland developed a new headquarters organization to prepare for beginning offensive operations in New Guinea. As he had sent him to the front on Bataan earlier, MacArthur sometimes dispatched Sutherland to consult combat commanders during the bloody Papuan campaign of July 1942–January 1943. For Sutherland, the half year following the conquest of Papua was a busy time of staff expansion and coordinating the rapid buildup of SWPA forces. That spring he represented the USAFFE commander at a Pacific strategy conference in Washington with the Joint Chiefs of Staff and with representatives from the other Pacific theater headquarters (Pearl Harbor and Noumea). Sutherland forcefully but futilely presented MacArthur's case for higher priority on SWPA operations and against opening a Central Pacific offensive.

By February 1944, when Sutherland became a lieutenant general, SWPA forces had taken Northeast New Guinea, the Admiralties, and part of New Britain. In the next seven months they would conquer Netherlands New Guinea and Morotai, advancing above the equator. Sutherland moved to Hollandia on the Dutch New Guinea coast to set up advance headquarters in April. That spring, too, he returned to Washington for another conference on future Pacific strategy; he defended MacArthur's plans strongly, if not always tactfully.

When MacArthur's forces secured the northeast coast of Leyte in the Philippines in October 1944, he told Sutherland to establish advance SWPA headquarters there, at Tacloban. He and Sutherland were nearly hit on several occasions during heavy Japanese air raids on Tacloban. Long regarded as the SWPA commander's principal confidant, Sutherland had an angry clash with him at Tacloban, and the two men were never close again.

In March 1945, Sutherland moved on to battle-devastated Manila, where SWPA headquarters was to be set up. He continued to display skill in planning and organizing but had lost much of his earlier dynamism. Nonetheless, MacArthur chose him as chief of staff for both of his new commands in the spring and summer of 1945—United States Army Forces, Pacific (USAFPAC), and Supreme Commander for the Allied Powers, Japan (SCAP). Sutherland had conspicuous roles at the Japanese surrender ceremony aboard the USS *Missouri* in Tokyo Bay and later at Tokyo headquarters in administering nonmilitary and military activities of the occupation. Faced with declining health, however, he obtained a transfer to the United States in December 1945 and retired in 1946 after a short stint at the headquarters of Army Ground Forces in Washington.

Following his first wife's death, he married Mrs. Virginia (Shaw) Root in 1962. He died in Washington and was buried at Arlington National Cemetery.

[Sutherland's official records and personal papers are located mainly in the National Archives, though some items are in the MacArthur Memorial Archives in Norfolk, Va. See Charles A. Willoughby and John Chamberlain, *MacArthur: 1941–1951* (1954); Courtney Whitney, *MacArthur: His Rendezvous with History* (1956); Louis Morton, *Strategy and Command* (1962); Douglas MacArthur, *Reminiscences* (1964); D. Clayton James, *The Years of MacArthur*, 3 vols. (1970–1985); Carol M. Petillo, *Douglas MacArthur: The Philippine Years* (1981); and Roger O. Egeberg, *The General* (1983). An obituary is in the *New York Times*, June 26, 1966.]

D. CLAYTON JAMES

SWING, RAYMOND EDWARDS (GRAM) (Mar. 25, 1887–Dec. 22, 1968), foreign correspondent and news commentator, was born in Cortland, N.Y., the son of Albert Temple Swing, a Congregationalist minister, and Alice Edwards Mead, the daughter of Elizabeth Storrs Mead, the first president of Mount Holyoke College. After Swing's father served several pastorates, in 1893 the family settled at Oberlin College in Ohio, where his father taught church history and his mother taught German. In this academic milieu, with its intellectual table talk, Raymond was reared under a strict discipline, which he broke frequently. He seemed destined for the ministry or for teaching, but when he entered Oberlin in 1904, he did not do well in his studies and was suspended after his first year. He was, however, influenced by Oberlin's social radicalism.

After leaving Oberlin, Swing tried a variety of stopgap jobs, and then, in 1906, he found his vocation when he became a cub reporter for the *Cleveland Press*. At that time American journalism was developing a new sense of public obligation, which took the form of "muckraking" examinations of political corruption and corporate misbehavior. Swing spent the next six years working for newspapers in Ohio and Indiana, and during this period frequently visited an uncle, George Herbert Mead, who was a University of Chicago professor of social psychology, a close friend of John Dewey, and an associate of Jane Addams. These acquaintances nourished his liberalism to the extent that during an interval between jobs in Indianapolis and Cincinnati, Swing did social work on Chicago's West Side. He married Suzanne Morin, a student from France, on July 9, 1912; they had two children.

When Swing married, his uncle gave the couple the wedding gift of a year in Europe, and while in Berlin, Swing became a foreign correspondent, joining the overseas service of the *Chicago Daily News*. When the outbreak of World War I transformed the lackadaisical foreign bureaus of American newspapers into vital informational outposts, Swing remained in Berlin, where he amply proved his journalistic aptitude. But his French-born wife was unhappy in a country at war with her own and returned to the United States, ending the marriage in 1915. Swing continued to report the war from Berlin but also toured Turkey and the Balkans, witnessing naval actions in the Dardanelles and visiting the trenches of Gallipoli. Upon American entry into the war, he returned home to serve with the War Labor Board in Washington.

After the war Swing wrote briefly for the liberal *Nation*, but he craved to return to Europe and so, in 1919, became correspondent for the *New York Herald* in Berlin. It was a time of volatile and violent politics, with rival extremist groups, inflation, strikes, and intense diplomatic and trade activity by the new and revolutionary Soviet Union, which, during six years of foreign and civil war, had barred foreign correspondents. But, in 1921, in anticipation of the American relief mission, Moscow finally allowed newsmen entry, and Swing was one of them.

Swing's vivid dispatches about the Volga famine and the Moscow of Lenin and Trotsky were not printed, since the *Herald*, like the United States government, preferred not to recognize the existence of the Bolshevik state, presumably believing that anything that was not in the *Herald* was not true. Swing's dissatisfaction with the paper was compounded at the Genoa Conference of 1922, from which Germany and Russia, the twin pariahs of Europe, adjourned to nearby Rapallo to sign a treaty of cooperation. The paper assigned him a collaborator to cover the Russian delegation, causing Swing to believe the *Herald* did not trust his objectivity. He therefore resigned to become London correspondent for the *Wall Street Journal*. On Jan. 10, 1920, he remarried, acquiring an additional name in the process: Betty Gram, a music student and ardent feminist from Oregon, intended to retain her maiden name after their marriage but agreed to the compromise of the use of both names by both parties. His byline became Raymond Gram Swing and so remained, in print and on the air, until they were divorced in 1942. (They had three children.)

In 1924, Swing joined the foreign-news service of the *Philadelphia Public Ledger* and the *New York Post*. The ensuing ten years in London found him in his element, reporting on Britain's first Labour government and the complex problems of Europe between the wars. He was also heard frequently on discussion and interview programs of the British Broadcasting Corporation (BBC). After the death in 1933 of the publisher Cyrus H. K. Curtis, the *Ledger-Post* service was discontinued and, with it, Swing's overseas tenure.

Back in Washington, Swing wrote for the *Nation* again and reported for the *London News-Chronicle* and Britain's weekly *Economist*. In 1935 he also took up the newest journalistic craft, becoming the American end of a weekly exchange of broadcasts with Britain undertaken by the BBC. These commentaries continued for ten years. Transmitted by shortwave, they made Swing's voice familiar around the world. During World War II the British-American exchange became one between two Americans, Swing and his London-based friend Edward R. Murrow of the Columbia Broadcasting System.

In 1936, Swing also began nightly commentaries on American networks—first, for the Mutual Broadcasting System and, later, for the National Broadcasting Company and the American Broadcasting Company. In his prewar broadcasts, he condemned the appeasement of Hitler, and long before Pearl Harbor he criticized American isolationism. A supporter of Wilson and a believer in "one world," he was said to be the Roosevelt administration's "favorite newscaster." On the air he spoke slowly, distinctly, and calmly, in a whispery voice. His broadcasts were intended as rational evaluations of events and situations but often sounded like sermons. One critic called him "a hair-shirt character." His radio style went with the man himself, for he was tall, stooped, scholarly in appearance, and reserved in manner. He was usually ranked in opinion polls among the most respected in a galaxy of commentators that included Murrow, H. V. Kaltenborn, Elmer Davis, and Quincy Howe. By the time the war ended, Swing was being heard on 120 stations. He had also been married again—on Jan. 3, 1945, to Mary S. Hartshorne—and had become active in the World Federalist movement.

Against the rising tide of anti-Soviet feeling in cold-war America, Swing supported "peaceful coexistence" between the two great powers and, for this, was widely criticized. Swing publicly and vigorously opposed the detractors as themselves "un-American."

He stopped his commercial broadcasting in 1951 to become the first political commentator for the government-operated Voice of America; but its restriction to narrow policy lines and Senator Joseph R. McCarthy's assault on it, during which Swing was among those interrogated by a Senate committee, impelled him to resign, though he had been exonerated and reconfirmed. He then joined Murrow in the writing of the latter's daily radio commentaries. The partnership lasted six years, until 1959, when Murrow began a final sabbatical and Swing returned to the Voice, which had been moved from the State Department to the less restrictive United States Information Agency (USIA). Voice management passed into Murrow's hands when he became USIA director in 1961, and the two men were together once more, though both were failing in health. In 1957, Swing married Meisung Euyang Loh, a coworker at the Voice. He retired at the end of 1963, when Murrow was also resigning. He died in Washington.

[Swing's papers, including typescripts of broadcasts, published articles, lectures, and some letters, are in the Manuscript Division of the Library of Congress. In the Library's Music Division are numerous recordings of broadcasts. Scores of broadcasts are also included in three of his books, *How War Came* (1939), *Preview of History* (1943), and *In the Name of Sanity* (1946). His other books are *Forerunners of American Fascism* (1935) and *Good Evening! A Professional Memoir* (1964). See also David Holbrook Culbert, *News for Everyman* (1976); and Irving E. Fang, *Those Radio Commentators!* (1977).

Obituaries are in the *New York Times* and the *Washington Post*, both Dec. 24, 1968.]

ALEXANDER KENDRICK

SZELL, GEORGE (June 7, 1897–July 30, 1970), orchestra conductor, was born in Budapest, Austria-Hungary, the son of Georg Charles Szell, a lawyer and businessman, and Margarethe Harmat. He displayed a remarkable ear for music at an early age and at six commenced formal piano study with Richard Robert in Vienna. In 1908, Szell made his public debut as pianist and composer in a concert with the Vienna Tonkünstler Orchestra, during which he performed several compositions, including his own Rondo for Piano and Orchestra. An immediate success, Szell next played in Dresden and in London, where the *Daily Mail* referred to him as "the new Mozart." His parents, however, refused to exploit him as a prodigy. Instead, they withdrew him from the stage so that he could study theory and composition with Josef Foerster, Eusebius Mandyczewski, and Max Reger.

In 1913, Szell conducted for the first time at a concert of the Vienna Konzertvereins-Orchester in Bad Kissingen. Exhilarated by this experience, Szell decided upon a conducting career. In 1914 he appeared with the Berlin Philharmonic Orchestra as piano soloist in Beethoven's *Emperor* Concerto and as conductor of Richard Strauss's *Till Eulenspiegels lustige Streiche* and a symphonic work of his own. Strauss was so impressed with Szell's musicianship that he engaged him as an assistant conductor and coach at the Berlin Royal Opera. From 1915 to 1917, Szell performed a variety of duties under Strauss's tutelage. He received no pay for his labor, but the learning experience was invaluable.

Upon Strauss's recommendation, Szell was signed to a five-year contract in 1917 as principal conductor of the Municipal Theater in Strassburg. A year later, however, French troops occupied the city and the theater closed. After intermittent engagements as guest conductor and concert pianist, Szell served from 1919 to 1921 as an assistant conductor of the German Opera in Prague. In 1920 he married Olga Band; they divorced in 1926.

In 1921–1922, Szell was principal conductor of the Darmstadt Court Theater, and from 1922 to 1924, principal conductor of the Municipal Theater in Düsseldorf. From 1924 to 1929, he was principal conductor of the Berlin State Opera under Generalmusikdirektor Erich Kleiber. Concurrently, he conducted the Berlin Radio Orchestra and taught at the Berlin Hochschule für Musik.

From 1929 to 1937, Szell resided in Prague as music director of the German Opera House, conducted Philharmonic concerts, and was professor at the Academy of Music and Dramatic Arts. During this period, he enhanced his musical reputation with numerous guest-conducting appearances throughout Europe, as well as his first American concert (Jan. 24, 1930, with the St. Louis Symphony Orchestra).

Alarmed in 1937 by Germany's militant aggressiveness, Szell hastened to Western Europe. From 1937 to 1939 he was simultaneously principal conductor of the Scottish Orchestra in Glasgow and conductor of the Residentie Orchestra in The Hague. On Jan. 25, 1938, he married Helene Schulz; they had no children.

During the summers of 1938 and 1939, Szell journeyed to Australia to conduct the Celebrity Concerts of the Australian Broadcasting Commission. While returning to Europe in September 1939, Szell received word in New York that the Scottish Orchestra had been disbanded because of the outbreak of World War II. Stranded in America and unable to find a full-time conducting post, Szell obtained employment as a teacher of composition at the Mannes School of Music and as director of an opera workshop at the New School for Social Research, both in New York City.

Appearances as conductor with Toscanini's NBC Symphony Orchestra in 1941 and early 1942 focused national attention upon Szell and produced several guest-conducting offers. On Dec. 9, 1942, Szell made his debut with the Metropolitan Opera, conducting a highly acclaimed performance of *Salome*. Szell remained with the Met until 1946 and returned for three performances of *Tannhäuser* during the 1953–1954 season. In all, he conducted there twelve operas a total of eighty-seven times. He specialized in Wagner and Strauss, but he also conducted Mussorgsky's *Boris Godunov*, Mozart's *Don Giovanni*, and Verdi's *Otello*.

Szell's first appearance with the New York Philharmonic (1943) marked the beginning of a fruitful twenty-seven-year association. (In 1969–1970 he served as its senior adviser and guest conductor.) Guest-conducting appearances with the Cleveland Orchestra in 1944 and 1945 led to Szell's appointment as music director of that organization in 1946, the year he became an American citizen. At the time of his engagement, Szell told the orchestra board that if given the necessary power, he would "make the orchestra second to none and establish Cleveland as one of the symphony capitals of the world."

Assured that full support would be forthcoming, Szell replaced recalcitrant and lethargic players, obtained the best available musicians for the first-chair positions, and expanded the orchestra to over 100 pieces. Furthermore, Szell demanded total concentration and commitment from his players. At rehearsals, which were as exhausting as concerts, Szell dissected each composition. He labored to produce a controlled orchestral sound based upon rhythmic integrity, a chamber-music cohesiveness within and among the sections of the orchestra, and, above all, a faithful adherence to the composer's text. His credo was, "Honesty and integrity in performance are matters of artistic morality."

During the 1950's, Szell's reputation and that of the Cleveland Orchestra grew apace as regional tours, phonograph records, and weekly radio broadcasts revealed the Cleveland sound to enthusiastic listeners. During the summer of 1957 the Cleveland Orchestra toured Europe and was acclaimed as one of the world's premier ensembles. From 1958 on, New York concerts evoked comparable accolades.

In the 1950's and 1960's, Szell guest-conducted regularly in Europe, including appearances at the Edinburgh, Lucerne, and Salzburg festivals and at La Scala and the Vienna State Opera. He served as co-conductor of the Amsterdam Concertgebouw Orchestra in 1958–1961. He took the Cleveland Orchestra to Europe during the summers of 1965 and 1967 and to the Orient in 1970.

Szell was a commanding figure on the podium. Nearly six feet tall, broad-shouldered and stern, he exuded confidence and authority. Eschewing exaggerated theatrical gestures, he conducted with short, concise beats and rapier-like thrusts, a style patterned on that of Richard Strauss. His memory was phenomenal, and he usually conducted without a score.

Szell admired most the Germanic composers of the classical and romantic periods, especially the works of Haydn, Mozart, Beethoven, Schubert, Schumann, Brahms, Mahler, and Strauss. These, too, were the composers he most frequently recorded (usually for Columbia or its Epic affiliate) in both Europe and America. He found much of extremely modern music "boring" and frequently delegated its performance to his associate or guest conductors.

A man of keen intellect and curiosity who read widely, Szell was well versed on a variety of subjects. For diversion, he enjoyed preparing ethnic cuisine and playing golf. But his consummate passion was music: "It is my conviction that to accomplish greatness one must love music more than oneself." He died in Cleveland.

[On Szell's life and work, see *High Fidelity*, Jan. 1965; *New Yorker*, Nov. 6, 1965; Robert C. Marsh, *The Cleveland Orchestra* (1967); *Saturday Review of Literature*, Aug. 29, 1970; David Ewen, ed., *Musicians Since 1900* (1978); and John L. Holmes, *Conductors on Record* (1982). See also William H. Seltsam, *Metropolitan Opera Annals: A Chronicle of Artists and Performers* (1947) and its *Supplement Number One* (1957); Quaintance Eaton, *Opera Caravan* (1957); Howard Shanet, *Philharmonic: A History of New York's Orchestra* (1975); and Frederick P. Fellers and Betty Meyers, *Discographies of Commercial Recordings of the Cleveland Orchestra and the Cincinnati Symphony Orchestra* (1978). Szell displays his erudition and wit in a recorded interview on Columbia BTS 31, a bonus accompanying Columbia M2-31313; he may also be heard on Epic PBC 1/PLC 1. An obituary is in the *New York Times*, July 31, 1970.]

LOUIS R. THOMAS

TAMIRIS, HELEN (Apr. 23, 1903–Aug. 4, 1966), dancer and choreographer, was born Helen Becker in New York City, the daughter of Isor Becker, a tailor, and Rose Simonoff, who immigrated to the United States in the 1890's. She grew up on New York's Lower East Side, beginning dance lessons at age eight.

Tamiris was trained in two forms of stage dance—the interpretative from Irene Lewisohn at the Henry Street Settlement and the natural from a Duncan descendant at Carnegie Hall. She studied Italian ballet with Rosina Galli and Russian ballet with Michel Fokine. After graduation from high school, she joined the Metropolitan Opera corps de ballet, with which she performed for three seasons. She also performed for one season as second première danseuse with the Bracale Opera Company during its South American tour in 1922–1923; for six months in the last *Music Box Revue*, in 1924–1925; and for one season in the presentations of John Murray Anderson in nightclubs and movie houses during 1925–1926.

During the late 1920's, Tamiris began her revolt against the traditional types of dance. She announced that artists in America, a new civilization, must create new art forms. She chose to present her new art within the open arena of concert dance. American modern dance was growing out of her innovations and those of Martha Graham and of Doris Humphrey, with Charles Weidman, and was aided by the writings of the critic John Martin and the musical forms of the accompanist Louis Horst. Her opening contribution to modern dance was made during 1927–1929 in twenty-seven solo dances for seven concerts—four in New York and three in Europe. She abandoned traditional mimed stories, theatricality, and atmosphere. Her dances were characteristically contemporary American, using jazz in *1927* (1927, with music by George Gershwin); uniquely no accompaniment for *The Queen Walks in the Garden* (1927); contemporary music in *Impressions of the Bull Ring* (1927, Gómez Calleja) and *Twentieth-Century Bacchante* (1928, Louis Gruenberg); and sounds such as the beating of piano strings in *Prize Fight Studies* (1928) and sirens in *Dance of the City* (1929). These dances made bold statements in both theme and accompaniment. They defined in dance, as others were doing in other arts, the dynamic spirit, vigor, speed, verve and motion of American life.

Tamiris, beautiful, splendidly vital, tall and statuesque, with golden hair, electrified her audiences as both dancer and choreographer. She spoke for humanity and democracy in her dances, most eloquently in a repertoire of solos based on "Negro spirituals" (by which term they are collectively known), which had for her an extemporaneous air of freely expressing the feelings of the moment. The theme of the suffering blacks was set to choral singing: "Nobody Knows de Trouble I Seen" and "Joshua Fit de Battle ob Jericho" (1928); "Swing Low, Sweet Chariot" (1929); "Crucifixion" (1931); and "Git on Board Lil Chillen" and "Go Down Moses" (1932).

Tamiris led in the formation of the Dance Repertory Theatre (her contributions were self-accompanied dances), which provided common theatrical support for her and the other modern dancers, but such cooperation among these artists in revolt against all traditional restraints existed for only two brief seasons, 1930 and 1931. In her School of the American Dance, opened in the fall of 1929, Tamiris approached students with a method later infused with ideas from method acting, which emphasized the innate ability of each student to be expressive. Thus, through the years, she developed no identifiable dance technique. Rather, students learned to be creative out of their own resources.

Tamiris formed her Group, for which she created the following New York productions: the joyous song *Walt Whitman Suite*, comprising *Salut au Monde, Song of the Open Road* (first movement), *I Sing the Body Electric, Song of the Open Road* (second movement), and *Halcyon Days* (1934, Genevieve Pitot); the socially conscious manifesto *Cycle of Unrest*, comprising *Protest* (Elie Siegmeister), *The Individual and the Mass* (Hindemith), *Affirmation* (Alexander Mossolov), *Camaraderie* (Siegmeister), and *Conflict* (Henry Brant) (1935); the antiwar dirge *Harvest, 1935*, comprising *Sycophants* (Hindemith), *Middle Ground* (Shostakovich), and *Maneuvers* (Hindemith-Debussy) (1935); and the percussion piece *Momentum*, comprising *Unemployed, SH!—SH—, Legion, Nightriders, Diversion*, and *Disclosure* (Herbert Haufreucht, 1936). In a 1935–1936 Midwest tour by Tamiris and ten dancers, Tamiris disseminated modern dance, now an identifiable dance genre, one that, she said, had the ability to express modern problems and to make audiences want to do something about them.

This sense of mission for dance in large part determined the effectiveness of the Federal Dance Theater of the Works Progress Administration, for which Tamiris choreographed works from 1936 to 1939. A leading figure in the Concert Dancers' League, a supporter of the New Dance League, chair of the American Dance Association, and a member of the Executive Committee of the New York Dance Project, Tamiris pushed dance into the federal project. She choreographed another major work on the plight of blacks, *How Long, Brethren?* (1937, Gellert-Siegmeister Collection), and one on the civil war in Spain, *Adelante* (1939, Pitot). By the time of this last production, the federal project lost funding and ceased to exist.

The onset of World War II canceled any further development of public support of the arts.

In the fall of 1941, Tamiris began a personal relationship with the dancer Daniel Nagrin, and they married on Oct. 6, 1946; they had no children. Success on Broadway came with *Up in Central Park* in 1945 and continued until 1957. She became known as a vital creator, unique in her skill at seeing a musical whole, with all its elements balanced to preserve its integrity. Bringing the drive of her new art to revivify dance in the commercial theater, Tamiris choreographed, staged, and directed dances in eighteen Broadway musicals, many of which had long runs: *Up in Central Park* (1945), which was notable for "The Skating Ballet" and which had national and European productions; *Annie Get Your Gun* (1946), notable for "Wild Horse Ceremonial Dance," danced by Nagrin, with New York City Center, London, and national productions; a new production of *Show Boat* (1946); *Inside U.S.A.* (1948), notable for "Haunted Heart" and "Tiger Lily," with Valerie Bettis as dancer; *Touch and Go* (1948), which was notable for "American Primitive" and "Under the Sleeping Volcano," danced by Nagrin and Pearl Lang, and for which Tamiris received an Antoinette Perry Award; *Fanny* (1954); and *Plain and Fancy* (1955), which was notable for "By Lantern Light" and "On the Midway," featuring Nagrin, and which toured nationally and was also produced in London. Tamiris directed and recreated her dances for the movie version of *Up in Central Park* (1948). She also created dances for the film *Just for You* (1952), with Nagrin as soloist.

Tamiris returned to concert work during the summers of 1957 and 1958 and taught during the summer at the Perry-Mansfield School of Theatre and Dance in Steamboat Springs, Colo., from 1956 to 1958 and at Connecticut College in 1959. The Tamiris-Nagrin Dance Company was formed in 1960 and existed until 1963. The two dancers separated in 1964. Tamiris died in New York City.

[Tamiris' papers are in the Daniel Nagrin Collection in Tempe, Ariz., and the Dance Collection of the New York Public Library at Lincoln Center. See Louis Horst, "Tamiris," *Dance Observer*, Apr. 1934; Margaret Lloyd, *The Borzoi Book of Modern Dance* (1949); and Christena L. Schlundt, *Tamiris: A Chronicle of Her Dance Career, 1927–1955* (1972). A seventeen-minute film, *Helen Tamiris in Her "Negro Spirituals"* (1958), was produced by William Skipper Corp. An obituary is in the *New York Times*, Aug. 5, 1966.]

CHRISTENA L. SCHLUNDT

TAYLOR, JOSEPH DEEMS (Dec. 22, 1885–July 3, 1966), composer, author, editor, and music critic, was born in New York City, the son of Joseph Schimmel Taylor, superintendent of schools in the Bronx, and Katherine Moore Johnson, a schoolteacher. He received his elementary education at the Ethical Culture School and graduated with a B.A. from New York University in 1906.

He took piano lessons in 1906, but he was largely self-taught. Taylor wrote the music for four comic operas with William Le Baron. *The Echo* was produced on Broadway in 1909 by Charles Dillingham, with the actress Bessie Love. On the advice of Victor Herbert, who was impressed by *The Oracle*, a comic opera, he studied harmony and counterpoint with Oscar Coon, a bandsman of Oswego, N.Y., in 1908–1911.

Taylor's early musical efforts included a library of traditional vocal music that he prepared for the Schumann Club and his friend Percy Rector Stephens, the conductor of the women's choral group. In 1913 he won first place in the National Federation of Music Clubs competition with *The Siren Song*, an orchestral composition. The following year, he contributed a setting for women's voices and orchestra of Alfred Noyes's poem *The Highwayman* to the MacDowell Festival at Petersboro, N.Y. He created one of his most celebrated works, *Through the Looking Glass*, for chamber orchestra in 1917, later arranging it for full orchestra.

Taylor was on the staff of the *Nelson Encyclopedia* in 1906–1907 and moved to the *Encyclopaedia Britannica* the following year. A man with a keen sense of wit, which found expression in his music as well as his writing, he wrote a humorous column for the *New York Press*. He also was an assistant editor of the *New York Tribune* Sunday magazine in 1916, becoming its war correspondent in France in 1916–1917. He was the music critic of the *New York World* (1921–1925), the editor of *Musical America* (1927–1929), and the music critic of the *New York American* (1931–1932).

In 1922, Taylor became interested in writing music for the Broadway theater. For two years he wrote incidental, thematic, and background music for such theatrical works as Molnar's *Liliom* (1921) and George S. Kaufman and Marc Connelly's *Dulcy* (1921) and *Beggar on Horseback* (1924). In 1925 he produced *Jurgen*, a symphonic poem based on James Branch Cabell's novel, and *Circus Day* for jazz orchestra, which was arranged for full orchestra by Ferde Grofé.

Taylor received a commission from the Metropolitan Opera in 1925. He turned to the great lyric poet Edna St. Vincent Millay for the libretto of what became known as *The King's Henchman*. Its premiere on Feb. 17, 1927, was described by the historian John Tasker Howard as "one of the most dazzling." The audience response was so strong that the work had fourteen performances between 1927 and 1929. His opera *Peter Ibbetson*, commissioned by the Met, was based on a novel by George du Maurier. Taylor wrote his own libretto. Although it was not well received by the critics, audiences loved the opera, which the Met performed sixteen times between 1931 and 1935. He wrote two other operas: *Ramuntcho* (1942) and *The Dragon* (1958).

In 1931, Taylor was invited to broadcast a series of radio talks on opera over the National Broadcasting Company, and from 1936 to 1943 he was an intermission commentator for national broadcasts of the New York Philharmonic Orchestra. He was also a regular panelist on the "Information Please" radio program and in 1940 served as the narrator for Walt Disney's *Fantasia*.

Taylor's published writings include *Of Men and Music* (1937), *The Well-Tempered Listener* (1940) and *Music to My Ears* (1949), which were all based on his radio talks, and *Some Enchanted Evenings: The Story of Rodgers and Hammerstein* (1953).

As a composer, Taylor found nothing attractive in twentieth-century avant-garde trends and resisted them, except in the area of orchestration. He said, "The test of music is not the mathematics behind it, but how it sounds. Too many modern composers are trying to make technical innovations take the place of musical ideas." Howard felt that he gained recognition "merely because he [wrote] beautiful music, worthy to rank with the great works of the world."

Taylor was married three times: in 1917 to Jane Anderson, from whom he was divorced after a few years; on July 11, 1921, to Mary Kennedy, from whom he was divorced in 1934; and on Apr. 17, 1945, to Lucille Watson-Little, a costume designer, a marriage that was annulled in 1952. He and Kennedy had one child.

Taylor received honorary degrees from New York University (1927), Dartmouth College (1939), the University of Rochester (1939), the Cincinnati Conservatory of Music (1941), Syracuse University (1944), and Juniata College (1931). He joined the American Society of Composers, Authors, and Publishers (ASCAP) in 1927 and was elected a director in 1933, serving until his death. From 1942 to 1948 he was president of ASCAP. Shortly after his death, the organization established the ASCAP–Deems Taylor Awards, given annually to writers and publishers of outstanding books on music.

[Some of Taylor's memorabilia are in the home of Michael Davis, Columbia, Md., and with a grandson of Taylor's sister. He wrote *Pictorial History of the Movies* (1943) and *The One-Track Mind* (1953). A comprehensive and analytical work is John Tasker Howard, *Deems Taylor* (1927). See also J. F. Porte, "Deems Taylor, an American Hope," *Sackbut*, 9 (1929); Irving Kolodin, *The Metropolitan Opera* (1966); and David Ewen, *Composers Since 1900* (1969). An obituary is in the *New York Times*, July 4, 1966.]

ARNOLD SHAW

TAYLOR, ROBERT (Aug. 5, 1911–June 8, 1969), actor, was born Spangler Arlington Brugh in Filley, Nebr., the only child of Spangler Andrew Brugh and Ruth Adelia Stanhope. Originally a grain dealer, the senior Brugh became a doctor in hopes of improving his wife's heart condition. Their son was a shy, lonely child dominated by his mother's poor health, varying moods, and possessiveness. He somewhat escaped this restrictive atmosphere in high school, where he excelled in tennis and track, won a state oratorical championship, and attracted female attention with his handsome appearance. In 1929 he entered Doane College in nearby Crete, planning to become a doctor. His mother insisted that he continue the cello lessons begun in childhood.

When Taylor's music teacher transferred from Doane to Pomona College in Claremont, Calif., he was permitted to follow. There he joined the undergraduate drama club and appeared in numerous productions. After seeing his portrayal of Captain Stanhope in *Journey's End*, a Metro-Goldwyn-Mayer (MGM) talent scout offered him a contract, which he did not immediately accept. After graduation and his father's death in 1933, his mother suggested that they move permanently to California, where he enrolled in the Neely Dixon Dramatic School in Hollywood. Although he made an unsuccessful MGM screen test, he attracted the attention of Oliver Tinsdell, an MGM drama coach.

In February 1934, Taylor signed a standard seven-year contract with MGM at $35 a week. As did other major studios, MGM freely gave contracts to aspiring actors and actresses in hopes of finding "stars." The studios risked little, because the contracts bound an actor for an extended period but committed the studio to no more than six months, with an option to renew. In Taylor's case, however, the agreement lasted until 1958—a record for a major star to remain with one studio.

Louis B. Mayer, head of MGM—whom Taylor, unlike most of his contemporaries, found "kind, fatherly, understanding, and protective"—arranged for intensive acting lessons and gave him the name Robert Taylor because it sounded "American." He lent Taylor to Fox for a minor role in a Will Rogers vehicle, *Handy Andy* (1934), and gave him a bit part in MGM's *Wicked Woman* (1935) along with other minor roles.

Taylor's opportunity came in 1935, when Universal borrowed him to portray a reformed playboy opposite Irene Dunne in *Magnificent Obsession*. Nearly overnight, he became a star, mobbed by female fans and the recipient of thousands of adoring letters each week. Mayer was quick to take advantage of his new celebrity by pairing him with MGM's leading actresses: Janet Gaynor in *Small Town Girl* (1936), Loretta Young in *Private Number* (1936), Barbara Stanwyck in *His Brother's Wife* (1936), Joan Crawford in *The Gorgeous Hussy* (1936), Greta Garbo in *Camille* (1937), and Jean Harlow in *Personal Property* (1937). Exhibitors voted him the fourth-biggest box-office attraction of 1936.

With his black wavy hair, blue eyes, classically handsome face, and sturdy physique, Taylor fascinated female moviegoers in a manner similar to Rudolph Valentino. Like his predecessor, he was also the object of male disdain and newspaper ridicule that he was a "pretty boy" who lacked virility. In hopes of countering an image that threatened his new star, Mayer gave Taylor the role of a cocky, breezy American who wins a scholarship to an Oxford college in *A Yank at Oxford* (1938). Taylor revealed a hairy chest, swaggered, and even engaged in fistfights. The new, more "masculine" image appealed to both sexes. A series of MGM films followed in which Taylor played soldiers, boxers, or tough guys: *Three Comrades* (1938), *The Crowd Roars* (1938), *Stand Up and Fight* (1939), *Waterloo Bridge* (1940), *Flight Command* (1941), and *Billy the Kid* (1941), his first western. These roles and his marriage to actress Barbara Stanwyck on May 14, 1939, secured the image that MGM wanted.

Taylor contributed to the war effort of the 1940's both in Hollywood and in the armed forces. He starred in two MGM war pictures, *Stand By for Action* and *Bataan* (both 1943); in the latter he gave a realistic portrayal as a hard-bitten sergeant who dies fighting the Japanese. Considered too old for combat duty, Taylor served as a flying instructor in the Naval Air Corps and directed seventeen training films. He narrated *The Fighting Lady* (1944), a documentary about a United States warship, which won an Academy Award.

Questioned in October 1947 by the House Un-American Activities Committee about Communist influence in Hollywood, Taylor complained that the original script of *Song of Russia* (1944), in which he starred, contained numerous pro-Communist references. He testified that a number of Hollywood performers were Communist sympathizers and should be deported to the Soviet Union.

By the late 1940's, Taylor's box-office appeal had waned. MGM executives had some difficulty finding vehicles and suitable leading ladies. They cast him in expensive costume spectaculars in which he played brave heroes who triumph over evil and win beautiful women: *Quo Vadis* (1951) with Deborah Kerr, *Ivanhoe* (1952) with Joan Fontaine and Elizabeth Taylor, *Knights of the Round Table* (1954) with Ava Gardner, and *Quentin Durward* (1955) with Kay Kendall. After leaving MGM in 1958, he formed his own company, Robert Taylor Productions, and appeared in eleven films between 1959 and 1967.

Like others with declining box-office appeal, Taylor turned to television, starring as the captain of an elite squad of New York City plainclothes detectives in "The Detectives" (1959–1961). In September 1966 he signed on as host, narrator, and occasional star of "Death Valley Days."

Taylor's private life was free of scandal, despite involvements with a number of movie actresses. His marriage to Barbara Stanwyck was quietly terminated in 1952. On May 24, 1954, he married Ursula Thiess, a German actress; they had two children.

Although Taylor appeared in seventy-four films between 1934 and 1967, no one, least of all himself, considered him a good actor. Modest and untemperamental, he once remarked to an interviewer, "I've never had an Oscar and probably never will. I'm content to do as well as I can." Yet, he exemplified what the Hollywood star system was intended to produce—a handsome personality who, while attracting large numbers of fans, would give competent, professional performances in "formula" films, ranging from gangster melodramas to westerns. Unlike such ambitious careerists as James Cagney and Bette Davis, Taylor did not even feel stifled by MGM but welcomed the control and direction its executives gave his career. He was in every sense "a Hollywood star." He died in Santa Monica, Calif.

[See Ronald L. Bowers, "Robert Taylor," *Films in Review*, Jan. 1967, which includes a complete list of his film roles; David Shipman, *The Great Movie Stars: The Golden Years* (1970); Jane Ellen Wayne, *The Life of Robert Taylor* (1973); and Lawrence J. Quirk, *The Films of Robert Taylor* (1975). An obituary is in the *New York Times*, June 9, 1969.]

G. F. GOODWIN

THOMAS, GEORGE ALLISON (1911–Oct. 18, 1968), Onondaga Indian chief and *tododáho* (spiritual leader) of the Longhouse religion of the Iroquois Confederacy, was born on the Onondaga Reservation, south of Syracuse, N.Y., the son of George Thomas, chief and *tadodáho*, and Margaret Greene. A lifelong resident of the Onondaga Reservation, George A. Thomas attended the Onondaga Valley Academy. His religious education came from his father and from attending and observing ceremonials at Iroquois longhouses, structures that served as houses of worship.

For much of his life, Thomas promoted Iroquoian culture and the spiritual welfare of the Iroquois's Six Nations—the Cayuga, Mohawk, Oneida, Onondaga, Seneca, and Tuscarora. He participated in the Onondaga Singing Society, which inculcated Native American traditions and values and provided aid to the poor. An imposing figure with a barrel chest and deep, pleasant voice, Thomas was a master speaker of the Onondaga language and of several other Iroquoian languages. He participated in meetings of the Cayuga County Historical Society, belonged to the Six Nations Agricultural Society, which encouraged farming and promoted Iroquois participation at the annual New York State Fair in Syracuse, and served as an adviser to the Boy Scouts Committee at Onondaga.

Iroquois chiefs do not pass on titles to their sons, but when Thomas' father died in October 1957 Thomas was selected, after the traditional ten-day condolence council, as *tadodáho*. Although as *tadodáho* Thomas had great prestige, he had limited authority and exercised no formal power over the Six Nations. As *tadodáho* Thomas served as a teacher, role model, and ceremonial leader of the *Gaiwiio* (Good Word or Code of Handsome Lake), a Native American religion. Thomas married Theresa Homer; the date of the marriage is unknown. They had one child.

Thomas was *tadodáho* at a time of great crisis in Iroquoia. Significant Iroquois lands—from 11,000 to 12,000 acres in all—were expropriated for the building of the St. Lawrence Seaway (1954–1959), the Niagara Power Project (1957–1961), and the Kinzua Dam (1957–1966) . As *tadoháho* of the Iroquois Confederacy, Thomas led several protests against these intrusions. In a message sent to President Eisenhower, the Iroquois insisted that the expropriations were illegal because the Six Nations were a sovereign entity not subject to the laws of New York, the United States, or Canada.

Thomas also led a protest against New York State's imposition of a sales tax on Native American lands, and, just prior to his death, called on the state to return to his people the sacred ceremonial Iroquois wampum belts housed at the New York State Museum. Thomas died in Syracuse, N.Y.

[See Laurence M. Hauptman, *The Iroquois Struggle for Survival* (1986); and Fred R. Wolcott, *Onondaga* (1986). See also the obituaries, *Syracuse Post-Standard* and *Syracuse Herald Journal*, both Oct.

23, 1968; and *New York Times*, Oct. 24, 1968; and William N. Fenton, "The Funeral of Tadodáho," *Indian Historian*, Spring 1970.]

LAURENCE M. HAUPTMAN

THOMAS, JOHN PARNELL (Jan. 16, 1895–Nov. 19, 1970), businessman and congressman, was born John Parnell Feeney, Jr., in Jersey City, N.J., the son of John Parnell Feeney and Georgianna Thomas. His father was serving as police commissioner of Jersey City at his death in 1905. In that year, the family moved to Allendale, N.J. After graduating from public high school, Feeney enrolled at the University of Pennsylvania in 1914 and two years later transferred to the New York University Law School. His formal schooling ended the next year when he enlisted in the army after America's entry into World War I. Commissioned a second lieutenant, he served overseas, where he became active in counterespionage work and achieved the rank of captain by the time of his discharge in 1919.

After the war Feeney obtained employment as a bond salesman with the Paine Webber Company, a New York investment house. He rose quickly, becoming manager of the bond department by 1924; he remained with the company until 1941. In 1920, Feeney, believing he could achieve greater recognition and business under his mother's maiden name, changed his last name to Thomas. On Jan. 21, 1921, he married Amelia Wilson Stiles; they had two children.

Thomas' business career steered him into conservative New Jersey Republican politics. In 1925, he won a seat on the Allendale Borough Council. From 1926 to 1930 he served as mayor of Allendale. In 1935 he was elected a representative from Bergen County to the New Jersey Assembly. Controversy and publicity surrounded him during his brief Assembly tenure. Opponents, questioning his political ethics, accused him of undue profits from the sale of bonds to the state. He also demonstrated an ability to react violently to ideas that he considered inimical to his own. For example, he called for the impeachment of the governor because of the latter's sales-tax theories. In the spring of 1936 the Republican state committee picked Thomas to run for the Seventh Congressional District seat. That fall he won the first of six successive terms in the United States House of Representatives.

Thomas became a member of the Military Affairs Committee. Originally he supported United States neutrality, but as world conflict seemed inevitable, he soon became an advocate of a strong preparedness program; he also favored the Selective Service Act of 1940 and the Lend-Lease Act of 1941. After World War II he emerged as a leading opponent of civilian control of peacetime atomic energy, maintaining that military control would prevent domination by "subversive" scientists.

As a freshman, Thomas had quickly established himself as a strident and vociferous critic of the New Deal and Democratic politics. Shortly after being appointed in 1938 to the special Dies Committee to investigate un-American activities, Thomas attacked the Works Progress Administration's Federal Theatre and Writers' projects as being Communist. He felt Communism had penetrated into all areas of American society, especially the government. He saw his mission as one of ferreting out Communists and liberal fellow travelers. He continually tried to link the New Deal to Communism. His partisan tirades, especially calling for the impeachment of Labor Secretary Frances Perkins, drew rebukes from colleagues of both parties, but he relentlessly continued to attack liberal Democrats. In committee hearings, he acquired a reputation as a tough and often abrasive interrogator.

After the 1946 congressional elections, in which the Republicans gained control of the House, Thomas became chairman of the Dies Committee, newly renamed the House Un-American Activities Committee (HUAC). He streamlined committee operations, increased investigatory personnel, and ran HUAC like a business with himself as board chairman. In 1947 the committee launched an investigation into the effects of the Communist party on the labor movement and other areas of American life. Thomas' deep-seated antipathy toward labor was unrestrained in the hearings. He began using a tactic that ultimately led to a series of contempt-of-Congress citations against uncooperative witnesses. When a witness proved unwilling to testify, the committee replaced him with one of its own investigators, who in turn disclosed what information it had on the witness. This tactic proved particularly useful when the committee turned its attention to investigating the movie industry in October 1947. Many noted Hollywood personalities, such as Louis B. Mayer, Gary Cooper, and Ronald Reagan, testified about alleged subversive activities of a group of screenwriters. These "friendly" witnesses were often vague in their testimony, but Thomas, relying on confidential information received from the Federal Bureau of Investigation, continued his attack. At times he became involved in heated arguments with "unfriendly" witnesses who questioned HUAC's right to subvert their civil liberties. The "Hollywood Ten," producers, directors, and screenwriters who refused to answer most questions, were found in contempt of Congress and received one-year prison sentences.

The famous Hiss-Chambers hearings were conducted before HUAC in 1948. Thomas, however, was absent during most of the hearings, yet his blatant partisanship and dictatorial tactics constantly drew criticism from the Truman administration and civil libertarians. Undaunted, Thomas launched an attack on Edward Condon, the director of the Bureau of Standards, claiming he was a weak link in America's atomic security. The committee could not substantiate the charges, and Condon was ultimately cleared. Finally, in August 1948 there appeared a series of articles by the columnist Drew Pearson that questioned Thomas' congressional-office payroll practices, and this led to his downfall. In October a federal grand jury began investigating the accusations, and in November, Thomas was indicted for padding his congressional payroll. After a series of delays due to his health problems, Thomas in late 1949 pleaded no contest. He was fined $10,000 and sentenced to prison. He resigned from the House on Jan. 2, 1950, and served nearly nine months in federal prison at Danbury, Conn., before being paroled by President Truman. Ironically, one of his fellow inmates was Ring Lardner, Jr., one of the Hollywood Ten.

Thomas consistently proclaimed his innocence and attempted a congressional comeback in 1954, but was soundly defeated. In 1956 he moved to St. Petersburg, Fla., where he died.

[Thomas' papers were destroyed in the 1950's; however, scattered correspondence can be found in the papers of some of his fellow congressmen. See August R. Ogden, *The Dies Committee* (1945); Robert E. Stripling, *The Red Plot Against America* (1949); Robert K. Carr, *The House Committee on Un-American Activities, 1945–1950* (1952); Lewis H. Carlson, "J. Parnell Thomas and the House Committee on Un-American Activities, 1938–1948" (Ph.D. diss., Michigan State University, 1967; Jane De Hart Mathews, *The Federal Theatre, 1935–1939* (1967); Alan D. Harper, *The Politics of Loyalty: The White House and the Communist Issue, 1946–1952* (1969); Robert F. Vaughn, *Only Victims: A Study of Show Business Blacklisting* (1972); Allen D. Weinstein, *Perjury: The Hiss-Chambers Case* (1978); and Kenneth O'Reilly, *Hoover and the Un-Americans* (1983). An obituary is in the *New York Times*, Nov. 20, 1970.]

CHARLES C. HAY III

THOMAS, NORMAN MATTOON (Nov. 20, 1884–Dec. 19, 1968), reformer and Socialist, was born in Marion, Ohio, the son of Welling Evan Thomas, a Presbyterian minister, and Emma Mattoon. Thomas attended Marion High School (1897–1901), Bucknell University (1901–1902), and Princeton University (1902–1905), which awarded him a B.A. and high academic honors. After briefly working in New York and traveling around the world, Thomas became an assistant to the pastor at the city's Christ Church and then associate minister of the Brick Presbyterian Church. He married Frances Violet Stewart on Sept. 1, 1910; they had six children. The following year he received a B.D. from the Union Theological Seminary, was ordained a Presbyterian minister, and became pastor of the East Harlem Presbyterian Church and chairman of the American Parish, a settlement house. In 1916 he joined the Fellowship of Reconciliation, an organization for religious pacifists, and later founded and edited its publication, *The World Tomorrow*. He also joined the American Union Against Militarism and in 1917 helped establish its Civil Liberties Bureau, which later became the American Civil Liberties Union (ACLU).

Thomas strongly opposed American entry into World War I, and in 1917 he supported the Socialist leader Morris Hillquit for mayor of New York, motivated both by the Socialist party's antiwar stand and by his growing belief that poverty could not be eliminated under capitalism. In 1918 he joined the Socialist party and gave up his pastorate, though he remained a minister until 1931. After serving as associate editor of the liberal *Nation* magazine, he became the codirector of the League for Industrial Democracy (1922–1937), an educational affiliate of the Socialist party, and, after the death of Eugene Debs in 1926, the head of the party itself. In 1924 he ran for governor of New York on the Socialist and Progressive tickets. Thereafter, he ran as a Socialist for mayor of New York City in 1925 and 1929, for the state senate in 1926, for alderman in 1927, and for borough president of Manhattan in 1931. Every four years from 1928 through 1948, he ran for the presidency of the United States.

The Socialist party emerged from World War I a shadow of its former self. Its opposition to American entry into the war cost it support, as did government persecution of Socialists during and after the war. Left-wing members charged party leaders with being too conservative and left the party, some to become revolutionary Communists. The Great Depression gave American socialism a last chance to rebuild itself, and thus, in 1932, Thomas received 884,781 votes for president, more than three times what he had polled in 1928. Even so, this was a weak showing at a time when national income had fallen by more than half and capitalism, in the eyes of many, was on its deathbed. The New Deal, by reviving hope and enacting reforms that Socialists had long advocated, destroyed the party's electoral base to such an extent that in 1936, Thomas polled only 187,572 votes. Though the Socialist party did not actually expire until 1960, it was, to all intents and purposes, finished. Many of the best younger members were drawn to the far left, some becoming Communists, others Trotskyists after the Socialist party's short-lived but disastrous merger with Leon Trotsky's American followers. Less-radical Socialists could not resist the opportunity to put cherished ideas into practice and therefore cast their lot with the New Deal.

In 1938, Thomas founded the Keep America Out of War Committee, beginning the most controversial phase of his career. Thomas was no longer an absolute pacifist, as he had been during World War I. In 1937 he had written that "one may be against both war and fascism, and yet find in every dispatch from Spain grim proof that practically, under conditions all too likely to occur again and again, resolute and effective opposition to fascism means war." But whereas Thomas preferred war to fascism in Spain, his position on America had not changed: he maintained that if America entered the next war, it would cease to be democratic, regardless of the outcome, and so must remain neutral at all costs. This belief, to which Thomas clung even after World War II broke out, put him in a compromising position. Soon he was appearing on the same platform with spokesmen for America First, a largely conservative anti-interventionist organization. Thomas stopped working with America First after Charles Lindbergh gave a speech for it that was widely regarded as anti-Semitic. Yet, he otherwise held his ground until Pearl Harbor, after which, further resistance being futile, he adopted a position that he described as one of giving "critical support" to the war effort. This meant paying special attention to civil liberties, which had in any case been a central interest of his since World War I. Thomas was particularly critical of the government's decision to intern Japanese-Americans, and he was one of the few to speak out immediately against the dropping of the atomic bomb on Japan. Above all, he worked at promoting world peace through international cooperation, establishing the Post-War World Council to support this effort.

Unlike many pacifists and civil libertarians, Thomas did not believe that his goals required him to ignore the evils of Communism. He had been sympathetic to it, but personal experience with American Communists during the depression and his observations of Spanish and Soviet Communism made while touring Europe in 1937 changed his mind. In 1940, Thomas led the successful effort to remove Communists from important positions in the ACLU, of which he was a longtime board member. During the McCarthy era he defended the civil liberties of Communists but not their right to hold sensitive offices or to serve as teachers.

Thomas had once believed that world peace would not be achieved until there was a world federation of democratic Socialist states. But World War II persuaded Thomas that neither Socialism nor democracy would be safe until an international organization was established capable of maintaining peace. To be workable, Thomas believed, such a union could ask only minimal concessions of power from its members. "Hence," Thomas wrote, "it has become my conviction that the most that can possibly be required of nations comprising a federation is abstention from aggression abroad and from the persecution of cultural and other minorities within their borders." Thomas never stopped working to that end and never ceased his opposition to war. Some of his last speeches were devoted to attacks upon the American military effort in Vietnam. He died in Huntington, N.Y.

Thomas was a tall, handsome man of great warmth and charm. A devoted husband and father, he was involved in family life to a degree unusual for one who led so demanding a public life. Friendly, outgoing, and humorous, he refused to engage in factional bickering but was an untiring advocate of the causes he believed in; he did not shrink from controversy, conflict, or even danger when principle was at stake. He was no stranger to the picket line and could not be intimidated by force or the threat of it, speaking wherever civil rights and civil liberties were most in danger.

Thomas' wife had private means, which enabled her husband to be a full-time activist. His income as a writer and speaker, which was often substantial, went to support his own work and the enterprises crucial to it. As a Christian for much of his life (he gave up organized religion during the 1930's) and a Socialist to the end, Thomas was bothered at times by his comparative affluence. But since his wife's money enabled him to give all his time and energy to public affairs, Thomas could not do without it. Not having to earn a living added much to his independence and effectiveness.

The place of Norman Thomas in American history owes little to his role as head of the Socialist party, for all its importance to him. A poor leader, Thomas was often criticized for failing to heal factional wounds, prevent defections, and attend to party work. Few historians believe that his organizational shortcomings made much difference, for Socialism had been defeated in America by the time he took over the party. Whatever small chance of success remained was foreclosed by the New Deal. The historical significance of Norman Thomas arises from his long years as a defender of unpopular people and causes. He was one of the country's leading orators and a fluent writer who composed hundreds of articles and twenty-one books. He devoted this great outpouring to three main themes, democratic Socialism, peace, and civil rights and liberties. Yet, his achievement cannot be measured in terms of ground won or lost by these causes. Thomas was a national treasure, and so recognized in his lifetime, because he served as the conscience of America.

[Thomas' papers, including an unpublished autobiography, are in the New York Public Library. The Columbia University Oral History Project contains three interviews with Thomas. Thomas wrote a vast number of pamphlets and articles in addition to his longer works, almost all of which were topical and not intended to stand the test of time. A representative selection of his books is *The Conscientious Objector in America* (1923); *America's Way Out: A Program for Democracy* (1931); *The Choice Before Us* (1934); *World Federation: What Are the Difficulties?* (1942); *A Socialist's Faith* (1951); *The Prerequisites for Peace* (1959); *Great Dissenters* (1961); and *Socialism Re-Examined* (1963). See Harry Fleischman, *Norman Thomas: A Biography* (1964); Daniel Bell, *Marxian Socialism in the United States* (1967); Murray B. Seidler, *Norman Thomas: Respectable Rebel* (1967); James C. Durman, *Norman Thomas* (1974); and W. A. Swanberg, *Norman Thomas: The Last Idealist* (1976). An obituary is in the *New York Times*, Dec. 22, 1968.]

William L. O'Neill

THOMAS, ROLAND JAY (June 9, 1900–Apr. 18, 1967), labor organizer and president of the United Automobile Workers (UAW), was born in East Palestine, Ohio, the son of Jacob William Thomas, a railroad worker, and Mary Alice Jackson. When Thomas was about seventeen, the family moved to Youngstown, Ohio, and in 1918 he graduated from high school in nearby Hubbard. From 1919 to 1921 he attended Wooster (Ohio) College, where he studied for the Presbyterian ministry, but he was too poor to complete his schooling.

Thomas worked for a while in the Youngstown steel mills and for the Ohio Bell Telephone Company and Western Electric. In 1923 he moved to Detroit to work in the auto factories there. He was first a metal finisher in a Fisher body plant and then became a welder at Cadillac Motors. In 1929 he took a welding job at a Detroit Chrysler plant.

In 1934, Thomas was elected employee representative of his plant to the Automobile Labor Board. Two years later he was made plant president and overall vice-president of the Automotive Industrial Workers of America. This independent union became a part of the UAW at the latter's 1936 convention, with Thomas as president of the new UAW Chrysler Local 7.

Thomas led his local in the sit-down strike against Chrysler in March 1937. On August 7 he married Mildred Wettergren, a sewing-machine operator in the trim division of the Chrysler plant where he worked; they had one child.

By the time the third UAW convention was called in Milwaukee in late August 1937, the union was already in the throes of internal warfare. Homer Martin, the UAW president, had alienated so many of his colleagues that the rival groups, collectively called "the Unity Caucus," had formed to defeat him. The caucus and the Martin supporters agreed that Thomas, who had remained aloof from the factional fighting, be chosen as one of several vice-presidents. Thus, in 1937, Thomas was made a UAW vice-president and placed in charge of all bargaining with the Chrysler Corporation.

Throughout most of the remainder of Martin's stormy presidency, Thomas managed to stay apart from the increasing dissension. Although Martin expelled several officers from the executive board in June 1938, Thomas was kept on. By the end of the year, however, he and Thomas had finally split, and Thomas was among the fifteen board members Martin suspended in January 1939.

The suspended officers, with the support of the Congress of Industrial Organizations (CIO), set up a second union headquarters in Detroit. Martin withdrew his UAW organization from the CIO at a convention in March 1939, while his UAW rivals held a convention in Cleveland. John L. Lewis of the CIO sent Philip Murray and others to this convention, and they persuaded the remaining UAW leaders to adopt Thomas, who had been acting UAW-CIO president since January, as their president. Thomas was regarded as sufficiently neutral to bring together the warring factions. He was elected UAW-CIO president in April 1939.

Because of the UAW split that spring, several corporations, General Motors (GM) among them, refused to bargain with either labor group. One of Thomas' first moves as union president was to appoint Walter Reuther, who was the head of a huge Detroit local and a former member of Martin's executive board, director of the UAW General Motors department. Within a few months, the auto workers had made it clear to GM that the UAW-CIO was their only legitimate representative.

In 1940 the UAW launched an intensive campaign to organize the Ford Motor Company, a task never completed under Martin. The effort was successful, and Thomas signed the first Ford contract in June 1941. That same year he was unanimously reelected UAW president. In 1942, President Franklin D. Roosevelt appointed Thomas to the Labor Advisory Committee and to the War Labor Board. Thomas made frequent trips overseas on behalf of both the War Department and the international labor movement, heading the American delegation to the World Trade Union Conference in London in 1945 and helping form what eventually became the International Confederation of Free Trade Unions.

American labor had adopted a "no-strike" pledge during wartime, and Thomas, who was familiar with the American feeling abroad against strikes, consistently opposed any repeal of this pledge. In 1945, just after V-J Day, the GM workers, under Reuther's direction, asked for a substantial wage increase, but GM refused. Reuther, insisting that higher wages for auto workers meant higher wages for all workers, led the workers out on a strike that lasted 113 days.

Thomas had only reluctantly supported the GM strike and, by late 1945, was moving away from his neutral position toward an anti-Reuther group within the UAW leadership, headed by secretary-treasurer George Addes. Unfortunately for Thomas, the Addes faction also included a small Communist element, which left Thomas vulnerable at the UAW convention in 1946. Moreover, just as the convention opened in March 1946, the GM dispute was settled with a raise, and Ford and Chrysler agreed to similar wage increases. Fresh from this victory and considered by some as the real leader of the union, Reuther presented the first serious challenge to Thomas for UAW leadership. While Thomas attacked Reuther's strike strategy as "fancy economics," Reuther, an articulate, even compelling orator, defended the strike and underscored the Communist support of the Thomas-Addes faction. These tactics worked. After hours of vote-taking, Reuther was elected the new president by 124 votes.

Thomas was made a vice-president again, and the Thomas-Addes group retained its ascendancy on the UAW board until November 1947, when Thomas was not reelected. He then joined the national CIO staff as an assistant to its head, Philip Murray. Thomas had already been a vice-president of the CIO since 1939 and the secretary-treasurer of the CIO Political Action Committee since 1944.

Murray had always had "a distinct fondness" for "the great big guy" and had even thrown his support publicly to Thomas during the 1946 convention. After Murray's death in 1952, Reuther became head of the CIO. Thomas remained with the organization, however, and became an assistant to George Meany in 1955 when the CIO merged with the American Federation of Labor (AFL). Although Thomas suffered a stroke in 1962, he became a troubleshooter for the AFL-CIO the next year but retired on Jan. 1, 1964. He and his wife moved to Muskegon, Mich., where he died in 1967.

Thomas was "a roaring bull of a man in his heyday" whose tobacco chewing and frank speech endeared him to the rank and file, from which he had sprung. He championed the rights of blacks to work in the auto plants. He was honest but unimaginative and unable to understand the new labor movement that emerged from World War II. He had led his union honorably all through the war only to find his blunt, rather simple style of leadership no longer adequate in the new and complex postwar America.

[Thomas' unpublished papers are in the R. J. Thomas Collection at the Archives of Labor and Urban Affairs, at Wayne State University, Detroit, which also is the repository of the R. J. Thomas Oral History. See also the UAW publicity department and "The History of Local 7" (1971) in the archives' vertical files. See Irving Howe and B. J. Widick, *The UAW and Walter Reuther* (1949); George Douglas Blackwood, "The United Automobile Workers of America, 1935–1951" (Ph.D. diss., University of Chicago, 1951); Warner Pflug, *The UAW in Pictures* (1971); and Labor Research Associates, *The Labor Fact Book*, III (1972). An obituary is in the *New York Times*, Apr. 19, 1967.]

SANDRA SHAFFER VAN DOREN

THYE, EDWARD JOHN (Apr. 26, 1896–Aug. 28, 1969), governor of Minnesota and United States senator, was born on a farm near Frederick, S.Dak., the son of Norwegian-American parents, Andrew John Thye and Bertha Wangan. In 1904 the family loaded its possessions into a freight car and returned to Minnesota, where his parents had met and married, and rented a farm near Northfield. In 1913 he attended classes at the Tractor and Internal Combustion School in Waterloo, Iowa, and the following year at the American Business College in Minneapolis, which awarded him a degree in 1916. When the United States entered World War I, he enlisted in the Aviation Section of the United States Army Signal Corps. He served in France, where he was commissioned a second lieutenant.

Following Thye's discharge in January 1919 he was employed by the Deere and Webber Company of Minneapolis as a tractor expert and, from 1920 to 1922, as a salesman. In the latter year he acquired a 280-acre farm near Northfield, which he operated for the rest of his life. Expanding the farm to 562 acres, he raised wheat, corn, hogs, and dairy cows, and maintained a 900-tree apple orchard. On June 21, 1921, he married Hazel Ramage; they had one child. Thye was elected in 1925 to the Sciota town council and later to the school board; he also served as president of the Dakota County Farm Bureau and as a director of the Twin City Milk Producers Association. In 1933 he became an appraiser for the Federal Land Bank in Minnesota. He resigned at the end of 1934 when his wife became ill; she died in 1936.

In 1938, Thye's longtime friend Harold Stassen, the Republican governor of Minnesota, appointed him deputy commissioner of agriculture. He was elected lieutenant governor in 1942. On November 12 of that year he married Myrtle Oliver. Thye succeeded Stassen as governor when Stassen resigned to serve in the United States Navy in 1943. Thye was elected to a full term as governor in 1944 by the largest vote and the largest majority ever received by a gubernatorial candidate in Minnesota up to that time; he was also the first farmer ever to hold that office.

As governor, Thye became popular by addressing the people over the radio and by traveling throughout the state. By insisting on sound finances and management, he reduced the state debt, increased old-age assistance and aid to blind and dependent children, and enlarged overcrowded state institutions. He also promoted better labor relations; labor stoppages during the war years were 70 percent below the years 1936–1938 and well below the national average during the war. He also launched plans for industrial expansion and postwar development of public institutions. He established a human-rights commission, began extensive highway construction programs, and approved a low-cost prepaid medical plan for state workers.

While serving his last year as governor, Thye was elected to the United States Senate, defeating Henrik Shipstead. Thye served in that body from 1947 to 1959. In the Senate, Thye chaired the Select Committee on Small Business during the Eighty-third Congress. He was liberal and internationalist in his outlook; though Republican, he often voted with the Democratic majority, especially when the measure had bipartisan support. In 1950 he was one of the seven cosigners of Senator Margaret Chase Smith's "Declaration of Conscience" against Senator Joseph R. McCarthy, who had sought to exploit "fear, bigotry, ignorance and intolerance" for political gain. In 1956, Thye again came to national prominence as a member of the Special Committee on Campaign Contributions, investigating the illegal use of oil money in the campaign of Francis H. Chase.

In 1952, Thye originally supported Harold Stassen for president but switched to Dwight D. Eisenhower. He became a strong supporter of Eisenhower on domestic and foreign policy issues and coauthored the Food for Peace program and the Soil Bank plan. Seeking a third term in 1958, Thye lost to Eugene J. McCarthy by 63,000 votes.

In 1959, Thye headed a Labor Department consultants' group recommending changes in the Mexican farm labor (bracero) program. He also registered as a lobbyist for the Spring Air Company.

In 1967, Thye suffered a heart attack and was stricken with pneumonia. Thereafter, he disposed of his cattle, sold his farm machinery, and, except for the orchards, leased his lands. He died at his farm near Northfield.

The *Minneapolis Tribune* recalled that even as a United States senator, Thye had remained close to his farm roots. Guiding a reporter around his farm, Thye said, "The greatest way of relaxing that I can find is to go to work on my farm, whether it's driving a tractor, working in the fields or just in the dooryard—and when I want to go to work here, no filibuster can stop me."

[Thye's papers, covering primarily the years of his public career, are in the Archives-Manuscript Division of the Minnesota Historical Society in St. Paul. The Norwegian-American Historical Association in Northfield has a small collection of materials covering his public career during the years 1948–1958. Thye participated in three oral-history projects: for the Library of Congress, for the Eisenhower Administration Project at Columbia University, and for the Minnesota Historical Society. An obituary is in the *New York Times*, Aug. 29, 1969.]

RICHARD LOWITT

TODD, WALTER EDMOND CLYDE (Sept. 6, 1874–June 25, 1969), ornithologist and museum curator, was born in Smithfield, Ohio, the son of William Todd, a school principal, and Isabella Hunter. As a boy, he became a careful and knowledgeable observer of birds and, at thirteen, published in the *Oölogist*, his first contribution to a scientific journal. His formal education ended with graduation from high school in Beaver, Pa., where the family had moved in 1877. He entered Geneva College in 1891 but within a few weeks withdrew to accept an apprenticeship in the Division of Ornithology and Mammalogy (later the Biological Survey) in the Department of Agriculture.

During his six years in Washington, Todd acquired not only specialized knowledge and skills but also, from study on his own, a good substitute for a college education. George M. Sutton, a younger ornithologist and later an associate, noted that what Todd "knew about physics, mathematics, and astronomy amazed me." While in Washington Todd became acquainted with a number of scientists and others in the emerging field of ornithology. But Washington offered neither the prospect of field experience nor chance of advancement, and in 1899 he resigned to become curator of birds at the newly founded Carnegie Museum in Pittsburgh. That association was to last seventy years, in the first twenty-five of which the director, less interested in the advancement of knowledge than in popular education, denied Todd support for research. To finance his expeditions and the preparation and publication of his books, Todd had to develop his own sources of support.

As curator, Todd classified large collections of neotropical birds acquired by the museum. From his pen came more than a thousand pages of articles describing these specimens. In 1896, after a severe bout of malaria, he was cautioned to avoid travel in the tropics, and so, he never visited some areas about which he published extensively.

Early in his career Todd recognized that the avifauna of northern Canada was almost entirely unknown and fixed on it as a field for study. In 1901 he made the first of eighteen expeditions to the region between Hudson's Bay and the Atlantic. Problems of transport, logistics, and weather were massive, and financial support was scant. With extraordinary persistence, even when past seventy, Todd did his share of the strenuous work in the unmapped wilderness, where travel was by canoe and backpack and where dogsleds and power boats were luxuries. A perfectionist, Todd wanted to produce a comprehensive treatise that would embrace the findings of other competent scholars who had invaded parts of the vast territory in which Todd felt that he had earned a monopoly. As a result, it was 1943 before *The Birds of the Labrador Peninsula and Adjacent Regions: A Distributional List* appeared. With more than 800 pages, each with two columns of small print, the volume is distinguished for its graceful and often spirited writing.

Todd's permanent residence in the upper Ohio Valley enabled him to extend fieldwork into the western half of Pennsylvania. In 1940 he succeeded in publishing, with support from friends and foundations, his exhaustive *Birds of Western Pennsylvania*, a work of more than 700 pages that incorporated, with appropriate acknowledgment, the work of others with his own observations and conclusions.

Todd's central interest all his life was the geographical distribution of bird life. As early as 1900, his field studies had made him skeptical of the concept of "life zones" put forward by C. H. Merriam and J. A. Allen, in which habitats are defined in terms of latitude and altitude. Todd found that his data could be better accommodated to the concept of the "biome," which characterizes habitat as an array of plant and animal forms at a particular period.

No ornithologist in Todd's long professional life could escape the controversy over recognizing as distinct species, rather than as subspecies, birds with minor differences in appearance or measurement. Todd was independent and judicious, but time has confirmed his reluctance to expand the list of species.

In 1907, Todd married Leila E. Eason of Beaver, Pa.; they had no children. The couple settled in a new house that he occupied until his death in Rochester, Pa.

[Todd's correspondence and manuscript autobiography of his first twenty-seven years are in the Carnegie Museum, Pittsburgh. A bibliography of his publications through 1939 appears in the *Cardinal*, 5 (1940); and, for the years 1940–1966, in *Auk*, 87 (1970). See Bayard Christie, "W. E. Clyde Todd," *Cardinal*, 5 (1940); Kenneth C. Parkes's memorial, *Auk*, 87 (1970); and George M. Sutton, *Bird Student* (1980). A review of Todd's *Birds of Western Pennsylvania* by Robert C. Murphy is in the *Cardinal*, 5 (1940); and Oliver L. Austin's review of *Birds of Labrador* is in *Auk*, 81 (1964). An obituary is in the *New York Times*, June 27, 1969.]

THOMAS LE DUC

TOKLAS, ALICE BABETTE (Apr. 30, 1877–Mar. 7, 1967), writer, was born in San Francisco, Calif., the daughter of Ferdinand Toklas, the owner of a merchandising establishment, and Emma Levinsky. She grew up, she said, in "necessary luxury." She attended one of the first kindergartens in the United States, a school that her mother had helped to establish and at which she studied German, English, geography, and arithmetic. Her grandmother took her to the opera and gave her piano lessons. In 1885–1886, Toklas and her family made an extended trip to Europe to visit her father's family, Poles who lived in Germany. On their return to America, she attended private schools in San Francisco and Mt. Rainier Seminary in Seattle, where the family lived for several years. After being tutored for the entrance examinations, she entered the music conservatory at the University of Washington in the fall of 1893. She later wrote that the parchment she finally received certified her "as a bachelor of music."

When her mother died in March 1897, Toklas and her father and brother went to live with her grandparents in a household that included several uncles and cousins. She became the housekeeper and learned how to ration supplies, plan menus, and deal with grocers. After the death of her grandfather in 1902, her family moved to smaller quarters. Although she worked toward a career as a concert pianist, she all but gave it up when her piano teacher died in 1904.

The San Francisco earthquake of April 1906 altered her life abruptly. When Michael Stein, the older brother of Gertrude Stein, and his wife came to San Francisco to see about repairs to their rental property, Toklas and her friend Harriet Levy, who had met the Steins in Europe, listened to their stories of life in Paris. Toklas resolved to go there, although she had to borrow the money from Levy. On the evening of their arrival in Paris in September 1907, Toklas met Gertrude Stein. Fascinated by Stein's large "golden brown presence" and by her "deep, full, velvety" voice, Toklas felt she was in the presence of genius. Almost at once she began correcting the proofs of Stein's latest book. They also went for walks together and traveled in Spain and Italy. When Levy returned to America, Toklas moved in at 27 rue de Fleurus, where the Stein-Toklas salon soon became one of the centers of intellectual life in Paris.

The friendship between Toklas and Stein developed into a closely knit family relationship. For nearly four decades, they entertained old friends, including Picasso, Matisse, Carl Van Vechten, and Edith Sitwell, and new ones, such as F. Scott Fitzgerald, Virgil Thomson, Ernest Hemingway, Sherwood Anderson, Charles Chaplin, Jo Davidson, Anita Loos, Thornton Wilder, Richard Wright, and the GIs of World War II. Although Stein was the dominant figure, Toklas seemed to be in command. She ran the house, ordered the meals, and did most of thc shopping and much of the cooking. For her, cooking was as much a cultivated art as was painting or writing.

As Stein's secretary, Toklas taught herself to type, transcribing everything that was written in the blue copybooks that Stein had "adopted from French schoolchildren." During World War I it was Toklas who proposed that they join the American Fund for French Wounded. In their Ford car, which they had shipped from New York, they distributed relief supplies, at Perpignan, Nîmes, and Strasbourg. Fame came to Stein with the publication of *The Autobiography of Alice B. Toklas* (1933), and both women became celebrities. When they organized the Plains Editions, their own publishing company, Toklas served as both publisher and distributor. On Oct. 17, 1934, they left for a triumphal six-month lecture tour of America; it was the only trip either of them made to the United States once they had met. During World War II they remained in France, living in the south at Bilignin and then at Culoz. They returned to Paris in mid-December 1944, opening their apartment on the rue Christine to soldiers and visitors.

After the death of Stein in 1946, Toklas remained in the apartment; Stein's will had specified that her friend should receive "proper maintenance and support" for the rest of her life. Toklas tried to carry on their old ways. She helped ready Stein's unpublished writings for publication, and she made herself available to writers and scholars.

Toklas then began her own writing career. In "They Who Came to Paris to Write" (*New York Times Book Review*, Aug. 6, 1951), she supplied her own keen and insightful comments on writers she had met and known. In "Fifty Years of French Fashions" (*Atlantic Monthly*, June 1958), she reviewed the history of haute couture as she had known it; she remembered warning Stein once not to reveal the fact that they were wearing clothes designed by Pierre Balmain. "We look like gypsies," she said. In "The Rue Dauphine Refuses the Revolution" (*New Republic*, Aug. 8, 1958), she predicted that there would be no revolution in France. In other pieces, she remembered Scott Fitzgerald, Sylvia Beach, and Matisse.

Toklas was famous for her rich cooking; her first published book was *The Alice B. Toklas Cookbook* (1954), which achieved popularity for both its gourmet recipes and her cryptic comments. The most famous recipe is for hashish fudge, contributed by her artist friend Brion Gysin. A second cookbook, *Aromas and Flavors of Past and Present* (1958), was assembled by Poppy Cannon, who altered it for American tastes. Toklas disapproved of the changes and said that she would never use it herself. In *What Is Remembered* (1963), she recalled her early days in San Francisco and Seattle and her life in Paris. *Staying on Alone: Letters of Alice B. Toklas*, edited by Edward Burns (1973), contains a detailed record of her last years.

Suffering from arthritis and cataracts, in December 1957, Toklas, whose family was Jewish, was admitted to the Catholic church, remembering, she said, that she was "baptized a Catholic as a small child with my mother's knowledge." In August 1960 she journeyed to Rome for a stay with the sisters in the Monastery of the Precious Blood. She returned to Paris in June 1961. Evicted from the old apartment, which had been sold, she moved to the rue de la Convention in 1964. Without money, she was aided by friends who organized a fund for her. She died in Paris.

[Most of the Stein-Toklas papers are in the Beinecke Library, Yale University; material about Toklas' early years in California and Washington is in the Bancroft Library, University of California at Berkeley. Additional material may be found in libraries of many universities; see the listing in *Staying on Alone*, cited in text.

Additional writings of Toklas include "Between

Classics," a review of *The Stories of F. Scott Fitzgerald*, edited by Malcolm Cowley, *New York Times Book Review*, Mar. 4, 1951; "Some Memories of Henri Matisse: 1907–1922," *Yale Literary Magazine*, Fall 1955; "Sylvia and Her Friends," *New Republic*, Oct. 19, 1959; *Dear Sammy*, edited with a memoir by Samuel M. Steward (1977); and "Three Unpublished Letters of Alice B. Toklas," edited by Hilbert H. Campbell, *English Language Notes*, 20 (1983).

Linda Simon, *The Biography of Alice B. Toklas* (1977), is a full-length study. See also Harriet Levy, *920 O'Farrell Street* (1947); Joseph Barry, "Miss Toklas on Her Own," *New Republic*, Mar. 30, 1963; Gilbert Harrison, "Alice B. Toklas," *New Republic*, Mar. 18, 1967; and Ray Lewis White, *Gertrude Stein and Alice B. Toklas: A Reference Guide* (1984). An obituary is in the *New York Times*, Mar. 8, 1967.]

JOHN E. HART

TONE, STANISLAS PASCAL FRANCHOT (Feb. 27, 1905–Sept. 18, 1968), actor, was born in Niagara Falls, N.Y., the son of Frank Jerome Tone, an applied chemist who later became president of the Carborundum Company of America, and Gertrude Franchot. Tone received his early education at private schools, including the Hill School in Pottstown, Pa. (1919–1923). He then attended Cornell University, where he earned Phi Beta Kappa honors and a B.A. in Romance languages in three years (1924–1927). Tone also played forty different roles in a variety of drama classes while at Cornell.

Following a summer of study at the University of Rennes in France, Tone returned to the United States intending to teach, but he gave in to his passion for the theater. He joined the Garry McGarry Players—a Buffalo stock company headed by his cousin, Pascal Franchot—as assistant stage manager. He first acted with the company when he replaced a juvenile lead who had become ill. In October 1927, Tone first appeared in New York City at the New Playwrights' Theatre in *The Belt*. He made his Broadway debut the following year with Katharine Cornell in *The Age of Innocence*. From 1929 to 1931, Tone appeared in Theatre Guild productions (*Red Dust*, *Meteor*, *Hotel Universe*) and played his first starring role in *Green Grow the Lilacs* (1931). He went with the Group Theatre when it split off from the Theatre Guild in 1931; with the Group, he appeared in *The House of Connelly* (1931), *Night over Taos* (1932), and *A Thousand Summers* (1932).

Tone, who was tall, witty, intelligent, and gracefully handsome, appeared to be a perfect matinee idol for his time. He enjoyed New York's nightlife and was frequently seen in the company of beautiful women at the city's finest nightclubs. In 1932, Tone made his film debut in Paramount's *Wiser Sex*, with Claudette Colbert. Some months later, while appearing as the lead in the play *Success Story* (1932), Tone was signed to a five-year contract by Metro-Goldwyn-Mayer (MGM). He played Walter Huston's secretary in *Gabriel over the White House* (1933) and Joan Crawford's brother in *Today We Live* (1933). Tone then appeared in a string of MGM romantic comedies: *The Stranger's Return* (1933, with Miriam Hopkins), *Dancing Lady* (1933, with Crawford), *Bombshell* (1933, with Jean Harlow), *Sadie McKee* (1934, with Crawford), and *The Girl from Missouri* (1934, with Harlow). He received top billing for the first time in *Straight Is the Way* (1934), with Gladys George. While on loan to other studios, Tone generally found meatier parts. He appeared in John Ford's *The World Moves On* (1934) at Fox; *Gentlemen Are Born* (1934) and *Dangerous* (1935) at Warner Brothers; and Henry Hathaway's *The Lives of a Bengal Lancer* (1935) at Paramount, in the last-named giving one of his best performances. On Oct. 11, 1935, Tone married the actress Joan Crawford, whom he had met during the filming of *Today We Live*.

After playing the midshipman in MGM's *Mutiny on the Bounty* (1935)—for which he received an Academy Award nomination as best actor—Tone appeared in a number of films for the studio in which his roles were routine: *One New York Night* (1935), *Reckless* (1935), *No More Ladies* (1935), *The King Steps Out* (1936), *Suzy* (1936), *Exclusive Story* (1936), and *The Gorgeous Hussy* (1936). In *Quality Street* (1937), Tone played period comedy opposite Katharine Hepburn. He was atypically cast as a vicious gangster in *They Gave Him a Gun* (1937).

One survey placed Tone seventh among Hollywood's top ten male stars in 1937. As an officer in the Screen Actors Guild, he earned a reputation as a "Red" among some producers because of his outspokenness. Tone's appearance in *Fast and Furious* (1939) marked the end of his contract with MGM; he had increasingly objected to the "stuffed shirt" roles in which the studio was casting him, and his parting with MGM was not amicable. In 1939, Tone and Crawford were divorced; they had no children.

Tone returned to the stage in New York, appearing in *The Gentle People* (1939) and *The Fifth Column* (1940). On Oct. 19, 1941, he married the actress Jean Wallace; they had two children. During the 1940's, Tone free-lanced as a film actor. Though he found more varied parts, his stock in Hollywood steadily declined. Two of Tone's better films of the decade were *Trail of the Vigilantes* (1940) and *Five Graves to Cairo* (1943). Often, however, he appeared in vehicles which were shallow and, on occasion, tasteless. Tone and Wallace were divorced in 1949. On Sept. 28, 1951, he married the starlet Barbara Payton. Their short-lived romance caused world headlines because of several nightclub brawls; they were divorced early in 1952.

Tone's film career was played out by the early 1950's. He returned to the stage, where he was sometimes able to appear in plays having the quality he desired: *The Second Man* in summer stock in 1950 and 1952; *Oh, Men! Oh, Women!* (1953) and a revival of *The Time of Your Life* (1955) on Broadway; *Uncle Vanya* (1956) off Broadway; and Eugene O'Neill's *A Moon for the Misbegotten* (1957) on Broadway. In 1958, Tone disclosed that he had married the actress Dolores Dorn-Heft in 1956; they were divorced in 1959. During the 1960's, Tone continued his occasional stage appearances in New York, notably in a revival of *Strange Interlude* (1963). There were also a few film parts, of which the most impressive was in *Advise and Consent* (1962), in which he played the President. At the time of his death in New York, Tone was trying to set up a film based on *Renoir, My Father*, by the French painter's son, the filmmaker Jean Renoir, with himself in the title role; he had also just given up his interest in an off-Broadway theater he had hoped to use for experimental work.

Throughout his career, Tone was devoted to the stage. Swept up by Hollywood from New York's radical theater in the early 1930's, he returned to the stage again and again. Nevertheless, he believed that the film was a better medium for telling a story. Charming and sympathetic, Tone played film comedy with ease. As a type, his confident, worldly screen character went out of fashion in the 1940's.

[See the *New Republic*, Nov. 16, 1932, and Mar. 25, 1940; *Collier's*, June 30, 1934, with photographs; *Photoplay*, Sept. 1935, May 1937, and June 1937; the *New York Herald-Tribune*, Mar. 2, 1940; the *New York World-Telegram*, Mar. 2 and Mar. 20, 1940; the *New Yorker*, Mar. 16, 1940; and David Shipman, *The Great Movie Stars: The Golden Years* (rev. ed., 1979), with photograph. An obituary is in the *New York Times*, Sept. 19, 1968.]

L. MOODY SIMMS, JR.

TRACY, SPENCER BONAVENTURE (Apr. 5, 1900–June 10, 1967), actor, was born in Milwaukee, Wis., the son of John Edward Tracy, a sales manager for a trucking firm, and Caroline Brown. A sensitive, quick-tempered, and impulsive child, Tracy was expelled from fifteen public and parochial grammar schools for truancy and fighting. After briefly attending two high schools in Kansas City, Mo., he entered Marquette Academy, a Jesuit preparatory school in Milwaukee. In early 1918 he enlisted in the United States Navy but never saw combat duty. He returned to Marquette after the war but was graduated from Northwestern Military and Naval Academy in Lake Geneva, Wis., in late 1920. Although he entered Ripon College in Wisconsin in January 1921 with the hope of becoming a doctor, he decided to become an actor after appearing in undergraduate dramatic productions.

In April 1922, Tracy left Ripon and enrolled at the American Academy of Dramatic Arts in New York City. His parents were disappointed, but they agreed to pay his tuition. He shared a room at a lodging house with his friend and fellow actor Pat O'Brien. He began to audition for parts, obtaining his first professional role, as a nonspeaking robot, in the Theatre Guild's production of Karel Čapek's *R.U.R.* in October 1922. After graduation from the American Academy in March 1923, he was hired as a bit player in a stock company in White Plains, N.Y. He married the company's leading lady, Louise Treadwell, on Sept. 12, 1923; they had two children, one of whom, John, was born deaf.

Tracy's first speaking part on Broadway was in an Ethel Barrymore vehicle, *A Royal Fandango*, which opened in November 1923. The play failed, and his performance passed unnoticed by critics. He returned to short-term engagements and one-night stands with stock and repertory companies. His next Broadway appearance was in *Yellow*, a George M. Cohan production, which opened in September 1926. The play received mixed reviews, but Tracy impressed Cohan, who wrote a part for him in *Baby Cyclone*, a comedy that opened on Broadway in September 1927. His performance in the hit established him as a promising newcomer, but he was unable to build on this success. It was not until early 1930, when *The Last Mile*, a prison melodrama in which he played a tough, cold-blooded murderer, opened on Broadway, that he achieved a critical and popular breakthrough. His performance was noticed by the film director John Ford, who had agreed to direct a comedy about prison life for Fox Films.

Fox executives, who had seen an earlier screen test of Tracy, regarded him as too "ugly" for leading-man roles and too young for character parts. Ford persuaded them to sign him to a one-picture contract. After moviegoers and critics praised his performance in *Up the River* (1930), Fox signed him to a five-year contract in January 1931.

Tracy's years at Fox were unhappy. Studio executives were unsure about his appeal to female fans, and when *Quick Millions* (1931) failed at the box office, they did not authorize the buildup that might have made him a star. He appeared in eighteen films for Fox, usually as a gangster or tough guy who got his comeuppance in the last reel. Critics praised his acting, but those films, with the exception of *The Power and the Glory* (1933), *20,000 Years in Sing Sing* (Warner Brothers, 1933), and *Man's Castle* (Columbia, 1933), are undistinguished.

A moody perfectionist with high professional standards, Tracy fought violently for script changes, engaged in heavy drinking bouts when he did not get what he wanted, and often disappeared during the production of films he disliked. Anguish and guilt over his son's congenital deafness aggravated his career frustrations. He lacked the patience needed to assist his wife's efforts to teach their son to talk. The Tracys separated in 1933, then reconciled, and then separated again, although Tracy continued to take a deep interest in his wife and children. In 1942, Mrs. Tracy, with her husband's financial support, established the John Tracy Clinic at the University of Southern California to train teachers and provide support for the deaf and their families.

On Apr. 8, 1935, Fox officials, tired of Tracy's excessive drinking and pugnacity, released him from his contract. That same day, he signed with Metro-Goldwyn-Mayer (MGM), where he was to remain for twenty years. He became part of an extraordinary star-making system created by Louis B. Mayer, MGM's shrewd but bullying and paternalistic chief executive. Mayer gave him three roles that raised him to the threshold of stardom: a priest in *San Francisco* (1936); an innocent man almost lynched by a mob in Fritz Lang's *Fury* (1936); and an unscrupulous newspaper editor in the farce *Libeled Lady* (1936), with Jean Harlow, Myrna Loy, and William Powell.

His new status was confirmed by his performance as Manuel, a Portuguese fisherman, in a film version of Rudyard Kipling's *Captains Courageous* (1937), for which he received his first Academy Award as best actor. He received his second Academy Award for his characterization of Father Edward J. Flanagan in *Boys Town* (1938), becoming the first actor to win an Oscar in two consecutive years. In *Boys Town* he created a characterization of a strong man of determination and integrity who battles against insurmountable odds, a type he was to play many times. He played similar roles in *Test Pilot* (1938), with Clark Gable and Myrna Loy; *Stanley and Livingstone* (Twentieth Century–Fox, 1939); *Northwest Passage* (1940); and *Edison the Man* (1940).

In 1941, Tracy began his professional and personal association with Katharine Hepburn in a deft and sparkling comedy, *Woman of the Year* (1942). They portrayed a down-to-earth sportswriter and a political columnist who after a series of mutual adjustments develop a complementary relationship. Moviegoers delighted in the obvious chemistry between them, and more thoughtful observers saw in their relationship an archetypal American marriage. Of their nine films together, *Woman of the Year*, *State of the Union* (1948), *Adam's Rib* (1949), and *Pat and Mike* (1952) were the best. Privately, they developed a close and enduring relationship. In late 1945, most likely influenced by Hepburn, Tracy returned to Broadway in *The Rugged Path*, a play written for him by Robert E. Sherwood. Although the play received mixed reviews, Tracy won critical praise.

In the 1950's, with white hair, a deeply lined

face, and considerable girth, Tracy was the first important leading man to recognize the inevitability of advancing years and to portray characters his own age. Although he made only one or two films a year, his performances were among the most impressive of his career. In the delightful family comedy *Father of the Bride* (1950) and its sequel, *Father's Little Dividend* (1951), he played the father with wry humor, charm, and warmth. He continued to sharpen his characterization of the isolated individual who struggles against adversity as a one-armed veteran who uncovers a murder in *Bad Day at Black Rock* (1955); as a poor and unlucky Cuban fisherman in *The Old Man and the Sea* (Warner Brothers, 1958), the screen version of Ernest Hemingway's novella; and as a Boston politician in *The Last Hurrah* (Columbia, 1958).

The revival of his career did not reconcile him to the changes that took place at MGM in the 1950's. Mayer had been forced to resign as studio head in 1951, and many of Tracy's fellow stars had either gone into retirement or left to work with independent producers. The perfectionism and acting insecurities that had made him difficult to work with intensified. MGM executives wanted him to make *Tribute to a Bad Man*, but he was not satisfied with the script or the director, Robert Wise. In June 1955 his erratic behavior on the set and excessive demands led to his dismissal from the film and the termination of his MGM contract after twenty years.

Beset by heart and respiratory difficulties, by the 1960's Tracy had become so cantankerous and irascible that he was difficult to direct. However, the director Stanley Kramer, a close friend, elicited fine performances from him in four films, apparently by giving him free rein. He portrayed a lawyer loosely based on Clarence Darrow in *Inherit the Wind* (United Artists, 1960); a judge presiding over the tribunal that tried Nazis for war crimes in *Judgment at Nuremberg* (United Artists, 1961); and an unscrupulous sheriff in the tedious farce *It's a Mad, Mad, Mad, Mad World* (United Artists, 1963). He was reunited with Hepburn in *Guess Who's Coming to Dinner* (Columbia, 1967), in which they portrayed liberal parents confronted by a daughter who plans to marry a black man.

To many of his contemporaries, Tracy was the greatest screen actor of his generation. His two Oscars and nine nominations as best actor support their conclusion. What they found appealing was the naturalness of his acting style. His underplaying of emotion and gesture inspired a generation of film actors. Although one story states that Tracy's advice to an aspiring young actor was simply "Learn your lines," in reality he was very serious about his acting. To develop a characterization, he would lock himself away with a script for weeks trying to understand how the character would think and talk. What appeared to be natural and effortless was the very opposite. His few critics claimed that his naturalness was easy because he played himself. More accurately, he discovered his range as an actor and brilliantly played many different roles within that range. Two weeks after completing *Guess Who's Coming to Dinner*, he died in Beverly Hills, Calif.

[See Donald Deschner, *The Films of Spencer Tracy* (1968), which contains a complete list of his film roles; Larry Swindell, *Spencer Tracy* (1969); Romano Tozzi, *Spencer Tracy* (1973); and Garson Kanin, *Tracy and Hepburn* (1971). An obituary is in the *New York Times*, June 11, 1967.]

G. F. GOODWIN

TUCKER, SOPHIE (Jan. 13, 1887–Feb. 9, 1966), singer and actress, was the daughter of Charles Kalish and Dolly Abuza. She was born in a farmhouse somewhere in Russia on a road leading to the Baltic Sea, for her mother was on her way to the United States to join her father (who took the name Charles Abuza when he arrived in America). The family lived in Boston for eight years and then moved to Hartford, Conn., where her father operated a restaurant. Tucker worked in the restaurant while attending school and occasionally earned small tips by singing for the customers. Shortly after graduation from the Brown School at the age of sixteen or seventeen (she was always intentionally vague about dates), she married Louis Tuck, a truck driver. The marriage was short-lived, and after the birth of a son, the couple separated.

Tucker left for New York City in 1906 to enter show business. After much difficulty finding work, she sang for her dinner at the Café Monopol. It was at this time that she changed her name to Tucker. Her next engagement was at the German Village, a beer garden on Fortieth Street near Broadway, where she sang more than fifty songs a night for $15 a week plus tips. She was a heavy, powerful blonde with a strong voice and an attractive personality.

After appearing in blackface in an amateur show at the 125th Street Theater, Tucker received a contract with the Park Circuit. She performed as a blackface singer in small towns and was billed as "World-Renowned Coon Singer." She then toured with the New England circuit of Hathaway Theaters. She developed a small reputation as a "coon shouter" and received an engagement at Tony Pastor's in New York City, where she sang such songs as "All I Get Is Sympathy," "Why Was I Ever Born Lazy?" and "Rosie, My Dusky Georgia Rose." To gain experience, she then joined Manchester and Hill's chain of burlesque houses at less pay, but she had the opportunity to appear in skits as well as sing. One day her trunk was lost, and she never again performed in blackface.

In 1909, Tucker was hired to sing in the Ziegfeld Follies. When the show opened in Atlantic City, her act competed with the star, Nora Bayes, and so, Tucker's part was reduced to one song. When the show got to New York City, Tucker lost her job when a new star, Eva Tanguay, took over her song. She returned to vaudeville and became a headliner. At theaters such as the American Music Hall in New York City and the Music Hall in Chicago she amused audiences with her song "There's Company in the Parlour, Girls, Come on Down." Tucker considered herself gawky and correctly reasoned that she could deliver songs with double meanings that would be accepted as humorous rather than indecent. Nevertheless, in Portland, Oreg., while she was singing on the Pantages Circuit, a warrant was sworn out for her arrest for "The Angle Worm Wiggle," which was called "immoral and indecent," but the district attorney threw out the case. By 1914, Tucker's first husband had died, and she married her pianist, Frank Westphal. That same year, she appeared at the Palace Theater in New York City, the epitome of success for vaudeville performers, and sang "Who Paid the Rent for Mrs. Rip Van Winkle When Rip Van Winkle Was Away?" In 1922, she toured England and was a big hit in music halls with such songs as "When They Get Too Wild for Everyone Else, They're Perfect for Me." At the same time, she entertained upper-class audiences at the supper club of the Metropole Hotel. In 1923 and 1924, she played in the better vaudeville houses of the Orpheum, Pantages, and Sullivan-Considine circuits in the United States.

The following year Tucker returned to England and sang at the exclusive Kit-Kat Club in London and in *Charlot's Revue*. That year she first sang "My Yiddishe Momma," which became closely identified with her. In 1926 she opened at Sophie Tucker's Playground, a cabaret in New York City, and in 1927 appeared in Earl Carroll's *Vanities*. At the Palace in 1928 she was billed as "The Last of the Red Hot Mamas," a title that remained with her for the rest of her career.

Tucker, determined, hardworking, and ambitious, carefully developed a style that was garish, raucous, and sentimental. She established a warm, personal relationship with her audiences. She was meticulous about her dress, spending large sums for brilliant gowns, diamonds, and white mink that helped define her image. She often shared billing with such stars as Will Rogers, W. C. Fields, Eddie Cantor, and Fanny Brice. Personal appearances were her great strength in show business. Although she made a few motion pictures, they did not add to her status as a performer. Among them were *Honky Tonk* (1929), *Broadway Melody of 1938* (1937), with Robert Taylor, Eleanor Powell, and Judy Garland, and *Follow the Boys* (1944). In 1930, after Tucker's second marriage had ended in divorce, she married her business manager, Al Lackey. This marriage also ended in divorce in 1934.

When vaudeville faded in popularity, Tucker performed at nightclubs in New York City, Las Vegas, Miami Beach, and the Catskills as well as abroad, where she was always in demand. In 1953, a testimonial dinner at the Waldorf-Astoria Hotel attended by 1,500 people celebrated her golden jubilee as a performer.

Tucker contributed time and energy to raise funds for charities that crossed racial and religious lines. In 1945 she established the Sophie Tucker Foundation. In 1955 Brandeis University announced the Sophie Tucker Chair of Theater Arts. Her popularity with the public persisted as she grew older. In the latter part of her career she was still able to make fun of herself and sang "I'm the 3-D Mama with the Big Wide Screen." Until shortly before her death in New York City, she appeared in clubs and on television.

[Materials on Tucker's career are in the Sophie Tucker Collection of the New York Public Library at Lincoln Center. Her autobiography, written with Dorothy Giles, is *Some of These Days* (1945). See D. Gilbert, *American Vaudeville: Its Life and Times* (1940); Abel Green and Joe Laurie, Jr., *Show Biz from Vaude to Video* (1951); and John E. Di Meglio, *Vaudeville USA* (1973).]

E. A. McKAY

TWEED, HARRISON (Oct. 18, 1885–June 16, 1969), lawyer and bar association officer, was born in New York City, the son of Charles Harrison Tweed, the general counsel for the Central Pacific, Chesapeake and Ohio, and affiliated railroad corporations, and Helen Minerva Evarts. His maternal grandfather, William M. Evarts, served successively from 1868 to 1891 as United States attorney general, secretary of state, and senator from New York and was one of the leaders of the American bar. Tweed graduated from St. Mark's School in Southborough, Mass., and received a B.A. from Harvard in 1907. At Harvard Law School he served on the law review and was awarded an LL.B. in 1910.

His career at the bar began with a clerkship in the office of Byrne and Cutcheon in New York City. After service as a captain in World War I he joined one of the predecessor firms to Milbank, Tweed, Hadley, and McCloy, with which he remained as a partner the rest of his life. Milbank, Tweed was the legal arm of the Chase bank and the Rockefeller family. Tweed specialized in drafting wills and trust agreements and in administering estates. He wrote briefs in litigation arising out of them and argued, and won, several notable appeals in the New York courts and the United States Supreme Court. Because he was born partially deaf, he never tried a case. In conferences with other lawyers he usually spoke last, and his views generally became the group's consensus. Imitating Justice Oliver Wendell Holmes, he had no desk in his office, writing instead at a lectern.

Tweed's appointment as chairman of the legal aid committee of the Association of the Bar of the City of New York in 1932 led to a continuing involvement in bar organizations. He became an enthusiastic convert to the necessity of providing competent legal services to all people. Legal aid, he wrote, was "operation equal justice," "an obligation of the bar," and essential to secure the success of the adversary system. He served as president of the Legal Aid Society of New York from 1936 to 1945, later publishing a history of its first seventy-five years, and of the National Legal Aid and Defender Association from 1949 to 1955.

In 1945, Tweed was elected president of the New York City bar association. To rejuvenate the staid organization, he brought in younger lawyers, established a bulletin, reorganized committees that issued reports, and created the position of executive secretary. All of this was done in a spirit of openness, equality, informality, and fun (a recurring word with Tweed). In this way, Tweed transformed a stuffy club into a strong progressive force for public service. C. C. Burlingham, the doyen of the New York bar, said that Tweed was "the best president the Bar Association has ever had."

In 1947, Tweed became president of the American Law Institute (ALI). He was a guiding force in its major labors—the updating of the institute's published *Restatements*, as well as the preparation of the Uniform Commercial Code, model codes and statutes on penal law and taxation, and the first restatement on the foreign-relations law of the United States. He took a light, subtle approach, usually talking around the matter at hand so as to envelop the object of his attention; only occasionally did he take a direct part in the proceedings over which he smoothly presided.

Starting in 1947, Tweed was chairman of the ALI–American Bar Association (ABA) joint committee on continuing legal education. Refreshment of the law, Tweed believed, was a professional responsibility. He wrote articles, spoke to lawyers' groups, buttonholed bar leaders, and organized conferences. For many years, a colleague noted, he "*was* the committee." The number of administrators of state continuing-legal-education programs increased markedly during his tenure.

Educational matters and public service occupied much of Tweed's time. He was a trustee of Sarah Lawrence College from 1940 to 1965, chairman of the board for eight years, and interim president of the college in 1959–1960. He served as an overseer of Harvard University during 1950–1956, and from 1951 to 1967 he was a trustee of the Cooper Union for the Advancement of Science and Art in New York City. New York governor Thomas E. Dewey in 1953 appointed him chairman of a commission to study reorganization of the state's courts; many of its recommendations, including the formation of a judicial conference of the state's judges, were later adopted. In 1963, at the request of President John F. Kennedy, Tweed became cochairman of the Lawyers' Committee for Civil Rights Under Law, a position he held for two years.

Tweed believed that lawyers' training to define complicated issues enabled them to play a special role outside the practice of law: "Even if he contributes nothing more than a sense of orderliness and an ability to organize thought and to pose the right questions, the lawyer will have pulled his weight in the boat." Of his year as president of Sarah Lawrence College, he wrote, "I think that I did manage to bring to the faculty an organization and an understanding of democratic procedures which no one but a lawyer could have done."

Tweed was married three times and divorced twice. By his first marriage, on June 14, 1914, to Eleanor Roelker, he had two children. Following his divorce in 1928, he married Blanche Oelrichs Barrymore, the former wife of John Barrymore and, as Michael Strange, an actress and writer; they were divorced in 1942. He and Barbara Banning, whom he married on Nov. 21, 1942, had one child.

Tall, erect, and lean, Tweed was "the most democratic of aristocrats." He was the only lawyer to be awarded medals for distinguished service from the New York City, New York State, and American bar associations. The ABA tribute noted that his was "the Horatio Alger story in reverse." "I have a high opinion of lawyers," Tweed said in 1945. "With all their faults, they stack up well against those in every other occupation or profession. They are better to work with or play with or fight with or drink with than most other varieties of mankind." He died in New York City.

[Tweed's history of the Legal Aid Society was published as *The Legal Aid Society, New York City, 1876–1951)* (1954). See his chapter, "One Lawyer's Life," in Albert Love and James Saxon Childers, eds., *Listen to Leaders in Law* (1963). A series of interviews dealing largely with his law practice are in the Columbia Oral History Collection.

Tributes to Tweed appear in the 1969 *Association of the Bar of the City of New York Yearbook* and the 1970 *American Law Institute Proceedings*. George Martin, *Causes and Conflicts* (1970), deals with Tweed's activities in the New York City bar association. An obituary is in the *New York Times*, June 17, 1969.]

ROGER K. NEWMAN

VAIL, ROBERT WILLIAM GLENROIE (Mar. 26, 1890–June 21, 1966), librarian, bibliographer, and historian, was born in Victor, N.Y., the son of James Gardiner Vail and Mary Elizabeth Boughton. Although as an adult he signed himself with the initials of his given names, or less often as Robert, Vail was known as Noah or Glen in his youth. Curiosity about the American past spiked Vail's ambition and shaped his career. As a student at Cornell University, he started compiling scrapbooks for the centennial of his hometown. He collected physical and literary items, such as a little-known account of an 1850 cross-country trip; this he edited and published in 1920 as his first work.

After receiving a B.A. from Cornell in 1914, he enrolled at the Library School of the New York Public Library and began work there as a reference assistant. While keeping up his bibliographic pursuits by visiting bookstores, he met Wilberforce Eames, who had begun his career as a bookseller in Brooklyn, N.Y. Eames, impressed with Vail's knowledge of Americana, acquainted him with a vast, unfinished bibliographical project initiated by Joseph Sabin in the 1850's.

Sabin's goal had been the compilation of a complete bibliographic record of all the titles in American history and literature. He had published the first volume shortly after the Civil War, at which time he estimated that he would finish the project by 1880. When he died in 1881, however, he was only up to the letter *P* in what he had called the *Dictionary of Books on American History*. Eames took over the project, reaching authors surnamed Smith before he abandoned the effort in 1892. Procedures had become complicated, and some scholars concluded that the attempt had been impossible even when Sabin had designed it. Eames and Vail nevertheless used the dormant Sabin files to check unusual imprints that Vail was discovering.

Vail's work was interrupted in 1916 when he entered the army. He spent his tour of duty at Fort Totten in New York. After military service, he returned to the New York Public Library for a short time, until he was hired as librarian of the Minnesota Historical Society in

St. Paul. He married Marie Rogers on Aug. 4, 1919; they had two children.

In 1921 Vail moved back to New York City to join the Roosevelt Memorial Association, which was trying to publish in a single edition a complete collection of Theodore Roosevelt's works. As librarian of Roosevelt House, Vail produced the *Memorial Edition of the Works of Theodore Roosevelt* (1923–1926) in twenty-four volumes, of which Vail edited the final twelve. Harvard Library later acquired the collection. Although Vail never finished a planned bibliography of Roosevelt's works, he did include separate bibliographies in some of the volumes of the *Memorial Edition*, and he published several of Roosevelt's writings that were hard to find, including *Who Should Go West* (1927) and *The Value of Athletic Training* (1929).

In 1928 the New York Public Library rehired Vail as Eames's coeditor in completing the Sabin project, which the Bibliographical Society of America had revived with donations from the Carnegie Corporation. The immense undertaking was progressing through Smith surnames when Vail began to sift through thousands of catalog slips from bookstores and auction houses. In 1930, as publication resumed, Vail was appointed editor of the project.

Vail soon gained repute for writing an article that solved a long-standing bibliographic mystery. Patrons had been beseeching librarians to appraise a Jan. 4, 1800, issue of a New York county newspaper that featured a notice of George Washington's death. Vail's article demonstrated that the issue had been reprinted many times throughout the nineteenth century. Indeed, thousands of copies had been distributed at the centennial exhibition in Philadelphia in 1876.

That thorough establishment of provenance prompted the American Antiquarian Society in Worchester, Mass., a group devoted to the collection and publication of American history, to hire Vail as their librarian. He continued working on the Sabin project and completed it in 1936, when it was published as *Bibliotheca Americana*. The work comprises twenty-nine volumes, the last nine by Vail. It includes references to more than 250,000 publications and identifies libraries throughout the world that own copies of these books. In 1940, Vail became director of the New York State Library in Albany. He remained there as state librarian until 1944, when he accepted the directorship of the New-York Historical Society in New York City, a position he considered the pinnacle of his career.

Vail's knowledge and ability flowered at the New-York Historical Society. He continued discovering manuscripts, one of which, to his delight, proved to be the original document that Napoleon signed authorizing the sale of the Louisiana Territory to the United States. In 1954, Vail published a sesquicentennial history of the society titled *Knickerbocker Birthday*. Although the volume was criticized for focusing too intently on the society's officers, it did succeed in attracting financial contributions. A practical function of scholarship among librarians, Vail explained, was to raise funds and acquire material. He also encouraged librarians to learn about book acquisition and printing in order to answer questions about book production from its earliest stages.

Although a dedicated scholar, Vail demonstrated the broad range of his interests by becoming an authority on the American circus. He frequently brightened the libraries he administered with circus paintings and exhibitions. He liked to clarify his philosophy of librarianship, manuscript curatorship, and archival administration by employing metaphors of circus life.

No master of synthesis, as a writer Vail usually failed when attempting a sustained, smooth narrative but nearly always succeeded in his bibliographies. His unusual talent for finding and listing every possible descriptive detail of rare works led to his reputation as a bibliographer's bibliographer. He retired from the society in 1960 and moved to Albuquerque, N.Mex., where he died.

[Vail's first published work was his edition of Charles W. Smith, *Journal of a Trip to California Across the Continent from Weston, Mo., to Weber Creek, Cal., in the Summer of 1850*. Vail's account of the production of the *Bibliotheca Americana* is in "Sabin's *Dictionary*," *Papers of the Bibliographical Society of America*, 1 (1937), and in "Wilberforce Eames," *Proceedings of the American Antiquarian Society*, Apr. 1938. Vail's bibliographical prowess was demonstrated in "The *Ulster County Gazette* and Its Illegitimate Offspring" and "The *Ulster County Gazette* Found at Last," *Bulletin of the New York Public Library*, Apr. 1930 and Apr. 1931. He considered his most valuable contribution to be his extensive Americana bibliographies, particularly *A Guide to the Resources of the American Antiquarian*

Society, a National Library of American History (1937) and *The Voices of the Old Frontier* (1949). His professional philosophy and administrative work are evidenced in his annual reports published in *Proceedings of the American Antiquarian Society* (1931–1939) and *New-York Historical Society Quarterly* (1945–1959). Most of his writings appeared in those journals and in the *Bulletin of the New York Public Library* (1929–1931). His interest in the making and selling of books can be seen in his biography of Isaiah Thomas in the *Dictionary of American Biography*, XVIII (1936).

Vail's studies of the American circus include "The Beginnings of the American Circus," *Colophon* (1934); "The Circus from Noah's Ark to New York," *Bulletin of the Museum of the City of New York*, Apr. 1938; and "This Way to the Big Top!" *Quarterly Bulletin of the New-York Historical Society*, July 1945.

Information about Vail is sparse, but see Frederick R. Goff, "R. W. G. Vail: A Bibliographical Appreciation," *Inter-American Review of Bibliography*, Sept. 1967; and Pamela Spence Richards, "The War Years and the Directorship of R. W. G. Vail (1944–1960)," in *Scholars and Gentlemen* (1984). An obituary is in the *New York Times*, June 23, 1966.]

DAVID JOHN MYCUE

VAN DE GRAAFF, ROBERT JEMISON (Dec. 20, 1901–Jan. 16, 1967), physicist and inventor, was born in Tuscaloosa, Ala., the son of Adrian Sebastian Van de Graaff, a jurist, and Minnie Cherokee Hargrove. He attended public school in Tuscaloosa from 1908 to 1918, studied mechanical engineering at the University of Alabama, where he received his B.S. degree in 1922 and his M.S. degree in 1923, and worked for a year as a research assistant for the Alabama Power Company.

Van de Graaff's interest in physics led him to continue his formal education. From 1924 to 1925 he studied at the Sorbonne in Paris, where he attended lectures given by Marie Curie. In 1925 he was awarded a Rhodes Scholarship at Oxford University (Queen's College). He received his B.S. degree in physics there in 1926 and his Ph.D. degree in 1928, the latter, under the direction of J. S. E. Townsend, for research on ion mobility. A fellowship from the International Education Board enabled him to remain at Oxford for an additional year. Finally, a fellowship from the National Research Council in 1929 led Van de Graaff to return to the United States.

While abroad, Van de Graaff had become interested in designing a device that could accelerate electrons, protons, or heavier atomic nuclei to high energies. After considering a variety of approaches, he came up with the invention now known as the Van de Graaff generator. He realized that if an electrical charge was sprayed onto a moving belt and then carried inside an insulated metal sphere and deposited there, the charge would accumulate on the sphere's outer surface. Applying the generator's high voltages to a suitably designed vacuum tube would turn the device into a particle accelerator.

At Princeton, where he chose to resume his research, the physicist Karl T. Compton encouraged him to build the first working models of his invention. In September 1931, Van de Graaff described the device at a meeting of the American Physical Society, and in November he demonstrated it publicly at the dinner held to celebrate the founding of the American Institute of Physics.

In the same year, Van de Graaff accepted an offer from Compton, then president of the Massachusetts Institute of Technology (MIT), to join him as a research associate. In addition, Compton helped him to secure a patent on his invention and a grant from the Research Corporation (the first of several in the 1930's) to build a machine with spheres fifteen feet in diameter.

The new device was erected in 1932–1933 in an airship hangar at Round Hill, near South Dartmouth, Mass., but difficulties with its operation in the open air led to its reconstruction in 1937–1938 in a pressurized chamber on the MIT campus. From the outset, the huge machine was popularly viewed as one of the classic "atom smashers" of the decade, and in the mid-1950's it was moved once again, this time to Boston's Museum of Science. On Aug. 12, 1936, he married Catherine Boyden; they had two children.

Meanwhile, Van de Graaff began pursuing the medical and industrial applications of his invention. The former arose primarily from his association with John G. Trump, an electrical engineer at MIT. In 1937 the first of his medical X-ray machines was ready for clinical use at the Collis P. Huntington Memorial Hospital of the Harvard Medical School. Attention to the generator's industrial applications came during World War II. Working at MIT under a contract from the Office of Scientific

Research and Development, he directed the High Voltage Radiographic Project, which developed X-ray machines for the nondestructive testing of naval ordnance.

After the war, Van de Graaff returned to nuclear-physics research. A grant from the Rockefeller Foundation in 1945 enabled him and his MIT coworkers, including W. W. Buechner, to build a more compact and more powerful Van de Graaff accelerator, which they used for an important experimental program. Trump decided to manufacture the device commercially and therefore established the High Voltage Engineering Corporation (HVEC) on Dec. 19, 1946. Denis M. Robinson was appointed president; Trump, technical director; and Van de Graaff, chief physicist. Financial backing from the American Research and Development Corporation enabled the company to start operating in early 1947. Initially it emphasized X-ray machines for medical purposes (Trump's interest) rather than accelerators for nuclear research (Van de Graaff's interest).

An unexpectedly strong postwar demand for Van de Graaff accelerators for studies of nuclear structure led Van de Graaff to increase his participation at HVEC. Following Luis W. Alvarez's discovery of the energy-doubling principle in 1951, the company decided to develop a new generation of research machines, tandem Van de Graaff accelerators, which proved highly successful.

The effect on Van de Graaff's career was equally pronounced. In 1960 he resigned his position as associate professor of physics at MIT, which he had held since 1934, to devote all his efforts to serving as HVEC's chief scientist, and at the time of his death in Boston, he was engaged in designing a machine that could accelerate very heavy nuclei, including uranium nuclei.

The unifying theme of Van de Graaff's career was the development of his invention as a technique for accelerating any desired element in a precisely controlled fashion to ever-higher energies and intensities. His courteous manners and the strength of his physical intuition combined to make him an effective leader of the teams engaged in that work. Although not inclined by temperament to promote his ideas aggressively, he consistently won the support of those who were willing to make sure he received adequate resources. Beginning in the 1940's, however, his personal participation was often limited by back pain arising from a high school football injury.

In the course of his career, Van de Graaff authored and coauthored numerous scientific articles and received numerous patents, including one for the insulating-core transformer. His work with Van de Graaff generators brought him several awards, notably the 1947 Duddell Medal of the Physical Society of Great Britain and the 1966 Tom W. Bonner Prize of the American Physical Society.

[Archival sources include the R. J. Van de Graaff Papers, the Papers of the High Voltage Engineering Corporation, and the Records of the Office of the President at the Institute Archives of MIT, as well as material at the MIT Museum, the W. S. Hoole Library of the University of Alabama, the Rockefeller Archive Center, the Research Corporation, the Library of Congress (the M. A. Tuve Papers), the Center for History of Physics of the American Institute of Physics, and the F. A. Countway Library of Medicine of Harvard University. A partial list of his published works follows the essay on Van de Graaff by E. A. Burrill in the *Dictionary of Scientific Biography*.

On his life and work, see E. A. Burrill, "Van de Graaff: The Man and His Accelerators," *Physics Today*, 20 (1967); L. G. H. Huxley, "Dr. R. J. Van de Graaff," *Nature*, Apr. 8, 1967; and P. H. Rose, "In Memoriam: Robert Jemison Van de Graaff, 20 December 1901–16 January 1967," *Nuclear Instruments and Methods*, 60 (1968). Also useful are the entries for A. S. Van de Graaff, A. C. Hargrove, and Robert Jemison (Van de Graaff's great-grandfather) in T. M. Owen, *History of Alabama and Dictionary of Alabama Biography* (1921); "Supervoltage Machines," *Fortune*, Apr. 1950; "The Management Style of Denis Robinson," *Innovation*, June 1969; and D. A. Bromley, "The Development of Electrostatic Accelerators," *Nuclear Instruments and Methods*, 122 (1974). An obituary is in the *New York Times*, Jan. 17, 1967.]

THOMAS DAVID CORNELL

VAN DOREN, IRITA BRADFORD (Mar. 16, 1891–Dec. 18, 1966), literary editor, was born in Birmingham, Ala., the daughter of John Taylor Bradford, a lumberman and merchant, and Ida Henley Brooks. When she was four, her family moved to Tallahassee, Fla., where her father owned a sawmill. Five years later, he was shot and killed by a discharged worker, and Irita's mother had to support the family by giving music lessons and selling preserves and jellies. All four children had a strong interest in literature, and while helping their mother put up jars of preserves, they took turns reading aloud from the classics.

At the age of seventeen, Van Doren graduated from Florida State College for Women, where she edited the school's literary magazine. The following year she received her master's degree and then embarked for New York to study English at Columbia University. While working on her doctorate, she taught part-time at Hunter College. On Aug. 23, 1912, she married a young Columbia instructor, Carl Van Doren, who went on to become a prominent literary critic and Pulitzer Prize–winning biographer. They bought a farm in West Cornwall, Conn., where they spent weekends and the summer. They had three children.

In the early years of their marriage, Van Doren assisted her husband in researching his books. And in 1919, when he became literary editor of the *Nation*, she also joined the editorial staff, succeeding him as book editor in 1923. Then, in 1924, her friend Stuart P. Sherman accepted the book editorship of the *New York Herald Tribune* on the condition that she be hired as his chief assistant. While Sherman wrote a weekly column and was primarily a critic, Van Doren helped launch and edited "Books," the paper's weekly book-review section. Following Sherman's death in 1926, Van Doren was named literary editor of the *Herald Tribune*, and for the next thirty-seven years, she ran the influential literary supplement, gaining an international reputation for shrewd editorial judgment and fairness.

Although the *Herald Tribune* was staunchly Republican in its editorial policies, Van Doren had autonomy and gave representation to a broad spectrum of contributors. "Since 'Books' is published as part of a large newspaper," she observed, "it must count among its potential readers people of every variety, taste and opinion. And since all kinds of books are published, it seems only fair to review them from the point of view from which they are written, so that they will ultimately find the audience for whom they are intended."

Within a short time at the *Herald Tribune*, Van Doren won recognition as a leading literary figure and one of the newspaper's most gifted editors. She hired distinguished writers as visiting critics, she initiated a national best-seller list, and despite a low budget that made it impossible to pay contributors more than a few cents a word, she attracted a wide range of celebrated writers and critics. Working with a much smaller staff than that at the rival *New York Times*, she built a literary supplement that was considered at least the equal of its local rival, and often livelier and better-written. A woman of strong principle, Van Doren did not hesitate to call publisher Alfred Knopf's bluff when he threatened to discontinue advertising in the *Herald Tribune* in retaliation for an unfavorable review. Knopf did not carry out his threat.

Enormously popular among literary people, Van Doren was an arresting personality, a woman of wit, intellect, warmth, vitality, and a special grace. She presided over a literary salon that included some of the most notable writers of the age. Among those in her circle were Carl Sandburg, Rebecca West, Virginia Woolf, John Erskine, André Maurois, James Thurber, Sinclair Lewis, Dorothy Thompson, Hugh Walpole, Stephen Vincent Benét, Aldous Huxley, and her brother-in-law Mark Van Doren. While her career prospered, her marriage soured, and in 1935 the Van Dorens were divorced.

Two years later, Van Doren met Wendell L. Willkie, who was then chairman of Commonwealth and Southern, the nation's largest public-utility holding company. One of the initial ties between them was a mutual interest in southern history. But they soon were romantically involved. Willkie spoke privately of divorcing his wife to marry Van Doren, but could not bring himself to ask her for a divorce. He also feared that a divorce might harm his political career. Van Doren encouraged his political ambitions and assisted him with his magazine articles and speeches; her efforts brought a new polish and vigor to his literary style. It was through Van Doren that Willkie developed his close friendship with *Herald Tribune* publishers Ogden and Helen Reid, who were to be among his earliest and most important sponsors for the 1940 Republican presidential nomination.

When Willkie campaigned for the presidency, Van Doren told him that he should keep his distance from her and make the most of his opportunity. Resentful of the hypocrisy of politics, Willkie nonetheless followed Van Doren's advice but stayed in daily contact with her by telephone during his campaign travels. After losing the election to Franklin D. Roosevelt, Willkie resumed his relationship with Van

Doren. She was the principal collaborator on Willkie's best-selling *One World* (1943) and also edited his book *An American Program* (1944). At the time of Willkie's death in 1944, Van Doren was his closest friend and confidante.

Van Doren retired from the *Herald Tribune* in the spring of 1963 and became literary consultant to the publishing firm of William Morrow. Although often encouraged by publishers to write her memoirs, she politely declined, referring to herself as "the nonwriting Van Doren."

Short, slender, and dark-haired, Van Doren spoke with a soft southern accent. "Among the kind-hearted editors I have known she was by far the kindest," recalled Malcolm Cowley. A *Herald Tribune* colleague, John K. Hutchens, added, "She had great skill and charm, and she also had a vein of iron."

[Van Doren's papers are in the Library of Congress. Her relationship with Willkie is described in Joseph Barnes, *Willkie* (1952); and Steve Neal, *Dark Horse* (1984). See also John K. Hutchens, "Irita Van Doren," *Authors Guild Bulletin*, Jan.–Feb. 1967. An obituary is in the *New York Times*, Dec. 19, 1966.]

STEVE NEAL

VINER, JACOB (May 3, 1892–Sept. 12, 1970), economist, was born in Montreal, Canada, the son of Samuel Viner and Rachel Smilovici. Both parents came from shopkeeping families in Romania and engaged in the same pursuit in Canada. Viner graduated from McGill University in 1914 and began graduate work at Harvard in the same year, obtaining his M.A. in economics in 1915; his doctorate was awarded in 1922 for a dissertation on Canada's international indebtedness, begun under the supervision of Frank Taussig, a teacher for whom Viner retained considerable respect. Viner was appointed instructor in the Department of Economics at the University of Chicago in 1916, but his career was interrupted during World War I by a period spent with the United States Tariff Commission and later with the Shipping Board. He returned to Chicago in 1919, and on September 15 he married Frances Viola Klein; they had two children.

Viner rapidly became a leading figure in the University of Chicago economics department, which included Henry Simons, Frank Knight, Paul Douglas, and Henry Schultz. Viner was promoted to a full professorship at the age of thirty-four, at which time he also became a United States citizen, while retaining personal and professional links with his Canadian background. As a teacher of economic theory Viner was known for his originality and thoroughness and for a rigor amounting to toughness. He edited the *Journal of Political Economy* with Frank Knight from 1929 until 1946, when he moved to Princeton. He remained there until his retirement in 1960. Viner served as a special assistant to the United States Treasury under Henry Morgenthau (1934–1939) and as a consultant to the State Department (1943–1952), where his knowledge of international affairs was put to good use.

Viner's earliest monographs dealt with an important problem bedeviling international trade—namely, the dumping of goods on the world market (*Dumping;* 1922). In *Canada's Balance of International Indebtedness, 1900–1939* (1923), based on his doctoral dissertation, Viner became one of the first to subject the classical theory of balance-of-payments adjustment to an empirical test. His next major contribution to this field was his authoritative *Studies in the Theory of International Trade* (1937), a rare combination of history and theory that traced the intellectual development of the subject from the seventeenth century to the present. Viner continued to work on international economics and commercial policy into the postwar period. His two most important works are *The Customs Union Issue* (1950) and *International Trade and Economic Development* (1952), based on lectures given in Brazil. He wrote from the cosmopolitan perspective of one who was deeply versed in the classical liberal position; but he was also fully conscious of those developments in the world economy and international relations that had made classical theory and its prescriptions less applicable than they had been in the pre-1914 era.

Viner made a significant early contribution to the theory of costs and pricing in his article "Cost Curves and Supply Curves" (*Zeitschrift für Nationalökonomie*, 3 [1931]), which anticipated much of the modern theory of the firm acting under imperfect competition. But the hallmark of his position was his mistrust of extended chains of deductive reasoning where elegance and generality were sought at the expense of empirical significance and the capacity to shed light on crucial policymaking questions. Such a preference for facts underlay his long-running defense of a "real-cost" approach to pure trade theory against the proponents of "opportunity-cost" methods. They are also manifest in his pioneering contribution, when dealing with customs unions, to the theory of second best—how to appraise partial movements toward an "ideal" solution in an imperfect world.

Parallel to his practical and pressing concerns as an economist and adviser, Viner sustained an impressive program of historical research that went well beyond the narrow confines of doctrinal history. The article "Adam Smith and Laissez-Faire" (*Journal of Political Economy*, 35 [1927]) established him as one of the world's authorities on Smith's social philosophy; and over time Viner wrote a series of studies revealing his mastery of the mercantilist literature, of the work of Mandeville and the Augustan satirists generally, and of the English liberal tradition from Bentham and Mill to Alfred Marshall.

In the fifteen years before his death in Princeton, Viner undertook an ambitious yet meticulous study of theological debate from the church fathers through the Scholastics to the Enlightenment and beyond, the results of which appeared posthumously in *The Role of Providence in the Social Order* (1972) and *Religious Thought and Economic Society* (1978). In all his scholarly writings Viner set the highest standards for the reporting and interpretation of past thinking, expressing his credo in "A Modest Proposal for Some Stress on Scholarship in Graduate Training," delivered at Brown University in 1950. Here Viner said that although scholarship does not rank with the creative arts and scientific discovery, learning has a place in the graduate curriculum as an antidote to narrow specialization.

Viner does not fit neatly into any of the available categories for classifying economists of his generation. He described himself as "a moderate liberal" but was far removed from "neoliberal" believers in the free market as a panacea. Similarly, although critical of Keynesianism, he never adopted a partisan anti-Keynesian position. Lionel Robbins described him as "the outstanding all-rounder of his time." Whether as economist or scholar, he contributed to a broad spectrum of what have become separate specialties without sacrificing his rigorous professional standards. He was tolerantly eclectic in his intellectual tastes, condemning only the more dogmatic claims to knowledge or political salvation. In the classroom and in conversation, he was witty and erudite; in conducting an argument, he was subtle and tenacious. Intellectual autonomy went along with punctiliousness in the performance of professional obligations, including correspondence with other scholars. By temperament, learning and choice he was a constructive skeptic and humanist.

[An extensive collection of correspondence and other unpublished material can be found at the Seeley G. Mudd Repository at Princeton University. Collections of Viner's articles are *International Economics* (1951) and *The Long View and the Short* (1958). For accounts of Viner's career, see Lionel Robbins, *Jacob Viner: A Tribute* (1971); Donald Winch, "Jacob Viner," *American Scholar*, 50 (Autumn, 1981), and "Jacob Viner as Intellectual Historian," in *Research in the History of Economic Thought and Methodology*, I (1983).]

DONALD WINCH

VLADIMIROFF, PIERRE (Feb. 1, 1893–Nov. 25, 1970), ballet dancer, was born Piotr Nikolaevich Vladimirov, in St. Petersburg (now Leningrad), Russia, the son of Nikolai Vladimiroff, a cossack, and his wife, Alexandra. Vladimiroff first showed enthusiasm for dancing when as a small boy he leaped up to join his father's regiment in the *lezginka*, a virtuosic folk dance. Soon after, his godmother took him to auditions for the Imperial School of Ballet, at that time supported by the tsar and connected to the Maryinsky Theater in St. Petersburg. Vladimiroff was accepted and studied with ballet masters Sergei Legat and Mikhail Oboukhoff. As a student, he was known for his vivacity and independence, frequently going around school with a cossack uniform and dagger instead of the required imperial uniform. In 1911 he graduated from the Ballet School and, like all graduates, was automatically accepted into the Imperial Ballet company.

In 1912 Vladimiroff joined Sergei Diaghilev's Ballets Russes when the company toured western Europe. Diaghilev's company, formed mainly of Maryinsky dancers, gave Europe its first taste of classical Russian dancing; the tour was a great success. On his return Vladimiroff began to get better roles at the Maryinsky, especially since Legat, premier danseur and teacher, was getting older and Vaslav Nijinsky, the Maryinsky's star, had left to dance for Diaghilev. After a quarrel with Diaghilev in 1914, however, Nijinsky left the company. Vladimiroff received another leave from the Maryinsky to dance Nijinsky's part of the Slave in Michel Fokine's *Cléopâtre*. According to Serge Grigoriev, a longtime regisseur of Diaghilev's Ballets Russes, Vladimiroff's execution of the role was brilliant.

In 1915 Vladimiroff became a premier danseur at the Maryinsky Theater. He created roles in Fokine's *Francesca da Rimini* and *Eros*. He also made several innovations in traditional male roles. Along with the director and conductor, he arranged a dramatic entrance for the male dancer in the coda of the Black Swan pas de deux in *Swan Lake*. Instead of beginning from the center of the stage, he entered with a leap from the wings after the music had begun. (Vladimiroff's variation is generally performed today.) Vladimiroff's repertoire also included classics such as *Paquita*, *Raymonda*, and *Giselle*.

When the Revolution occurred in Russia in 1917, the Imperial School closed for a year, although the company continued performing. Conditions were poor: there was not enough to eat, the theaters were unheated, and many dancers left. Prima ballerina Matilda Kshesinska, who had powerful political connections, offered to help Vladimiroff escape. At first he refused, preferring to stay in Russia, but later he changed his mind. On Easter night in 1920 he crossed the border into Finland disguised as a peasant. He brought with him Felia Doubrovska, a Maryinsky dancer, and her mother. For a time Vladimiroff and Doubrovska danced in Paris. They joined Diaghilev's company in 1921, and were immediately cast in his production of the Russian classic *The Sleeping Princess* (*Sleeping Beauty*) in London. Vladimiroff was given the part of Florestan and Doubrovska danced a solo. Vladimiroff and Doubrovska were married on Jan. 11, 1922. Although he could have remained with the Diaghilev company, Vladimiroff knew that Diaghilev had other favorites and would not give him the roles he wanted. In 1922 Vladimiroff left to dance with Tamara Karsavina, also originally of the Maryinsky, on a tour through Eastern Europe; Doubrovska remained with Diaghilev. Vladimiroff returned in 1925 for one season with Diaghilev, then left in 1926 to join Mikhail Mordkin's Russian Ballet tour of America. In 1927 he rejoined Karsavina for another tour of Eastern Europe.

Vladimiroff joined Anna Pavlova's company, his last, in 1928. Pavlova, like Vladimiroff, had left the Maryinsky to dance with Diaghilev before forming her own company. As the partner of Pavlova, the most famous dancer in the world, Vladimiroff toured Egypt, India, and Europe. He often urged Pavlova to attempt more original and inspiring productions, but she conceived of her company primarily as a vehicle for herself and was interested only in presenting old favorites. After Diaghilev's death in 1929, Doubrovska also joined Pavlova's company. Pavlova's death in 1931 greatly depressed Vladimiroff, who decided to stop performing at the age of thirty-eight, still young for a male dancer. He then served as regisseur for a small touring company in the United States headed by Serge Lifar. In 1934 George Balanchine, who had been impressed with Vladimiroff's fine classical technique, invited him to teach at the newly formed School of American Ballet in New York City. Vladimiroff taught advanced classes and coached dancers, such as André Eglevsky, in classical repertoire. Although Vladimiroff was a guest teacher with other companies for brief periods, he remained at the School of American Ballet until 1967, when he retired. Vladimiroff died in New York City.

Called by Lincoln Kirstein in 1935 "one of the noblest living exponents of pure classic style," Vladimiroff was a splendid partner and a virile, exciting dancer known better in Russia than in America. He constantly sought more challenging and demanding roles and was willing to leave familiar surroundings to further develop his artistic abilities. According to his wife he always missed Russia and spoke often of returning, although he never did. Vladimiroff enjoyed teaching and found that it came easily to him. He was known for the careful progression of his classes, which helped students develop exceptionally well-balanced and strong techniques. He also provided the vital link with the great Russian tradition that is in part responsible for the speed and dazzling precision for which Balanchine's dancers are known. Vladimiroff's example encouraged the development of male dancers in America, and he left a legacy of pure classical dancing to those who pass through the School of American Ballet today.

[See Marion Horosko, "In the Shadow of the Russian Tradition," *Dance*, Feb. 1971; Abbie Relkin, "In Pavlova's Shadow," *Ballet News*, Jan. 1981; and Victoria Huckenpaler, "Felia Doubrovska," *Dance Chronicle*, V, 4, 1982–1983. Obituaries are in the *New York Times*, Nov. 26, 1970; and *Dance*, Jan. 1971. A source in Russian is Vera Krasnovskaya, *Russian Ballet Theater of the Twentieth Century*, II (1972).]

DAPHNE POWELL

VON STERNBERG, JOSEF (May 29, 1894–Dec. 22, 1969), motion-picture director, was born Jonas Sternberg in Vienna, Austria-Hungary, the son of Maurice Sternberg, a businessman, and Serafine Singer. In 1897 his father immigrated to the United States, and Josef and his mother followed four years later. The father took his family back to Vienna in 1904, but four years later the family returned to New York City. The young Sternberg's sporadic education included a period at Jamaica High School in Queens, N.Y., but he dropped out in 1909 to work in the garment industry. In 1911, Sternberg became a film patcher, occasionally working as a projectionist. Later he found employment at the World Film Corporation in Fort Lee, N.J., and in time became the chief assistant to the company's president.

When the United States entered World War I in 1917, Sternberg became involved in the production of army training films and subsequently served in the Signal Corps and the Medical Corps. After the war he briefly returned to his job in New Jersey before undertaking what he described as his "apprenticeship"—working as a cutter, editor, title writer, and assistant director in New Jersey, New York, Austria, and England. In 1922, Sternberg, who was usually called Jo, adapted into English the Austrian Karl Adolph's novel *Töchter* (1914); the translation, entitled *Daughters of Vienna*, was published in 1923. By then, he was in Hollywood. The 1924 release *By Divine Right*, on which he worked as assistant director and scenario writer, is the first known instance of the name Josef von Sternberg being used in a screen credit. According to him, his name was "elongated" without his knowledge or approval by the director of the film.

During 1924, von Sternberg wrote, produced, and directed *The Salvation Hunters*. Consciously realistic, with arty overtones of social significance, the film was shot on the mud flats south of Los Angeles. This simple tale of a boy who wins a worldly girl from a brute was produced for less than $5,000, most of which came from George K. Arthur, the young, unknown English actor who played the boy. It won lavish praise from Douglas Fairbanks and Charlie Chaplin, whose United Artists Corporation subsequently distributed the film, and was chosen by one critic as among the ten best of the year.

While a projected collaboration with Mary Pickford never materialized, von Sternberg landed a multiple-picture contract with Metro-Goldwyn-Mayer (MGM). Executives who did not like his first film for the studio partially reshot it, and von Sternberg stalked off the set of the second film after two weeks, unhappy with the assignment. MGM soon terminated his contract. In 1926, Chaplin employed von Sternberg to direct a comeback film for the comedian's former leading lady Edna Purviance. *The Sea Gull* (retitled *A Woman of the Sea* to avoid confusion with the Chekhov play) was partly reshot by Chaplin, previewed once, and then suppressed by the comedian, who supposedly destroyed the negative. The reasons for Chaplin's actions remain a mystery.

Von Sternberg again joined the ranks of the assistant directors. In 1927, Paramount assigned him to reshoot *Children of Divorce*. He completed a substantial number of retakes in only three days, salvaged the film, and earned a project of his own. Between 1927 and 1935 (when he left the studio) he directed fourteen films—one-half of all the films he finished during his career.

Von Sternberg began auspiciously with *Underworld* (1927), a tough, violent melodrama credited with initiating that era's cycle of gangster films. His next film, *The Last Command* (1928), deals with an émigré czarist general who is cast in a bit role as a general in a film about the Russian Revolution. Emil Jannings, the eminent German actor, played the general in what proved to be the best film of his brief American career.

Von Sternberg's other 1928 releases were *The Dragnet*, a mystery, and *The Docks of New York*, a harsh but romantic melodrama. He had two films released in 1929: *The Case of Lena Smith*, a bitter tale of a mother and her illegitimate child set in fin-de-siècle Vienna; and *Thunderbolt*, a gangster film that was his first talkie and made striking use of asynchronous sound. During 1928–1929 he also wrote the story for another Jannings film, and at Paramount's behest—and with the director Erich von Stroheim's approval—he recut *The Wedding March* (1928).

Jannings, in his homeland to make his talkie debut, persuaded the German production company UFA, which had ties to Paramount, to engage von Sternberg. The director arrived in Germany in August 1929, and after some discussion among all parties, it was decided to film Heinrich Mann's 1905 novel *Professor Unrat*, which deals with the decline of a teacher who becomes involved with a loose-living entertainer at the Blue Angel cabaret. Von Sternberg had little interest in Mann's social criticism and emphasized (as in most of his previous films) the sexual relationships between the protagonists. The entertainer, Lola Lola, a callous femme fatale, degrades the teacher, who finds release only in death. Filmed in both German and English versions, *Der blaue Engel* (*The Blue Angel*; 1930), von Sternberg's best-known film, won critical acclaim and commercial success.

Much of that triumph lay in von Sternberg's use of Marlene Dietrich, then a little-known but experienced actress, as the erotic Lola Lola. His career was inextricably wound up with hers until 1935, and he made only one movie without her during that time—an uneven 1931 adaptation of Theodore Dreiser's novel *An American Tragedy* that outraged the author and disappointed the critics. In a succession of movies, von Sternberg molded Dietrich's image to such an extent that he was accused of being a Svengali to her Trilby. In *Morocco* (1930), *Dishonored* (1931), *Shanghai Express* (1932), *Blonde Venus* (1932), *The Scarlet Empress* (1934), and *The Devil Is a Woman* (1935), von Sternberg used his considerable skills to create in each film a variation of the femme fatale portrayed by Dietrich in *The Blue Angel*.

A master of light and shadow, von Sternberg was the only director at the time admitted to the American Society of Cinematographers. He had a distinct visual style that intriguingly utilized various textures, ranging from lace to smoke. In all his films he made unusual use of symbols, reflections, and dissolves (one scene beginning while the previous one ends). Prior to *The Blue Angel* he had been known as a director who clearly and quickly developed plot and characterizations. But von Sternberg's concentration on Dietrich came at the expense of exposition. He also became profligate, spending hours on a shot that would show Dietrich onscreen for a few seconds. The result was intriguing and she was ravishing, but the films suffered and costs soared.

Their last three films, though beautifully crafted, were neither critically nor commercially successful. In 1935, during the last days of shooting *The Devil Is a Woman*, von Sternberg announced an end to their collaboration. But he never again accomplished what he had created before her or with her.

After leaving Paramount, von Sternberg made few films, but many of his projects never materialized. He completed three films during the 1930's, including an iconoclastic but fascinating version of *Crime and Punishment* (1935), with Peter Lorre. An abortive project was his attempt to film Robert Graves's *I, Claudius* in 1937 with Charles Laughton, an effort detailed in the 1965 BBC-TV documentary *The Epic That Never Was*. His last major film, *The Shanghai Gesture* (1941), was based on a vintage theatrical shocker. In the early 1950's, at the invitation of Howard Hughes, he shot two potboilers for RKO; both *Macao* (1952) and *Jet Pilot* (1957) were extensively reshot. Von Sternberg financed his last film, which received little distribution: *Anatahan* (1953) dealt with a group of Japanese soldiers and one woman stranded on a Pacific island during and after World War II. He spent most of the 1950's and 1960's teaching at universities and appearing at retrospectives of his work around the world. He received various honors, including the George Eastman House Medal of Honor (1957). He died in Los Angeles.

Von Sternberg married the actress Riza Royce in July 1926. In 1927, an interlocutory divorce decree was granted. They reconciled but then were divorced in June 1930. On July 30, 1943, von Sternberg married his twenty-one-year-old secretary, Jeanne Avette McBride; she divorced him in 1945. On Oct. 2, 1948, he married a twenty-eight-year-old war widow, Meri Ottis Wilner; they had one child.

A major talent who in his best films displayed a remarkable visual bravura, von Sternberg was a great craftsman but unfortunately not a commercial filmmaker. His avowedly personal style of filmmaking proved too enigmatic, too evasive, too exotic. His films, with a few exceptions, failed at the box office, and the industry turned its back on him.

[Von Sternberg's autobiography, *Fun in a Chinese Laundry* (1965), is fascinating but vague. Critical studies include Herman Weinberg, *Josef von Sternberg* (1966); Andrew Sarris, *The Films of Josef von Sternberg* (1967); and John Baxter, *The Cinema of Josef von Sternberg* (1973). See also Kevin Brownlow, *The Parade's Gone By . . .* (1968); and Peter Baxter, ed., *Sternberg* (1980). An obituary is in the *New York Times*, Dec. 23, 1969.]

DANIEL J. LEAB

VORIS, JOHN RALPH (June 6, 1880–Jan. 12, 1968), minister and social reformer, was born in Franklin, Ind., the son of George Washington Voris, a contract carpenter, and Anna L. Tucker. He attended grade and high school in Anderson after the family moved there in 1889. When the family returned to Franklin in 1898, he entered the Baptist Franklin College, from which he received a B.A. degree in 1901.

Voris' youthful attraction to Christian service as a pastor, teacher, or social worker was turned in the direction of the ministry by a local pastor who encouraged him to give up plans for graduate study in sociology in favor of pursuing a ministerial degree at the University of Chicago's School of Divinity. He completed studies by 1904 for the B.D. degree, which was conferred in 1906, having met tuition expenses through service as pastor of a local German Methodist church. Voris' practical introduction to social work was as a staff member assigned to youth work at the Twenty-third Street Young Men's Christian Association (YMCA) in New York City from 1904 to 1909. In 1905–1906 he took graduate courses in sociology at Columbia University.

Voris filled a succession of pastorates during the years immediately before and after World War I, ably supported by his wife, Edith DeMotte Walker, a former high school teacher, whom he married on June 19, 1906; they had three children. The altruism and concern for children and youth that had drawn him to social service ultimately persuaded him to exchange pastoral for social work. He filled a summer pastorate at the Wading River Congregational Church on Long Island, N.Y., in 1908–1909. Following a teaching interlude from 1909 to 1911, which he spent lecturing on biblical literature and directing the campus YMCA at the University of Indiana, he was formally received into the Presbyterian church. He served as pastor in New Albany, Ind., from 1911 to 1913 and was president of the Social Welfare Association of New Albany. From 1913 to 1916 he was pastor of the Union Presbyterian Church in Laramie, Wyo., and served as chaplain at the University of Wyoming and as an officer for the Presbyterian Synod of Wyoming. In Manhattan, Kans., from 1916 to 1917, he was pastor of the First Congregational Church. Although not an imposing figure, he had a commanding presence and a forceful speaking style that led to an invitation to lecture on the Chautauqua summer circuit in 1917. He had given eighty-four lectures in several states before responding to an urgent request to administer programs for army recruits when the United States entered World War I.

As general secretary of the YMCA, Voris organized services at Camp Kearney, Calif., in 1917–1918 and then worked for the National War Work Council of the YMCA out of its San Francisco office from 1918 to 1920 as director of religious work and later as supervisor of the council's western United States operations. Further experiences as associate national field director for the Inter-church World Movement (1919–1920) and as associate general secretary and director of church and other relations for the Near East Relief Program exposed Voris to postwar needs. His Near East relief duties involved biennial trips in 1921–1925 to study famine conditions in Russia, Armenia, and Greece and to assist clergymen in charge of orphanages in the Near East. In 1929–1931 he served as executive secretary of the Golden Rule Foundation and in 1929–1930 as honorary executive secretary of the Committee on Relations with Eastern Churches.

The Save the Children Federation, incorporated in New York City by Voris and a few close associates in January 1932, was designed to relieve suffering caused by poverty without creedal, racial, or regional restrictions. Self-help methods were invented to employ rural teachers and volunteer aids in southern Appalachia to improve living conditions in that region. Voris guided the federation from its inception until his retirement in 1952, and under his direction it expanded to serve needy children of the world by means of fund-raising and a network of field offices in various parts of the United States, Latin America, Europe, Asia, and Africa, as well as through affiliation with other national and international relief organizations. The British and French governments honored him for his international relief work, making him an honorary Officer of the Order of the British Empire in 1946, awarding him the French Legion of Honor, and making him an Officier d'Académie in 1948. An honorary doctor of divinity degree was awarded by Franklin College for his efforts in furthering Christian unity and interracial goodwill. He was elected a vice-president of the International Union of Child Welfare in 1945 and participated in its biennial conference at Stockholm in 1948. In the 1930's and 1940's the *Christian Century* and other church publications carried articles by him on conditions in the Near East and Russia and on the work of the federation.

Tireless in his dedication and keenly aware of the sufferings that World War II and the subsequent displacement of families had inflicted on children, Voris retired from Save the Children in 1952 and formed Seniors in Philanthropic Service, a Los Angeles–based program through which retired persons collected and distributed clothing to needy children. As with Save the Children, for which Edith Voris had conducted infant clothing drives and other projects, his wife was an active partner in the practical implementation of the new service. Voris died in Duarte, Calif.

[Among Voris' articles is "The Russia I Saw," *Christian Century*, Sept. 22, 1943. An obituary is in the *New York Times*, Jan. 18, 1968.]

KAREN M. KENNELLY

VORSE, MARY HEATON (Oct. 9, 1874–June 14, 1966), author, journalist, and labor activist, was born Mary Heaton in New York City, the daughter of Hiram Heaton, a retired innkeeper, and Ellen Cordelia Blackman. Her parents, who both came from old New England families, provided Vorse with an upbringing that was financially comfortable and culturally stimulating, but politically sheltered. The Heaton family resided in Amherst, Mass., but often spent winters in Europe. Vorse attended private schools, but much of her education came from travel and her mother's tutoring.

Vorse hoped to become an artist and studied for several years in Paris and in New York City. Once she realized that her art would never be more than merely competent, she turned to other outlets. In 1898 she married Albert White Vorse, a newspaperman and aspiring writer with a deep interest in boating and exploration. They had two children. The Vorses eagerly participated in Bohemian life in New York City's Greenwich Village, but in 1903 they moved to Europe for several years in the hope that cheaper living costs would enable Albert White Vorse to launch a literary career. His ambitions were not fulfilled, but Mary Heaton Vorse discovered that she had a natural talent for writing. Her first triumph came in August 1905 when the *Atlantic Monthly* published her comic sketch "The Breaking-in of a Yachtman's Wife." The story was eventually developed into a novel with the same title and published in 1908. Popular magazines began buying virtually everything Vorse wrote, and she wrote prolifically. Her specialty was the warm, humorous sketch focusing on family life. She became so successful that she was invited to contribute a chapter to *The Whole Family* (1908), a composite novel featuring the work of twelve writers, including such distinguished figures as William Dean Howells and Henry James.

Upon their return to the United States, the Vorses helped establish the A Club, an experiment in cooperative housing in New York City that attracted liberal intellectuals and writers. In 1907 they bought an old house in Provincetown, Mass., which became a vital part of Mary Heaton Vorse's life. The genial treatment of domestic life that characterized her fiction did not reveal the truth about her marriage, which was often strained. Vorse separated from her husband in 1909. On June 14, 1910, he died suddenly, and the next day Vorse's mother died. Vorse heard of both deaths while crossing the Atlantic.

The next years were marked by Vorse's determination to support her family through freelance writing and her increasing interest in political reform and the labor movement. She continued to write light fiction and tied some of her magazine sketches together with episodic frameworks, publishing them as novels. The most representative of these was Vorse's affectionate study of American family life, *The Prestons* (1918), but her most original and most interesting work of fiction was *The Autobiography of an Elderly Woman* (1911), which offered a moving portrait of an old woman's struggle to maintain an active and independent life. Vorse's historical importance, however, stems more from her work on behalf of organized labor than from her literary efforts. She regarded the textile mill strike at Lawrence, Mass., in 1912 as the turning point of her life. Her dismay at the deplorable living conditions of workers and their families led to her fervent determination to aid the cause of labor.

Vorse's devotion to reform was shared and encouraged by Joe O'Brien, a journalist who became her second husband in 1912; they had one child. O'Brien seemed to have been the ideal mate for Mary Heaton Vorse (the name she used throughout her professional career); their homes in Greenwich Village and Provincetown became important centers for the radical intelligentsia. Vorse did much to turn Provincetown into a refuge for writers from New York City. She helped found the Provincetown Players, the repertory company that revitalized the American theater in the early twentieth century. The group's first production was given on her wharf in 1915. O'Brien's death in 1915 was a serious blow to Vorse, but she kept busy as a writer and a political activist. Little is known about her relationship with Robert Minor, a political cartoonist and radical, whom Vorse apparently married in 1920 and divorced in 1922.

Vorse aptly described herself as "a woman who in early life got angry because many children lived miserably and died needlessly." She was associated with various left-wing movements and edited *The Masses* for a while, but she had little interest in abstract ideological questions. The distinguishing mark of her journalism, which appeared in major newspapers and in magazines such as *Harper's*, the *Nation*, the *New Republic*, and the *Advance*, was an insistence on recognizing the realities of human suffering. Her articles contained facts and statistics, but their power stemmed from Vorse's ability to arouse the reader's compassion and indignation. Her most impressive book of nonfiction, *Men and Steel* (1920), was a vivid account of the great steel strike of 1919 and a compelling portrayal of human beings victimized by impersonal forces.

Vorse's labor reporting took her throughout the United States and spanned four decades. After the Lawrence strike of 1912 she wrote about and often actively participated in most of the labor movement's crucial struggles, including the attempt of the Industrial Workers of the World (IWW) to organize New York City's unemployed in 1914, the miners' strike in Minnesota's Mesabi Range in 1916, the steel strike of 1919, the Passaic, N.J., textile strike of 1926 (for which Vorse served as publicity director), the efforts throughout the 1920's and 1930's to organize southern mills and mines, and the major victory of the United Automobile Workers (UAW) in their Flint, Mich., strike of 1937. Her writings helped to make organized labor and the right to strike accepted parts of American life. Next to *Men and Steel*, her most important book about labor was *Labor's New Millions* (1938), which reflected Vorse's deep admiration for the Congress of Industrial Organizations (CIO). She also wrote *Strike* (1930), a novel about the attempt of the National Textile Workers' Union to organize the textile mills in Gastonia, N.C. Her last major article, an exposé of union corruption on the New York City waterfront, appeared in *Harper's* in 1952. A decade later she was among the first recipients of the United Automobile Workers' Social Justice Award.

Vorse's work took her to Europe frequently, where her writing focused on victims of war, injustice, and political disorder. While attending international conferences on woman's suffrage and world peace in 1915, Vorse witnessed the effects of World War I. She produced a few propaganda reports for the American government and later wrote about postwar conditions in Europe for the Red Cross, the American Relief Association, and American periodicals. She also covered the Russian famine of 1921–1922 for the Hearst newspapers. Her other European reporting included accounts of Adolf Hitler's rise to power in 1933, the beginnings of World War II, and her service in Italy with the United Nations Relief and Rehabilitation Administration from 1945 to 1947.

Vorse's *Footnote to Folly* (1935) provided a vivid picture of the events she witnessed in America and Europe from 1912 to 1922. *Time and the Town* (1942) contained reminiscences of her beloved Provincetown. These autobiographical writings revealed little about her personal life, but Vorse's courage, dedication, and compassion won the admiration of many. Ill health limited her activities during the final years of her long life. At the time of her death in Provincetown she was virtually forgotten.

[The Vorse papers are in the Archives of Labor History and Urban Affairs, Wayne State University,

Detroit, Mich. See the Rusty Byrne bibliography, Schlesinger Library, Radcliffe College, Cambridge, Mass. The Oral History Collection at Columbia University contains a transcript of "The Reminiscences of Mary Heaton Vorse" (1957). The introduction to *Rebel Pen* (1968), Dee Garrison's collection of Vorse's writings, provides the only reliable guide to Vorse's personal life. See also "The Rebel Girl," in Murray Kempton, *Part of Our Time* (1955). An obituary is in the *New York Times*, June 15, 1966.]

ALFRED BENDIXEN

WALLACE, LURLEEN BURNS (Sept. 19, 1926–May 7, 1968), governor of Alabama, was born in Tuscaloosa, Ala., the daughter of Henry Morgan Burns, a lumber grader and later a shipyard worker, and Estelle Burroughs. She attended local schools, graduating early from high school, and received a diploma from the Tuscaloosa Business College in 1942. That year she met George Corley Wallace in the local Kress variety store, where she worked as a clerk. They were married on May 21, 1943; they had four children. After his discharge from the Army Air Forces in 1945, the Wallaces settled in Clayton, Ala.

George Wallace was elected to the state legislature in 1946, and thus began his political career. Lurleen Wallace, the model of the busy, middle-class housewife, was active in the Methodist church, where she taught Sunday school. Wallace enjoyed needlework, water-skiing, horseback riding, and flying light airplanes, although she never received a pilot's license. Politics, though, were left to her husband.

This would begin to change in 1958, when Wallace's husband first ran for governor of Alabama. Then she made a few campaign appearances with him. Although he lost the primary election, his ambition to become governor remained keen. In 1962, with his attractive though shy wife at his side, he emerged as a hard-line segregationist candidate, and a successful one. He became the foremost example of a states'-rights governor. As Alabama's first lady, Lurleen Wallace presided graciously over the usual round of receptions and teas.

Lurleen Wallace was thrust onto the center stage of politics because of a provision in Alabama's constitution forbidding a governor from succeeding himself in office. Failing in his attempt to change the state constitution on this point and not wanting to relinquish his authority, he asked his wife to consider running for governor in 1966. After giving the question much thought, Wallace decided to do so, even though her husband had reportedly cooled on the matter.

On Feb. 24, 1966, Lurleen Wallace announced her candidacy for governor. There never was any doubt that she was running as her husband's surrogate. He declared that if she were elected, "I shall be by her side and shall make the policies and decisions affecting the next administration." She added, "My election would enable my husband to carry on his programs for the people of Alabama." Moreover, she made it clear that she would assist him in forwarding his growing presidential ambitions. In their numerous joint appearances, she dealt with state and local issues and he chiefly with national issues. She usually spoke first and then introduced her husband by saying, "If you elect me, he will be my number-one adviser." She showed sparkle and ability in speaking, and she increasingly spoke longer during her appearances and contributed to the writing of her speeches. Her chief campaign issue, as was her husband's, was opposition to outside interference in state affairs.

Wallace had to face some election factors that her husband had not encountered in 1962. Not only had a substantial number of blacks become registered voters since then, but also the Republicans had become a force with which to reckon. Moreover, she was running against nine other Democrats in the 1966 gubernatorial primary election. Wallace swept all before her, however, winning the primary election with 54.1 percent of the votes cast. She won the general election against a segregationist Republican congressman and an independent candidate, polling 63.4 percent of the vote. Thus, she became only the third woman—and the first since the 1930's—to be elected a governor in the United States.

Wallace's tenure of office was memorable, if short. She was inaugurated on Jan. 16, 1967. Wallace reiterated her vow to carry on her husband's programs, adding that Alabama's "principles of self-government will not be suppressed by force—force from China, from Russia, from Cuba, or from Washington, D.C." When in March 1967 a federal court ordered the desegregation of the state's public schools, she asked the legislature for complete control over the schools. In May she cut off state funds to all-black Tuskegee Institute. Wallace also followed her husband's drives to improve state highways, expand trade-school training, combat tuberculosis, and encourage Alabama's industrial development. Her own contribution was to secure funding to improve mental hospitals. She was a working governor, however much her husband set the policies of her administration.

Wallace had had an operation for cancer before she ran for governor. In July 1967 she had to undergo surgery for a new malignancy. From then on, she was able to devote little time to her official duties, although she did find time to make out-of-state appearances with her husband in the following November and January in connection with his independent candidacy for the presidency. Her health deteriorated rapidly, though, until her death in Montgomery.

During her time on the public scene, Wallace made a favorable impression on many Americans. Her verve, diligence, and wit gave her considerable credibility, and her early death made her seem a tragic figure. During the resurgence of the women's movement in America, she was a symbol, despite her segregationism and her husband's domination, of womanly success for many. Indeed, she placed sixth on a list of the nation's most-admired women in a December 1966 Gallup poll.

[Archival material on Wallace is in the Alabama Department of Archives and History. There are two biographies: Jack D. House, *Lady of Courage* (1969); and Anita Smith, *The Intimate Story of Lurleen Wallace* (1969). See also Ray Jenkins, "Mr. and Mrs. Wallace Run for Governor of Alabama," *New York Times Magazine*, Apr. 24, 1966, and "The Queen of Alabama and the Prince Consort," *New York Times Magazine*, May 21, 1967; Marshall Frady, *Wallace* (1968); George Wallace, Jr., *The Wallaces of Alabama* (1975); and George C. Wallace, *Stand Up for America* (1976). An obituary is in the *New York Times*, May 7, 1968.]

DONALD R. MCCOY

WANGER, WALTER (July 11, 1894–Nov. 18, 1968), theater and motion-picture producer, was born Walter Feuchtwanger in San Francisco, Calif., the son of Sigmund Feuchtwanger, a wealthy manufacturer of denim overalls, and Stella Stettheimer. He attended Pacific Heights Grammar School. The family frequently went to the theater, opera, and ballet and traveled regularly to Europe, providing Wanger with a cosmopolitan background that became one of his strengths as a producer.

In 1905, Sigmund Feuchtwanger died and the family moved to New York and shortened the name to Wanger. Walter attended the Cascadilla School in Ithaca, N.Y., and entered Dartmouth College in 1911. He fell into academic difficulties and left the college to study in Europe. He met George Bernard Shaw, the English actor and producer Harley Granville-Barker, and others who introduced him to the designs of Léon Bakst and the theories of the New Theater movement. Wanger, excited by these ideas, returned to Dartmouth and transformed the theater program there. Discovering his powers as a producer, he influenced a donor to build a theater, established a scene-building organization, freed his plays from faculty supervision, and expanded the number of plays produced, coupling serious works with vaudeville. This diversity became a hallmark of Wanger's work.

In December 1914, when Dartmouth declared Wanger academically ineligible for theater activities, he left to become an assistant to Granville-Barker, then directing plays in New York City. The following year Wanger joined the Elisabeth Marbury agency, negotiating Irene Castle's appearance in the serial film *Patria*. In January 1917 he successfully produced a Broadway play, *'Ception Shoals*, starring Alla Nazimova.

Wanger enlisted in the army in June 1917 and, though trained in the Air Corps, spent the war working on propaganda in Rome. A newsreel he promoted so impressed him with its power to change public opinion that he decided to make a career in film. After serving as an aide at the Paris Peace Conference, he returned to New York and on Sept. 13, 1919, married Justine Johnstone, a Ziegfeld Follies actress; they had no children.

After a dinner party at which he met Jesse L. Lasky, the head of the Famous Players–Lasky film company, the predecessor of Paramount Pictures, Wanger worked on several scripts for Lasky, who made him general manager of Paramount Pictures' Long Island studios. Wanger's outspoken criticisms aggravated a feud between Paramount's New York and Hollywood units, and after a dispute in 1920, he left Paramount and went to England.

In London, Wanger supervised the opening

of new cinemas for Provincial Cinematograph Theatres, produced three plays by Frederick Lonsdale, and arranged the American tour of a major revue. Lasky rehired Wanger in 1923 to supervise all of Paramount's productions. Wanger remained with the studio until 1931, demonstrating considerable showmanship and a gift for artistic innovation. He convinced Elinor Glyn to write *It* so that Clara Bow could be the "It" girl. He also helped the director Rouben Mamoulian to develop the revolutionary soundtrack of the film *Applause* in 1929.

When Emmanuel Cohen took over Paramount in 1931, Wanger left. After several unhappy months at Columbia Pictures, he became an executive producer at Metro-Goldwyn-Mayer, where he stayed until 1934. His work there included Garbo's *Queen Christina* (1933) and the political fantasy *Gabriel Over the White House* (1933). After conflicts with Mayer, Wanger returned to Paramount as an independent producer. He made what is held to be the first outdoor Technicolor film, *The Trail of the Lonesome Pine* (1936); *Every Night at Eight* (1935), a widely imitated musical; *The President Vanishes* (1935), a controversial political thriller; and eleven others.

These films enhanced Wanger's reputation as a trendsetter. Many of the stars he used were under contract to him; some, like Charles Boyer, owed their careers to Wanger's management. Wanger negotiated a long-term contract at United Artists, where he made several highly regarded films. With some, including *You Only Live Once* (1937), he planned the production; with others, like *Stagecoach* (1939), he was only nominally associated.

In 1938, Wanger was divorced. On Jan. 12, 1940, he married the actress Joan Bennett; they had two children. From 1939 to 1945, the period of his greatest prestige, he served as president of the Academy of Motion Picture Arts and Sciences, and he and Bennett were leaders of Hollywood society. Dartmouth belatedly awarded him a degree in 1938, and the next year, *Foreign Affairs* published his article on the increasing threat of censorship and the influence of American films abroad.

Wanger resigned from United Artists in 1941 and set up his own production company allied with Universal Pictures. From 1942 to 1945 he made a number of minor but successful films. In 1945, in partnership with his wife and the director Fritz Lang, he produced *Scarlet Street*, considered one of Lang and Bennett's best films.

Wanger filmed Ingrid Bergman in 1948 in *Joan of Arc*, a financial and artistic failure. Although the following year he produced three successful films, he remained in debt and without prospects. In January 1951 he was sued for bankruptcy. Forced to seek employment at a second-rate studio, Wanger was dependent on his wife's earnings and resented the television work she undertook to support the family. His resentment focused on Bennett's agent, Jennings Lang, with whom the actress was rumored to be having a love affair. On Dec. 13, 1951, Wanger accosted Bennett and Lang in a parking lot and shot the agent. Lang recovered and Wanger received a four-month jail sentence.

Wanger capitalized on his notoriety by making a prison film, *Riot in Cell Block 11* (1954), directed by Don Siegel. He continued to produce successful films, including *Invasion of the Body Snatchers* (1956), again with Siegel directing and considered by many to be Siegel's best film, and *I Want to Live* (1958), for which Susan Hayward won an Academy Award.

Wanger, then in ill health, turned to a long-planned dramatization of the life of Cleopatra. He convinced Twentieth Century–Fox to make a lavish spectacle with Elizabeth Taylor. Hampered by illness, bad weather, political infighting, and raucous publicity, *Cleopatra* (1963) proved, at $37 million, the costliest picture that had yet been made, nearly bankrupting the studio. Though Wanger was removed from the film's production staff, he retained credit as producer and published an account of his troubles in *My Life with Cleopatra* (1963).

During the last five years of his life, Wanger was unable to produce another project. Divorced from Bennett in 1965, he lived in New York, dining out, visiting friends, vacationing with his children, and planning new movies. He died in New York City.

In an era when sophistication was rare among film producers, Wanger supplied an erudition and love of innovation that made him a leader in the industry. He produced more than sixty pictures, and even his routine films have a distinctive character. His memorable films are usually attributed to their directors, but Wanger's contribution was substantial. As Siegel said, "Walter inspires one; he encourages creativity. I was working with a man who was educating me."

[The Academy of Motion Picture Arts and Sciences, Beverly Hills, Calif., and the Dartmouth College Archives and Alumni Records Office, Hanover, N.H., maintain files on Wanger. An article about him is in the *Dartmouth College Library Bulletin*, Apr. 1983. See also Jesse L. Lasky, *I Blow My Own Horn* (1957); Joan Bennett, *The Bennett Playbill* (1970); Bernard Rosenberg and Harry Silverstein, *The Real Tinsel* (1970); Stuart Rosenthal and Judith M. Cass, *Tod Browning, Don Siegel* (1975); and Tino Balio, *United Artists: The Company Built by the Stars* (1976). An obituary is in the *New York Times*, Nov. 19, 1968.]

ALAN BUSTER

WARBURG, JAMES PAUL (Aug. 18, 1896–June 3, 1969), financier, author, and government official, was born in Hamburg, Germany, the son of Paul Moritz Warburg, a banker, and Nina Jenny Loeb. His parents brought him to the United States in 1901, and he was naturalized in 1911. He attended Columbia Grammar School, New York City, and Middlesex School, Concord, Mass., until 1913. He graduated in 1917 with a B.A. from Harvard University.

After working briefly as a passenger agent for the Baltimore and Ohio Railroad, he joined the navy in 1917 as a seaman; he was later commissioned a lieutenant in the Navy Flying Corps. While in training as a combat pilot, he developed a new type of aero compass and was assigned to Washington, D.C., to supervise its production. On June 1, 1918, he married Katharine Faulkner Swift, from whom he was divorced in 1934. They had three children.

Warburg began his banking career with the National Metropolitan Bank in Washington, D.C., in 1918. He moved to the First National Bank of Boston in 1919 as a bookkeeper and rose to assistant cashier by 1921, when he left to become vice-president of the International Acceptance Corporation in New York City, a firm founded by his father. International Acceptance specialized in financing international trade by means of bankers' acceptances issued under letters of credit. In 1928 International Acceptance was amalgamated with the Bank of Manhattan Company, the securities affiliate of the Bank of Manhattan. In 1931 and 1932 Warburg was president of the International Acceptance Bank, and from 1932 through 1935 he served as vice-chairman of the board of the Bank of Manhattan Company.

In 1933 Warburg, a lifelong Democrat, joined President Franklin D. Roosevelt's first "brain trust" as a financial adviser. His initial assignment was to determine which banks were sufficiently sound to merit reopening after the bank holiday. He assisted in reforming the banking system and analyzed industrial recovery proposals. Warburg prepared the agenda for the World Economic Conference in London and served as monetary adviser to the American delegation to the conference but resigned when President Roosevelt rejected a return to the gold standard. Warburg began to criticize Roosevelt's fiscal policies in best-selling books such as *The Money Muddle* (1934) and *It's Up to Us* (1934). In 1936 he opposed Roosevelt's reelection in a series of syndicated newspaper columns and in two books, *Hell Bent for Election* (1935) and *Still Hell Bent* (1936). In April 1935 Warburg married Phyllis Baldwin Browne. They had no children and were divorced in 1947.

In 1937 Warburg began a career as a free-lance originator of industrial financing in New York City. His greatest success was finding financing for Edwin H. Land, the inventor of the Polaroid process, which reduced the intensity of light passing through plastic. Warburg invested heavily in the Polaroid Corporation (eventually making a fortune) and served on its board of directors.

In 1939 Warburg grew concerned about American isolationism and neutrality. Despite his earlier disagreements with Roosevelt, he supported the president's foreign policy in two books, *Peace in Our Time* (1940) and *Our War and Our Peace* (1941). He became a leading spokesman for the Committee to Defend America by Aiding the Allies and helped found the Fight for Freedom Committee, which called for immediate American entry into World War II. In 1941 Warburg debated Charles Lindbergh of America First, an isolationist organization, at Madison Square Garden in New York City.

Appointed special assistant in the Office of Coordinator of Information, Warburg worked in the development of propaganda and assembled a foreign-language staff for the Foreign Information Service. In July 1942 he was appointed deputy director of the overseas branch of the Office of War Information in London, with responsibility for propaganda aimed at the Axis powers and at occupied European nations.

Warburg left government service in February 1944 and wrote the first of a series of books in which he advocated the continuation of Roosevelt's policies as the best means of maintaining peace. He also worked for Roosevelt's reelection that year.

Warburg became critical of the foreign policy of President Harry S Truman, who, Warburg believed, had moved away from Roosevelt's cooperation with the Soviet Union and from adherence to the Atlantic Alliance. Warburg was an early and vocal critic of the Truman Doctrine and of the idea of the United States as a global policeman.

In 1947 Warburg helped form and became director of the United World Federalists (UFW), an organization skeptical of the United Nations' ability to maintain peace. The Federalists called for a stronger international organization with universal membership and weighted representation, world government, total disarmament, abolition of national armies, and world law.

On August 28, 1948, Warburg married Joan Melber. They had four children. Frustrated by the unwillingness of many members to speak out on government actions, Warburg distanced himself from the UWF and began a series of books examining American foreign policy. He opposed containment and favored accommodation with the Soviet Union and Communist China in the interest of peace.

In 1960 Warburg supported John F. Kennedy for president, and in 1961 he was appointed to assist John McCloy, who was forming a new Arms Control and Disarmament Agency and was negotiating with the Soviet Union. Warburg provided the president with ideas for speeches on disarmament and on the establishment of world peace. Warburg received the Gandhi Peace Prize in 1962. He died in Greenwich, Conn.

[The Warburg papers are at the John F. Kennedy Presidential Library, Boston, Mass. See Stephen Birmingham, *Our Crowd* (1967); and Vincent P. Carosso, *Investment Banking in America* (1970). There is an obituary in the *New York Times*, June 4, 1969.]

STEPHEN D. BODAYLA

WARD, HARRY FREDERICK (Oct. 15, 1873–Dec. 9, 1966), religious educator, author, and social critic, was born near London, England, in Brentford, Middlesex County, the son of Harry Ward, a prosperous butcher and provisions merchant and a Methodist lay minister, and Florence ("Fanny") Jeffery. Ward worked in the family business and was appalled by his father's callous attitude toward employees. This early contact with capitalism influenced his later sympathy with labor.

Ward attended a boys' school befitting his father's status as a tradesman. Realizing the educational limitations imposed upon him by his social class, he immigrated to the United States in 1891. He lived for a time with relatives in Utah and Idaho and worked at odd jobs, including lay preaching (which he had done in England) and missionary work. He enrolled at the University of Southern California in 1893 but then transferred to Northwestern University in Evanston, Ill., the strong Methodism of which reinforced his earlier evangelism and probably determined his career. He received his bachelor's degree in 1897 and won a scholarship to Harvard, from which he received a master's degree in philosophy in 1898.

Ward, a disciple of the Social Gospel, was named head resident of the Northwestern Settlement House in Chicago in 1898. He also studied for certification as a Methodist minister. On Apr. 20, 1899, he married Harriet Mae ("Daisy") Kendall, the daughter of a Kansas City manufacturer, whom he had met at Northwestern; they had three children.

In 1900, Ward was abruptly dismissed from the settlement house in a dispute with the governing council over administrative authority. He was accredited as a minister in 1902 and continued preaching at the Wabash Avenue Methodist Church in Chicago between 1900 and 1902. He served two more inner-city churches and one suburban church during the next decade. The spread of social and economic reform, the rise of organized labor, and the challenge of Socialist thought during the Progressive era paralleled his personal experiences and observations of the miseries of Chicago; to these factors Ward applied his own religious and philosophical insights.

In 1907, Ward drafted "The Social Creed of the Churches," a landmark church program for the benefit of workers. The statement invoked the Golden Rule and Christ's precepts and committed the Methodist Episcopal church to "equal rights and complete Justice for all men in all stations of life." It also promoted most of the contemporary aims of labor advocates: conciliation and arbitration, health and safety for laborers, abolition of child labor, regulation of the labor of women, suppression of sweatshops, reduced working hours, expanded leisure, full employment, a six-day work week, a living wage, and fairer distribution of goods and services. This led to the formation in December 1907 of the Methodist Federation for Social Service (later, Social Action) as a propaganda agency for the creed among Methodists, but endorsements soon came from many other religious organizations. Ward served the federation as editor (1907–1911) and general secretary (1911–1944). The work of the federation is considered his most enduring contribution.

For half a century, Ward remained a major social critic and activist. He composed manifestos, policy pronouncements, petitions, and letters to the editor, and wrote more than two hundred books and articles. Representative of his writings on religion and economics are *The Labor Movement* (1917), *The New Social Order* (1919), *Our Economic Morality* (1929), and *Which Way Religion?* (1931), while *In Place of Profit* (1933) reveals his view of the Soviet system. He also worked constantly through conferences, committees, and organizations and their internal networks. Most of Ward's articles were commentary on, or restatements of, his social vision; only a few of his full-length books contain original ideas. He generally eschewed traditional organized politics and participation in labor-union affairs.

In 1913, Ward was appointed professor of social service at Boston University's School of Theology. In 1918 he was named professor of Christian ethics at Union Theological Seminary in New York City, from which he retired in 1941.

Ward's faith in advocacy organizations is exemplified in four major commitments: to civil liberties, to the peace movement, to racial equality, and to a united antifascist front. He served as chairman of the national board of the American Civil Liberties Union (ACLU) during its first twenty years (1920–1940). His contribution to the early ACLU is obscured by his controversial resignation, personality and ideological clashes among board members, and the dominance of Roger Baldwin as director.

The American League Against War and Fascism (after 1936 the League for Peace and Democracy) was founded in 1933 as a united front for farm, labor, church, minority, civil rights, and consumer organizations alarmed by the threat of international war and the rise of European fascism. Ward served as national chairman from 1934 until the league was dissolved in 1940. It was beset by internal dissension and external attacks throughout its brief history, and Ward was unable to create sufficient cohesion among its intellectuals, writers, and activists to permit real accomplishments. Even less successful was Ward's involvement from 1933 to 1938 with *New America*, which he launched among intellectuals to draw a blueprint for a new social order derived from the American revolutionary tradition.

By the 1930's, Ward was increasingly on the defensive. His strong prolabor views, his interest in Marxism and socialism, and his defense of the rights of all, including American Communists and Communist sympathizers, led to charges of anticapitalism and pro-Communism. His invariable response was that he was a member of no party. This did not satisfy his opponents, who knew of his frequent association with, and defense of, Communists and Communist organizations and of his admiration for the Soviet economic system and his sympathy with Russian policies.

Ward viewed Jesus Christ as a revolutionary historical figure, only one of many such figures, whose basic ideas were added to, and even corrupted, in organized Christianity. He was intrigued by Karl Marx, whom he saw less as an economic theorist than as a humanitarian. Visits to India, China, and Russia also influenced his international outlook. He remained active as a speaker, agitator, and writer until a few years before his death in Palisades, N.J.

[The Union Theological Seminary Library in New York City contains the personal papers of Ward, his wife, and several faculty associates. The Drew Theological Seminary Library in Madison, N.J., holds the papers of the Methodist Federation for Social Service; Princeton University Library contains papers of the ACLU; and the Swarthmore College Library Peace Collection in Swarthmore, Penn., holds the papers of the American League Against War and Fascism. Eugene P. Link, *Labor-Religion Prophet: The Times and Life of Harry F. Ward* (1984), a sympathetic portrait, lists more than 200 books and articles by Ward. An obituary is in the *New York Times*, Dec. 10, 1966.]

FREDERICK I. OLSON

WARING, JULIUS WATIES (July 27, 1880–Jan. 11, 1968), lawyer, federal judge, and civil rights activist, was born in Charleston, S.C., the son of Edward Perry Waring, a railroad official, and Anna Thomasine Waties. Both the Waring and Waties families had long provided South Carolina with socially and politically prominent people. For eight generations Waring's ancestors had been, in his words, "fine, decent slaveholders."

Waring attended a private secondary school in Charleston and got his B.A. at the College of Charleston in 1900. After graduation, he clerked with a prestigious Charleston law firm. Once a lawyer, he built a thriving practice. A handsome, genial six-footer, Waring enjoyed the life of an eligible bachelor for several years. On Oct. 30, 1913, he married Annie S. Gammell, a hometown belle from a well-established family; they had one child.

From 1914 to 1921, Waring served as assistant United States attorney, a job he owed to his vigorous campaigning for Woodrow Wilson in 1912. In this position he gained extensive knowledge of federal law, which heightened his longtime ambition to be a federal judge. In the 1920's working mainly for corporate interests, his law firm prospered. His social status on the rise, he joined the elitist Charleston Light Dragoons, a kind of upper-class American Legion that traced its roots back to the American Revolution, and the even more exclusive St. Cecilia Society. In the 1930's he became more involved in politics. From 1933 to 1942 he was corporate counsel for the depression-ravaged city of Charleston, working under the opportunistic New Deal mayor, Burnett Maybank.

In 1938, Waring directed the senatorial campaign of "Cotton" Ed Smith, a notorious baiter of blacks. By 1940 he was a solid fixture of the Democratic establishment in South Carolina, and in 1942, Senators Maybank and Smith, his former bosses, secured his appointment as a federal district judge.

Waring donned his judicial robes with great emotion. It was "like being born again," he said. He soon gained a reputation as a stern, efficient, and dignified judge. No longer a partisan, he claimed that he "gradually acquired a passion for justice." Nevertheless, had he not changed his racial views and handed down a series of liberal civil rights decisions between 1945 and 1951, he undoubtedly would have escaped historical notice.

In his first civil rights case, *Thompson* v. *Gibbes* (1945), Waring ordered the equalization of pay for black and white teachers. *Thompson* alerted him to the pervasive discrimination against blacks. He next raised local eyebrows by including blacks on jurors' lists and demanding that lawyers in his courtroom address all blacks as "Mr.," "Mrs.," or "Miss." He also hired a brawny black man as his bailiff.

Despite such actions, for some time Waring's outlook remained essentially that of a paternalistic gradualist. By 1947, however, he had begun to move leftward. Gradualism seemed inadequate in a state where officials employed every conceivable subterfuge to maintain the banned white primary. Thus, in 1947, Waring issued a decision on South Carolina's illegal disfranchisement of blacks that jolted the state. In a fiery opinion (*Rice* v. *Elmore*), he declared, "It is time for South Carolina to rejoin the Union. It is time . . . to adopt the American way of conducting elections."

Waring's bombshell brought him instant ostracism. No local whites, not even relatives, visited his stately home after 1947. Night riders burned crosses on his lawn and fired shots through his windows. Hundreds of scurrilous letters and scores of obscene telephone calls deluged him. Politicians threatened to impeach him. *Time* called him "the man they love to hate."

Hostility only pushed Waring further leftward. By 1949, in fact, he felt compelled to help demolish segregation. He now considered desegregation as the necessary first step to racial progress and maintained that it could only be achieved by federal intervention. Sitting on the special three-man court in 1951 that heard *Briggs* v. *Elliot* (one of the four school desegregation cases finally decided by the Supreme Court in 1954), Waring argued passionately in dissent that segregation in public schools harmed blacks and was unconstitutional. "*Segregation*," he underscored, "*is per se inequality*."

Waring retired in 1952 and moved to New York City, where he was a much-sought-after hero. On the night of May 17, 1954, Walter White, the head of the National Association for the Advancement of Colored People, and a host of noted racial liberals held an impromptu party at Waring's apartment to celebrate the *Brown* v. *Board of Education* decision and honor the judge. He spent his remaining years in New

York, lending his hand to many civil rights causes.

Because Waring never questioned racial caste until his sixties, southern whites were perplexed by his transformation. Most interpreted his conversion as revenge for the hostile reaction encountered when he divorced his first wife in 1945 in order to marry Elizabeth Hoffman, a twice-divorced northerner. Actually, his change of heart was far more complex. Several factors were responsible: his appointment to the bench significantly altered his perspective on the law, and his marriage to a northern woman forced him to see the South through her shocked eyes. His new spouse introduced him to the writings of Wilbur J. Cash and Gunnar Myrdal, two severe critics of the South, and to many of her liberal northern friends. Waring also had a self-righteous streak that grew stronger with age. It was enhanced by the adulation he received from blacks and northern whites for his bold fight against Jim Crow. Furthermore, the timing of Waring's appointment to the court was crucial. It came when the race problem loomed large as a national issue. This forced him to deal with the matter. Addressing the issue with courage and dramatic fervor, he thrust himself into the limelight and into the nation's conscience at a crucial time in American race relations.

[Waring's personal papers are in the Moorland Spingarn Research Center at Howard University, Washington, D.C. See also his article "The Struggle for Negro Rights," *Lawyers Guild Review*, Winter 1949.

Popular accounts of Waring can be found in "The Man They Love to Hate," *Time*, Aug. 23, 1948; Samuel Grafton, "The Lonesomest Man in Town," *Collier's*, Apr. 29, 1950; and Carl Rowan, "How Far from Slavery?" *Look*, Jan. 15, 1952. The best scholarly accounts of Waring are Robert L. Terry, "J. Waties Waring: Spokesman for Racial Justice in the New South" (Ph.D. diss., University of Utah, 1970); William B. Scott, "Judge J. Waties Waring: Advocate of 'Another' South," *South Atlantic Quarterly*, Summer 1978; and David W. Southern, "Beyond Jim Crow: Waring's Fight Against Segregation in South Carolina, 1942–52," *Journal of Negro History*, Fall 1981. Useful information is also offered in Jack W. Peltason, *Fifty-eight Lonely Men* (1961); and Richard Kluger, *Simple Justice* (1976). For a memoir about Waring by fellow southern liberals, see Marion Wright and Arnold Shankman, *Human Rights Odyssey* (1978).

Waring contributed to the Columbia University Oral History Project in 1957. An obituary is in the *New York Times*, Jan. 12, 1968.]

DAVID W. SOUTHERN

WARNER, WILLIAM LLOYD (Oct. 26, 1898–May 23, 1970), social anthropologist, was born in Redlands, Calif., the son of William Taylor Warner, a rancher, engineer, and owner of a gold mine, and Clara Belle Carter. After graduating from high school in San Bernardino, Calif., he tried to write Tin Pan Alley jazz. During World War I, he served in the infantry and then attended the University of California at Berkeley. In 1925 he graduated with a B.A. in anthropology.

Warner's teachers Robert Lowie and Alfred Kroeber, both of whom became his good friends, encouraged him to study native non-Western peoples. Bronislaw Malinowski, another anthropologist of the British functionalist school, lectured at Berkeley shortly before Warner entered the field, an event that strengthened Warner's developing interest in functionalism. Warner told his colleagues that one day he would apply similar methods to an analysis of modern industrial society.

In 1926, Warner received a grant from the Rockefeller Foundation to study the Murgnin aborigines of northeastern Arnhem Land, Australia. Warner's functionalist education was completed under Alfred Radcliffe-Brown, who became his mentor in Australia. Radcliffe-Brown introduced Warner to the works of Émile Durkheim and Marcel Mauss, French sociologists who argued that social life and symbolism represented distinct "social," not "psychological," phenomena. Durkheim's scientific approach to measuring social behaviors also contributed to Warner's later work. Radcliffe-Brown helped Warner to obtain funds for two more years of research from the Australian National Research Council.

In his study Warner incorporated the then-standard anthropological research interest in technology with Radcliffe-Brown's stress on kinship and with the Durkheimian interest in symbolism as a metaphor for social structure. Warner's was one of the earliest efforts to understand the linkages between social-structural and cultural-symbolic phenomena. Throughout the rest of his career he further expanded his understanding of these relationships between the symbolic, structural, technological, economic, and ecological components of human social communities. His doctoral dissertation is the classic *A Black Civilization: A Social Study of an Australian Tribe* (1937). Warner never defended the dissertation, however.

After returning from Australia in 1929, Warner became assistant professor in the Department of Anthropology and in the School of Business at Harvard. Elton Mayo, a physiological psychologist, helped bring Warner to Harvard, where the two served on the Committee on Industrial Psychology. Warner's work, which moved him into the forefront of modern American anthropology, took two major but interrelated directions. One involved his affiliation with Mayo's studies of worker relationships, unrest, and fatigue at the Hawthorne Western Electric plant in Chicago. Warner employed anthropological methods to show that worker fatigue could be reduced by altering relationships in the workplace. The other resulted in the Yankee City studies, which remain the most comprehensive studies of an American community.

The Yankee City studies began in 1930, and the fieldwork ended five years later. The research, also coordinated with Mayo, was conducted in Newburyport, Mass. While Mayo's group had largely conducted biological and psychological research on industrial workers, Warner convincingly argued that an anthropological study of an industrial setting would add an important social dimension. People are products of their social environments, he believed. Behaviors learned within the home and community influence the interactions observed in the workplace. Yankee City was Warner's opportunity to apply the techniques of study used and refined with the Murgnin to a modern social setting and, more important, to help improve factory conditions.

The Yankee City studies employed a work force of graduate students and collaborating professors. Reams of quantitative data from censuses, surveys, and various local documents were collected, along with detailed life histories. Special studies examined the factories, ethnic groups, and symbols. This comprehensive approach was based on Warner's evolving concept of community. Reflecting Radcliffe-Brown's structuralism, Durkheim's concepts of social interdependence, concepts of social self developed by Georg Simmel and George Meade, and Malinowski's emphasis upon social means of meeting biological demands, Warner conceptualized community as the ordered, social relationships and values shared by a human group and passed on from generation to generation. Individuals receive "identity" through participation in community processes—the rituals, family life, and other aspects of daily living. Relationships noted in the factory, for example, were traced to community patterns in general, such as social mobility, class, and ideals.

The Yankee City studies led to Warner's definitions of social class and status. Class refers to social levels within communities associated with particular attitudes and life-styles. Status represents the position a person occupies within a given social context, as defined by such culturally meaningful variables as occupation, age, kinship, power, and sex.

The Yankee City studies were published in six volumes between 1941 and 1959. They have been criticized for being overly generalized, and some claim that Warner's concept of community is of little use when analyzing the dynamics of American and other industrial societies. C. Wright Mills described Warner's discussions of class and status as being confusing, ahistorical, unconcerned with power, and of little theoretical value. Solon T. Kimball argued in 1979 that Warner's concepts emphasize human relationships, not static entities like individuals or particular social groups, and, further, that Warner's community and status concepts are cross-cultural and dynamic and have been misunderstood by sociologists.

Warner also initiated or oversaw a number of community studies patterned after Yankee City. The more famous of these include Arensberg and Kimball's study in Ireland, Burleigh and Mary Gardner and Allison Davis' studies of southern racial-caste relations, and Warner's studies of the Midwest. On Jan. 10, 1932, Warner married Mildred Hall; they had three children.

In 1935, Warner took a position as associate professor in sociology and anthropology at Chicago. There he became involved with the Committee on Human Development. He investigated social-class influences on educational achievement, presenting data particularly useful in explaining the generally lower academic scores of black children. He also made studies of agricultural policy and worked with the Federal Extension Service in incorporating social-science findings into their educational approaches. He conducted studies on Navaho personality and tribal patterns under John Collier in the mid-1940's. These activities reflect Warner's continuing concern that social science be used to combat social problems and inequities.

In 1946, Warner and Gardner formed Social Research, Inc., a consulting firm offering social-science analysis of managerial and human-relations problems in business. The techniques employed in the Hawthorne studies and Yankee City were refined through this organization. Warner combined this activity with a series of studies of the personality, behavior, and general character of bureaucratic workers and executives, interests that led him to focus on corporate society.

Warner became professor of social research at Michigan State University in 1959, a position he held until his death. In 1961 he identified the components of what he called "the emergent American society." He believed that the corporation is the most integrative influence upon American society as a whole. In *The American Federal Executive* (1967), he compared the personality, mobility, attitudes, and behavior of corporate executives with American ideals, goals, and expectations; a second volume was never completed.

Warner always encouraged students to be innovative, but he worked closely with them. He was a lively teacher, filling blackboards with diagrams and exchanging ideas in the classroom on anything from his ongoing fieldwork to the theories of Marx, Malinowski, and others. His conceptualizations of the way cultural norms and worldview interact to influence technology, organization, and ecological relations influenced the theories of Leslie White and Julian Steward. His discussions of class, family, and community influenced Talcott Parsons, Gunnar Myrdal, Robert Havighurst, Conrad Arensberg, Solon Kimball, and countless others. It is fair to say that by the time of his death in Chicago, Warner had achieved his goal of bringing anthropology into the modern world and making it a meaningful mechanism for understanding and exploring human relationships and problems.

[A collection of Warner's correspondence, reviews of his works, personal notes, and bibliographies are housed at the Special Collections branch of the Milbank Memorial Library, Teachers College, Columbia University. Warner's research on the Murgnin is summarized in *A Black Civilization: A Social Study of an Australian Tribe* (1937). His best-known works are the Yankee City series, published under joint authorship as *The Social Life of the Modern Community* (1941), *The Status System of the Modern Community* (1942), *The Social Systems of American Ethnic Groups* (1945), *The Social System of the Modern Factory* (1947), and *The Living and the Dead* (1959). Warner's major studies of American values and religious life include *Democracy in Jonesville* (1949), *American Life: Dream and Reality* (1953), and *The Family of God: A Symbolic Study of Christian Life in America* (1961). Warner's important industrial-relations studies include *Occupational Mobility in American Business and Industry* (1955), *Industrial Man: Businessmen and Business Organizations* (1959), and *The Corporation in the Emergent American Society* (1962). *The Emergent American Society: Large-Scale Organizations* (1967) was part of a planned but never completed two-volume set on modern corporate-industrial America.

On Warner's contributions, see Conrad Arensberg and Solon Kimball, *Culture and Community* (1965); and Elizabeth Eddy and William Partridge, eds., *Applied Anthropology in America* (1978). An obituary is in the *New York Times*, May 24, 1970.]

DWIGHT L. SCHMIDT

WATERMAN, ALAN TOWER (June 4, 1892–Dec. 1, 1967), physicist and federal scientific administrator, was born in Cornwall, N.Y., into a middle-class academic family of modest means, the son of Frank Alan Waterman, who taught physics at Smith College, and Florence Tower. Waterman developed wide-ranging interests in outdoor activities such as camping, in sports, and in music. Throughout his life he pursued these activities avidly, as if to suggest that he sought a life of balance and diversity as a well-rounded person. This was indeed to become a key to his persona.

After attending public schools in Northampton, Mass., he entered Princeton University in 1909. Waterman almost did not become a scientist; it was not until his second year at Princeton that he enrolled in a science course. His fascination with the techniques and satisfactions of scientific experimentation convinced him to be a scientist. He took his B.A. in 1913, his M.A. in 1914, and his Ph.D. in 1916 from Princeton in experimental physics. As an instructor of physics at the University of Cincinnati the next academic year, he met Mary Mallon of Cincinnati, who came from an upper-middle-class family with roots in Columbus, Ohio, and graduated second in her class at Vassar. They married on Aug. 19, 1917; they had five children. In the fall of 1917 he enlisted as a private in the United States Army and was assigned to the Science and Research Division of the Signal Corps, in which he did meteorological work. He rose to the rank of first lieutenant. In the fall of 1919, he became an instructor in physics at Yale University, where he spent the next twenty-seven years, attaining the rank of assistant professor in 1923 and associate professor in 1931. A full professorship at Yale eluded him.

At Yale, Waterman was a researcher of modest productivity. He published fifteen technical papers between 1923 and 1937, chiefly in two major journals, the *Physical Review* and the *Philosophical Magazine*. Much of his work centered on the conduction of electricity through solids. It demonstrated a flair for experimental physics and an adequacy in physical theory. Students and colleagues alike judged Waterman a demanding and rigorous teacher who was effective in his presentations and fair in his judgments. He led an active life while at Yale. Thus, he served as chief reader for the College Entrance Examination Board between 1930 and 1942, and chief examiner of physics from 1937 to 1949. Between 1935 and 1942 he was a member of the editorial board of the *American Journal of Science,* America's oldest continuous scientific journal, published at Yale.

Waterman also pursued his other interests. He qualified as a guide to the Maine woods. With great relish he camped in the remote wilds; he was an expert hiker and canoeist. He participated in such sports as tennis and skiing. He also played viola in a string quartet. Later in life, he took up the bagpipes. He took pride in being self-taught in such activities. Of slight build, erect stature, and medium height, he was always trim, for he was never given to excess in these or any other aspects of his life, as, for example, in his political views, which were characteristically patriotic for his generation but also those of an optimistic, moderate liberal who wished to believe the best of others. In contact with others, he often played the role of the moderator and the guide, as if he projected onto others his conception of a personal life of judicious balance and proportion.

Waterman was well suited by temperament and experience to become a widely respected scientific administrator. In 1942 he went to Washington to work with the National Defense Research Committee, soon renamed the Office of Scientific Research and Development, the agency headed by Vannevar Bush that mobilized science and technology for World War II. The move from New Haven to Washington, seemingly only for the duration, in actuality thrust him upon a new stage, that of the rapidly developing system or establishment of leading science universities and federal agencies. He retained his Yale affiliation until 1948, but for all practical purposes, he had left in 1942.

During the war, Waterman was deputy to Karl T. Compton in the Office of Scientific Research and Development. Until 1943 he worked in Division D, becoming deeply involved in reviewing weapons research on projects relating to such things as guided missiles, electronic communications and radio, chemical engineering, and, above all, radar. He assisted Compton in directing the development and application of radar from the original British work in that field. This became an enormous enterprise in which more than 150 different systems were developed for land-based, water-borne, and aircraft radar machines and in which thousands were employed in research and development (almost 5,000 by the war's end). Radar facilitated the defeat of Axis military forces in multiple ways, and its development forms a fascinating picture of the interplay of science, technology, and governmental institutions.

In 1943, Waterman was appointed deputy chief of the Office of Field Service, within the Office of Scientific Research and Development; he succeeded Compton as chief in 1945–1946. He assigned hundreds of scientific advisers to commanders in the field, thus deploying his talents in institutional diplomacy and personal relationships but generating large numbers of contacts. Waterman's technical expertise as a physicist was appropriate to his responsibilities in the Office of Scientific Research and Development, as was his ability to command widespread trust. Compton regarded Waterman as his indispensable deputy, his "first and best move" at the Office of Scientific Research and Development. Waterman guided and persuaded rather than cajoled and dominated.

Following World War II, Waterman, as a federal scientific administrator, helped oversee the completion of the new postwar system of relationships between Washington and the nation's scientists and research institutions. Always a strong apostle of basic research, a natural position for a professor of science who also loved the beauties of nature, he insisted upon what has been called the assembly-line notion of the relations of technology and science, which holds that technological "progress" comes only from basic scientific research and that there is no such thing as a distinct knowledge base in technology. What would guarantee economic growth and political stability, then, was disinterested scientific research, not immediately directed toward practical ends, the result of which would be, at the assembly line's terminus, gadgetry, prosperity, and peace through military strength. Such a view buttressed the power and prestige of the nation's scientific elite, to say the least, and it possessed hidden, if powerful, implications for decision-making in public policy.

Waterman was appointed deputy chief of the newly established Office of Naval Research in 1946 and rose to chief by 1951. He helped work out a new system of research contracts with universities, experimenting with procedures of review and evaluation that he took with him to the National Science Foundation when appointed its first director in 1951. The Office of Naval Research received much praise for having sponsored "basic" research in many fields when Waterman was there, including electronics, which included some research on computers and undersea acoustics, such as investigation of communication among dolphins. Given Waterman's values and commitments, the Office of Naval Research under his leadership may be more sensibly regarded as having been deeply interested in ultimate military applications at the end of the assembly line of basic research and technological development. And the scientists who won grants were presumably delighted to have support for research.

In the new post–World War II era, no longer did private individuals, states, corporations, or philanthropic foundations alone support science and science education. Ineluctably the new scientific establishment was instantaneously politicized. President Harry Truman's appointment of Waterman as the National Science Foundation's first director in 1951 was as astute as it was inevitable, given Waterman's extensive network of allies in leading universities and the federal government. Waterman set many precedents within the foundation. He worked out the complex peer review and panel system in ways that guaranteed the nation's scientific elite and its favored institutions virtual hegemony over priorities and programs. When the National Science Foundation was created in 1950, its annual budget was $400,000, but so effective an advocate of the agency was Waterman that when he retired on June 30, 1963, its annual budget was almost $500 million. Waterman made "basic science" the National Science Foundation's policy and its public ideology in national politics. This basic-science idea—essentially the assembly-line notion of the relations of science and technology—was ably articulated by Harvard University president James B. Conant, who insisted that applied research was a dead end, mere tinkering by the unschooled. Conant's position appears highly problematic; arguably technology has always had its knowledge base. Conant's thesis became the national scientific establishment's "pure" or "basic" science ideology. As the foundation's public representative, Waterman consistently deployed this ideology of national science, whether appearing before congressional committees, at press conferences, or on ceremonial occasions. The ideology of national pure science enabled Waterman to present a far different picture of science than that suggested by the weapons of mass destruction of the age. Waterman's public relations efforts as director were tireless indeed; his 162 publications and addresses as director extolled the virtues of national science as fully capable of meeting the many needs of the complex industrial society that America had become in peace and in war. He warned that all the nation's intellectual resources should be marshaled, calling for an equitable balance between spending on nonscientific and scientific education.

Waterman received many honors and awards as recognition of his service during the war and, especially, of his tenure as director of the National Science Foundation, when he received twenty-four honorary degrees from colleges and universities. The National Academy of Sciences finally recognized him when it bestowed its Public Welfare Medal on him in 1960. So did the nation's scientific elite in 1962, when its members and allies elected him president of the American Association for the Advancement of Science. In December 1963,

President Lyndon Johnson awarded him the Presidential Medal of Freedom. Waterman was a member of many scientific societies and served on numerous boards of directors of scientific and governmental organizations and institutions. In retirement he pursued his other interests. He died in Washington, D.C.

[Waterman's papers are located at the Manuscripts Division, Library of Congress, and in the archives of the National Science Foundation. His technical papers include "An Equilibrium Theory of Conduction," *Physical Review*, 22 (1923); "Extension of Fowler's Theory of Photoelectronic Sensitivity as a Function of Temperature," ibid., 44 (1933); and "The Fundamental Properties of the Electron," *Electrical Engineering*, 53 (1934). Among the 162 publications he wrote while the National Science Foundation's director are "Government-Supported Research," *Journal of Engineering Education*, 43 (1952); "The National Science Foundation: Its Organization and Purpose," *American Journal of Physics*, 20 (1952); and "What Lies Ahead for Science in the Sixties," *Science Digest*, 49 (1961).

On Waterman and the institutions and issues with which he associated, see Vannevar Bush, *Science, the Endless Frontier* (1945); James Phinney Baxter III, *Scientists Against Time* (1946); Irvin Stewart, *Organizing Scientific Research for War* (1948); James B. Conant, *Science and Common Sense* (1951); A. Hunter Dupree, *Science in the Federal Government* (1957); Ronald C. Tobey, *The American Ideology of Science, 1919–1930* (1971); Daniel J. Kevles, *The Physicists* (1978); J. Merton England, A *Patron for Pure Science* (1982); and Sally G. Kohlstedt and Margaret W. Rossiter, eds., *Historical Writing on American Science, Osiris*, 2nd ser., I (1985), especially the essays by Albert Moyers, Alex Roland, Rossiter, and George Wise. An obituary is in the *New York Times*, Dec. 2, 1967.]

HAMILTON CRAVENS

WAXMAN, FRANZ (Dec. 24, 1906–Feb. 24, 1967), composer and conductor, was born Franz Wachsmann at Königshütte in Upper Silesia, Germany (now Chorozów, Poland), the son of Otto Wachsmann, a salesman for the steel industry, and Rosalie Perl. His father actively discouraged his son's desire for a musical career. But Wachsmann, who had attained a respectable pianistic ability by the age of twelve, was adamant. After serving briefly as a bank teller, he switched to full-time musical study at the age of sixteen. In 1923 he enrolled at the Dresden Music Academy, but shortly thereafter he switched to the more ambitious program of the Berlin Conservatory. In Berlin he pursued composition and conducting studies by day while supporting himself as a café pianist by night.

Wachsmann's association with the popular Weintraub Syncopaters brought him into contact with the composer Friedrich Hollaender, who enlisted him to work in the new field of providing music for the sound cinema. One of Wachsmann's very first assignments at the UFA studios in Berlin was to orchestrate and conduct Hollaender's music for *The Blue Angel* (1930), which became an international success. His first major original score was for Fritz Lang's French-made *Liliom* (1933), for which he utilized chorus, orchestra, and the ondes martenot, probably the first use of an electronic instrument in films.

In 1933, Wachsmann, who was Jewish, was beaten by a Nazi youth gang on a Berlin street. Shortly thereafter he moved to Paris and then the United States when the German producer Erich Pommer invited him to work on *Music in the Air* (1934) in Hollywood. It was on his arrival in the United States that he adopted the spelling "Waxman." He married Alice Pauline Schachmann, another émigré and the former wife of attorney Alfred Apfel, in October 1934; they had one child. Waxman became an American citizen in 1939.

In Hollywood, Waxman was soon asked by the director James Whale to score his sequel to *Frankenstein*. Whereas earlier films in Universal's nascent horror cycle had largely employed late-romantic classics, Waxman composed for *The Bride of Frankenstein* (1935) a completely original symphonic score that became a landmark in the developing art of film music. Its themes became familiar to millions when Universal recycled them in many subsequent films and in the *Flash Gordon* serials of the late 1930's.

Waxman soon became music director of the Universal studios, where the most important film he scored during his brief tenure was *Magnificent Obsession* (1935); but he preferred composition to administrative work and soon resigned to work solely as a composer. Among his scores for Metro-Goldwyn-Mayer (MGM), Selznick, and Warner Brothers were *Captains Courageous* (1937), *Three Comrades* (1938), *Rebecca* (1940), *The Philadelphia Story* (1940), *Dr. Jekyll and Mr. Hyde* (1941), *Suspicion* (1941), *Objective, Burma!* (1945), and *Humoresque* (1947).

It was in the 1950's, when Waxman worked on a free-lance basis, that his career blossomed fully. The demented tango that expresses a silent-movie queen's delusions in *Sunset Boulevard* (1950) and the haunting, rhapsodic saxophone music of *A Place in the Sun* (1951) are among his best-remembered works. Waxman received Academy Awards for each of these scores, the only composer to have been so honored in successive years. His other major works of the 1950's include the scores for *The Silver Chalice* (1954), *Rear Window* (1954), *Sayonara* (1957), and *Peyton Place* (1957). *Crime in the Streets* (1956) demonstrates Waxman's continuing fascination with American jazz, which he pioneered in Germany during his Weintraub period. *The Spirit of St. Louis* (1957) contains a brilliantly mechanistic fugal passage for the building of Lindbergh's airplane. *The Nun's Story* (1959), arguably his masterpiece, integrates Gregorian antiphons into a modern harmonic context to express the anguish of a woman's spiritual crisis. In all, Waxman scored nearly 200 films, plus a good deal of television. His last film was *Lost Command* (1966).

Waxman was a strong believer in the use of tone color for its ability to alter mood instantaneously. His flair for unusual instrumentation—such as the electric violin in *Suspicion* and the solo piccolo in *Hemingway's Adventures of a Young Man* (1962)—plus the intense angularity of his style (Prokofiev has been cited as a major influence) made Waxman a particularly effective composer for films of psychological disorientation (*Rebecca*, *Suspicion*, and *Sunset Boulevard*) and for stories of interior conflict (*The Spirit of St. Louis* and *The Nun's Story*). Nevertheless, he also had great success with such extravagant outdoor adventures as *Prince Valiant* (1954) and *Taras Bulba* (1962).

Although Waxman never took a musical degree, he maintained his connection with the concert world throughout his life. In Europe, Bruno Walter furthered his career; in Hollywood he studied with Arnold Schoenberg. In 1947, Waxman founded the Los Angeles International Music Festival in order to bring contemporary music to the West Coast. This annual summer event at Royce Hall at the University of California at Los Angeles endured until the year of his death. Raising the funds himself—and contributing the proceeds from many of his film commissions—Waxman gave American or West Coast premieres of works by Mahler, Schoenberg, Shostakovich, Stravinsky, Vaughan Williams, and many others. He also made numerous guest-conducting appearances in Western Europe, the Soviet Union, and Israel. Of his own concert compositions, the *Carmen* Fantasie (1947; first written for the film *Humoresque*) was recorded by Jascha Heifetz and achieved great popularity. The Sinfonietta for Strings and Timpani (1955) was also successful. Other works include the oratorio *Joshua* (1959); the song cycle *The Song of Terezin* (1965), on poems by young concentration-camp victims; and an unfinished opera based on his film music for *Dr. Jekyll and Mr. Hyde*.

Waxman's first wife died in 1957, and in August 1958, he married the pianist Lella Saenger-Sethe. They were divorced in 1965. During the last decade of his life Waxman resided for six months a year in New York City, accepting fewer film commissions in order to concentrate on his concert activities. He died in Los Angeles.

Waxman was a passionately serious musician in a milieu where such qualities were not always appreciated. His music did not escape the condescension that was frequently bestowed on serious film music. For example, a *Time* critic in 1963 dismissed his *Taras Bulba* score as a mixture of "Showstakovich and Messorgsky and . . . Minsky-Korsetoff." Yet, that music has since become sufficiently popular to have been recorded three times. Numerous other Waxman scores have been recorded or reissued since his death. Although only a few of his concert works have won favor, his stature as a film-music pioneer and champion of new music seems secure.

[The Waxman papers, including many scores and recordings, are at the George Arents Research Library of Syracuse University. The fullest study is Page Cook, "Franz Waxman," *Films in Review*, Aug.–Sept. 1968. See also Tony Thomas, *Music for the Movies* (1973) and *Film Music: The View from the Podium* (1979); and Alfred Frankenstein, "Franz Waxman's Music for *The Silver Chalice*," *Film Music Notebook*, Spring 1975. An interview is in *Hollywood Quarterly*, 5 (1950), repr. in *Pro Musica Sana*, 8 (1979–1980). Little of the concert music has been recorded, but many film sound tracks and anthologies are available. An obituary is in the *New York Times*, Feb. 26, 1967.]

JOHN FITZPATRICK

WEBB, CLIFTON (Nov. 19, 1893–Oct. 13, 1966), singer, dancer, and actor, was born Webb Parmalee Hollenbeck in Indianapolis, Ind. In 1896 his family moved to New York City, and there, when he was seven, "Young Webb," as his mother liked to call him, accompanied a neighbor girl to dancing school. By chance, Malcolm Douglas of the Children's Theatre visited the school that day looking for a boy to play a role in one of his productions. He asked Webb if he would like to do some acting. Webb's mother had aspired to be an actress in her youth, and she readily gave her approval. She would become the most famous stage mother of her time, transferring her own theatrical ambitions to her young son. Webb's father apparently was not enthusiastic about the decision, and the parents soon separated. (Webb's mother once said of her husband, "We never speak of him, he didn't care for the theatre.")

Webb made his formal theatrical debut in 1900 at the Carnegie Hall Theatre in *The Brownies*. He next played the title role in a dramatization of *Oliver Twist*. *The Master of Carlton Hall*, in which he played a little southern boy, followed. After appearing in several more children's plays, Webb retired from acting for a while and resumed his education. An extremely bright student, he was able to graduate from grammar school in New York at the age of thirteen. He then studied painting with Robert Henri and singing with Victor Maurel. He gave his first one-man art show at the age of fourteen. He also soon acquired a love of opera and learned some fifteen operatic roles in French and Italian. This led to a contract with Boston's Aborn Opera Company in 1911, and he appeared in their production of *Mignon* when he was but seventeen. He later appeared in *La boheme*, *Madame Butterfly*, and *Hansel and Gretel*. In 1913 he played in a musical comedy entitled *The Purple Road* at the Liberty Theater in New York.

A dance craze was sweeping the country at this time, and Webb teamed up with Bonnie Glass and, later, Mae Murray as his dancing partner. Within a short time, the slender six-footer with the slightly upturned nose became one of the most popular ballroom dancers in New York City. In addition, Webb conducted private dancing classes, with his mother serving as secretary and manager of the Webb Dance Studio. He appeared in another musical comedy, *Love o' Mike*, in 1917. This was followed by *Listen, Lester* (1918) and *As You Were* (1920). In 1921 the noted English producer Charles B. Cochran invited him to London. Webb spent two seasons in that city as well as one in Paris. He achieved great success in both places.

He then returned to the United States and appeared in the musical comedy *Jack and Jill* (1923). However, Webb yearned to play some straight roles and resented being known only as a hoofer. He decided to put away his dancing shoes forever. Working toward that goal, he appeared in a straight comedy, *Meet the Wife* (1923), and received excellent reviews. He worked in films during these years, too. He was a dapper costar of such films as *Polly with a Past* (1920), *New Toys* (1925), and *The Heart of a Siren* (1925). But Webb could not lay his dancing shoes aside for very long, and he had them on again when he appeared on the stage in *Sunny* (1925), which had a then fabulously successful run of ninety-two weeks. His nimble footwork was a highlight of other productions, including *She's My Baby* (1928), *Treasure Girl* (1928), the first *Little Show* (1929), *Three's a Crowd* (1930), *Flying Colors* (1932), and *As Thousands Cheer* (1933).

There followed an interlude in Hollywood when Metro-Goldwyn-Mayer put Webb on a salary of $3,000 a week. While socially it turned out to be a pleasant experience, professionally it was a disaster. For eighteen months, he swam, attended gala parties, met all the important people, but never once appeared in a motion picture. He referred to Hollywood as "a land of endowed vacations." Webb was able to get his five-year contract terminated, and returned again to New York. In 1936 he appeared in the Theatre Guild's production of *And Stars Remain*. Webb also played in a revival of Oscar Wilde's comedy *The Importance of Being Earnest* (1939) and in the summer of 1939 worked in a stock revival of *Burlesque*. For the next year and a half he went on tour as Sheridan Whiteside in *The Man Who Came to Dinner*. In 1942 he played the lead in Noel Coward's *Blithe Spirit*.

While Webb was touring the country in *Blithe Spirit*, he received his second call to Hollywood. Otto Preminger at Twentieth Century–Fox wanted the actor to portray the caustic and arrogant columnist Waldo Lydecker in *Laura* (1944). His performance was a tour de force in nastiness, and it earned him an Oscar nomination for best supporting actor and a long run as a Fox star. His acerbic character in *Laura* set the pattern for many subsequent roles. In his films, Webb epitomized the sophisticated, cosmopolitan, pompous, know-it-all type, with old-maid ways and an acid tongue. For instance, in *The Dark Corner* (1946) he played an uncle who secretly yearned to do away with his nephew. In *The Razor's Edge* (1946) he played Elliott Templeton, the archsnob and social tyrant, and earned another Oscar nomination as best supporting actor. He played these roles so superbly that he faced the danger of being stereotyped.

A much-needed change of pace came in 1948 when he portrayed a haughty gentleman-genius named Lynn Belvedere, who becomes a rather atypical nurse and baby-sitter to a brood of noisy children in *Sitting Pretty*. The film gained him excellent reviews and an Oscar nomination for best actor. He reprised this role in *Mr. Belvedere Goes to College* (1949) and *Mr. Belvedere Rings the Bell* (1951) and again was well received by the public and reviewers. He gave outstanding performances as Papa Gilbreth in *Cheaper by the Dozen* (1950) and an angel returned to earth in *For Heaven's Sake* (1950). In these pictures, his skill at nastiness was well mixed with sentimental comedy, and the public loved it. In 1950 he was selected by American motion-picture exhibitors as one of the year's top ten money-making stars.

Webb greatly enjoyed all this fame and fortune, which came to him in middle age. He was a bachelor and lived in Beverly Hills with his mother. Webb's taste in clothes, as well as his command of the social graces, was impeccable. He was a very sociable man and loved to entertain and go to parties. As in his Broadway years, his mother, Maybelle, was his constant companion, and they were one of the most popular "couples" in the Hollywood social set.

In the years after 1950, Webb also appeared in *Elopement* (1951), *Dreamboat* (1952), *Stars and Stripes Forever* (as John Philip Sousa; 1952), *Titanic* (1953), *Mister Scoutmaster* (1953), *Three Coins in the Fountain* (1954), *Woman's World* (1954), *The Man Who Never Was* (1956), *Boy on a Dolphin* (1957), *The Remarkable Mr. Pennypacker* (1959), *Holiday for Lovers* (1959), and *Satan Never Sleeps* (1962). Except for *Dreamboat, Titanic,* and *Mister Scoutmaster,* these films were of generally mediocre quality, and Webb's acting was not much praised by the critics. Part of the reason for so many unfavorable reviews was that he had become the exclusive property of Fox. Because he was gold at the box office, the studio put him in as many pictures as possible, but unfortunately, it had a dearth of distinguished writers and directors. Many of its pictures during this period emphasized Technicolor, Cinemascope, and spectacular location scenery over plot, dialogue, and character development. Part of the problem, too, was that Webb tended to play the familiar waspish character over and over. It worked well in several pictures, but was not well received in a number of others. He retired after *Satan Never Sleeps* and had serious health problems during the next several years. Webb died in Beverly Hills.

[There are no book-length studies of Webb. See Daniel Blum, *Great Stars of the American Stage: A Pictorial Record* (1952); Paul Michael and James Robert Parish, *The American Movies Reference Book: The Sound Era* (1969); Bill Libby, *They Didn't Win the Oscars* (1980); and David Thomson, *A Biographical Dictionary of Film* (1981). An obituary is in the *New York Times*, Oct. 14, 1966.]

J. MICHAEL QUILL

WERTENBAKER, THOMAS JEFFERSON (Feb. 6, 1879–Apr. 22, 1966), historian and university professor, was born in Charlottesville, Va., the son of Charles Christian Wertenbaker, a landholder and cigar manufacturer, and Frances Thomas Leftwich. The Wertenbakers came from unpretentious Huguenot and German origins. In America, Wertenbaker men often married Englishwomen of higher social status. Wertenbaker's paternal grandfather, William, was appointed by Thomas Jefferson in 1826 as secretary to the faculty and first librarian of the University of Virginia, an institution he served for more than fifty years before he died in 1882. He also unfurled one of the first Confederate flags in Charlottesville on Mar. 23, 1861, weeks before Virginia seceded, and he bequeathed to his descendants a store of anecdotes about Jefferson, James Madison, James Monroe, and other great men of the early Republic, all of whem he knew personally. Wertenbaker's father, a Confederate veteran, sent his sons to the University of Virginia. The family ambience is subtly portrayed in *To My Father* (1936), the autobiographical novel of

Wertenbaker's nephew Charles, in which Thomas appears briefly as "Uncle Paul."

Wertenbaker read Edward Gibbon through at thirteen and attended local public schools, the Jones' University School, and Charlottesville Public High School. He entered the University of Virginia in 1896 and interrupted his studies to teach for a year at St. Matthew's School in Dobbs Ferry, N.Y. He graduated Phi Beta Kappa, receiving both his B.A. and M.A. degrees in 1902. He then served briefly as editor of the *Charlottesville Morning News* and the *Baltimore News* before enrolling as a doctoral student at the University of Virginia in 1906. He supported himself as associate professor of history and economics at the Agricultural and Mechanical College at Texas (1907–1909) and then as an instructor in American history at the University of Virginia (1909–1910) until he received his Ph.D. in 1910 and published, at his own expense, his dissertation, *Patrician and Plebeian in Virginia; or The Origin and Development of the Social Classes of the Old Dominion*. This study, which powerfully challenged the romantic myth of the cavalier origins of Virginia's great planter dynasties, advanced a new methodology for understanding the social history of colonial America. He later improved this technique through a sophisticated use of rent rolls, tax lists, and headright records.

Wertenbaker's reputation attracted the attention of Woodrow Wilson, who was then president of Princeton and was campaigning for the governorship of New Jersey; Wilson persuaded him to move to Princeton in 1910. On July 10, 1916, Wertenbaker married Sarah Rossetter Marshall of Lexington, Ky.; they had one child. From 1917 to 1923, Wertenbaker earned supplementary income as a member of the editorial staff of the *New York Evening Sun*.

Wertenbaker rose through the ranks at Princeton—assistant professor of history in 1914, associate in 1921, and Edwards Professor of History from 1925 until his retirement in 1947. From 1928 to 1936 he served as department chairman. Always a popular lecturer both on campus and off, he also played a role in building the doctoral program of his department, mostly through the appointments that he encouraged.

Wertenbaker's national and international reputation grew as he published a steadily growing number of important books over nearly half a century. *Virginia Under the Stuarts* (1914) and *The Planters of Colonial Virginia* (1922) further developed his argument that seventeenth-century Virginia offered liberty and great opportunity to small planters until the Navigation Acts and the growth of slavery created a much less open society. His textbook *The American People: A History* (1926) did not romanticize the slave regime, showed sympathy for Confederate men and motives even though he considered "their task almost hopeless from the start," shared the prevailing white view that Reconstruction had been a carnival of misrule and corruption, but explicitly refused to blame the freedmen for these problems. His book *The First Americans, 1607–1690* (1927) was one of the earliest volumes to be completed for the innovative series A History of American Life, edited by Arthur M. Schlesinger, Sr., and Dixon Ryan Fox. In *Norfolk: Historic Southern Port* (1931), he tried to rescue local history from "the antiquarian and the genealogist," while *Torchbearer of the Revolution: The Story of Bacon's Rebellion and Its Leader* (1940) returned to his first love, the seventeenth-century Virginia rebel who, he believed, came closer than anyone else to anticipating Jeffersonian values.

These accomplishments won Wertenbaker a high degree of recognition. In 1931 he taught at the University of Göttingen, where he saw something of the rise of Nazism. Oxford University named him Harmsworth Professor in 1939, but he could not go to England because of the outbreak of World War II. After delivering the Anson G. Phelps Lectures at New York University in 1942 (published in that year as *The Golden Age of Colonial Culture*), he finally got to England and the Harmsworth Professorship in 1944–1945. By then, he was beginning to receive honorary degrees almost every year, and in 1947 he served as president of the American Historical Association. During this period he became active in organizing the Institute of Early American History and Culture at Williamsburg, Va. After his 1947 retirement, he taught briefly at the University of Delaware, Emory University, the University of Virginia, and Hampden-Sydney College, but his most important stint was at the University of Munich (1950–1951), where he helped to organize American-civilization programs throughout the German Federal Republic.

Wertenbaker's publications continued into the 1950's. Between 1938 and 1947 he completed an impressive trilogy on each of the regions that contributed to the Founding of American Civilization series: *The Middle Colonies* (1938), *The Old South* (1942), and *The Puritan Oligarchy* (1947). The first volume was the most innovative of the three, with its broad emphasis on pluralism and cultural diversity as essential American traits, themes also reflected in *Father Knickerbocker Rebels: New York City During the Revolution* (1948). His New England volume was less forgiving than the others. He shared none of Perry Miller's fascination with the severe ambiguities at the core of the Puritan mind; in Wertenbaker's judgment, New Englanders before 1700 contributed little of significance to the triumph of liberty in America. His presidential address to the American Historical Association argued that no one could make sense of the Midwest without seeing it as a crucible that brought together and transformed each of these colonial subcultures. He also produced an excellent history of higher education, *Princeton, 1746–1896* (1946), for the university's bicentennial. His last studies, particularly *Bacon's Rebellion: 1676* (1957) and *Give Me Liberty: The Struggle for Self-Government in Virginia* (1958), reveal some of the defensiveness of a man who realized that his own profession was beginning to destroy what he held most sacred. By then, his Princeton successor, Wesley Frank Craven; Wilcomb Washburn; and Bernard Bailyn were all challenging Nathaniel Bacon's place in the history of American liberty.

Wertenbaker wrote vigorous, graphic prose. An unashamed advocate of the Whig interpretation of history, he celebrated the triumph of liberty in Anglo-America and deplored its tardy arrival in militaristic Germany. His best writing drew from his richly diverse family heritage to broader American themes and revealed him as a Virginian convinced that his state had done more than any other to establish the nation's democratic tradition, a southerner committed to the superiority of free labor over any slave system, an American rooted in his multiethnic past, and a Protestant suspicious of any denomination's claim to possess final truth.

Wertenbaker took seriously the civic responsibilities of a prominent historian. Despite a flirtation with the neutrality movement of the 1930's, which in turn may well reveal second thoughts about Wilson's intervention in 1917, he ardently supported America's efforts in both world wars. "Great Britain," he declared, "was the United States' first line of defense." Yet, he retained his ancestral sympathy for Germany and believed by 1950 that the fates of America and West Germany were inextricably intertwined. He hoped he could persuade Germans to study serious American texts before Hollywood and pulp fiction misled them completely.

Wertenbaker was spare, erect, and somewhat angular. His voice, his nephew observed, "was gentle and he laughed a lot, but when he laughed he never made a sound, just opened his mouth wide and wrinkled up his eyes." Close Princeton friends and many students called him "the Colonel," a reflection of his refined southern manners. A talented amateur architect, he designed the Phi Kappa Psi Fraternity House at the University of Virginia and his home, Thoroughgood, in Princeton. He died in Princeton.

[Wertenbaker's faculty file in the Princeton University Archives at the Seeley G. Mudd Library contains clippings and some correspondence. Writings not cited in the text include *The United States of America: A History* (1931), with Donald E. Smith; and *The Government of Virginia in the Seventeenth Century* (1957). An obituary is in the *New York Times*, Apr. 23, 1966.]

JOHN M. MURRIN

WHITE, EDWARD HIGGINS, II (Nov. 14, 1930–Jan. 27, 1967), United States Air Force officer and astronaut, was born in San Antonio, Tex., the son of Edward H. White, a career air force officer and a pioneer army balloonist and aviator, and Mary Haller. The family was often transferred and lived in Washington, D.C., when White was in high school. Having no representative in Congress, he won appointment to the United States Military Academy by making himself known to as many congressmen as possible while attending high school. He graduated from the academy in 1952 with a commission as a second lieutenant in the air force and married Patricia Elaine Finegan shortly thereafter; they had two children.

While serving as a fighter pilot in Germany, White followed with interest the development of the manned space-flight program and set out to qualify as an astronaut. With air force support, he earned a master's degree in aeronautical engineering from the University of Michigan in 1959 and then completed the course at the Air Force Test Pilot School at

Edwards Air Force Base in the same year. He was then assigned to Wright-Patterson Air Force Base as a test pilot. Among his duties at Wright-Patterson was piloting the KC-135 transport plane in which several of the original seven astronauts trained for the weightless conditions of orbital flight. By the time he was selected as an astronaut, White had spent more time in weightlessness than most of the other astronauts.

White applied for the astronaut program as soon as the National Aeronautics and Space Administration (NASA) announced openings for a second group of trainees and was accepted on Sept. 17, 1962. He was the pilot on *Gemini IV*, commanded by James A. McDivitt, the second mission in the Gemini project and the first long-duration flight (sixty-two revolutions on June 3–7, 1965) in the American manned space-flight program. During this mission he became the first American to perform extravehicular activity, floating for twenty minutes over a distance of some 7,500 miles. On Mar. 21, 1966, White was named to the crew of the first Apollo flight.

For the circumstances of his death, see the article on Virgil Ivan Grissom.

W. D. COMPTON

WHITE, GEORGE (1890–Oct. 11, 1968), producer, director, actor, librettist, and lyricist, was born George Alviel Weitz, in a Lower East Side tenement in New York City, the son of Lena White. His father, whose full name is not known, was an extremely religious and improvident Jewish garment manufacturer. White had little formal education and was essentially on his own from the age of five. When White was about ten, his father's business failed. The family then moved to Toronto, Canada, where White joined a gang of street hoodlums who pilfered and spent their leisure hours buck dancing on the sidewalks.

About a year later White ran away from home, going to Buffalo and later to Detroit, where he made money dancing in the streets while playing his own accompaniment on a harmonica. During this period he worked as mascot to a regiment, stable boy, jockey, newsboy, and bellhop. By the age of thirteen he was back in New York working as a messenger for the Postal Telegraph Company. Assigned to the late shift, White delivered a telegram early one morning to a Bowery honky-tonk run by "Piggy" Donovan. When he saw a young black dancer there being showered with coins, he requested his own hoofing time and picked up $12.30 from the floor. Although he never returned to his office, he did keep the uniform and was soon called Swifty White, the Dancing Messenger-Boy.

For the next several months White danced in various Bowery saloons for pennies and nickels until he teamed with another dancer, Benny Ryan. Samuel Scribner, who became the president of the Columbia Burlesque Wheel, saw them and put them in a burlesque show called *Gay Morning Glories*. After several other burlesque and vaudeville engagements, Ryan and White, who had become headliners, joined the cast of Charles Dillingham's show *The Echo* in 1910 at the Globe Theater, with White making his Broadway debut. White and Ryan separated after this show.

White's subsequent appearances included a brief engagement in the 1911 *Ziegfeld Follies;* a Winter Garden revue, *Vera Violetta* (1911), with Al Jolson, in which he helped to popularize the turkey trot; a tour of *The Red Widow* (1912), with Raymond Hitchcock; *The Whirl of Society* (1912), as a dancer; another Winter Garden revue, *The Pleasure Seekers* (1913), in the role of Jack Heminway; *The Midnight Girl* (1914), as François; the 1915 *Ziegfeld Follies;* and in 1917 a role in the revue *Miss 1917*. At about this time, White produced one of the first elaborate miniature revues for vaudeville.

In 1919, with $12,000 in cash and $35,000 in credit, White produced the first of his musical revues called the *Scandals*. In all, White produced, directed, and often performed in, thirteen editions of his revue up to 1939. Between 1926 and 1931 the *Scandals* were the paragon of annual revues, reaching their high point with the 1926 edition, in which Ann Pennington introduced White's dance invention, the black bottom. His revues, lavish shows for the edification of the tired businessman, captured for many Americans the giddy 1920's. He never owned his own theater; most of the *Scandals* were presented at the Apollo on Forty-second Street. The *Scandals* sometimes earned White as much as $20,000 a week, much of which was left at racetracks. The 1921 edition netted $400,000, despite bad reviews, typified by Burns Mantle's famous comment that White's *Scandals* "prove that a hoofer should stick to his dancing." After 1931 many of

White's ventures failed and he was in and out of bankruptcy.

White also produced and directed *Runnin' Wild* (1923), in which the Charleston was introduced; *Manhattan Mary* (1927), with Ed Wynn and designs by Erté; *Flying High* (1930), with Bert Lahr; *George White's Music Hall Varieties* (1932 and 1933); and Sigmund Romberg's *Melody* (1933). White became interested in films, and produced, directed, wrote, and performed in film versions of the *Scandals,* in 1934, 1935, and 1945. He also appeared as himself in the 1945 film biography of George Gershwin, *Rhapsody in Blue*.

White found little success during the last twenty-five years of his life. In 1940 he opened a theater-restaurant called George White's Gay White Way on the site later occupied by the Latin Quarter, but he had to close it in 1941 and then moved to California. In 1942 he filed a voluntary bankruptcy petition in which he listed his liabilities as $500,000 and his assets as $500 and a Rolls-Royce. A hit-and-run conviction in 1946 led to his serving almost nine months of a year's sentence.

After this dark period, his most successful ventures were several cabaret revues produced at New York's Versailles Club in the early 1950's. In 1960 he put all of his money into a revue for El Rancho Vegas in Las Vegas, but the casino and café burned down prior to its opening. He tried his luck again in New York with a revue at Jack Silverman's International Restaurant, without success.

White, an authentically Runyonesque character, was a small, neat man known for his raffish style, cockiness, showmanly instincts, and tirelessness. He claimed never to have missed a performance of one of his shows and was frequently seen selling tickets at the box office. Despite his good looks, White never married.

As the last of the three best-known purveyors of the American revue, along with Florenz Ziegfeld and Earl Carroll, White made unique contributions to the form, placing it undeniably in the machine age. His shows were known for their simplicity, cleanness, and fast pace, reflecting his love of dancing. No other revue produced as many durable musical standards, including Gershwin's "I'll Build a Stairway to Paradise" (1922) and "Somebody Loves Me" (1924); De Sylva, Brown, and Henderson's "Birth of the Blues" (1926); and Brown and Henderson's "Life Is Just a Bowl of Cherries" (1931). Although his casts were relatively small compared to those of Ziegfeld or Carroll, he featured such performers as Ann Pennington, the Howard Brothers, Harry Richman, Ethel Merman, Rudy Vallee, Ray Bolger, Eleanor Powell, Helen Morgan, and Ann Miller. As a dancer and choreographer, he will be remembered for his creation of the turkey trot, the Charleston, and the black bottom. White died in Los Angeles.

[The Performing Arts Research Center of the New York Public Library at Lincoln Center has extensive files, including scrapbooks, and files of reviews are available in the Harvard Theatre Collection. See O. O. McIntyre, "He Had No Chance, But—," *Cosmopolitan*, Oct. 1926; Nanette Kutner, "The Hoofer Who Became a Producer," *Theatre Magazine*, July 1927; and Alexander Woollcott, "The Rise of Swifty White," *Collier's*, May 19, 1928. Background on White and his shows can be found in Gerald Bordman, *American Musical Theatre: A Chronicle* (1978) and *American Musical Revue* (1985); and Robert Baral, *Revue* (1962), which includes a good summary of each of the editions of the *Scandals*. Obituaries are in the *New York Times*, Oct. 12, 1968; and *Variety*, Oct. 16, 1968.]

DON B. WILMETH

WHITE, JOSH (Feb. 11, 1915–Sept. 5, 1969), guitarist and folksinger who also performed as Tippy Barton, Pinewood Tom, and the Singing Christian, was born Joshua Daniel White in Greenville, S.C., the son of Dennis White, a preacher, and Daisy Elizabeth Humphrey. He sang in the choir of the Church of God in the Saints of Christ in Greenville. His mother hoped that he would become a preacher, but at the age of seven he began guiding and singing with blind black street singers. From that point his schooling became erratic. He later commented, "I never got beyond the sixth grade," although he is recorded as having attended Stirling High School in Greenville between 1928 and 1932. He wandered the streets of southeastern cities and Chicago, leading a series of blind street singers and learning their songs.

Among the street singers White led were Blind Joe Taggart, with whom he first recorded on the Paramount label in Chicago in 1928, as well as Blind Lemon Jefferson, who, White recalled, taught him to sing "lonely" songs. In 1932 he first went to New York City to record many of Lemon's songs. There he joined a folk group, Clarence Williams' "Southernaires," performing as the Singing Christian, at $18 a performance. He appeared with them on the "Harlem Fantasy" radio show and made recordings with them on the Banner/ARC label.

In 1936, White's career nearly ended when, as the result of a fall on an icy pavement, he injured his fingers so severely that doctors predicted he would never play again. He worked as an elevator operator and then gradually began to play again at Harlem rent parties, experiences that he later referred to in his hit recording of "One Meatball," which sold a million copies.

In 1939, White formed the Josh White Singers, with which he appeared at Café Society Downtown. He began to perform there alone in 1943. In 1940 he appeared as Blind Lemon Jefferson in the Broadway play *John Henry*, which starred Paul Robeson. In the early 1940's he recorded on the Columbia label and appeared with Leadbelly (Huddie Ledbetter) at the Village Vanguard jazz club and on the radio. He played again on Broadway in *Blue Holiday* in 1945 and in *A Long Way from Home* in 1948. After a government-sponsored tour of Mexico in 1942, he became a favorite performer of President Franklin D. Roosevelt, frequently entertaining at the White House. He gave Library of Congress concerts during the 1940's, recorded on the Library of Congress label, and performed on weekly radio shows for the Office of War Information (OWI).

In the last years of the war, White toured and recorded with Libby Holman, performed with Paul Robeson in the Langston Hughes operetta *The Man Who Went to War* on OWI radio, and in a salute to Fats Waller at Carnegie Hall in 1944. In January 1945 he performed at President Roosevelt's inaugural ball, appeared in the film *Crimson Canary*, and began the concert career that would keep him on tour and in recording studios in America and abroad for the rest of his life. In 1950 he toured Europe with Eleanor Roosevelt.

White's own songs were often strongly critical of society, and in an appearance before the House Committee on Un-American Activities in 1950 he testified that his opposition to racial discrimination had led him to become a "sucker" in performing for organizations later determined to be Communist fronts. He also said that he had never been a Communist. Some critics felt that White failed to support Paul Robeson and by implication criticized him to the committee.

White married Carol Carr on Dec. 23, 1934; they had five children, two of whom, Beverly White Saunders and Joshua Donald White, became folksingers, appearing frequently with White in the late 1950's and early 1960's. His son later performed as Josh White, Jr. White suffered a heart attack in June 1961 but continued to perform. He appeared at the March on Washington for Jobs and Freedom on Aug. 28, 1963. An automobile accident in 1966 forced him to limit his activities. He died in Manhasset on Long Island, N.Y.

Critical assessment of White's talents and performances varied widely, ranging from Don McLean's obituary statement in *Sing Out* (Winter 1960) that "he was one of the finest artists America ever produced" (generally considered an exaggeration) to Arnold Shaw's description of him in *The World of Soul* (1970) as "a pre-Belafonte black sex idol. To folk singing, if not the blues, he brought matinee sexuality, bell-like diction, and pop appeal." Carter B. Horsley called him in the *New York Times* (Sept. 6, 1969) "a leading popularizer of the blues [who] captivated audiences with his casual charm and his authoritatively sensual style."

White's performances were notable for his smooth baritone and his clear diction, but they emphasized, too, the wide range of emotions demanded by his repertoire: songs that ranged from his own compositions and from those sung by Georgia chain-gang prisoners to spirituals, pre–Civil War songs, and the ballads that had been passed down from English and Scotch-Irish settlers in the mountains of the South.

As a collector, composer, and performer, White was a major contributor to the blues and to American folk music that drew its substance from city streets, urban and rural honky-tonks, and American concert halls by way of the sophisticated urban cabarets that were a feature of American society at midcentury. His best-known songs include "Ball and Chain Blues," "Delia," "Hard Times Blues," "Jim Crow Train," "Silicosis Blues," "Uncle Sam Says," and "Welfare Blues." He was also a major influence on the emerging style of younger performers, including Harry Belafonte, Oscar Brown, Jr., and Dave Van Ronk.

[There is no full biographical or critical study of White. Peter Link has written "Josh: The Man and

His Music," a musical biography, which has been performed in regional theaters, featuring Josh White, Jr., as his father. White collaborated with Ivor Maroints on *The Josh White Guitar Method* (1956), and many of his own songs and arrangements, as well as a biographical introduction, are in *The Josh White Song Book* (1963), edited by Robert Shelton and Walter Raim. Other biographical and critical material appears in *Blues Unlimited*, July–Sept. 1968. An obituary is in the *New York Times*, Sept. 6, 1969.]

DAVID D. ANDERSON

WHITEMAN, PAUL SAMUEL ("POPS") (Mar. 28, 1890–Dec. 29, 1967), bandleader, was born in Denver, Colo., the son of Wilberforce James Whiteman, a music teacher and the director of music education in the Denver school system, and Elfrida Dallison, a vocalist. At the age of six, he began taking violin lessons from his father. Following graduation from East Denver High School in 1907, he joined the Denver Symphony Orchestra as a violist. A year later he eloped with a chorus girl, Nellie Stack; the marriage was annulled in 1910.

The next year, Whiteman moved to San Francisco, where he eventually found work in that city's symphony orchestra. He resigned from the position in 1916 to study and perform jazz, which was just starting to become popular. In this he was unsuccessful because he lacked the proper technique. He did, however, discover that improvisation, or "faking," was the basis for the style as then played. Thereupon, he decided to try to make it acceptable for skilled musicans to perform jazz without losing the spontaneity of "faked" presentations.

After World War I service as a navy bandmaster, Whiteman reentered the field of popular music and in 1919 opened in Los Angeles with what came to be referred to as the "original" Paul Whiteman orchestra. At about this time he hired the composer Ferde Grofé as his arranger. The following spring Whiteman and his musicians began appearing in theatrical productions and nightclubs in Atlantic City and New York and started recording for the Victor Company in Camden, N.J.

In 1921, Whiteman married showgirl Africa ("Jimmie") Smith, but the marriage ended in a few months. On Nov. 4, 1922, he married dancer Mildred Vanderhoff (known professionally as Vanda Hoff); they had one child and were divorced in 1931.

As the physically imposing Whiteman's fame grew in the early 1920's his picture often appeared in the newspapers, and his round face, double chin, pencil-thin moustache, and receding hairline soon became widely recognized. These characteristics were incorporated into a distinctive, copyrighted sketch that identified him for the remainder of his life.

Whiteman considered his men as more than just hired employees and, in a manner unusual in the 1920's, worked to achieve social acceptance for dance-band performers. In 1923 the Whiteman orchestra embarked on the first of two successful tours to England, and in the same year, he became one of the earliest leaders to add vocal choruses to dance-band recordings.

Whiteman further dignified jazz by presenting the famous Feb. 12, 1924, concert in New York's Aeolian Hall, featuring the number thereafter most associated with him, *Rhapsody in Blue*. Its composer, George Gershwin, performed the piano part. At this time, Whiteman came to be called "the King of Jazz."

After his introduction to radio in the mid-1920's, Whiteman starred in numerous programs, beginning in 1928. Two years later he appeared in the first of his motion pictures, *The King of Jazz*, while continuing to work on improving the unmistakable orchestral sound of his band, which he maintained despite personnel changes. Among other noted performers who were with the Whiteman organization was the vocalist Mildred Bailey, whom he hired in 1929. She is credited with originating the nickname "Pops" for the conductor.

Although the Great Depression affected the band business, Whiteman kept his musicians employed. On Aug. 18, 1931, he married the film actress Margaret Livingston, after going on a strenuous weight-reducing program in response to her wishes. They eventually adopted four children. In addition to her other duties, the new Mrs. Whiteman began managing her husband's financial affairs.

As the Swing Era developed in the 1930's Whiteman, as always, changed with the times and formed the "Swing Wing" within his orchestra. Because of severe physical and emotional exhaustion, the conductor broke up his band in 1940, and after farming briefly in New Jersey, he reorganized his musicians the following year and returned to radio work. In 1943 he began the "Philco Radio Hall of Fame" program and became musical director of the Blue Network, later known as the American Broadcasting Company (ABC). He appeared as himself in the film biography of George Gershwin, *Rhapsody in Blue* (1945).

In accord with another national trend, that of using recordings extensively on radio, Whiteman in 1947 broadcast the first network disc-jockey show. He also made his final movie appearance, in *The Fabulous Dorseys* (1947). During the late 1940's he entered the field of television with "The Dave Garroway Show," "TV Teen Club," and a musical series, "Paul Whiteman's Goodyear Revue," on ABC-TV. He was a vice-president of the ABC network from 1947 to 1955.

Whiteman continued his earlier interest in auto racing and other pursuits, as well as music, until nearly the end of his life. Following his death in Doylestown, Pa., a funeral service was held at which some of his former musicians played the slow theme from *Rhapsody in Blue* and his favorite song, "When Day Is Done."

Although Whiteman was known as the King of Jazz, this was technically a misnomer. He did, however, employ many jazz musicians and bring arrangements of popular, semiclassical, and symphonic music with jazz overtones (including Gershwin's famous work and Grofé's *Grand Canyon Suite*) to millions of listeners. Moreover, the list of musicians, vocalists, composers, and arrangers associated with Whiteman comprises a veritable who's who of American music. The conductor was eulogized by Stanley Adams as having "raised popular music from the basement to the penthouse." Duke Ellington said that Whiteman "made a lady out of jazz."

[The Paul Whiteman Collection is at Williams College, Williamstown, Mass. Whiteman wrote three books: *Jazz* (1926), *How to Be a Bandleader* (1941), and *Records for the Millions: A Guide to Record Collecting* (1948). Margaret Livingston Whiteman, *Whiteman's Burden* (1933), deals mainly with her husband's weight problem.

On his life and work, see Leo Walker, *The Wonderful Era of the Great Dance Bands* (1964) and *The Big Band Almanac* (1978); George T. Simon, *Simon Says* (1971) and *The Big Bands* (1981); John Chilton, *Who's Who of Jazz* (1972); Roger D. Kinkle, *The Complete Encyclopedia of Popular Music and Jazz: 1900–1950* (1974); Brian Rust, *The American Dance Band Discography: 1917–1942* (1975); Carl Johnson, *Paul Whiteman: A Chronology* (1977); David Meeker, *Jazz in the Movies* (1977); and Thomas De Long, *Pops* (1983). An obituary is in the *New York Times*, Dec. 30, 1967.]

BARRETT G. POTTER

WHITNEY, COURTNEY (May 20, 1897–Mar. 21, 1969), army officer, was born in Takoma Park, Md., the son of Milton Whitney, the first director of the United States Department of Agriculture's Bureau of Soils, and Annie Cushing Langdon. Whitney attended public schools in Washington, D.C. In August 1917, after serving briefly in the National Guard, he joined the Aviation Section of the Army Signal Corps, soon earning a second lieutenant's commission. In the next nine years, he was stationed at airfields in Louisiana, Mississippi, the District of Columbia, and the Philippines. He became a section chief in the Office of the Chief of the Army Air Corps in 1926. He married Evelyn Ewart Jones on Oct. 20, 1920; they had two children.

While stationed at Bolling Field, Whitney studied law in the evenings at the National University in Washington, where he earned an LL.B. in 1923. Resigning from the Air Corps in 1927, he established a lucrative law practice in Manila. His friends included many influential Filipinos as well as General Douglas MacArthur, commander of the United States Army's Philippine Department from 1928 to 1930 and military adviser to the Commonwealth government from 1935 to 1941.

In the autumn of 1940, Whitney returned to active duty in Washington as a major. He became assistant chief of the Legal Division of the Army Air Corps and, in February 1943, assistant judge advocate of the Army Air Force. In May, Whitney was transferred to MacArthur's Southwest Pacific–theater headquarters in Australia. By then a colonel, he was selected to head the Philippine Regional Section, which provided logistical assistance to the resistance movements, dispatched American personnel to train guerrillas, collected intelligence, and disseminated propaganda among the Filipinos. MacArthur was pleased with Whitney's work and with the strong support the guerrillas gave United States forces later. Whitney soon became MacArthur's confidant and eventually almost his alter ego. Elevated to brigadier general in January 1945, Whitney assisted Filipino officials in restoring government and order in the wake of the advancing American forces.

In late August 1945, Whitney moved to

Japan with MacArthur, who had become supreme commander for the Allied powers there. In December, Whitney became chief of the Government Section, the most powerful of the occupation agencies. Whitney assembled an able group of officers and civilian experts to oversee the demilitarization and democratization of Japan. Whitney's staff was largely responsible for drafting Japan's constitution of 1946, which incorporated liberal, democratic features from various Western constitutions. Whitney and his colleagues also advised the Japanese on the legislative measures necessary to revise statutes and codes for the new constitution. They were also responsible for purging ultranationalists and militarists; decentralizing administrative, fiscal, and police authority; promoting woman's suffrage; supervising election procedures and political-party activities; maintaining liaison between MacArthur's headquarters and the Japanese government; and modernizing the civil service.

When the Korean War erupted in June 1950, Whitney was named military secretary of the United Nations Command, which MacArthur headed. He accompanied MacArthur to the conference with President Truman on Wake Island that October. When Truman relieved MacArthur of his commands in April 1951, Whitney returned to America with the general.

That spring Whitney retired as a major general, to serve as MacArthur's personal secretary in New York City, where the five-star general maintained an office. When MacArthur became board chairman of Remington Rand in 1952, Whitney was employed as an executive by the firm. In 1956, Whitney published an adulatory book on the 1941–1951 period of MacArthur's career. After MacArthur's death in 1964, Whitney moved back to Washington, where he died.

Although he was hardworking and intelligent, Whitney was also considered abrasive by some, especially colleagues who envied his unique bond with MacArthur and correspondents who were critical of the five-star officer. Particularly after World War II, Whitney probably became more essential to MacArthur than Colonel House had been to Woodrow Wilson or Harry Hopkins to Franklin Roosevelt.

[Whitney's personal papers are in the archives of the MacArthur Memorial in Norfolk, Va., and his official records are located both there and in the Washington National Records Center. Whitney wrote *MacArthur: His Rendezvous with History* (1956), and he edited *Political Reorientation of Japan*, 2 vols. (1948), as well as other Government Section reports. Obituaries are in the *New York Times* and *Washington Post*, both Mar. 22, 1969.]

D. Clayton James

WICKARD, CLAUDE RAYMOND (Feb. 28, 1893–Apr. 29, 1967), United States secretary of agriculture, was born on a 200-acre corn farm near Flora, Ind., the son of Andrew Jackson Wickard, a dirt farmer, and Iva Lenora Kirkpatrick. Wickard's childhood was typical of rural youth at the turn of the century and made him acutely conscious of being thought of as a "hayseed." Thus, when he graduated from high school, he insisted, over his father's strenuous objections, that he be financed in the pursuit of a degree in agriculture. Upon graduation from Purdue with a B.S. in 1915, he took over the management of his father's land, added another 100 acres to it, and named it Fairacre Farms.

As America entered World War I, Wickard modernized the farm, introducing bathroom plumbing and electric lights. On Apr. 17, 1918, he married Louise Eckert; they had two children. Occupationally deferred from the army, Wickard cash-cropped the farm to pay off his debts. When the war ended, he started to draw on the knowledge of "scientific agriculture" he had gained at Purdue. He refertilized his soil in the 1920's and started raising fine hogs to process his corn crops into pork and bacon. He received awards and gained fame for his extraordinarily high yields in both corn and meat, and in 1928 he was granted the coveted Master Farmer citation.

His agricultural expertise led to a close relationship with the Indiana State Extension Service and to leadership in the state Farm Bureau; this in turn led to Democratic party politics. In November 1932, when Franklin D. Roosevelt won the presidency, Wickard won a seat in the Indiana State Senate. A corn-belt Democrat was rarity enough, but one who had both administrative and political experience was certain to be noticed by Secretary of Agriculture Henry A. Wallace, who was at that moment creating a vast army of people to manage the first Agricultural Adjustment Administration (AAA) programs. Wickard had served less than a year in the state senate when he was called to Washington, D.C., to begin his twenty-year government career as an assistant in the Corn-Hog Section of the AAA.

Although it was widely assumed that Wickard's appointment had been a "political" one, he came to be regarded as an effective administrator. He was a stocky, balding man with the hands of a farmer, gruff and abrupt one moment but then self-deprecating and uncertain the next. His leadership came from the power of office, not from charm or charisma. When Wallace first aspired to the vice-presidency in January 1940, he named Wickard as undersecretary of agriculture. Seven months later, on Sept. 5, 1940, Roosevelt agreed that Wickard should succeed Wallace as secretary of agriculture in a semitemporary arrangement while Wallace went on the campaign trail.

In January 1941, with Roosevelt a third-term president and Wallace his vice-president, the agriculture portfolio fell to Wickard. But now everything had changed. In 1933, Wickard and the AAA created scarcity by plowing under crops so as to raise prices. With the coming of World War II, the burgeoning arms economy meant full agricultural production, rising farm prices and industrial wages, and the hovering threat of inflation. If Wickard were to keep his congressional and farm backing, he would have to raise farm prices as high as they would go. If the secretary of agriculture were to keep his job in the cabinet, he would have to keep food prices down. Wickard was a loyal, liberal New Deal Democrat. But he was also an Indiana corn-hog farmer who remembered the dreaded surplus and the specter of agricultural ruin. Wickard viewed the conflict with the Axis powers from the perspective of a back-forty war between too much and too little.

As Wickard trod the taut line between glut and plenty, he began to overreach himself administratively. Roosevelt had said that the New Deal was gone and that winning the war was all that mattered. Whereas most cabinet members had already deferred to war-production, price, and allocation directors, Wickard wanted to be both a secretary and a director. He asked to be named food administrator, and in December 1942, Roosevelt reluctantly gave in to him. Within four months, Wickard had made a series of disastrous staffing decisions and so was superseded as "food czar" by someone else. He retained his position as secretary of agriculture, however, throughout the war.

By the time the war in Europe ended, Roosevelt was dead and the new president, Harry Truman, had made it clear that he wanted to select his own cabinet. Not yet ready to return permanently to the farm, Wickard was given his choice of Agriculture Department programs. He chose the Rural Electrification Administration (REA). When Congress created the REA in 1936, only 10 percent of American farms had electricity. When Wickard became REA administrator in May 1945, 46 percent of farms had been electrified. His administration of the REA was an unqualified success. By the time he left Washington in January 1953 and returned to Indiana, over 88 percent of all farms in the nation had electric lights.

Three years later, Wickard campaigned to unseat Republican Senator Homer Capehart and lost. He spent the balance of his life as a trustee of Purdue University and as the proprietor of Fairacre Farms. He died in a car crash near Delphi, Ind.

[Wickard's diary and papers are in the Franklin D. Roosevelt Presidential Library, Hyde Park, N.Y. His reminiscences are included in the Columbia University Oral History Project. See Dean Albertson, *Roosevelt's Farmer* (1961). An obituary is in the *New York Times*, Apr. 30, 1967.]

DEAN ALBERTSON

WILEY, ALEXANDER (May 26, 1884–Oct. 26, 1967), lawyer and United States senator, was born in Chippewa Falls, Wis., the son of Alexander Wiley, a Norwegian immigrant farmer who had changed his name from Hvila, and Sophia Ekern. From 1902 to 1904 he attended Augsburg College in Minneapolis, where he studied for the Lutheran ministry. Abandoning that course of study, he enrolled in law school at the University of Michigan in 1904 but then transferred to the University of Wisconsin Law School, where he received his LL.B. in 1907. He returned to Chippewa Falls to establish his law practice, and in 1909 he was elected district attorney for Chippewa County. He married May Jenkins on Nov. 25, 1909; they had four children. In 1915 he resumed his private law practice. He also owned a dairy farm as well as banking and business interests; however, he lost much of his wealth in the economic collapse of 1929.

In 1933, Wiley was elected president of the Kiwanis International for the Wisconsin–Upper Michigan district. Through his Kiwanis work, he won public recognition, and partly as a result of this, the Republican party chose him as its gubernatorial candidate in 1936. He was defeated by the incumbent Progressive-party governor, Philip La Follette, with the Democratic candidate running third. The Republicans, impressed by his showing, nominated him for the United States Senate in 1938. He easily defeated the Democratic candidate, F. Ryan Duffy, and the Progressive candidate, Herman Ekern.

When he entered the Senate in 1939, Wiley was a dedicated isolationist who voted against selective service, lend-lease, and repeal of portions of the Neutrality Acts. As he became increasingly alarmed by the international situation, he began to support preparedness legislation. Ten months before the Japanese attack on Pearl Harbor, he called in vain for the secretary of state to appear before the Senate to report on the status of American defenses in the Pacific. With the advent of World War II, Wiley completed his shift from isolationist to internationalist. He said he was "able to make the switch because I like to think I'm big enough of a man to change my mind when I see I've been wrong."

Wiley easily won reelection in 1944, first defeating Joseph R. McCarthy in the Republican primary and then defeating Democrat Howard McMurray in the fall election. At the conclusion of World War II, he consistently supported the concept of collective security, voting in 1945 for the Bretton Woods Monetary Agreement and for ratification of the United Nations Charter. In 1945 he also became a member of the Foreign Relations Committee, where he was greatly influenced by the Republican senator Arthur Vandenberg's pleas for bipartisanship in foreign policy. Wiley supported the 1946 loan to Great Britain, aid to Greece and Turkey under the Truman Doctrine, the Marshall Plan, and American membership in the North Atlantic Treaty Organization (NATO).

Wiley served from 1947 to 1948 as chairman of the Senate Judiciary Committee and established the precedent of consulting local bar associations on the qualifications of nominees. In 1950 he was reelected by nearly 80,000 votes over Democrat Thomas Fairchild. When the United States became involved in military action in Korea, he at first supported the president's decision to send troops, but he later disagreed with the manner in which the war was being waged. He questioned the wisdom of Truman's decision to remove General Douglas MacArthur from command in Korea but conceded the president's right to do so. From 1952 to 1953 he served as United States delegate to the United Nations General Assembly, appointed first by Truman and then by Eisenhower.

In May 1952 (Wiley kept the exact date secret), Wiley, whose wife had died in August 1948, married Dorothy McBride Kydd. That same year, he made a significant speech in the Senate, calling for the entry of West Germany into the NATO alliance and attacking conservative Republicans, led by Robert Taft, for their lack of support of bipartisan foreign policy. This speech was widely regarded as an attempt to assume the leadership of the internationalist wing of the party, left vacant by Senator Vandenberg's death. When the Republicans again controlled the Senate in 1953–1954, Wiley became chairman of the Foreign Relations Committee.

Despite strong isolationist sentiment in Wisconsin, Wiley's attention to the needs of his constituents on domestic matters had kept his popularity strong in the state. In 1953, however, isolationists controlling the Republican state convention in Wisconsin obtained a vote of censure against him for his opposition to the proposed Bricker amendment, which would have limited the president's treaty-making powers. In 1956 the Republican state convention endorsed the isolationist Glenn R. Davis for Wiley's Senate seat. Denouncing the convention delegates as "Eisenhower haters," Wiley campaigned vigorously and defeated Davis in the primary. He then easily defeated Democrat Henry W. Maier in the fall election.

Wiley's political problems resulted largely from his disagreements with fellow Wisconsin senator Joseph R. McCarthy. A stalwart anti-Communist, Wiley usually swallowed his distaste for McCarthy and his methods. In the face of McCarthy's opposition, he did, however, support Eisenhower's appointment of Charles E. Bohlen as ambassador to the Soviet Union, and he also criticized McCarthy's attack in 1953 on the British Labour-party leader Clement Attlee. Wiley was one of only three senators who failed to vote on McCarthy's censure.

In 1962, Wiley lost his bid for a fifth term in the Senate to Democrat Gaylord Nelson. Wiley continued to live for some years in Washington. A Lutheran in his youth, he increasingly turned to Christian Science, and in 1967 entered a Christian Science nursing home in Philadelphia, where he died. Wiley was known for his folksy humor, for his garrulous personality, and particularly for the cheese parties he gave to promote his state's dairy industry; he once unveiled a bust of the former vice-president John Nance Garner sculpted in cheddar cheese.

[A large collection of Wiley's papers is at the State Historical Society of Wisconsin. He wrote *Laughing with Congress* (1947); and "Reflections on the Seaway," in *Proceedings of a Special One-Day Institute, "Wisconsin and the Seaway"* (1955). On his career, see Hugh Morrow, "Big Wind from Wisconsin," *Saturday Evening Post*, Oct. 20, 1951; Arnold Heidenheimer, "Wiley: Another Vandenberg?" *New Republic*, June 2, 1952; Richard H. Rovere, "Letter from Washington," *New Yorker*, June 21, 1952; Edwin R. Bayley, "Wisconsin: The War Against Eisenhower," *New Republic*, July 6, 1953; T. L. Hills, *The St. Lawrence Seaway* (1959); Ronald J. Caridi, *The Korean War and American Politics* (1968); Robert Griffith, *The Politics of Fear* (1970); and Thomas C. Reeves, *The Life and Times of Joe McCarthy* (1982). Oral-history interviews with him are on deposit at Princeton and Columbia universities. Obituaries are in the *New York Times* and the *Washington Post*, both Oct. 27, 1967.]

MELBA PORTER HAY

WOOD, CRAIG RALPH (*ca.* 1901–May 7, 1968), professional golfer, was born in Lake Placid, N.Y. Little is known of his family or his early life. When he joined the professional golf circuit in the late 1920's he was one of the few college-educated players. Wood was best known as a powerful driver whose smooth and effortless swing enabled him consistently to hit drives further than other players. His tee shot of 430 yards on the fifth hole of the course at Saint Andrews, Scotland, in the 1933 British Open, is commemorated by a concrete slab on the spot where it landed.

Despite his ability, Wood failed to win major championships in the 1930's. His successes came in smaller tournaments, such as the Galveston (Texas) Open of 1934, where he beat Byron Nelson. He and his sixteen-year-old protégé, Bobby Jacobson, who was the New Jersey Junior Champion, won the Pro/Am Best Ball Tournament in August 1934, and Wood won again in the New Jersey Open the same month. These and other successes during the 1930's kept Wood among the top money winners each year. In 1932–1933 he led the winter tour in earnings.

Wood's frequent selection as a member of the United States Ryder Cup team also reflected his consistent play during the 1930's. Yet victory regularly eluded him. He finished second to Densmore Shute in the British Open in 1933, losing in a thirty-six-hole playoff, and was the runner-up in the United States Professional Golfers Association Championship in 1934. He had previously finished second on two occasions and third on two others in the New Jersey Open before he won it in 1934 on his eighth attempt. In the Masters Championship of 1935 he lost in a playoff to Gene Sarazen, whose remarkable double-eagle two on the fifteenth hole of the last round forged a tie after regulation play. Because of these near misses, he became known as "number-two Wood."

Wood was a popular player, drawing large galleries wherever he appeared. A congenial man who was knowledgeable about contemporary issues, he loved to chat with the crowd about any topic except golf. He was a successful club professional, serving successively at the Forest Hills (N.Y.) Field Club in the 1920's, and at the Deal, N.J., and Hollywood, Fla., golf clubs in the 1930's. In 1939 he became club pro at the Winged Foot Club in Mamaroneck, N.Y.

Wood's fortunes turned around in 1940 when he won the Metropolitan Open with the remarkable score of 264, then the world record for the fewest shots in a four-round tournament. The following year he captured the Masters Championship, won the United States National Open, and, in head-to-head play in what was deemed to be the "unofficial world championship," defeated Vic Ghezzi, who had won the Professional Golfers Association title that year. These victories assured Wood's selection as captain of the United States Ryder Cup team for 1942.

After World War II Wood appeared only occasionally, last competing in 1948. From 1945 until 1963 he was successively a sales representative for several companies and a car dealer in New Jersey and Westchester County, N.Y. In 1963 he moved to Grand Bahama Island, where he established the Lucayan Country Club and became its first resident professional. Wood married Jacqueline Valentine on April 7, 1934. He died while visiting Palm Beach, Fla.

[Wood wrote "The Pro Has 'Em Too," *New York Times Magazine*, June 15, 1941. See *Newsweek*, June 22, 1964, and May 20, 1968; *Time*, May 17, 1968; Len Elliott and Barbara Kelley, *Who's Who in Golf* (1976); and Michael Hobbs, *50 Masters of Golf* (1983). An obituary is in the *New York Times*, May 9, 1968.]

CHARLES R. MIDDLETON

WOOD, JOHN STEPHENS (Feb. 8, 1885–Sept. 12, 1968), United States congressman, was born near Ball Ground, Ga., the son of Jessie L. Wood, a farmer, and Sarah Holcomb. After attending local schools, he worked in a factory and later as a teacher. He was educated at North Georgia Agricultural College and Mercer University, from which he received an LL.B. in 1910. Admitted to the bar that year, he practiced law in Jasper and later Canton. He married Margurete Roberts on Sept. 3, 1913. After her death, he married Louise Jones on May 23, 1926. Wood had one child with his first wife and three with his second.

Wood entered politics when he served as a delegate to the Democratic National Convention in 1912. He was Canton city attorney in 1915–1916. In the latter year, he was elected to the Georgia House of Representatives, from which he resigned in 1918 for duty with the Army Air Service. Wood afterward combined law and politics, serving as solicitor general of the Blue Ridge judicial circuit from 1921 to 1926 and as superior court judge from 1926 to 1931. In 1930 he defeated the dean of the Georgia congressional delegation, Thomas M. Bell, in the Democratic primary; then and in 1932, Wood won election to the United States House of Representatives. He represented the state's Ninth Congressional District, which was known as one of the most isolated in the nation. Although generally a loyal Democrat, he opposed some home- and farm-relief legislation, which probably contributed to his defeat for renomination in 1934. Wood then resumed law practice in Canton. When B. Frank Whelchel, who had narrowly defeated him in 1934 and again in 1936, announced his retirement in 1944, Wood successfully sought election to Congress again. He was reelected in 1946, 1948, and 1950.

In 1945 chance propelled Wood to prominence. He had quickly established himself as a conservative member of the House, except on international affairs, voting more often with Republicans than with his fellow Democrats. Wood allied himself with one of the leading conservative Democrat congressmen, John E. Rankin of Mississippi. In particular, he supported Rankin's successful crusade to establish the House Un-American Activities Committee (HUAC) as a standing committee. When the chairman of that committee, Edward J. Hart of New Jersey, resigned in July, Wood was chosen to fill his place. It was unusual for a junior member of the House to become chairman of a standing committee, but Rankin, who did not want to surrender his chairmanship of the Veterans Affairs Committee, dictated the move. In Wood he found a compliant man who let Rankin do whatever he wanted with HUAC. The committee thus became notorious for the broad scope of its investigations and its sensationalism in 1945–1946. Wood contributed to this by probing radio news commentators and introducing legislation designed to control their remarks.

Wood was also a member of the House Education and Labor and, briefly, Foreign Affairs committees. During his last three terms in Congress he moderated his position on some economic issues. He was particularly known for his unsuccessful effort in 1949 to modify the terms of the Labor-Management Relations (Taft-Hartley) Act. Although he now more often voted with other Democrats, Wood was still considered a conservative, albeit an independent one. He was also a staunch opponent of civil rights legislation.

Wood's reputation was based primarily on his connection with HUAC. Although he was not chairman of the committee during the Republican Eightieth Congress (1947–1949), he resumed that role from 1949 to 1953. Rankin had left the committee because of a new rule in 1949 that the chairman of another House committee could not serve on HUAC. Thus, Wood became chairman of the committee in fact as well as in name. As such, he contributed to the formulation of the controversial Internal Security Act of 1950 (popularly known as the McCarran Act). More important, Wood toned down his committee's sensationalism, allowed witnesses to make statements and be accompanied by counsel, and restrained somewhat the issuance of contempt citations. His handling of the committee's proceedings was usually gentlemanly. He sometimes was unable, however, to control the aggressive behavior of some of his fellow members. Moreover, Wood acquiesced in, and even initiated, controversial investigations of alleged subversion in government, labor unions, academic life, entertainment, and the medical profession.

Upon becoming chairman of HUAC in 1945, Wood had announced that he would not engage in "either 'whitewashing' or witch-hunting." Personally, he strove to adhere to this, although he made it clear that the committee's rules in getting maximum exposure of subversive activities in American life would be enforced. When the playwright Lillian Hellman in 1952 declared that there were limits to what she would tell the committee, Wood replied that "the committee cannot permit witnesses to set forth the terms under which they will testify." This exchange was part of HUAC's most publicized action, an investigation in 1951–1952 of subversive influences in the motion-picture industry. The subsequent public hearings were sometimes covered on television. One result was that the film industry blacklisted at least two dozen actors, writers, and other employees. Twenty-three of these people later sued Wood, the committee, and various motion-picture studios for $51 million, without success.

Wood did not run for reelection to Congress in 1952. He resumed his law practice in Canton the following year and he returned to public notice only once, in 1955, when President Dwight D. Eisenhower nominated him for a three-year term on the Subversive Activities Control Board. The National Association for the Advancement of Colored People, among others, strenuously objected to his appointment. After Wood admitted that as a young man he had applied for membership in the Ku Klux Klan, although he had not joined, the Senate failed to act on his confirmation. Illness later forced him to retire from law practice. He died in Marietta, Ga.

Wood was typical of many southern Democratic congressmen of his time, mild-mannered and even courtly in person but outspoken on issues, often controversial, of concern to white southerners. Wood opposed racial equality, adopted an independent and often conservative position on economic questions, and ardently defended what he regarded as American national security.

[Data about Wood can be found in the biographical files of the Georgia Department of Archives and History, Atlanta. Sources for Wood's work with HUAC are Robert K. Carr, *The House Committee on Un-American Activities, 1945–1950* (1952); Carl Beck, *Contempt of Congress* (1959); and Walter Goodman, *The Committee* (1968). Obituaries are in the *Atlanta Constitution*, Sept. 13, 1968; and the *New York Times*, Sept. 14, 1968.]

DONALD R. MCCOY

WOOD, ROBERT ELKINGTON (June 13, 1879–Nov. 6, 1969), army officer and merchant, was born in Kansas City, Mo., the son of Robert Whitney Wood, a coal and ice merchant who had been one of John Brown's raiders and a Union captain in the Civil War, and Lillie Marian Collins. Unable to attend Yale University because of financial reverses suffered by his father during the early 1890's, Wood obtained an appointment to West Point, from which he graduated thirteenth in a class of fifty-four in 1900.

After duty with the army in the Philippines and on the western frontier, Wood volunteered for service in Panama in 1905, after the United States had taken over from the French the construction of the Panama Canal. He demonstrated an aptitude for organization and management and was assigned the purchasing of all supplies and equipment for the canal and the feeding, housing, and governing of the canal's 50,000 workers and their families. He rose to the rank of major and saw the canal through to its completion in 1915. He then took early retirement granted by a special act of Congress in recognition of his service. On Apr. 30, 1908, he married Mary Butler Hardwick; they had five children.

Wood rejoined the army in 1917 (when the United States entered World War I) and was commissioned a colonel. Posted to Europe to prepare for the arrival of American troops, he brought order to the operation of French ports, which were overwhelmed by the increase in traffic; incoming ships often waited weeks in the harbor before docking. His success led to his appointment as acting quartermaster general (with the rank of brigadier general) and responsibility for all supply services for the American Expeditionary Force. He was awarded the Distinguished Service Medal for his work.

Released from service in 1919, Wood became vice-president for merchandising of Montgomery Ward and Company. He saw that the automobile and improved roads were creating great changes in consumer markets, and he urged his superiors to capitalize on them by adding retail stores to the company's mail-order system. Wood's persistence in this idea led to his dismissal. Julius Rosenwald, head of the other large mail-order enterprise in Chicago, Sears, Roebuck, and Company, hired Wood in November 1924, and Wood opened his first store two months later. His strategy was an immediate success; other stores followed rapidly. By January 1928, when Wood became president and chief executive, he had created a nationwide chain of retail stores. Sears's 1931 retail sales surpassed its mail-order sales, and from then on it dominated the business.

Under Wood the 1930's were a decade of economic and managerial progress. Building and directing the affairs of a far-flung mail-order and retail business required innovative responses to unprecedented problems. He integrated mass production with mass distribution to serve the rapidly urbanizing mass market; he devised organizational arrangements to promote high levels of morale and motivation; and he fashioned policies to maintain public support during a time of virulent anti–chain store agitation.

Wood was unorthodox in his business priorities, insisting that Sears's responsibility was first to the customer, then to the employee, then to the community (whose purchasing power was vital), and last to the stockholder, who, Wood argued, was best served if the others came first. In 1939 Wood gave up the responsibilities of day-to-day management and became chairman. Gravely concerned about war in Europe and convinced that America should stay out of the conflict, he accepted the chairmanship of the America First movement but he disbanded that organization immediately after Pearl Harbor. He was unsuccessful in his effort to volunteer for active duty but aided Gen. Henry Harley ("Hap") Arnold as a civilian adviser on supply matters. For these efforts, Wood was awarded the Legion of Merit.

Wood foresaw the vast economic expansion that would follow World War II and invested Sears's capital in new, expanded, and more efficient facilities. In the eight years following World War II, Wood opened 134 new stores, relocated 83, enlarged 149 others, and put millions of dollars into larger parking lots, warehouses, and mail-order plants. During this period he also built retail stores in Latin America and moved into Canada, in a joint venture with Simpson's Ltd. During these years Sears's sales almost doubled.

After retiring in April 1954, Wood remained an active member of the Sears board for another fourteen years. During the first six of these he greatly influenced the selection of senior officers. He relinquished his director's post to become honorary board chairman in May 1968. He died in Lake Forest, Ill.

From a little over $200 million in 1924, when Woods joined Sears, sales rose to over $3 billion in 1954, when he retired. Sears's net profits grew from $14 to $141 million, and its net worth from $126 million to $1.141 billion. Employees increased from 23,000 to 200,000. By the time Wood retired Sears had become the world's largest general merchandise distributor and one of America's largest employers. Sears, under Wood, contributed significantly to the emergence of a new American middle class and to upgrading the quality of life for American workers. His move into Latin America speeded progress there in industrialization, improved living standards, and accelerated the development of a new middle class. Wood's most important contribution was his demonstration in practical terms that human and economic values are not necessarily conflictive but that, with proper care, they can be mutually supportive.

[Wood wrote *Mail Order Retailing Pioneered in Chicago* (1948) and *Monument for the World* (1963). See also Boris Emmet and John E. Jeuck, *Catalogues and Counters* (1950); Alfred D. Chandler, Jr., *Strategy and Structure* (1962); Justus D. Doenecke, "The Isolationism of General Robert E. Wood," John N. Schacht, ed., in *Three Faces of Midwest Isolationism* (1981); and James C. Worthy, *Shaping an American Institution* (1984). "The Reminiscences of General Robert E. Wood" are in the Oral History Collection, Columbia University, New York City (1961).]

JAMES C. WORTHY

WOODRING, HARRY HINES (May 31, 1887–Sept. 9, 1967), governor of Kansas and secretary of war, was born in Elk City, Kans., the son of Hines Woodring, a grain dealer, and Melissa Jane Cooper. Woodring's early life was influenced by his family's poverty and the overprotectiveness of five older sisters. As a youth, he swept floors and did odd jobs at the First National Bank of Elk City. He attended the Elk City grade and high schools and Montgomery County High School until 1904, when he began to take classes at Lebanon (Ind.) Business University. After returning from Indiana in 1905, he became an assistant cashier at the First National. In 1909 he accepted an assistant cashier's position at the First National Bank of nearby Neodesha, Kans., and soon became a cashier.

In 1918, Woodring enlisted in the Army Tank Corps and was sent to Camp Colt, Pa., where he served as a personnel clerk. He was recommended for officers' school, and in October 1918 he was commissioned a second lieutenant in the Tank Corps. Before he could be shipped overseas, the war ended.

Woodring then worked briefly at the Mid-West National Bank in Kansas City before returning to Neodesha as managing director of the First National Bank. Throughout the 1920's the quiet yet personable bachelor was involved in civic activities, his church (Disciples of Christ), and the American Legion, of which he was elected state commander in 1928. His leadership of the 19,000-member legion whetted his political appetite and provided contacts throughout the state.

In March 1929, Woodring, who had gained controlling interest in the bank, decided to sell out and retire. The following January, with little backing and no political experience, he announced he would seek the Democratic nomination for governor. An effective orator and campaigner, he won the Democratic nomination. When the Republican party split and John Brinkley ran as an independent, Woodring carried the election by 251 votes over his Republican opponent, Frank Haucke.

Although new to politics, Woodring performed extremely well as governor. Under his leadership the Republican-controlled legislature adopted a state income tax and limited property taxes, measures that provided considerable relief to residents of the depression-racked state. Woodring also established the Crippled Children's Commission; expanded road construction; outlawed large-scale corporation farming, which threatened the small family farm; and strictly controlled holding companies and stock transactions. His well-publicized battle with large utility companies resulted in major reductions in gas rates.

In 1932, Woodring ran for reelection against Republican Alf M. Landon and, again, independent John Brinkley. The Republican wounds of two years before had healed enough to enable Landon to edge out Woodring by less than 6,000 votes.

But Woodring, who had been one of the first governors to champion the presidential nomination of New York governor Franklin D. Roosevelt, returned to public life in 1933 when Roosevelt named him assisant secretary of war. When Woodring arrived in Washington, he was touted as one of the city's most highly sought-after bachelors. He married Helen Coolidge, the daughter of the Massachusetts democratic senator Marcus A. Coolidge, on July 25, 1933; they had three children.

As assistant secretary, Woodring instituted many reforms in military procurement procedures that promoted competitive bidding and improved quality at reduced cost. He also advocated that the Army Air Corps play a major role in the establishment of the General Headquarters Air Force and in the development of a four-engine bomber—the B-17 of World War II fame.

In the fall of 1936, Secretary of War George Dern died and Woodring was given a recess appointment as secretary. The following April the assignment was made permanent. For the next three years, Woodring helped improve the army's state of readiness by developing the Protective Mobilization Plan and revising the Industrial Mobilization Plan. The plans ultimately served as the basis for America's World War II mobilization. He was also instrumental in establishing the Enlisted Reserve and the Triangular Infantry Division.

As Europe moved closer to war in 1939 and early 1940, Woodring increasingly came into conflict with President Roosevelt over whether American-built military aircraft (including the relatively few B-17's just coming off the assembly line) and army "surplus" should be made available to Britain and France so that they could resist Nazi Germany. Roosevelt favored such action, but Woodring argued that it would leave the nation vulnerable if the United States went to war. Roosevelt tolerated the war secretary's obstructiveness until June 19, 1940, when he asked for, and received, Woodring's resignation. Woodring thus earned the dubious distinction of being the only cabinet member ever removed by Roosevelt. Woodring's term as secretary was marred by a well-publicized feud with his assistant secretary of war, Louis Johnson, an able but ambitious man whose pursuit of the secretaryship divided the War Department at a time when unity and order were needed.

Following his dismissal, Woodring returned to Kansas. In 1946 he won the Democratic nomination for governor but was defeated in the general election by Republican Frank Carlson. Ten years later, in his final campaign, he again sought the gubernatorial nomination but lost to George Docking by less that 900 votes. In 1946 his twelve-year-old son Marcus died of polio. In 1960 he and his wife were divorced. To those setbacks were added financial difficulties and health problems. In September 1967 he was seriously burned when his pajamas caught fire; he died of a stroke brought on by the burns several days later.

[Woodring's personal papers, which cover his prepolitical career, gubernatorial service, years in the War Department and post-Washington career, are in the Spencer Research Library, University of Kansas at Lawrence. His official papers as governor are at the Kansas State Historical Society in Topeka, while his official correspondence as assistant secretary of war and secretary of war is found at the National Archives, Washington, D.C.

The only full-length biography is Keith McFarland, *Harry H. Woodring* (1975). On his pre-Washington career, see Donald McCoy, *Landon of Kansas* (1966); Francis W. Schruben, *Kansas in Turmoil, 1930–1936* (1969); and Keith McFarland, "Secretary of War Harry Woodring: Early Career in Kansas," *Kansas Historical Quarterly*, 37 (1973). For his Washington years, see Forrest C. Pogue, *George C. Marshall*, I (1963) and II (1965). An obituary is the *New York Times*, Sept. 10, 1967.]

KEITH D. MCFARLAND

WOOLMAN, COLLETT EVERMAN (Oct. 8, 1889–Sept. 11, 1966), airline executive, was born in Bloomington, Ind., the son of Albert Jefferson Woolman, a professor of physics, and Daura Campbell. He was reared principally in Champaign-Urbana, Ill., graduating from high school there in 1908. Commonly known as C. E., he enrolled at the University of Illinois the same year. He sang in a glee club and, being tall and rawboned, went out for varsity football. Exposure to aviation came early; in 1909 he worked his way to France on a cattle boat to attend the first major international flying meet at Reims, France. After graduating from the University of Illinois in 1912 with a B.S. in agriculture, Woolman managed a plantation in northeastern Louisiana. Then, following passage of the Smith-Lever Agricultural Extension Act in 1914, he became an early county agent, serving Ouachita Parish until his promotion to district supervisor for the Louisiana State Extension Service in 1916 took him from Monroe to Baton Rouge. On Aug. 8, 1916, he married Helen Fairfield, a home-economics teacher; they had two children, whom their workaholic father tended to neglect.

One of Woolman's main concerns in Louisiana, the annual depredations of the boll weevil, was addressed in the early 1920's by the United States Department of Agriculture's Delta laboratory at Tallulah, where entomologist Bert R. Coad experimented in aerial crop-dusting. Coad's work, utilizing army planes and personnel, came to the attention of the Huff Daland aircraft manufacturing company of New York, which introduced the first commercial crop-dusting planes and, in 1924, formed a dusting division. The following year it hired Woolman to sell its services to planters in the Delta. Woolman was a great salesman, having both charisma and the common touch. From the division's Monroe base, the company conducted dusting not only in the Delta but as far away as California and Peru.

Woolman and his immediate superior, Harold R. Harris, were among the pioneers of airline service in South America, helping to secure concessions for the financiers controlling both Huff Daland (subsequently known as Keystone) and Pan American Airways. When its owners sold the dusting division's assets in 1928, Woolman won financial backing from Monroe-area businessmen to purchase control, and he founded an independent dusting company, Delta Air Service. The parent company of Delta Air Lines, this firm added passenger service in 1929 when Woolman secured a secondhand six-passenger Travel Air biplane to operate between Monroe and Dallas, Tex. By 1930, with additional aircraft, service was expanded to Atlanta, Ga.

When Postmaster General Walter F. Brown

realigned airmail service in 1930, Delta failed to win an airmail contract, then indispensable for successful airline operations. Returning to crop-dusting during the next four years of the Great Depression, Woolman kept the company alive by employing a trait for which he became famous—frugality. After the Roosevelt administration in 1934 canceled most airmail contracts because of irregularities discovered by a congressional investigation into Brown's methods, Woolman led Delta back into airline operations by winning an airmail route from Fort Worth, Tex., to Charleston, S.C. Crop-dusting revenues still carried the company until the late 1930's, but gradually airline profits expanded and Woolman emerged as a shrewd general manager.

Woolman's astuteness was instrumental in Delta's subsequent climb from regional status to that of a major carrier. When logic dictated a move from Monroe to a major financial center, Woolman prevailed over board members who wanted Dallas as headquarters; in 1941, Delta moved to Woolman's choice, Atlanta, which had been for several years the hinge of the company's system and the base of most of its flight personnel. About this time Delta acquired some Douglas DC-3's, the airliner that revolutionized the industry, and began what became a long series of new route acquisitions in cases decided by the Civil Aeronautics Board. World War II impeded Delta's growth in civilian operations, but the company revived with the return of peace. Woolman led negotiations producing a merger in 1953 with Chicago and Southern, an airline with mainly north-south routes that complemented Delta's basically east-west system.

Firm but benevolent, Woolman instilled in Delta's personnel a feeling that they belonged to an extended family to which they owed love and loyalty. Aided by the firm's southern location and heritage, he kept Delta essentially nonunionized, except for its pilots, thus sparing the company from the rash of postwar strikes. He also insisted that Delta's flight engineers be certified pilots, thereby avoiding jurisdictional conflict in the cockpit. When the jet age arrived in the 1950's, Woolman and Delta were ready; the company pioneered the operation of such aircraft as the DC-8, in 1959, and the DC-9, in 1964.

Woolman's salary, like that of other Delta executives, was low in comparison to the sums paid to airline executives elsewhere, but Woolman became wealthy through the acquisition of company stock. He was also a civic leader in Atlanta and raised orchids for a hobby. Despite failing health, he remained a key figure in the airline industry, which became almost the sole focus of his life after the death of his wife in 1962; during his last few years he relied upon Delta for emotional support just as the company had always relied upon him for leadership. He died in Houston, Tex.

[The Woolman files are in the Delta general offices at Hartsfield International Airport in Atlanta. The University of Illinois Alumni Association has a collection of obituaries and other materials. The years 1935–1941 are covered in the papers of Laigh Parker at Delta headquarters. See also articles in Delta's in-house publication, *Delta Digest;* and W. David Lewis and Wesley Phillips Newton, *Delta* (1979).]

W. David Lewis
Wesley Phillips Newton

WRIGHT, THEODORE PAUL (May 25, 1895–Aug. 21, 1970), aeronautical engineer and administrator, was born in Galesburg, Ill., the son of Philip Green Wright and Elizabeth Quincy Sewall. Wright's father was professor of mathematics at Lombard College, a respected poet and mentor of Carl Sandburg, and a social activist. Motivated to excel by the example of his two older brothers, a geneticist and an expert on international law, Wright received a B.S. from Lombard College in 1915. In 1918 he obtained a B.S. in architectural engineering from the Massachusetts Institute of Technology (MIT). That year, on December 4, he married Margaret McCarl; they had two children.

Wright later termed his association with aviation "fortuitious." Uninterested in aeronautics prior to World War I, nevertheless he enrolled in the United States Naval Reserve Flying Corps at MIT in September 1917. Following graduation, he was given two months of instruction in aeronautical engineering and was then assigned as a naval aircraft inspector. In 1919 Wright became chief inspector for four Curtiss NC-4 flying boats being built for a planned transatlantic flight. One of them went from Newfoundland to Portugal via the Azores in May, becoming the first airplane to fly across the Atlantic Ocean.

Wright resigned from the navy in November

1921 and joined the Curtiss Aeroplane and Motor Company as an engineer. In 1925 he became chief engineer of the airplane division. Wright held a variety of positions following the formation of the Curtiss-Wright Corporation in 1928; he became vice-president and director of engineering in 1937.

During his twenty years in private industry, Wright supervised the design and production of numerous military and commercial aircraft, including the Hawk, Helldiver, Condor, and C-46. He took special interest in the Tanager, a pioneering short-takeoff-and-landing (STOL) airplane that employed a combination of slats, flaps, and floating ailerons to give outstanding low-speed stability and handling characteristics. In 1930 the Tanager won the $100,000 prize in the Guggenheim Safe Aircraft Competition, bringing Wright the prestigious Wright Brothers Medal of the Society of Automotive Engineers.

Concerned with development and production as well as design, Wright established a project engineer system at Curtiss that became the standard for the aircraft industry. Under this system one individual took responsibility for a new aircraft, from approval of the basic design, through the drafting phases, to final production. Wright also developed the widely used learner's curve, an important statistical device used to predict production costs.

In June 1940, following President Franklin D. Roosevelt's call for 50,000 aircraft, Wright joined the National Defense Advisory Commission. Nine months later he became assistant chief of the aircraft section in the Office of Production Management, the successor to the commission. After Pearl Harbor, Wright served as chairman of the Joint Aircraft Committee (an Anglo-American body that scheduled delivery of all aircraft), as director of the Aircraft Resources Control Office, and as a member of the Aircraft Production Board of the War Production Board. In these positions Wright played a key role in expanding aircraft production, especially in developing essential statistical tools that provided accurate information on industrial capacity and measurements of worker efficiency.

In September 1944, as aircraft production approached 100,000 planes a year, Wright accepted a presidential appointment as administrator of the Civil Aeronautics Administration (CAA). His first task was to decentralize an organization whose personnel had become increasingly dependent upon Washington for day-to-day decisions. While retaining policymaking at headquarters, Wright delegated administrative authority to regional offices. He also institutionalized the designee program, under which the CAA allowed certified private individuals to act as safety inspectors for aircraft and airmen. This freed the aeronautical industry from unnecessary delays and permitted major savings of CAA personnel and expenditures, an important consideration during the budgetary restraints after World War II.

During his three-and-a-half years as administrator, Wright fostered private aviation to a greater extent than did his predecessors, simplifying regulations for private pilots and directing regional administrators to be more responsive to their problems. He also supervised the modernization of radio aids to navigation, including the replacement of low-frequency radio ranges with very-high-frequency (VHF) omnidirectional ranges and the installation of instrument landing systems. Although he lacked the toughness needed to implement a thorough reorganization of personnel at the CAA, Wright brought order and equilibrium to civil aviation.

Discouraged when not promoted to assistant secretary of commerce and no longer willing to accept the financial burden of public office, Wright resigned in April 1948. Rejecting attractive offers from industry, he became vice-president for research of Cornell University and president of the Cornell Aeronautical Laboratory. In 1950, after persuading Harry F. Guggenheim to collaborate with Cornell in establishing a facility to investigate and promote aviation safety, he became chairman of the Cornell-Guggenheim Aviation Safety Center. In 1959–1960 he administered a research budget of over $33 million, approximately half of which came from government contracts with the aeronautical laboratory for work on helicopters, missiles, weapon systems, and other defense projects.

Wright continued to work in aeronautical and community affairs following his retirement in 1960. He took a special interest in environmental and conservation problems. His last paper, a treatise on overpopulation, was published six months before his death, in Ithaca, N.Y.

[The Wright papers are in the Cornell University Library, Ithaca, N.Y. The best source is Wright's

Articles and Addresses of Theodore P. Wright (1969–1970). See also Irving B. Holley, Jr., *Buying Aircraft* (1964); Richard P. Hallion, *Legacy of Flight* (1977); and John R. M. Wilson, *Turbulence Aloft* (1979).]

WILLIAM M. LEARY

WYNN, ED (Nov. 9, 1886–June 19, 1966), comedian and actor, was born Isaiah Edwin Leopold in Philadelphia, Pa., the son of Joseph Leopold, a prosperous manufacturer of women's hats, and his wife, Minnie (her maiden name is unknown), immigrants from, respectively, Czechoslovakia and Turkey. From a young age, he demonstrated a gift for comedy. One story of his childhood concerns his early habit of entering one of his father's retail shops and drolly mimicking customers as they tried on merchandise. His first taste of professional theater, a performance of *Dr. Jekyll and Mr. Hyde*, whetted his appetite for more. Another story, perhaps apocryphal, relates that on days when he knew he was to go to the theater, his mother would often find him sobbing, "I want eight o'clock."

By his early teens, Leopold knew that he wanted to make entertainment his life. At fifteen, he abandoned any thought of finishing his education at Philadelphia's Central High School and ran away to join the Thurber-Nasher Repertoire Company as a general utility boy. Earning about $10 a week, he was mainly charged with distributing handbills and looking after luggage. But he also had an opportunity to play bit parts, and after adopting the stage name Ed Wynn (from the syllables of his middle name), he landed the role of an old retainer in *American Grit*. The company went broke, and Wynn had to return home, where his father tried to interest him in selling hats. The effort was wasted, however; in 1902, Wynn was off to New York, where he and Jack Lewis formed a comedy act called the Rah! Rah! Boys. The team had difficulty in obtaining engagements, and Wynn had to live on money sent to him by his mother. But after performing at a benefit, the pair received a booking at New York's leading vaudeville house, the Colonial, where Wynn found himself earning $200 a week. In 1904, after playing with Lewis for nearly two years, Wynn decided to develop an act featuring only himself. The venture proved successful almost from the start, and he was soon a headliner on the vaudeville circuit.

In these early days, Wynn cultivated a comic style that in large degree set a pattern for the rest of his career. Writing his own material, he carefully avoided off-color jokes and instead rested his comedy on a combination of outrageous costumes and clever timing and delivery. In retrospect, many of his gags seem sophomoric, but coming from him, they had the power to engender laughter that sometimes lasted for minutes on end. In a routine of 1913, for example, Wynn played a hapless court jester facing certain death if he should fail to make his humorless monarch laugh. The king remained silently impassive throughout, but as a critic from *Variety* noted, audiences did not share his self-control in the face of Wynn's desperate antics.

In 1914 and 1915, Wynn performed in the *Ziegfeld Follies*, where he is best remembered for hiding under a pool table used in the act of W. C. Fields and upstaging the unwary Fields by pretending to catch flies. On Sept. 5, 1914, Wynn married Hilda Keenan, the daughter of the Irish-American actor James Francis ("Frank") Keenan. The couple's only child, Keenan, became a noted film actor.

In 1919, after several years of starring in one successful comedy or revue after another, Wynn's career took a sudden turn for the worse when he openly supported an Actors' Equity strike. Blacklisted for taking the union's part, Wynn soon found that no theater in New York would book him. But the setback was short-lived. Risking much of his financial security, he undertook to write and produce his own musical comedy revue. The result was *Ed Wynn's Carnival*, which opened in 1920 and proved an instantaneous hit. A year later, he realized even greater success with his creation and staging of *The Perfect Fool*—a title that eventually became his nickname. By now Wynn, with his crazy costumes, lisping voice, and growing supply of zany inventions, was becoming an institution. In the next several years he triumphed in two more vehicles of his own making, *The Grab Bag* (1924) and *Laugh Parade* (1931), and enjoyed much success in productions such as *Manhattan Mary* (1927) and *Simple Simon* (1930).

Between 1932 and 1935, Wynn appeared on the radio as the Texaco Fire Chief, and because he felt that the only way to perform effectively was before real people, he became one of the first performers in that medium to work in costume before a live audience. Adopting a falsetto that he did not normally use on the stage, Wynn also introduced the practice of making both his sponsor and his announcer, Graham McNamee, the butt of jokes. These innovative high jinks delighted America, and it was estimated at one point that Wynn had more than 20 million listeners.

By the late 1930's, Wynn's life had become an emotional maelstrom. Two months after divorcing his wife in 1937, he married the showgirl Frieda Mierse, and within two years divorced her; they had no children. Compounding his difficulties yet further, his large investment in a new radio chain went bad, and he faced claims from the Internal Revenue Service for back taxes that amounted to more than $500,000. In the wake of these adversities, Wynn suffered a nervous breakdown. Late in 1940, however, he returned to Broadway in *Boys and Girls Together*, where he uttered his famous exit line, "I'll be back in a flash with more trash," and introduced his eleven-foot pole for people he would not touch with a ten-foot pole. Of this production critic Brooks Atkinson declared, "It is funny to the point of tears."

In 1944, Wynn returned to radio as King Bubbles in "Happy Island," but the show was a failure. In 1946 he married Dorothy Nesbitt, whom he divorced in 1955; they had no children. Wynn turned to television in the late 1940's, and from October 1949 to July 1950 he was the star of his own weekly variety show on the Columbia Broadcasting System (CBS). From 1950 to 1953 he appeared every fourth week on the National Broadcasting Company (NBC) program "Four-Star Revue." But now Wynn's brand of comedy was beginning to seem passé, and when NBC dropped him after 1953, it appeared that his career was over.

In 1955, prodded by his son, Keenan, who was now a successful character actor, Wynn took a role in the movie *The Great Man* (released in 1956), and in the process demonstrated his considerable potential for straight drama. Shortly thereafter, he appeared with his son in the widely acclaimed television drama *Requiem for a Heavyweight*, and over the next ten years, he played characters in a number of motion pictures, including *Marjorie Morningstar* (1958), *The Diary of Anne Frank* (1959), and *Mary Poppins* (1964). For his supporting performance in *Anne Frank*, he was nominated for an Academy Award. Not long after finishing his last film, *The Gnome-Mobile* (1967), Wynn died in Beverly Hills, Calif.

Wynn once declared that "a comedian is not a man who opens a funny door—a comedian is one who opens a door in a funny way." But perhaps a more insightful explanation for his popularity as a funnyman over so many years came from fellow comedian Jack Benny. "When Wynn said anything funny," Benny noted, "you believed everything he said. It made no difference how ridiculous the joke was. If he said he had an uncle who was walking around without his head, you absolutely believed it."

[A small collection of Wynn's personal papers, consisting primarily of news clippings and original musical scores, is in the University Research Library of the University of California at Los Angeles. The most extensive published source on Wynn is Keenan Wynn, *Ed Wynn's Son* (1959). Shorter treatments include "Gag Tycoon," *Time*, Oct. 3, 1932; S. J. Woolf, "How to Hatch a Joke," *New York Times Magazine*, July 5, 1942; and Anthony Slide, *The Vaudevillians* (1981). Obituaries are in the *New York Times*, June 20, 1966; and *Time*, July 1, 1966.]

FREDERICK S. VOSS

YATES, HERBERT JOHN (Aug. 24, 1880–Feb. 3, 1966), motion-picture executive, was born in Brooklyn, N.Y., the son of Charles Henry Yates, an English-born accountant and seller of religious literature, and Emma Worthing. After completing his secondary education in the local public schools, Yates attended Columbia University's night school briefly in the late 1890's but soon abandoned his pursuit of a higher education for a career in business.

Yates began as an office boy for the American Tobacco Company, rose rapidly in that firm, and became sales manager for the eastern region by the age of thirty. In 1914, three years after the Supreme Court decision dissolving the tobacco trust, he became a sales executive in the newly formed company of Liggett and Myers. On Nov. 14, 1910, he married Petra Antonsen; they had four children.

In the early 1910's, Yates invested in the motion-picture production company organized by silent-screen star Roscoe ("Fatty") Arbuckle. Within three years he reportedly made a profit of 200 percent on his initial capital outlay. His early investments, however, primarily involved the manufacture and processing of motion-picture film. In 1916 he resigned his position with Liggett and Myers, and a year later, with his brother George, organized Republic Film Laboratories. In 1922 he established, and became chairman of, Consolidated Film Industries, which brought together several rival firms. By the early 1930's, Consolidated, with its main plant at Fort Lee, N.J., served many Hollywood studios and had become one of the nation's largest producers and developers of motion-picture film.

During the 1930's, Yates gradually shifted his main interest from film laboratory services to moviemaking. A number of minor film studios had become indebted to Consolidated Film Industries, and in 1935, Yates acquired the assets of the Monogram, Mascot, and Liberty studios to establish Republic Productions, with headquarters in the old Mack Sennett studios in North Hollywood, Calif. Yates served as chairman and, after 1938, also as president of the new firm, which was reorganized in 1945 as Republic Pictures Corporation and included as subsidiaries Consolidated Film Industries and other Yates enterprises. Under Yates's leadership, Republic quickly became a major producer of movie serials and, more significantly, of B-films—features that filled the lower half of the double bills then offered by most of the nation's theaters.

Republic, assured of a steady market for its B films, profited from low budgets made possible by the utilization of short shooting schedules, minimal sets, formulaic plots, and relatively inexpensive actors and directors. Although the studio produced a wide variety of films, its standard fare was the western—both the action film and the so-called "singing western." In the former category, John Wayne emerged as Republic's main attraction, while its "horse operas" made stars of Gene Autry and Roy Rogers.

After World War II, Republic encountered growing financial difficulties. Though its gross revenues increased fourfold during the 1940's, profits declined because of soaring production costs. A new and more sophisticated generation of moviegoers was less interested in Republic's standard offering. Yates sought to change the studio's image by producing more-expensive A films, the best of which are three John Wayne films, *The Wake of the Red Witch* (1948), *The Sands of Iwo Jima* (1949), and *The Quiet Man* (1952), nominated for an Academy Award as best film; yet these efforts generally garnered little prestige or profit.

The rapid growth of television in the 1950's posed insurmountable difficulties for Republic. The new medium lured America's youth away from the Saturday double-feature matinee, thus lessening the demand for the studio's B features. Yates was the first Hollywood studio executive to make his old movies available for television, but his arrangements for that purpose led to an acrimonious boycott against Republic by the Screen Actors Guild over residual payments to performers whose films appeared on television. The studio posted net losses in excess of $1 million in both 1957 and 1958. At the annual stockholders' meeting in the latter year Yates bluntly announced, "We have one problem—getting out of the motion-picture business." Before Yates sold out his interests in the firm and resigned the chairmanship in July 1959, Republic had indeed ceased its moviemaking activities. Its last film, a B western entitled *Plunderers of Painted Flats*, had been released the previous January.

Although millions of Americans annually attended Republic's pictures during Yates's twenty-four-year tenure as its chairman, his name was hardly a household word. He ruled the studio with an iron hand. In his early years he took pride in the fact that he was a businessman primarily interested in a healthy balance sheet. Yet he clearly allowed his heart to overrule his head in his stubborn, costly, and unsuccessful campaign in the late 1940's and early 1950's to make a film star of his protégée, Vera Hruba Ralston, a former Czech ice-skating champion with limited dramatic talents. In 1949, Yates's first wife died; he and Ralston were married on Mar. 15, 1952. He died in Sherman Oaks, Calif.

[Yates's career is appraised briefly in Todd McCarthy and Charles Flynn, eds., *Kings of the Bs* (1975), and more fully in Richard Maurice Hurst, *Republic Studios* (1979). An obituary is in the *New York Times*, Feb. 5, 1966.]

EDWIN A. MILES

ZIMMERMAN, HENRY ("HEINIE") (Feb. 10, 1886–Mar. 14, 1969), baseball player, usually known as Heinie or Zim, was born in the Bronx, N.Y., the son of a traveling fur salesman and his wife. Zimmerman completed an eighth-grade education in the public schools of the Bronx and became apprenticed to a plumber. Although for a number of years he worked at his craft in the winter, he soon found baseball irresistible. Quickly he graduated from local sandlot ball to semiprofessional ball, able to earn $25 a week with one team on Wednesdays and Saturdays and an additional $8 with another club on Sundays. He was a standout at several positions. In 1906 he was signed by Wilkes-Barre of the New York State League at a salary of $150 per month. He played second base and hit .314 in 1907. Late that year he was sold to the Chicago Cubs for $1,250. He could not break into the Cubs lineup because the famous infielders Joe Tinker, Hoot Evers, and Frank Chance seemed immovable. Opportunity finally arrived in 1911 when he became the team's regular second baseman. The following spring he was switched to third base. That year he led the National League in hitting with a .372 average, his career high. In 1916, recognized as the best third baseman in the league, he was traded to the New York Giants for Larry Doyle, their second baseman, who had led the league in batting in 1915, and two other players. The Cubs had apparently grown tired of the annual salary disputes with their right-handed slugger.

Standing five feet, eleven-and-a-half inches tall and weighing 185 pounds in his prime, Zimmerman was handsome, broad-shouldered, and sometimes swaggering. When he joined the Giants at their hotel in St. Louis, he walked up to the room clerk and asked, "Any mail for the Great Zim?" He could also be irascible. In 1917 he was fined by the league for cursing at an umpire in a dispute and throwing a ball at him. One day the following year he failed to run out a fly ball that was dropped by an outfielder, and upon being bawled out by the manager, John McGraw, Zimmerman promptly walked off the field in a huff.

Zimmerman's impulsiveness may have been responsible for the "bonehead" play that made him a baseball "immortal." It took place at the Polo Grounds in New York on Oct. 15, 1917, in the fourth inning of the sixth and, as it turned out, final game of the World Series between the Giants and the Chicago White Sox. Eddie Collins, the peerless second baseman of the Sox, led off the inning with a roller to Zimmerman, who threw wide past first baseman Walter Holke for a two-base error. With Collins now on second base, Joe Jackson, the left fielder, hit an easy fly to Dave Robertson in right field, who dropped the ball for an error, sending Collins to third. The pitcher, Rube Benton, induced the next batter, the hard-hitting Hap Felsch, to bounce back to him. Seeing Collins way off third, Benton threw the ball to Zimmerman, apparently trapping Collins between third and home. In the ensuing rundown, Collins, seeing the plate unguarded, took off for home like a scared rabbit, with Zimmerman, holding the ball in his hand and his arm outstretched, in desperate, fruitless pursuit. A few moments later a single drove in Jackson and Felsch, and the White Sox, with three runs in, had put the game on ice. Zimmerman, ever after known as "the man who chased Eddie Collins across the plate," insisted always that he could have done nothing else. "What was I supposed to do with the ball, eat it?" he used to ask plaintively. "There wasn't anybody to throw it to except Klem." (Bill Klem, the renowned umpire, was behind the plate.)

Some observers said that Holke and Benton deserved the blame for not backing up catcher Bill Rariden. Rariden may have been out of position, but the White Sox manager and third-base coach, Clarence ("Pants") Rowland, afterward said that he had heard Zimmerman shout to Rariden, "Get out of the way, I'll get this monkey myself." The next day the *New York Times* reported, "The great crowd shook with laughter and filled the air with cries of derision at one of the stupidest plays that has ever been seen in a world's series." The newspaper explained, "Heinie could just as well have thrown the ball to Bill Rariden and squelched Collins, but Zim thought it was a track meet instead of a ball game and wanted to match his lumber-wagon gait against the fleetest sprinter in the game."

Years later Collins said that Zimmerman had not deserved the lambasting he received in the press and that Holke and Rariden were responsible for the blunder. "They left the plate uncovered. I saw my chance and shot for home. What could Zimmerman have done but dash after me?" A widely printed newspaper photograph seemed to substantiate this verdict.

Zimmerman's career ended in 1919 when he was suspended for having thrown games. Zimmerman denied the accusation, but in an affidavit he gave the *New York American* two years later he admitted that he had been a go-between for a gambler offering $100 each to three Giants ballplayers if they would see to it that their team lost the final series with the Cubs in 1919. Zimmerman in his thirteen years in the big leagues went to bat 5,304 times and compiled a .295 batting average, with a slugging percentage of .419.

Zimmerman dropped out of the public gaze after retiring, although for a time he played on a semipro club. He reappeared suddenly in 1935 when he was named in an income-tax evasion case against "Dutch" Schultz, the notorious bootlegger and racketeer. Zimmerman, it was revealed, was a partner of Schultz's in a speakeasy in the Bronx in 1929 and 1930 and had a joint account with him, containing at one time almost $16,000. Possibly this connection had been arranged by Zimmerman's brother-in-law, Joe Noe, a prominent Bronx bootlegger, whose body, riddled with bullets, was found in front of one of the best-known Prohibition-era nightclubs in 1928. Noe was reputed to have been in business with Schultz.

Zimmerman had married Helene Chasar in 1912, when she was sixteen years old; they had one child. Three years later his wife sued him for nonsupport, and they were divorced in 1916. Zimmerman's second wife, Bertha Noe, stated at the time of her husband's death in a Bronx hospital that in his later years he had been a steamfitter.

[A collection of newspaper clippings about Zimmerman in the library of the National Baseball Hall of Fame and Museum at Cooperstown, N.Y., is invaluable. The statistics of Zimmerman's baseball career are in Joseph L. Reichler, ed., *The Baseball Encyclopedia* (1969). Published accounts of his exploits are in Frank Graham, *McGraw of the Giants: An Informal Biography* (1944); John Durant, *Highlights of the World Series* (1963); and Charles Einstein, *The Fireside Book of Baseball* (1956). A report of Zimmerman's relationship with "Dutch" Schultz is in the *New York Times*, Apr. 17, 1935. An obituary is in the *New York Times*, Mar. 15, 1969.]

HENRY F. GRAFF

ZORACH, WILLIAM (Feb. 28, 1889–Nov. 15, 1966), sculptor, was born Zorach Samovich, in Euberick, Lithuania, the son of Orchick Samovich, a barge keeper on the Nieman River, and Toba Getal. Zorach's father immigrated to the United States in 1892 and became a peddler in Port Clinton, Ohio. Zorach, his mother, and five siblings joined his father the next year. In 1896 the family settled in Cleveland and subsisted on his father's earnings as a junk dealer.

Zorach grew up in a slum amid other immigrants; his parents could neither read nor write, although they spoke five languages. Shy and serious, Zorach regarded public school as a mystery. In the first grade he reported his name, Zorach, to his teacher, who decided to call him Willie—hence the name William Zorach. In the third grade he began selling newspapers and shining shoes to supplement the family income. At the end of the seventh grade he left school to become an apprentice lithographer for the W. J. Morgan Lithography Company, where he was employed from 1902 to 1912.

Zorach enjoyed woodcarving and took drawing classes at the Educational Alliance in Cleveland. Encouraged by a colleague at the lithography company, he enrolled in night classes at the Cleveland School of Art, where he studied from 1905 to 1908. Resolving to become a "real" artist, he spent the winters of 1908–1910 in New York City, studying painting and drawing at the National Academy of Design; he returned to Cleveland in the summers to work as a lithographer. He became a competent draftsman and in 1910 decided to continue his studies in Paris. (He was naturalized as an American citizen before 1910.)

Since Zorach did not speak French, he enrolled in Jacques Émile Blanche's La Palette, where criticism was given in English. There he was impressed by the Scottish artist John Duncan Fergusson's painting classes and by an American student, Marguerite Thompson, who introduced Zorach to Gertrude Stein, Alice B. Toklas, and Pablo Picasso. Zorach and Thompson took in exhibitions of fauvist, cubist, and Postimpressionist painting.

Exhausting his funds, Zorach returned to his lithography job in Cleveland late in 1911. After saving for a year he moved to New York City. On Dec. 24, 1912, he married Thompson and moved into a small studio that they decorated with murals and a red floor. They had two children. Both artists exhibited in the 1913 Armory Show and participated in a variety of activities associated with the fledgling New York avant-garde. From 1913 to 1919 they experimented with modernist painting styles derived from Henri Matisse and fauvism, and then cubism. Zorach's most sophisticated and satisfying accomplishments as a painter, exuberant watercolor studies of Yosemite Valley, were created during a visit to California in 1920–1921.

The Zorachs spent winters in New York and summers in New England. In 1915 they met John Reed, Louise Bryant, and Eugene O'Neill in Provincetown, Mass., where Zorach made sets for O'Neill's *Bound East for Cardiff.* Zorach's family summered in New Hampshire in 1917. There Zorach began a series of woodblock prints. Incising a butternut panel, he became intrigued with the carving process and developed the panel into a sculptural relief, *Waterfall.*

Although not formally trained as a sculptor, Zorach executed several wooden panels between 1917 and 1922. By 1922 he had "realized that sculpture, not painting, would have to become my lifework. . . . I could not take it or leave it. It consumed me and I lived it." He had undertaken his first stone carvings in 1921, teaching himself the requisite techniques. His initial efforts reflect an enthusiasm for African, Aztec, and Mayan forms, but he quickly settled upon a more naturalistic figurative style not unrelated to that of his friend Gaston Lachaise.

Traditional sculptors in the late nineteenth and early twentieth centuries modeled their designs in clay; these models were then enlarged and copied in stone by professional cutters. Zorach was one of the first American sculptors to advocate direct carving—realization of form by the artist himself. "It's a metaphysical sort of thing," he wrote, "almost like a sailor's relationship to the sea in which he becomes part of the elements." Among Zorach's preferred materials were the granite boulders of Maine, where he bought a summer home in 1923.

Zorach advanced quickly and intuitively as a sculptor. In 1927 he began one of his most well known compositions, *Mother and Child,* carved from a three-ton block of rose marble; it was acquired by the Metropolitan Museum of Art in 1952. Zorach regarded this rhythmic complex of simplified anatomical forms as his finest sculpture, not only on formal grounds but also because the figures express maternal tenderness and family unity, universal themes that came to represent for Zorach the raison d'être of art. Traditional subject matter and direct carving were the cornerstones of his mature oeuvre and of his instruction at New York's Art Students League, where he taught from 1929 to 1960.

Zorach's reputation as a sculptor grew in the 1930's, and he received several major commissions. For private patrons he carved animal figures, family groups, sensuous female torsos, and visionary heads, many of which call to mind the contemporaneous work of Jacob Epstein, the sculptor whom Zorach regarded as "the greatest of this age."

Zorach was known for his peasantlike bluntness, straightforward approach to aesthetic problems, and lack of guile, a quality sometimes disadvantageous in executing public commissions. Zorach encountered the first of several public controversies in 1932, when he created a nude female figure symbolizing the dance for Radio City Music Hall. The sculpture was refused on the ground that its nudity rendered it unfit for public exhibition. Art organizations protested, and the work was eventually installed. Zorach's most painful contretemps began in 1956, when a nearly completed monumental relief commissioned by the Second National Bank of Houston, Tex., was suddenly rejected because of a rumor that Zorach was a Communist sympathizer. Zorach denied the allegation, but the controversy followed him for more than a decade.

On the occasion of his major retrospective exhibition at the Whitney Museum of American Art in 1959, the curator John Baur described Zorach as one of those who rescued American sculpture "from the neo-classical inanities and illustrative modeling which dominated it at the end of the century. . . . Zorach probably did the most to establish here the practice of direct carving and the aesthetic concepts which grew out of it, just as he had the greatest influence, by teaching and example, on a following generation." Zorach died in Bath, Maine.

[Many Zorach photographs, scrapbooks, and letters are at the Zorach Studio in Brooklyn, N.Y. William and Marguerite Zorach's correspondence is in the Library of Congress. Zorach's papers are in the Archives of American Art, Smithsonian Institution, Washington, D.C. Zorach wrote *Zorach Explains Sculpture* (1947) and *Art Is My Life* (1967). See Paul Wingert, *The Sculpture of William Zorach* (1938); John Baur, *William Zorach* (1959); and Roberta Tarbell, "Catalogue Raisonné of William Zorach's Carved Sculpture" (Ph.D. diss., University of Delaware, 1976). An obituary is in the *New York Times,* Nov. 17, 1966.]

PATRICIA FAILING

INDEX GUIDE

TO THE SUPPLEMENTS

Index Guide to the Supplements

Index Guide to the Supplements

Index Guide to the Supplements

Index Guide to the Supplements

Index Guide to the Supplements

Index Guide to the Supplements

Index Guide to the Supplements

Index Guide to the Supplements

Index Guide to the Supplements

Index Guide to the Supplements

Index Guide to the Supplements